Also included in Massey's collection were plays by Isabel Ecclestone Mackay, Canada's major female playwright of the 1920s, and Carroll Aikins, who would take over running Hart House Theatre later in the decade. Aikins's own experimental Home Theatre, built in the middle of an apple orchard in British Columbia's Okanagan Valley, lasted from 1920–22. Another Hart House participant of note was Roy Mitchell, its first artistic director, a guru of creative, non-commercial theatre and a seminal figure in both Toronto and New York's Little Theatres.

Throughout the 1920s and into the '30s, amateur theatre flourished under the umbrella of the Little Theatre movement, a burgeoning of homegrown playmaking in communities on both sides of the Canada-U.S. border. Little theatres sprouted in dozens of cities and towns across Canada. Those committed to the idea of a National Theatre found hope even in such humble institutions, "because they build the foundation for more mature creative theatres and develop an audience for the Ultimate National Canadian theatre."[9] That lofty goal seemed to move a step closer to realization with the establishment in 1932 of the Dominion Drama Festival, a nationwide competition organized by the new Governor General, Lord Bessborough, and chaired by the ubiquitous Vincent Massey. The festival would consist of an annual series of regional playoffs climaxing in a final (held in a different city each year) at which awards would be given for production and performance. Community theatres, school and university drama groups, and established companies like Hart House would all be eligible, and adjudicators would provide helpful feedback as well as award trophies. The DDF aimed to showcase theatre in Canada and at the same time upgrade the quality of Canada's theatrical arts and crafts through competition and cross-fertilization.

During the years of its existence (1933–70, with a hiatus from 1940–46 due to the war), the Dominion Drama Festival helped institutionalize amateur theatre in Canada. Whether it accomplished much more than that has been a matter of debate. It provided a proving ground for Canadian talent which often went on to New York, London, Hollywood, or by the 1950s to Stratford or other areas of the nascent Canadian professional theatre. Through trophies and cash prizes, the DDF also encouraged the writing and production of Canadian plays, an encouragement that proved at least statistically impressive. In 1934, festival organizers could come up with just nine Canadian titles for its list of suggested plays sent out to participating groups; by 1966, the list contained 240 Canadian titles in English alone. But the quality and adventurousness of the work the festival inspired were often questionable. As late as 1967, the DDF would refuse to allow Michel Tremblay's contentious *Les Belles-Soeurs* to be produced as part of its all-Canadian celebrations.[10]

An earlier indictment of the DDF's limitations was its inability to contend with the multimedia expressionism of Herman Voaden's plays, which consistently failed to advance beyond regional competitions in the 1930s. Ironically, Voaden had been a vocal advocate of a national drama league like the DDF to help cement Canada's theatrical development and serve as a bulwark against the dangerous "pressure of American influence" threatening to "override our national and British character."[11] An ardent cultural nationalist and theatrical innovator, he advocated a Canadian dramatic art as distinctive as the paintings of the Group of Seven. To that end, in 1929 he sponsored a playwriting competition requiring that each play be set in the Canadian North with the play's subject or mood based on the writer's favourite Canadian painting. Voaden's own plays combined a mystical vision of the Canadian landscape with modern dance, Wagnerian opera, and symbolist dramatic techniques, resulting in a synaesthetic form he called "symphonic expressionism" in titles like *Rocks*, *Earth Song*, and *Hill-Land*. Voaden's Play Workshop in Toronto produced twenty-five new Canadian plays from 1934–36. But for all his extensive work as playwright, producer, director, and educator, Voaden's greatest contribution to the development of Canadian theatre may have been his persistent lobbying for government support for the arts. In 1945, he was elected first president of the new Canadian Arts Council.

The Play Workshop and Hart House were not the only centres of Canadian playwriting activity. A group of women journalists organized the Playwrights' Studio Group in Toronto in 1932 and by the end of the decade had produced more than fifty new plays, mainly society comedies. At the other end of the spectrum were the Progressive Arts Clubs in Toronto, Montreal, Winnipeg, and Vancouver, leftist workers' theatre groups that created and performed agitprop and social protest plays throughout the Depression years. In Alberta, the Banff School of the Theatre was founded in 1933, evolving into the Banff School of Fine Arts, still an important centre for theatre training and workshop production. Alberta's Elsie Park Gowan and Gwen Pharis Ringwood wrote some of the strongest Canadian plays of the period. Ringwood, who would later teach playwriting at Banff to George Ryga among others, created stark prairie tragedies such as "Still Stands the House" and *Dark Harvest*. Gowan's *The Last Caveman* (1946) would be one of the first Canadian plays produced professionally in postwar Canada.[12]

Perhaps the most significant development for English-Canadian drama in the 1930s and '40s was the rise of radio. The Canadian Broadcasting Corporation (CBC) had been established in 1932, in part to resist the powerful tide of American commercial radio flowing across the border. In 1936, it began broadcasting radio plays for which it paid writers, producers, actors, musicians, and technicians. What came to be known as "The Golden Age" of Canadian radio – Canada's equivalent of a national professional theatre – began when Andrew Allan became supervisor of drama for CBC and producer of its weekly *Stage* series. Under Allan from 1944 to 1955, hundreds of original scripts and adaptations by house writers such as Lister Sinclair and Len Peterson were produced for live broadcast on *Stage* and *Wednesday Night*: consistently bold and imaginative drama that maintained high standards of excellence while proving broadly popular. At one time only *Hockey Night in Canada* drew more listeners than *Stage*. The stable of writers and actors that Allan assembled, including performers like John Drainie, Don Harron, and Frances Hyland, who would become mainstays of the new professional theatre, was "far and away the most exciting repertory group that can be heard," wrote the *New York Times* radio critic in 1946.[13] Although radio's golden age faded with the coming of television in the 1950s, and CBC has been slowly eviscerated by budget cuts since the 1980s, radio drama continued to provide an important source of work and income for Canadian actors and playwrights to the end of the century and beyond.

Despite the varied successes of the DDF and the CBC, neither amateur theatricals nor radio drama could satisfy the need for a vibrant, professional domestic stage culture. John Coulter, who became an award-winning DDF playwright and a frequently produced CBC dramatist soon after emigrating from Ireland to Canada in 1936, was a vocal critic of the Canadian theatre scene. In a magazine article published in 1938, he held up Dublin's Abbey Theatre as a model for Canadians, a theatre "showing the Irish to themselves ... Irish mugs in Irish mirrors."[14] Canadian audiences, too, he argued, could see their lives reflected in the work of their playwrights if the writers would find their subject matter in Canadian stories. After a series of plays set in Ireland, Coulter took his own advice and turned to writing radio plays about Canadian history. He achieved his greatest success with a trilogy of stage plays about Louis Riel. First produced in 1950, Coulter's *Riel* would serve as a paradigm for the history plays of James Reaney and the Theatre Passe Muraille dramatists of the 1970s: revisionist Canadian history with the rebel or underdog as hero, presented as a synthesis of documentary and myth.

Coulter was fortunate that by the time *Riel* was ready, he had a professional company available to produce it: the New Play Society (NPS), founded by Dora Mavor Moore in 1946. Moore had been the first Canadian to attend London's Royal Academy of Dramatic Arts, and she had directed extensively at Hart House and other Toronto amateur theatres. When World War Two ended, she founded a professional company, paying actors fifteen dollars per production. The NPS opened with a classic of the Abbey Theatre, Synge's *Playboy of the Western World*, but it also produced new Canadian work by writers like Coulter, Lister Sinclair, Harry Boyle, and Dora's son Mavor, who played the title role in *Riel* and would become a major figure in Canadian arts. Mavor Moore created the company's most substantial success, *Spring Thaw*, a satirical musical revue on Canadian topics, first staged in 1948 and remounted with increased popularity annually for the next twenty years. The NPS remained active until 1971, but its prime years were 1946–50 when its full seasons of plays in the Royal Ontario Museum Theatre (a basement auditorium) proved to many skeptics the viability of a professional Canadian stage.[15]

Other professional companies followed, among them Sydney Risk's Everyman Theatre in Vancouver (1946–53), which toured throughout western Canada, and Ottawa's Canadian Repertory Theatre (1948–56), whose casts featured future Canadian stars Christopher Plummer, William Shatner, Amelia Hall, and William Hutt, among others. The co-founders of Toronto's Jupiter Theatre (1951–54) included Lorne Greene and John Drainie. In 1954 Toronto brothers Donald and Murray Davis founded Crest Theatre, which presented quality work in continuous repertory for thirteen seasons. The major Canadian playwright associated with the Crest was Robertson Davies, whose *A Jig for the Gypsy* and *Hunting Stuart* premiered there in 1954–55. Davies was already English Canada's foremost playwright on the amateur circuit with "Eros at Breakfast," "Overlaid," and *Fortune, My Foe* in 1948–49, satires of Canadian philistinism and what he considered the national disease, "emotional understimulation." He remained a significant force in Canadian theatre until the mid-1960s when his playwriting career gave way to his work as a novelist.[16]

Aside from his playwriting, Davies's journalism made a strong contribution to the developing Canadian theatre in the postwar era. Under both his own name and the pseudonym Samuel Marchbanks, he railed in protest like Voaden and Coulter against the conditions under which would-be Canadian theatre professionals had to labour – what he called in 1952 "the seedy amateurism which has afflicted the arts here for so long."[17] With fond reminiscences of his experience as a young actor in England, Davies reacted with enthusiasm to the idea of a world-class Shakespearean festival theatre in Stratford, Ontario. Along with Dora Mavor Moore and festival organizer Tom Patterson, he was instrumental in arranging for innovative British producer-director Tyrone Guthrie to head the venture, which held its first season of two plays under a tent in the summer of 1953. Guthrie imported stars Alec Guinness and Irene Worth to play the leads and fleshed out the rest of the company with Canadian actors, a policy that by and large remained standard for Stratford well into the 1980s.

Reviewing that first season, Davies concluded that it had given Canadians "a new vision of the theatre":

> This cannot help but have its effect on work everywhere in the country. For one thing, many of our best Canadian actors are working at Stratford ... Are these actors, who have tasted the wine of true theatre, ever again to be satisfied with the sour slops of under-rehearsed, under-dressed, under-mounted, under-paid, and frequently ill-considered and ill-financed theatre projects? ... The Stratford Festival is an artistic bombshell, exploded just at the time when Canadian theatre is most ready for a break with the dead past and a leap into the future.[18]

The Stratford Festival did have an enormous impact on theatre and the idea of theatre in Canada. It became an event of international importance and influence (its new non-proscenium thrust stage designed by Guthrie and Tanya Moisiewitsch made waves in theatres worldwide). It raised the profile of theatre in Canada as nothing else had been able to do and served as a focus of national cultural pride. The festival also became a training ground for many of the best actors who emerged in Canada over the next three decades. Moreover,

> Stratford created a model for indigenous Canadian theatre: a non-profit organization, unconcerned with the values of New York, unashamedly using imported personnel where Canadian expertise was lacking, equally unashamedly welcoming

subsidy support in return for placing its destiny – at a policy-making level – in the hands of a volunteer citizen Board of Governors, and representatives of the community in which it found itself.[19]

But Stratford did little to support the development of Canadian playwriting. Writers like John Herbert and James Reaney would receive workshop and small-scale public performances of their plays there in the late 1960s. In 1971 a Third Stage was added, in part to produce Canadian work. But by that time, with its huge financial operation, Stratford had become in many eyes a cultural dinosaur, devouring large subsidies at the expense of the smaller theatres whose productions of Canadian plays, often on shoestring budgets, were more central to an emerging national drama than was a theatre run by British artistic directors and devoted to Shakespeare. Ironically, while Stratford feasted, Canadian drama came of age in the early 1970s as a kind of poor theatre nourished on just those "sour slops" that Davies had complained of in 1953. Six decades after its creation – now with four stages – Stratford remains a central element of Canada's theatrical ecology. Even with a fully Canadian contingent of lead actors, directors, and designers, and Canadian artistic directors for the past thirty years, the festival continues to elicit ambivalent responses from the Canadian theatrical community.[20]

By 1956 Mavor Moore could write, "the Canadian theatre ... like the stock market, is bullish these days ..."[21] The success of Stratford and the other new professional theatres was augmented by CBC television, which from its inception in 1952 gave starts to a number of important dramatists who would later go on to write for the stage, including George Ryga, David French, and Michel Tremblay. The Canadian economy was booming. And on the horizon was the Canada Council, whose founding in 1957 would change the nature of theatre in Canada more than any other single development, providing a massive influx of government funding for buildings, companies, and individuals engaged in the arts.

The Canada Council was the most concrete manifestation of the Royal Commission on National Development in the Arts, Letters, and Sciences appointed by Prime Minister Louis St. Laurent in 1949 with Vincent Massey as chairman. While Canada had established its economic and military bona fides in both war and peace, it remained seriously underdeveloped culturally and artistically. Why had Canada so few creative artists of note compared to other major nations, and so relatively little in the way of arts, including theatre? The Massey Commission, as it came to be called, aimed to find out.

The Commission found that "the forces of geography" had conspired to put a nation of fourteen million (at the time) alongside a behemoth ten times as populous and many times more culturally aggressive. As the Cold War had replaced the postwar peace, the growing threat of nuclear conflict between the United States and the Soviet Union, the outbreak of the Korean War, and the military and economic weakness of postwar Britain had all drawn Canada increasingly into the American orbit. Canada and the United States were partners in NATO (the North Atlantic Treaty Organization) and NORAD (the North American Air Defense Agreement), fought together in Korea, and shared in the Red scare. Despite continued discomfort among some Canadian artists, politicians, and educators about the overwhelming influence of American culture, the two nations had become increasingly integrated since the United States had replaced Britain as Canada's leading trading partner in 1921. Between 1948 and 1953 Canada's military expenditures grew from 7 per cent of its federal budget to 43 per cent. Yet, the Commission's 1951 *Report* argued, Canadians lacked "the advantages of what soldiers call defense in depth" against the "American invasion by film, radio, and periodical." Continuing the metaphor, the *Report* concluded, "Our military defences must be made secure, but our cultural defences equally demand national attention ..."[22]

Even if, as some have argued, the Massey Commission proceeded from certain British-imported, elitist cultural biases, it proved a game-changer. Because it found that Canadian culture was being stifled not just by the omnipresence of American influences but also by the lack of support and facilities for artists in Canada, it concluded that the nation's cultural defences could only be secured through significant government financial aid for artists and infrastructure. Modelled along the lines of the British Arts Council, the Canada Council for the Encouragement of the Arts, Letters, Humanities, and Social Sciences would support Canadian culture at home and abroad. From an outlay of $2.6 million in arts grants in its first year, 1957, the Canada Council's investment in individuals and groups grew to more than $60 million by 1970, a quantum leap in the funds available to fuel the engine of Canadian cultural nationalism.

Money wasn't the only catalyst for change. In 1958 in Winnipeg, Tom Hendry and John Hirsch merged their amateur Theatre 77 with the Winnipeg Little Theatre to create a regional professional theatre, the Manitoba Theatre Centre (MTC), with Hirsch as its first artistic director. From the start, the MTC "was meant to be more than a theatre, something that could in fact become a focus for all theatrical energy and resources in one community."[23] Combining mainstage productions in Winnipeg with a touring company, children's theatre, and school, the MTC succeeded so well in galvanizing the support and resources of its constituency that it became the basis for a new concept: a decentralized, regional Canadian version of a national theatre.[24] With support and encouragement from the Canada Council a network of regional theatres spread across the country: Vancouver's Playhouse and Halifax's Neptune in 1963, Edmonton's Citadel in 1965, and Regina's Globe in 1966. By 1970 Montreal, Calgary, Fredericton, and Toronto also had theatres catering to regional communities.

Canada, it seemed, had indeed become bullish on theatre. To train and supply actors for the new national theatre network, the National Theatre School was opened in Montreal in 1960 with separate French and English programs. At Niagara-on-the-Lake the Shaw Festival began operation in 1962, and Prince Edward Island's Charlottetown Festival was inaugurated in 1964, specializing in Canadian musical theatre. St. John's got its Arts and Culture Centre in 1967. And in 1969–70, the completion of three major Centennial construction projects – Ottawa's National Arts Centre, Toronto's St. Lawrence Centre, and a new building for the MTC – rounded out a decade of extraordinary growth for the Canadian theatre.

With the superstructure essentially intact, the missing link now was the plays. Where were the plays that might crystallize the new drama in English Canada the way John Osborne's *Look Back in Anger* had done in Britain and Gélinas's *Tit-Coq* in Quebec (and the way Tremblay's *Les Belles-Soeurs* would do again in Quebec, in a different way, in 1968). Those plays had in common vernacular speech, anti-establishment anger, and characters, settings, and situations definitively of their own time and place. So too had the play that finally touched the nerve of English Canada. *The Ecstasy of Rita Joe* premiered at the Vancouver Playhouse on November 23, 1967, in a landmark production remounted for the opening of the National Arts Centre in 1969. That year the play was also broadcast on CBC-TV and produced in a French translation by Gratien Gélinas in Montreal. In 1971 choreographer Norbert Vesak adapted the play for the Royal Winnipeg Ballet. *Rita Joe* reverberated through the nation's collective consciousness. In a review of a later theatrical production, critic Jamie Portman recalled, "*Rita Joe* happened during Centennial year when Canadians were anxious to look at themselves. But the look that this play provided was an unsettling one. It punctured the euphoria and the smug complacency of Canada's birthday celebrations and declared unequivocally that all was not well with this country and its institutions." Its implications for Canadian playwriting were equally dramatic:

> This was an indigenous Canadian drama that surfaced and succeeded at a time when indigenous Canadian drama was generally considered to be an aberration. It was a play of merit, worthy of production in any Canadian theatre. It prompted an awareness of the existence of other plays potentially worthy of production. It provided resounding evidence that it was not necessary for any Canadian theatre to rely solely on imported fare. With the arrival of *The Ecstasy of Rita Joe*, Canadian plays ceased to be a rarity in English-speaking Canada. Companies dedicated to the production of new Canadian drama sprang up, and in so doing nurtured the further growth of playwriting activity. Canada's regional theatres – some of them grudgingly – found themselves forced to take the Canadian playwright seriously for the first time.[25]

Yet the battle for credibility was not so easily won. Just how grudgingly the theatre establishment received the Canadian playwright was vividly registered by a study that found that, in 1970, the seven major regional theatres had produced the work of a total of two Canadian dramatists, and paid them less than $5,000 out of combined budgets of more than $2 million.[26] Consider the case of the once pioneering Manitoba Theatre Centre. Despite its success with Winnipeg writer Ann Henry's *Lulu Street* in 1967, more than a decade would pass before the MTC presented another new play by a local playwright. The flurry of Canadian play production in 1967 had been in some respects no more than Centennial Year tokenism.

The stage history of John Herbert's *Fortune and Men's Eyes* reveals the challenges faced by Canadian playwrights. *Fortune* had been work-shopped at Stratford in 1965. Denied a full production there or anywhere else in Canada, the play opened in New York in 1967 and ran for a year off-Broadway. In 1968, it had a long run in London and become a full-scale international hit. By 1969, it was already being revived in New York. The play's impact on other Canadian dramatists was immediate and inspirational: "the ice-breaker in the channel," George Ryga called it.[27] But for all that, professional productions of *Fortune and Men's Eyes* in Canada to 1970 consisted of a week at the Vancouver Playhouse's Stage 2 and a brief run in the MTC's Studio Theatre. There was not a mainstage production to be seen. Herbert's hometown of Toronto would have to wait until 1975 to see the play at all.

What had gone wrong? The expectations and struggles of more than a half-century had resulted in a Canadian theatre that by the late 1960s had already become entrenched and conservative. Rather than living up to the original promise of the regionals to create new models adapted to the distinctive needs of their communities, which should have meant presenting plays written about those communities from within them, the large subsidized theatres tried to emulate Broadway and London's West End. When artistic directors were asked about Canadian plays and playwrights, their responses were often remarkably similar:

> I don't see how a play can be Canadian.
> I don't think there are any plays that you could call strictly Canadian.
> But if you start to define what is a Canadian and what is a Canadian playwright, what do you end up with?
> What does the phrase mean?[28]

With few exceptions the regionals served up homogenized theatre: safe, commercial seasons of British and American hits plus a smattering of world classics. Moreover, it was theatre as Cultural Event, like the opera or the symphony, the kind of thing you got dressed up for.

But the late 1960s was the Age of Aquarius and the Generation Gap. Theatre artists – many of them in the first wave of Baby Boomers graduating from university – and much of their potential audience were evolving in a different direction. The Canadian Centennial and the emergence of a Canadian professional theatre community just happened to coincide with the most radical cultural upheaval of the century in the Western world. There was a sexual revolution, a musical revolution, a drug revolution; long hair, peace marches, and a Summer of Love. By 1968 in Chicago, Paris, and Prague the revolution would spill over into the streets. Canada wasn't immune to these forces nor could its theatre be, no matter how stubbornly middle-aged and middle-class it tried to remain.

That the most significant Canadian plays of the decade should have appeared in 1967–68 was not coincidental. *The Ecstasy of Rita Joe, Fortune* and *Men's Eyes*, and *Les Belles-Soeurs* are plays very much of their age, marked by strong social consciousness and anti-establishment anger. Alienated from the mainstream themselves, the playwrights were in sync with the temper of the times. Herbert and Tremblay were gay men. Ryga and Herbert were outspoken and uncompromising in their social and political views. It was characteristic of their outsider status that neither was initially allowed entry into the United States to see his own play in production; characteristic that Herbert refused the Dominion Drama Festival's Massey Award (and its $1,000 prize) for Best Play for *Fortune and Men's Eyes* in 1968; characteristic that Ryga's 1970 play *Captives of the Faceless Drummer* would so upset the Vancouver Playhouse board, which had commissioned it, that they would refuse its production. It was ironic but perhaps inevitable that the two writers whose plays brought modern English-Canadian drama into existence would eventually find themselves virtually unproduced by the major Canadian theatres.[29]

Modern Canadian drama was born out of an amalgam of the new consciousness of the age – social, political, and aesthetic – with the new Canadian self-consciousness. Since the larger theatres were generally unsympathetic and unaccommodating to both these forces, an even newer Canadian theatre had to be invented, an alternate theatre. One of its prime movers in Toronto was Martin Kinch, who claimed that those first heady days had little to do with nationalism:

> The real influences were Fritz Perls and Timothy Leary, Peter Brook and Jerzy Grotowski, Tom O'Horgan, Café La Mama, Julian Beck, Judith Malina, and the ensemble of the Living Theatre; in short, a host of European and American artists, most of them primarily dedicated to the ethic and the aesthetic of "doing your own thing" ... It was an exciting time, a time of experiment and exploration ... expressionism, hallucination, confrontation, and audience participation flourished. Perhaps most important, however, there existed a definite bond between the theatres and their audience; an audience that was characterized by long hair, beards, bells, and babies in the front rows of the most outrageous plays. Its concerns were the concerns of "the sixties": the breaking of sexual taboo, the problems of individual freedom, and the yearning for community.[30]

In 1969, Kinch became a co-director of Toronto's Theatre Passe Muraille, founded the previous year by Jim Garrard. As its name suggests, Passe Muraille was to be a theatre without walls: neither the traditional fourth wall between actors and audience nor necessarily even the walls of a theatre building. Garrard envisioned "a guerrilla theatre": "Theatre in the subways, get a truck and do theatre in small towns, real circuses, grab people in the streets ... I'd like to make theatre as popular as bowling."[31] A milestone for the new alternate theatre movement was Passe Muraille's production of American playwright Rochelle Owens's *Futz* in February 1969. A play about a man in love with a pig, in both style and content it established the parameters of the alternate theatre's self-conscious anti-conventionality. The sex, obscenity, and nudity it featured would become almost obligatory. When the show was shut down by the morality squad, and the company charged and subsequently acquitted, the new movement had its red badge of courage.

Nationalism soon joined, and to some extent eclipsed, sensationalism in Toronto's new alternate theatre scene, largely through the efforts of Ken Gass and Paul Thompson. Gass set out to prove that Canadian playwrights indeed existed, and were just waiting to be discovered and encouraged. His Factory Theatre Lab was both a factory and a laboratory, presenting polished new plays as well as experimental works-in-progress. Most importantly, it would be "The Home of the Canadian Playwright." His concept paid off with a string of notable new plays: David Freeman's *Creeps*, Herschel Hardin's *Esker Mike and His Wife, Agiluk*, and George Walker's *Prince of Naples* all in 1971; most of Walker's other plays over the next dozen years; and exciting (though not necessarily enduring) work by Hrant Alianak, Larry Fineberg, Bryan Wade, and Gass himself. Gass remained artistic director of Factory Lab until 1979, then returned to the post again in 1996 to save the company, now called simply Factory Theatre, from imminent demise.

Paul Thompson became artistic director of Theatre Passe Muraille after working in France with Roger Planchon, whose process-oriented, political brand of theatre contrasted dramatically with Thompson's experiences during a brief apprenticeship at Stratford. Rejecting the Stratford model, Thompson focused his company on local subject matter and collective creation, involving his actors in first-hand research, improvisation, and continual revision, and utilizing their individual skills as key elements in the play wherever possible. When Thompson took over Passe Muraille, there was already a precedent for this kind of theatre in Toronto. George Luscombe had worked with Joan Littlewood's Theatre Workshop in England in the mid-1950s and had founded Toronto Workshop Productions in 1959 based on Littlewood's political and stylistic principles: left-wing politics and an eclectic style that integrated improvisation, documentary, commedia dell'arte, and often collective scripting. In the late 1960s and early '70s TWP produced potent socio-political theatre with its agitprop pieces, *Mister Bones* and *Chicago '70* on race and politics in America, and its bittersweet evocation of the Canadian Depression, *Ten Lost Years*. The partnership of Luscombe and Toronto Workshop Productions lasted for thirty years until the company folded in 1989 and its building passed on to Sky Gilbert's Buddies in Bad Times Theatre.[32]

Under Thompson's stewardship, Theatre Passe Muraille became the most important Canadian theatre of the early 1970s. Creations like *Doukhobors*, *The Farm Show* (first staged in a Clinton, Ontario barn), and *The Adventures of an Immigrant* (performed in Toronto streetcars) made often stirring theatrical poetry out of material that was sometimes mundane and always local. Docudrama with a high degree of theatricality became the Passe Muraille trademark: a small company of actors using little but their own bodies and voices to create ingenious stage metaphors.

They inspired countless imitators across the country, although in less talented hands the deceptively rigorous demands of collective scripting and a presentational style sometimes had unfortunate results. Among the best of their offshoots were Newfoundland's CODCO and Twenty-Fifth Street House Theatre in Saskatoon, whose *Paper Wheat*, a play about the founding of the co-op movement on the prairies, was in the finest Passe Muraille tradition. The company also specialized in resurrecting, popularizing, dramatizing, and often mythicizing Canadian history in collective scripts or in conjunction with a writer. *Buffalo Jump* with Carol Bolt, *1837: The Farmers' Revolt* with Rick Salutin, *Them Donnellys* with Frank MacEnany, and *Far as the Eye Can See* with Rudy Wiebe were some of the best of the collaborations. Later in the decade, Passe Muraille company members John Gray (now John MacLachlan Gray) and Eric Peterson would create *Billy Bishop Goes to War*, and Linda Griffiths would write and perform *Maggie & Pierre*. Perhaps the most exciting Canadian playwright to emerge in the 1980s, Judith Thompson, also came out of Passe Muraille with her extraordinary first play, *The Crackwalker*, and Sally Clark was playwright-in-residence there in 1985–86. Theatre Passe Muraille and Factory Theatre remain to the present day two of the primary loci of Canadian theatrical production and development.

Not everything was happening in Toronto. In Vancouver, where Sidney Risk had pioneered postwar professional touring with his Everyman Theatre, and where John Juliani's experimental Savage God project had been operating since 1966, John MacLachlan Gray, Larry Lillo, and a group of other University of British Columbia graduates formed Tamahnous Theatre in 1971, a collective that would remain Vancouver's most original and progressive company for the next ten years. Among its most important productions were the small-cast musicals *Billy Bishop Goes to War* and Morris Panych's "post-nuclear cabaret," *Last Call!* Vancouver's New Play Centre had come into being in 1970 dedicated to developing new scripts by local writers. Under the direction of Pamela Hawthorn from 1972 until 1989, the New Play Centre (NPC) had a hand in most of the drama to come out of British Columbia, including the work of Margaret Hollingsworth, Tom Walmsley, Ted Galay, John Lazarus, Sheldon Rosen, Betty Lambert, Eric Nicol, and Sherman Snukal. In the late 1990s, the NPC metamorphosed into Playwrights Theatre Centre, which continues its predecessor's work.

Seeded by government grants from Local Initiatives Programs (LIP) and Opportunities for Youth (OFY), new companies doing indigenous theatre sprouted everywhere in 1971–72: Edmonton's Theatre 3, Calgary's Alberta Theatre Projects, Pier One in Halifax, the Mummers Troupe in St. John's. Festival Lennoxville in Quebec presented all-Canadian summer seasons of plays by the likes of Michael Cook, Herschel Hardin, and Sharon Pollock from 1972 until its demise in 1982, a victim of poor demographics and Parti Québécois cultural policy.

Most of the action, though, was in Toronto, and nothing did more to cement its position at the centre of the new movement than Tarragon Theatre. Founded in 1971 by Bill Glassco, who had directed David

Freeman's *Creeps* at the Factory Lab earlier in the year, Tarragon opened with a revised version of Creeps that proved even more successful than the original. The first Tarragon season ended with a new work that was to become the single most influential Canadian play of the 1970s, David French's *Leaving Home*. Its story of generational conflict and a singularly Canadian form of immigrant alienation (ex-Newfoundlanders spiritually adrift in Toronto) elicited strong audience identification, and its straight-forward, accessible style had broad appeal. *Leaving Home* created a vogue for domestic realism that some saw as a debilitating counterforce to the more adventurous directions Canadian drama seemed to be taking at the time. Tarragon soon became identified with that particular style, especially in light of Glassco's productions of subsequent realist plays by Freeman and French. But Tarragon also introduced English Canada to the plays of Michel Tremblay with Glassco as director and co-translator – plays domestic in setting but hardly realistic in style. Moreover, from 1973–75 Tarragon produced James Reaney's Donnelly trilogy, including *Sticks and Stones: The Donnellys, Part I*, a work far removed from stylistic realism or naturalism. Unlike the great majority of companies devoted to Canadian plays, Tarragon managed both to combine artistic and commercial suc-cess and to sustain it over many years. More than any other theatre it succeeded in bringing Canadian drama into the mainstream. After Glassco left Tarragon in 1985, its status was maintained under the artistic director-ship of former theatre critic Urjo Kareda, followed by Richard Rose. The many playwrights in this volume of *Modern Canadian Plays* whose work is associated with Tarragon – not only James Reaney, but also Michel Tremblay, David French, Joan MacLeod, Ann-Marie MacDonald, and Judith Thompson – testify to the continued influence, importance, and adventurousness of the company.

The wave of new alternate theatres in Toronto crested in 1972 with the founding of Toronto Free Theatre by Tom Hendry, Martin Kinch, and John Palmer. Subsidized by LIP grants, performances were literally free until 1974 when the impossible economics of that policy led to gradually increasing admissions. Toronto Free's reputation rested on its excellent ensemble of actors and a distinctive taste for the psychologically bizarre. Many of its early successes were plays by its in-house triumvirate – especially Hendry and Palmer – along with Carol Bolt. George F. Walker and Erika Ritter were among the most noteworthy later additions to Toronto Free's playwriting corps, with *Zastrozzi: The Master of Discipline* premiering there in 1977.

Notwithstanding the dynamism of the alternate companies, Cana-dian theatre in the early 1970s was in danger of falling victim to an insidious form of ghettoization. Canadian plays were relegated to small, low-budget theatres that lacked the financial and technical resources avail-able to the heavily subsidized festivals and regionals. While non-Canadian works had access to lush productions, large casts, and relatively well paid actors, Canadian plays were doomed to what George Ryga called "beggars theatre"[33] – the same conditions about which Robertson Davies had com-plained in 1953 – and Canadian playwrights were denied opportunities to make a living by their craft. In an attempt to remedy this situation a group of playwrights met in the summer of 1971 to consider "The Dilemma of the Playwright in Canada." Their most contentious recommendation called for a 50 per cent Canadian content quota for all theatres receiving government funding. Most artistic directors and editorialists were predictably outraged. "If it ever happened, then critics should also get Canada Council grants for sitting through the plays," was one wit's response.[34] Though no formal quota system was ever adopted, the controversy led to an informal policy decision by the Canada Council to "appeal" to its client theatres to do more Canadian plays. The results were startling. By the 1972–73 season, nearly 50 per cent of the plays produced by subsidized theatres in both English and French were Canadian.

Among the most tangible consequences of this new policy was a return to one of the original precepts of the regional ideal, the commissioning by regional theatres of new plays from local playwrights. These arrangements proved mutually fruitful to Sharon Pollock with the Vancouver Playhouse and Theatre Calgary, John Murrell and W.O. Mitchell also with Theatre Calgary, Ken Mitchell and Rex Deverell with Regina's Globe, and David Fennario with the Centaur in Montreal. The Blyth and Kawartha Summer Festivals, in cultivating playwright Anne Chislett, proved the value of a homegrown product even in the traditionally more commercial milieu of summer theatre. In each of these cases plays written with specific associations for local audiences made their way into theatres across the country. Canadian writers and producers may have finally learned what John Coulter had called, back in 1938, "the paradoxical truth that the most effective way to keep an eye on Broadway is to keep on looking attentively at the life passing under your own nose in your own home town."[35]

Another way "to keep an eye on Broadway" and London was to strengthen and nationalize the organizational infrastructure of Canadian theatre. In 1976, the Professional Association of Canadian Theatres (PACT) and the Association for Canadian Theatre History, a national academic organization (now called Canadian Association for Theatre Research) were founded, and Canadian Actors' Equity Association declared its independence from American Actors' Equity.

Given the tremendous expansion Canadian theatre had undergone since 1967, a certain amount of retrenchment was inevitable by the 1980s. Theatres as widely divergent as Saskatoon's Twenty-Fifth Street and the Stratford Festival had to weather financial and artistic crises that threatened their survival. Some went under: Vancouver's Westcoast Actors, Edmonton's Theatre 3, Montreal's Saidye Bronfman. Facing new audience expectations and a changing ideological climate, Toronto and Vancouver's major "alternates" (no longer an accurate term) underwent structural reorganization and found new artistic directors. Toronto Free would soon disappear in a merger and Tamahnous would disappear altogether. But Passe Muraille, Tarragon and Factory, along with the resurgent regionals and successful middle-of-the-road theatres like Vancouver's Arts Club, continued to provide a springboard for Canadian plays. And across the country a new generation of neo-alternates arose: the Vancouver East Cultural Centre, Prairie Theatre Exchange in Winnipeg, Ottawa's Great Canadian Theatre Company, Nova Scotia's Mulgrave Road Co-op and Ship's Company, and Rising Tide Theatre in St. John's. Nakai Theatre Ensemble in Whitehorse and Tununiq Arsarniit Theatre Group in what is now Nunavut ensured the exposure of lively theatrical voices in the Canadian North. Touchstone joined the scene in Vancouver along with Green Thumb, which set the pattern for hard-hitting young people's theatre.

Edmonton was particularly fertile ground. Theatre Network, Northern Light, Catalyst, Workshop West, and Phoenix Theatre all came on stream before 1982, the year the Edmonton Fringe Festival was born. Modelled on the Edinburgh Fringe, Edmonton's festival has become a hugely successful affair with annual attendance in the quarter-million range, and a prototype for the many other Canadian Fringes that have sprung up in its wake.

Meanwhile, Toronto's theatrical expansion continued to the point where it could soon claim second-place only to New York as a mecca for theatre in North America. Among its important new companies were Necessary Angel, Nightwood (which became Canada's foremost feminist theatre and producer of *Goodnight Desdemona (Good Morning Juliet)*, among other seminal works), Buddies in Bad Times (soon the country's most important gay company as well as a centre for new play development with its spin-off Rhubarb Festival), clown-based Theatre Columbus, multicultural Cahoots, and Native Earth Performing Arts, which led the 1980s renaissance of First Nations theatre in Canada. The Toronto International Theatre Festival, and its successor, Harbourfront, showcased Canadian plays and productions alongside some of the best theatre companies in the world.

Canadian theatre's growing cultural prominence was signified by a series of new awards and textbooks. Joining the prestigious Chalmers Award, given by the Toronto Drama Bench since 1972 for best Canadian play produced each year in Toronto, were the Canadian Authors' Association Award for Drama (1975) and, in 1981, the Governor General's Award in Drama for the best new Canadian plays in publication in French and English. The Doras in Toronto (after Dora Mavor Moore), the Jessies in Vancouver (after Jessie Richardson), the Sterlings in Edmonton (after Elizabeth Sterling Haynes), and the Bettys in Calgary (after Betty Mitchell) celebrate the best work done on those cities' stages in the name of a local theatrical pioneer. The Nathan Cohen Award for excellence in theatre criticism commemorated a legendary theatre critic. The publication of three Canadian drama anthologies in 1984–85, including the first version of this one, made Canadian plays more accessible to high school and post-secondary students, more entrenched in curricula, more academically respectable.

By the mid-1980s, the nationalism that had largely inspired and in some ways kick-started the new Canadian theatre had pretty much gone out of vogue. Free trade and globalism were soon to become the new keywords. Even the old keywords had new meanings. As Alan Filewod points out, "in 1974 the terms 'native' and 'indigenous' meant 'Canadian' as opposed to British or American; by 1984 they had acquired a much more specific value (pertaining to aboriginal peoples) which challenged the very meaning of 'Canadian' as it was understood only a decade earlier."[36]

Nevertheless, the next few years were marked by an unprecedented series of theatrical coups led by what John MacLachlan Gray has called the Old Warriors of Canadian Nationalism. Tarragon pioneer Bill Glassco became artistic director of southern Ontario's major regional theatre, CentreStage, in 1985, then engineered a merger with Guy Sprung and Toronto Free Theatre to create the Canadian Stage Company in 1988. That year Tamahnous co-founder and west coast alternate-theatre icon Larry Lillo made a triumphant return to Vancouver to run B.C.'s flagship regional theatre, the Playhouse, and Sharon Pollock took over her hometown regional, Theatre New Brunswick. The Stratford Festival's controversial attempt to hire a non-Canadian artistic director in 1980 was resolved in favour of the appointment of John Hirsch, who had co-founded Manitoba Theatre Centre back in 1958. Canadian actor Richard Monette, who had once played Hosanna at Tarragon, took over the festival's reins in 1992. With such apparent victories the nationalist agenda receded in importance. In relative terms this was the case even in Quebec.

But as economic issues superseded nationalism on the larger political landscape, economics also assumed greater political and artistic impact in the theatre. Canada's non-profit, publicly subsidized theatre system had to deal with shrinking government support in the face of growing deficits and an unsympathetic Conservative regime under Brian Mulroney. Theatre was increasingly perceived as just another commodity, forced to find its niche in a competitive and fragmented cultural marketplace battered by recessions and dominated by home video. Theatre boards run by businessmen assumed more and more power, and corporate sponsorships to replace lost government funding became the norm. Conflicts between the artistic and corporate agendas led to a series of crises. If 1988 had seen the apparent victory of the cultural nationalists, 1989 showed how fragile the new theatrical order really was. Canada's longest-running alternate theatre, Toronto Workshop Productions, shut down in a struggle between its artists and its board. Canadian Stage Company's board forcibly removed artistic director Guy Sprung, and Sharon Pollock resigned from Theatre New Brunswick in frustration. *Canadian Theatre Review* titled its Summer 1990 issue, "Surviving the Nineties." A 1996 issue would be titled "Survivors of the Ice Age."

For a few playwrights the commercialization of Canadian theatre meant not just surviving but thriving, as hit plays from small non-profit stages got remounted in large, long-run commercial venues. Toronto led the way with George F. Walker's *Love and Anger* and Brad Fraser's *Unidentified Human Remains and the True Nature of Love* crossing over into commercial production in 1990, and Tomson Highway's *Dry Lips Oughta Move to Kapuskasing* in 1991.

By far the most significant commercial development was the arrival of the mega-musical. In 1985, to accommodate Andrew Lloyd Webber's

Cats, Toronto's old Elgin Theatre–Winter Garden complex was restored to its former glory and *Cats* ran for two years. In 1989, entertainment mogul Garth Drabinsky renovated another magnificent old Toronto vaudeville house, the Pantages, for Lloyd Webber's *Phantom of the Opera*, which ended up running for ten years and selling over seven million tickets. Producers Ed and David Mirvish opened *Les Misérables* at their historic Royal Alexandra Theatre. The extraordinary success of these huge imported shows, not just in Toronto but in their spin-off tours across Canada, led to more of the same. In the early 1990s, the Mirvishes built the Princess of Wales theatre to house *Miss Saigon* and Drabinsky's Livent became North America's largest theatrical production company. Livent opened its new North York Performing Arts Centre with a production of *Show Boat,* then in a strictly commercial exchange renamed it the Ford Centre for the Performing Arts. While still importing shows, Canadian mega-musical producers also began creating their own versions of musical theatre classics for export (*Show Boat, Joseph and His Amazing Technicolor Dreamcoat*), as well as commissioning new shows like Drabinsky's *Kiss of the Spider Woman* and *Ragtime*, and an all-Canadian *Napoleon*.

The mega-musical boom had the virtue of fueling the theatrical economy, creating international stars of Canadian actors like Brent Carver and Jeff Hyslop, and spin-off opportunities for a few Canadian non-musical plays. Drabinsky was responsible for the commercial remount of *Love and Anger*, and the Mirvishes for *Dry Lips*. But on the whole it posed severe challenges for Canadian non-profit theatres. Rather than benefitting from a trickle-down of the new audiences created and abetted by the megas, low-budget companies found themselves in difficult competition for the theatre-going dollar. The success of these shows also shaped audience expectation and demand, and fostered pressures, subtle and unsubtle, from boards, funding agencies, and others to conform to the mega-musical aesthetic: high on spectacle, low on content, lacking in Canadian reference, and empty of political challenge. "Megamusicals can kill intelligent theatre," Sky Gilbert complained. "Megamusicals actually make you stupid."[37] Intelligence eventually triumphed. With the novelty of the genre waning, his overextended empire straining, and Drabinsky himself accused of cooking the books, Livent collapsed in 1998. Drabinsky would go to prison for fraud. The non-profit theatres, where most Canadian plays are born and performed, would survive the challenge.

New festivals and companies continued to emerge. Montreal's Festival de théâtre des Amériques (now Festival TransAmérique) (1985) and Toronto's du Maurier World Stage (1986) became important showcases for innovative theatre from Canada and around the world. Two Calgary festivals, Alberta Theatre Projects' New PlayRites (1986) and One Yellow Rabbit's experimental High Performance Rodeo (1987), as well as Native Earth's Weesageechik Begins to Dance festival (1988), joined established new play development organizations like the Banff Centre, Playwrights' Workshop Montreal, Vancouver's New Play Centre / Playwrights Theatre Centre, and the Rhubarb Festival. Nova Scotia's Festival Antigonish (1988) and a number of new summer Shakespeare festivals set up shop:

Shakespeare-on-the-Saskatchewan in Saskatoon (1985), Repercussion Theatre in Montreal (1988), Edmonton's Shakespeare-in-the-Park (1989), and Bard on the Beach in Vancouver (1991).

Social upheavals marked the 1980s and early '90s, where this volume of plays leaves off. Gay liberation, the AIDS epidemic, and second-wave feminism had powerful effects on Canadian life and art, manifested in new notions of selfhood, relationships, gender construction, and family configurations. These forces are evident in all the plays that make up the second half of this volume – Sharon Pollock's *Blood Relations*, Sky Gilbert's *Drag Queens on Trial*, Kelly Rebar's *Bordertown Café*, Joan MacLeod's *Toronto, Mississippi*, Ann-Marie MacDonald's *Goodnight Desdemona (Good Morning Juliet)*, Tomson Highway's *Dry Lips Oughta Move to Kapuskasing*, Judith Thompson's *Lion in the Streets*, and Sally Clark's *Life Without Instruction*. Gay, lesbian, and feminist theatre organizations like Buddies in Bad Times, Nightwood Theatre, and Vancouver's Women in View (1988–97) were instrumental in developing and producing work that dramatized those issues. The era was also notable for a new consciousness among Canadians of First Nations, due in part to the terrible revelations about residential schools that began leaking out in the late 1980s. Native theatrical artistry played a more positive role. De-ba-jeh-mu-jig Theatre on Manitoulin Island in Ontario and Native Earth Performing Arts, both founded in the early 1980s, nurtured and developed Tomson Highway's *The Rez Sisters* and *Dry Lips Oughta Move to Kapuskasing*. Under Highway's artistic directorship, 1986–90, and subsequently under the direction of Floyd Favel, Drew Hayden Taylor, and Yvette Nolan, Native Earth has fostered the work of a whole generation of Aboriginal Canadian theatre artists.

Read these plays against the backdrop of the decades during which Canadians struggled to make a theatre of their own. The fifteen in this volume represent, of course, only one of numerous possible samplings of the plays written and produced in Canada in the quarter-century after 1967. They will lead you, I hope, to want to read and see others, including those in Volume Two, which continues the eventful history of Canadian theatre through 2012.

NOTES

1. The story of pre-twentieth century Canadian theatre has been told only in bits and pieces. For a general overview see Eugene Benson and L.W. Conolly, *English-Canadian Theatre* (Toronto: Oxford UP, 1987). Anton Wagner and Richard Plant, ed., *Canada's Lost Plays* (Toronto: CTR, 1978–81) is an excellent anthology in four volumes presenting plays from the nineteenth through the mid-twentieth century with extensive historical introductions. See also, among others, Jerry Wasserman, *Spectacle of Empire: Marc Lescarbot's Theatre of Neptune in New France* (Vancouver: Talonbooks, 2006); Leonard E. Doucette, *Theatre in French Canada: Laying the Foundations, 1606–1867* (Toronto: U of Toronto P, 1984); Yashdip S. Bains, *English Canadian Theatre, 1765–1826* (NY: Peter Lang, 1998); Mary Elizabeth Smith, *Too Soon the Curtain Fell: A History of Theatre in Saint John, 1789–1900* (Fredericton: Brunswick, 1981); Murray D. Edwards, *A Stage in Our Past: English-Language Theatre in Eastern Canada from the 1790s to 1914* (Toronto: U of Toronto P, 1968); Franklin Graham, *Histrionic Montreal: Annals of the Montreal Stage, with Biographical and Critical Notices of the Plays*

and *Players of a Century*, 2nd ed. (Montreal: John Lovell & Son, 1902); Chad Evans, *Frontier Theatre: A History of Nineteenth-Century Theatrical Entertainment in the Canadian Far West and Alaska* (Victoria: Sono Nis, 1983); E. Ross Stuart, *The History of Prairie Theatre: The Development of Theatre in Alberta, Manitoba, and Saskatchewan, 1833–1982* (Toronto: Simon & Pierre, 1984); John Orrell, *Fallen Empires: Lost Theatres of Edmonton, 1881–1914* (Edmonton: NeWest, 1981); Ann Saddlemyer, ed., *Early Stages: Theatre in Ontario, 1800–1914* (Toronto: U of Toronto P, 1990); Kym Bird, *Redressing the Past: The Politics of Early English-Canadian Women's Drama, 1880–1920* (Montreal: McGill-Queen's UP, 2004).

2. Nathan Cohen, "Theatre Today: English Canada," *Tamarack Review* 13 (Autumn 1959): 28.

3. Thomas B. Hendry, "Trends in Canadian Theatre," *Tulane Drama Review* 10:1 (Fall 1965): 62–70. That same year Michael Tait concluded his survey of "the grey wastes of Canadian drama," 1920–60, by noting "perhaps the most depressing feature of theatre in Canada: the lack of any vital and continuing relationship between theatrical activity and the work of the Canadian playwright." "Drama and Theatre," *Literary History of Canada*, ed. Carl F. Klinck. 2nd ed. (Toronto: U of Toronto P, 1976), II, 159, 167.

4. Betty Lee, *Love and Whisky: The Story of the Dominion Drama Festival* (Toronto: McClelland & Stewart, 1973), 296.

5. For an important collection of articles documenting twentieth-century Canadian theatre, see Don Rubin, ed., *Canadian Theatre History: Selected Readings* (Toronto: Playwrights Canada, 2004). See also Jerry Wasserman, "Early English-Canadian Theater and Drama, 1918–1967," *History of Literature in Canada: English-Canadian and French-Canadian*. Ed. Reingard M. Nischik (Rochester: Camden House, 2008), 207–21.

6. Alan Filewod, "National Theatre/National Obsession," *Canadian Theatre Review* 62 (Spring 1990): 6; rpt. Rubin, ed., *Canadian Theatre History*, 410. Cf. Patrick B. O'Neill, "The British Canadian Theatrical Organization Society and the Trans-Canada Theatre Society," *Journal of Canadian Studies* 15:1 (Spring 1980): 56–67; and Anthony Vickery, "Two Patterns of Touring Canada: 1896 to 1914," *Theatre Research in Canada* 31 (Spring 2010): 1–19; Robertson Davies, "Mixed Grill: Touring Fare in Canada, 1920–1935," *Theatrical Touring and Founding in North America*. Ed. L.W. Conolly (Westport, CT: Greenwood, 1982), 41–56.

7. Fred Jacobs, "Waiting for a Dramatist," *Canadian Magazine* 43 (June 1914): 146. On the relationship between Canada's theatre critics and Canadian theatrical development, see Anton Wagner, ed., *Establishing Our Boundaries: English-Canadian Theatre Criticism* (Toronto: U of Toronto P, 1999).

8. Vincent Massey, "The Prospects of a Canadian Drama," *Queen's Quarterly* 30 (Oct. 1922): 200; rpt. Rubin, ed, *Canadian Theatre History*, 55.

9. Rupert Caplan, "The Ultimate National Theatre," *Canadian Forum* 9 (Jan. 1929): 143–44; rpt. Rubin, ed, *Canadian Theatre History*, 78.

10. Lee, 287–98; Gaetan Charlebois, "*Les Belles-Soeurs*," *Canadian Theatre Encyclopedia*. www.canadiantheatre.com. Betty Lee's *Love and Whisky*, the primary source for information on the DDF and the only book on the subject, is packed with information. But it lacks footnotes and often quotes inaccurately. Cf. Herbert Whittaker, "Dominion Drama Festival," *Oxford Companion to Canadian Theatre*. Ed. Eugene Benson and L.W. Conolly (Toronto: Oxford UP, 1989), 144–45.

11. H.A. Voaden, "A National Drama League," *Canadian Forum* 9 (Dec. 1928): 105; rpt. Rubin, ed., *Canadian Theatre History*, 76. Anton Wagner maintains an excellent website, *The Worlds of Herman Voaden*, containing twenty-two of Voaden's plays, nearly thirty of his articles, and numerous articles about him. http://www.lib.unb.ca/Texts/Theatre/voaden/index.htm

12. See Anton Wagner, ed. *Canada's Lost Plays, Volume Three: The Developing Mosaic: English-Canadian Drama to Mid-Century* (Toronto: CTR, 1980); Benson and Conolly, *English-Canadian Theatre*, Ch. 2; Rubin, ed., *Canadian Theatre History*, Sec. 3; Alan Filewod, *Committing Theatre: Theatre Radicalism and Political Intervention in Canada* (Toronto: Between the Lines, 2011), Ch. 4; Susan McNicoll, *The Opening Act: Canadian Theatre History 1945–1953* (Vancouver: Ronsdale, 2012); Geraldine Anthony, *Gwen Pharis Ringwood* (Boston: Twayne, 1981); Moira Day, ed., *The Hungry Spirit: Selected Plays and Prose by Elsie Park Gowan* (Edmonton: NeWest, 1992).

13. Jack Gould, "Canada Shows Us How," *New York Times* (1 Sept. 1946): Sec. II: 7. Cf. Howard Fink and John Jackson, ed., *All the Bright Company: Radio Drama Produced by Andrew Allan* (Kingston & Toronto: Quarry/CBC, 1987); N. Alice Frick, *Image in the Mind: CBC Radio Drama, 1944 to 1954* (Toronto: Canadian Stage & Arts, 1987).

14. John Coulter, "The Canadian Theatre and the Irish Exemplar," *Theatre Arts Monthly* 22 (July 1938): 503; rpt. Rubin, ed., *Canadian Theatre History*, 119.

15. See Paula Sperdakos, *Dora Mavor Moore: Pioneer of the Canadian Theatre* (Toronto: ECW, 1995); Mavor Moore, *Reinventing Myself: Memoirs*

(Toronto: Stoddart, 1994); Allan Boss, *Identifying Mavor Moore: A Historical and Literary Study* (Toronto: Playwrights Canada, 2011).

16. See McNicoll, *The Opening Act*; James Hoffman, "Sydney Risk and the Everyman Theatre," *BC Studies* 76 (Winter 1987–1988): 33–57; Amelia Hall, *Life before Stratford: The Memoirs of Amelia Hall* (Toronto: Dundurn, 1989); Paul Illidge, *Glass Cage: The Crest Theatre Story* (Toronto: Creber Monde, 2005); Susan Stone-Blackburn, *Robertson Davies, Playwright: A Search for the Self on the Canadian Stage* (Vancouver: UBC Press, 1985).

17. Robertson Davies, *The Well-Tempered Critic: One Man's View of Theatre and Letters in Canada*, ed. Judith Skelton Grant (Toronto: McClelland & Stewart, 1981), 66.

18. Davies, 74.

19. Hendry, "Trends in Canadian Theatre," 64–65; rpt. Rubin, ed., *Canadian Theatre History*, 246.

20. See Tom Patterson and Allan Gould, *First Stage: The Making of the Stratford Festival* (Toronto: McClelland & Stewart, 1987); John Pettigrew and Jamie Portman, *Stratford: The First Thirty Years* (Toronto: Macmillan, 1985); Martin Hunter, *Romancing the Bard: Stratford at Fifty* (Toronto: Dundurn, 2001); Robert Cushman, *Fifty Seasons at Stratford* (Toronto: Madison, 2002).

21. Mavor Moore, "A Theatre for Canada," *University of Toronto Quarterly* 26 (Oct. 1956): 2; rpt. Rubin, ed., *Canadian Theatre History*, 233.

22. *Report of the Royal Commission on National Development in the Arts, Letters, and Sciences* (Ottawa: Edmond Cloutier, 1951), 13, 18, 275. On Massey cf. Alan Filewod, *Performing Canada: The Nation Enacted in the Imagined Theatre* (Kamloops, BC: Textual Studies in Canada, 2002), Ch. 3; and Karen A. Finlay, *The Force of Culture: Vincent Massey and Canadian Sovereignty* (Toronto: U of Toronto P, 2004).

23. Tom Hendry, "MTC: A View from the Beginning," *Canadian Theatre Review* 4 (Fall 1974): 16.

24. See Fraidie Martz and Andrew Wilson, *A Fiery Soul: The Life and Theatrical Times of John Hirsch* (Montreal: Véhicule, 2011).

25. Jamie Portman, "*Ecstasy of Rita Joe* Still Manages to Shock and Scourge," *Vancouver Province* (12 April 1976): 10. Cf. Neil Carson, "Towards a Popular Theatre in English Canada," *Canadian Literature* 85 (Summer 1980): 64–65.

26. David Gustafson, "Let's Really Hear It for Canadian Theatre," *Maclean's* 84 (Oct. 1971): 84.

27. George Ryga, "Contemporary Theatre and Its Language," *Canadian Theatre Review* 14 (Spring 1977): 8.

28. Quoted verbatim from a series of interviews with artistic directors of regional theatres in *The Stage in Canada*: Edward Gilbert (Manitoba Theatre Centre), 3 (May 1967), 14; Robert Glenn (Citadel [Edmonton]), 3 (June 1967), 7; Joy Coghill (Vancouver Playhouse), 3 (Sept. 1967), 10; Kurt Reis (MTC), 5 (Nov. 1969), 13.

29. See Bryan D. Palmer, *Canada's 1960s: The Ironies of Identity in a Rebellious Era* (Toronto: U of Toronto P, 2009); Benson & Conolly, *English-Canadian Theatre*, Ch. 3; James Hoffman, *The Ecstasy of Resistance: A Biography of George Ryga* (Toronto: ECW, 1995); Erin Hurley, *National Performance: Representing Quebec from Expo 67 to Céline Dion* (Toronto: U of Toronto P, 2011), Ch. 3–4.

30. Martin Kinch, "The Canadian Theatre: In for the Long Haul," *This Magazine* 10 (Nov.–Dec. 1976): 4–5.

31. Qtd in Robert Wallace, "Growing Pains: Toronto Theatre in the 1970s," *Canadian Literature* 85 (Summer 1980): 77. Cf. Johnston, *Up the Mainstream*.

32. See Neil Carson, *Harlequin in Hogtown: George Luscombe and Toronto Workshop Productions* (Toronto: U of Toronto P, 1995). For Thompson and Theatre Passe Muraille, see Alan Filewod, *Collective Encounters: Documentary Theatre in English Canada* (Toronto: U of Toronto P, 1987), Ch. 1–2; Denis Johnston, *Up the Mainstream: The Rise of Toronto's Alternative Theatres, 1968–1975* (Toronto: U of Toronto P, 1991); Diane Bessai, *Playwrights of Collective Creation* (Toronto: Simon & Pierre, 1992); Judith Rudakoff, ed., *Dangerous Traditions: A Passe Muraille Anthology* (Winnipeg: Blizzard, 1992).

33. George Ryga, "Theatre in Canada: A Viewpoint on Its Development and Future," *Canadian Theatre Review* 1 (Winter 1974): 30; rpt. Rubin, ed., *Canadian Theatre History*, 340.

34. Bill Thomas in the *Times Colonist* (Victoria), quoted in "Playwrights," *The Stage in Canada* 6 (Jan. 1972): 17.

35. Coulter, 123.

36. Alan Filewod, "Between Empires: Post-Imperialism and Canadian Theatre," *Essays in Theatre* 11 (Nov. 1992): 11.

37. Sky Gilbert, "Gotta Sing, Gotta Dance, Gotta Cry," *Globe and Mail* (3 Nov. 1997): C1.

GEORGE
RYGA

1932–1987

"Playwright George Ryga Thursday night peeled a cicatrice off Canadian society and showed the bleeding flesh beneath." Reviewing the first performance of *The Ecstasy of Rita Joe* in November 1967, *Vancouver Sun* critic Jack Richards zeroed in on the nasty, unacknowledged wound of Canadian racism that Ryga's play revealed to its stunned opening night audience. In his eloquent "Lament for Confederation," a speech he gave in Vancouver on July 1, 1967, Canada's hundredth birthday, Coast Salish Chief Dan George had publicly challenged the self-congratulatory nature of the Centennial celebrations: "in the long hundred years since the white man came, I have seen my freedom disappear like the salmon going mysteriously out to sea ... When I fought to protect my life and my home, I was called a savage ... My nation was ignored in your history textbooks ... I was ridiculed in your plays and motion pictures... Oh Canada, how can I celebrate with you this Centenary...?" For First Nations people, their wounds still open, their scars still raw, there seemed little to celebrate. Ryga's play bluntly and powerfully reinforced that message – not least because Dan George, one of Canada's best-known actors and its most respected Aboriginal spokesman, played the key role of Rita's father, David Joe, in the Vancouver production as well as in the remounts in Ottawa and Washington that followed. *The Ecstasy of Rita Joe* would go on to be both an important political consciousness-raiser and an enduring Canadian theatrical classic.

Richards's review also identified an essential quality of Ryga's work that proved to be one of his major strengths and most serious difficulties as a writer and public figure. With stubborn integrity and single-mindedness, Ryga made a career of tearing at sensitive wounds, often stirring up controversy and making himself unpopular in the process. Outspoken, abrasive, and always fiercely committed to social justice and the defence of human dignity, he created an impressive body of dramatic work that is less well known than it should be in Canada.

Ryga gave warning of his uncompromising political views soon after leaving the Ukrainian community in northern Alberta where he had grown up. At the Banff School of Fine Arts in 1950, he was barred from future scholarships for writing a poem critical of the Korean War. Three years later, he lost his job at an Edmonton radio station because of his public protests against the Cold War trial and subsequent execution for treason of Ethel and Julius Rosenberg in the United States. When in 1962, after a decade of poetry and fiction, Ryga turned his hand to drama, the imprint of his convictions was immediately clear.

His first play, *Indian*, written for television, is an austere, powerful work that announced a remarkable dramatic talent. The nameless Indian of the title initially seems a stereotype but gradually reveals a desperate humanity in whose light his white employer and the complacent government agent (a recurrent character type in Ryga's work) seem bloodless ciphers. The abrupt plunges into memory that punctuate the naturalism of *Indian* look forward to the more sophisticated stylization of Ryga's stage plays. The tone of combined anger and sadness would mark the best of Ryga's work to come.

In 1963, Ryga settled permanently in Summerland, British Columbia. After publishing two novels about the harshness of prairie life, *Hungry Hills* (1963) and *Ballad of a Stonepicker* (1966), he was commissioned to write a Centennial play for the Vancouver Playhouse. *The Ecstasy of Rita Joe* was the result. He followed it with the commercially successful *Grass and Wild Strawberries* (1969), a multimedia exploration of the conflict between 1960s youth culture and the adult establishment. When his third commission from the Playhouse coincided with Quebec's October Crisis in 1970, Ryga reshaped his work-in-progress into a confrontation between a government mandarin and the terrorist holding him hostage. Upset by the script, the Playhouse board refused to produce it, scheduling instead a Neil Simon play and firing artistic director David Gardner. Months of bitter public controversy ensued, and for a short time *Captives of the Faceless Drummer* (1971) became a *cause célèbre*. But long after the play was forgotten, the bitterness lingered and Ryga became increasingly alienated from the mainstream of Canadian theatre.

Ryga's subsequent plays were produced in the relative obscurity of Banff – *Sunrise on Sarah* (1972) and *Portrait of Angelica* (1977); Edmonton's Theatre Network – *Seven Hours to Sundown* (1977); Western Canada Theatre Company in Kamloops – *Ploughmen of the Glacier* (1977); Kam Theatre Lab of North Bay, Ontario – the excellent *A Letter to My Son* (1984); and Vancouver's Firehall Theatre – *One More for the Road* (1985). Few of the larger theatre companies have ever done any of his work except *Rita Joe*. One of his most ambitious plays, *Paracelsus*, first published in 1974, didn't receive a professional production until 1986.

Ryga wrote two more novels, *Night Desk* (1976) and *In the Shadow of the Vulture* (1985), and a book about his trip to China, *Beyond the Crimson Morning* (1979). Two volumes of his uncollected writings were published after his 1987 death. *The Athabasca Ryga* (1990) and *Summerland* (1992) include stories, essays, TV and radio plays, and his last poem. A volume of sixteen of his plays, other than *The Ecstasy of Rita Joe*, was published as *The Other Plays* (2004). *Hungry Hills, Ballad of a Stonepicker*, and *Night Desk* were republished in a one-volume edition as *The Prairie Novels* (2004), and a film version of *Hungry Hills*, titled *George Ryga's Hungry Hills*, was produced in 2009. Ryga's Summerland home became a writers' retreat called The Ryga Centre in 1996, and since 2004 the George Ryga Award for Social Awareness in Literature has been given annually to a British

Columbia writer. In 2009, Okanagan College founded a literary journal called *Ryga: A Journal of Provocations.*

For much of his career, Ryga's work was more popular on radio and stages in Europe than in Canada. This may in part reflect the European sensibility in his writing, especially *The Ecstasy of Rita Joe*. The quality of Rita's suffering, her passivity, and sense of spiritual homelessness are evocative of Dostoevsky (whom Ryga claimed to have read in full). The nightmarishness of Rita's experience, her feelings of entrapment and unaccountable guilt have roots that go back through Kafka to early Expressionist drama – to Georg Büchner's *Woyzeck* and Eugene O'Neill's *The Hairy Ape*. Rita takes her place in that tradition: the outsider perceived as a freak, struggling to preserve her integrity in the face of a system socially and politically designed to frustrate her every attempt to make sense of her life; struggling to avoid internalizing the guilt imposed by a world that grows increasingly monstrous until it completes its inevitable process of destruction.

Central to Rita's torment is the cultural and epistemological schism between whites and Native people, represented in its extreme form by the contrast between the Magistrate's mechanical, life-denying pseudo-rationalism and the humane, intuitive impressionism of David Joe (perhaps excessively romanticized – there are definite traces of the Noble Savage in his character). These ways of seeing and understanding the world are so fundamentally different that the results of their clashes are sometimes comical. When Rita claims to have seen God in the sky, she is told to call the Air Force. When Jaimie Paul sees a TV commercial that shows a knife "cutting up good shoes like they were potatoes," he reacts with comic bewilderment (edged with the bitter irony that he and Rita have nothing to eat). But Rita's inability to assimilate is also the real crime of which the white Witnesses, the Teacher and Priest, the Magistrate, and Mr. Homer take turns accusing her. In court, while the Magistrate rambles on about "the process of legal argument," Rita asks him if she can bum a cigarette; in the stage direction, the Policeman "smiles and exits" – he rests his case. Later, the Magistrate tells Rita, "the obstacles to your life are here … in your thoughts … possibly even in your culture," and he suggests that she fix her hair, tame her accent, "perhaps even change your name."

But Rita won't be helped and can't be saved. She certainly gets no help from the hollow paternalism of the Priest, the Magistrate, or the ironically named Mr. Homer. Nor can Rita be aided by her own father. For all the sympathy Ryga invests in him, David Joe is impotent to save his people, just as Jaimie Paul says. When her father comes to take Rita home to the reserve from the city, she refuses to go. Rita is trapped. The rural past, though pastoral in her memory, she knows is a dead end. The urban present holds only degradation and the promise of an early death. And what about the future? The circular ramp that comprises the set, according to the stage directions, traces Rita's futile journey through the play; the shadowy Murderers who appear and reappear symbolize her doom, immanent from the start; the Brechtian Singer who sings of the fate of Rita and Jaimie forecloses any hope of salvation. The one rich fantasy she and

Jaimie indulge turns quickly sour: their dream of having children in the city collides with the ugly fact that Clara Hill has had to give her children away. The scene that begins with the implied promise of lovemaking in Jaimie's room ends in frustration, disgust, and despair. Like all tragedies, the ending holds at least a suggestion of hope for the future, in the protest and implied resistance of Eileen and the young Indian men.

But is Rita Joe tragic? Does she retain something of her selfhood with a stubborn persistence that somehow transforms her death from a sordid ritual of rape and murder into the "ecstasy" of a martyr? Or is she a passive victim doomed by birth, culture, and her own resignation? The play's articulation of these questions is complicated by the problems inherent in a white male writer's depiction of an Aboriginal woman's experience – a character represented onstage in the original production by classically trained white actress Frances Hyland. That Native actors Dan George and August Schellenberg had major roles was a sign of some progress at the time. Not until 1981, however, would a production of the play use Aboriginal performers in all the Native roles, with Margo Kane as Rita and Tom Jackson as Jaimie. By the mid-1980s, an increasingly strong contingent of First Nations actors and playwrights would begin telling their theatrical stories themselves.

George Ryga's probing of this terrible wound near the heart of Canadian society, radical in 1967, continues to resonate with its own dark truths. This was made clear in two celebrated fortieth-anniversary productions, at Vancouver's Firehall Arts Centre in 2007 and in a Western Canada Theatre / National Arts Centre co-production in 2009. Both starred Lisa C. Ravensbergen as Rita; in the latter production August Schellenberg returned to the play, this time as David Joe.

The Ecstasy of Rita Joe

George Ryga

The Ecstasy of Rita Joe opened at the Vancouver Playhouse Theatre on November 23, 1967, with the following cast:

RITA JOE	Frances Hyland
JAIMIE PAUL	August Schellenberg
DAVID JOE	Chief Dan George
MAGISTRATE	Henry Ramer
MR. HOMER	Walter Marsh
PRIEST	Robert Clothier
EILEEN JOE	Patricia Gage
OLD INDIAN WOMAN	Rae Brown
TEACHER	Claudine Melgrave
POLICEMAN	Bill Clarkson
WITNESS, MURDERER	Merv Campone
WITNESS, MURDERER	Alex Bruhanski
WITNESS	Jack Leaf
MURDERER	Jack Buttrey
YOUNG INDIAN MEN	Leonard George
	Robert Hall
	Frank Lewis
	Paul Stanley
GUITARIST	Willy Dunn
SINGER	Ann Mortifee

Directed by George Bloomfield
Set and Lighting Design by Charles Evans
Costume Design by Margaret Ryan
Music by Willy Dunn and Ann Mortifee
Lyrics by George Ryga
Choreography by Norbert Vesak

CHARACTERS

RITA JOE
JAIMIE PAUL
DAVID JOE, *Rita's father*
MAGISTRATE
MR. HOMER
FATHER ANDREW, *a priest*
EILEEN JOE, *Rita's sister*
OLD INDIAN WOMAN
MISS DONOHUE, *a teacher*
POLICEMAN
WITNESSES
MURDERERS
YOUNG INDIAN MEN
SINGER

SET

*A circular ramp beginning at floor level stage left and continuing downward below floor level at stage front, then rising and sweeping along stage back at two-foot elevation to disappear in the wings of stage left. This ramp dominates the stage by wrapping the central and forward playing area. A short approach ramp, meeting with the main ramp at stage right, expedites entrances from the wings of stage right. The **MAGISTRATE**'s chair and representation of court desk are situated at stage right, enclosed within the sweep of the ramp. At the foot of the desk is a lip onstage right side. The **SINGER** sits here, turned away from the focus of the play. Her songs and accompaniment appear almost accidental. She has all the reactions of a white liberal folklorist with a limited concern and understanding of an ethnic dilemma, which she touches in the course of her research and work in compiling and writing folk songs. She serves, too, as an alter ego to **RITA JOE**.*

*No curtain is used during the play. At the opening, intermission, and conclusion of the play, the curtain remains up. The onus for isolating scenes from the past and present in **RITA JOE**'s life falls on highlight lighting.*

Backstage, there is a mountain cyclorama. In front of the cyclorama there is a darker maze curtain to suggest gloom and confusion, and a cityscape.

ACT ONE

The house lights and stage work lights remain on. Backstage, cyclorama, and maze curtains are up, revealing wall back of stage, exit doors, etc.

CAST and SINGER enter offstage singly and in pairs from the wings, from the exit doors at the back of the theatre, and from the auditorium side doors. The entrances are workmanlike and untheatrical. When all the CAST is onstage, they turn to face the audience momentarily. The house lights dim.

The cyclorama is lowered into place. The maze curtain follows. This creates a sense of compression of stage into the auditorium. Recorded voices are heard in a jumble of mutterings and throat clearings. The MAGISTRATE enters as the CLERK begins.

CLERK: (*recorded*) This court is in session. All present will rise ...

The shuffling and scraping of furniture is heard. The CAST repeat "Rita Joe, Rita Joe." A POLICEMAN brings on RITA JOE.

MAGISTRATE: Who is she? Can she speak English?

POLICEMAN: Yes.

MAGISTRATE: Then let her speak for herself!

He speaks to the audience firmly and with reason.

MAGISTRATE: To understand life in a given society, one must understand laws of that society. All relationships ...

CLERK: (*recorded*) Man to man ... man to woman ... man to property ... man to the state ...

MAGISTRATE: ... are determined and enriched by laws that have grown out of social realities. The quality of the law under which you live and function determines the real quality of the freedom that was yours today.

The rest of the CAST slowly move out.

MAGISTRATE: Your home and your well-being were protected. The roads of the city are open to us. So are the galleries, libraries, the administrative and public buildings. There are buses, trains ...

going in and coming out. Nobody is a prisoner here.

RITA: (*with humour, almost a sad sigh*) The first time I tried to go home I was picked up by some men who gave me five dollars. An' then they arrested me.

The POLICEMAN retreats into the shadows. The SINGER crosses down.

MAGISTRATE: Thousands leave and enter the city every day ...

RITA: It wasn't true what they said, but nobody'd believe me ...

SINGER: (*singing a recitivo searching for a melody*)
Will the winds not blow
My words to her
Like the seeds
Of the dandelion?

MAGISTRATE: (*smiling, as at a private joke*) Once ... I saw a little girl in the Cariboo country. It was summer then and she wore only a blouse and skirt. I wondered what she wore in winter?

The MURDERERS hover in the background on the upper ramp. One whistles and one lights a cigarette – an action which will be repeated at the end of the play.

RITA: (*moving to him, but hesitating*) You look like a good man. Tell them to let me go, please!

The MAGISTRATE goes to his podium.

MAGISTRATE: Our nation is on an economic par with the state of Arkansas ... We are a developing country, but a buoyant one. Still ... the summer report of the Economic Council of Canada predicts a reduction in the gross national product unless we utilize our manpower for greater efficiency. Employed, happy people make for a prosperous, happy nation ...

RITA: (*exultantly*) I worked at some jobs, mister!

The MAGISTRATE turns to face RITA JOE. The MURDERERS have gone.

MAGISTRATE: Gainful employment. Obedience to the law ...

RITA: (*to the MAGISTRATE*) Once I had a job ...

He does not relate to her. She is troubled. She talks to the audience.

RITA: Once I had a job in a tire store ... an' I'd worry about what time my boss would come ... He was always late ... and so was everybody. Sometimes I got to thinkin' what would happen if he'd not come. And nobody else would come. And I'd be all day in this big room with no lights on an' the telephone ringing an' people asking for other people that weren't there ... What would happen?

As she relates her concern, she laughs. Toward the end of her monologue she is so amused by the absurdity of it all that she can hardly contain herself.

Lights fade on the MAGISTRATE who broods in his chair as he examines his court papers.

Lights up on JAIMIE PAUL approaching on the backstage ramp from stage left. He is jubilant, his laughter blending with her laughter. At the sound of his voice, RITA JOE runs to him, to the memory of him.

JAIMIE: I seen the city today and I seen things today I never knew was there, Rita Joe!

RITA: (*happily*) I seen them too, Jaimie Paul!

He pauses above her, his mood light and childlike.

JAIMIE: I see a guy on top of a bridge, talkin' to himself ... an' lots of people on the beach watchin' harbour seals ... Kids feed popcorn to seagulls ... an' I think to myself ... Boy! Pigeons eat pretty good here!

RITA: In the morning, Jaimie Paul ... very early in the morning ... the air is cold like at home ...

JAIMIE: Pretty soon I seen a little woman walkin' a big black dog on a rope ... Dog is mad ... Dog wants a man!

JAIMIE PAUL moves to RITA JOE. They embrace.

RITA: Clouds are red over the city in the morning. Clara Hill says to me, "If you're real happy ... the clouds make you forget you're not home ..."

They laugh together. JAIMIE PAUL breaks from her. He punctuates his story with wide, sweeping gestures.

JAIMIE: I start singin' and some hotel windows open. I wave to them, but nobody waves back! They're watchin' me, like I was a harbour seal! (*He laughs.*) So I stopped singin'!

RITA: I remember colours, but I've forgot faces already ...

JAIMIE PAUL looks at her as her mood changes. Faint light on the MAGISTRATE brightens.

RITA: A train whistle is white, with black lines ... A sick man talkin' is brown like an overcoat with pockets torn an' string showin' ... A sad woman is a room with the curtains shut ...

MAGISTRATE: Rita Joe?

She becomes sobered, but JAIMIE PAUL continues laughing. She nods to the MAGISTRATE, then turns to JAIMIE PAUL.

RITA: Them bastards put me in jail. They're gonna do it again, they said ... Them bastards!

JAIMIE: Guys who sell newspapers don't see nothin' ...

RITA: They drive by me, lookin' ...

JAIMIE: I'm gonna be a carpenter!

RITA: I walk like a stick, tryin' to keep my ass from showin' because I know what they're thinkin' ... Them bastards!

JAIMIE: I got myself boots an' a new shirt ... See!

RITA: (*worried now*) I thought their jail was on fire ... I thought it was burning.

JAIMIE: Room I got costs me seven bucks a week ...

RITA: I can't leave town. Every time I try, they put me in jail.

A POLICEMAN enters with a file folder.

JAIMIE: They say it's a pretty good room for seven bucks a week ...

JAIMIE PAUL begins to retreat backward from her, along the ramp to the wings of stage left. She is isolated in a pool of light away from the MAGISTRATE. The isolation between her and JAIMIE PAUL deepens, as the scene turns into the courtroom again.

MAGISTRATE: Vagrancy ... You are charged with vagrancy.

JAIMIE: (*with enthusiasm, boyishly*) First hundred bucks I make, Rita Joe ... I'm gonna buy a car so I can take you every place!

RITA: (*moving after him*) Jaimie!

He retreats, dream-like, into the wings. The spell of memory between them is broken. Pools of light between her and the MAGISTRATE spread and fuse into a single light area. She turns to the MAGISTRATE, worried and confused.

MAGISTRATE: (*reading the documents in his hand*) The charge against you this morning is vagrancy ...

The MAGISTRATE continues studying the papers he holds. She looks up at him and shakes her head helplessly, then blurts out to him.

RITA: I had to spend last night in jail ... Did you know?

MAGISTRATE: Yes. You were arrested.

RITA: I didn't know when morning came ... there was no windows ... The jail stinks! People in jail stink!

MAGISTRATE: (*indulgently*) Are you surprised?

RITA: I didn't know anybody there ... People in jail stink like paper that's been in the rain too long. But a jail stinks worse. It stinks of rust ... an' old hair ...

MAGISTRATE: (*looking down at her for the first time*) You ... are Rita Joe?

She nods quickly. A faint concern shows in his face. He watches her for a long moment.

MAGISTRATE: I know your face ... yet ... it wasn't in this courtroom. Or was it?

RITA: I don't know ...

MAGISTRATE: (*pondering*) Have you appeared before me in the past year?

RITA: (*turning away from him, shrugging*) I don't know. I can't remember ...

The MAGISTRATE throws his head back and laughs. The POLICEMAN joins in.

MAGISTRATE: You can't remember? Come now ...

RITA: (*laughing with him and looking to the POLICEMAN*) I can't remember ...

MAGISTRATE: Then I take it you haven't appeared before me. Certainly you and I would remember if you had.

RITA: (*smiling*) I don't remember ...

The MAGISTRATE makes some hurried notes, but he is watching RITA JOE, formulating his next thought.

RITA: (*naively*) My sister hitchhiked home an' she had no trouble like I ...

MAGISTRATE: You'll need witnesses, Rita Joe. I'm only giving you eight hours to find witnesses for yourself ...

RITA: Jaimie knows ...

She turns to where JAIMIE PAUL had been, but the back of the stage is in darkness. The POLICEMAN exits suddenly.

RITA: Jaimie knew ...

Her voice trails off pathetically. The MAGISTRATE shrugs and returns to studying his notes. RITA JOE chafes during the silence that follows. She craves communion with people, with the MAGISTRATE.

RITA: My sister was a dressmaker, mister! But she only worked two weeks in the city ... An' then she got sick and went back to the reserve to help my father catch fish an' cut pulpwood. (*smiling*) She's not coming back ... that's for sure!

MAGISTRATE: (*with interest*) Should I know your sister? What was her name?

RITA: Eileen Joe.

EILEEN JOE appears spotlit behind, a memory crowding in.

MAGISTRATE: Eileen ... that's a soft, undulating name.

RITA: Two weeks, and not one white woman came to her to leave an order or old clothes for her to fix. No work at all for two weeks, an' her money ran out ... Isn't that funny?

MAGISTRATE: (*again studying RITA JOE, his mind elsewhere*) Hmmmmm ...

EILEEN JOE disappears.

RITA: So she went back to the reserve to catch fish an' cut pulpwood!

MAGISTRATE: I do know your face ... yes! And yet ...

RITA: Can I sit someplace?

MAGISTRATE: (*excited*) I remember now ... Yes! I was on holidays three summers back in the Cariboo country ... driving over this road with not a house or field in sight ... just barren land, wild and windblown. And then I saw this child beside the road, dressed in a blouse and skirt, barefooted ...

RITA: (*looking around*) I don't feel so good, mister.

MAGISTRATE: My God, she wasn't more than three or four years old ... walking toward me beside the road. When I'd passed her, I stopped my car and then turned around and drove back to where I'd seen her, for I wondered what she could possibly be doing in such a lonely country at that age without her father or mother walking with her ...

When I got back to where I'd seen her, she had disappeared. She was nowhere to be seen. Yet the land was flat for over a mile in every direction ... I had to see her. But I couldn't ... (*He stares down at RITA JOE for a long moment.*) You see, what I was going to say was that this child had your face! Isn't that strange?

RITA: (*with disinterest*) Sure, if you think so, mister ...

MAGISTRATE: Could she have been ... your daughter?

RITA: What difference does it make?

MAGISTRATE: Children cannot be left like that ... It takes money to raise children in the woods as in the cities ... There are institutions and people with more money than you who could ...

RITA: Nobody would get my child, mister!

She is distracted by EILEEN JOE's voice in her memory. EILEEN's voice begins in darkness, but as she speaks a spotlight isolates her in front of the ramp, stage left. EILEEN is on her hands and knees, two buckets beside her. She is picking berries in mime.

EILEEN: First was the strawberries an' then the blueberries. After the frost ... we picked the cranberries ... (*She laughs with delight.*)

RITA: (*pleading with the MAGISTRATE, but her attention on EILEEN*) Let me go, mister ...

MAGISTRATE: I can't let you go. I don't think that would be of any use in the circumstances. Would you like a lawyer?

Even as he speaks, RITA JOE has entered the scene with EILEEN picking berries. The MAGISTRATE's light fades on his podium.

RITA: You ate the strawberries an' blueberries because you were always a hungry kid!

EILEEN: But not cranberries! They made my stomach hurt.

RITA JOE goes down on her knees with EILEEN.

RITA: Let me pick ... You rest. (*holding out the bucket to EILEEN*) Mine's full already ... Let's change. You rest ...

During the exchange of buckets, EILEEN notices her hands are larger than RITA JOE's. She is both delighted and surprised by this.

EILEEN: My hands are bigger than yours, Rita ... Look! (*taking RITA JOE's hands in hers*) When did my hands grow so big?

RITA: (*wisely and sadly*) You've worked so hard ... I'm older than you, Leenie ... I will always be older.

The two sisters are thoughtful for a moment, each watching the other in silence. Then RITA JOE becomes animated and resumes her mime of picking berries in the woods.

RITA: We picked lots of wild berries when we were kids, Leenie!

They turn away from their work and lie down alongside each other, facing the front of the stage. The light on them becomes summery, warm.

RITA: In the summer, it was hot an' flies hummed so loud you'd go to sleep if you sat down an' just listened.

EILEEN: The leaves on the poplars used to turn black an' curl together with the heat ...

RITA: One day you and I were pickin' blueberries and a big storm came ...

A sudden crash of thunder and a lightning flash. The lights turn cold and blue. The three MURDERERS stand in silhouette on a riser behind them. EILEEN cringes in fear, afraid of the storm, aware of the presence of the MURDERERS behind them. RITA JOE springs to her feet, her being attached to the wildness of the atmosphere. Lightning continues to flash and flicker.

EILEEN: Oh no!

RITA: (*shouting*) It got cold and the rain an' hail came ... the sky falling!

EILEEN: (*crying in fear*) Rita!

RITA: (*laughing, shouting*) Stay there!

A high flash of lightning silhouettes the MURDERERS harshly. They take a step forward on the lightning flash. EILEEN dashes into the arms of RITA JOE. She screams and drags RITA JOE down with her. RITA JOE struggles against EILEEN.

RITA: Let me go! What in hell's wrong with you? Let me go!

MAGISTRATE: I can't let you go.

The lightning dies, but the thunder rumbles off into the distance. EILEEN subsides, and pressing herself into the arms of RITA JOE as a small child to her mother, she sobs quietly.

RITA: There, there ... (*with infinite tenderness*) You said to me, "What would happen if the storm hurt us an' we can't find our way home, but are lost together so far away in the bush?"

EILEEN looks up, brushing away her tears and smiling at RITA JOE.

RITA & EILEEN: (*in unison*) Would you be my mother then?

RITA: Would I be your mother?

RITA JOE releases EILEEN, who looks back fearfully to where the MURDERERS had stood. They are gone. She rises and, collecting the buckets, moves hesitantly to where they had been. Confident now, she laughs softly and nervously to herself and leaves the stage. RITA JOE rises and talks to EILEEN as she departs.

RITA: We walked home through the mud an' icy puddles among the trees. At first you cried, Leenie ... and then you wanted to sleep. But I held you up an' when we got home you said you were sure you would've died in the bush if it hadn't been for us being together like that.

EILEEN disappears from the stage. The MAGISTRATE's light comes up. RITA JOE shakes her head sadly at the memory, then comes forward to the apron of the stage. She is proud of her sister, and her next speech reveals this pride.

RITA: She made a blouse for me that I wore every day for one year, an' it never ripped at the armpits like the blouse I buy in the store does the first time I stretch. (*She stretches languidly.*) I like to stretch when I'm happy! It makes all the happiness go through me like warm water ...

The PRIEST, the TEACHER, and a YOUNG INDIAN MAN cross the stage directly behind her. The PRIEST wears a Roman collar and the checked bush jacket of a worker-priest. He pauses before passing RITA JOE and goes to meet her.

PRIEST: Rita Joe? When did you get back? How's life?

RITA: (*shrugs noncommittally*) You know me, Father Andrew ... could be better, could be worse ...

PRIEST: Are you still working?

She smiles at him. Her gestures are not definite.

RITA: (*still noncommittal.*) I live.

PRIEST: (*serious and concerned*) It's not easy, is it?

RITA: Not always.

The TEACHER and the YOUNG INDIAN MAN exit.

PRIEST: A lot of things are different in the city. It's easier here on the reserve ... life is simpler. You can be yourself. That's important to remember.

RITA: Yes, Father ...

The PRIEST wants to ask and say more, but he cannot. An awkward moment between them and he reaches out to touch her shoulder gently.

PRIEST: Well ... be a good girl, Rita Joe ...

RITA: (*without turning after him*) Goodbye, Father.

MAGISTRATE: (*more insistently*) Do you want a lawyer?

The PRIEST leaves stage right. As he leaves, cross light to where a happy JAIMIE PAUL enters from stage left. JAIMIE PAUL comes down to join RITA JOE.

JAIMIE: This guy asked me how much education I got, an' I says to him, "Grade six. How much education a man need for such a job?" ... An' the bum, he says it's not good enough! I should take night school. But I got the job, an' I start next Friday ... like this ...

JAIMIE PAUL does a mock sweeping routine as if he was cleaning a vast office building. He and RITA JOE are both laughing.

JAIMIE: Pretty good, eh?

RITA: Pretty good.

JAIMIE: Cleaning the floors an' desks in the building ... But it's a government job, and that's good for life. Work hard, then the government give me a raise ... I never had a job like that before ...

RITA: When I sleep happy, I dream of blueberries an' sun an' all the nice things when I was a little kid, Jaimie Paul.

The sound of an airplane is heard. JAIMIE PAUL looks up. RITA JOE also stares into the sky of her memory. JAIMIE PAUL's face is touched with pain and recollection. The TEACHER, RITA JOE's FATHER, an OLD WOMAN, four YOUNG INDIAN MEN, and EILEEN JOE come into the background quietly, as if at a wharf watching the airplane leave the village. They stand looking up until the noise of the aircraft begins to diminish.

JAIMIE: That airplane ... a Cessna ... (*He continues watching the aircraft and turns, following its flight path.*) She said to me, maybe I never see you again, Jaimie Paul.

There is a faint light on the MAGISTRATE in his chair. He is thoughtful, looking down at his hands.

MAGISTRATE: Do you want a lawyer?

RITA: (*to JAIMIE PAUL*) Who?

JAIMIE: Your mother ... I said to her, they'll fix you up good in the hospital. Better than before ... It was a Cessna that landed on the river an' took her away ... Maybe I never see you again, Jaimie, she says to me. She knew she was gonna die, but I was a kid and so were you ... What the hell did we know? I'll never forget ...

JAIMIE PAUL joins the village group on the upper level.

SINGER: (*singing an indefinite melody developing into a square-dance tune*)

There was a man in a beat-up hat
Who runs a house in the middle of town,
An' round his stovepipe chimney house
The magpies sat, just a-lookin' round.

The Indian village people remain in the back of the stage, still watching the airplane that has vanished. JAIMIE PAUL, on his way, passes MR. HOMER, a white citizen who has the hurried but fulfilled appearance of the socially responsible man. MR. HOMER comes to the front of the stage beside RITA JOE. He talks directly to the audience.

MR. HOMER: Sure, we do a lot of things for our Indians here in the city at the Centre ... Bring 'em in from the cold an' give them food ... The rest ... well, the rest kinda takes care of itself.

RITA JOE lowers her head and looks away from him. MR. HOMER moves to her and places his hand on her shoulders possessively.

MR. HOMER: When your mother got sick we flew her out ... You remember that, Rita Joe?

RITA: (*nodding, looking down*) Yes, Mr. Homer ... Thank you.

MR. HOMER: And we sent her body back for the funeral ... Right, Rita Joe?

The people of the village leave except for the YOUNG INDIAN MEN who remain and mime drinking.

MR. HOMER: And then sometimes a man drinks it up an' leaves his wife an' kids and the poor dears come here for help. We give them food an' a place to sleep ... Right, Rita?

RITA: Yes.

MR. HOMER: Clothes, too ... White people leave clothes here for the Indians to take if they need 'em. Used to have them all up on racks over there ... just like in a store ... (*pointing*) But now we got them all on a heap on a table in the basement. (*He laughs and RITA JOE nods with him.*) Indian people ... 'specially the women ... get more of a kick diggin' through stuff that's piled up like that ...

MR. HOMER chuckles and shakes his head. There is a pale light on the MAGISTRATE, who is still looking down at his hands.

MAGISTRATE: There are institutions to help you ...

MR. HOMER: (*again speaking to the audience, but now angry over some personal beef*) So you see, the Centre serves a need that's real for Indians who come to the city. (*wagging his finger at the audience angrily*) It's the do-gooders burn my ass, you know! They come in from television or the newspaper ... hang around just long enough to see a drunken Indian ... an' bingo!

JAIMIE: Bingo!

MR. HOMER: That's their story! Next thing, they're seeing some kind of Red Power ...

The YOUNG INDIAN MEN laugh and RITA JOE gets up to join them.

MR. HOMER: ... or beatin' the government over the head! Let them live an' work among the Indians for a few months ... then they'd know what it's really like ...

The music comes up sharply.

SINGER: (*singing*)

Round and round the cenotaph,
The clumsy seagulls play.
Fed by funny men with hats
Who watch them night and day.

The four YOUNG INDIAN MEN join with RITA JOE and dance. Leading the group is JAIMIE PAUL. He is drunk, dishevelled. Light spreads before them as they advance onstage. They are laughing rowdily. RITA JOE moves to them.

RITA: Jaimie Paul?

MR. HOMER leaves. JAIMIE PAUL is overtaken by two of his companions who take him by the arms, but he pushes them roughly away.

JAIMIE: Get the hell outa my way! ... I'm as good a man as him any time ... (*crossing downstage to confront a member of the audience*) You know me? ... You think I'm a dirty Indian, eh? Get outa my way! (*He puts his hands over his head and continues staggering away.*) Goddammit, I wanna sleep ...

The YOUNG INDIAN MEN and JAIMIE PAUL exit. RITA JOE follows after JAIMIE PAUL, reaching out to touch him, but the SINGER stands in her way and drives her back, singing.

Music up tempo and volume.

SINGER: (*singing*)

Oh, can't you see that train roll on,
Its hot black wheels keep comin' on?
A Kamloops Indian died today.
Train didn't hit him, he just fell.
Busy train with wheels on fire!

The music dies. A POLICEMAN enters.

POLICEMAN: Rita Joe!

He repeats her name many times. The TEACHER enters ringing the school handbell and crosses through.

TEACHER: (*calling*) Rita Joe! Rita Joe! Didn't you hear the bell ring? The class is waiting ... The class is always waiting for you. (*She exits.*)

MAGISTRATE & POLICEMAN: (*sharply, in unison*) Rita Joe!

The POLICEMAN grabs and shakes RITA JOE to snap her out of her reverie.

Light up on the MAGISTRATE who sits erect, with authority.

MAGISTRATE: I ask you for the last time, Rita Joe ... Do you want a lawyer?

RITA: (*defiantly*) What for? ... I can take care of myself.

MAGISTRATE: The charge against you this morning is prostitution. Why did you not return to your people as you said you would?

The light on the backstage dies. RITA JOE stands before the MAGISTRATE and the POLICEMAN. She is contained in a pool of light before them.

RITA: (*nervous, with despair*) I tried ... I tried ...

MAGISTRATE: (*settling back into his chair and taking a folder from his desk, which he opens and studies*) Special Constable Eric Wilson has submitted a statement to the effect that on June 18th he and Special Constable Schneider approached you on Fourth Avenue at nine forty in the evening ...

POLICEMAN: We were impersonating two deckhands newly arrived in the city ...

MAGISTRATE: You were arrested an hour later on charges of prostitution.

The MAGISTRATE holds the folder threateningly and looks down at her. RITA JOE is defiant.

RITA: That's a goddamned lie!

MAGISTRATE: (*sternly, gesturing to the POLICEMAN*) This is a police statement. Surely you don't think a mistake was made?

RITA: (*peering into the light above her, shuddering*) Everything in this room is like ice ... How can you stay alive working here? ... I'm so hungry I want to throw up ...

MAGISTRATE: You have heard the statement, Rita Joe ... Do you deny it?

RITA: I was going home, trying to find the highway ... I knew those two were cops, the moment I saw them ... I told them to go f ... fly a kite! They got sore then an' started pushing me around ...

MAGISTRATE: (*patiently now, waving down the objections of the POLICEMAN*) Go on.

RITA: They followed me around until a third cop drove up. An' then they arrested me.

MAGISTRATE: Arrested you ... Nothing else?

RITA: They stuffed five-dollar bills in my pockets when they had me in the car ... I ask you, mister, when are they gonna charge cops like that with contributing to ...

POLICEMAN: Your worship ...

MAGISTRATE: (*irritably, indicating the folder on the table before him*) Now it's your word against this! You need references ... people who know you ... who will come to court to substantiate what you say ... today! That is the process of legal argument!

RITA: Can I bum a cigarette someplace?

MAGISTRATE: No. You can't smoke in court.

The POLICEMAN smiles and exits.

RITA: Then give me a bed to sleep on, or is the sun gonna rise an' rise until it burns a hole in my head?

Guitar music cues softly in the background.

MAGISTRATE: Tell me about the child.

RITA: What child?

MAGISTRATE: The little girl I once saw beside the road!

RITA: I don't know any girl, mister! When do I eat? Why does an Indian wait even when he's there first thing in the morning?

The pool of light tightens around the MAGISTRATE and RITA JOE.

MAGISTRATE: I have children ... two sons ...

RITA: (*nodding*) Sure. That's good.

MAGISTRATE: (*groping for words to express a message that is very precious to him*) My sons can go in any direction they wish ... into trades or university ... But if I had a daughter, I would be more concerned ...

RITA: What's so special about a girl?

MAGISTRATE: I would wish ... well, I'd be concerned about her choices ... her choices of living, school ... friends ... These things don't come as lightly for a girl. For boys it's different ... But I would worry if I had a daughter ... Don't hide your child! Someone else can be found to raise her if you can't!

RITA JOE shakes her head, a strange smile on her face.

MAGISTRATE: Why not? There are people who would love to take care of it.

RITA: Nobody would get my child ... I would sooner kill it an' bury it first! I am not a kind woman, mister judge!

MAGISTRATE: (*at a loss*) I see ...

RITA: (*a cry*) I want to go home ...

Quick up-tempo music is heard. Suddenly, the lights change.

JAIMIE PAUL and the YOUNG INDIAN MEN sweep over the backstage ramp, the light widening for them. RITA JOE moves into this railway station crowd. She turns from one man to another until she sees JAIMIE PAUL.

EILEEN JOE and an OLD WOMAN enter.

RITA: Jaimie!

EILEEN: (*happily, running to him*) Jaimie Paul! God's sakes ... When did you get back from the North? ... I thought you said you wasn't coming until breakup ...

JAIMIE: (*turning to EILEEN*) I was comin' home on the train ... had a bit to drink and was feeling pretty good ... Lots of women sleeping in their seats on the train ... I'd lift their hats an' say, "Excuse me, lady ... I'm lookin' for a wife!" (*turning to the OLD WOMAN*) One fat lady got mad, an' I says to her, "That's all right, lady ... You got no worries ... You keep sleepin'!"

Laughter.

JAIMIE PAUL and the OLD WOMAN move away. EILEEN sees RITA JOE who is standing watching.

EILEEN: Rita! ... Tom an' I broke up ... did I tell you?

RITA: No, Leenie ... you didn't tell me!

EILEEN: He was no good ... He stopped comin' to see me when he said he would. I kept waiting, but he didn't come ...

RITA: I sent you a pillow for your wedding!

EILEEN: I gave it away ... I gave it to Clara Hill.

RITA: (*laughing bawdily and miming pregnancy*) Clara Hill don't need no pillow now!

JAIMIE: (*smiling, crossing to her, and exiting*) I always came to see you, Rita Joe ...

RITA JOE looks bewildered.

OLD WOMAN: (*exiting*) I made two Saskatoon pies, Rita ... You said next time you came home you wanted Saskatoon pie with lots of sugar ...

EILEEN and the OLD WOMAN drift away. JAIMIE PAUL moves on to the shadows. The THREE MURDERERS enter in silhouette; one whistles. RITA JOE rushes to the YOUNG INDIAN MEN downstage.

RITA: This is me, Rita Joe, God's sakes ... We went to the same school together ... Don't you know me now, Johnny? You remember how tough you was when you was a boy? ... We tied you up in the Rainbow Creek and forgot you was there after recess ... An' after school was out, somebody remembered. (*laughing*) And you was blue when we got to you. Your clothes was wet to the chin, an' you said, "That's a pretty good knot ... I almost gave up trying to untie it!"

> *The music continues. RITA JOE steps among the YOUNG INDIAN MEN and they mime being piled in a car at a drive-in.*

Steve Laporte? ... You remember us goin' to the drive-in and the cold rain comin' down the car windows so we couldn't see the picture show anyhow?

> *She sits beside STEVE LAPORTE. They mime the windshield wipers.*

> *A cold white light comes up on the playing area directly in front of the MAGISTRATE's chair. A MALE WITNESS of dishevelled, dirty appearance steps into the light and delivers testimony in a whining, defensive voice. He is one of the MURDERERS, but apart from the other three he is nervous.*

FIRST WITNESS: I gave her three bucks ... an' once I got her goin' she started yellin' like hell! Called me a dog, pig ... some filthy kind of animal ... So I slapped her around a bit ... Guys said she was a funny kind of bim- ... would do it for them standing up, but not for me she wouldn't ... So I slapped her around ...

> *The MAGISTRATE nods and makes a notation. The light on the FIRST WITNESS dies. RITA JOE speaks with urgency and growing fear to STEVE LAPORTE.*

RITA: Then you shut the wipers off an' we were just sitting there, not knowing what to do ... I wish ... we could go back again there an' start livin' from that day on ... Jaimie!

> *RITA JOE looks at STEVE LAPORTE as at a stranger. She stands and draws away from him. JAIMIE PAUL enters behind RITA JOE.*

> *There is a cold light before the MAGISTRATE again and another MALE WITNESS moves into the light, replacing the FIRST WITNESS. He, too, is one of the MURDERERS. This SECOND WITNESS testifies with full gusto.*

SECOND WITNESS: Gave her a job in my tire store ... took her over to my place after work once ... She was scared when I tried a trick, but I'm easy on broads that get scared, providin' they keep their voices down ... After that, I slipped her a fiver ... Well, sir, she took the money, then she stood in front of the window, her head high an' her naked shoulders shakin' like she was cold. Well,

sir, she cried a little an' then she says, "Goddammit, but I wish I was a school teacher ..."

> *He laughs and everyone onstage joins in the laughter. The light dies out on the SECOND WITNESS. JAIMIE PAUL enters and crosses to RITA JOE. They lie down and embrace.*

RITA: You always came to see me, Jaimie Paul ... The night we were in the cemetery ... you remember, Jaimie Paul? I turned my face from yours until I saw the ground ... an' I knew that below us ... they were like us once, and now they lie below the ground, their eyes gone, the bones showin' ... They must've spoke and touched each other here ... like you're touching me, Jaimie Paul ... an' now there was nothing over them, except us ... an' wind in the grass an' a barbwire fence creaking. An' behind that, a hundred acres of barley. (*JAIMIE PAUL stands.*) That's something to remember, when you're lovin', eh?

> *The sound of a train whistle is heard. JAIMIE PAUL goes and the lights onstage fade.*

> *The music comes up and the SINGER sings. As JAIMIE PAUL passes her, the SINGER pursues him up the ramp, and RITA JOE runs after them.*

SINGER: (*singing*)

Oh, can't you see that train roll on,
Gonna kill a man, before it's gone?
Jaimie Paul fell and died.
He had it comin', so it's all right.
Silver train with wheels on fire!

> *The music dies instantly. RITA JOE's words come on the heels of the music as a bitter extension of the song. She stands before the MAGISTRATE, again in the court, but looks back to where JAIMIE PAUL had been in the gloom. The POLICEMAN enters where JAIMIE PAUL has exited, replacing him, for the fourth trial scene.*

RITA: Jaimie, why am I here? ... Is it ... because people are talkin' about me and all them men ... Is that why? I never wanted to cut cordwood for a living ... (*with great bitterness*) Never once I thought ... it'd be like this ...

MAGISTRATE: What are we going to do about you, Rita Joe? This is the seventh charge against you in one year ... Laws are not made to be violated in this way ... Why did you steal?

RITA: I was hungry. I had no money.

MAGISTRATE: Yet you must have known you would be caught?

RITA: Yes.

MAGISTRATE: Are you not afraid of what is happening to you?

RITA: I am afraid of a lot of things. Put me in jail. I don't care ...

MAGISTRATE: (*with forced authority*) Law is a procedure. The procedure must be respected. It took hundreds of years to develop this process of law.

RITA: I stole a sweater ... They caught me in five minutes!

> *She smiles whimsically at this. The* **MAGISTRATE** *is leafing through the documents before him. The* **POLICEMAN** *stands to one side of him.*

MAGISTRATE: The prosecutor's office has submitted some of the past history of Rita Joe ...

POLICEMAN: She was born and raised on a reservation. Then came a brief period in a public school off the reservation ... at which time Rita Joe established herself as something of a disruptive influence ...

RITA: What's that mean?

MAGISTRATE: (*turning to her, smiling*) A trouble-maker!

> *RITA JOE becomes animated, aware of the trap around her closing even at moments such as this.*

RITA: Maybe it was about the horse, huh? (*She looks up at the* **MAGISTRATE** *who is still smiling, offering her no help.*) There was this accident with a horse ... It happened like this ... I was riding a horse to school an' some of the boys shot a rifle an' my horse bucked an' I fell off. I fell in the bush an' got scratched ... The boys caught the horse by the school and tried to ride him, but the horse bucked an' pinned a boy against a tree, breaking his leg in two places ... (*She indicates the place the leg got broken.*) They said ... an' he said I'd rode the horse over him on purpose!

MAGISTRATE: Well ... did you?

RITA: It wasn't that way at all, I tell you! They lied!

> *The* **POLICEMAN** *and the* **SINGER** *laugh.*

MAGISTRATE: Why should they lie, and Rita Joe alone tell the truth? ... Or are you a child enough to believe the civilization of which we are a part ... (*He indicates the audience as inclusive of civilization from his point of view.*) ... does not understand Rita Joe?

RITA: I don't know what you're saying.

MAGISTRATE: (*with a touch of compassion*) Look at you, woman! Each time you come before me you are older. The lines in your face are those of ...

RITA: I'm tired an' I want to eat, mister! I haven't had grub since day before yesterday ... This room is like a boat on water ... I'm so dizzy ... What the hell kind of place is this won't let me go lie down on grass?

> *She doubles over to choke back her nausea.*

MAGISTRATE: This is not the reservation, Rita Joe. This is another place, another time ...

RITA: (*straining to remember, to herself*) I was once in Whitecourt, Alberta. The cops are fatter there than here. I had to get out of Whitecourt, Alberta ...

MAGISTRATE: Don't blame the police, Rita Joe! The obstacles to your life are here ... (*He touches his forefinger to his temples.*) ... in your thoughts ... possibly even in your culture ...

> *RITA JOE turns away from him, searching the darkness behind her.*

MAGISTRATE: What's the matter?

RITA: I want to go home!

MAGISTRATE: But you can't go now. You've broken a law for which you will have to pay a fine or go to prison ...

RITA: I have no money.

MAGISTRATE: (*with exasperation*) Rita Joe ... It is against the law to solicit men on the street. You have to wash ...

> *RITA JOE begins to move away from him, crossing the front of the stage along the apron, her walk cocky. The light spreads and follows her.*

MAGISTRATE: You can't walk around in old clothes and running shoes made of canvas ... You have to have some money in your pockets and an address where you live. You should fix your hair ... perhaps even change your name. And try to tame that accent that sounds like you have a mouthful of sawdust ... There is no peace in being extraordinary!

> *The light dies on the* **MAGISTRATE** *and the* **POLICEMAN.**

RITA JOE is transported into another memory. JAIMIE PAUL enters and slides along the floor, left of centre stage. He is drunk, counting the fingers on his outstretched hands. MR. HOMER has entered with a wagon carrying hot soup and mugs. Four YOUNG INDIAN MEN come in out of the cold. MR. HOMER speaks to the audience in a matter-of-fact, informative way.

MR. HOMER: (*dispensing soup to the YOUNG INDIAN MEN*) The do-gooders make something special of the Indian ... There's nothing special here ... At the Centre here, the quick cure is a bowl of stew under the belt and a good night's sleep.

JAIMIE: Hey, Mister Homer! How come I got so many fingers? Heh?

He laughs. MR. HOMER ignores JAIMIE PAUL and continues talking to the audience.

MR. HOMER: I wouldn't say they were brothers or sisters to me ... no, sir! But if you're ...

JAIMIE: (*getting up and embracing RITA JOE*) I got two hands an' one neck ... I can kill more than I can eat ... If I had more fingers I would need mittens big as pie plates ... Yeh?

MR. HOMER: (*to JAIMIE PAUL*) Lie down, Jaimie Paul, an' have some more sleep. When you feel better, I'll get you some soup.

RITA JOE laughs. JAIMIE PAUL weaves his way uncertainly to where MR. HOMER stands.

JAIMIE: (*laughing*) I spit in your soup! You know what I say? ... I say I spit in your soup, Mister Homer ...

He comes to MR. HOMER and seems about to do just what he threatens.

MR. HOMER: (*pushing him away with good humour*) I'll spit in your eyeball if you don't shut up!

JAIMIE: (*breaking away from MR. HOMER, taunting*) You ... are not Mister Homer!

MR. HOMER: I'm not what?

JAIMIE: You're not Mister Homer ... You're somebody wearing his pants an' shirt ... (*stumbling away*) But you're not Mister Homer ... Mister Homer never gets mad ... No, sir, not Mister Homer!

MR. HOMER: I'm not mad ... What're you talkin' about?

JAIMIE PAUL turns and approaches the YOUNG INDIAN MEN. He threatens to fall off the apron of the stage.

JAIMIE: No ... not Mister Homer! An' I got ten fingers ... How's that?

MR. HOMER: For Chrissake, Jaimie ... go to sleep.

JAIMIE PAUL stops and scowls, then grins knowingly. He begins to mime a clumsy paddler paddling a boat.

JAIMIE: (*laughing again*) I know you ... Hey? I know you! ... I seen you up Rainbow Creek one time ... I seen you paddling! (*He breaks up with laughter.*)

MR. HOMER: (*amused, tolerant*) Oh come on ... I've never been to Rainbow Creek.

JAIMIE: (*controlling his laughter*) Sure you been to Rainbow Creek ... (*He begins to mime paddling again.*) Next time you need a good paddler, you see me. I have a governmen' job, but screw that. I'm gonna paddle! I seen you paddle ...

Again he breaks up in laughter as he once more demonstrates the quality of paddling he once saw. RITA JOE is fully enjoying the spectacle. So are the YOUNG INDIAN MEN. MR. HOMER is also amused by the absurdity of the situation.

JAIMIE: I have seen some paddlers ... but you!

JAIMIE PAUL turns but chokes up with laughter and waves his hand derisively, laughing.

MR. HOMER: It must've been somebody else ... I've never been to Rainbow Creek.

JAIMIE: Like hell, you say!

JAIMIE PAUL paddles the soup wagon out. Guitar music comes in with an upbeat tempo. RITA JOE and the YOUNG INDIAN MEN dance to the beat. The YOUNG INDIAN MEN then drift after MR. HOMER.

The light fades slowly on centre stage and the music changes.

RITA JOE, happy in her memory, does a circling butch walk in the fading light to the song of the SINGER. At the conclusion of the song, she is on the apron, stage right, in a wash of light that includes the MAGISTRATE and the SINGER.

SINGER: (*singing*)

I woke up at six o'clock
Stumbled out of bed,

Crash of cans an' diesel trucks
Damned near killed me dead.
Sleepless hours, heavy nights,
Dream your dreams so pretty.
God was gonna have a laugh
An' gave me a job in the city!

RITA JOE is still elated at her memory of JAIMIE PAUL and his story. With unusual candour, she turns girlishly before the MAGISTRATE, and in mild imitation of her own moment of drunkenness, begins telling him a story.

Faint guitar music in the background continues.

RITA: One night I drank a little bit of wine, an' I was outside lookin' at the stars ... thinking ... when I was a little girl how much bigger the trees were ... no clouds, but suddenly there was a light that made the whole sky look like day ... (*Guitar out.*) ... just for a moment ... an' before I got used to the night ... I saw animals, moving across the sky ... two white horses ... A man was takin' them by the halters, and I knew the man was my grandfather ...

She stares at the MAGISTRATE, unsure of herself now.

MAGISTRATE: Yes! Is that all?

RITA: No ... But I never seen my grandfather alive, and I got so sad thinkin' about it I wanted to cry. I wasn't sure it was him, even ... (*She begins to laugh.*) I went an' telephoned the police and asked for the chief, but the chief was home and a guy asks what I want.

MAGISTRATE: (*mildly amused*) You ... called the police?

RITA: I told the guy I'd seen God, and he says, "Yeh? What would you like us to do about it?" An' I said, "Pray! Laugh! Shout!"

MAGISTRATE: Go on ...

RITA: He ... asked where I'd seen God, an' I told him in the sky. He says you better call this number ... It's the Air Force. They'll take care of it! (*She laughs and the MAGISTRATE smiles.*) I called the number the guy gave me, but it was nighttime and there was no answer! If God was to come at night, after office hours, then ...

A terrible awkwardness sets in. There is a harsh light on her. She turns away, aware that she is in captivity.

The MAGISTRATE stirs with discomfort.

RITA: (*with great fear*) How long will this be? Will I never be able to ...

MAGISTRATE: (*annoyed at himself, at her*) There is nothing here but a record of your convictions ... nothing to speak for you and provide me with any reason to moderate your sentence! What the hell am I supposed to do? Violate the law myself because I feel that somehow ... I've known and felt ... No! (*turning from her*) You give me no alternative ... no alternative at all!

The MAGISTRATE packs up his books.

RITA: I'll go home ... jus' let me go home. I can't get out of jail to find the highway ... or some kind of job!

MAGISTRATE: (*standing*) Prison and fines are not the only thing ... Have you, for instance, considered that you might be an incurable carrier? There are people like that ... They cannot come into contact with others without infecting them. They cannot eat from dishes others may use ... They cannot prepare or touch food others will eat ... The same with clothes, cars, hospital beds! (*He exits.*)

RITA JOE shakes her head with disbelief. The idea of perpetual condemnation is beyond her comprehension. She falls to the floor. Guitar music is heard in the background.

She turns away from the MAGISTRATE and the light comes up over the ramp at the back of the stage. Another light comes up on centre stage left. Here, EILEEN JOE and the OLD WOMAN mime washing clothes using a scrubbing board. They place the wash into woven baskets. The woman and the girl are on their knees, facing each other.

On the ramp above them, JAIMIE PAUL is struggling with a POLICEMAN, who is scolding him softly for being drunk, abusive, and noisy. JAIMIE PAUL is jocular; the POLICEMAN, harassed and worried. They slowly cross the ramp from stage left.

SINGER: (*singing*)
Four o'clock in the morning,
The sailor rides the ship
An' I ride the wind!
Eight o'clock in the morning,
My honey's scoldin' the sleepyheads
An' I'm scoldin' him.

JAIMIE: (*to the* POLICEMAN) On the Smoky River ... four o'clock in the morning ... Hey? There was nobody ... just me ... You know that?

POLICEMAN: No, I don't. Come on. Let's get you home.

JAIMIE PAUL moves forward and embraces the POLICEMAN.

JAIMIE: You wanna see something? (*He takes out a coin to do a trick.*)

OLD WOMAN: (*to* EILEEN) Your father's been very sick.

EILEEN: He won't eat nothing ...

OLD WOMAN: Jus' sits and worries ... That's no good.

JAIMIE PAUL: (*finishing his coin trick*) You like that one? Hey, we both work for the government, eh?

They exit laughing.

JAIMIE PAUL: Watch the rough stuff ... just don't make me mad.

OLD WOMAN: If Rita Joe was to come and see him ... maybe say goodbye to him ...

RITA: (*calling from her world to the world of her strongest fears*) But he's not dying! I saw him not so long ago ...

The women in her memory do not hear her. They continue discussing her father.

OLD WOMAN: He loved her an' always worried ...

RITA: I didn't know he was sick!

OLD WOMAN: You were smart to come back, Eileen Joe.

RITA: (*again calling over the distance of her soul*) Nobody told me!

SINGER: (*singing*)

Nine o'clock in the evening,

Moon is high in the blueberry sky

An' I'm lovin' you.

JAIMIE: (*now passing along the apron beside* RITA JOE, *talking to the* POLICEMAN) You seen where I live? Big house with a mongolia in front ... Fancy place! You wanna see the room I got?

POLICEMAN: (*gruffly, aware that* JAIMIE PAUL *can become angry quickly*) When I get holidays, we'll take a tour of everything you've got ... but I don't get holidays until September!

From the apron they cross upstage diagonally, between the OLD WOMAN with EILEEN, and RITA JOE.

JAIMIE: You're a good man ... good for a laugh. I'm a good man ... you know me!

POLICEMAN: Sure, you're first class when you're sober!

JAIMIE: I got a cousin in the city. He got his wife a stove an' washing machine! He's a good man ... You know my cousin maybe?

Fading off. They leave the stage.

The OLD WOMAN has risen from her knees and wearily collected one basket of clothes. She climbs the ramp and moves to the wings, stage right. EILEEN is thoughtful and slower, but she also prepares her clothes wash and follows.

OLD WOMAN: Nothing in the city I can see ... only if you're lucky. A good man who don't drink or play cards ... that's all.

EILEEN: And if he's bad?

OLD WOMAN: Then leave him. I'm older than you, Eileen ... I know what's best.

The OLD WOMAN exits. The guitar music dies out. JAIMIE PAUL's laughter and voice is heard offstage.

JAIMIE: (*offstage, loud, boisterous*) We both work for the gov'ment! We're buddies, no? ... You think we're both the same?

Laughter. The lights on the ramp and centre stage die.

RITA: (*following* JAIMIE PAUL's *laughter*) Good or bad, what difference? So long as he's a livin' man!

RITA JOE and EILEEN giggle. The light spreads around her into pale infinity.

The TEACHER enters on the ramp. She rings a handbell and stops a short distance from the wings to peer around. She is a shy, inadequate woman who moves and behaves jerkily, the product of incomplete education and poor job placement.

TEACHER: (*in a scolding voice*) Rita! Rita Joe! (*The bell rings.*) The class is waiting for you. The class is always waiting.

RITA JOE is startled to hear the bell and see the woman. She comes to her feet, now a child before the TEACHER, and runs to join EILEEN. JAIMIE PAUL and YOUNG INDIAN MEN have entered with the bell and sit cross-legged on the floor as school children.

RITA: The sun is in my skin, Miss Donohue. The leaves is red and orange, and the wind stopped blowin' an hour ago.

The TEACHER has stopped to listen to this. RITA JOE and EILEEN, late again, slip into class and sit on the floor with the others.

TEACHER: Rita! What is a noun? (*No answer. The kids poke RITA JOE to stand up.*) Did you hear what I asked?

RITA: (*uncertain*) No ... yes?

TEACHER: There's a lot you don't know ... That kind of behaviour is exhibitionism! We are a melting pot!

RITA: A melting pot?

TEACHER: A melting pot! Do you know what a melting pot is?

RITA: It's ... (*She shrugs.*) ... a melting pot!

The class laughs.

TEACHER: Precisely! You put copper and tin into a melting pot and out comes bronze ... It's the same with people!

RITA: Yes, Miss Donohue ... out comes bronze ...

Laughter again. The TEACHER calls RITA JOE over to her. The light fades on the other children.

TEACHER: Rita, what was it I said to you this morning?

RITA: You said ... wash my neck, clean my fingernails ...

TEACHER: (*cagey*) No, it wasn't, Rita!

RITA: I can't remember. It was long ago.

TEACHER: Try to remember, Rita.

RITA: I don't remember, Miss Donohue! I was thinkin' about you last night, thinkin' if you knew some ...

TEACHER: You are straying off the topic! Never stray off the topic!

RITA: It was a dream, but now I'm scared, Miss Donohue. I've been a long time moving about ... trying to find something! ... I must've lost ...

TEACHER: No, Rita. That is not important.

RITA: Not important?

TEACHER: No, Rita ... Now you repeat after me like I said or I'm going to have to pass you by again. Say after me ...

RITA: Sure. Say after you ...

TEACHER: Say after me ... "A book of verse underneath the spreading bough ..."

RITA: "A book of verse underneath the spreading bough ..."

TEACHER: "A jug of wine, a loaf of bread, and thou beside me ... singing in the wilderness."

RITA: (*the child spell broken, she laughs bawdily*) Jaimie said, "To heck with the wine an' loaf ... Let's have some more of this here thou!"

Her laughter dies. She wipes her lips, as if trying to erase some stain there.

TEACHER: (*peevish*) All right, Rita ... All right, let's have none of that!

RITA: (*plaintively*) I'm sorry, Miss Donohue ... I'm sure sorry!

TEACHER: That's all right.

RITA: I'm sorry!

TEACHER: All right ...

RITA: Sorry ...

TEACHER: You will never make bronze! Coming from nowhere and going no place! Who am I to change that?

RITA JOE grips the edge of the desk with both hands, holding on tightly.

RITA: No! They said for me to stay here, to learn something!

TEACHER: (*with exasperation*) I tried to teach you, but your head was in the clouds, and as for your body ... Well! I wouldn't even think what I know you do!

The TEACHER crosses among the other children.

RITA: I'm sorry ... please! Let me say it after you again ... (*blurting it out*) "A book of verse underneath the spreading ..."

TEACHER: Arguing ... always trying to upset me ... and in grade four ... I saw it then ... pawing the ground for men like a bitch in heat!

RITA: (*dismayed*) It ... isn't so!

TEACHER: You think I don't know? I'm not blind ... I can see out of the windows.

*The **TEACHER** marches off into the wings and the class runs after her, leaving **RITA JOE** alone onstage.*

RITA: That's a lie! For God's sake, tell the judge I have a good character ... I am clean an' honest ... Everything you said is right, I'm never gonna argue again ... I believe in God ... an' I'm from the country and lost like hell! Tell him! (*She shakes her head sadly, knowing the extent of her betrayal.*) They only give me eight hours to find somebody who knows me ... An' seven and a half hours is gone already!

The light on the scene dies.

SINGER: (*recitivo*)

Things that were ...

Life that might have been ...

A pale backlight on the back of the ramp comes up. Recorded sounds of crickets and the distant sound of a train whistle are heard.

RITA JOE's FATHER and JAIMIE PAUL enter on the ramp from stage left. The FATHER leads the way. JAIMIE PAUL is behind, rolling a cigarette. They walk slowly, thoughtfully, following the ramp across and downstage. RITA JOE stands separate, watching.

SINGER: (*singing*)

The blue evening of the first

Warm day

Is the last evening.

There'll not be another

Like it.

JAIMIE: No more handouts, David Joe ... We can pick an' can the berries ourselves.

FATHER: We need money to start a cooperative like that.

JAIMIE: Then some other way!

Standing still, the old man listens to the sounds of the train and the night.

FATHER: You're a young man, Jaimie Paul ... young an' angry. It's not good to be that angry.

JAIMIE: We're gonna work an' live like people ... not be afraid all the time ... stop listening to an old priest an' Indian Department guys who're working for a pension!

FATHER: You're a young man, Jaimie Paul ...

JAIMIE: I say stop listening, David Joe! ... In the city they never learned my name. It was "Hey, fella" ... or "You, boy" ... that kind of stuff.

Pause. The sound of the train whistle is heard.

FATHER: A beautiful night, Jaimie Paul.

JAIMIE: We can make some money. The berries are good this year!

JAIMIE PAUL is restless, edgy, particularly on the train-whistle sound.

FATHER: Sometimes ... children ... you remember every day with them ... Never forget you are alive with children.

JAIMIE: (*turning away and beginning to retrace his steps*) You want us all to leave an' go to the city? Is that what you want?

The FATHER shakes his head. He does not wish for this, but the generation spread between them is great now. JAIMIE PAUL walks away with a gesture of contempt.

The sounds die. The light dies and isolates the FATHER and RITA JOE.

RITA: You were sick, an' now you're well.

FATHER: (*in measured speech, turning away from RITA JOE, as if carefully recalling something of great importance*) You left your father, Rita Joe ... never wrote Eileen a letter that time ... Your father was pretty sick man that time ... pretty sick man ... June 9th he got the cold, an' on June 20th he ...

RITA: But you're alive! I had such crazy dreams I'd wake up laughing at myself!

FATHER: I have dreams, too ...

RITA JOE moves forward to him. She stops talking to him, as if communicating thoughts rather than words. He remains standing where he is, facing away from her.

RITA: I was in a big city ... so many streets I'd get lost like nothin' ... When you got sick I was on a job ...

FATHER: June 9th I got the cold ...

RITA: Good job in a tire store ... Jaimie Paul's got a job with the government, you know?

FATHER: Pretty sick man, that time ...

RITA: A good job in a tire store. They was gonna teach me how to file statements after I learned the telephone. Bus ticket home was twenty dollars ...

But I got drunk all the same when I heard an' I went in and tried to work that day ... (*smiling and shaking her head*) Boy, I tried to work! Some day that was!

FATHER: I have dreams ... Sometimes I'm scared ...

They finally look at each other.

RITA: (*shuddering*) I'm so cold ...

FATHER: Long dreams ... I dream about Rita Joe ... (*sadly*) Have to get better. I've lived longer, but I know nothing ... nothing at all. Only the old stories.

RITA JOE moves sideways to him. She is smiling happily.

RITA: When I was little, a man came out of the bush to see you. Tell me why again!

The FATHER hesitates, shaking his head, but he is also smiling. The light of their separate yearnings fades out and the front of the stage is lit with the two of them together. The FATHER turns and comes forward to meet her.

FATHER: You don't want to hear that story again.

He sits on the slight elevation of the stage apron. RITA JOE sits down in front of him and snuggles between his knees. He leans forward over her.

RITA: It's the best story I ever heard!

FATHER: You were a little girl ... four years old already ... an' Eileen was getting big inside your mother. One day it was hot ... sure was hot. Too hot to try an' fish in the lake, because the fish was down deep where the water was cold.

RITA: The dog started to bark ...

FATHER: The dog started to bark ... How!

FATHER & RITA: (*in unison*) How! How! How!

FATHER: Barking to beat hell an' I says to myself why ... on such a hot day? Then I see the bushes moving ... somebody was coming to see us. Your mother said from inside the house, "What's the matter with that dog?" An' I says to her, "Somebody coming to see me." It was big Sandy Collins, who ran the sawmill back of the reserve. Business was bad for big Sandy then ... but he comes out of that bush like he was being chased ... his clothes all wet an' stickin' to him ... his cap in his hands, an' his face black with the heat and dirt from hard work ... He says to me, "My little Millie got a cough last night an' today she's dead." ... "She's dead," big Sandy says to me. I says to him, "I'm

sorry to hear that, Sandy. Millie is the same age as my Rita." And he says to me, "David Joe ... look, you got another kid coming ... won't make much difference to you ... Sell me Rita Joe like she is for a thousand dollars!"

RITA JOE giggles. The FATHER raises his hand to silence her.

FATHER: "A thousand dollars is a lot of money, Sandy," I says to him ... "Lots of money. You got to cut a lot of timber for a thousand dollars." Then he says to me, "Not a thousand cash at once, David Joe. First I give you two hundred fifty dollars ... When Rita Joe comes ten years old and she's still all right, I give you the next two hundred fifty ... An' if she don't die by fifteen, I guarantee you five hundred dollars cash at once!"

RITA JOE and the FATHER break into laughter. He reaches around her throat and draws her close.

FATHER: So you see, Rita Joe, you lose me one thousand dollars from big Sandy Collins!

They continue laughing.

A harsh light on the MAGISTRATE, who enters and stands on his podium.

MAGISTRATE: Rita Joe, when was the last time you had dental treatment?

RITA JOE covers her ears, refusing to surrender this moment of security in the arms of her FATHER.

RITA: I can't hear you!

MAGISTRATE: (*loudly*) You had your teeth fixed ever?

RITA: (*coming to her feet and turning on him*) Leave me alone!

MAGISTRATE: Have you had your lungs X-rayed recently?

RITA: I was hungry, that's all!

MAGISTRATE: (*becoming staccato, machine-like in his questions*) When was your last Wassermann taken?

RITA: What's that?

RITA JOE hears the TEACHER's voice. She turns to see the approaching TEACHER give the MAGISTRATE testimony. The stage is lit in a cold blue light now.

TEACHER: (*crisply to the MAGISTRATE as she approaches, her monologue a reading*) Dear Sir ... In reply to your letter of the twelfth, I cannot in all sincerity provide a reference of good character for one Rita Joe ...

The WITNESSES do not see her and the testimony takes on the air of a nightmare for RITA JOE. She is baffled and afraid. The TEACHER continues to quietly repeat her testimony. RITA JOE appeals to the MAGISTRATE.

RITA: Why am I here? What've I done?

MAGISTRATE: You are charged with prostitution.

Her FATHER stands and crosses upstage to the ramp to observe. He is joined by EILEEN JOE, the OLD WOMAN, and the PRIEST. MR. HOMER approaches briskly from stage left.

MR. HOMER: She'd been drinking when she comes into the Centre ... Nothing wrong in that I could see, 'specially on a Friday night. So I give her some soup an' a sandwich. Then all of a sudden in the middle of a silly argument, she goes haywire ... an' I see her comin' at me ... I'll tell you, I was scared! I don't know Indian women that well!

MAGISTRATE: Assault!

RITA JOE retreats from him. The TEACHER and MR. HOMER now stand before the MAGISTRATE as if they were frozen. MR. HOMER repeats his testimony under the main dialogue. JAIMIE PAUL staggers in from stage right, over the ramp, heading to the wings of lower stage left.

JAIMIE: (*to himself*) What the hell are they doing?

RITA: (*running to him*) Say a good word for me, Jaimie!

JAIMIE: They fired me yesterday ... What the hell's the use of living?

JAIMIE PAUL leaves the stage as the SCHOOL BOARD CLERK enters to offer further testimony to the MAGISTRATE.

SCHOOL BOARD CLERK: I recommended in a letter that she take school after grade five through correspondence courses from the Department of Education ... but she never replied to the form letter the school division sent her ...

RITA: (*defending herself to the MAGISTRATE*) That drunken bastard Mahoney used it to light fire in his store ... He'd never tell Indians when mail came for us!

SCHOOL BOARD CLERK: I repeat ... I wish our position understood most clearly ... No reply was

ever received in this office to the letter we sent Rita Joe!

RITA: One letter ... one letter for a lifetime?

TEACHER: Say after me! "I wandered lonely as a cloud, that floats on high o'er vales and hills ... When all at once I saw a crowd ... a melting pot ..."

A POLICEMAN and a MALE WITNESS enter. The PRIEST crosses downstage. The testimonies are becoming a nightmare babble. RITA JOE is stung, stumbling backward from all of them as they face the MAGISTRATE with their condemnations.

POLICEMAN: We were impersonating two deckhands ...

The PRIEST is passing by RITA JOE. He makes the sign of the cross and offers comfort in a thin voice, lost in the noise.

PRIEST: Be patient, Rita ... The young are always stormy, but in time, your understanding will deepen ... There is an end to all things.

WITNESS: I gave her a job, but she was kind of slow ... I can't wait around, there's lots of white people goin' lookin' for work ... so I figure, to hell with this noise ...

MAGISTRATE: (*loudly over the voices*) Have your ears ached?

RITA: No!

MAGISTRATE: Have you any boils on your back? Any discharge? When did you bathe last?

The MURDERERS appear and circle RITA JOE.

MAGISTRATE: Answer me! Drunkenness! Shoplifting! Assault! Prostitution, prostitution, prostitution, prostitution!

RITA: (*her voice shrill, cutting over the babble*) I don't know what happened ... but you got to listen to me and believe me, mister!

The babble ceases abruptly. RITA JOE pleads with them as best she knows.

RITA: You got rules here that was made before I was born ... I was hungry when I stole something ... an' I was hollerin' I was so lonely when I started whoring ...

The MURDERERS come closer.

MAGISTRATE: Rita Joe ... has a doctor examined you? ... I mean, really examined you? Rita Joe ... you might be carrying and transmitting some disease and not aware of it!

RITA: (*breaking away from the MURDERERS*) Bastards! (*to the MAGISTRATE*) Put me in jail ... I don't care ... I'll sign anything. I'm so goddamn hungry I'm sick ... Whatever it is, I'm guilty!

She clutches her head and goes down in a squat of defeat.

MAGISTRATE: Are you free of venereal disease?

RITA: I don't know. I'm not sick that way.

MAGISTRATE: How can you tell?

RITA: (*lifting her face to him*) I know ... A woman knows them things ...

Pause.

MAGISTRATE: Thirty days!

The POLICEMAN leads RITA JOE off and the house lights come up. The ACTORS and the SINGER walk off the stage, leaving emptiness as at the opening of the act.

House lights up.

ACT TWO

The house lights dim. A POLICEMAN brings RITA JOE in downstage centre. She curls up in her jail cell and sleeps. RITA JOE's FATHER enters on the ramp and crosses down to the audience. The stage work lights die down. Lights isolate RITA JOE's FATHER. Another light with prison-bar shadows isolates RITA JOE in her area of the stage.

FATHER: (*looking down on RITA JOE*) I see no way ... no way ... It's not clear like trees against snow ... not clear at all ... (*to the audience.*) But when I was fifteen years old, I leave the reserve to work on a threshing crew. They pay a dollar a day for a good man ... an' I was a good strong man. The first time I got work there was a girl about as old as me ... She'd come out in the yard an' watch the men working at the threshing machine. She had eyes that were the biggest I ever seen ... like fifty-cent pieces ... an' there was always a flock of geese around her. Whenever I see her I feel good. She used to stand an' watch me, an' the geese made a helluva lot of noise. One time I got off my rick an' went to get a drink of water ... but I walked close to where she was watching me. She backed away, and then ran from me with the geese chasin' after her, their wings out an' their feet no longer touching the ground ... They were white geese ...

The last time Rita Joe come home to see us ... the last time she ever come home ... I watched her leave ... and I seen geese running after Rita Joe the same way ... white geese ... with their wings out an' their feet no longer touching the ground. And I remembered it all, an' my heart got so heavy I wanted to cry ...

The light fades to darkness on the FATHER, as he exits up the ramp and off. RITA JOE wakes from her dream, cold, shaking, desperate.

SINGER: (*singing*)

The blue evening of the
First warm day
Is the last evening.
There'll not be another
Like it.

The POLICEMAN and the PRIEST enter from darkness. The PRIEST is dressed in a dark suit that needs pressing. He stops in half-shadow outside RITA JOE's prison light. The scene between them is played out in the manner of two country people meeting in a time of crisis. Their thoughts come slowly, incompletely. There is fear and helplessness in both characters.

PRIEST: I came twice before they'd let me see you ...

RITA JOE jumps to her feet. She smiles at him.

RITA: Oh, Father Andrew!

PRIEST: Even so, I had to wait an hour.

A long pause. He clumsily takes out a package of cigarettes and matches from his pocket and hands them to her, aware that he is possibly breaking a prison regulation.

PRIEST: I'm sorry about this, Rita.

RITA JOE tears the package open greedily and lights a cigarette. She draws on it with animal satisfaction.

RITA: I don't know what's happening, Father Andrew.

PRIEST: They're not ... hurting you here?

RITA: No.

PRIEST: I could make an appointment with the warden if there was something ...

RITA: What's it like outside? ... Is it a nice day outside? I heard it raining last night ... Was it raining?

PRIEST: It rains a lot here ...

RITA: When I was a kid, there was leaves an' a river ... Jaimie Paul told me once that maybe we never see those things again.

A long pause. The PRIEST struggles with himself.

PRIEST: I've never been inside a jail before ... They told me there was a chapel ... (*He points indefinitely back.*)

RITA: What's gonna happen to me? ... That judge sure got sore ... (*She laughs.*)

PRIEST: (*with disgust, yet unsure of himself*) Prostitution this time?

RITA: I guess so ...

PRIEST: You know how I feel ... City is no place for you ... nor for me ... I've spent my life in the same surroundings as your father!

RITA: Sure ... but you had God on your side!

She smiles mischievously. The PRIEST angers.

PRIEST: Rita, try to understand ... Our Lord Jesus once met a woman such as you beside the well ... He forgave her!

RITA: I don't think God hears me here ... Nobody hears me now, nobody except cops an' pimps an' bootleggers!

PRIEST: I'm here. I was there when you were born.

RITA: You've told me lots of times ... I was thinkin' about my mother last night ... She died young ... I'm older than she was ...

PRIEST: Your mother was a good, hard-working woman. She was happy ...

A pause between them.

RITA: There was frost on the street at five o'clock Tuesday morning when they arrested me ... Last night I remembered things flyin' and kids runnin' past me trying to catch a chocolate wrapper that's blowin' in the wind ... (*She presses her hands against her bosom.*) It hurts me here to think about them things!

PRIEST: I worry about you ... Your father worries, too ... I baptized you ... I watched you and Leenie grow into women!

RITA: Yes ... I seen God in what you said ... in your clothes! In your hair!

PRIEST: But you're not the woman I expected you to be ... Your pride, Rita ... your pride ... may bar you from heaven.

RITA: (*mocking him*) They got rules there, too ... in heaven?

PRIEST: (*angry*) Rita! ... I'm not blind ... I can see! I'm not deaf ... I know all about you! So does God!

RITA: My uncle was Dan Joe ... He was dyin' and he said to me, "Long ago the white man come with Bibles to talk to my people, who had the land. They talk for hundred years ... then we had all the Bibles, an' the white man had our land ..."

PRIEST: Don't blame the Church! We are trying to help ...

RITA: (*with passion*) How? I'm looking for the door ...

PRIEST: (*tortured now*) I ... will hear your confession ...

RITA: But I want to be free!

PRIEST: (*stiffly*) We learn through suffering, Rita Joe ... We will only be free if we become humble again. (*pause*) Will you confess, Rita Joe? (*a long pause*) I'm going back on the four o'clock bus. (*He begins walking away into the gloom.*) I'll tell your father I saw you, and you looked well. (*He is suddenly relieved.*)

RITA: (*after him as he leaves*) You go to hell!

The PRIEST turns sharply.

RITA: Go tell your God ... when you see him ... tell him about Rita Joe an' what they done to her! Tell him about yourself, too! ... That you were not good enough for me, but that didn't stop you tryin'! Tell him that!

The PRIEST hurries away. Guitar in. RITA JOE sits down, brooding.

SINGER: (*singing*)

I will give you the wind and a sense of wonder
As the child by the river, the reedy river.
I will give you the sky wounded by thunder
And a leaf on the river, the silver river.

A light comes up on the ramp where JAIMIE PAUL appears, smiling and waving to her.

JAIMIE: (*shouting*) Rita Joe! I'm gonna take you dancing after work Friday ... That job's gonna be all right!

RITA: (*springing to her feet, elated*) Put me back in jail so I can be free on Friday!

> *A sudden burst of dance music. The stage lights up and JAIMIE PAUL approaches her. They dance together, remaining close downstage centre.*

SINGER: (*singing*)

Round an' round the cenotaph,
The clumsy seagulls play.
Fed by funny men with hats
Who watch them night and day.
Sleepless hours, heavy nights,
Dream your dreams so pretty.
God was gonna have a laugh
An' gave me a job in the city!

> *The music continues for the interlude.*

> *Some YOUNG INDIAN MEN run onto the stage along the ramp and join JAIMIE PAUL and RITA JOE in their dance. The MURDERERS enter and elbow into the group, their attention specifically menacing toward JAIMIE PAUL and RITA JOE. A street brawl begins as a POLICEMAN passes through on his beat. The MURDERERS leave hastily.*

I woke up at six o'clock,
Stumbled out of bed.
Crash of steel and diesel trucks
Damned near killed me dead.
Sleepless hours, heavy nights,
Dream your dreams so pretty.
God was gonna have a laugh
An' gave me a job in the city!

> *Musical interlude. RITA JOE and JAIMIE PAUL continue dancing languidly. The YOUNG INDIAN MEN exit.*

I've polished floors an' cut the trees,
Fished and stooked the wheat.
Now "Hallelujah, Praise the Lord,"
I sing before I eat!
Sleepless hours, heavy nights,
Dream your dreams so pretty.
God was gonna have a laugh
An' gave me a job in the city!

> *Musical interlude.*

> *The music dies as the YOUNG INDIAN MEN wheel in a brass bed, circle it around, and exit. The stage darkens except for a pool of light where RITA JOE and JAIMIE PAUL stand, embracing. JAIMIE PAUL takes her hand and leads her away.*

JAIMIE: Come on, Rita Joe ... you're slow.

RITA: (*happy in her memories, not wishing to forget too soon, hesitating*) How much rent ... for a place where you can keep babies?

JAIMIE: I don't know ... maybe eighty dollars a month.

RITA: That's a lot of money.

JAIMIE: It costs a buck to go dancin' even ...

> *They walk slowly along the apron to stage left, as if following a street to JAIMIE PAUL's rooming house.*

JAIMIE: It's a good place ... I got a sink in the room. Costs seven bucks a week, that's all!

RITA: That's good ... I only got a bed in my place ...

JAIMIE: I seen Mickey an' Steve Laporte last night.

RITA: How are they?

JAIMIE: Good ... We're goin' to a beer parlour Monday night when I get paid ... the same beer parlour they threw Steve out of! Only now there's three of us goin' in!

> *They arrive at and enter his room. A spot illuminates the bed near the wings of stage left. It is old, dilapidated. JAIMIE PAUL and RITA JOE enter the area of light around the bed. He is aware that the room is more drab than he would wish it.*

JAIMIE: How do you like it ... I like it!

RITA: (*examining room critically*) It's ... smaller than my place.

JAIMIE: Sit down.

> *She sits on the edge of the bed and falls backward into a springless hollow. He laughs nervously. He is awkward and confused. The ease they shared walking to his place is now constricted.*

JAIMIE: I was gonna get some grub today, but I was busy ... Here ...

> *He takes a chocolate bar out of his shirt pocket and offers it to her. She opens it, breaks off a small piece, and gives the remainder to him. He closes the wrapper and replaces the bar in his pocket. She eats ravenously. He walks around the bed nervously.*

JAIMIE: No fat D.P.'s gonna throw me or the boys out of that beer parlour or he's gonna get this!

He holds up a fist in a gesture that is both poignant and futile. She laughs and he glowers at her.

JAIMIE: I'm tellin' you!

RITA: If they want to throw you out, they'll throw you out.

JAIMIE: Well, this is one Indian guy they're not pushing around no more!

RITA: God helps them who help themselves.

JAIMIE: That's right! (*laughing*) I was lookin' at the white shirts in Eaton's and this bugger comes an' says to me, "You gonna buy or you gonna look all day?"

RITA: (*looking around her*) It's a nice room for a guy, I guess ...

JAIMIE: It's a lousy room!

RITA JOE lies back lengthwise in the bed. JAIMIE PAUL sits on the bed beside her.

RITA: You need a good job to have babies in the city ... Clara Hill gave both her kids away they say ...

JAIMIE: Where do kids like that go?

RITA: Foster homes, I guess.

JAIMIE: If somebody don't like the kid, back they go to another foster home?

RITA: I guess so ... Clara Hill don't know where her kids are now.

JAIMIE: (*twisting sharply in his anger*) Goddamn it!

RITA: My father says –

JAIMIE PAUL rises, crosses round the bed to the other side.

JAIMIE: (*harshly*) I don't want to hear what your father got to say! He's like ... like the kind of Indian a white man likes! He's gonna look wise and wait forever ... for what? For the kids they take away to come back?

RITA: He's scared ... I'm scared ... We're all scared, Jaimie Paul.

JAIMIE: (*lying face down and miming a gun through the bars*) Sometimes I feel like takin' a gun and just ... (*He waves his hand as if to liquidate his environment and all that bedevils him. He turns over on his back and lies beside RITA JOE.*) I don't know ... Goddammit, I don't know what to do. I get mad an'

then I don't know what I'm doing or thinkin' ... I get scared sometimes, Rita Joe.

RITA: (*tenderly*) We're scared ... everybody ...

JAIMIE: I'm scared of dyin' ... in the city. They don't care for one another here ... You got to be smart or have a good job to live like that.

RITA: Clara Hill's gonna have another baby ...

JAIMIE: I can't live like that ... A man don't count for much here ... Women can do as much as a man ... There's no difference between men and women. I can't live like that.

RITA: You got to stop worrying, Jaimie Paul. You're gonna get sick worryin'.

JAIMIE: You can't live like that, can you?

RITA: No.

JAIMIE: I can't figure out what the hell they want from us!

RITA: (*laughing*) Last time I was in trouble, the judge was asking me what I wanted from him! I could've told him, but I didn't!

They both laugh. JAIMIE PAUL becomes playful and happy.

JAIMIE: Last night I seen television in a store window. I seen a guy on television showing this knife that cuts everything it's so sharp ... He was cutting up good shoes like they were potatoes ... That was sure funny to see!

Again they laugh in merriment at the idea of such a demonstration. JAIMIE PAUL continues with his story, gesturing with his hands.

JAIMIE: Chop ... chop ... chop ... A potful of shoes in no time! What's a guy gonna do with a potful of shoes? Cook them?

They continue laughing and lie together again. Then JAIMIE PAUL sobers. He rises from the bed and walks around it. He offers his hand to RITA JOE, who also rises.

JAIMIE: (*dryly*) Come on. This is a lousy room!

SINGER: (*reprise*)

God was gonna have a laugh,
And gave me a job in the city!

The light goes down on RITA JOE and JAIMIE PAUL. The YOUNG INDIAN MEN clear the bed. Cross-fade to the rear ramp of the stage. RITA JOE's FATHER and the PRIEST enter and cross the stage.

PRIEST: She got out yesterday, but she wouldn't let me see her. I stayed an extra day, but she wouldn't see me.

FATHER: (*sadly*) I must go once more to the city ... I must go to see them.

PRIEST: You're an old man ... I wish I could persuade you not to go.

FATHER: You wouldn't say that if you had children, Andrew ...

The lights go down on them.

The lights come up downstage centre. Carrying a table between them, three YOUNG INDIAN MEN precede MR. HOMER, who follows with a hamper of clothes under his arm.

MR. HOMER: Yeh ... right about there is fine, boys. Got to get the clutter out of the basement ... There's mice coming in to beat hell.

MR. HOMER empties the clothes hamper on the table. The YOUNG INDIAN MEN step aside and converse in an undertone.

On the ramp, a YOUNG INDIAN MAN weaves his way from stage left and down to centre stage where the others have brought the table. He is followed by JAIMIE PAUL and RITA JOE, who mime his intoxicated progress.

MR. HOMER: (*speaking to the audience*) The Society for Aid to the Indians sent a guy over to see if I could recommend someone who'd been ... well, through the mill, like they say ... an' then smartened up an' taken rehabilitation. The guy said they just wanted a rehabilitated Indian to show up at their annual dinner. No speeches or fancy stuff ... just be there.

The YOUNG INDIAN MAN lies down carefully to one side of MR. HOMER.

MR. HOMER: Hi, Louie. Not that I would cross the street for the Society ... They're nothing but a pack of do-gooders out to get their name in the papers ...

The YOUNG INDIAN MAN begins to sing a tuneless song, trailing off into silence.

MR. HOMER: Keep it down, eh, Louie? I couldn't think of anybody to suggest to this guy ... so he went away pretty sore ...

RITA JOE begins to rummage through the clothes on the table. She looks at sweaters and holds a

red one thoughtfully in her hands. *JAIMIE PAUL is in conversation with the YOUNG INDIAN MEN to one side of the table. MR. HOMER turns from the audience to see RITA JOE holding the sweater.*

MR. HOMER: Try it on, Rita Joe ... That's what the stuff's here for.

JAIMIE PAUL turns. He is in a provocative mood, seething with rebellion that makes the humour he triggers both biting and deceptively innocent. The YOUNG INDIAN MEN respond to him with strong laughter. JAIMIE PAUL takes a play punch at one of them.

JAIMIE: Whoops! Scared you, eh? (*He glances back at MR. HOMER, as if talking to him.*) Can't take it, eh? The priest can't take it. Indian Department guys can't take it ... Why listen to them? Listen to the radio if you want to hear something.

The YOUNG INDIAN MEN laugh.

JAIMIE: Or listen to me! You think I'm smart?

YOUNG INDIAN MAN: You're a smart man, Jaimie Paul.

JAIMIE: Naw ... I'm not smart ... (*pointing to another YOUNG INDIAN MAN*) This guy here ... calls himself squaw-humper ... he's smart! ... Him ... he buys extra big shirts ... more cloth for the same money ... That's smart! (*laughter*) I'm not smart. (*seriously*) You figure we can start a business an' be our own boss?

YOUNG INDIAN MAN: I don't know about that ...

JAIMIE PAUL leaves them and goes to lean over the YOUNG INDIAN MAN, who is now asleep on the floor.

JAIMIE: Buy a taxi ... be our own boss ...

He shakes the sleeping YOUNG INDIAN MAN, who immediately begins his tuneless song.

JAIMIE: Aw, he's drunk.

JAIMIE PAUL goes over to the table and stares at the YOUNG INDIAN MAN beyond the table.

JAIMIE: (*soberly*) Buy everything we need ... Don't be bums! Bums need grub an' clothes ... Bums is bad for the country, right Mr. Homer?

MR. HOMER: (*nodding*) I guess so ... (*to RITA JOE who is now wearing the old sweater*) Red looks good on you, Rita Joe ... Take it!

JAIMIE PAUL goes over and embraces RITA JOE, then gently pushes her away.

JAIMIE: She looks better in yellow. I never seen a red dandelion before.

He and the YOUNG INDIAN MEN laugh, but the laughter is hollow.

MR. HOMER: Come on, Jaimie! Leave the girl alone. That's what it's here for ... Are you working?

JAIMIE: (*evasive, needling*) Yeh! ... No! ... "Can you drive?" the guy says to me. "Sure, I can drive," I says to him. "Okay," he says, "then drive this broom until the warehouse is clean."

They all laugh.

MR. HOMER: That's a good one ... Jaimie, you're a card ... Well, time to get some food for you lot ...

MR. HOMER leaves. RITA JOE feels better about the sweater. She looks to one of the YOUNG INDIAN MEN for approval. JAIMIE PAUL becomes grim-faced.

RITA: Do you like it?

YOUNG INDIAN MAN: Sure. It's a nice sweater ... Take it.

JAIMIE: Take it where? Take it to hell ... Be men! (*pointing after MR. HOMER*) He's got no kids ... Guys like that get mean when they got no kids ... We're his kids an' he means to keep it that way! Well, I'm a big boy now! (*to RITA JOE*) I go to the employment office. I want work an' I want it now. "I'm not a goddamned cripple," I says to him. An' he says he can only take my name! If work comes, he'll call me! "What the hell is this," I says to him. "I'll never get work like that ... There's no telephone in the house where I got a room!"

MR. HOMER returns, pushing a wheeled tray on which he has some food for sandwiches, a loaf of bread, and a large cutting knife. He begins to make some sandwiches.

RITA: (*scolding JAIMIE PAUL*) You won't get work talking that way, Jaimie Paul!

JAIMIE: Why not? I'm not scared. He gets mad at me an' I say to him ... "You think I'm some stupid Indian you're talkin' to? Heh? You think that?"

JAIMIE PAUL struts and swaggers to demonstrate how he faced his opponent at the employment office.

MR. HOMER: (*cutting bread*) You're a tough man to cross, Jaimie Paul.

JAIMIE: (*ignoring MR. HOMER, to the YOUNG INDIAN MEN*) Boy, I showed that bastard who he was talkin' to!

RITA: Did you get the job?

JAIMIE: (*turning to her, laughing boyishly*) No! He called the cops an' they threw me out!

They all laugh. The YOUNG INDIAN MEN go to the table now and rummage through the clothes.

MR. HOMER: Take whatever you want, boys ... there's more clothes comin' tomorrow.

JAIMIE PAUL impulsively moves to the table where the YOUNG INDIAN MEN are fingering the clothes. He pushes them aside and shoves the clothes in a heap, leaving a small corner of the table clean. He takes out two coins from his pockets and spits in his hands.

JAIMIE: I got a new trick ... Come on, Mister Homer ... I'll show you! See this! (*He shows the coins, then slams his hands palms down on the table.*) Which hand got the coins?

MR. HOMER: Why ... one under each hand ...

JAIMIE: Right! (*turning up his hands*) Again? (*He collects the coins and slaps his hands down again.*) Where are the coins now? Come on, guess!

MR. HOMER is confident now and points to the right hand with his cutting knife. JAIMIE PAUL laughs and lifts his hands. The coins are under his left hand.

MR. HOMER: Son of a gun.

JAIMIE: You're a smart man.

He puts the coins in his pockets and, laughing, turns to RITA JOE who stands uncertainly, dressed in the red sweater. She likes the garment, but she is aware JAIMIE PAUL might resent her taking it. The YOUNG INDIAN MEN again move to the table, and MR. HOMER returns to making sandwiches.

MR. HOMER: There's a good pair of socks might come in handy for one of you guys!

A YOUNG INDIAN MAN pokes his thumbs through the holes in the socks and laughs.

JAIMIE: Sure ... take the socks! Take the table! (*He slaps the table with his hands and laughs.*) Take Mister Homer cutting bread! Take everything!

MR. HOMER: Hey, Jaimie!

JAIMIE: Why not? There's more comin' tomorrow, you said!

RITA: Jaimie!

MR. HOMER: You're sure in a smart-assed mood today, aren't you?

JAIMIE: (*pointing to the YOUNG INDIAN MAN with the socks, but talking to MR. HOMER*) Mister, friend Steve over there laughs lots ... He figures ... the way to get along an' live is to grab his guts an' laugh at anything anybody says. You see him laughing all the time. A dog barks at him an' he laughs ... (*laughter from the YOUNG INDIAN MAN*) Laughs at a fence post fallin' ... (*laughter*) Kids with funny eyes make him go haywire ... (*laughter*) Can of meat an' no can opener ...

MR. HOMER watches the YOUNG INDIAN MEN and grins at JAIMIE PAUL.

MR. HOMER: Yeh ... he laughs quite a bit ...

JAIMIE: He laughs at a rusty nail ... Nice guy ... laughs all the time.

MR. HOMER: (*to JAIMIE PAUL, holding the knife*) You wanted mustard on your bread or just plain?

JAIMIE: I seen him cut his hand and start laughin' ... isn't that funny?

The YOUNG INDIAN MEN laugh, but with less humour now.

MR. HOMER: (*to JAIMIE PAUL*) You want mustard? ... I'm talkin' to you!

JAIMIE: I'm not hungry.

The YOUNG INDIAN MEN stop laughing altogether. They become tense and suspicious of JAIMIE PAUL, who is watching them severely.

MR. HOMER: Suit yourself. Rita?

RITA: (*shaking her head slowly, her gaze on JAIMIE PAUL's face*) I'm not hungry.

MR. HOMER looks from RITA JOE to JAIMIE PAUL, then to the YOUNG INDIAN MEN. His manner stiffens.

MR. HOMER: I see ...

JAIMIE PAUL and RITA JOE touch hands and come forward to sit on the apron of the stage, front. A pale light is on the two of them. The stage lights behind them fade. A low light that is diffused and shadowy remains on the table where MR. HOMER has prepared the food. The YOUNG INDIAN MEN move slowly to the table and begin eating the sandwiches MR. HOMER offers to them. The light on the table fades very low. JAIMIE PAUL hands a cigarette to RITA JOE and they smoke.

Light comes up over the rear ramp. RITA JOE's FATHER enters onto the ramp from the wings of stage right. His step is resolute. The PRIEST follows behind him a few paces. They have been arguing. Both are dressed in work clothes: heavy trousers and windbreakers.

JAIMIE: When I'm laughing, I got friends.

RITA: I know, Jaimie Paul ...

PRIEST: That was the way I found her, that was the way I left her.

JAIMIE: (*bitterly*) When I'm laughing, I'm a joker ... a funny boy!

FATHER: If I was young ... I wouldn't sleep. I would talk to people ... let them all know!

JAIMIE: I'm not dangerous when I'm laughing ...

PRIEST: You could lose the reserve and have nowhere to go!

FATHER: I have lost more than that! Young people die ... young people don't believe me ...

JAIMIE: That's all right ... that's all right ...

The light dies out on JAIMIE PAUL and RITA JOE. The light also dies out on MR. HOMER and the YOUNG INDIAN MEN.

PRIEST: You think they believe that hotheaded ... that troublemaker?

FATHER: (*turning to face the PRIEST*) Jaimie Paul is a good boy!

PRIEST: David Joe ... you and I have lived through a lot. We need peace now, and time to consider what to do next.

FATHER: Eileen said to me last night ... she wants to go to the city. I worry all night ... What can I do?

PRIEST: I'll talk to her, if you wish.

FATHER: (*angry*) And tell her what? ... Of the animals there ... (*gesturing to the audience*) who sleep with sore stomachs because ... they eat too much?

PRIEST: We mustn't lose the reserve and the old life, David Joe ... Would you ... give up being chief on the reserve?

FATHER: Yes!

PRIEST: To Jaimie Paul?

FATHER: No ... to someone who's been to school ... maybe university ... who knows more.

PRIEST: (*relieved by this, but not reassured*) The people here need your wisdom and stability, David Joe. There is no man here who knows as much about hunting and fishing and guiding. You can survive ... What does a youngster who's been away to school know of this?

FATHER: (*sadly*) If we only fish an' hunt an' cut pulpwood ... pick strawberries in the bush ... for a hundred years more, we are dead. I know this, here ... (*He touches his breast.*)

The light dies on the ramp. A light rises on JAIMIE PAUL and RITA JOE sitting at the apron of the stage. MR. HOMER is still cutting bread for sandwiches. The three YOUNG INDIAN MEN have eaten and appear restless to leave. The fourth YOUNG INDIAN MAN is still asleep on the floor. RITA JOE has taken off the red sweater, but continues to hold it in her hand.

JAIMIE: (*to MR. HOMER*) One time I was on a trapline five days without grub. I ate snow an' I walked until I got back. You think you can take it like me?

MR. HOMER: (*approaching JAIMIE PAUL and holding out a sandwich to him*) Here ... have a sandwich now.

JAIMIE PAUL ignores his hand.

RITA: Mister Homer don't know what happened, Jaimie Paul.

MR. HOMER shrugs and walks away to his sandwich table.

JAIMIE: Then he's got to learn ... Sure he knows! (*to MR. HOMER*) Sure he knows! He's feedin' sandwiches to Indian bums ... He knows. He's the worst kind!

The YOUNG INDIAN MEN freeze and MR. HOMER stops.

MR. HOMER: (*coldly*) I've never yet asked a man to leave this building.

RITA JOE and JAIMIE PAUL rise to their feet. RITA JOE goes to the clothes table and throws the red sweater back on the pile of clothes. JAIMIE PAUL laughs sardonically.

MR. HOMER: (*to RITA JOE*) Hey, not you, girl ... You take it!

She shakes her head and moves to leave.

RITA: I think we better go, boys.

The sleeping YOUNG INDIAN MAN slowly raises his head, senses there is something wrong, and is about to be helped up when ...

JAIMIE: After five days without grub, the first meal I threw up ... stomach couldn't take it ... But after that it was all right ... (*to MR. HOMER, with intensity*) I don't believe nobody ... no priest nor government ... They don't know what it's like to ... to want an' not have ... to stand in line an' nobody sees you!

MR. HOMER: If you want food, eat! You need clothes, take them. That's all ... But I'm runnin' this Centre my way, and I mean it!

JAIMIE: I come to say no to you ... That's all ... that's all!

He throws out his arms in a gesture that is both defiant and childlike. The gesture disarms some of MR. HOMER's growing hostility.

MR. HOMER: You've got that right ... no problems. There's others come through here day an' night ... No problems.

JAIMIE: I don't want no others to come. I don't want them to eat here! (*indicating his friends*) If we got to take it from behind a store window, then we break the window an' wait for the cops. It's better than ... than this!

He gestures with contempt at the food and the clothes on the table.

MR. HOMER: Rita Joe ... where'd you pick up this ... this loudmouth anyway?

RITA: (*slowly, firmly*) I think ... Jaimie Paul's ... right.

MR. HOMER looks from face to face. The three YOUNG INDIAN MEN are passive, staring into the distance. The fourth is trying hard to clear his head. JAIMIE PAUL is cold, hostile. RITA JOE is determined.

MR. HOMER: (*decisively*) All right! You've eaten ... looked over the clothes ... Now clear out so others get a chance to come in! Move!

He tries to herd everyone out and the four YOUNG INDIAN MEN begin to move away. JAIMIE PAUL mimics the gestures of MR. HOMER and steps in front of the YOUNG INDIAN MEN herding them back in.

JAIMIE: Run, boys, run! Or Mister Homer gonna beat us up!

RITA JOE takes JAIMIE PAUL's hand and tries to pull him away to leave.

RITA: Jaimie Paul ... you said to me no trouble!

JAIMIE PAUL pulls his hand free and jumps to the back of the clothes table. MR. HOMER comes for him, unknowingly still carrying the slicing knife in his hand. An absurd chase begins around the table. One of the YOUNG INDIAN MEN laughs, and, stepping forward, catches hold of MR. HOMER's hand with the knife in it.

YOUNG INDIAN MAN: Hey! Don't play with a knife, Mister Homer!

He gently takes the knife away from MR. HOMER and drops it on the food table behind. MR. HOMER looks at his hand, an expression of shock on his face. JAIMIE PAUL gives him no time to think about the knife and what it must have appeared like to the YOUNG INDIAN MEN. He pulls a large brassiere from the clothes table and mockingly holds it over his breasts, which he sticks out enticingly at MR. HOMER. The YOUNG INDIAN MEN laugh. MR. HOMER is exasperated and furious. RITA JOE is frightened.

RITA: It's not funny, Jaimie!

JAIMIE: It's funny as hell, Rita Joe. Even funnier this way!

JAIMIE PAUL puts the brassiere over his head, with the cups down over his ears and the straps under his chin. The YOUNG INDIAN MEN are all laughing now and moving close to the table. MR. HOMER makes a futile attempt at driving them off.

Suddenly JAIMIE PAUL's expression turns to one of hatred. He throws the brassiere on the table, and gripping its edge, throws the table and clothes over, scattering the clothes. He kicks at them. The YOUNG INDIAN MEN all jump in and, picking up the clothes, hurl them over the ramp.

RITA JOE runs in to try and stop them. She grips the table and tries lifting it up again.

MR. HOMER: (*to JAIMIE PAUL*) Cut that out, you son of a bitch!

JAIMIE PAUL stands watching him. MR. HOMER is in a fury. He sees RITA JOE struggling to right the table. He moves to her and pushes her hard.

MR. HOMER: You slut! ... You breed whore!

RITA JOE recoils. With a shriek of frustration, she attacks MR. HOMER, tearing at him. He backs away, then turns and runs. JAIMIE PAUL overturns the table again. The others join in the melee with the clothes. A POLICEMAN enters and grabs JAIMIE PAUL. RITA JOE and the four YOUNG INDIAN MEN exit, clearing away the tables and remaining clothes.

A sharp, tiny spotlight comes up on the face and upper torso of JAIMIE PAUL. He is wild with rebellion as the POLICEMAN forces him, in an arm lock, down toward the audience.

JAIMIE: (*screaming defiance at the audience*) Not jus' a box of cornflakes! When I go in, I want the whole store! That's right ... the whole goddamned store!

Another sharp light on the MAGISTRATE standing on his podium looking down at JAIMIE PAUL.

MAGISTRATE: Thirty days!

JAIMIE: (*held by POLICEMEN*) Sure, sure ... Anything else you know?

MAGISTRATE: Thirty days!

JAIMIE: Gimme back my truth!

MAGISTRATE: We'll get larger prisons and more police in every town and city across the country!

JAIMIE: Teach me who I really am! You've taken that away! Give me back the real me so I can live like a man!

MAGISTRATE: There is room for dialogue. There is room for disagreement and there is room for social change ... but within the framework of institutions and traditions in existence for that purpose!

JAIMIE: (*spitting*) Go to hell! ... I can die an' you got nothing to tell me!

MAGISTRATE: (*in a cold fury*) Thirty days! And after that, it will be six months! And after that ... God help you!

The MAGISTRATE marches off his platform and offstage. JAIMIE PAUL is led briskly in the other direction offstage.

The lights change. RITA JOE enters, crossing the stage, exchanging a look with the SINGER.

SINGER: (*singing*)
Sleepless hours, heavy nights,
Dream your dreams so pretty.

God was gonna have a laugh
An' gave me a job in the city!

> RITA JOE *walks the street. She is smoking a ciga-*
> *rette. She is dispirited.*

> *The light broadens across the stage.* RITA JOE'*s*
> FATHER *and* JAIMIE PAUL *enter from the wings*
> *stage left. They walk slowly toward where* RITA JOE
> *stands. At the sight of her* FATHER, RITA JOE *moans*
> *softly and hurriedly stamps out her cigarette. She*
> *visibly straightens and waits for the approaching*
> *men, her expression one of fear and joy.*

FATHER: I got a ride on Miller's truck ... took me
two days ...

JAIMIE: It's a long way, David Joe.

> *The* FATHER *stops a pace short of* RITA JOE *and*
> *looks at her with great tenderness and concern.*

FATHER: (*softly*) I come ... to get Rita Joe.

RITA: Oh ... I don't know ...

> *She looks to* JAIMIE PAUL *for help in deciding what*
> *to do, but he is sullen and uncommunicative.*

FATHER: I come to take Rita Joe home ... We got
a house an' some work sometime ...

JAIMIE: She's with me now, David Joe.

RITA: (*very torn*) I don't know ...

JAIMIE: You don't have to go back, Rita Joe.

> RITA JOE *looks away from her* FATHER *with humil-*
> *ity. The* FATHER *turns to* JAIMIE PAUL. *He stands*
> *ancient and heroic.*

FATHER: I live ... an' I am afraid. Because ... I
have not done everything. When I have done
everything ... know that my children are safe ...
then ... it will be all right. Not before.

JAIMIE: (*to* RITA JOE) You don't have to go. This
is an old man now ... He has nothing to give ...
nothin' to say!

> RITA JOE *reacts to both men, her conflict*
> *deepening.*

FATHER: (*turning away from* JAIMIE PAUL *to* RITA
JOE) For a long time ... a very long time ... she was
in my hands ... like that! (*He cups his hands into*
the shape of a bowl.) Sweet ... tiny ... lovin' all the
time and wanting love ... (*He shakes his head sadly.*)

JAIMIE: (*angrily*) Go tell it to the white men! They're
lookin' for Indians that stay proud even when they
hurt ... just so long's they don't ask for their rights!

> *The* FATHER *turns slowly, with great dignity, to*
> JAIMIE PAUL. *His gestures show* JAIMIE PAUL *to*
> *be wrong; the old man's spirit was never broken.*
> JAIMIE PAUL *understands and looks away.*

FATHER: You're a good boy, Jaimie Paul ... a good
boy ... (*to* RITA JOE, *talking slowly, painfully*) I once
seen a dragonfly breakin' its shell to get its wings ...
it floated on water an' crawled up on a log where
I was sitting ... It dug its feet into the log an' then
it pulled until the shell bust over its neck. Then it
pulled some more ... an' slowly its wings slipped
out of the shell ... like that!

> *He shows with his hands how the dragonfly got*
> *his freedom.*

JAIMIE: (*angered and deeply moved by the* FATHER)
Where you gonna be when they start bustin' our
heads open an' throwing us into jails right across
the goddamned country?

FATHER: Such wings I never seen before ... folded
like an accordion so fine, like thin glass an' white
in the morning sun ...

JAIMIE: We're gonna have to fight to win ... there's
no other way! They're not listenin' to you, old
man! Or to me.

FATHER: It spread its wings ... so slowly ... an' then
the wings opened an' began to flutter ... just like
that ... see! Hesitant at first ... then stronger ...
an' then the wings beatin' like that made the
dragonfly's body quiver until the shell on its back
falls off ...

JAIMIE: Stop kiddin' yourself! We're gonna say no
pretty soon to all the crap that makes us soft an'
easy to push this way ... that way!

FATHER: ... An' the dragonfly ... flew up ... up ...
up ... into the white sun ... to the green sky ... to
the sun ... faster an' faster ... Higher ... higher!

> *The* FATHER *reaches up with his hands, releasing*
> *the imaginary dragonfly into the sun, his final*
> *words torn out of his heart.* RITA JOE *springs to*
> *her feet and rushes against* JAIMIE PAUL, *striking*
> *at him with her fists.*

RITA: (*savagely*) For Chrissakes, I'm not goin'
back! ... Leave him alone ... He's everything we
got left now!

> JAIMIE PAUL *stands, frozen by his emotion which*
> *he can barely control. The* FATHER *turns.* RITA JOE
> *goes to him. The* FATHER *speaks privately to* RITA
> JOE *in Indian dialect. They embrace. He pauses*

for a long moment to embrace and forgive her everything. Then he goes slowly off into the wings of stage left without looking back.

FATHER: Goodbye, Rita Joe ... Goodbye, Jaimie Paul ...

RITA: Goodbye, Father.

JAIMIE PAUL watches RITA JOE, who moves away from him to the front of the stage.

JAIMIE: (*to her*) You comin'?

She shakes her head to indicate no, she is staying. Suddenly JAIMIE PAUL runs away from her diagonally across to the wings upstage. As he nears the wings, the four YOUNG INDIAN MEN emerge, happily on their way to a party. They stop him at his approach. He runs into them, directing them back, his voice breaking with feelings of love and hatred intermingling.

JAIMIE: (*shouting at them*) Next time ... in a beer parlour or any place like that ... I'll go myself or you guys take me home ... No more white buggers pushin' us out the door or he gets this!

He raises his fist. The group of YOUNG INDIAN MEN, elated by their newly found determination, surround JAIMIE PAUL and exit into the wings. The light dies in back and at stage left.

The MAGISTRATE enters. There is a light on RITA JOE where she stands. There is also a light around the MAGISTRATE. The MAGISTRATE's voice and purpose are leaden. He has given up on RITA JOE. He is merely performing the formality of condemning her and dismissing her from his conscience.

MAGISTRATE: I sentence you to thirty days in prison.

RITA: (*angry, defiant*) Sure, sure ... Anything else you know?

MAGISTRATE: I sentence you to thirty days in prison, with a recommendation you be examined medically and given all necessary treatment at the prison clinic. There is nothing ... there is nothing I can do now.

RITA: (*stoically*) Thank you. Is that right? To thank you?

MAGISTRATE: You'll be back ... always be back ... growing older, tougher ... filthier ... looking more like stone and prison bars ... the lines in your face will tell everyone who sees you about prison windows and prison food.

RITA: No child on the road would remember you, mister!

The MAGISTRATE comes down to stand before her. He has the rambling confidence of detached authority.

MAGISTRATE: What do you expect? We provide schools for you and you won't attend them because they're out of the way and that little extra effort is too much for you! We came up as a civilization having to ... yes, claw upward at times ... There's nothing wrong with that ... We give you chest X-ray clinics ...

He turns away from her and goes to the apron of the stage and speaks directly to the audience.

MAGISTRATE: We give them chest X-ray clinics and three-quarters of them won't show up ... Those that do frequently get medical attention at one of the hospitals ...

RITA: (*interjecting*) My mother died!

MAGISTRATE: (*not hearing her*) But as soon as they're released they forget they're chronically ill and end up on a drinking party and a long walk home through the snow ... Next thing ... they're dead!

RITA: (*quietly*) Oh, put me in jail an' then let me go.

MAGISTRATE: (*turning to her*) Some of you get jobs ... There are jobs, good jobs, if you'd only look around a bit ... and stick with them when you get them. But no ... you get a job and promise to stay with it and learn, and two weeks later you're gone for three, four days without explanation ... Your reliability record is ruined and an employer has to regard you as lazy, undependable ... What do you expect!

RITA: I'm not scared of you now, bastard!

MAGISTRATE: You have a mind ... you have a heart. The cities are open to you to come and go as you wish, yet you gravitate to the slums and skid rows and the shanty-town fringes. You become a whore, drunkard, user of narcotics ... At best, dying of illness or malnutrition ... At worst, kicked or beaten to death by some angry white scum who finds in you something lower than himself to pound his frustrations out on! What's to be done! You Indians seem to be incapable of taking action to help yourselves. Someone must care for you ... Who! For how long!

RITA: You don't know nothin'!

MAGISTRATE: I know ... I know ... It's a struggle just to stay alive. I know ... I understand. That struggle is mine, as well as yours, Rita Joe! The jungle of the executive has as many savage teeth ready to go for the throat as the rundown hotel on the waterfront ... Your days and hours are numbered, Rita Joe ... I worry for the child I once saw ... I have already forgotten the woman! (*He turns away from her and exits into the wings stage right.*)

The lights on RITA JOE fade. Lights of cold, eerie blue wash the backdrop of the stage faintly. RITA JOE stands in silhouette for a long moment. Slowly, ominously, the three MURDERERS appear on the ramp backstage, one coming from the wings of stage right; one from the wings of stage left; and one rising from the back of the ramp, climbing it. One of the MURDERERS is whistling, a soft nervous noise throughout their scene onstage. RITA JOE whimpers in fear, and as the MURDERERS loom above her, she runs along the apron to stage left. Here she bumps into JAIMIE PAUL who enters. She screams in fear.

JAIMIE: Rita Joe!

RITA: (*terrorized*) Jaimie! They're comin'. I seen them comin'!

JAIMIE: Who's coming! What's the matter, Rita Joe?

RITA: Men I once dreamed about ... I seen it all happen once before ... an' it was like this ...

JAIMIE PAUL laughs and pats her shoulders reassuringly. He takes her hand and tries to lead her forward to the apron of the stage, but RITA JOE is dead, her steps wooden.

JAIMIE: Don't worry ... I can take care of myself!

A faint light on the two of them.

RITA: You been in jail now too, Jaimie Paul ...

JAIMIE: So what! Guys in jail was saying that they got to put a man behind bars or the judge don't get paid for being in court to make the trial ... Funny world, eh, Rita Joe!

RITA: (*nodding*) Funny world.

The light dies on them. They come forward slowly.

JAIMIE: I got a room with a hot plate ... We can have a couple of eggs and some tea before we go to see the movie.

RITA: What was it like for you in jail?

JAIMIE: So-so ...

JAIMIE PAUL motions for RITA JOE to follow him and moves forward from her. The distant sound of a train approaching is heard. She is wooden, coming slowly after him.

RITA: It was different where the women were ... It's different to be a woman ... Some women was wild ... and they shouted they were riding black horses into a fire I couldn't see ... There was no fire there, Jaimie!

JAIMIE: (*turning to her, taking her arm*) Don't worry ... we're goin' to eat and then see a movie ... Come on, Rita Joe!

She looks back and sees the MURDERERS rise and slowly approach from the gloom. Her speech becomes thick and unsteady as she follows JAIMIE PAUL to the front of the ramp.

RITA: One time I couldn't find the street where I had a room to sleep in ... forgot my handbag ... had no money ... An old man with a dog said hello, but I couldn't say hello back because I was worried an' my mouth was so sticky I couldn't speak to him ...

JAIMIE: Are you comin'?

RITA: When you're tired an' sick, Jaimie, the city starts to dance ...

JAIMIE: (*taking her hand, pulling her gently along*) Come on, Rita Joe.

RITA: The streetlights start rollin' like wheels an' cement walls feel like they was made of blanket cloth ...

The sound of the train is closer now. The lights of its lamps flicker in back of the stage. RITA JOE turns to face the MURDERERS, one of whom is whistling ominously. She whimpers in fear and presses herself against JAIMIE PAUL. He turns and sees the MURDERERS hovering near them.

JAIMIE: Don't be scared ... Nothing to be scared of, Rita Joe ... (*to the MURDERERS*) What the hell do you want?

One of the MURDERERS laughs. JAIMIE PAUL pushes RITA JOE back behind himself. He moves toward the MURDERERS, taunting them.

JAIMIE: You think I can't take care of myself?

With deceptive casualness, the MURDERERS approach him. One of them makes a sudden lurch at JAIMIE PAUL as if to draw him into their circle. JAIMIE PAUL anticipates the trap and takes a flying kick at the *MURDERER, knocking him down. They close around JAIMIE PAUL with precision, then attack. JAIMIE PAUL leaps, but is caught mid-air by the other two. They bring him down and put the boots to him. RITA JOE screams and runs to him. The train sound is loud and immediate now.*

One of the MURDERERS has grabbed RITA JOE. The remaining two raise JAIMIE PAUL to his feet and one knees him viciously in the groin. JAIMIE PAUL screams and doubles over. The lights of the train are upon them. The MURDERERS leap off the ramp leaving JAIMIE PAUL in the path of the approaching train. JAIMIE PAUL's death cry becomes the sound of the train horn. As the train sound roars by, the MURDERERS return to close in around RITA JOE.

One MURDERER springs forward and grabs RITA JOE. The other two help to hold her, with nervous fear and lust. RITA JOE breaks free of them and runs to the front of the stage. The three MURDERERS come after her, panting hard. They close in on her leisurely now, playing with her, knowing that they have her trapped.

Recorded and overlapping voices.

CLERK: The court calls Rita Joe ...

MAGISTRATE: Who is she? ... Let her speak for herself ...

RITA: In the summer it was hot, an' flies hummed ...

TEACHER: A book of verse, a melting pot ...

MAGISTRATE: Thirty days!

FATHER: Barkin' to beat hell ... How! How!

JAIMIE: (*laughing, defiant, taunting*) You go to hell!

PRIEST: A confession, Rita Joe ...

Over the voices she hears, the MURDERERS attack. Dragging her down backward, they pull her legs open and one MURDERER lowers himself on her.

RITA: Jaimie! Jaimie! Jaimie!

RITA JOE's head lolls over sideways. The MURDERERS stare at her and pull back slightly.

MURDERER: (*thickly, rising off her twisted, broken body*) Shit ... she's dead ... We hardly touched her.

He hesitates for a moment, then runs, joined by the SECOND MURDERER.

SECOND MURDERER: Let's get out of here!

They run up onto the ramp and watch as the THIRD MURDERER piteously climbs onto the dead RITA JOE.

Sounds of a funeral chant. MOURNERS appear on riser backstage. RITA JOE's FATHER enters from the wings of stage left, chanting an ancient Indian funeral chant, carrying the body of JAIMIE PAUL. The MURDERER hesitates in his necrophilic rape and then runs away. The YOUNG INDIAN MEN bring the body of JAIMIE PAUL over the ramp and approach. The body is placed down on the podium, beside RITA JOE's. All the Indians, young and old, kneel around the two bodies. The FATHER continues his death chant. The PRIEST enters from the wings of stage right reciting a prayer. The TEACHER, SINGER, POLICEMAN, and MURDERERS come with him forming the outside perimeter around the Indian funeral.

PRIEST: Hail Mary, Mother of God ... pray for us sinners now and at the hour of our death.

Repeated until finally EILEEN JOE slowly rises to her feet and turns to the PRIEST and WHITE MOURNERS.

EILEEN: (*softly, over the sounds of chanting and praying*) No! ... No! ... No more!

The YOUNG INDIAN MEN rise one after another facing the outer circle defiantly, and the CAST freezes onstage, except for the SINGER.

SINGER: (*singing*)

Oh, the singing bird

Has found its wings

And it's soaring!

My God, what a sight!

On the cold fresh wind of morning! ...

During the song, EILEEN JOE steps forward to the audience. As the song ends, she says –

EILEEN: When Rita Joe first come to the city, she told me ... the cement made her feet hurt.

END

MICHEL TREMBLAY

When Michel Tremblay saw his first play, *Le Train*, televised in 1964, he realized he had written "a bad French play." As he recalls in the interview collection *Stage Voices*, "When I began to write drama, I wrote bad *French* plays because what I had seen on TV were good *French* plays!" He resolved to write about the people he knew in ways that would reflect their lives and experience as Quebeckers, and in the language they really spoke – not French or even "French-Canadian," but Québécois. With the tremendous success of *Les Belles-Soeurs* in 1968, Tremblay changed the face of theatre in Quebec, becoming an icon of Québécois nationalism and launching a career that would make him Quebec's – and Canada's – foremost dramatist.

The attempt to write modern Quebec onto the stage had begun in 1948 with Gratien Gélinas's *Tit-Coq*, a well-made, sentimental melodrama that pitted an outsider (the "little rooster" of the title, a young soldier played by Gélinas himself) against the established order in the form of church and family. Tit-Coq's illegitimacy, his colloquial language, the realist backdrop of working-class Montreal, all these struck powerful chords in the Quebec audience and made the play an unprecedented success. Led by writers like Gélinas and Marcel Dubé, whose *Zone* (1953) depicted the tragedy of a teenage gang in the Montreal slums, indigenous French-language theatre thrived in 1950s Quebec, aided by the popularity of television drama. But by the end of the decade, Gélinas, Dubé, and the other mainstays of the new theatre seemed to have abandoned Québécois idioms for more standardized Parisian language and style, writing the "good French plays" Tremblay inadvertently took as his own early models. It remained for Tremblay to break the mould by grounding his plays in a radically localized, de-romanticized Montreal milieu. Beginning with *Les Belles-Soeurs*, his characters would speak not in "proper French" but, for the first time ever on the stage, entirely in joual, the bastardized local slang that was for some Quebeckers an embarrassing sign of their cultural degradation, but for others a symbol of their uniqueness as a people.

Tremblay wrote *Le Train* in 1959, his playwriting debut coinciding with the death of Premier Maurice Duplessis and the end of the deeply conservative political regime that had ruled Quebec through the entire postwar era. *Les Belles-Soeurs* premiered the same year René Lévesque founded the nationalist Parti Québécois. The decade framed by these two plays saw the beginning of the period of social renaissance dubbed the Quiet Revolution, as well as the not-so-quiet revolutionary campaign for Quebec independence mounted by the FLQ (Front de libération du Québec) and French President Charles de Gaulle's famous "Vive le Québec libre" speech in Montreal. As the redefinition of Quebec's political identity intensified, the articulation of its culture played an increasingly important role in the ferment of the times. Michel Tremblay was right in the midst of that ferment.

He grew up in a working-class neighbourhood in east end Montreal, the Plateau Mont-Royal, raised by an extended family of women. Though a gifted student, Tremblay eventually left school to work as a printer, his father's profession, before turning to writing full time. In 1964, he met young director André Brassard, who became his lifelong collaborator and primary dramatic interpreter. The next year, Brassard staged several short stories from what would be Tremblay's first published book, *Stories for Late Night Drinkers* (1966). Tremblay wrote *Les Belles-Soeurs* in 1965, and during the three years it took to get produced, he revised and expanded some earlier one-acts into *En Pièces Détachées*, which opened in 1969 at Théâtre de Quat'Sous, the Montreal venue that became most closely identified with his work.

By this time, the parameters of Tremblay's dramatic world had been clearly laid out. The unhappy women of *Les Belles-Soeurs* and *En Pièces Détachées*, and the broken men of the latter play, live on a street very much like the rue Fabre on which Tremblay himself grew up, festering in severely dysfunctional families, sexually and emotionally frustrated and desperate to escape their alienation. Their fantasies of escape are often directed at another street: boulevard Saint-Laurent, a.k.a. "The Main," a fringe society of clubs and bars, hookers, and drag queens, where anything seems possible. But ultimately it proves to be a world of false glamour and shattered dreams. Eventually, the "Cycle of Les Belles-Soeurs" would comprise more than a dozen plays mapping the rich human territory around these two streets.

La Duchesse de Langeais (1969), the lengthy monologue of an aging transvestite, provides Tremblay's first direct introduction to the world of The Main, elaborated again in the musical *Demain matin, Montréal m'attend* (1970), and in *Hosanna* (1973), one of his most popular and enduring plays. The poignant story of a hairdresser-cum-drag queen with a biker lover and the burning desire to be Elizabeth Taylor in the movie *Cleopatra*, the play had productions in Paris, New York, and London between 1978 and 1981, and has been frequently revived in both English Canada and Quebec. An engaging human drama about homosexual love – Tremblay was among Canada's first openly gay playwrights – *Hosanna* also functions as cultural allegory. "We submitted to a foreign culture and this turned us into transvestites," Tremblay has said. "Finally, in the sixties, we began taking off our foreign clothes and trying to rediscover the centre of our Quebec reality ..."

The family plays, too, speak to Tremblay's sense of the broader Québécois condition. *Forever Yours, Marie-Lou* (1971), his most brutal portrait of the self-destructive family, is an image of colonized Quebec torn by internecine warfare and self-hatred. In the play, two sisters, Carmen and

Manon, live haunted by the ghosts of their dead parents, paralyzed by the dead hand of the past. Carmen flees to the clubs of The Main and becomes a country singer, returning in Tremblay's *Sainte-Carmen of the Main* (1976) as a martyr to cultural authenticity. Manon, whom Tremblay has said he loves most of all his characters, becomes a religious fanatic, appearing again in *Damnée Manon, Sacrée Sandra* (1977) along with her alter ego, the transvestite Sandra, Hosanna's archrival. In 1991, the three plays appeared together in Montreal under the title *La Trilogie des Brassard*. A National Arts Centre remount of *Sainte-Carmen of the Main* in Ottawa in 2011 featured, according to *Maclean's* magazine, "a Pakistani-Canadian lead and Icelandic throat singing."

Forever Yours, Marie-Lou initiated the popularization of Tremblay's plays in English, premiering at Toronto's Tarragon Theatre in 1972, directed by Bill Glassco in a translation by Glassco and John Van Burek. Five years later, it became his first play to get an English-language production in Quebec when the election of the Parti Québécois prompted Tremblay to lift his prohibition against English-language productions in his home province. By that time, *En Pièces Détachées, Les Belles-Soeurs*, and *Hosanna* had also entered the English-Canadian repertoire, as had *Bonjour, là, Bonjour* (1974), in which brother-sister incest and the ability of a son to tell his father he loves him indicated Tremblay's more positive feelings about the possibilities of healing within both the microcosm and macrocosm of modern Quebec. It quickly became one of his most popular plays, produced across the United States over the next decade.

After *Damnée Manon*, Tremblay felt he had temporarily said all he had to say in drama and turned his attention to a semi-autobiographical cycle of novels set on the same rue Fabre from the 1940s to the early 1960s. The magic-realist Chronicles of Plateau Mont-Royal include *The Fat Woman Next Door Is Pregnant* (1978) – the title character is Tremblay's mother, pregnant with him; *Thérèse and Pierrette and the Little Hanging Angel* (1980); *The Duchess and the Commoner* (1982); *News from Édouard* (1984); *The First Quarter of the Moon* (1989); and *A Thing of Beauty* (1998). *The Heart Laid Bare* (1986) is the first of a number of his novels about gay love. In 2005, Tremblay completed a fictional trilogy about the cultural transformation of Montreal in the 1960s as seen through the eyes of waitress Céline Poulin and her transvestite friends on The Main: *The Black Notebook* (2003), *The Red Notebook* (2004), and *The Blue Notebook* (2005). *Crossing the Continent* (2007) is the first of his latest series of novels to be translated (the others are *La Traversée de la ville* [2008] and *La Traversée des sentiments* [2009]).

But Tremblay was far from through with the stage. He remained consistently prolific as a playwright for another three decades, continually revisiting his favourite characters and opening new vistas in his exploration of Québécois life with one hit production after another in French and English. In *The Impromptu of Outremont* (1980), he visited the bourgeois drawing room of four sisters who discuss the scandalous opening night of *Les Belles-Soeurs*; an artsy gay couple is his subject in *Remember Me* (1981), and a Québécoise opera singer in *Impromptu on Nun's Island* (2002).

Albertine in Five Times (1984) returned to the gritty emotional landscapes of his early plays, five actresses simultaneously playing the desperate Albertine at different decades in her life. The play had a gala twenty-fifth anniversary English-language production at the Shaw Festival in 2009. In *Past Perfect* (2003), Albertine and her brawling family return again. The *Globe and Mail* called its 2006 Tarragon Theatre production "emotionally breathtaking." In *The Real World?* (1987), Tremblay metatheatrically examines the ways he exploited his own family for his dramatic art. *La Maison Suspendue* (1990) celebrates reconciliation and the imagination in a dreamy, sentimental weaving together of three generations from both the play and novel cycles. *Marcel Pursued by the Hounds* (1992), a prequel to *En Pièces Détachées*, once again finds the tawdry Main a beacon of hope for escape from the misery of family and neighbourhood. *Solemn Mass for a Full Moon in Summer* (1996) poetically treats three sets of lovers on a Montreal summer evening. It had popular productions in England, Ireland, and Australia.

Paying homage to his late mother, Nana, *For the Pleasure of Seeing Her Again* (1998) proved a great popular and critical success in both French- and English-Canada, including a bravura revival at Stratford in 2010. It earned Tremblay another Floyd S. Chalmers Canadian Play Award thirty years after the premiere of *Les Belles-Soeurs*. *Assorted Candies for the Theatre* (2006) revisits Albertine, Nana, and other Tremblay favourites. In 2008, Tremblay gave Nana a monologue from beyond the grave in *Le Paradis à le fin de vos jours* to mark the fortieth anniversary of *Les Belles-Soeurs*. Few hints of paradise are evident in the bitter father-son confrontations of *The Driving Force* (2003). *Fragments de mensonges inutiles* (2009) imagines a homosexual relationship between two young men living fifty years apart.

Tremblay's substantial opus also includes adaptations of plays by Aristophanes, Chekhov, Tennessee Williams, Dario Fo, and Paul Zindel. *Les Gars de Québec* (1985) sets Gogol's *The Inspector General* in rural Quebec during the Duplessis era. Tremblay has written the Québécois pop opera *Nelligan* (1990) and four autobiographical memoirs: *Bambi and Me* (1990), *Twelve Opening Acts* (1992), *Birth of a Bookworm* (1994), and *Bonbons assortis / Assorted Candies* (2002). His screenwriting includes *Il était une fois dans l'est* (1974), a cinematic extension of his early dramatic material in collaboration with André Brassard.

Tremblay's numerous honours include six Floyd S. Chalmers Canadian Play Awards in Toronto, the Governor General's Performing Arts Award, the Ontario Lieutenant Governor's Medal, the Blue Metropolis International Literary Grand Prix, and the Prix France–Québec (twice). In 1984, France named him Chevalier de l'Ordre des Arts et des Lettres, and he has received honorary degrees in English Canada, Quebec, and Scotland. In 2005, the Manitoba Theatre Centre celebrated Tremblay Fest with productions of fifteen of his plays by different companies, making Tremblay the first Canadian playwright to be so honoured. In 2011, he was awarded the Révolution Tranquille medal, given to artists, creators, and artisans who began their careers between 1960 and 1970 and still have an influence in their field of practice.

Les Belles-Soeurs remains his most celebrated work, in French and in translation. In 1991–93 alone, it played in English at the Stratford Festival, in Spanish in Buenos Aires, in Yorkshire dialect in Sheffield, and in French, Yiddish, and Scots in Montreal. In Scots dialect, as *The Guid Sisters,* it has been one of Scotland's most popular plays since 1988. France's prestigious literary magazine *Lire* named *Les Belles-Soeurs* one of the forty-nine plays in its ideal repertoire of world theatre since antiquity. John N. Smith directed an English-language film adaptation, *Geraldine's Fortune,* in 2004. A stage musical version by René Richard Cyr and Daniel Bélanger, titled *Belles-Soeurs*, was the smash hit of the 2010 Montreal theatre season, with an English version being workshopped.

Initially the play met with great resistance. Rejected by the Dominion Drama Festival for its 1967 all-Canadian showcase, *Les Belles-Soeurs* finally gained public attention through a reading at Montreal's recently founded Centre d'Essai des Auteurs Dramatiques, the most important laboratory for new play development in Quebec. The play's premiere, directed by André Brassard at Théâtre du Rideau-Vert in August 1968, elicited howls of protest. Its antagonists complained of the play's unflattering portrayal of Québécoise womanhood, family, and religion. But they focused their attacks on the use of joual with its crudity and vulgarity ("a filthy bathroom language," wrote one reviewer), its incorporation of English words and phrases, and its implications of Quebec's inferiority to the imperial French standard of language and culture. (Tremblay seems to have anticipated these criticisms in the play itself, as the affected character Lisette de Courval gushes over how refined and polite Europeans are, and how beautifully everyone speaks in Paris: "There they talk real French ... Not like here.") For Tremblay, the language established his characters' authenticity. It reflected the frustrations of their daily existence and emblemized Quebec's historical legacy of bitterness and defeat echoed at the end of the play in the ironic singing of "O Canada," which Tremblay has called "an anthem of submission."

Along with the protests there were also torrents of praise, and in short order the play's champions overcame its critics. Following two popular revivals in Montreal, *Les Belles-Soeurs* had a triumphant production in Paris in 1973. That same year Brassard directed its English-language debut at Toronto's St. Lawrence Centre to rave reviews. Seattle hosted the American premiere in 1979. The play's successes in English have come despite the severe difficulties of translating a language whose precise flavour and cultural particularities can only be roughly approximated.

Literally translated, "*les belles-soeurs*" means "the sisters-in-law," but it's hard to miss the additional ironic suggestion of "beautiful sisters." Like the creators of other well-known stage sisters, Anton Chekhov and Tomson Highway, and like his favourite playwright, Samuel Beckett, Tremblay writes tragicomedy. The play opens with Germaine Lauzon celebrating her good fortune. She has won a million stamps – the 1960s equivalent of points you can exchange for products, except these are physical stamps you had to paste individually into booklets before you could exchange them. And for Germaine and her mostly working-class women relatives, friends, and neighbours, the products that can be attained (greatly exaggerated by Germaine) represent a bourgeois consumerist dream of domestic heaven. Tremblay satirizes the manners and dissects the values of the female society gathered in Germaine's kitchen on the rue Fabre – their philistine tastes, greed and envy, social and religious hypocrisy – through sharply comic character portraits and often hilarious ensembles like the "Ode to Bingo." But at the same time he details the fifteen women's painfully repressed desires and thwarted aspirations. They span three generations, but profound unhappiness and pessimism is their common lot. Lacking joy ("I've never laughed in my life"), desperate for affection ("I need ... to love someone"), resigned to futility ("Do I look like someone who's ever won anything?"), they turn their bitterness to resentment. No one can be allowed to snatch a little happiness, not friend or sister, mother-in-law or daughter. The lives of the young – Linda, Lise, and Ginette – promise only to repeat the patterns of the old. The clubs on the Main offer the illusion of hope but no long-term escape, as Pierrette's sad story reveals. Even Germaine's apparent good fortune only leads her down the classic tragic path of dramatic irony, through pride to a fall. No one ever gets to Moscow and Godot never comes.

Tremblay's admiration for the Greek tragic chorus is reflected in the play's choral interludes. In typical Tremblayan fashion, the chorus of women lamenting "this stupid, rotten life" combines pain ("My husband bitches. The kids scream. We all fight") and comic painkiller ("But at night we watch TV"). But Tremblay suggests that the chorus has yet another function: "One woman saying she is unhappy with her life is pitiful, but five women saying at the same time that they are unhappy with their lives is the beginning of a revolution" (*Stage Voices*). The kitchen setting and the absence of men in the play (the image, Tremblay has suggested, of a politically emasculated Quebec) provide a feminized space for the women to voice their complaints and frustrations, many of them regarding sex or domestic oppression linked directly to gender. But they fail to find allies in each other. Their solo turns, when they come downstage to speak to the audience in monologue, occur far more frequently than any choral solidarity. "They're women who should have rebelled but it was still too early in our history for that to happen," Tremblay told Donald Smith in 1986. "They know why they're unhappy and they'd like it to change, but they still don't have the means to do it. All they can do is give in and go on accepting it."

Michel Tremblay

Les Belles-Soeurs

Translated by John Van Burek
& Bill Glassco

Les Belles-Soeurs was first produced at
Le Théâtre du Rideau-Vert in Montreal on
August 28, 1968, with the following cast:

GERMAINE LAUZON	Denise Proulx
LINDA LAUZON	Odette Gagnon
ROSE OUIMET	Denise Filiatrault
GABRIELLE JODOIN	Lucille Bélair
LISETTE DE COURVAL	Hélène Loiselle
MARIE-ANGE BROUILLETTE	Marthe Choquette
YVETTE LONGPRÉ	Sylvie Heppel
DES-NEIGES VERRETTE	Denise de Jaguère
THÉRÈSE DUBUC	Germaine Giroux
OLIVINE DUBUC	Nicole Leblanc
ANGÉLINE SAUVÉ	Anne-Marie Ducharme
RHÉAUNA BIBEAU	Germaine Lemyre
LISE PAQUETTE	Rita Lafontaine
GINETTE MENARD	Josée Beauregard
PIERRETTE GUÉRIN	Luce Guilbeault

Directed and Designed by André Brassard

Les Belles-Soeurs was first performed in English,
translated by John Van Burek and Bill Glassco,
at the St. Lawrence Centre in Toronto on
April 3, 1973, with the following cast:

GERMAINE LAUZON	Candy Kane
LINDA LAUZON	Elva Mai Hoover
ROSE OUIMET	Monique Mercure
GABRIELLE JODOIN	Araby Lockhart
LISETTE DE COURVAL	Mia Anderson
MARIE-ANGE BROUILLETTE	Deborah Packer
YVETTE LONGPRÉ	Louise Nichol
DES-NEIGES VERRETTE	Maureen Fitzgerald
THÉRÈSE DUBUC	Irene Hogan
OLIVINE DUBUC	Lilian Lewis
ANGÉLINE SAUVÉ	Patricia Hamilton
RHÉAUNA BIBEAU	Nancy Kerr
LISE PAQUETTE	Trudy Young
GINETTE MENARD	Suzette Couture
PIERRETTE GUÉRIN	Melanie Morse

Directed and Designed by André Brassard

CHARACTERS

GERMAINE LAUZON
LINDA LAUZON, *Germaine's daughter*
ROSE OUIMET, *Germaine's sister*
GABRIELLE JODOIN, *another sister*
LISETTE DE COURVAL
MARIE-ANGE BROUILLETTE | *neighbours*
YVETTE LONGPRÉ
DES-NEIGES VERRETTE
THÉRÈSE DUBUC, *Germaine's sister-in-law*
OLIVINE DUBUC, *Thérèse's mother-in-law*
ANGÉLINE SAUVÉ
RHÉAUNA BIBEAU | *neighbours*
LISE PAQUETTE
GINETTE MENARD, *Linda's friends*
PIERRETTE GUÉRIN, *Germaine's youngest sister*

SCENE

*The kitchen of a Montreal tenement, 1965. Four
enormous boxes occupy centre stage.*

ACT ONE

*LINDA LAUZON enters. She sees four boxes in the
middle of the kitchen.*

LINDA: God, what's that? Ma!

GERMAINE: (*offstage*) Is that you, Linda?

LINDA: Yeah! What are all these boxes in the kitchen?

GERMAINE: (*offstage*) They're my stamps.

LINDA: Already? Jeez, that was fast.

GERMAINE LAUZON enters.

GERMAINE: Yeah, it surprised me, too. They came this morning right after you left. The doorbell rang. I went to answer it and there's this big fellow standing there. Oh, you'd have liked him, Linda. Just your type. About twenty-two, twenty-three, dark curly hair. Nice little moustache. Real handsome. Anyway, he says to me, "Are you the lady of the house, Mme Germaine Lauzon?" I said, "Yes that's me." And he says, "Good, I've brought your stamps." Linda, I was so excited. I didn't know what to say. Next thing I knew, two guys are bringing in the boxes and the other one's giving me this speech. Linda, what a talker. And such manners. I'm sure you would have liked him.

LINDA: So, what did he say?

GERMAINE: I can't remember. I was so excited. He told me the company he works for was real happy I'd won the million stamps. That I was real lucky ... Me, I was speechless. I wish your father had been here, he could have talked to him. I don't even know if I thanked him.

LINDA: That's a lot of stamps to glue. Four boxes! One million stamps, that's no joke!

GERMAINE: There's only three boxes. The other one's booklets. But I had an idea, Linda. We're not gonna do all this alone! You going out tonight?

LINDA: Yeah, Robert's supposed to call me ...

GERMAINE: You can't put it off 'til tomorrow? Listen, I had an idea. I phoned my sisters, your father's sister, and I went to see the neighbours. And I've invited them all to come and paste stamps with us tonight. I'm gonna give a stamp-pasting party. Isn't that a great idea? I bought some peanuts, and your little brother went out to get some Coke ...

LINDA: Ma, you know I always go out on Thursdays! It's our night out. We're gonna go to a show.

GERMAINE: You can't leave me alone on a night like this. I've got fifteen people coming ...

LINDA: Are you crazy! You'll never get fifteen people in this kitchen! And you can't use the rest of the house. The painters are here. Jesus, Ma! Sometimes you're really dumb.

GERMAINE: Sure, that's right, put me down. Fine, you go out, do just as you like. That's all you ever do anyway. Nothing new. I never have any pleasure. Someone's always got to spoil it for me. Go ahead, Linda, you go out tonight, go to your goddamned show. Jesus Christ Almighty, I'm so fed up.

LINDA: Come on, Ma, be reasonable ...

GERMAINE: I don't want to be reasonable, I don't want to hear about it! I kill myself for you and what do I get in return? Nothing! A big fat nothing! You can't even do me a little favour! I'm warning you, Linda, I'm getting sick of waiting on you, you and everyone else. I'm not your servant, you know. I've got a million stamps to paste and I'm not about to do it myself. Besides, those stamps are for the whole family, which means everybody's gotta do their share. Your father's working tonight, but if we don't get done, he says he'll help tomorrow. I'm not asking for the moon. Help me for a change, instead of wasting your time with that jerk.

LINDA: Robert is not a jerk.

GERMAINE: Sure, he's a genius! Boy, I knew you were stupid, but not that stupid. When are you going to realize your Robert is a bozo? He doesn't even make sixty bucks a week. All he can do is take you to the local movie house Thursday nights. Take a mother's advice, Linda, keep hanging around with that dope and you'll end up just like him. You want to marry a shoe-gluer and be a strapper all your life?

LINDA: Shut up, Ma! When you get sore, you don't know what you're saying. Anyway, forget it ... I'll stay home ... just stop screaming, okay? And by the way, Robert's due for a raise soon and he'll be making lots more. He's not as dumb as you think. Even the boss told me he might start making big money 'cause they'll put him in charge of something. You wait. Eighty bucks a week is nothing to laugh at. Anyway ... I'm gonna go phone him and tell him I can't go to the show ... Hey, why don't I tell him to come and glue stamps with us?

GERMAINE: Mother of God, I just told you I can't stand him and you want to bring him home tonight. Where the hell are your brains? What did I do to make God in heaven send me such idiots? Just this afternoon, I send your brother to get me a bag of onions and he comes home with a quart of milk. It's unbelievable! You have to repeat everything ten times around here. No wonder I lose my temper. I told you, Linda. The party's for girls. Just girls. Your Robert's not queer, is he?

LINDA: Okay, Ma, okay, don't flip your wig. I'll tell him not to come. Jesus, you can't do a thing around here. You think I feel like gluing stamps after working all day. (*She starts to dial a number.*) Why don't you go dust in the living room, eh? You don't have to listen to what I'm going to say ... Hello, may I speak to Robert? When do you expect him? ... Okay, will you tell him Linda phoned? ... Fine, Mme Bergeron, and you? ... That's good ... Okay, thanks a lot. Bye. (*She hangs up. The phone rings right away.*) Hello? ... Ma, it's for you.

GERMAINE: Twenty years old and you still can't say "One moment please" when you answer a phone.

LINDA: It's only Aunt Rose. Why should I be polite to her?

GERMAINE: (*putting her hand over the receiver*) Will you be quiet! What if she heard you?

LINDA: Who gives a shit?

GERMAINE: Hello? Oh, it's you, Rose ... Yeah, they're here ... How 'bout that? A million of 'em! They're sitting right in front of me and I still can't believe it. One million! One million! I don't know how much that is, but who cares. A million's a million ... Sure, they sent a catalogue. I already had one but this one's for this year, so it's a lot better. The old one was falling apart ... They've got the most beautiful stuff, wait 'til you see it. It's unbelievable! I think I'll be able to take everything they've got. I'll re-furnish the whole house. I'm gonna get a new stove, new fridge, new kitchen table and chairs. I think I'll take the red one with the gold stars. I don't think you've seen that one ... Oh, it's so beautiful, Rose. I'm getting new pots, new cutlery, a full set of dishes, salt and pepper shakers ... Oh, and you know those glasses with the "caprice" design. Well, I'm taking a set of those, too. Mme de Courval got a set last year and she paid a fortune for them, but mine will be free. She'll be mad as hell ... What? ... Yeah, she'll be here tonight. They've got those chrome tins for flour and sugar, coffee, and stuff ... I'm taking it all. I'm getting a colonial bedroom suite with full accessories. There's curtains, dresser covers, one of those things you put on the floor beside the bed ... No, dear, not that ... New wallpaper ... Not the floral, Henri can't sleep with flowers ...

I'm telling you, Rose, it's gonna be one beautiful bedroom. And the living room! Wait 'til you hear this ... I've got a big TV with a built-in stereo, a synthetic nylon carpet, real paintings ... You know those Chinese paintings I've always wanted, the ones with the velvet? ... Aren't they though? Oh, now get a load of this ... I'm gonna have the same crystal platters as your sister-in-law, Aline! I'm not sure, but I think mine are even nicer. There's ashtrays and lamps ... I guess that's about it for the living room ... there's an electric razor for Henri to shave with, shower curtains. So what? We'll put one in. It all comes with the stamps. There's a sunken bathtub, a new sink, bathing suits for everyone ... No, Rose, I am not too fat. Don't get smart. Now listen, I'm gonna re-do the kid's room, completely. Have you seen what they've got for kids' bedrooms? Rose, it's fabulous! They've got Mickey Mouse all over everything. And for Linda's room ... Okay, sure, you can just look at the catalogue. But come over right away, the others will be here any minute. I told them to come early. I mean it's gonna take forever to paste all those stamps.

MARIE-ANGE BROUILLETTE enters.

GERMAINE: Okay, I've gotta go. Mme Brouillette's just arrived. Okay, yeah ... Yeah ... Bye! (*hangs up the phone*)

MARIE-ANGE: Mme Lauzon, I just can't help it, I'm jealous.

GERMAINE: Well, I know what you mean. It's quite an event. But excuse me for a moment, Mme Brouillette, I'm not quite ready. I was talking to my sister, Rose. We can see each other across the alley, it's handy.

MARIE-ANGE: Is she gonna be here?

GERMAINE: You bet! She wouldn't miss this for love nor money. Here, have a seat and while you're waiting, look at the catalogue. You won't believe all the lovely things they've got. And I'm getting them all, Mme Brouillette. The works! The whole catalogue. (*She goes into her bedroom.*)

MARIE-ANGE: You wouldn't catch me having luck like that. Fat chance. My life is shit and it always will be. A million stamps! A whole house. If I didn't bite my tongue, I'd scream. Typical. The ones with all the luck least deserve it. What did Mme Lauzon do to deserve this, eh? Nothing. Absolutely nothing! She's no better looking than me. In fact, she's no better period. These contests shouldn't be allowed. The priest the other day was right. They ought to be abolished. Why should she win a million stamps and not me? Why? It's not fair. I work, too, I've got kids, too, I have to wipe their asses, just like her. If anything, my kids are cleaner than hers. I work like a slave, it's no wonder I'm all skin and bones. Her, she's fat as a pig. And now, I'll have to live next door to her and the house she gets for free. It burns me up, I can't stand it. What's more, there'll be no end to her smart-assed comments 'cause it'll all go straight to her head. She's just the type, the loud-mouthed bitch. We'll be hearing about her goddamned stamps for years. I've a right to be angry. I don't want to die in this shit while Mme Fatso here goes swimming in velvet! It's not fair! I'm sick of knocking myself out for nothing! My life is nothing. A big fat zero. And I haven't a cent to my name. I'm fed up. I'm fed up with this stupid, rotten life.

During the monologue, GABRIELLE JODOIN, ROSE OUIMET, YVETTE LONGPRÉ, and LISETTE DE COURVAL have entered. They take their places in the kitchen without paying attention to MARIE-ANGE. The five women get up and turn to the audience. The lighting changes.

THE FIVE WOMEN: (*together*) This stupid, rotten life! Monday!

LISETTE: When the sun with his rays starts caressing the little flowers in the fields and the little birdies open wide their little beaks to send forth their little cries to heaven ...

THE OTHERS: I get up and I fix breakfast. Toast, coffee, bacon, eggs. I nearly go nuts trying to get the others out of bed. The kids leave for school, my husband goes to work.

MARIE-ANGE: Not mine, he's unemployed. He stays in bed.

THE FIVE WOMEN: Then I work. I work like a demon. I don't stop 'til noon. I wash ... Dresses, shirts, stockings, sweaters, pants, underpants, bras. The works. I scrub it, wring it out, scrub it again, rinse it ... My hands are chapped. My back is sore. I curse like hell. At noon, the kids come home. They eat like pigs, they wreck the house, they leave. In the afternoon, I hang out the wash, the biggest pain of all. When that's finished, I start the supper. They all come home. They're tired and grumpy. We all fight. But at night, we watch TV. Tuesday ...

LISETTE: When the sun with his rays ...

THE OTHERS: I get up and I fix breakfast. The same goddamn thing. Toast, coffee, bacon, eggs. I drag the others out of bed and I shove them out the door. Then it's the ironing. I work, I work, I work, and I work. It's noon before I know it and the kids are mad because lunch isn't ready. I make 'em baloney sandwiches. I work all afternoon. Suppertime comes, we all fight. But at night, we watch TV. Wednesday ... Shopping day. I walk all day, I break my back carrying parcels this big, I come back home exhausted. But I've still got to make supper. When the others get home, I look like I'm dead. I am. My husband bitches, the kids scream. We all fight. But at night, we watch TV. Thursday and Friday ... Same thing ... I work. I slave. I kill myself for my pack of morons. Then I spend the day Saturday tripping over the kids and we all fight. But at night, we watch TV. Sunday we go out, the whole family, we get on the bus and go for supper with the mother-in-law. I have to watch the kids like a hawk, laugh at the old man's jokes, eat the old lady's food, which everyone says is better than mine ... At night, we watch TV. I'm fed up with this stupid, rotten life! This stupid, rotten life! This stupid, rotten life. This stup- ...

The lights return to normal. They sit down suddenly.

LISETTE: On my last trip to Europe ...

ROSE: There she goes with her Europe again. We're in for it now. Once she gets started, there's no shutting her up!

DES-NEIGES VERRETTE comes in. Discreet little greetings are heard.

LISETTE: I only wished to say that in Europe they don't have stamps. I mean, they have stamps, but not like these ones. Only letter-stamping stamps.

DES-NEIGES: That's no fun! So they don't get presents like us? Sounds pretty dull to me, Europe.

LISETTE: Oh no, it's very nice despite that ...

MARIE-ANGE: Mind you, I've got nothing against stamps, they're useful. If it weren't for the stamps, I'd still be waiting for that thing to grind my meat with. What I don't like is the contests.

LISETTE: But why? They can make families happy.

MARIE-ANGE: Maybe, but they're a pain in the ass for the people next door.

LISETTE: Mme Brouillette, your language! I speak properly, and I'm none the worse for it.

MARIE-ANGE: I talk the way I talk, and I say what I got to say. I never went to Europe, so I can't afford to talk like you.

ROSE: Hey, you two, cut it out! We didn't come here to fight. You keep it up, I'm crossing the alley and going home.

GABRIELLE: What's taking Germaine so long? Germaine!

GERMAINE: (*from the bedroom*) Be there in a minute. I'm having a hard time getting into my ... Well, I'm having a hard time ... Is Linda there?

GABRIELLE: Linda! Linda! No, she's not here.

MARIE-ANGE: I think I saw her go out a while ago.

GERMAINE: Don't tell me she's snuck out, the little bugger.

GABRIELLE: Can we start pasting stamps in the meantime?

GERMAINE: No, wait! I'm going to tell you what to do. Don't start yet, wait 'til I get there. Chat for a bit.

GABRIELLE: "Chat for a bit?" What are we going to chat about ...

The telephone rings.

ROSE: My God, that scared me! Hello ... No, she's out, but if you want to wait, I think she'll be back in a few minutes. (*She puts the receiver down, goes out on the balcony and shouts.*) Linda! Linda, telephone!

LISETTE: So, Mme Longpré, how does marriage agree with your daughter Claudette?

YVETTE: Oh, she loves it. She's having a ball. She told me about her honeymoon, you know.

GABRIELLE: Where did they go to?

YVETTE: Well, he won a trip to the Canary Islands, eh? So you see, they had to put the wedding ahead a bit ...

ROSE: (*laughing*) The Canary Islands! A honeymoon in bird shit, eh?

GABRIELLE: Come on, Rose!

ROSE: What?

DES-NEIGES: The Canary Islands, where's that?

LISETTE: We stopped by there, my husband and I, on our last trip to Europe. It's a real ... It's a very pleasant country. The women only wear skirts.

ROSE: The perfect place for my husband!

LISETTE: And I'm afraid the natives are not very clean. Of course, in Europe, people don't wash.

DES-NEIGES: It shows, too. Look at those Italians next door to me. You wouldn't believe how that woman stinks.

They all burst out laughing.

LISETTE: (*insinuating*) Did you ever notice her clothesline, on Monday?

DES-NEIGES: No, why?

LISETTE: Well, all I know is this ... Those people don't have any underwear.

MARIE-ANGE: You're kidding!

ROSE: I don't believe it!

YVETTE: You gotta be joking!

LISETTE: It's the God's truth! Take a look for yourselves next Monday. You'll see.

YVETTE: No wonder they stink.

MARIE-ANGE: Maybe she's too modest to hang them outside.

The others laugh.

LISETTE: Modest! A European? They don't know what it means. Just look at their movies you see on TV. It's appalling. They stand right in the middle of the street and kiss. On the mouth, too! It's in their blood, you know. Take a look at that Italian's daughter when she brings her friends around ... Her boyfriends, that is ... It's disgusting what she does, that girl. She has no shame! Which reminds me, Mme Ouimet. I saw your Michel the other day ...

ROSE: Not with that slut, I hope!

LISETTE: I'm afraid so.

ROSE: You must be mistaken. It couldn't have been him.

LISETTE: I beg your pardon, but the Italians are my neighbours, too. The two of them were on the front balcony ... I suppose they thought no one could see them ...

DES-NEIGES: It's true, Mme Ouimet, I saw them myself. I tell you, they were necking like crazy.

ROSE: The little bastard! As if one pig in the family's not enough. By "pig" I mean my husband. Can't even watch a girl on TV without getting a ... Without getting worked up. Goddamn sex! They never get enough, those Ouimets. They're all alike, they ...

GABRIELLE: Rose, you don't have to tell the whole world ...

LISETTE: But we're very concerned ...

DES-NEIGES & MARIE-ANGE: Yes, we are ...

YVETTE: To get back to my daughter's honey-moon ...

GERMAINE: (*entering*) Here I am, girls! (*greetings, "how are yous," etc.*) So, what have you all been talking about?

ROSE: Oh, Mme Longpré was telling us about her daughter Claudette's honeymoon ...

GERMAINE: Really? (*to YVETTE*) Hello, dear ... (*to ROSE*) And what was she saying?

ROSE: Sounds like they had a great trip. They met all these people. They went on a boat. They were visiting islands, of course, the Canary Islands ... They went fishing and they caught fish this big. They ran into some couples they knew ... Old friends of Claudette's. Then they came back together and, oh yes, they stopped over in New York. Mme Longpré was giving us all the details ...

YVETTE: Well ...

ROSE: Eh, Mme Longpré, isn't that right?

YVETTE: Well, as a matter of fact ...

GERMAINE: You tell your daughter, Mme Longpré, that I wish her all the best. Of course, we weren't invited to the wedding, but we wish her well anyway.

There is an embarrassed silence.

GABRIELLE: Hey! It's almost seven! The rosary!

GERMAINE: Dear God, my novena for Sainte Thérèse. I'll get Linda's radio. (*She goes out.*)

ROSE: What does she want with Sainte Thérèse, especially after winning all that?

DES-NEIGES: Maybe she's having trouble with her kids ...

GABRIELLE: No, she would have told me ...

GERMAINE: (*from the bedroom*) Goddamn it! Where did she put that frigging radio?

ROSE: I don't know, Gaby. Our sister usually keeps things to herself.

GABRIELLE: Not with me. She tells me everything. You, you're such a blabbermouth ...

ROSE: You've got a lot of nerve! What do you mean "blabbermouth"? Gabrielle Jodoin! My mouth's no bigger than yours.

GABRIELLE: Come off it, you know you can't keep a secret!

ROSE: Well, I never ... If you think ...

LISETTE: Wasn't it you, Mme Ouimet, who just said we didn't come here to quarrel?

ROSE: Hey, you mind your own business. Besides, I didn't say "quarrel." I said "fight."

GERMAINE: (*coming back in with a radio*) What's going on? I can hear you at the other end of the house!

GABRIELLE: Nothing, it's our sister again ...

GERMAINE: Settle down, Rose. You're supposed to be the life of the party ... No fighting tonight.

ROSE: You see! In our family we say "fight."

GERMAINE turns on the radio. We hear a voice saying the rosary. All the women get down on their knees. After a few "Hail Marys" a great racket is heard outside. The women scream and run to the door.

GERMAINE: Omigod! My sister-in-law Thérèse's mother-in-law just fell down three flights of stairs!

ROSE: Did you hurt yourself, Mme Dubuc?

GABRIELLE: Rose, shut up! She's probably dead!

THÉRÈSE: (*from a distance*) Are you all right, Mme Dubuc? (*A faint moan is heard.*) Wait a minute. Let me get the wheelchair off you. Is that better? Now I'm gonna help you get back in your chair. Come on, Mme Dubuc, make a little effort. Don't be so limp! Ouch!

DES-NEIGES: Here, Mme Dubuc. Let me give you a hand.

THÉRÈSE: Thanks, Mlle Verrette. You're so kind.

The other women come back into the room.

ROSE: Germaine, shut off the radio. I'm a nervous wreck!

GERMAINE: What about my novena?

ROSE: How far have you gotten?

GERMAINE: I'm only up to seven, but I promised to do nine.

ROSE: So, pick it up tomorrow and you'll be finished on Saturday.

GERMAINE: It's not for nine days, it's for nine weeks.

THÉRÈSE DUBUC and DES-NEIGES VERRETTE enter with OLIVINE DUBUC, who is in a wheelchair.

GERMAINE: My God, she wasn't hurt bad, I hope.

THÉRÈSE: No, no, she's used to it. She falls out of her chair ten times a day. Whew! I'm all out of breath. It's no joke, hauling this thing up three flights of stairs. You got something to drink, Germaine?

GERMAINE: Gaby, give Thérèse a glass of water. (*She approaches* OLIVINE DUBUC.) And how are you today, Mme Dubuc?

THÉRÈSE: Don't get too close, Germaine. She's been biting lately.

> *In fact,* OLIVINE DUBUC *tries to bite* GERMAINE's *hand.*

GERMAINE: My God, you're right! She's dangerous! How long has she been doing that?

THÉRÈSE: Shut off the radio, Germaine, it's getting on my nerves. I'm too upset after what's happened.

GERMAINE: (*reluctantly shuts off the radio*) It's all right, Thérèse, I understand.

THÉRÈSE: Honestly, you don't know what it's like, I'm at the end of my tether! You can't imagine my life since I got stuck with my mother-in-law. It's not that I don't love her, the poor woman, I pity her. But she's sick, and so temperamental. I've gotta watch her like a hawk!

DES-NEIGES: How come she's out of the hospital?

THÉRÈSE: Well, you see, Mlle Verrette, three months ago my husband got a raise, so welfare stopped paying for his mother. If she'd stayed there, we would have had to pay all the bills ourselves.

MARIE-ANGE: My, my, my ...

YVETTE: That's awful.

DES-NEIGES: Dreadful!

> *During* THÉRÈSE's *speech,* GERMAINE *opens the boxes and distributes the stamps and books.*

THÉRÈSE: We had to bring her home. It's some cross to bear, believe me! Don't forget, that woman's ninety-three years old. It's like having a baby in the house. I have to dress her, undress her, wash her ...

DES-NEIGES: God forbid!

YVETTE: You poor thing.

THÉRÈSE: No, it's no fun. Why only this morning, I said to Paul ... he's my youngest ... "Maman's going shopping, so you stay here and take good care of Granny." Well, when I got home, Mme

Dubuc had dumped a quart of molasses all over herself and was playing in it like a kid. Of course, Paul was nowhere to be seen. I had to clean the table, the floor, the wheelchair ...

GERMAINE: What about Mme Dubuc?

THÉRÈSE: I left her like that for the rest of the afternoon. That'll teach her. If she's gonna act like a baby, I'll treat her like one. Do you realize I have to spoon-feed her?

GERMAINE: My poor Thérèse. How I feel for you.

DES-NEIGES: You're too good, Thérèse.

GABRIELLE: Much too good, I agree.

THÉRÈSE: What can you do, we all have our crosses to bear.

MARIE-ANGE: If you ask me, Thérèse, you've got a heavy one!

THÉRÈSE: Oh well, I don't complain. I just tell myself that our Lord is good and He's gonna help me get through.

LISETTE: I can't bear it, it makes me want to weep.

THÉRÈSE: Now, Mme de Courval, don't overdo it.

DES-NEIGES: All I can say, Mme Dubuc, is you're a real saint.

GERMAINE: Well, now that you've got stamps and booklets, I'll put a little water in some saucers and we can get started, eh? We don't want to spend the night yakking.

> *She fills a few saucers and passes them around. The women start pasting stamps in the books.* GERMAINE *goes out on the balcony.*

GERMAINE: If Linda were here, she could help me! Linda! Linda! Richard, have you seen Linda? I don't believe it! She's got the nerve to sit and drink Coke while I'm slaving away! Be an angel, will you, and tell her to come home right away? Come see Mme Lauzon tomorrow and she'll give you some peanuts and candy, if there's any left, okay? Go on, sweetie, and tell her to get home this minute! (*She comes back inside.*) The little bitch. She promised to stay home.

MARIE-ANGE: Kids are all the same.

THÉRÈSE: You can say that again! They got no respect.

GABRIELLE: You're telling me. At our house, it's unbearable. Ever since my Raymond started his *cours classique* he's changed something awful ... We don't recognize him! He walks around with his nose in the air like he's too good for us. He speaks Latin, at the table! We have to listen to his awful music. Can you imagine, classical music in the middle of the afternoon? And when we don't want to watch his stupid TV concerts, he throws a fit. If there's one thing I hate it's classical music.

ROSE: Ah! You're not the only one.

THÉRÈSE: I agree. It drives me crazy. Clink! Clank! Bing, bang, bong!

GABRIELLE: Of course, Raymond says we don't understand it. As if there's something to understand! Just because he's learning all sorts of nonsense at school, he thinks he can treat us like dirt. I've got half a mind to yank him out and put him to work.

ALL THE WOMEN: Kids are so ungrateful! Kids are so ungrateful!

GERMAINE: Be sure to fill those books, eh, girls? Stamps on every page.

ROSE: Relax, Germaine, you'd think we'd never done it before.

YVETTE: Isn't it getting a little warm in here? Maybe we could open the window a bit ...

GERMAINE: No, no, not with the stamps. It'll make a draft.

ROSE: Come on, Germaine, they're not birds. They won't fly away. Oh, speaking of birds, last Sunday I went to see Bernard, my oldest. Well, you've never seen so many birds in one house. The house is one big birdcage. And it's her doing, you know. She's nuts about birds! And she doesn't want to kill any. Too soft-hearted, but surely to God there's a limit. Listen to this, it's a scream.

Spotlight on ROSE OUIMET.

ROSE: I'm telling you the woman's nuts. I joke about it but really, it's not funny. Anyway, last Easter, Bernard picked up this birdcage for the two kids. Some guy at the tavern needed money, so he sold it to him cheap ... Well, the minute he got it in the house, she went bananas. Fell head over heels in love with his birds. No kidding. She took better care of them than she did her kids. Of course, in no time at all the females were laying eggs ... And when they started to hatch, Manon thought they were so cute. She didn't have the heart to get rid of them. You've got to be crazy, eh? So she kept them! The whole flock! God knows how many she's got. I never tried to count 'em ... But, believe me, every time I set foot in the place

I nearly go out of my mind! But wait, you haven't heard anything yet. Every day around two, she opens up the cage and out come her stupid birds. What happens? They fly all over the house. They shit all over everything, including us, and we run after them cleaning it all up. Of course, when it's time to get them back in the cage, they don't want to go. They're having too much fun! So Manon starts screaming at the kids, "Catch Maman's little birdies, Maman's too tired." So the kids go charging after the birds and the place is a frigging circus. Me, I get the hell out! I go sit on the balcony and wait 'til they've all been caught. (*The women laugh.*) And those kids! God, what brats! Oh, I like them okay, they're my grandchildren. But Jesus, do they drive me nuts. Our kids weren't like that. Say what you like. Young people today, they don't know how to bring up their kids.

GERMAINE: You said it!

YVETTE: That's for sure.

ROSE: I mean, take the bathroom. Now we wouldn't have let our kids play in there. Well, you should have seen it on Sunday. The kids went in there like they were just going about their business and in no time flat they'd turned the place upside down. I didn't say a word! Manon always says I talk too much. But I could hear them all right and they were getting on my nerves. You know what they were doing? They took the toilet paper, and they unrolled the whole goddamn thing. Manon just yelled, "Look, you kids, Maman's gonna get angry." A lot of good that did. They didn't pay any attention. They kept right on going. I would've skinned 'em alive, the little buggers. And were they having a ball! Bruno, the youngest ... Can you imagine calling a kid "Bruno"? ... Anyway, Bruno climbed into the bathtub fully dressed and all rolled up in toilet paper and turned on the water. Listen, he was laughing so hard he nearly drowned! He was making boats out of soggy paper and the water was running all over the place. A real flood! Well, I had to do something. I mean, enough is enough, so I gave them a licking and sent them off to bed.

YVETTE: That's exactly what they needed!

ROSE: Their mother raised a stink, of course, but I'll be damned if I was gonna let them carry on like that. Manon, the dim-wit, she just sits there peeling potatoes and listening to the radio. Oh, she's a winner, that one! But I guess she's happy. The only thing she worries about is her birds.

Poor Bernard! At times I really feel sorry for him, being married to that. He should have stayed home with me. He was a lot better off ... (*She bursts out laughing. Lights return to normal.*)

YVETTE: Isn't she a riot! There's no stopping her.

GABRIELLE: Yeah, there's never a dull moment with Rose.

ROSE: I always say, when it's time to laugh, might as well have a good one. Every story has a funny side, you know? Even the sad ones ...

THÉRÈSE: You're damn lucky if you can say that, Mme Ouimet. It's not everyone ...

DES-NEIGES: We understand, dear. It must be hard for you to laugh with all your troubles. You're far too good, Mme Dubuc! You're always thinking of others ...

ROSE: That's right, you should think of yourself sometimes. You never go out.

THÉRÈSE: I don't have time! When would you have me go out? I have to take care of her ... Ah! if only that was all ...

GERMAINE: Thérèse, don't tell me there's more.

THÉRÈSE: If you only knew! Now that my husband's making some money the family thinks we're millionaires. Why only yesterday, a sister-in-law of my sister-in-law's came to the door with her hand out. Well, you know me. When she told me her story it just broke my heart. So I gave her some old clothes I didn't need anymore ... Ah, she was so happy ... weeping with gratitude ... she even kissed my hands.

DES-NEIGES: I'm not surprised. You deserve it!

MARIE-ANGE: Mme Dubuc, I really admire you.

THÉRÈSE: Oh, don't say that ...

DES-NEIGES: No, no, no. You deserve it.

LISETTE: You certainly do, Mme Dubuc. You deserve our admiration and I assure you, I shan't forget you in my prayers.

THÉRÈSE: Well, I always say, "If God put poor people on this earth, they gotta be encouraged."

GERMAINE: When you're through filling your books there instead of piling them on the table, why don't we put them back in the box? ... Rose, give me a hand. We'll take out the empty books and put in the full ones.

ROSE: Good idea. My God! Look at all these books. We gotta fill all them tonight?

GERMAINE: Sure, why not? Besides, everyone's not here yet, so we ...

DES-NEIGES: Who else is coming, Mme Lauzon?

GERMAINE: Rhéauna Bibeau and Angéline Sauvé are supposed to come by after the funeral parlour. One of Mlle Bibeau's old girlfriends has a daughter whose husband died. His name was ... Baril, I think ...

YVETTE: Not Rosaire Baril.

GERMAINE: Yeah, I think that's it ...

YVETTE: But I knew him well! I used to go out with him for God's sake. How do you like that! I'd have been a widow today.

GABRIELLE: Guess what, girls? I got the eight mistakes in last Saturday's paper. It's the first time I ever got 'em all and I've been trying for six months ... I sent in the answer ...

YVETTE: Did you win anything yet?

GABRIELLE: Do I look like someone who's ever won anything?

THÉRÈSE: Hey, Germaine, what are you going to do with all these stamps?

GERMAINE: Didn't I tell you? I'm going to redecorate the whole house. Wait a minute ... Where did I put the catalogue? ... Ah, here it is. Look at that, Thérèse. I'm gonna have all that for nothing.

THÉRÈSE: For nothing! You mean it's not going to cost you a cent?

GERMAINE: Not a cent! Aren't these contests wonderful?

LISETTE: That's not what Mme Brouillette said a while ago ...

GERMAINE: What do you mean?

MARIE-ANGE: Mme de Courval, really!

ROSE: Well, come on, Mme Brouillette. Don't be afraid to say what you think. You said earlier you don't like these contests because only one family wins.

MARIE-ANGE: Well, it's true! All these lotteries and contests are unfair. I'm against them.

GERMAINE: Just because you never won anything.

MARIE-ANGE: Maybe, maybe, but they're still not fair.

GERMAINE: Not fair, my eye! You're jealous, that's all. You said so yourself the minute you walked in.

Well, I don't like jealous people, Mme Brouillette. I don't like them one bit! In fact, if you really want to know, I can't stand them!

MARIE-ANGE: Well! In that case, I'm leaving!

GERMAINE: No, no don't go! Look I'm sorry ... I'm all nerves tonight, I don't know what I'm saying. We'll just forget it, okay? You have every right to your opinions. Every right. Just sit back down and keep pasting.

ROSE: Our sister's afraid of losing one of her workers.

GABRIELLE: Shut up, Rose! You're always sticking your nose where it don't belong.

ROSE: What's eating you? I can't even open my mouth?

MARIE-ANGE: All right, I'll stay. But I still don't like them.

*From this point on, **MARIE-ANGE BROUILLETTE** will steal all the books she fills. The others will see what she's doing right from the start, except for **GERMAINE**, obviously, and they will decide to follow suit.*

LISETTE: Well, I figured out the mystery charade in last month's *Chatelaine.* It was very easy ... My first syllable is a Persian king ...

ROSE: Onassis?

LISETTE: No, a *Persian* king ... It's a "shah" ...

ROSE: That's a Persian?

LISETTE: Why, of course ...

ROSE: (*laughing*) That's his tough luck!

LISETTE: My second is for killing bugs ... No one? ... Oh well, "Raid" ...

ROSE: My husband's a worm, do you think it would work on him? ... She's really nuts with all this stuff, eh?

LISETTE: And the whole thing is a social game ...

ROSE: Spin the bottle!

GABRIELLE: Rose, will you shut up for God's sake! (*to LISETTE*) Scrabble?

LISETTE: Oh come now, it's simple ... Shahraid ... Charade!

YVETTE: Ah ... What's a charade?

LISETTE: Of course, I figured it out in no time ... It was so easy ...

YVETTE: So, did you win anything?

LISETTE: Oh, I didn't bother to send it in. I just did it for the challenge ... Besides, do I look like I need to win things?

ROSE: Well, I like mystery words, hidden words, crosswords, turned-around words, bilingual words. All that stuff with words. It's my specialty. I'm a champ, you know, I've broken all the records! Never miss a contest ... Costs me two bucks a week just for stamps!

YVETTE: So did you win yet?

ROSE: (*looking at GERMAINE*) Do I look like somebody who's ever won anything?

THÉRÈSE: Mme Dubuc, will you let go of my saucer? ... There, now you've done it! You've spilled it! That's the last straw!

She socks her mother-in-law on the head and the latter settles down a little.

GABRIELLE: Wow! You don't fool around! Aren't you afraid you'll hurt her?

THÉRÈSE: No, no. She's used to it. It's the only way to shut her up. My husband figured it out. If you give her a good bash on the head, it seems to knock her out a while. That way she stays in her corner and we get some peace.

Blackout. Spotlight on YVETTE LONGPRÉ.

YVETTE: When my daughter Claudette got back from her honeymoon, she gave me the top part of her wedding cake. I was so proud! It's such a lovely piece. A miniature sanctuary all made of icing. It's got a red velvet stairway leading up to a platform and on top of the platform stand the bride and groom. Two little dolls all dressed up like newlyweds. There's even a priest to bless them and behind him there's an altar. It's *all* icing. I've never seen anything so beautiful. Of course, we paid a lot for the cake. After all, six levels! It wasn't *all* cake though. That would have cost a fortune. Just the first two levels were cake. The rest was wood. But it's amazing, eh? You'd never have guessed. Anyway, when my daughter gave me the top part, she had it put under this glass bell. It looked so pretty, but I was afraid it would spoil ... you know, without air. So I took my husband's glass knife ... He's got a special knife for cutting glass ... And I cut a hole in the top of the bell. Now the air will stay fresh and the cake won't go bad.

Lights up.

DES-NEIGES: Me, too. I took a stab at a contest a few weeks ago. You had to find a slogan for some bookstore ... I think it was Hachette or something ... Anyway, I gave it a try ... I came up with "Hachette will chop the cost of your books." Not bad, eh?

YVETTE: Yeah, but did you win anything?

DES-NEIGES: Do I look like somebody who's ever won anything?

GERMAINE: By the way, Rose, I saw you cutting your grass this morning. You should buy a lawn mower.

ROSE: What for? I get along fine with scissors. Besides it keeps me in shape.

GERMAINE: You were puffing away like a steam engine.

ROSE: I'm telling you, it's good for me. Anyway, I can't afford a lawn mower. Even if I could, that's the last thing I'd buy.

GERMAINE: I'll be getting a lawn mower with my stamps ...

DES-NEIGES: Her and her stamps, she's starting to get on my nerves! (*She hides a booklet in her purse.*)

ROSE: What are you gonna do with a lawn mower on the third floor?

GERMAINE: You never know, it might come in handy. And who knows, we might move someday.

DES-NEIGES: I suppose she's going to tell us she needs a new house for all the stuff she's gonna get with her lovely stamps.

GERMAINE: You know, we probably will need a bigger place for all the stuff I'm gonna get with my stamps.

DES-NEIGES VERRETTE, THÉRÈSE DUBUC, and MARIE-ANGE BROUILLETTE all hide two or three books each.

GERMAINE: Rose, if you want, you can borrow my lawn mower.

ROSE: No way! I might bust it. I'd be collecting stamps for the next two years just to pay you back.

The women laugh.

GERMAINE: Don't be smart.

MARIE-ANGE: Isn't she something! Can you beat that!

THÉRÈSE: Hey, I forgot to tell you. I guessed the mystery voice on the radio ... It was Duplessis ...

My husband figured it out 'cause it was an old voice. I sent in twenty-five letters just to be sure they'd get it. And for extra luck, I signed my youngest boy's name, Paul Dubuc ...

YVETTE: Did you win anything yet?

THÉRÈSE: (*looking to GERMAINE*) Do I look like someone who's ever won anything?

GABRIELLE: Say, do you know what my husband's gonna get me for my birthday?

ROSE: Same as last year. Two pairs of nylons.

GABRIELLE: No, siree! A fur coat. Of course, it's not real fur, but who cares? I don't think real fur's worth buying anymore. The synthetics they make nowadays are just as nice. In fact, sometimes nicer.

LISETTE: Oh, I disagree ...

ROSE: Sure, we all know who's got a fat mink stole!

LISETTE: Well, if you ask me, there's no substitute for authentic, genuine fur. Incidentally, I'll be getting a new stole in the autumn. The one I have now is three years old and it's starting to look ... well, a bit ratty. Mind you, it's still mink, but ...

ROSE: Shut your mouth, you bloody liar! We know goddamn well your husband's up to his ass in debt because of your mink stoles and trips to Europe! She's got no more money than the rest of us and she thinks her farts smell like perfume!

LISETTE: Mme Jodoin, if your husband wants to buy my stole, I'll sell it to him cheap. Then you'll have real mink. After all, between friends ...

YVETTE: You know the inflated objects game in the paper, the one where you're supposed to guess what the objects are? Well, I guessed them. There was a screw, a screwdriver, and some kind of bent-up hook.

THE OTHERS: So ...

YVETTE sits down.

GERMAINE: You know Daniel, Mme Robitaille's little boy? He fell off the second-floor balcony the other day. Not even a scratch! How 'bout that?

MARIE-ANGE: Don't forget he landed on Mme Turgeon's hammock. And Monsieur Turgeon was in it at the time ...

GERMAINE: That's right. He's in hospital for three months.

DES-NEIGES: Speaking of accidents, I heard a joke the other day ...

ROSE: Well, aren't you gonna tell us?

DES-NEIGES: Oh, I couldn't. It's too racy ...

ROSE: Come on, Mlle Verrette! We know you've got a stack of them ...

DES-NEIGES: No. I'm too embarrassed. I don't know why, but I am ...

GABRIELLE: Don't be such a tease, Mlle Verrette. You know darn well you're gonna tell us anyway ...

DES-NEIGES: Well ... All right ... There was this nun who got raped in an alley ...

ROSE: Sounds good!

DES-NEIGES: And the next morning they found her lying in the yard, a real mess, her habit pulled over her head, moaning away ... So this reporter comes running over and he says to her, "Excuse me, Sister, but could you tell us something about this terrible thing that's happened to you?" Well, she opens her eyes, looks up at him and in a very small voice she says, "Again, please."

All the women burst out laughing except for LISETTE DE COURVAL, who appears scandalized.

ROSE: Christ Almighty, that's hysterical! I haven't heard such a good one for ages. I'm gonna pee my pants! Mlle Verrette, where in the world do you get them?

GABRIELLE: You know where, from her travelling salesman ...

DES-NEIGES: Mme Jodoin, please!

ROSE: That's right, too. Her travelling salesman ...

LISETTE: I don't understand.

GABRIELLE: Mlle Verrette has a travelling salesman who comes to sell her brushes every month. I think she likes him more than his brushes.

DES-NEIGES: Mme Jodoin, honestly!

ROSE: One thing's for sure, Mlle Verrette has more brushes than anyone in the parish. Hey, I saw your boyfriend the other day ... He was sitting in the restaurant ... He must have been to see you, eh?

DES-NEIGES: Yes, he was – but I assure you, there's nothing between us.

ROSE: That's what they all say.

DES NEIGES: Really, Mme Ouimet, you're always twisting things to make people look bad. Monsieur Simard is a very nice man.

ROSE: Yeah, but who's to say you're a nice lady? Now, now, Mlle Verrette, don't get angry. I'm only pulling your leg.

DES-NEIGES: Then don't say things like that. Of course, I'm a nice lady, a thoroughly respectable one, too. By the way, the last time he was over, Henri ... er ... Monsieur Simard was telling me about a project he has in mind ... And he asked me to extend you all an invitation. He wants me to organize a demonstration next week ... at my house. He chose me because he knows my house ... It'd be for a week Sunday, right after the rosary. I need at least ten people if I'm gonna get my gift ... You know, they give away those fancy cups to the one who holds the demonstration ... Fantasy Chinaware ... You should see them, they're gorgeous. They're souvenirs he brought back from Niagara Falls ... They must have cost a fortune.

ROSE: You bet, we'll go, eh, girls? I love demonstrations! Any door prizes?

DES-NEIGES: I don't know. I suppose. Maybe ... Anyway, I'll provide snacks ...

ROSE: That's more than you get around here. We'll be lucky to see a glass of water!

OLIVINE DUBUC tries to bite her daughter-in-law.

THÉRÈSE: Mme Dubuc, if you don't stop that I'm gonna lock you in the bathroom and you can stay there for the rest of the evening.

Blackout. Spotlight on DES-NEIGES VERRETTE.

DES-NEIGES: The first time I saw him I thought he was ugly ... it's true. He's not good-looking. When I opened the door he took off his hat and said, "Would you be interested in buying some brushes, Madame?" I slammed the door in his face. I never let a man in the house! Who knows what might happen ... The only one who gets in is the paper boy. He's still too young to get any wrong ideas. Well, a month later my friend with the brushes came back. There was a terrible snowstorm outside, so I let him stand in the hall. Once he was in the house, I was frightened, but I told myself he didn't look dangerous, even if he wasn't good-looking ... He's always well-dressed ... Not a hair out of place ... He's a real gentleman ... And so polite! Well, he sold me a couple of brushes and then he showed me his catalogue. There was one that I wanted, but he didn't have it with him, so he said I could place an order. Ever since then, he's come back once a month. Sometimes I don't buy a thing. He just comes in and we chat for a while. He's such a nice man. When he speaks, you forget he's ugly. And he knows so many interesting things! The man must travel all over the province! I think ... I think I'm in love with him ... I know it's crazy. I only see him once a month, but it's so nice when we're together. I'm so happy when he comes. I've never felt this way before. Never. Men never paid much attention to me. I've always been ... unattached. But he tells me about his trips, and all kinds of stories ... Sometimes they're a bit risqué, but honestly, they're so funny! I must admit, I've always liked stories that are a bit off-colour ... And it's good for you to tell them sometimes. Not all his jokes are dirty, mind you. Lots of them are clean. And it's only lately that he's been telling me the spicy ones. Sometimes they're so dirty I blush! The last time he came he took my hand when I blushed. I nearly went out of my mind. My insides went all funny when he put his big hand on mine. I need him so badly! I don't want him to go away! Sometimes, just sometimes, I dream about him. I dream ... that we're married. I need him to come and see me. He's the first man that ever cared about me. I don't want to lose him! I don't want to! If he goes away, I'll be all alone again, and I need ... someone to love ... (*She lowers her eyes and murmurs.*) I need a man.

The lights come on again. LINDA LAUZON, *GINETTE MENARD, and LISE PAQUETTE enter.*

GERMAINE: Ah, there you are!

LINDA: I was at the restaurant.

GERMAINE: I know you were at the restaurant. You keep hanging around there, you're gonna end up like your Aunt Pierrette ... In a whorehouse.

LINDA: Lay off, Ma! You're making a stink over nothing.

GERMAINE: I asked you to stay home ...

LINDA: Look, I went to get cigarettes and I ran into Lise and Ginette ...

GERMAINE: That's no excuse. You knew I was having company, why didn't you come right home. You do it on purpose, Linda. You do it just to make my blood boil. You want me to blow my stack in front of my friends? Is that it? You want me to swear in public? Well, Jesus Christ Almighty, you've succeeded! But don't think you're off the hook yet, Linda Lauzon. I'll take care of you later.

ROSE: This is no time to bawl her out, Germaine!

GABRIELLE: Rose, you mind your own business.

LINDA: So, I'm a little late, my God, it's not the end of the world!

LISE: It's our fault, Mme Lauzon.

GINETTE: Yeah, it's our fault.

GERMAINE: I know it's your fault. And I've told Linda a hundred times not to run around with tramps. But you think she gives a damn? Sometimes I'd like to strangle her!

ROSE: Now, Germaine ...

GABRIELLE: Rose, I told you, stay out of this! You got that? It's their business. It's nothing to do with you.

ROSE: Hey, get off my back! What's with you anyway? Linda's getting bawled out and she hasn't done a goddamn thing!

GABRIELLE: It's none of our business!

LINDA: Leave her alone, Aunt Gaby. She's only trying to defend me.

GABRIELLE: Don't you tell me what to do! I'm your godmother!

GERMAINE: You see what she's like! Day in and day out! I never brought her up to act this way.

ROSE: Now that you mention it, how do you bring up your kids?

GERMAINE: Hah! You should talk! ... Your kids ...

LINDA: Go on, Aunt Rose, tell her. You're the only one who can give it to her good.

GERMAINE: So, you're siding with your Aunt Rose now, are you? You've forgotten what you said when she phoned a while ago, eh? You've forgotten about that? Come on, Linda, tell Aunt Rose what you said about her.

LINDA: That was different ...

ROSE: Why, what did she say?

GERMAINE: Well, she answered the phone when you called, right? And she was too rude to say, "One moment, please," so I told her to be more polite with you ...

LINDA: Will you shut up, Ma! That has nothing to do with it.

ROSE: I want to know what you said, Linda.

LINDA: It's not important, I was mad at her.

GERMAINE: She said, "It's only Aunt Rose. Why should I be polite to her?"

ROSE: I don't believe it ... You said that?

LINDA: I told you, I was mad at her!

ROSE: I never thought that of you, Linda. There, you've let me down. You've really let me down.

GABRIELLE: Let them fight it out themselves, Rose.

ROSE: You bet I'll let 'em fight. Go on, Germaine. Knock her silly, the little brat! You wanna know something, Linda? Your mother's right. If you're not careful, you'll end up like your Aunt Pierrette. I've got a good mind to slap your face!

GERMAINE: Just you try it! You don't lay a hand on my kids! If they need a beating, I'll do it. Nobody else!

THÉRÈSE: Will you please stop bickering, I'm tired!

DES-NEIGES: Lord, yes, you're wearing us out.

THÉRÈSE: You'll wake up my mother-in-law and get her going again.

GERMAINE: She's your problem, not mine! Why didn't you leave her at home?

THÉRÈSE: Germaine Lauzon!

GABRIELLE: Well, she's right. You don't go out to parties with a ninety-three-year-old cripple.

LISETTE: Mme Jodoin, didn't I just hear you tell your sister to mind her own business?

GABRIELLE: Keep your big nose out of this, you stuck-up bitch! Shut your yap and keep pasting or I'll shut it for you.

LISETTE: (*getting up*) Gabrielle Jodoin!

OLIVINE DUBUC spills the saucer she has been playing with.

THÉRÈSE: Mme Dubuc, for God's sake!

GERMAINE: Aw, shit, my tablecloth!

ROSE: She's soaked me, the old bag!

THÉRÈSE: That's not true! You weren't even close!

ROSE: Sure, call me a liar right to my face!

THÉRÈSE: Rose Ouimet, you are a liar!

GERMAINE: Look out, she's falling out of her chair!

DES-NEIGES: Oh no, she's on the floor, again!

THÉRÈSE: Somebody give me a hand.

ROSE: Not me, no way!

GABRIELLE: Pick her up yourself.

DES-NEIGES: Here, I'll help you, Mme Dubuc.

THÉRÈSE: Thank you, Mlle Verrette.

GERMAINE: And you, Linda, you watch your step for the rest of the evening.

LINDA: I feel like going back to the restaurant.

GERMAINE: Do that and you won't set foot in this house again, you hear?

LINDA: Sure, I've heard it a thousand times.

LISE: Can it, Linda …

THÉRÈSE: For God's sake, Mme Dubuc, make a little effort. You go limp like that on purpose.

MARIE-ANGE: I'll hold the chair.

THÉRÈSE: Thank you …

ROSE: If it was me, I'd take that lousy chair and …

GABRIELLE: Rose, don't start again!

THÉRÈSE: Whew! What I go through …

GABRIELLE: Hey, will you get a load of de Courval, still pasting her stamps … The bloody snob. As if nothing had happened! I guess we're not good enough for her.

Blackout. Spotlight on LISETTE DE COURVAL.

LISETTE: It's like living in a barnyard. Léopold told me not to come and he was right. I should have stayed home. We don't belong with these people. Once you've tasted life on an ocean liner and have to return to this, well … It's enough to make you weep … I can still see myself, stretched out on the deck chair, a Book of the Month in my lap … And that lieutenant who was giving me the eye … My husband says he wasn't, but he didn't see what I saw … Mmmmm … That was some man. Maybe I should have encouraged him a little more … (*She sighs.*) … And Europe! Everyone there is so refined! So much more polite than here. You'd never meet a Germaine Lauzon in Europe. Never! Only people of substance. In Paris, you know, everyone speaks so beautifully and there they talk *real* French … Not like here … I despise every one of them. I'll never set foot in this place again! Léopold was right about these people. These people are *cheap*. We shouldn't mix with them. Shouldn't talk about them … They should be hidden away somewhere. They don't know how to live! We broke away from this and we must never, ever go back. Dear God, they make me so ashamed!

The lights come back up.

LINDA: I've had it. I'm leaving …

GERMAINE: The hell you are! I'm warning you Linda! …

LINDA: "I'm warning you, Linda!" Is that all you know how to say?

LISE: Linda, don't be stupid.

GINETTE: Let's stay.

LINDA: No, I'm leaving. I've listened to enough crap for one night.

GERMAINE: Linda, I forbid you to leave!

VOICE OF A NEIGHBOUR: Will you stop screaming up there. We can't hear ourselves think!

ROSE: (*going out on the balcony*) Hey, you! Get back in your house.

NEIGHBOUR: I wasn't talking to you!

ROSE: Oh yes, you were. I'm just as loud as the rest of them!

GABRIELLE: Rose, get in here!

DES-NEIGES: (*referring to the neighbour*) Don't pay any attention to her.

NEIGHBOUR: I'm gonna call the cops!

ROSE: Go right ahead, we need some men up here.

GERMAINE: Rose Ouimet, get back in this house! And you, Linda ...

LINDA: I'm leaving. See ya! (*She goes out with GINETTE and LISE.*)

GERMAINE: She's gone! Gone! Walked right out! I don't believe it! That kid will be the death of me. I'm gonna smash something. I'm gonna smash something!

ROSE: Germaine, control yourself.

GERMAINE: Making a fool of me in front of everyone! (*She starts sobbing.*) My own daughter ... I'm so ashamed!

GABRIELLE: Come on, Germaine. It's not that bad ...

LINDA'S VOICE: Hey, if it isn't Mlle Sauvé. How are you doing?

ANGÉLINE'S VOICE: Hello, sweetheart, how are you?

ROSE: Germaine, they're here. Blow your nose and stop crying.

LINDA'S VOICE: Not bad, thanks.

RHÉAUNA'S VOICE: Where are you off to?

LINDA'S VOICE: I was gonna go to the restaurant, but now that you're here, I think I'll stay.

LINDA, GINETTE, and LISE enter with ANGÉLINE and RHÉAUNA.

ANGÉLINE: Hello, everybody.

RHÉAUNA: Hello.

THE OTHERS: Hello, hello. Come on in, how have you been ... *etc.*

RHÉAUNA: What an awful climb, Mme Lauzon. I'm all out of breath.

GERMAINE: Well, have a seat ...

ROSE: You're out of breath? Don't worry, my sister's getting an elevator with her stamps.

They all laugh except RHÉAUNA and ANGÉLINE, who don't understand.

GERMAINE: Very funny, Rose! Linda, go get some more chairs ...

LINDA: Where? There aren't any more.

GERMAINE: Go ask Mme Bergeron if she'll lend us some ...

LINDA: (*to the girls*) Come on, guys ...

GERMAINE: (*low to LINDA*) We make peace for now, but wait 'til the others have gone ...

LINDA: I'm not scared of you. If I came back it's because Mlle Sauvé and Mlle Bibeau showed up, not because of you. (*LINDA goes out with her friends.*)

DES-NEIGES: Here, take my seat, Mlle Bibeau ...

THÉRÈSE: Yes, come and sit next to me ...

MARIE-ANGE: Sit down here, Mlle Bibeau ...

ANGÉLINE & RHÉAUNA: Thank you. Thanks very much.

RHÉAUNA: I see you're pasting stamps.

GERMAINE: We sure are. A million of 'em!

RHÉAUNA: Dear God, a million! How are you getting on?

ROSE: Not bad ... But my tongue's paralyzed.

RHÉAUNA: You've been doing it with your tongue?

GABRIELLE: Of course not, she's just being smart.

ROSE: Good old Bibeau. Sharp as a tack!

ANGÉLINE: Why don't we give you a hand?

ROSE: Okay. As long as you don't give us some tongue! (*She bursts out laughing.*)

GABRIELLE: Rose, don't be vulgar!

GERMAINE: So, how was the funeral parlour?

Blackout. Spotlight on ANGÉLINE and RHÉAUNA.

RHÉAUNA: I tell you, it came as a shock ...

ANGÉLINE: But I thought you hardly knew him.

RHÉAUNA: I knew his mother. So did you. Remember, we went to school together. I watched that man grow up ...

ANGÉLINE: Such a shame. Gone, just like that. And us, we're still here.

RHÉAUNA: Ah, but not for long ...

ANGÉLINE: Rhéauna, please ...

RHÉAUNA: I know what I'm talking about. You can tell when the end is near. I've suffered. I know.

ANGÉLINE: Ah, when it comes to that, we've both had our share. I've suffered, too.

RHÉAUNA: I've suffered a lot more than you, Angéline. Seventeen operations! A lung, a kidney, one of my breasts ... Gone! I'm telling you, there's not much left.

ANGÉLINE: And me with my arthritis that won't let up. But Mme ... What was her name ... You know, the wife of the deceased ... She gave me a recipe ... She says it works wonders.

RHÉAUNA: But you've tried everything. The doctors have all told you, there's nothing you can do. There's no cure for arthritis.

ANGÉLINE: Doctors, doctors! ... I've had it with doctors. All they think about is money. They bleed you to death and go to California for the winter. You know, Rhéauna, the doctor said he'd get well, Monsieur ... What was his name again? The one who died?

RHÉAUNA: Monsieur Baril ...

ANGÉLINE: That's it. I can never remember it. It's easy enough, too. Anyhow, the doctor told Monsieur Baril that he had nothing to worry about ... And look what happened ... Only forty years old ...

RHÉAUNA: Forty years old! That's young to die.

ANGÉLINE: He sure went fast ...

RHÉAUNA: She told me how it happened. It's so sad ...

ANGÉLINE: Really? I wasn't there. How did it happen?

RHÉAUNA: When he got home from work on Monday night, she thought he was looking a bit strange. He was white as a sheet, so she asked him how he felt. He said he felt okay and they started supper ... Well, now, the kids were making a fuss at the table and Monsieur Baril got mad and had to punish Rolande. That's his daughter ... Of course, after that, he looked like he was ready to drop ...

she didn't take her eyes off him for a second ... But she told me later that it happened so fast she didn't have time to do a thing. All of a sudden he said he felt funny and over he went ... His face right in the soup. That was it!

ANGÉLINE: Lord, have mercy. So sudden! I tell you, Rhéauna, it's frightening. It gives me the shivers.

RHÉAUNA: Isn't it the truth? We never know when God's going to come for us. He said it Himself, "I'll come like a thief."

ANGÉLINE: Don't talk like that, it scares me. I don't want to die that way. I want to die in my bed ... have time to make my confession ...

RHÉAUNA: Oh God forbid that I should die before confessing! Angéline, promise me you'll call the priest the minute I'm feeling weak. Promise me that.

ANGÉLINE: You know I will. You've asked me a hundred times. Didn't I get him there for your last attack? You had Communion and everything.

RHÉAUNA: I'm so afraid to die without the last rites.

ANGÉLINE: But what do you have to confess, Rhéauna?

RHÉAUNA: Don't say that, Angéline. Don't ever say that! We're never too old to sin.

ANGÉLINE: If you ask me, Rhéauna, you'll go straight to heaven. You've got nothing to worry about. Hey! Did you notice Baril's daughter? The way she's changed! She looks like a corpse.

RHÉAUNA: Isn't it the truth. Poor Rolande. She's telling everyone that she killed her father. It's because of her that he got mad, you see, at supper ... Oh, I feel so sorry for her ... And her mother. What a tragedy! Such a loss for everyone. They'll miss him so ...

ANGÉLINE: You're telling me ... The father. Mind you, it's not as bad as the mother, but still ...

RHÉAUNA: True. Losing the mother is worse. You can't replace a mother.

ANGÉLINE: Did you see how nice he looked? ... Like a young man. He was even smiling ... I could have sworn he was asleep. But I still think he's better off where he is ... You know what they say, it's the ones who stay behind who most deserve the pity. Him, he's fine now ... Ah, I still can't get over how good he looked. Almost like he was breathing.

RHÉAUNA: Yeah! But he wasn't.

ANGÉLINE: But I can't imagine why they put him in that suit ...

RHÉAUNA: What do you mean?

ANGÉLINE: Didn't you notice? He was wearing a blue suit. You don't do that when you're dead. A blue suit is much too light. Now, navy blue would be okay, but powder blue ... Never! When you're dead, you wear a black suit.

RHÉAUNA: Maybe he didn't have one. They're not that well off, you know.

ANGÉLINE: Dear God, you can rent a black suit! And look at Mme Baril's sister! In green! At a funeral parlour! And did you notice how much she's aged? She looks years older than her sister ...

RHÉAUNA: She is older.

ANGÉLINE: Don't be silly, Rhéauna, she's younger.

RHÉAUNA: No, she isn't.

ANGÉLINE: Why sure, Rhéauna, listen! Mme Baril is at least thirty-seven, but her sister ...

RHÉAUNA: She's well over forty!

ANGÉLINE: Rhéauna, she isn't!

RHÉAUNA: She's at least forty-five ...

ANGÉLINE: That's what I'm telling you. She's aged so much, she looks a lot older than she is ... Listen, my sister-in-law, Rose-Aimée, is thirty-six and the two of them went to school together ...

RHÉAUNA: Well, anyway, it doesn't surprise me she's aged so fast ... What with the life she leads ...

ANGÉLINE: I'm not sure they're true, all those stories.

RHÉAUNA: They must be! Mme Baril tries to hide it 'cause it's her sister ... But the truth always comes out. It's like Mme Lauzon and her sister, Pierrette. Now, if there's one person I can't stand, it's Pierrette Guérin. A shameless hussy! Nothing but shame to her whole family. I tell you, Angéline, I wouldn't want to see her soul. It must be black as coal.

ANGÉLINE: You know, Rhéauna, deep down inside, Pierrette isn't all bad.

Spotlight on GERMAINE LAUZON.

GERMAINE: My sister, Pierrette, I've had nothing to do with her for a long time. Not after what she did. When she was young, she was so good, and so pretty. But now, she's nothing but a whore.

My sisters and I were nuts about her. We spoiled her rotten. And look what it got us ... I don't understand. I don't understand. Papa used to call her his pepper pot. He was so crazy about his little Pierrette. When he'd put her on his knee, you could tell he was happy. And the rest of us weren't even jealous ...

ROSE: We'd say, "She's the youngest. It's always that way, it's the youngest who gets the attention." When she started school, we dressed her like a princess. I was already married, but I remember as if it were yesterday. Oh, she was so pretty! Like Shirley Temple! And so quick at school. A lot better than me, that's for sure. I was lousy at school ... I was the class clown, that's all I was ever good for ... But her, the little bugger, always coming home with prizes. First in French, first in arithmetic, first in religion ... Yeah, religion! She was pious as a nun, that kid. I tell you, the Sisters were nuts about her! But to see her today ... I almost feel sorry for her. She must need help sometimes ... She must get so lonely ...

GABRIELLE: When she finished school, we asked her what she wanted to do. She wanted to be a teacher. She was all set to begin her training ... And then she met her Johnny.

THE THREE SISTERS: Goddamn Johnny! He's a devil out of hell! It's all his fault she turned out the way she did. Goddamn Johnny! Goddamn Johnny!

RHÉAUNA: What do you mean, not all bad! You've got to be pretty low to do what she did. Do you know what Mme Longpré told me about her?

ANGÉLINE: No, what?

THÉRÈSE: Ow!

The lights come back up. THÉRÈSE DUBUC gives her mother-in-law a sock on the head.

GERMAINE: Beat her brains out if you have to, Thérèse, but do something!

THÉRÈSE: Sure, beat her brains out! Look, I'm doing all I can to keep her quiet. I'm not about to kill her just to make you happy.

ROSE: If it was up to me, I'd shove her off the balcony ...

THÉRÈSE: What? Say that again, Rose. I didn't hear you!

ROSE: I was talking to myself.

THÉRÈSE: You're scared, eh?

ROSE: Me, scared?

THÉRÈSE: Yes, Rose. Scared!

MARIE-ANGE: Don't tell me there's gonna be another fight.

ANGÉLINE: Has there been a fight?

RHÉAUNA: Oh, who was fighting?

ANGÉLINE: We should have come sooner.

THÉRÈSE: I won't stand for that. She insulted my mother-in-law! My husband's mother!

LISETTE: There they go again!

ROSE: She's so old! She's useless!

GERMAINE: Rose!

GABRIELLE: Rose, that's cruel! Aren't you ashamed?

THÉRÈSE: Rose Ouimet, I'll never forgive you for those words! Never!

ROSE: Ah, piss off!

ANGÉLINE: Who had a fight?

ROSE: You want to know everything, eh, Mlle Sauvé? You want all the gory details?

ANGÉLINE: Mme Ouimet!

ROSE: So you can blab it all over town, eh? Isn't that it?

RHÉAUNA: Rose Ouimet, I don't lose my temper often, but I will not allow you to insult my friend.

MARIE-ANGE: (*to herself*) I'll just grab a few more while no one's looking.

GABRIELLE: (*who has seen her*) What are you doing there, Mme Brouillette?

ROSE: Fine, I've said enough. I'll shut up.

MARIE-ANGE: Shhhh! Take these and keep quiet!

LINDA, GINETTE, and LISE arrive with the chairs. There is a great hullaballoo. All the women change places, taking advantage of the occasion to steal more stamps.

MARIE-ANGE: Don't be afraid, take them!

DES-NEIGES: Aren't you overdoing it?

THÉRÈSE: Hide these in your pocket, Mme Dubuc ... No! Damn it! Hide them!

GERMAINE: You know that guy who runs the meat shop, what a thief!

The door opens suddenly and PIERRETTE GUÉRIN comes in.

PIERRETTE: Hi, everybody!

THE OTHERS: Pierrette!

LINDA: Great! It's Aunt Pierrette!

ANGÉLINE: Omigod, Pierrette!

GERMAINE: What are you doing here? I told you I never wanted to see you again.

PIERRETTE: I heard that my big sister, Germaine, had won a million stamps, so I decided to come over and have a look. (*She sees ANGÉLINE.*) Well, I'll be goddamned! Angéline! What are you doing here?

Everyone looks at ANGÉLINE.

Blackout.

ACT TWO

The second act begins with PIERRETTE's entrance. Hence the last six speeches of Act One are repeated now. The door opens suddenly and PIERRETTE GUÉRIN comes in.

PIERRETTE: Hi, everybody!

THE OTHERS: Pierrette!

LINDA: Great! It's Aunt Pierrette!

ANGÉLINE: Omigod, Pierrette!

GERMAINE: What are you doing here? I told you I never wanted to see you again.

PIERRETTE: I heard that my big sister, Germaine, had won a million stamps, so I decided to come over and have a look. (*She sees ANGÉLINE.*) Well, I'll be goddamned! Angéline! What are you doing here?

Everyone looks at ANGÉLINE.

ANGÉLINE: My God! I'm caught.

GERMAINE: What do you mean, Angéline?

GABRIELLE: How come you're talking to Mlle Sauvé?

ROSE: You oughta be ashamed!

PIERRETTE: Why? We're real good friends, eh, Géline?

ANGÉLINE: Oh! I think I'm going to faint! (*She pretends to faint.*)

RHÉAUNA: Good heavens, Angéline!

ROSE: She's dead!

RHÉAUNA: What?

GABRIELLE: Don't be ridiculous! Rose, you're getting carried away again.

PIERRETTE: She hasn't even fainted. She's only pretending. (*PIERRETTE approaches ANGÉLINE.*)

GERMAINE: Don't you touch her!

PIERRETTE: Mind your own business! She's my friend.

RHÉAUNA: What do you mean, your friend?

GERMAINE: Don't try to tell us Mlle Sauvé is a friend of yours!

PIERRETTE: Of course she is! She comes to see me at the club almost every Friday night.

ALL THE WOMEN: What!

RHÉAUNA: That's impossible.

PIERRETTE: Ask her! Hey, Géline, isn't it true what I'm saying? Come on, stop playing dead and answer me. Angéline, we all know you're faking! Tell them. Isn't it true you come to the club?

ANGÉLINE: (*after a silence*) Yes, it's true.

RHÉAUNA: Oh, Angéline! Angéline!

SOME OF THE WOMEN: Dear God, this is dreadful!

SOME OTHER WOMEN: Dear God, this is horrible!

LINDA, GINETTE & LISE: Holy shit, that's great!

The lights go out.

RHÉAUNA: Angéline! Angéline!

Spotlight on ANGÉLINE and RHÉAUNA.

ANGÉLINE: Rhéauna, you must understand ...

RHÉAUNA: Don't you touch me! Get away!

THE WOMEN: Who would have thought ... such a horrible thing!

RHÉAUNA: I'd never have thought this of you. You, in a club. And every Friday night! It's not possible. It can't be true.

ANGÉLINE: I don't do anything wrong, Rhéauna. All I have is a Coke.

THE WOMEN: In a club! In a nightclub!

GERMAINE: God only knows what she does there.

ROSE: Maybe she tries to get picked up.

ANGÉLINE: But I tell you, I don't do anything wrong!

PIERRETTE: It's true. She doesn't do anything wrong.

ROSE, GERMAINE & GABRIELLE: Shut up, you demon. Shut up!

RHÉAUNA: You're no longer my friend, Angéline. I don't know you.

ANGÉLINE: Listen to me, Rhéauna, you must listen! I'll explain everything and then you'll see!

ROSE, GERMAINE & GABRIELLE: A club! The fastest road to hell!

ALL THE WOMEN: (*except the girls*) The road to hell, the road to hell! If you go there, you'll lose your soul! Cursed drink, cursed dancing! That's the place where our men go wrong and spend their money on women of sin!

ROSE, GERMAINE & GABRIELLE: Women of sin like you, Pierrette!

ALL THE WOMEN: (*except the girls*) Shame on you, Angéline Sauvé, to spend your time in this sinful way!

RHÉAUNA: But, Angéline, a club! It's worse than hell!

PIERRETTE: (*laughing heartily*) If hell's anything like the club I work in, I wouldn't mind eternity there!

ROSE, GERMAINE & GABRIELLE: Shut up, Pierrette. The devil has your tongue!

LINDA, GINETTE & LISE: The devil? Come on! Get with the times! The clubs are not the end of the world! They're no worse than any place else. They're fun! They're lots of fun. The clubs are lots of fun.

THE WOMEN: Ah! Youth is blind! Youth is blind! You're gonna lose yourselves and then you'll come crying to us. But it'll be too late! It'll be too late! Watch out! You be careful of these cursed places! We don't always know when we fall, but when we get back up, it's too late!

LISE: Too late! It's too late! Omigod, it's too late!

GERMAINE: I hope at least you'll go to confession, Angéline Sauvé!

ROSE: And to think that every Sunday I see you at Communion ... Communion with a sin like that on your conscience!

GABRIELLE: A mortal sin!

ROSE, GERMAINE & GABRIELLE: How many times have we been told ... It's a mortal sin to set foot in a club!

ANGÉLINE: That's enough. Shut up and listen to me!

THE WOMEN: Never! You've no excuse!

ANGÉLINE: Rhéauna, will you listen to me! We're old friends. We've been together for thirty-five years. You mean a lot to me, but there are times when I want to see other people. You know how I am. I like to have fun. I grew up in church basements and I want to see other things. Clubs aren't all bad, you know. I've been going for four years and I never did anything wrong. And the people who work there, they're no worse than us. I want to meet people, Rhéauna! Rhéauna, I've never laughed in my life!

RHÉAUNA: There are better places to laugh. Angéline, you're going to lose your soul. Tell me you won't go back.

ANGÉLINE: Listen, Rhéauna, I can't! I like to go there, don't you understand. I like it!

RHÉAUNA: You must promise or I'll never speak to you again. It's up to you. It's me or the club. If you only knew how much that hurts, my best friend sneaking off to a nightclub. How do you think that looks, Angéline? What will people say when they see you going there? Especially where Pierrette works. It's the lowest of them all! You must never go back, Angéline, you hear? If you do, it's finished between us. Finished! You ought to be ashamed!

ANGÉLINE: Rhéauna, you can't ask me not to go back ... Rhéauna, answer me!

RHÉAUNA: Until you promise, not another word!

The lights come up. ANGÉLINE sits in a corner. PIERRETTE joins her.

ANGÉLINE: Why did you have to come here tonight?

PIERRETTE: Let them talk. They love to get hysterical. They know damn well you don't do anything wrong at the club. In five minutes, they'll forget all about it.

ANGÉLINE: You think so, eh? Well, what about Rhéauna? You think she'll forgive me just like that? And Mme de Courval, who's in charge of recreation for the parish, also president of the Altar Society at Our Lady of Perpetual Help! You think she'll continue speaking to me? And your sisters, who can't stand you because you work in a club! I'm telling you it's hopeless! Hopeless!

GERMAINE: Pierrette!

PIERRETTE: Listen, Germaine, Angéline feels bad enough. So let's not fight, eh? I came here to see you and paste stamps and I want to stay. And I don't have the plague, okay? Just leave us alone. Don't worry. The two of us'll stay out of your way. After tonight, if you want, I'll never come back again. But I can't leave Angéline alone.

ANGÉLINE: You can leave if you want, Pierrette ...

PIERRETTE: No, I want to stay.

ANGÉLINE: Okay, then I'll go.

LISETTE: Why don't they both leave!

ANGÉLINE gets up.

ANGÉLINE: (*to RHÉAUNA*) Are you coming? (*RHÉAUNA doesn't answer.*) Okay. I'll leave the door unlocked ...

She goes toward the door. The lights go out. Spotlight on ANGÉLINE SAUVÉ.

ANGÉLINE: It's easy to judge people. It's easy to judge them, but you have to look at both sides of the coin. The people I've met in that club are my best friends. No one has ever treated me so well ... Not even Rhéauna. I have fun with those people. I can laugh with them. I was brought up by nuns in the parish halls who did the best they could, poor souls, but knew nothing. I was fifty-five years old when I learned to laugh. And it was only by chance. Because Pierrette took me to her club one night. Oh, I didn't want to go. She had to drag me there. But, you know, the minute I got in the door, I knew what it was to go through life without having any fun. I suppose clubs aren't for everyone, but me, I like them. And of course, it's not true that I only have a Coke. Of course, I drink liquor! I don't have much, but still, it makes me happy. I don't do anyone any harm and I buy myself two hours of pleasure every week. But this was bound to happen someday. I knew I'd get caught sooner or later. I knew it. What am I going to do now? Dear God, what am I going to do? (*pause*) Damn it all! Everyone deserves to get some fun out of life! (*pause*) I always said that if I got caught I'd stop going ... But I don't know if I can ... And Rhéauna will never go along with that. (*pause*) Ah, well, I suppose Rhéauna is worth more than Pierrette. (*She gives a long sigh.*) I guess the party's over ...

She goes off. Spotlight on YVETTE LONGPRÉ.

YVETTE: Last week, my sister-in-law, Fleur-Ange, had a birthday. They had a real nice party for her. There was a whole gang of us there. First there was her and her family, eh? Oscar David, her husband, Fleur-Ange David, that's her, and their seven kids: Raymonde, Claude, Lisette, Fernand, Réal, Micheline, and Yves. Her husband's parents, Aurèle David and his wife, Ozéa David, were there, too. Next, there was my sister-in-law's mother,

Blanche Tremblay. Her father wasn't there 'cause he's dead ... Then there were the other guests: Antonio Fournier, his wife, Rita, Germaine Gervais, also Wilfred Gervais, Armand Campeau, Daniel Lemoyne and his wife, Rose-Aimée, Roger Joly, Hormidas Guay, Simmone Laflamme, Napoleon Gauvin, Anne-Marie Turgeon, Conrad Joanette, Léa Liasse, Jeanette Landreville, Nona Laplante, Robertine Portelance, Gilbert Morrissette, Lilianne Beaupré, Virginie Latour, Alexandre Thibodeau, Ovila Gariépy, Roméo Bacon and his wife, Juliette, Mimi Bleau, Pit Cadieux, Ludger Champagne, Rosaire Rouleau, Roger Chabot, Antonio Simard, Alexandrine Smith, Philémon Langlois, Eliane Meunier, Marcel Morel, Grégoire Cinq-Mars, Théodore Fortier, Hermine Héroux, and us, my husband, Euclide, and me. And I think that's just about everyone ...

The lights come back up.

GERMAINE: Okay, now let's get back to work, eh?

ROSE: On your toes, girls. Here we go!

DES-NEIGES: We're not doing badly, are we? Look at all I've pasted ...

MARIE-ANGE: What about all you've stolen ...

LISETTE: You want to hand me some more stamps, Mme Lauzon.

GERMAINE: Sure ... coming right up ... Here's a whole bunch.

RHÉAUNA: Angéline! Angéline! It can't be true!

LINDA: (*to PIERRETTE*) Hi, Aunt Pierrette.

PIERRETTE: Hi! How're you doing?

LINDA: Oh, not too hot. Ma and I are always fighting and I'm really getting sick of it. She's always bitching about nothing, you know? I'd sure like to get out of here.

GERMAINE: The retreats will be starting pretty soon, eh?

ROSE: Yeah! That's what they said last Sunday.

MARIE-ANGE: I hope we won't be getting the same priest as last year ...

GERMAINE: Me, too! I didn't like him either. What a bore.

PIERRETTE: Well, what's stopping you? You could come and stay with me ...

LINDA: Are you kidding? They'd disown me on the spot!

LISETTE: No, we've got a new one coming this year.

DES-NEIGES: Oh yeah? Who's it gonna be?

LISETTE: A certain Abbé Rochon. They say he's excellent. I was talking to l'Abbé Gagné the other day and he tells me he's one of his best friends ...

ROSE: (*to GABRIELLE*) There she goes again with her l'Abbé Gagné. We'll be hearing about him all night! You'd think she was in love with him. L'Abbé Gagné this, l'Abbé Gagné that. Well, if you want my opinion, I don't like l'Abbé Gagné.

GABRIELLE: I agree. He's too modern for me. It's okay to take care of parish activities, but he shouldn't forget he's a priest! A man of God!

LISETTE: Oh, but the man is a saint ... You should get to know him, Mme Dubuc. I'm sure you'd like him ... When he speaks, you'd swear it was the Lord himself talking to us.

THÉRÈSE: Don't overdo it ...

LISETTE: And the children! They adore him. Oh, that reminds me, the children in the parish are organizing a variety night for next month. I hope you can all make it because it should be very impressive. They've been practising for ages ...

DES-NEIGES: What's on the programme?

LISETTE: Well, it's going to be very good. There'll be all sorts of things. Mme Gladu's little boy is going to sing ...

ROSE: Again! I'm getting sick of that kid. Besides, since he went on television, his mother's got her nose in the air. She thinks she's a real star!

LISETTE: But the child has a lovely voice.

ROSE: Oh yeah? Well, he looks like a girl with his mouth all puckered up like a turkey's ass.

GABRIELLE: Rose!

LISETTE: Diane Aubin will give a demonstration of aquatic swimming ... We'll be holding the event next door to the city pool, it will be wonderful ...

ROSE: Any door prizes?

LISETTE: Oh yes, lots. And the final event of the evening will be a giant bingo.

THE OTHER WOMEN: (*except the girls*) A bingo!

Blackout.

When the lights come back up, the women are all at the edge of the stage.

LISETTE: Ode to Bingo!

While ROSE, GERMAINE, GABRIELLE, THÉRÈSE, and MARIE-ANGE recite the "Ode to Bingo," the four other women call out bingo numbers in counterpoint.

ROSE, GERMAINE, GABRIELLE, THÉRÈSE & MARIE-ANGE: Me, there's nothing in the world I like more than bingo. Almost every month we have one in the parish. I get ready two days ahead of time; I'm all wound up, I can't sit still, it's all I can think of. And when the big day arrives, I'm so excited, housework's out of the question. The minute supper's over, I get all dressed up, and a team of wild horses couldn't hold me back. I love playing bingo! I adore playing bingo! There's nothing in the world can beat bingo! When we arrive at the apartment where we're going to play, we take off our coats and head straight for the tables. Sometimes it's the living room the lady's cleared, sometimes it's the kitchen. Sometimes it's even the bedroom. We sit at the tables, distribute the cards, set up the chips and the game begins!

The women who are calling the numbers continue alone for a moment.

ROSE, GERMAINE, GABRIELLE, THÉRÈSE & MARIE-ANGE: I'm so excited, I go bananas. I get all mixed up, I sweat like a pig, screw up the numbers, put my chips in the wrong squares, make the caller repeat the numbers, I'm in an awful state! I love playing bingo! I adore playing bingo! There's nothing in the world can beat bingo! The game's almost over. I've got three more tries. Two down and one across. I'm missing the B14! I need the B14! I want the B14! I look at the others. Shit, they're as close as I am. What am I gonna do? I've gotta win! I've gotta win! I've gotta win!

LISETTE: B14!

THE OTHERS: Bingo! Bingo! I've won! I knew it! I knew I couldn't lose! I've won! Hey, what did I win?

LISETTE: Last month we had Chinese dog doorstops. But this month, this month, we've got ashtray floor lamps!

THE OTHERS: I love playing bingo! I adore playing bingo! There's nothing in the world beats bingo! What a shame they don't have 'em more often. The more they have, the happier it makes me! Long live the Chinese dogs! Long live the ashtray floor lamps! Long live bingo!

Lights to normal.

ROSE: I'm getting thirsty.

GERMAINE: Oh God, I forgot the drinks! Linda, get out the Cokes.

OLIVINE: Coke ... Coke ... Yeah ... Yeah, Coke ...

THÉRÈSE: Relax, Mme Dubuc. You'll get your Coke like everyone else. But drink it properly! No spilling it like last time.

ROSE: She's driving me up the wall with her mother-in-law ...

GABRIELLE: Forget it, Rose. There's been enough fighting already.

GERMAINE: Yeah! Just keep quiet and paste. You're not doing a thing!

Spotlight on the refrigerator. The following scene takes place by the refrigerator door.

LISE: (*to LINDA*) I've got to talk to you, Linda ...

LINDA: I know, you told me at the restaurant ... But it's hardly a good time ...

LISE: It won't take long and I've got to tell somebody, I can't hide it much longer. I'm too upset. And Linda, you're my best friend ... Linda, I'm going to have a baby.

LINDA: What! But that's crazy! Are you sure?

LISE: Yes, I'm sure. The doctors told me.

LINDA: What are you gonna do?

LISE: I don't know. I'm so depressed! I haven't told my parents yet. My father'll kill me, I know he will. When the doctor told me, I felt like jumping off the balcony ...

PIERRETTE: Listen, Lise ...

LINDA: You heard?

PIERRETTE: Yeah! I know you're in a jam, kid, but ... I might be able to help you ...

LISE: Yeah? How?

PIERRETTE: Well, I know a doctor ...

LINDA: Pierrette, she can't do that!

PIERRETTE: Come on, it's not dangerous ... He does it twice a week, this guy.

LISE: I've thought about it already, Linda ... But I didn't know anyone ... And I'm scared to try it alone.

PIERRETTE: Don't ever do that! It's too dangerous! But with this doctor ... I can arrange it, if you like. A week from now you'll be all fixed up.

LINDA: Lise, you can't do that!

LISE: What else can I do? It's the only way out. I don't want the thing to be born. Look what happened to Manon Belair. She was in the same boat and now her life's all screwed up because she's got that kid on her hands.

LINDA: What about the father? Can't he marry you?

LISE: Are you kidding! I don't even know where he is. He just took off somewhere. Sure, he promised me the moon. We were gonna be happy. He was raking it in, I thought everything was roses. One present after another. No end to it. It was great while it lasted ... but goddamn it, this had to happen. It just had to. Why is it always me who ends up in the shit? All I ever wanted was a proper life for myself. I'm sick of working at Kresge's. I want to make something of myself, you know, I want to be somebody. I want a car, a decent place to live, nice clothes. My uniforms for the restaurant are all I own, for Chrissake. I never have any money, I always have to scrounge, but I want that to change. I don't want to be cheap anymore. I came into this world by the back door, but by Christ I'll go out by the front! Nothing's gonna stop me. Nothing. You watch, Linda, you'll see I was right. Give me two or three years and you'll see that Lise Paquette is a somebody. And money, she's gonna have it, okay?

LINDA: You're off to a bad start.

LISE: That's just it! I've made a mistake and I want to correct it. After this I'll start fresh. You understand, don't you, Pierrette?

PIERRETTE: Sure, I do. I know what it is to want to be rich. Look at me. When I was your age, I left home because I wanted to make some money. But I didn't start by working in a dime store. Oh no! I went straight to the club. Because that's where the money was. And it won't be long now before I hit the jackpot. Johnny's promised me ...

ROSE, GERMAINE & GABRIELLE: Goddamn Johnny! Goddamn Johnny!

GINETTE: What's going on over here?

LISE: Nothing, nothing. (to PIERRETTE) We'll talk about it later ...

GINETTE: Talk about what?

LISE: Forget it. It's nothing!

GINETTE: Can't you tell me?

LISE: Look, will you leave me alone?

PIERRETTE: Come on, we can talk over here ...

GERMAINE: What's happening to those Cokes?

LINDA: Coming, coming ...

The lights come back up.

GABRIELLE: Hey, Rose, you know that blue suit of yours? How much did you pay for it?

ROSE: Which one?

GABRIELLE: You know, the one with the white lace around the collar?

ROSE: Oh, that one ... I got it for $9.98.

GABRIELLE: That's what I thought. Imagine, today I saw the same one at Reitman's for $14.98.

ROSE: No kidding! I told you I got it cheap, eh?

GABRIELLE: I don't know how you do it. You always find the bargains.

LISETTE: My daughter Micheline just found a new job. She's started to work with those FBI machines.

MARIE-ANGE: Oh yeah! I hear those things are tough on the nerves. The girls who work them have to change jobs every six months. My sister-in-law, Simonne's daughter, had a nervous breakdown over one. Simonne just called today to tell me about it.

ROSE: Omigod, I forgot, Linda, you're wanted on the phone!

LINDA runs to the phone.

LINDA: Hello? Robert? How long have you been waiting?

GINETTE: Tell me.

LISE: No. Beat it, will you? I want to talk to Pierrette ... Go on, get lost!

GINETTE: Okay, I get the message! You're happy to have me around when there's nobody else, eh? But when someone more interesting comes along ...

LINDA: Listen, Robert, how many times do I have to tell you, it's not my fault! I just found out!

THÉRÈSE: Here, Mme Dubuc, hide these!

ROSE: How are things at your place, Ginette?

GINETTE: Oh, same as usual, they fight all day long ... Nothing new. My mother still drinks ... And my father gets mad ... And they go on fighting ...

ROSE: Poor kid ... And your sister?

GINETTE: Suzanne? Oh, she's still the brainy one. She can't do anything wrong, you know? "Now there's a girl who uses her head. You should be more like her, Ginette. She's making something of her life" ... Nobody else even counts, especially me. But they always did like her best. And, of course, now she's a teacher, you'd think she was a saint or something.

ROSE: Hey, come on, Ginette. Isn't that a bit much?

GINETTE: No, I'm serious ... My mother's never cared about me. It's always, "Suzanne's the prettiest. Suzanne's the nicest" ... Day in, day out till I'm sick of it! Even Lise doesn't like me anymore!

LINDA: (*on the phone*) Oh, go to hell! If you're not gonna listen, why should I talk? Call me back when you're in a better mood! (*She hangs up.*) For Chrissake, Aunt Rose, why didn't you tell me I was wanted on the phone? Now he's pissed off at me!

ROSE: Isn't she polite! You see how polite she is?

Spotlight on PIERRETTE GUÉRIN.

PIERRETTE: When I left home, I was head over heels in love, I couldn't even see straight. No one existed for me but Johnny. He made me waste ten years of my life, the bastard. I'm only thirty now and I feel like sixty. The things that guy got me to do! And me, the idiot, I listened to him. Did I ever. Ten years I worked his club for him. I was a looker, I brought in the customers, and that was fine as long as it lasted ... But now ... now I'm fucked. I feel like jumping off a bridge. All I got left is the bottle. And that's what I've been doing since Friday. Poor Lise, she thinks she's done for just 'cause she's pregnant. She's young, I'll give her my doctor's name ... He'll fix her up. It'll be easy for her to start over. But not me. Not me. I'm too old. A girl who's been at it for ten years is washed up. Finished. And try telling that to my sisters. They'll never understand. I don't know what I'm gonna do now. I don't know.

LISE: I don't know what I'm gonna do now. I don't know. An abortion, that's serious. I've heard enough stories to know that. But I guess I'm better off going to see Pierrette's doctor than trying to do it myself. Ah, why do these things always happen to me? Pierrette, she's lucky. Working in the same club for ten years, making a bundle ... And she's in love! I wouldn't mind being in her shoes. Even if her family can't stand her, at least she's happy on her own.

PIERRETTE: He dumped me, just like that! "It's finished," he said. "I don't need you anymore. You're too old and too ugly. So pack your bags and beat it." That son of a bitch! He didn't leave me a nickel! Not a goddamn nickel! After all I did for him. Ten years! Ten years for nothing. That's enough to make anyone pack it in. What am I gonna do now, eh? What? Become a waitress at Kresge's like Lise? No thanks! Kresge's is fine for kids and old ladies, but not for me. I don't know what I'm gonna do. I just don't know. And here I've gotta pretend everything's great. But I can't tell Linda and Lise I'm washed up. (*Silence.*) Yeah ... I guess there's nothing left but booze ... Good thing I like that ...

LISE: (*interspersed throughout PIERRETTE's last speech*) I'm scared, dear God, I'm scared! (*She approaches PIERRETTE.*) Are you sure this'll work, Pierrette? If you only knew how scared I am!

PIERRETTE: (*laughing*) 'Course it will. It'll be fine, kid. You'll see ...

The lights come back up.

MARIE-ANGE: It's not even safe to go to the show anymore. I went to the Rex the other day to see Belmondo in something, I forget what. I went alone, 'cause my husband didn't wanna go. Well, all of a sudden, right in the middle of the show this smelly old bum sits down next to me and starts grabbing my knee. You can imagine how embarrassed I was but that didn't stop me. I stood up, took my purse and smashed him right in his ugly face.

DES-NEIGES: Good for you, Mme Brouillette! I always carry a hatpin when I go to the show. You never know what'll happen. And the first one who tries to get fresh with me ... But I've never used it yet.

ROSE: Hey, Germaine, these Cokes are pretty warm.

GERMAINE: When are you gonna stop criticizing, eh? When?

LISE: Linda, you got a pencil and paper?

LINDA: I'm telling you, Lise, don't do it!

LISE: I know what I'm doing. I've made up my mind and nothing's gonna make me change it.

RHÉAUNA: (*to THÉRÈSE*) What are you doing there?

THÉRÈSE: Shh! Not so loud! You should take some, too. Two or three books, she'll never know.

RHÉAUNA: I'm not a thief!

THÉRÈSE: Come on, Mlle Bibeau, it's not a question of stealing. She got these stamps for nothing and there's a million of 'em. A million!

RHÉAUNA: Say what you will, she invited us here to paste her stamps and we've got no right to steal them!

GERMAINE: (*to ROSE*) What are those two talking about? I don't like all this whispering ...

She goes over to RHÉAUNA and THÉRÈSE.

THÉRÈSE: (*seeing her coming*) Oh ... Yeah ... You add two cups of water and stir.

RHÉAUNA: What? (*noticing GERMAINE*) Oh! Yes! She was giving me a recipe.

GERMAINE: A recipe for what?

RHÉAUNA: Doughnuts!

THÉRÈSE: Chocolate pudding!

GERMAINE: Well, which is it? Doughnuts or chocolate pudding? (*She comes back to ROSE.*) Listen, Rose, there's something fishy going on around here.

ROSE: (*who has just hidden a few books in her purse*) Don't be silly ... You're imagining things

GERMAINE: And I think Linda's spending too much time with Pierrette. Linda, get over here!

LINDA: In a minute, Ma ...

GERMAINE: I said come here! That means now. Not tomorrow!

LINDA: Okay! Don't get in a flap ... So, what do you want?

GABRIELLE: Stay with us a bit ... You've been with your aunt long enough.

LINDA: So what?

GERMAINE: What's going on between her and Lise there?

LINDA: Oh ... Nothing ...

GERMAINE: Answer when you're spoken to!

ROSE: Lise wrote something down a while ago.

LINDA: It was just an address ...

GERMAINE: Not Pierrette's, I hope! If I ever find out you've been to her place, you're gonna hear from me, got that?

LINDA: Will you lay off! I'm old enough to know what I'm doing! (*She goes back to PIERRETTE.*)

ROSE: Maybe it's none of my business, Germaine, but ...

GERMAINE: Why, what's the matter now?

ROSE: Your Linda's picking up some pretty bad habits ...

GERMAINE: You can say that again! But don't worry, Rose, I can handle her. She's gonna straighten out fast. And as for Pierrette, it's the last time she'll set foot in this house. I'll throw her down the goddamn stairs!

MARIE-ANGE: Have you noticed Mme Bergeron's daughter lately? Wouldn't you say she's been putting on weight?

LISETTE: Yes, I've noticed that ...

THÉRÈSE: (*insinuating*) Strange, isn't it? It's all in her middle.

ROSE: I guess the sap's running a bit early this year.

MARIE-ANGE: She tries to hide it, too. It's beginning to show, though.

THÉRÈSE: And how! I wonder who could have done it?

LISETTE: It's probably her stepfather ...

GERMAINE: Wouldn't surprise me in the least. He's been after her ever since he married her mother.

THÉRÈSE: It must be awful in that house. I feel sorry for Monique. She's so young ...

ROSE: Maybe so, but you must admit, she's been looking for it, too. Look how she dresses. Last summer, I was embarrassed to look at her! And you know me, I'm no prude. Remember those red shorts she had on, those short shorts? Well, I said it then, and I'll say it again, "Monique Bergeron is gonna turn out bad." She's got the devil in her, that girl, a real demon. Besides, she's a redhead ... No, you can say what you like, those unwed mothers deserve what they get and I got no sympathy for 'em.

LISE starts to get up.

PIERRETTE: Take it easy, kid!

ROSE: It's true! It's their own damn fault! I'm not talking about the ones who get raped. That's different. But an ordinary girl who gets herself knocked up, uh! uh! ... She gets no sympathy from me. It's too goddamn bad! I tell you, if my Carmen ever came home like that, she'd go sailing right through the window! Not that I'm worried about her, mind you. She's not that kind of girl ... Nope, for me unwed mothers are all the same. A bunch of depraved sluts. You know what my husband calls 'em, eh? Cockteasers!

LISE: I'll kill her if she doesn't shut up!

GINETTE: Why? If you ask me, she's right.

LISE: You shut your trap and get out of here!

PIERRETTE: Isn't that a bit much, Rose?

ROSE: Listen, Pierrette, we know you're an expert on these matters. We know you can't be shocked. Maybe you think it's normal, but we don't. There's one way to prevent it ...

PIERRETTE: (*laughing*) There's lots of ways. Ever heard of the pill?

ROSE: It's no use talking to you! That's not what I meant! I'm against free love! I'm a Catholic! So leave us alone and stay where you belong, filthy whore!

LISETTE: I think perhaps you exaggerate, Mme Ouimet. There are occasions when girls can get themselves in trouble and it's not entirely their fault.

ROSE: You! You believe everything they tell you in those stupid French movies!

LISETTE: What have you got against French movies?

ROSE: Nothing. I like English ones better, that's all. French movies, they're too realistic, too farfetched. You shouldn't believe what they say. They always make you feel sorry for the girl who gets pregnant. It's never anyone else's fault. Well, do you feel sorry for tramps like that? I don't! A movie's a movie and life's life!

LISE: I'll kill her, the bitch! Stupid fucking jerk! She goes around judging everyone – and she's got the brains of a ... And as for her Carmen. Well, I happen to know her Carmen and believe me, she does a lot more than tease! She oughta clean her own house before she shits on everyone else.

*Spotlight on **ROSE OUIMET**.*

ROSE: That's right. Life is life and no goddamn Frenchman ever made a movie about that! Sure, any old actress can make you feel sorry for her in a movie. Easy as pie! And when she's finished work, she can go home to her big fat mansion and climb into her big fat bed that's twice the size of my bedroom, for Chrissake! But the rest of us, when we get up in the morning ... When I wake up in the morning he's lying there staring at me ... Waiting. Every morning, I open my eyes and there he is, waiting! Every night, I get into bed and there he is, waiting! He's always there, always after me, always hanging over me like a vulture. Goddamn sex! It's never that way in the movies, is it? Oh no, in the movies it's always fun! Besides, who cares about a woman who's gotta spend her life with a pig just 'cause she said yes to him once? Well, I'm telling you, no fucking movie was ever this sad. Because movies don't last a lifetime! (*Silence.*) Why did I ever do it? Why? I should have said no. I should have yelled no at the top of my lungs and stayed an old maid. At least I'd have had some peace. I was so ignorant in those days. Christ, I didn't know what I was in for. All I could think of was "the Holy State of Matrimony"! You gotta be stupid to bring up your kids like that, knowing nothing. My Carmen won't get caught like that. Because I've been telling her for years what men are really worth. She won't be able to say I didn't warn her! (*on the verge of tears*) She won't end up like me, forty-four years old, with a two-year-old kid and another one on the way, with a stupid slob of a husband who can't understand a thing, who demands his "rights" at least twice a day, 365 days a year. When you get to be forty and you realize you've got nothing behind you and nothing ahead of you, it makes you want to dump everything and start all over ... But women ... women can't do that ... They get grabbed by the throat, and they stay that way, right to the end!

The lights come back up.

GABRIELLE: Well, I like French movies. They sure know how to make 'em good and sad. They make me cry every time. And you must admit, Frenchmen are a lot better looking than Canadians. They're real men!

GERMAINE: Now wait just a minute! That's not true.

MARIE-ANGE: Come on! The little peckers don't even come up to my shoulder. And they act like girls! Of course, what do you expect? They're all queer!

GABRIELLE: I beg your pardon. Some of them are men! And I don't mean like our husbands.

MARIE-ANGE: After our husbands, anything looks good.

LISETTE: You don't mix serviettes with paper napkins.

GERMAINE: Okay, so our husbands are rough, but our actors are just as good and just as good-looking as any one of those French fairies from France.

GABRIELLE: Well, I wouldn't say no to Jean Marais. Now there's a real man!

OLIVINE: Coke ... Coke ... More ... Coke ...

ROSE: Hey, can't you shut her up? It's impossible to work! Shove a Coke in her mouth, Germaine. That'll keep her quiet.

GERMAINE: I think I've run out.

ROSE: Jesus, you didn't buy much, did you? Talk about cheap!

RHÉAUNA: (*as she steals some stamps*) Oh, what the heck. Three more books and I can get my chrome dustpan.

ANGÉLINE: (*comes in*) Hello ... (*to RHÉAUNA*) I've come back ...

THE OTHERS: (*coldly*) Hello ...

ANGÉLINE: I went to see Father Castelneau ...

PIERRETTE: She didn't even look at me!

MARIE-ANGE: What does she want with Mlle Bibeau?

DES-NEIGES: I'm sure it's to ask forgiveness. After all, Mlle Sauvé is a good person and she knows what's right. It'll all work out for the best, you'll see.

GERMAINE: While we're waiting, I'm gonna see how many books we've filled.

The women sit up in their chairs. GABRIELLE hesitates, then speaks.

GABRIELLE: Oh, Germaine, I forgot to tell you. I found a corset-maker. Her name's Angélina Giroux. Come over here, I'll tell you about her.

RHÉAUNA: I knew you'd come back to me, Angéline. I'm very happy. You'll see, we'll pray together and the Good Lord will forget all about it. God's not stupid, you know.

LISE: That's it, Pierrette, they've made up.

PIERRETTE: I'll be goddamned!

ANGÉLINE: I'll just say goodbye to Pierrette and explain ...

RHÉAUNA: No, you'd best not say another word to her. Stay with me and leave her alone. That chapter's closed.

ANGÉLINE: Whatever you say.

PIERRETTE: Well, that's that. She's won. Makes me want to puke. Nothing left for me to do here. I'm getting out of here.

GERMAINE: Gaby, you're terrific. I'd almost given up hope. It's not everyone can make me a corset. I'll go see her next week. (*She goes over to the box that is supposed to hold the completed books. The women follow her with their eyes.*) My God, there isn't much here! Where are all the booklets? There's no more than a dozen in the box. Maybe they're ... No, the table's empty! (*Silence. GERMAINE looks at all the women.*) What's going on here?

THE OTHERS: Well ... Ah ... I don't know ... Really ...

They pretend to search for the books. GERMAINE stations herself in front of the door.

GERMAINE: Where are my stamps?

ROSE: I don't know, Germaine. Let's look for them.

GERMAINE: They're not in the box and they're not on the table. I want to know what's happened to my stamps!

OLIVINE: (*pulling stamps out from under her clothes*) Stamps? Stamps ... Stamps ... (*She laughs.*)

THÉRÈSE: Mme Dubuc, hide that ... Goddamn it, Mme Dubuc!

MARIE-ANGE: Holy Sainte Anne!

DES-NEIGES: Pray for us!

GERMAINE: But her clothes are full of them! What the ... She's got them everywhere! Here ... and here ... Thérèse ... Don't tell me it's you.

THÉRÈSE: Heavens, no! I swear, I had no idea!

GERMAINE: Let me see your purse.

THÉRÈSE: Really, Germaine, if that's all the faith you have in me.

ROSE: Germaine, don't be ridiculous!

GERMAINE: You too, Rose. I want to see your purse. I want to see all your purses. Every one of them!

DES-NEIGES: I refuse! I've never been so insulted!

YVETTE: Me neither.

LISETTE: I'll never set foot in here again!

GERMAINE grabs THÉRÈSE's bag and opens it. She pulls out several books.

GERMAINE: Ah hah! I knew it! I bet it's the same with all of you! You bastards! You won't get out of here alive! I'll knock you to kingdom come!

PIERRETTE: I'll help you, Germaine. Nothing but a pack of thieves! And they look down their noses at me!

GERMAINE: Show me your purses. (*She grabs ROSE's purse.*) Look at that ... And that! (*She grabs another purse.*) More here. And look, still more! You too, Mlle Bibeau? There's only three, but even so!

ANGÉLINE: Oh Rhéauna, you too!

GERMAINE: All of you, thieves! The whole bunch of you, you hear me? Thieves!

MARIE-ANGE: You don't deserve all those stamps.

DES-NEIGES: Why you more than anyone else?

ROSE: You've made us feel like shit with your million stamps!

GERMAINE: But those stamps are mine!

LISETTE: They ought to be for everyone!

THE OTHERS: Yeah, everyone!

GERMAINE: But they're mine! Give them back to me!

THE OTHERS: No way!

MARIE-ANGE: There's lots more in the boxes. Let's help ourselves.

DES-NEIGES: Good idea.

YVETTE: I'm filling my purse.

GERMAINE: Stop! Keep your hands off!

THÉRÈSE: Here, Mme Dubuc, take these! Here's some more.

MARIE-ANGE: Come on, Mlle Verrette. There's tons of them. Here. Give me a hand.

PIERRETTE: Let go of that!

GERMAINE: My stamps! My stamps!

ROSE: Help me, Gaby, I've got too many!

GERMAINE: My stamps! My stamps!

A huge battle ensues. The women steal all the stamps they can. PIERRETTE and GERMAINE try to stop them. LINDA and LISE stay seated in the corner and watch without moving. Screams are heard as some of the women begin fighting.

MARIE-ANGE: Give me those, they're mine!

ROSE: That's a lie, they're mine!

LISETTE: (*to GABRIELLE*) Will you let go of me! Let me go!

They start throwing stamps and books at one another. Everybody grabs all they can get their hands on, throwing stamps everywhere, out the door, even out the window. OLIVINE DUBUC starts cruising around in her wheelchair singing "O Canada." A few women go out with their loot of stamps. ROSE and GABRIELLE stay a bit longer than the others.

GERMAINE: My sisters! My own sisters!

GABRIELLE and ROSE go out. The only ones left in the kitchen are GERMAINE, LINDA, and PIERRETTE. GERMAINE collapses into a chair.

GERMAINE: My stamps! My stamps!

PIERRETTE: (*putting her arms around GERMAINE's shoulders*) Don't cry, Germaine.

GERMAINE: Don't talk to me. Get out! You're no better than the rest of them!

PIERRETTE: But ...

GERMAINE: Get out! I never want to see you again!

PIERRETTE: But I tried to help you! I'm on your side, Germaine!

GERMAINE: Get out and leave me alone! Don't speak to me. I don't want to see anyone!

PIERRETTE goes out slowly. LINDA also heads toward the door.

LINDA: It'll be some job cleaning all that up!

GERMAINE: My God! My God! My stamps! There's nothing left! Nothing! Nothing! My beautiful new home! My lovely furniture! Gone! My stamps! My stamps!

She falls to her knees beside the chair, picking up the remaining stamps. She is crying very hard. We hear all the others outside singing "O Canada." As the song continues, GERMAINE regains her courage. She finishes "O Canada" with the others, standing at attention, with tears in her eyes. A rain of stamps falls slowly from the ceiling ...

END

DAVID FRENCH

(1939–2010)

If a single playwright could be said to have shaped Canadian drama in the 1970s and '80s, it would be David French. From his apprenticeship with the CBC and his early identification with alternate theatre in Toronto to the success of his plays as a mainstay of the regional theatres and a cultural export, his career coincided with the late twentieth-century growth and maturation of Canadian theatrical art. For thirty years French wrote broadly popular, commercially appealing realist plays rooted in his own life and experience. His Mercer family saga, which brought a version (and vision) of Newfoundland onto the Canadian stage, has been compared to the autobiographically based plays of Eugene O'Neill, Tennessee Williams, and Arthur Miller. The Mercer plays and French's hugely successful backstage comedy *Jitters* are painful, funny, affectionate examinations of conditions that are widely recognizable yet at the same time distinctively local and emphatically Canadian.

French was born in Coley's Point, Newfoundland, but moved to Toronto with his parents and four brothers when he was six, their emigration part of a generation of postwar Newfoundlanders "goin' down the road" to mainland Canada in search of economic opportunity. After finishing high school in 1958 he studied acting for two years in Toronto and Pasadena, California, and from 1960 to 1965 worked as an actor, mostly for CBC-TV. Meanwhile, he was also writing. In 1962, CBC bought his first play, "Behold the Dark River," and over the next decade broadcast seven more of his half-hour television scripts. Through the late 1960s, French supported his writing by working at a variety of jobs, including a two-year stint in the Regina post office.

While summering on Prince Edward Island in 1971, he decided to try writing a stage play about his family's experience of adjusting to life outside Newfoundland in the late 1950s. By autumn, he had a one-act called "Behold This House," which he offered to Tarragon Theatre's artistic director Bill Glassco after seeing Glassco's production of David Freeman's *Creeps* at the theatre. Retitled and expanded to full length, *Leaving Home* opened in May 1972 and immediately made French a Canadian theatrical star. The play has since enjoyed well over a hundred productions. It also marked the start of a rich collaboration that saw each of French's plays premiere under Glassco's direction until the latter's death in 2004.

At the end of *Leaving Home*, young Ben Mercer sets out on his own after a terrible row with his father, Jacob, leaving the rift between them as unresolved as Jacob's own sense of manhood and feelings of cultural alienation. *Of the Fields, Lately* (1973) picks up two years later with Ben's temporary return to his parents' home in Toronto, ending with Jacob's death. The play is gentler and more elegiac but also slighter than its predecessor. It won the Floyd S. Chalmers Canadian Play Award for 1973 and has been very successful in its own right with productions across Canada and the United States, including a brief Broadway run in 1980.

After a number of abortive attempts to write a third Mercer play, French altered his focus to the sleazy underworld of cheap hoods, hookers, and con men, but *One Crack Out* (1975) was a disappointment. Glassco then suggested that he try translating Chekhov. French's version of *The Seagull* (1977) seemed to get him back on track creatively, running for two months on Broadway in 1992–93. Now inspired to write a full-out comedy, he returned to a subject he knew well, this time the world of Canadian theatre itself. *Jitters* (1979), a self-referential backstage comedy set in a small, low-budget Toronto theatre, is both a conventional genre play – "an almost perfect comedy of its kind," the *New York Times* called it – and a hilarious rendering of Canadian cultural schizophrenia. To the standard insecurities and insanities common to show-biz people everywhere are added those peculiar to a culture which continually looks across its southern border for approval and in which, at the same time, according to one of the play's characters, "success is like stepping out of line." *Jitters* was a smash hit in Toronto, then had productions in nearly every regional theatre across Canada and a successful run in New Haven prior to a planned Broadway opening in 1981. Ironically, like the play-within-the-play itself, *Jitters* never made it to that Promised Land. But it remains French's most popular play.

The Riddle of the World (1981) – a comedy of ideas about the sexual and spiritual lives of urban sophisticates – failed to catch fire with audiences or critics. But French found his way once again by returning to the Mercer family. *Salt-Water Moon* (1984), a prequel to his two earlier Mercer plays, chronicles the courtship of young Jacob and Mary in rural Newfoundland in 1926. A lyrical romantic comedy featuring only the two characters, it has proven as substantial a success as its predecessors and has probably had more productions in the past decade than the two earlier plays combined. A Los Angeles production in 1985 earned it the Hollywood Drama-Logue Critics Award for best play, and the published text won the Canadian Authors Association Literary Award for drama the following year.

In 1989, the Mercer trilogy became a tetralogy with what French insisted at the time would be the last play in the series, *1949*. For three days before Newfoundland officially joins Canada, Jacob and Mary host in their Toronto home a large, politically divided extended family of expatriate Newfoundlanders whose personal dramas unfold against the larger issue of cultural survival. By turns comedy and melodrama, *1949* brings onstage for the first time important out-characters from the earlier Mercer plays and provides rich subtext for the domestic events, a decade later, of *Leaving Home*.

In 1993, French shifted gears again with *Silver Dagger*, a mystery thriller produced in Toronto by Canadian Stage, the company that premiered *1949*. *That Summer*, a memory play about sisters in 1950s Ontario, opened at the Blyth Festival in 1999, and in 2006 French published his final work before his death, a translation and adaptation of Strindberg's *Miss Julie*.

In the intervening period, *Soldier's Heart* (2001), the fifth and final Mercer play, premiered at the Tarragon. Set in 1924, on the eighth anniversary of the Newfoundland Regiment's terrible day of reckoning on the French battlefield at Beaumont Hamel in the First Battle of the Somme, it is chronologically the earliest play in the series. Sixteen-year-old Jacob learns from his father, Esau, what leaving home to fight in the Great War meant for Esau and his Newfoundland compatriots. Hearing of Esau's profoundly traumatic experiences on the Somme, Jacob becomes, in his father's words, "a man." *Soldier's Heart* establishes much of the near-mythic cultural and personal history that resonates through the other Mercer plays.

French's major plays remain firmly in the Canadian repertory, most evidently in Newfoundland and Toronto, the primary poles of his life and work. In 2009, Theatre Newfoundland Labrador produced all five Mercer plays at the Gros Morne Theatre Festival in their temporal order, beginning with *Soldier's Heart* and ending with *Of the Fields, Lately*. Toronto's Soulpepper Theatre Company presented a David French play in four successive seasons from 2007 to 2010: *Leaving Home; Salt-Water Moon; Of the Fields, Lately;* and *Jitters*. The three Mercer plays in that series were republished in one volume in 2009 with an introduction by Soulpepper's artistic director, Albert Schultz.

The Mercer plays are driven by archetypal energies: the difficult passage into manhood, the fierce protective love of one sister for another, the tangled dynamics of family. What make the plays special are the cultural circumstances that shape those energies, especially the conflict between the characters who remain bound by the powerful pull of Newfoundland and those who make the perilous choice of "leaving home." Understood in the context of all five plays, that phrase resonates with emotional, psychological, political, and cultural complexities in addition to its generational and geographical meanings. In *Leaving Home,* Jacob asks Minnie about her boyfriend, Harold: "What is he, Minnie? Newfie?" "No, boy –" she answers. "Canadian." After ten years of Confederation and even longer living in Toronto, Jacob and his expatriate contemporaries still think in terms of us and them.

Harold is a brilliant comic symbol of the "Canadian" Other as the Newfoundlanders see him: the grey, humourless undertaker who speaks not at all but carries a very big stick. Harold's comic potency serves as foil for Jacob's sense of impotence and patriarchal failure. His own sons, after all, are colourless, fully assimilated Canadians for whom Newfoundland exists not even as memory but only in their father's embarrassing prejudices and oft-told tall tales. As Chris Johnson has argued, Jacob's cultural identity is closely tied to his patriarchal self-image. In order to sustain the legend on which his own sense of self is based ("I was out fishing on the Labrador when I was ten years old, six months of the year for ten dollars, and out of that ten dollars had to come my rubber boots"), he must per-petuate it in his sons. So he tests Ben's manhood by demanding that Ben drink not Canadian whisky but Newfie "screech." Jacob tries desperately to keep Ben from leaving by showing him photos of the family back "home." Leaving home literally as they already have figuratively, the sons shatter Jacob's hope of sustaining and defending his cultural heritage within the garrison of the family.

Lacking the colourful language and theatrical vitality of Jacob, Mary, and Minnie, the younger characters (Ben, Billy, and Kathy) are some-what pale and conventional by comparison. French himself seems to lose interest in the Bill-Kathy subplot, abruptly resolving it in a single stage direction. Ben's story is more compelling in its Oedipal twists and turns and dramatic conclusion. In the context of the youth culture's ongoing generational battles and the nationalist impulse driving the new Canadian theatre in the early 1970s, Ben's thrust for independence made a powerful statement. But in the end the play's focus is fixed firmly on Jacob and on Mary, who gets the last word and makes the final adjustment to our emotional allegiance.

Leaving Home

David French

Leaving Home was first performed May 16, 1972, at the Tarragon Theatre, Toronto, with the following cast:

MARY MERCER	Maureen Fitzgerald
BEN MERCER	Frank Moore
BILLY MERCER	Mel Tuck
JACOB MERCER	Sean Sullivan
KATHY JACKSON	Lyn Griffin
MINNIE JACKSON	Liza Creighton
HAROLD	Les Carlson

Directed by Bill Glassco
Designed by Dan Yarhi and Stephen Katz
Costume Design by Vicky Manthorpe

CHARACTERS

MARY MERCER
JACOB MERCER
BEN MERCER ⎤
BILLY MERCER ⎦ *their sons*
KATHY JACKSON, *BILLY's fiancée*
MINNIE JACKSON, *her mother*
HAROLD, *MINNIE's boyfriend*

SCENE

The play is set in Toronto on an early November day in the late 1950s.

SET

The lights come up on a working-class house in Toronto. The stage is divided into three playing areas: kitchen, dining room, and living room. In addition, there is a hallway leading into the living room. Two bedroom doors lead off the hallway, as well as the front door, which is offstage.

The kitchen contains a fridge, a stove, cupboards over the sink for everyday dishes, and a small drop-leaf table with two wooden chairs, one at either end. A plastic garbage receptacle stands beside the stove. A hockey calendar hangs on a wall, and a kitchen prayer.

The dining room is furnished simply with an oak table and chairs. There is an oak cabinet containing the good dishes and silverware. Perhaps a family portrait hangs on the wall – a photo taken when the sons were much younger.

The living room contains a chesterfield and an armchair, a TV, a record player and a fireplace. On the mantel rests a photo album and a silver-framed photo of the two sons – then small boys – astride a pinto pony. On one wall hangs a mirror. On another, a seascape. There is also a small table with a telephone on it.

ACT ONE

It is around five thirty on a Friday afternoon, and MARY MERCER, aged fifty, stands before the mirror in the living room, admiring her brand new dress and fixed hair. As she preens, the front door opens and in walk her two sons, BEN, eighteen, and BILL, seventeen. Each carries a box from a formal rental shop and schoolbooks.

MARY: Did you bump into your father?

BEN: No, we just missed him, Mom. He's already picked up his tux. He's probably at the Oakwood. (*He opens the fridge and helps himself to a beer.*)

MARY: Get your big nose out of the fridge. And put down that beer. You'll spoil your appetite.

BEN: No, I won't. (*He searches for a bottle opener in a drawer.*)

MARY: And don't contradict me. What other bad habits you learned lately?

BEN: (*teasing*) Don't be such a grouch. You sound like Dad. (*He sits at the table and opens his beer.*)

MARY: Yes, well just because you're in university now, don't t'ink you can raid the fridge any time you likes.

BILL crosses the kitchen and throws his black binder and books in the garbage receptacle.

MARY: What's that for? (*BILL exits into his bedroom and she calls after him.*) It's not the end of the world, my son. (*pause*) Tell you the truth, Ben. We always figured you'd be the one to land in trouble, if anyone did. I don't mean that as an insult. You're more ... I don't know ... like your father.

BEN: I am?

Music from BILL's room.

MARY: (*calling, exasperated*) Billy, do you have to have that so loud? (*BILL turns down his record player. To BEN*) I'm glad your graduation went okay last night. How was Billy? Was he glad he went?

BEN: Well, he wasn't upset, if that's what you mean.

MARY: (*slight pause*) Ben, how come you not to ask your father?

BEN: What do you mean?

BILL: (*off*) Mom, will you pack my suitcase? I can't get everything in.

MARY: (*calling*) I can't now, Billy. Later.

BEN: I want to talk to you, Mom. It's important.

MARY: I want to talk to you, too.

BILL: (*comes out of the bedroom, crosses to kitchen*) Mom, here's the deposit on my locker. I cleaned it out and threw away all my old gym clothes. (*He helps himself to an apple from the fridge.*)

MARY: Didn't you just hear me tell your brother to stay out of there? I might as well talk to the sink. Well, you can t'row away your old school clothes – that's your affair – but take those books out of the garbage. Go on. You never knows. They might come in handy sometime.

BILL: How? (*He takes the books out, then sits at the table with BEN.*)

MARY: Well, you can always go to night school and get your senior matric, once the baby arrives and Kathy's back to work ... Poor child. I talked to her on the phone this morning. She's still upset, and I don't blame her. I'd be hurt myself if my own mother was too drunk to show up to my shower.

BILL: (*a slight ray of hope*) Maybe she won't show up tonight.

MARY: (*glances anxiously at the kitchen clock and turns to check the fish and potatoes*) Look at the time. I just wish to goodness he had more t'ought, your father. The supper'll dry up if he don't hurry. He might pick up a phone and mention when he'll be home. Not a grain of t'ought in his head. And I wouldn't put it past him to forget his tux in the beer parlour. (*Finally, she turns and looks at her two sons, disappointed.*) And look at the two of you. Too busy with your mouths to give your mother a second glance. I could stand here till my legs dropped off before either of you would notice my dress.

BEN: It's beautiful, Mom.

MARY: That the truth?

BILL: Would we lie to you, Mom?

MARY: Just so long as I don't look foolish next to Minnie. She can afford to dress up – Willard left her well off when he died.

BEN: Don't worry about the money. Dad won't mind.

MARY: Well, it's not every day your own son gets married, is it? (*to BILL as she puts on a large apron*) It's just that I don't want Minnie Jackson looking all decked out like the *Queen Mary* and me the tug that dragged her in. You understands, don't you, Ben?

BEN: Sure.

BILL: I understand, too, Mom.

MARY: I know you do, Billy. I know you do. (*She opens a tin of peaches and fills five dessert dishes.*) Minnie used to go with your father. Did you know that, Billy? Years and years ago.

BILL: No kidding?

BEN: (*at the same time*) Really?

MARY: True as God is in heaven. Minnie was awful sweet on Dad, too. She t'ought the world of him.

BILL: (*incredulously*) Dad?

MARY: Don't act so surprised. Your father was quite a one with the girls.

BEN: No kidding?

MARY: He could have had his pick of any number of girls. (*to BILL*) You ask Minnie sometime. Of course, in those days I was going with Jerome McKenzie, who later became a Queen's Counsel in St. John's. I must have mentioned him.

The boys exchange smiles.

BEN: I think you have, Mom.

BILL: A hundred times.

MARY: (*gently indignant – to BILL*) And that I haven't!

BILL: She has, too. Hasn't she, Ben?

MARY: Never you mind, Ben. (*to BILL*) And instead of sitting around gabbing so much you'd better go change your clothes. Kathy'll soon be here. (*as BILL crosses to his bedroom*) Is the rehearsal still at eight?

BILL: We're supposed to meet Father Douglas at the church at five to. I just hope Dad's not too drunk. (*He exits.*)

MARY: (*studies BEN a moment*) Look at yourself. A cigarette in one hand, a bottle of beer in the other, at your age! You didn't learn any of your bad habits from me, I can tell you. (*pause*) Ben, don't be in such a hurry to grow up. (*She sits across from him.*) Whatever you do, don't be in such a hurry. Look at your poor young brother. His whole life ruined. Oh, I could weep a bellyful when I t'inks of it. Just seventeen, not old enough to sprout whiskers on his chin, and already the burdens of a man on his t'in little shoulders. Your poor father hasn't slept a full night since this happened. Did you know that? He had such high hopes for Billy. He wanted you both to go to college and not have to work as hard as he's had to all his life. And now look. You have more sense than that, Ben. Don't let life trap you.

BILL enters. He has changed his pants and is buttoning a clean white shirt. MARY goes into the dining room and begins to remove the tablecloth from the dining room table.

BILL: Mom, what about Dad? He won't start picking on the priest, will he? You know how he likes to argue.

MARY: He won't say a word, my son. You needn't worry. Worry more about Minnie showing up.

BILL: What if he's drunk?

MARY: He won't be. Your father knows better than to sound off in church. Oh, and another t'ing – he wants you to polish his shoes for tonight. They're in the bedroom. The polish is on your dresser. You needn't be too fussy.

BEN: I'll do his shoes, Mom. Billy's all dressed.

MARY: No, no, Ben, that's all right. He asked Billy to.

BILL: What did Ben do this time?

MARY: He didn't do anyt'ing.

BILL: He must have.

MARY: Is it too much trouble to polish your father's shoes, after all he does for you? If you won't do it, I'll do it myself.

BILL: (*indignantly*) How come when Dad's mad at Ben, I get all the dirty jobs? Jeez! Will I be glad to get out of here! (*Rolling up his shirt sleeves, he exits into his bedroom.*)

MARY takes a clean white linen tablecloth from a drawer in the cabinet and covers the table. During the following scene she sets five places with her good glasses, silverware, and plates.

BEN: (*slight pause*) Billy's right, isn't he? What'd I do, Mom?

MARY: Take it up with your father. I'm tired of being the middleman.

BEN: Is it because of last night? (*slight pause*) It is, isn't it?

MARY: He t'inks you didn't want him there, Ben. He t'inks you're ashamed of him.

BEN: He wouldn't have gone, Mom. That's the only reason I never invited him.

MARY: He would have went, last night.

BEN: (*angrily*) He's never even been to one lousy Parents' Night in thirteen years. Not one! And he calls *me* contrary!

MARY: You listen to me. Your father never got past grade t'ree. He was yanked out of school and made to work. In those days, back home, he was lucky to get that much and don't kid yourself.

BEN: Yeah? So?

MARY: So? So he's afraid to. He's afraid of sticking out. Is that so hard to understand? Is it?

BEN: What're you getting angry about? All I said was –

MARY: You say he don't take an interest, but he was proud enough to show off your report cards all those years. I suppose with you that don't count for much.

BEN: All right. But he never goes anywhere without you, Mom, and last night you were here at the shower.

MARY: Last night was different, Ben, and you ought to know that. It was your high school graduation. He would have went with me or without me. If you'd only asked him. (*A truck* horn blasts twice.) There he is now in the driveway. Whatever happens, don't fall for his old tricks. He'll be looking for a fight, and doing his best to find any excuse. (*calling*) Billy, you hear that? Don't complain about the shoes, once your father comes!

BEN: (*urgently*) Mom, there's something I want to tell you before Dad comes in.

MARY: Sure, my son. Go ahead. I'm listening. What's on your mind?

BEN: Well ...

MARY: (*smiling*) Come on. It can't be that bad.

BEN: (*slight pause*) I want to move out, Mom.

MARY: (*almost inaudibly*) ... What?

BEN: I said I want to move out.

MARY: (*softly, as she sets the cutlery*) I heard you. (*pause*) What for?

BEN: I just think it's time. I'll be nineteen soon. (*pause*) I'm moving in with Billy and Kathy and I'll help pay the rent. (*pause*) I won't be far away. I'll see you on weekends. (*MARY nods.*) Mom?

MARY: (*absently*) What?

BEN: Will you tell Dad? (*slight pause*) Mom? Did you hear me?

MARY: I heard you. He'll be upset, I can tell you. By rights you ought to tell him yourself.

BEN: If I do, we'll just get into a big fight and you know it. He'll take it better, coming from you.

The front door opens and JACOB MERCER enters whistling "I's the B'y." He is fifty, though he looks older. He is dressed in a peaked cap, carpenter's overalls, thick-soled workboots, and a lumberjack shirt over a T-shirt. Under one arm he carries his black lunch pail.

MARY: Your suit! I knowed it!

JACOB: Don't get in an uproar, now. I left it sitting on the front seat of the truck. (*He looks at BEN, then back to MARY.*) Is Billy home?

MARY: He's in the bedroom, polishing your shoes.

JACOB: (*crosses to the bedroom door*) Billy, my son, come out a moment. (*BILL enters, carrying a shoe brush.*) Put down the brush and go out in my truck and bring back the tux on the seat.

BILL: What's wrong with Ben? He's not doing anything.

JACOB: Don't ask questions. That's a good boy. I'd ask your brother, but he always has a good excuse.

BEN: I'll go get it. (*He starts for the front door.*)

JACOB: (*calling after BEN*) Oh, it's too late to make up now. The damage is done.

MARY: Don't talk nonsense, Jacob.

JACOB: (*a last thrust*) And aside from that – I wouldn't want you dirtying your nice clean hands in your father's dirty old truck!

The front door closes on his last words. BILL returns to his room. JACOB sets his lunch pail and his cap on the dining room table.

JACOB: Did he get his diploma?

MARY: Yes. It's in the bedroom.

JACOB: (*breaks into a smile and lifts his cap*) And will you gaze on Mary over there. When I stepped in the door, I t'ought the Queen had dropped in for tea.

MARY: You didn't even notice.

JACOB: Come here, my dear, and give Jacob a kiss.

MARY: (*She darts behind the table, laughing.*) I'll give Jacob a swift boot in the rear end with my pointed toe. (*JACOB grabs her, rubs his rough cheek against hers.*) You'll take the skin off! Jake! You're far too rough! And watch my new dress! Don't rip it.

JACOB: (*releases her and breaks into a little jig, singing*)
I's the b'y that builds the boat
And I's the b'y that sails her,
I's the b'y that catches the fish
And takes 'em home to Lizer.
Sods and rinds to cover your flake
Cake and tea for supper
Codfish in the spring of the year
Fried in maggoty butter.
I don't want your maggoty fish
Cake and tea for winter
I could buy as good as that
Down in Bona Vista.
I took Lizer to a dance
And faith but she could travel
And every step that she did take
Was up to her ass in gravel.

JACOB ends the song with a little step or flourish.

MARY: There's no mistakin' where you've been to, and it's not to church.

JACOB: All right, now, I had one little glass, and don't you start.

MARY: (*as she re-enters the kitchen*) How many?

JACOB: I can't lie, Mary. (*He puts his hand on his heart.*) As God is my witness – two. Two glasses to celebrate the wedding of my youngest son. (*He follows her into the kitchen.*)

MARY: Half a dozen's more like it, unless you expects God to perjure Himself for the likes of you. Well, no odds: you're just in time. Kathy'll soon be here, so get cleaned up.

JACOB: I washed up on the job.

MARY: Well, change your clothes. You're not sitting down with the likes of that on. (*She returns to the dining room with bread and butter for the dining room table.*)

JACOB: I suppose it's fish with Kathy coming and him now a bloody Mick. Next t'ing you knows he'll be expecting me to chant grace in Latin.

MARY: And I'll crown you if you opens your yap like that around Kathy. Don't you dare.

JACOB: (*Following MARY, he sits at the dining room table.*) 'Course we could have the priest drop by and bless the table himself. (*He makes the sign of the cross.*)

MARY: Jacob!

JACOB: Though I doubts he could get his Cadillac in the driveway.

MARY: (*back to kitchen*) If you comes out with the likes of that tonight, I'll never speak to you again. You hear?

JACOB: Ah, go on with you. What do you know? If you had nothing in your pockets but holes, a priest wouldn't give you t'read to sew it with.

BEN: (*enters with the box*) I put your toolbox down in the basement while I was at it, Dad. And rolled up the windows in your truck, in case it rains tonight.

JACOB: Did you, now? And I'm supposed to forget all about last night, is that it? Pretend it never occurred? Your brother's good enough for you but not your own father. (*as BEN crosses to kitchen*) Well, it would take more time than that to stitch up the hurt, I can assure you. And a long time before it heals. Don't be looking to your mother for support.

BEN: I wasn't. (*He sits at the kitchen table.*)

JACOB: Or for sympathy, either.

MARY: Jacob, it don't serve no purpose to look for a fight.

JACOB: (*to MARY*) You keep your two cents' worth out of it. Nobody asked you. You got too much to say.

BILL: (*enters, carrying the shined shoes, which he gives to his father*) Hey, Dad, do me a favour? When Kathy gets here, no cracks about the Pope's nose and stuff like that. And just for once don't do that Squid-Jiggin' thing and take your teeth out. Okay? (*He sits at the table across from his father and reads the evening paper.*)

JACOB: Well, listen to him, now. (*to MARY*) Who put him up to that? You? Imagine. Telling me what I can say and do in my own house.

MARY: (*returning to the dining room*) Billy, my son, I got a feeling you just walked into it. (*She takes a polishing cloth from a cabinet and rubs her good silverware, including a large fish-knife.*)

JACOB: (*to BILL*) If you only knowed what my poor father went t'rough with the Catholics. Oh, if you only knowed, you wouldn't be doing this. My own son a turncoat. And back home, when we was growing up, you wouldn't dare go where the Catholics lived after dark. You'd be murdered, and many's the poor boy was. Knocked over the head and drownded, and all they done was let night catch them on a Catholic road. My father's brother was one. Poor Isaac. He was just fifteen, that summer. Tied with his arms behind him and tossed in the pond like a stone. My poor father never forgot that to his dying day. (*The family waits out the harangue.*) And here you is j'ining their ranks! T'ree weeks of instructions. By the jumping Jesus Christ you don't come from my side of the family. I'm glad my poor father never lived to see this day, I can tell you. The loyalest Orangeman that ever marched in a church parade, my father. He'd turn over in his grave if he saw a grandson of his kissing the Pope's ass. Promising to bring up your poor innocent babies Roman Catholics and them as ignorant of Rome as earthworms.

Oh, it's a good t'ing for you, my son, that he ain't around to see it, because sure as you'm there he'd march into that church tomorrow with his belt in his hand, and take that smirk off your face! Billy, my son, I never expected this of you, of all people. No, I didn't. Not you. If it was your brother, now, I could understand it. He'd do it just for spite ...

MARY: Hold your tongue, boy. Don't you ever run down? I just hope to goodness Ben don't call on you at the wedding to toast the bride and groom. We'll all be old before it's over. (*slight pause*) Did you try on your tux?

JACOB: No, boy, it was too crowded.

MARY: Then try it on. You're worse than the kids. (*She hands him the box.*) Go on.

JACOB: (*to BILL, referring to the shoes*) T'anks. (*He exits into his bedroom.*)

MARY: Ben, do your mother a favour? Fill up the glasses. I left the jug in the kitchen. (*She sits at the dining room table, checks and folds five linen napkins.*) Look at him, Ben. The little fart. My baby. (*to herself*) How quick it all goes ... I can still see us to this day ... the t'ree of us ... coming up from Newfoundland ... July of 1945 ... the war not yet over ... Father gone ahead to look for work on construction ... that old train packed with soldiers, and do you t'ink a single one would rise off his big fat backside to offer up his seat? Not on your life. There we was, huddled together out on the brakes, a couple, t'ree hours ... with the wind and the soot from the engine blowing back ... until a lady come out and saw us. "Well, the likes of this I've never seen," she says. "I've got four sons in the war, and if one of mine was in that carriage, I'd disown 'im!"

We've never had anyt'ing to be ashamed of, my sons. We've been poor ... but we've always stuck together. (*to BILL*) Is you frightened, my son?

BILL: No. Why should I be?

MARY: Don't be ashamed of it. Tomorrow you'll most likely wish you was back with your mother and father in your own soft bed.

BEN: He's scared shitless, Mom. (*to BILL*) Tell the truth.

MARY: Ben, is that nice talk?

BILL: (*to BEN*) I'll trade places.

MARY: Well, as long as you loves her, that's all that matters. Without that there's nothing, and with it what you don't have can wait. But a word of warning, Billy – don't come running to us with your squabbles, because we won't stick our noses into it. And before I forgets – you'd better not say a word to your father about moving out. I'll tell him myself after the wedding.

JACOB: (*off*) Mary!

MARY: (*calling*) What is it, boy?

JACOB: (*off*) Come here! I can't get this goddamn button fast!

MARY: (*shaking her head*) It's one of those mysteries how he made it t'rough life this far. If he didn't have me, he wouldn't know which leg of his pants was which. (*She exits.*)

BILL: (*slight pause*) You told her, huh? She doesn't seem to mind.

BEN: Keep your voice down. You want Dad to hear?

BILL: What did she say? Is she going to tell him?

BEN: Yeah, but do you think I ought to let her?

BILL: What do you mean?

BEN: Well, maybe I should tell him myself.

BILL: Are you crazy?

BEN: If I don't, you know what'll happen. Mom'll get all the shit.

BILL: (*pause*) Ben, you really want to do this? Are you sure?

BEN: Look – my books and tuition're paid for. All I got to worry about is the rent. I can handle that, waiting on tables. I'll make out. Listen, whose idea was it anyhow? Mine or yours? I wouldn't do it if I didn't want to.

BILL: Okay.

BEN: I need to, Billy. Christ, you know that. Either Dad goes, or I do.

BILL: I wish I felt that way. I don't want to move out. I don't want to get married. I don't know the first thing about girls. I mean, Kathy's the first girl I ever did it with. No kidding. The very first. We've only done it four or five times. The first time was in a cemetery, for Chrissake!

BEN: Well, at least you've been laid, Billy. I never.

BILL: Really? (*He laughs. Pause.*) I like Kathy. I like her a lot. But I don't know what else. What do you think Dad would do, if he was in my shoes? I think if Kathy was Mom he'd marry her, don't you?

MARY: (*enters*) Listen to me, you two. I don't want either one of you to say one word or snicker even when your father comes out. Is that understood?

BEN: What's wrong?

MARY: They gave him the wrong coat. I suppose he was in such a rush to get to the Oakwood he didn't bother trying it on.

JACOB enters singing, now dressed in the rental tux and polished shoes. The sleeves are miles too short for him, the back hiked up. He looks like a caricature of discomfort.

JACOB: (*singing*)

Here comes the bride,

All fat and wide,

See how she wobbles

From side to side.

> *The boys glance at one another and try to keep from breaking up.*

JACOB: Well, boys, am I a fit match for your mother?

BEN: Dad, I wish I had a camera.

JACOB: Is you making fun?

MARY: No, he's not. The sleeves are a sight, but – (*giving BEN a censorious look*) – aside from that it's a perfect fit. Couldn't be better. Could it, Billy?

BILL: Made to measure, Dad.

JACOB: I t'ink I'll kick up my heels. I'm in the right mood. (*as he crosses to the record player*) What do you say, Mary? Feel up to it? (*He selects a record.*)

MARY: I'm willing, if you is, Jake.

JACOB: All right, boys, give us room. (*The record starts to play – a rousing tune with lots of fiddles.*) Your mother loves to twirl her skirt and show off her drawers! (*He seizes his wife and they whirl around the room, twirling and stomping with enjoyment and abandon.*)

BEN: Go, Mom! (*He whistles. BILL and BEN clap their hands to the music.*) Give her hell, Dad!

MARY: Not so fast, Jacob, you'll make me dizzy!

> *JACOB stops after a few turns. He is slightly dizzy. He sits.*

JACOB: (*to BILL*) Dance with your mother. I galled my heel at work. (*BILL does.*) You ought to have seen your mother in her day, Ben. She'd turn the head of a statue. There wasn't a man from Bareneed to Bay Roberts didn't blink when she passed by.

MARY: Come on, Ben. Before it's over. (*She takes BEN, and they dance around the room.*)

JACOB: That's one t'ing about Ben, Mary. He won't ever leave you. The day he gets married himself he'll move in next door.

Finally, MARY collapses laughing on the chesterfield. The music plays on.

JACOB: (*expansively*) I t'ink a drink's in order. What do you say, boys? To whet the appetite. (*He searches in the bottom of the cabinet. To MARY*) Where's all the whisky to? You didn't t'row it out, did you?

MARY: You t'rowed it down your t'roat, that's where it was t'rowed.

JACOB: Well, boys, looks like there's no whisky. (*He holds up a bottle.*) How does a little "screech" sound?

BEN: Not for me, Dad.

JACOB: Why not?

BEN: I just don't like it.

JACOB: (*sarcastically*) No, you wouldn't. I suppose it's too strong for you. Well, Billy'll have some, won't you, my son? (*He turns down the music.*)

BILL: (*surprised*) I will?

JACOB: Get two glasses out, then, and let's have a quick drink. (*BILL does and hands a glass to his father.*) Don't suppose you'd have a little drop, Mary, my love? (*He winks at BILL.*)

MARY: Go on with you. You ought to have better sense, teaching the boys all your bad habits. And after you promised your poor mother on her death-bed you'd warn them off alcohol …

JACOB: Don't talk foolishness. A drop of this won't harm a soul. Might even do some good, all you know.

MARY: Yes, some good it's done you.

JACOB: At least I'd take a drink with my own father, if he was alive. I'd do that much, my lady.

MARY: (*quickly*) Pay no attention, Ben. (*to JACOB*) And listen, I don't want you getting tight and making a disgrace of yourself at the rehearsal tonight. You hear?

JACOB: Oh, I'll be just as sober as the priest, rest assured of that. And you just study his fingers, if they'm not as brown as a new potato from nicotine. I dare say if he didn't swallow Sen-Sen, you'd know where all that communion wine goes to. (*to BILL*) How many drunks you suppose is wearing Roman collars? More than the Pope would dare admit. And all those t'ousands of babies they keep digging up in the basements of convents. It's shocking.

BEN: That's a lot of bull, Dad.

JACOB: It is, is it? Who told you that? Is that more of the stuff you learns at university? Your trouble is you've been brainwashed.

BEN: You just want to believe all that.

MARY: And you'd better not come out with that tonight, if you knows what's good for you.

JACOB: (*to BILL*) Mind – I'm giving you fair warning. I won't sprinkle my face with holy water or make the sign of the cross. And nothing in this world or the next can persuade me.

BILL: You don't have to, Dad. Relax.

JACOB: Just so you knows.

BEN: All you got to do, Dad, is sit there in the front row and look sweet.

JACOB: All right, there's no need to get saucy. I wasn't talking to you! (*He pours a little "screech" in the two glasses. To BILL*) Here's to you, boy. You got the makings of a man. That's more than I can say for your older brother. (*JACOB downs his drink. BILL glances helplessly at BEN. He doesn't drink.*) Go on. (*BILL hesitates, then downs it, grimacing and coughing.*) You see that, Mary? (*his anger rising*) It's your fault the one's the way he is. It's high time, my lady, you let go and weaned him away from the tit!

MARY: (*angrily*) You shut your mouth. There's no call for that kind of talk!

JACOB: He needs more in his veins than mother's milk, goddamn it!

BEN: (*shouting at JACOB*) What're you screaming at her for? She didn't do anything!

JACOB: (*a semblance of sudden calm*) Well, listen to him, now. Look at the murder in his face. One harsh word to his mother and up comes his fists. I'll bet you wouldn't be so quick to defend your father.

MARY: Be still, Jacob. You don't know what you're saying.

JACOB: He t'inks he's too good to drink with me!

BEN: All right, I will, if it's that important. Only let's not fight.

MARY: He's just taunting you into it, Ben. Don't let him.

JACOB: (*sarcastically*) No, my son, your mother's right. I wouldn't wish for your downfall on my account. To hear her tell it I'm the devil tempting Saul on the road to Damascus.

MARY: Well, the devil better learn his scripture, if he wants to quote it. The devil tempted our Lord in the wilderness, and Saul had a revelation on the road to Damascus.

JACOB: A revelation! (*He turns off the record.*) I'll give you a revelation! I'm just a piece of shit around here! Who is it wears himself out year after year to give him a roof over his head and food in his mouth? Who buys his clothes and keeps him in university?

MARY: He buys his own clothes, and he's got a scholarship.

JACOB: (*furious*) Oh, butt out! You'd stick up for him if it meant your life, and never once put in a good word for me.

MARY: I'm only giving credit where's credit due.

JACOB: Liar.

MARY: Ah, go on. You're a fine one to talk. You'd call the ace of spades white and not bat an eye.

JACOB: (*enraged*) It never fails. I can't get my own son to do the simplest goddamn t'ing without a row. No matter what.

BEN: It's never simple, Dad. You never let it be simple or I might. It's always a test.

JACOB: Test!

MARY: Ben, don't get drawn into it.

JACOB: (*to BEN*) The sooner you learns to get along with others, the sooner you'll grow up. Test!

BEN: Do you ever hear yourself? "Ben, get up that ladder. You want people to think you're a sissy?" "Have a drink, Ben. It'll make a man out of you!"

JACOB: I said no such t'ing, now. Liar.

BEN: It's what you meant. "Cut your hair, Ben. You look like a girl." The same shit over and over, and it never stops!

JACOB: Now it all comes out. You listening to this, Mary?

BEN: No, you listen, Dad. You don't really expect me to climb that ladder or take that drink. You want me to refuse, don't you?

JACOB: Well, listen to him. The faster you gets out into the real world the better for you. (*He turns away.*)

BEN: Dad, you don't want me to be a man, you just want to impress me with how much less of a man I am than you. (*He snatches the bottle from his father and takes a swig.*) All right. Look. (*He rips open his* *shirt.*) I still haven't got hair on my chest, and I'm still not a threat to you.

JACOB: No, and you'm not likely ever to be, either, until you grows up and gets out from under your mother's skirts.

BEN: No, Dad – until I get out from under yours.

The doorbell rings.

MARY: That's Kathy. All right, that's more than enough for one night. Let's have no more bickering. Jake, get dressed. And not another word out of anyone. The poor girl will t'ink she's fallen in with a pack of wild savages.

JACOB: (*getting in the last word*) And there's no bloody mistakin' who the wild savage is. (*With that he exits into his bedroom.*)

MARY: Billy, answer the door. (*to BEN*) And you – change your shirt. You look a fright.

BEN exits. BILL opens the front door, and KATHY enters. She is sixteen, very pretty, but at the moment her face is pale and emotionless.

KATHY: Hello, Mrs. Mercer.

MARY: You're just in time, Kathy. (*MARY gives her a kiss.*) Take her coat, Billy. I'll be right out, dear. (*She exits.*)

KATHY: Where is everyone?

BILL: (*taking her coat*) Getting dressed. (*As he tries to kiss her, she pulls away her cheek.*) What's wrong? (*He hangs up her coat.*)

KATHY: Nothing. I don't feel well.

BILL: Why not? Did you drink too much at the party?

KATHY: What party?

BILL: Didn't the girls at work throw a party for you this afternoon?

KATHY: I didn't go to the office this afternoon.

BILL: You didn't go? What do you mean?

KATHY: Just what I said.

BILL: What did you say?

KATHY: Will you get off my back!

BILL: What did I say? (*slight pause*) Are you mad at me?

KATHY: (*looks at him*) Billy, do you love me? Do you? I need to know.

BILL: What's happened, Kathy?

KATHY: I'm asking you a simple question.

BILL: And I want to know what's happened.

KATHY: If I hadn't been pregnant, you'd never have wanted to get married, would you?

BILL: So?

KATHY: I hate you.

BILL: For Chrissake, Kathy, what's happened?

KATHY: (*sits on the chesterfield*) I lost the baby ...

BILL: What?

KATHY: Isn't that good news?

BILL: What the hell happened?

KATHY: I started bleeding in the ladies' room this morning.

BILL: Bleeding? What do you mean?

KATHY: Hemorrhaging. I screamed, and one of the girls rushed me to the hospital. I think the people at work thought I'd done something to myself.

BILL: Had you?

KATHY: Of course not. You know I wouldn't.

BILL: What did the doctor say?

KATHY: I had a miscarriage. (*She looks up at him.*) You're not even sorry, are you?

BILL: I am, really. What else did the doctor say?

KATHY: I lost a lot of blood. I'm supposed to eat lots of liver and milk, to build it up. You should have seen me, Billy. I was white and shaky. I'm a little better now. I've been sleeping all afternoon.

BILL: (*slight pause*) What was it?

KATHY: What was what?

BILL: The baby.

KATHY: Do you really want to know?

BILL doesn't answer.

BILL: What'll we do?

KATHY: Tell our folks, I guess. My mother doesn't know yet. She's been at the track all day with her boyfriend. (*slight pause*) I haven't told anyone else, Billy. Just you.

Enter JACOB and MARY. He is dressed in a pair of slacks and a white shirt. He carries a necktie in his hand. MARY wears a blouse and skirt.

JACOB: Billy, my son, tie me a Windsor knot. That's a good boy. (*He hands BILL the necktie and BILL* *proceeds to make the knot. Shyly, to KATHY*) Hello, my dear. (*KATHY nods.*) Lovely old day.

MARY: Come on. We may as well sit right down before it colds off. I'll serve up the fish and potatoes. (*She transfers the fish and potatoes into serving dishes.*)

JACOB: (*calling*) Ben! (*to KATHY, referring to the tie*) I'm all t'umbs or I'd do it myself.

BEN: (*enters, his shirt changed*) Hi, Kathy.

KATHY: Hi, Ben. Congratulations.

BEN: For what?

KATHY: Didn't you graduate last night?

BEN: Oh. Yeah.

JACOB: I suppose if Ben ever becomes Prime Minister, I'll be the last to know unless I reads it in the newspapers.

MARY: Kathy, you sit right down there, dear. Billy, you sit next to her. And Ben's right here. (*BILL hands his father the tie. JACOB slips it on as he approaches the table.*) Father, why don't you say grace?

JACOB: Maybe Kathy would like to.

KATHY: We never say grace at our house.

JACOB: Is that a fact? Imagine.

BILL: (*jumping in*) "Bless this food that now we take, and feed our souls for Jesus' sake. Amen."

ALL: Amen. (*They dig in.*)

JACOB: Have an eye to the bones, Kathy. (*slight pause*) You was born in Toronto, wasn't you? Someday you'll have to take a trip home, you and Billy, and see how they dries the cod on the beaches. He don't remember any more than you. He was just little when he come up here.

MARY: That was a long time ago, Kathy. 1945.

KATHY: (*slight pause*) Have you been home since, Mr. Mercer?

JACOB: No, my dear, and I don't know if I wants to. A different generation growing up now. (*glancing at BEN*) A different brand of Newfie altogether. And once the old-timers die off, that'll be the end of it. Newfoundland'll never be the same after that, I can tell you. (*slight pause*) Do you know what flakes is?

KATHY: No.

JACOB: Well, they'm spread over the shore – these wooden stages they dries the codfish on. Sometimes – and this is no word of a lie, is it, Mary? – the fishflies'll buzz around that codfish as t'ick as the hairs on your arm. (*slight pause*) T'icker. T'ick as tarpaper.

MARY: Jacob, we're eating. (*to KATHY*) He's just like his poor mother, Jacob is. She'd start on about the tapeworm as you was lifting the pork to your mouth. (*to JACOB*) Let the poor girl eat in peace, Father. (*to KATHY*) You've hardly touched your food, dear. Has he spoiled your appetite? It wouldn't be the first time.

KATHY: I'm just not too hungry, Mrs. Mercer.

MARY: I understands. Big day tomorrow. I was the same way, my wedding day. It's a wonder I didn't faint.

JACOB: (*slight pause – to KATHY*) You notice Ben don't look my way? He's sore. (*KATHY glances at BEN, who goes on eating, oblivious.*) Oh, he knows how to dish it out with the best, but he can't take it. You can joke with Billy, he likes a bit of fun, but with the other one you don't dare open your mouth.

BEN: Will you shut up, Dad?

JACOB: (*to KATHY*) I'll bet you didn't get sore with your poor father and talk back all the time when he was alive, did you, my dear? No, that's what you didn't. You had more respect. And I bet now you don't regret it.

MARY: Don't ask the child to choose sides, Jacob. You've got no right to do that. Anyhow, Kathy's got more sense than to get mixed up in it. Don't you, Kathy?

JACOB: The Bible says to honour thy father and thy mother …

MARY: (*exasperated*) Oh, hold your tongue, for goodness sake. Don't your jaw ever get tired?

JACOB: (*to KATHY*) Well, you can see for yourself what happens, my dear. Anyone in this room is free to say what they likes about the old man, but just let him criticize back and you'd t'ink a fox had burst into the chicken coop, the way Mother Mercer here gathers her first-born under her wing. (*slight pause – to KATHY, but meant for his wife*) I suppose by now you've heard your mother and me once went together? I suppose Minnie's mentioned it often enough? Fine figure of a woman, Minnie. Still looks as good as ever.

BILL: I hear you used to be a real woman's man, Dad.

JACOB: Who told you that?

BILL: Mom.

MARY: (*quickly*) Liar. I told you no such t'ing.

BILL: You did so. Didn't she, Ben?

BEN smiles at his mother.

JACOB: Well, contrary to what your mother tells, that particular year I had only one sweetheart, and that was Minnie Jackson. Wasn't it, Mary?

MARY: (*nodding*) She was still a Fraser then. That was the same year I was going with Jerome McKenzie. Wasn't it, Jacob?

JACOB: Oh, don't forget the most important part, Mary, the Q.C., the Queen's Counsel. Jerome McKenzie, Q.C. (*to KATHY*) Jerome's a well-known barrister in St. John's, and Mrs. Mercer's all the time t'rowing him up in my face. Ain't you Mary? Never lets me forget it, will you? (*to KATHY*) You see, my dear, she might have married Jerome McKenzie, Q.C. and never had a single worry in the world, if it wasn't for me. Ain't that so, Mary?

MARY: If you insists, Jacob.

BILL and KATHY stare silently at their plates, embarrassed. BEN looks from his father to his mother and then to BILL.

BEN: Did you get the boutonnieres and the cuff links for the ushers?

MARY: It's all taken care of, my son. (*pause*) What kind of flowers did your mother order, Kathy?

KATHY: Red roses.

MARY: How nice.

KATHY: I like yellow roses better, but – (*She stops abruptly.*)

BILL: But what?

KATHY: Nothing.

MARY: Yellow roses mean tears, my son.

KATHY: Did you carry roses, Mrs. Mercer?

MARY: I did. Red butterfly roses. And I wore a gown of white satin, with a lace veil. I even had a crown of orange blossoms.

KATHY: I'll bet you were beautiful.

JACOB: My dear, she lit up that little Anglican church like the Second Coming. I suppose I told you all about the wedding ring?

MARY: No, you didn't, and she don't want to hear tell of it, and neither do the rest of us. Don't listen to his big fibs, Kathy.

JACOB: I still remembers that day. I had on my gabardine suit, with a white carnation in the lapel. In those days Mary t'ought I was handsome.

MARY: Get to the point, Father.

JACOB: We was that poor I couldn't afford a ring, so when the Reverend Mr. Price got t'rough with the dearly beloveds and asked for the ring, I reached into my pocket and give him all I had – an old bent nail.

MARY: Last time it was cigar band.

JACOB: (*still to KATHY*) And if you was to ask me today, twenty years later, if it's been worth it – my dear, my answer would still be the same, for all her many faults – that old rusty nail has brung me more joy and happiness than you can ever imagine. And I wouldn't trade the old woman here, nor a blessed hair of her head, not for all the gold bullion in the Vatican.

BILL: Dad.

JACOB: And my name's not Jerome McKenzie, Q.C., either. And the likes of Ben here may t'ink me just an old fool, not worth a second t'ought – (*BEN shoves back his plate, holding back his temper.*) – and run me down to my face the first chance he gets –

BEN: Ah, shut up.

JACOB: – and treat me with no more respect and consideration than you would your own worst enemy! –

BEN: Will you grow up! (*He knocks over his chair and exits into his bedroom.*)

JACOB: (*shouting after him*) – but I've always done what I seen fit, and no man can do more! (*The door slams – slight pause.*) I won't say another word.

MARY: You've said enough, brother. (*slight pause*) What Kathy must t'ink of us! (*slight pause*) And then you wonders why he's the way he is, when you sits there brazen-faced and makes him feel like two cents in front of company. You haven't a grain of sense, you haven't!

JACOB: Did I say a word of a lie? Did I?

MARY: No, you always speaks the gospel truth, you do.

JACOB: I never could say two words in a row to that one, without he takes offence. Not two bloody words! (*MARY collects the supper plates. BILL and KATHY remain seated.*) Look. He didn't finish half his plate. (*calling*) Come out and eat the rest of your supper, Ben. There's no food wasted in this house. (*slight pause*) Take it to him, Mary.

MARY: (*picking up BEN's chair*) You – you're the cause of it. You're enough to spoil anyone's appetite.

JACOB: Ah, for Chrissake, he's too damn soft, and you don't help any. I was out fishing on the Labrador when I was ten years old, six months of the year for ten dollars, and out of that ten dollars had to come my rubber boots. (*to KATHY*) Ten years old, and I had to stand up and take it like a man. (*to MARY*) That's a lot tougher than a few harsh words from his father!

MARY: (*as she serves the dessert*) And you'll make him hard, is that it, Jacob? Hard and tough like yourself? Blame him for all you've suffered. Make him pay for all you never had.

JACOB: Oh, shut up, Mary, you don't understand these matters. He won't have you or me to fall back on once he gets out into the world. He'll need to be strong or – (*He winks at BILL.*) – he'll end up like your cousin Israel.

MARY: And don't tell *that* story, Jacob. You're at the table.

JACOB: (*to KATHY*) Israel Parsons was Mrs. Mercer's first cousin.

MARY: Might as well talk to a log.

JACOB: He was a law student at the time, and he worked summers at the pulp and paper mill at Corner Brook, cleaning the machines. Well, one noon hour he crawled inside a machine to clean the big sharp blades, and someone flicked on the switch. Poor young Israel was ground up into pulp. They didn't find a trace of him, did they Mary? Not even a hair. Mary's poor mother always joked that he was the only one of her relatives ever to make the headlines – if you knows what I mean.

MARY: She knows. And just what has Israel Parsons got to do with Ben, pray tell?

JACOB: Because that's what the world will do to Ben, Mary, if he's not strong. Chew him up alive and swallow him down without a trace. Mark my words. (*He lifts the bowl to his mouth and drinks the peach juice.*)

The front door bursts open.

MINNIE: (*off*) Anybody home?

JACOB: Minnie! (*He glances at MARY, then rises.*)

MINNIE enters. She is in her late forties, boisterous and voluptuous, a little flashily dressed.

MINNIE: Is you still eating?

JACOB: No, come in, come in.

MINNIE: If you is – guess what? – I brung along me new boyfriend to spoil your appetites ... Where's he to? Can't keep track of the bugger! (*She returns to the hallway, and shouts offstage.*) For Chrissake, you dirty t'ing, you! You might have waited till you got inside!

KATHY: (*to BILL*) What's she doing here?

MINNIE: (*off*) Come on. There's no need to be shy.

HAROLD enters with MINNIE. He is conservatively dressed but sports a white carnation.

MINNIE: (*to HAROLD*) That's Jacob and Mary. This here's Harold. (*They shake hands.*)

JACOB: Here give me your coats. (*He takes the coats.*)

MINNIE: T'anks, boy. (*to KATHY*) Hello, sister! Still mad at me? (*KATHY doesn't answer. To MARY.*) Harold works in a funeral parlour. He's an embalmer. Imagine. We met when poor Willard died. He worked on his corpse.

MARY: (*incredulously*) You made that up, Minnie. Confess.

MINNIE: As God is my witness, maid!

JACOB: Just as long as you'm not drumming up business, Harold.

HAROLD doesn't crack a smile.

MINNIE: He ain't got an ounce of humour in his body, Harold. (*looking at JACOB*) But he's got two or t'ree pounds of what counts. Don't you, Lazarus?

KATHY: (*sharply*) Mother!

MINNIE: "Mother" yourself. (*sitting on an arm of the chesterfield next to HAROLD*) I calls him Lazarus because he comes to life at night. And what a resurrection. Ah, I'm so wicked, Mary. To tell you the truth, I haven't been exactly mourning since Willard died, as sister over there can testify. And I'll tell you why. I took a good solid look at Willard – God rest his soul! – stretched out in his casket the t'ree days of his wake, all powdered and rouged and made up like a total stranger, and I says to myself, Minnie, live it up, maid. This is all there is, this life. You're dead a good long time. (*to JACOB*) And I for one wouldn't bet a t'in dime on the hereafter, and God knows I've t'rowed hundreds of dollars away on long shots in my day.

JACOB: Now, Minnie, enough of the religion. Would you both care for a whisky? (*MARY reacts.*)

MINNIE: (*meaning HAROLD*) Look at his ears pick up. Sure, Jake. That's one of the reasons we come early. (*JACOB crosses to the cabinet during MINNIE's speech and brings out a bottle of whisky. He pours three drinks.*) And Mary, I got to apologize for last night. I suppose I'll never live it down. I don't know what happened, maid. I laid down with a drink in me hand after supper and the next t'ing I know it's this morning and I'm in the doghouse.

MARY: That's okay, Minnie. (*She sits.*)

JACOB: Billy, my son, bring me the ginger ale. That's a good boy. (*During the dialogue BILL fetches the ginger ale from the fridge and returns to the dining room table.*) How do you like your drink, Minnie?

MINNIE: A little mix in mine, and not'ing in Harold's. The ginger ale tickles his nose and gets him all excited.

JACOB: What is he, Minnie? Newfie?

MINNIE: No, boy – Canadian.

JACOB: Harold, there's only two kinds of people in this world – Newfies and them that wishes they was.

MINNIE: That's what I tells him, boy.

JACOB: Why else would Canada have j'ined us in '49? Right, Minnie? (*JACOB crosses to the chesterfield with the drinks.*)

MARY: I t'ought you didn't have no whisky? I t'ought all you had in the house was "screech"? Do you mean to tell me that was deliberate, what you put Ben t'rough?

JACOB: (*quickly changing the subject*) Minnie, don't you want to see the shower gifts?

MINNIE: Sure, boy. Where's they to?

JACOB: They're in the bedroom. Show her, Mary. Now's a good time.

> MARY rises and crosses to the bedroom door. MINNIE follows.

MINNIE: (*indicating HAROLD*) Don't give him any more to drink, Jacob, till I gets back. The bugger likes to get a head start.

> They exit.

MINNIE: (*off*) Maid, will you look! A gift shop! Jesus!

JACOB: (*slight pause – to HAROLD, embarrassed*) Well.

> HAROLD nods. They drink.

MINNIE: (*off*) Even a rolling pin! (*She pokes out her head.*) My Jesus, Harold, I finally found somet'ing that compares!

> JACOB glances at HAROLD. HAROLD glances at JACOB. They drink.

JACOB: (*after a moment*) Grand old day.

> HAROLD nods. Silence.

JACOB: (*after a moment*) Couldn't ask for better.

> HAROLD nods. Silence.

JACOB: (*after a moment*) Another grand day tomorrow.

> HAROLD clears his throat.

JACOB: Pardon?

> HAROLD shakes his head. Silence.

JACOB: (*embarrassed*) Well, why don't we see what mischief the women are up to?

> HAROLD nods. With visible relief both men exit together.

BILL: Tomorrow's off! We've got to tell them, Kathy! And right now!

KATHY: We don't have to call it off.

BILL: What do you mean?

KATHY: You know what I mean.

BILL: You mean you'd get married without having to?

KATHY: I work, you know. I'll be getting a raise in two months, and another six months after that. I'll be making good money by the time you get into university. I could help put you through. (*slight pause*) I wouldn't be in the way. (*slight pause*) Billy! Don't you even care for me?

BILL: Sure.

KATHY: How much?

> Enter HAROLD. During the dialogue he helps himself to another drink from the dining room and crosses to the chesterfield.

BILL: A lot. But I still don't want to get married. I'm not ready. We're too young. Christ, you can't even cook!

KATHY: And you're just a mama's boy!

> HAROLD is now seated. KATHY stares at him a moment. Then she smiles.

KATHY: Well, Harold wants me, even if you don't. Don't you, Harold? (*She rises and crosses to the chesterfield, flaunting herself.*)

BILL: Kathy!

KATHY: (*to HAROLD*) I've seen the way you look at me. (*She drops on the chesterfield beside HAROLD.*) You'd like to hop in the sack with me, wouldn't you? Tell the truth.

BILL: Why are you doing this?

KATHY: You think he's any different than you?

BILL: What do you mean?

KATHY: This makes you jealous, Billy? (*She caresses the inside of HAROLD's thigh.*)

BILL: (*grabbing her by the wrist*) I don't understand you, Kathy.

KATHY: I understand you, Billy. Only too well. Poor trapped Billy.

BILL: I'm not trapped.

KATHY: Aren't you?

BILL: No! I'll call it off!

KATHY: Yes! Why don't you?

BILL: I will!

KATHY: I wouldn't want you to waste your life. I'll bet now you wished you'd never met me, don't you? You wish you'd never touched me. All this trouble because you didn't have the nerve to go to the drugstore!

BILL: Well, why did you let me do it if it wasn't a safe time? Answer me that?

Enter MINNIE, JACOB, and MARY.

MINNIE: Well, kids, you're well off now. More than we got when we started out, heh, Mary? Willard and me didn't have a pot to piss in or a window to t'row it out. (*to JACOB, as she sits*) Where's your eldest? I ain't met him yet.

JACOB: Ben? Oh, he's in his bedroom – (*He glances at MARY who is now sitting in the armchair.*) – studying. He's in university, Minnie. (*He calls to BEN's door.*) Ben, come out. (*slight pause*) And bring your diploma. (*He glances sheepishly at MARY and looks away. MARY shakes her head, amused.*)

Enter BEN, dressed in a sport jacket. He carries his rolled-up diploma tied with a ribbon.

JACOB: Graduated from grade t'irteen last night, Minnie. That's Ben. Ben, this is Mrs. Jackson, and that's Harold.

They all nod hello.

MINNIE: (*appraising BEN with obvious delight*) So this is the best man, heh? Well. Well, well, well. What a fine-looking boy, Jacob. He'll be tall.

JACOB: A little too t'in, Minnie. And not much colour to his face.

MINNIE: What odds? You was a skeleton yourself at his age. Tell you what, Ben. Be over some Saturday night and give you a scrubbing down in the tub. We'll send your father and mother to the pictures. (*to MARY*) Oh, how wicked, maid. Don't mind me, I've got the dirtiest tongue. The t'ings I comes out with. That's what comes of hanging around racetracks and taverns with the likes of the Formaldehyde Kid here. (*slight pause*) You looks like your mother's side of the family, Ben.

JACOB: I kind of t'ought he looked like my side. (*to BEN*) Show Minnie your diploma.

BEN hands the diploma to MINNIE.

MINNIE: (*to BEN*) Proud father.

BEN: (*to JACOB*) I thought you didn't have any whisky?

JACOB: (*ignoring BEN and glancing over MINNIE's shoulder as she reads the diploma*) He got honours all the way t'rough high school, Minnie. He got a scholarship.

MINNIE: Where'd he get his brains to? (*embarrassed silence – to BEN*) Told you you look like your mother's side. (*She hands back the diploma, rises, and hands her glass to JACOB.*) Next round less ginger ale, Jacob. Gives me gas. (*crossing to the record player*) And I'd hate to start cracking off around Father Douglas. (*She puts on a record – "Moonglow" theme from* Picnic.) What a face he's on him, already, the priest. Pinched little mouth. You'd t'ink he just opened the Song of Solomon and found a fart pressed between the pages like a rose. (*She starts to move slowly to the music.*)

KATHY: Mother, do you have to?

MINNIE: Do I have to what, sister?

KATHY: Make a fool of yourself.

MINNIE: Listen to who's talking! (*slight pause*) I'd dance with Harold except the only tune he knows is the "Death March." And the only step he knows is the foxtrot. Imagine foxtrotting to the "Death March." (*to JACOB*) Jacob, you was a one for dancing years ago. Wasn't he, Mary?

MARY: He still is, Minnie.

MINNIE: Did he ever tell you how I first got to go out with him?

MARY: I don't believe he did.

MINNIE: He didn't? Well, remember Georgie Bishop? He took me out one night – to the Salvation Army dance at Bay Roberts. It was in the wintertime, and cold as a nun's tit. I saw Jacob there, hanging about, and now and then he'd look my way and I'd wink. Oh, I was some brazen.

JACOB: I t'ought you had somet'ing in your eye, Minnie.

MINNIE: Yes, boy, the same as was in yours – the devil! ... To make a long story short, Mary, when it come time to go home, Georgie and me went outside where his horse and sled was hitched to the post. He'd tied it fast with a knot, and do you know what this bugger had gone and done?

JACOB: Now don't tell that, Minnie.

MINNIE: Pissed on the knot! He had, maid. A ball of ice as big as me fist. And who do you suppose walks up large as life and offers to drive me home in his sled? (*pause*) Poor Georgie. The last I remembers of him he was cursing the dirty son of a bitch that had done it and was stabbing away at the knot with his jackknife! (*She notices BEN's amused reaction to her story.*) Come dance with me, Ben. Don't be shy. Come on. If I'm not mistaken, you've got the devil in your eye, too. Just like your father. (*She puts BEN's arm around her waist and they dance.*) Look, Harold. You might learn a t'ing or two. (*She presses close against BEN.*) Mmm. You know, Jacob, this is no longer a little boy. He's coming of age.

KATHY: Mother, you're dirty.

MINNIE: How fast you've grown, Ben. How tall and straight. Do you want to hear a funny one? I could have been your mother. Imagine. But your grandfather – Jacob's father – put his foot down. I was a Catholic, and that was that in no uncertain terms. Wasn't it, Jacob? (*slight pause*) So I married Willard ... (*They break apart. To JACOB, as she sits.*) Ah, well, boy, I suppose it all worked out for the best. Just t'ink, Jacob – if you had married me it might have been you Harold pumped full of fluids.

JACOB: That it might, Minnie. That it might.

MINNIE: But you can't help marvel at the way t'ings work out. Makes you wonder sometimes.

JACOB: (*turns off music*) What's that, Minnie?

MINNIE: Your son marrying my daughter and turning Catholic in the bargain. Serves you right, you old bugger. The last laugh's on you. And your poor old father.

JACOB: You'm not still carrying that grudge around inside you, is you? I'm getting a fine girl in the family. That's the way I looks at it.

MINNIE: (*rising to help herself to another drink*) I don't mind telling you, Jacob, I've had my hands full with *that* one. Not a moment's peace since the day poor Willard died. She was kind of stuck on her father, you know. Jesus, boy, she won't even speak to Harold. Won't let him give her away tomorrow, will you, sister? Her uncle's doing that. Oh, she snaps me head off if I as much as makes a suggestion. T'inks she knows it all. And now look. All I can say is I'm glad her father ain't alive, this night.

JACOB: Now, Minnie, you knows you don't mean all that. Own up to it.

MINNIE: Oh, I means it, boy, and more. T'ank God it's only the second month. At least she don't show yet. If she's anyt'ing like me, she'll have a bad time. Well, a little pain'll teach her a good lesson.

KATHY: I wish you wouldn't talk about me like that, Mother.

MINNIE: Like what?

KATHY: Like I was invisible. I don't like it; I've told you before.

JACOB: Now, now, Kathy.

MINNIE: Listen to her, will you? Invisible. Sister, you may soon wish you *was* invisible, when the girls from work start counting back on the office calendar.

KATHY: Let them count!

MINNIE: See, Jacob? See what I'm up against? No shame!

JACOB: Minnie, let's not have any hard feelings. It's most time for church. I'll get the coats.

MARY: Yes, do.

JACOB gets MINNIE's and MARY's coats.

MINNIE: (*crossing to BEN*) You don't know, Mary, how fortunate you is having sons. That's the biggest letdown of me life, not having a boy ... We couldn't have any but the one ... (*bitterly*) and that had to be the bitch of the litter. How I curse the day. A boy like this must be a constant joy, Mary.

MARY: And a tribulation, maid.

MINNIE: Yes, but look at all the worry a daughter brings. (*as JACOB helps her into her coat*) This is the kind of fix she can get herself into.

KATHY: Mother, I just asked you not to.

BILL: Tell her, Kathy.

MINNIE: And then to top it off who gets the bill for the wedding? Oh, it's just dandy having a daughter, just dandy. I could wring her neck.

BILL: Kathy.

KATHY: (*to BILL*) You tell her.

MINNIE: If I had my own way I know what I'd do with all the bitches at birth. I'd do with them exactly what we did back home with the kittens –

KATHY: I'm not pregnant!

MINNIE: What?

KATHY: (*bitterly*) You heard me. I'm not pregnant.

MINNIE: What do you mean you're not? You are so, unless you've done somet'ing to yourself ...

KATHY: I didn't.

MARY: Kathy.

MINNIE: I took you to the doctor myself. I was in his office. Why in hell do you suppose you're getting married tomorrow, if it's not because you're having a baby?

KATHY: (*turning to MARY*) Mrs. Mercer, I had a miscarriage ...

MINNIE: A miscarriage ...

MARY: When, Kathy? (*She puts her arms around KATHY.*)

KATHY: This morning. I went to the doctor. There's no mistake. And I didn't do anything to myself, Mother.

MINNIE: (*quietly*) Did I say you did, sister?

MARY: Sit down, dear. (*She helps KATHY sit – long pause.*) This may not be the right moment to mention it, Minnie, but ... well, it seems to me t'ings have altered somewhat. (*She looks at BEN.*) T'ings are back to the way they used to be. The youngsters don't need to get married. There's no reason to, now.

Pause. No one moves except HAROLD who raises his glass to drink.

Blackout.

ACT TWO

A moment later. As the lights come up, the actors are in the exact positions and attitudes they were at the end of Act One. The tableau dissolves into action.

JACOB: Sit down, Minnie. We've got to talk this out. (*to KATHY*) Can I get you anyt'ing, my dear?

KATHY shakes her head. MINNIE sits.

MINNIE: (*slight pause*) What time is it getting to be?

BEN: Seven fifteen.

MINNIE: The priest expects us there sharp at eight. He's got a mass to say at half-past.

MARY: Now wait just a minute. I t'ink you're being hasty, Minnie. The children can please themselves, now, what they wants to do. Maybe they don't want to get married.

JACOB: Mary's right, Minnie. Ask them.

MINNIE: For someone who don't like to butt in, maid, you got a lot to say sometimes. Stay out of it or I might say somet'ing I'm sorry for.

MARY: I can't stay out of it. I wouldn't advise my worst enemy to jump into marriage that young, and neither would you, Minnie. They'd be far better off waiting till Billy finishes university ...

MINNIE: Well, maybe *they* can afford to put it off, but *I* sure as hell can't. The invitations are out ... the cake's bought, and the dress ... the flowers arranged for ... the photographer ... the priest and organist hired ... the church and banquet hall rented ... the food –

KATHY: (*jumping up*) I don't want to get married!

MARY: What?

MINNIE: What? Don't believe her, Mary. She do so. She's got a stack of love comics a mile high. (*to KATHY*) Now you shut your mouth, sister, or I'll shut it for you.

KATHY: I won't.

MINNIE: You knows what'll happen if you backs out now? I'll be made a laughing stock. Is that what you wants, you little bitch?

KATHY: Don't call me a bitch, you old slut!

MARY: Kathy.

MINNIE: (*to JACOB*) Did you hear that? Why, I'll slap the face right off her! (*She goes after KATHY.*)

JACOB: (*keeping MINNIE away from her daughter*) All right, now. This is no way to behave. Tonight of all nights!

KATHY: That's what you are, an old cow! He only wants you for your money. (*indicating HAROLD*)

MINNIE: That's a lie.

KATHY: Is it?

MINNIE: That's a lie. Let me at her, Jacob. I'll knock her to kingdom come.

JACOB: Enough, goddamn it! Both of you! (*Silence.*) That's better. Let's all ca'm down. We could all learn a lesson from Harold here. He's civilized. (*slight pause*) What we need's a drink.

MINNIE: (*as JACOB refills the glasses*) Imagine. My own flesh and blood, and she's got it in for me. She's never had much use for me, and even less since I took up with Harold here. She'll say anyt'ing to get back at me. Anyt'ing!

JACOB: Kathy's had a bad time of it, Minnie. No doubt she's upset. (*to MARY*) Remember how you was, when we lost our first? Didn't care if she lived or died. Didn't care if she ever laid eyes on me again, she was that down in the dumps. And I'm surprised, Billy. Not once have you come to her defence or spoken a word of comfort. You've got to be more of a man than that.

BEN: Why can't they get married and Billy still go to school?

MARY: (*to BEN*) Mind your business.

MINNIE: You hear that, Jacob? That's the one with all the brains.

BEN: (*to MARY*) I'm just trying to help.

MARY: Who? Yourself?

KATHY: I want him to, Mrs. Mercer. He doesn't have to quit school. I like to work. Honest.

MARY: Well, Billy, you're the only one we haven't heard from. What do you say?

JACOB: Ah, what's it matter if he gets married now or after university? He won't do much better than Kathy.

MINNIE: She's a good girl, in spite of what I said about her. A hard worker. She always pays her board sharp. And clean as a whistle.

JACOB: That's settled, then.

MARY: Is it, Billy?

JACOB: For God's sake, Mary.

MARY: He's got a tongue of his own. Let him answer. The poor child can't get a word in edgewise.

JACOB: Stop smothering him. He's a man now. Let him act like one. (*amused*) Besides, he's just getting cold feet. Ain't you, my son?

BEN: Did you get cold feet, Dad?

JACOB: All men do. (*MARY glances at JACOB who nudges her.*) Even the best of us. He'll be fine after tomorrow.

MINNIE: T'anks, Jacob. I could kiss you. Now, Harold, wait your turn, and don't be jealous. (*She crosses to the record player and selects a record.*) The mother of the bride and the father of the groom will now have the next dance. With your permission, Mary?

MARY: With my blessing, maid.

JACOB: (*glancing at MARY*) I don't know whether I'm up to it, Minnie.

MINNIE: Go on, Jacob. You'll be dancing a jig at your own wake.

Music: "Isle of Newfoundland." JACOB takes MINNIE in his arms and they dance. BILL goes to KATHY, takes her hand and leads her into the darkened kitchen. They make up.

MINNIE: Ah, Jacob, remember when we'd hug and smooch in the darkest places on the dance floor? The way he stuck to the shadows, Mary, you'd swear he was a bat. Dance with her, Harold. (*indicating MARY*) He's some wonderful dancer, boy. Went to Arthur Murray's. He's awful shy, though.

MARY and HAROLD exchange glances. HAROLD clears his throat.

MINNIE: Ah, boy, Jacob, I'd better give Harold a turn. He'd sit there all night looking anxious. He likes a good foxtrot. Fancies himself Valentino. Come on, Lazarus.

MINNIE and HAROLD dance. JACOB crosses to MARY who is sitting behind the dining room table.

JACOB: Dance, Mary?

MARY: You'll make a good match, the two of you.

JACOB: Mary, I t'ink you'm jealous.

MARY: Don't be foolish. And don't start showing off. That's the next step.

JACOB: "How beautiful are thy feet with shoes, O prince's daughter! The j'ints of thy t'ighs are like jewels, the work of the hands of a cunning workman. Thy navel is like a round goblet, which wanteth not liquor: thy belly is like –"

MARY: (*sharply*) Jacob!

JACOB: "– an heap of wheat set about with lilies. Thy two breasts –"

MARY: All right, boy – enough!

JACOB: (*sitting*) Do you remember, Mary, when you was just a piss-tail maid picking blueberries on the cliffs behind your father's house, your poor knees tattooed from kneeling? Did you ever t'ink for a single minute that one day you'd be the mother of grown-up sons and one of 'em about to start a life of his own?

MARY: No, and that I didn't. In those days I couldn't see no further ahead than you charging down Country Road on your old white horse to whisk me away to the mainland.

JACOB: Any regrets?

MARY: What does you t'ink?

JACOB: Ah, go on with you. (*pause*) The old house seems smaller already, don't it?

MARY: Empty.

MINNIE: (*still dancing*) Tomorrow's a landmark for us all, Jacob. I lose me only daughter and you lose your two sons. (*JACOB reacts.*) Somehow I don't envy you, boy. I t'ink it'll be harder on you. If I had sons ...

> *JACOB crosses quickly to the record player and switches it off.*

JACOB: What was that you just said, Minnie? Did I hear you correct? Whose sons?

MINNIE: Yours.

JACOB: Mine? Only one's going.

MINNIE: Didn't anybody tell you?

JACOB: Tell me what? I'm lucky to get the time of day. (*to MARY*) Tell me what?

MARY: Ben's moving in with Bill and Kathy. Taking their spare room.

JACOB: He is like hell!

BEN: I am!

JACOB: You'm not!

BEN: I am!

JACOB: Don't be foolish!

MINNIE: I t'ought he knowed, Mary. I t'ought the kids had told him.

JACOB: No, Minnie, they neglected to mention it. I'm not surprised!

MINNIE: I wouldn't have put me big foot in me mouth otherwise.

JACOB: Why should I know any more what goes on in my own house than the stranger on the street? I'm only his father. I'm not the one they all confides in around this house, I can tell you. I'm just the goddamn old fool. That's all! The goddamn fool.

BEN: I wanted to tell you after the wedding.

JACOB: Yes, you did so.

BEN: I would have sooner, but this is what happens.

JACOB: Oh, so now it's all my fault?

BEN: I didn't say that. Stop twisting what I say.

JACOB: How quick you is to shift the blame, my son. (*to MARY*) How come you to know? He was quick enough to run to you with the news, wasn't he?

MARY: I can't help that.

JACOB: Yes, you can. I'm always the last to find out, and you'm the reason, Mary. You'm the ringleader. The t'ree of you against the one of me.

MARY: And you talks about shifting the blame.

JACOB: Wasn't I the last to find out Billy was getting married? He told you first, but did you come and confide in me? That you didn't. If I hadn't found that bill from Ostrander's for Kathy's engagement ring ...!

BILL: We would have told you ...

JACOB: A lot of respect you show for your father. A lot of respect. You'm no better than your brother.

MARY: Ca'm down, boy. You're just getting yourself all worked up.

JACOB: I won't ca'm down. Ca'm down. All I ever does is break my back for their good and comfort, and how is it they repays me? A slap in the face! (*to BEN*) What did you have in mind to do, my son? Sneak off with all your belongings, like a thief, while your father was at work?

BEN: Go to hell.

JACOB: What did you say?

BEN: You heard me. I don't have to take shit like that from anyone. And I don't care who's here!

JACOB takes a threatening step toward his son. MARY steps between.

JACOB: I'll knock your goddamn block off!

MARY: Now just stop it, the both of you! Stop it!

MINNIE: I'd never have gotten away with that from my father. He'd have tanned me good.

MARY: And Minnie – mind your own business. This is none of your concern.

JACOB: Talking like that to his own father ...

BEN: And if you ever hit me again ...!

JACOB: I'll hit you in two seconds flat, if you carries on. Just keep it up. Don't t'ink for one minute you'm too old yet!

BEN: Come on. Hit me. I'm not scared. Hit me. You'd never see me again!

MARY: (*slapping BEN*) Shut right up. You're just as bad as he is!

MINNIE: Two of a kind, maid. Two peas in a pod. That's why they don't get on.

JACOB: Why the hell do you suppose we slaved to buy this house, if it wasn't for you two? And now you won't stick around long enough to help pay back a red cent. You'd rather pay rent to a stranger!

BILL: Dad, I'm leaving to get married, in case you forgot.

JACOB: You don't need to. Put it off. Listen to your mother!

BILL: A minute ago you said –

JACOB: Forget a minute ago! This is now!

BEN: He'll have converted for nothing, if he does!

JACOB: You shut your bloody mouth! (*to BILL*) Put it off, my son. There's no hurry. Don't be swayed by Minnie. She's just t'inking of herself. Getting revenge for old hurts.

MINNIE: And you're full of shit, Jacob.

JACOB: You goddamn Catholics, you don't even believe in birth control. Holy Jumping Jesus Christ. The poor young boy'll be saddled with a gang of little ones before he knows it! And all because my poor father hated the Micks!

MINNIE: Come on, sister, we don't need that. Get your coat. You too, Harold. Let's go, Billy. The priest can't wait on the likes of us.

BILL and KATHY move to go.

JACOB: Don't go, Billy. There's no need!

BILL: First you say one thing, Dad, and then you say something else. Will you please make up your mind! (*to BEN*) Ben, what should I do? Tell me.

BEN: I can't help you, Billy.

KATHY looks at BILL, then runs out, slamming the door.

MARY: (*to BILL*) Go after her, my son. Now's the time she needs you. We'll see you in church. Go on, now.

BILL: Ben?

BEN: In a minute. I'll see you there.

BILL: Dad? (*JACOB turns away. BILL runs out.*)

MINNIE: I'll take the two kids with me, Mary. See you in a few minutes.

JACOB: You won't see me there tonight, Minnie, and you can count on that. And not tomorrow, either.

MINNIE: That's up to you, Jacob, though I hope you changes your mind for Billy's sake. (*slight pause*) We oughtn't to let our differences interfere with the children. (*slight pause*) Come along, Lazarus. It's time we dragged our backsides to the church.

They exit. Silence. MARY removes her coat, then slowly begins to clear the table. BEN looks over at his father. Finally, he speaks.

BEN: Dad ...

JACOB: What?

BEN: I want to explain. Will you let me?

JACOB: I should t'ink you'd be ashamed to even look at me, let alone open your mouth. (*slight pause*) Well? What is it? I suppose we'm not good enough for you?

BEN: Oh come on.

JACOB: (*to MARY*) If you's going to the church, you'd better be off.

BEN: We still have a few minutes.

JACOB: (*to MARY*) And no odds what, I won't go to church. They can do without me.

MARY: Suit yourself. But I'm going. Just don't come back on me afterward for not coaxing you to.

JACOB: You can walk in that church tonight, feeling the way you does? Oh, you'm some two-faced, Mary.

MARY: Don't you talk. You was quite willing to see Billy go, till it slipped out that Ben was going, too.

JACOB: That's a lie!

MARY: Is it?

JACOB: That's a damn lie!

MARY: I'll call a cab. (*She crosses to the phone, picks up the receiver. To JACOB.*) We can't always have it our way. (*She dials and ad libs softly while dialogue continues between father and son.*)

JACOB: A lifetime spent in this house, and he gives us less notice than you would a landlord! And me about to wallpaper his room like a goddamn fool! (*slight pause*) And don't come back broke and starving in a week or two and expect a handout, 'cause the only way you'll get t'rough that door is to break it in! (*slight pause*) You'll never last on your own. You never had to provide for yourself.

BEN: I'll learn.

JACOB: You'll starve.

BEN: All right, I'll starve. And then you can have the satisfaction of being right. (*slight pause*) You're always telling me it's time I got out on my own and grew up.

JACOB: Sure, t'row up in my face what I said in the past!

BEN: Dad, will you listen to me for once? It's not because home's bad, or because I hate you. It's not that. I just want to be independent, that's all. Can't you understand that? (*slight pause*) I had to move out sometime.

JACOB: Was it somet'ing I said? What was it? Tell me. I must have said somet'ing!

BEN: No, it was nothing you said. Will you come off it?

JACOB: Can you imagine what our relatives will say, once they hears? They'll say you left home on account of me.

BEN: Well, who the hell cares?

JACOB: And you any idea what this'll do to your mother? You'm her favourite. (*The last syllable rhymes with "night."*)

MARY: Jacob! That's not fair!

JACOB: What odds? It's true, and don't deny it. (*to BEN*) Your mother's always been most fond of you. She even delivered you herself. Did you know that?

MARY: There's no time for family history, Father.

JACOB moves quickly to the mantel and takes the photo album. He is slightly desperate now. He flicks open the album.

JACOB: (*intimately, to BEN*) Look. Look at that one. You could scarcely walk. Clinging for dear life to your mother's knee. (*turning the page*) And look at this. The four of us. Harry Saunders took that of us with my old box camera the day the Germans marched into Paris. (*turns the photo over*) There. You'm good with dates. June 14th, 1940. Look how lovely your mother looks, my son. No more than ninety pounds when she had you.

MARY: Ninety-one.

JACOB: She was that t'in, you'd swear the wind would carry her off. We never believed we'd have another, after the first died. He was premature. Seven months, and he only lived a few hours.

MARY: Enough of the past, boy.

JACOB: That was some night, the night you was born. Blizzarding to beat hell. The doctor lived in Bay Roberts, and I had to hitch up the sled –

MARY: He's heard all that.

JACOB: Some woman, your mother. Cut and tied the cord herself. Had you scrubbed to a shine and was washed herself and back in bed, sound asleep, before we showed up.

MARY: Took all the good out of me, too.

JACOB: And wasn't she a picture? She could have passed for her namesake in the stained glass of a Catholic window, she was that radiant.

MARY: Get on with you.

JACOB: Your mother'd never let on, but you can imagine the state she'll be in if you goes. You'm all that's left now, Ben. The last son. (*a whisper*) I t'ink she wishes you'd stay.

MARY: I heard that. Look, you speak for yourself. I've interfered enough for one night.

JACOB: Your mother has always lived just for the two of you.

MARY: (*pained*) Oh Jacob.

JACOB: Always.

BEN: Come on, Dad, that's not true.

JACOB: It is so, now. It is so.

MARY: Well it's not, and don't you say it is. The likes of that!

JACOB: Confess, Mary. I don't count, I've never counted. Not since the day they was born.

BEN: If that's true, Dad, you should be glad to get rid of both of us. Have Mom all to yourself again.

JACOB: Don't be smart.

MARY: Who's the one making all the fuss? Me or you? Answer me that.

JACOB: No, you'd sit by silent and let me do it for you and take all the shit that comes with it. I'm wise to your little games.

MARY: I can't stop him, if he wants to go. I don't like it any more than you do. I can't imagine this house without our two sons. But if what Ben wants is to go, he's got my blessing. I won't stand in his way because I'm scared. And if you can't speak for yourself, don't speak for me. I'm out of it.

JACOB: If he's so dead set on going, he can march out the door this very minute.

MARY: He will not! Don't be foolish!

JACOB: He will so, if I say so! (*He charges into BEN's bedroom and returns with a suitcase which he sets on the floor.*) There! Pack your belongings right this second, if we'm not good enough for you.

MARY: Ben, don't pay him no mind.

JACOB: I don't want you in this house another minute, if you'm that anxious to be elsewhere. Ingrate!

MARY: If you don't shut your big yap, he just might, and then you'd be in some state.

JACOB: Oh, I would, would I? Well, we'll just see about that. I'll help him pack, if he likes! (*He charges into BEN's bedroom.*)

MARY: Ben, don't talk back to him when he's mad. It only makes it worse, you knows that.

JACOB: (*comes out with a stack of record albums which he hurls violently to the floor*) There. Enough of that goddamn squealing and squawking. Now I can get some peace and quiet after a hard day's work.

BEN: Dad, I think I ought to ...

JACOB: Don't open your mouth. I don't want to hear another word!

BEN: All right, make a fool of yourself!

JACOB: (*to MARY*) And that goes for you, too! (*He charges back into the bedroom.*)

BEN: What'll we do, Mom? We got to get out of here. Can't you stop him?

MARY: All you can do, when he gets like this, is let him run down and tire himself out. His poor father

was the same. He'd hurl you t'rough the window one minute and brush the glass off you the next.

JACOB: (*comes out with a stack of new shirts still in the cellophane*) And look at this, will you? Talk about a sin. I walks around with my ass out, and here's six new shirts never even opened. (*He hurls the shirts on the pile of records.*)

BEN: I don't want to spoil your fun, Dad, but so far all that stuff belongs to Billy. (*JACOB stares at the scattered records and shirts, alarmed.*)

MARY: Now you've done it, boy. Will you sit down now? You're just making a bigger fool of yourself the longer you stands.

JACOB: (*Her reproach is all he needs to get back in stride.*) Sure, mock me when I'm down. Well, I'll show you who the fool is. We'll just see who has the last laugh! (*He charges into his own bedroom. MARY picks up the records and shirts.*)

BEN: (*pause*) I wanted to tell him, Mom, a week ago. I kept putting it off.

MARY: I wish you had, Ben. This mightn't have happened.

BEN: It's all our fault, anyhow.

MARY: What do you mean?

BEN: We've made him feel like an outsider all these years. The three of us. You, me, Billy. It's always been him and us. Always. As long as I can remember.

MARY: Blame your father's temper. He's always had a bad temper. All we done was try our best to avoid it.

BEN: Yeah, but we make it worse. We feed it. We shouldn't shut him out the way we do.

MARY: And what is it you're not saying, that's it's my fault somehow? Is that what you t'inks? Say it.

BEN: I didn't say that.

MARY: Your father believes it. He calls me the ringleader.

BEN: Well, you set the example, Mom, a long time ago. When we were little.

MARY: Don't you talk, Ben. You're some one to point fingers. (*slight pause*) Perhaps I did. Perhaps your father's right all along. But you're no little child any longer, and you haven't been for years. You're a man now, and you never followed anyone's example for too long unless you had a mind to. So don't use that excuse.

BEN: I'm not. I'm just as much to blame as anybody. I know that.

MARY: I always tried to keep the peace. And that wasn't always easy in this family, with you and your father at each other's t'roats night and day. And to keep the peace I had to sometimes keep a good many unpleasant facts from your father. Small, simple t'ings, mostly.

BEN: You were just sparing yourself.

MARY: I was doing what I considered the most good! And don't tell me I wasn't. Oh, Ben, you knows yourself what he's like. If you lost five dollars down the sewer, you didn't dare let on. If you did, he'd dance around the room like one leg was on fire and the other had a bee up it. It was just easier that way, not to tell him. Easier on the whole family. Yes, and easier on myself.

BEN: But it wasn't easier when he found out. On him or us.

MARY: He didn't always, Ben.

BEN: No, but when he does, like tonight – it's worse!

JACOB enters the room from the bedroom, slowly, carrying a small cardboard box. He removes the contents of the box – a neatly folded silk dressing gown – and throws the box to one side.

JACOB: I won't be needing the likes of this. Take it with you. I've got enough old junk cluttering up my closet.

BEN: I don't want it, either.

MARY: He gave you that for your birthday. You've never even worn it.

JACOB: Take it! (*He hurls it violently in BEN's face. Then he notices the diploma lying on the table. He grabs it.*)

MARY: Not the diploma, Jacob! No!

BEN says nothing. He just stares at his father, who stares back the whole time he removes the ribbon, unfolds the diploma, and tears it into two pieces, then four, then eight. He drops the pieces to the floor.

MARY: God help you. This time you've gone too far.

Pause. Then BEN crosses to the suitcase. He picks it up.

BEN: I'll pack. (*He exits into his bedroom.*)

MARY: All right. You satisfied? You've made me feel deeply ashamed tonight, Jacob, the way you treats Ben. I only hopes he forgives you. I don't know if I would, if it was me.

JACOB: I always knowed it would come to this one day. He's always hated me, and don't say he hasn't. Did you see him tonight? I can't so much as lay a hand on his shoulder. He pulls away. His own father, and I can't touch him. All his life long he's done nothing but mock and defy me, and now he's made me turn him out in anger, my own son. (*to MARY, angrily*) And you can bugger off, too, if you don't like it. Don't let me keep you. Just pack your bag and take him with you. Dare say you'd be happier off. I don't give a good goddamn if the whole lot of you deserts me.

MARY: You don't know when to stop, do you? You just don't know when to call a halt. What must I do? Knock you senseless? You'd go on and on until you brought your whole house tumbling down. I suppose it's late in the day to be expecting miracles, but for God's sake, Jacob, control yourself. For once in your life would you just t'ink before you speaks? Please! (*slight pause*) I have no sympathy for you. You brought this all on yourself. You wouldn't listen. Well, listen now. Have you ever in your whole life took two minutes out to try and understand him? Have you? Instead of galloping off in all directions? Dredging up old hurts? Why, not five minutes ago he stood on that exact spot and stuck up for you!

JACOB: (*surprised, slightly incredulous*) Ben did ...?

MARY: Yes, Ben did, and don't look so surprised. Now it may be too late, but there are some t'ings that just have to be said, right now, in the open. Sit down and listen. Sit down. (*JACOB sits.*) For twenty years now I've handled the purse strings in this family, and only because you shoved it off on me. I don't like to do it any more than you do. I'm just as bad at it, except you're better with the excuses. (*JACOB rises.*) I'm not finished. Sit down. (*He does – slight pause.*) Last fall you tumbled off our garage roof and sprained your back. You was laid up for six months all told – November to May – without a red cent of Workmen's Compensation, because the accident didn't happen on the job. And I made all the payments as usual – the mortgages, your truck, the groceries, life insurance, the hydro and oilman, your union dues. All that, and more. I took care of it all. And where, Jacob, do you suppose the money came from? You never once asked. Did you ever wonder?

JACOB: Where? From the bank.

MARY: The bank! We didn't have a nickel in the bank. Not after the second month.

JACOB: What is you getting at, Mary?

MARY: Just this. (*She lowers her voice.*) If Ben hadn't got a scholarship, he wouldn't have went to college this fall. He couldn't have afforded to. It was his money that took us over the winter. All those years of working part-time and summers. All of it gone.

JACOB: Ben did that?

MARY: And you says he hates you!

JACOB: I don't want no handouts from him. I'll pay him back every cent of it.

MARY: Shut up. He'll hear you! He never wanted you to know, so don't you dare let on that I told you, you hear? He knowed how proud you is, and he knowed you wouldn't want to t'ink you wasn't supporting your family. (*slight pause*) Now, boy, who's got the last laugh? (*MARY takes her coat and puts it on as she crosses to BEN's door.*) Hurry up, Ben. The taxi ought to be here any second. (*She turns and looks at JACOB. There is anguish in her face. When she speaks her voice is drained.*) I'm tired, Jacob. And you ought to be, too, by all rights. It's time to quit it. A lifetime of this is enough, you and Ben. Declare it an even match for your own sake, boy, if for nothing else. I don't want to see you keep getting the worst of it. You always did and you still do.

Enter BEN, carrying his suitcase.

BEN: (*to MARY*) Isn't the cab here yet? It's almost eight.

MARY: He'll beep his horn. (*slight pause*) You don't need to take that now, my son. Pick it up Later.

BEN: That's okay, Mom. I've got all I want. The rest you can throw out. (*He sits on his suitcase.*)

JACOB: Your mother told me what you done last winter. I –

MARY: (*sharply*) Jacob!

JACOB: I wants to t'ank you. I'll pay you back.

MARY: You promised you – (*She stops, shakes her head in exasperation.*)

JACOB: (*slight pause*) I'm sorry what happened here tonight. I wants you to know that. I'll make it up to you. I will.

BEN: (*meaning it*) It's nothing. Forget it.

MARY: Let him say he's sorry, Ben. He needs to.

JACOB: Maybe I've been wrong. I suppose I ain't been the best of fathers. I couldn't give you all I'd like to. But I've been the best I could under the circumstances.

BEN: Dad.

JACOB: Hear me out, now. We never seen eye to eye in most cases, but we'm still a family. We've got to stick together. All we got in this world is the family – (*He rises.*) – and it's breaking up, Ben. (*slight pause*) Stay for a while longer. For a few more years.

BEN: I can't.

JACOB: You can. Why not?

BEN: I just can't.

JACOB: Spite! You'm just doing this out of spite! (*BEN shakes his head.*) Then reconsider ... like a good boy. Let your brother rent his room to a stranger, if he's that hard up. Don't let him break us up.

The taxi sounds its horn.

MARY: There's the taxi now.

JACOB: (*desperately*) You don't have to go, my son. You knows I never meant what I said before. You'm welcome to stay as long as you likes, and you won't have to pay a cent of rent. (*even more desperately*) Come back afterward!

BEN: No, Dad.

JACOB: Yes, come back. Like a good boy. I never had a choice in my day, Ben. You do.

BEN: I don't!

JACOB: You do so! Don't contradict me!

BEN: What do you know? You don't know the first thing about me, and you don't want to. You don't know how I feel, and you don't give a shit!

JACOB: In my day we had a duty to –

BEN: In your day! I'm sick of hearing about your fucking day! This is *my* day, and we're strangers. You know the men you work with better than you do me! Isn't that right? Isn't it?

JACOB: And you treats your friends better than you do me! I know that much, I can tell you. A whole lot better! And with more respect. Using language like that in front of your mother!

The taxi honks impatiently. BEN moves to go. JACOB grabs the suitcase.

MARY: Jacob! The taxi's waiting!

JACOB: (to BEN) You're not taking that suitcase out of this house! Not this blessed day! (He puts the suitcase down at a distance.)

MARY: That's okay, Ben. Leave it. You can come back some other time. (MARY exits.)

JACOB: He will like hell. Once he goes, that's it. He came with nothing, he'll go with nothing!

BEN: (slight pause) Do you know why I want to be on my own? The real reason?

JACOB: To whore around!

BEN: Because you're not going to stop until there's nothing left of me. It's not the world that wants to devour me, Dad – it's you!

JACOB whips off his belt.

JACOB: (as he brings it down hard on BEN's back) Then go!

BEN instinctively covers his head, crouching a little, unprotesting.

JACOB: (sobbing, as he brings the belt down again and again) Go! Go! Go! Go! Go!

Finally, as JACOB swings again for the sixth time, BEN whirls and grabs the belt from his father's hand. Then with a violent motion he flings it aside.

BEN: You shouldn't have done that, Dad. You shouldn't. (He exits.)

Silence. JACOB retrieves his belt. A slight pause.

JACOB: (fiercely striking the chesterfield with his belt) Holy Jumping Jesus Christ!

Silence. MARY enters from the hallway. JACOB begins to put on his belt. He notices MARY.

JACOB: What's you doing here? Isn't you going?

He crosses into the dining room and sits at the table. Slowly MARY puts down her purse and enters the dining room, crossing behind JACOB and sitting at the table beside him. She says nothing.

JACOB: (anguished) In the name of Jesus, Mary, whatever possessed you to marry the likes of me over Jerome McKenzie? (MARY says nothing. Pause.) I've never asked you before, but I've always wondered.

Pause.

MARY: It was that day you, me, and Jerome McKenzie was all sitting around my mother's kitchen and in walked my brother Clifford. He was teaching grade six in St. John's that year, and he told of a story that occurred that very morning at school. You've most likely forgotten. A little girl had come into his class with a note from her teacher. She was told to carry the note around to every class in the school and wait till every teacher read it. Clifford did, with the child standing next to him. The note had t'ree words on it: *Don't she smell?* Well, Jacob, boy, when you heard that, you brought your fist down so hard on the tabletop it cracked one of Mother's good saucers, and that's when I knowed Jerome McKenzie hadn't a hope in hell. (slight pause) Q.C. or no Q.C.!

Slowly MARY lifts one foot then the other onto the chair in front of her. The lights slowly dim into darkness.

END

JAMES REANEY

(1926–2008)

Observing how "life reflected art" in Stratford, Ontario, near where he was born and grew up, James Reaney wrote in a 1962 poem, "Let us make a form out of this: documentary on one side and myth on the other." No other Canadian dramatist has so successfully transmuted the stuff of documentary into the material of myth. Reaney makes of the life and history of Souwesto – the small towns and farms of southwestern Ontario – a rich poetic brew steeped in Blake and the Brontës, Walt Disney and the Bible, and leavened with a childlike propensity to treat everything as creative play. In his hands, the story of the Donnellys, local history and legend, emerges as an experience of extraordinary theatrical scope and complexity, a trilogy of plays that many consider the finest achievement of the Canadian theatre in the 1970s.

Reaney was well established as a poet and academic before he began writing for the stage. In 1949, he earned an M.A. in English at the University of Toronto and a Governor General's Literary Award for his first book of poetry, *The Red Heart*. After teaching at the University of Manitoba for seven years, he returned to the University of Toronto to pick up his Ph.D. in 1958 along with another Governor General's Literary Award for his second book of verse, *A Suit of Nettles*. Reaney began teaching English at the University of Western Ontario in 1960, a position he would hold for three decades. That year also marked his founding of the innovative journal *Alphabet,* which he edited until 1971, and his remarkable debut in the theatre with *The Killdeer*. Mavor Moore hailed it as "the first Canadian play of real consequence, and the first demonstration of genius among us." *The Killdeer* won five awards at the 1960 Dominion Drama Festival and a third Governor General's Literary Award for Reaney upon its publication in 1962. The play's eclectic symbolist style, melodramatic plot, and archetypal struggle between the forces of innocence and corruption signalled the shape of much of Reaney's work to come, including *The Donnellys*.

He continued writing poetry – *Twelve Letters to a Small Town* (1962) and *The Dance of Death at London, Ontario* (1963) – but most of his subsequent work was in theatre. *The Killdeer* was followed by *Night-Blooming Cereus* and *One-Man Masque* (1960), *The Easter Egg* (1962), and a series of fantastical plays for children commencing with the Manitoba Theatre Centre's 1963 production of *Names and Nicknames*. With *The Sun and the Moon* (1965) at the London Summer Theatre, Reaney began his long association with Keith Turnbull, a key development in the evolution of Reaney's stagecraft. In *Listen to the Wind* (1966), produced by Turnbull and directed by Reaney himself, from his sickbed the young protagonist "dreams out" a play-within-a-play. The complex action unfolds on a bare stage with a props table, a few actors, and a chorus of children providing visual metaphors and sound effects. The presentational style reminds us that acting is merely formalized play, a revelation of the power of imagination to transform reality. Out of *Listen to the Wind* came the Listeners' Workshop. Once a week for two years, Reaney led groups of local children and adults through elaborate play exercises designed to stretch their imaginations by, for example, improvising the Book of Genesis. From these workshops grew what he called the embryonics of *Colours in the Dark*, commissioned by the Stratford Festival in 1967. A Joycean epic revealing the macrocosm of human history in the microcosm of an individual life, the play is described by Reaney as a theatrical experience "designed to give you that mosaic – that all-things-happening-at-the-same-time-higgledy-piggledy feeling that rummaging through a play box can give you."

The embryonics of *The Donnellys* also arose out of the Listeners' Workshop, although Reaney had been fascinated since childhood by this dramatic story that had played out only twenty miles from where he was born. He began researching the project in 1967; and except for a major revision of *The Killdeer* in 1968, *The Donnellys* remained his sole dramatic concern for the next eight years. In 1973, Reaney took what was by then a massive script to Halifax, where Keith Turnbull and a group of actors that included Jerry Franken and Patricia Ludwick (the future Mr. and Mrs. Donnelly) put it through a series of workshops from which three separate plays emerged. Bill Glassco agreed to produce them at Toronto's Tarragon Theatre with Turnbull directing. *Sticks and Stones: The Donnellys, Part I,* opened in 1973. *The St Nicholas Hotel, Wm Donnelly Prop.: The Donnellys, Part II*, premiered in 1974 and won the Floyd S. Chalmers Canadian Play Award. *Handcuffs: The Donnellys, Part III,* opened in March 1975. Later that year, the newly christened NDWT Company – Reaney, Turnbull, et al. – toured all three plays across Canada. *Fourteen Barrels from Sea to Sea* (1977) is Reaney's highly personal account of the tour. *Sticks and Stones* would later receive major productions at the Blyth Festival (1989) and in a National Arts Centre–Stratford Festival co-production (2005). The full trilogy had a notable revival at Banff in 1996. *The Donnellys* was first published as a trilogy in 1983, republished in 2000, and again in 2008.

Reaney used the workshop preparation method with the NDWT Company for his next series of plays, all based on local Ontario history or pseudo-history: *Baldoon* (1976), written with C.H. Gervais; *The Dismissal* (1977), featuring Mackenzie King as a scheming undergraduate; *Wacousta!* (1978) and its sequel *The Canadian Brothers* (1983), products of nearly two years' intensive workshops (some led by Tomson Highway); *King Whistle* (1979); and *Antler River* (1980). In *Gyroscope* (1981), Reaney returned to more personal dramatic material. With his libretto for John Beckwith's opera *The Shivaree*, first performed in 1982, he was reunited with the composer for whose music he had written *Night-Blooming Cereus* twenty years earlier. In 1989, Reaney and Beckwith collaborated on another opera, *Crazy to Kill*, for the Guelph Spring Festival, and in 1990 Reaney's historical opera *Serinette* (music by Harry Somers) premiered at the Sharon (Ontario) Music Festival. During this particularly productive period Reaney also wrote *Performance Poems* (1990); a short-story collection, *The Box Social* (1996); and a stage adaptation of Lewis Carroll's *Alice through the Looking Glass*, produced at Stratford in 1994 and again in 1996. John Beckwith edited Reaney's collected librettos in *Scripts: Librettos for Operas and Other Musical Works* (2004), and Reaney's friend, Stan Dragland, edited his final collection of poems, *Souwesto Home* (2005). Publications since Reaney's death in 2008 include a collection of poetry – *The Essential James Reaney* (2009) – and a volume of plays, *Reaney Days in the West Room* (2009), edited by David Ferry, one of the original actors in *The Donnellys*.

Reaney's *Performance Poems* includes "Imprecations," a poem for two voices that celebrates the arts of cursing and name-calling, a fitting celebration for a writer who always held names to be as tangible as sticks and stones, and even more powerful. The Donnelly story as Reaney tells it is very much about the power of names. To carry the Donnelly name is both curse and blessing, sacrament and doom. In *The St Nicholas Hotel*, Will Donnelly looks into the future and sees how his enemies "smeared our name for all time so that when children are naughty their mothers still say to them be quiet, or the Black Donnellys will get you." Historically, the Donnellys were Irish Catholic immigrants who settled in Biddulph Township near Lucan, Ontario, in 1844. James and Johannah and their seven sons and a daughter almost immediately became embroiled in conflicts with their neighbours, and much of the violence that wracked the region – barn burnings, assaults, mutilations of farm animals – was attributed to the Donnelly family. In 1857 James Donnelly killed a man in a fight and went to prison for seven years. In 1879 son Mike was stabbed to death in a hotel bar-room, his assailant imprisoned for only two years. Finally, on the night of February 3, 1880, a mob of vigilantes burst into the Donnelly home and murdered Mr. and Mrs. Donnelly, son Tom and niece Bridget, and later that night son John. Though an eyewitness identified many of the killers, no one ever went to prison for the crimes.

In researching the plays, Reaney discovered that his source material embodied opposing views of the principals. The evil Donnellys of popular history and local lore were incarnated in Thomas P. Kelley's 1954 best-seller, *The Black Donnellys: The True Story of Canada's Most Barbaric Feud*, a potboiler that presented the family as "the most vicious and heartless bunch of devils that ever drew the breath of human life." In Kelley's version, the depraved family members, led by monstrous Johannah, terrorize the district for the sheer malicious joy of it and get only what they deserve in the end. Kelley published a second, even more sensationalized account, *Vengeance of the Black Donnellys: Canada's Most Feared Family Strikes Back from the Grave* (1962), and the two books together sold over a million copies. A more sympathetic and objective treatment was Orlo Miller's *The Donnellys Must Die* (1962). Miller argued that the Donnellys were essentially victims of a nasty vendetta that had carried over from

Ireland where they had refused to join the secret anti-Protestant society of Whiteboys (or Whitefeet). As a result, in the largely Irish settlement of Biddulph they were branded with the hated name "Blackfeet," made scapegoats, and persecuted for a great deal of local violence which was not of their doing. Reaney ultimately followed Miller's lead but went even further. He doesn't just exonerate the Donnellys. He celebrates them.

Part I, *Sticks and Stones*, covers the period 1857–67, opening with an expository flashback showing the Donnellys' stubborn refusal to bend to Whitefeet pressures in Ireland. We see them struggling to make a place for themselves in Biddulph, caught between the Roman (Catholic) and Protestant Lines of settlers, uncomfortable with both. They lose half their farm in a bitter dispute with the Fat Woman and her husband, and Mr. Donnelly is goaded into fighting with the Fat Woman's brother, Pat Farl, who won't stop calling him "Blackfoot." When Mr. Donnelly kills Farl, a heroic effort by Mrs. Donnelly gets her husband's sentence commuted to seven years in prison. At the end, the Biddulph Whitefeet burn the Donnellys' barn and try to intimidate them into leaving the township, but Mr. Donnelly (described in a stage direction as *a small square chunk of will*) refuses, reiterating what he told them in Ireland, "Donnellys don't kneel." In a prefatory note, Reaney writes, "It was at this time that the Donnellys decided to be Donnellys."

To be a Donnelly in Reaney's portrayal is to be strong, proud, stubborn, forthright, heroic. The Chorus in Act Three asks, in one of the many catechisms in *Sticks and Stones*, "Why was I a Donnelly?" Jennie and the other women answer, "Because ... you chose to be a Donnelly ... Because you were tall; you were different / and you weren't afraid ..." To be a Donnelly is to choose to be true to your own values no matter how much pain that may cause you. It is to stand up against the mob, the community, the church, and even the law if they pressure you to be what you are not. It is to show intense loyalty to your own family and generosity as a family to others who have been rejected or betrayed by theirs. To be a Donnelly, for Reaney, is to have the kind of integrity lacking in almost every character or institution that opposes them throughout the trilogy, from the corrupt magistrates George Stub and Tom Cassleigh in Part I to the churchmen who organize the vigilantes in Part III and the jury that finds mob leader Jim Carroll not guilty of their murder. Reaney seems to have romanticized the historical Donnellys almost as much as Kelley demonized them.

The second play, *The St Nicholas Hotel, Wm Donnelly Prop.*, takes place twenty-four years after the final events of *Sticks and Stones*. Will, the Donnelly known as "Cripple," now proprietor of a hotel near Biddulph, gets asked the trilogy's key question, "Why did they all hate you so much?" The play stages his memories as the complicated answer. Beginning in 1873, when Will and Mike torment their competitors by using their charm and daring to run a successful stage line, and ending six years later when Mike is stabbed to death by an envious rival, Will's tale indicates that the hatred is generated by the volatile combination of Donnelly pride and mischief and their neighbours' jealousy and corruption. Brimming with positive energy, the Donnellys provide a constant unwelcome challenge to the negativity and complacency of so much of their community. Young Tom Ryan explains that he ran away from his brutal home to the Donnellys (making his humiliated father another of their lifelong enemies) "because they're brave ... they're handsome," and "there's love there." Meanwhile, pranks result in tragic accidents and bitter retaliations. Violence escalates rapidly. Fights break out, stagecoaches crash, animals are mutilated. James dies of alcohol and illness. And the powers-that-be in Biddulph recruit first an ineffectual private detective and finally sly, vengeful mob leader Jim Carroll to blacken the Donnelly name and arrange for Mike's murder. In the play's final scene, Mike's ghost looms silently over two maids who try to scrub his bloodstain out of a barroom floor – an uneasy symbol of the Donnellys' stubborn staying power.

Part III, *Handcuffs*, focuses on the 1880 massacre and the few months immediately preceding and following it, filling in the details of what the first two plays have already told us will happen. The Donnellys *must* die; their pride and stubbornness cannot be endured. They are tragic.

Sticks and Stones is an extraordinary achievement, rich and dense as both literary text and theatrical script. Reaney weaves into the tale the symbolism of fertility myth – the Donnellys are naturalized in the Barleycorn ballad, "planted" and "harvested" such that they become archetypes; immortalized, though they will die as individuals. (See the last line and final stage direction of the play, in which the cast leaves a pile of sticks and a pile of stones on the stage.) Symbols such as the catechism, wheel, cat's cradle, and of course sticks and stones further enrich the play's literary texture.

But even more evident upon reading is the play's remarkable theatricality. All those symbols appear either as physical props or constructions of the actors themselves. Among other things, *The Donnellys* is a quintessential artifact of the popular "poor theatre" style of the late 1960s, carried over into the 1970s. Utilizing a bare stage, minimal costume pieces, and homely or homemade props, these plays relied heavily on the imaginations of their artist-creators (playwright, director, actors) and rely heavily still on their audiences. The style was ideally suited to the anti-materialist counterculture of the age, as well as to a newly emergent alternative Canadian theatre that was short on money and material resources. Showcased by *The Donnellys*, this brand of stagecraft was fully implanted in the Canadian theatrical imagination of the era through the influence of Toronto's Theatre Passe Muraille under Paul Thompson (about which more in the introduction to *Billy Bishop Goes to War*).

Mark the play's use of choral work and the fiddle, whistle, and dance (all actors' resources); the way the actors "*should look like an old document*" or map; the multi-casting required of a company of only eleven actors playing dozens of parts. Note the playful metatheatricality: the characters' references to their being in a play; the travesty of the Black Donnellys Medicine Show, ripped straight from the pages of

Thomas P. Kelley's potboilers. The motto for this kind of theatre might be "Anything Goes." Look for the appearance of Mrs. Donnelly's ghost, and for Jenny, as a grown-up in Act Three, narrating the events of the 1860s from the future. And notice in Act Two, the stage direction indicating how the Governor General and his wife might be distinguished from the other characters: *"perhaps he and his lady should be in period dress ... Perhaps marionettes."* The word "perhaps" is key here. Reaney has built flexibility and improvisational creativity into his text, allowing ample artistic freedom for those who (re)produce the play onstage or, like ourselves, in the theatre of our minds.

Sticks and Stones: The Donnellys, Part I

James Reaney

Sticks and Stones: The Donnellys, Part I, was first performed at Tarragon Theatre, Toronto, on November 24, 1973, with the following cast:

MR. DONNELLY	Jerry Franken
MRS. DONNELLY	Patricia Ludwick
PATRICK / PAT	Richard Carson
WILLIAM / WILL	David Ferry
MICHAEL / MIKE	Rick Gorrie
JANE / JENNY	Carol Lazare
MR. FAT	Bob Aarron
MRS. FAT	Miriam Greene
JIM FEENY	Ian Langs
CONSTABLE	Don McQuarrie
SURVEYOR, FRIAR,	
SHOWMAN, CONSTABLE	
and **SIR EDMUND**	Fletcher T. Williamson

Directed by Keith Turnbull
Lighting Design by John Stammers

PLAYWRIGHT'S NOTE

The play is based on the story of an actual family that came out from Ireland in 1844 to Biddulph Township eighteen miles from London, Ontario, and was annihilated by a secret society formed among their neighbours thirty-six years later. In the text that follows, the reader will meet Mr. and Mrs. Donnelly, their son William and their only daughter, Jenny. The other six sons are there, but they appear most clearly in the form of their shirts on Mrs. Donnelly's washing line. Watch for friends of the Donnellys – Andrew Keefe, the taverner, and Jim Feeny, the traitor. Their neighbours form a Catholic road of farmers' names and a Protestant road. Then there are enemies: George Stub, a Protestant merchant in the nearby village; and Tom Cassleigh, a neighbour who was tried several times for killing an Englishman named Brimmacombe. Both these gentlemen are also local magistrates! Two more enemies are close neighbours – called here Mr. and Mrs. Fat; also Pat Farl, whom Mr. Donnelly killed at a logging bee. There is a Medicine Showman who puts on a rival play to mime how fiendish the Donnellys were; there are constables, census takers, gaolers, black settlers, surveyors, the pyromaniac eight Gallagher boys, Mrs. Farl, priests, a bishop, and many others.

The complete story of the Donnelly tragedy is too large for one evening. This play gets you started and takes you as far as one of those moments after which things will never be the same again. When "persons unknown" burnt down his barn in 1867, James Donnelly defied this invitation to get out of the neighbourhood. He swore that he would stay in Biddulph Township forever. He is still there. It was at this time that the Donnellys decided to be Donnellys.

When you immerse yourself in this play, you may find that your experience matches my own when I immersed myself some eight years ago in documents that had lain for years in the attics of two local courthouses. After a while, I couldn't stop thinking about them.

– James Reaney

CHARACTERS

MRS. DONNELLY (*Johannah*)
MR. DONNELLY (*James / Jim*)
JAMES
WILLIAM / WILL
JOHN
PATRICK / PAT
MICHAEL / MIKE *their sons*
ROBERT / BOB
THOMAS / TOM
JANE / JENNY, *their daughter*
SURVEYOR

BOY, *his son*
CENSUS TAKER (*Mr. Darcy*)
PRIEST
GEORGE STUB, *ultra-Protestant merchant and*
enemy of THE DONNELLYS
JOHN GRACE, THE DONNELLYS' *landlord*
ANDREW KEEFE, *tavern keeper and friend of*
THE DONNELLYS
NEGRO WOMAN
A STICKSMAN
TOM CASSLEIGH, *Catholic neighbour and*
THE DONNELLYS' *enemy*
FRIAR
GEORGE ARMSTRONG
BRIMMACOMBE
MARKSEY
MAN ONE
MAN TWO
CHILD
FAT WOMAN / FAT LADY
MR. FAT (*Mike*), *her husband*
FARL, *her brother and* DONNELLYS' *enemy*
GAOLER
SHOWMAN
FALSE MR. DONNELLY
FALSE MRS. DONNELLY
FALSE JOHN
GROG BOSS
MAN THREE
MULOWNEY
CONSTABLE
OLD MRS. KEEFE
SIR EDMUND, *Governor General*
LADY HEAD, *his wife*
WOMAN ONE
WOMAN TWO
FAT GIRL
MAGGIE, FAT LADY'*s niece*
DONEGAN
MRS. GALLAGHER
SARAH FARL, FARL'*s widow,* DONEGAN'*s sister*
JIM FEENY, TOM DONNELLY'*s best friend*
SHOWMAN'S SON
FALSE JIM (*Feeny*)
FALSE PAT (*Donnelly*)
MRS. DONNELLY'S GHOST
CARPENTER

ACT ONE

The room in which the story is presented contains
all of the objects and properties required – ladders,
barrels, sticks, stones, noisemakers, chairs, etc. The
central area is bare except for a pile of sticks on
one side and a pile of stones on the other, and
possibly a pile of four boulders at the back in the
centre. In the distance, there is the drunken and
rowdy singing of a tavern song.

Oh, three men went to Deroughata
To sell three loads of rye.
They shouted up and they shouted down
The barley grain should die.

   (*refrain*)

Tiree igery ary ann, Tiree igery ee,
Tiree igery ary ann, The barley grain for me.

Then the farmer came with a big plough,
He ploughed me under the sod.
Then winter it being over
And the summer coming on,
Sure, the barley grain shot forth his head
With a beard like any man.

Then the reaper came with a sharp hook;
He made me no reply.
He caught me by the whiskers and
Cut me above the thigh.

Then the binder came with her neat thumb;
She bound me all around
And then they hired a handyman
To stand me on the ground.

Then the pitcher came with a steel fork;
He pierced it through me heart.
And like a rogue or highwayman
They bound me to the cart.

Then they took me to the barn and
Spread me out on the floor.
They left me there for a space of time
And me beard grew through the door.

Then the thresher came with a big flail;
He swore he'd break me bones

But the miller he used me worse
He ground me between two stones.

Then they took me out of that and
Threw me into a well.
They left me there for a space of time,
And me belly began to swell.

Then they sold me to the brewer
And he brewed me on the pan
But when I got into the jug
I was the strongest man.

Then they drank you in the kitchen
And they drank you in the hall,

(said, not sung)

But the drunkard he used you worse;
He pissed you against the wall.

Now the stage turns the deep green of primeval forest; someone imitates the whistle of a deep forest bird – the peewee – and then a boy, WILL DONNELLY, limps across the stage to sit down on the pile of stones with his catechism book. His mother, MRS. DONNELLY, a tall woman, enters the forest looking for her son. She comes over to him, accepts his book, and says, after refusing his offer of a seat on the stones:

MRS. DONNELLY: Which are the sacraments that can be received only once?

WILL: The sacraments that can be received only once are Baptism, Confirmation, and Holy Orders.

MRS. DONNELLY: Now, Will, why can Baptism, Confirmation, and Holy Orders be received only once?

WILL: Baptism, Confirmation, and Holy Orders can be received only once because they imprint on the soul – a spiritual mark, called a character, which lasts forever.

OTHERS: (at back of theatre, singing softly)

Oh, three men went to Deroughata
To sell three loads of rye.
They shouted up and they shouted down
The barley grain should die.

MRS. DONNELLY: Now where's your shoes? They were on your feet when we left the chapel.

WILL: I know where they are. Mother, I just don't want them to wear out so fast.

MRS. DONNELLY: Who's making you feel shame of your feet?

WILL: Nobody.

MRS. DONNELLY: Were the boys calling you names in the churchyard then?

WILL: Yes. They threw stones at me and they called me – cripple. I'm used to that, Mother, but there was a new boy there and do you want to know what he called me, Mother? (She nods.) Blackfoot!

MRS. DONNELLY: Did they call us that then?

WILL: Yes. And me myself – the Blackfoot. Cripple, I know. But what do they mean by Blackfoot?

MRS. DONNELLY: I suppose across the sea even it would come following us.

WILL: What come following us, Mother?

Enter MR. DONNELLY and stands with his back to us far upstage at the centre. The mob moves a step or two closer to the stage. As if made of forest branches and leaves behind them and above them, a silhouette map of Ireland appears towering on the backstage wall.

OTHERS: (singing, a step or two closer)

Then the farmer came with a big plough,
He ploughed me under the sod.
Then winter it being over
And the summer coming on,
Sure, the barley grain shot forth his head
With a beard like any man.

Someone in a dress rolls a barrel onstage; "she" covers it with a sheet of rusty tin and then places on top of the tin a model of the Sheas' house. As "she" departs, two men disguised in dresses, bonnets, and masks or veils strike matches and burn down the house. The fire makes their shadows grow into the branch map of Ireland. All this proceeds under MRS. DONNELLY's speech and illustrates it.

MRS. DONNELLY: In the old country, Will, where your father and your brother James and your mother were born – you were called a Blackfoot if you wouldn't join the Whitefeet.

WILL: Who were the Whitefeet?

MRS. DONNELLY: Who, indeed. They were a faction, they were a secret society, a secret people.

MALE VOICE: (*from the OTHERS*) Six eggs to you, Rody, and half a dozen of them rotten.

GIRL'S VOICE: The landlords are tyrants – English robbers and murderers that rob the people of their little spots, and turn 'em out to perish. 'Tis justice to punish the bloody robbers!

MRS. DONNELLY: Oh, indeed it was justice and the Whitefeet rode around at night dressed up like ladies, mind you, so they couldn't be recognized. They made it hot for landlords and bailiffs. The trouble was they made it hot for everybody. Will, there was one family – the Sheas – they lived twenty miles off, they said no to the Whitefoot Society, no, they wouldn't give up the farm they'd just rented, and a good farm it was in those hard times, just because the Whitefeet wanted nobody ever to rent that farm at all to spite the landlord. So no, says the Sheas. Well what the Whitefeet did to the Sheas one night is so terrible I'm going to whisper it to you and don't ever talk about it again.

OTHERS: (*singing*)

Then the reaper came with a sharp hook;
He made me no reply.
He caught me by the whiskers and
Cut me above the thigh.

WILL: Even the baby was dead then?

MRS. DONNELLY: Despite all the mother did she would have had to drown it altogether to save him from the fire and that baby died, Will, because his father wouldn't join the secret people, because his father would not do what they done, do what they told him to do.

Men start preparing a barrel for a human occupant by putting thorn branches into it.

WILL: It's better to join them then?

MRS. DONNELLY: And have to help burn whole families alive in their beds then? Sure, Will, terrible and filthy as the name of Blackfoot is – worse than scab, or leper or nigger or heretic have they made it, they, the clean, just, and secret people – I'd rather be called scab, or leper or nigger or heretic or Blackfoot than do what they did to the Sheas. At first they'd ride by and you'd find a note at your doorway that said – "signed by Matthew Midnight."

OTHERS: (*whispering*) Signed by Matthew Midnight.

WILL: Who was he?

MRS. DONNELLY: Oh, the pretend name of their Chief. The Great Chief of the Secret Society and the note would say –

MALE VOICE: (*under and over*) Jim Donnelly –

OTHERS: (*singing*)

Then the binder came with her neat thumb;
She bound me all around.

MALE VOICE: Jim Donnelly!

OTHERS: (*singing*)

And then they hired a handyman
To stand me on the ground.

MALE VOICE: Jim Donnelly!

A man is put into the barrel; they roll it back and forth in time to the singing and the speech. Another man rolls on the floor – back and forth.

MALE VOICE: If you don't help us cut off the bailiff's ears tomorrow night, you are a Blackfoot and we'll cut off yours an' fill a barrel first with thorns and nails and then – with – you.

MRS. DONNELLY: Yes. So if you were afraid, Will, you joined them and they made you kneel down and swear and drink – faith to them forever.

BARREL ROLLERS: (*repeat under*) Terry Morgan's in the barrel.

OTHERS: (*galloping under*)

Then the pitcher came with a steel fork;
He pierced it through me heart.
And like a rogue or a highwayman
They bound me to the cart. (*knocking*)

MRS. DONNELLY and WILL have climbed a great stepladder at the back of the stage.

MRS. DONNELLY: One night, Will, your father was up the road visiting a farmer he was to do some work for the next morning. They followed him there.

The barrel rollers join the mob, barrel tumbling down off the stage where DONEGAN will fall down later, but is hoisted up again; we begin to focus on MR. DONNELLY's back.

OTHERS: Come out, Jim Donnelly.

MRS. DONNELLY: They said to your father –

OTHERS: Put on you my good fellow and come out till two or three of your neighbours that wish you well gets a sight of your purty face, you babe of grace.

MRS. DONNELLY: Your father stood behind the door and he says –

MR. DONNELLY: Who are you that wants me at all?

MRS. DONNELLY: And they says –

OTHERS: Come out first, avourneen.

> *OTHERS prepare a Bible and candle. MR. DONNELLY turns to us for the first time. He is a small square chunk of will.*

MRS. DONNELLY: He opened the door and came out.

OTHERS: Oh, Jim Donnelly. Jim, the Whitefeet hear that you let one of your mares stand to Johnson's stallion last Monday coming home from the fair.

MRS. DONNELLY: To which your father replied –

MR. DONNELLY: (*He comes toward us and them with affability.*) It was love at first sight. Sure, Johnson's stallion was mounting my one mare before I could stop him. Would you have me break up a pair of true lovers? Would you? And I had my back turned for the merest minute getting the other mare's tail out of a thorn bush.

OTHERS: Did you not know, Jim Donnelly, that no Whitefoot is to have any dealings with the Protestant and the heretic Johnson?

MR. DONNELLY: Yes, but it was –

OTHERS: (*They extend two lighted candles to him.*) Kneel, Donnelly. Get down on your knees. (*But he stands. The barrel is rolled back and forth in front of him.*) Swear (*striking a book*) by the holy evangelists that you will always be joined to this society known as the Whitefeet and that you will forever and forever obey –

MR. DONNELLY: But you see I won't kneel. And I won't, I will not swear that.

HALF OF OTHERS: (*singing*)

Hrump hrumpety bump brump brump

Terry's in the barrel

Hrump hrumpety bump brump brump

Jim Donnelly's in it, too,

We'll roll you right up Keeper's Hill

it's true, it's true … (*repeat under*)

> *This "it's true" with malign stamping of feet goes on under the speech of the remaining half of OTHERS.*

HALF OF OTHERS: If you refuse, Jim Donnelly – if you refuse, Donnelly, you won't know the day nor

the hour nor the night nor the hour when we'll come to –

MR. DONNELLY: No, I'm not! Kneel! No! Swear! No! I will not kneel.

> *We still hear Terry Morgan in the barrel saying, "It's true, it's true, it's true."*

MRS. DONNELLY: So they cursed your father and called him a –

OTHERS: Blackfoot!

> *The barrel is rolled at MR. DONNELLY, who catches it. As they yell the name at him, they turn their backs on him, hiding their eyes as if he's too foul to see. They lie down in two rows on either side of the stage – these will become the "roads" of Biddulph in the next scene.*

MR. DONNELLY: (*singing like one of those John L. McCormack records*)

Then they took me to the barn and

Spread me out on the floor.

They left me there for a space of time

And me beard grew through the door.

The shadow map shows Ireland drifting away.

OTHERS: (*singing into the floor*)

Then the thresher came with a big flail;

> *MR. DONNELLY lets Terry Morgan out of the barrel, rolls it aside, where it now becomes a hollow tree, and, assisting Morgan, goes straight upstage, then over to stage left where both figures melt into the CHORUS there.*

He swore he'd break me bones

But the miller he used me worse

He ground me between two stones.

MRS. DONNELLY: What day is it today of all days, William Donnelly?

WILL: It's my birthday.

MRS. DONNELLY: Tell me one wish.

WILL: Well, Mother, 'tis something other than a prayer book. I'd like a horse – a black stallion. And a sword. Then I'd ride up and down the line and I'd cut the heads off all those who call me – us – names.

MRS. DONNELLY: Go over to the old tree the storm fell down, Will, what would you call this big black horse?

WILL: Lord Byron. But he wouldn't be lame, you see.

MRS. DONNELLY: Now see what you find there hidden among the roots. (*He searches, crawling into the barrel, searching around it.*)

OTHERS: (*singing softly and rolling over*)

Then they took me out of that and

Threw me into a well.

They left me there for a space of time,

And me belly began to swell.

WILL: It's a parcel. (*Actually it is just two sticks.*)

MRS. DONNELLY: But it's not likely your father and I would give you a brown paper parcel for your twelfth birthday. What's it a parcel of, Will?

WILL: A fiddle. Is it just for today, Mother? Just mine for my birthday? But tomorrow will my brothers get at it?

MRS. DONNELLY: No, Will, it is for you – and only you. To be your music for your entire lifetime. Remember what I've told you today.

> *WILL mimes the fiddle with two sticks; at edge of stage, a real fiddler follows.*

WILL: (*as he tunes*) What did happen to father when he wouldn't kneel and he wouldn't swear?

MRS. DONNELLY: Nothing's happened.

WILL: Nothing's happened yet?

MRS. DONNELLY: Nor ever will.

WILL: Are there some of them followed us here then?

MRS. DONNELLY: Your father outfaced them in the old country, and if they were ever to come after him up the roads of Biddulph, he'd do the same to them again. We're not there anymore, Will. We're where *you* were born – not an old country, but a new country these Canadas. Only bullies and blowhards say at you: "You won't know the day nor the hour nor the night when we'll come to – " Aye, yes – come to a tap with our fists on their chests at our gateway that'll send them rolling down the line like ninepins. (*She picks up a stone and bowls it down the aisle.*) What do your father and mother care if they should follow us – whisper me who called you the name. (*He does quickly and –*)

OTHERS: (*softly*) A high grey hill –

MRS. DONNELLY: Uh, it's his tattletale mother is a fat woman has to be raised in and out and onto her bed with a pulley. No-Feet-at-All should be her name and his – the No-Feet-with-All-the-Belly. She's got wind of something and the child has overheard. Will, after this harvest, I'm telling you your father will own this very ground we're standing on and shortly after that we'll own to another heir, not our fifth boy, pray, but our first girl may it please heaven and when he owns the very ground we stand on and the fields he has made, you'll see they'll never drive us off. We won't be druv!

OTHERS: (*whistling wind noises*) – that's Keeper's Hill.

MRS. DONNELLY: Here we stay.

OTHERS: In Ireland.

> *The map silhouettes the coasts of Iceland, Greenland, Newfoundland, the River, Lake Ontario, Hamilton, and then the province of Upper Canada where it comes to rest.*

MRS. DONNELLY: Not in Ireland. No, not there. With old names – Blackfoot, Whitefoot, slavery and fear. Here is a new fiddle, Will (*She takes the fiddle.*) and we're free as it is to play all the tunes. (*She uses the fiddle and speaks this verse, the CHORUS whistling the tune under.*)

Then they sold me to the brewer

And he brewed me on the pan

But when I got into the jug

I was the strongest man.

If you're afraid you should be – (*fills the whole theatre*)

OTHERS: – Ireland – (*just barely there, but there*)

MRS. DONNELLY:

– If you're not you'll live.

> (*They leave the forest and she turns from us, singing.*)

Then they drank you in the kitchen

And they drank you in the hall,

> (*said, not sung*)

But the drunkard he used you worse;

He pissed you against the wall.

OTHERS: Ten years before this the Township of Biddulph was surveyed.

> *SURVEYOR and BOY enter with chain, stakes and mallet, and book. Two OTHERS stretch out blue brook cloth across stage-water music. The rest return to their lines stage right and stage left to make Jacob's ladders, or cats' cradles.*

BOY: So what's this lot, Pa?

SURVEYOR: Concession Six, Lot Eighteen.

BOY: I wonder who'll come to live here. (*Driving in stakes that indicate the borders of the* **DONNELLY** *farm.*)

SURVEYOR: You're always wondering about that, aren't you, Davie? Well, it won't be any more coloured settlers. The Company's tired of them. So it will be Irish squatters more than likely – Big Jim Johnson is bringing over a horde of his relatives from Tipperary and he's bringing every sort evidently so he'll feel at home again.

BOY: I wonder what they'll be like.

SURVEYOR: Oh, Paddy will fight the coloured folks and drive them out if he can. Then he'll fight his Paddy neighbours and then he'll fight himself and then he'll move on somewhere and repeat the process.

BOY: What'll they fight about, Pa? (*His father washes his face in the stream.*)

SURVEYOR: Well, to begin with the way this lot is laid out, there's a small creek enters it from the next farm, crosses it and then flows into the next farm. Farm that is to be. It'll be the subject of a lawsuit, quarrels about water rights, flooding – they'll love that little creek.

BOY: Couldn't you stop that?

SURVEYOR: Well, now, what would you suggest?

BOY: Make the farms a different shape?

SURVEYOR: I'm not allowed to do that, Davie. The laws of geometry are the laws of geometry. (*Looping the chain so as to measure the next lot: we begin to focus on the next scene.*) No, people must make do with what right angles and Euclid and we surveyors and measurers provide for them.

BOY: (*moving on*) So what's this lot, Pa?

SURVEYOR: Concession Six, Lot Seventeen.

OTHERS: (*Using ropes and making cats' cradles [Jacob's ladders] out of them and their bodies; fates with string entangling people's lives. Distribute the following phrases with differing textures.*)

Wild lands   wild lands   wild lands

   Cut into concessions   cut into farms

Canada West   Canada West

In the New World   the new world

       the new world

CHORUS whistles to the "Temple House Reel." They dance with pieces of wood that they join together into the **DONNELLY** *shanty, which stands a bit aslant centre stage and behind which appears an* early map of Biddulph Township showing the net of concessions, roads, farms with owners' names on them, and a feeling that we have come from Ireland to a closer look at what is happening here. As if to a tree at the side of the stage, someone hammers up a notice with a stone.

A **CENSUS TAKER** *carrying another big book approaches the* **DONNELLY** *place and is met by* **MR. DONNELLY**. **MRS. DONNELLY** *comes out of their shanty with a baby. She puts it down in a cradle and walks over to the tree, takes down the notice.*

CENSUS TAKER: A fine morning, Jim Donnelly. Now this has nothing to do with taxes. What it is, is this: they're enumerating the population of Canada West in 1848 so what returns will I make for you, Jim Donnelly?

CENSUS TAKER asks the row of questions in left-hand column; **MR. DONNELLY** *answers with words in right-hand column.*

CENSUS TAKER:	MR. DONNELLY:
Situation – Lot?	Eighteen
Concession?	Six
Religion?	Church of Rome
Natives of Ireland in each family?	Three
Total number of persons resident in the house where the Census is taken?	Four
Lands – Number of acres held by each family?	One hundred
Uncultivated, of wood in wild land?	One hundred
Neat cattle	None
Horses	None
Hogs	Three
Proprietor or Non-Proprietor?	Non-Proprietor
Landlord?	John Grace, carpenter, London Township

CENSUS TAKER: You want to keep track of your landlord, Mr. Donnelly. Someone was asking Mr. Grace about his land up here and he said no one was living on it.

MR. DONNELLY: It's a funny thing then, Mr. Darcy, that he recognizes our money when we go into town to give him his yearly rent then. Does he think it's ghosts that are improving his land for him?

CENSUS TAKER: Good day to you, Jim Donnelly. And Mrs. Donnelly, too.

MRS. DONNELLY: Good day to you, Mr. Darcy. (*She comes to her husband with the notice from the tree.*)

MR. DONNELLY: Read it aloud for me, Mrs. Donnelly.

OTHERS:

Squatters and Trespassers. Notice is hereby given.

Squatters and Trespassers. Notice is hereby given.

MRS. DONNELLY: Oh, did you know this now, Mr. Donnelly. There are now again many people going about the country in search of Improved Lands, occupied by Squatters with the intention of –

OTHERS: – Purchasing over their heads.

MR. DONNELLY: Over my head is under my feet. Old John Grace is not going to sell it from either over us nor under us till he considers our offer and his promise. He won't even own it himself till eight years from now, and if it goes up in value, it's my work and yours, Judith, has made it go up. He agreed to that and he's going to stick by it.

A PRIEST interrupts MR. & MRS. DONNELLY.

PRIEST: Who are punished in Purgatory?

MR. & MRS. DONNELLY: Those are punished for a time in Purgatory who die in state of grace but are guilty of venial sin or have not fully satisfied for the temporal punishment due to their sins.

PRIEST: Who are punished in hell?

MR. DONNELLY: Not I. No, not James Donnelly. I'm not in hell though my friends in Biddulph thought to send me there, but after thirty-five years in Biddulph who would find hell any bigger a fire than that fire I died in? I'm not in hell for I'm in a play (*ladders begin to register on us, poking up behind*) and it's my duty to – (*pause*) Name the roads of Biddulph!

OTHERS:

Front Road   Coursey Line   Gulley Road

Sauble Line   Revere Road   Granton Line

Swamp Line   Roman Line

At the back of the stage are raised five ladders. Stage-right ladder is the tallest; then they get

smaller to quite a stubby one – their shadows and patterns matching the map of Biddulph, which is a triangle.

MR. DONNELLY: Yes, those are the roads of Biddulph. I was one of the path masters for the Roman Line. My neighbours and myself for three days in the spring and three days in the late summer would dig and pick and scrape and shovel gravel so there'd be a smoother road for my enemies to come and club me, and these roads of Biddulph – you're right to see them as ladders, yes, ladders that we crawled up and down on and up other ladders – up to Goderich for justice, down to London to pay our rent.

The ladders have been laid before MR. DONNELLY and he uses their rungs to illustrate.

MR. DONNELLY: Why are the roads here rather than here? Why do I live here rather than here? Wild lands cut by surveyors into people – with your chain you decided that it would be here, my farm – that people say I squatted on Concession Six, Lot Eighteen – and you decided –

BOY: So what's this lot, Dad?

MR. DONNELLY: That's Mulowney's. At his five-acre slashing I should kill Farl and there –

SURVEYOR: Concession Six, Lot Fifteen.

MR. DONNELLY: – I should be caught. Caught in the lines and the roads and the farms they made and the quarrels about fences and ditches – the Protestant Line, now who settled that line?

OTHERS: (*Use a long ladder as the core for this: whistle "Lilliburlero" under – this tune will meet the banjo tune behind the NEGRO settlers' protest – the CHORUS forms a double line that faces us with one black in its midst.*)

	Who settled the third and fourth concessions?
Protestants	Johnstons
STICKS HALF CHORUS:	**STONES HALF CHORUS:**
Big Jim, Little Jim, Jerry Jim	Johnson
Big John's John's George	Johnson
Big Tom's John's George	Johnson
and	
Attery	Stub

Armwright	Latchett
Courcey	Blackwell
	Protestants

and pioneers!

The Guernseys	and the Cobbetts
came with them it appears	And then –

NEGRO: (*banjo; distribute the following names*)

What about the Mescoes	and the Washingtons
Taylors	Runcimans
Delkeys (*humming*)	and the Bells –

MR. DONNELLY: Yes, the coloured settlers had come to those concessions ten years before any of us came from Ireland and it was their bad luck to have farms just where the new railroad slated to cross the Proof Line Road from London to Goderich.

The burning-of-house-on-barrel routine is set up with men disguised in women's clothes. In bowler hat and suspenders, ultra-Protestant GEORGE STUB comes forward.

STUB: Darkie, if you don't sell me that corner five acres you've squatted on there I'm going to heat it hotter than hell, and something else so serious might happen that they'll have to erect a gallows for me.

Pinned by a ladder, the NEGRO cannot prevent them from burning his property.

ALL: Proclamation!

WOMEN: Robert Baldwin, Attorney General –

MALE VOICE: Whereas about midnight of Thursday the nineteenth day of October now last past, certain Barns, the properties of Bell, Ephraim Taylor, and the Reverend Daniel A. Turner, Coloured Inhabitants of the Township of Biddulph in our province of Canada, were destroyed by fire.

STUB ET AL.: (*derisively*) And whereas there is reason to believe that the said fire was not caused by accident, but was the act of Incendiaries at present unknown. Now know ye, that a reward of –

MALE VOICE: – fifty pounds will be paid to any person –

FEMALE VOICES: – Witness. Our right trusty and right well beloved Cousin Earl of Elgin and Kincardine and Governor General of British North America. (*pause*) A true copy.

MR. DONNELLY: Arhh, Stub and his pals got off and it came out that a few coloured settlers stayed where they had first settled, but drifted away south to London, down the ladder – *shhh!*

The following inserts are like mugshots suddenly cut into the other imagery.

GAOLER:	**STUB:** (*from behind bars of gaol ladder*)
Name	George Stub
Date When Committed	October 20th, 1848
Height	Six feet
Colour of Eyes	Grey
Place of Birth	Tipperary
Religion	Church of England
For What Committed	Suspicion of arson, burning the coloured settlers' barns
Occupation	Senator
Mr. Stub!	I'm a storekeeper now, but that's what I'll ask Macdonald for in '78, if I get his Catholic candidate all the Orangemen's votes.
Colour of Eyes	Grey

MR. DONNELLY: So the road you lived on could destroy you just like that, and the road you lived on might not turn on you, but decide to have a go at another road. What other road? Why the sixth and seventh concession where I lived. My road. Who settled the Roman Line? Church Line? Chapel Line?

The whistled "Temple House Reel" goes under here; we begin to have a kind of music for each social group.

STICKS:	**STONES:**
Barry	Trehy
Feeny	O'Halloran
Cahill	Cassleigh
McCann	Flynn
Grace	

WILL and JENNY run up and down the ladder that represents the Roman Line.

WILL: No, that's wrong now. You should say Donnelly's. Not Grace's farm. John Grace never cleared that farm.

STICKS: But John Grace has the deed to this farm, Cripple.

JENNY: When he was my father's landlord, but it was my father cleared the land and made it a farm of value.

STUB: Where's your deed, Donnelly?

WILL: But don't you see that we had something better than a deed? We had his *word* as a *friend* of my mother and father's over in the old country. Mr. Grace told my father he'd get him started on a farm up in Biddulph if Paddy with a hod wasn't good enough for him. He'd pay the taxes, we'd pay him rent and at the end of ten years we'd have the first chance to buy at a fair price.

GRACE: (*while sawing a stick in two*) But how in the devil's name was I to know that at the end of the ten years the war would have driven the price so high and wheat at two dollars a bushel?

STONES: Did he get the promise in handwriting?

STICKS: Squatters can't read.

WILL: When my father was promised that land –

WOMEN: Concession Six, Lot Eighteen.

WILL: He took a handful of it back to my mother and she said –

MR. DONNELLY walks down the Roman Line (i.e., the two lines of STICKS & STONES like the lineup of a reel, to MRS. DONNELLY at the upstage end). This is one of the most important design images of the story, a man caught between the lines of his neighbours, caught in a ladder, and the big dance at the end of the play will emphasize this quality of THE DONNELLYS being planted in rows of people they can't get away from.

MRS. DONNELLY: James. What have you there in your hand?

WILL: He said –

WILL & MR. DONNELLY: – Mrs. Donnelly, this is the farm that's going to be ours.

BOYS: Concession Six, Lot Eighteen.

WILL: Start again, please. If you walked south down the Roman Line –

They say their names with a crouch, and a secret meaning, since most of them are Protestant misunderstandings for Gaelic names. This contrasts the Roman Line with the Protestant Line, who are more aggressive and sure of themselves.

STICKS:	STONES:
Barry	Trehy
Feeny	O'Halloran
Cahill	Cassleigh
McCann	Flynn
Pause.	
Donnelly	Mulowney
Egan	Marksey
Quinn	Farl
Gallagher	Duffy
Clancy	Donovan
(*bell*) and Father Flynn's church	
	and Andy Keefe's tavern (*jug sound*)

WILL & JENNY:

Brother and sister we walk down the road
We were born on and lived there
The road our father helped build
When his killers were babies.

The road chant can be repeated with variations. THE DONNELLYS walk down the line and it is hard to do so because the line sways out and is wide; then it sprouts perspectives; MRS. DONNELLY stands at the end before kneeling. MR. DONNELLY then turns to tell us something. Actors have been drifting off to view some offstage disturbance.

BOY: The *London Inquirer* September 20th, 1844.

VOICE: The Huron Assizes is to be congratulated on not having a single prisoner stand for trial and aside from –

MRS. DONNELLY: (*folding a newspaper*) And indeed they were to be congratulated while there was still time because his Lordship never wore a pair of white gloves again, not at least while Biddulph Township was part of Huron County – from 1844 to 1863.

ALL: Return of convictions made by Her Majesty's Justices of the –

The following "Return of Convictions" sequence needs stone-clicking rhythms, and a chopping block might be brought in to show how they axed out clubs for their battles. The rubrics "Name of Prosecutor," etc. need not be repeated each time but can be represented by a gesture illustrative to each. The whole cast is drawn up in three files to say and illustrate the three columns. The company should look like an old document that suddenly bristles with stones that hurt as they come zinging through the air.

STONES: Peace within the Township of Biddulph –

STICKS:	STONES:	OTHERS:
Name of Prosecutor	Name of Defendant	Nature of Charge
George Campbell	Thomas Cain	throwing stones at the premises
William Hogan	James Nugent	evading toll, stealing hoops

Illustrate the crimes with noise and mime and props.

The Queen	Thomas Cassleigh	Murdering an Englishman

As indicated above, but with new variation that the OTHERS should carry.

STICKS:	OTHERS:	STONES:	OTHERS:
Thomas Hogshaw	accuses	William Harleton	of milking a cow – furtively
Dennis Devlin	accuses	Paul Quinlan	of assault and battery

STICKS:	STONES:	OTHERS:
Name of Prosecutor	Name of Defendant	Nature of Charge
Gerald Quinn	Timothy Egan	Tearing down his house

*Now the **STICKS** [Protestant Line] face the **STONES** [Roman Line] and whistle "Lilliburlero" at them. The **ROMAN LINERS** reply with their theme.*

STICKS: The Biddulph Riot –

OTHERS: which took place –

STONES: – at Andrew Keefe's tavern –

KEEFE: (*in apron with tray of bottles*) A friend of the Donnellys, my name is Andy Keefe and I own the tavern at the first tollgate into Biddulph just across from St. Patrick's church. On Christmas Eve, 1857, just after the election in which Mr. Holmes defeated Mr. Cayley, the Blackmouth Proddies paid me a visit.

STICKS:	STONES:
ten or twelve sleighs	one hundred persons
Hurrah for the Tips	Hurrah for the Grits
Hurrah for the Tories	Hurrah for Holmes

This choral account of a riot should be counterpointed to a riot mime perhaps in slow motion where the Protestants drive the Catholics offstage with their clubs. But the Catholics secretly return to the stone pile and throw all the stones offstage at pursuing Protestants. Women take off their black woollen stockings, put a stone in each, and wave them around their heads. Use sounds from saws on wood, rended wood, sounds of broken glass.

NEGRO WOMAN: (*with lantern directly in front of us*) On the night of December 24th, I was at the barn feeding my cattle about six or seven o'clock after night. Heard some sleighs coming up from –

A STICKSMAN: Strike him – strike him –

NEGRO WOMAN: Bar-room door lying on the ground and some men pounding him. I went to the house thinking my children might be frightened. I was all alone, afraid they might molest me.

KEEFE: Shame, shame. Have mercy, boys.

A STICKSMAN: There's a man killed. One of us.

A STICKSMAN: Give us a light to find Ryan and Keefe, the bloody Papists.

NEGRO WOMAN: (*now at the ladder behind the DONNELLY house*) Went upstairs in my house, drew out the board in the Gavel end of the house and looked out and saw the moon rising.

KEEFE: Did then and there break and destroy all the windows in the lower part of my house –

WOMEN: – Sticks stones and axes. (*Repeat under until indicated.*)

KEEFE: Household furniture, breaking, tearing, burning it, cut down the signpost, cut the spokes of the wagons, cut down the water pump, threw sticks, stones, and the water pail into the house. (*Throw a pail of water on the stage floor at this point.*

Some kneel down to scoop up the liquor.) Broke the taps off my liquor casks, suffered the liquor –

A STICKSMAN: Don't burn this, his house, he's a good fellow.

STONESMAN: Run away.

KEEFE: Alex Fraser, John Bell, Peter Cody, my mother, my mother, my two barkeepers, Tim Casey and Bill Ryan.

WOMAN: Sticks stones and axes. (*end of repeat*)

A STICKSMAN: Hurrah for Holmes – let's go back and kill them all.

KEEFE: Hurrah for the Grits! Rushed upstairs to hide for our lives –

STICKS: Hurrah for Holmes, ye bloody Papists –

STONES: Hurrah for Cayley –

STONES throw stones at STICKS – stones are left covering the stage. This sequence ends with all crawling back onstage groaning and lying down. A man rolls a wheel across the stage. This will soon reappear. Now a sweet-voiced PRIEST drones on about diocesan history. A shuffling FRIAR with staff will eventually meet TOM CASSLEIGH and his wagon wheel.

PRIEST: The diocese in which the wretched Donnelly family lived had a troubled inception. The first bishop moved the see from London, that was but eighteen miles away, to a border town some 150 miles away at least. The first bishop built himself a barge in which he planned to visit the hinterland of his diocese, but as it was being launched it sank. Four Dominican friars from Kentucky he left behind to take care of the spiritual affairs of his people in Middlesex and Huron Counties. These friars would tramp the countryside sometimes meeting an old farmer whom they would confess through one of the wheels of his hay wagon.

CASSLEIGH reaches through the spokes of his wagon wheel toward the wandering FRIAR, who comes over to him. This man is young, very sure of himself, and violent. His scene with the FRIAR contains both truth and mockery in a mixture for which we can't find a recipe.

CASSLEIGH: Bless me, Father, for I have sinned.

FRIAR: When did you last confess, my son?

CASSLEIGH: Back in the old country, Father.

FRIAR: How far away in time would that be now?

CASSLEIGH: (*pause*) I want to confess the sin of murder, Father.

FRIAR: Oh, my son, that is a mortal sin.

CASSLEIGH: It was, Father, indeed it was mortal to him. But, Father, I didn't kill the man.

FRIAR: Oh? Then how are you guilty of the crime?

CASSLEIGH: A friend of mine did the deed – for me. It was the Englishman who was killed on our road last February, sure, you must have heard about it, caused quite a stir, but I didn't kill him, oh no.

FRIAR: Why did you hate the Englishman so much?

With the men of the cast, re-enact the story. CASSLEIGH goes over and tumbles on the ground with GEORGE ARMSTRONG. Use a ladder as a sort of memory curtain. Follow the lead of what action the speeches suggest, but cut to the bone. Candles for the lights in farmhouses, paper for snow.

BRIMMACOMBE: (*directly to us*) What have I done to you, man?

CASSLEIGH: At your barn raising north of our settlement where you Cornishes live in Usborne Township, Mr. Brimmacombe –

VOICE: – He attacked me and was taken away. There was a fight between George Armstrong and Thomas Cassleigh. Brimmacombe and two others of us parted them. Brimmacombe told his hired man to hold Cassleigh down until he'd promise to be quiet. When Cassleigh got up, he took off his coat and struck the hired man, saying to Brimmacombe –

CASSLEIGH: – And you will be marked yet sometime between this and the London road.

BRIMMACOMBE: Me, man, what have I done to you?

FRIAR: What is the fifth commandment of God?

CASSLEIGH: The fifth commandment of God is: Thou, Brimmacombe – should not have seen me beaten so badly. (*The Roman Line forms for CASSLEIGH to skulk up and down, hiding behind people as if they were houses, shanties, trees, and barns.*) Where are they now? Brimmacombe and his man. I seen them go down the road in the morning. When are they coming back? Perhaps they'll get a knock somewhere when they were not looking for it.

Try a Roman Line formation that goes across the stage rather than up and down it.

MRS. DONNELLY: The whole settlement knew several weeks beforehand that if Brimmacombe came back up the Roman Line he would never reach home alive.

*There is a flurry of snowflakes. The Roman Line has candles for its thin row of lamps and candles in the winter twilight. We focus on **ANDREW KEEFE** and **BRIMMACOMBE**, perhaps at the end of the name sequence for the Roman Line, which can go on softly under.*

ALL: The sixth of February, 1857.

KEEFE: Take my advice, Mr. Brimmacombe, cut the bells off your sleigh now that your hired man has gone ahead and you're all alone. Not wise, Mr. Brimmacombe, not wise. How the devil did your sleigh upset so – och, it's that big snowdrift that comes between the church and my tavern – and you've got two cows as companions – take the other road home.

BRIMMACOMBE: Andy Keefe, how can I do that? I've sent my hired man ahead of me. He's to meet me at Donnelly's schoolhouse. How can I tell the roads apart in the twilight and the snow? They're just two lines of sparks where the settlers have lit their lamps and candles. Ah, this is the other road that's safe for a Protestant to drive his cattle up.

ALL: The snow was on the ground.

The theatre gets very dark; we see two ladders with their shadows.

BRIMMACOMBE: What road am I on then?

STICKS: *(softly)* Donovan **STONES:** Clancy

BRIMMACOMBE: Not Courcy and Blackwell?

STICKS: Gallagher **STONES:** Duffy

BRIMMACOMBE: Not Armwright Latchett?

ALL: Quinn Marksey

BRIMMACOMBE: Then I'm not on the Protestant Road?

MARKSEY: Brimmacombe, we told you you'd be marked between your house and the London road and I mark you here.

Silhouette ladder clubbing and whistle under the Roman Line reel.

WOMAN:

whick whack	sticks and clubs
crick crack	stones they threw
sticks and stones	stones and sticks

Whisper this under. Lanterns come from all sorts of places in the theatre.

MAN ONE: He had a small bit uv a stick in his hand.

MAN TWO: Coming home about eight or nine o'clock at night, I saw his whip and cap beside him where he lay on the road. My wife was with me and sez she –

WOMAN: – Och, Paddy, is this a log or a man in the shnow?

MAN TWO: An sez she –

WOMAN: – I think he's an Englishman name of Brummygum.

MAN ONE: I didn't hear anyone say it was Brummygum. Dannelly that's now in the Pinitinshery – was the first man that towld me. (*The lanterns converge over the dead body.*)

WOMAN: It was then just sunset and growing dark –

CHILD: A man was dead on the road –

MAN TWO: Saw the body lying up the road, oh! He must have been killed.

*Shadows of people, confessional wheel, then a slow retreat and disappearance of lanterns until we are left with the **FRIAR** and his penitent in the summer afternoon light.*

ALL: It's a dangerous thing to find a dead body.

WOMAN: Sell your land, Joe.

MAN ONE: People moved away if they could.

MRS. DONNELLY: The Cassleighs and the Markseys were near and dreaded neighbours.

MAN TWO: Tom Cassleigh and his great friend, Will Marksey, shortly after this bought up some of the deserted farms.

FRIAR: Are you sorry then that you took his life?

CASSLEIGH: *(pause)* I didn't take it, Father.

FRIAR: You and your friend must give yourselves up to the magistrates.

CASSLEIGH: I'm sworn to my friend, Father.

FRIAR: Why is it two years since the deed was done and still they have not caught you? Or was it that you were taken but each time you terrified the constables into letting you go?

CASSLEIGH: Why, Father, they've been and tried me for it, but I've got a friend who stole the witness papers from the courthouse and I believe they can't try me again till they get them all sworn and copied out again.

FRIAR: What friends are these?

CASSLEIGH: Friends of my ribbon, Father.

MAN ONE: Did not say I heard Marksey say he had given Brimmacombe a tap?

FRIAR: Did not those who saw your friend strike the blow bear witness?

CASSLEIGH: They saw him. They saw him seeing them seeing him and they saw me seeing him seeing them seeing them seeing him. Can we help it if they have a mortal fear of us?

FRIAR: You are not sorry for what you have done then?

CASSLEIGH: Am I not then? I didn't do it. I can't tell on my friend. And he may have hit the Englishman a bit uv a tap, but he didn't hate the man.

FRIAR: And I cannot absolve you of your mortal sin. But may God soon move you to true repentance for your sins – that you may receive His sacred absolution. In nomine Patris et Filii et Spiritus Sancti.

We watch CASSLEIGH weaving back and forth behind the wheel as the FRIAR walks up the Roman Line.

GAOLER:	CASSLEIGH:
Name?	Tom Cassleigh
Number?	551
Age?	Twenty-seven
Height?	Five feet eight and a half inches
Colour of eyes?	Grey
Crime?	Suspicion of murder

As the FRIAR walks up the Roman Line, they kneel to him and so reveal the CENSUS TAKER and MR. DONNELLY.

CENSUS TAKER:	MR. DONNELLY:
How many natives of Canada?	Five, five boys
How many acres?	One hundred
In cultivation?	Thirty in crop, seventy acres of wild land
Wheat?	Twenty-eight acres, yielded fifteen bushels per acre
Potatoes?	Two acres – thirty bushels

CENSUS TAKER: Good day to you, Jim Donnelly.

MR. DONNELLY: Good day to you, Mr. Hodgins.

A very tinny bell rings the angelus.

FRIAR: Angelus Domini nuntiavit Mariae.

POPULUS: Et concepit de Spiritu Sancto. Ave Maria.

FRIAR: Ecce ancilla Domini.

POPULUS: Fiat mihi secundum verbum tuum. Ave Maria.

FRIAR: And the word was made flesh.

POPULUS: And dwelt among us. Hail Mary.

FRIAR: Ora pro nobis, sancta Dei Genitrix.

POPULUS: That we may be made worthy of the promises of Christ. Gratium tuam.

This prayer goes under the scene with the FRIAR. A mix of Latin and English swells up when there are chances.

Angelus Domini nuntiavit Mariae	The angel of the Lord declared unto Mary
Et concepit de Spiritu Sancto	And she conceived of the Holy Ghost.
Ave Maria ...	Hail Mary ...
Ecce ancilla Domini.	Behold the handmaid of the Lord.
(Fiat mihi secundum verbum tuum)	(Be it done unto me according to Thy word.)
Ave Maria ...	Hail Mary ...
Et Verbum caro factum est.	And the Word was made flesh.
(Et habitavit in nobis.)	(And dwelt among us.)
Ave Maria ...	Hail Mary ...
Ora pro nobis, sancta Dei Genitrix	Pray for us, O Holy Mother of God
(Ut digni efficiamur promissionibus Christi.)	(That we may be made worthy of the promises of Christ.)
Oremus: – Gratiam tuam quaesumus, Domine, mentibus nostris infunde; ut qui angelo nuntiante, Christi Filii tui incarnationem cognovimus, per passionem ejus et	– Let us pray: Pour forth, we beseech Thee, O Lord, Thy grace into our hearts, that we, to whom the Incarnation of Christ Thy Son was made known by the message of an Angel, may, by His passion

passionem ejus et crucem ad resurrectionis gloriam perducamur. Per eundem Christum Dominum nostrum Amen

and cross, be brought to the glory of His Resurrection. Through the same Christ Our Lord. Amen

FRIAR: A letter for you, Mr. Donnelly, from Ireland. And one for you, Mrs. Donnelly. (*They thank him under the continuation of the angelus prayer.*) Do you ever wish sometimes to be where this letter came from, Mrs. Donnelly? (*They shake their heads and murmur "No, Father" under the prayer.*) May I purloin one of your five sons for a moment, Mrs. Donnelly? William, I have something for you as well as for your parents. William Donnelly, the bishop will visit this mission on the Saturday after St. John's Day. Will you be ready for his questions and his presence, do you think? I have with me your confirmation ticket.

They have come down the Roman Line and out into the downstage area where there are trees (ladders) for WILL to climb up, swing from as the FRIAR tries to tempt him into the priesthood.

WILL: There is a question, Father, I want to ask the bishop.

FRIAR: And what is that question, my son?

WILL: People call me Cripple, Father. What I want to know is: why was I created lame? I'm going to ask him that.

FRIAR: I wonder, Will, if I might try to answer for him. That's a good question, Will, but first let me ask you a question. What is it you want most to give to yourself?

WILL: I used to want to give myself a horse – and a sword, Father. For when I'm riding, I'm not a cripple then. I used to want to give myself a fiddle. Then I received one for my birthday. Now I want to play my fiddle so well that people will ask me to play at their weddings because when I play or when I dance, why then you see, Father, I'm not crippled then.

FRIAR: Are you crippled then when you're praying?

WILL: (*pause*) No, Father.

FRIAR: What the bishop may say to you is that your lameness is God's marking you for His own. Your condition is a badge of His favour.

WILL: Father, if you had been lame could you have confessed as many souls as you have this week?

FRIAR: No, my son. No. Will, here is the piece of paper you will need to be able to receive the holy sacrament of confirmation.

WILL: Thank you, Father.

FRIAR: Will, would you know then how to address the bishop with the proper form of his title if you should decide to ask him this question of yours? (*After a pause, WILL shakes his head.*)

ALL: Per eundem Christum Dominum nostrum. Amen. (*The prayer under ends. The missals rustle shut and then the angelus mood is broken by one of the ladders crashing to the floor.*)

Axes and wood-chopping sounds.

CORONER: In the year 1847, eight men were accidentally killed. Two men were murdered by falling trees.

MR. DONNELLY: Yes, it got so you didn't have to use knife or club, why a tree would do it for you. There was one farm I was chopping on in the winter of 1855 where an accident happened (*all the ladders are lowered by ropes in slow motion on top of MR. DONNELLY*) to me. I wasn't hurt. I just sat there in the snow thinking for a while as they chopped through the branches to get at me. There's two men here I don't know well at all at all, and they done that. There were two families came to our line that fall, just fresh out from the old country – one of them had a wife who was as broad as she was long, the other was a man who was helping the fat woman's husband get my farm away from me and his name was – Farl.

WILL & JENNY: Why is our father's farm so narrow?

DONNELLY BOYS (STONES): (*advancing across the stage picking up stones; the stage is the front field of the DONNELLY farm*) Picking up stones in our father's front field. Where do we put them, Pa?

MR. DONNELLY: At the line fence over there and the line fence over there. (*Points and illustrates with the extreme edges of the playing area.*)

They toss the smaller stones into these two lines. Use quite big stones for some of the boys to lug. Underline with whistled reel. Now enters the FAT WOMAN. We never really catch her name, but she is the arch-enemy of THE DONNELLYS. Her

husband is also fairly fat and they have a certain on-the-ground quality that materializes everything, while with THE DONNELLYS there is just the opposite feeling. She enters carrying a small laundry stove, which she crashes down.

FAT WOMAN: Husband. (*pause*) If you're the boss, prove it. Prove it by putting on your mitts. Go out and get me some wood.

MR. FAT: I asked my old woman where'd I get the kind of wood she wanted.

FAT WOMAN: I need some more-than-dry wood for my little darling of a laundry stove here. Did you really buy that hundred acres Donnelly is squatting on, or who's the boss?

FARL: (*springs up from nowhere*) Shure, Mike. You're the boss. We'll get some of the best dried kindling for your old woman she ever seen. Come on. (*Out they go.*)

FAT WOMAN: Now there goes the boss. At last. There goes the boss.

WILL & JENNY: Why is our father's farm so narrow?

JENNY: I remember the census taker came up the road again.

DONNELLY BOYS (STONES): Ten years we picked up the stones.

The two lines of people move toward each other.

STICKS: Widening and clearing

STONES: Our father and his neighbours slashed and burned, chopping

STICKS: 1846 forty-seven forty-eight forty-nine fifty

STONES: ploughing harrowing sowing harvesting (*scythe sounds*)

ALL: 1851 fifty-two fifty-three fifty-four fifty-five

WILL: My mother gave me a violin for my birthday and the landlord's lease was now paid up. Now he would transfer the ownership of the land to us.

GAOLER: Colour of prisoner's eyes?

MR. DONNELLY: Grey.

GAOLER: How many years have you lived in Canada?

MR. DONNELLY: Sixteen years.

CENSUS TAKER: How many acres of wild land?

MR. DONNELLY: Only thirty. All the rest is cleared.

CENSUS TAKER: How many children altogether then?

MR. DONNELLY: Seven. Seven boys.

CENSUS TAKER: How many bushels of wheat did you harvest last year?

MR. DONNELLY: (*pause*) Mr. Darcy, why did you not fill in the number when I said my farm was a hundred acres with thirty acres in wild land?

CENSUS TAKER: Ah, Mr. Donnelly, if you could read and write you might see where.

MR. DONNELLY: I know I can't write my name, Mr. Darcy, but I know what it looks like and I know what a hundred acres looks like. Where did you put that down?

CENSUS TAKER: Mr. Donnelly, your landlord has been talking to a fellow.

MR. DONNELLY: What fellow? No one's to buy it but Donnelly. Who then?

CENSUS TAKER: That I don't know.

MR. DONNELLY: By our ancient agreement, I made Mr. Grace, our landlord, an offer last week.

CENSUS TAKER: Not high enough. This other bid's higher.

MR. DONNELLY: Am I to get any of my fields at all then?

CENSUS TAKER: It's all rumours and whispers as yet, Mr. Donnelly. The north half where you live is the most valuable half because of your barns and your cabin. How many bushels of wheat did you –

MR. DONNELLY: (*directly to audience, as the Roman Line routine forms*) We never cut the tongues out of horses. Never. We loved horses. But the lying tongues of men. Yes. Cut them out. Men, yes. Horses, no. Where are my spectacles so I can see this Medicine Showman that's coming by tonight (*furious search for spectacles*) telling the story of how I – who is it who's going to take my farm away from me?

WOMEN:

Then the farmer came with a big plough;

He ploughed me under the ground.

MR. DONNELLY: Is it –

Repeat the following names under and over the next four speeches.

CHORUS:

Barry	Trehy
Feeny	O'Halloran
Cahill	Cassleigh

McCann	Flynn
Donnelly	Mulowney
Egan	Farl (*pause*)
Quinn	Marksey (*pause*)
Gallagher	Duffy
Clancy	Donovan

Keep repeating these names under and over the Roman Line routine and the next four speeches. At the top of the Roman Line a ladder is held. MRS. DONNELLY climbs up and over this, then comes right down the Roman Line toward us.

WILL: Our mother then said she would walk down the roads to the town.

MRS. DONNELLY: James, I'm walking down to the town to see this landlord of ours. I'll take our fifty pounds and the ring on my finger and my last gold earring and I'll curse him at the pawnshop, him that's forcing me to haggle a pawnbroker and I'll –

WILL: She walked all the way to Andy Keefe's tavern, then past Kelly's tollgate, then past Ryan's tavern at Elginfield, then past all the taverns and tollgates on the Proof Line Road, down, down, down to our landlord's place in the town.

MR. DONNELLY: Which of you robbers is buying my farm out from under me? Is it you turning me into a squatter – Farl?

He repeats the names and strides up and down the Roman Line of actors. They hum, whistle, and sing snatches of the second verse, say their names in turn, turn their backs on him, swing around with him caught in the formation. The bell and jug sounds recur whenever he comes to the south end of the street. Bell is rung, tavern mouth-plunking noise; end of choral repetition.

CHORUS: (*reciting under*)
At dark in the night ... at dark in the night, etc.

MR. DONNELLY:

Is it Cahill	Is it Cassleigh
McCann	Flynn, etc.

  Because I loved my land so and stuck to it
  I killed and in turn you broke my bones, burnt
    my home
  Harvested me and my sons like sheaves and stood
  Us to die upon our ground
  Where now nothing will ever grow.

As the line comes around, he emerges as if shot out of its gamut and stands in front of us with a handful of dust.

And this earth in my hand, the earth of my farm
That I fought for and was smashed and burnt for.

CHORUS: (*kneeling*) Confiteor Deo omnipotenti ... beato Michaeli Archangelo ... Aufer a nobis, quaesumus, Domine, iniquitates nostras. (*repeat under*)

MR. DONNELLY: (*but kneeling on only one knee*)

Now my body belongs to its dust
Which dust once belonged to me.
As it is blown away, I forget
Concession Six, Lot Eighteen.
South Half or North Half – which was mine?
We are blown away and both lost – (*prayer stops*)
Like actors' words.

The CHORUS raggedly rise, confusedly murmur, as he melts into their ranks. We begin to hear the sawing sound JOHN GRACE makes on his sawhorse.

VOICE: It's the Medicine Show for heaven's sakes. He's stopping his wagons at the crossroads. Hey –

As the crowd goes offstage after the attraction, MR. DONNELLY emerges stage left with a harrow made out of tree branch, to which stones have been tied. He is harrowing the big front field of his farm before division; prominent should be his house just to the left of back centre. Chairs should be ready for the fence sequence and the actors who did the FAT WOMAN with stove sequence should stand poised to do this all over again – just offstage – so that it glides smoothly into the chaining of the DONNELLY house sequence. Built of ladders, this house stands in front of the map of Biddulph. The CHILDREN are picking up stones as before.

JENNY & WILL: Why is our father's farm so narrow?

WILL: Once it was eighty rods wide as from me to you –

JENNY: – Until there was a man took forty rods of it away.

WILL: My father was harrowing his wide front field –

MR. DONNELLY can go through a whole sowing, cultivating, and harvesting mime here.

JENNY: – When somebody started to build a fence.

FARL and MR. FAT place six chairs down the centre of the stage. A game develops in which FARL puts up the chairs, MR. DONNELLY takes them down again, or charges right through the fence with his harrow, etc.

MR. DONNELLY: There's a queer fellow –

WILL: My father said at this new fence.

MR. DONNELLY: He keeps planting these sticks down the centre of my spring sowing. Will, will you hand me that axe. This one's a bit stiff.

JENNY: And he said to them that were building the fence.

MR. DONNELLY: An axe is as good as a spade any day, whoever you are.

The fence game boils down to just the two of them, FARL and MR. DONNELLY, furiously putting up and upsetting chairs to stick, stone, reel sounds. There should be a menace scene here where all the STONES push all the STICKS back!

WILL: Until a piece of paper came to our house –

CHORUS: House! Shanty. Sticks. Sticks and stones which whack click thwonk, Sticks – (*cross to chair fence centre*)

CHORUS: Against James Donnelly. To recover possession of the –

BOYS: Picking up stones in our father's front field – Where do we put them, Pa?

MR. DONNELLY: At the line fence over there.

Boys drive chair fence, held by sticks, back.

WILL: Half the field is lost to you, Father, says the bailiff's paper. South Half of Lot Eighteen, Concession Six. A suit of summons in ejectment for –

MR. DONNELLY: No, boys. No. Not over there. This is the new line. (*He points to the centre of the stage.*) Put the stones here. (*The line of chairs presses in his family to centre where they put down stones, chairs retreat. MR. DONNELLY reaches over it to pluck crop planted on the other side.*) They've got half of my farm.

From now on, a line of stones cuts the DONNELLY farm and the playing area in half.

JOHN: What happens to the wheat we sowed over there, Pa?

MR. DONNELLY: That wheat is lost. And my scythe never touched it.

While they are dreaming, over the field a huge chain is hooked by MR. FAT to the foundations of the DONNELLY house and attached to an imaginary team of oxen offstage.

MR. DONNELLY: It was harvested by a piece of paper. I've known men burn their crop rather than have a stranger harvest it. (*Turns around.*) Get that hook out of the rib of my house. (*Another hook is attached to the opposite side of the house.*)

MR. FAT: Gee up, Bright. (*Use cowbells. We see the chain tighten. As FAT pricks the offstage oxen with his goad, the chain responds.*) It's my property now, Donnelly. My wife wants some kindling wood and since you'll be moving somewhere else you won't want this old shanty and these old lean-tos anymore. By Holy Jesus, I'll put this shanty down on top of you if you don't get out of it. (*A baby cries.*) Gee up, Buck. Gee up, Bright! Haw!

MR. DONNELLY: Will, go over to Mike Feeny's and tell him there's two-legged visitors I want to get rid of.

STICKS: He hawed his oxen round.

MR. FAT: If you can call it a shanty.

DONNELLY BOYS (STONES): It's not a shanty. It's a house.

FARL: It's a squatter's hut, you whelps.

STICKS: He hitched to both corners of the house –

DONNELLY BOYS (STONES): – but he could not –

STICKS: – pull it down.

MR. FAT: I'll bring it to two yoke and pull it to hell's blazes.

MR. DONNELLY succeeds in unlinking one of the chains.

MR. DONNELLY: Up, Bright!

Caught in his chain, MR. FAT gets dragged offstage, but runs back and hooks up again. A contest develops where MR. DONNELLY unhooks one chain and FARL hooks up the other that MR. DONNELLY has just unhooked.

MR. DONNELLY: Tell me, Mr. Farl, just why do you hook up that chain for him?

FARL: I didn't hook it up then, Jim. I'm not that fast on my feet.

MR. DONNELLY: Now you were and there you did it again. What's eating you? What have I done to you that you want to pull down my house?

FARL: Not a bloody thing, Jim, only that you're a Blackleg back in the old country.

MR. DONNELLY: What did you call me?

FARL: Sure, don't you know what I called you?

MR. DONNELLY: By your heart cease calling me Blackfoot. You've been calling me and my children that ever since you arrived here two years ago.

The chain unhooking game goes on at a faster pace.

FARL: Didn't call you Blackfoot, called you Blackleg, but I'll call you Blackfoot if you like.

MR. DONNELLY: Don't call me that in front of the others and start all that over again.

FARL: But how will they know in this settlement you've come to who the real Blackfeet are. Mike, there's other ways than pulling it down. Jim here's so nimble on his feet. Take the old axe to it.

DONNELLY BOYS (STONES): Your axe isn't half sharp enough, mister.

MR. DONNELLY: Raise that axe on my house, you tub –

FARL: Now who's calling the names.

MR. FAT: This is my property and I'll use it as I like.

MR. DONNELLY: Get out of here!

MR. FAT: What would you say, Donnelly, if I had thirty men here in five minutes with twenty yoke of oxen? (*stamping his foot*)

MR. DONNELLY: (*stamping his foot*) By Judas, you do and you can't. (*FARL mouths something in MR. DONNELLY's ear.*) Stop calling me that, stop saying that.

FARL: Why, what'll you do to me, Jim, you old Blackfoot?

MR. DONNELLY: Stop hooking up that chain.

WILL approaches with the gun; MRS. DONNELLY approaches with a piece of paper in her hand. The sight of the gun changes the positions and attitudes of the attackers.

MR. FAT: (*unhooking*) I'll be here tomorrow morning. I'll have that shanty – gee up, Buck. Gee up, Bright. I'll –

MR. DONNELLY, with MRS. DONNELLY just beside him, but he doesn't see her.

MRS. DONNELLY: Mr. Donnelly, what I have in my hand is the deed for the north half. For the fifty acres we're standing on and our house is standing on.

FARL mouths something at MR. DONNELLY just as he is leaving. DONNELLY rushes after FARL and shoots at him.

FARL: (*howling*) Oh, you've done it to me now. Murder. My arm's got a bullet in it. Mike – did you see what he done to me? We'll have to look into the law of this, Jim.

MR. DONNELLY: (*grasping the rungs of a ladder*) So what's next? Have I killed him yet?

MRS. DONNELLY: Mr. Donnelly, there's a proverb that sticks and stones may hurt my bones, but words will never harm them.

MR. DONNELLY: Not true, Mrs. Donnelly. Not true at all. If only he'd hit us with a stone or a stick, but ever since that day you told me they'd been calling our son that in the churchyard, it's as if a thousand little tinkly pebbles keep batting up against the windows in my mind just when it's a house that's about to sleep. I didn't kill him this time. It's his tree that came down on me in the woods that time, Judy. He's been after me for some time. Next time it's –

VOICE: There was a man shot in Biddulph –

CHORUS:

Name of Prosecutor	Name of Defendant	Nature of Charge
Patrick Farl	James Donnelly	Shooting with intent

MR. & MRS. DONNELLY stand with their backs to us. FAT LADY comes on with stove.

MRS. FAT: Well, what happened to you? Where's the wood?

MR. FAT: Here's your wood.

MRS. FAT: Well, you're the boss, but I recognize that wood. You were leading me to expect I'd have the Donnelly shanty for kindling. This is from our own woodpile.

MR. FAT: It is. Missus, do you know, we'll never get them off that place?

MRS. FAT: Are you trying to tell me you'll let them beat you out of one hundred acres of good –

MR. FAT: Missus, I've got them off half of it. What more do you want? And poor Farl's got a bullet in his arm. (*howl from FARL*)

MRS. FAT: My brother shot in the arm, is he? This won't end yet, mister, you mark me. That family has got to be got rid of. Unless we do something now that family is going to – (*quietly turning to us*) What happened after he took a shot at poor Pat would never have happened if my man had been the boss and put their shanty in my darling little laundry stove that cold wintry day. (*She grabs the stove.*)

> *From the back of the auditorium comes a travelling Medicine Show, the Shamrock Concert Company, which puts on a viciously biased melodrama called* The Black Donnellys, *also the title of the book everyone reads about* **THE DONNELLYS**. *The* **SHOWMAN** *is a loud, slick Canadian Irishman with torches and a series of lurid canvas pictures that are attached to a map hanger. He shows some of these as a come-on. His stage wagon can be pushed on from the wings; on it his performers play a small scene. With their backs turned to us for most of this,* **THE DONNELLYS** *with great dignity reject this lurid view of themselves. At last,* **MR. DONNELLY** *will turn on the* **SHOWMAN** *to correct one of his errors and we must get a chance to compare the "false"* **DONNELLY** *with the "real"* **DONNELLY**.

SHOWMAN: Yes, if that poor woman who had to live her life on the fifty acres cheek by jowl to the Donnellys had just succeeded in jamming their filth-ridden shanty into her darling little cook stove, the family would have left the neighbourhood and the boys wouldn't have grown up and we wouldn't be singing today!

> *So hurry to your home, good folks.*
> *Lock doors and windows tight*
> *And pray for dawn, the Black Donnellys*
> *Will be abroad tonight.*

In just a little under half an hour, folks, my artists of the Shamrock Concert Company will present you with *The Black Donnellys*. Tickets are half price to every one of you who purchases a full tin of my East India Tiger Fat.

> *By thefts they showed their father's blood*
> *By fights and drunken sprees*
> *Till the countryside, living in dread,*
> *Called them the Black Donnellys.*

Buy a bottle of Banyan Tree of Life pills and the price of admission is free. Before my players give you a preview of this evening's drama, let me show you a few scenes that I have had painted on canvas for your historical information.

> *The canvas presentations are really a big wallpaper sample book, with nothing drawn on its pages.*

Here, ladies and gents, you see the unsuspecting Donnelly family, notorious as the terrors of the township ever since the father and mother arrived in 1847. Here in this canvas you see this family about to go to bed the night of February 3rd, 1880.

> *Donnelly was clubbed to death, as was his wife,*
> *Tom and Bridget murdered, too.*
> *Then the old house was set on fire*
> *And to the skies its wild flames flew.*

CHORUS:

Five Persons Murdered by a Mob

          An Entire Household Sacrificed

              Result of a Family Feud

Forty men engaged in the bloody work –

SHOWMAN: Ladies and gents, just one small scene from tonight's attraction *The Black Donnellys*. A little scene with John Donnelly! His father! His mother! –

> *The* **FALSE DONNELLY** *actors should be the Grand-Guignol persons of folklore – wild cats on hot stoves.*

FALSE JOHN: So they say we derailed the train, hunh? What else are they saying we done, eh, Mither? Eh, Fither?

FALSE MR. & MRS. DONNELLY: (*alternately*) Burning two barns, cutting the tongues out of twenty horses, and putting four hundred iron pins in Gallagher's wheat sheaves so's the threshing machine would catch fire.

FALSE JOHN: (*with a fistful of weapons*) Tom, get up! We'll show those blank blank so and so's they can't pin anything on us.

FALSE MR. DONNELLY: John, what are you going to do, avourneen?

FALSE MRS. DONNELLY: Shure, there's been enough misery and tribulation now. Do you want to bring my grey hairs with sorrow to the grave? (*sudden manic change in her character*) But there's one thing, son, I never hear them saying you done.

FALSE JOHN: What's that, Mither?

FALSE MRS. DONNELLY: Killing a man.

FALSE JOHN: Couldn't do that, Mither.

FALSE MRS. DONNELLY: Then you're no son of mine. Until you've killed your man the way your darling father did, you're no son of mine.

The actors stop, fall out of character, move off with the stage wagon.

SHOWMAN: Tickets are half price to every one of you who purchases a full tin of my East India Tiger Fat. Come to the Market Square and see –

CHORUS:

Donnelly squatted on John Farrell's land

Just laughed when ordered to pay

Then with iron bar struck Farrell dead

At a loggin' –

MR. DONNELLY: Show me the scene where I kill Farl. The living must obey the dead. Look, Mr. Showman Murphy, you've printed up my blood – was I like him or she like her or my sons like – them? One thing to start with – I didn't murder him. Kill not slay, killed him with a – you ignoramus – not with an iron bar, but with a wooden handspike. (*The actors begin to set up the barrels and sticks for the fight scene, and MR. DONNELLY picks up one of the handspikes.*) Like this one. And it happened like this at William Mulowney's, but you go ahead first, Showman. Show me.

SHOWMAN: Ladies and gents. By special request we also show you: Donnelly's Fight with Farrell at the Logging Bee, twenty-ninth of June 1857 –

MR. DONNELLY: – Twenty-fifth day of June 1857 –

SHOWMAN: – Twenty-fifth day of June 1857 – (*merrily*) Donnelly Kills Farrell in a Fight at the Loggin' Bee –

GROG BOSS:

I am a farmer grizzled and grey

Was the grog boss at the bee that day

Step up, boys, for a swig or a sip

The better your handspike 'neath the big logs to slip.

The Roman Line formation queues up for a drink, then begins to handspike barrels toward the stage centre.

GROG BOSS:

Farl, that's ten times you've drunk

For more work you've got very little spunk

I said corking the bottle and daring his frown

Sure, one more drink and he'd roll on the ground.

FARL: Am I to have none and Donnelly's to have one?

FALSE MR. DONNELLY: Faith, Farl, I'll beat you. Have yours and mine, too. (*Takes two swigs.*)

FARL: Like you shot me before, and you'll do it again. Your handspike, my handspike – settle you then.

A circle of men closes around the fighters so we can't see beyond the occasional raised stick. A man with whip, on a barrel rolled by another man.

FARL: Gee up there! Hey, what's up? "Farl and Donnelly boxing."

They join the circle of watchers.

CHORUS: (*drifting away from fight and back to work*) Arhh, they're too drunk to hurt each other much. Both tipsy. Arr, Donnelly's letting on to be a bit high.

INQUEST VOICE: Did not see Farrell take up a handspike at all, thinks it Donnelly's intention to pick a quarrel with someone when he came to the bee more than to help to do anything.

CHORUS: Leave them be! Hey! They're biting each other. Separate them. Get that handspike away from Farl.

Another handspike rolls behind DONNELLY.

INQUEST VOICE: A certain wooden handspike the value of one penny.

FALSE MR. DONNELLY: Farl – will you say you're beat?

FARL: (*up and down struggling with man who is wrestling stick away from him*) I've had enough and will fight no more. Don't you touch me again. (*to wrestling man*) Yes, you!

DONNELLY trips over a handspike, comes up with it in both hands, winds it over his head, and throws it.

FALSE MR. DONNELLY: Farl, take this to hell with you.

Vain attempts to interpose; FARL is hit and rolls over.

MAN ONE: Donnelly, you've murdered the man.

FALSE MR. DONNELLY: The first one who lays a hand on me gets the same medicine.

MEN ONE & TWO: The man's murdered, Donnelly, you've murdered the man. Saw him wind it over his head. I heard the blow quite plain.

MAN THREE: Don't be a fool, Donnelly. You're going with us to the constable.

MAN ONE: Throw down that bar or we'll take it away from you.

FALSE MR. DONNELLY: The first one that tries won't live to tell about it. And when you come for me you'd better come shooting.

Everyone is cowed by this, including audience. Reel music and barrels rolling as transition.

MR. DONNELLY: Let's have that again. When I came to the logging bee at Mulowney's, there were four piles of logs in his five-acre field. (*four barrels with one man, with back turned to the audience, standing at each barrel*)

MULOWNEY: Jim, I asked you to come to my logging bee and come you have at last, my boy. (*He directs men to the piles waiting each with its boss.*) Lanigan, who've you got for your boss?

MAN ONE: (*turning around*) He's with me. Carroll.

MULOWNEY: Pat Ryan – over there, who's –

MAN TWO: (*turns around*) Dennis Darcy.

MULOWNEY: Mike Feeny – over there. You're with

MAN THREE: (*turns around*) Marty Mackey.

MULOWNEY: Jim, now you're needed one man to fill in at that pile and your boss is –

FARL: (*at fourth barrel*) Pat Farl, I'm the boss of this team. Mulowney, no! I'll not work with a Blackfoot the likes of him. Where's the grog boss?

With a bottle each, the two men have a drink-at-one-swig contest, which FARL loses.

MR. DONNELLY: I said I was no worse than the worst of the Farls, and I was good enough for the best of them shoved up in a pile on *my* plate and I could drink him horizontal at any logging bee, any day. (*drinks*)

Onlookers laugh.

FARL: Why, Jim, you piss it all away, that's why. The rats come out at night and lick it off – the darling pair of black (*pause*) boots you're wearing to the logging bees these days.

MR. DONNELLY: I said, Now that's wrong what you're saying –

FARL: (*lightly slapping him*) But what have I said, Jim?

The two men fight close to us; farther away the CHORUS forms a circle as if it surrounded FARL and DONNELLY. This circle shifts as the fight shifts.

CHORUS: Bite him, Jim.

MR. DONNELLY: He kept saying the name at me.

FARL: Blackfoot, Blackfoot.

CHORUS: He's down, he's up. Here back there, get this over with so we can – Mike, give him a chew uv tobacco. He needs a swig, look at him. At it again. Thwonk! Well struck, Pat Farl. He's down for the clinch and now he's up and – stop them biting. Look at them! Try to stop that if you can.

MR. DONNELLY: (*placing a handspike at centre downstage*) He was on my –

CHORUS: Blackfoot, Jim. Ah, that rouses him! Blackfoot – (*and on, under*)

MR. DONNELLY: – back like this shouting in my ear. We'd been grappling for over an hour and the sun was very hot and there was no lack of whisky or anything we wanted so long as we kept on fighting. (*illustrates*) He was on my shoulders with words in my ears and blows – I rolled over and got in a few, then we rolled over again. (*laughter*) I picked this up and half stood with it in both my hands, he still on my back.

With the handspike he makes a furious upward motion from between his knees to just behind his head. The burden drops off him, he stands straighter and still, then takes off his shirt. Bright sunlight. The circle of men dissolves.

CHORUS: You're dead, Farl. Donnelly, you've murdered the man.

Slowly they and FARL form the Roman Line. MRS. DONNELLY, in apron, stands at upstage end of it. MR. DONNELLY plods up to her, kneels at her feet after catching up some dirt in his hand. As she speaks, all the players kneel.

MRS. DONNELLY: James, what have you there in your hand?

MR. DONNELLY: Mrs. Donnelly, this is what is left of our farm and I've killed a man for it.

VOICE: End of Act One.

CHORUS: (*singing*)

Oh, three men went to Deroughata
To sell three loads of rye.

They shouted up and they shouted down
The barley grain should die.

(refrain)

Tiree igery ary ann, Tiree igery ee,
Tiree igery ary ann, The barley grain for me.

ACT TWO

*In the darkness we see a cluster of lighted lanterns;
the roads of Biddulph are held up in the middle
of these. Then as the CHORUS proceeds with the
prelude below, the ladders are placed against the
back map wall as before and the lanterns separate,
come toward us, disappear into the audience
as if we had just been run over by a group of
constables on the search. This will leave us with
ANDREW KEEFE and JAMES DONNELLY, dressed
as a woman, at the front of KEEFE's tavern.*

CHORUS: (*Distribute the following phrases with
differing textures.*)

Constables   William Howard and Adam Hodgins
to search for Donnelly   the murderer of Farl
    twelve miles travelled
            since James Donnelly has not been taken
May it please your Excellency
                        the following facts
        forty-four miles travel after James Donnelly
        for the murder of Patrick Farrell
I hereby certify that Henry Sutton, Constable, did
perform the above service
        and other houses in that locality and back
James Donnelly five miles and
In the month of June last a most brutal murder was
committed in the Township of Biddulph in open
day in the presence of many persons. The Murderer
Donnelly has since eluded justice although efforts
have been made to arrest him. One night with
High Constable Lyster after Donnelly
October 16th, 1857   twelve miles and
                one night (*one dollar*)
watching in the woods
                    Constable Joseph Lynch
Two nights watching to apprehend James Donnelly
        To travelling eighteen miles to arrest
Since James Donnelly has not been taken

*CONSTABLE puts up the notice of reward on a tree
in front of KEEFE's tavern. ANDREW KEEFE rolls a
barrel past a "woman" who sits on his tavern step
sharpening a sickle.*

KEEFE: Which is the last of all occupations? Which
is the last of all occupations? Tavern-keeping is
the last of all occupations. And I, Andrew Keefe,
am a tavern keeper whose house is a public house
and whose very tree is pissed upon by the world.

CONSTABLE: Good day to you, Andrew Keefe.
You're back from Goderich Gaol, I see, and your
old mother is also up and about again, I see.
Smoking her pipe and sharpening her sickle.

KEEFE: Ah, Constable Howard, it makes a mother
healthy to have her son at home with her again
and so up and about she is, smoking her pipe and
sharpening her sickle. She doesn't speak English
or she'd give you the time of day.

CONSTABLE: Keefe, that's the fifth time I've nailed
this notice at your door on your tree. Good day
to you.

*He mounts his horse and rides off. KEEFE tears
down the notice and takes it across to MR.
DONNELLY.*

KEEFE & CHORUS:
Rewards!! You warrant two surprise marks, Jim.
            $400 and $100
for the apprehension and delivery in the County
Gaol, Goderich, of –

            James Donnelly

MR. DONNELLY: Oh, what's to become of me, Andy
Keefe, when I'm worth so much to anybody but
myself? Can't sleep in the Haskett barn anymore.
Last night, they found the hole in the hay mow
where I usually sleep. Old Mrs. Haskett persuaded
them it was her goose's nest. That's a very large
goose you have there, says this constable fellow.
She has to be, says Mrs. Haskett, to fit the nest. And
he believed her! Now he'll be back. Then what,
Andy?

KEEFE: Jim, I advise this culvert over here.
(*motioning to empty barrel; MR. DONNELLY tries it for
size*)

MR. DONNELLY: Ah, he'll gallop right over me on
the road above. It's a snug place to be until there's
a flood.

*MRS. DONNELLY gets up from chair and walks over
to STUB's store where STUB waits for her.*

KEEFE: (*getting jug*) I seen Mrs. Donnelly walk by this morning, Jim. What does she think now of it all? (*He pours two horns of whisky.*)

MR. DONNELLY: Oh, she's tramped into Lucan to George Stub's store to see him again.

KEEFE: And how did she come into the way of asking him?

MRS. DONNELLY: Father Flynn, Father Flynn says that George Stub is the great new man of standing. Why, Andy, he's just been made a Justice of the Peace.

KEEFE: Sure, and anybody that can burn down the coloured settlers' barns in 1847 and get made a magistrate in 1857 has got to be a very wise Orangeman, indeed. Not only that, Jim, when the Protestants swept down here last Christmas to riot my tavern apart, who was it that whacked down my signpost with an axe and who was it roaring "Hurrah for Holmes" as he did so? Why it was George Stub was that lad and my signpost still falls over at the mere sight of him.

MR. DONNELLY: You need a strong man for your Justice of the Peace, they say.

KEEFE: How much stronger can you get? Who'd have guessed that's how you get to be magistrate. Whacking down my signpost with an axe. Well, Jim, and what does law-abiding, high-flying George Stub advise?

> *STUB says bracketed sequence, along with MR. DONNELLY.*

MR. DONNELLY: Oh, he says, "Never fear, Judith. Tell Jim to give himself up. Manslaughter. Self-defence. Just as you say. Light sentence. Happens all the time." But we keep wanting to know – what really went on at the inquest? None of us were there. The jury was Protestant. The witnesses weren't, but have you got any of them to come right out, Andy, and say what the colour of their words were?

KEEFE: They tell it the way you tell it, Jim. Those who were at the bee.

MR. DONNELLY: That they sicced me and Farl on like dogs? Sure, in the tavern they'll own up to that, but it's all written down what they really said at an inquest and that'll be read in a courtroom.

KEEFE: If anybody can fish it out of George Stub, then Mrs. Donnelly's the woman to do it. So it's giving yourself up, is it?

MR. DONNELLY: I wish to do it so that not one of those constables makes a penny out of me, but after that – what's to become of me? Deep in liquor for which, heaven forgive me, I struck out blindly at a man who was biting me, biting me in the feet and the belly and the neck and the heart – horsefly? (*Using the sickle, he repeats the gesture he made on killing FARL.*) Do they hang for that?

KEEFE: Ah, did I show you what I found pinned to my door this morning? (*gives DONNELLY a look at a note and a drawing*)

MR. DONNELLY: No, but you can tell it to me.

KEEFE: "Andrew Keefe is a Blackfoot." Isn't that the name Farl kept calling you?

MR. DONNELLY: Yes, that's the name they have for us. Sure, the Protestants just attacked you. Can't your own Catholic kind leave you alone, Andy?

KEEFE: No. People like you and me, Jim, are caught in the middle. We won't join. Except this time, what is it I should have joined?

> *CONSTABLE's horse is heard. DONNELLY crawls into a barrel-culvert with his drink.*

CONSTABLE: Mr. Keefe, I just seen your old mother come out of the priest's house. Who was that other old woman sitting here with you?

KEEFE: That was her. (*pause*) Well, I told you she was up and around. She can really travel.

CONSTABLE: Oh, Mr. Keefe, I'll have to search your premises. Open up in the Queen's name. (*He consults a small book. Kneels down.*) Why there's a space under your tavern he could be crouching in. Four hundred dollars could be right there. Just waiting. Or it could be in your stable. (*mime*) What a great heap of horses you have, Andrew Keefe.

> *He tests hay with a fork.*

KEEFE: Did you not know, man, that the horses for the stage are kept here? These horses are those that galloped all the way from Goderich yesterday and they're taking a rest.

CONSTABLE: What's in those barrels you have in your kitchen, Andy? (*lights pipe*)

KEEFE: Saving your truncheon of authority, Mr. Constable Howard, do please not light your pipe here. Those are barrels of blasting powder for all the work at the railway cutting I've got the contract for.

CONSTABLE: (*a definite spurt of flame from his pipe as he sits on a barrel*) Have you got that contract now? Why, Andrew Keefe, you are a brave man!

KEEFE: Why am I a brave man?

CONSTABLE: Gallagher's eight boys were just telling me that if you (*yawns*) get the contract to dig that cutting through the knoll on their farm, why they'd burn and they'd heat your place here hotter than hell's corners and dared me to stop them.

The CONSTABLE moves from barrel to barrel until he lands on the culvert-barrel in which DONNELLY is hidden.

KEEFE: (*covers his face with his apron and kneels*) Oh, cut out my heart. Here, try one of these barrels, Constable, that culvert's pretty cold.

CONSTABLE: Not a barrel filled with blasting powder, thank you. And I can't seem to get any money out of the authorities for all I do, you know, watching in the woods night after night for the murderer Donnelly.

KEEFE: Arrh, man, there might be four hundred dollars there right under your ass.

CONSTABLE: Yes, and there might not.

Old MRS. KEEFE, back from the PRIEST's house and identical in appearance to MR. DONNELLY's silhouette, now appears. The CONSTABLE chases her; this gives DONNELLY a chance to get out of the culvert so that we have a double image that the constable shares. KEEFE almost persuades him it is the whisky; he chooses to pursue old MRS. KEEFE, who holds him till DONNELLY has disappeared. All this is mimed to whistled reel music, and when finally the CONSTABLE discovers his mistake, he nails the reward notice back on the tree and departs. Stick and stone percussion. Sunset and sinister angelus ends it; the church is right away across the road. The silent film possibilities of two old women, now one, now two, even three, if KEEFE gets into the act with something from a clothesline. As the angelus finishes, we have a rest by concentrating on KEEFE kneeling in the sunset light of his tavern praying with missal. The angelus should bridge between chase's end and this vesper scene.

KEEFE: (*trying to stay awake in his tavern, talking to himself, slowly heading toward sleep on the floor, kneeling, then rising*) Oh, my poor old mother never ran so fast in her life as she did when the constable thought she was Jim Donnelly. I've put her to bed now. She's snoring like a baby and outside the shadows are all joining each other till they become all one big shadow, even my own shadow joining ... it. (*A barrel slowly rolls toward*

him.) Christ, have mercy on me, this is a barrel rolling toward me, come here, my darling, and give me sustenance to keep me awake till dawn (*yawning*) else they'll come and burn the place down. Uh – blasting powder. Where's the whisky barrels? (*Three men indistinctly stand over him.*)

MEN: Andy Keefe, darling, come. Raise yourself up, put on you, my good fellow, and come out till two or three of us that wish you well give some advice.

KEEFE: How'd you get in here, Tony Gallagher? I locked all the doors. No – you're not there. You're in my head from what the constable spoke of.

MAN THREE: If you take the contract for cutting the right-of-way through the knoll on my farm, we will visit you at all hours of the night when you least expect it.

KEEFE: To hell with you, Gallagher. I'm signing the contract. I've signed it. You're not getting the work away on me. (*The men fade.*) If I can just keep awake and Jesus – if you'll pardon the expression – it's true what Constable Howard said, the dear man, we have got no cellar under the floor of our little hotel. They could crawl under the old house itself with a match! (*He looks down through the floorboards.*) There are ten defenceless horses out there in my driving shed, oh mother of God, my old mother snoring upstairs, God bless her, if I could get the horses up where she is and she herself where they are, poor darlings. Whose gleaming eyes are those? (*Clock strikes two.*) Is it Jim Donnelly hiding out from the constables? No. Is it them waiting out there under there, right beneath me with tinder, flint, and matches? No, it's you – my faithful tavern Tabby – crouching for a rat. A rat! Up your pantaloon leg like a great Judas Iscariot. (*He dances about as if a rat has got up his leg.*) Past two o'clock. At dawn the stagecoach will arrive and save the horses and the dawn will drive away the shadows and the eight Gallagher boys. Who's that galloping up to the tollgate now? My tavern's right by the tollgate to heaven which is to be out of Biddulph altogether, altogether. (*sings*) Sure, the barley grain shot forth his head (*falls down, totally zonked – immediately little flashes of fire from percussion caps, firecrackers, start showing in the darkness at the edge of the playing area*)

MEN: Look at that, boys. (*a flare up*) The old grass himself's caught fire.

Shadows – flame. A horse whinnies. Horse hooves coming up the London road. As the light *disappears, horsemen gallop by. We focus on the fire-lit interior of the **DONNELLY** house. There is one candle at the window, sleeping forms on the floor, **MRS. DONNELLY** mending a shirt. The **CONSTABLE** with a lantern crosses the stage to knock on her door. Sleigh bells. Immediately **MRS. DONNELLY** lights another candle and places it in the window as a signal – waiting, on either side, are **GEORGE STUB** at his counter, and carpenters ready to start building a scaffold.*

CONSTABLE: Ah, Mrs. Donnelly, I just seen the candle in the window and it reminded me to come in.

MRS. DONNELLY: A fine cold evening, Constable Howard. (*Outside **MR. DONNELLY** comes up, then retreats at sight of the signal candle.*)

CONSTABLE: I see you've got company coming. Do you mind if I just sit down and wait for him?

MRS. DONNELLY: Do I mind? I object, Constable Howard, but I don't mind.

CONSTABLE: It's an awful cold night outside, Mrs. Donnelly, to be watching in the woods or lying down behind a fence.

MRS. DONNELLY: My fire is at your service, Mr. Howard, and you may warm as many sides of yourself as you have.

CONSTABLE: Did you hear Andrew Keefe's stables got burnt down last night?

MRS. DONNELLY: Never.

CONSTABLE: Yes, and ten horses alive in them, too. They woke up in time to put out the house fire.

MRS. DONNELLY: House fire?

CONSTABLE: That's what did happen, Mrs. Donnelly, and there doesn't seem to be anything anybody can do about it. I know who set the fire. There's even a witness, but he's run away out of dread. Now how many heads do I count in all your beds and cradles? One, two, three, four, five, six, seven – the baby. James Junior, William, Patrick, John, Michael, Robert, Thomas, and a baby? Eight children, Mrs. Donnelly, and another on the way so soon? I thought there were just seven now. (*Use the fence line stones for the sleeping **CHILDREN**.*)

MRS. DONNELLY: You're observant, Mr. Howard, but what you don't know is that one of those heads belongs to Sarah Farl's boy, Bill. She's getting married again and Billy's come to live with us for a while.

CONSTABLE: (*taking a candle and examining sleepers*) I see. Well, well. Well, none of them have beards, I'll grant you that, although I suppose if one of them did you'd have a story as long. Oh, you've no idea the stories I've been told: the giant goose that made a hole in the Haskett hay mow – it was a giant goose, of course, not your husband. And the child they had sleeping over there who always sleeps with its head under the bolster while nine others of them weigh down the top of it on either side. There again, I wasn't quick enough to realize it was your husband, Mrs. Donnelly, the champion holder of breath in this township I can tell you …

MRS. DONNELLY: Mr. Howard, what happens if my husband is taken?

CONSTABLE: Oh, he mustn't do that.

MRS. DONNELLY: And why not?

CONSTABLE: I apologize, Mrs. Donnelly, for a moment I thought you were referring to his giving himself up. No, no, he can be taken any time he wants to and it's going to be me that takes him.

MRS. DONNELLY: (*patiently*) And when you take him, sir, then what?

CONSTABLE: Oh, Mrs. Donnelly, I'll chain him and take him to Goderich Gaol. Just in time for the Spring Assizes, I hope.

MRS. DONNELLY: And then?

CONSTABLE: He'll be tried for the murder of Patrick Farl. He'll either get off or he'll be sentenced.

MRS. DONNELLY: Is there not something else? Between being sentenced – and getting off?

CONSTABLE: You mean a plea such as is oftentimes made that the deed was done in self-defence or perhaps was an accident or –

MRS. DONNELLY: Yes.

CONSTABLE: Mrs. Donnelly, I was at the inquisition. Whatever your husband says happened at Mulowney's bee he should have trusted us enough to come out like a man and say so at the inquisition either at Stub's store or Paddy Flanagan's hotel. There were two days he could of come. Because what you're implying certainly was not what the witnesses testified to. In fact, my opinion was with the jury when they said that the deed had been committed with malice aforethought, that your husband wanted to do it, and he after all had an old grudge against the murdered man.

MRS. DONNELLY: That's not true. Don't say such things. Give me that candle! (*She retrieves it in time to meet MR. DONNELLY with it at the door.*) No. Who could we trust – not our landlords or our neighbours. We're alone. (*She meets her husband coming in the door.*) Here's the candle, Mr. Donnelly, that should have warned you we had a British peace-making constable in our house. Something he's just told me, Jim, makes me wonder.

MR. DONNELLY: Howard? Constable Howard, I'm giving myself up.

MRS. DONNELLY: Is what you're doing right? Run for it.

CONSTABLE: (*grasping at his instruction book*) Four hundred dollars! Lost!

MR. DONNELLY: I'm giving myself up for nothing and I want a warm by my own fire first.

CONSTABLE: I wish I could have apprehended you properly, Donnelly. It seems by the book that if you give yourself up I don't get the reward.

MR. DONNELLY: Deliver me to the gaol, Mr. Howard. I'll back you up there and they'll give you a pound or two for that surely.

MRS. DONNELLY: Whirlwind! What will happen to us, Mr. Donnelly? Do you know what's been said here tonight? Shall I wake the children, Jim?

MR. DONNELLY: One candle or two, Mrs. Donnelly, I'd have come in you know. No, I'll see them again. (*He bends down over the sleepers.*) Oh God, he looks like his father! (*Not knowing what he's doing after seeing the face of FARL again, MR. DONNELLY lunges up with a candle in the FARL gesture.*) Handcuff me, Howard. No, don't you dare! Not yet till I've said farewell to my wife. (*He takes MRS. DONNELLY's hands in his.*) Under the snow I was scraping away, the wheat in our fields looks green, Mrs. Donnelly. The boys are getting old enough to cradle most of it. Ask the Keefes and Feenys to help. They're our friends. No one asked them for their opinion at the inquest either. Well, I will now, and get a girl to help you with the binding of the wheat, Mrs. Donnelly. Don't try to do any of it by yourself. (*He thrusts out his hands for the cuffs.*) And if they decide, Mr. Howard, to choke me off, there are seven men there under the blankets waiting to sprout up and show the world that I live.

In contrast to the paper snow used for the BRIMMACOMBE murder, here use milkweed-down. MRS. DONNELLY stands at the doorway listening to the bells of the sleigh as the CONSTABLE takes her husband away. Reel whistling and sudden bright, fully lit stage with all the company present. Onstage right, STUB's store and he waiting at the counter for MRS. DONNELLY's attack; to stage left, sticks are going to be used by a gallows builder. MRS. DONNELLY downstage centre; CHORUS in between her and MR. DONNELLY, the effect is of crash! from sleigh bells to the reality of the verdict. Forming a circle around DONNELLY and pointing at him.

CHORUS: Jury returned to Court with verdict Guilty. Sentenced to be taken to the gaol whence he came thence on the seventeenth of September to the place of execution there to be hanged by the neck until dead.

STUB with assistance starts building a scaffold. MRS. DONNELLY surges over to STUB's store with a stick and begins to lay about her – lots of stones fall off counter as she makes her sweep. Barrels fall over.

MRS. DONNELLY: You lied to me, you grocer. You registry rat, George Stub, the lease eel and blackmouth deedpoll worm – you lied to me when you said my husband would get off if he turned himself in, and after you lied, sir, Sir Grocer, you rode into town and you bought our mortgage because if my husband hanged we'd lose the fifty acres, our last, and it would be yours for a while until they bought it from you. Did the Fat Woman put you up to this?

Most of the actors kneel as if at church.

STUB: (*starting the scaffold-building sequence with sticks and boards*) Eight days' work of carpenters at two dollars per day, sixteen dollars.

MRS. DONNELLY: Well, sirs, you're wasting your time because he shall not, will not, hang.

DONNELLY BOYS (STONES) bring to centre stage a roll of paper, which they unroll until it extends to the edges of the stage.

MRS. DONNELLY: He will not be hanged either, do you hear that, inhabitants of Biddulph. There, children, if we can fill that much paper with names and get it to the Governor General in time he will not be … for, you see, he did not kill the man intentionally. It was an unlucky stroke given in liquor. If – thank you, Father Flynn – if you do not wish to sign this petition for my husband's life, then remain kneeling.

She moves about as if visiting countless people. From time to time someone stands up, goes over to the roll of paper, which is unwound until at the end of the scene it is completely extended again.

MRS. DONNELLY: Yes, stand if you can see your way at all at all to helping a woman with seven boys and one more child on the way. Thank you. Mr. Grace, shure, it's the least he could do after selling half of the farm out from under us in the first place. My Father in heaven if this eighth child is an eighth boy I'll go hang myself from that elm.

It's got to be a girl, pray God send me a little girl. Thank you, Mrs. Marksey, oh, oh, her husband is in the same gaol as Jim is, for burning down Andrew Keefe's stables. I better go easy on talk about gaol, if her husband doesn't get off it might cheer her up to see my husband get hanged.

It was an unlucky stroke given in liquor, you won't sign, I know why. You're a cousin of Farl's and you stand to gain by his tricking us out of half our farm. I still can't get used to our front field looking so narrow. Well, so you won't sign, good day to you, but privately in my own mind I'll curse you as I pull my shadow down the road in the sunlight: may the devil when you arrive in hell take your shinbone – and make it a flute and play nothing but the merriest jigs and reels upon it. But I'll keep that private you've taken half our farm from us, but you shall not take half our family from us, which is my husband. Now we've got – four hundred names.

There are still a few obstinate kneelers who will only disappear in the going-to-Goderich sequence; the paper is rolled up and given to MRS. DONNELLY.

MRS. DONNELLY: And now I'll walk with these names to Goderich.

WILL: When my mother heard that the Governor General was to be there for the celebration opening the railroad from Goderich to Brantford to Buffalo, she determined that she would meet him with the petitions we had helped and friends had helped her gather up.

The road from Biddulph to Goderich is represented by a series of short and long ladders held up firmly by the cast. MRS. DONNELLY climbs over these ladders. We hear road sounds – barking of dogs, etc. – that accompany her journey.

MRS. DONNELLY: At Marystown the dogs barked at me –

CHORUS: And people who had signed wished her good luck.

Generally repeat this solo and choral response arrangement between MRS. DONNELLY and the other actors.

MRS. DONNELLY: At Irishtown the grain wagons were all going south –

CHORUS: North she was going, north through their dust.

MRS. DONNELLY: There at St. Peter's is he buried whom my husband killed –

CHORUS: His cold hands reached across the road and held back her feet.

MRS. DONNELLY: I dare not enter there to pray for his soul –

CHORUS: The chapel has no shadow. It is noon.

VOICE: Last spring a man and a woman came to a sudden death … it is not known how, and were buried in their own field in Biddulph.

STUB: Twelve hundred feet of pine lumber at ten dollars per M.

MRS. DONNELLY: Now I've reached the borders of Biddulph –

VOICE: Sarah Stratton, an old woman who was found dead … on the north boundary of Biddulph going to Exeter out of Biddulph.

MRS. DONNELLY: Well, she almost made it, but once past this tollgate and I am –

CHORUS: – out of Biddulph! Past two tollgates, there are twelve still to –

MRS. DONNELLY: Oak tree with your shadow Indian dark –

CHORUS: Lie and rest beneath my speaking saying leaves –

MRS. DONNELLY: The whip of that carter touched my cheek. I look like a beggar woman tramping the roads –

CHORUS: Clean white tower clouds walk in the sky –

STUB: Nine hundred feet of hemlock scantlings, seven dollars per M, six dollars and thirty cents.

MRS. DONNELLY: Tollgate of the setting sun show me your latch –

CHORUS: Twilight rain on this roof from those clouds –

MRS. DONNELLY: Falling down, down as I sleep till the earth wheels –

CHORUS: Down to the dawn whose tollgate opens to all –

MRS. DONNELLY: I'll pray for the dawn with these winter stars –

CHORUS: In the chill dark starting out before there were proper shadows –

STUB: Detlor and Sons for nails, hinges, and bolts, two dollars and ninety cents.

CHORUS:

Francistown	Rogersville	Hensall	Kippen
Brucefield	Rattenbury's	Clinton	and turn

MRS. DONNELLY: I'm on the Huron Road now and I turn west to –

CHORUS: Holmesville where her Member of Parliament lived.

MRS. DONNELLY: Yes, Mr. Holmes. Hurrah for Holmes will be our cry from now on in. Our family's vote is Grit forever and I've seven sons who'll agree or else. Why, sir, you've garnered almost as many names from this township as I have from Biddulph. My family's blessing on you and your family forever. And our eight votes, sir, someday. Except the one I'm carrying, God bless her.

STUB: Nolan's account for Staples Ring & Co.

MRS. DONNELLY: The road's like a knife I cut through the bush with –

CHORUS: She climbed up the hill, the last tavern hill before –

STUB: Rope from W.E. Grace, twenty-four cents. Four long polls at one dollar each.

MRS. DONNELLY: From this hill I see the river. I see the blue lake –

CHORUS: The ship in the harbour flew a red-and-gold flag –

STUB: Twenty cedar posts, one piece of five-by-six maple scantling.

MRS. DONNELLY: I'll have time to see the mayor of the town. I'll change my dress, comb my hair somewhere. Somewhere. I won't see Mr. Donnelly till I've delivered the petitions. What's that hammering sound I hear? My own heart more than likely.

STUB: One mask, twelve and a half cents. One white cap for prisoner, fifty cents.

CHORUS: The evening of July 7th, 1858.

*The **GOVERNOR GENERAL** has already made his entry, walking slowly along the railing of his yacht. Unlike nearly all the others in the play, perhaps he and his lady should be in period dress – they are out of the play, both in fact and effect. Perhaps marionettes. They look down at us – at them – their subjects. Distant salon music of the 1857 period. LADY HEAD enters.*

LADY HEAD: Edmund, won't you join us for the music?

SIR EDMUND: Perhaps in half an hour, Mary. I'm held out here by some rather grim official business. It's the convict Donnelly's wife. She's just come aboard.

LADY HEAD: How very, very curious. May I stay to watch?

SIR EDMUND: You find someone begging for her husband's life of interest, do you?

LADY HEAD: I'm not just idly curious, Edmund. I wish to see her.

SIR EDMUND: She is reported to have walked every step of the way from her township, Biddulph, which is forty miles away back there somewhere in the bush.

LADY HEAD: How do we know this fact for sure?

SIR EDMUND: Well, my dear, the mayor of this town told it to me at dinner tonight and also presented me on the spot with a petition for Donnelly's life from the citizens of Goderich.

LADY HEAD: You were having much more interesting conversation than I was, my dear. You've no idea what I suffered through. I think living in such an out-of-the-way place jellies the brain. The palm trees we had last time, Edmund, were so much more interesting than these pines.

SIR EDMUND: You find it dull and I'm sorry for that, my dear. They and we have done all that's humanly possible to make it of interest. New railroad opens tomorrow – railway celebration, four hundred to dinner and a ball for thousands, fireworks. Mary, I do wish you wouldn't –

LADY HEAD: Why?

SIR EDMUND: These scenes with the condemned convicts' wives are, can be, extremely embarrassing. They usually kneel, try to grasp my knees, and there are tears.

LADY HEAD: What are the extenuating circumstances, Edmund? Was he guilty or innocent or is it just that he's her husband?

SIR EDMUND: I don't think you can call him innocent. But my feelings are, from what the locals say, that he did not present his part of the story soon enough, or could not present it, since he eluded the constables for a year or two. Now he has almost got himself hanged.

An AIDE-DE-CAMP approaches and whispers in his ear. Our eye takes in MRS. DONNELLY at extreme stage left. Her dress is exactly right – it embodies will – and grows out of the dusty, road-fighting woman we have just seen, but is also miles apart from that. An obscure tapping sound. Walking across, she curtsies ever so slightly.

MRS. DONNELLY: Your Excellency, I have three petitions to present, praying that the life of my husband might be spared.

SIR EDMUND: Mrs. Donnelly? Pray be seated. As you might probably have learned, a decision as to royal clemency is made by my advisers after consultation with the judge who sentenced your husband.

MRS. DONNELLY: Nevertheless, sir, you might give to your advisers some impression of the petitioners' present view of the case. There are names among the hundreds who signed these addresses to Your Excellency, names of men who could have prevented the whole tragedy except they were drunk and such was their hilarity that they liked nothing better than to watch two men who were even more drunk attempt to destroy each other, sicced on by their howls of encouragement. They were not men enough to admit to this – neither at the inquest nor at the trial where they heard their earlier lies read out to them. Faced with Donnelly's wife, however, they signed their names or made their marks to the truth at last. I shall bring the truth out of Biddulph yet and my husband alive back some day to his seven children and his farm. I wish you and your lady good night, sir, and I beg you to consider what is written on scraps of paper my friends and (*She gives him the petitions.*) myself have caught pity and truth in, name by name, and then pasted together – by my children – into the sincere prayers you hold in your hands.

As she leaves, neatly backing up and then turning, a ladder has been set up with MR. DONNELLY behind it. She goes over to see him; at another ladder she will wait for the letter from the Executive Council – at her front door back in Biddulph.

LADY HEAD: What will she do now, Edmund?

SIR EDMUND: (*pause*) She'll say goodbye to her husband at the gaol over there and then start walking back to their shanty back somewhere in the bush. The Executive Council meets a fortnight from tomorrow. God knows what the Attorney General will decide. If I know Macdonald's mind, he'll be appalled at the number of votes he might lose. (*He unfolds the petitions.*)

LADY HEAD: Ah, this hand was learnt a long time ago from a priest who'd been trained abroad, wouldn't you say? I haven't seen an M like that since I was at school. Some of them put capital letters in the centre of their names. Oh, it's a Norman name – D'Arcy.

SIR EDMUND: This is the third or fourth murder in that locality, although in his favour I will say that this man at least gave himself up. Now she'll wait at her doorstep for a letter with our seal upon it.

LADY HEAD: What do you think, Edmund?

SIR EDMUND: What does it matter, my dear?

LADY HEAD: It does matter, Edmund. (*They walk along the railing back to the music.*) I feel that I shall remember that woman for the rest of my life.

SIR EDMUND: Oh, I believe her. But you asked me and what I think is this. Something in her presence seems to say – that she's not fated to save her husband from his sentence.

We now focus on MRS. DONNELLY standing in front of her house in bright summer sunlight, the cicadas strumming away with the heat. A galloping horseman throws the letter with a red seal at her feet. One of her CHILDREN picks it up for her – she throws it on the ground again. Humming sound of cicadas.

MRS. DONNELLY: I walked all the way to Goderich. I met him. I gave him the three petitions and now they've all turned into this letter and I won't open it. It's so hot and bright, the cicadas shrill shrill shrill away. Everything turns into a letter. That letter. It's like the handspike he saw on the ground and then he picked it up. I hate the fact that there's moments each like a bridge of dread, and why does there have to be an earth that goes round and round? There. My hand feels the letter. How heavy the seal makes it. I'd like to seal my letters with that heavy a red wax. If it says no, we'll throw the farm, what's left of it. We'll throw it away and move into town, get John Grace to put us up again, take in washing, cook. (*opens letter*) If it says yes, your husband may live, I'll give one cry against my doorframe here and then – wait for him to come home, get going on the next petition to get his sentence shortened.

She reads the letter, gives a brief cry, and turns to her family. Some of them reply from offstage or from the CHORUS. The seven sons can be represented by two lines hung with shirts – one for now, the other for when they are grown up.

MRS. DONNELLY: Boys, how old are you now?

As they tell her their ages, in the background the CHORUS (as if a legal clerk and assistant) go on about expenses. A train whistle. Very shadily, the trip MR. DONNELLY takes to Kingston lies under the boys' recital of their ages.

CHORUS:	BOYS:
James	Seventeen
William	Thirteen
John	Twelve
Patrick	Ten
Michael	Nine
Robert	Six
Thomas	Five

WOMAN ONE: Expenses taking convict James Donnelly to the penitentiary. Cab from gaol to station at Goderich –

WOMAN TWO: Two shillings, two sixpence –

WOMAN ONE: Paid railway fare from Goderich to Paris –

WOMAN TWO: For three –

WOMAN ONE: Railway fare from Toronto to Kingston for three –

WOMAN TWO: Cab from station to penitentiary and back –

WOMAN ONE: Dinner for two at Kingston –

WOMAN TWO: Three shillings, nine pence –

WOMEN: Expenses taking convict James Donnelly to the penitentiary.

MRS. DONNELLY: Children, yesterday was July 28th and that day your father was sentenced to seven years in prison. How old will you be when your father comes back?

CHORUS:	BOYS:
James	Twenty-four
William	Twenty
John	Nineteen
Patrick	Seventeen
Michael	Sixteen

MRS. DONNELLY: Robert, you'll be thirteen and Thomas will be twelve when Mr. Donnelly comes back to live with us again. Back from prison where he'll have been seven years of his life.

A girl comes running in.

JENNY: My name is Jenny and I'm seven years old when my father gets out of prison.

ALL: Seven years. (*the line fence; the boys kick the stones of the line fence this way and that*)

JAMES & JOHN: Why is our father's farm so narrow? Because he was cheated by the farrow. Of the pig and the sow, the fat woman who now snores as the moon lights our labours.

WILL: There are other ways of getting that fence down than that, James and John. As a matter of fact, that's the poorest way I ever saw and you'll drive our mother mad with the lawsuit over it.

JAMES: We thought a while. (*The church bell rings midnight and they put the fence up again.*) So what's your better way, Will?

WILL: I'll make the fence disappear by playing my fiddle at it. Someday. (*The two brothers look at each other.*) I'm practising up for it. You'll see, the fence will dance away, away.

JAMES: We believed him. And it almost happened.

The Christening Scene will already have started to merge in, but beginning to be established should be the GIRL with the Sword [MAGGIE], the FAT LADY with her turnips and grindstone.

ALL: Six years.

PRIEST: (*In white vestments, standing beside MRS. DONNELLY with a baby in her arms, he gives her a candle.*) Receive this burning light and see thou guard the grace of thy baptism without blame. Keep the commandments of God so that when the Lord shall come to call thee to the nuptials, thou mayest meet Him with all the saints in the heavenly courts, there to live forever and ever.

ALL: Amen.

PRIEST: Jane Donnelly, vade in pace et Dominus sit tecum.

ALL: Amen.

Jane [JENNY], the small girl, simultaneously puts four small stones on the ground by the doorstep and plays house.

JENNY:

> Here I'm sitting sewing
>
> In my little housey
>
> No one comes to see me
>
> Except my little mousey

ALL: Five years.

> *WILL DONNELLY limps to centre stage pursued by a mob of jeerers, led by the FAT WOMAN as a girl, with a cap on her head.*

MOB: (*singing*)

> *Cain killed Abel, Donnelly killed Farrell*
>
> *Your old man killed Farrell, Will*
>
> *Where's your father, they asked young Cripple*
>
> *He's down at Kingston on the old treadmill*

> *With tree branches TOM and JOHN DONNELLY appear. The mob runs jeering away, all save the FAT GIRL, who trips. They beat her and tear her cap.*

JAMES & JOHN: Tell us your names.

GIRL: Jim Donnelly and John Donnelly.

JAMES & JOHN: If you'll repeat what you said to our brother Will just now, we won't give you a licking. You were singing it, weren't you? Well, let's just hear you sing it again.

GIRL: I won't.

JAMES & JOHN: You won't, eh?

GIRL: I won't do a thing the sons of a murderer want.

JAMES & JOHN: Then you'll have to take a licking from us then. (*they beat her off*)

> *Reaching for his fiddle as if to heal wounds, WILL plays far upstage on his side of the fence. His playing produces a girl from the enemy farm who dances, whirling a sword.*

MAGGIE: This may be the last time I can show you the sword, Will. Oh, please stop playing so I can stop dancing. (*He doesn't.*)

WILL: Maggie, why? (*finally stopping*)

MAGGIE: My brother says I'm not to let you see it again or he'll tell my Aunt Theresa.

WILL: In that case, let's begin my last look. (*She takes the fiddle and plays, while he practises swordplay.*) Does no one in your family that took half our land away from us be able, Maggie, to read the writing on this sword?

MAGGIE: No, Grandmother says the man's not born yet can read that sword. Her father's father found it on the battlefield a hundred years ago. (*The FAT LADY rolls grindstone out and darts her eyes about suspiciously.*) Now it's your turn of the promise. (*He plays and she dances.*) Oh ... oh, I must run back home. Will, please don't play or they'll hear you. Play, play! Don't stop. I can't stop dancing. (*She disappears, to reappear at the "front of the farm" by her aunt with her grindstone.*)

FAT LADY: When I needed it to chop up turnips for the pigs, where were you with that old sword, Maggie?

MAGGIE: Playing, Aunt Theresa. Looking for the black hen's nest. (*She dances whenever her aunt is not looking.*)

FAT LADY: Don't go too near the line fence we have to share with those squatters, Maggie. They'll try to pull you over and insult you. I can hear that damn cripple's fiddle playing back there. He'll make our red cow with the brass tip on one horn bear a freemartin, between him and his mother cursing us. Why this sword's too dull to cut even turnips with. Whatever have you been doing with it? Here, turn the grindstone while I – (*sharpens the sword*)

MAGGIE: You'll grind off the old writing that way, Aunt Theresa.

FAT LADY: Dull as the dead it is. (*grinds*) What writing?

> *WILL covers his face; then we watch the FAT LADY turn her big buttocks to the DONNELLY front door and chop up turnips. Out of the DONNELLY house steals a younger kid with a slingshot, which begets a routine underlining the story of THE DONNELLYS' seven years with father in prison told by the sweet PRIEST we have previously heard on the subject of diocesan history. It is almost as if the boy might also ping the PRIEST.*

PRIEST: While the father was away in the penitentiary and taking away with him, I might add, the useful and fruitful influence a father always has, e.g., there was no one to put the fear of God into the seven boys with a big or little stick. The wretched family managed to survive by the genuinely heroic efforts of Mrs. Donnelly. Three times she gathered petitions for remission of her husband's sentence and sent them to the government.

VOICE: With regard to this request for further clemency, "altogether premature."

PRIEST: George Stub, who now held a mortgage on the Donnelly farm, sent a letter intimating that –

STUB: The time for the payment of a large sum overdue on this mortgage thereon has elapsed –

MRS. DONNELLY: (*emerging from the house with household chores*) We sold the pigs and took out a second mortgage from a railway conductor. (*overlap*)

PRIEST: Now it is rather interesting to relate that the family who had bought up the south half of the Donnelly farm in 1856 and very nearly chased the Donnellys off all of their property – this family decided to move away. The south half of the farm was up for sale –

MRS. DONNELLY: The children begged me to try to buy it back, but there was just enough money to send Will down to school in the town. No, we would wait, would have to wait for the years to go by before our farm would heal itself from being cut in half by that turnip chopper over there.

*The stone finds its target and **FAT LADY** emits a howl. **MRS. DONNELLY** takes a stick and pursues **ROBERT DONNELLY**, but even under her arm he manages another direct hit. This should somehow lead to a routine with whistle accompaniment where both women pursue the scamp, with the **FAT LADY** almost crossing the fence. Then silence and –*

MRS. DONNELLY: Mrs. Ryan, you have dropped your sword over the fence. (*pause*) Do not attempt to come over the fence or I shall charge you with trespass. Here – I shall throw the sword over the fence and I am shamed to see that glory used to chop turnips, but the fox has so long fouled the badger's den I shouldn't be surprised. And I shall punish my own child.

*A magistrate's court is set up in **STUB**'s store in Lucan. Fluidly, you should be able to establish this out of the line-fence chairs. Kneeling in rows, holding ladders, the courtroom audience reacts with loud heehaws and ladder motions.*

CHORUS: Four years.

STUB: Remember, that in magistrate's court, Will Donnelly, you must speak the truth. Why, for what reason did you lead these other boys of the neighbourhood to steal six fleeces of wool from the premises of Patrick Ryan, entering and breaking the curtilage?

WILL: I can't tell you, Mr. Stub.

STUB: How much is the value of a fleece of wool, Will?

WILL: Five dollars.

STUB: So how much would six fleeces bring you on the market down at London?

WILL: Don't know. I think it would be thirty dollars.

STUB: You think it would be thirty dollars. You know it would be thirty dollars. Where is your father, Will?

WILL: I think he's in prison.

STUB: You think he's in prison. My boy, you know he's in prison and your little gang will soon join him and he can break a few of your skulls together while he's at it. Johannah, what have you to say for your son's behaviour?

MRS. DONNELLY: Sir, there's a pair of special shoes this lad has wanted for some time that cost quite a penny. Have you any notion how quickly his shoes wear out?

STUB: Then let him go barefoot, Johannah Donnelly.

MRS. DONNELLY: And have him the barefoot hobbledehoy of the school, I suppose.

STUB: Take him out of the school. Since you can't quite afford it with your fifty acres, you maybe shouldn't be trying. Between you and your high notions and your crippled son, you've corrupted half the youth in the settlement. Shirts from clotheslines and stamps from the post office is how it started. Next fleeces of wool and next –

WILL: Maybe it was we wanted to buy the horse.

STUB: And all six of you were to take turns riding it, or were you to climb up on it all at once? What horse?

WILL: The one the king of the Indians had when they were camping over by the river. He said we could have his grey horse for thirty dollars.

STUB: The king of the Indians? You mean an Indian chief, I presume. Has anyone seen Indians camping over by the river lately? Let alone a king of them? (*pause*) Will, did he wear a crown?

WILL: They'd come up along the river for the flax picking and he was the king of them.

STUB: Will, this is like the story you told about the old sword that disappeared for a while on your road. When it was found again it was seen to be nothing but a rusty turnip knife. Will Donnelly not only – is always into a new one each day, a new strange story. Look at him. Just as he stands is he not a strange story?

MRS. DONNELLY: (*puncturing*) No stranger than your own story, Mr. Stub. That you should be a Justice of the Peace in 1864 when in 1848 in October of that year you led a mob to burn down the Africans' barns, to steal their land, not steal their shirts or their fleeces, but their very existence. (*laughter*) But that was some time ago, and with the profit from that bold adventure you've supported the party that gave you a commission of the peace, aye, and your arsonist brother a place on the Grand Jury. Yes, Donnelly is a strange story, sir, but you law-abiding high-flyer, never as strange as – could never compete with yours.

STUB: Silence, Johannah Donnelly. I'll send you both down, mother and son. Down to the Quarter Sessions. Too are charged you!

ALL: The Queen against Johannah Donnelly.

MRS. DONNELLY: Let us hear the charge against me then. How many fleeces of wool did Judith Donnelly get away with?

STUB: Can no one here think of what she should be charged with?

FAT LADY: I can. I can think of what to charge her with. I'm willing to swear out an information, at this very moment, that I saw on the Friday following the Thursday the fleeces were reported to be missing. I saw this woman out in her backyard washing something white. And it looked like fleeces to me, Mr. Stub.

ALL: The Queen against Johannah Donnelly. Receiving stolen goods.

MRS. DONNELLY: You'd even gore your own ox to goad me, wouldn't you? Because your son is charged as well and I've read somewhere there's a lovely penalty for perjury and malicious arrest, but perhaps you'd like to take back that charge. (*pause*) Anything goes, I see, if you can plunge your horn into me, into us – up to the very last wrinkle.

A small girl comes with a note for MRS. DONNELLY, which she reads while keeping an eye on the BAILIFF who, carrying a staff, conducts WILL to behind a ladder. To read the note, MRS. DONNELLY puts on glasses.

ALL: Three years.

MRS. DONNELLY: My dear girl, have you not heard the trouble we're in? You'll have to tell your mother I cannot come to help her for I'm waiting to hear how my son's trial goes. And my own trial promises to be next. (*pause*) And Farl's wife will be there at this raising bee. Her marrying again does not make her any less the widow of the man my husband killed. I can't bear her looking at me. (*pause, a bell at a prison*)

We now focus on WILL as a prisoner, his body behind a ladder.

CHORUS: The Queen against William Donnelly et aliter.

VOICE: Indictment withdrawn. No bill. Insufficient evidence.

MRS. DONNELLY: I'll go, sweetheart. I'll take your mother this bread and some meat. I'll walk back with you, darling.

We now lose sight of MRS. DONNELLY as the cast expands into the crowd of people at Gallagher's bee.

CHORUS: The raising bee at Gallagher's on the Cedar Swamp Line.

The crowd is spaced out over the stage held by something that is happening just offstage left. TOM CASSLEIGH is dealing out whisky to men as they finish washing their faces and hands in a horse trough. There's a towel they dry themselves with, but one of the men reaches for the apron of a woman. A small tense scream. Some of the men are deeply drunk and occasionally stagger or fall over. As someone rolls a wagon wheel down stage left and leans it up over a chair, a man throws some water at another, flicking it out of a dipper.

MAN TWO: Six eggs to you, Rody, and half a dozen of them rotten.

These two men square off for a fight, but CASSLEIGH, who is as powerful among these people as STUB is in the village, walks between them.

CASSLEIGH: Why waste your time on each other, Rody and Dan, when there's more fun to be had over here? Donegal! (*to a man sitting on the edge of the stage rather out of it all*) After all, would you like a drop now from my jug – Mr. Donegan?

DONEGAN: No, I would not, Cassleigh. I said you and your gang stole my oak tree and, until we settle that, I'll not drink from your jug. If you want to know I'm going home.

CASSLEIGH: D'ye hear him, men? He's going home.

Suddenly we and DONEGAN are faced by a gang of men with sticks, one of them turning his hand-spike into a torch. Not all join CASSLEIGH's mob. Some hang back; the women bunch in fear – save for the FAT LADY who calmly gathers some wood.

CASSLEIGH: Donegan, we stole your oak tree, eh? Say that to our faces, eh? Now you're afraid to, darling, aren't you?

A barrel is rolled over and filled with sharp objects.

DONEGAN: (*backing up offstage as the men push him over*) I only want fair play about my oak tree. It's sorry I am I mentioned it. What d'you want with me at all?

Whatever does happen to DONEGAN, perhaps we should be dimly aware that he is being put into the barrel. We see nothing nor hear anything of the usual cruelty paraphernalia – just silence; the men and women onstage come over gingerly to take a look, then register – shame, disgust, fascination, even joining in.

MEN: What about your oak tree now, Donegan!

Just as one does join the offstage mob, MRS. DONNELLY enters stage right with girl. Opposition – she – the non-joiner as against the tormentors – in the darkness of the cellar or underneath a wagon.

MRS. GALLAGHER: Oh, Mrs. Donnelly. I'm sorry I asked you to come. Some of the men have too much drink into them and they're tormenting the life out of Donegan who asked about – why would he mention it when they're so – asked about his oak tree he says Tom Cassleigh stole on him.

MRS. DONNELLY: Complaining to that man about your oak tree is a mistake surely. He'd brain you with it.

SARAH FARL: What is to be done, Judith Donnelly?

MRS. DONNELLY: What's to be done – are they not letting him go yet?

SARAH FARL: They're saying they'll clip off his ears.

MRS. DONNELLY: Are there no men to stop this?

SARAH FARL: They're afraid of Cassleigh. Or they like watching.

MRS. DONNELLY: Where's Mrs. Cassleigh?

SARAH FARL: Not here, Mrs. Donnelly. But in the same churchyard as my Patrick lies buried.

MRS. DONNELLY: Sarah Farl. I cannot help calling you that although I know that your name is now Sarah Flannery. And once a very long time ago, I knew you as Sarah Donegan.

SARAH FARL: Judith Donnelly who were once Judith Magee. You alone of anyone here can save my brother. Tell them to stop.

MRS. DONNELLY: (*kneeling*) Sarah Flannery that was Sarah Farl. Very well then. (*covering her face*) Have you forgiven me and mine then for what we did to your man? And for what my husband is now in prison for?

SARAH FARL: (*pause*) You won't let them go on, will you?

MRS. DONNELLY: (*getting up*) Yes, Sarah Farl. Sarah Donegan that was, that I used to see running up Keeper's Hill in her bare feet. I will save your brother. (*She pauses at the lip of the stage. As she begins her speech to the tormentors below, slowly STUB and his counter fade in at stage right. The PRIEST will soon begin to mount a centre-back pulpit, which is in effect the roof of the DONNELLY house.*) Leave that man alone. What in heaven's name and the name of hell do you think you're about with him? Have you, Mr. Cassleigh, tortured him enough? Put that knife back where it belongs, Mr. Cassleigh, if you still know what pockets are for, or do you carry the knife permanently stuck in your hand like a thorn? (*CASSLEIGH comes toward her with his knife, but her glance forces him to weave out from the wheel, through it, and around the barnyard.*) Get back, you savage. Have you not killed enough when you got your friend to tap the Englishman over the head at our doorstep on our road? Tom, let me see the knife. (*He – click! – gives her the knife.*) Give Mr. Donegan back his clothes ... raise him up out of that mud. Dung! There's fields of grain to garner with bread for you all and you'd rather be thorns to each other. There's tables of food for you to eat and you won't come and sit down at them. Well, you won't sit down at them. Get back to work, you fools. You tribe!

For a moment she stands isolated: STUB on one side, CASSLEIGH on the other. She has won and DONEGAN is rescued. She disappears to help him. As the PRIEST begins, the people all enter centre area and kneel. Slowly everyone kneels but it would be hard to tell at what point we saw MRS. DONNELLY kneeling. Candles.

PRIEST: When I turned this poor man in his bed last evening, the flesh actually fell from his bones. I looked to heaven, my friends of Biddulph, my friends of St. Patrick's parish, and I was, and I still am, afraid that the hand of God will fall on Biddulph someday and fall with great weight. I want all those who tormented and burnt and cut this man to come in the presence of all the congregation and ask God's pardon.

A pause during which one man rises. Before he rises there is silence filled with the buzzing of a fly against a window.

GALLAGHER: Father Crinnon, I come forward in the presence of all the congregation and ask God's pardon. I stood by while the crime was done. Nor did I even offer to help the woman who risked her life to save the man. I ask God to pardon me – and to pardon me, too, for ever being in such company.

PRIEST: (*coming down from pulpit*) Domine exaudi vocem meam.

CHORUS: Si iniquitates observaveris, Domine, Domine quis sustinebit. (*candles*)

PRIEST: For Thine arrows stick fast in me. And Thou hast laid Thy hand heavily upon me.

They move upstage where they face us as the audience of the Medicine Show. Their candles are its footlights. The DONNELLY house lies between us and the stage of the show. STUB becomes the SHOWMAN counting his take; on him we also see the front gate of the DONNELLY house where TOM and JIM FEENY prepare their scene.

CHORUS: There is no health in my flesh because of Thy wrath. There is no peace in my bones because of my sins.

TOM: Two years. (*He is sharpening a jackknife on a stone.*) My name is Tom Donnelly and my best friend was a boy who lived up the road called Jim Feeny.

JIM: What're you doing with the knife, Tom?

TOM: See, I can cut my name on my arm. T-O-M.

JIM: What about your last name.

TOM: Haven't got any more arm. Your turn, Jim.

JIM: Ouch! How'd you get it so sharp?

TOM: Whetted it for half a day on the doorstep. I. Now for your M.

JIM: Uh.

TOM: Don't you want me to finish it?

JIM: No! You know I can't stand pain, Tom. (*Screams as TOM grabs his arm and finishes it anyhow.*)

TOM: Now – cross your arm with mine. Your blood, my blood, mixed in brotherhood. (*train whistle*)

Their arms crossed, the boys freeze. We focus on the SHOWMAN counting his take while the last scene of the Medicine Show's The Black Donnellys play is winding up. This last scene is played on ladders held up by the footlight holders.

SHOWMAN: Shamrock Liniment?

SON: Must have sold forty bottles.

WOMAN: So how many tins of the East India Tiger Fat?

SON: Fifty-five.

SHOWMAN: So … $252.35 off these yokels tonight that came to see our little penniless dreadful – *The Black Donnellys, Or the Biddulph Horror.*

SON: Pa, we sure scared it out of them tonight.

SHOWMAN: Yeah. Which part do you think, my boy, scares them the most?

SON: The part where they draw lots to see who'll kill the girl?

SHOWMAN: That's worth sixteen bottles of Shamrock Liniment right there, isn't it? (*He takes out his watch.*) Oh, it's the Jim Feeny weeps over his betrayal of Tom Donnelly for five hundred bucks and he never even got the money scene. Listen to him whine.

FALSE JIM: Pat, you have always used me white.

FALSE PAT: What's on your mind, Jim Feeny?

FALSE JIM: Pat Donnelly, you are as square a man as ever I met. Pat, I can't sleep nights for thinking what I done to Tom. I didn't know they was going to murder them. I thought it was just to scare them or at the worst shake him up a little.

SHOWMAN: Christy Dominy, that's my cue. (*He rushes out to be ready.*)

FALSE PAT: Jim, what was the one thing you ever done that you're sorry for?

FALSE JIM: I sold Tom Donnelly, Tom Donnelly, the best friend I ever had.

SHOWMAN: (*on a shorter ladder held up by his son*) Showing, folks, that there were those who loved the Donnellys as well as loathed them. Will it ever be known who killed them that dark night of February 4th, 1880? One thing is known – after the Donnellys left Biddulph at last there was peace. No more fires, no more mysterious outrages, and who today would guess that in that tranquil countryside such dire events had once took place. In the words of the "Old Song" we close. (*He sings with banjo, fiddle.*)

Oh, all young folks take warning
Never live a life of hate,
Of wickedness or violence, lest
You share the Donnellys' fate.
Their murdered bodies lie today,
A mile from Lucan town
But the memories of the awful feud
Time never will live down. (*applause, train whistle, scream*)

We focus again on the boys with crossed arms.

TOM: Now – cross your arm with mine, Jim Feeny. Your blood, my blood, mixed in brotherhood. (*train whistle*)

MRS. DONNELLY: (*coming out of the house*) What is this unearthly silence out here, boys? John or Mike, before you go out to the fields again, hold the lamp for me while I hang out your shirts. The moonlight doesn't reach over the washhouse yet on this side of the house. But it will. Rising pretty full moon you are. Why are you two boys hiding your arms, eh? Jim Feeny and Tom Donnelly, the two scamps. What month is this we're in, Tom?

TOM: July, Mother.

MRS. DONNELLY: And, Mike, what's the date yesterday?

MIKE: Twenty-eighth –

MR. DONNELLY: So it is the twenty-ninth of July. There's your seven shirts all hanging on the line for you to put on for mass tomorrow if Father comes back. So you'll look like seven gentlemen instead of the seven devils I've raised.

TOM: They let Father out yesterday.

MRS. DONNELLY: I was wondering if any of you'd remember that he was sentenced on July 28th, seven years ago. He could be here tonight.

MIKE: Not if he's walking, Mother. (*train whistle*)

MRS. DONNELLY: Do you see your father tramping the roads with a bundle on his back? No, he'll take the cars. And the stage. Oh, he'll come walking up the road from the chapel where he'll get off the London Road. Now I'll wait for him here by the gate with this lamp. Bring sheaves with you when you've finished the field. Your father will want to see what his farm's been doing, right away. I'll stand out here with my lamp. You will come

tonight. I know you will. I'll hold this lamp until either its oil runs dry or you're home. Moon, you hold your lamp, stars. I hold mine. (*night sounds*) I stand. I'll stand here years after tonight – a seal in the air – long after my house and my gate and my curtilage have become dust. A lamp hanging in the air, held by a ghost lady.

In the half-light, MRS. DONNELLY'S GHOST comes up behind her and eventually takes the lamp from her. They stand back to back, move away from each other, but they never face each other. In effect, we are looking at another deep-down, dead-leaf self of MRS. DONNELLY.

GHOST: Mention me, Judith, and I float up from the culvert where I'll hide to frighten travellers years from now. A ghost lady with a lamp, no – a lamp floating in midair up and down by the fence by the road.

MRS. DONNELLY: Who is that behind me?

GHOST: It's no good to turn around because you cannot see me or even hear me, but only sense me with the drumming eye of your heart.

MRS. DONNELLY: Yes, I can hear you. My heart can hear you. What will –

GHOST: You'll die unconfessed, Judith Donnelly. And wander these roads for a certain while. Dead leaf. Float light.

MRS. DONNELLY: What have I got ready for him to come back to? Were there –

GHOST: There were ladders with certain rungs, Judith, you could have avoided, you know.

MRS. DONNELLY: Seven years I've waited for my husband to return.

GHOST: Your first mistake was to stay here at all.

MRS. DONNELLY: And give up my husband's farm that we've fought for?

GHOST: Well, its ground loves you. But why did you have to talk back to that Orangeman Stub?

MRS. DONNELLY: I should have been weak and let him call my son a thieving cripple?

GHOST: Oh yes, and lived.

MRS. DONNELLY: When she asked me to save her brother at the bee –

GHOST: You should have said, "Save your brother yourself," and you should have let Donegan then be cut to ribbons by Cassleigh.

MRS. DONNELLY: Will Cassleigh never forget that then?

GHOST: During the day, but not at night.

MRS. DONNELLY: Why should we be afraid? Look at all the neighbours who signed their names for my husband's life.

GHOST: Stub and Cassleigh can change that with –

MRS. DONNELLY: How! –

GHOST: With their tongues and their words. Did you see that boy who's such a friend of Tom's?

MRS. DONNELLY: Yes, Jim Feeny. My sons have many such loyal friends.

GHOST: (*laughing*) From where I stand tonight wandering through, crossing times and places as I please, I saw some cheap Medicine Show put on a play in which that very Jim Feeny grown up to be a weak young wastrel sold your son Tom for five hundred dollars. And he had Tom's name written on his arm.

MRS. DONNELLY: Oh, if only we could get out of the pound we're locked in – it's like a house with twisty windows – what is it out there coming down the road?

GHOST: It still may not happen. Ah, I can see him before you do. The darkness and the shadows changing into a traveller. Your husband. Coming back to you as one day his ghost will come back to me – with a ticket that confirms us across the river and finally out of Biddulph.

MRS. DONNELLY: Sleep voice within me. If I wait long enough, my husband will come from where he has journeyed.

GHOST: (*As MRS. DONNELLY walks away from her to meet MR. DONNELLY down in the audience corridor; by the time MR. & MRS. DONNELLY come up to the clothesline scene, the GHOST has vanished.*) Yes, sleep here if you can. Mrs. Shea held her child in the rain barrel while a mob of four hundred set fire to their house. She held and held until past the borders of life. I hold this. Past life. Past death!

All but the lamp fades, then we are back in 1865 again; the line of seven shirts, the harvest moon, the woman with the lamp, crickets singing loudly, then fading as someone walks through them. MR. DONNELLY walks up to his wife and takes the lamp from her.

MRS. DONNELLY: Boys, line up to see if your father can say your names still.

We see sheaves through the shirts, and the seven boys partly through them, although as the naming goes on the shadows of the seven DONNELLYS grow huge and by themselves towering over the theatre.

MR. DONNELLY: James – Will – John – Patrick – Michael – Robert – Thomas. (*to the shirts; train whistle faraway; MRS. DONNELLY brings out the sleeping JENNY in her arms*) Jenny?

MRS. DONNELLY: She's still asleep.

MR. DONNELLY: Judith Donnelly, mother of Jane Donnelly.

MRS. DONNELLY: James Donnelly, senior, father of Jane Donnelly and these ... seven.

MR. DONNELLY: Mrs. Donnelly, I was thinking what fair seed we have sown and I have come back at last to harvest. (*train whistle*)

ALL: (*singing*)

Then they sold me to the brewer
And he brewed me on the pan
(softly) But when I got into the jug
I was the strongest man.

VOICE: End of Act Two.

ACT THREE

JENNY: (*as a grown-up to tell us the rest of the story*) When I woke up the next morning, I was to see my father for the very first time.

Behind her narration the entire company mimes groupings that go through the story backward and forward; they make the Roman Line; they do the ladder journey format; they suddenly kneel, cross themselves ... people caught in the Roman Line.

JENNY: No, I did not know it at the time, but in those few months and years after my father returned from seven years in prison, we – the entire Donnelly family – mother, father, seven sons, and one daughter – were up for confirmation in a church called the Roman Line. No, it was a bigger church than that for it involved Protestants, too. We were going to be tested for confirmation in a church called – Biddulph. Most of the people liked us at that time. That doesn't matter, though. Those with power did not. Our confirmation came up, and although we had known our catechism well, we failed.

CHORUS: (*tossing sticks and stones in patterned throwing and catching*) Which are the sacraments that can be received only once?

JENNY: Your mother, your father, your brothers.

CHORUS: Why can they be received only once?

JENNY: Just a minute, Your Lordship. I'm not ready for that one yet, but there's also the rungs of the ladder they've climbed that we can't see down, down, down, and there's also the other people and what they think.

CHORUS: So what lot is this, Pa?

JENNY: It was my father's farm. Half of its fields were lost to his enemies.

CHORUS: What about the Mescoes and the Washingtons?

JENNY: Better to be black all over than just to have black feet.

CHORUS: Who settled the Roman Line, Church Line, Chapel Line? (*form line*)

JENNY: Who owns it now, you mean?

CHORUS:

Barry	Trehy
Feeny	Cassleigh
Cahill	Cassleigh
McCann	Marksey
Donnelly	Mulowney
Egan	Marksey
Quinn	

JENNY: Now that's not right. The Quinns were burnt out in '66, and they left. That was how you knew that you hadn't passed the catechism. A burning barn is a good strong hint with your house left over.

CHORUS: Who bought up the Quinn place?

JENNY: Guess.

CHORUS: Cassleigh.

CHORUS: What have I done to you, man?

JENNY: Nothing, for a while. All was quiet. No bad names were even used. Everything seemed to be all right.

CHORUS: Do you desire any one thing other than fiddle, sword, and horse?

JENNY: Yes, to get back the other half of my father's farm. But when it came up for sale again our friend was afraid to sell it to us. The Fat Lady's family offered him so much money – where did they get all the money so suddenly? We had the Fat Lady for a neighbour again.

CHORUS: Which of you robbers is buying my farm out from under me?

JENNY: There's fifty acres you'll never get and across the road the Mulowney brothers who'd never married offered to sell my father either one of their twenty-five-acre lots.

CHORUS: Where's the grog boss?

JENNY: He couldn't buy both of them. One of the lots had blood on it, blood he had spilled. Meanwhile we all went to mass together and several New Years and Lents went by.

CHORUS: Which is the last of all the occupations?

JENNY: To be the fence viewers who had to decide our tile-and-ditch dispute with the Fat Lady's husband and nephews. There was a small creek ran through their farm, at the back, and our farm and then across into the next farm. But our back field kept flooding. (*The CHORUS hold up a line of tile that more or less fits together.*) They were applying the flood-'em-out-test by plugging our tile with straw and rags. (*Furious activity of plugging and unplugging. Lanterns – watchings, reel whistlings, a blue gauze sheet for the water. THE DONNELLYS decide to use bigger tile and a line of this meets the line of smaller tile.*) After we put in some bigger tile that would be impossible to plug up so easily, their back field got flooded and they sued.

CHORUS: We, the Fence Viewers of the Township of Biddulph in the County of Middlesex, have been nominated to view and arbitrate between William –

JENNY: We won the case and the fence viewers made the Fat Lady put in the same kind of tile we had at a dollar a rod. But it was a dangerous victory. (*A bell rings.*) Time to put a stone in one of the fence viewer's threshing machines, and that is why, as they all had things happen to them of more than just mischief, I call fence-viewing the last of all the occupations.

CHORUS: What are the extenuating circumstances, Edmund?

JENNY: We couldn't be flooded out, so something else had to be tried. Rumours were spread at market, mill, tavern, and church that we were selling up and leaving the neighbourhood. Then a true report was also spread that we were fixing up our log house and adding a back kitchen. We had been seen talking to a house framer.

CHORUS: Is there nobody here can think what she should be charged with?

JENNY: Charged I was to sweep out the school, because there was to be a wedding dance there that night and it was potato-picking time, in the fall of '67 and all our harvest was up at the barn or in stacks close by. Ah, everyone was coming to that dance because we would be there and the bishop in his flame-red robes would appear to say whether we could join the church of Biddulph. The bride has asked you to play, Will. That's been a wish he's had since boyhood.

The dance involves all the actors and extras if possible, maybe not. Go through several reels, particularly those involving MR. & MRS. DONNELLY dancing down Roman Line formations. Let audience just soak in the experience of watching them all dance – something black about it, something funny. Then the back of the stage goes red, or the windows of the hall go red. There is growing confusion and then voices saying –

CHORUS: Your barn's on fire, Donnelly.

A burning-barn model is carried down the line of dancers. We watch THE DONNELLYS looking down at this till it is almost out. WILLIAM breaks his fiddle, picks up a horseshoe.

JENNY: And what happened when my father and my brothers went to our well?

CHORUS: They found the pump broken.

JENNY: But there was a flowing spring, so there was still water to be had, but what did it say chalked on a board over the spring?

CHORUS: Over Donnelly's Spring it is written in chalk –

MRS. DONNELLY: No Water for Blackfeet.

This should be chalked on the floor of the stage. The CHORUS chants this around JENNY and other DONNELLYS in circles, then as suddenly kneel with their backs to JENNY. Pause. Scene with STUB and MR. DONNELLY set up.

STUB: Good morning, Jim. Bad news about your barn last night. I hear you're leaving us.

MR. DONNELLY: Why would I do that, Mr. Stub, when I've just bought some land across the road and need your notary stamp, so they tell me, on this piece of paper?

STUB: The Mulowney property.

CARPENTER: Are you giving up on the idea of making your house larger, Mr. Donnelly, or do you still want me to –

MR. DONNELLY: I'm not giving up anything, Mr. Thompson. Come over for tea this evening and we'll have a talk. I've got a house and a barn for you

to work at. And you can start right now by being witness for my signature. Where is it, Mr. Stub, that I make my mark? (*He puts on his spectacles.*)

STUB: Hold on a minute, Jim, before you sign. There was a man just in here swearing out an information against your eldest son – James Donnelly Junior.

MR. DONNELLY: Ah, they're still disputing my son's farm over there.

STUB: So you say, but this man says your boys are squatting on property that is his.

MR. DONNELLY: My son has to live somewhere, Mr. Stub, and although the land is a bit swampy, he went ahead and made a heavy investment in that property a full year before your informant was heard of.

STUB: My God, Donnelly, is it to start all over again? There'll be a fight and each one of your boys'll have seven sons – you shouldn't be buying land in this township, Jim, you should be selling it.

MR. DONNELLY: The way you talk, I'm doing the right thing. Seven times seven is forty-nine, they told me once, and we'll need all the property we can get to house the overflow. Why selling my land here would be just what those who burnt down my barn want.

STUB: Here's where you make your mark, Jim. (*pause*) There isn't enough land in this township for seven Donnellys, Jim.

As MR. DONNELLY is holding the pen, the company makes a big sound with sticks on the floor – the sound of his pen scratching.

JENNY: My father walked out of the store and down the roads of Biddulph.

CHORUS: But first he paused and flung back –

MR. DONNELLY: Gallagher has eight boys. Do you want to know, Mr. Stub, why we never hear you complaining of hordes of Gallaghers bursting this township at the seams? Because the Gallaghers vote Tory the way you do now. And I guess it's only Grits who mustn't multiply (*pause*) like myself. Andy Keefe, wherever are you rolling that barrel to?

KEEFE: Up the road apiece.

MR. DONNELLY: You heard about my barn?

KEEFE: I saw the glow in the sky.

MR. DONNELLY: Andy. What's in the barrel?

KEEFE: I'm shamed to admit it, Jim, but it's buttermilk.

MR. DONNELLY: Why be ashamed. Until they burnt it down you were running a beautiful cheese factory down there on the ruins of your tavern.

KEEFE: This is the one thing, Jim Donnelly, that's left behind from that beautiful cheese factory, the third occupation I tried since I came to this settlement of Cain. It alone did not catch fire.

MR. DONNELLY: Well, then, Andy, why are you rolling it along the road here and so far from home? Are you going to see somebody with it or –

KEEFE: I've got a ticket on the five o'clock train tonight, tickets for my mother and myself, tickets to Michigan and I'm just rolling this first down the road and down their lane and if they're not home I'm leaving it with a note saying: "You forgot to burn this."

MR. DONNELLY: And if they're home, Andy?

KEEFE: I've a pretty speech prepared, a speech of thanks prepared for leaving a Blackfoot at the very least a barrel of buttermilk from his cheese factory. (*sound*) There's Tom Cassleigh galloping after us. I think I'll roll my barrel down this side road so you can talk and keep him by you for it's his house I'm delivering this to, Jim.

> *CASSLEIGH drives up in a wagon and stops to address MR. DONNELLY. This wagon can be mimed with two actors supporting CASSLEIGH in a ladder, and one actor as horse.*

CASSLEIGH: Is it Jim Donnelly whose barn was burnt up last evening?

JENNY: What did my father reply?

MR. DONNELLY: Tom Cassleigh, it is that Donnelly whose barn was burnt up last night when he and his family were away at the wedding.

CASSLEIGH: We're at the crossroads, Jim, and there's empty roads for miles with nothing on them, no one coming toward us. Let's have a talk, Jim.

MR. DONNELLY: (*examining*) Tom, you've got yourself a new wagon. Sure, get down from it and we'll have a talk.

CASSLEIGH: New position in the world, Jim, new wagon.

MR. DONNELLY: (*lifting up horses' hooves*) New position?

CASSLEIGH: Haven't you heard? I'm now the first Catholic Justice of the Peace in this township.

MR. DONNELLY: Sure, Tom, the bench needs someone of your experience to tell us how it is from all the sides. Why, Tom, there's one new shoe on this horse – it's clean from the forge.

CASSLEIGH: What of that?

MR. DONNELLY: Well, as you know, that horse lost a shoe last night. By the light from our blazing granary my sons found it for you. (*Holding up the horseshoe, DONNELLY uses it as bait to lure CASSLEIGH down from his perch, play soccer with it, kick it under the wagon, etc.*)

CASSLEIGH: Donnelly, give that to me. Yes, we want you out of the township. Last month at haying time, we offered you good money for your miserable fifty acres, so see what happened, you Blackfoot face of a dog. You went into town to buy even more land today. (*Perhaps MR. DONNELLY has got the horseshoe on the end of CASSLEIGH's whip and dangles it up on the wagon, making CASSLEIGH jump.*) Do we have to make the offer again?

MR. DONNELLY: Oh, make the offer again, Tom, and see what we say.

CASSLEIGH: We say? Who's on your side?

MR. DONNELLY: A great many people with good hearts into them.

CASSLEIGH: We can change that. For one thing the next drainage dispute won't go your way, with me on the bench.

MR. DONNELLY: But, Tom, maybe we'll take your offer. Tell me what it is. We're at the crossroads. There's no one coming toward us for miles. Let us talk.

CASSLEIGH: (*panting*) Would you believe it. We're willing to buy you out at the same price we offered at haying time.

MR. DONNELLY: And when the Donnellys are gone the whole line will be yours, won't it? No one else to stand up to you or stand up to Mr. Stub. There's a thing I said in Ireland once that perhaps you heard.

CASSLEIGH: We let you go then, Donnelly, but fathers swore sons to follow you and show you up for the Blackfoot be-by-yourself you were that night.

MR. DONNELLY: I said something that night and I'll say it again.

CASSLEIGH: Donnelly, there's one more turn. (*pause*) Come and join us again, Jim. We can use your seven sons. Don't count on your Protestant friends. It could have been Stub who burnt you out. They use you, Jim, don't you see? Already your sons are blamed for things they do to us. And when we do things to them we're spreading the word it's you.

MR. DONNELLY: (*visibly affected by this, he throws the horseshoe under the wagon*) You damn weasel, sneaking in and out behind the wheels of your cart. Yes, let me out of Biddulph.

CASSLEIGH: (*silky*) We'll let you out of Biddulph, Jim. Follow your other Blackfoot friend to Michigan if you like.

Pause.

MR. DONNELLY: No, this is a new country we live in. It's not back in the old country we're living. Mrs. Donnelly and myself are free to do as we please. No one has to be afraid of secret societies, secret people. We're not in Ireland, do you hear, Tom Cassleigh?

DONNELLY is now after CASSLEIGH.

CASSLEIGH: In the daytime, Jim. But at night – confess, you dream your dream you are back under Keeper's Hill and the Whitefeet knock on your door to ask you some questions.

MR. DONNELLY: No.

CASSLEIGH: This is your last chance then. Get out. You killed one of us and you must pay in exile or kind.

JENNY: But in crawling under the wagon after the horseshoe my father had thrown there, Mr. Cassleigh in reaching for it jammed his shoulder in the spokes of his wagon wheel, his horses moved a bit and he was pinned.

MR. DONNELLY: Aye, I killed, shure, I killed – fighting for my name and my family and my land in hot blood. On this very road down at the tracks you killed – by cold proxy. Having myself seven sons and a girl, I ask you what children have you? What have you got between your legs, Cassleigh – a knife? And you're afraid of us. (*searching around for a stick*) You're so afraid of not having that horseshoe you've got yourself stuck beneath your own wagon, haven't you? My wife, Tom, is the only person in this settlement who ever stood up to you. She stopped you from cutting up Donegan and until she's afraid and wants to leave, I'm not either. Now, I'll beat your horses with this stick and

they'll gallop off with your face down in the gravel. (*Once he finds the stick, some gesture with it parallels the stick action in the scene with FARL.*)

CASSLEIGH: Donnelly!

The horses shift, but CASSLEIGH is still trapped.

MR. DONNELLY: Hush. Not so loud or they'll bolt. There, there, my beauties. Why you caught your arm trying to reach for the horseshoe. Here I'll put it a bit closer. I'll jam it right into your mouth, Cassleigh. Bite on to it, there. (*He frees him and pushes him up onto his wagon.*) Did you think, Cassleigh, my boy, that after being away from my land for seven years I was going to run away from it because you faction of sneaks said so? Look at this road. (*scooping up gravel*) This part of the road your grand new cart rolls on I was the first path master of. I built this road before you were ever heard of or the Fat Woman and her husband who got half our farm away from us. Before Stub drove out the Africans and you killed the Englishman, I helped make this road with Andy Keefe who you've finally chased out, to your shame. Well, Tom, there's some horse dung. I didn't put that in my road, but have it anyhow. You drove out Donegan, but you'll never get Donnelly's oak tree nor drive out his wife. Hold tight to your seat. Here, take the reins, because I'm going to larrup your horses one great larrup to show their master who's the master of this road. (*whack*) You ask me to kneel, do you? And swear? (*He throws stones after the retreating wagon.*) Donnellys don't kneel.

CHORUS: Where is your father, Will?

JENNY: A dozen years after this, a mob led by Tom Cassleigh – and by this time he had turned nearly everyone against us – at night, this mob broke into my father's house, clubbed them to death and then burnt the house down over my mother and father's heads. (*She is looking directly through ladder rungs at CASSLEIGH.*)

CHORUS: Boys, how old are you now?

JENNY: Two of us were old enough to see what had happened. Patrick left when he married, so did I. Old enough, coward enough, I mean. We could see that we could never join that church that the bishop had finally come to with fire for mitre and a torch for a crook and had not just slapped us all lightly on either cheek as token for the sufferings we must endure as followers of Jesus. No, the old ruffian had knocked us on the floor, to the floor, and kicked us with his hooved boot and punched us with his thistle mitts and said, "Get the hell out, you bugger Donnellys. No water for you, but we've fire."

CHORUS: Why was I created lame?

JENNY: Let me think about the answer to that one, Will. Is it –

Distribute this speech among the women; some men join in later.

CHORUS: Why was I a Donnelly?

JENNY: Because from the courts of heaven, when you're there, you will see that however the ladders and sticks and stones caught you and bruised you and smashed you, and the bakers and brewers forced you to work for them for nothing, from the eye of God in which you will someday walk you will see (*use ladders held up and moved back and forth by ALL THE CAST*) that once, long before you were born (*sometimes together with CHORUS, sometimes solo*) you chose to be a Donnelly and laughed at what it would mean, the proud woman put to milking cows, the genius trotting around with a stallion, the old sword rusted into a turnip knife. You laughed and lay down with your fate like a bride, even the miserable fire of it. So that I am proud to be a Donnelly against all the contempt of the world. I am proud that my mother confirmed my brother in the forest with the fiddle, long before the bishop and the friar could get hold of him, and I wish now I had shared my mother's fate beside her.

(*solo*) But, oh, still would it have been different. I loved my mother and I nearly saved her even three days before they burnt her with their coal oil.

Because you were tall; you were different / and you weren't afraid, that is why they burnt you first with their tongues / then with their kerosene.

Train whistle.

JENNY: And there were other times I tried and there was this dream about the time I tried and was to try. And the dream I am going to show you repeats itself to me like a creed I have learned I cannot tell when.

Barking of a dog. MR. & MRS. DONNELLY appear very neatly dressed as for a journey, or like figures in a legend.

JENNY: I dream that I've come up to visit the farm, my mother and father are all alone, the boys are all away, and I persuade them to leave with me. Before something happens. Good. Because if they

leave, then the boys can leave. But if they stay, then the boys have to fight for their parents and their work all the time. There's a train we have tickets for and – it stops at the crossing near Andy Keefe's tavern. We have lots of time, except –

MR. DONNELLY: Jenny, we can't leave. The little dog you sent us for a present. Where is he? (*whistles*) The devil a dog is he. He doesn't seem to want to come with us.

JENNY: We spent five minutes catching the dog.

Train whistle.

JENNY: And we start walking down the road, when my mother looks back.

Raise the clothesline of shirts here.

MRS. DONNELLY: Jenny, the boys' shirts are all left out on the line. I was sure we took them in and it's going to rain. (*barking*)

MRS. DONNELLY folds up the clothesline.

JENNY: So we take in the shirts, but the little dog I gave them –

MRS. DONNELLY: No, no, Jenny. There's lots of time. The train will wait. Now you watch, Mr. Donnelly. He'll come to me. He likes a piece of bread. Now there. Hold on to him this time, Jim.

The shirts appear on the line again.

JENNY: I knew it to be a dream even in the dream because there was still time to catch the train but – there they were on the line again. "Mother, come anyhow. We'll wait at the station for the next train."

MR. DONNELLY: (*helping his wife take in the shirts*) Your mother's bringing her sons into the house out of the rain. Will our daughter not come in as well?

JENNY: (*kneeling*) Mother – Father – you've changed your minds about leaving then?

MRS. DONNELLY: About leaving – oh yes, Jenny.

MR. DONNELLY: We're not to buy the farm in Michigan after all, Jenny. Wait till next year and this wheat the boys have sown is harvested.

MRS. DONNELLY: Jenny, your father and I will never leave Biddulph.

The parents stand watching JENNY. Singing the "Barley Corn Ballad," the cast make a pile of sticks and a pile of stones on the stage and leave them.

END

GEORGE F. WALKER

(b. 1947)

In the 1970s, when many Canadian playwrights were busy examining the Canadian character and family, the country's regional and national history, and the experiences and meanings of being Canadian, George F. Walker's gaze was elsewhere. Avoiding the subjects and styles of the Canadian theatrical mainstream, Walker staked out his own distinctive territory, drawing from the generic fringes of present-day popular culture (cartoons, film noir) and the revenge tragedy and gothic melodrama of the past. Even as his plays grew steadily more naturalistic and domestic in the 1980s and '90s, they remained peopled with obsessive characters living in extremity and given to philosophical musings about the need to wrench order out of chaos. Walker's work exists, he has said, along "that fine line between the serious and the comic." No play of his occupies that black-comic territory with greater stylishness or command than *Zastrozzi*.

Walker grew up in the working-class east end of Toronto. He was driving taxi in 1970 (so the story goes) when he saw a flyer soliciting scripts for Ken Gass's new Factory Theatre Lab. The play he submitted, *Prince of Naples*, was his first attempt at writing drama, and when he attended its opening in 1971, it was only the second play he had ever seen. Despite Walker's inexperience, Gass made him resident playwright from 1971–76, an invaluable apprenticeship and the start of an enduring association that has seen most of Walker's plays premiere at the Factory.

Prince of Naples and *Ambush at Tether's End* (1971) were absurdist exercises, derivative of Ionesco and Beckett. With *Sacktown Rag* (1972) and *Bagdad Saloon* (1973), Walker began to find his own voice, planting increasingly exotic landscapes of the mind with pop icons like Gary Cooper and Gertrude Stein. This phase of his work climaxed with *Beyond Mozambique* (1974) and *Ramona and the White Slaves* (1976). The former features a B-movie jungle locale populated by a drug-addicted priest, a disgraced Mountie, a porn-film starlet, and a demonic Nazi doctor whose wife thinks she is Olga in Chekhov's *Three Sisters*. *Ramona*, a murder mystery-cum-opium dream that marked Walker's directing debut, takes place in a Hong Kong brothel in 1919.

Walker took his next three plays to Toronto Free Theatre. *Gossip* (1977), *Zastrozzi* (1977), and *Filthy Rich* (1979) were less obscure, more accessible, and more popular than his previous work. Indebted to Humphrey Bogart and Raymond Chandler, *Gossip* and *Filthy Rich* were the first of his plays in film-noir style. Along with *The Art of War* (1983), they were published under the title *The Power Plays* (1986), featuring a character named Tyrone Power as a cynical, shabby investigative reporter or private eye, reluctantly involved in sorting out political intrigue and murder. Related in theme and mood is the Floyd S. Chalmers Canadian Play Award–winning *Theatre of the Film Noir* (1981), a bizarre murder mystery set in wartime Paris.

Exotic locales feature prominently in *Rumours of Our Death* (1980), an antiwar parable directed by Walker as a rock musical, and *Science and Madness* (1982), a turn-of-the-century gothic melodrama. But Walker increasingly focused his attention on the modern city he had explored in the first two Power plays. *Criminals in Love*, winner of the 1984 Governor General's Literary Award; *Better Living* (1986); and *Beautiful City* (1987) were published as *The East End Plays* (1988), this time transparently the east end of Toronto itself. The nihilism of Walker's earlier work gives way in these political comedies to tenuous hope for a life of simple happiness in a city salvaged from the powerful and greedy.

Love and Anger (1989) and *Escape from Happiness* (1991), a sequel to *Better Living*, continue Walker's championing of women, the oppressed, and the marginal against the patriarchal centre. These two Chalmers Award–winning comedies have had critical and popular success across the United States as well as Canada. But the play that first cemented Walker's reputation outside Canada was *Nothing Sacred* (1988), his adaptation of Turgenev's 1862 novel, *Fathers and Sons*. Set in pre-revolutionary Russia, it won a batch of major Canadian theatre awards and became so popular among American regional theatres that the *Los Angeles Times* named it play of the year. In 1993, Walker wrote *Tough!* for Vancouver's Green Thumb Theatre, a comedy about sex and gender relations among three young people.

After taking time off from theatre to write TV scripts for *The News-room* and *Due South*, Walker returned in triumph to his first theatrical home. Having nearly folded, Toronto's Factory Theatre was once more under the artistic directorship of Ken Gass, who presented Walker's six new one-act plays, all set in the same shabby motel room. Running the gamut from bitter drama to wacky comedy, *Suburban Motel* (1997–98) played in repertory format, two plays a night, directed by Walker himself. It was a major success, winning multiple Chalmers and Dora Awards and acclaim for subsequent productions in Montreal, Vancouver, and elsewhere. Walker also wrote the screenplay for its 2006 film adaptation, *Niagara Motel*.

He rang in the millennium with *Heaven* (2000), a bitter ethical-revenge comedy whose characters come back from the dead, premiered by Toronto's Canadian Stage. Since then, Walker has worked primarily in television, co-writing (with Dani Romain) and producing series very much in sync with the themes of his later plays: *This Is Wonderland* (2004–05) chronicles the law and disorder of the Canadian legal system with its victims and minions in a Toronto court; *The Line* (2008) is a gritty cop show; and *Living in Your Car* (2010) looks at corporate corruption and the urban underclass. But he hasn't forsaken the theatre. *And So It Goes* (Factory, 2010) concerns an unemployed middle-class couple, their schizophrenic daughter, and the ghost of Kurt Vonnegut. *King of Thieves*, adapted from the eighteenth-century classic *The Beggar's Opera*, premiered at Stratford in 2010, commissioned by Festival artistic director Des McAnuff, Walker's old friend from the Toronto alternate theatre scene of the 1970s.

Widely produced domestically and internationally, *Zastrozzi* was Walker's most popular play in that era and has remained so. It was produced by Joseph Papp for the New York Shakespeare Festival in 1982 at the end of Walker's year as playwright-in-residence there. Walker himself directed an acclaimed Toronto revival in 1987, and its 2009 remount was a major success at Stratford. Walker's personal successes include his appointment as the National Theatre School of Canada's first resident playwright in 1991, the Order of Canada in 2006, and the Governor General's Performing Arts Award for Lifetime Achievement in 2009.

Zastrozzi is prototypical 1970s Walker. Trying to assert order or impose meaning in the face of chaos, his early protagonists come in three versions. First is the artist who dreams up his own reality without much success, as in the "cartoon" plays *Sacktown Rag* and *Bagdad Saloon*. Verezzi is Walker's portrait of the artist as narcissist, a silly man who believes himself the messenger of God. Second is the justicer: the detective-heroes of *Ramona* and the film-noir plays who specialize in making things clear and putting them right. Like them, Victor is "an ordinary man" obsessed with balance and committed to justice, playing superego to Verezzi's ego. In Walker's later plays, "ordinary" men and women will increasingly occupy centre stage. But in *Zastrozzi*, Victor is merely a foil for the much more potent forces of darkness embodied in the third of Walker's protagonist types, the arch-criminal atheist. Assuming a metaphysical void in which, according to Zastrozzi, "life is a series of totally arbitrary and often meaningless events," he fills it with the unfettered self ("I am the absence of God," proclaims Rocco in *Beyond Mozambique*). Unlike the reformist protagonists of the later plays, Zastrozzi does not try to oppose the fundamental disorder he sees at the heart of things. Rather, he makes himself its agent. In a world defined by what Zastrozzi calls "negative spirituality," chaos is the natural condition, evil the most powerful motive force, and crime the only meaningful action. Rocco puts it succinctly: "there's something about committing crimes against humanity that puts you in touch with the purpose of the universe."

Unique among Walker's protagonists, Zastrozzi is both master criminal and justicer, the revenger in obsessive pursuit of Verezzi for the murder of his mother. But vengeance turns out to be only a secondary matter. Zastrozzi's real vocation is "making everyone answerable" to his own dark truth. As self-appointed "Master of Discipline," he is both judge and executioner. He singles out Verezzi for special attention because of Verezzi's facile religious optimism, artistic impressionism, and smile – the incarnation of everything "pleasantly vague" that Zastrozzi abhors about the modern age relentlessly dawning in 1893.

The play asks us to sympathize with this diabolical Don Quixote, despite his abhorrent crimes, possibly because he suffers the fate of all anachronisms unwilling to adapt in a time of transition. A giant among pygmies, Zastrozzi sees his "student" Bernardo as a mere thug without artistry or imagination. Weary, preoccupied, and dogged by nightmares in which he is overwhelmed by goodness and weakness, he begins increasingly to show cracks in his façade of invincibility, losing interest in satanic soulmate Matilda and falling in love with the purity and innocence of Julia. Surveying his victories at the end, he knows he is only marking time. He has won another battle but will surely lose the war.

None of this is as solemn as it sounds. Like all good comedy, *Zastrozzi* is at heart a serious play. At the same time its inflated Grand-Guignol style sends up an array of literary and theatrical sources: the baroque conventions of Jacobean revenge tragedy; Shelley's overheated gothic romance; the nihilism of Nietzschean philosophy; the stark dichotomies of melodrama; Artaud's Theatre of Cruelty. All these share a dramatic excessiveness that tends toward self-parody. *Zastrozzi* celebrates their excesses – and its own – with elegant deadpan humour and a self-conscious inversion of values that rings of Oscar Wilde and Joe Orton, but should ultimately be called Walkeresque.

Zastrozzi: The Master of Discipline

George F. Walker

Zastrozzi opened on November 2, 1977, at Toronto Free Theatre with the following cast:

ZASTROZZI	Stephen Markle
BERNARDO	George Buza
VEREZZI	Geoffrey Bowes
VICTOR	David Bolt
MATILDA	Diane D'Aquila
JULIA	Valerie Warburton

Directed by William Lane
Set Design by Doug Robinson
Lighting Design by Gerry Brown
Sound Design by Wes Wraggett
Fights Arranged by Patrick Crean

PLAYWRIGHT'S NOTE

This play is not an adaptation of Shelley's *Zastrozzi*. The playwright read a brief description of this novella in a biography of Shelley and that provided the inspiration for *Zastrozzi: The Master of Discipline*, something quite different from Shelley's work.

CHARACTERS

ZASTROZZI, *a master criminal, German*
BERNARDO, *his friend*
VEREZZI, *an Italian, an artist, a dreamer*
VICTOR, *his tutor*
MATILDA, *a gypsy, a raven-haired beauty*
JULIA, *an aristocrat, a fair-haired beauty*

SCENE

Europe. Probably Italy. The 1890s.

SET

It should combine a simplified version of a Piranesi drawing of a prison and the ruins of an ancient city. There are interesting and varied chambers within and the walls are crumbling. The tops of several trees are visible and weeds are growing out of the stones.

PROLOGUE

*Just before the storm. **BERNARDO** is looking up at the sky.*

BERNARDO: It is not a passion. Passion will eventually reward the soul. It is not an obsession. Obsession will sustain you for a lifetime. It is not an idea. An idea is the product of an ordinary mind. It is not an emotion. It cannot be purged. It is not greed or lust or hate or fear. It is none of those things. It is worse. The sky is swelling. And all those with timid natures had better go hide. It will conspire with the sky, and the air will explode, and the world will break apart and get thrown around like dust. But it is not the end of the world. It is easily worse. It is revenge.

*Blackout followed by a loud sustained volley of thunder. Deadly calm. **ZASTROZZI** lights an oil lamp and stands rigidly. His face is twisted with hatred.*

ZASTROZZI: You are looking at Zastrozzi. But that means very little. What means much more is that Zastrozzi is looking at you. Don't make a sound. Breathe quietly. He is easily annoyed. And when he is annoyed, he strikes. Look at his right arm. (*holding it up*) It wields the sword that has killed two hundred men. Watch the right arm constantly. Be very careful not to let it catch you unprepared. But while watching the right arm (*suddenly producing a dagger with his left hand*), do not forget the left arm. Because this man Zastrozzi has no weaknesses. No weakness at all. Remember that. Or he will have you. He will have you any way he wants you.

Lightning. A long pause. **ZASTROZZI**'s *face and body relax. He looks around almost peacefully. He smiles.*

I am Zastrozzi. The master criminal of all Europe. This is not a boast. It is information. I am to be feared for countless reasons. The obvious ones of strength and skill with any weapon. The less-obvious ones because of the quality of my mind. It is superb. It works in unique ways. And it is always working because I do not sleep. I do not sleep because if I do I have nightmares, and when you have a mind like mine, you have nightmares that could petrify the devil. Sometimes because my mind is so powerful I even have nightmares when I am awake, and because my mind is so powerful, I am able to split my consciousness in two and observe myself having my nightmare. This is not a trick. It is a phenomenon. I am having one now. I have this one often. In it, I am what I am. The force of darkness. The clear, sane voice of negative spirituality. Making everyone answerable to the only constant truth I understand. Mankind is weak. The world is ugly. The only way to save them from each other is to destroy them both. In this nightmare, I am accomplishing this with great efficiency. I am destroying cities. I am destroying countries. I am disturbing social patterns and upsetting established cultures. I am causing people such unspeakable misery that many of them are actually saving me the trouble by doing away with themselves. And even better, I am actually making them understand that this is, in fact, the way things should proceed. I am at the height of my power. I am lucid, calm, organized, and energetic. Then it happens. A group of people come out of the darkness with sickly smiles on their faces. They walk up to me and tell me they have discovered my weakness, a flaw in my power, and that I am finished as a force to be reckoned with. Then one of them reaches out and tickles me affectionately under my chin. I am furious. I pick him up and crack his spine on my knee then throw him to the ground. He dies immediately. And after he dies he turns his head to me and says, "Misery loves chaos. And chaos loves company." I look at him, and even though I know that the dead cannot speak, let alone make sense, I feel my brain turn to burning ashes and all my control run out of my body like mud and I scream at him like a maniac (*whispering*), "What does that mean."

Blackout.

SCENE 1

A vicious series of lightning bolts flash, illuminating the entire stage. A bedchamber. **ZASTROZZI** *is reeling about violently.*

ZASTROZZI: Where is the Italian Verezzi. Tell him I have come to send him to hell. Tell him that Zastrozzi is here. Tell him I am waiting. He can hide no more. He can run no farther. I am here. And I am staying. (*grabbing a flask of wine and drinking*) Ah, Jesus, this wine tastes like it was made by amateurs. I hate amateurs. Death to all of them. Remember that.

BERNARDO bursts into the chamber. ZASTROZZI throws a sabre at him like a spear. BERNARDO ducks. The two men look at each other.

BERNARDO: It's Bernardo.

ZASTROZZI: Step closer. The light is tricky.

BERNARDO: It *is* Bernardo, sir.

ZASTROZZI: Ah, Jesus! (*turning and violently ripping all the coverings from the bed*) I thought I saw an Italian to be killed.

BERNARDO: Not this one I hope. Please be more careful.

ZASTROZZI: Don't worry, Bernardo. Of all the Italians worthy of killing I am interested in only one. (*sitting on the bed*) But my mind is becoming clearer by the minute and unless I get some satisfaction I may come to the inevitable conclusion that all Italians are worthy of killing for one reason or another.

BERNARDO: Yes, I like your threats. They keep me alert.

ZASTROZZI: Learn to smile when you are being ironic. It might save your life some day.

BERNARDO: (*smiling*) The best advice is that of the best advised.

ZASTROZZI: Remind me to order you to say that again when I'm not preoccupied.

BERNARDO: It doesn't –

ZASTROZZI: Have you found him.

BERNARDO: He is here.

ZASTROZZI: Where.

BERNARDO: At least he was here. He has gone off into the countryside. But he is expected back.

ZASTROZZI: How soon.

BERNARDO: Eventually.

ZASTROZZI advances on BERNARDO.

BERNARDO: That is what I was told. And that is what I am reporting.

ZASTROZZI: Told by whom.

BERNARDO: The innkeeper where he stays.

ZASTROZZI: Then you were at his rooms?

BERNARDO: Yes.

ZASTROZZI: How do they smell. What do they look like. Describe them to me. No, wait, first, are you sure it is the same man. Verezzi the poet.

BERNARDO: Now Verezzi the painter.

ZASTROZZI: Yes, yes. And before that Verezzi the dramatist. And before that Verezzi the dancer. His vocation makes no difference. Always changing. Always pleasantly artistic. But the man himself, Bernardo. A description.

BERNARDO: The innkeeper described the same man.

ZASTROZZI: Even so. Possibly a coincidence. But the important things.

BERNARDO: Those as well.

ZASTROZZI: A religious man?

BERNARDO: Very.

ZASTROZZI: Always praying?

BERNARDO: Before and after every meal. Often during the meal. Occasionally throughout the meal.

ZASTROZZI: And the ladies. Does he have a way with them.

BERNARDO: Many ladies have visited him in his room. Most come back again.

ZASTROZZI: What about the smile. The smile that I see clearly in my head even though I have never met the man who wears it. That smile is an unnatural thing, Bernardo. Empty.

BERNARDO: "He smiles an annoying much of the time." I quote the innkeeper directly.

ZASTROZZI: Then it is him. It is Verezzi the artiste. The Christian. The great lover. The optimist. I will have him soon. Are you happy for me, my friend.

BERNARDO: I have watched you wanting him for a long time. I have grown fond of the force behind the search for revenge. I think I'll miss it.

ZASTROZZI: At first, I wanted him just for myself. For what he did to my mother. But what I have learned of this man, Verezzi, makes me want him for another reason. That smile, Bernardo, I will remove it from the earth. It is a dangerous thing.

It raises a bigger issue than revenge. (*repeating this last sentence in German [Es wirft ein größeres Problem als Rache]*)

BERNARDO: Is this a new development.

ZASTROZZI: Actually, it is still revenge. But in a larger sense. In fact, it is revenge in its true and original meaning. And, therefore, some other word is probably necessary. It is 1893 and language, like everything else, has become pleasantly vague.

BERNARDO: I'm not sure I understand.

ZASTROZZI: Naturally. Because if you did then there would be two of us and there is only need for one. No. Call it revenge, Bernardo. Tell everyone else to call it revenge. If it will make you happy I'll even call it revenge.

Blackout.

SCENE 2

The countryside, a light rain is falling. VEREZZI is sitting behind an easel, paintbrush in hand. VICTOR holds an umbrella over VEREZZI's head and examines the painting in silence for a while.

VICTOR: Always tell the truth. Except when under pressure.

VEREZZI: What does that mean.

VICTOR: How can you paint a German landscape when you have never been to Germany.

VEREZZI: My father was in Germany. He told me all about it.

VICTOR: That's silly. You present a false image.

VEREZZI: Perhaps. But my heart is in the right place.

VICTOR: Unsuspecting people will look at your art and think they see the truth.

VEREZZI: Perhaps my Germany is the real Germany. And if not, then perhaps it is what the real Germany should be.

VICTOR: What is that supposed to mean.

VEREZZI: I'm not quite sure. Yes, I am. Perhaps Germany is ugly. Or perhaps Germany is bland. What is the point of creating bland or ugly art.

VICTOR: To illustrate the truth.

VEREZZI: Art has nothing to do with truth.

VICTOR: Then what is its purpose.

VEREZZI: To enlighten.

VICTOR: How can you enlighten if you don't serve the truth.

VEREZZI: You enlighten by serving God.

VICTOR: Then God is not serving the truth.

VEREZZI: Is that a question or a statement.

VICTOR: Both.

VEREZZI: Then you are a heretic.

VICTOR: And you are a liar.

VEREZZI: A dreamer, Victor. A dreamer.

VICTOR: The same thing.

VEREZZI: Enough. I don't even remember asking your opinion.

VICTOR: If I waited to be asked you would never receive my criticism and, therefore, no education.

VEREZZI: You weren't hired as a tutor. You were hired as a servant.

VICTOR: That was before either of us realized how monumentally ignorant you are.

VEREZZI: Enough. What colours do you mix to make ochre.

VICTOR: Ochre is unnecessary.

VEREZZI: That hill should be shaded with ochre.

VICTOR: On some other planet perhaps. On earth it's green.

VEREZZI: Earth is boring.

VICTOR: Why don't you ask God to move you.

VEREZZI: Don't make fun of God.

VICTOR: I was making fun of Verezzi.

VEREZZI: The two are interchangeable.

VICTOR: That sounds slightly narcissistic to me.

VEREZZI: I am His messenger on earth.

VICTOR: What.

VEREZZI: (*a revelation*) I *am* His messenger on earth.

VICTOR: This is a new development. Until recently you were His servant.

VEREZZI: Through devotion and regular prayer, I have attained a new position.

VICTOR: Then God encourages linear growth.

VEREZZI: I beg your pardon.

VICTOR: When will you be made Messiah.

VEREZZI: Atheist. How do you sleep without fear.

VICTOR: A secret. Besides, I am not an atheist. I just have a more pragmatic relationship with God than you do.

VEREZZI: What is it.

VICTOR: It is based on reality, Verezzi. You wouldn't comprehend it.

VEREZZI: I should dismiss you. I think you mean to corrupt me.

VICTOR: Can I ask you a question.

VEREZZI: No.

VICTOR: Not even a sincere one?

VEREZZI: In all the time I've known you, you've never once been sincere on the subject of my religious experiences.

VICTOR: Be patient. At least I don't laugh in your face anymore.

VEREZZI: Ask your question.

VICTOR: How do you reconcile being God's messenger on earth with the fact that you find earth boring.

VEREZZI: That is my cross. I bear it.

VICTOR: (*sadly*) Yes. Of course you do. You probably do.

VEREZZI: Besides, I am an artist. Even if I was not a religious artist I would be dissatisfied. That is the nature of an artist.

VICTOR: That is the opinion of a very silly man.

VEREZZI: Enough. I have to finish.

VICTOR: When are we going back to the village.

VEREZZI: When I have completed my painting.

VICTOR: And what will you do with the painting.

VEREZZI: It contains His message. I'll give it to someone.

VICTOR: Not sell it?

VEREZZI: His message should not be sold. It's a gift. Besides I have no need of money.

VICTOR: That's because your father was very rich.

VEREZZI: Yes. So what.

VICTOR: I was just wondering how a messenger of God would get by if he weren't independently wealthy.

VEREZZI: You are a subversive.

VICTOR: And you are a saint.

VEREZZI: Oh. Thank you.

VICTOR: No. It wasn't a compliment.

Blackout.

SCENE 3

A dining chamber. Occasional thunder, lightning, and rain outside. MATILDA and ZASTROZZI are some distance apart preparing to fight. They cut the air with their sabres. On the table are the remnants of a meal. BERNARDO sits in a chair, munching a chicken leg, his legs on the table. He describes VEREZZI's room.

BERNARDO: The room smelled of lilacs, incense, and mint tea. This Verezzi is an orderly fellow for sure. Nothing about the room was haphazard. Everything was neat and clean. In fact, the place appeared to have been arranged by a geometrist, for all objects were placed at perfectly right angles to each other. And between the two halves of the room – one used for work and the other for play – there was a perfect symmetry.

ZASTROZZI: Then he has someone with him. A man like Verezzi is not capable of symmetry. (*pause*) Balance. A dangerous opponent in regulated combat. But get him in an alley or a dark street and you have him disoriented. Nevertheless, out of respect for his inclination, I'll cut him up into thirty-two pieces of equal size. Are you ready, Matilda.

MATILDA: First I want to make one thing clear. I do not suffer from rapier envy. I just like to fight.

MATILDA and ZASTROZZI cross swords and begin to fight. As they progress it becomes clear that MATILDA is very good even though ZASTROZZI is not trying very hard.

BERNARDO: There were several of his paintings in the room. For the most part he is a mediocre artist but occasionally he exhibits a certain flair. It's naive but it's there. One painting in particular caught my eye. An informal unrecognizable series of swirls and circles in white, off-white, and beige. He seems very fond of it himself. He has given it a title.

ZASTROZZI: What does he call it then.

BERNARDO: *God's Stomach.*

MATILDA: The man is a fool.

BERNARDO: I would tend to agree.

ZASTROZZI: Then how has he evaded us for three years.

BERNARDO: I've been thinking about that.

ZASTROZZI: Thinking?

BERNARDO: Perhaps he doesn't know we've been chasing him.

ZASTROZZI: Nonsense. He's a clever man.

BERNARDO: But surely there are none more clever than the guileless.

ZASTROZZI: Stop thinking, Bernardo. It causes you to have absurd poetic fantasies. I am clever. I am the most accomplished criminal in Europe. Matilda is clever. She is the most accomplished seductress in Europe. Do either of us seem guileless to you.

BERNARDO: No. But you, sir, are motivated by a strange and powerful external force and Matilda has certain physical assets which allow her activities a certain ease.

MATILDA: I also have a first-class mind, Bernardo, and it gives me self-confidence. But if I didn't and I heard that patronizing comment about my body, I would take off your head.

BERNARDO: If I ever have my head taken off, I hope you'll be the one who does it. But not with your sword. I would like you to use your teeth.

MATILDA: Are comments like that what you use to show sexual interest in someone.

BERNARDO: Excuse me. (*standing and starting off*)

MATILDA: Don't be shy, Bernardo. Are you being shy, Bernardo.

BERNARDO: If you wish.

MATILDA: Actually all I wish is that men in general could perform with the same intensity that they lust with.

BERNARDO: I might surprise you.

MATILDA: You might. But I think we both doubt that.

BERNARDO: Excuse me. I think I'll go visit the inn again. (*starting off again*) Oh, I forgot. Here is one of his drawings. I took it from his room.

ZASTROZZI: You stole it.

BERNARDO: Yes.

ZASTROZZI: Why.

BERNARDO: Zastrozzi asks why someone steals something. Zastrozzi, who has stolen more than any man alive.

ZASTROZZI: Put it back.

BERNARDO: Why.

ZASTROZZI: We are not thieves anymore.

BERNARDO: Then what are we.

ZASTROZZI: We are not thieves.

BERNARDO leaves.

MATILDA: I don't want to do this anymore. (*throwing down her sabre*) Let's make love.

ZASTROZZI: I'm preoccupied.

MATILDA: With what.

ZASTROZZI: The image of Verezzi's painting.

MATILDA: You didn't even look at it.

ZASTROZZI: I saw it in my head. It is a colourful pastoral. An impression of a landscape. Impressionism. Distortion.

MATILDA: Very interesting. Great material for preoccupation, I'm sure. But you were preoccupied the last time I came to you. And the time before that as well. We haven't made love in over a year.

ZASTROZZI: Then go somewhere else. Making love is not an accurate description of what we do anyway.

MATILDA: I realize that. I know what we do. We ravage each other. Nevertheless, I miss it. Don't you?

ZASTROZZI: No.

MATILDA: Zastrozzi is hollow. I have come three hundred miles just to be reminded once again that Zastrozzi is hollow.

ZASTROZZI: Drink. (*picking up a flask and drinking*)

MATILDA: Don't you ever get physically aroused anymore.

ZASTROZZI: No. All sexual desire left me the moment I realized I had a purpose in life.

MATILDA: So now you have a purpose. I thought you just wanted to make people suffer.

ZASTROZZI: Can't that be a purpose.

MATILDA: I don't know. But I do know it can't stop you from desiring me. There's something you're not telling me.

ZASTROZZI: Very well. I swore a vow of chastity.

MATILDA: To whom.

ZASTROZZI: The Emperor of Spain's mistress.

MATILDA: Nonsense. When would you have met her.

ZASTROZZI: When I robbed the Emperor's country estate. His mistress was there alone. One thing led to another and I raped her. Just as I was leaving she looked up and said, "I can live with this if you vow never to be intimate with another woman." I shrugged my shoulders, said, "All right," and left. (*MATILDA laughs.*) I knew you would understand.

MATILDA: I'm the only woman alive who could. We belong together. It would be delicious while it lasted. There's no one alive we couldn't victimize in one way or another. And when we're finally caught, we can go to hell together.

ZASTROZZI: No, not hell. Some place less specific. Atheists don't go to hell. They don't know where it is. The Christians invented it and the only decent thing they've done is to keep its whereabouts a secret to outsiders.

MATILDA: Then forget hell. Let's go to Africa instead.

ZASTROZZI: Later. I have things to do.

MATILDA: Ah, yes. This search for revenge on some God-obsessed Italian. You are letting it change your personality.

ZASTROZZI: He murdered my mother.

MATILDA: So find him. Then kill him. It's a simple matter. It should not be your purpose in life. Revenge is an interesting obsession but it isn't worthy of the powers of Zastrozzi.

ZASTROZZI: I know. But Verezzi represents something which must be destroyed. He gives people gifts and tells them they are from God. Do you realize the damage that someone like that can do.

MATILDA: Damage to what. (*ZASTROZZI makes a dismissive gesture.*) I don't understand.

ZASTROZZI: I don't need your understanding.

MATILDA: Yes. I know that. I haven't been coming to you all these years because I think you need anything from me. It's that I need something from you.

ZASTROZZI: Really. What.

MATILDA: The whore sleeps with the devil so she can feel like a virgin?

ZASTROZZI: Something like that. Yes. What a comfortable little solution to guilt. Except that your devil is unpredictable.

ZASTROZZI hits MATILDA and knocks her down.

ZASTROZZI: Get out.

MATILDA: Let me stay.

ZASTROZZI: Get out. Or your devil might slit your throat just to show the flaw in your argument.

MATILDA: If I crawl across to you and beg, will you let me stay.

ZASTROZZI looks at her silently for a moment.

ZASTROZZI: First, let's see how you crawl.

MATILDA crawls slowly over to him, wraps her arms around his legs, and rests her head on his boot.

MATILDA: Let me stay. Do what you have to. Go send this Italian Verezzi to hell and then let me stay forever.

ZASTROZZI: Shush. (*thinking, breaking away from her, and pacing slowly*) Send this Verezzi to hell. (*chuckling*) Yes.

ZASTROZZI paces some more, stops, and looks at MATILDA.

ZASTROZZI: I will. He is a Christian. He can go to hell. Or at least he thinks he can. And the pain. Such excruciating pain. Much, much more than if I were to merely kill him. He must be made to send himself in his mind to hell. By killing himself. The most direct route to hell is by suicide. Over a woman. The most desirable woman in the world. She will entrap him then destroy him. And his destruction will be exquisitely painful and it will appear to everyone to have happened naturally as if it were meant to be. (*pause*) You will do this for me, won't you, Matilda.

MATILDA looks at him. Stands. Straightens her clothes.

MATILDA: First, let's see how you crawl.

They stare at each other. Finally, ZASTROZZI gets down and slowly crawls over to her. He wraps his arms around her legs.

ZASTROZZI: Entrap him. Then destroy him.

BERNARDO walks in, sees them, smiles.

BERNARDO: He's back.

Blackout.

SCENE 4

Street scene. A light rain is falling. JULIA is sitting on some steps, holding an umbrella above her head. VEREZZI is standing centre stage, looking up, smiling, hitting himself on the head with both his hands, and moving about delicately.

VEREZZI: I'm so happy. Life has once again given me the giggles. What a surprise. In the ruins of an ancient city, on a foul, damp day in spring, the soggy young artist, walking aimlessly about in search of something to draw, meets the most beautiful and sensitive woman alive.

JULIA: You are kind. But you flatter me.

VEREZZI: Not yet. But I will. I am growing silly with delight. (*reeling around a few times*)

JULIA: Good heavens. What's wrong with you. Why can't you just come sit down and have a pleasant conversation.

VEREZZI: You want me to be sober.

JULIA: If you'd just stay still for a moment. We only met a minute ago. All we said to each other was hello. And you started prancing about and giggling.

VEREZZI: Yes. A less perceptive person would think I was insane.

JULIA: Well, you might be insane for all I know. Can't you even introduce yourself.

VEREZZI: (*sobering*) Yes. Of course. (*walking over*) I am Verezzi.

JULIA: My name is Julia.

VEREZZI: (*spinning around*) Of course it is! Could it be anything else. You are spectacular and your name is a song.

JULIA: Sir. You will sit down. You will stop talking like a frenzied poetic moron and will make rational conversation. It can be pleasant conversation. It can even be romantic conversation. But it will be rational or I am leaving.

VEREZZI: (*sitting*) I am Verezzi.

JULIA: Yes, you've said that.

VEREZZI: And you are Julia.

JULIA: And I have said that.

VEREZZI: Will you marry me.

JULIA: No.

VEREZZI: I am depressed.

JULIA: How old are you.

VEREZZI: Twenty-five.

JULIA: You have the emotions of a ten-year-old.

VEREZZI: That is often the case with a visionary.

JULIA: So you have visions.

VEREZZI: (*a revelation*) I am a visionary.

JULIA: So you ... have visions.

VEREZZI: Yes. But don't tell anyone. I'm not ready to meet my followers yet.

JULIA: Visions of what nature.

VEREZZI: Religious.

JULIA: Visions of God?

VEREZZI: Of God. By God. For God. Through God.

VEREZZI smiles. JULIA just stares silently at him for a while.

JULIA: You are the first visionary I have met. At least the first one who has told me that he was one.

VEREZZI: I hope you're not thinking I'm bragging.

JULIA: No, that's not what I'm thinking.

VEREZZI: Good. Because I worked hard to be what I am. At first I was just a person, then a religious person, then a servant of God, then a messenger of God.

JULIA: And now a visionary.

VEREZZI: Yes.

JULIA: When did you have your first vision.

VEREZZI: I haven't had one yet.

JULIA: I don't understand.

VEREZZI: Neither do I. I suppose I'll just have to be patient.

Pause.

JULIA: But you told me you had visions. Of God. By God. For God et cetera.

VEREZZI: Yes. I was speaking hypothetically.

JULIA: I'm sorry. But I don't think that makes any sense.

VEREZZI: No. Then I was speaking metaphorically.

JULIA: That neither.

VEREZZI: Symbolically.

JULIA: No.

VEREZZI: Will you marry me.

JULIA: No. (*standing*)

VEREZZI: Where are you going.

JULIA: Home.

VEREZZI: May I call on you.

JULIA: No. (*exiting*)

VEREZZI: I love her. She is just the right kind of woman for me. She has no imagination and she takes her religion very seriously. God is creating a balance.

VICTOR enters.

VICTOR: Who was that woman.

VEREZZI: Her name is Julia. She lives here. She is very bright. She is an aristocrat. She thinks I'm insane. I gave her that impression intentionally by making fun of religious states of mind. It was a test. She passed. I'm going to marry her.

VICTOR: Shut up.

VEREZZI: I won't shut up. You are my servant. You shut up.

VICTOR: You're getting worse daily. You're almost insensate. There is danger here and you can't appreciate it.

VEREZZI: There is no danger here. There is only love here.

VICTOR: You are insane.

VEREZZI: Who says so.

VICTOR: I do.

VEREZZI: You are my servant. You are not to say I am insane. I say you are insane. Yes, Victor, you are insane. So there.

VICTOR: Shut up.

VEREZZI: You shut up.

VICTOR grabs VEREZZI by the throat and shakes him.

VICTOR: Shut up, shut up, shut up.

VEREZZI raises a hand and VICTOR lets him go.

VICTOR: Now are you ready to listen to me.

VEREZZI: You hurt me.

VICTOR: I'm sorry. You were in a daze.

VEREZZI: I was?

VICTOR: Yes. How do you feel now.

VEREZZI: My throat hurts.

VICTOR: But are you sensible.

VEREZZI: Of course.

VICTOR: I found out from the innkeeper that someone has been making inquiries about you. Do you know what that means.

VEREZZI: Yes. My followers are beginning to gather.

VICTOR: Shut up. You don't have any followers.

VEREZZI: As of last count, my followers numbered 454. I can describe each of them to you in detail.

VICTOR: You've hallucinated every one of them. The man making inquiries about you was probably a friend of that man Zastrozzi.

VEREZZI: Zastrozzi. Zastrozzi, the German? The master criminal? The man who seeks revenge upon me?

VICTOR: Yes.

VEREZZI: He does not exist! He is a phantom of your mind. For three years, you have been telling me I have been hunted by Zastrozzi and yet I have never seen him.

VICTOR: Because I have kept us ahead of him. I have evaded him.

VEREZZI: As only you could. Because he is a phantom of your mind.

VICTOR: He was making inquiries about you.

VEREZZI: That was one of my followers.

VICTOR: Your followers do not exist. It was Zastrozzi.

VEREZZI: Zastrozzi does not exist! I have 454 followers. Follower number one is short and bald. Follower number two is tall with a beard. Follower number three is ...

VICTOR: Shut up. You are insane. And you grow worse every day. But I promised your father I would take care of you, so I will.

VEREZZI: You didn't know my father. I hired you. As a servant. You must be feverish in your brain. But I will save you. You are a challenge.

VICTOR: Very well. But let's move on. You can save me at some other place.

VEREZZI: I can't. The birds are here.

VICTOR: I beg your pardon.

VEREZZI: Look up. What do you see.

VICTOR: A flock of birds.

VEREZZI: Yes. They are the sign.

VICTOR: What sign.

VEREZZI: The one my followers will be able to see in order to know where I am.

VICTOR: I don't believe this.

VEREZZI: Try. Please.

VICTOR: I will not.

VEREZZI: Very well. But when my followers arrive you're going to feel very out of place. They all believe it.

VICTOR gestures in disgust and leaves. VEREZZI drifts off in his mind.

VEREZZI: Follower number 54 is of medium height but he limps. Follower number 101 is blind. Follower number 262 is ... a Persian immigrant.

BERNARDO comes on, dragging MATILDA by the hair. He is carrying a whip.

BERNARDO: Here's a nice quiet place for a beating. Strip to the waist.

MATILDA: No, sir. Please forgive me. I won't do it again.

BERNARDO: For sure you won't. Not after this.

MATILDA tries to run away. He intercepts and throws her down. VEREZZI raises his hand.

VEREZZI: Excuse me.

BERNARDO: What do you want.

VEREZZI: A little human kindness, sir.

BERNARDO: Mind your own business.

BERNARDO raises the whip. VEREZZI approaches them.

VEREZZI: Leave her alone.

BERNARDO: You have been warned. (*drawing his sabre*) Defend yourself.

VEREZZI: Do I look like an angel of God, sir.

BERNARDO: No.

VEREZZI: Then you are in for a big surprise.

VEREZZI draws his sabre. Swishes it about. Trying to impress BERNARDO with his style. BERNARDO laughs. They fight. BERNARDO allows himself to be disarmed. VEREZZI has his sabre at BERNARDO's chest. Suddenly, VEREZZI drifts off in his mind.

VEREZZI: No. This is violence, isn't it. I shouldn't be doing this. This is wrong. I am an artist. I am in touch with Him.

BERNARDO slips away. MATILDA goes to VEREZZI and seductively runs her fingers through his hair.

MATILDA: Thank you.

VEREZZI: (*looking up*) You're welcome.

MATILDA: No. Thank you very, very much.

MATILDA smiles. VEREZZI smiles.

Blackout.

SCENE 5

*Evening. A secluded place. **ZASTROZZI** is sitting inert. **JULIA** comes on with a picnic basket.*

JULIA: Excuse me, sir. But do you mind if I sit here.

***ZASTROZZI** slowly turns toward her and looks at her impassively for a moment.*

ZASTROZZI: It would be best if you did not.

JULIA: But I always come here at this time on this particular day of the week to have my picnic.

ZASTROZZI: Without fail?

JULIA: Yes.

ZASTROZZI: Well, today you have been broken of a very silly habit. Move on.

JULIA: Why should I.

ZASTROZZI: I want to be alone.

JULIA: Then you move on.

ZASTROZZI: I want to be alone. And I want to be alone exactly where I am.

JULIA: Well, today you are not going to get what you want. I am sitting and I am eating.

***JULIA** eats and **ZASTROZZI** watches her for a moment.*

ZASTROZZI: You are an only child from a very wealthy family.

JULIA: Perhaps.

ZASTROZZI: You don't have a worry in the world.

JULIA: Perhaps not.

ZASTROZZI: You don't have a thought in your head.

JULIA: I have one or two.

ZASTROZZI: And you are a virgin. (*pause*) Well, are you or are you not a virgin.

JULIA: Why. Are you looking for one.

ZASTROZZI: Go away.

JULIA: In good time. Perhaps when I'm finished eating this piece of cheese. Perhaps after I eat my apple. In good time.

Pause.

ZASTROZZI: Do you know who I am.

JULIA: No. Who are you.

ZASTROZZI: I am the man who is going to take away your virginity.

JULIA: Many have tried. All have failed. It will never be taken away. It will be given. In good time.

ZASTROZZI: Yes. Before you eat your apple to be exact.

JULIA: I'll scream.

ZASTROZZI: If you scream, it will be the last sound you ever hear.

JULIA: Then I'll go limp. You won't enjoy it.

ZASTROZZI: It's not important that I enjoy it. It's important that you enjoy it.

JULIA: Impossible.

ZASTROZZI: Look at me.

JULIA: No. I don't think I will.

ZASTROZZI: Why not. Don't you find me attractive.

JULIA: That's not the point. You've threatened to rape me.

ZASTROZZI: Surely you knew I was joking.

JULIA: You didn't sound like you were joking.

ZASTROZZI: I was only trying to hide the embarrassing truth.

JULIA: And what might that be.

ZASTROZZI: That, like so many other men, I have admired you from a distance and could never gather the courage to approach you.

JULIA: So you waited here knowing I was coming on this particular day.

ZASTROZZI: Yes.

JULIA: And you adopted an aggressive attitude to disguise your true and romantic feelings for me.

ZASTROZZI: Yes.

JULIA: Yes. I can believe that. Men have done sillier things for me. Do you still want me to look at you.

ZASTROZZI: No. I'm too embarrassed.

JULIA: I understand.

ZASTROZZI: Just look ahead.

JULIA: If you wish.

Pause.

ZASTROZZI: I hope you don't mind that I'm doing this.

JULIA: What.

ZASTROZZI: Running my hand through your hair.

***ZASTROZZI** does nothing. He will do nothing.*

JULIA: Oh. I don't feel anything.

ZASTROZZI: I am running my hand through your hair. Very softly.

JULIA: Well, I guess it's all right.

ZASTROZZI: You have a very soft neck.

JULIA: Are you touching my neck. (*looking at him*)

ZASTROZZI: Please just look ahead. (*looking at her*) Please.

JULIA: All right. (*turning away*)

ZASTROZZI: Very soft neck. Very soft shoulders, too. And if I may just lower my hand a little.

JULIA: Please, sir.

ZASTROZZI: I'm sorry you spoke too late. Yes, your breast is also soft. But firm.

JULIA: Please. No one has ever –

ZASTROZZI: Both breasts so wonderfully firm. And my face so nice against your neck. If I could just reach down.

JULIA: No, sir –

ZASTROZZI: You should have said so earlier. Your stomach. My God. This is such a wonderful feeling, isn't it.

JULIA: I'm not quite –

ZASTROZZI: That's it. Lean back a little.

JULIA: I shouldn't be doing this.

JULIA does nothing. She will do nothing.

ZASTROZZI: Back a little farther. Lie down.

JULIA: All the way?

ZASTROZZI: Yes.

JULIA: But –

ZASTROZZI: Lie down.

JULIA: Like this?

ZASTROZZI: Yes.

JULIA: What are you doing now.

ZASTROZZI: Kissing you on your mouth.

Pause.

JULIA: Yes. And now?

Pause.

ZASTROZZI: Your breasts.

Pause.

JULIA: Yes. And now?

Pause.

ZASTROZZI: Relax.

Pause.

JULIA: Yes.

Blackout.

SCENE 6

The sky is rumbling again. ZASTROZZI is drunk. He is at the doorway of his bedchamber. He drinks the last of the wine in his flask and throws it on the floor.

ZASTROZZI: Where is my wine. I called for that wine an hour ago. I warn you it is in your best interest to keep me drunk. I am at my mellowest when drunk. Innkeeper!

A VOICE: Coming, sir.

ZASTROZZI grunts. He goes and sits in a chair near the bed, picks up a book, reads, grunts, grunts louder, throws the book across the room.

ZASTROZZI: Liar! (*standing, pacing*) They're all liars. Why do I read books. What is this new age of optimism they're all talking about. It's a lie sponsored by the Church and the government to give the people false hope. The people. I care less about the people than I do about the Church or the government. Then what do you care about sin. I care that I should not ask myself questions like that. I care to be dumb and without care. I care that I should not ask myself questions like that ever again. (*sitting, pausing*) Sad. (*standing*) Wine! (*sitting*) Sad.

VICTOR comes in with the wine.

ZASTROZZI: Who are you.

VICTOR: I own this inn.

ZASTROZZI: No. I've met the owner.

VICTOR: The former owner. I won it from him in a card game last night.

ZASTROZZI: Congratulations. Put the wine down and get out.

VICTOR: (*putting the wine down*) You are the great Zastrozzi, aren't you.

ZASTROZZI: I am a lodger in your inn.

VICTOR: Are you ashamed of being Zastrozzi.

ZASTROZZI: If you were to die in the near future would many people attend your funeral.

VICTOR: No.

ZASTROZZI: Then save yourself the embarrassment. Get out.

VICTOR: I heard that Zastrozzi once passed through Paris like the plague. Leaving the aristocracy nearly bankrupt, their daughters all defiled and diseased, the police in chaos and the museums ransacked. And all because, it is said, he took a dislike to the popular French taste in art.

ZASTROZZI: A slight exaggeration. He took a dislike to a certain aristocratic artist who happened to have a very willing daughter and one painting in one museum.

VICTOR: And did Zastrozzi kill the artist, rape his daughter, and destroy the painting.

ZASTROZZI: The daughter was not touched. She had syphilis. Probably given to her by the father. The painting was not worth destroying. It was just removed from the illustrious company it had no right to be with. (*taking a drink*)

VICTOR: But the artist was killed.

ZASTROZZI: Yes. Certainly.

VICTOR: Why.

ZASTROZZI: To prove that even artists must answer to somebody.

VICTOR: And what has Zastrozzi come to this obscure place to prove.

ZASTROZZI: Zastrozzi is starting some new endeavour. He is going to murder only innkeepers for a year.

VICTOR: I am not afraid of you.

ZASTROZZI: Then you are stupid. (*pause*) And you are not an innkeeper.

VICTOR: They say that all Europe has no more cause to fear Zastrozzi. They say that for three years he has been single-minded in a search for revenge on one man and that all the rest of Europe has been untouched.

ZASTROZZI: They think and say only what Zastrozzi wants them to think and say.

VICTOR: They also say that any man can cross him, that any woman can use him. Because the master criminal, the great Zastrozzi, is in a trance.

ZASTROZZI: Ah. But then there are trances ... (*drawing his sword, he does four or five amazing things with it*) ... and there are trances. (*putting the sword to VICTOR's throat*) Now, who are you.

VICTOR: (*stepping back, afraid*) Your revenge upon Verezzi will be empty.

ZASTROZZI: Who is he to you.

VICTOR: I'm his tutor.

ZASTROZZI: His what.

VICTOR: Tutor. I teach him things.

ZASTROZZI: Is that so. And what, for example, do you teach him.

VICTOR: How to evade the man who wants to destroy him.

ZASTROZZI: You are the one responsible for stretching my search to three years.

VICTOR: Yes.

ZASTROZZI: Interesting. You don't look capable of having done it. You look ordinary.

VICTOR: I am.

ZASTROZZI: No. In your case the look might actually be deceiving. But we'll soon find out. Where is your weapon.

VICTOR: I don't have one.

ZASTROZZI: Then why the innkeeper disguise. You must be here to intervene for your student.

VICTOR: Intervention doesn't have to be violent.

ZASTROZZI: I'm afraid it does. Haven't you been reading the latest books. The world is in desperate need of action. The most decisive action is always violent. (*repeating this last sentence in German [Die entscheidende Aktion ist immer heftiger]*)

VICTOR: Interesting. But all I'm saying is that I didn't think killing you would necessarily have to be the only way to stop you. I thought I could try common sense with you.

ZASTROZZI: You were wrong. Try something else.

VICTOR: Verezzi is insane.

ZASTROZZI: I don't care.

VICTOR: But revenge on an insane man can't mean anything.

ZASTROZZI: Wrong. I don't share the belief that the insane have left this world. They're still here. They're just hiding.

VICTOR: But he thinks he is a visionary.

ZASTROZZI: Well, perhaps he is. I don't care about that either. That's between him and his God. This matter is between him and me.

Pause.

VICTOR: I know why you seek revenge on Verezzi.

ZASTROZZI: No one knows!

VICTOR: I know of the crime that he and his father committed upon your mother.

ZASTROZZI: Ah, yes. The crime. What version have you heard.

VICTOR: The real one.

ZASTROZZI: Is that so.

VICTOR: I was a friend of his father. I was away studying. Hadn't seen him for years. Had never even met his son. A letter arrived. He said he was dying. And asked if I would protect his son who would probably be in danger.

ZASTROZZI: And the letter described what they had done?

VICTOR: Yes.

ZASTROZZI: What did you think.

VICTOR: It was horrible, of course.

ZASTROZZI: Describe exactly what you mean by horrible.

VICTOR: Bloody. Vicious. Unforgivable.

ZASTROZZI: Wrong. Not even close. Horrible is when things proceed unnaturally. When people remain unanswerable for their actions.

VICTOR: But the letter also told me why they had done it. This woman's son had killed my friend's daughter. Verezzi's sister.

ZASTROZZI: No. It wasn't me.

VICTOR: Then who was it.

ZASTROZZI: Never mind. But even if I had killed her, then the quarrel would be with me. Not my mother. That is usually the way with revenge, isn't it.

VICTOR: You couldn't be found.

ZASTROZZI: I was away. Studying. I was called back to examine my mother's corpse. And the father's letter actually did describe what they had done to her?

VICTOR: Yes.

ZASTROZZI: Imagine that. How could he bring himself to tell anyone. I thought he was a Christian.

VICTOR: It was a confession, I think.

ZASTROZZI: Are you a priest.

VICTOR: I was at the time.

ZASTROZZI: And you left the Church just to protect Verezzi?

VICTOR: It doesn't matter why I left the Church.

ZASTROZZI: Yes. That's correct. Only two things should matter to you. That Verezzi killed my mother in a horrible manner. And that I, her son, have a legitimate claim to vengeance.

VICTOR: But he has no memory of the crime. He never has had. He must have blocked it out almost immediately.

ZASTROZZI: I don't care. I seek revenge. Revenge is a simple matter. You shouldn't have turned it into such an issue by hiding him from me for all this time.

VICTOR: But there's something else, isn't there.

ZASTROZZI: I beg your pardon.

VICTOR: I think there's another reason altogether why you want to destroy Verezzi.

ZASTROZZI: What is your name.

VICTOR: Victor.

ZASTROZZI: No. You are not an ordinary man, Victor. But you would be wise to become one within the next few hours.

VICTOR: When are you coming to take him.

ZASTROZZI: I am here now. Are you going to run off again.

VICTOR: No. He won't leave. He's waiting for his followers. Listen. I don't care much for violence. But to get to him you will have to go around me.

ZASTROZZI: I have already done that. And I didn't even know you existed.

VICTOR: How.

ZASTROZZI: Never mind. Concern yourself with this. If what I plan doesn't work I will not be going around you or anyone or anything else. I will be coming directly at him. And if you are in the way you will be killed. Now go away. I'm tired. Tired of the chase. The explanation of the chase. Of everything. Of you specifically at this moment.

ZASTROZZI turns around. VICTOR pulls a knife from inside his shirt, raises it to ZASTROZZI's back, and holds it there. Finally, VICTOR lowers it.

ZASTROZZI: Go away.

VICTOR exits, passing BERNARDO coming in.

BERNARDO: He had a knife about six inches away from your back.

ZASTROZZI: Why didn't you stop him. He could have killed me.

BERNARDO: I doubt it.

ZASTROZZI: Did you arrange for the introduction.

BERNARDO: Yes.

ZASTROZZI: I wonder now if it is a good enough plan.

BERNARDO: Probably not. (*starting off*)

ZASTROZZI: It doesn't matter. It's almost over. I sense it. One way or the other I have him. This way would be less violent but more satisfying. Where are you going.

BERNARDO: A young woman in the village smiled at me. She's very pretty. And obviously well off. I think I'll seduce her and rob her blind.

ZASTROZZI: You know, Bernardo, that you don't have to do these things just to impress me.

BERNARDO: Thank you.

ZASTROZZI: You could try to become the nice young man you were before your one little mistake.

BERNARDO: And what was that.

ZASTROZZI: You murdered Verezzi's sister. Don't tell me you had forgotten.

BERNARDO: Yes, I had. I've murdered so many others since then.

ZASTROZZI: You really are a seedy little butcher, aren't you.

BERNARDO: Once you make your one little mistake, sir, you must continue or be destroyed. The insulation of evil is the only thing that makes you survive. I learned that from watching you.

ZASTROZZI: But sometimes your crimes are heartless enough to shock even me. Who is the dark personality here after all.

BERNARDO: You, sir. But I strive hard to be your shadow.

ZASTROZZI: Good. That man with the knife to my back. His name is Victor. He is Verezzi's tutor. He looks harmless, doesn't he.

BERNARDO: Yes.

ZASTROZZI: He isn't. I give him to you. He'll probably present a challenge.

BERNARDO: Thank you. (*starting off*)

ZASTROZZI: Oh, Bernardo.

BERNARDO: Yes.

ZASTROZZI: I don't expect you to understand why you are killing him. But I do expect you to do it with some imagination!

BERNARDO leaves. ZASTROZZI takes a long drink.

Blackout.

Intermission.

SCENE 7

VEREZZI's room. VEREZZI and MATILDA are making love. He is delirious. We know they are finished when he makes an absurdly loud and sustained groaning sound. MATILDA gets out of bed and looks at him in disbelief. She is clothed. He is naked.

VEREZZI: I am in love.

MATILDA: So soon?

VEREZZI: I am enthralled. You were wonderful. What a new treat. Usually I am the one who is wonderful and the women are enthralled. Where did you get this strange power.

MATILDA: It's something I was born with.

VEREZZI: How do you know.

MATILDA: What else could it be. It's not something you get from practice. I'm not a whore.

VEREZZI: No. But you're not a saint either. I'd know if you were. Because ... (*a revelation*) *I'm* a saint.

MATILDA: Of course you are.

VEREZZI: Don't be intimidated. Saints are human.

MATILDA: Why should I be intimidated. Saint or no saint. You are the one who loves me.

VEREZZI: You mean you don't love me?

MATILDA: No. Of course not.

VEREZZI: I don't understand. Explain. But be kind about it.

MATILDA: I love someone else.

VEREZZI: Who.

MATILDA: You saw him earlier.

VEREZZI: That man who was going to beat you?

MATILDA: Yes. Bernardo.

VEREZZI: That's disgusting. How can you love someone who beats you.

MATILDA: It's not *that* he beats me. It's *how* he beats me.

VEREZZI: I don't understand. Explain. But be kind.

MATILDA: He beats me like he could kill me. And I love him for that.

VEREZZI: You should love me instead. I'm gentle. I'm an artist. I'm a saint. And I love you.

MATILDA: Could you kill me. If you could kill me I might love you.

VEREZZI: You're very strange. And you're very exciting. But I don't think you're very healthy. That's a challenge. I can help you. Stay with me.

MATILDA: I can't! I love someone else.

VEREZZI: Then why did you make love to me.

MATILDA: A part of me is gentle. It wanted to thank you. But a larger part of me is something else. It wants to be beaten. (*starting off*)

VEREZZI: Stay. I could beat you. A little.

MATILDA: If you really loved me you could do better.

VEREZZI: But I'm a saint. I love things. I can't hurt things. How could I face my followers. They're coming soon. Some of them are very vulnerable. Some of them are swans. Some of them are tiny little caterpillars who have been crawling for weeks to get here. I can't disappoint them. How can I preach love and human kindness to all my followers then go into the privacy of my bedroom and beat a woman unconscious.

MATILDA: If you are a saint, you can take certain liberties. People will understand.

VEREZZI: But will the caterpillars. They are dumb. I love them. Honestly I do. But they are dumb. Crawl, crawl. That's all they do. Crawl. Life's dilemmas are multiplied for a saint. He has to deal with too many things at once. One of my followers is a Turk. I don't even speak his language. When he comes, how am I going to give him the message. I keep waiting for the gift of tongues but it never comes. God is handicapping me. And now you want me to beat you. I abhor violence. It makes me retch. But I love you. I'll die if you leave me.

MATILDA starts off. VEREZZI crawls out of the bed and over to her.

VEREZZI: Please don't go. I know. You can beat me instead.

MATILDA: That just won't do.

VEREZZI: But won't you even try.

VICTOR comes in.

VICTOR: What's this. Get up.

VEREZZI stands.

VICTOR: (*to MATILDA*) Who are you.

VEREZZI: She is the woman I love.

VICTOR: And why were you grovelling on the floor.

VEREZZI: Because she doesn't love me. What can I do, Victor. She's breaking my heart.

VICTOR: It seems to me that I met the woman you love earlier. That virgin God sent for you.

VICTOR starts to pack.

VEREZZI: Yes. Julia. That's right. I love her. I'd forgotten. Oh, thank God. For a moment there I didn't know what I was going to do. It's all right, Matilda. You can go now.

MATILDA: So you don't love me after all.

VEREZZI: But I do. It's just that I also love Julia. And she's less of a challenge. She just thinks I'm insane. I can deal with that. But I don't know if I can ever deal with you, Matilda. You want me to want to kill you. That's unique. But it's not healthy. But I do love you. And if it weren't for Julia I would probably destroy myself over you. Or something to that effect.

MATILDA: (*with clenched teeth*) Or something to that effect. (*starting off*)

VEREZZI: Oh. Say hello to Bernardo for me. I think he likes me.

MATILDA looks at him oddly, shakes her head, and leaves.

VICTOR: What was that all about.

VEREZZI: One of the tests of sainthood, I imagine.

VICTOR: Did you pass.

VEREZZI: I don't know. Tell me, Victor, how do you suppose I can find out.

VICTOR: Oh, shut up. Get packed. We're leaving.

VEREZZI: Why.

VICTOR: Zastrozzi is here.

VEREZZI: Who.

VICTOR: Zastrozzi. Zastrozzi!

VEREZZI: Oh yes. The phantom of your brain. You've dreamt him up again, have you.

VICTOR: I've seen him. I was at his rooms.

VEREZZI: Oh really. And what does he look like. Does he have fangs. Does he have horns. Does he have eyes dripping blood.

VICTOR: No. He's a man. Just a man. Calm. Purposeful. And very experienced. Just a man. But a very dangerous one.

VEREZZI: Well then bring him along and I'll deal with him. A little human understanding should get him to leave you alone.

VICTOR: You're no match for him.

VEREZZI: Why not.

VICTOR: Because he's perfectly sane. And you're a delirious lunatic.

VEREZZI: And if I am, is it good and right for you to be telling me so. Would it not be more good and more right for you to be more understanding. That's an hypothesis of a religious nature. I have decided that your degeneration has gone far enough. And I am commencing spiritual guidance with you immediately. (*sitting on the bed*) Now come sit at my feet.

VICTOR: Get packed.

VEREZZI: Lesson number one. When the Messiah speaks, listen.

VICTOR: When did you become the Messiah.

VEREZZI: Did I say Messiah. No.

VICTOR: I heard you.

VEREZZI: No. Not me. God. God said Messiah.

VICTOR: I don't understand. Are you God or are you the Messiah.

VEREZZI: I am Verezzi. I am whoever He wants me to be.

VICTOR: You are exploring new dimensions of the human mind, Verezzi. But I don't think the world is ready for you yet. Get packed. We're leaving.

VEREZZI: No.

VICTOR: Please! I promised your father. It's the only promise in my life I've ever kept. It keeps me sane. Please get packed!

VEREZZI: No. I have to go find Julia. I have to tell her that God is talking to me. I know she'll marry me now.

VICTOR: Let me try to explain it to you in a way you will understand.

VICTOR drops to his knees.

VEREZZI: Don't patronize me, Victor. I am not a moron. I am just a good and lovely man.

VICTOR: Well, that could be a matter of opinion. But let us suppose you are in fact just a good man.

VEREZZI: And lovely.

VICTOR: Yes.

VEREZZI: And very tidy as well.

VICTOR: Yes. All those things. A good lovely tidy man. Who is gentle to all things living and dead, et cetera, and wishes only to carry about the positive uplifting spirit of God. Then doesn't it make sense that in order to do that you should become aware of the obstacles that lie naturally in your path. The forces of evil that wish to stop you. In effect, doesn't it make sense that a good man should also be a cunning man.

VEREZZI: No.

VEREZZI leaves. VICTOR sits on the bed. Shakes his head.

VICTOR: I give up. Zastrozzi will get his revenge on the lunatic Verezzi. After three years he will finally destroy a vegetable. I don't know who to pity more. Zastrozzi, the poor vegetable, or whatever it was that created them both. Sad. (*shrugging*) No. I can't give up. I promised. I must save him. Even if I must hurt him a little.

VICTOR stands and searches the room for something heavy. He finds something, takes it, and runs out.

Blackout.

SCENE 8

A lull in the storm. VICTOR is walking through a dark alley. Suddenly a torch is lit. It is held by BERNARDO. He is standing with sword drawn in VICTOR's way.

VICTOR: Excuse me. Did a man pass by here recently. A young man.

BERNARDO: Forget him. His time is almost here. You have business with me.

VICTOR: What do you want.

BERNARDO: I am from Zastrozzi.

VICTOR: And what does Zastrozzi want from me.

BERNARDO: Your life.

VICTOR: A bizarre request. Do you understand the reason for it.

BERNARDO: No. I am a more simple man than Zastrozzi. I can only understand simple reasons for killing a man. And very simple ways of going about it.

VICTOR: Interesting. What, for example, are the simple reasons for killing a man.

BERNARDO: To get his money.

VICTOR: I have none.

BERNARDO: If he has done some wrong to me.

VICTOR: I don't even know you.

BERNARDO: Or if he presents some kind of threat.

VICTOR: Surely you can tell just by looking at me that I'm harmless.

BERNARDO: Zastrozzi says you are not.

VICTOR: Zastrozzi flatters me.

BERNARDO: Zastrozzi sees things that others cannot.

VICTOR: Perhaps that is because he is insane.

BERNARDO: He is not the least bit insane.

VICTOR: Are you absolutely sure of that.

BERNARDO: Yes.

VICTOR: Oh.

BERNARDO: In fact, he is the sanest man I have ever met. He is also the most perverse. The combination makes him very dangerous. You do not upset a man like this. When he tells you to kill someone, you do it. Even though you personally have nothing to gain from it. When he tells you to do it with imagination, you try to do so. Even though you do not know why or even how to go about it.

VICTOR: Poor fellow. You're in quite a fix.

BERNARDO: While you on the other hand are not, is that it.

VICTOR: I am probably going to die. That I can understand. You are going to spend the rest of your life fulfilling someone else's wishes that you do not understand. That, sir, is a state of mental chaos usually associated with purgatory. I pity you.

BERNARDO: Shut up.

VICTOR: I pity you like I would a diseased dog.

BERNARDO: I said shut up.

VICTOR: You are out of your element. Zastrozzi is the master of evil and you are just a thug.

BERNARDO: I am more than that, I know.

VICTOR: A thug. And a murderer. You cannot think of an imaginative way to kill me because you have no imagination. You stand there with a sword and threaten a man who is unarmed. That is the posture of a cheap murderer.

BERNARDO: I could use my hands. Would you feel better about that.

VICTOR: I am only thinking of you.

BERNARDO: (*throwing down the sword*) It will take a little longer this way. (*approaching VICTOR*) I'm going to have to strangle you.

VICTOR: Well, it's not exactly inspired. But it's better than just cutting me down with a sword. Congratulations.

BERNARDO: Thank you.

VICTOR: But before you start, I have a confession to make.

> *VICTOR quickly takes out the heavy object he has taken from the room in the previous scene and hits BERNARDO over the head. BERNARDO falls unconscious to the ground.*

VICTOR: I lied about not being armed.

> *VEREZZI comes on in a daze.*

VEREZZI: Victor. I'm glad you're here. I can't find any of my followers. They must have gotten lost.

VICTOR: (*pointing off*) No. There's one now.

> *VEREZZI turns and VICTOR hits him over the head with his object. VEREZZI falls unconscious. VICTOR picks him up under the arms.*

VICTOR: A place to hide. Some place quiet. I have to think about what is happening to me. That vacant prison I saw this morning. (*dragging VEREZZI away*) What's this. He's smiling. Even in pain he smiles.

> *Blackout.*

SCENE 9

> *ZASTROZZI's room. ZASTROZZI is standing in the middle of the room shivering, a blanket wrapped around him.*

ZASTROZZI: I am having a nightmare. It involves the final battle over control of the world between the forces of good and evil. It is the most terrifying nightmare I have ever had. Something so extremely unusual has happened that my mind in all its power cannot even begin to comprehend it. I am in charge of the forces of good. And I am winning. I think there is just the slightest possibility that there might be something wrong with my mind after all. The nightmare continues. I lead the forces of good with their toothy, God-obsessed smiles into the fortress of the commander of the forces of evil. We easily overcome the fortress and become gracious victors – not raping or murdering or even taking prisoners. We just smile and wish goodness and mercy to rain down on everyone. And I am smiling and wishing out loud for goodness and mercy as well except that inside I am deeply ill and feel like throwing up. And then we are taken to meet the commander of the forces of evil and he walks through a large wooden door and I see that he looks familiar. And he should. Because it is Zastrozzi. And even though I know that I am Zastrozzi, I cannot help but feel extremely confused. And he reinforces this confusion when he opens his mouth and says, "I am Zastrozzi." At which point I feel myself smile even wider, so wide that I feel my skin tighten and I know that my face will become stuck forever like this in the widest, stupidest, most merciful and good smile ever worn by a human being. Then I die. But before I die I remember thinking – they are going to make me a saint. They are going to make me a Christian saint. The patron saint of smiles. The nightmare ends. I need a drink. I need to sit down. I need more than anything to stop having nightmares. They're getting worse every day. There might be something wrong with my mind. (*shivering*) The nightmare continues. Again. (*smiling*)

MATILDA comes on dragging a whip along the floor. She is furious.

MATILDA: Zastrozzi! (*swinging the whip around above her head, cracking it*) Zastrozzi! I'm going to whip you. I'm going to whip you for making a fool out of me. For sending me to entrap a man who is an idiot and feels nothing except idiotic things. (*pause*) The nightmares. (*sighing and starting off, seeing him shaking*) No. (*turning back*) Zastrozzi, I have failed. Whip me.

ZASTROZZI: I can't be bothered. (*turning to her, smiling stupidly*)

MATILDA: Zastrozzi, you have a stupid empty smile on your face. Just like the one the idiot wears. You are standing there shivering under a blanket like a sick old man. You don't look like Zastrozzi. You look like an ass.

ZASTROZZI: (*trying to concentrate*) And now.

MATILDA: You are still shivering.

ZASTROZZI: (*closing his eyes and concentrating*) And now.

MATILDA: You are still smiling like an idiot.

ZASTROZZI: (*closing his eyes and concentrating*) Now? (*approaching her slowly*) Now?!

MATILDA: Now I feel like whipping you for threatening me. (*She begins to whip him. ZASTROZZI doesn't move.*) Don't ever make a fool of me again. Don't ever threaten me again. Who do you think I

am. I am not one of those who quiver when they hear your name. I am your match, sir. I am every bit your match. (*She throws the whip down.*)

ZASTROZZI: Are you.

MATILDA: In every way.

ZASTROZZI: In every way?

MATILDA: Yes.

ZASTROZZI: Ah, well. You must know. And if you know, then I must agree. Correct?

MATILDA: Yes. So you will let me stay? We'll be together?

ZASTROZZI: I'm afraid that's impossible.

MATILDA: Why.

ZASTROZZI: We're too much alike. You've just said so. I am in love with someone else.

MATILDA: Impossible.

ZASTROZZI: Life is strange, isn't it. I met her just a short while ago. She is quite different from me. That is probably why I love her. She is pure and innocent and possesses a marvellous, gentle sensuality that I have never experienced before. In fact, just thinking about her arouses me. I am thinking about her now and I am getting aroused now.

ZASTROZZI grabs MATILDA.

MATILDA: What are you doing.

ZASTROZZI: I am going to make love to you. Haven't you wanted me to for a long time.

MATILDA: Not while you are thinking about another woman.

ZASTROZZI: I'm sorry. But that is the way it must be.

MATILDA: I couldn't bear it.

ZASTROZZI: But you are a match for me in all ways. And I could bear it. I could even enjoy it. In fact that is the way people like us should enjoy it. Try to enjoy it.

MATILDA: I can't.

ZASTROZZI: Try.

MATILDA: No.

ZASTROZZI: Are you crying.

MATILDA: No.

ZASTROZZI: You are crying, aren't you.

MATILDA: No.

ZASTROZZI: Are you sure.

MATILDA: Yes.

ZASTROZZI: Are you crying.

MATILDA: Yes.

ZASTROZZI hits her and she is propelled across the room and falls.

MATILDA: What are you doing.

ZASTROZZI: Making a point.

MATILDA: You treat me this way because I am a woman.

ZASTROZZI: Nonsense. Women, men, children, goats. I treat them all the same. I ask them to be answerable.

BERNARDO walks on, his head bandaged.

ZASTROZZI: (*to MATILDA*) Here. I'll show you what I mean. (*walking over to BERNARDO.*) I take it from your wound that you have failed.

BERNARDO: Yes, I'm sorry.

ZASTROZZI: That's not necessary. I don't want you to feel sorry. I don't want you to feel anything. Do you understand.

BERNARDO: I think so.

ZASTROZZI: Try to understand. Try to feel nothing. Are you feeling nothing now.

BERNARDO: I'm not sure.

ZASTROZZI: Try. Feel nothing. Are you feeling nothing.

BERNARDO: Yes.

ZASTROZZI: Good.

ZASTROZZI hits BERNARDO's face viciously with the back of his hand. BERNARDO staggers back, but doesn't fall.

ZASTROZZI: Fall down when I hit you, Bernardo.

BERNARDO: Why.

ZASTROZZI: Because it makes it appear that you are resisting when you don't. And you have nothing to gain from resisting.

ZASTROZZI hits BERNARDO again. BERNARDO staggers back but doesn't fall. He looks at ZASTROZZI and drops to his knees.

ZASTROZZI: Some advice for both of you. Get to know your limitations. Then remember that as you go through life there are only two things worth knowing. The first is too complex for you to understand. The second is that life is a series of totally arbitrary and often meaningless events

and the only way to make sense of life is to forget that you know that. In other words, occupy yourselves. Matilda, go seduce Verezzi, and if he is preoccupied, remove his preoccupations. The plan to drive him to suicide is not the most inspired I have ever thought of but it will do to keep us occupied for a while. After you have done that, come looking for me, and if I am in the mood, we can play your silly whipping games. And as for you, Bernardo, go do something you at least understand. Commit some foul, meaningless crime. That village girl you mentioned earlier. Go abuse her and steal everything she values. And enjoy it as much as possible because eventually you will be made accountable. And now if you will excuse me, I am going to visit the local prison. It hasn't been used in years. But I'm sure it is still full of wondrous sensations. I do some of my best thinking in prisons. Did you know that.

MATILDA: Yes.

BERNARDO: No.

ZASTROZZI: It's true though. I've visited some of the best prisons in Europe. I find it invigorating. It helps to confirm my sanity. Only a sane person could function in those places as well as I do. Does that make sense.

BERNARDO: Yes.

MATILDA: No.

ZASTROZZI: You see I must visit these prisons. It is the only way to make myself answerable. I have never been apprehended and I never will be. So I have to voluntarily submit to a prison in order to make myself experience judgment. When I have experienced enough, I escape. Do you understand.

BERNARDO: Yes.

MATILDA: Yes.

ZASTROZZI: No, you don't.

ZASTROZZI smiles and leaves.

BERNARDO: He *is* crazy.

MATILDA: Of course he is. He has always been crazy.

BERNARDO: Not always.

MATILDA: How would you know. You are crazy yourself. For that matter so am I. For wanting him the way I do. I should find a more simple man.

BERNARDO stands and goes to MATILDA.

BERNARDO: I am a more simple man.

MATILDA: That's the problem. It is men like you who make me want men like him.

BERNARDO: I could surprise you.

MATILDA: You would have to.

BERNARDO: I would like to make love to you.

MATILDA: I know.

BERNARDO: May I.

MATILDA: I will be thinking of Zastrozzi.

BERNARDO: I might surprise you.

MATILDA: Well, you can try at least.

BERNARDO grabs her and kisses her.

MATILDA: Harder.

She grabs him savagely and kisses him.

Blackout.

SCENE 10

For the first time the focus is on the full set. Stripped of all furnishings, it should appear like an old dungeon. BERNARDO comes on pulling JULIA, who he has chained at the wrists. He takes her into one of the chambers.

JULIA: What are you doing this for.

BERNARDO: You smiled at me.

JULIA: It was just an invitation for polite conversation.

BERNARDO: What would that mean to me. What was I supposed to do after the conversation. Marry you? Settle into a wonderful, lawful, domestic life?

JULIA: I really had no plans beyond conversation, sir.

BERNARDO: You wouldn't. You spend too much time with civilized men. This will teach you never to smile at strangers.

JULIA: Have I offended you.

BERNARDO: No. I'm just accepting your invitation and using it in the only way I can.

JULIA: What are you going to do with me.

BERNARDO: Anything I please.

JULIA: What is this place. I've never been here.

BERNARDO: No, you wouldn't have. It's an old prison. It used to house the criminally deranged but now it's vacant. More or less. A friend of mine

found it. He has a way of finding places like these. What do you think of it.

JULIA: It's horrible.

BERNARDO: Yes. It is, isn't it. It will do very nicely.

JULIA: For what.

BERNARDO: For whatever I please.

JULIA: You're going to rape me, aren't you. You're going to rape me and murder me.

BERNARDO: Not necessarily in that order, though.

JULIA: You appeared to be such a nice young man.

BERNARDO grabs her hair.

BERNARDO: Nice? What would I do if I was nice. If a pretty woman smiled at me and we had a polite conversation, could I marry her and be lawful and decent? No, I wouldn't do that now. My mind would explode. Yet I am a man. When a woman smiles, I must do something. So I do what I am doing.

JULIA: You don't have to do this. Let me go. We'll start again from the beginning. We'll meet in the fresh air on a sunny day. Talk about healthy things. Develop a respectful attitude toward each other. Eventually fall in love on just the right terms.

BERNARDO: Impossible. You're not the woman I could be in love with.

JULIA: I could try.

BERNARDO: Impossible. I can tell from your smile. There is a woman I love, though, who could love me on the right terms. But she loves someone else. His name is Zastrozzi. Have you heard of him.

JULIA: I ... I think so.

BERNARDO: He is the one they talk about in whispers in your circles. I am the one who follows him around like a dog. (*starting off*)

JULIA: Where are you going.

BERNARDO: Back to your house. To rob it of everything of any value at all. And to kill your parents.

JULIA: Please don't.

BERNARDO: Why not. And give me a reason I can understand.

JULIA: They're dreadful people. You would only be putting them out of their misery.

BERNARDO: Not bad. That's interesting. So there is something else behind that civilized smile. I'll be back.

JULIA: If you leave me alone I'll scream until someone finds me.

BERNARDO: (*walking to her*) You shouldn't have said that. That was a mistake.

BERNARDO hits JULIA. She falls, unconscious. He unlocks the chain.

BERNARDO: She doesn't need these now. And I might have to use them. (*sadly*) I might want to use them. I might love to use them.

He leaves. In another corner of the set, VICTOR comes on carrying the unconscious VEREZZI on his shoulders. He takes him into a chamber, puts him down, and examines his head.

VICTOR: Perhaps I hit you too hard. You're barely breathing. Well, you were doomed anyway. At least this way you have a chance. (*looking around*) This place is horrible. But he'll be safe here I suppose. (*sitting*) Now what am I to do. The only way I can get him to run is to keep him unconscious and that's just not practical. I could leave him here and forget the whole matter. That's practical. Leave him here! Forget the whole matter! That's practical! But I did make that promise. And it's the only promise I've ever kept. I certainly didn't keep my promise to God. But I don't feel so bad about that, having met this Zastrozzi. If he is one of God's creatures, then God must be used to disappointment. On the other hand, I just don't like the man. Everything he does, everything he represents unsettles me to the bone. Zastrozzi decides that an artist must be judged by someone so he kills him. Zastrozzi is to blame for his own mother's death in a crime of passion but hounds a poor lunatic because he cannot accept the blame himself. Zastrozzi steals, violates, and murders on a regular basis, and remains perfectly sane. Verezzi commits one crime of passion then goes on a binge of mindless religious love and becomes moronic. Something is wrong. Something is unbalanced. I abhor violence. But I also abhor a lack of balance. It shows that the truth is missing somewhere. And it makes me feel very, very uneasy. Uneasy in a way I have not felt since I was … Yes, Verezzi, I will restore a truth to your lunatic mind and your lunatic world. (*taking VEREZZI's sword*) Zastrozzi.

VICTOR exits. JULIA groans then slowly regains consciousness and gets up. She makes her way around the dungeon, sees VEREZZI, and goes to him. She kneels down and takes his pulse.

JULIA: What's happening to me. I go for a series of walks in the street. Smile at two young men. One of them tells me he is a visionary. The other one abducts me and tells me he is going to rape and murder me, not necessarily in that order. Then he hits me like he would a man and knocks me unconscious. I wake up and find the young man who thinks he is a visionary lying on the ground bleeding to death from a head wound. What's happening to me.

MATILDA enters.

MATILDA: You must be the virgin. The one with the marvellous, gentle sensuality.

JULIA: Who are you.

MATILDA: My name is Matilda. I am your competition. I have a sensuality which is not the least bit gentle.

JULIA: Really. What do you want.

MATILDA: I want to kill all the virgins in the world.

JULIA: Oh no. What's happening to me.

MATILDA: Unfortunately for you, we are both in love with the same man.

JULIA: (*pointing to VEREZZI*) Him? I don't love him. I don't even like him.

MATILDA: Not him. Zastrozzi.

JULIA: I've heard of him. He's the one who is whispered about in polite society.

MATILDA: He is the evil genius of all Europe. A criminal. And I am a criminal, too. We belong together. So we must fight and I must kill you.

JULIA: Why can't I just leave.

MATILDA: That won't do. Besides, I will enjoy killing you. It is women like you who make me look like a tart.

JULIA: Nonsense. It's the way you dress.

MATILDA: Stand up, you mindless virgin.

JULIA: (*standing*) Madame, I am neither mindless nor a virgin. I am merely a victim of bizarre circumstance. A product of healthy civilization thrown into a jungle of the deranged.

MATILDA: Yes, get angry. You are better when you are angry. If I were a man I would seduce you on the spot.

JULIA: That's perverse!

MATILDA: (*taking a knife from under her skirts*) Yes, get indignant. You are quite provocative when you are upset. Take off your clothes.

JULIA: Why.

MATILDA: We are going to make love.

JULIA: Oh no, we are not.

MATILDA: Yes, get confused. You are quite ridiculous when you are confused. And it is exactly the way someone like you should die.

MATILDA advances.

JULIA: What are you doing.

MATILDA: We are going to fight. And we are only going to stop fighting when one of us is dead.

JULIA: I would rather not. I would rather discuss some other possibility. I'm only seventeen years old. People tell me I have so much to live for.

MATILDA: Oh. Name something worth living for and I might spare your life.

JULIA: But how could I. A woman like you could never appreciate what I think is worth living for. No offence. But take your dress for example. I would live to dress much better than that.

MATILDA: You mindless, coy, disgusting virgin!

MATILDA attacks and they struggle. The knife falls and JULIA scrambles after it. MATILDA leaps on her and somehow MATILDA is stabbed. She falls over dead. JULIA feels her pulse.

JULIA: Dead. Omigod. (*standing*) What is happening to me. First a victim. Now a murderer! And I don't even know her. This is grossly unfair. I'm young. I've had the proper education. My future was a pleasant rosy colour. I could see it in my head. It was a rosy colour. Very pretty. This is truly grossly unfair.

BERNARDO comes in. He sees MATILDA's body and rushes to it.

BERNARDO: You killed her.

JULIA: I had no choice. She attacked me.

BERNARDO: She was the only woman I could have been in love with on the right terms. You have blocked out my future.

JULIA: I'm sorry. But she didn't love you anyway. She loved that Zastrozzi.

BERNARDO: You have closed off my life from my brain. It is exploding!

JULIA: Well, if you'll pardon me expressing an opinion, I think she was not entirely a rational person. Not at all the kind of person you need. You are not a rational person either and you would

be better off with someone who could tame your tendency toward violence. If you'll pardon my opinion, I mean.

BERNARDO approaches her.

JULIA: What are you going to do.

BERNARDO: Stay still.

JULIA: (*backing away*) No. This isn't fair. I shouldn't be involved in any of this. I didn't love him. I didn't hate her. I've only a strange and vague recollection of this Zastrozzi. And all I did was smile at you.

BERNARDO: Stay very still.

JULIA: Please.

BERNARDO strangles her. ZASTROZZI appears out of the darkness.

ZASTROZZI: Bernardo.

BERNARDO drops JULIA, who falls to the floor lifeless. He turns to face ZASTROZZI.

ZASTROZZI: Another victim, Bernardo?

BERNARDO: She murdered Matilda.

ZASTROZZI: She was merely defending herself.

BERNARDO: You saw?

ZASTROZZI: I have been here for hours.

BERNARDO: Why didn't you do something.

ZASTROZZI: I was preoccupied.

BERNARDO: Matilda is dead.

ZASTROZZI: I didn't know you had such deep feelings for her.

BERNARDO: It wouldn't have mattered to you. You only have one thought. Well, there he is. Verezzi the Italian. Take him. I am going to bury Matilda.

ZASTROZZI: Verezzi will wait. You are not going anywhere. You have to face your judgment.

BERNARDO: It will come.

ZASTROZZI: It has.

BERNARDO: From you?

ZASTROZZI: Is there anyone better at it.

BERNARDO: Judgment for what exactly.

ZASTROZZI: For all your crimes. All the people you have murdered have spoken to me in my nightmares and asked that you be made answerable.

BERNARDO: I am just a student to the master.

ZASTROZZI: And only the master is qualified to judge. Draw your sword, Bernardo. Let us have the formality of a contest. But know now that you are dead.

BERNARDO: Sir. Let me go.

ZASTROZZI: No.

ZASTROZZI draws his sword. BERNARDO draws his. They fight. Viciously. Expertly. BERNARDO is good. ZASTROZZI is the master, though, and eventually he pierces BERNARDO's chest. BERNARDO drops to his knees.

BERNARDO: Sir.

ZASTROZZI: You are dead.

ZASTROZZI knocks BERNARDO over with his foot. BERNARDO is dead. ZASTROZZI walks over to VEREZZI and stands silently looking down at him for a while, then sits down and cradles VEREZZI's head.

ZASTROZZI: Verezzi. Finally. Not dying at all. It's just a flesh wound. Your breathing becomes stronger. Soon you will wake up. I want you to be awake for this. It would have been more satisfying to have you destroy yourself. But you are too clever for that. Everyone thinks you are out of your mind. But I know you have just been hiding. Hiding from your crimes, Verezzi. Hiding from the crime of telling people you are giving them gifts from God. The crime of letting them think there is happiness in that stupid smile of yours. The crime of making language pleasantly vague and painting with distorted imagination. The crime of disturbing the natural condition in which the dark side prevails. Wake up, Verezzi. Zastrozzi is here to prove that you must be judged. You can hide no more.

A VOICE : And what is Zastrozzi hiding from.

ZASTROZZI: (*standing*) What do you want.

VICTOR comes out of the darkness carrying VEREZZI's sabre.

VICTOR: Sir. Tell me. What is this about. (*looking around*) All this death.

ZASTROZZI: It is a continuing process of simplification. I am simplifying my life. These people came here to be judged.

VICTOR: By you?

ZASTROZZI: Is there anyone better at it.

VICTOR: Apparently not. Well then, I too want to be judged by Zastrozzi, who judges for a profession.

ZASTROZZI: Then step closer.

VICTOR: Is there a fee.

ZASTROZZI: Yes. But I take it from you quickly. You'll never even know it's gone.

VICTOR: I have another idea. I think a man who enjoys his profession as much as you should be the one to pay the fee.

ZASTROZZI: Perhaps. But I have never met anyone who would collect from me.

VICTOR: You have now, sir.

ZASTROZZI: I doubt it very much. You don't even hold your weapon properly.

VICTOR: I have an unorthodox style. But it serves.

ZASTROZZI: Let's see.

He draws his sword. VICTOR begins a short prayer in Latin which ZASTROZZI finishes for him. VICTOR looks at ZASTROZZI. Pause.

ZASTROZZI: Did you not know that I could see into your heart. (*repeating this last sentence in German [Haben Sie nicht wissen, dass ich in dein Herz zu sehen]*)

VICTOR: (*in any Romance language*) Yes. But I can see into your heart as well.

ZASTROZZI: (*in the same Romance language*) Then it will be an interesting battle.

Pause.

VICTOR: So.

ZASTROZZI: So.

They approach each other, cross swords, and begin to fight. The fight will continue and move across the entire stage at least once.

ZASTROZZI tests VICTOR. He responds well but his moves are very unusual. VICTOR will gradually get better by observing ZASTROZZI's moves.

ZASTROZZI: What are all these strange things you are doing designed for.

VICTOR: To keep me alive.

ZASTROZZI: Eventually I will find a way to penetrate your unorthodox style.

VICTOR: That might be difficult. Since I am making it up as I go along.

ZASTROZZI: You look silly.

VICTOR: But I am alive.

ZASTROZZI: Perhaps more alive than you have ever been. That is sometimes the way a person faces death.

VICTOR: I intend to live.

ZASTROZZI: Then you should have taken my advice and become an ordinary man.

VICTOR: Sir. The point is that I *am* an ordinary man.

ZASTROZZI: An ordinary man does not challenge Zastrozzi.

ZASTROZZI attacks him viciously. VICTOR defends himself well.

VICTOR: I am still alive. I am still waiting to be judged.

ZASTROZZI: And growing arrogant as well.

VICTOR: You talk about arrogance. The man who kills on a whim. Who kills an artist simply because he is mediocre. Who commits crimes against people because he believes he is the thing to which they must be answerable.

ZASTROZZI: They must be answerable to something.

VICTOR: There is always God, you know.

ZASTROZZI: I am an atheist. If a man who is an atheist believes that people must be answerable, he has a duty to make them answerable to something.

VICTOR: Answerable to your own demented personality.

ZASTROZZI: I am what they are. They answer to themselves.

VICTOR: All right, forget God. A man is responsible to humanity.

ZASTROZZI: And I am part of humanity.

VICTOR: The irresponsible part.

ZASTROZZI: No. It is my responsibility to spread out like a disease and purge. And by destroying everything make everything safe.

VICTOR: Explain exactly what you mean by safe.

ZASTROZZI: Alive. Untouched by expectation. Free of history. Free of religion. Free of everything. And soon to be free of you.

ZASTROZZI attacks and VICTOR defends himself very well.

VICTOR: I am still alive.

ZASTROZZI: But you are totally on the defensive.

VICTOR: I don't have to kill you. I only have to survive. By merely surviving I neutralize you.

ZASTROZZI: You cannot neutralize something you do not understand.

VICTOR: We are approaching a new century, and with it a new world. There will be no place in it for your attitude, your behaviour.

ZASTROZZI: This new world, what do you suppose it will be like.

VICTOR: Better.

ZASTROZZI: Describe what you mean by better.

VICTOR: More humane. More civilized.

ZASTROZZI: Wrong. Better is when the truth is understood. Understanding the truth is understanding that the force of darkness is constant.

VICTOR: No, it is not. Your time is over.

ZASTROZZI: Wrong again.

ZASTROZZI attacks him viciously. VICTOR defends himself and is ebullient.

VICTOR: I am alive! Everything I said was true. You are neutralized. I am the emissary of goodness in the battle between good and evil. I have found God again.

VICTOR lunges forward wildly. ZASTROZZI plunges his sabre through VICTOR's heart.

VICTOR: I am alive.

VICTOR falls down and dies.

ZASTROZZI: Ah, Victor. You understood what was in your heart. But you did not know your limitations.

ZASTROZZI throws down his sabre. VEREZZI groans and slowly wakes up. He sits, then stands, while ZASTROZZI watches him. VEREZZI staggers around looking at the bodies and slowly regaining his equilibrium.

VEREZZI: Look at all these dead people. What happened.

ZASTROZZI: A series of unfortunate accidents.

VEREZZI: Who are you.

ZASTROZZI: Zastrozzi.

VEREZZI freezes.

VEREZZI: I thought you didn't exist.

ZASTROZZI: Nonsense. You know me well.

VEREZZI: Are you responsible for all these dead people.

ZASTROZZI: No. You are.

VEREZZI: That's quite impossible. I am a servant of God.

ZASTROZZI: You are dead.

ZASTROZZI has drawn a knife.

VEREZZI: What are you going to do.

ZASTROZZI: Cut open your stomach.

VEREZZI: You can't. I'm immune. I am in touch with Him. Protected by Him. Loved by Him.

VEREZZI closes his eyes. ZASTROZZI approaches him.

VEREZZI: You can't hurt me. I'll just wait here. Nothing will happen.

ZASTROZZI: Do you feel anything.

VEREZZI: Yes.

ZASTROZZI: Do you feel fear.

VEREZZI: Yes.

ZASTROZZI: Now who am I.

VEREZZI: Zastrozzi.

ZASTROZZI: And what is Zastrozzi.

VEREZZI: The devil.

ZASTROZZI: Nonsense. What is he.

VEREZZI: A man.

ZASTROZZI: What kind of man.

VEREZZI: I don't know.

ZASTROZZI: A sane man. What kind of man.

VEREZZI: A sane man.

ZASTROZZI: And what kind of man are you.

VEREZZI: I don't know.

ZASTROZZI: You feel fear when you are about to be murdered. And you are no longer smiling. You are a sane man, too. From this moment on and forever. Do you understand. Perfectly sane and very, very afraid.

VEREZZI: Yes.

ZASTROZZI: Now get going.

VEREZZI: Where.

ZASTROZZI: You have to hide. I am giving you a day and I am coming after you. And do you know why I am coming after you.

VEREZZI: No.

ZASTROZZI: Because it will keep me preoccupied. Now leave. And hide well. I wish to be preoccupied for a long time.

VEREZZI slowly leaves. ZASTROZZI looks at all the corpses.

ZASTROZZI: (*smiling*) I like it here. Sad. No. I like it here.

ZATROZZI takes a cape off one of the corpses and wraps himself with it.

ZASTROZZI: I think I'll visit here again. It will help me stay sane.

Pause.

ZASTROZZI: Yes. I like it here.

Blackout.

END

JOHN MACLACHLAN GRAY

(b. 1946)

with ERIC PETERSON

(b. 1946)

As a theatrical term, "musical" has traditionally evoked visions of Broadway extravaganzas like *Oklahoma* or *Annie*. In the 1980s and '90s the megamusical gained ascendancy. Big-budget spectacles like *Cats, Les Miserables,* and *Phantom of the Opera* were mass-marketed on an international scale. Canada's long musical theatre tradition, according to Mel Atkey in *Broadway North: The Dream of a Canadian Musical Theatre*, traces its roots all the way back to 1606 and *The Theatre of Neptune in New France*. But until the extraordinary Broadway success in 2006–07 of *The Drowsy Chaperone* (book by Bob Martin and Don McKellar, music and lyrics by Lisa Lambert and Greg Morrison), Canadian theatre's musical tradition had been more modest and offbeat. Its major creations from 1948–78 included the satirical revue *Spring Thaw, Anne of Green Gables, Ten Lost Years,* and Ken Mitchell's *Cruel Tears*, a country and western adaptation of *Othello* set in Saskatchewan.

For about fifteen years dating from the late 1970s, the unchallenged master of the small, offbeat Canadian musical was John Gray, now known as John MacLachlan Gray. As writer, composer, director, and performer, Gray created literate and immensely entertaining plays bridging "legitimate" theatre and the stage musical. The play that defined his career and became a prototype for Canadian musicals was *Billy Bishop Goes to War*. By any criteria it has been one of the most successful Canadian plays ever written.

Born in Ottawa and raised in Truro, Nova Scotia, Gray was one of three brothers who all became professional musicians. While attending Mount Allison University from 1965–68, he played organ and trumpet with The Lincolns, a local rock 'n' roll band. After graduating with a B.A. in English, Gray headed for Vancouver where he studied theatre at the University of British Columbia, receiving his M.A. in directing in 1971. He subsequently co-founded Tamahnous Theatre and over the next four years directed eight of the plays that made Vancouver's Tamahnous one of the most exciting experimental companies in the country. Gray moved to Toronto in 1975, joining Paul Thompson's Theatre Passe Muraille as a composer and sometime director, and writing music for a half-dozen Passe Muraille shows.

Gray's first play, *18 Wheels*, was produced by Passe Muraille and Tamahnous in 1977 under his own direction. Its all-night truckers and truck-stop waitress tell their stories in country and western song. With its simple set, witty lyrics, affection for the ordinary guy, and keen sense of Canadian identity, *18 Wheels* established Gray's musical and dramatic signature, including its dark existential streak. The trucker, like Billy Bishop, rides out alone, "Where the night is all around, as thick as clay, / And death is riding shotgun all the way."

Billy Bishop Goes to War first appeared in November 1978, co-produced by the Vancouver East Cultural Centre and Tamahnous after a workshop earlier in the year at Theatre Passe Muraille. It had its genesis in 1971 when Gray and Eric Peterson first met at the University of British Columbia. Saskatchewan-born Peterson had spent two years in British repertory theatre before arriving on the west coast. After two years with Tamahnous he preceded Gray to Toronto and quickly gained a reputation as one of Passe Muraille's most imaginative actors. In 1976, Peterson discovered Bishop's autobiography, *Winged Warfare*, and co-developed the show with Gray. Though Gray is the writer of record, Peterson's skilled character work and virtuoso acting have been essential ingredients in the play's success – and in his own substantial career in Canadian theatre and television, including lead roles in the popular series *Street Legal, Corner Gas,* and *This Is Wonderland.*

Gray's third hit musical, *Rock and Roll*, opened under his own direction in 1981, co-produced by the Vancouver East Cultural Centre and National Arts Centre. In this semi-autobiographical play about a 1960s Nova Scotia dance band, Gray once again tells an exuberant comic tale of small-town Canadian boys who look back slightly disillusioned and nostalgic at their coming of age. The play won the 1988 Canadian Authors' Association Literary Award for Drama. Two children's plays followed: *Bongo from the Congo* (with Eric Peterson) and *Balthazar and the Mojo Star.* Halifax's Neptune Theatre premiered Gray's only non-musical, *Better Watch Out, Better Not Die* (1983), a farcical thriller, and *Don Messer's Jubilee* (1985), Gray's homage to the legendary Maritime folk band and his fourth successive musical smash. *18 Wheels, Rock and Roll,* and *Don Messer's Jubilee* were published together in 1987 as *Local Boy Makes Good.* A paean to the pains and lusts of the middle-aged male body, *Health, The Musical* (1989) premiered at the Vancouver Playhouse starring Peterson. Gray returned to the skies in 1993 with *Amelia!*, a musical about Amelia Earhart, co-produced by Vancouver's Carousel Theatre and the National Arts Centre. CBC Radio produced *The Tree, the Tower, the Flood,* a musical about the Creation, in 1997.

In 1984, Gray scripted and co-directed a prize-winning TV version of *Rock and Roll* titled *The King of Friday Night,* and published his first novel, *Dazzled,* a comic saga about growing up absurd in the 1970s. He wrote and performed satirical music videos for CBC-TV's *The Journal* from 1987 to

1990, and wrote the screenplay for the feature film *Kootenay Brown* (1990). His eclectic publications include an irreverent history of tattooing titled *I Love Mom* (1995) and a collection of essays on Canadian culture, *Lost in North America* (1995). He has written award-winning columns for *West* and *Western Living* magazines and for the online newspaper the *Tyee*, as well as for the *Vancouver Sun* and *Globe and Mail*.

He published his second novel, *A Gift for the Little Master*, in 2000 and since then has worked primarily as a novelist, writing thrillers set in Victorian England and mid-nineteenth-century America: *The Fiend in Human* (2003), *White Stone Day* (2005), and *Not Quite Dead* (2007). A long-time resident of Vancouver, Gray now goes by John MacLachlan Gray to distinguish himself, he has said, from the author of *Men Are from Mars, Women Are from Venus* and a well-known Canadian journalist, both named John Gray.

Following its initial Vancouver run in 1978, Gray and Peterson took *Billy Bishop Goes to War* on a sixteen-month Canadian tour. Then in 1980, with Mike Nichols as co-producer, they opened in Washington as a prelude to four months in New York on and off Broadway, where Peterson won the Clarence Derwent Award for Most Promising Actor. Next, the show went to the Edinburgh Festival and to Los Angeles, where it won both Best Play and Best Actor awards. Subsequently, the play has enjoyed hundreds of productions across North America. Gray and Peterson starred in a BBC-TV version in 1982, the year the published script won the Governor General's Literary Award for Drama.

In 1998 Gray and Peterson, both having just turned fifty, toured Canada in a highly acclaimed twentieth-anniversary production, revised to frame the original play as the now fifty-year-old Bishop's retrospective look at his own story. In 2009 they performed it for Soulpepper Theatre in Toronto, a sold-out production remounted again in 2010, with the performers now in their sixties making further changes to the script. The script of the play printed here includes Gray's latest revisions and alternatives for playing Billy as either a young man or an older one. A successful 2010 production of the play in Vancouver and Saskatoon featured John's musician son Zachary Gray in the role of the Narrator, playing electric guitar as well as piano. John and Eric starred again in a feature film version directed by Barbara Willis-Sweete in 2011.

The theatrical and ideological strategies of *Billy Bishop Goes to War* derive at least partly from the model Paul Thompson established in the 1970s at Theatre Passe Muraille, where Gray and Peterson were working when they conceptualized the show. The essence of Thompson's nationalist dramaturgy, Brian Arnott has pointed out, "was a conscientious effort to give theatrical validity to sounds, rhythms and myths that were distinctively Canadian." His mode of collective creation brought actors directly into the process and explicitly incorporated their skills in both script and production. Thompson's form of "poor theatre" minimized sets, props, and costumes; the voices, bodies, talent, and imagination of the performers became paramount. Consequently, the theatricality of a Passe Muraille show often reflected its theme of Can-Do Canadianism.

Canadian audiences watched plays about Canadian characters with minimal resources who imaginatively overcome severe obstacles. Those characters were played by Canadian actors facing analogous challenges on the stage.

Billy Bishop Goes to War sharply focuses the Passe Muraille style and theme in a tour de force for one actor. Apart from the Narrator / Piano Player who provides mostly musical support, the actor playing Bishop is alone onstage telling his story, creating all the other characters without changes of costume or makeup, and nearly all the sound effects (the Piano Player does the rest). He works on a set bare except for the piano and is equipped with a minimum of props. The essence of the play can be found in the extraordinary scene where Bishop describes his first solo flight, accompanying his narrative with his own vocal effects and (in the original production) only a hand-held model airplane for illustration. This is theatre pared down to its essentials: a skilled actor on a bare stage creating a world before our eyes. Reading this kind of play demands of us an imaginative reconstruction.

Hearing *Billy Bishop Goes to War* makes one aware of the subtle modulations of tone effected by Gray's music and songs. Most of the criticism directed at the play when it was first performed, only a few years after the end of the Vietnam war, concerned Bishop's attitude toward war and his own part in it as well as the play's attitude toward Bishop. Does Gray celebrate war by glamorizing Bishop and his bloodlust or trivialize war by showing it as a game? Does Bishop have any doubts about his own cold-bloodedness?

Gray insists in a preface published in the first edition that the play "does not address itself to the issue of whether or not war is a good thing or a bad thing." But colouring Bishop's ascendancy to the status of war hero is the terrific melancholy of the opening song in Act One, "We Were Off to Fight the Hun," which resonates through the play, belying his naive idea that war would be "lots of fun." Many of the songs share that tone. The play's most beautiful song, "In the Sky," is as much a poignant lament as a romantic celebration of aerial warfare; and "Friends Ain't S'posed to Die" makes blatant, in melody and lyrics, the shame Bishop felt in surviving when "most of us never got old."

Of course the spirited anthems also reflect Bishop's joy in his work. He did love flying and he makes us share in his exhilaration. But he came to love killing, too. We watch the comic innocent of Act One develop in Act Two into the icy professional who stays "as calm as the ocean" and goes up even on his days off because he likes it so much. Gray never allows Bishop to be totally unconscious of the ironies in his situation. The fact that the "Survival" song at the top of Act Two is sung by Bishop in the voice of a French chanteuse, the "Lovely Hélène," gives it an edge of self-mockery; maybe Bishop is even a little embarrassed about his new-found cynicism. "The Dying of Albert Ball" is Bishop's (and Gray's) brilliant post-colonial response to his manipulation by Lady St. Helier and the rest of the British ruling class who "like their heroes / Cold and dead." Finally, the rousing "Empire Soirée" provides a bitter counterpoint to the celebrations of victory. The personal heroism and sacrifice of the brave men dancing and dying in the sky is superseded by the pointless and impersonal "dance of history" as one war is followed by another.

"Makes you wonder what it was all for," Bishop mutters in 1941. Though not very introspective, he is far from blind to the insanity of war. His visions of No Man's Land and of the two German flyers falling out of their plane are among the most chilling moments in Canadian theatre. But ultimately, Billy Bishop's reminiscence is not so much about his experience of horror and death as it is about being young and the most intensely alive he ever felt. "One thing's for sure," he sings. "We'll never be that young again." He sings not only for himself but for a world that would never be the same.

John MacLachlan Gray
with Eric Peterson

Billy Bishop
Goes to War

Billy Bishop Goes to War opened on November 3, 1978, at the Vancouver East Cultural Centre, produced by the Vancouver East Cultural Centre in association with Tamahnous Theatre.

BILLY BISHOP   Eric Peterson
NARRATOR /
PIANO PLAYER   John MacLachlan Gray

Directed by John MacLachlan Gray
Set and Lighting Design by Paul Williams
Music and Lyrics by John MacLachlan Gray

PLAYWRIGHT'S NOTES

Billy Bishop Goes to War is dedicated to all those who didn't come back from the war, and to those who did and wondered why.

– JOHN MACLACHLAN GRAY (1981)

The script that follows is necessarily two scripts, depending on the age of the storyteller. Differences in the two versions appear as explanatory stage directions. The dialogue is identical throughout, except for the ending: in one case, the younger Bishop flashes forward to World War Two, as he rallies the troops while in his mid-forties; in the other, the elder Bishop writes a last letter to Margaret at age sixty-two. But really, it is the same play it always was – just as Peterson and Gray are the same people we were at age thirty-two. The difference is in the telling.

– JOHN MACLACHLAN GRAY (2012)

CHARACTERS

    NARRATOR / PIANO PLAYER
    BILLY BISHOP, *who also plays*

    AN UPPERCLASSMAN
    ADJUTANT PERRAULT
    AN AIRMAN
    SIR HUGH CECIL
    LADY ST. HELIER
    CEDRIC, *her butler*
    A DOCTOR
    OFFICER ONE
    OFFICER TWO
    GENERAL JOHN HIGGINS, *Brigade Commander*
    A TOMMY
    THE LOVELY HÉLÈNE
    ALBERT BALL
    WALTER BOURNE, *Bishop's mechanic*
    A GERMAN
    GENERAL HUGH M. TRENCHARD
    AN ADJUTANT
    SECOND OFFICER
    KING GEORGE V

ACT ONE

*Lights up on **BILLY BISHOP** and the **PIANO PLAYER**, on a stage containing memorabilia, much of it from the Great War. The setting could be an officer's mess, a Legion bar, a cluttered room in Bishop's house, or the attic of a veteran's hospital. **BISHOP** sits in a vintage chair. The **PIANO PLAYER** – he could be an old friend or a memory – sits at the piano and sings.*

BISHOP & PIANO PLAYER: (*singing*)
We were off to fight the Hun,
We would shoot him with a gun.
Our medals would shine
Like a sabre in the sun.
We were off to fight the Hun

And it looked like lots of fun,
Somehow it didn't seem like war
At all, at all, at all.
Somehow it didn't seem like war at all.

> *BISHOP speaks both to the audience and to the*
> *PIANO PLAYER, who continues to accompany*
> *him with a nostalgic chord sequence – amused or*
> *poignant, depending on the man's age.*

BISHOP: I think when you haven't been in a war for a while … you've got to take what you can get. I mean, Canada? 1914? They must have been pretty desperate. Take me, for instance. Twenty years old, a convicted liar and cheat – I mean, I'm on record as the worst student RMC – Royal Military College in Kingston, Ontario – I'm on record as the worst student they ever had. I join up, they made me an officer! A lieutenant in the Mississauga Horse. All I can say is, they must have been scraping the bottom of the barrel.

BISHOP & PIANO PLAYER: (*singing*)

We were off to fight the Hun,
Though hardly anyone
Had ever read about a battle,
Much less seen a Lewis gun.
We were off to fight the Hun
And it looked like lots of fun,
Somehow it didn't seem like war
At all, at all, at all.
Somehow it didn't seem like war at all.

BISHOP: Yeah, it looked like it was going to be a great war. I mean, all my friends were very keen to join up – they were. Not me. Royal Military College was enough for me. Now the reason I went to RMC was … (*tries to remember*)

PIANO PLAYER: Well, you could ride a horse.

BISHOP: I could ride a horse. And I was a good shot. I mean, I am a really good shot. I've got these tremendous eyes, you see. And Royal Military College had an entrance exam – which was good because my previous scholastic record wasn't that hot. In fact, when I told my principal that indeed I was going to RMC, he said, "Bishop, you don't have the brains." But I studied real hard, sat for the exams, and got in.

> *The PIANO PLAYER beats a military snare-drum*
> *pattern on his knees.*

BISHOP: (*as officer*) Recruits! Recruits will march at all times, they will not loiter, they will not window-shop. Recruits! Recruits will run at all times through the parade square. Recruits! Recruits will be soundly trounced every Friday night, whether they deserve it or not! (*as himself*) I mean those guys were nuts! They were going to make leaders out of us – the theory being that before you could lead, you had to learn to obey. So because of this we were all assigned to an upperclassman as a kind of, well, slave. And I got assigned to this real sadistic SOB, this guy named Vivian Bishop – that's right, it's the same surname as me; and because of this, I had to tuck him in at night, kiss him on the forehead, and say, "Goodnight, sir!"

PIANO PLAYER: Daddy. Goodnight, Daddy.

BISHOP: (*mortified*) Goodnight, Daddy. I mean, it was pretty hard to take some of this stuff seriously. One of my punishments: I'm s'posed to clean out this old Martello tower by the edge of the lake. I mean it's filthy, hasn't been cleaned in years. Now I do a real great job. I clean it up really well. This upperclassman comes along to inspect it.

> *BISHOP becomes both the UPPERCLASSMAN and*
> *himself.*

UPPERCLASSMAN: What's this in the corner, Bishop?

BISHOP: That? (*looks carefully*) That's a spider, sir.

UPPERCLASSMAN: That's right, Bishop. That's a spider. Now you had orders to clean this place up. You haven't done it. Now you get down on your hands and knees and you eat that spider.

BISHOP: (*to the audience*) I had to eat a spider, in front of all my classmates. You ever had to eat a spider? In public? I doubt it. Nuts! Now whenever I'm not happy, whenever I'm not having a really good time, I do one of three things: I get sick, I get injured, or I get in an awful lot of trouble. My third year at RMC, I got into a lot of trouble. This friend of mine, Townsend? One night we got a bottle of gin and we stole a canoe. Well, we'd arranged to meet these girls out on … what was it?

PIANO PLAYER: Cedar Island. Dead Man's Bay.

BISHOP: Cedar Island out on Dead Man's Bay. Of course, the canoe tips over. Now it's early spring, it's really cold. We get back to shore somehow, and we're just like this (*shivering violently*), and Townsend says, "Bish, Bish, I've got to go to the infirmary, I think I've got pneumonia." And I say to him, "Well, whatever you do, you silly bugger, put on some dry clothes." Because we couldn't let on what we were doing – I mean, we're absent without leave, in possession of alcohol, and we stole a canoe. What I didn't know was, the officer on duty witnessed this whole thing. Townsend goes to the infirmary, he's confronted with these charges, he admits everything. I didn't know that. I'm rudely awakened out of my sleep and hauled before old Adjutant Perrault.

*At attention, he addresses **ADJUTANT PERRAULT**, who is French-Canadian.*

Sir? I've been in my bed all night, sir. I really don't know what you're talking about, sir –

PERRAULT: Come on, come on now, Bishop. We have the testimony of the officer on duty. We also have the confession of your accomplice implicating you fully in this. Now what is your story, Bishop?

BISHOP: (*to the audience*) Well, I figure I'm in too deep to change my story. (*to PERRAULT*) Sir, I still maintain –

PERRAULT: Bishop! I'm going to say the worst thing I can say to a gentleman cadet: You are a liar, Bishop!

*The **PIANO PLAYER** winces and looks away. **BISHOP** is momentarily sobered by the memory.*

BISHOP: I got twenty-eight days restricted leave for that. It's like house arrest. Then they caught me cheating on my final exams – well, I handed in the crib notes with the exam paper! And that's when they called me the worst student RMC ever had. They weren't going to tell me what my punishment was until the next fall, so I could stew about it all summer, but I knew what it was going to be. Expulsion. With full honours. But then the war broke out and I enlisted and was made an officer – I mean, for me, it was the lesser of two evils. But everyone else was very keen on the whole thing. They were!

BISHOP & PIANO PLAYER: (*singing*)

We were off to fight the Hun,
Though hardly anyone
Had ever seen a Hun,
Wouldn't know one if we saw one.
We were off to fight the Hun
And it looked like lots of fun,
Somehow it didn't seem like war
At all, at all, at all.
Somehow it didn't seem like war at all.

*More military rhythm from the **PIANO PLAYER**.*

BISHOP: October 1st, 1914! The First Contingent of the Canadian Expeditionary Force left for England! I wasn't with them. I was in the hospital. Thinking of Margaret.

*The **PIANO PLAYER** plays the "Dear Margaret" theme while **BISHOP** narrates a letter to an old photograph.*

BISHOP: Dear … Dearest Margaret. I am in the hospital with pneumonia. I also have an allergy. The doctors don't know what I am allergic to. Maybe it's horses. Maybe it's the army. The hospital is nice, so am in good spirits. Thinking of you constantly, I remain …

*Again the **PIANO PLAYER** slaps out a military rhythm.*

BISHOP: March 1915! The Second, Third, Fourth, Fifth, and Sixth Contingents of the Canadian Expeditionary Force left for England! I wasn't with them either. I was back in the hospital. Thinking of Margaret.

Another letter, spoken to the "Dear Margaret" musical theme.

Dearest Margaret. Please excuse my writing, as I have a badly sprained wrist. Yesterday my horse reared up and fell over backward on me. It was awful, I could have been killed. My head was completely buried in the mud. My nose is of course broken and quite swollen, I can't see out of one eye, I have two broken ribs, and am pretty badly bruised, but the doctor figures I'll be up and around by Monday. The hospital is nice, so am in fine spirits. Thinking of you constantly, I remain …

*The **PIANO PLAYER** slaps out a military rhythm once again.*

BISHOP: July 1915! The Seventh Contingent of the Canadian Expeditionary Force left for England! And I was with them!

*The **PIANO PLAYER** plays a steady, timpani-like bass roll.*

Now this was aboard a cattle boat, called the *Caledonia*, in Montreal. There was this big crowd came down to the pier to see us off, I mean, hundreds and hundreds of people, and for a while there, I felt like the whole thing was worth doing. I mean it's pretty impressive when you look out there and you see hundreds and hundreds of people waving - at you. When you're from a small town, the numbers get to you. And you're looking out at them, and they're looking at you, and you think, "Boy, I must be doing something right!"

The PIANO PLAYER breaks into "God Save the King."

And they play "God Save the King," and everybody is crying and waving and cheering, and the boat pulls out, and they start to yell like you never heard anybody yell before – I mean, you feel good, you really do! And we're all praying, "Please, God, don't let the fighting be over before I can take part in it!" (*He gets carried away.*) "On the edge of destiny, you must test your strength!" (*pause, as he comes to his senses*) What the hell am I talking about?

The PIANO PLAYER plays a monotonous bass pattern suggesting the roll of a ship.

BISHOP: The good ship *Caledonia* quickly changed its name to the good ship Vomit. It was never meant to hold people. Even the horses didn't like it. Up. Down. Up. Down. And they're siphoning brandy down our throats to keep us from puking our guts up on deck. It was a big joke. Whenever someone would puke, which was every minute or so, everyone would point and laugh like it was the funniest thing you ever saw. I mean puke swishing around the deck two inches deep, har, har, har! (*ship's bells on piano suggest a calm sea*) You couldn't sleep, even when it was calm, because every time you closed your eyes, you had this nightmare about torpedoes (*demonstrates a torpedo to ominous accompaniment*). Every time I closed my eyes I could see this torpedo coming through the water, through the hull of the ship, and ... BOOM!

The PIANO PLAYER plays a crash of clustered bass notes.

And we were torpedoed just off the coast of Ireland. I was scared shitless. All you could do was stand at the rail and watch the other ships get hit and go down. Bodies ... floating around like driftwood in the water. But we made it through. The Good Ship *Caledonia*, latrine of the Atlantic, finally made it through to Portsmouth, full of dead horses and sick Canadians. When we got off, they thought we were a boatload of Balkan refugees.

BISHOP & PIANO PLAYER: (*singing*)
We were off to fight the Hun,
We would shoot him with a gun.
Our medals would shine

Like a sabre in the sun.
We were off to fight the Hun
And it looked like lots of fun,
Somehow it didn't seem like war
At all, at all, at all.
Somehow it didn't seem like war at all.

BISHOP: A few days later, we marched into Shorncliffe Military Camp, right on the Channel. On a clear night you could see the artillery flashes from France.

Distant explosions on piano.

I took it as a sign of better things to come. It wasn't.

BISHOP narrates another letter to the "Dearest Margaret" theme.

Dearest Margaret. Shorncliffe Military Camp is the worst yet. The wind brings two kinds of weather – either it rains or it doesn't. When it rains, you've got mud like I've never seen before. Your horse gets stuck in a foot and a half of mud, you get off – and you're knee deep. The rain falls in sheets; you're never, never dry. Then the rain stops and the ground dries out – what a relief, you say. But then the wind gets the dust going and you've got dust storms for days. The sand is like needles hitting you: a lot of the men are bleeding from the eyes. I don't know which is worse – going blind or going crazy. The sand gets into your food, your clothes, your tent, your ... body orifices. A lot of the guys have something called desert madness, which is really serious. As I write this letter, the sand is drifting across the page. Thinking of you constantly, I remain ...

The PIANO PLAYER brings "Dearest Margaret" theme to a melancholy end while BISHOP ruefully ponders his fate.

Being buried alive in the mud. I was seriously considering this prospect one day, when a funny thing happened. (*demonstrating*) You see, I got my horse stuck in the middle of the parade ground. The horse is up to its fetlocks, I'm up to my knees, mud, sweat, and horse shit from head to toe ...

The PIANO PLAYER plays an ethereal "flying" theme, reminiscent of Ravel or Debussy.

Then suddenly, out of the clouds comes this little single-seater scout, this little fighter plane. It circles a couple of times. – I guess the pilot had lost his way and was coming down to ask for directions. He does this turn, then lands on an open space, like a dragonfly on a rock. The pilot jumps out – he's in this long sheepskin coat, helmet, goggles ... Warm and dry. He gets his directions, then jumps back into the machine and up in the air, with the mist blowing off him. All by himself. No superior officer. No horse. No sand, no mud – what a beautiful picture. I don't know how long I stood there watching, until he was long gone. Out of sight.

The music ends. BISHOP abruptly breaks the mood.

I mean, this war was going on a lot longer than anyone expected. A lot more people were getting killed than anyone expected, too. Now I sure as hell wasn't going to spend the rest of the war in the mud. And I wasn't going to die in the mud!

The PIANO PLAYER strikes up a sentimental tune while BISHOP sets up two chairs, gets a glass, then drunkenly joins in the chorus.

PIANO PLAYER: (*singing*)

Thinking of December nights

In the clear Canadian cold,

Where the winter air don't smell bad,

And the wind don't make you old.

Where the rain don't wash your heart out,

And the nights ain't filled with fear.

Oh, those old familiar voices

Whisper in my ears.

Chorus

Oh, Canada,

Sing a song for me.

Sing one for your lonely son,

So far across the sea.

The PIANO PLAYER breaks into a fast-stride dance tune. BISHOP's reverie is interrupted by a drunken, half-mad Scottish AIRMAN. (He can be portrayed as Cockney.) BISHOP, as always, plays both parts.

AIRMAN: Ye don't fancy the Cavalry then, eh mate?

BISHOP: What?!

AIRMAN: I said, ye don't fancy the Cavalry then. It's worse at the front, mate. There ye got Heinie shootin' at ye ... with machine guns. DAKAKAKAKAK! Har, har! It's a bloody shooting gallery with you in the middle of it, mate.

BISHOP: This is awful. Something must be done. Jeez, I was a casualty in training!

AIRMAN: Take a word of advice from me, mate. The only way out ... is up.

BISHOP: Up?

AIRMAN: Up. Join the Royal Flying Corps. I did. I used to be in the Cavalry. I joined the RFC, and I like it. It's good, clean work. Mind you, the machines barely stay in the air an' the life expectancy of the new lads is about eleven days, but I like it. It's good, clean work.

BISHOP: Just a minute. How can I get into the Royal Flying Corps? I'm Canadian. I'm cannon fodder. You have to practically own your own plane to join the RFC.

AIRMAN: Au contraire, mate. Au contraire. The upper classes are depressed by the present statistics, so they're not joining with their usual alacrity. Now, anyone who wants to can get blown out of the air. Even Canadians.

BISHOP: Well, what do I have to do?

AIRMAN: Ye go down, see them at the War Office – daft bunch of twits, but they're all right. Now you act real eager, see? Like you crave the excitement, any old rubbish. But they're not going to know what to ask you because they don't know a bleeding thing about it. So they'll ask you whatever comes into their heads, which isn't much, then they'll say you can't be a pilot, you got to be an observer.

BISHOP: What's an observer?

AIRMAN: He's the laddie who goes along for the ride. Looks about.

BISHOP: Oh.

AIRMAN: Now you act real disappointed – like your mum always wanted you to be a pilot. Then you get your transfer ...

BISHOP: Just a minute, just a minute. So I'm an observer. I'm the guy that looks about. So what? How do I get to be a pilot?

AIRMAN: (*thinks about this*) I dunno. Sooner or later you just get to be a pilot. Plenty of vacancies these days. Check the casualty lists, wait for a bad one. (*He becomes inexplicably enraged.*) You have to go in by the back door, you know what I mean? Nobody gets to be a pilot right away – 'specially not fucking Canadians!

The music stops cold. BISHOP speaks to the audience.

BISHOP: Did you ever trust your entire future to a drunken conversation in a bar? Two days later, I went down to see them at the War Office.

The PIANO PLAYER plays a martial intro as BISHOP faces SIR HUGH CECIL at the War Office. SIR HUGH is getting on in years and the technology of modern war has confused him.

SIR HUGH: So. You wish to transfer to the Royal Flying Corps. Am I right? Am I correct?

BISHOP: Yes, sir. I want to become a fighter pilot, sir.

SIR HUGH: I thought as much. Well done. Jolly good.

BISHOP: It's what my mother always wanted, sir.

SIR HUGH: It's what your mother always ... oh. (*impressed*) Oh. Oh I see. Well, the situation is this, Bishop. We need good men in the Royal Flying Corps, but they must have the correct ... er, qualifications. Now while the War Office has not yet ascertained what qualifications are indeed necessary for flying a ... er ... an aeroplane, we must see to it that all candidates possess the correct qualifications – should the War Office ever decide what those qualifications ... are. Do you understand that, Bishop?

BISHOP: Perfectly, sir.

SIR HUGH: Jolly good. Excellent. Well done. That's more than I can say. Shall we begin, then?

BISHOP: Ready when you are, sir.

SIR HUGH: Oh, that's good, too! Shows keenness, you see. Excellent. Well done. Jolly good. (*aside*) Good lord, what on earth should I ask him? (*pause while he collects his thoughts; finally*) Do you ski?

BISHOP: (*nonplussed*) Ski, sir?

SIR HUGH: Yes. Do you ski?

BISHOP: (*to the audience*) Here was an Englishman asking a Canadian whether or not he skied. Now, if the Canadian said he didn't ski, the Englishman might find that somewhat ... suspicious. (*to SIR HUGH*) Ski, sir? Yes, sir! (*to the audience*) Never skied in my life.

SIR HUGH: Thought you might. Well done. Excellent ... Oh dear .... (*thinks up another question*) Do you ride a horse?

BISHOP: I'm an officer in the Cavalry, sir!

SIR HUGH: Doesn't necessarily follow. But let's put down that you ride, shall we? Now what about sports? Run, jump, throw the ball, play the game, eh what?

BISHOP: Sports, sir? All sports!

SIR HUGH: Oh, I say! Bishop, I am most impressed!

BISHOP: Does this mean I can become a fighter pilot, sir?

SIR HUGH: Who knows, Bishop? Who knows? All full-up with fighter pilots at the moment, I'm afraid, take six months, a year to get in. Terribly sorry, old man. Nothing I can do.

BISHOP: I see, sir.

SIR HUGH: However: We have an immediate need for observers – you know, that's the fellow who goes along for the ride. Looks about, I suppose. What do you say, Bishop?

BISHOP: (*to the audience*) I thought about it. I wanted to be a pilot. I couldn't. So in the fall of 1915, I joined the Twenty-One Squadron as an observer. You see, that's what they were using the machines for at that time. Observation. You could take pictures of enemy troop formations, direct artillery fire, stuff like that. And I was really good at the aerial photography. I've got these great eyes – remember?

The PIANO PLAYER reprises the ethereal "flying" theme.

BISHOP: And to fly! You're in this old Farnham trainer. Sounds like a tractor. Coughs, wheezes, chugs its way up to one thousand feet. You're in a kite with a motor that can barely get off the ground – but even so, you're in the air. You're not ... on the ground. You're above everything.

The ethereal piano theme becomes carnival-like.

It was a different world up there, a different war. And a different breed of men fighting that war. Flyers! During training we heard all the stories: if you went down behind enemy lines and were killed, they'd come over – the Germans, that is – under a flag of truce, and drop a photograph of your grave. Nice. If you were taken prisoner, it was the champagne razzle in the mess, talking and drinking all night. It was a different war they were fighting up there – and from where I stood it looked pretty darn good!

The PIANO PLAYER introduces a mess-hall sing-along song reminiscent of Flanders and Swann.

PIANO PLAYER: Could you be a tiny bit more specific, please?

BISHOP: Certainly.

BISHOP & PIANO PLAYER: (*speaking alternate lines, then singing together for the chorus*)

I see two planes in the air,

A fight that's fair and square,

With dips and loops and rolls

That would scare ya. (I'm scared already.)

We will force the German down,

And arrest him on the ground,

A patriotic lad from Bavaria. (Jawohl!)

He'll surrender willingly,

And salute our chivalry,

For this war was none of our creation. (Damn right about that.)

But before it's prison camp,

And a bed that's cold and damp,

We'll have a little celebration.

Chorus

Oh we'll toast our youth

On champagne and vermouth,

For all of us know what it's like to fly.

Oh the fortunes of war

Can't erase esprit de corps,

And we'll all of us be friends 'til we die.

PIANO PLAYER: Be so good as to elaborate on that general theme.

BISHOP: I shall do so. (*singing*)

Oh, we'll drink the night away,

And when the Bosch is led away,

We'll load him down with cigarettes and wine.

(Of course we will.)

Both sing.

We'll drink a final toast goodbye,

But for the grace of God go I,

And we'll vow that we'll be friends ... another time.

Chorus

Oh, we'll toast our youth

On champagne and vermouth,

For all of us know what it's like to fly.

Oh the fortunes of war

Can't erase esprit de corps

And we'll all of us be friends 'til we die.

BISHOP: You want chivalry? You want gallantry? You want nice guys? Well, that's your flyer – and, jeez, I was going to be one of them!

The PIANO PLAYER returns to the carnival theme.

BISHOP: January 1st, 1916, I crossed the Channel as a flyer ... well, an observer, anyway. And that's when I found out that Twenty-One Squadron was known as the "suicide squadron." That awful nickname preyed on my mind, you know?

The carnival theme darkens.

And the Archies? The anti-aircraft guns? (*shudders*) Not tonight, Archibald! You're tooling around over the line, doing your observation work, a sitting duck, when suddenly you're surrounded by these little black puffs of smoke ... Then bam! Whiz! Shrapnel shrieking all around you. I was hit on the head by a piece of shrapnel – just a bruise, but a couple of inches lower and I could have been killed. And we were all scared stiff of this new German machine – the Fokker. It had this interrupter gear, so the pilot could shoot straight through the propeller without actually shooting the propeller off – all he had to do was aim his plane at you!

Carnival music dies.

And casualties? Lots and lots and lots of casualties. It was a grim situation – but we didn't know how grim it could get until we saw the R.E.7. The Reconnaissance Experimental Number Seven: our new plane.

BISHOP mimes the following, using furniture and whatever props are at hand.

To look at it, what you saw was a mound of cables and wires, with a thousand pounds of equipment hanging onto it. Four machine guns. A five-hundred-pound bomb, for God's sake! Cameras, reconnaissance equipment ... Roger Neville (that's my pilot), he and I are ordered into the thing to take it up. (*imitates a sputtering, floundering airplane that will not fly*) Of course, the thing doesn't get off the ground. Anyone could see that. We think fine, good riddance. Uh-oh. The officers go into a huddle.

OFFICER ONE: Well, what do you think the problem is?

OFFICER TWO: I don't know, sir. Maybe we should try taking the bomb off.

OFFICER ONE: A splendid idea. Take the bomb off.

OFFICER TWO: Take the bomb off!

PIANO PLAYER: Take the bomb off!

BISHOP: Take the bomb off! So we take the bomb off and try again. This time the thing sort of flops down the runway like a crippled duck. (*imitates the floundering airplane*) Finally, by taking everything off but one machine gun, the thing sort of flopped itself into the air and chugged along. It was a pig. We were all scared stiff of it. So they put us on active duty – as *bombers*! They give us two bombs each, tell us to fly over Hunland and drop them on somebody. But in order to accommodate for the weight of the bombs? They took our machine gun away!

The PIANO PLAYER breaks into a sort of ragtime blues.

BISHOP: Dearest Margaret. We are dropping bombs on the enemy from unarmed machines. It is exciting work. It's hard to keep your confidence in a war when you don't have a gun. Somehow we get back in one piece and we start joking around and inspecting the machine for shrapnel damage. You're so thankful not to be dead. Then I go back to the barracks and lie down ... and a kind of terrible loneliness comes over you. It's like waiting for the firing squad. You want to cry, you feel so frightened, and so alone. I think all of us who aren't dead think these things. Thinking of you constantly, I remain ...

BISHOP takes a rest while the PIANO PLAYER sings:

Nobody shoots no one in Canada,
At least nobody they don't know.
Nobody shoots no one in Canada,
Last battle was a long, long time ago.

Nobody picks no fights in Canada,
Not with nobody they ain't met.
Nobody starts no wars in Canada,
Folks tend to work for what they get.

BISHOP joins in.

Take me under
That big blue sky,
Where the deer and the black bear play.
May not be heaven,
But heaven knows we try,
Wish I was in Canada today.

Nobody drop no bombs on Canada,
Don't want no one to go to hell.
Nobody drops no bombs on Canada,
Where folks tend to wish each other well.

The music continues, interrupted by sound effects where appropriate.

BISHOP: Of course, in this situation it wasn't long before the accidents started happening again. You know, it's kind of spooky, but I think being accident-prone actually saved my life. I'm driving a truckload of parts a couple of miles from the aerodrome and I run into another truck. (*crash!*) I'm inspecting the undercarriage of my machine when a cable snaps (*ping!*) and hits me on the head. I'm unconscious for two days. I had a tooth pulled? It got infected. I was in the hospital for two weeks. Then Roger does this really bad landing. (*crash!*) I hit my knee on a metal brace inside the plane so hard I could barely walk! Then I got three weeks in London, none too soon. On the boat back to England we all got into the champagne and cognac pretty heavy, and by the time we arrived we were all pretty tight, and this game developed, to see who would be the first to touch foot on English soil. I'm leading the race down the gangplank, and I trip and fall. (*multiple crashes!*) Everyone else falls on top of me – right on the knee I hurt in the crash! God, the pain was awful. But I'd be damned if I'd spend my leave in the hospital, so I just poured down the brandy until the thing was pretty well numb, had a hell of a time. If the pain got to me in the night and I couldn't sleep, I'd just pour down the brandy. But around my last day of leave, I started thinking about the bombing runs, the Archies, the Fokkers, and I thought, jeez, maybe I better have someone look at this knee! The doctor found I had a cracked kneecap, which meant I'd be in the hospital for a couple of weeks. But he also found that I had a badly strained heart, which meant I would be in the hospital for an indefinite period. As far as I was concerned, I was out of the war.

BISHOP & PIANO PLAYER: (*singing*)
Take me under
That big blue sky,
Where the deer and the black bear play.
May not be heaven,
But heaven knows we try,
Wish I was in Canada today.

I'm dreaming of the trees in Canada,
Northern lights are dancing in my head.
If I die, then let me die in Canada,
Where there's a chance I'll die in bed.

The music becomes restful.

BISHOP: The hospital is nice. People don't shoot at you. People don't drop things on you. I thought it would be a nice place to spend the war. I went to sleep for three days.

A crash on piano, followed by distorted marching music.

I had this nightmare. A terrible dream. I am in the lobby of the Grand Hotel in London. The band is playing military music, and the lobby is full of English and German officers, and they're dancing – together. And their medals jingle like sleigh bells in the snow – ching, ching! Ching-ching! Ching-ching! The sound is deafening. I've got to get out of there. I start to run, but my knee gives out underneath me. As I get up, I get kicked in the stomach by a Prussian boot. As I turn to run, I get kicked in the rear by an English boot. Then I turn around, and all the officers have formed a chorus line, like the Follies, and they are heading for me – kicking! I scream as a hundred boots kick me high in the air, as I turn over and over in the air, shouting, "Help me! Help me! They're trying to kill me!"

The music reaches a climax. He stops abruptly when he hears a voice.

LADY ST. HELIER: My goodness, Bishop, you'll not get any rest screaming at the top of your lungs like that.

BISHOP: In front of me was a face I'd never seen before – very old, female, with long white hair pulled back tightly in a bun, exposing two of the largest ears I had ever seen.

LADY ST. HELIER: You would be the son of Will Bishop of Owen Sound, Canada, would you not? Of course you are – the resemblance is quite startling. Your father was a loyal supporter of a very good friend of mine – Sir Wilfrid Laurier. It was in that connection that I first met your father in Ottawa ... A gaping mouth is most impolite, Bishop. No, I am not a clairvoyant. I am Lady St. Helier: Reform alderman, poetess, friend of Churchill, and the woman who will save your life.

BISHOP: (*speechless*) Er, um ... I mean, ahhh ...

LADY ST. HELIER: Enough of this gay banter, Bishop. Time runs apace and my life is not without its limits. You have been making rather a mess of it, haven't you? You're a rude young man behaving like cannon fodder. Perfectly acceptable characteristics in a Canadian – but you are different. You are a gifted Canadian. And that gift belongs to a much older and deeper tradition than Canada can ever provide. Quite against your own wishes, you will be released from this wretched hospital in two weeks' time. Promptly at three o'clock on that afternoon, you will present yourself before my door at Portland Place, dressed for tea and in a positive frame of mind. Please be punctual. Good day, Mr. Bishop.

BISHOP: (*to the audience*) Well, jeez, that old girl must have known something I didn't, because two weeks later I find myself in front of her door at Portland Place, in my best uniform, shining my shoes on my trousers. (*He mimes knocking on the door, which creaks open; he looks up – way up.*) Hi.

CEDRIC the butler looks down at him with distaste.

CEDRIC: Madam. The colonial is here. Shall I show him in?

LADY ST. HELIER: (*muffled in the distance*) Yes, Cedric, please. Show him in.

CEDRIC: Get in.

BISHOP: I'm shown into the largest room I have ever seen. A fireplace eight feet high; a staircase that must have had a hundred steps in it. I'm not used to dealing with nobility: servants, grand ballrooms, pheasant hunting on the heath, fifty-year-old brandy over billiards, breakfast in bed – shit, what a life!

CEDRIC: Madam is in the study. Get in.

BISHOP: The study: books, books, more books than I'll ever read. Persian rug. Tiger's head over the mantle. African spears in the corner. (*sings*) "Rule Britannia, Britannia rules the ..." I stood at the door. I'm on edge. Out of my element.

LADY ST. HELIER: Very punctual, Mr. Bishop. Please sit down.

BISHOP: I sit in this chair that is all carved lions ... (*winces*) One of the lions stuck in my back.

CEDRIC: Would our visitor from Canada care for tea, Madam?

LADY ST. HELIER: Would you care for something to drink, Bishop?

BISHOP: (*unenthusiastic*) Tea? Ahhh, sure. Tea would be fine.

LADY ST. HELIER: A tea for Bishop, Cedric. And I'll have a gin.

BISHOP: *Gin?* I wonder if I might change mine to ... (*notes CEDRIC's intimidating presence*) No, no, no, tea would be, tea would be fine. (*to the audience*) Tea is served. I sip my tea. Lady St. Helier sips her gin. And Cedric looms over me – afraid I was going to drool on the rug or something. Lady St. Helier stared at me through these thick spectacles. Then suddenly her ears twitched, like she was honing in on something.

LADY ST. HELIER: I have written a poem in your honour, Bishop. I can but hope that your rustic mind will appreciate its significance. (*to the PIANO PLAYER*) Cedric!

She performs a recitative to piano accompaniment.

You're a typical Canadian,
You're modesty itself,
And you really wouldn't want to hurt a flea.
But you're just about to go
The way of the buffalo.
You'd do well to take this good advice from me.

I'm awfully sick and tired,
Being constantly required
To stand by and watch Canadians make the best of it;
For the colonial mentality
Defies all rationality.
You seem to go to lengths to make a mess of it.

Why don't you grow up,
Before I throw up?
Do you expect somebody else to do it for you?
Before you're dead out,
Get the lead out,
And seize what little life still lies before you.

Do you really expect Empire
To settle back, retire,
And say, "Colonials, go on your merry way"?
I'm very tired of your whining
And your infantile maligning.
Your own weakness simply won't be whined away.

Oh, don't be so naive,
And take your heart off your sleeve,
For a fool and his life will soon be parted.
War's a fact of life today
And it will not be wished away.
Forget that fact and you are dead before you've started.

So Bishop, grow up
Before I throw up.
Your worst enemy is yourself, as you well know.
Before you're dead out,
Get the lead out,
You have your own naivety to overthrow.

The PIANO PLAYER ends with a flourish.

LADY ST. HELIER: (*to the PIANO PLAYER*) Thank you, Cedric. (*to BISHOP*) Do I make myself clear, Mr. Bishop? You will cease this mediocrity that your record only too clearly reveals. You will become the pilot that you wished to be – and were lamentably content to settle for less. Now this will take time, for you must recover the health that you have so seriously undermined. To that end, you will become a lodger at Portland Place – top of the stairs, third floor, seventh door on the left. (*to CEDRIC*) Cedric, be kind to Bishop. And ignore his bad manners. For cultivation exacts a price – the loss of a certain ... vitality. Beneath this rude colonial exterior there beats a power you will never know. Properly harnessed, that power will win wars for you. Churchill knows it, and I know it, too. (*to BISHOP*) Good day, Mr. Bishop.

A pause while BISHOP digests this.

BISHOP: (*to the audience*) Now there are one or two Canadians who would have taken offence at that. But not me. Staying at Portland Place, I found out some things right away. For example, life goes much smoother when you have influence. Take this pilot business, for example. Lady St. Helier gets on the phone to Churchill himself. The very next day I'm called down to the War Office. The atmosphere is much different.

The PIANO PLAYER plays a martial intro as once again BISHOP faces SIR HUGH CECIL.

SIR HUGH: Bishop! Jolly good, well done, excellent, good to see you! Well, my boy, your mother's wish is finally going to come true.

BISHOP: Oh really, sir?

SIR HUGH: Yes, yes, you are going to become a pilot. No problem, pas de problème. Medical examination in two days' time, then report for training.

BISHOP: (*to the audience*) Medical examination!? What about my weak heart? What about the fact that two weeks ago I was on the verge of medical discharge?

> An overworked, preoccupied *DOCTOR* deals with his case.

DOCTOR: Ah yes, Bishop – strip to the waist. Good. Stick out your tongue and say ninety-nine – good. (*inserts finger below*) Cough twice – that's good, too. Now turn around ten times – eight ... nine ... ten ... Attention! Still on your feet, Bishop? You're fit as a fiddle and ready to fly!

> The *PIANO PLAYER* plays a kind of polka. *BISHOP* sings a merry tune with macabre overtones.

Gonna fly ...
Gonna fly so high
Like a bird in the sky,
With the wind in my hair
And the sun burning in my eyes.
Flying Canadian,
Machine gun in my hand,
First Hun I see's the first Hun to die.

Gonna fly ...
In my machine,
Gonna shoot so clean,
Gonna hear them scream
When I hit them between the eyes.
Flying Canadian,
Machine gun in my hand,
First Hun I see's the first Hun to die.

> Chorus

Flying ...
What have I been waiting for?
What a way to fight a war!
Flying Canadian,
Machine gun in my hand,
First Hun I see's the first Hun to die.

Gonna fly ...
Gonna shoot them down
'Til they hit the ground
And they burn with the sound
Of bacon on the fry. (Sssss!)

Flying Canadian,
Machine gun in my hand,
First Hun I see's the first Hun to die.

> Chorus

Flying ...
What have I been waiting for?
What a way to fight a war!
Flying Canadian,
Machine gun in my hand,
First Hun I see's the first Hun to die.

> The song ends abruptly, then *BISHOP* launches into a sequence that can be done in many different ways, all of which – whether involving an ashtray, a model plane, or some other device – involve a good deal of mime; as well, *BISHOP* performs sound effects vocally, much as a boy of about age ten might do.

BISHOP: I'll never forget my first solo flight. Lonely? Jesus. You're sitting at the controls, all by yourself – trying to remember what they're all for. Everyone has stopped doing what they're doing – to watch you. There's an ambulance parked across the field – with its engines running, you know why. You also know that there's a surgical team in the hospital, just ready to rip.

PIANO PLAYER: Switch off!

BISHOP: (*at the controls*) Switch off.

PIANO PLAYER: Petrol on!

BISHOP: Petrol on.

PIANO PLAYER: Suck in!

BISHOP: Suck in.

PIANO PLAYER: Switch on!

BISHOP: Switch on.

PIANO PLAYER: Contact!

BISHOP: Contact! The propeller is given a sharp turn and the engine starts with a roar. (*He makes an engine sound, then coughs.*) Coughs a few times, then starts hitting on all cylinders. (*steady engine noise*) You signal for them to take away the chocks.

Then you're bouncing across the field, under your own power, and head her up into the wind. (*checks his foot controls*) Rudder (*click, click*). Elevators (*click, click*). Ailerons (*squeak, squeak*). Heart (*ba-BOOM! ba-BOOM! Ba-BOOM!*) I open the throttle all the way (*engine accelerates*) ... and you're off! Pull back on the stick – easy – easy! (*He demonstrates as the plane bumps violently along, then finally becomes airborne.*) Once I was in the air, I felt a lot better. In fact, I felt like a king! Mind you, I'm not fooling around, I'm flying straight as I can, climbing steadily. (*looks about*) All by yourself! What a feeling! ... (*alarmed*) I've got to turn. I execute a gentle turn ... skidding like crazy, but what the hell. I bank it a little more – too much. Too much! ... But all in all, I'm having a hell of a time – until I remember I've to land! What do I do now? Keep your head, that's what you do. Pull back on the throttle. (*engine has a coughing fit*) Too much! I put the nose down into a steep dive ... too steep! I bring it up again, down again, up, down ... and in a series of steps, I descend to earth. Then I execute everything I remember you have to do to make a perfect landing ... forty feet off the ground! I put the nose down and do another perfect landing ... This time, I'm only eight feet off the ground. But now I have no room left to do another nose down manoeuvre. The rumpty takes things into her own hands and just pancakes the rest of the way to the ground. (*piano crashes*) First solo flight! Greatest day in a man's life!

BISHOP & PIANO PLAYER: (*singing*)

Flying ...

What have I been waiting for?

What a way to fight a war.

Flying Canadian,

Machine gun in my hand,

First Hun I see's the first Hun to die,

The song ends abruptly.

NOTE: *When BISHOP is portrayed as an old man, the following scene is deleted entirely, the principal reason being that Bishop's tendency to error has been well established. By moving from his first solo flight directly to his first kill, there is a continuum to the old man's memory. With the younger BISHOP, however, there is value in reminding the audience that his future status was by no means a foregone conclusion, that a superior officer could justifiably regard him as a jackass.*

BISHOP: In the early part of 1916, I was posted back to France – as a fighter pilot. Sixty Squadron, Third British Brigade. I worked like a Trojan for those wings – and I just about lost them before I really began. I was returning from my first O.P. – Operational Patrol – and I crashed my Nieuport on landing. I wasn't hurt, but the aircraft was pretty well pranged, and that was bad because General John Higgins, the Brigade Commander, saw me do it. Well, he couldn't help but see me do it. I just about crashed at his feet!

HIGGINS: I watched you yesterday, Bishop. You destroyed a machine – a very expensive, very nice machine. Doing a simple landing on a clear day. That machine was more valuable than you'll ever be, bucko.

BISHOP: Sir, it was a gust of wind from the hangar. Ask Major Scott, our patrol leader, it could have happened to anyone ...

HIGGINS: Bishop, I was on the field.

BISHOP: Yes, sir.

HIGGINS: There was no wind.

BISHOP: No wind. Yes, sir.

HIGGINS: I have your record here before me, Bishop. It's not a very impressive document, is it? On the positive side ... you were wounded. And you scored well in target practice, without having ever actually fired upon the enemy. The list of your negative accomplishments, however, is longer, isn't it? Much longer. Conduct unbecoming an officer, breaches of discipline, a lot of silly accidents – suspicious accidents, if I might say so – a trail of wrecked machinery in your wake. You are a terrible pilot, Bishop, and a liability to the RFC, and I wish to God you were back in Canada where you belong – or failing that, digging a trench in some unstrategic valley. In short, you're finished, Bishop, finished. When your replacement arrives, he will replace you. That is all.

BISHOP: (*to the audience*) That was the lowest point in my career. Then came March 25th, 1917.

*The following scene is performed with **BISHOP** creating the sound effects in the manner of his first solo flight, but with a growing sense of menace, as a boy's adventure story takes on real adult fear and aggression, and as the adrenalin rush takes over.*

Four Nieuport scouts in diamond formation climb to nine thousand feet, crossing the line somewhere between Arras and St. Léger. Our patrol is to crisscross the lines, noting Heinie's positions and troop movements.

The drone of an airplane. RRRrrr.

I'm the last man in the patrol – tough place to be because if you fall too far behind, the headhunters are waiting for you. It starts out cloudy, then gradually clears up. We fly for half an hour and don't see anything, just miles and miles of nothing.

The drone continues, RRRrrr – then a warning chord on piano.

Suddenly, I see four specks, above and behind us – perfect place for an enemy attack. I watch as the specks get larger ... I can make out the black crosses – Huns!

The piano underscore becomes more rhythmic – like the approaching torpedo earlier in Act One.

It's hard to believe that they are real, and alive, and hostile. I want to circle around and have a better look at them. Albatros V-Strutters, beautiful with their sweptback planes, powerful and quick. RRRrrr. We keep flying steadily – Jack Scott, our leader, either hasn't seen them or wants them to think he hasn't seen them. They're getting closer and closer. We keep flying straight. They're two hundred yards behind us, getting closer and closer ...

The piano follows the action like a movie score.

Suddenly, Rrrr! Jack Scott opens up into a sharp climbing turn to get above and behind them. (*gesturing*) The rest of us follow – Rrrr! Rrrr! Rrrrr! I'm slower than the rest and come out about forty yards behind. In front of me a dogfight is happening right in front of my very eyes, real pandemonium, planes turning every which way – Rrrr! Rrrr! Machine-gun fire – AKAKAKAK!

The piano underscore becomes surreal and discordant.

Suddenly – Rrrr! Jack Scott sweeps below me with an Albatros on his tail, raking his wings and fuselage with gunfire! For a moment I'm just frozen there, not knowing what to do, my whole body just shaking! ... Then I throw the stick forward and dive on the Hun. I keep him in my Aldis sight until he completely fills the lens – AKAKAKAK! What a feeling, as he flips onto his back and falls out of control ...

The piano stops cold.

But wait! Wait! Grid Caldwell told me about this. He's not out of control, he's faking it! He's going to level out at two-thousand feet and escape. Bastard! (*battle music resumes*) I dive after him with my engine full on. Sure enough, he comes out of it, but I'm still there – AKAKAKAK! Again, my tracers smash into his machine – God, I've got to be hitting him! He flips over on his back and is gone again, but this time I'm right on him. EEEEEEEEE! The wires on my machine scream in protest. Nieuports have had their wings come off at 150 miles an hour, I must be doing 180, but I just don't give a shit! I keep firing on the tumbling Hun – AKAKAKAKAAK! (*huge crash on piano*) He just crashes into the earth and explodes in flames! BAA-WHOOSH! I pull back on the stick, and level out, screaming at the top of my lungs – I WIN, I WIN, I WIN!

Abrupt silence, followed by the sound of wind. No engine, no nothing.

Jesus, my engine stopped! It must have filled with oil on the dive. I try every trick in the book to get it going again. Nothing. Oh God, I'm going to go in!

*Gunfire from the **PIANO PLAYER**.*

Ground fire! I must still be over Hunland. Just my luck to do something right and end up being taken prisoner. Lower and lower. I pick out what seems to be a level patch and I put her down.

*The plane lands with a bouncing crash. **BISHOP** ends up on the floor, crouched behind a prop or a piece of furniture.*

I got out of the plane into what seemed to be a shell hole. I took my Very light pistol with me. I wasn't exactly sure what I was going to do with it ...

TOMMY: (*in a Newfoundland accent*) Well, you're just in time for a cup of tea there, my son.

BISHOP: (*panic*) Arrgh! (*relieved*) Jeez, you spoke English! Hey, look, where am I?

TOMMY: Yer at the bottom of Signal Hill in downtown St. John's. You want to keep down, duckie? Heinie's just over there. Well gol, that was a nice bit of flying you did there – yer a hundred yards our side of the line.

BISHOP: Look, can you do me a favour? I'd like to try and get the plane up again.

TOMMY: Not tonight, my son. No, you're going to have to take the Bridal Suite here at the Avalon Hotel.

The shriek of shelling and the crash of explosions get louder.

BISHOP: I spent the night in a trench, in six inches of water. (*shriek! crash!*) The Tommies seemed to be able to sleep. I sure couldn't.

The barrage reaches a peak, then fades into the distance.

Next morning at first light, I crawled out to see how my plane was. Miraculously, it hadn't been hurt ... And that's when I got my first look at no man's land. Jesus what a mess. Hardly a tree left standing. And the smell! It was hard to believe you were still on earth. I saw a couple of Tommies sleeping in a trench nearby. (*to the Tommies*) Hey, you guys. I wonder if you could give me a hand with ...

The Tommies aren't sleeping. He recoils from what he sees.

Oh my God.

The PIANO PLAYER sings. BISHOP joins in.

O the bloody earth is littered
With the fighters and the quitters,
O what could be more bitter
Than a nameless death below;
See the trenches, long and winding,
See the battle, slowly grinding,
Don't you wonder how good men can live so low.

Up above the sun is burning,
Up above the clouds are turning,
You can hear those soldiers yearning:
"O if only I could fly!"
From the burning sun, I'll sight you,
In the burning sun, I'll fight you –
O let us dance together in the sky.

    Chorus

In the sky,
In the sky,
Just you and I up there together –
Who knows why?
One the hunter, one the hunted;
A life to live, a death confronted –
"O let us dance together in the sky."

For you the bell is ringing,
And for you the bullets stinging,
My Lewis gun is singing –
O my friend, it's you or I!
And I'll watch your last returning
To the earth, the fire burning.
Look up and you will see me wave goodbye.

    Chorus

In the sky,
In the sky,
Just you and I up there together –
Who knows why?
One the hunter, one the hunted;
A life to live, a death confronted –
O let us dance together in the sky.

ACT TWO

The PIANO PLAYER plays and sings "The Bold Aviator." This mordant little song (the lyrics are authentic from the period) can be performed as a drinking song, as a singalong, or as a plaintive ballad.

O the bold Aviator lay dying,
As 'neath the wreckage he lay,
To the sobbing mechanic beside him
These last parting words he did say:

"Two valves you'll find in my stomach,
Three sparkplugs are safe in my lung;
The prop is in splinters inside me,
To my fingers, the joystick has clung.

Then get you six brandies and sodas,
And lay them all out in a row;
And get you six other good airmen
To drink to this pilot below.

Take the cylinders out of my kidneys,
The connecting rod out of my brain;
From the small of my back take the crankshaft,
And assemble the engine again."

The song ends. Immediately the PIANO PLAYER launches into the "Survival" theme, as a much-altered BISHOP speaks as though giving advice to a novice pilot.

BISHOP: Survival. That's the important thing. And the only way to learn survival – is to survive. Success depends on accuracy and surprise: how well you shoot, how you get into the fight, and how well you fly – in that order. I can't fly worth a shit compared to someone like Barker or Ball, but I don't care. If I get a kill, it's usually in the first few seconds. Any longer than that and you might as well get the hell out. You've got to be good enough to get him in the first few bursts; so practise your shooting as much as you can – after patrols, between patrols, on your day off. If I get a clear shot at a guy, he's dead. Ever heard of "flamers"? That's when you bounce a machine and it just bursts into flames. Now I don't want to sound bloodthirsty or anything, but when that happens, it's very satisfying. But it's almost always pure luck, you hit a gas line or something like that. If you want the machine to go down every time, you aim for one thing – the man. I always go for the man.

The music stops and the PIANO PLAYER takes the part of the M.C. in a French cabaret.

PIANO PLAYER: (*French accent*) Ladies and Gentlemen. Mesdames et Messieurs. Charlie's Bar, Amiens, proudly presents ... Ze Lovely Hélène!

BISHOP takes the part of a Dietrich-like cabaret singer. He and the PIANO PLAYER sing:

HÉLÈNE:

Johnny was a Christian, he was humble and humane.

His conscience was clear and his soul without a stain.

PIANO PLAYER:

He was contemplating heaven when –

HÉLÈNE:

– ze wings fell off his plane.

PIANO PLAYER:

And he never got out alive?

HÉLÈNE:

Non. He did not survive.

HÉLÈNE:

George was patriotic, his country he adored,

He was the first to volunteer when his land took up the sword;

PIANO PLAYER:

And a half a dozen medals were –

HÉLÈNE:

His posthumous reward.

PIANO PLAYER:

And he never got out alive?

HÉLÈNE:

Non. He did not survive.

They sing chorus together.

So when you fight, stay as calm as the ocean,
And watch what's going on behind your shoulder
Remember, war's not the place for deep emotion ...

HÉLÈNE:

And maybe you'll get ... a little older.

The "Survivial" theme resumes. BISHOP, as himself, continues the lesson.

BISHOP: Come into a fight with an advantage – height, speed, surprise. Come at him out of the sun, he'll never see you. Get on his tail, his blind spot, so you can shoot him without too much risk to yourself. Generally, patrols don't watch behind them as much, so sneak up on the last man, he'll never know what hit him ... Hunt them! Like Hell's handmaiden! If it's one on one, you come at the bugger, guns blazing, he chickens out and you get him as he comes across your sights. If you both veer the same way ... you're dead. So it's tricky. You have to keep your nerve.

The song resumes.

HÉLÈNE:

Geoffrey made a virtue out of cowardice and fear,
The first to go on sick leave and the last to volunteer.

PIANO PLAYER:

He was running from a fight ...

HÉLÈNE:

When they attacked him from the rear.

PIANO PLAYER:

And he never got out alive?

HÉLÈNE:

Non. He did not survive.

Back to the "Survival" theme. BISHOP resumes the lesson.

BISHOP: The other thing is your mental attitude. It's not like the infantry, where a bunch of guys work themselves up into a screaming rage and tear off over the top, yelling and waving their bayonets – it's not like that. You're part of a machine, so you have to stay very calm and cold, so that you and your machine work together to bring the other fellow down. You get so you don't feel anything after a while ... until the moment you start firing, then that old dry-throat, heart-throbbing thrill comes back. It's a great feeling!

BISHOP: (*as the LOVELY HÉLÈNE, singing*)

Jimmy hated Germans with a passion cold and deep.

He cursed them when he saw them, he cursed them in his sleep.

PIANO PLAYER:

He was cursing when his plane went down

HÉLÈNE:

And landed in a heap.

PIANO PLAYER:

And he never got out alive?

HÉLÈNE:

Non. He did not survive.

Both sing chorus.

So when you fight, stay as calm as the ocean,

And watch what's going on behind your shoulder.

Remember, war's not the place for deep emotion,

HÉLÈNE:

And maybe you will get ... (*softly*) *a little older.*

The PIANO PLAYER plays a series of minor chords.

BISHOP: Bloody April, we lost just about everyone I started with: Knowles, Hall, Williams, Townsend, Chapman. Steadman – shot down the day he joined the squadron. You see, the Hun has better machines than ours, and some of their pilots are very, very good. But practice makes perfect – if you can stay alive long enough to practice. It gets easier and easier to stay alive because hardly anyone has the same experience as you ... (*silence*) Oh yeah, and another thing: you take your fun where you can find it.

The PIANO PLAYER begins a variation of the "Survival" theme – slower and more gently.

BISHOP: He has noticed the lovely Hélène. She has noticed him. They meet outside. Without a

word, she signals him to follow. Silently, they walk down an alleyway, through an archway, and up a darkened stairway. They are in her room. He watches as she lights a candle. Then she turns to him and says, "I should not be doing this. My lover is a colonel at the front. But you are so beautiful ... and so, so young." An hour later they kiss in the darkened doorway. She says, "If you see me, you do not know me." And she is gone.

He meets his friends, who have had the same good luck. It's late. They've missed the last bus to the aerodrome ... Arm in arm, they walk in the moonlight, silently sharing a flask of brandy, breathing in that warm spring air. As they approach Filescamp, they begin to sing, loudly: "Mademoiselle from Armentières, parlez-vous. Mademoiselle from Armentières, parlez-vous" ... as if to leave behind the feelings they have had that night. In an hour, they will be on patrol. They go to bed. They sleep.

Sudden crashing piano chords. BISHOP writes a letter to Margaret.

BISHOP: Dearest Margaret. It is the merry month of May, and today I sent another merry Hun to his merry death. I'm not sure you would appreciate the bloodthirsty streak that has come over me in the past months. How I hate the Hun. He has killed so many of my friends. I enjoy killing him now. I go up as much as I can, even on my day off. My score is getting higher and higher – because I like it. (*chord change on piano*) Yesterday, I had a narrow escape. A bullet came through the windshield – ping! – creased my helmet. But a miss is as good as a mile, and if I am for it, then I am for it. But I do not believe that I am for it. (*chord change*) My superiors are pleased. Not only have I been made captain, they are recommending me for the Military Cross. (*chord change*) Thinking of you constantly, I remain ...

The PIANO PLAYER segues to the "Lovely Hélène" waltz. BISHOP speaks the verse.

You may think you've something special that will get you through this war,

But the odds aren't in your favour, that's a fact you can't ignore.

PIANO PLAYER: (*singing*)

Chances are the man will come, knocking at your door –

BISHOP:

And you'll never get out alive.

You won't survive.

Both sing chorus.

So when you fight, stay as calm as the ocean,
And watch what's going on behind your shoulder.
Remember, war's not the place for deep emotion,
And maybe you will get ...

BISHOP: A little older.

End song. Pause, as BISHOP produces a picture, a memento of ALBERT BALL.

BISHOP: Albert Ball, Britain's highest-scoring ace, sat before me. His black eyes gleamed at me – very pale, very intense. Back home we would have said he had eyes like two pissholes in the snow. But that's not very romantic. And Albert Ball was romantic, Jesus, if anybody was.

BISHOP performs a scene, playing himself and ALBERT BALL.

BALL: Compatriots in glory! Oh, Bishop, I have an absolutely ripping idea. I want you to try and picture this: two pilots cross the line in the dim, early dawn. It is dark. A slight fog. They fly straight for the German aerodromes at Douai – ghosts in the night. The Hun, unsuspecting, sleeps cosily in his lair. The sentries are sleeping. Perhaps the Baron von Richthofen himself is there, sleeping, dreaming of eagles and ... Wiener schnitzel. Suddenly, he is awakened by the sound of machine-gun fire! He rushes to his window to see four, maybe five, of his best machines in flames! He watches as the frantic pilots try to take off, and one by one are shot down! The two unknown raiders strike a devastating blow! Bishop, you and I are those two unknown raiders.

BISHOP: Jeez, I like it! It's a good plan! (*pause*) How do we get out?

BALL: Get out?

BISHOP: Yeah, get out. You know – escape.

BALL: I don't think you quite get the picture, Bishop. It's an heroic exploit ... Getting out has nothing to do with it.

BISHOP: Oh. (*pause*) Well, it's a good plan. It's got a few holes I'd like to see plugged. I'd like to think about it.

BALL: All right, Bishop, you think about it. But remember this: Compatriots in glory!

BISHOP: (*to the audience*) Quite a fellow.

The PIANO PLAYER performs a chord sequence, then an announcement:

PIANO PLAYER: The Dying of Albert Ball.

BISHOP recites a ballad in the style of Robert Service.

He was only eighteen
When he downed his first machine,
And any chance of living through this war was small;
He was nineteen when I met him,
And I never will forget him,
The pilot by the name of Albert Ball.

No matter what the odds,
He left his fate up to the gods,
Laughing as the bullets brushed his skin.
Like a medieval knight,
He would charge into the fight
And trust that one more time his pluck would let him win.

O he courted the Reaper
Like the woman of his dreams,
And the Reaper smiled each time he came to call;
But the British like their heroes
Cold and dead, or so it seems,
And their hero in the sky was Albert Ball.

But long after the fight,
Way into the night,
Cold thoughts, as dark as night would fill his brain.
For bloodstains never fade,
And there are debts to be repaid
For the souls of all those men who died in vain.

So when the night was dark and deep,
And the men lay fast asleep,
An eerie sound would filter through the night.
It was a violin,
A sound as soft as skin,
Someone was playing in the dim moonlight.

There he stood, dark and thin,
And on his violin
Played a song that spoke of loneliness and pain;
It mourned his victories,
It mourned dead enemies
And friends that he would never see again.

Yes, he courted the Reaper
Like the woman of his dreams,
And the Reaper smiled each time he came to call;
But the British like their heroes
Cold and dead, or so it seems,
And their hero in the sky was Albert Ball.

It's an ironic twist of fate
That brings a hero to the gate,
And Ball was no exception to the rule;
Fate puts out the spark
In a way as if to mark
The fine line between a hero and a fool.

Each time he crossed the line,
Albert Ball would check the time
By an old church clock reminding him of home.
The Hun came to know
The man who flew so low
On his way back to the aerodrome.

It was the sixth of May,
He'd done bloody well that day;
For the forty-fourth time, he'd won the game.
As he flew low to check the hour,
A hail of bullets from the tower –
And Albert Ball lay dying in the flames.

But through his clouded eyes
Maybe he realized,
This was the moment he'd been waiting for.
For the moment that he died,
He was a hero, bona fide –
There are to be no living heroes in this war.

For when a country goes insane,
Obsessed with blood and pain,
Just to be alive is something of a sin.
A war's not satisfied

Until all the best have died –
And the Devil take the man who saves his skin.

But sometimes, late at night,
When the moon is cold and bright,
I sometimes think I hear that violin.
Death is waiting, just outside,
And my eyes are open wide,
As I lie and wait for morning to begin.

For I'm courting the Reaper
Like the woman of my dreams,
And the Reaper smiles each time I come to call;
But the British like their heroes
Cold and dead, or so it seems,
And my name will take the place of Albert Ball.

BISHOP and the *PIANO PLAYER* sing "Friends Ain't S'posed to Die."

Look at the names on the statues,
Anywhere you go,
Someone was killed
A long time ago.
I remember the places;
I remember a time –
Those were the names of friends of mine.

The statues are old now
And they're fading fast;
Something big must have happened
Way in the past.
The names are so faded
You can hardly see –
The faces are always young to me.

　　　Chorus

Friends ain't s'posed to die 'til they're old,
And friends ain't s'posed to die in pain;
No one should die alone when he is twenty-one,
And living shouldn't make you feel ashamed.

I can't believe how young we were back then.
One thing's for sure, we'll never be that young again.
We were daring young men, with hearts of gold,
And most of us never got old.

*The song ends. Abruptly the **PIANO PLAYER** raps repeatedly on the piano as **BISHOP** assumes the character of **CEDRIC** the butler.*

CEDRIC: Wakey, wakey, Bishop! Wakey, wakey! Rise and shine!

BISHOP: (*drowsy and hungover*) Cedric? What's the idea, waking me up in the middle of the night.

CEDRIC: It's bloody well eleven o'clock. And Madam has a bone to pick with you.

BISHOP: All right, all right, I'll be right there.

*He stands and faces the chair where, presumably, **LADY ST. HELIER** is seated.*

BISHOP: Good morning, Granny.

LADY ST. HELIER: Bishop. Sit down. I have a bone to pick with you. Cedric, the colonial is under the weather. Bring tea and Epsom salts. (*to BISHOP*) Where were you last night?

BISHOP: I was ... I was out.

LADY ST. HELIER: Very good. Very specific. Well, I have my own sources, and the picture that was painted for me is not fit for public viewing: disgusting, unmannered, and informal practices, in company that is unworthy even of you. But what concerns me is not where you were, but where you were not – to wit, you were not at a party which I personally arranged, at which you were to meet Bonar Law, Chancellor of the Exchequer. What do you have to say in your defence?

BISHOP: Now look, Granny –

LADY ST. HELIER: I'll thank you not to call me Granny. The quaintness quite turns my stomach.

BISHOP: Look, that was the fourth darn formal dinner this week – first it's General Haig, then what's-his-name, the parliamentary secretary ... I wanna have some fun!

LADY ST. HELIER: (*a severe pause*) Bishop, I am only going to say this once: It is not for you to be interested, amused, or entertained. You are no longer a rather short colonial with poor taste and a bad service record. You are a figurehead. A dignitary. The people of Canada, England, the Empire, the world, look to you as a symbol of victory – and you will act the part. You will shine your shoes and press your trousers. You will refrain from spitting, swearing, public drunkenness – and I say this with emphasis: you will keep your appointments with your betters! Now, tonight you are having dinner with Lord Beaverbrook, tomorrow with Attorney General F.E. Smith. Need I say more?

BISHOP: No. No. I'll be there ... Granny.

LADY ST. HELIER: Good. Oh, and Bishop, I had the occasion to pass the upstairs bathroom, and I took the liberty of inspecting your toilet kit. There is what I can only describe as moss growing on your hairbrush, and your after-shave smells like cat urine. I believe the implications are clear? (*to the PIANO PLAYER*) Cedric, a difficult road lies before us. Empire must rely for her defences on an assemblage of Canadians, Australians, and blacks. And now the Americans.

CEDRIC: Oh no.

LADY ST. HELIER: Exactly. Our way of life is in peril!

*The **PIANO PLAYER** plays a bouncy tune while **BISHOP**, slightly drunk, composes a letter to Margaret.*

BISHOP: Dearest Margaret. I'm not sure I can get through this evening. In the next room is Princess Marie-Louise and four or five lords and ladies I can't even remember. I drank a little bit too much champagne at supper tonight and told the princess a lot of lies. Now I'm afraid to go back in there because I can't remember what the lies were, and I'm afraid I'll contradict myself and look like an idiot. Being rich, you've got a lot more class than me. They'd like you. Maybe we ought to get married. Thinking of you constantly, I remain ...

*The **PIANO PLAYER** sings "Who Wants to Go Back Home," joined by **BISHOP**.*

Oh, when you steal a girl
From an English Earl,
Who wants to go back home?
Just a Canadian boy,
England's pride and joy,
Who wants to go back home?
You may be a king on English ground,
But when you go back to your old hometown,
They'll find ways to shoot you down –
Who wants to go back home?

Oh baby, I'm so far from home,
And I'm all alone,
And I'm saving England's ass,
And although I'm not your class,

I've got a chest that's full of brass.
Why don't you
Give me a kiss before I hit the sky.
One if I live, two if I die,
And maybe a third before we say goodbye –
Who wants to go back home?

PIANO PLAYER: (*singing*)

The prime of life,
The best of men,
It will never be like this again.
Who wants a life of remember when –
Who wants to go back home?
Who wants to go back home?

> *The song ends. Abruptly, the music takes on a more sinister quality. The following sequence is told and acted out to music in much the same way as the Act One air battle, except the quality of the boy's adventure story is entirely gone now. What remains is adrenaline and fear and deadly concentration.*

BISHOP: I woke up at three o'clock in the morning, and Jesus was I scared – very tense, you know? I mean, Albert Ball said you couldn't do it with just one guy, and Albert Ball was a maniac. But I figure it's no different than what we do every day, so what the hell. I mean, it's no worse. I don't think. Trouble is, nobody has ever attacked a German aerodrome single-handedly, so it's chancy – you know what I mean? I put my flying suit over my pyjamas, grab a cup of tea, and out I go. It's raining. Lousy weather for it, but what can you do? Walter Bourne, my mechanic, is the only other man up. He has the engine running and waiting for me.

He takes the part of BOURNE.

BOURNE: Bloody stupid idea if you ask me, sir. I would put thumbs down on the whole thing and go back to bed if I was you, sir.

BISHOP: Thanks a lot, Walter. That's really encouraging.

BOURNE: It's pissing rain, sir. Bleeding pity to die in the pissing rain. I can see it all now, right before me very eyes. First, Albert Ball gets it. Then Captain Bishop gets it. I mean, it's a balls-up from beginning to end. Why don't you just take my advice and go back to bed like a good lad, sir?

BISHOP: Why don't you shut up, Walter. Ready?

BOURNE: Ready, sir!

The plane takes off to music.

BISHOP: God, it's awful up here. Pale grey light, cold, lonely as hell. My stomach's bothering me. Nerves? Naw, forgot to eat breakfast, just one more thing to put up with. RRRrrr. I climb to just inside the clouds as I go over the line. No trouble? Good. Everybody is asleep. Let's find the German aerodrome. RRRrrr. Where is it? Should be right around here. (*Musical sting as he spots something.*) All right: a quick pass, a few bursts inside those sheds just to wake them up, then pick them off one by one as they try and come up. (*He starts the attack, then stops abruptly.*) Wait a minute! Wait a minute! There's no planes! There's no people – the bloody place is deserted! Well shit, that's that, isn't it? I mean, I can't shoot anyone if there's nobody there to shoot. Bloody stupid embarrassment, that's what it is. RRRrrr. Feeling really miserable now, I cruise around looking for some troops to shoot them. Nothing! What the hell's going on around here, is everyone on vacation? (*musical sting*) Suddenly I see the sheds of another German aerodrome, ahead and slightly to the left. Dandy. Trouble is, it's a little far behind the lines, and I'm not exactly sure where I am, but it's either that or go back. My stomach's really bothering me now – why didn't I eat breakfast? And why didn't I change out of my pyjamas? That's going to be great if I'm taken prisoner, real dignified – spend the rest of the war in my bloody pyjamas. RRRrrr. Over the aerodrome at about three hundred feet – Jesus, we've got lots of planes here, lots and lots of planes: six scouts – and a two-seater. Hope that two-seater doesn't come up for me. I'll have a hell of a time getting him from the rear. It's a little late to think about that now!

Engine noise and machine-gun fire from the PIANO PLAYER.

AKAKAKAKAKAKAK! RRRRRrrrrr!

I don't know how many guys I got on that first pass, a lot of guys went down, a lot of guys stayed down. I shot up some of their planes pretty bad –

Gunfire from the PIANO PLAYER.

I forgot about the machine guns guarding the aerodrome! Bullets all around me, tearing up the canvas on my machine; just so long as they don't hit a wire. Keep dodging! Rrrr! Rrrr! I can't get too far away or I'll never pick them off as they try and come up – come on, you guys, come on! One of them's starting to taxi now. I come right down on the deck about fifteen feet behind him. AKAKAKAKAK! He gets about six feet off the ground, does this weird somersault, and smashes into the end of the field. I pull her around as quick as I can – RRRrrr – just in time to pick up another fellow as he tries to come up. AKAKAKAKAK! My tracers are going wide but the guy is so frightened he doesn't watch where he's going and smashes into some trees at the end of the field. I put a few rounds into him and pull back on the stick. RRRrrr! I'm feeling great now, I don't feel scared, I don't feel nothing, just ready to fight. Come on, you bastards, come on! (*musical sting*) Wait a minute, wait a minute. This is what Ball was worried about – two of them are taking off from opposite directions at the same time. Now I feel scared – what do I do now? Get the hell out, that's what you do!

Gunfire from the PIANO PLAYER.

One of them is close enough behind me to start firing. Where's the other one? Still on the ground. All right, you wanna fight? We'll fight! I put her into a tight turn, he stays right with me – but not quite tight enough. As he comes in for his second firing pass, I evade him with a lateral loop, rudder down off the top, and drop on his tail – AKAKAKAK! I hit the man. The plane goes down and crashes in flames on the field. Beautiful.

Gunfire from the PIANO PLAYER.

The second man is closing with me. I have just enough time to put on my last drum of ammunition. I fly straight at him, the old chicken game. I use up all my ammunition –

Both BISHOP and the PIANO PLAYER fire.

AKAKAKAKAKAK! I miss him, but he doesn't want to fight. Probably thinks I'm crazy. I've got to get out of here, they will have telephoned every aerodrome in the area, there will be hundreds of planes after me. I climb and head for home. RRRrrr.

The music becomes eerie.

All by myself again, at last. Am I going the right way? Jesus my stomach! Sharp pains like I've been shot. (*feels his stomach and looks at his hand*) Nope, no blood. Good, I haven't been shot. It's just the excitement, on an empty stomach. Being frightened. Jeez, I think I'm going to pass out. Don't pass out, don't pass out ...

Silence on piano, followed by ominous punctuation.

Then I look up, and my heart just stops dead then and there. I'm not kidding. One thousand feet above me, six Albatros scouts. And me with no ammunition. I think I'm going to puke – don't puke, don't puke! Fly under them, maybe they won't see you. RRRrrr. I try to keep up. For a mile I fly under them, just trying to keep up. RRRrrr. I've got to get away. They're faster than me, and if they see me they got me, but I've got to get away! I dive and head for the line ... (*sudden silence*) I can feel the bullets smashing into my back any second, into my arms, into my legs, into my ... (*He looks up. A chord on piano.*) Nothing. Jeez, they didn't see me. RRRrrr. Filescamp. Home. Just land it, take it easy. I land. Walter Bourne is there with a group of the others.

BOURNE: I'm standing around, waiting for him to be phoned in missing, when there he comes. Like he's been sightseeing. He lands with his usual skill, cracking both wheels, then comes to a halt, just like usual – 'cept there's nothing left of his bloody machine. It's in pieces, bits of canvas flopping around like laundry in the breeze. Beats me how it stayed together. Captain Bishop sits there, quiet-like. Then he turns to me and he says, "Walter, I did it."

BISHOP: (*completes the speech as himself*) I DID IT. Never had so much fun in my life!

A minor chord on the piano. It's not all triumph.

BISHOP: That was the best fight I ever had. Everybody made a very big deal of it – but I just kept fighting all summer, my score kept getting higher and higher, and I was feeling good. By the middle of August, I had forty-three – one less than Albert Ball. And that's when the generals and colonels started treating me funny.

Reprise of going-to-war music from Act One. BISHOP plays himself and GENERAL TRENCHARD.

TRENCHARD: Bishop! We have lots of medals for you, lots and lots of medals – and that's not all. You will receive your medals, you will go on extended Canada leave, and you won't fight again.

BISHOP: Excuse me, sir, what did you say?

TRENCHARD: Have I got a speech impediment, Bishop? I said you won't fight again.

BISHOP: Not fight again? I gotta fight again! I've got forty-three, Ball had forty-four, all I need is one more of those sons of ...

TRENCHARD: Bishop! You have done very well. You will receive the Victoria Cross, the Distinguished Service Order, the Military Cross. No English pilot has done that – not even Albert Ball, God rest his soul. Leave it at that, Bishop. You have done England a great service. Thank you very much. Now you don't have to fight anymore. I should think you'd be delighted.

BISHOP: You don't understand, sir. I like it.

TRENCHARD: Well, of course you like it. That is hardly the point. You see, Bishop, you have become a colonial figurehead.

BISHOP: I know, sir. A dignitary.

TRENCHARD: A *colonial* dignitary, Bishop. There is a difference. You see, Bishop, the problem with your colonial is that he has a morbid enthusiasm for life. You might call it a *life wish*. Now, what happens when your colonial figurehead gets killed? I'll tell you what happens. Colonial morale plummets. Despair is in the air. Fatalism rears its ugly head. But a living colonial "hero" – that's a different cup of tea. The men are inspired. They say: "He did it and he lived. I can do it, too." Do you get the picture, Bishop?

BISHOP: I believe I do, sir.

TRENCHARD: Good lad. You shall leave Sixty Squadron, never to return, on the morning of August 17th. That is all.

BISHOP: (*to the audience*) Well, that still gives me a week. A lot can be done in a week.

In the next six days, I shot down five planes. I really was Number One now. And the squadron, they gave me a big piss-up on my last night. But something happened in that last week that made me fairly glad to get out of it for a while. It was number forty-six.

Spoken to the "Lovely Hélène" waltz.

It's dusk. Around eight o'clock. I'm returning to Filescamp pretty leisurely because I figure this is my last bit of flying for a bit. It's a nice clear evening, and when it's clear up there in the evening, it's very, very ... pretty. Suddenly, I see this German Aviatik two-seater heading right for me. It's a gift: I don't even have to think about this one. I put the plane down into a steep dive and come underneath him and just rake his belly with bullets. Well, I don't know how they built those things, but the whole thing just fell apart before my very eyes. The wings came off, bits of the fuselage just collapsed ... and the pilot and the gunner, they fall free! Now I'm pretty sure I didn't hit them, so they are alive and there is nothing I can do to help them or shoot them or anything. All I can do is just sit there and watch those two men fall, wide awake ... to die. It's awful! I know I've killed lots of them, but this is different. I watch them falling, down, down, down, one minute, two minutes, three minutes ...

The music descends.

It's like I can feel them looking at me.

The PIANO PLAYER hits a soft bass note. He takes a moment to recover.

So when I leave for London the next day, I'm pretty glad to be going after all.

The PIANO PLAYER plays part of "You're a Typical Canadian," indicating a return to London and LADY ST. HELIER.

LADY ST. HELIER: Bishop, today you will meet the King. This represents a high-water mark for us all, and you must see to it that you do not make a balls-up of it. I understand the King is particularly excited today. It seems this is his first opportunity of presenting three medals to the same gentleman. Furthermore, the King is amused that that gentleman is from the colonies. The King, therefore, may speak to you. Should you be so honoured, you will respond politely, in grammatically cogent sentences, with neither cloying sentimentality nor rude familiarity. You shall speak to the King with dignity and restraint. Do you think you can manage that, Bishop? Is it possible that the safest course would be for you to keep your mouth shut?

Again, a phrase from "You're a Typical Canadian" on piano.

BISHOP: I arrived at Buckingham Palace – late. It is very confusing.

ADJUTANT: Excuse me, sir, but where do you think you're going?

BISHOP: Oh. Um. I'm supposed to get a medal or something around here.

ADJUTANT: Oh, you're way off, you are, sir. This is His Majesty's personal reception area. You just about stumbled into the royal loo!!!

OFFICER: What seems to be the problem around here?

ADJUTANT: (*to* **OFFICER**) Well, the colonial here wants a medal. But his sense of direction has failed him.

OFFICER: Come along, Bishop, we've been looking all over for you. Now, the procedure is this: ten paces to the centre, turn, bow ...

The PIANO PLAYER strikes up "Land of Hope and Glory."

It's started already. Bishop, you're just going to have to wing it!

The music continues as a processional.

BISHOP: Here comes the King with his retinue, Order of St. Michael, Order of St. George, and here's me. The King pins three medals on my chest. Then he says ...

The PIANO PLAYER takes the part of KING GEORGE.

KING GEORGE: Well, Captain Bishop! You've been a busy bugger!

BISHOP: (*to the audience*) I'm not kidding. The King is standing here and I'm standing here. The King speaks to me for fifteen minutes. I can't say a word. But after the investiture come the parties, the balls, the photographers, the newspaper reporters, the Lords and Ladies, the champagne, the filet mignon and the fifty-year-old brandy. And here's me. Billy Bishop, from Owen Sound, Canada, and I know one thing – this is my day! There will never be another day like it! I think of this as we dance far into the night, as we dance to the music of ... the Empire Soirée.

BISHOP & PIANO PLAYER: (*singing alternate lines, then singing together for the chorus*)

Civilizations come and go (don't you know),
Dancing on to oblivion (oblivion),
The birth and death of nations,
Of civilizations,
Can be viewed down the barrel of a gun.

   Chorus

You're all invited to the Empire Soirée,
We'll see each other there, just wait and see
   (wait and see);
Attendance is required at the Empire Soirée,
We'll all dance the dance of history.

Revolutions come and go (come and go).
New empires will take each other's place
   (take their place);
The song may be fun,
But a new dance has begun,
When someone points a gun at someone's face.

Alexander and Julius had their dance
   (had their chance),
'Til somebody said: "May I cut in?" (with a grin).
All you and I can do,
Is put on our dancing shoes,
And wait for the next one to begin.

   Chorus

You're all invited to the Empire Soirée,
We'll see each other there, just wait and see
   (wait and see);
Attendance is required at the Empire Soirée,
We'll all dance the dance of history.

The song ends abruptly, followed by the opening chords to "We Were Off to Fight the Hun," and the PIANO PLAYER sings:

We were off to fight the foe,
We would change the world, although
How little had we travelled,
And how little did we know.

Now the young will fight the foe,
And we watch them as they go.
Somehow it doesn't seem like war
At all, at all, at all;
Somehow it didn't seem like war at all.

At this point there are two alternate concluding scenes, depending on whether the part is being played by a young or an old man.

FOR A YOUNG ACTOR

BISHOP exits during the song to reappear as a middle-aged man in a World War Two uniform. He faces the audience and gives a speech as though to rally the troops.

BISHOP: I have seen you go, and my heart is very proud. Once again, in the brief space of twenty years, our brave young men rush to the defence of the Mother Country. Again you must go forward, with all the courage and vigour of youth, to wrest mankind from the grip of the Iron Cross and the Swastika. Once again, on the edge of destiny, you must test your strength. I know you of old, I think. God speed you. God speed you, the Army, on feet and on wheels, a member of which I was for so many happy years of my life. God speed you the Air Force, where, in the crucible of battle, I grew from youth to manhood. God speed you and God bless you. For, once again, the freedom of mankind rests in you: in the courage, the skill, the strength and the blood of our indomitable youth.

The speech ends on a grand note. Then BISHOP stops and looks at the audience with a certain amount of bewilderment. He speaks to the audience as though to an old friend.

You know, I pinned the wings on my own son this week. Margaret and I are very proud of him. And our daughter. Three Bishops in uniform, fighting in the same war. Well, I guess I'm on the sidelines cheering them on ...

FOR AN OLD ACTOR

The PIANO PLAYER segues from "Off to Fight the Hun" to a gentle reprise of the "Dearest Margaret" theme as BISHOP narrates a last letter.

Dearest Margaret. I think when you haven't been in a war for a while, it comes as a bit of a surprise ... how much you miss it. That survival is really just a reprieve. And so you watch your children, and other people's children, go to war. And you're on the sidelines – cheering them on ... And now the faithful Lethbridge will put me to bed. I haven't felt this good in weeks. Thinking of you constantly, I remain ...

The ending of the play is the same, whether the actor playing BISHOP is young or old. The PIANO PLAYER plays a haunting, discordant version of "In the Sky."

BISHOP: You know, it comes to me as a surprise that there is another war on. We didn't think there was going to be another war, back in 1918. Makes you wonder what it was all for. But then again, none of us are in control of these things, are we? And all in all I'd have to say ... it was a hell of a time.

BISHOP sings, a cappella.

O the bloody earth is littered
With the fighters and the quitters;
You can hear those soldiers yearning,
"O if only I could fly!"
In the burning sun I'll sight you,
In the burning sun I'll fight you –
O let us dance together in the sky.

BISHOP & PIANO PLAYER: (*singing quietly*)

In the sky,
In the sky,
Just you and I up there together,
Who knows why?
One the hunter, one the hunted,
A life to live, a death confronted,
O let us dance together in the sky.

The PIANO PLAYER plays a closing series of chords.

END

DAVID
FENNARIO

(b. 1947)

One of the distinguishing features of modern Canadian drama has been its tendency to give a stage voice to the dispossessed, those living outside or on the fringes of the Canadian mainstream. In the 1960s and '70s, important plays like *The Ecstasy of Rita Joe*, *Les Belles-Soeurs*, *Fortune and Men's Eyes*, and *Creeps* drew their protagonists from worlds marginal to the lives of the middle class. George F. Walker, Judith Thompson, Tomson Highway, and others have continued to dramatize the other Canada. But no Canadian playwright has focused on a single marginalized community as consistently as David Fennario. Fennario's world is "the Pointe," the primarily anglophone working-class district of Pointe-Saint-Charles in Montreal. His characters are a politically disenfranchised urban proletariat locked into a culture of poverty by socio-economic circumstances and their own sense of futility. Fennario's plays show them coping with the daily indignities at work and at home. And he shows us what happens when they are pushed beyond the point at which apathy, jokes, or another beer are enough to kill the pain. In *Balconville*, Fennario presents a vision of working-class Quebec in microcosm, a sharply etched, richly human portrait of French and English divided by language though joined in most other significant ways, seemingly unable to recognize their common cause. In the process, he created Canada's first truly bilingual play.

Fennario himself comes from the world he writes about. Born David Wiper in the Pointe, he was raised, he claims in *The Work: Conversations with English-Canadian Playwrights* (1982), to be stupid: "That's about survival; if I think I'm stupid I'll be able to last forty years working at Northern Electric ... That was basic Pointe training." He dropped out of school at age seventeen, took the name "Fennario" from a Bob Dylan song, and temporarily became part of the hippie subculture. In 1968, he went to work in a Montreal dress factory and then in a Simpson's warehouse – experiences he would use in his first two plays – meanwhile becoming an active member of the Socialist Labour Party.

Hoping to avoid the dead end for which he seemed destined, Fennario enrolled at Montreal's Dawson College in 1970. His English teacher recognized the astonishing raw talent shown in a journal Fennario had been keeping, and she helped him have it published. *Without a Parachute* (1972), Fennario's impressions of life in the Pointe from 1969 to 1971, came to the attention of Maurice Podbrey, artistic director of the Centaur Theatre, who commissioned Fennario to write a play. Fennario had seen only one play before. So Podbrey helped get him a Canada Council grant to spend two years sitting in on rehearsals and learning theatre from the inside as writer-in-residence at the Centaur. Fennario remained the Centaur's resident playwright for nearly a decade.

On the Job (1975), his powerful debut, brought Fennario theatrical success and personal notoriety. Gary, the young worker from the Pointe whose revolutionary politics initiate a wildcat strike in the dress-factory shipping room, was obviously the playwright himself. Fennario became a media darling, Canadian theatre's angry young working-class hero. That had an effect on his next play, *Nothing to Lose* (1976), which suffers from the gross intrusion of autobiography. This time the workers are on a lunch break at a tavern. Job action is brewing when in walks Jerry, once a fellow worker but now a celebrity writer, back with tales from that other world. Jerry is back yet again in *Toronto* (1978), Fennario's most self-indulgent and least successful play.

Balconville (1979) distilled the best of Fennario's early work. He wrote himself into the play only peripherally in aspects of young Tom; brought the crazy worker and Pointe legend Jackie from the two early plays into the foreground as Johnny Regan; increased the role of the francophone characters, an important but subordinate element in the earlier plays; and moved his setting from the workplace to the home, giving women a central role in his drama for the first time. But the real *coup de théâtre* was writing nearly a third of the dialogue in French. More than fifty thousand Montrealers saw *Balconville* during its two runs in January 1979 and a year later. A revised version with a new ending broke attendance records at the St. Lawrence Centre for the Arts in Toronto in the fall of 1979, toured Canada, and won the Floyd S. Chalmers Canadian Play Award in 1980. In 1981, the Centaur took its production to Belfast, Bath, and London, the first Canadian company ever to play the Old Vic. In 1992, the play had a major Montreal revival at the Centaur, directed by Paul Thompson.

Following *Balconville*, Theatre Passe Muraille produced an adaptation of *Without a Parachute* (1979), and from that came *Changes* (1980), an autobiographical one-man show. Fennario was back at the Centaur for his next major play, *Moving* (1983), in which a family becomes the battleground for the social and political wars of contemporary Quebec. Fennario walked away from middle-class professional theatre in the mid-1980s to devote himself to working with Black Rock Theatre in Pointe-Saint-Charles, where he still lives. For Black Rock, he wrote and directed a series of plays examining Montreal's ruling elite and their victimization of the city's working classes: the historical satires *Joe Beef* (1984), for which he received the Prix Pauline Julien from the United Steelworkers' Union; *Doctor Thomas Neill Cream (Mystery at McGill)* (1985); and *The Murder of Susan Parr* (1989). He returned to the Centaur in 1991 with *The Death of René Lévesque*, a controversial play condemning the Parti Québécois leader for betraying his social democratic principles.

In 1994, Fennario wrote and performed *Banana Boots* for Toronto's Annex Theatre and subsequently for television. In this one-man show, Fennario describes his changing feelings about his own role in the theatre while on tour with *Balconville* in Belfast. He also performed solo *Mysteries of Montreal: A Hidden History of Canada* (a.k.a. *Gargoyles*, 1997), a walking tour of Old Montreal in which he presented an alternative to conventional local history. (James McGill was "a slave owner who made a fortune ripping off the native peoples.") *Fessenden's Follies*, his play about the Canadian who invented radio in 1906, was broadcast over community radio stations in Canada, the United States, and Britain in 2006. *Bolsheviki*, a solo anti-war play debunking the myths around Canada's involvement in World War One, premiered at Montreal's Infinithéâtre in 2010. And in 2005, the Centaur premiered *Condoville*, a sequel to *Balconville* with some of the same characters (and a couple of the original actors) now dealing with the gentrification of the old neighbourhood.

In the plays leading up to *Balconville*, the politics are mostly a veneer behind which the young workers act out their frustration and rage against the repressive system with wild releases of anarchic energy. *On the Job* and *Nothing to Lose* show us the last hurrahs of 1960s rebelliousness. With *Balconville*, everyone has grown older. Elvis is dead and the 1960s are just a dim memory. Johnny was a "rebel. A real teen angel," but he's grown up to be a drunk. The Parti Québécois is in power but nothing has really changed for the Montreal poor except that now the *maudits anglais* are in the same boat as the French. "That's one good thing now," Paquette tells Tom. "We're all equal. Nobody's got a chance." This kind of bitter fatalism ("the psychology of the poor," Fennario calls it) seems borne out in the play not only when Paquette loses his job, but by the future apparently in store for the young people, Tom and Diane. Tom tries unsuccessfully to escape but can't get across the border. By the end, he's on the treadmill working at an unskilled job he already hates. Diane will help out her family by going to work as a waitress. But we see from Irene's life where that is likely to lead her: through the same bleak cycle of futility and despair.

Fennario dismisses "the myth of the happy poor," and indeed, except for simple-minded Thibault, his characters are not happy. But they are funny and resilient in the tradition of what might be called tenement naturalism shared by playwrights such as Michel Tremblay and Sean O'Casey. Like them, Fennario finds great strength in his women. Although they all have desperate moments, they are not easily fazed. Cécile persists in feeding her "air force" and cultivating her plants no matter how often the cats piss on them. Irene never stops trying to rally her neighbours to political activism no matter how great their apathy.

Toward the end, there are real signs of hope. Despite the heat that makes everyone irritable and despite the strong sense of two solitudes evoked by separate flags, separate languages, and separate TV sets side by side, some progress occurs. Johnny stops drinking and commiserates with Paquette *in French*. The broken step, the play's most conspicuous symbol of the disrepair in the life of this community, gets fixed. It can only happen one small step at a time, Fennario seems to be saying. But this ending appears only in a revised version of the play. The ending of the original production was a contrivance of wishful thinking: "the characters suddenly fall misty-eyed into each other's arms, ready to enter some nebulous franglophone workers' paradise," Fred Blazer reported in his *Globe and Mail* review. In rethinking the ending, Fennario replaced his Marxist answer with a Brechtian question that the characters ask in their own separate languages. "I think maybe the other ending is more enjoyable," Fennario has said, "but this one seems more true."

Because the French dialogue is such an essential component of this play, the text has been presented here as it was in production, intact and untranslated. Bilingualism is at the very heart of *Balconville*. A unilingual anglophone audience or one with only minimal French is in the same relationship to the play as an anglophone working-class Quebecker like Johnny Regan is to the francophone culture that surrounds him. The audience's experience of *Balconville* reiterates one of the things the play is about: language differences are a serious obstacle to communication but can be overcome with effort. If its French passages were translated, this would be a different play. Of course a theatre audience has access to vocal inflection, gesture, facial expression, and body language that can communicate eloquently even when words are not understood, whereas the reader of a play has only stage directions and her own imagination to help fill in the blanks. So the reader who knows little or no French will have to work hard for a full understanding of *Balconville*. But the rewards are well worth the effort.

David Fennario

Balconville

Balconville was first performed at the Centaur
Theatre in Montreal on January 2, 1979, with
the following cast:

CLAUDE PAQUETTE	Marc Gélinas
CÉCILE PAQUETTE	Cécile St-Denis
DIANE PAQUETTE	Manon Bourgeois
MURIEL WILLIAMS	Terry Tweed
TOM WILLIAMS	Robert Parson
JOHNNY REGAN	Peter MacNeill
IRENE REGAN	Lynn Deragon
THIBAULT	Jean Archambault
GAËTAN BOLDUC	Gilles Tordjman

Directed by Guy Sprung
Set and Costume Design by Barbra Matis
Lighting Design by Steven Hawkins
Sound Design by Peter Smith
Stage Managed by Erika Klusch

CHARACTERS

CLAUDE PAQUETTE

CÉCILE PAQUETTE, *his wife*

DIANE PAQUETTE, *their daughter*

MURIEL WILLIAMS

TOM WILLIAMS, *her son*

JOHNNY REGAN

IRENE REGAN, *his wife*

THIBAULT

GAËTAN BOLDUC, *a politician*

SET

*The back of a tenement in the Pointe-Saint-Charles
district of Montreal. We see a flight of stairs leading
up to two balconies set side by side, one belonging
to the Regans and the other, to the Paquettes.
The balcony belonging to the Paquettes is directly
below the ground-floor balcony of the Williams.*

ACT ONE

SCENE 1

It is night. **TOM** *is sitting on his back balcony trying
to play "Mona" on his guitar. The sound of a car
screeching around a corner is heard. The car beeps
its horn.* **DIANE** *enters.*

VOICE: Diane, Diane ...

DIANE: J'savais que t'avais une autre blonde.

VOICE: Mais non, Diane, c'était ma soeur.

DIANE: Oui, ta soeur. Mange d'la merde. Fuck you!

*CÉCILE comes out of her house and stands on her
balcony.*

CÉCILE: C'est-tu, Jean-Guy? Diane?

DIANE: Oh, achale-moi pas.

The car screeches away.

MURIEL: (*from the screen door behind* **TOM**)
Goddamn teenagers, they don't stop until they
kill someone. Tommy, what are you doing there?

*The sound of the car screeching is heard on the
other side of the stage.*

VOICE: Hey, Diane. Diane ...

DIANE: Maudit crisse, va-t'en, hostie.

CÉCILE: Diane, c'est Jean-Guy.

VOICE: Hey, Diane. Viens-t'en faire un tour avec
moi. Diane?

The car beeps its horn.

DIANE: Jamais, jamais. J't'haïs, j't'haïs.

VOICE: Hey, Diane.

The car beeps its horn again.

PAQUETTE: (*from inside his house*) Qu'est-ce qu'y
a? Qu'est-ce tu veux, hostie?

VOICE: Diane, viens ici.

PAQUETTE: (*yelling from the upstairs window*) Si tu
t'en vas pas, j'appelle la police.

MURIEL comes out of her house, goes down the alley, and yells after the car.

MURIEL: Get the hell out of here, you goddamn little creep!

The car screeches away. MURIEL returns to her house.

MURIEL: Tom, you gotta get up tomorrow.

TOM: Yeah, yeah.

MURIEL goes into her house.

PAQUETTE: Maudit crisse, j'te dis que t'en as des amis toi. C'est la dernière fois que je te préviens. Cécile, viens-tu t'coucher?

CÉCILE: Oui, oui, Claude, j'arrive. Diane, Jean-Guy devrait pas venir si tard.

DIANE: Ah, parle-moi pu d'lui.

CÉCILE: Son char fait bien trop de train, y devrait faire réparer son muffler.

CÉCILE goes into her house with DIANE. JOHNNY enters. He is drunk and singing "Heartbreak Hotel." He finds that the door to his house is locked.

JOHNNY: Hey, Irene ... Irene, open the fuckin' door.

IRENE opens the door.

PAQUETTE: (*from inside his house*) Hey! Ferme ta gueule, toi-là.

JOHNNY: Fuck you!

He goes into his house and slams the door shut.

Blackout.

SCENE 2

The next day. It is morning. THIBAULT enters wheeling his Chez Momo's delivery bike down the lane. TOM comes out of the house with toast, coffee, cigarettes, and his guitar. When he is finished his toast and coffee, he begins to practise his guitar.

MURIEL: (*from inside her house*) Tom, you left the goddamn toaster on again.

TOM: Yeah?

MURIEL: Yeah well, I'm the one who pays the electric bills.

THIBAULT: (*looking at the tire on his delivery bike*) Câlice, how did that happen? The tire, c'est fini.

TOM: A flat.

THIBAULT: Eh?

TOM: A flat tire.

THIBAULT: Ben oui, un flat tire. The other one, she's okay ... That's funny, eh? Very funny, that.

TOM: Don't worry, Thibault, it's only flat on the bottom.

THIBAULT: You think so? Well, I got to phone the boss.

He goes up the stairs and steps over the broken step.

TOM: Hey, watch the step!

THIBAULT: (*knocking on PAQUETTE's door*) Paquette, Paquette ...

PAQUETTE: (*from inside his house*) Tabarnac, c'est quoi?

THIBAULT: C'est moi, Paquette. J'ai un flat tire.

PAQUETTE: Cécile, la porte ...

CÉCILE: (*from inside the house*) Oui, oui ... Une minute ...

THIBAULT: C'est moi, Paquette.

CÉCILE: (*at the screen door*) Allô, Thibault. Comment ça va?

THIBAULT: J'ai un flat tire sur mon bicycle.

CÉCILE: Oh, un flat tire.

PAQUETTE: Que c'est qu'y a?

CÉCILE: C'est Thibault, Claude.

PAQUETTE: Thibault? Thibault?

THIBAULT: Oui. Bonjour.

PAQUETTE: Es-tu tombé sur la tête, tabarnac? Il est sept heures et demie du matin, hostie de ciboire.

CÉCILE: Claude a travaillé tard hier soir.

THIBAULT: That's not so good, eh?

PAQUETTE: Que c'est qu'y veut?

CÉCILE: Y veux savoir c'que tu veux.

THIBAULT: (*yelling at PAQUETTE through the window*) J'ai un flat tire. Je voudrais téléphoner à mon boss.

PAQUETTE: Cris pas si fort, j'suis pas sourd. Cécile, dis-lui rentrer.

JOHNNY: (*from inside his house*) What the fuck's going on?

THIBAULT: C'est-tu, okay?

CÉCILE: Oui, oui. Entre.

THIBAULT goes into PAQUETTE's house. JOHNNY comes out on his balcony.

JOHNNY: What's going on?

TOM: (*from below*) Thibault's got a flat tire.

JOHNNY: Flat tire? Big fuckin' production!

He goes back into his house.

THIBAULT: (*inside PAQUETTE's house*) Allô, Paquette. J'vas téléphoner à mon boss. C'est-tu, okay? C'est-tu, okay?

PAQUETTE: (*from inside his house*) Ferme ta gueule! Tu m'as réveillé asteure. Fais ce que t'as à faire.

THIBAULT: (*on the telephone*) Oui, allô, Monsieur Kryshinsky ... This is the right number? This is Monsieur Kryshinsky? ... Bon. C'est moi, Thibault ... Oui ... Quoi? ... Yes, I'm not there. I'm here ...

CÉCILE: (*from inside the house*) Veux-tu ton déjeuner, Claude?

PAQUETTE: Non, fais-moi un café. Ça va faire.

THIBAULT: Un flat tire, oui ... Okay. Yes, sir. I'll be there ... Oui. I'll be there tout de suite ... Okay, boss. Bye ... Allô? Bye. (*He hangs up the telephone.*) Faut que j'm'en aille. C'était mon boss. Tu le connais, "I don't like it when you're late. When I get to the store, I want you there at the door. Right there at the door."

PAQUETTE: (*at the door, pushing THIBAULT outside*) Salut, Thibault. Salut, Thibault.

THIBAULT: Okay, salut.

Coming down the stairs, THIBAULT trips on the broken step and loses his cap.

TOM: (*from below*) Watch the step!

THIBAULT: Hey, that was a close one. Very close, that one.

THIBAULT exits on his bike.

PAQUETTE: (*on his balcony*) Cécile, est-ce que Diane veut un lift pour aller à l'école?

CÉCILE: (*at the screen door*) Diane?

DIANE: (*from inside the house*) Non.

PAQUETTE: Pourquoi faire?

DIANE: Parce que j'aime pas la manière qu'y chauffe son char.

CÉCILE: Elle a dit que ...

PAQUETTE: J'suis pas sourd. Qu'elle s'arrange pas pour manquer ses cours, c'est moi qui les paye cet été.

DIANE: Inquiète-toi pas avec ça.

JOHNNY comes out on his balcony.

PAQUETTE: (*to JOHNNY*) Hey, people gotta sleep at night, eh?

JOHNNY: You talking to me?

PAQUETTE: (*pointing to the wall*) No, him. Hostie.

CÉCILE: Claude, j'pense que ce soir, je vais te faire des bonnes tourtières. Tu sais celles que t'aimes, celles du Lac Saint-Jean.

PAQUETTE: Encore des tourtières.

CÉCILE: Claude, t'aimes ça des tourtières.

PAQUETTE: Oui, j'aime ça des tourtières, mais pas tous les jours.

DIANE: (*from inside the house*) Maman, où sont mes souliers ... mes talons hauts?

CÉCILE: J'n'sais pas. Où est-ce que tu les as mis hier soir?

She disappears into the house.

PAQUETTE: Cécile, j'm'en vas.

JOHNNY: Watch the step!

PAQUETTE: (*coming down the stairs*) C'est qui a encore laissé les vidanges en dessous des escaliers?

TOM: (*from below*) Not me.

PAQUETTE: It's me who got the trouble with the landlord, eh?

CÉCILE comes running out on the balcony with PAQUETTE's lunch bucket.

CÉCILE: Claude, Claude ... T'as oublié ton lunch.

PAQUETTE: C'est l'affaire de Thibault ... Pitch moi-la.

CÉCILE tosses him his lunch.

JOHNNY: Baloney sandwiches again, eh, Porky?

PAQUETTE exits. IRENE comes out on her balcony to take the underwear off the clothesline.

JOHNNY: What time is it, Irene?

IRENE: (*looking at him*) You look a wreck.

JOHNNY: You don't look so hot yourself.

IRENE: You're beginning to look like a boozer. Ya know that?

JOHNNY: Hey, all I want is the time.

DIANE comes out on the balcony carrying her school books.

DIANE: J'perds mon temps avec ce maudit cours stupide, surtout l'été.

CÉCILE: Diane, est-ce que tu vas venir souper?

DIANE: Peut-être.

CÉCILE goes back into her house. DIANE comes down the stairs. She is wearing shorts and high heels. JOHNNY and TOM both look at her.

JOHNNY: Hey, Diane, ya look like a flamingo in those things.

DIANE makes a face at him and exits down the lane.

IRENE: You like that, eh?

JOHNNY: Just looking.

IRENE: Well, no more meat and potatoes for you.

JOHNNY: Eh?

IRENE: You know what I mean.

JOHNNY: What?

IRENE goes back into the house.

JOHNNY: Fuck!

TOM: She's mad, eh?

JOHNNY: Ya ask her for the time and she tells you how to make a watch.

He listens to TOM practising his guitar.

JOHNNY: Hey, softer on the strings. Strum them, don't bang them.

TOM: (*trying to strum*) Like that?

JOHNNY: Yeah, sort of ...

TOM: You used to play, eh?

JOHNNY: Yeah. Ever heard of "J.R. and the Falling Stars"?

TOM: No.

JOHNNY: You're looking at "J.R."

MURIEL comes out of her house carrying a bag of garbage.

MURIEL: (*to TOM*) What are you doing?

TOM: The UIC don't open till nine o'clock.

MURIEL: Yeah, but there's gonna be a lineup.

TOM: It's a waste of time. They never get ya jobs anyhow.

MURIEL: Well, don't think you're gonna hang around here doing nothing.

TOM: Okay, okay. Ma, I need some bus fare and some money for lunch.

MURIEL: You can come home for lunch.

TOM: Ma ...

MURIEL: I'm not giving you any money to bum around with.

TOM goes into the house with his guitar.

MURIEL: And you leave my purse alone in there, too.

TOM: (*coming back out with her purse*) Ma, I want my allowance.

MURIEL: What allowance? You don't go to school no more.

TOM: I want my money.

MURIEL: Gimme that purse. Gimme that goddamn purse.

She snatches her purse away from TOM, opens it, and gives him some bus tickets.

MURIEL: That's it ... that's all you get.

TOM: Fuck!

MURIEL: Don't you swear at me. Don't you ever swear at me.

TOM exits.

JOHNNY: (*singing*) "Heigh-ho, heigh-ho, it's off to work we go."

MURIEL: (*to JOHNNY*) You're not funny.

JOHNNY: You're a little hard on the kid, aren't ya, Muriel?

MURIEL: Yeah well, look what happened to you.

JOHNNY: Fuck! What's with everybody today? Is it the heat or what?

He goes into his house. CÉCILE comes out on her balcony. She notices MURIEL's wash hanging from the clothesline.

CÉCILE: It's so nice to see that, madame.

MURIEL: See what?

CÉCILE: To see you put up the washing the right way. First the white clothes, then the dark ones. The young girls, they don't care anymore.

MURIEL: Yeah well, why should they?

CÉCILE: Having children is not easy today? Eh?

MURIEL: Ah, they don't know what's good for them.

CÉCILE: Oui, I suppose.

MURIEL: When I was a kid, you just did what you were told and that was it.

CÉCILE: Yes, I remember that, too.

MURIEL: Everybody got along all right. Now, nobody knows their ass from their elbow.

CÉCILE: Elbow? ... Yes ...

THIBAULT enters on his bike again. He is looking for his cap.

CÉCILE: Allô, Thibault. Comment ça va?

THIBAULT: Ma casquette ...

CÉCILE: Ta casquette?

THIBAULT: Ben oui, j'ai perdu ma casquette. Oh, elle est en bas.

He looks under the stairs and finds his cap.

J'veux pas la perdre. J'ai payé quatre dollars chez Kresge.

CÉCILE: Eh, Thibault, ton boss était pas trop fâché?

THIBAULT: Il a sacré un peu après moi, but so what, eh? Il est jamais content anyway. Qu'tu fasses n'importe quoi.

CÉCILE: C'est la vie, hein ça?

THIBAULT: Oh oui. C'est la vie. (*He checks his transistor radio.*) Hey, thirty-two degrees. That used to be cold. Now, it's hot.

CÉCILE: Comment va ta mère? Est-ce qu'elle va toujours à Notre-Dame-des-Sept-Douleurs?

THIBAULT: Oh oui. Tous le jours. Mes frères sont tous partis, mais moi, j'suis toujours avec.

CÉCILE: C'est bien ça. Ta mère doit être contente.

THIBAULT: J'fais toute pour elle. Toute. Dans un an, elle va recevoir sa old-age pension et puis on va pouvoir s'payer un plus grand logement. On va déménager à Verdun.

CÉCILE: À Verdun. Ça va être bien ça. Thibault, ton boss.

THIBAULT: Oh oui. Mon boss. I better go now.

THIBAULT exits. MURIEL's phone rings. She goes into her house to answer it. CÉCILE goes into her house.

MURIEL: (*on the telephone*) Yeah, hello ... Who? ... Bill, where the hell are ya? ... On the docks ... shipping out to Sault Ste. Marie ... Are you coming back or what? ... Don't give me that crap. What's her name, eh? ... Yeah, I'm getting the cheques ... Tom? No, he's not here ... Yeah ... Yeah ... Look, I'm busy ... Bye. (*She hangs up the telephone.*) Christ, I wish I knew for sure.

IRENE and JOHNNY come out on their balcony. JOHNNY is sipping a cup of coffee. IRENE is wearing her waitress uniform. She is on her way to work.

IRENE: I want to talk to you when I get back, Johnny.

JOHNNY: Yeah, yeah. (*sipping his coffee*) Agh! What are you trying to do, poison me?

IRENE: I used brown sugar instead of white.

JOHNNY: Shit.

IRENE: It's healthier for you ... You going down to the UIC?

JOHNNY: Yeah.

IRENE: Today?

JOHNNY: Yeah, today.

IRENE starts to come down the stairs.

JOHNNY: Irene, what shift are you on?

IRENE: Ten to six this week.

JOHNNY: Why don't you quit that fucking job? Get something else.

IRENE: (*stopping*) Like what?

JOHNNY: Like anything except a waitress.

IRENE continues down the stairs and exits down the lane.

JOHNNY: (*shouting after her*) Pick me up a carton of smokes, I'm sick of these rollies.

Blackout.

SCENE 3

TOM and JOHNNY enter from the alley. JOHNNY is carrying a case of beer.

JOHNNY: I'm telling ya, they're all fucking separatists at the UIC. If you're English, you're fucked.

TOM: The phones are always ringing and nobody ever answers them. Ever notice that?

JOHNNY: Too busy having coffee breaks. (*He hands TOM a beer.*) Unenjoyment Disappointment Office.

JOHNNY sits at the foot of the stairs. TOM leans on the railing.

TOM: Hey, I went down to Northern Electric. I figured I've been breathing in their smoke all my life, so the least they could do is give me a job. Didn't get one ... They're automating.

MURIEL comes out of her house.

JOHNNY: Hi, Muriel.

MURIEL: (*to TOM*) What are you doing?

TOM: Standing up.

JOHNNY: Wanna brew, Muriel?

MURIEL: I told you to keep your goddamn beer to yourself. Tom, come here.

TOM: What?

MURIEL: Never mind what. Just come here. (*TOM moves toward her.*) So, did you go to that job interview?

TOM: Yeah.

MURIEL: So?

TOM: So the guy didn't like me.

MURIEL: He didn't like you? How come?

TOM: I dunno.

MURIEL: What do you mean, you dunno?

TOM: He wanted to send me to some stupid joe job way out in Park Extension. Minimum wage.

MURIEL: Since when can you afford to be fussy?

TOM: I'd have to get up at five in the morning.

MURIEL: There's a lot of things I don't like either, but I do them.

TOM: Well, I don't.

MURIEL: Anyhow, your father phoned. He's not coming home.

TOM: I don't blame him.

MURIEL: What's that?

TOM: Forget it.

MURIEL: Don't you get into one of your moods, mister, 'cause I'll give it to you right back.

MURIEL goes into her house.

TOM: Fuckin' bitch!

JOHNNY: Hey, don't worry about it.

TOM: Just 'cause she's frustrated, don't mean she's gotta take it out on me.

JOHNNY: Let them scream, that's what I do.

JOHNNY leaves TOM and starts up the stairs for his balcony. TOM goes into his house to get his guitar. CÉCILE comes out on her balcony with a handful of bread crumbs. She starts to feed the birds.

CÉCILE: Hi, Johnny.

JOHNNY: Hi, Cécile.

CÉCILE: Nice day, eh?

JOHNNY: Yeah, but it's too hot.

CÉCILE: Oh yes, too hot.

She continues to feed the birds.

JOHNNY: Feeding your Air Force?

CÉCILE: My what?

JOHNNY: Your Air Force ... Cécile's Air Force.

CÉCILE: Ah oui. Air Force.

JOHNNY: Just kidding ya, Cécile.

He sits on his balcony with his beer.

CÉCILE: You just kidding me, eh, Johnny?

She throws some more bread crumbs over the railing. They fall on MURIEL as she comes out of her house carrying a basket of washing.

MURIEL: Jesus Murphy!

CÉCILE: Oh, excuse me, madame. Excuse me. Hello!

MURIEL: Yeah, hello ...

CÉCILE: Aw, it's so nice, eh?

MURIEL: What?

CÉCILE: The sun. It's so nice.

MURIEL: Yeah, I guess it is.

CÉCILE: It's so good for my plants.

JOHNNY: How are your tomatoes?

CÉCILE: My tomatoes? Very good. This year, I think I get some big ones. Last year, I don't know what happened to them.

JOHNNY: The cat pissed on them.

CÉCILE: The what?

JOHNNY: The big tomcat that's always hanging around with Muriel. He pissed on them.

CÉCILE: You think so?

JOHNNY: Sure.

CÉCILE sits on her balcony. TOM comes out of the house again and sits practising his guitar.

JOHNNY: (*to TOM*) Too heavy on the strings ...

PAQUETTE enters carrying his lunch bucket. He is coming home from work.

JOHNNY: Hey, the working man!

PAQUETTE: Somebody has to work, eh?

He starts to climb the stairs. JOHNNY stops him.

JOHNNY: Have a brew here.

PAQUETTE: Okay.

He takes a pint from JOHNNY and sits down on JOHNNY's balcony.

PAQUETTE: Hey, my car, it's not working again. That goddamn carburetor ... (*to CÉCILE, on her balcony*) Cécile ... Hey, Cécile.

CÉCILE: Oui.

PAQUETTE: J'vas manger plus tard.

CÉCILE: Quoi?

PAQUETTE: (*shouting at her*) J'vas manger plus tard.

CÉCILE: Tu vas manger plus tard?

PAQUETTE: Oui, tabarnac!

CÉCILE: T'as pas besoin de sacrer, Claude.

PAQUETTE: C'est correct. As-tu appelé Chez Momo pour faire venir de la bière?

CÉCILE: Oui, Claude.

JOHNNY: Hot, eh? Can't breathe in the fuckin' house ... Can't sleep.

PAQUETTE: Hey, don't talk about it. Today in work one guy, he faints.

JOHNNY: Oh yeah?

PAQUETTE: No, the bosses say there's some energy crisis or something, so they stop the air conditioning in the factory, eh? Not in the office, of course.

JOHNNY: Tell the union.

PAQUETTE: Hey, the union. It's too hot to laugh, câlice.

JOHNNY: Another fire last night, eh?

PAQUETTE: Ah oui. What street?

JOHNNY: On Liverpool.

PAQUETTE: Liverpool encore. Tabarnac.

JOHNNY: Fuckin' firebugs, man. This block is gonna go up for sure.

PAQUETTE: Oui, that's for sure.

JOHNNY: Soon as I get my cheque, I'm gonna pull off a midnight move. Fuck this shit!

PAQUETTE: Oui, midnight move, for sure. Hey, just like the Arsenaults en bas. Fuck the landlords! It's the best way.

JOHNNY: Yeah ... Whew, hot. Going anywhere this summer?

PAQUETTE: Moi? Balconville.

JOHNNY: Yeah. Miami Bench.

THIBAULT wheels in on his Chez Momo's delivery bike.

THIBAULT: Chez Momo's is here.

JOHNNY: Hey, Thibault T-bone.

TOM: Hey, ya fixed the flat?

THIBAULT gets off his bike. He takes a case of beer from the bike.

THIBAULT: Oui. Hey me, I know the bike, eh? I know what to do.

JOHNNY: Hey, T-bone.

THIBAULT: Chez Momo's is here.

Coming up the stairs, he trips on the broken step.

JOHNNY: Watch the step!

PAQUETTE: Watch the beer!

JOHNNY: You okay?

THIBAULT: Me? I'm okay. But my leg, I don't know.

PAQUETTE: Why don't you read the sign?

THIBAULT: Eh?

PAQUETTE: The sign ...

THIBAULT reads the sign on the balcony. It reads, "Prenez garde."

THIBAULT: Prenez garde. Okay, prenez garde. So what? Tiens, ta bière.

He puts the case of beer down next to PAQUETTE, who gives him some money for the beer.

PAQUETTE: As-tu fini pour à soir?

THIBAULT: Oui, fini. C'est mon dernier voyage. (*shaking the change in his pocket*) Hey, des tips.

JOHNNY: Had a good day, eh?

THIBAULT: Hey, Johnny. Johnny B. Good. Long time no see, like they say.

JOHNNY: Yeah.

THIBAULT: Bye-bye, Johnny B. Good. You remember that?

JOHNNY: Remember what?

THIBAULT: Hey, there in the park, when they used to have the dances. You used to sing all the time like Elvis. (*He does an imitation of Elvis.*) Tutti-frutti, bop-bop-aloo, bop-a-bop, bam-boom. Like that, in the park.

JOHNNY: Yeah, yeah.

THIBAULT: C'était le fun. Me, I like that, but the girls grew up. They got old. You, too. Paquette, too. He's so fat now. Very fat.

PAQUETTE: Hey, hey.

JOHNNY: You remember all that shit?

THIBAULT: Me? Sure. I remember everything. Everything. Everybody forgets but me. I don't. It's funny, that, eh?

JOHNNY: Yeah.

THIBAULT: But you, you don't sing no more.

JOHNNY: No, I don't sing no more.

THIBAULT: Well, everybody gets old. It's funny, I watch it all change, but it's still the same thing ... I don't know. So what, eh?

PAQUETTE takes THIBAULT's nude magazine out of his back pocket and flips through it.

PAQUETTE: Hey, Thibault. You have a girlfriend?

THIBAULT: Me? Sure. I got two of them. Deux.

PAQUETTE: Deux?

THIBAULT: (*taking back his magazine*) Sure. I got one on Coleraine and the other one, she lives on Hibernia. Two girls. It's tough. (*He comes down the stairs.*) English, too. That surprise me. English, they do it, too.

THIBAULT exits on his bike. PAQUETTE takes his beer and moves over to his balcony.

JOHNNY: (*pointing to his head, referring to THIBAULT*) The lights are on, but nobody's home.

PAQUETTE: He might as well be crazy, eh? It helps.

JOHNNY: Thinking's no good, man. I wish I could have half my brain removed. Boom! No more troubles. Just like Thibault.

CÉCILE: Pauvre homme. He was such a good boy when he was young. Remember?

PAQUETTE: It's easy to be good when you're young.

CÉCILE: He should have become a priest.

PAQUETTE: Cécile, nobody becomes a priest anymore.

He bumps into one of CÉCILE's plants.

CÉCILE: Claude, fais attention à mes plantes!

PAQUETTE: Toi, pis tes câlices de plantes. Y'en a partout sur le balcon.

IRENE enters. She is wearing her waitress uniform, coming home from work. She stops at MURIEL's house.

IRENE: Hi, Tommy. Your mother home?

TOM: Yeah.

IRENE: (*knocking on MURIEL's door*) Yoo-hoo, Muriel. It's me ... Pointe Action Committee meeting tonight at seven thirty, eh?

MURIEL: (*at the screen door*) I don't think I'll be going, Irene.

IRENE: It's an important meeting, Muriel. We're going down to City Hall to demand more stop signs on the streets. Kids are getting hurt.

MURIEL: Yeah, I know.

IRENE: The more of us there, the better.

MURIEL: Yeah. I'm just not in the mood.

IRENE: You okay?

MURIEL: Yeah.

IRENE: Well, okay.

MURIEL goes back into her house. IRENE goes up the stairs, avoiding the broken step.

IRENE: Shit, why doesn't somebody fix that goddamn step?

JOHNNY: I didn't break it.

PAQUETTE: Hey, if I fix it, the landlord will raise the rent.

IRENE: (*at the top of the stairs, looking at JOHNNY and his beer*) Having fun?

JOHNNY: Just having a couple of brews, Irene.

IRENE: Yeah sure.

JOHNNY: (*offering her a beer*) Here, have one.

She pushes his arm out of the way.

JOHNNY: Hey, don't get self-righteous, okay? I get bored, all right? Bored!

IRENE: (*giving him his carton of cigarettes*) Did you go down to the UIC?

JOHNNY: "The cheque's in the mail," unquote.

IRENE: They said that last week.

JOHNNY: They'll say it again next week, too ... Irene, relax. Have a brew.

IRENE: Let me by.

She goes into the house.

PAQUETTE: (*from his balcony*) Hey, there's always trouble when a woman gets a job, eh?

JOHNNY: Yeah, fuckin' UIC slave market, people lined up like sheep. I hate lines.

PAQUETTE: Me, I don't know what's worse, working or not working. Sometimes I wish they'd lay me off for maybe a month.

JOHNNY: Factory getting to ya?

PAQUETTE: Hey, I even dream of it at night, hostie. Click, clack, bing, bang. It's bad enough being there in the day, but I see it at night, too, hostie.

JOHNNY: Twelve weeks I've been waiting for that cheque ... Four weeks' penalty for getting fired, four weeks for filing the claim late, and another four weeks for them to put the cheque in the fuckin' mail.

PAQUETTE: Hey, if they treat a dog like that, the SPCA would sue them.

DIANE enters, prancing along in her shorts and high heels.

JOHNNY: Love that walk, Diane.

DIANE: Fuck you!

PAQUETTE: Hey, watch ton langage, toi.

DIANE climbs the stairs. When she has passed PAQUETTE, she turns and mouths the words, "Fuck you, too." She goes into the house.

JOHNNY: (*shouting after her*) Hey, you're gonna break a leg in those things.

PAQUETTE: Maudit.

JOHNNY: She's starting to look good.

PAQUETTE: Oui. Too good.

JOHNNY: Lots of nice young pussy around the neighbourhood, man. Breaks my heart to see it all.

PAQUETTE: (*reaching for his wallet*) Johnny, I have something ...

He comes over and shows JOHNNY a photograph from his wallet.

PAQUETTE: Hey. Look at that ...

JOHNNY: Who's that? Cécile?

PAQUETTE: Oui ... She was nice, eh?

JOHNNY: Yeah. (*looking at the photograph again*) Who's that?

PAQUETTE: That? That's me. Moi.

JOHNNY: You're not serious?

PAQUETTE: Hey. Okay, okay.

He snatches back his wallet and returns to his balcony. From DIANE's room, the record "Hot Child in the City" can be heard.

PAQUETTE: Hey, Cécile ... Cécile, dis à Diane de baisser sa musique de tuns.

CÉCILE: (*shouting into the house*) Diane, baisse la musique juste un peu.

The music fades away. IRENE comes out on her balcony to hang up her waitress uniform. JOHNNY goes over to her and starts to hug her.

IRENE: Stop it.

JOHNNY: Honey, don't be mad.

IRENE: I'm not mad, Johnny. Stop it. You smell of beer.

JOHNNY: Okay. I'll hold my breath, Irene.

IRENE: Johnny, you've got to do something ... anything ... Keep yourself busy.

JOHNNY: Yeah, I'm gonna call up some people, try to get something together, as soon as I get my first cheque.

IRENE: That goddamn cheque!

JOHNNY: Well, I don't want to give up now. Those bastards owe me that money, Irene.

IRENE: Well, why don't you come down to our Unemployment Committee meetings?

JOHNNY: You know that I don't like meetings.

IRENE: Yeah, yeah. Ya'd rather watch *Charlie's Angels*.

JOHNNY: Irene, it's gonna be all right, okay? Say "okay." Say "okay."

IRENE: Okay.

JOHNNY: All right.

IRENE: I don't know why I have to nag. I don't want to nag. Don't want to sound like my mother.

JOHNNY: Hey, what's the matter? (*tickling her*) You sensitive, eh? You sensitive?

IRENE: Johnny.

JOHNNY: Come on, a Québec quickie.

PAQUETTE: (*from his balcony*) Hey, Jean. It's too hot for that, eh?

JOHNNY: Aw, the heat makes me horny ...

An election campaign truck passes by playing Elvis Presley music and broadcasting in French and English.

VOICE: Vote for Gaëtan Bolduc. Gaëtan Bolduc's the man for you. The man of the people. Bolduc is on your side.

JOHNNY: Fuck you, Bolduc!

IRENE: Bolduc is on *his* side.

VOICE: Remember, on the sixth, vote for progress, vote for change, vote for a winner. Vote for Bolduc, the man for you ... available and dynamic ...

The sound fades away.

JOHNNY: Circus is starting early this year. A month away from the election and he's already doing his fuckin' number.

IRENE: Bolduc, the boss. Did ya see the size of his new house?

JOHNNY: Once a year, he buys hot dogs for the kids on the boardwalk. Big fuckin' deal!

TOM: Yeah ... stale hot dogs.

PAQUETTE: Those guys are all the same crooks.

IRENE: I don't know what's worse, Joe Who or René Quoi?

She goes and gets the mail.

PAQUETTE: Bolduc, he was okay ... until he got the power. Then, that's it. He forgets us.

JOHNNY: Any mail for me?

IRENE: (*looking through the mail*) No. Aw, shit. La merde.

JOHNNY: What?

IRENE: Water tax. Eighty-four dollars for water. Christ, it tastes like turpentine and they charge us like it's champagne.

JOHNNY: Hey, all the bills are in French anyhow, separatist bastards. Tell them we're paying in English.

PAQUETTE: Hey, I don't like that.

JOHNNY: What?

PAQUETTE: There's a lot of English bastards around, too, eh?

JOHNNY: Yeah, but they're not forcing ya out of the province.

PAQUETTE: Learn how to speak French, that's all.

CÉCILE: You know, Irene, there was another fire last night.

IRENE: Another one?

CÉCILE: Oui. Last night. A big one.

IRENE: The Pointe Action Group thinks the landlords are setting the fires themselves.

PAQUETTE: The landlords? Burning down their own houses?

IRENE: For the insurance.

JOHNNY: Yeah, I believe that.

PAQUETTE: It's the punk kids that do it. They got no father. The mother, she drinks in the taverns. What do they care, eh? They should make them work. Stop all the welfare.

IRENE: There *is* no work.

PAQUETTE: There's jobs, if they want them. They don't try hard enough.

JOHNNY: Yeah, there's jobs, but who wants to be a busboy all their lives?

PAQUETTE: It's a job.

JOHNNY: Yeah well, I'm no fuckin' immigrant. I was born here.

PAQUETTE: That's the trouble ... too many people. "Overpopulation," they call it. We need another war or something. Stop all the welfare and make the lazy bums work.

IRENE: How come people always blame the poor? They never blame the rich.

PAQUETTE: Hey you, tell me, who's got the money, eh? Who's got all the money?

JOHNNY: Not me.

PAQUETTE: It's the English and the Jews.

IRENE: Hey!

PAQUETTE: They control everything, the goddamn Jews. That's the trouble.

IRENE: Hey, my mother was Jewish, so don't give me that shit, okay?

PAQUETTE: Hey, I don't talk about the good Jews ...

JOHNNY: What the fuck's going on?

PAQUETTE: Hey me, I work all my life. All my life, me. Since I was ten years old.

JOHNNY: Yeah, so why cry about it?

PAQUETTE: Hey, John, that's not what I'm talking about.

JOHNNY: Hey, fuck the politics!

CÉCILE: Who knows what is true, eh? What is the truth?

PAQUETTE: You, you go light candles in the church. Me, I know what is the truth. A piece of shit, câlice.

CÉCILE: Claude.

PAQUETTE: Ah oui, Claude.

IRENE: Anyhow, forget it.

JOHNNY: Yeah, fuck the politics. Nobody has fun in the Pointe anymore. We should have a party or something.

IRENE: A party, on what?

JOHNNY: Next week, I get my cheque, right? We'll have a party, just like the old days. Invite everybody on the block. We'll have a ball.

IRENE: You'll have a ball. I'll clean up the mess.

IRENE goes into the house.

JOHNNY: Irene, fuck!

He exits after her.

MURIEL: (*from inside her house*) Tom, your supper's on the table.

TOM: Yeah, yeah.

MURIEL: (*coming out of the house carrying a pot of spaghetti*) Tommy, I'm not going to tell you again.

TOM: What is it? Spaghetti?

MURIEL: Yeah, spaghetti.

TOM: I'm not hungry. I don't want any.

MURIEL: You don't want it? You don't want it? Well here, take it!

*She dumps the spaghetti on **TOM**'s head.*

TOM: Ma! Shit!

He exits down the alley.

PAQUETTE: That woman, she's a little bit crazy, I think.

CÉCILE: T'as pas faim, Claude?

PAQUETTE: Y fait trop chaud. Fais-moi une limonade.

CÉCILE goes to get him a lemonade. DIANE comes out on the balcony and sits in the rocking chair. She is reading a magazine. PAQUETTE starts in on her.

PAQUETTE: Où est-ce que t'étais hier soir?

DIANE: Dehors.

PAQUETTE: Où ça dehors?

DIANE: Dehors. J't'ai dit dehors.

PAQUETTE: Dehors avec Jean-Guy pis toute la gang. Vous avez fumé, vous avez bu, vous avez fourré, vous avez en du fun, hein?

DIANE: Oui, on a eu ben de fun.

PAQUETTE: Il est même pas pusher. Qu'est-ce qu'y fait pour vivre d'abord?

DIANE: Il travaille des fois. J'sais pas. Demande-lui si tu veux savoir.

PAQUETTE: Diane, tu vois pas que c'est un hostie de pas-bon.

DIANE: Parce que toi tu sais ce qui est bon pour moi. Tu t'es pas regardé.

PAQUETTE: Pis tu t'penses smart. Tu penses que t'as inventé le monde. Eh. Diane, regarde les femmes dans la rue. C'est ça que tu veux? Te marier, avoir un petit par année, devenir large de même, t'écraser devant la télévision, manger des chips et pis attendre le welfare et le mari. C'est ça que tu veux avec Jean-Guy?

DIANE: Tant qu'à ça pourquoi pas?

PAQUETTE: Bon. Ben tant que tu vas rester ici, tu vas rentrer à minuit. Tu vas à l'école. C'est pour te sortir de cette câlice de merde-là.

DIANE: Tu vas à l'école, pis y a même pas de job en sortant.

PAQUETTE: Diane, pense. Sers-toi de ta tête, pas de ton cul, crisse.

CÉCILE: (*returning with the lemonade*) Claude.

PAQUETTE: Comment, Claude? Tabarnac, t'es sa mère, parles-y.

CÉCILE: Mais elle est jeune.

PAQUETTE: Oh. Oh, elle est jeune. Parce qu'est jeune, elle a droit de tout faire, pis quand elle va nous arriver en ballon.

DIANE: Fais-toi en pas, parce que j'prends la pillule.

She shows him her pill dispenser.

PAQUETTE: Maudit crisse. (*He comes down the stairs and exits into the shed.*) Va chez-toi.

CÉCILE: Tu l'as fait fâcher.

DIANE: Il est stupide.

CÉCILE: Mais, c'est ton père, Diane.

DIANE: Il est stupide pareil.

CÉCILE: Il essaye de t'aider. Y s'inquiète pour toi.

DIANE: Ça, Cécile, c'est ton problème. C'est pas le mien. J'suis pas obligée de l'endurer.

CÉCILE: C'est la job qui fait qu'y est fatigué. Y voudrait être fin avec toi des fois, mais il en peut plus, il est trop fatigué.

DIANE: Tu le gâtes trop, Cécile. C'est de ta faute. Tu le gâtes trop.

CÉCILE: Faut bien vivre.

DIANE: Dis-y donc non des fois, peut-être qu'il serait plus fin avec toi.

They hear a hammering noise coming from the shed. PAQUETTE is in there working on his car.

DIANE: Regarde, y passe plus d'temps avec son maudit Buick qu'il passe avec toi.

CÉCILE: Mon erreur moi-là, ça a été d'avoir juste un enfant. Si tu te maries, Diane, arrange-toi pas pour avoir juste un enfant parce que tu vas te sentir bien toute seule.

DIANE: Maman, t'aurais dû rester au Lac Saint-Jean à la campagne avec ta famille. C'était là ta place, pas ici. C'est vrai, ça.

IRENE and JOHNNY come out of their house. IRENE is on her way to her Pointe Action Committee meeting.

IRENE: You wanna come to the meeting?

JOHNNY: No.

IRENE: Why not?

JOHNNY: 'Cause they're boring.

IRENE: Boring?

JOHNNY: Yeah, everybody's sitting around with a long face ... Boring!

IRENE: We're planning our next action.

JOHNNY: Yeah, sure. Another demonstration. Big fuckin' deal!

IRENE: We gotta start somewhere.

JOHNNY: Yeah well, they got a long fuckin' ways to go.

IRENE: (*coming down the stairs*) If you're waiting for Superman, you're gonna wait a long, long time.

JOHNNY: If you wanna fight politicians, go out and shoot a couple of them. All this talking drives me nuts.

He goes back into the house.

IRENE: (*starting after him*) I'll be back at ten. There's some supper in the fridge.

IRENE sees MURIEL crying as she cleans up the spaghetti.

IRENE: Muriel, you okay? You all right, girl?

MURIEL: Oh, go away.

IRENE: What's wrong? ... What's right? Guess that's an easier question, eh?

MURIEL: Oh, I feel stupid.

IRENE: Here, I got a Kleenex.

MURIEL: Thanks.

IRENE: You're not pregnant, are you?

MURIEL: Don't be crazy.

IRENE: Got the blues?

MURIEL: I'm worried about my stomach. It's acting up again.

IRENE: Maybe it's ulcers.

MURIEL: I don't know.

IRENE: Go to the hospital.

MURIEL: I'm afraid.

IRENE: You're afraid of what the doctor might say?

MURIEL: Yeah.

IRENE: Well, at least you'll know what you've got ... You'll feel better once you do.

MURIEL: I dunno.

IRENE: I'll go with ya.

MURIEL: Irene, you don't have to.

IRENE: Listen, I wouldn't want to go alone either. So, how about, uh, Tuesday?

MURIEL: I don't know. All they do is give ya pills, dope ya up, and send ya back home again.

IRENE: Well, let them take a look at ya anyhow.

MURIEL: Tuesday?

IRENE: Yeah.

MURIEL: Sick or not, what's the difference?

IRENE: When is your old man due back from the boats?

MURIEL: Him? Oh, he's taking his time. Don't worry, he's in no hurry to come back. It's the perfect life for him. He can drink all he wants, screw around ... and he gets paid for it.

IRENE: Well, still it'll be nice to have him back.

MURIEL: Come off it! And your old man isn't much better. I'd dump him so quick, it wouldn't be funny. You're too good for him, Irene.

IRENE: Oh well, ya know how it is? Ya marry a prince and he turns into a frog.

MURIEL: Yeah, Bill was always great for a good time. But he was no good for nothing else.

IRENE: He still sends the cheques?

MURIEL: Yeah. Aw, it's nobody's fault ... everybody's fault ... Ever think about what we'll be doing in ten years?

IRENE: Ten years? Ugh, I don't think about it. Maybe we'll win the Super Loto or something ... You know, you gotta get out of the house more. Ya make a lousy housewife. Try something else.

MURIEL: Like what?

IRENE: I don't know. School?

MURIEL: Jesus Christ, they threw me out of grade eight for punching out the teacher.

IRENE: Yeah, I remember that.

MURIEL: Yeah. Old man Breslin with the wandering hands.

IRENE: Pow, pow! Love it!

MURIEL: He had it coming.

IRENE: He sure did and you gave it to him. People still talk about it, eh? Sure.

MURIEL: Yeah, eh?

IRENE: Yeah ... Tuesday?

MURIEL: Yeah, Tuesday ... Thanks, Irene.

IRENE: Aw, us girls got to stick together, eh?

CÉCILE starts to water her plants. The water drips down on IRENE and MURIEL below.

IRENE: Aw, shit. When she's not feeding her Air Force, she's watering her jungle ... Bye.

IRENE exits. The broadcast VOICE is heard again.

VOICE: Gaëtan Bolduc, the man for you. The man of today, the man of the people, the man who cares. Vote for action, vote for a winner, vote for Bolduc. Gaëtan Bolduc ... available and dynamic ... the man for you.

FIRST VOICE: (*from the truck*) Yeah, yeah. Bolduc, Bolduc, Bolduc. Câlice, how many more times do we have to drive around the block?

SECOND VOICE: (*from the truck*) We got three more hours, hostie.

FIRST VOICE: (*from the truck*) That shithead. Bolduc. Bolduc. Me, I'm so sick of his fuckin' name. Bolduc. Bolduc. Fuck you, Bolduc! You cheap son of a bitch.

SECOND VOICE: (*from the truck*) Next time, we'll ask for forty bucks a day.

FIRST VOICE: (*from the truck*) Hey, fifty. Fifty bucks a day.

SECOND VOICE: (*from the truck*) Oui, fifty.

FIRST VOICE: (*from the truck*) Crisse, François. The speaker is still on. They can hear us.

SECOND VOICE: (*from the truck*) The speaker? What? The speaker!? Câlice.

The voices stop. Elvis Presley music comes on.

Blackout.

SCENE 4

It is night. The sound of a record playing rock music is heard. DIANE, CÉCILE, IRENE, MURIEL, THIBAULT, and TOM are dancing in the street.

THIBAULT: Hey, look. I got one. The Mashed Potato Duck.

IRENE: Hey, come on, everybody, make a circle. Take turns in the middle. Come on.

DIANE steps into the circle and does a dance, then TOM takes his turn.

MURIEL: Move your feet. Move your feet.

THIBAULT: (*stepping into the circle*) Hey, the duck. Look, I got one. The Mashed Potato Duck.

They push him out of the circle.

IRENE: Hey, Cécile. Come on.

They push Cécile into the circle. She moves a bit. They applaud.

IRENE: Hey, shake that thing. All right, Muriel. Come on, your turn. Come on.

MURIEL: Aw, that's kids' stuff.

IRENE: Come on.

Just as MURIEL starts to dance, the record ends.

MURIEL: Well, that's it.

THIBAULT: It's hot, eh? Hot ... whew.

TOM: Hey, where's Johnny?

IRENE: Him? He's always late. He's the star, right?

MURIEL: That's one word for him.

IRENE: Hey, Muriel. Tell that joke. The one you told me this morning.

MURIEL: Naw, naw. You tell it.

IRENE: Come on.

MURIEL: No. You tell it better.

IRENE: Okay. You ready? Okay, this guy is going to bed with a girl for the first time ...

THIBAULT: Oh, dirty joke! Hey!

MURIEL: Don't worry, Thibault. You'll never get it.

IRENE: Yeah, and he takes off his socks and shoes, and his feet are deformed, and she says, "What's wrong with your feet?" And he says, "Well, when I was a kid, I had toelio."

TOM: "Toelio."

IRENE: And she says, "You mean, polio." "No, toelio." And well, then, he takes off his pants …

THIBAULT whistles.

MURIEL: Down, Thibault. Down.

IRENE: And … and his knees are all, you know, bulgy.

DIANE: C'est quoi ça, "bulgy"?

IRENE: Tout enflé … And the girl says, "What's wrong with your knees?" "Well, when I was a kid, I had the kneasles." "You mean, measles." "No, kneasles." Then, he takes off his underwear …

THIBAULT whistles again.

IRENE: And she says, "Oh no, don't tell me you had smallcocks, too." Small cocks.

They all laugh.

MURIEL: Thibault, ya got it now?

CÉCILE: Diane. "Smallcocks," c'est quoi?

DIANE: P'tite bizoune.

CÉCILE: Oh bizoune. Oui.

MURIEL: Shit, it's been so long I forgot what they look like.

The girls all laugh.

THIBAULT: Hey, that's funny, that, eh?

TOM: Hey, ya wanna see my Elvis Presley imitation? Eh?

DIANE: Oui.

TOM: Ya wanna see it?

MURIEL: No.

IRENE: Sure.

TOM: Okay? Ya ready?

IRENE: Ready.

TOM: Elvis!

He bends his head back and crosses his arms like a laid-out corpse. They all groan.

DIANE: I like that. (*She copies his Elvis imitation.*) Elvis!

THIBAULT: That's all?

TOM: Yeah.

DIANE puts another record on. It is "Hot Child in the City." THIBAULT grabs her and begins to dance.

THIBAULT: Cha-cha-cha, hostie.

DIANE: Hey, not so close, okay? Not so close. J'vas te puncher.

THIBAULT: Hey, let's dance. Dansons.

IRENE: (*cutting in*) Here, Diane. You take Tom.

She grabs THIBAULT. TOM and DIANE dance.

IRENE: Come on, Thibault, you sexy thing.

THIBAULT: Cha-cha-cha, hostie.

IRENE and THIBAULT dance.

IRENE: (*turning to MURIEL*) Christ, hey Muriel, look. (*referring to herself and THIBAULT*) The last tango in the Pointe.

MURIEL: Careful. You'll get him so excited, he'll piss himself.

PAQUETTE and JOHNNY enter with their arms around one another's shoulders. They are drunk and singing.

PAQUETTE & JOHNNY: (*singing*)
Jesus saves his money at
the Bank of Montréal.
Jesus saves his money at
the Bank of Montréal.
Jesus saves his money at
the Bank of Montréal.
Jesus saves, Jesus saves –
Jesus saves.

IRENE: Shit, he's drunk already.

PAQUETTE: Hey, les femmes. Nous sommes ici.

DIANE mimics him.

THIBAULT: Hey, Paquette. Watch me dance.

JOHNNY: (*singing with PAQUETTE*)
Irene, goodnight,
Irene, goodnight,
Goodnight, Irene,
Goodnight, Irene,
I'll see you in my dreams.

PAQUETTE: Hey, les femmes. C'est moi.

JOHNNY: Hey, Irene. I'm a little late. Had a few drinks with what's his name.

PAQUETTE: Paquette.

JOHNNY: Pole-quette.

PAQUETTE: Naw. Paw-quette.

JOHNNY: Okay, tell the people your name (*together*) ... Paquette.

THIBAULT: Thibault. My name, Thibault.

PAQUETTE and JOHNNY start to climb the stairs. JOHNNY stumbles on the broken step.

PAQUETTE: Eh, Johnny? Un autre p'tit step. La bière est en haut.

IRENE: Fais attention à sa tête.

She goes to help JOHNNY up the stairs. She is followed by MURIEL, THIBAULT, DIANE, and TOM.

PAQUETTE: C'est sa tête carrée. C'est les coins qui accrochent.

When JOHNNY gets up the stairs, he grabs IRENE.

JOHNNY: Irene, I love ya, love ya, love ya ...

THIBAULT: We have fun, eh? Watch me dance.

JOHNNY: Yeah, we're gonna rock this joint. Where's the beer?

MURIEL: You've had enough.

PAQUETTE: Hey, Johnny. Dansons, dansons.

He does a dance step.

JOHNNY: Where *is* everybody?

IRENE: This is it. We're all here.

JOHNNY: What do ya mean? Where are they? Danny? Jerry?

IRENE: Guess they couldn't make it.

JOHNNY: I knew the fuckers wouldn't come.

IRENE: Maybe they'll come later.

JOHNNY bangs into his house.

IRENE: Johnny ...

PAQUETTE: Put on some music. Hey, what's wrong? Put on some music. We'll have a good time.

He goes into his house and puts on the record "Hot Child in the City."

THIBAULT: Tutti-frutti, hostie. Let's twist some more.

JOHNNY: (*inside his house*) What's Jerry's number? What's his fuckin' number?

IRENE: I dunno.

PAQUETTE: Hey, Diane. C'est ta tune. (*to MURIEL*) Hey, let's dance ... Why not?

MURIEL: Ask your wife.

PAQUETTE: Come on. I don't bite.

MURIEL: You're drunk.

They dance on the balcony.

PAQUETTE: Eh? Not bad, eh? I dance good, eh?

MURIEL: Yeah, sure. Terrific.

PAQUETTE: Not bad for a peasoup, eh?

JOHNNY: (*inside the house, on the phone*) Jerry, that you? What are ya doing at home? You're supposed to be here ... What? ... Hey, turn that fuckin' music down ... What? ... Fuck that shit, man. This is supposed to be a get-together and nobody's here. Nobody! Just the Pepsi's next door ... What? ... What? ... I don't want to hear that shit, Jerry. You coming? You coming? ... Maybe later? Fuck you!

He slams down the receiver and bangs his way out onto the balcony.

IRENE: Johnny, Johnny ...

JOHNNY: The party's over. Fuck off! Everybody, fuck off!

PAQUETTE: Hey, Jacques. We'll have a good time, eh?

JOHNNY: (*pushing PAQUETTE*) Get on your own fuckin' side.

PAQUETTE: Hey. Hey.

JOHNNY: Fuckin' gorf. Pepper. Get on your own side.

PAQUETTE: Hey, watch that, eh? Fais attention, okay?

JOHNNY: We were here first, ya fuckin' farmer. Go back to the sticks.

PAQUETTE: Hey, reste tranquille, eh?

JOHNNY: You wanna fight? Wanna fight?

JOHNNY swings at PAQUETTE, but misses him. He falls down. IRENE and MURIEL push him toward the door of his house.

PAQUETTE: Keep your garbage on your side.

JOHNNY: (*stumbling*) The party's over. No more parties. No more.

IRENE: Get him into the house.

MURIEL: Stupid men.

They carry him into his house.

JOHNNY: Jerry. Where's Jerry? Jerry?

MURIEL: Good old days ... Never was any good old days.

They exit into the house.

THIBAULT: Johnny, he gets a little drunk tonight, eh?

TOM: Hey, a little.

DIANE: It's fun for them. That's the way they have fun.

CÉCILE: It's a full moon. That's why everyone is so crazy.

PAQUETTE: What's wrong? Hey, what's wrong?

He puts the record back on. It is "Hot Child in the City" once again.

THIBAULT: Away, Paquette. Let's twist some more.

TOM: (*to MURIEL, as she comes out of JOHNNY's house*) Is he okay?

MURIEL: He's okay. You wanna end up just like him? That's the way you're going.

TOM: Yeah, yeah.

PAQUETTE goes over to MURIEL, who isn't interested in dancing, so he starts dancing with DIANE. He begins to slobber all over her. She pushes him away, goes down the stairs, and exits down the lane.

CÉCILE: Diane. Diane.

PAQUETTE: Who wants to dance? Hey.

He heads toward MURIEL.

MURIEL: (*pushing him aside*) Get lost. Beat it.

PAQUETTE: Quoi?

MURIEL: Ya make me sick.

PAQUETTE: Hey, parle-moi en français, eh? Parle-moi en français.

MURIEL: Go on. Hit me. Hit me. Try it.

PAQUETTE: Maudits anglais. Throw them all out. Toute le gang. On est au Québec. On est chez-nous.

MURIEL: I was born here, too, ya bigmouth Frenchman.

PAQUETTE: It's our turn now, eh? Our turn. And Ottawa, Ottawa can kiss my Pepsi ass.

MURIEL: Ferme ta gueule, toi.

THIBAULT: Fuck the Queen!

MURIEL: Fuck Lévesque!

MURIEL goes back into IRENE's house. PAQUETTE knocks over one of CÉCILE's plants by accident.

CÉCILE: Claude, fais attention à mes plantes. Claude.

PAQUETTE picks up one of her plants and throws it over the railing.

PAQUETTE: Tiens, ta câlice de plante.

CÉCILE runs into the house crying.

PAQUETTE: (*opening another beer*) It's crying time again, eh? Crying time again.

THIBAULT: Me, I don't hate the English. I just don't like them, that's all.

PAQUETTE: Maudits anglais!

THIBAULT: They got funny heads. Square heads.

PAQUETTE: (*to TOM*) You. Hey you. Think maybe you got a chance, eh? No more. That's one good thing now. We're all the same now, eh? We're all equal. Nobody's got a chance. Nobody.

THIBAULT: Fuck the Queen!

PAQUETTE: Maybe you got dreams, eh? Me, too. I had dreams. Thibault, too. He had dreams.

THIBAULT: Oui, me, too.

PAQUETTE: If you knew what I know, you'd go jump in the river right now. Tonight.

THIBAULT: Oui, tonight. The river. No joke, that.

PAQUETTE: (*hugging THIBAULT*) Thibault, you're a bum ... a bum and a drunk.

THIBAULT: Oui, a bum.

PAQUETTE: You know what? Me, I work all my life. All my life.

THIBAULT: That's too bad.

PAQUETTE: When I was young, I was going to do this and that, but the job, the fuckin' job, it took my life away. What can you do? Everybody says, "What can you do?" That's the way it goes.

THIBAULT: That's the way it goes.

PAQUETTE: You get old and ugly and you die ... and that's all.

THIBAULT: That's all.

PAQUETTE: I try, but it don't help. No matter what you do.

TOM comes down the stairs and goes into his house to get his guitar.

PAQUETTE: No matter what you do.

THIBAULT: So what? That's what I say. So what?

PAQUETTE: So what? Maudits anglais.

THIBAULT: Oui. So what? (*looking into the case of beer*) Hey, no more beer.

IRENE and MURIEL come out on the balcony.

THIBAULT: Eh, y a plus de bière?

PAQUETTE: On va aller en chercher en ville.

THIBAULT: Comment?

PAQUETTE: Ben ... avec mon char.

THIBAULT: Ton char?

PAQUETTE: Ben oui. Mon char, hostie.

They come down the stairs.

THIBAULT: Ah oui. Ton char dans le garage. Prenez garde. Watch the step.

They pick up some tools and exit for the shed to fix the car.

IRENE: They're gonna get themselves killed.

MURIEL: Don't worry, they'll never get that car to start.

IRENE: Well, Johnny's out for the night. He'll wake up tomorrow, drink a bottle of Coke, and ask me what he did.

MURIEL: He needs a kick in the ass ... and fast.

IRENE: He told me he wants me to find another man ... Yeah ... Here I am, thirty-four years old, and he wants me to go find another man. Fat chance.

MURIEL: I dunno. You're still in pretty good shape.

IRENE: Aw, I'm no spring chicken anymore ... I'm a broiler.

MURIEL: You're better off without a man. Who needs them?

IRENE: Aw, I guess I love the creep.

MURIEL: Love? Love never got through the Wellington Tunnel.

IRENE: I had this guy who was nuts about me ... always phoning me up, calling on me. He's a teacher now in NDG ... But I fell for Johnny. He was a rebel. A real teen angel, ya know what I mean?

MURIEL: Yeah, so they grow up to be drunks.

IRENE: I can't blame him. He's been trying.

MURIEL: No, guess you can't blame the poor ignorant stupid bastards.

IRENE: I'm scared for him.

MURIEL: It never pays to be too nice, Irene. I used to be nice, but it never got me nowhere.

IRENE: Yeah ... But why, Muriel? Why? How do you change it?

MURIEL: They're all the same, Irene ... all of them.

IRENE: The doctor's still taking tests?

MURIEL: Yeah ... you know doctors. They never tell ya nothing. All they do is poke your stomach, take your blood, give ya some pills, and tell ya to come in next week. Makes ya feel like a goddamn guinea pig.

IRENE: Yeah well, meanwhile there's the late movie, eh? What's on anyhow?

MURIEL: I dunno.

IRENE: See ya ...

MURIEL: Yeah, Irene ... don't let him walk on you. That's what I'm trying to say anyhow.

IRENE: 'Night.

MURIEL: Yeah.

IRENE goes into her house. MURIEL comes down the stairs. She sees TOM sitting on her balcony with his guitar.

MURIEL: I'm locking the door at twelve o'clock.

TOM: Yeah.

MURIEL: I mean it.

TOM: Yeah, yeah.

MURIEL goes into her house.

PAQUETTE: (*yelling at THIBAULT in the shed*) Non, non. Le wrench. Donne-moi le wrench qui est sur la valise.

THIBAULT: La valise.

PAQUETTE: Oui, tabarnac.

THIBAULT: Y fait noir. Ouch!

PAQUETTE: Le hood. Fais attention au hood. Ta tête.

A slamming sound is heard.

PAQUETTE: Maudit, tabarnac de câlice de Sainte-Vierge. Hostie, que t'es cave! Tiens la lumière.

THIBAULT: La lumière. Okay.

TOM: (*playing his guitar and singing*)
Tell you, Mona, what I'm gonna do,
Build a house next door to you,
Then I can see you in the summertime,
We can blow kisses through the blinds.
Come on, Mona, out in the front,
Listen to my heart go bumpetity-bump.

DIANE enters. When TOM has finished playing, she applauds.

TOM: Uh, hi ... Want some beer? ... Go ahead, I got an extra bottle. (*DIANE takes a sip.*) The party's over, eh?

DIANE: The party. Oui.

TOM: Uh ... everybody got drunk and crazy, eh?

DIANE: Quoi?

TOM: Drunk, crazy ... like that ...

He mimes "drunk."

DIANE: Drunk? Ah oui ... Mon anglais est pas tellement bon.

TOM: My French is, uh ... comme ci, comme ça ... Like that ... So, uh ... what's new?

DIANE: What's new?

TOM: Yeah, what's new?

DIANE: You tell me? ... Bon? ... Well?

She moves toward the stairs.

TOM: Hey, uh ... where ya going?

DIANE: I don't speak the good English.

TOM: Look, finish your beer. I mean, uh ... why not?

DIANE: (*stopping at the foot of the stairs*) I don't want to go home.

TOM: Yeah. I know the feeling. You, uh ... never look too happy.

DIANE: Happy? What's that? ... Something on TV?

TOM: Yeah well, I dunno ... You're so pretty. Ya should be happy. (*DIANE groans.*) That's a dumb thing to say, eh? Yeah ... So, uh ... what do you do?

DIANE: Me? I still go to school ... I write poems sometimes.

TOM; Yeah, that figures ... Uh ... what kind of poems?

DIANE: Sad ones.

TOM: I'm asking 'cause, well ... ya look like a girl who writes poems. Guess I could do it, too, but I wouldn't know why. I flunked English. French, too ... Babysitting, that's all school is ...

DIANE: Do you like films? ... Me, I like films. But they make me feel bad, too. I don't want them to stop.

TOM: Hey, cinemascope. In living colour. Diane Paquette.

DIANE: No, I'll never use that name. Not Paquette.

TOM: Okay, Diane, uh ...

DIANE: Diane Desmarchais. Why not Diane Desmarchais?

TOM: Yeah. Okay. Boulevard Desmarchais. Sounds good ...

DIANE: So, you don't go to school no more?

TOM: Naw. I mean, I know my ABCs ... most of them ... Looking for work ... I dunno, it's crazy. I mean, if someone wanted me to work for them, why don't they ask me. I mean, I don't know why I've got to go looking for work when I don't even want it.

DIANE: No job, no money. No money, no nothing.

TOM: Yeah, money ... Hey, uh ... don't you ever blink?

DIANE: Never.

TOM: Once a year or what? ...

DIANE: Your hair, it makes you look funny.

TOM: Funny? What do you mean?

DIANE: I think it's too short.

TOM: Oui, too short.

DIANE: I think you have to grow it longer ...

TOM: Yeah well, I'm getting out. I'm leaving ... Ever think of doing that? Goodbye, Pointe-Saint-Charles.

DIANE: Where will you go?

TOM: I dunno ... anywhere. New York City.

DIANE: New York City?

TOM: Yeah, sure.

DIANE: They got jobs down there?

TOM: I dunno ... It's a big place. Ya never know. I might find a job as a musician, ya know? Once I learn about, uh, major chords, minor chords. Shit like that ...

DIANE: Well, salut. Bonne chance.

She starts up the stairs.

TOM: Hey, Diane. Wait. Attends peu ... You wanna come with me?

DIANE: Avec toi? Pourquoi?

TOM: Well, I figure you wanna get out, too ... Anyhow, forget it. It's stupid. Ya don't even know me ... I'm a bit stoned ... Well, see ya.

DIANE: Bye ... Write me a letter, okay?

She goes into her house.

TOM: Aw, forget it. It's stupid ... stupid.

TOM exits with his guitar. PAQUETTE and THIBAULT are heard banging away in the shed.

PAQUETTE: Verrat de tabarnac de crisse de ciboire.

THIBAULT: J'pense que c'est pas le spark plug, eh?

PAQUETTE: Fuck you. Où est le pipe wrench?

THIBAULT: Le pipe wrench?

PAQUETTE: Oui, le pipe wrench. Je pense que j'l'ai laissé sur le balcon.

THIBAULT: Le balcon. Okay, okay, okay, okay. Okay, so what?

He comes in from the shed and goes up the stairs. While he is looking for the pipe wrench, he drinks some beer from some discarded beer bottles.

Le pipe wrench, le pipe wrench. So what? On se rendra jamais en ville.

PAQUETTE: Thibault ... Hostie ...

THIBAULT: Oui, j'cherche. J'cherche. (*He takes a slug of beer from one of the beer bottles and gags on a cigarette butt.*) Agh. Touf. Une cigarette, hostie.

PAQUETTE gets the car started, guns the engine, then chokes it.

PAQUETTE: Tu veux pas partir. Tu veux pas partir. Ben. J'vas t'arranger ça.

PAQUETTE takes a hammer to the car. The sound of smashing is heard. CÉCILE comes out on her balcony.

CÉCILE: Mais, qu'est-ce qui se passe? Claude? ...

PAQUETTE comes out of the shed carrying a hammer. He throws the hammer to the ground and climbs the stairs.

THIBAULT: (*to PAQUETTE*) You fix it?

PAQUETTE: (*to CÉCILE*) Pas un mot s'a game. Pas un mot.

PAQUETTE and CÉCILE exit into their house, leaving THIBAULT standing alone on the balcony.

THIBAULT: Okay, on ira jamais en ville. So what? Thibault, he's okay. I go find my own beer. So what?

He comes down the stairs and exits. MURIEL comes out on her balcony.

MURIEL: Tommy, I'm gonna lock this door. Tommy? ... All right.

She shuts the door and bolts it closed.

Blackout.

ACT TWO

SCENE 1

It is night. JOHNNY and THIBAULT enter singing. Both of them are drunk. JOHNNY is riding THIBAULT's delivery bike.

JOHNNY & THIBAULT: (*singing*)
We don't care about
All the rest of Canada,
All the rest of Canada,
All the rest of Canada.
We don't care for
All the rest of Canada,
We're from Pointe-Saint-Charles.

MURIEL: (*from inside her house*) Shut up out there!

JOHNNY: Fuck you!

THIBAULT: So what, eh? Get off my bike, you ... Away.

JOHNNY: (*getting off THIBAULT's bike*) Hey, Thibault, you're not a separatist, are ya?

THIBAULT: FLQ, moi. Boom! I blow everything up. (*He kicks a garbage can.*) Boom!

MURIEL: (*from inside her house*) Jesus Murphy.

THIBAULT: (*taking a magazine out of his back pocket*) We have a good time, eh? Good time. Look, big tits.

He sits down on a bench. JOHNNY sits down beside him.

JOHNNY: You're my friend, eh, Thibault?

THIBAULT: Sure, if that's what you say.

JOHNNY: You're my only, only friend.

THIBAULT: I'm your only friend ... and I'm not even your friend.

JOHNNY: So whose friend are ya?

THIBAULT: I don't know.

JOHNNY: You wanna know whose friend you are? You're my friend.

THIBAULT: Sure ... My mother, once she takes me to the Oratoire, because I got the polio. So, she takes me there. She prays to Saint-Joseph, but the polio, it don't go away ...

JOHNNY: Fuck off.

THIBAULT: Eh, so what?

JOHNNY: What, so what?

THIBAULT: What so what?

JOHNNY: Yeah, you say, "So what?" and I say, "What, so what?"

THIBAULT: You crazy, you.

JOHNNY: Fuckin' right, I'm crazy. (*yelling*) I'm trying, Irene. I'm trying ... I'm dying.

THIBAULT: Hey, Johnny. Do Elvis. Do Elvis ... "I'm all shook up."

JOHNNY: (*snapping into an Elvis imitation*) "I'm all shook up."

IRENE comes out on her balcony.

IRENE: Johnny.

JOHNNY: Irene, remember me when I was eighteen? (*He does more of his Elvis imitation.*) "Be-bop-a-lula."

IRENE: Come on up to bed, Johnny. I've got to work tomorrow.

JOHNNY: Tomorrow? Fuck tomorrow! Everybody's worried about tomorrow. I'm worried about right now.

THIBAULT: Hey, do Elvis. Do some more Elvis ... "You ain't nothing but a hound dog."

JOHNNY: Elvis is dead, ya dumb Pepsi. He's dead. Don't ya understand that? He's dead.

He goes to the stairs and starts to climb them. He collapses.

IRENE: Come on, Johnny.

She comes down and tries to get him up the stairs. He grunts.

IRENE: Shit. La merde ... Muriel? Muriel?

MURIEL: (*from inside her house*) Leave him there, it'll do him good.

CÉCILE: (*coming out on her balcony*) Madame, you need some help?

IRENE: Thanks.

CÉCILE comes down the stairs. Together, she and IRENE carry JOHNNY up the stairs and into his house.

JOHNNY: Irene, I love you ... Gonna buy ya a house, Irene.

CÉCILE comes back out. She sees THIBAULT sitting on the steps looking at one of his magazines.

THIBAULT: Paquette, Paquette, tu t'souviens? Toi et moi à la Rodéo? Big Fat Babette ... "Please Help Me I'm Falling in Love with You." Big tits ... big tits.

CÉCILE: Shhhhhh, Thibault. Claude dort.

THIBAULT: (*looking at his magazine*) Tits ... big tits.

He rips a page out of the magazine. He goes and sits on his bike. IRENE comes out on the balcony carrying two Cokes.

IRENE: Veux-tu un Coke, Cécile?

CÉCILE: Yes, that would be nice.

CÉCILE sits down on her rocking chair. IRENE comes and sits down beside her.

CÉCILE: It's so quiet, eh? This is my favourite time, when it's quiet.

IRENE: Yeah.

CÉCILE: Look, there's the Big Dipper.

IRENE: Oh yeah?

CÉCILE: Right there. Right next to that shed.

IRENE: You know, I haven't looked at the sky in years.

CÉCILE: When I was a little girl in Lac Saint-Jean, I knew the names of all the stars ... the Great Bear, the Swan, the Hunter ...

IRENE: They've got names, eh?

CÉCILE: Of course. Everything has a name.

IRENE: How did you meet Paquette? Uh ... Claude?

CÉCILE: He had a truck. He was a truck driver ... So handsome ... At first, we thought he would marry one of my older sisters, but she didn't want him because he was too loud ... And my mother, too, she didn't like him. But ...

IRENE: You liked him.

CÉCILE: I was a young girl ...

IRENE: So was I ... I had a dream last night ...

CÉCILE: A dream? Tell me. I love dreams.

IRENE: I ... I dreamed I saw Jacob wrestling the angel. Imagine that.

CÉCILE: Jacob?

IRENE: Yeah, you know? Jacob ... in the Bible.

CÉCILE: Jacob. Ah oui.

IRENE: Anyhow, I woke up feeling good ... Well, it's been one of those years, eh?

CÉCILE: Johnny and Claude, right now ... they not getting along so good?

IRENE: Well, they're both being stupid. But Johnny started it. He's such a goddamn redneck sometimes.

CÉCILE: It's strange ... Before, Claude, he wants to be like the English ... and now, he puts everything on them.

DIANE enters.

CÉCILE: Diane, il est passé minuit. Ton père va être fâché.

DIANE: (*coming up the stairs*) Irene, I have something ...

IRENE: Oh?

DIANE: Une lettre de Tom.

IRENE: Tom. He wrote you?

DIANE: Oui, but I can't understand all the words.

IRENE: Let me see it. (*She takes the letter and looks at the postmark.*) Ormstown? What's the silly bugger doing in Ormstown? ... You want me to read it?

DIANE: Oui.

IRENE: "Hi, Diane ... Took me a day hitchhiking to get this far so far. Tomorrow, guess I'll reach the border and cross over into the land of Jimmy Carter and Mickey Mouse."

DIANE: (*laughing*) Mickey Mouse.

IRENE: "I can feel New York City down there, pulling me like a magnet." Tu comprends? Magnet?

IRENE mimes "magnet," banging the fist of one hand into her other hand.

DIANE: Oui.

IRENE: "Pull at him." Shit, it's gonna hit him on the head.

DIANE: Quoi?

IRENE: Uh ... okay. "I don't have no money, but a faggot bought me a meal." Faggot? C'est une tapette.

DIANE: Oui.

IRENE: "I'm glad we had that talk, even if I did sound kind of crazy ... I think you're beautiful. I mean, how do you say something like that? But it's true." Wow! Hot stuff!

DIANE: (*taking back the letter*) It's okay ... I understand the rest.

IRENE: Hey, sounds like Tom really likes ya, girl.

DIANE: Hey, I know what he wants.

IRENE: Yeah, so is he gonna get some?

DIANE: He's cute ... a bit.

IRENE: New York City.

DIANE: Me, I want to go there.

IRENE: Yeah?

DIANE: Sure. Go there and live like in the movies. It would be fun, eh?

IRENE: Yeah ... like the movies. Poor Muriel.

DIANE: His mother? ... What for? ... She was going to throw him out anyhow.

IRENE: Well, I've got to work tomorrow. Bye.

DIANE: Bye.

CÉCILE: Goodnight, Irene.

IRENE exits into her house.

CÉCILE: Diane, viens-tu coucher?

DIANE: Non.

CÉCILE exits into her house. DIANE sits at the top of the stairs. THIBAULT is still sitting on his bike at the bottom of the stairs.

THIBAULT: Diane. Diane.

DIANE: Va-t'en chez-vous, Thibault.

THIBAULT: Eh, Diane? J'vas m'acheter une Honda 750. C'est vrai, Diane. Brammmmm, brammmmm. Honda. J'vas m'en acheter une.

DIANE: Oui, oui.

THIBAULT: J'vas t'faire des rides, eh?

DIANE: Va-t'en chez-vous, Thibault.

THIBAULT: C'est vrai, Diane. Une 750. Brammmmmm, brammmmm.

He exits on his bike. DIANE remains at the top of the stairs looking at her letter.

Blackout.

SCENE 2

The next day. It is a very hot Sunday afternoon. JOHNNY, PAQUETTE, and DIANE are on the balcony watching the ball game on TV – on separate TVs. MURIEL is sweeping her balcony.

JOHNNY: (*watching TV*) Aw, shit ... bunch of bums!

PAQUETTE: (*watching TV*) Maudits Expos!

IRENE enters yawning. She is coming home from work, wearing her waitress uniform. She sees MURIEL sweeping her balcony.

IRENE: Boy, this heat ...

MURIEL: Couple more days of this and we'll be having riots.

IRENE: Yeah.

MURIEL: Sorry about last night ... I was in one of my moods.

IRENE: Aw, forget it. Hey, Diane got a letter from Tom, eh? ... Yeah.

MURIEL: He writes to her, but he doesn't write to his mother?

IRENE: He's in Ormstown.

MURIEL: Ormstown? Where's that?

IRENE: Somewhere in the bush.

MURIEL: Well, as soon as he gets hungry, he'll come home ... just let him try to get through the door.

IRENE: Aw, don't worry. Young guys are like tomcats. They always land on their feet.

MURIEL: Who says I'm worried?

IRENE: Okay.

PAQUETTE: (*watching TV*) Away, away ... câlice.

JOHNNY: (*watching TV*) Aw, shit! Le merde! Move your ass! Move your ass!

PAQUETTE: (*watching TV*) Il est temps, tabarnac!

JOHNNY: (*seeing IRENE coming up the stairs*) Hey, did you pick me up some smokes?

IRENE dumps a pack of smokes in his lap and goes on into the house. CÉCILE enters. She is wearing her church clothes. She comes up behind MURIEL.

CÉCILE: Bonjour, Madame Williams.

MURIEL: (*jumping in fright*) Oh God, don't creep up on me like that.

CÉCILE: How are you? ... Nice day, eh?

MURIEL: Too hot.

CÉCILE: Ah yes, too hot ... It's so nice to see people together in the church. Being together makes people feel so good.

PAQUETTE and **JOHNNY:** (*together*) Grimsley, ya bum! ... Aux douches!

MURIEL: Yeah ... (*looking at where CÉCILE is standing*) Move ...

CÉCILE moves and MURIEL continues sweeping. CÉCILE goes up the stairs. DIANE notices her hat.

DIANE: Maman, les femmes n'ont plus besoin de porter de chapeau pour aller à la messe.

CÉCILE: Je sais, Diane, mais je suis habituée de même.

PAQUETTE and JOHNNY both react to something in the baseball game on TV.

CÉCILE: Diane, tu devrais venir avec moi dimanche prochain.

DIANE: C'est toujours le même show. Quand ils changeront le programme, peut-être que j'irai.

PAQUETTE: (*to CÉCILE and DIANE*) Tabarnac, y a tu moyen d'écouter ma game tranquille? Ça fait une semaine que j'attends après ça. Cécile, va me chercher une bière.

CÉCILE: Oui, Claude ...

She goes to get him a beer.

JOHNNY: Hey, Irene? ... Irene? ...

IRENE: (*at the screen door*) Yeah?

JOHNNY: Get me a Coke.

IRENE: What's the matter, you break your leg?

JOHNNY: It's too hot to move.

IRENE: I'm moving.

PAQUETTE: (*watching TV*) Merde!

JOHNNY: (*watching TV*) Shit!

PAQUETTE: Un autre foul ball, hostie!

CÉCILE: (*bringing PAQUETTE a beer*) Claude, veux-tu un sandwich?

PAQUETTE: Quoi?

CÉCILE: Un sandwich?

PAQUETTE: (*watching TV*) Away ... away là!

She goes to get him a sandwich.

JOHNNY: (*watching TV*) Faster! Get under it! Get under it! ... No, fuck!

PAQUETTE: (*watching TV*) Shit! La merde!

CÉCILE comes back and puts a sandwich in one of PAQUETTE's hands and a beer in his other hand.

DIANE: Paquette est assez grand pour se mouvoir tout seul, Cécile.

PAQUETTE: « Cécile » ... c'est ta mère que t'appelles « Cécile ». Tu vas me faire le plaisir de l'appeler « Maman ».

DIANE: (*to PAQUETTE*) You are a piece of shit.

She throws a bag of potato chips at him and stomps off into the house.

PAQUETTE: Voyons. Qu'est-ce qu'y lui prend?

CÉCILE: J'sais pas. J'pense qu'elle s'est chicanée avec sa chum.

JOHNNY: (*watching TV*) Go, go, go!

PAQUETTE: (*watching TV*) Vite, vite, vite! ... Bonne. That's it ... Oui.

JOHNNY: (*watching TV*) About time ...

Inside the house, DIANE puts on a record. It is "Hot Child in the City."

PAQUETTE: Cécile, dis-lui de baisser sa câlice de musique de hot child in the city, hostie.

CÉCILE goes into the house. The music fades away. IRENE comes out and hands JOHNNY a Coke.

IRENE: Johnny, I want to talk to you.

JOHNNY: Yeah, yeah.

IRENE: What happened last night?

JOHNNY: Last night? ... Hey, I'm watching the game.

IRENE: When does it end?

JOHNNY: Eh? ... Ten minutes.

IRENE: I want to talk to you before I go out.

JOHNNY: Yeah, yeah ... talk. Okay.

IRENE: I mean it.

JOHNNY: Don't do the martyr, okay? Not the martyr, please.

IRENE exits into the house. THIBAULT enters on his bike. He starts putting "Gaëtan Bolduc ... Available and Dynamic" campaign posters all over the walls.

MURIEL: (*watching THIBAULT*) What's this?

THIBAULT: Dix piastres pour la journée ... Me and four other guys are putting them up all over. Bolduc, he wants to win this time, eh?

MURIEL: (*ripping down one of the posters*) Not on my wall ...

THIBAULT: Eh? Not on your wall?

MURIEL: No.

THIBAULT: No?

MURIEL: No, you stupid little jerk.

She crumples up the poster and throws it at him.

THIBAULT: No? ... Okay, no.

He goes up the stairs with his posters and sees PAQUETTE and JOHNNY watching TV. He sits beside PAQUETTE.

THIBAULT: Hey, c'est quoi l'score? What's the score?

PAQUETTE: Huit à cinq.

JOHNNY: (*shouting across at them*) The Expos got five.

THIBAULT: Hey. Good game, eh? ... Hot, eh? Hot ... very hot. Très chaud ... Agh ... hard to breathe. (*He coughs.*) Agh, my throat ... Hot ...

PAQUETTE: (*calling to CÉCILE*) Cécile, apporte-moi deux autres bières.

CÉCILE: (*at the screen door*) Deux?

PAQUETTE: Oui.

THIBAULT: Ah oui ... Good game, eh?

PAQUETTE: Ferme ta gueule, toi. Okay?

THIBAULT: Hey, regarde.

He shows PAQUETTE a poster.

PAQUETTE: Ôte-toi d'là. C'est quoi ça? Bolduc?

THIBAULT: Oui. Prends-en une.

PAQUETTE: Tu vas laisser tes cochonneries ailleurs.

He crumples up the poster and throws it over the balcony.

THIBAULT: Eh, tu votes pas Libéral cette année?

MURIEL: (*from downstairs*) Hey ... watch the garbage, okay?

CÉCILE: (*bringing out two beer*) Ah, bonjour, Thibault. Comment va ta mère?

THIBAULT: Oui, ça va bien.

JOHNNY: (*watching TV*) Slide, for fuck's sake! Slide!

PAQUETTE: (*watching TV*) C'est pas un coursier, c'est un cheval de labo!

CÉCILE: Claude, j'aurais besoin de cinq piastres.

PAQUETTE: Cinq piastres, pourquoi? Diane? Dis-y de venir les demander à sa piece of shit, okay?

CÉCILE exits into the house.

THIBAULT: (*looking at both TVs*) Hey, hey, it's the same game! The same game!

The broadcast VOICE is heard again.

VOICE: N'oubliez pas dans deux semaines, votez Gaëtan Bolduc. Bolduc est sur votre côté, toujours disponible et dynamique ... Bolduc ...

The broadcast truck plays Elvis Presley music. The music fades away.

THIBAULT: (*referring to the broadcast VOICE*) Oui, that's him right there.

PAQUETTE: (*watching TV*) Maudit, même pas capable de regarder sa game tranquille.

THIBAULT: (*watching TV*) Trois hommes sur les buts.

PAQUETTE: (*watching TV*) Y sont capables, si y veulent.

IRENE comes out on the balcony.

IRENE: Can we talk now?

JOHNNY: Shit, it bugs me when goofs like Bolduc use good Elvis music.

IRENE: Johnny, you got drunk again last night.

JOHNNY: Yeah ...

IRENE: Four nights in a row ... You said you were gonna stop. I thought we had all that settled.

JOHNNY: Listen ... this is not the right time.

IRENE: It's never the right time. I'm tired of waiting for the right time. Let's talk now ... Let's try to talk.

JOHNNY: Talk ... Look, I just need one more night to straighten out.

IRENE: Straighten out what?

JOHNNY: I'm not working, so you think you can pick on me, is that it? Is that it?

IRENE: This is not a contest.

JOHNNY: I got a hangover ... I'm in a bad mood.

IRENE: So, you're gonna go out tonight, too?

JOHNNY: Yeah, that's right ... Yeah.

IRENE: Well, don't count on me being here to wipe up your puke forever.

JOHNNY: Nobody's asking you to.

IRENE: I'm tired of being the wife in your life, Johnny. I'm not gonna hang around here and watch you wreck yourself ... No, thanks.

JOHNNY: I don't want to hear this.

IRENE: From now on, every time you get drunk, that's one more step toward goodbye ... Not tomorrow or next week, but soon, because it's not doing either of us any good.

JOHNNY: Irene, it's too hot to get mad.

IRENE: Wish I was mad. Can't even cry about it anymore.

JOHNNY: Look, I'm going up to the hospital next week. There's a pill they got, it makes ya sick every time ya take a drink.

IRENE: Johnny, you got to do it yourself.

JOHNNY: Okay, that's it for now. Okay? ... You're right, but it's the wrong time, okay? Okay?

IRENE goes into the house.

JOHNNY: (*shouting after her*) Hey, Irene, is there any more Coke in the fridge? Irene? ... Fuck!

CÉCILE comes out to water her plants.

CÉCILE: Mes plantes. They get thirsty, too.

JOHNNY: Eh?

CÉCILE: (*holding up a plant*) See? ... They're smiling.

JOHNNY shrugs and gets up and turns off the TV. CÉCILE goes back into her house.

JOHNNY: Goddamn bums don't know how to win ...

THIBAULT: (*to JOHNNY*) They're losing in French, too.

PAQUETTE: (*watching TV*) Nos champions! L'ont encore dans le cul, hostie.

JOHNNY: (*to PAQUETTE*) So, Paquette, what do ya think of the game? Eh?

THIBAULT: He don't speak the English no more.

JOHNNY: Oh yeah?

THIBAULT: Oui, and me, too. I don't speak the English since last week. Maybe a few times, but that's all.

JOHNNY: Yeah well, fuck the both of yas!

He goes into his house and comes out with a Canadian flag which he starts nailing up above his window.

THIBAULT: (*looking at JOHNNY's flag*) As-tu vu ça, Paquette?

PAQUETTE: Tu t'as pompé là, hostie!

PAQUETTE dashes into his house and comes out with a huge Québec flag, which THIBAULT staples to the wall.

PAQUETTE: Tabarnac! Tu m'en spotteras pas avec ça. Thibault, viens m'aider, prends ton bord.

THIBAULT goes over to help JOHNNY staple his flag above the window. When JOHNNY turns around, he sees PAQUETTE's huge Québec flag.

JOHNNY: Fuck!

He exits into his house. PAQUETTE and THIBAULT laugh. They turn off their TV set and exit into PAQUETTE's house. The broadcast VOICE is heard again.

VOICE: Gaëtan Bolduc, the man for you ... available and dynamic ... Gaëtan Bolduc, the man for you ... available and dynamic ...

The sound fades away. GAËTAN BOLDUC enters and knocks on MURIEL's door.

MURIEL: (*coming to the door*) Yeah, yeah. Hold your horses. (*She opens the door and sees BOLDUC.*) Holy shit!

BOLDUC: Ah, bonjour ... Tu parles anglais? English?

MURIEL: Yeah.

BOLDUC: Ah ... I'm Gaëtan Bolduc, your Member of Parliament. We all know that something is wrong with Québec right now, eh?

MURIEL: You're goddamn right.

BOLDUC: Well, I would like to help fix it ... Bon. Here's my card with information ... Don't be afraid to call, eh?

MURIEL: Yeah, yeah.

BOLDUC: Don't forget me on the sixth.

MURIEL: Don't worry, I will.

She slams the door shut in his face. He goes up the stairs and knocks on JOHNNY's door.

IRENE: (*inside the house*) Johnny ... there's someone at the door, Johnny. I'm in the tub.

JOHNNY: (*inside the house*) Shit! (*He opens the door.*) You!

BOLDUC: Ah, bonjour ... Tu parles anglais? English?

JOHNNY: Yeah.

BOLDUC: Ah, I'm Gaëtan Bolduc, your Member of Parliament ...

JOHNNY: Oh, "Gaëtan Bolduc, the man for you ... available and dynamic." So what can I do for you?

BOLDUC: No ... What can *I* do for you?

JOHNNY: You mean, what can I do *to* you?

BOLDUC: Bon. Here is my card with information. Don't forget, a vote for Gaëtan Bolduc is a vote for me ... Bonjour.

JOHNNY: Hey! Wait a minute ... I'm not finished yet. I only get to see you once every four years.

BOLDUC: Is there something you'd like to know?

JOHNNY: Yeah ... Houses are still burning down, there's no jobs ... What happened to all them promises?

BOLDUC: It takes time ... We're working on it ...

JOHNNY: Yeah? Eh, well, you got a lot of nerve walking around here ... and quit using Elvis music, okay? What's the matter, you got no respect for the dead?

JOHNNY exits into his house.

IRENE: (*from inside the house*) Johnny, what's that all about?

JOHNNY: (*from inside the house*) It's fuckface Bolduc.

IRENE: (*from inside the house*) Bolduc?

BOLDUC knocks on PAQUETTE's door. DIANE answers the door.

DIANE: Oui?

BOLDUC: Êtes-vous la femme de la maison?

DIANE: Moi? Jamais ... Paquette? Paquette, c'est Bolduc.

PAQUETTE: Quoi?

THIBAULT sneaks out the window and goes downstairs, where he starts putting up more Bolduc posters. PAQUETTE comes to the door.

BOLDUC: Bonjour. Je suis Gaëtan Bolduc, votre député au parlement.

PAQUETTE: Salut, Gaëtan.

BOLDUC: Allô?

PAQUETTE: Tu me reconnais? Claude Paquette? ... École de Notre-Dame-des-Sept-Douleurs?

BOLDUC: Ah oui ... Oui ...

PAQUETTE: Claude Paquette ...

BOLDUC: Claude Paquette? ... Oui, c'est ça ...

PAQUETTE: Tu sais que t'as l'air de pas t'arranger, mon Bolduc.

BOLDUC: Je travaille fort, tu sais ... On fait ce qu'on peut ...

PAQUETTE: Moi aussi ... J'travaille fort. Tu sais qu'j'ai jamais été sur le welfare. Moi, jamais. Les jeunes y se câlicent de ça, mais y faut que quelqu'un paye les taxes. Ces crisses de jeunes-là, y devraient toutes les câlicer dans l'armée. Comme ça y travailleraient.

BOLDUC: Alors, tu vas voter pour moi, eh, Claude?

PAQUETTE: Fuck you! Tu me poigneras pas une deuxième fois!

JOHNNY comes out and goes down the stairs. When he reaches the bottom of the stairs, he turns around and throws some eggs back at BOLDUC. They miss him and hit PAQUETTE.

PAQUETTE: Hey!

BOLDUC: C'est un joke, ça? Tu vas entendre parler de mes avocats, toi.

BOLDUC comes down the stairs and exits hurriedly. JOHNNY hands the eggs to THIBAULT to make it seem as if he had thrown them. He exits after BOLDUC.

PAQUETTE: Qu'est-ce que c'est ça? Qu'est-ce que c'est ça?

CÉCILE comes out. She looks at PAQUETTE.

CÉCILE: Claude, c'est quoi? Un oiseau?

THIBAULT starts coming up the stairs.

PAQUETTE: (*to THIBAULT*) Thibault, est-ce que t'as qu'que chose sur la toiture?

THIBAULT: La toiture?

PAQUETTE: Oui ... la toiture.

THIBAULT: (*looking up at the roof*) Non.

PAQUETTE sees the eggs that JOHNNY has given to THIBAULT.

PAQUETTE: C'est quoi ça?

He takes the eggs from THIBAULT and starts throwing them at him. THIBAULT runs down the stairs.

THIBAULT: Hey! Hey! ...

PAQUETTE: Ah, mon petit, tabarnac ...

JOHNNY enters and goes up the stairs to his balcony.

THIBAULT: C'est pas moi. C'est pas moi ... (*He points to JOHNNY.*) C'est lui. C'est lui.

JOHNNY stands on his balcony laughing.

PAQUETTE: C'est toi ça, eh? Big joke, eh? Big joke.

He throws an egg at JOHNNY.

JOHNNY: You watch yourself ... Okay?

JOHNNY crosses to PAQUETTE's balcony.

PAQUETTE: Hey, keep on your own side! Keep on your own side!

JOHNNY: You and Bolduc, eh? Ya suck!

PAQUETTE: Hey, c'est toi qui vote pour les Libérals, eh? Pas moi.

JOHNNY: Yeah, eh?

They start shoving each other. IRENE comes out and she and CÉCILE try to break up the fight.

CÉCILE: Claude ...

IRENE: Johnny, stop it ...

IRENE starts hitting JOHNNY with a towel.

JOHNNY: What are ya hitting me for?

IRENE exits into the house with JOHNNY in tow. DIANE laughs at PAQUETTE from inside the house.

PAQUETTE: La petite crisse, elle trouve ça drôle? Ça t'fait rire? Ça t'fait rire?

DIANE: (*from inside the house*) Oui, je trouve ça drôle ... Lâche ça ... Lâche ça ...

PAQUETTE goes into the house, takes one of DIANE's records, and throws it out the window.

PAQUETTE: Est-ce tu trouves ça drôle?

DIANE: (*from inside the house*) Sors de ma chambre ... Va-t'en d'ici ...

TOM enters and knocks at MURIEL's door.

MURIEL: (*coming to the door*) Yeah, yeah. (*She opens the door.*) You're back.

TOM: Yeah.

MURIEL: Well, you better wash up ... There's some food in the fridge.

TOM: Ma?

MURIEL: Yeah?

TOM: Uh ... nothing ...

He walks into the house. DIANE comes out of the house and sits in the rocking chair. She is crying. JOHNNY comes out of his house and sits on the balcony. CÉCILE comes out on her balcony.

CÉCILE: J'ai hâte qu'il fasse froid. Ton père peut pas dormir quand il fait trop chaud. Ça le rend de mauvaise humeur. (*She checks her plants.*) C'est vrai. Il y a de la place ici. Je pense que je vais déménager mes plantes sur le balcon d'en avant.

She sees that DIANE is crying.

Diane ... Diane, qu'est-ce qu'y a?

DIANE: Y a rien.

CÉCILE: Tu vas voir, ton père va être malheureux de ce qu'il a fait, il va être gentil avec toi.

DIANE: Oui, mais j'suis pas un jouet, moi, maman.

CÉCILE: Diane ...

DIANE: Laisse-moi tranquille ...

CÉCILE goes back into her house.

JOHNNY: Irene? Hey, Irene? ...

IRENE: (*coming to the screen door*) Yeah?

JOHNNY: Lend me a few bucks. I wanna go uptown ... Yeah, yeah, I know ... Look, why don't you just tell me to leave. Ya know, tell me to leave and it's all over.

IRENE: You're so weak.

JOHNNY: Just tell me it's over and I'm gone.

IRENE: I have to be strong for the both of us.

JOHNNY: It's so easy for you. You do this because of that. You do that because of this. It's not that easy for me.

IRENE: (*throwing him five dollars, yelling*) I hate you ... I hate you ...

She goes back into the house and slams the door.

JOHNNY: One more night, Irene ...

He exits. MURIEL comes out and throws a pair of boots in the garbage can. TOM follows her out. He has nothing on his feet.

TOM: Hey, Ma ... what are you doing?

MURIEL: You're not wearing these. They stink.

TOM: What do ya mean?

MURIEL: They stink and I'm throwing them out.

TOM: Ma, it's the only pair of boots I've got.

MURIEL: You're not wearing them in the house ... and just because your father is a bum, doesn't mean you have to be one, too.

She goes back into the house. TOM takes the boots out of the garbage can and puts them back on.

TOM: She's nuts. I mean, she's clinical ...

DIANE: You? ... You're back again?

TOM: Yeah. Did a circle ...

DIANE: Why did you come back here?

TOM: I had no choice ... Same old shit, eh?

DIANE: They drive me crazy, all these people ...

TOM: I know what you mean.

DIANE: They're not happy, so they want everybody else to be the same way.

TOM: Yeah ...

DIANE: Me? I want to get out ... But how? Where do you go?

TOM: Not to Ormstown, I'll tell ya that ... Bunch of farmers ...

DIANE: You don't like New York City?

TOM: Never got there ... Wouldn't let me cross the border ... No money.

DIANE: You need money, eh?

TOM: Yeah.

DIANE: Always the same thing ...

TOM: Yeah. They don't make it easy for ya.

DIANE: They? ... Oui ... they.

TOM: You, uh ... get my letter?

DIANE: Oui.

TOM: So ... what do ya think?

DIANE: Why do you worry about what I think?

TOM: I don't know ...

DIANE: The letter was ... okay.

TOM: Oh yeah? I meant what I said, ya know? ... in the letter.

DIANE: I'm not beautiful.

TOM: I don't know ... Girls that never blink turn me on.

DIANE: That's too bad for you.

TOM: Hey, uh ... I'm gonna look for work here, and when I got some money, maybe I'll try New York again.

DIANE: What for? It's the same thing everywhere.

TOM: Hey, uh ... you're in a good mood, eh?

PAQUETTE comes out carrying some pop bottles down the stairs.

PAQUETTE: Hey, Diane. Je m'en vais au magasin. As-tu besoin de qu'que chose?

DIANE: Je veux rien qui vient de toi.

PAQUETTE: Tu pourrais au moins d'être polie, câlice, apart de ça. J't'ai pas dit que j'voulais pas que tu t'tiennes avec les têtes carrées.

DIANE: You don't tell me what to do.

PAQUETTE: Crisse, parle-moi en français, par exemple.

DIANE: Fuck you!

PAQUETTE: (*to TOM*) Et toi-là. Keep on your own side.

He exits.

TOM: Good to be home again ...

DIANE: Nobody tells me what to do ... Nobody.

TOM: All those French guys over thirty ... Grease!

DIANE: Et toi, tête carrée. What do you look like, eh?

TOM: Don't know ... Have to wear a box for a hat, I guess.

DIANE: That's right ... Aw, it's so hot!

TOM: You, uh, want to take a walk? ... No, eh?

DIANE: A walk?

TOM: Yeah, a walk.

DIANE: Where?

TOM: I don't know ... the boardwalk? I always walk there.

DIANE: Okay.

TOM: Uh ... which way?

DIANE: I don't care.

TOM: This way ...

They begin to exit. MURIEL comes out of the house.

MURIEL: Tom?

TOM: Yeah?

MURIEL: Just look at you ... You're a mess!

TOM: We're going for a walk.

MURIEL: Tom, come here ... I want to speak to you ...

TOM: What?

MURIEL: Do you think this is fair to me?

TOM: What?

MURIEL: All of this? ...

TOM: I guess not.

MURIEL: You guess not?

TOM: Look, I had nothing to do with this. I was just born here, that's all.

MURIEL: Listen, don't think you can start in all over, hanging around here daydreaming, 'cause I won't have it. Either you get a job or you get out. It's one or the other ...

TOM: Job! Job! Job! I'm gonna get a job!

MURIEL: I've heard that one before.

TOM: This time I'm gonna look.

MURIEL: Sure ... and then, you'll move out with your first cheque.

TOM: Ma?

MURIEL: Don't you "Ma" me.

TOM: Ma? I don't wanna fight with ya, Ma.

MURIEL: So, don't fight ...

MURIEL exits into her house.

TOM: Home, sweet home ...

He bangs a garbage can and exits down the lane with DIANE.

Blackout.

SCENE 3

The sound of sawing is heard offstage. JOHNNY is in the shed working. PAQUETTE enters carrying his lunch bucket. He is coming home from work early. CÉCILE is watering her plants on the balcony.

CÉCILE: Claude, t'es de bonne heure. Qu'est-ce qui arrive? Es-tu malade?

PAQUETTE: Non, je ne suis pas malade.

CÉCILE: Qu'est-ce qu'y a qui va pas?

PAQUETTE: J'ai perdu ma job. Je suis revenu à pied.

CÉCILE: Veux-tu une chaise, Claude?

PAQUETTE: Pas une crisse d'avertissement. Je suis allé voir le boss en haut. Il a dit que ça lui faisait ben de la peine, mais il pouvait rien faire. Là, je suis allé voir le gars de l'union. Tu sais ce qu'il m'a dit, le gars de l'union, eh? "There's nothing we can do. The company is stopping their operation in Montreal. They're going to relocate it in Taiwan." ... Taïwan!

CÉCILE: Taïwan? C'est au Vermont, ça?

PAQUETTE: Treize ans de ma vie ... Treize ans de ma câlice de vie ...

CÉCILE: Quatorze, Claude. Je me souviens. Quand t'as eu ta job, c'était en octobre.

PAQUETTE: J'ai quarante-deux ans, tabarnac. J'peux pas recommencer à zéro. Qu'est-ce que j'vas faire?

CÉCILE: Tu l'aimais pas ta job de toute façon.

PAQUETTE: J'sais que je l'aimais pas, mais y faut ben manger.

CÉCILE: Oui.

PAQUETTE: Les crisses y sont ben toutes pareils. Les tabarnacs. Y s'servent de toi pis quand y'ont pu besoin de toi, y te câlicent dehors comme un vieux torchon sale. Pis, fuck you! Mange d'la merde. Pis si tu meures, c'est encore mieux. Y'ont pu de welfare à payer.

CÉCILE: Welfare? Mais on a jamais été sur le welfare, Claude.

PAQUETTE: Cécile, c'est pas de ma faute. C'est pas de ma faute.

CÉCILE: Je sais que je dis des choses stupides, mais je sais pas quoi dire.

The broadcast VOICE is heard.

VOICE: Don't forget tomorrow. Voting day ... Re-elect Gaëtan Bolduc, the man for you ... available and dynamic ...

The sound fades away. DIANE *and* TOM *enter together.*

DIANE: *Apocalypse Now?* C'est quoi, *Apocalypse Now?*

TOM: It's a film about that war there in the States.

DIANE: What war?

TOM: Uh ... China ... Somewhere over there ... Wanna go? Tonight?

DIANE: Okay ... Salut ... (*She goes up the stairs.*)

TOM: See ya ... (*He goes into his house.*)

DIANE: (*at the top of the stairs*) Allô, Maman. Ça va?

PAQUETTE: Diane, tu peux oublier ton école.

DIANE: Qu'est-ce qu'y lui prend lui?

CÉCILE: Ton père a perdu sa job.

DIANE: Sa job?

CÉCILE: Oui, Diane.

DIANE: Bon. Y a pas d'quoi se plaindre.

CÉCILE: Ah, Diane.

DIANE: C'est bien mieux de même. Comme ça, on l'entendra plus chicaner. Cette job-là, nous a toutes rendus fous. C'est vrai.

CÉCILE: Elle est jeune, Claude.

PAQUETTE: Laisse-la faire.

DIANE: Je vais m'en trouver une job, moi. Inquiète-toi pas. C'est facile. Ils ont toujours besoin de waitress cute. Puis moi, je suis cute. Je vais en parler avec Irene, okay?

PAQUETTE: Moi, il faut que je fasse quelque chose.

DIANE: Va quelque part avec Cécile. Vous êtes libres, là. C'est le temps ou jamais. Oubliez ça pour un bout de temps.

PAQUETTE: Oh non.

CÉCILE: Mais où est-ce qu'on irait?

PAQUETTE: Diane, tu te souviens quand tu étais petite, petite de même, on montait en haut sur la montagne, eh? On regardait les beaux arbres, les beaux oiseaux. C'était beau, hein? Diane, j'ai toujours voulu ce qu'il y avait de mieux pour toi. Je suis fatigué. Je ne sais plus quoi dire.

CÉCILE: Viens t'allonger, Claude. Viens t'allonger.

CÉCILE helps PAQUETTE to the door.

DIANE: Papa.

They exit into the house. DIANE *sits on a chair on the balcony.* MURIEL *and* IRENE *enter.*

IRENE: So what did they say this time?

MURIEL: Ah, you know doctors ... They just try to scare ya ...

IRENE: Hey, you're going to be okay.

MURIEL: Nope. They said it was serious.

IRENE: Yeah? How serious?

MURIEL: I'm gonna have an operation.

IRENE: Oh no, Muriel.

MURIEL: Yeah ... on the stomach. Ulcers.

IRENE: Oh no.

MURIEL: Aw, now that I know what they're gonna do, I'm not worried about it. It's just thinking about it that drives ya nuts.

IRENE: Ulcers ... Hey, so I was right, eh?

MURIEL: Yeah. Now, I'm gonna have to drink lots of milk ... Yuk!

IRENE: Does Tom know?

MURIEL: Yeah, he seems worried about it.

IRENE: Well, of course.

MURIEL: Ya know what those bastard doctors told me? Told me, I had to stop being so nervous ... Yeah, there's this fat pig making eighty thousand dollars a year, living in Côte Saint-Luc, telling me not to be a nervous wreck ... Well, I got so mad, I tell ya ... I got so mad, I couldn't talk.

IRENE: I can't blame ya.

MURIEL: It makes ya wanna kill yourself just out of spite.

IRENE: Ya oughta go to the clinic in the Pointe. The doctors there treat ya like a human being.

MURIEL: I dunno ... I heard they're all Commies or something.

IRENE: So what?

MURIEL: Yeah well, guess they couldn't be any worse ... Oh Irene, wait ... I wanna show ya something. (*She takes a small box out of her purse and opens it.*) Look.

IRENE: A brooch ... That's beautiful.

MURIEL: Tom bought it for me with his first pay.

IRENE: It's beautiful.

MURIEL: Yeah ... stupid kid. Now, he doesn't have enough money for car fare.

JOHNNY enters from the shed carrying some lumber and tools. He has built a new step for the stairs.

IRENE: Does he like his new job?

MURIEL: Well, he's lasted a month. That's some kind of record. (*She sees JOHNNY and the step.*) Holy shit! Hey, watch your thumbs!

JOHNNY glares at her.

MURIEL: Just a joke ... (*She goes into her house.*)

JOHNNY: Irene, gimme a hand with this ... Yeah, I know, officially, we ain't talking, but I need a hand ...

IRENE: I don't believe it.

She goes over to help JOHNNY put the new step in place.

JOHNNY: So, what's new? ... How are ya?

IRENE: I don't know ... Haven't been talking to myself lately.

JOHNNY: I've been off the sauce for a week now, right?

IRENE: Yeah.

JOHNNY: Yeah.

IRENE: You want a medal or what?

JOHNNY: Irene ... It's not easy, okay?

IRENE: Try being a woman for a while ...

DIANE: (*from upstairs*) Oui, that's right.

JOHNNY: (*taking IRENE over to one side*) Irene, all that crap about you being strong for the both of us ...

IRENE: It's not crap.

JOHNNY: Yeah, okay ... it's true, but I didn't make up the rules of the game, okay? I mean, it wasn't me.

IRENE: It wasn't me.

JOHNNY: I'm sorry, Irene. You know that? ... I'm sorry.

IRENE: I was worried ...

JOHNNY: About what?

IRENE: I've never seen you that bad before ...

JOHNNY: Hey, I don't melt in the rain ... I don't get diarrhea in the snow. I'm a survivor.

IRENE: Yeah ... (*They embrace.*) So, what are you gonna do?

JOHNNY: Maybe I can get back into music.

IRENE: You've been miserable ever since ya quit playing.

JOHNNY: You're the one who nagged me to quit.

IRENE: All I wanted you to do was stop drinking and screwing around so much ... Music had nothing to do with it.

JOHNNY: What do you know about the nightlife, Irene?

IRENE: Yeah well ... Anyhow, no matter what happens, we'll always be friends, eh?

JOHNNY: Is that a threat?

TOM comes out with his guitar and starts to play a song.

IRENE: Hi, Tommy.

IRENE goes up the stairs and into the house. JOHNNY comes over to talk to TOM.

JOHNNY: So, how's the new job?

TOM: Aw, Troy Laundry ... What can I say? Some guys been there twenty years and I'm there twenty days and already going nuts.

JOHNNY: Bad news, eh?

TOM: Hey. Can't talk to anybody ... They're all deaf from the noise.

JOHNNY: They probably got nothing to say anyhow.

TOM: Ya don't get a watch when you retire, ya get a hearing aid.

CÉCILE comes out on her balcony to speak to DIANE.

CÉCILE: Tu sais, Diane, j'ai vu ton père pleurer juste une fois. C'est quand t'étais petite puis bien malade.

DIANE: Je ne me souviens pas de ça.

CÉCILE: Ça fait longtemps. On restait sur la rue Joseph.

TOM plays a tune on his guitar.

TOM: (*to DIANE*) Hi, Diane ... You like that? ...

DIANE: No ... Know any disco?

TOM: Disco! ... "Disco Duck" ... I don't got the right buttons on this thing.

MURIEL: (*from inside the house*) Tommy?

TOM: Yeah?

MURIEL: I'm gonna need a hand in here ... I'm moving out your old man's junk into the shed.

TOM: You're moving it out?

MURIEL: Yeah ... He's never here and we can use the room.

TOM: Okay.

He goes in to help her move the things out to the shed. IRENE comes out of her house and goes down the stairs.

IRENE: All the trouble that step caused us over the last year and look at that, it's fixed.

JOHNNY: Yeah, I'm gonna send Giboux the bill.

DIANE: (*to IRENE*) Irene, is there any jobs at your place?

IRENE: What?

DIANE: I have to find work. My father, he lost his job.

IRENE: He lost his job?

CÉCILE: Yes. The company is going to Taiwan, but they don't want to take Claude.

IRENE: The bastards.

JOHNNY: He got the axe, eh?

IRENE: How is he?

DIANE: Not so good ... Maybe you can talk to him, Irene.

IRENE: Be better if you talk to him, Johnny.

JOHNNY: What the fuck am I gonna say? He don't even want to speak my language.

IRENE: (*shouting*) Hey, Muriel. Paquette lost his job.

MURIEL comes out of her house.

MURIEL: What? Another one for your Unemployment Committee. (*to CÉCILE*) Sorry, madame. I really am.

IRENE: We can get him out on our next demonstration.

JOHNNY: Another one?

IRENE: We're gonna march in front of the UIC building. Let them know we don't like the 40 per cent unemployment down here.

JOHNNY: Demonstration in the Pointe? That's not news.

MURIEL: We should do it in Westmount. That's where all the money is. Go up there and sit on their goddamn front lawns.

DIANE: Oui. Go right up there and let them know what we look like.

TOM: Yeah.

CÉCILE: It's very nice up in Westmount ... It's very nice.

JOHNNY: Yeah, you can take Thibault and leave him up there ... Boom! Into the woodwork ... Westmount's infested ... Thousands of little Thibaults running around ... Boom! Another Pointe-Saint-Charles!

MURIEL: Thibault ... our secret weapon.

TOM: So secret, he don't even know.

IRENE: Johnny, talk to Paquette ...

JOHNNY: You talk to him ...

IRENE: Johnny?

JOHNNY: Look, it's the principle of the thing ...

IRENE: Principle of what?

JOHNNY: Well, he started it, right?

IRENE: Started what?

DIANE: Maudit crisse, Johnny!

JOHNNY: All right. Ya want me to be the nice guy ... Why do I always got to be the nice guy?

He goes up the stairs and knocks on PAQUETTE's door.

JOHNNY: Hey, Porky ... Peace in the valley, okay?

PAQUETTE: (*from inside his house*) Quoi?

JOHNNY: Let's kiss and make up.

PAQUETTE: Quoi?

IRENE: Tell him you're sorry he lost his job.

JOHNNY: Look, I'm sorry you lost your job ...

IRENE: Tell him in French.

JOHNNY: I don't know how.

IRENE: Try ... J'ai de la peine ...

JOHNNY: J'ai de la peine ...

IRENE: J'ai de la peine que tu as perdu ... que tu as perdu ...

JOHNNY: J'ai de la peine que tu as perdu ...

IRENE: Ta job.

JOHNNY: Ta fuckin' job ... He's not talking.

IRENE: He's upset.

JOHNNY: Diane, how do you say, "Together, we can fuck Bolduc"?

DIANE: "Ensemble on peut fourrer Bolduc."

JOHNNY: Hey, Paquette ... "Ensemble ..."

PAQUETTE: (*at his screen door*) Hey, you go away with the bullshit, okay? Take it somewhere else ...

It's just another Pepsi who loses his job. T'es content ... Alors, viens pas m'écoeurer avec ça.

He slams the door shut.

JOHNNY: Irene!

He goes into his house and slams the door shut.

IRENE: Oh boy!

She goes up the stairs to PAQUETTE's door and knocks on it. There is no answer.

MURIEL: Talking's easy, Irene, but try to get people together ... Ppphht!

IRENE: What does it take to move you guys? ... We gotta help ourselves. That's easy to understand, isn't it?

DIANE: They don't want to understand ... it's easier to eat shit.

IRENE: I don't know why I bother.

MURIEL: Ah, we can still do the demonstration without them.

CÉCILE: We need the government to help us.

MURIEL: What are you talking about? Bolduc is the government!

IRENE: Well ... I'm tired ...

THIBAULT enters on his bike. He has a case of beer for PAQUETTE.

THIBAULT: Chez Momo's is here.

TOM: Hey, Thibault. How's the girls?

THIBAULT: Oh boy, don't talk to me about that ... Trouble all the time ...

He goes up the stairs and discovers the new step.

Hey! (*He dances on the new step.*) Où est Paquette? (*He puts the case of beer down on the balcony.*)

CÉCILE: Claude est pas bien aujourd'hui. Il a perdu sa job.

THIBAULT: Il a perdu sa job? Aw, everybody's got trouble now, eh? Me, last week, I got hit by a Cadillac.

MURIEL: By a what?

THIBAULT: A Cadillac, oui ... Big car, eh? ... So, I phone the boss and he says, "How's the bike?" "How's the bike?" hostie ... Hey me, I know the boss. Sometimes he talks nice, but he's still the boss, eh?

MURIEL: Aw, bosses ... they're all the same, Thibault.

THIBAULT: Sure, I know that ... Maybe I'm crazy, but I'm not stupid, eh?

MURIEL: They do what they want, the bastards. They always do what they want.

She starts ripping down Bolduc posters.

THIBAULT: Hey, Bolduc won't like that ...

MURIEL: Ppphht on Bolduc.

THIBAULT: Okay ... He won't like that, that's all.

DIANE: Irene, do you smell something?

IRENE: Yeah ...

TOM: Probably someone burning garbage.

MURIEL: Do you see any smoke?

IRENE: Yeah, but I don't know where it's coming from.

CÉCILE: C'est un feu.

THIBAULT: Un feu? Où ça un feu?

IRENE: (*to JOHNNY, inside the house*) Johnny, go down the lane and take a look.

JOHNNY: (*coming out of his house*) Why do I always have to do everything around here?

He dashes off down the lane, followed by TOM and DIANE. They all yell. "Fire!" JOHNNY comes running back on.

JOHNNY: Irene, call the cops! It's a big one! Just a few houses down ...

He runs back down the lane.

CÉCILE: Claude? Claude, y a un feu!

IRENE: I can't get the cops. The lines are busy ...

PAQUETTE comes running out of his house.

CÉCILE: Claude, dis à Diane de ne pas aller trop proche ...

He exits down the lane.

IRENE: It's a big one.

CÉCILE: Oh yes ... a big one ...

MURIEL: Those old houses go up like matchsticks ...

PAQUETTE: (*yelling offstage*) Ça s'étend aux sheds d'à côté!

CÉCILE: Mon Dieu!

MURIEL: What did he say?

IRENE: It's spreading ...

MURIEL: Where the hell are the firemen?

IRENE: If this were Westmount, there wouldn't be a fire.

MURIEL: Yeah, right ...

PAQUETTE comes running back on.

PAQUETTE: Ça continue à s'étendre!

MURIEL: What's he saying?

PAQUETTE: Cécile, on va sortir les meubles!

JOHNNY comes running back on, followed by TOM and DIANE.

JOHNNY: Hey, Irene, start moving our stuff out!

There is general running around and shouting. THIBAULT gets in everyone's way. JOHNNY and PAQUETTE carry down their TV sets and their beer first. CÉCILE carries down her plants.

MURIEL: Tom, move your ass!

TOM: Aw, we're insured anyhow ...

MURIEL: Move it!

PAQUETTE: (*to CÉCILE*) C'est pas le temps toi et pis tes hostie de plantes.

MURIEL: Thibault, get your bike out of the way!

THIBAULT: Hey, don't touch my bike!

MURIEL: Then get it out of the way!

THIBAULT: Eh, Madame Paquette, y a un gros feu là-bas! Hey, good thing we fix that step, eh?

JOHNNY: (*to PAQUETTE*) Keep your shit on that side ...

PAQUETTE: Va donc chier, câlice!

JOHNNY and PAQUETTE collide at the top of the stairs. They start pushing and shoving each other to see who will go down the stairs first.

PAQUETTE: Ote-toi de là, hostie!

JOHNNY: Get out of my way!

IRENE, CÉCILE, and DIANE rush in to break up the fight.

IRENE: Don't be so stupid ... Now, get out of the way ... both of you. Come, you guys ... Hey, Muriel, Tom ... we'll do a relay ... We'll move them out upstairs, then we'll do you.

MURIEL: Why upstairs first?

IRENE: Muriel, come on!

The relay begins. They all start passing stuff down. It comes at them through the windows and through the doors. PAQUETTE calls JOHNNY over to give him a hand with the sofa.

PAQUETTE: Lève-toi ... Lève-le ...

JOHNNY: Irene, he's speaking French!

IRENE: Lift it!

PAQUETTE: Tourne-le ... Tourne-le ...

JOHNNY: Yeah, yeah ... tour-ney ...

PAQUETTE: À droite ...

IRENE: To the right.

PAQUETTE: Laisse-le slyer sur la rampe ... la rampe ...

JOHNNY: What???

IRENE: Slide it down the banister!

They slide the sofa down the banister. JOHNNY hurts himself when he and PAQUETTE put the sofa down at the foot of the stairs.

PAQUETTE: Okay, allez, Johnny ... We go move ton sofa ...

He helps JOHNNY up the stairs. When they get halfway up, a huge crashing noise is heard.

TOM: There goes the roof!

CÉCILE: Mon Dieu!

IRENE: Here it comes ...

MURIEL: Christ, we're next!

The broadcast VOICE is heard once again.

VOICE: Citizens of Pointe-Saint-Charles, we live in a time when we need a strong government, a just government, one that is not afraid to deal harshly with disrupters, sabotage, corruptions, and criminals. Remember, a vote for Gaëtan Bolduc is a vote for security, for justice, for law and order ... and for the future. Le futur ...

JOHNNY, IRENE, MURIEL, and TOM: (*turning to the audience*) What are we going to do?

PAQUETTE, CÉCILE, DIANE, and THIBAULT: (*turning to the audience*) Qu'est-ce qu'on va faire?

Blackout.

END

SHARON POLLOCK

(b. 1936)

Sharon Pollock was a pioneer of the new Canadian theatre in the early 1970s, and she remains a living force in Canadian theatre today. In 2012, her seventy-fifth birthday was celebrated in Calgary with a major scholarly conference that also showcased her distinguished theatrical career, a career notable for the many powerful plays she has written about injustice in both the public and private spheres, about the oppression of women and minorities, about violence, and about the abuses of power. A fiercely outspoken woman of the theatre, she has also acted and directed, run theatres, and advocated for them. Her most frequently produced work remains *Blood Relations*, the play that launched her international reputation. Its complex dramatic and psychological structure combined with its feminist imperative, autobiographical resonances, and revisionist treatment of an almost mythic figure in Lizzie Borden has cemented its place in the contemporary theatrical canon.

Pollock's stage work includes history plays, family plays, and later in her career, plays that clearly bridge the personal and political. But as Pollock herself has said more than once, she has in some sense been writing the same play over and over: a play about fathers or father figures betraying the trust of those who depend on them, driven to those betrayals by their adherence to a rigid set of external, systemic values, and usually refusing to acknowledge responsibility for the damage they do. Often in Pollock's plays, women are on the receiving end. Sometimes, as in *Blood Relations*, repression and injustice produce a corresponding violence in return.

Sharon Pollock was born Mary Sharon Chalmers in Fredericton, where she first became involved in theatre while at the University of New Brunswick. With the Prairie Players in 1966, she toured British Columbia and Alberta and was voted Best Actress at the Dominion Drama Festival. She settled in Calgary the next year, and while pregnant with her sixth child she began writing her first play. The absurdist farce *A Compulsory Option* won the 1971 Alberta Playwriting Competition and was produced in 1972 by the New Play Centre in Vancouver, where Pollock and her family were then living. *Walsh* (1973) explored the relationship between the North-West Mounted Police major of the title and Sitting Bull's Sioux on the Canadian prairies in the 1870s. Its Theatre Calgary premiere and 1974 production at the Stratford Festival brought Pollock to wide public attention. A productive association with the Vancouver Playhouse resulted in six plays for children between 1973 and 1976, as well as *The Komagata Maru*

Incident (1976), which dissects the politics of racism behind the Canadian government's refusal to admit Sikh immigrants into Vancouver in 1914. Pollock herself played the title role of Lizzie Borden in the Douglas College production of her next play, *My Name Is Lisbeth* (1976), which after much revision would become *Blood Relations*.

Pollock moved to Edmonton in 1976 to teach playwriting at the University of Alberta, but except for a few brief periods since 1977, she has made her home in Calgary. From 1977–79, she ran the summer Playwrights' Colony at Banff and was playwright-in-residence for Alberta Theatre Projects, which produced her fine study of a family of prairie farmers, *Generations*, in 1980. That year, Edmonton's Citadel Theatre mounted *One Tiger to a Hill*, her dramatization of a fatal hostage-taking at the B.C. Penitentiary. She spent 1981–82 as artist-in-residence at the National Arts Centre, returning to Theatre Calgary where she served briefly as artistic director in 1984. Theatre Calgary premiered *Whiskey Six Cadenza* (1983), a tale of rum-running, coal mining, and sexual abuse in 1920s Alberta, and *Doc* (1984), the powerful play that most overtly reflects her own biography.

Doc is based on her family during the years she was growing up in Fredericton: the father in the play, with her father's real name, Everett Chalmers, devotes himself to his work as a respected physician and pillar of the community while the alcoholic mother (bearing Pollock's mother's real name) slowly comes apart at home. Pollock writes herself into the play as the daughter, who appears in two time frames: as an adult and as the child watching the unfolding of this terrible drama of guilt, recrimination, and eventual suicide. Pollock's own daughter Amanda made her professional stage debut in the role of the young daughter. In 1986, *Doc* won Pollock her second Governor General's Award for Drama.

After a couple of unhappy years as artistic director of Theatre New Brunswick, Pollock returned to performing in 1989, premiering her one-woman play *Getting It Straight* at the International Women's Festival in Winnipeg. A lyrical feminist monologue about male aggression and abuses of power, spoken by an apparent madwoman beneath a rodeo grandstand ("I am not mad, I am getting it straight"), the play was remounted at Toronto's Factory Theatre in 1990. Pollock's ongoing concern with feminist and Aboriginal issues was reflected in *The Making of Warriors* (1990), one in a long line of radio plays that includes the 1980 ACTRA Best Radio Drama Award winner, *Sweet Land of Liberty*. The Stratford Festival produced *Fair Liberty's Call* (1993), the tale of a Loyalist family's travails in New Brunswick following the American Revolution. Pollock herself directed *Saucy Jack* (1993), a metatheatrical examination of Jack the Ripper, at her own Garry Theatre in Calgary, which she ran from 1992 to 1997.

Calgary's Theatre Junction produced the historically based dramas *Moving Pictures* (1999), about Canadian silent-film actress Nell Shipman; *End Dream* (2000), Pollock's study of a notorious murder case in 1920s Vancouver involving race, class, and gender matters; and *Angel's Trumpet* (2001), a play about F. Scott and Zelda Fitzgerald and Zelda's psychiatrist. *Man Out of Joint* (2007), premiered by Calgary's Downstage Performance

Society, focuses on a Canadian lawyer defending a group of Muslims accused of terrorism.

Blood Relations was first staged in 1980 by Edmonton's Theatre 3, and the volume Blood Relations and Other Plays won the inaugural Governor General's Literary Award for Drama in 1981. The play had numerous productions in the 1980s across Canada, with major revivals at London's Grand Theatre in 1989, directed by Martha Henry, and at the Shaw Festival in 2004. It has played in New York, Australia, and England, and at many Canadian and American universities. It appeared in French as Liens de sang (1986) in Quebec and has had at least three productions in Japan. Blood Relations has been a magnet for many of Canada's finest actresses, including Patricia Collins, Shirley Douglas, Clare Coulter, Diana Leblanc, and Frances Hyland. Pollock herself has directed two productions and she performed the role of Miss Lizzie / Bridget at Theatre Calgary in 1981. The play has been widely republished, including in Cynthia Zimmerman's three-volume Sharon Pollock: Collected Works (Playwrights Canada Press, 2005–08). The version printed here is Sharon Pollock's most recent revision of the play (2012), including a couple of significantly expanded scenes.

Pollock took the central event of Blood Relations and most of its characters from history. The real-life, thirty-two-year-old Lizzie Borden was accused, tried, and acquitted in Fall River, Massachusetts, in 1892, of the sensational crime of murdering her father and stepmother with a hatchet. She became something of a folk figure; many decades later, American children (I among them) still chanted the singsong rhyme, "Lizzie Borden took an axe / And gave her mother forty whacks ..." Following her acquittal, due largely to testimony provided by the Bordens' maid, Bridget, Lizzie remained living in the family home, estranged from her sister, Emma, and was rumoured to have a scandalous relationship with Boston actress Nance O'Neill.

Other than changing Lizzie's age to thirty-four, Pollock remains true to the historical facts. But she complicates any sense of straightforward narrative by telling the story of Lizzie's family relations and the killing of her stepmother and father within a metatheatrical frame. Lizzie and her friend, the Actress, in 1902, re-enact the events of 1892 in what Pollock calls the "dream thesis," with the Actress playing the role of Miss Lizzie and Lizzie herself acting the part of Bridget. Both actors also serve as directors, giving each other notes and commentary as they step in and out of the frame. By the end of the play, although it seems pretty clear whodunit, the densely performative, linguistically rich investigation into Lizzie Borden's psychology and family reveals a deep, bitter, complex nexus of liability, implicating multiple characters, the social structure, and even the audience.

Much of the play's power comes from the intense feeling of entrapment experienced by Lizzie, an unmarried adult woman living in her father's house and severely constrained by the gendered Victorian mores of late nineteenth-century New England. Her father treats her like a child, refuses to let her work, tries to force her to marry a man in whom she has no interest, and doesn't trust her or Emma to inherit the family home and business, which Mrs. Borden and her brother Harry plot to get for themselves. Even talking to, much less flirting with, married Dr. Patrick is taboo. In one sense, *Blood Relations* is a feminist parable. Like Ibsen's Nora in *A Doll's House*, Lizzie needs to break free of the patriarchal home and its values if she is to live as an authentic adult. Like Nora, Lizzie despairs to the point where she considers suicide. But unlike Nora, Lizzie doesn't have the wherewithal – or maybe the courage – simply to walk out the door. Whether she liberates herself at all remains ambiguous at play's end.

In her "Afterword" to *Blood Relations* in a 1984 collection by Methuen (*Plays by Women*, vol. 3), Pollock wrote, "Prior to working in the theatre, I was married for some years to a violent man. I spent a great deal of time devising, quite literally, murderous schemes to rid me of him ... I would have killed to maintain my sense of self ... And so it is with Lizzie." The autobiographical resonances of Sharon Pollock's relationship with Lizzie Borden go well beyond this connection. As Pollock's biographer, Sherrill Grace, puts it, "there are many other subterranean parallels between the Fall River world of the Bordens and the Fredericton world of the Chalmers." I have argued (see "Daddy's Girls") that Pollock in this play and others was working through some deep-seated psychosexual issues involving herself and her own parents. Other critics have argued vociferously about *Blood Relations* from very different perspectives, more so than probably any other drama in the Canadian canon. After more than thirty years, *Blood Relations* remains passionately in play.

Blood Relations

Sharon Pollock

Blood Relations was first performed March 12, 1980, at Theatre 3, Edmonton, with the following cast:

MISS LIZZIE	Janet Daverne
THE ACTRESS	Judith Mabey
EMMA	Barbara Reese
DR. PATRICK / THE DEFENCE	Wendell Smith
HARRY	Brian Atkins
MRS. BORDEN	Paddy English
MR. BORDEN	Charles Kerr

Directed by Keith Digby
Set and Prop Design by J. Fraser Hiltz
Costume Design by Kathryn Burns
Lighting Design by Luciano Iogna
Stage Managed by Maureen A. Dool

CHARACTERS

MISS LIZZIE, *who will play* **BRIDGET**, *the Irish maid*
THE ACTRESS, *who will play* **LIZZIE BORDEN**
HARRY, *Mrs. Borden's brother*
EMMA, *Lizzie's older sister*
ANDREW (MR. BORDEN), *Lizzie's father*
ABIGAIL (MRS. BORDEN), *Lizzie's stepmother*
DR. PATRICK, *the Irish doctor;*
    sometimes **THE DEFENCE**

SCENE

The time proper is late-fall Sunday afternoon and evening, in Fall River, 1902. The year of the "dream thesis," if one might call it that, is 1892. There is a dining room and parlour area within the Borden house, an exit from the dining area to the kitchen, and a flight of stairs from the parlour leading to the second floor, plus a walkway outside the Borden house with some indication of where the birds are kept.

PRODUCTION NOTES

The set should accommodate free-flowing action. There should be no division of the script into scenes by blackouts, movement of furniture, or sets. There are often soft freezes of some characters while other scenes are being played. **THE DEFENCE** *may be seen directly, may be a shadow only, or may appear as a figure behind a scrim. Unless* **MISS LIZZIE** *is exiting or entering with her* **BRIDGET** *business, she is present (often with* **THE ACTRESS**), *observing unobtrusively as "herself," except for those occasions when she, as* **BRIDGET**, *is taking part in the action, or as noted in Act Two, when she is absent from the entrance of* **DR. PATRICK** *to her reappearance as* **BRIDGET** *after washing the windows. The murders of which* **MISS LIZZIE** *was accused took place in August 1892; her trial and acquittal, in June of the following year.*

ACT ONE

Lights up on the figure of a woman (THE ACTRESS) standing centre stage. It is a somewhat formal pose. A pause. She speaks:

"Since what I am about to say must be but that
Which contradicts my accusation, and
The testimony on my part no other
But what comes from myself, it shall scarce boot me
To say 'Not Guilty.'
But, if Powers Divine
Behold our human action as they do,
I doubt not then but innocence shall make
False accusation blush and tyranny
Tremble at ... at ..."

She wriggles the fingers of an outstretched hand searching for the word.

"Aaaat" … Bollocks!!

She raises her script, takes a bite of chocolate.

"Tremble at 'Patience'," patience, patience! …

MISS LIZZIE enters from the kitchen with tea service. THE ACTRESS's attention drifts to MISS LIZZIE. THE ACTRESS watches MISS LIZZIE sit in the parlour and proceed to pour two cups of tea. THE ACTRESS sucks her teeth a bit to clear the chocolate as she speaks.

THE ACTRESS: Which … is proper, Lizzie?

MISS LIZZIE: Proper?

THE ACTRESS: To pour first the cream, and add the tea – or first tea and add cream. One is proper. Is the way you do the proper way, the way it's done in circles where it counts?

MISS LIZZIE: Sugar?

THE ACTRESS: Well, is it?

MISS LIZZIE: I don't know. Sugar?

THE ACTRESS: Mmmn. (*MISS LIZZIE adds sugar.*) I suppose if we had Mrs. Beeton's book of etiquette, we could look it up.

MISS LIZZIE: I do have it. Shall I get it?

THE ACTRESS: No … You could ask your sister, she might know.

MISS LIZZIE: Do you want this tea or not?

THE ACTRESS: I hate tea.

MISS LIZZIE: You drink it every Sunday.

THE ACTRESS: I drink it because you like to serve it.

MISS LIZZIE: Pppuh.

THE ACTRESS: It's true. You've no idea how I suffer from this toast-and-tea ritual. I really do. The tea upsets my stomach and the toast makes me fat because I eat so much of it.

MISS LIZZIE: Practise some restraint then.

THE ACTRESS: Mmmmm … Why don't we ask your sister which is proper?

MISS LIZZIE: You ask her.

THE ACTRESS: How can I? She doesn't speak to me. I don't think she even sees me. She gives no indication of it. (*She looks up the stairs.*) What do you suppose she does up there every Sunday afternoon?

MISS LIZZIE: She sulks.

THE ACTRESS: And reads the Bible, I suppose, and Mrs. Beeton's book of etiquette. Oh Lizzie … What a long day. The absolutely longest day … When does that come anyway, the longest day?

MISS LIZZIE: June.

THE ACTRESS: Ah yes, June. (*She looks at MISS LIZZIE.*) June?

MISS LIZZIE: June.

THE ACTRESS: Mmmmmm …

MISS LIZZIE: I know what you're thinking.

THE ACTRESS: Of course you do … I'm thinking … shall I pour the sherry – or will you.

MISS LIZZIE: No.

THE ACTRESS: I'm thinking … June … in Fall River.

MISS LIZZIE: No.

THE ACTRESS: August in Fall River? (*She smiles.*)

Pause.

MISS LIZZIE: We could have met in Boston.

THE ACTRESS: I prefer it here.

MISS LIZZIE: You don't find it … a trifle boring?

THE ACTRESS: Au contraire.

MISS LIZZIE gives a small laugh at the affectation.

THE ACTRESS: What?

MISS LIZZIE: I find it a trifle boring … I know what you're doing. You're soaking up the ambience.

THE ACTRESS: Nonsense, Lizzie. I come to see you.

MISS LIZZIE: Why?

THE ACTRESS: Because … of us.

MISS LIZZIE: You were a late arrival last night. Later than usual.

THE ACTRESS: Don't be silly.

MISS LIZZIE: I wonder why.

THE ACTRESS: The show was late, late starting, late coming down.

MISS LIZZIE: And?

THE ACTRESS: And – then we all went out for drinks.

MISS LIZZIE: We?

THE ACTRESS: The other members of the cast.

MISS LIZZIE: Oh yes.

THE ACTRESS: And then I caught a cab … all the way from Boston … Do you know what it cost?

MISS LIZZIE: I should. I paid the bill, remember?

THE ACTRESS: (*laughing*) Of course. What a jumble all my thoughts are. There're too many words running 'round inside my head today. It's terrible.

MISS LIZZIE: It sounds it.

THE ACTRESS: ... You know ... you do this thing ... you stare at me ... You look directly at my eyes. I think ... you think ... that if I'm lying ... it will come up, like lemons on a slot machine. (*She makes a gesture at her eyes.*) Tick. Tick ... (*pause*) In the alley, behind the theatre the other day, there were some kids. You know what they were doing?

MISS LIZZIE: How could I?

THE ACTRESS: They were playing skip rope, and you know what they were singing? (*She sings, and claps her hands to*):

"Lizzie Borden took an axe,

Gave her mother forty whacks.

When the job was nicely done,

She gave her father forty-one."

MISS LIZZIE: Did you stop them?

THE ACTRESS: No.

MISS LIZZIE: Did you tell them I was acquitted?

THE ACTRESS: No.

MISS LIZZIE: What did you do?

THE ACTRESS: I shut the window.

MISS LIZZIE: A noble gesture on my behalf.

THE ACTRESS: We were doing lines – the noise they make is dreadful. Sometimes they play ball, ka-thunk, ka-thunk, ka-thunk against the wall. Once I saw them with a cat and –

MISS LIZZIE: And then you didn't stop them?

THE ACTRESS: That time I stopped them. (*She crosses to a table where there is a gramophone and prepares to play a record. She stops.*) Should I?

MISS LIZZIE: Why not?

THE ACTRESS: Your sister, the noise upsets her.

MISS LIZZIE: And she upsets me. On numerous occasions.

THE ACTRESS: You're incorrigible, Lizzie.

THE ACTRESS holds out her arms to MISS LIZZIE. They dance the latest "in" dance, a Scott Joplin composition. It requires some concentration, but they chat while dancing rather formally in contrast to the music.

THE ACTRESS: ... Do you think your jawline's heavy?

MISS LIZZIE: Why do you ask?

THE ACTRESS: They said you had jowls.

MISS LIZZIE: Did they.

THE ACTRESS: The reports of the day said you were definitely jowly.

MISS LIZZIE: That was ten years ago.

THE ACTRESS: Imagine. You were only thirty-four.

MISS LIZZIE: Yes.

THE ACTRESS: It happened here, this house.

MISS LIZZIE: You're leading.

THE ACTRESS: I know.

MISS LIZZIE: ... I don't think I'm jowly. Then or now. Do you?

THE ACTRESS: Lizzie? ... Lizzie!

MISS LIZZIE: What?

THE ACTRESS: Did you?

MISS LIZZIE: Did I what?

Pause.

THE ACTRESS: You never tell me anything. (*She turns off the music.*)

MISS LIZZIE: I tell you everything.

THE ACTRESS: No, you don't!

MISS LIZZIE: Oh yes, I tell you the most personal things about myself, my thoughts, my dreams, my –

THE ACTRESS: But never that one thing ... (*She lights a cigarette.*)

MISS LIZZIE: And don't smoke those – they stink.

THE ACTRESS ignores her, inhales, and then exhales a volume of smoke in MISS LIZZIE's direction.

MISS LIZZIE: Do you suppose ... people buy you drinks ... or cast you even ... because you have a "liaison" with Lizzie Borden? Do you suppose they do that?

THE ACTRESS: They cast me because I'm good at what I do.

MISS LIZZIE: They never pry? They never ask? What's she really like? Is she really jowly? Did she? Didn't she?

THE ACTRESS: What could I tell them? You never tell me anything.

MISS LIZZIE: I tell you everything.

THE ACTRESS: But that! (*pause*) You think everybody talks about you – they don't.

MISS LIZZIE: Here they do.

THE ACTRESS: You think they talk about you.

MISS LIZZIE: But never to me.

THE ACTRESS: Well ... you give them lots to talk about.

MISS LIZZIE: You know you're right, your mind is a jumble.

THE ACTRESS: I told you so.

Pause.

MISS LIZZIE: You remind me of my sister.

THE ACTRESS: Oh God, in what way?

MISS LIZZIE: Day in, day out, ten years now, sometimes at breakfast as she rolls little crumbs of bread in little balls, sometimes at noon, or late at night ... "Did you, Lizzie? Lizzie, did you?"

THE ACTRESS: Ten years, day in, day out?

MISS LIZZIE: Oh yes. She sits there where Papa used to sit and I sit there, where I have always sat. She looks at me and at her plate, then at me, and at her plate, then at me and then she says, "Did you Lizzie? Lizzie, did you?"

THE ACTRESS: (*a nasal imitation of EMMA's voice*) "Did-you-Lizzie – Lizzie-did-you?" (*laughing*)

MISS LIZZIE: Did I what?

THE ACTRESS: (*continuing her imitation of EMMA*) "You know."

MISS LIZZIE: Well, what do you think?

THE ACTRESS: "Oh, I believe you didn't; in fact, I know you didn't. What a thought! After all, you were acquitted."

MISS LIZZIE: Yes, I was.

THE ACTRESS: "But sometimes when I'm on the street ... or shopping ... or at the church even, I catch somebody's eye, they look away ... and I think to myself, "Did-you-Lizzie –Lizzie-did-yoooou?"

MISS LIZZIE: (*laughing*) Ah, poor Emma.

THE ACTRESS: (*dropping her EMMA imitation*) Well, did you?

MISS LIZZIE: Is it important?

THE ACTRESS: Yes.

MISS LIZZIE: Why?

THE ACTRESS: I have ... a compulsion to know the truth.

MISS LIZZIE: The truth?

THE ACTRESS: Yes.

MISS LIZZIE: ... Sometimes I think you look like me, and you're not jowly.

THE ACTRESS: No.

MISS LIZZIE: You look like me, or how I think I look, or how I ought to look ... sometimes you think like me ... do you feel that?

THE ACTRESS: Sometimes.

MISS LIZZIE: (*triumphant*) You shouldn't have to ask then. You should know. "Did I, didn't I?" You tell me.

THE ACTRESS: I'll tell you what I think ... I think ... that you're aware there is a certain fascination in the ambiguity ... You always paint the background but leave the rest to my imagination. Did Lizzie Borden take an axe? ... If you didn't, I should be disappointed ... and if you did, I should be horrified.

MISS LIZZIE: And which is worse?

THE ACTRESS: To have murdered one's parents, or to be a pretentious small-town spinster? I don't know.

MISS LIZZIE: Why're you so cruel to me?

THE ACTRESS: I'm teasing, Lizzie, I'm only teasing. Come on, paint the background again.

MISS LIZZIE: Why?

THE ACTRESS: Perhaps you'll give something away.

MISS LIZZIE: Which you'll dine out on.

THE ACTRESS: Of course. (*laughing*) Come on, Lizzie. Come on.

MISS LIZZIE: Come on what?

THE ACTRESS: Tell me!

Pause.

MISS LIZZIE: Sooo – a game.

THE ACTRESS: What?

MISS LIZZIE: A game? ... And you'll play me.

THE ACTRESS: Oh –

MISS LIZZIE: It's your stock in trade, my love.

THE ACTRESS: All right ... A game!

MISS LIZZIE: Let me think ... let me ... Bridget ... yes – Brrridget.

THE ACTRESS: Bridget?

MISS LIZZIE: We had a maid then, yes, and her name was Bridget. Bridget, she was a great one for stories, telling stories – and stood like this, very straight back, and her hair was all ... and there she was – in the courtroom! In her new dress on the stand. "Do you swear to tell the truth, the whole truth, and nothing but the truth, so help you God?" (*imitating an Irish accent*)

"I do, sir," she said.

"Would you give the court your name."

"Bridget O'Sullivan, sir."

Very faint echo of the voice of THE DEFENCE under MISS LIZZIE's next line.

"And occupation."

"I'm like what you'd call a maid, sir. I do a bit of everything, cleanin' and cookin' and –"

The actual voice of THE DEFENCE is heard alone; he may also be seen.

THE DEFENCE: You've been in Fall River how long?

MISS LIZZIE: (*continuing as BRIDGET, while THE ACTRESS, who will play LIZZIE, observes*) Well now, about five years, sir, ever since I came over. I worked up on the hill for a while but it didn't – well, you could say, suit me, too la-di-dah – so I –

THE DEFENCE: Your employer in June of 1892 was?

BRIDGET: Yes, sir. Mr. Borden, sir. Well, more rightly, Mrs. Borden, for she was the one who –

THE DEFENCE: Your impression of the household?

BRIDGET: Well … the man of the house, Mr. Borden, was a bit of a … tightwad, and Mrs. B. could nag you into the grave. Still, she helped with the dishes and things (*BRIDGET begins arranging things at the table*) which not everyone does when they hires a maid. (*HARRY appears on the stairs; approaches BRIDGET stealthily. She is unaware of him.*) Then there was the daughters, Miss Emma and Lizzie, and that day, Mr. Wingate, Mrs. B.'s brother who'd stayed for the night and was – (*As BRIDGET bends over the table, HARRY grabs her ass with both hands. She screams.*) Get off with you!

HARRY: Come on, Bridget, give me a kiss!

BRIDGET: I'll give you a good poke in the nose if you don't keep your hands to yourself.

HARRY: Ohhh-hh-hh, Bridget!

BRIDGET: Get away, you old sod!

HARRY: Haven't you missed me?

BRIDGET: I have not! I was pinched black and blue last time and I'll be sufferin' the same before I see the end of you this time.

HARRY: (*tilting his ass at her*) You want to see my end?

BRIDGET: You're a dirty old man.

HARRY: If Mr. Borden hears that, you'll be out on the street. (*grabbing her*) Where's my kiss!

BRIDGET: (*dumping a glass of water on his head*) There! (*HARRY splutters.*) Would you like another? You silly thing you – and leave me towels alone!

HARRY: You've soaked my shirt.

BRIDGET: Shut up and pour yourself a cup of coffee.

HARRY: You got no sense of fun, Bridget.

BRIDGET: Well now, if you tried actin' like the gentleman farmer you're supposed to be, Mr. Wingate –

HARRY: I'm tellin' you, you can't take a joke.

BRIDGET: If Mr. Borden sees you jokin', it's not his maid he'll be throwin' out on the street, but his brother-in-law, and that's the truth.

HARRY: What's between you and me's between you and me, eh?

BRIDGET: There ain't nothin' between you and me.

HARRY: … Finest cup of coffee in Fall River.

BRIDGET: There's no gettin' on the good side of me now, it's too late for that.

HARRY: … Bridget? … You know what tickles my fancy?

BRIDGET: No, and I don't want to hear.

HARRY: It's your Irish temper.

BRIDGET: It is, is it? … Can I ask you something?

HARRY: Ooohhh – anything.

BRIDGET: (*innocently*) Does Miss Lizzie know you're here? … I say, does Miss Lizzie –

HARRY: Why do you bring her up?

BRIDGET: She don't then, eh? (*teasing*) It's a surprise visit?

HARRY: No surprise to her father.

BRIDGET: Oh?

HARRY: We got business.

BRIDGET: I'd of thought the last bit of business was enough.

HARRY: It's not for – (*He stops before saying "you to say."*)

BRIDGET: You don't learn a thing, from me or Lizzie, do you?

HARRY: Listen here –

BRIDGET: You mean you've forgotten how mad she was when you got her father to sign the rent from the mill house over to your sister? Oh my.

HARRY: She's his wife, isn't she?

BRIDGET: (*lightly*) Second wife.

HARRY: She's still got her rights.

BRIDGET: Who am I to say who's got a right? But I can tell you this – Miss Lizzie don't see it that way.

HARRY: It don't matter how Miss Lizzie sees it.

BRIDGET: Oh, it matters enough – she had you thrown out last time, didn't she? Bejesus that was a laugh!

HARRY: You mind your tongue.

BRIDGET: And after you left, you know what happened?

HARRY: Get away.

BRIDGET: She and sister Emma got her father's rent money from the other mill house to make it all even-steven – and now, here you are back again? What kind of business you up to this time? (*whispering in his ear*) Mind Lizzie doesn't catch you.

HARRY: Get away!

BRIDGET: (*laughing*) Ohhhh – would you like some more coffee, sir? It's the finest coffee in all Fall River! (*She pours it.*) Thank you, sir. You're welcome, sir. (*She exits to the kitchen.*)

HARRY: There'll be no trouble this time!! Do you hear me!

BRIDGET: (*off*) Yes, sir.

HARRY: There'll be no trouble. (*sees a basket of crusts*) What the hell's this? I said is this for breakfast!

BRIDGET: (*entering*) Is what for – oh no – Mr. Borden's not economizin' to that degree yet, it's the crusts for Miss Lizzie's birds.

HARRY: What birds?

BRIDGET: Some kind of pet pigeons she's raisin' out in the shed. Miss Lizzie loves her pigeons.

HARRY: Miss Lizzie loves kittens and cats and horses and dogs. What Miss Lizzie doesn't love is people.

BRIDGET: *Some* people. (*She looks past HARRY to THE ACTRESS / LIZZIE. HARRY turns to follow her gaze. BRIDGET speaks encouragingly to THE ACTRESS, inviting THE ACTRESS to join her.*) Good mornin', Lizzie.

THE ACTRESS: (*She's a trifle tentative as she takes on the role of LIZZIE with the information she's gleaned from watching MISS LIZZIE's BRIDGET scene.*) Is the coffee on?

BRIDGET: Yes, ma'am.

LIZZIE: I'll have some then.

BRIDGET: Yes, ma'am. (*She makes no move to get it, but watches as LIZZIE stares at HARRY.*)

HARRY: Well ... I think ... maybe I'll ... just split a bit of that kindling out back. (*He exits.*)

LIZZIE: Silly ass.

BRIDGET: Oh Lizzie. (*She laughs. She enjoys THE ACTRESS / LIZZIE's comments as she guides her into her role by continuing to "paint the background."*)

LIZZIE: Well, he is. He's a silly ass.

BRIDGET: Can you remember him last time with your papa? Oh, I can still hear him: "Now, Andrew, I've spent my life raisin' horses and I'm gonna tell you somethin' – a *woman* is just like a *horse*! You keep her on a tight rein, or she'll take the bit in her teeth and, next thing you know, road, destination, and purpose is all behind you, and you'll be damn lucky if she don't pitch you right in a sewer ditch!"

LIZZIE: Stupid bugger.

BRIDGET: Oh Lizzie, what language! What would your father say if he heard you?

LIZZIE: Well ... I've never used a word I didn't hear from him first.

BRIDGET: Do you think he'd be congratulatin' you?

LIZZIE: Possibly. (*BRIDGET gives a subtle shake of her head.*) Not.

BRIDGET: Possibly not is right ... And what if Mrs. B. should hear you?

LIZZIE: I hope and pray that she does ... Do you know what I think, Bridget? I think there's nothing wrong with Mrs. B. ... that losing eighty pounds and tripling her intellect wouldn't cure.

BRIDGET: (*loving it*) You ought to be ashamed.

LIZZIE: It's the truth, isn't it?

BRIDGET: Still, what a way to talk of your mother.

LIZZIE: Stepmother.

BRIDGET: Yes, still, you don't mean it, do you?

LIZZIE: Don't I? (*louder*) She's a *silly ass*, too!

BRIDGET: Shhhh.

LIZZIE: It's all right, she's deaf as a picket fence when she wants to be ... What's he here for? (*increasingly secure in her role*)

BRIDGET: Never said.

LIZZIE: He's come to worm more money out of Papa I bet.

BRIDGET: Lizzie.

LIZZIE: What.

BRIDGET: Your sister, Lizzie.

BRIDGET indicates EMMA. LIZZIE turns to see her on the stairs.

EMMA: You want to be quiet, Lizzie, a body can't sleep for the racket upstairs.

LIZZIE: Oh?

EMMA: You've been makin' too much noise.

LIZZIE: It must have been Bridget. She dropped a pot, didn't you, Bridget.

EMMA: A number of pots from the sound of it.

BRIDGET: I'm all thumbs this mornin', ma'am.

EMMA: You know it didn't sound like pots.

LIZZIE: Oh.

EMMA: Sounded more like voices.

LIZZIE: Oh?

EMMA: Sounded like your voice, Lizzie.

LIZZIE: Maybe you dreamt it.

EMMA: I wish I had, for someone was using words no lady would use.

LIZZIE: When Bridget dropped the pot, she did say "pshaw!" Didn't you, Bridget.

BRIDGET: Pshaw! That's what I said.

EMMA: That's not what I heard.

BRIDGET exits to the kitchen.

LIZZIE: Pshaw?

EMMA: If mother heard you, you know what she'd say.

LIZZIE: She's not my mother or yours.

EMMA: Well, she married our father twenty-seven years ago, if that doesn't make her our mother –

LIZZIE: It doesn't.

EMMA: Don't talk like that.

LIZZIE: I'll talk as I like.

EMMA: We're not going to fight, Lizzie. We're going to be quiet and have our breakfast.

LIZZIE: Is that what we're going to do?

EMMA: Yes.

LIZZIE: Oh.

EMMA: At least that's what I'm going to do.

LIZZIE: (*yelling very loudly*) Bridget, Emma wants her breakfast!

EMMA: I could have yelled myself.

LIZZIE: You could, but you never do.

BRIDGET enters and serves EMMA, who is reluctant to argue in front of BRIDGET.

EMMA: Thank you, Bridget.

LIZZIE: Did you know Harry Wingate's back for a visit? … He must have snuck in late last night so I wouldn't hear him. Did you? (*EMMA shakes her head. LIZZIE studies her.*) Did you know he was coming?

EMMA: No.

LIZZIE: No?

EMMA: But I do know he wouldn't be here unless Papa asked him.

LIZZIE: That's not the point. You know what happened last time he was here. Papa was signing property over to her.

EMMA: Oh Lizzie.

LIZZIE: Oh Lizzie, nothing. It's bad enough Papa's worth thousands of dollars, and here we are, stuck in this tiny bit of a house on Second Street, when we should be up on the hill and that's her doing. Or hers and Harry's.

EMMA: Shush.

LIZZIE: I won't shush. They cater to Papa's worst instincts.

EMMA: They'll hear you.

LIZZIE: I don't care if they do. It's true, isn't it? Papa tends to be miserly, he probably has the first penny he ever earned – or more likely she has it.

EMMA: You talk rubbish.

LIZZIE: Papa can be very warm-hearted and generous – but he needs encouragement.

EMMA: If Papa didn't save his money, Papa wouldn't have any money.

LIZZIE: And neither will we if he keeps signing things over to her.

EMMA: I'm not going to listen.

LIZZIE: Well, try thinking.

EMMA: Stop it.

LIZZIE: (*not a threat, a simple statement of fact*) Someday Papa will die –

EMMA: Don't say that.

LIZZIE: Someday Papa will die. And I don't intend to spend the rest of my life licking Harry Wingate's boots, or toadying to his sister.

MRS. BORDEN: (*from the stairs*) What's that?

LIZZIE: Nothing.

MRS. BORDEN: (*making her way downstairs*) Eh?

LIZZIE: I said, nothing!

BRIDGET holds out a basket of crusts. LIZZIE looks at it.

BRIDGET: For your birds, Miss Lizzie.

LIZZIE: (*taking the basket*) You want to know what I think? I think she's a fat cow and I hate her. (*She exits to watch the scene.*)

EMMA: ... Morning, Mother.

MRS. BORDEN: Morning, Emma.

EMMA: ... Did you have a good sleep?

BRIDGET will serve breakfast.

MRS. BORDEN: So-so ... It's the heat you know. It never cools off proper at night. It's too hot for a good sleep.

EMMA: ... Is Papa up?

MRS. BORDEN: He'll be down in a minute ... So-o-o ... what's wrong with Lizzie this morning?

EMMA: Nothing.

MRS. BORDEN: Has Harry come down?

EMMA: I'm not sure.

MRS. BORDEN: Bridget, has Harry come down?

BRIDGET: Yes, ma'am.

MRS. BORDEN: And?

BRIDGET: And he's gone out back for a bit.

MRS. BORDEN: Lizzie see him?

BRIDGET: Yes, ma'am.

BRIDGET beats it back to the kitchen to join LIZZIE and watch. EMMA concentrates on her plate.

MRS. BORDEN: You should have said so. She have words with him?

EMMA: Lizzie has more manners than that.

MRS. BORDEN: She's incapable of disciplining herself like a lady and we all know it.

EMMA: Well, she doesn't make a habit of picking fights with people.

MRS. BORDEN: That's just it. She does.

EMMA: Well ... she may –

MRS. BORDEN: And you can't deny that.

EMMA: (*louder*) Well, this morning she may have been a bit upset because no one told her he was coming and when she came down he was here. But that's all there was to it.

MRS. BORDEN: If your father wants my brother in for a stay, he's to ask Lizzie's permission, I suppose.

EMMA: No.

MRS. BORDEN: You know, Emma –

EMMA: She didn't argue with him or anything like that.

MRS. BORDEN: You spoiled her. You may have had the best of intentions, but you spoiled her.

MISS LIZZIE / BRIDGET is speaking to THE ACTRESS / LIZZIE.

MISS LIZZIE / BRIDGET: I was thirty-four years old, and I still daydreamed ... I did ... I daydreamed ... I dreamt that my name was Lisbeth ... and I lived up on the hill in a corner house ... and my hair wasn't red. I hate red hair. When I was little, everyone teased me ... When I was little, we never stayed in this house for the summer, we'd go to the farm ... I remember ... my knees were always covered with scabs, God knows how I got them, but you know what I'd do? I'd sit in the field, and haul up my skirts, and my petticoat and my bloomers and roll down my stockings and I'd *pick* the scabs on my knees! And Emma would catch me! You know what she'd say? "Nice little girls don't have scabs on their knees!"

They laugh.

LIZZIE: Poor Emma.

MISS LIZZIE / BRIDGET: I dreamt ... someday I'm going to live ... in a corner house on the hill ... I'll have parties, grand parties. I'll be ... witty, not biting, but witty. Everyone will be witty. Everyone who is *anyone* will want to come to my parties ... and if ... I can't ... live in a corner house on the hill ... I'll live on the farm, all by myself on the farm! There was a barn there, with barn cats and barn kittens and two horses and barn swallows that lived in the eaves ... The birds I kept here were pigeons, not swallows. They were grey, a dull grey ... but ... when the sun struck their feathers, I'd see blue, a steel blue with a sheen, and when they'd move in the sun they were bright blue and maroon and, over it all, an odd sparkle as if you'd ... grated a new silver dollar and the gratings caught in their feathers ... Most of the time they were dull ... and stupid perhaps ... but they weren't really. They were ... hiding I think ... They knew me ... They liked me. The truth ... is –

THE ACTRESS / LIZZIE: The truth is ... thirty-four is too old to daydream.

MRS. BORDEN: The truth is she's spoilt rotten. (*MR. BORDEN will come downstairs and take his place at the table. MRS. BORDEN continues for his benefit. MR. BORDEN ignores her. He has learned the fine art of tuning her out.*) And we're paying the piper for that. In most of the places I've been, the people who pay the piper call the tune. Of course, I haven't had the advantage of a trip to Europe with a bunch of lady friends like our Lizzie had three years ago, all expenses paid by her father.

EMMA: Morning, Papa.

MR. BORDEN: Mornin'.

MRS. BORDEN: I haven't had the benefit of that experience ... Did you know Lizzie's seen Harry?

MR. BORDEN: Has she.

MRS. BORDEN: You should have met him downtown. You should never have asked him to stay over.

MR. BORDEN: Why not?

MRS. BORDEN: You know as well as I do why not. I don't want a repeat of last time. She didn't speak civil for months.

MR. BORDEN: There's no reason for Harry to pay for a room when we've got a spare one ... Where's Lizzie?

EMMA: Out back feeding the birds.

MR. BORDEN: She's always out at those birds.

EMMA: Yes, Papa.

MR. BORDEN: And tell her to get a new lock for the shed. There's been someone in it again.

EMMA: All right.

MR. BORDEN: It's those little hellions from next door. We had no trouble with them playin' in that shed before, they always played in their own yard before.

EMMA: ... Papa?

MR. BORDEN: It's those damn birds, that's what brings them into the yard.

EMMA: ... About Harry ...

MR. BORDEN: What about Harry?

EMMA: Well ... I was just wondering why ... (*She stops before saying "he's here."*)

MR. BORDEN: You never mind Harry – did you speak to Lizzie about Johnny MacLeod?

EMMA: I ah –

MR. BORDEN: Eh?

EMMA: I said I tried to –

MR. BORDEN: What do you mean, you tried to.

EMMA: Well, I was working my way 'round to it but –

MR. BORDEN: What's so difficult about telling Lizzie Johnny MacLeod wants to call?

EMMA: Then why don't you tell her? I'm always the one that has to go running to Lizzie telling her this and telling her that, and taking the abuse for it!

MRS. BORDEN: We all know why that is, she can wrap her father 'round her little finger, always has, always could. If everything else fails, she throws a tantrum and her father buys her off, trip to Europe, rent to the mill house, it's all the same.

EMMA: Papa, what's Harry here for?

MR. BORDEN: None of your business.

MRS. BORDEN: And don't you go runnin' to Lizzie stirring things up.

EMMA: You know I've never done that!

MR. BORDEN: What she means –

EMMA: (*with anger but little fatigue*) I'm tired, do you hear? Tired! (*She gets up from the table and leaves for upstairs.*)

MR. BORDEN: Emma!

EMMA: You ask Harry here, you know there'll be trouble, and when I try to find out what's going on, so once again good old Emma can stand between you and Lizzie, all you've got to say is "none of your business!" Well then, it's *your* business, you look after it, because I'm not! (*She exits.*)

MRS. BORDEN: ... She's right.

MR. BORDEN: That's enough. I've had enough. I don't want to hear from you, too.

MRS. BORDEN: I'm only saying she's right. You have to talk straight and plain to Lizzie and tell her things she don't want to hear.

MR. BORDEN: About the farm?

MRS. BORDEN: About Johnny MacLeod! Keep your mouth shut about the farm and she won't know the difference.

MR. BORDEN: All right.

MRS. BORDEN: Speak to her about Johnny MacLeod.

MR. BORDEN: All right!

MRS. BORDEN: You know what they're saying in town. About her and that doctor.

MISS LIZZIE / BRIDGET speaks to THE ACTRESS / LIZZIE.

MISS LIZZIE / BRIDGET: They're saying if you live on Second Street and you need a house call, and you don't mind the Irish, call Dr. Patrick. Dr. Patrick is very prompt with his Second Street house calls.

THE ACTRESS / LIZZIE: Do they really say that?

MISS LIZZIE / BRIDGET: No, they don't. I'm telling a lie. But he is very prompt with a Second Street call. Do you know why that is?

THE ACTRESS / LIZZIE: Why?

MISS LIZZIE / BRIDGET: Well – he's hoping to see someone who lives on Second Street – someone who's yanking up her skirt and showing her ankle so she can take a decent-sized step – and forgetting everything she was ever taught in Miss Cornelia's School for Girls, and talking to the Irish as if she never heard of the Pope! Oh yes, he's very prompt getting to Second Street ... Getting away is something else ... (*She watches what follows.*)

DR. PATRICK: Good morning, Miss Borden!

LIZZIE: I haven't decided ... if it is ... or it isn't ...

DR. PATRICK: No, you've got it all wrong. The proper phrase is, "Good morning, Dr. Patrick," and then you smile, discreetly of course, and lower the eyes just a titch, twirl the parasol –

LIZZIE: The parasol?

DR. PATRICK: The parasol, but not too fast; and then you murmur in a voice that was ever sweet and low, "And how are you doin' this morning, Dr. Patrick?" Your education's been sadly neglected, Miss Borden.

LIZZIE: You're forgetting something. You're married – and Irish besides – I'm supposed to ignore you.

DR. PATRICK: Nooo.

LIZZIE: Yes. Don't you realize Papa and Emma have fits every time we engage in "illicit conversation." They're having fits right now.

DR. PATRICK: Well, does Mrs. Borden approve?

LIZZIE: Ahhh. She's the real reason I keep stopping and talking. Mrs. Borden is easily shocked. I'm hoping she dies from the shock.

DR. PATRICK: (*laughing*) Why don't you ... run away from home, Lizzie?

LIZZIE: Why don't you "run away" with me?

DR. PATRICK: Where'll we go?

LIZZIE: Boston.

DR. PATRICK: Boston?

LIZZIE: For a start.

DR. PATRICK: And when will we go?

LIZZIE: Tonight.

DR. PATRICK: But you don't really mean it, you're havin' me on.

LIZZIE: I do mean it.

DR. PATRICK: How can you joke – and look so serious?

LIZZIE: It's a gift.

DR. PATRICK: (*laughing*) Oh Lizzie –

LIZZIE: Look!

DR. PATRICK: What is it?

LIZZIE: It's those little beggars next door. Hey! Hey, get away! Get away there! ... They break into the shed to get at my birds and Papa gets angry.

DR. PATRICK: They're kids, it's a natural thing.

LIZZIE: Well, Papa doesn't like it.

DR. PATRICK: They just want to look at the birds.

LIZZIE: Papa says what's his is his own – you need a formal invitation to get into our yard ... (*pause*) How's your wife?

DR. PATRICK: My wife.

LIZZIE: Shouldn't I ask that? I thought nice polite ladies always inquired after the wives of their friends or acquaintances or ... whatever.

HARRY enters and observes them.

DR. PATRICK: You've met my wife, my wife is always the same.

LIZZIE: How boring for you.

DR. PATRICK: Uh-huh.

LIZZIE: And for her.

DR. PATRICK: Yes, indeed.

LIZZIE: And for me.

DR. PATRICK: Do you know what they say, Lizzie? They say if you live on Second Street, and you need a house call, and you don't mind the Irish, call Dr. Patrick. Dr. Patrick is very prompt with his Second Street house calls.

LIZZIE: I'll tell you what I've heard them say – Second Street is a nice place to visit, but you wouldn't want to live there. I certainly don't.

HARRY: Lizzie.

LIZZIE: Well, look who's here. Have you had the pleasure of meeting my uncle, Mr. Wingate.

DR. PATRICK: No, Miss Borden, that pleasure has never been mine.

LIZZIE: That's exactly how I feel.

DR. PATRICK: Mr. Wingate, sir.

HARRY: Dr. ... Patrick is it?

DR. PATRICK: Yes it is, sir.

HARRY: Who's sick? (*In other words, "What the hell are you doing here?"*)

LIZZIE: No one. He just dropped by for a visit; you see, Dr. Patrick and I are very old, very dear friends, isn't that so?

HARRY stares at DR. PATRICK.

DR. PATRICK: Well ... (*LIZZIE jabs him in the ribs.*) Ouch! It's her sense of humour, sir ... a rare trait in a woman.

HARRY: You best get in, Lizzie, it's gettin' on for lunch.

LIZZIE: Don't be silly, we just had breakfast.

HARRY: You best get in!

LIZZIE: ... Would you give me your arm, Dr. Patrick? (*She moves away with DR. PATRICK, ignoring HARRY.*)

DR. PATRICK: Now see what you've done?

LIZZIE: What?

DR. PATRICK: You've broken two of my ribs and ruined my reputation all in one blow.

LIZZIE: It's impossible to ruin an Irishman's reputation.

DR. PATRICK: I'll be seeing you, Lizzie ...

MISS LIZZIE / BRIDGET: They're sayin' it's time you were married.

LIZZIE: What time is that?

MISS LIZZIE / BRIDGET: You need a place of your own.

LIZZIE: How would getting married get me that?

MISS LIZZIE / BRIDGET: Though I don't know what man would put up with your moods!

LIZZIE: What about me putting up with his!

MISS LIZZIE / BRIDGET: Oh Lizzie!

LIZZIE: What's the matter, don't men have moods?

Their laugh is interrupted by HARRY and they watch the following.

HARRY: I'm tellin' you, as God is my witness, she's out in the walk talkin' to that Irish doctor, and he's fallin' all over her.

MRS. BORDEN: What's the matter with you. For her own sake you should speak to her.

MR. BORDEN: I will.

HARRY: The talk around town can't be doin' you any good.

MRS. BORDEN: Harry's right.

HARRY: Yes, sir.

MRS. BORDEN: He's tellin' you what you should know.

HARRY: If a man can't manage his own daughter, how the hell can he manage a business – that's what people say, and it don't matter a damn whether there's any sense in it or not.

MR. BORDEN: I know that.

MRS. BORDEN: Knowin' is one thing, doin' something about it is another. What're you goin' to do about it?

MR. BORDEN: Goddamn it! I said I was goin' to speak to her and I am!

MRS. BORDEN: Well, speak good and plain this time!

MR. BORDEN: Jesus Christ, woman!

MRS. BORDEN: Your "speakin' to Lizzie" is a ritual around here.

MR. BORDEN: Abbie –

MRS. BORDEN: She talks, you listen, and nothin' changes!

MR. BORDEN: That's enough!

MRS. BORDEN: Emma isn't the only one that's fed up to the teeth!

MR. BORDEN: Shut up!

MRS. BORDEN: You're gettin' old, Andrew! You're gettin' old! (*She exits.*)

An air of embarrassment from MR. BORDEN at having words in front of HARRY. MR. BORDEN fumbles with his pipe.

HARRY: (*offering his pouch of tobacco*) Here ... have some of mine.

MR. BORDEN: Don't mind if I do ... Nice mix.

HARRY: It is.

MR. BORDEN: ... I used to think ... by my seventies ... I'd be bouncin' a grandson on my knee ...

HARRY: Not too late for that.

MR. BORDEN: Nope ... never had any boys ... and girls ... don't seem to have the same sense of family ... You know it's all well and good to talk about speakin' plain to Lizzie, but the truth of the matter is, if Lizzie puts her mind to a thing, she does it, and if she don't, she don't.

HARRY: It's up to you to see she does.

MR. BORDEN: It's like Abigail says, knowin' is one thing, doin' is another ... You're lucky you never brought any children into the world, Harry, you don't have to deal with them.

HARRY: Now that's no way to be talkin'.

MR. BORDEN: There's Emma ... Emma's a good girl ... when Abbie and I get on, there'll always be Emma ... Well! You're not sittin' here to listen to me and my girls, are you, you didn't come here for that. Business, eh, Harry?

HARRY whips out a sheet of figures. The men study them.

MISS LIZZIE / BRIDGET: I can remember distinctly ... that moment I was undressing for bed, and I looked at my knees – and there were no scabs! At last! I thought I'm the nice little girl Emma wants me to be! But it wasn't that at all. I was just growing up. I didn't fall down so often ... (*She smiles.*) Do you suppose ... do you suppose there's a formula, a magic formula for being "a woman"? Do you suppose every girl baby receives it at birth, it's the last thing that happens just before birth, the magic formula is stamped indelibly on the brain – Ka Thud!! (*Her mood of amusement changes.*) ... And through some terrible oversight ... perhaps the death of my mother ... I didn't get that "Ka Thud"!! I was born ... defective.

LIZZIE: (*low*) No.

MISS LIZZIE / BRIDGET: Not defective?

LIZZIE: Just ... born.

THE DEFENCE: Gentlemen of the Jury! I ask you to look at the defendant, Miss Lizzie Borden. I ask you to recall the nature of the crime of which she is accused. I ask you – do you believe Miss Lizzie Borden, the youngest daughter of a scion of our community, a recipient of the fullest amenities our society can bestow upon its most fortunate members, do you believe Miss Lizzie Borden capable of wielding the murder weapon – thirty-two blows, gentlemen, thirty-two blows – fracturing Abigail Borden's skull, leaving her bloody and broken body in an upstairs bedroom; then, Miss Borden, with no hint of frenzy, hysteria, or trace of blood upon her person, engages in casual conversation with the maid, Bridget O'Sullivan, while awaiting her father's return home, upon which, after sending Bridget to her attic room, Miss Borden deals thirteen blows to the head of her father, and minutes later – in a state utterly compatible with that of a loving daughter upon discovery of murder most foul – Miss Borden calls for aid! Is this the aid we give her? Accusation of the most heinous and infamous of crimes? Do you believe Miss Lizzie Borden capable of these acts? I can tell you I do not!! I can tell you these acts of violence are acts of madness!! Gentlemen! If this gentlewoman is capable of such an act – I say to you – look to your daughters – if this gentlewoman is capable of such an act, which of us can lie abed at night, hear a step upon the stairs, a rustle in the hall, a creak outside the door? ... Which of you can plump your pillow, nudge your wife, close your eyes, and sleep? Gentlemen, Lizzie Borden is not mad. Gentlemen, Lizzie Borden is not guilty.

ACTRESS / LIZZIE steps into the scene.

MR. BORDEN: Lizzie?

LIZZIE: Papa ... have you and Harry got business?

HARRY: 'Lo, Lizzie. I'll, ah ... finish up later. (*He exits with the figures. LIZZIE watches him go.*)

MR. BORDEN: Lizzie?

LIZZIE: What?

MR. BORDEN: Could you sit down a minute?

LIZZIE: If it's about Dr. Patrick again, I –

MR. BORDEN: It isn't.

LIZZIE: Good.

MR. BORDEN: But we could start there.

LIZZIE: Oh Papa.

MR. BORDEN: Sit down, Lizzie.

LIZZIE: But I've heard it all before, another chat for a wayward girl.

MR. BORDEN: (*gently*) Bite your tongue, Lizzie.

She smiles at him. There is affection between them. She has the qualities he would like in a son but deplores in a daughter.

MR. BORDEN: Now ... first off ... I want you to know that I ... understand about you and the doctor.

LIZZIE: What do you understand?

MR. BORDEN: I understand ... that it's a natural thing.

LIZZIE: What is?

MR. BORDEN: I'm saying there's nothing unnatural about an attraction between a man and a woman. That's a natural thing.

LIZZIE: I find Dr. Patrick ... amusing and entertaining ... if that's what you mean, is that what you mean?

MR. BORDEN: This attraction ... points something up – you're a woman of thirty-four years –

LIZZIE: I know that.

MR. BORDEN: Just listen to me, Lizzie. I'm choosing my words, and I want you to listen. Now ... in most circumstances ... a woman of your age would be married, eh? Have children, be running her own house, that's the natural thing, eh? (*pause*) Eh, Lizzie?

LIZZIE: I don't know.

MR. BORDEN: Of course you do.

LIZZIE: You're saying I'm unnatural. Am I supposed to agree, is that what you want?

MR. BORDEN: No, I'm not saying that! I'm saying the opposite to that! ... I'm saying the feelings you have toward Dr. Patrick –

LIZZIE: What feelings?

MR. BORDEN: What's ... what's happening there, I can understand, but what you have to understand is that he's a married man, and there's nothing for you there.

LIZZIE: If he weren't married, Papa, I wouldn't be bothered talking to him! It's just a game, Papa, it's a game.

MR. BORDEN: A game.

LIZZIE: You have no idea how boring it is looking eligible, interested, and alluring, when I feel none of the three. So I play games. And it's a blessed relief to talk to a married man.

MR. BORDEN: What're his feelings for you?

LIZZIE: I don't know, I don't care. Can I go now?

MR. BORDEN: I'm not finished yet! ... You know Mr. MacLeod, Johnny MacLeod?

LIZZIE: I know his three little monsters.

MR. BORDEN: He's trying to raise three boys with no mother!

LIZZIE: That's not my problem! I'm going.

MR. BORDEN: Lizzie!

LIZZIE: What!

MR. BORDEN: Mr. MacLeod's asked to come over next Tuesday.

LIZZIE: I'll be out that night.

MR. BORDEN: No, you won't!

LIZZIE: Yes, I will! Whose idea was this?

MR. BORDEN: No one's.

LIZZIE: That's a lie. She wants to get rid of me.

MR. BORDEN: I want what's best for you!

LIZZIE: No, you don't! 'Cause you don't care what I want!

MR. BORDEN: You don't know what you want!

LIZZIE: But I know what you want! You want me living my life by the *Farmers' Almanac*; having everyone over for Christmas dinner; waiting up for my husband; and *serving at socials*!

MR. BORDEN: It's good enough for your mother!

LIZZIE: She is *not* my *mother*!

MR. BORDEN: ... John MacLeod is looking for a wife.

LIZZIE: No, goddamn it, he isn't!

MR. BORDEN: Lizzie!

LIZZIE: He's looking for a housekeeper and it isn't going to be me!

MR. BORDEN: You've a filthy mouth!

LIZZIE: Is that why you hate me?

MR. BORDEN: You don't make sense.

LIZZIE: Why is it when I pretend things I don't feel, that's when you like me?

MR. BORDEN: You talk foolish.

LIZZIE: I'm supposed to be a mirror. I'm supposed to reflect what you want to see, but everyone wants something different. If no one looks in the mirror, I'm not even there, I don't exist!

MR. BORDEN: Lizzie, you talk foolish!

LIZZIE: No, I don't, that isn't true.

MR. BORDEN: About Mr. MacLeod –

LIZZIE: You can't make me get married!

MR. BORDEN: Lizzie, do you want to spend the rest of your life in this house?

LIZZIE: No! No. I want out of it, but I won't get married to do it.

MRS. BORDEN: (*on her way through to the kitchen*) You've never been asked.

LIZZIE: Oh listen to her! I must be some sort of failure, then, eh? You had no son and a daughter that failed! What does that make you, Papa!

MR. BORDEN: I want you to think about Johnny MacLeod!

LIZZIE: To hell with him!

MR. BORDEN appears defeated. After a moment, LIZZIE goes to him, holds his hand, strokes his hair.

LIZZIE: Papa? ... Papa, I love you, I try to be what you want, really I do try, I try ... but ... I don't want to get married. I wouldn't be a good mother, I –

MR. BORDEN: How do you know –

LIZZIE: I know it! ... I want out of all this ... I hate this house, I hate ... I want out. Try to understand how I feel ... Why can't I do something? ... Eh? I mean ... I could ... I could go into your office ... I could ... learn how to keep books, I could –

MR. BORDEN: Lizzie.

LIZZIE: Why can't I do something like that?

MR. BORDEN: For God's sake, talk sensible.

LIZZIE: All right then! Why can't we move up on the hill to a house where we aren't in each other's laps!

MRS. BORDEN: (*returning from kitchen*) Why don't you move out!

LIZZIE: Give me the money and I'll go!

MRS. BORDEN: Money.

LIZZIE: And give me enough that I won't ever have to come back!

MRS. BORDEN: She always gets 'round to money!

LIZZIE: You drive me to it!

MRS. BORDEN: She's crazy!

LIZZIE: You drive me to it!

MRS. BORDEN: She should be locked up!

LIZZIE: (*beginning to smash the plates in the dining room*) There!! There!!

MR. BORDEN: Lizzie!

MRS. BORDEN: Stop her!

LIZZIE: There!

MR. BORDEN attempts to restrain her.

MRS. BORDEN: For God's sake, Andrew!

LIZZIE: Lock me up! Lock me up!

MR. BORDEN: Stop it! Lizzie!

LIZZIE: (*collapsing against him, crying*) Oh Papa, I can't stand it.

MR. BORDEN: There, there, come on now, it's all right, listen to me, Lizzie, it's all right.

MRS. BORDEN: You may as well get down on your knees.

LIZZIE: Look at her. She's jealous of me. She can't stand it whenever you're nice to me.

MR. BORDEN: There now.

MRS. BORDEN: Ask her about Dr. Patrick.

MR. BORDEN: I'll handle this my way.

LIZZIE: He's an entertaining person, there're very few around!

MRS. BORDEN: Fall River ain't Paris and ain't that a shame for our Lizzie!

LIZZIE: One trip three years ago and you're still harping on it; it's true, Papa, an elephant never forgets!

MR. BORDEN: Show some respect!

LIZZIE: She's a fat cow and I hate her!

MR. BORDEN slaps LIZZIE. There is a pause as he regains control of himself.

MR. BORDEN: Now ... now ... you'll see Mr. MacLeod Tuesday night.

LIZZIE: No.

MR. BORDEN: Goddamn it!! I said you'll see Johnny MacLeod Tuesday night!!

LIZZIE: No.

MR. BORDEN: Get the hell upstairs to your room!

LIZZIE: No.

MR. BORDEN: I'm telling you to go upstairs to your room!!

LIZZIE: I'll go when I'm ready.

MR. BORDEN: I said, Go!

He grabs her arm to move her forcibly. She hits his arm away.

LIZZIE: No! ... There's something you don't understand, Papa. You can't make me do one thing that I don't want to do. I'm going to keep on doing just what I want just when I want – like always!

MR. BORDEN shoves her to the floor to gain a clear exit from the room, stops on the stairs, looks back to her on the floor. He'd like to say "sorry" but is unable. He continues off.

MRS. BORDEN: You know, Lizzie, your father keeps you. You know you got nothing but what he gives you. And that's a fact of life. You got to come to deal with facts. I did.

LIZZIE: And married Papa.

MRS. BORDEN: And married your father. You never made it easy for me. I took on a man with two little ones, and Emma was your mother.

LIZZIE: You got stuck so I should too, is that it?

MRS. BORDEN: What?

LIZZIE: The reason I should marry Johnny MacLeod.

MRS. BORDEN: I just know, this time, in the end, you'll do what your papa says, you'll see.

LIZZIE: No, I won't. I have a right. A right that frees me from all that.

MRS. BORDEN: No, Lizzie, you got no rights.

LIZZIE: I've a legal right to one-third because I am his flesh and blood.

MRS. BORDEN: What you don't understand is your father's not dead yet, your father's got many good years ahead of him, and when his time comes, well, we'll see what his will says then ... Your father's no fool, Lizzie ... Only a fool would leave his money to you. (*She exits.*)

After a moment, BRIDGET enters from the kitchen.

BRIDGET: Ah Lizzie ... you outdid yourself that time. (*comforting LIZZIE*) ... Yes, you did ... an elephant never forgets!

LIZZIE: Oh Bridget.

BRIDGET: Come on now.

LIZZIE: I can't help it.

BRIDGET: Sure you can ... sure you can ... stop your cryin' and come and sit down ... you want me to tell you a story?

LIZZIE: No.

BRIDGET: Sure, a story. I'll tell you a story. Come on now ... now ... before I worked here I worked up on the hill and the lady of the house ... are you listenin'? Well, she swore by her cook, finest cook in creation, yes, always bowin' and scrapin' and smilin' and givin' up her day off if company arrived. Oh, the lady of the house, she loved that cook – and I'll tell you her name! It was Mary! Now listen! Do you know what Mary was doin'? (*LIZZIE shakes her head.*) Before eatin', the master'd serve drinks in the parlour – and out in the kitchen, Mary'd be spittin' in the soup!

LIZZIE: What?

BRIDGET: She'd spit in the soup! And she'd smile when they served it!

LIZZIE: No.

BRIDGET: Yes. I've seen her cut up hair for an omelette.

LIZZIE: You're lying.

BRIDGET: Cross me heart. They thought it was pepper!

LIZZIE: Oh Bridget!

BRIDGET: These two eyes have seen her season up mutton stew when it's off and gone bad.

LIZZIE: Gone bad?

BRIDGET: Oh and they et it, every bit, and the next day they was hit with ... *stomach flu*! So cook called it. Bejesus, Lizzie, I daren't tell you what she served up in their food, for fear you'd be sick!

LIZZIE: That's funny ... (*A fact – LIZZIE does not appear amused.*)

BRIDGET: (*starting to clear up the dishes*) Yes, well, I'm tellin' you I kept on the good side of cook.

LIZZIE: (*watching her for a moment*) ... Do you ... like me?

BRIDGET: Sure, I do ... You should try bein' more like cook, Lizzie. Smile and get 'round them. You can do it.

LIZZIE: It's not ... *fair* that I have to.

BRIDGET: There ain't nothin' fair in this world.

LIZZIE: Well then ... well then, I don't want to!

BRIDGET: You dream, Lizzie ... you dream dreams ... Work? Be sensible. What could you do?

LIZZIE: I could –

MISS LIZZIE / BRIDGET: No.

LIZZIE: I could –

MISS LIZZIE / BRIDGET: No.

LIZZIE: I could –

MISS LIZZIE / BRIDGET: No!

LIZZIE: I ... dream.

MISS LIZZIE / BRIDGET: You dream ... of a carousel ... you see a carousel ... you see lights that go on and go off ... you see yourself on a carousel horse, a red-painted horse with its head in the air, and green staring eyes, and a white flowing mane, it looks wild! ... It goes up and comes down, and the carousel whirls round with the music and lights, on and off ... and you watch ... watch yourself on the horse. You're wearing a mask, a white mask like the mane of the horse, it looks like your face except that it's rigid and white ... and it changes! With each flick of the lights, the expression, it changes, but always so rigid and hard, like the flesh of the horse that is red that you ride. You ride with no hands! No hands on this petrified horse, its head flung in the air, its wide staring eyes like those of a doe run down by the dogs! ... And each time you go 'round, your hands rise a fraction nearer the mask ... and the music and the carousel and the horse, they all three slow down, and they stop ... You can reach out and touch ... you ... you on the horse ... with your hands so at the eyes ... You look into the eyes! (*A sound from LIZZIE: she is horrified and frightened. She covers her eyes.*) There are none! None! Just black holes in a white mask ... (*pause*) The eyes of your birds ... are round ... and bright ... a light shines from inside ... they ... can see into your heart ... they're pretty ... they love you.

MR. BORDEN: I want this settled, Harry, I want it settled while Lizzie's out back.

MISS LIZZIE / BRIDGET draws LIZZIE's attention to the MR. BORDEN–HARRY scene. LIZZIE listens and will move closer.

HARRY: You know I'm for that.

MR. BORDEN: I want it all done but the signin' of the papers tomorrow, that's if I decide to –

HARRY: You can't lose, Andrew. That farm's just lyin' fallow.

MR. BORDEN: Well, let's see what you got.

HARRY: (*getting out his papers*) Look at this ... I'll run horse auctions and a buggy rental – now I'll pay no rent for the house or pasturage but you get 20 per cent, eh? That figure there –

MR. BORDEN: Mmmn.

HARRY: From my horse auctions last year, it'll go up on the farm and you'll get 20 per cent off the top ... My buggy rental won't do so well ... that's that figure there, approximate ... but it all adds up, eh? Adds up for you.

MR. BORDEN: It's a good deal, Harry, but ...

HARRY: Now I know why you're worried – but the farm will still be in the family, no worry there 'cause aren't I family? And whenever you or the girls want to come over for a visit, why I'll send a buggy from the rental, no need for you to have the expense of a horse, eh?

MR. BORDEN: It looks good on paper.

HARRY: There's ... ah, something else, it's a bit awkward but I got to mention it. I'll be severin' a lot of my present connections, and what I figure I've a right to is some kind of guarantee ...

MR. BORDEN: You mean a renewable lease for the farm?

HARRY: Well – what I'm wondering is ... No offence, but you're an older man, Andrew ... now if something should happen to you, where would the farm stand in regards to your will? That's what I'm wondering.

MR. BORDEN: I've not made a will.

HARRY: You know best – but I wouldn't want to be in a position where Lizzie would be havin' anything to do with that farm. The less she knows now the better, but she's bound to find out – I don't feel I'm steppin' out of line by bringin' this up.

LIZZIE is within earshot. She is staring at HARRY and MR. BORDEN. They do not see her.

MR. BORDEN: No.

HARRY: If you mind, you come right out and say so.

MR. BORDEN: That's all right.

HARRY: Now ... if you ... put the farm – in Abbie's name, what do you think?

MR. BORDEN: I don't know, Harry.

HARRY: I don't want to push.

MR. BORDEN: ... I should make a will ... I want the girls looked after, it don't seem like they'll marry ... and Abbie, she's younger than me, I know Emma will see to her, still ... moneywise I got to consider these things ... It makes a difference, no men in the family.

HARRY: You know you can count on me for whatever.

MR. BORDEN: If ... *If* I changed title to the farm, Abbie'd have to come down to the bank, I wouldn't want Lizzie to know.

HARRY: You can send a note for Abbie when you get to the bank; she can say it's a note from a friend, and then come down and meet you. Simple as that.

MR. BORDEN: I'll give it some thought.

HARRY: You see, Abbie owns the farm, it's no difference to you, but it gives me protection.

MR. BORDEN: Who's there?

HARRY: It's Lizzie.

MR. BORDEN: What do you want? ... Did you lock the shed? ... Is the shed locked! Did – You – Lock – the Shed! (*LIZZIE makes a slow motion which MR. BORDEN takes for assent.*) Well, you make sure it stays locked! I don't want any more of those damned kids in this yard! (*an awkward pause as MR. BORDEN and HARRY exchange a look*) ... I ... ah ... I think ... we about covered everything, Harry, we'll, ah, we'll let it go till tomorrow.

HARRY: Tomorrow then. Good enough ... well ... I'll just finish choppin' that kindlin', give a shout when it's lunchtime. (*He exits.*)

LIZZIE and MR. BORDEN stare at each other for a moment.

LIZZIE: (*very low*) What are you doing with the farm?

MR. BORDEN slowly picks up the papers and places them in his pocket.

LIZZIE: Papa? ... Papa! ...

The faint sound of children in the yard at the shed and the birds. It will grow in volume under the dialogue.

MR. BORDEN: What?

LIZZIE: Papa –

MR. BORDEN: What!

LIZZIE: I would like you to show me, what you put, in your pocket.

MR. BORDEN: It's none of your business.

A faint yell from HARRY out in the yard as the sound of the children is growing more frenzied. Sounds from outside happen simultaneously with the argument between LIZZIE and MR. BORDEN.

LIZZIE: I want you to show me!

MR. BORDEN: I said, it's none of your business!

LIZZIE: The farm is my business!

Another faint cry from HARRY attempting in vain to drive the children away.

MR. BORDEN: It's nothing.

LIZZIE: You show me!

MR. BORDEN: I said it's nothing!

LIZZIE makes a quick move toward her father to seize the paper from his pocket. Even more quickly and smartly he slaps her face. The voices of the children build in volume.

HARRY: (*bursts in carrying the hatchet*) Kids in the shed!

MR. BORDEN: Jesus Christ!

LIZZIE: What about the farm!

MR. BORDEN: You! You and those goddamn birds! I've told you! I've told you!

LIZZIE: What about the farm!

MR. BORDEN: Jesus Christ ... You never listen! Never!

HARRY: Andrew!

MR. BORDEN: I've told you time and again!

LIZZIE: (*still attempting to get the paper*) What about the farm!

MR. BORDEN: You never listen!

HARRY: Those kids!

MR. BORDEN: Never!

LIZZIE: Papa –

MR. BORDEN: (*He grabs the hatchet from HARRY and turns on LIZZIE.*) There'll be no more of your goddamn birds in this yard!!

LIZZIE: No, Papa ...

MR. BORDEN raises the hatchet and smashes it into the table as LIZZIE screams. The sound of the children's voices is at its loudest.

LIZZIE: Nooo!!

Silence. The sound of the voices is gone. The hatchet is embedded in the table. MR. BORDEN and HARRY assume a soft freeze as THE ACTRESS / LIZZIE turns to see MISS LIZZIE observing the scene.

THE ACTRESS / LIZZIE: No.

MISS LIZZIE: I loved them.

Blackout.

ACT TWO

Lights come up on THE ACTRESS / LIZZIE sitting at the dining-room table. She is very still, her hands clasped in her lap. MISS LIZZIE / BRIDGET is near her. She too is very still. A pause.

THE ACTRESS / LIZZIE: (*very low*) Talk to me.

MISS LIZZIE / BRIDGET: I remember ...

THE ACTRESS / LIZZIE: (*very low*) No.

MISS LIZZIE / BRIDGET: On the farm, Papa's farm, Harry's farm, when I was little and thought it was my farm and I loved it, we had some puppies, the farm dog had puppies, brown soft little puppies with brown ey– (*She does not complete the word "eyes."*) And ... one of the puppies got sick. I didn't know it was sick, it seemed like the others, but the mother, she knew. It would lie at the back of the box, she would lie in front of it while she nursed all the others. They ignored it, that puppy didn't exist for the others ... I think inside it was different, and the mother thought the difference she sensed was a sickness ... and after a while ... anyone could tell it was sick. It had nothing to eat! And Papa took it and drowned it. That's what you do on a farm with things that are different.

THE ACTRESS / LIZZIE: Am I different?

MISS LIZZIE / BRIDGET: You kill them.

THE ACTRESS / LIZZIE looks at MISS LIZZIE / BRIDGET, who looks toward the top of the stairs. MISS LIZZIE / BRIDGET gets up and exits to the kitchen. EMMA appears at the top of the stairs. She is dressed for travel and carries a small suitcase and her gloves. She stares down at LIZZIE still sitting at the table. After several moments LIZZIE becomes aware of that gaze and turns to look at EMMA, who then descends the stairs. She puts down her suitcase. She is not overjoyed at seeing LIZZIE, having hoped to get away before she arose; nevertheless, she begins with an excess of enthusiasm to cover the implications of her departure.

EMMA: Well! You're up early ... Bridget down? ... Did you put the coffee on? (*She puts her gloves on the table.*) My goodness, Lizzie, cat got your tongue? (*She exits to the kitchen. LIZZIE picks up the gloves. EMMA returns.*) Bridget's down, she's in the kitchen ... Well, looks like a real scorcher today, doesn't it?

LIZZIE: What's the bag for?

EMMA: I ... decided I might go for a little trip, a day or two, get away from the heat ... The girls've rented a place out beach way and I thought ... with the weather and all ...

LIZZIE: How can you do that?

EMMA: Do what? ... Anyway, I thought I might stay with them a few days ... Why don't you come with me?

LIZZIE: No.

EMMA: Just for a few days, come with me.

LIZZIE: No.

EMMA: You know you like the water.

LIZZIE: I said no!

EMMA: Oh Lizzie.

Pause.

LIZZIE: I don't see how you can leave me like this.

EMMA: I asked you to come with me.

LIZZIE: You know I can't do that.

EMMA: Why not?

LIZZIE: Someone has to *do* something, you just run away from things.

EMMA: ... Lizzie ... I'm sorry about the – (*She stops before saying "birds."*)

LIZZIE: No!

EMMA: Papa was angry.

LIZZIE: I don't want to talk about it.

EMMA: He's sorry now.

LIZZIE: Nobody *listens* to me, can't you hear me? I said *don't* talk about it. I don't want to talk about it. Stop talking about it!!

BRIDGET enters with the coffee.

EMMA: Thank you, Bridget.

MISS LIZZIE / BRIDGET sits in the parlour and watches.

EMMA: Well! ... I certainly can use this this morning ... Your coffee's there.

LIZZIE: I don't want it.

EMMA: You're going to ruin those gloves.

LIZZIE: I don't care.

EMMA: Since they're not yours.

LIZZIE bangs the gloves down on the table. A pause. Then EMMA picks them up and smooths them out.

LIZZIE: Why are you leaving me?

EMMA: I feel like a visit with the girls. Is there something wrong with that?

LIZZIE: How can you go now?

EMMA: I don't know what you're getting at.

LIZZIE: I heard them. I heard them talking yesterday. Do you know what they're saying?

EMMA: How could I?

LIZZIE: "How could I?" What do you mean "How could I?" Did you know?

EMMA: No, Lizzie, I did not.

LIZZIE: *Did-not-what.*

EMMA: Know.

LIZZIE: But you know now. How do you know now?

EMMA: I've put two and two together and I'm going over to the girls' for a visit!

LIZZIE: Please, Emma!

EMMA: It's too hot.

LIZZIE: I need you, don't go.

EMMA: I've been talking about this trip.

LIZZIE: That's a lie.

EMMA: They're expecting me.

LIZZIE: You're lying to me!

EMMA: I'm going to the girls' place. You can come if you want, you can stay if you want. I planned this trip and I'm taking it!

LIZZIE: Stop lying!

EMMA: If I want to tell a little white lie to avoid an altercation in this house, I'll do so. Other people have been doing it for years!

LIZZIE: You don't understand, you don't understand anything.

EMMA: Oh, I understand enough.

LIZZIE: You don't! Let me explain it to you. You listen carefully, you listen ... Harry's getting the farm, can you understand that? Harry is here and he's moving on the farm and he's going to be there, on the farm, living on the farm. *Our farm.* Do you understand that? ... Do you understand that!

EMMA: Yes.

LIZZIE: Harry's going to be on the farm. That's the first thing. No ... no, it isn't ... The first thing ... was the mill house, that was the first thing! And *now* the farm. You see there's a pattern, Emma, you can see that, can't you?

EMMA: I don't –

LIZZIE: You can see it! The mill house, then the farm, and the next thing is the papers for the farm – do you know what he's doing, Papa's doing? He's signing the farm over to her. It will never be ours, we will never have it, not ever. It's ours by rights, don't you feel that?

EMMA: The farm – has always meant a great deal to me, yes.

LIZZIE: Then what are you doing about it! You can't leave me now ... but that's not all. Papa's going to make a will, and you can see the pattern, can't you, and if the pattern keeps on, what do you suppose his will will say. What do you suppose, answer me!

EMMA: I don't know.

LIZZIE: Say it!

EMMA: He'll see we're looked after.

LIZZIE: I don't want to be looked after! What's the matter with you? Do you really want to spend the rest of your life with that cow, listening to her drone on and on for years! That's just what they think you'll do. Papa'll leave you a monthly allowance, just like he'll leave me, just enough to keep us all living together. We'll be worth millions on paper, and be stuck in this house and by and by Papa will die and Harry will move in and you will wait on that cow while she gets fatter and fatter and I – will – sit – in my room.

EMMA: Lizzie.

LIZZIE: We have to do something, you can see that. We have to do something.

EMMA: There's nothing we can do.

LIZZIE: Don't say that!

EMMA: All right, then, what can we do?

LIZZIE: I ... I ... don't know. But we have to do something, you have to help me, you can't go away and leave me alone, you can't do that.

EMMA: Then –

LIZZIE: You know what I thought? I thought you could talk to him, really talk to him, make him understand that we're people. *Individual people,* and we have to live separate lives, and his will should make it possible for us to do that. And the farm can't go to Harry.

EMMA: You know it's no use.

LIZZIE: I can't talk to him anymore. Every time I talk to him I make everything worse. I hate him, no. No, I don't. I hate *her.* (*EMMA looks at her brooch watch.*) Don't look at the time.

EMMA: I'll miss my connections.

LIZZIE: No!

EMMA: (*putting on her gloves*) Lizzie. There's certain things we have to face. One of them is, we can't change a thing.

LIZZIE: I won't let you go!

EMMA: I'll be back on the weekend.

LIZZIE: He killed my birds! He took the axe and he killed them! Emma, I ran out and held them in my hands, I felt their hearts throbbing and pumping and the blood gushed out of their necks, it was all over my hands, don't you care about that?

EMMA: I ... I ... have a train to catch.

MISS LIZZIE: He didn't care how much he hurt me, and you don't care either. Nobody cares.

EMMA: I have to go now.

MISS LIZZIE: That's right. Go away. I don't even like you, Emma. Go away! (*EMMA leaves. LIZZIE runs after her, calling.*) I'm sorry for all the things I told you! Things I really felt! You pretended to me, and I don't like you!! Go away!!

LIZZIE looks after EMMA's departing figure. After a moment, she slowly turns back into the room. MISS LIZZIE / BRIDGET is there.

LIZZIE: I want to die ... I want to die, but something inside won't let me ... inside something says no. (*She shuts her eyes.*) I can do anything.

THE DEFENCE: Miss Borden. (*Both LIZZIEs turn, mirror images of each other.*) Could you describe the sequence of events upon your father's arrival home?

MISS LIZZIE: (*unemotional and flat recital*) Papa came in ... we exchanged a few words ... Bridget and I spoke of the yard-goods sale downtown, whether she would buy some. She went up to her room ...

THE DEFENCE: And then?

MISS LIZZIE: I went out back ... through the yard ... I picked up several pears from the ground beneath the trees ... I went into the shed ... I stood looking out the window and ate the pears ...

THE DEFENCE: How many?

LIZZIE: Four.

THE DEFENCE: It wasn't warm, stifling in the shed?

LIZZIE: No, it was cool.

THE DEFENCE: What were you doing, apart from eating the pears?

LIZZIE: I suppose I was thinking. I just stood there, looking out the window, thinking, and eating the pears I'd picked up.

THE DEFENCE: You're fond of pears?

LIZZIE: (*a small smile*) Otherwise, I wouldn't eat them.

THE DEFENCE: Go on.

LIZZIE: I returned to the house. I found – Papa. I called for Bridget.

MRS. BORDEN descends the stairs. LIZZIE and MISS LIZZIE / BRIDGET turn to look at her. MRS. BORDEN is only aware of LIZZIE's stare. Pause.

MRS. BORDEN: ... What're you staring at? ... I said what're you staring at?

LIZZIE: Bridget?

MISS LIZZIE / BRIDGET: Yes, ma'am.

Pause.

MRS. BORDEN: Just coffee and a biscuit this morning, Bridget, it's too hot for a decent breakfast.

BRIDGET: Yes, ma'am.

She exits for the biscuit and coffee. LIZZIE stares at MRS. BORDEN, who senses something amiss.

MRS. BORDEN: ... Tell Bridget I'll have it in the parlour.

LIZZIE is making an effort to be pleasant, to be "good." MRS. BORDEN is more aware of this as unusual behaviour from LIZZIE than were she to be rude, biting, or threatening. LIZZIE, at the same time, feels caught in a dimension other than the one in which the people around her are operating. For LIZZIE, a bell-jar effect: simple acts seem filled with significance. LIZZIE is trying to fulfill other people's expectations of "normal."

LIZZIE: It's not me, is it?

MRS. BORDEN: What?

LIZZIE: You're not moving into the parlour because of me, are you?

MRS. BORDEN: What?

LIZZIE: I'd hate to think I'd driven you out of your own dining room.

MRS. BORDEN: No.

LIZZIE: Oh good, because I'd hate to think that was so.

MRS. BORDEN: It's cooler in the parlour.

LIZZIE: You know, you're right.

MRS. BORDEN: Eh?

LIZZIE: It is cooler ... (*BRIDGET enters with the coffee and biscuit.*) I will. Bridget.

She takes the coffee and biscuit, gives it to MRS. BORDEN. LIZZIE watches her eat and drink. MRS. BORDEN eats the biscuit delicately. LIZZIE's attention is caught by it. MISS LIZZIE / BRIDGET sits in the dining room and watches.

LIZZIE: Do you like that biscuit?

MRS. BORDEN: It could be lighter.

LIZZIE: You're right.

MR. BORDEN enters, makes his way into the kitchen. LIZZIE watches him pass.

LIZZIE: You know, Papa doesn't look well, Papa doesn't look well at all. Papa looks sick.

MRS. BORDEN: He had a bad night.

LIZZIE: Oh?

MRS. BORDEN: Too hot.

LIZZIE: But it's cooler in here, isn't it? ... (*not trusting her own evaluation of the degree of heat*) Isn't it?

MRS. BORDEN: Yes, yes, it's cooler in here.

MR. BORDEN enters with his coffee. LIZZIE goes to him.

LIZZIE: Papa? You should go in the parlour. It's much cooler in there, really it is.

He goes into the parlour. Silence except for the loud and slow tick-tock of a grandfather clock which continues under the scene. LIZZIE remains in the dining room. She sits at the table, folds her hands in her lap, a mirror image of MISS LIZZIE / BRIDGET. MR. BORDEN reads the paper. Pause.

MRS. BORDEN: I think I'll have Bridget do the windows today. (*pause*) They need doing. (*pause*) Get them out the way first thing. (*pause*) Anything in the paper, Andrew?

MR. BORDEN: (*intent on his paper*) Nope.

MRS. BORDEN: There never is ... I don't know why we buy it.

Pause.

MR. BORDEN: (*still reading*) Yup.

MRS. BORDEN: You going out this morning?

Pause.

MR. BORDEN: (*looking up from the paper, a quick sly glance to LIZZIE, then a longer look to MRS. BORDEN*) Business.

MRS. BORDEN: (*low*) Business ... well ... Harry must be having a bit of a sleep-in.

Pause.

MR. BORDEN: (*back at his paper*) Yup.

MRS. BORDEN: He's always up by – (*HARRY starts down the stairs.*) Well, speak of the devil – coffee and biscuits?

HARRY: Sounds good to me.

MRS. BORDEN starts off to get it. LIZZIE looks at her, catching her eye. MRS. BORDEN stops

abruptly. *The clock stops ticking and tocking. A silence fills the air. LIZZIE breaks it.*

LIZZIE: (*Her voice is too loud.*) Emma's gone over to visit at the girls' place. (*MR. BORDEN lowers his paper to look at her. HARRY looks at her. Suddenly aware of the loudness of her voice, she continues softly, too softly.*) ... Till the ... till the weekend.

MR. BORDEN: She didn't say she was going, when'd she decide that?

LIZZIE looks down at her hands, doesn't answer. An awkward pause. Then MRS. BORDEN continues out to the kitchen.

HARRY: Will you be, ah ... going downtown today?

MR. BORDEN: This mornin'. I got ... business at the bank.

A look between them. They are very aware of LIZZIE's presence.

HARRY: This mornin', eh? Well now ... that works out just fine for me. I can ... I got a bill to settle in town myself.

LIZZIE looks at them.

HARRY: I'll be on my way after that.

MR. BORDEN: Abbie'll be disappointed you're not stayin' for lunch.

HARRY: 'Nother time.

MR. BORDEN: (*aware of LIZZIE's gaze*) I, ah ... I don't know where she is with that coffee. I'll –

HARRY: Never you mind, you sit right there, I'll get it. (*Glad to escape, he exits.*)

LIZZIE and MR. BORDEN look at each other. Long pause with unspoken thoughts. Finally –

LIZZIE: Good mornin' Papa.

MR. BORDEN: Mornin', Lizzie.

LIZZIE: Did you have a good sleep?

MR. BORDEN: Not bad.

LIZZIE: Papa?

MR. BORDEN: Yes, Lizzie.

LIZZIE: You're a very strong-minded person, Papa, do you think I'm like you?

MR. BORDEN: In some ways ... perhaps.

LIZZIE: I must be like someone.

MR. BORDEN: You resemble your mother.

LIZZIE: I look like my mother?

MR. BORDEN: A bit like your mother.

LIZZIE: But my mother's dead.

MR. BORDEN: Lizzie –

LIZZIE: I remember you told me she died because she was sick ... I was born and she died. Did you love her?

MR. BORDEN: I married her.

LIZZIE: Can't you say if you loved her.

MR. BORDEN: Of course I did, Lizzie.

LIZZIE: Did you hate me for killing her?

MR. BORDEN: You don't think of it that way, it was just something that happened.

LIZZIE: Perhaps she just got tired and died. She didn't want to go on, and the chance came up and she took it. I could understand that ... Perhaps she was like a bird, she could see all the blue sky, and she wanted to fly away but she couldn't. She was caught, Papa, she was caught in a horrible snare, and she saw a way out and she took it ... Perhaps it was a very brave thing to do, Papa, perhaps it was the only way, and she hated to leave us because she loved us so much, but she couldn't breathe all caught in the snare ... (*long pause*) Some people have very small wrists, have you noticed. Mine aren't ...

> *There is a murmur from the kitchen, then muted laughter.* MR. BORDEN *looks toward it.*

LIZZIE: Papa! ... I am a very strong person.

MRS. BORDEN: (*off, laughing*) You're tellin' tales out of school, Harry!

HARRY: (*off*) God's truth. You should have seen the buggy when they brought it back.

MRS. BORDEN: (*off*) You've got to tell Andrew. (*She pokes her head in.*) Andrew, come on out here, Harry's got a story. (*off*) Now you'll have to start at the beginning again, oh my goodness.

> MR. BORDEN *starts for the kitchen. He stops, and looks back at* LIZZIE.

LIZZIE: Is there anything you want to tell me, Papa?

MRS. BORDEN: (*off*) Andrew!

LIZZIE: (*softly, an echo*) Andrew.

MR. BORDEN: What is it, Lizzie?

LIZZIE: If I promised to be a good girl forever and ever, would anything change?

MR. BORDEN: I don't know what you're talkin' about.

LIZZIE: I would be lying ... Papa! ... Don't do any business today. Don't go out. Stay home.

MR. BORDEN: What for?

LIZZIE: Everyone's leaving. Going away. Everyone's left.

MRS. BORDEN: (*off*) Andrew!

LIZZIE: (*softly, an echo*) Andrew.

MR. BORDEN: What is it?

LIZZIE: I'm calling you.

> MR. BORDEN *looks at her for a moment, then leaves for the kitchen.* DR. PATRICK *is heard whistling very softly.*

LIZZIE: Listen ...

MISS LIZZIE / BRIDGET: Listen?

LIZZIE: Can't you hear it ... Can't you?

MISS LIZZIE / BRIDGET: I ... (*beginning to shake her head "no," then*) ... I ... I can hear it ... (*whistling stops*) It's stopped ...?

> DR. PATRICK *can't be seen. Only his voice is heard.*

DR. PATRICK: Lizzie?

LIZZIE: (*realization*) I could hear it before – (*LIZZIE stops before saying "you."*) It sounded so sad I wanted to cry.

MISS LIZZIE / BRIDGET: You mustn't cry. (*She picks up the pail and exits, leaving* LIZZIE *alone.*)

LIZZIE: I mustn't cry.

DR. PATRICK: (*off*) I bet you know this one. (*He whistles an Irish jig.*)

LIZZIE: I know that! (*She begins to dance.*)

> DR. PATRICK *enters whistling. He claps in time to the dance.* LIZZIE *finishes the jig.* DR. PATRICK *applauds.*

DR. PATRICK: Bravo! Bravo!!

LIZZIE: You didn't know I could do that, did you?

DR. PATRICK: You're a woman of many talents, Miss Borden.

LIZZIE: You're not making fun of me?

DR. PATRICK: I would never do that.

LIZZIE: I can do anything I want.

DR. PATRICK: I'm sure you can.

LIZZIE: If I wanted to die – I could even do that!

DR. PATRICK: Well now, I don't think so.

LIZZIE: Yes, I could!

DR. PATRICK: Lizzie –

LIZZIE: You wouldn't know! You can't see into my heart.

DR. PATRICK: I think I can.

LIZZIE: Well, you can't!

DR. PATRICK: It's only a game.

LIZZIE: I never play games.

DR. PATRICK: Sure you do.

LIZZIE: I hate games.

DR. PATRICK: You're playin' one now.

LIZZIE: You don't even know me!

DR. PATRICK: Come on, Lizzie, we don't want to fight. I know what we'll do ... we'll start all over ... Shut your eyes, Lizzie. (*She does so.*) Good mornin', Miss Borden ... Good mornin', Miss Borden ...

LIZZIE: ... I haven't decided ... (*She slowly opens her eyes.*) ... if it is or it isn't.

DR. PATRICK: Much better ... and now ... would you take my arm, Miss Borden? How about a wee promenade?

LIZZIE: There's nowhere to go. (*It seems sadness has replaced anger.*)

DR. PATRICK: That isn't so ... What about Boston? ... Do you think it's too far for a stroll? ... I know what we'll do, we'll walk 'round to the side and you'll show me your birds ... I waited last night but you never showed up ... there I was, travellin' bag and all, and you never appeared ... I know what went wrong! We forgot to agree on an hour! Next time, Lizzie, you must set the hour ... Is this where they're kept?

LIZZIE nods, she opens the cage and looks in it.

DR. PATRICK: It's empty. (*He laughs.*) And you say you never play games.

LIZZIE: They're gone.

DR. PATRICK: You've been havin' me on again, yes, you have.

LIZZIE: They've run away.

DR. PATRICK: Did they really exist?

LIZZIE: I had blood on my hands.

DR. PATRICK: What do you say?

LIZZIE: You can't see it now. I washed it off. See?

DR. PATRICK: (*taking her hands*) Ah Lizzie ...

LIZZIE: Would you ... help someone die?

DR. PATRICK: Why do you ask that?

LIZZIE: Some people are better off dead. I might be better off dead.

DR. PATRICK: You're a precious and unique person, Lizzie, and you shouldn't think things like that.

LIZZIE: Precious and unique? (*The phrase resonates for her.*)

DR. PATRICK: All life is precious and unique.

LIZZIE: I am precious and unique? ... I *am* precious and unique. You said that.

DR. PATRICK: Oh, I believe it.

LIZZIE: And I am! I know it! People mix things up on you, you have to be careful. I am a person of worth!

DR. PATRICK: Sure you are.

LIZZIE: Not like that fat cow in there!

DR. PATRICK: Her life too is –

LIZZIE: No!

DR. PATRICK: Liz –

LIZZIE: Do you know her!

DR. PATRICK: That doesn't matter.

LIZZIE: Yes it does, it does matter.

DR. PATRICK: You can't be –

LIZZIE: You're a doctor, isn't that right?

DR. PATRICK: Right enough there.

LIZZIE: So, tell me, tell me, if a dreadful accident occurred ... and two people were dying ... but you could only save one ... Which would you save?

DR. PATRICK: You can't ask questions like that.

LIZZIE: Yes I can, come on, it's a game. How does a doctor determine? If one were old and the other were young – would you save the younger one first?

DR. PATRICK: Lizzie.

LIZZIE: You said you liked games! If one were a bad person and the other was good, was trying to be good, would you save the one who was good and let the bad person die?

DR. PATRICK: I don't know.

LIZZIE: Listen! If you could go back in time ... what would you do if you met a person who was evil and wicked?

DR. PATRICK: Who?

LIZZIE: I don't know, Attila the Hun!

DR. PATRICK: (*laughing*) Oh my.

LIZZIE: Listen! If you met Attila the Hun, and you were in a position to kill him, would you do it?

DR. PATRICK: I don't know.

LIZZIE: Think of the suffering he caused, the unhappiness.

DR. PATRICK: Yes, but I'm a doctor, not an assassin.

LIZZIE: I think you're a coward.

Pause.

DR. PATRICK: What I do is try to save lives.

LIZZIE: But you put poison out for the slugs in your garden.

DR. PATRICK: You got something mixed up.

LIZZIE: I've never been clearer. Everything's clear. I've lived all of my life for this one moment of absolute clarity! If war were declared, would you serve?

DR. PATRICK: I would fight in a war.

LIZZIE: You wouldn't fight, you would kill – you'd take a gun and shoot people, people who'd done nothing to you, people who were trying to be good, you'd kill them! And you say you wouldn't kill Attila the Hun, or that that stupid cow's life is precious – *My life is precious!!*

DR. PATRICK: To you.

LIZZIE: Yes to me, are you stupid!?

DR. PATRICK: And hers is to her.

LIZZIE: I don't care about her! – I'm glad you're not my doctor, you can't make decisions, can you? You are a coward. (*DR. PATRICK starts off.*) You're afraid of your wife ... you can only play games ... If I really wanted to go to Boston, you wouldn't come with me because you're a coward! *I'm not a coward!!*

LIZZIE turns to watch MRS. BORDEN enter the parlour and sit with needlework. After a moment MRS. BORDEN looks at LIZZIE, aware of her scrutiny.

LIZZIE: ... Where's Papa?

MRS. BORDEN: Out.

LIZZIE: And Mr. Wingate?

MRS. BORDEN: He's out, too.

LIZZIE: So what are you going to do, Mrs. Borden?

MRS. BORDEN: I'm going to finish up.

LIZZIE: You do that ... (*pause*) Where's Bridget?

MRS. BORDEN: Out back, washing windows ... You got clean clothes to go upstairs, they're in the kitchen.

Pause.

LIZZIE: Did you know Papa killed my birds with the axe? He chopped off their heads. (*MRS. BORDEN is uneasy.*) ... It's all right. At first I felt bad, but I feel better now. I feel much better now ... I am a woman of decision, Mrs. Borden. When I decide to do things, I do them, yes, I do. (*Smiles.*) How many times has Papa said – when Lizzie puts her mind to a thing, she does it – and I do ... It's always me who puts the slug poison out because they eat all the flowers and you don't like that, do you? They're bad things, they must die. You see, not all life is precious, is it?

After a moment, MRS. BORDEN makes an attempt casually to gather together her things, to go upstairs. She does not want to be in the room with LIZZIE.

LIZZIE: Where're you going?

MRS. BORDEN: Upstairs ... (*an excuse*) The spare room needs changing.

A knock at the back door.

LIZZIE: Someone's at the door ... (*a second knock, MRS. BORDEN makes a move*) I'll get it.

LIZZIE exits to the kitchen. MRS. BORDEN waits. LIZZIE returns. She's a bit out of breath. She carries a pile of clean clothes, which she puts on the table. She looks at MRS. BORDEN.

LIZZIE: Did you want something?

MRS. BORDEN: Who was it? – At the door?

LIZZIE: Oh yes. I forgot. I had to step out back for a moment and – it's a note. A message for you.

MRS. BORDEN: Oh.

LIZZIE: Shall I open it?

MRS. BORDEN: That's all right. (*She holds out her hand.*)

LIZZIE: Looks like Papa's handwriting ... (*She passes over the note.*) Aren't you going to open it?

MRS. BORDEN: I'll read it upstairs.

LIZZIE: Mrs. Borden! ... Would you mind ... putting my clothes in my room? (*She gets some clothes from the table. MRS. BORDEN takes them, something she would never normally do. Before she can move away, LIZZIE grabs her arm.*) Just a minute ... I would like you to look into my eyes. What's the matter? Nothing's wrong. It's an experiment ... Look right into them. Tell me ... what do you see ... can you see anything?

MRS. BORDEN: ... Myself.

LIZZIE: Yes. When a person dies, retained on her eye is the image of the last thing she saw. Isn't that interesting? (*pause*)

MRS. BORDEN slowly starts upstairs. LIZZIE picks up the remaining clothes on the table. The hand hatchet is concealed beneath them. She follows MRS. BORDEN up the stairs.

LIZZIE: Do you know something? If I were to kill someone, I would come up behind them very slowly and quietly. They would never even hear me, they would never turn around. (*MRS. BORDEN stops on the stairs. She turns around to look at LIZZIE, who is behind her.*) They would be too frightened to turn around even if they heard me. They would be so afraid they'd see what they feared. (*MRS. BORDEN makes a move, an effort to go past LIZZIE back down the stairs, to get away. LIZZIE stops her.*) Careful. Don't fall. (*MRS. BORDEN turns and slowly continues up the stairs with LIZZIE behind her.*) And then, I would strike them down. With them not turning around, they would retain no image of me on their eye. It would be better that way.

LIZZIE and MRS. BORDEN disappear at the top of the stairs. The stage is empty for a moment. Faint sound of a grandfather clock chiming the three-quarter hour. BRIDGET enters. She carries the pail for washing the windows. She sets the pail down, wipes her forehead. She stands for a moment, looking toward the stairs as if she might have heard a sound. She picks up the pail and exits to the kitchen. LIZZIE appears on the stairs. She is slightly out of breath, a few strands of her hair are out of place. She is carrying the pile of clothes she carried upstairs. LIZZIE descends the stairs. She seems calm, self-possessed, despite the hair and the deep breathing. She places the clothes on the table. After a moment she moves to a chair, pauses a moment, then sits. She sits there, straight back, hands in lap, an appearance of strong self-possession. BRIDGET enters from the kitchen and sees LIZZIE. BRIDGET tidies the room. She casts a glance at LIZZIE every once in a while, increasingly aware of her silence and stillness.

BRIDGET: Lizzie? ... Lizzie!?

LIZZIE gives a small slow shake of her head. BRIDGET, dismissed, returns to tidying. LIZZIE gently grasps BRIDGET's arm as BRIDGET passes near her. LIZZIE doesn't look at BRIDGET; she seems still deep in thought.

LIZZIE: We must hurry.

BRIDGET: (*a small laugh*) And why would we be hurryin'?

LIZZIE: We must –

BRIDGET: Too hot to hurry, Miss Lizzie.

LIZZIE: We must hurry – (*She looks directly at BRIDGET.*) – before papa gets home.

A moment as BRIDGET senses something not quite right about LIZZIE, but her discomfort fades somewhat and she returns to work, picking up the pile of clothes from the table.

BRIDGET: Oh Lizzie, your papa won't be coming home – (*The weight of the clothes is unusual. She puts the pile down, lifts the clothes to see what's beneath them.*) – not till it's – (*She sees the hatchet.*)

LIZZIE: Bridget?

BRIDGET: Oh, Lizzie.

LIZZIE: We must hurry – (*She looks directly at BRIDGET.*) – before papa gets home.

A moment as BRIDGET senses something not quite right about LIZZIE, but her discomfort fades somewhat and she returns to work, picking up the pile of clothes from the table.

BRIDGET: Oh Lizzie, your papa won't be coming home – (*The weight of the clothes is unusual. She puts the pile down, lifts the clothes to see what's beneath them.*) – not till it's – (*She sees the hatchet.*)

LIZZIE: Bridget?

BRIDGET: Oh, Lizzie.

LIZZIE: We must hurry – before Papa gets home.

BRIDGET: Lizzie?

LIZZIE: Before Papa Gets Home!

BRIDGET: (*quickly covering the hatchet*) What have you done.

LIZZIE: I have it all figured out.

BRIDGET: What have you done!

LIZZIE: But you have to help me!

BRIDGET: Oh no, Lizzie, no.

LIZZIE: You know he'd never leave me the farm – not with her on his back! But now (*She gets up; BRIDGET moves a bit away from her.*) I will have the farm! And I will have the money, yes, to do what I please! And you too, Bridget. (*She's moving toward, stalking BRIDGET, who is avoiding her.*) I'll give you some of my money, but you've got to help me!

BRIDGET: No, don't, keep away!

LIZZIE: Don't be afraid, it's me. (*She grabs BRIDGET.*) It's Lizzie, it's Lizzie, you like me!

BRIDGET: What have you done?

Pause. LIZZIE slowly releases BRIDGET, who begins to move toward the stairs.

LIZZIE: Don't – go up there.

BRIDGET: (*looking up the stairs and back at LIZZIE*) Oh Lizzie, you've –

LIZZIE: No no no no no, someone broke in –

BRIDGET: No, Lizzie –

LIZZIE: Someone broke in and they killed her.

BRIDGET: They'll know!

LIZZIE: Not if you help me.

BRIDGET: I can't, Miss Lizzie, I can't!

LIZZIE: (*grabbing BRIDGET*) Do you want them to hang me! Is that what you want! Want them to kill me! Oh Bridget, look! Look! (*She falls to her knees, clutching at BRIDGET.*) I'm begging for my life, I'm begging, on my knees I am begging, deny me and they will kill me, help me, Bridget, please help me, please, I'm begging you, please.

Pause.

BRIDGET: ... But ... (*She touches LIZZIE's face.*) but there's nothing we can do there's nothin' ... what ... could we do?

LIZZIE: (*up off her knees*) I have it all figured out –

BRIDGET: No –

LIZZIE: – I'll go downtown as quick as I can –

BRIDGET: No –

LIZZIE: – and you leave the doors open –

BRIDGET: – but I can't –

LIZZIE: – and go back outside –

BRIDGET: – but Lizzie –

LIZZIE: – and work!! Work on the windows!

BRIDGET: I've finished them, Lizzie.

LIZZIE: Then do them again!!! (*pause*) Remember last year when the burglar broke in? (*pause*) Today, someone broke in, and she caught them.

BRIDGET: They'll never believe us.

LIZZIE: Have coffee with Lucy next door.

BRIDGET: They'll –

LIZZIE: Stay with her till Papa gets home –

BRIDGET: But –

LIZZIE: He'll find her, then each of us swears! Both of us swear she was fine when we left, she was all right when we left! – It's going to work, Bridget, I know it!

BRIDGET: Your papa will guess.

LIZZIE: Never guess!!

BRIDGET: Your papa –

LIZZIE: (*getting ready to leave for downtown*) If he found me here he might guess, but he won't.

BRIDGET: Your papa will know!

LIZZIE: Papa loves me!!! ... If he has another story to believe, he'll believe it. He'd want to believe it. He'd have to believe it.

BRIDGET: Your papa will know.

LIZZIE: Why aren't you happy?! I'm happy. We both should be happy! (*LIZZIE embraces BRIDGET and steps back a pace.*) Now – how do I look?

MR. BORDEN enters. BRIDGET sees him. LIZZIE slowly turns to see what BRIDGET is looking at.

LIZZIE: Papa?

MR. BORDEN: What is it? Where's Mrs. Borden?

BRIDGET: I ... don't know ... sir ... I ... just came in, sir.

MR. BORDEN: Did she leave the house?

BRIDGET: Well, sir . . .

LIZZIE: She went out. Someone delivered a note. A message. And she left. (*LIZZIE takes off her hat and looks at her father.*) ... You're home early, Papa.

MR. BORDEN: I wanted to see Abbie. She's gone out, has she? ... Well, which way did she go? (*LIZZIE shrugs, he continues, as if thinking aloud.*) Well ... I ... I ... best wait for her here. I don't want to miss her again.

LIZZIE: Help Papa off with his coat, Bridget ... (*BRIDGET is reluctant to do so.*) Bridget! (*BRIDGET takes his coat.*) I hear there's a sale of dress goods on downtown. Why don't you go buy yourself a yard?

BRIDGET: Oh ... I don't know, ma'am.

LIZZIE: You don't want any?

BRIDGET: I don't know.

LIZZIE: Then ... why don't you go upstairs and lie down. Have a rest before lunch.

BRIDGET: I don't think I should.

LIZZIE: Nonsense.

BRIDGET: Lizzie, I –

LIZZIE: You go up and lie down. I'll look after things here.

LIZZIE smiles at BRIDGET, who starts up the stairs, then suddenly stops, reluctant to continue. She looks back at LIZZIE.

LIZZIE: It's all right ... go on ... it's all right.

BRIDGET continues a bit up the stairs, stops, and – as MISS LIZZIE – turns to watch. MR. BORDEN lowers the paper he's reading. LIZZIE looks at him.

LIZZIE: Hello, Papa. You look so tired ... I make you unhappy ... I don't like to make you unhappy. I love you.

MR. BORDEN: (*smiling and taking her hand*) I'm just getting old, Lizzie.

LIZZIE: You've got on my ring ... Do you remember when I gave you that? ... When I left Miss Cornelia's – it was in a little blue velvet box, you hid it behind your back, and you said, "Guess which hand, Lizzie!" And I guessed. And you gave it to me and you said, "It's real gold, Lizzie, it's for you because you are very precious to me." Do you remember, Papa? (*MR. BORDEN nods.*) And I took it out of the little blue velvet box, and I took your hand, and I put my ring on your finger and I said, "Thank you, Papa, I love you." ... You've never taken it off ... see how it bites into the flesh of your finger. (*She presses his hand to her face.*) I forgive you, Papa, I forgive you for killing my birds ... You look so tired, why don't you lie down and rest, put your feet up, I'll undo your shoes for you. (*She kneels and undoes his shoes.*)

MR. BORDEN: You're a good girl.

LIZZIE: I could never stand to have you hate me, Papa. Never. I would do anything rather than have you hate me.

MR. BORDEN: I don't hate you, Lizzie.

LIZZIE: I would not want you to find out anything that would make you hate me. Because I love you.

MR. BORDEN: And I love you, Lizzie, you'll always be precious to me.

LIZZIE: (*looking at him, then smiling*) Was I – when I had scabs on my knees?

MR. BORDEN: (*laughing*) Oh yes. Even then.

LIZZIE: (*laughing*) Oh Papa! ... Kiss me! (*He kisses her on the forehead.*) Thank you, Papa.

MR. BORDEN: Why're you crying?

LIZZIE: Because I'm so happy. Now ... put your feet up and get to sleep ... that's right ... shut your eyes ... go to sleep ... go to sleep.

She starts to hum and continues humming as MR. BORDEN falls asleep. Still humming, LIZZIE moves to the table, slips her hand under the clothes, withdraws the hatchet. She approaches her father with the hatchet behind her back. She stops humming. A pause, then she slowly raises the hatchet very high to strike him. Just as the hatchet is about to start its descent, there is a blackout.

MISS LIZZIE: (*screaming from the stairs*) Noooooo!

At the same time children's voices are heard singing. Their singing will grow increasingly discordant:

"Lizzie Borden took an axe,
Gave her mother forty whacks.
When the job was nicely done,
She gave her father forty-one!
Forty-one!
Forty-one!"

The singing increases in volume and distortion as it nears the end of the verse until the last words are very loud but discernible, just. Silence. Then the sound of slow, measured, heavy breathing growing into a wordless sound of hysteria. Light returns to the stage, dim light from late in the day. THE ACTRESS stands with the hatchet raised in the same position in which we saw her before the blackout, but the couch is empty. Her eyes are shut. The sound comes from her. MISS LIZZIE moves to THE ACTRESS and reaches up to take the hatchet from her. When MISS LIZZIE's hand touches the hand of THE ACTRESS, THE ACTRESS releases the hatchet and whirls around to face MISS LIZZIE, who is left holding the hatchet. THE ACTRESS backs away from MISS LIZZIE. There is a flickering of light at the top of the stairs.

EMMA: (*from upstairs*) Lizzie! Lizzie! You're making too much noise!

An older EMMA in a dressing gown slowly descends the stairs carrying an oil lamp. THE ACTRESS backs away from LIZZIE and moves into the shadows. MISS LIZZIE turns to see EMMA. The hatchet is behind MISS LIZZIE's back, concealed from EMMA, who pauses for a moment.

EMMA: Where is she?

MISS LIZZIE: Who?

EMMA: You know who. (*Pause and a standoff.*) It's late.

MISS LIZZIE: I know.

EMMA: Almost morning.

MISS LIZZIE: I know.

EMMA: (*Blowing the lamp out, leaving the room shadowed. In early morning light, she sits.*) Lizzie.

MISS LIZZIE: Yes?

EMMA: I want to speak to you, Lizzie.

MISS LIZZIE: Yes, Emma.

EMMA: That ... "actress" who's come up from Boston.

MISS LIZZIE: What about her?

EMMA: People talk.

MISS LIZZIE: You needn't listen.

EMMA: In your position you should do nothing to inspire talk.

MISS LIZZIE: People need so little in the way of inspiration. And Miss Cornelia's classes didn't cover "Etiquette for Acquitted Persons."

EMMA: Common sense should tell you what you ought or ought not do.

MISS LIZZIE: Common sense is repugnant to me. I prefer uncommon sense.

EMMA: I forbid her in this house, Lizzie!

> Pause.

MISS LIZZIE: Do you?

EMMA: (*backing down, softly*) It's just ... disgraceful.

MISS LIZZIE: I see.

EMMA: I simply cannot –

MISS LIZZIE: You could always leave.

EMMA: Leave?

MISS LIZZIE: Move. Away. Why don't you?

EMMA: I –

MISS LIZZIE: You could never, could you?

EMMA: If I only –

MISS LIZZIE: Knew.

EMMA: Lizzie. Lizzie did you?

MISS LIZZIE: Oh Emma, do you intend asking me that question from now till death us do part?

EMMA: It's just –

MISS LIZZIE: For if you do, I may well take something sharp to you.

EMMA: Why do you joke like that!

> *MISS LIZZIE turns away from EMMA who, for the first time, sees the hatchet held by MISS LIZZIE behind her back. EMMA's reaction is not any verbal or untoward movement. She freezes like a mouse as MISS LIZZIE, realizing what EMMA has seen, turns and advances on EMMA, who scurries away.*

MISS LIZZIE: Did you never stop and think that if I did, then you were guilty, too?

EMMA: (*caught and trapped*) What?

MISS LIZZIE: It was you who brought me up, like a mother to me. Almost like a mother. Did you never stop and think that I was like a puppet? Your puppet? My head your hand, yes, your hand working my mouth, me saying all the things you felt like saying, me doing all the things (*in her agitation MISS LIZZIE is raising the hatchet*) you felt like doing! Me spewing forth! Me hitting out! And you, you – ! (*She appears about to strike EMMA.*)

THE ACTRESS: Lizzie!

> *MISS LIZZIE regains control of herself.*

EMMA: (*whispering*) I wasn't even here that day.

MISS LIZZIE: (*lowering the hatchet*) I can swear to that.

EMMA: Do you want to drive me mad?

MISS LIZZIE: Oh yes.

EMMA: You didn't ... did you?

MISS LIZZIE: Poor ... Emma.

THE ACTRESS: Lizzie. (*She takes the hatchet from MISS LIZZIE.*) Lizzie, you did.

MISS LIZZIE: I didn't. You did.

> *THE ACTRESS looks to the hatchet, then out to the audience.*

> *Blackout.*

END

SKY
GILBERT

(b. 1952)

Sky Gilbert says he wrote *Drag Queens on Trial* when he "began to realize that the drag queen was the most potent and eloquent symbol of the 'otherness' which is, I think, the gay man's most enduring wound, and his prize, also." On opening night of the play in 1985, he recalls, "I strode into the theatre dressed in hopeless drag" – he had never worn drag publically before – "and plopped myself down right next to the critics. I truly thought my career might be over ..." Instead, even the critics from Toronto's straight press were delighted. In retrospect, Gilbert concluded that "they missed the political point, but loved the traditional characterization of gay men as campy queens. The gay community got the point, but was not so certain about its response."

Over the course of his controversial career as playwright and actor, director and artistic director, radical queer activist and drag queen, Gilbert has elicited uncertain responses from both ends of the political and sexual spectrums. He has been celebrated and vilified. R.M. Vaughan writes: "Critics on the left denounce his work as exploitative and hypersexual, liberals simply find it confusing, and right-wingers believe Gilbert is satanic, and possibly poisoning their children." Outspoken and outrageous, he has been a central character in his own drama onstage and off, a prolific and underrated playwright, a key figure in Canadian new play development, and altogether one of the most dynamic individuals in contemporary Canadian theatre.

Schuyler Lee Gilbert Jr. was born in Norwich, Connecticut, his father an insurance company manager, his mother the scion of a family with deeply conservative American roots. (Gilbert travesties family life in 1950s Norwich in his drag comedy *Lola Starr Builds Her Dream Home*, published in *Canadian Theatre Review* 59 [Summer 1989].) When Gilbert was twelve, he moved to Toronto with his mother and sister following his parents' divorce. He completed an arts degree at York University before co-founding Buddies in Bad Times Theatre and the Rhubarb Festival of new plays (its philosophy, "opportunity without interference") in 1979. He served as artistic director of both the theatre and the festival until 1997. Gilbert describes his two decades at Buddies in a memoir, *Ejaculations from the Charm Factory* (2000). Buddies and Rhubarb soon became identified primarily, though not exclusively, with gay and lesbian work, especially after 1985 when Gilbert instituted Buddies' 4-Play Festival, which commissions four new plays each year by gay and lesbian writers.

Gilbert himself came out as a gay writer in 1979 with *Lana Turner Has Collapsed!*, one of dozens of plays he wrote, directed, and/or performed at Buddies and Rhubarb while moving himself and his theatre in increasingly radical directions over the next two decades. At the same time as the quality of his work was being acknowledged by Dora and Chalmers Award nominations, the Pauline McGibbon Award for Directing (1985), and invitations to direct at the Shaw Festival, Gilbert was pushing the envelope hard. Drag, pedophilia, sado-masochism, and explicit gay sex came to mark his plays. He often appeared as his drag-queen alter ego, Jane, for highly publicized political protests in shopping malls and city council meetings. He vigorously attacked the homophobia of straights as well as what Marjorie Garber, in her book *Vested Interests: Cross-Dressing and Cultural Anxiety*, has called the transvestophobia of mainstream gays and lesbians who feel their status threatened by high-profile deviance. Soon he was calling his work "queer theatre." "If I was a sweeter nicer guy," Gilbert wrote in 1993, "I'd call Buddies in Bad Times Theatre a 'gay and lesbian theatre for all people.' But I'm not that nice. I'm an orgiastic poet and a drag queen ..." Yet his successes were practical as well as ideological. In 1992, he managed to leverage more than two million dollars from various levels of government to move Buddies into the defunct Toronto Workshop Productions' former theatre.

Some of the more than fifty produced plays of his own that Gilbert has directed include *The Postman Rings Once* (1987); *The Whore's Revenge* (1989); *Ban This Show* (1990), a response to the Robert Mapplethorpe controversies; and *Ten Ruminations on an Elegy Attributed to William Shakespeare*, which toured the United Kingdom in the late 1990s. His plays in print include three collections: *This Unknown Flesh* (1995); *Painted, Tainted, Sainted* (1996); and *Avoidance Tactics* (2001). In *Painted, Tainted, Sainted* can be found *Drag Queens on Trial*; its less successful sequel *Drag Queens in Outer Space* (1986), which featured Gilbert himself as Lana Lust in its 1990 San Francisco production; and the *Austin Powers*–ish drag musical *Suzie Goo: Private Secretary* (1991), which climaxes, so to speak, in the anthemic Gilbertian line, "Let the liquids spurt." These plays celebrate transgressive sexuality and critique the fears and hypocrisies of mainstream society through parodic, self-conscious camp comedy. The excellent *I Have AIDS!* (2009) reprises some of the key themes of *Drag Queens on Trial* almost a quarter-century later.

Another group of Gilbert's plays focuses on the power of illicit desire acting on and through the gay artist–intellectual. *Pasolini / Pelosi, or The God in Unknown Flesh* (1983), a sequel *In Which Pier Paolo Pasolini Sees His Own Death in the Face of a Boy* (1991), and *More Divine* (1994), about Roland Barthes and Michel Foucault, are among the best. Others concern David Hockney, Truman Capote, Frank O'Hara, Tennessee Williams, Constantine Cavafy, Mapplethorpe, and Shakespeare. Related in theme, *Theatrelife* (1987), *Play Murder* (1995), and *Bad Acting Teachers* (2006) explore the metatheatrical underpinnings of all Gilbert's work: the performative elements of gender and sexuality. Gilbert has published prolifically in poetry and fiction as well. His metaliterary novels *I Am Kaspar Klotz* (2001), *An*

English Gentleman (2004), *Brother Dumb* (2007), and *Wit in Love* (2008) are well worth reading. He has also made short films which have played the North American gay festival circuit, and has written essays on theatre and queer culture for publications as varied as *Canadian Theatre Review*, *This Magazine*, and the *National Post*. In 2006, Gilbert received his Ph.D. from the University of Toronto and is currently Associate Professor of Theatre at the University of Guelph.

In *Drag Queens on Trial*, Gilbert puts his own spin on material that has precedent and resonance in the Canadian theatre. Queenie in John Herbert's *Fortune and Men's Eyes* (1967) and the title character of Michel Tremblay's *Hosanna* (1973) are Gilbert's queens' older sisters in drag, both tried and found guilty – the latter of living inauthentically as a gay man by pretending to be a woman. But as heroic as they might have been in their embrace of drag's radical otherness in the 1960s and '70s, Queenie and Hosanna were also sad and defeated. In the 1980s, Michel Marc Bouchard's baroque romantic cross-dressers, in plays such as *Lilies*, appeared noble but melancholy and somewhat otherworldly. But there's nothing sad or otherworldly about Gilbert's three queens. They are triumphant and unapologetic, streetwise, and foul-mouthed. Their explicit, aggressive sexual language, still pretty shocking even today, would have seemed a lot more raw to Canadian audiences in 1985 before the mainstream theatrical success a few years later of plays such as Brad Fraser's similarly overt *Unidentified Human Remains* and *Poor Super Man*.

The structure of *Drag Queens* is highly schematic, not unlike the B-movie melodramas starring Joan Crawford or Lana Turner that it shamelessly parodies. In each of the three sections, Judy, Lana, and Marlene sit in front of their mirrors bitching and arguing while they make up and dress up for the three courtroom scenes. Each has her day in court where she is accused of the crime of being a drag queen while the other two play the prosecutor, the surprise witness, and the judge. (In the original production, a male judge spoke from a video screen.) The fourth actor is a taped voice, "male and authoritative," which sometimes sounds like the preview of a bad movie or prime-time soap ("they lived by the skin of their spike heels"), sometimes like a stage manager calling the actors in a play to their places, and sometimes like Charlie commanding his Angels, who in this case respond with hilarious, un-angelic obscenity.

The style of the play, like that of the queens themselves, is hyper-consciously theatrical: "Another day, another performance," says Lana as they take off their makeup. Art, Oscar Wilde averred, is a beautiful lie, ultimately truer than the so-called truth. (In my favourite Wildean moment in the play, the prosecutor challenges the accused: "How do you explain the fact that you sit before us, wearing breasts which are obviously not your own?" Marlene answers, "I hope that you do not wish to imply that I stole these breasts. They are mine. I bought them.") Marlene admits at her trial that lies are the essence of a drag queen's life. But the obvious artifice that aspires to something different and better than the ordinary, unglamorous "reality" that it rejects is "somehow the lie that tells the truth." Marlene and Judy both offer improved fictionalized versions of their pasts and impassioned confessions of guilt for being true to themselves rather than to the straight Canadian norm. (Marlene's diatribe against "cold, puritanical, sad, grey" Canada recalls similar complaints in Robertson Davies's dramatic comedies of the late 1940s.) But any moment in the play that threatens to become maudlin is instantly deflated, either by the queens themselves (Judy's tragedy-queenish mock suicide) or by the declaiming Voice: "DRAG QUEENS ON TRIAL!"

In an essay called "Closet Plays," Gilbert asserts that "in the language of camp, humour is terribly serious." This becomes evident in Act Two at Lana's trial. She has taken great pride in her drag queen's lifestyle. (Prosecutor: "Do you have sleazy sex with men in back alleys, toilets, steam baths ...?" Lana: "As often as humanly possible.") But when her doctor reveals that Lana is dying of AIDS and blames it on her homosexual promiscuity, Lana has a moment of self-doubt. This is the play's Big Scene, Lana's aria in which she faces down her doubt and embraces her truth. The rhetoric of her speech is both genuinely stirring in its unrepentant forthrightness and hopelessly campy in its melodramatic excess – music from *Tristan und Isolde*, a spotlight, and "spontaneous, taped, thunderous applause."

Suddenly turning *Drag Queens on Trial* into an AIDS play is one of Gilbert's more audacious moves, but he makes it work wonderfully. Staring into the apocalypse, the queens end the play with a chorus from drag queendom's favourite diva, Judy Garland. The last lines resonate with both the joy and terror of being alive and queer in the mid-1980s: "Shout hallelujah, come on, get happy / Get ready for the Judgment Day."

Sky Gilbert

Drag Queens on Trial

Drag Queens on Trial premiered on October 17, 1985, at the Metro Cinema in Toronto, produced by Buddies in Bad Times Theatre, with the following cast:

JUDY GOOSE	Leonard Chow
LANA LUST	Kent Staines
MARLENE DELORME	Doug Millar
JUDGE (in video)	Bill Zaget

Directed by Sky Gilbert
Set Design by Tanuj Kohli
Costume Design by Laura Divilio
Lighting Design by Patsy Lang
Video by Christopher Gerrard-Pinker

As truth is nonexistent it can never be anything but illusion – but illusion, the by-product of revealing artifice, can reach the summits nearer the unobtainable peak of Perfect Truth. For example, female impersonators. The impersonator is in fact a man (truth) until he re-creates himself as a woman (illusion) and, of the two, the illusion is truer.

– TRUMAN CAPOTE, *Answered Prayers*

CHARACTERS

MARLENE DELORME, *a tall, dignified blonde;*
   also plays Dr. Dimchick
JUDY GOOSE, *a short, undignified blonde;*
   also plays Anita Hrupki
LANA LUST, *a romantic redhead;*
   also plays Hermione Rosemount
CLERKS, JUDGES, PROSECUTING ATTORNEYS,
   all played by the three drag queens

PLAYWRIGHT'S NOTE

Although both *Drag Queens on Trial* and *Drag Queens in Space* were originally performed in Toronto during the 1980s, they have since been performed throughout the United States. It's a small gay world, and every city has its own landmark gay pubs and institutions. I give the director total freedom in changing local Canadian and Toronto references to specific places and institutions in your own town or city. Here is a glossary of some of these Toronto terms, from the 1980s, that will help the creative director to transpose the local terms:

Church and Wellesley – The core of the gay community. Church Street is Toronto's Castro or Christopher Street.

The Body Politic – Toronto's gay and lesbian newspaper.

Rites – Toronto's politically correct lesbian and gay newspaper.

Wellesley Fitness – The local gym where *all* the fags hang out.

Queen's Dairy – Greasy spoon where drag-queen hookers have breakfast and fags bring their tricks the morning after.

Cornelius – Premiere drag club in the city.

Chaps – Premiere butch–preppie bar in the city.

ACT ONE

In the black, we hear a musical chord, then a taped VOICE speaks in the dark. The voice is very deep, male, and authoritative.

VOICE: Scorned by home, church, family, and their best friends, they lived by the skin of their spike heels, they were –

Lights up on the drag queens in poses.

ALL: DRAG QUEENS ON TRIAL!

Blackout.

VOICE: Chosen outcasts by fate or by design, they fed on scraps of discarded desire. Unwanted, lonely, and more dangerous than you might imagine, they were –

Lights up, they pose.

ALL: DRAG QUEENS ON TRIAL!

Blackout.

VOICE: Poised on the precipice between immortality and irrelevance, they filed their nails until their fingers fell off. They were –

Lights up, they pose.

ALL: DRAG QUEENS ON TRIAL!

Blackout, pose again.

MARLENE: Painted.

JUDY: Tainted.

LANA: And, some say, nearly sainted.

MARLENE: Flaunted.

JUDY: Haunted.

LANA: And quite unnecessarily taunted.

MARLENE: Hated.

JUDY: Fated.

LANA: And rarely, rarely mated.

MARLENE: Sick.

JUDY: Chic.

LANA: And much too fond of dick.

ALL: They were – DRAG QUEENS ON TRIAL!

The three take various poses of pain and suffering and then groan one by one.

MARLENE: Ughghghghghgh!

JUDY: Arghghghghghgh!

LANA: Ahhhhhhhhhhh!

Blackout.

VOICE: See ... maudlin denials of almost certain guilt.

MARLENE: (*on the stand*) I didn't do it. I promise you, I didn't do it. If I'm guilty please please let the good Lord above put a run in my stocking! (*Looking down at her stocking, she screams in pain.*) AHHHHH!

Blackout.

VOICE: See ... careless confessions of brazen behaviour.

JUDY: (*on the stand*) All right ... so I did let him buy me a Coke. What of it? That doesn't mean anything does it? A girl has a right to let a boy buy her a Coke doesn't she? It doesn't make her a tramp does it? Well, does it? (*She looks around, paranoid.*) Well?

Blackout.

VOICE: See ... unexpected breakdowns in which the truth is finally told.

LANA: All right, yes, I did it, I killed him. But I didn't mean to. Besides, he treated me like a human turd. Everything I did was inadequate, wrong, double-plus ungood. The lovemaking, the cooking, yes, even the cocktail parties. It seemed I could do nothing right, and finally it all got too much for me and ... the doors did it ... it wasn't me (*She goes crazy.*) it was the doors, they killed him not me – the doors! (*She screams.*) The electric seeing-eye doors! (*She breaks down.*) ARGGGHGHGHGHGH!

ALL: DRAG QUEENS ON TRIAL!

Blackout. Voice in the dark.

VOICE: In the tenuous existence, the tortured life term of a drag queen, there are many trials. But perhaps the most arduous trial of all, and indeed the most important, is the premiere trial of the day, that is, getting out of bed and facing the morning ahead. Many a drag queen has faltered, nay died, while enduring this strenuous ordeal, fraught with dangers. And here, for the first time, live onstage, we allow you to witness this heroic act. Ladies and gentlemen, three drag queens, getting up in the morning and confronting their own faces in the dreaded bathroom mirror.

The sound of three alarm clocks ringing. Lights up on the three drag queens, each in their own beds. They are all wearing sleeping masks. They reach out to find the clocks and turn off the alarm. The overture to Tannhäuser begins. They spend the beginning of the overture – the horn section – sitting up in bed, taking off their sleeping masks, and pulling on robes. When the strings begin, they start crawling along the floor toward their mirrors. Then the strings and horns join triumphantly, and they are finally at their mirrors. When they face their own images, they turn away with cries of horror. They spend most of the triumphal march brushing teeth and wiping faces, mouthwash, etc. The music fades. They are ready for makeup and costumes. But first all three get up and sing.

ALL:

Forget your troubles, come on, get happy,
You better chase all your cares away.
Shout hallelujah, come on, get happy,
Get ready for the Judgment Day.

> *They tap dance, taps having been glued to their spike heels. Their high heels are permanently attached to their feet and are skin colour, thus looking like extensions of their legs. After this song, quite an ordeal, they collapse, tired, annoyed, and bored, into their chairs and begin putting on their makeup and costumes for the first trial scene. It's just three girls here, "shooting the shit."*

MARLENE: So, do you girls want to hear about last night or what?

LANA & JUDY: Yes!

MARLENE: Well, I was mortified, I almost wet my pants I was so pissed off –

JUDY: What what what what what.

MARLENE: Well, it was Chaps, right?

JUDY: I told you not to go to Chaps. They're prejudiced.

MARLENE: But that's just the point, I don't care.

LANA: What happened.

MARLENE: Well, he wouldn't let me in.

JUDY: Omigod!

LANA: Which one was this.

MARLENE: The little beefy one with the tattoos for days.

JUDY: Oh, you mean Frank.

MARLENE: I don't know what his fucking name is.

LANA: Yes, Frank.

JUDY: Oh God, he is so cute.

LANA: He is not cute.

JUDY: I would die to make it with him.

LANA: He is a pig, Judy, and if I ever see you go anywhere near him in a sexual way I will cut your balls off and use them for earrings.

JUDY: I've seen you flirt with him.

LANA: Only in my tragic past. So what happened?

MARLENE: Well, first of all, I was wearing the white sweater, with the tight black skirt – I mean I looked positively business-like and I had spent about two hours on my makeup and hair – well, I looked fantastic –

LANA: We'll take your word for it –

MARLENE: Lana.

LANA: What?

MARLENE: What do you mean by that?

LANA: I mean, we'll take your word for it you looked like Jessica Lange, darling, so get on with the story.

MARLENE: Well, whether or not my outfit was perfect has a direct bearing on the outcome of my little moral tale if you don't mind.

LANA: I don't. (*turning*) Do you have any real red, Judy?

JUDY: Red what?

LANA: Lipstick.

JUDY: I have Jungle Red.

LANA: Sounds great.

JUDY: I think maybe it's fluorescent.

LANA: Are you kidding?

JUDY: No.

LANA: Let me see.

MARLENE: Is anybody listening, does anybody care?

JUDY: I'm listening. I care.

LANA: (*looking at the lipstick*) Where did you get this lipstick?

JUDY: At a second-hand store on Queen Street.

MARLENE: You guys. I am like talking about the most important thing to happen to me since I decided not to have a sex change practically and all you guys can talk about is Jungle Red –

LANA: This stuff is lethal.

JUDY: What?

LANA: This lipstick is filled with radiation.

MARLENE: Oh come on, what are you –

LANA: No, honey, really look. Come here ... (*as they gather round*) It says on the label that this lipstick contains radium. Judy, if you're putting this gunk on your mouth, it's equivalent to eating nuclear waste.

JUDY: The guy told me it was like antique lipstick. And that it was made in the fifties. And it cost me twenty dollars.

LANA: Are you serious?

JUDY: Yes.

MARLENE: Let me see that. (*pause*) Omigod, she's right.

LANA: (*grabbing it*) Of course I'm right. Judy, you don't need this. (*raising her arm to throw it*)

JUDY: (*screaming*) WAIT! WHAT ARE YOU DOING!

LANA: I'm saving your fucking life, darling, I'm getting rid of this lipstick for once and for all –

JUDY: But – WAIT!

LANA: What is it?

JUDY: That's Jungle Red, that's the reddest lipstick I've ever had!

LANA: You don't understand.

MARLENE: Here, bitch. Let me explain. Judy, honey, you know – well, you've heard of the Second World War, haven't you?

LANA: Oh God, this is going to take hours.

MARLENE: Shut up, will you, I can communicate with her, if anybody can. Now you've heard of World War Two.

JUDY: Yeah, but I don't –

MARLENE: Now you just shush yourself and listen. You know the big mushroom cloud that happens when they drop one of those atomic bombs?

JUDY: Yeah, I know.

MARLENE: Well, the stuff that they put in those atomic bombs is the same stuff they put in this lipstick.

JUDY: Oh wow. (*pause*) It must be fantastic lipstick, eh?

LANA: (*to MARLENE*) Wonderful. You should work for the U.N. Give it to me. (*grabbing it*) Listen, Judy, I'm throwing this fucking lipstick in the garbage because it will rot your mouth.

LANA throws it.

JUDY: Ahhh. (*Pause; she stares out sadly.*) I'll never get lipstick that red again.

LANA: People are starving in Africa and you're crying over shades of red.

MARLENE: Oh, leave her alone. You, who invented the word *superficial*, should talk.

LANA: You, who blow old men in alleys, should talk.

MARLENE: I only blew one old man and I was desperate and very drunk. And it wasn't in an alley. It was at the Club Baths.

LANA: I never cruise public thoroughfares. Never after one a.m.

MARLENE: Yeah, but you live in the toilets.

LANA: (*suddenly turning into Joan Crawford in* Mildred Pierce) Veda. I feel as if I'm seeing you for the first time, and you're cheap, and horrible!

MARLENE: (*turning into Veda, horrified*) You think just because you get a little bit of money, you can get a fancy hairdo and buy some expensive clothes and turn yourself into a lady, well, you can't – you'll never be anything but a common frump ...

LANA: (*as if slapped*) Ahh!

MARLENE: ... whose father lived above a shop, and whose mother took in the washing –

LANA: Veda! Get out before I throw you out! Get out – before I kill you.

They hiss at each other.

JUDY: Are you guys going to stop arguing or not?

They look at each other.

LANA: She sure told us.

JUDY: Well, I get tired of it, that's all. Marlene, finish your story.

MARLENE: Well, as I was saying before I was so rudely interrupted by this overly glamorous refugee from the peace movement –

LANA: Oh, fuck off, cunt –

MARLENE: I was refused admission to Chaps.

LANA: Listen, bitch, haven't you figured out yet why you keep getting thrown out of bars?

MARLENE: I wasn't thrown out, I was refused admission.

LANA: *La même chose.* It has nothing to do with being in drag. I go to Chaps all the time in drag. It's because you're a rude, bitchy cunt.

MARLENE: Fuck off, toilet queen.

LANA: Well, the truth hurts. I've heard you ordering your drinks, Marlene, at the bar (*imitating MARLENE, putting on a truck-driver voice*): Could I have a gin and Sprite, please – you call that a slice of lemon – I'm sorry, dear, but that's not a full shot. (*resuming her own voice*) If I was a bartender, I'd throw your drink in your face.

MARLENE: Lana, just because you're pushing forty and well hung doesn't mean you're talented. (*JUDY giggles.*) And Judy, you've been in more hotel rooms than the Bible. (*JUDY stops giggling.*)

VOICE: DRAG QUEENS ON TRIAL. Scene One.

LANA: Omigod, I haven't got my hair combed.

JUDY: What am I going to use for lipstick?

MARLENE: Use blood, it's not nuclear.

LANA: Speak for yourself, I'm constantly aglow.

JUDY: Oh, I look so awful, I hate this costume.

VOICE: I repeat. DRAG QUEENS ON TRIAL. Scene One.

MARLENE: All right already, keep your nuts on.

LANA: Oh God, I can't find my beauty mark.

MARLENE: A beauty mark does not an Alexis Carrington Colby Dexter make.

LANA: Fuck off, Crystal, or else I'll induce another miscarriage.

MARLENE: (*as they find their places*) Let's go, girls.

JUDY: All right. I look ucky.

LANA: We all do, but that's our zany wacky charm. Go, girl.

They are set. The lights come up full on the courtroom. It is a vast chamber of marble. The judge's podium is huge – twice normal size – as is the vast witness box. The courtroom should dwarf these pitiful specimens of humanity, the drag queens. The opening of Wagner's Tristan und Isolde *– "Liebestod," "Love Death." LANA plays the prosecuting attorney. JUDY plays the judge and sits on the podium with the huge gavel. JUDY will play the surprise witness Anita Hrupki later in the scene. She also plays the clerk. MARLENE is on trial and stands – stoic, silent, and arrogant – with her back to the audience.*

Note: Each drag queen playing the surprise witness later in each of the three trials should exit after she is finished playing the clerk or judge. MARLENE is on trial; JUDY is the judge, clerk, and surprise witness; and LANA is prosecuting attorney.

JUDY: (*as judge*) Toronto District Court No. 345 now in session. (*bangs gavel*) The court will now come to order.

LANA: (*as prosecuting attorney*) The prosecution calls Marlene Delorme to the stand.

JUDY: (*as clerk*) Marlene Delorme. Marlene Delorme.

MARLENE turns. There is a look of defiance on her face. She is proud and radiantly beautiful. She takes her place on the stand.

Marlene Delorme, do you swear to tell the whole truth and nothing but the truth, so help you God.

MARLENE: I do.

JUDY: (*as clerk*) Please be seated.

MARLENE: Thank you.

The clerk looks at her oddly. She looks at him oddly.

LANA: Marlene Delorme, you are accused of being a drag queen. How do you plead?

MARLENE: (*after a pause*) Not guilty.

There is a taped sound effect of reaction in the courtroom. MARLENE smiles perceptibly.

JUDY: (*as judge*) Silence in the courtroom. (*She bangs her gavel.*) You may proceed.

Pause.

LANA: Miss Delorme – may I call you Miss?

MARLENE: Certainly.

LANA: Miss Delorme. You were born in 1960 in Winnipeg, Manitoba, of natural parents?

MARLENE: That is true.

LANA: A simple yes or no will be sufficient. Now, Miss Delorme, can you tell me something about your childhood?

MARLENE: I had a depraved childhood.

LANA: Pardon me, but don't you mean deprived?

MARLENE: I mean … depraved.

LANA: Now, Miss Delorme, in your own words, tell us something about your childhood in Winnipeg, Manitoba.

MARLENE: Well, at first, my childhood was much like that of any blonde-headed little boy. I played volleyball by the river near our thatched cottage with my chums, Mary, Ellen, and Louise. I had a pink Harley motor scooter, and a pet frog named Desirée. Life was carefree then – there was school and the usual after-school circle jerks, evenings being consumed by my overwhelming, almost embarrassing passion for my long, red train. In the afternoons there were pot parties on the lawn, and my father would serve us schnapps and tell us dirty stories. He was French and German in extraction.

LANA: I see. A life not unlike that of many other immigrant Winnipeg children.

MARLENE: You could say that, yes.

LANA: I find your story almost too idyllic to believe.

MARLENE: Well, that's your problem, isn't it?

LANA: I have no problems, Miss Delorme. It is you who have the "problems." That is why you are here today, on trial.

MARLENE: I don't agree.

LANA: That is irrelevant. (*pause*) Now, although your childhood was idyllic and, to quote you, much like that of any blonde-headed little boy, you made some fatal, ultimately tragic decisions in Winnipeg, did you not?

MARLENE: Why, I do not know to what you refer.

LANA: (*lashing out*) Perhaps I am referring to your decision to move to Toronto and become the rudest, most obnoxious drag queen in Eastern Canada?

MARLENE: I made no such conscious decision.

LANA: Well, if you made no such conscious decision, how do you explain the fact that you sit before us wearing breasts which are obviously not your own?

MARLENE: I hope you do not wish to imply that I stole these breasts. They are mine. I bought them.

LANA: (*leaning in for the kill*) Don't toy with me, Miss Delorme. If you made no such fatal decision, how did you turn into this monster that we see before us?

MARLENE: (*clearing her throat*) I became the horrible monster, to which you refer, not because of any fatal decision of my own, but due to tragic circumstances – in fact my own lethally accurate colour sense.

LANA: Colour sense?

MARLENE: Yes, you see, as a child, my mother would dress me up in, for instance, mauve shorts with a pink shirt and purple dickie, with perhaps blue accents in the socks and the usual white-and-black Oxfords and, of course, I would be forced to point out to her that her colour schemata was quite simply not going anywhere. Yes, perhaps pink with the mauve – though this is a trifle obvious, but the blue accents in the socks lead the eye to expect the wrong things and with the addition of the purple dickie, we have what must be quite simply termed a riot of colour. I refused to wear the outfit.

LANA: Was your mother outraged, then?

MARLENE: Outraged, no. Confused perhaps. But I base my not-guilty plea on what I consider to be my God-given traits – my colour sense and, of course, my passion for accessorizing, which was inherited from my grandmother who, not unlike Isadora Duncan, died when her scarf was caught in a pickup truck door. But I am a drag queen, and proud of my inherited traits. Indeed, to die because a purse or a scarf was caught in the doorway of any vehicle, particularly one driven by a handsome and masculine sort of man, would be a suitable death, a death I would treasure.

LANA: I don't think I understand the term "suitable death."

MARLENE: But then again, you aren't a drag queen, are you? Unless, of course, you are hiding something from us!

Laughter in the courtroom.

LANA: (*caught off guard*) I do not know to what you refer.

From the back of the theatre, JUDY suddenly enters. She is now Anita, MARLENE's hairdresser from Winnipeg.

JUDY: Marlene Delorme!

MARLENE: (*reflex action*) What – I –

JUDY: Marlene Delorme –

MARLENE: Anita, what are you – (*She stops, covers her mouth.*)

LANA: Marlene Delorme, do you know this woman?

MARLENE: No, I've never seen her before in my life.

JUDY: Don't try and lie, Bobby.

MARLENE: (*going crazy*) Bobby, she called me Bobby –

LANA: Miss Delorme, I think you are lying, I think you do, in fact, know this woman.

JUDY: You know me, admit it, you know me –

MARLENE: No, you are a complete stranger to me –

JUDY: You're lying, Bobby. At one time I was … I was little Bobby Fitch's hairdresser. And Marlene Delorme is really Bobby Fitch –

MARLENE: No, it's not true, I was never Bobby Fitch … it's not true, it's all vicious, pernicious lies.

LANA: Marlene Delorme – (*archly*) if that is, in fact, your name – will you leave the stand?

MARLENE: (*head held high*) Yes.

LANA: Anita, will you take the stand?

JUDY: Yes, Your Prosecutor.

She sits, crosses legs, smiles at non-existent judge.

LANA: Will you tell us your name, please, and what has caused you to interrupt these proceedings?

JUDY: My name is Anita Hrupki. I interrupted these proceedings because I had an important truth to tell.

JUDY smiles at the non-existent judge.

LANA: And what might that truth be?

JUDY: Well, you see, this silly Bobby Fitch is making up these lies about his background just so that he can get off scot-free. But he is guilty of being a drag queen. (*She smiles at the non-existent judge again; this is all memorized.*) The reason I say this is because this so-called Marlene Delorme was never the blonde-headed little boy she, sorry – *he* claims to be. In fact, he once had brown hair, and I was the first one to dye it. (*to the judge*) And I am sure there has been many a dye job since, Your Honour.

MARLENE: (*rising suddenly*) You vicious bitch! Who paid you? How much did they pay you? You can't even get your story straight.

LANA: Miss Delorme, please control yourself. It is only too obvious to the courtroom that the truth hurts. Continue, Miss Hrupki.

JUDY: Well, that is it, Your Honour. And Marlene Delorme is guilty of being a drag queen. Totally and completely guilty. Because she had her hair dyed blonde when she was thirteen. Through her own choice. And I did it.

LANA: And you have not been coached or paid any money to make this unexpected surprise confession.

JUDY: (*very memorized*) No, Your Prosecutor. I have not been coached. (*She looks at judge, smiles.*) Not to my knowledge.

LANA: Thank you, Miss Hrupki. You may leave the stand.

JUDY: You're welcome.

She steps down and then stops to talk to the prosecutor, who slips her some money. She smiles at the judge and moves on. Pause. MARLENE is weeping. LANA looks at her.

LANA: Marlene Delorme, will you take the stand?

MARLENE: (*wiping away the tears, dragging herself up*) Yes.

As MARLENE walks to the stand, Wagner music and a voiceover come up.

MARLENE: (*voiceover*) As I approached the stand, every nerve in my body quivering, I reviewed the accusations. They said I had lied, and I began to think about the lies, the years of lies, of living like a non-person in Winnipeg, of gazing up at the vast blue sky and feeling small, ever so small. Yes, my life had been lies, nothing but lies, but wasn't that the essence of being a drag queen? And wasn't the life of a drag queen somehow the lie that tells the truth? The words of Picasso and Norman Mailer swirled around in my head and then I finally decided, yes, I had to take the stand and finally tell the truth, the truth in all its bitterness, its violence, its sordid detail. I had entered that courtroom a proud Marlene Delorme, and whatever the outcome, I refused to leave it a cringing Bobby Fitch.

LANA: Now, Miss Delorme, I am going to ask you again if that is your name, and I will remind you that you are under oath.

MARLENE: Yes, my name is Marlene Delorme, but I was born Bobby Fitch.

LANA: So your name is really Bobby Fitch.

MARLENE: No, it is really Marlene Delorme –

LANA: So you continue to lie –

MARLENE: (*passionately*) How can I make you understand? When a drag queen lies, she tells the truth. That is what defines a drag queen. Yes, I was a boring little boy named Bobby Fitch; yes, I lived in a horrid little house, not a thatched cottage; yes, I had a pet frog, and his name wasn't Desirée – it was Fred; and my motor scooter wasn't pink, it was green like the motor scooters of other children. Yes, I made up those lies about my past, but only because my past could never be my past, because I am too fascinating and romantic a human being to have ever had a normal upbringing in Winnipeg.

LANA: I'm sorry, but in a court of law there is only truth and lies, and it seems obvious to me –

MARLENE: Don't talk to me about what is obvious. This may be a court of law but what about the court of the human heart. (*a murmur in the courtroom*) Let me tell you something. Yes, I admit I … (*pause*) I was born a brunette. But to quote Norman Mailer:

"Any lady who chooses to be a blonde is truly a blonde."

LANA: I'm sorry, the testimony of Norman Mailer is not admissible in a court of law.

MARLENE: What is admissible? Just think for a minute. What was admissible for me, a little boy with dusty brown hair, for I had light-coloured roots, who was a blonde in his heart? Don't let anyone tell you anything else, blondes do have more fun, and I made a pact with myself as a child that I would live my life as a blonde, no matter how much money I had to spend on conditioner. Before you condemn me, before you condemn the other little drag queens in the world, I want you to think about me – to the world outside, a brunette, yes, but born blonde, sitting in the living room of our two-bedroom house in Winnipeg in the middle of a bitter Winnipeg winter, and it's two o'clock in the morning and I'm sitting in front of the TV with the sound turned down to nothing, watching the sign-off signal. And do you know why?

LANA: Well, I don't really feel it's relevant –

MARLENE: No, it isn't relevant to anyone, but it is to me, and all the other little drag queens in the world, because the last thing to appear on that screen was the Canadian national anthem and a collage about Canada, with pictures of the Royal Family, and the Prairies, and the Rockies and finally what I had been waiting for, two ballet dancers. A woman, blonde, who I imagined myself to be, and a man with his buttocks almost naked, holding her. Imagine me, at seven years old waiting for the station to sign off, terrified that my father would find me, for this was the image that kept me alive, the image of those ballet dancers during the "O Canada" sign-off, during those lonely, bitter Winnipeg years. Find me guilty if you wish, guilty of being true to myself, guilty of being true to my innermost instincts instead of repressing everything honest, alive, and real that is inside of me, like the rest of the population of this cold, puritanical, sad, grey country where people have forgotten how to experience real joy, where bars close at one o'clock and marijuana is illegal, where people feel guilty for touching one another, where the only real happiness seems to be getting together on Saturday night and watching a bunch of idiots get their heads bashed in, in a stupid and savage sport they call hockey!

Taped applause.

LANA: Well, Marlene, or Bobby, or whatever your name is, the fact remains that you have lied on this witness stand, and in a court of law. That is perjury. I cannot see how any jury, however impassioned your plea, could acquit a liar.

MARLENE: Unless, of course, I have a jury of drag queens.

LANA: I rest the case for the moment. I call the second drag queen to the stand. Judy Goose.

The three drag queens break out of their characters and walk to their mirrors to start changing for the next courtroom drama.

MARLENE: So, anyway, when this guy told me he was not going to let me into Chaps I told him I was going to let him have it.

LANA: Marlene – how butch!

JUDY: So did you?

MARLENE: No, I chickened out. He has such big arms. So, anyway, I decided to lodge this formal letter of protest with *The Body Politic* and –

LANA: Marlene, darling, dearest.

MARLENE: Yes, Lana, lovelorn, lonely.

LANA: Are we to spend the whole evening being treated to boring stories of your tawdry melodramatic encounters with burly doormen?

MARLENE: Why, I suppose we don't really *have* to.

LANA: No?

MARLENE: No, I mean I suppose we could sit around and listen to your maudlin self-indulgent stories about the last man to beat you up in bed.

LANA: Oh Marlene, you're a card.

MARLENE: Oh Lana, you're a toilet queen.

LANA: I can't believe what a bitch you are. I tell you in confidence that I did, as a confused and effeminate young man, on occasion, cruise the toilets, and you insist on torturing me about it for the rest of my life.

MARLENE: I guess what bothers me is every time I stand on the corner of Jarvis and Wellesley, you insist on screeching at me at the top of your lungs – did you make any good tricks, honey? One thing I have never been is a prostitute.

LANA: Well, my philosophy is men are going to abuse you anyway, so you might as well make them pay cold hard cash for doing it.

JUDY: I had this guy really abuse me last night.

MARLENE: (*suddenly interested*) You did?

LANA: Who was it.

JUDY: His name was Dirk.

MARLENE: Oh God. Dirk. I've never met a Dirk I didn't hate.

LANA: Not that waiter at Buddies.

JUDY: Yup.

LANA: Judy, he's luscious.

JUDY: I know. And he has the dick of death, too.

LANA: Stomach muscles?

JUDY: For days.

MARLENE: Lana, please. I cannot believe the superficiality of your remarks. The tone of this conversation is reaching gutter level. (*pause, to JUDY*) Did he fuck you?

JUDY: I wouldn't let him. You know. AIDS.

MARLENE: I know. I always make them wait until the second date before I let them fuck me. And then they have to use a condom – ribbed.

JUDY: Ohhhhhh. Condoms, I hate them.

MARLENE: But it is the only thing that saves you from AIDS, besides not fucking, and you can forget that.

LANA: Yes, darling. It's one thing being fashionably self-destructive, but actually killing yourself and other people, well, I draw the line there –

JUDY: But don't you have trouble getting them on?

MARLENE: No, and you can accessorize, see? (*pulling out a pack of Fiesta condoms*) They come in lovely different vibrant colours to go with your bracelets and lingerie. I am particularly fond of a black bra with black condoms. I think the accents go quite nicely with my new dark lashes –

LANA: So get to the punchline, dear. Did he hit you?

JUDY: No, nothing like that. But this guy, Dirk, he was really rude.

LANA: Hmmm. I don't know if really rude actually counts as abuse.

MARLENE: Well, if you haven't been abused for days, it kind of makes you feel warm and cuddly and alive inside again. So what did he say, dear.

JUDY: Well. When we were all done and, it took a while, it takes him a long time to come, and when he finally did and he was lying in bed, and I asked him if he wanted a drink or a coffee and he said, yes, a drink.

MARLENE: How like a Dirk.

JUDY: So I went up to get him one but I was like naked, so I went to my closet to get a robe and I opened it up and there was all my stuff –

MARLENE: He saw the dresses –

LANA: The primal moment of a drag queen's existence. (*pause*) Was he shocked?

JUDY: Well, like at first he didn't get it, right, and he asked me if I had a roommate –

LANA: (*scoldingly*) Judy.

JUDY: What.

LANA: You didn't tell him you had a roommate.

JUDY: No. I was like really proud of myself, Lana, because I said, "No, I don't have a roommate – those dresses are mine," and then, just like that, I said, "I am a drag queen," because you said it's better to say it yourself than have them say it, right? So I did.

LANA: I'm proud of you, dear. If there's one thing a drag queen should be honest about, it's that she's a liar. So what did he do.

JUDY: He started yelling at me.

LANA: What did he say.

JUDY: He started saying drag queens were the lowest of lows and that he'd never go out with a drag queen and wasn't I a man or what.

LANA: So you told him off, right?

JUDY: Well –

LANA: I told you –

MARLENE: Lana darling, give it a rest.

LANA: I will not give it a rest. She should have told him off. He maligned our race.

MARLENE: Lana, look, it's hopeless, drag queens will always be thought of as the lowest scum on the face of the earth and the best thing to do is just accept that salient fact. It's called going with the flow. It's very Zen.

LANA: We may have a lot of bad press. But that doesn't mean we have to take it lying down.

MARLENE: Your favourite position –

LANA: Judy, listen to me –

MARLENE: Stop lecturing her. She doesn't have to confront everybody with the facts all the time –

LANA: Marlene, after what you said on the witness stand. I'm surprised at you.

MARLENE: I have my principles, but that doesn't mean I go around making a fool of myself in daily life.

LANA: Well, I have my principles and I live them every day of my life –

MARLENE: Please, Lana, don't start, I mean –

LANA: Don't ...

She breaks into her own powerful rendition of "Don't Rain on My Parade" from Funny Girl.

MARLENE: (*interrupting her*) Oh God, Saint Babs again.

LANA: And you just wait, Marlene Delorme, when it comes time for my trial, there will be no surprise witnesses.

MARLENE: You wanna bet?

VOICE: DRAG QUEENS ON TRIAL. Scene Two. Drag Queens on Trial.

JUDY: Oh shit.

MARLENE: It's all your fault, bitch.

LANA: What, cunt –

MARLENE: I've been so busy talking I haven't got my makeup straight.

JUDY: I'm really helpless without my Jungle Red.

LANA: (*to MARLENE*) Have you been using my cold cream?

MARLENE: No.

LANA: Then why is it all greasy?

MARLENE: Don't talk to me. You're the one with all the pores, darling.

VOICE: DRAG QUEENS ON TRIAL. Scene Two.

MARLENE: All right already. Hold on to your tits. God, I hate that voice.

LANA: It sounds like Orson Welles. I always loved him, fat or no fat. It's talent that really counts in this world, thank God.

MARLENE: Let's go, girls.

They enter the trial area again. This time JUDY is on trial; LANA is the judge, clerk, and surprise witness; and MARLENE is prosecuting attorney.

LANA: (*as judge*) Toronto District Court No. 878 now in session. (*She bangs the gavel.*) The court will now come to order.

MARLENE: The prosecution calls Judy Goose to the stand.

LANA: (*as clerk*) Judy Goose. Judy Goose.

JUDY stands up and fixes her stockings. She is still the dumb, guileless, sweet, and flirtatious girl she always is, only in this scene she has a Brooklyn accent and sounds a lot like Judy Holliday. She walks up to the witness stand.

LANA: Judy Goose, do you swear to tell the whole truth and nothing but the truth, so help you God.

JUDY: You bet.

LANA: (*as clerk*) Please be seated.

JUDY: Yeah.

LANA looks at JUDY oddly. JUDY looks at LANA oddly.

MARLENE: Judy Goose, you are accused of being a drag queen. How do you plead?

JUDY: Not guilty. With extenuating circumstances.

A murmur in the courtroom. JUDY looks around, confused.

JUDY: What's that?

LANA: (*as judge*) A murmur in the courtroom.

JUDY: Oh. I thought it was the pipes or something.

MARLENE: Now, Miss Goose, I may call you miss?

JUDY: (*nonplussed*) Yeah.

MARLENE: Miss Goose, you said you are pleading not guilty with extenuating circumstances.

JUDY: That's right.

MARLENE: And what might those extenuating circumstances be?

JUDY: (*as if by rote*) My tortured existence.

MARLENE: What?

JUDY: Are you deaf?

MARLENE: Pardon me, and what might that tortured existence be?

JUDY: Well, in the sad and sorry tale of my bizarre hurly-burly life story, I hardly know where to start. (*clearing her throat*) I was born many, many years ago, twenty-five to be exact, on a remote sled in the Yukon.

MARLENE: Excuse me, you were born on a sled?

JUDY: (*looking at her as if she's crazy*) Yeah.

MARLENE: Somehow I find that hard to believe.

JUDY: (a small laugh) Ha ha. (pause) So?

MARLENE: (annoyed) Please continue.

JUDY: My father was a cruel and heartless monster who beat me. Repeatedly. Hince, there was little choice –

MARLENE: I'm sorry, what was that you said?

JUDY: Where?

MARLENE: Before "there was little choice."

JUDY: Hince?

MARLENE: Ah. You mean *hence.*

JUDY: Hince. Hence. Jeez. *Hence*, there was little choice but for me to escape. Thus I ran away to Switzerland. At the age of seventeen. At that tender age, I was an innocent virgin unschooled in the ways of men. I found myself drinking alone on trains. A lot. And soon, unbeknownst to my own conscious mind, I had plunged myself into a snowdrift. I thought there was little hope, then, lo and behold, someone found me. The next thing I knew, I woke up in a lovely bed with coopids –

MARLENE: With what?

JUDY: Coopids – you know, those little fat babies – coopids around my head. My benefactor was none other than Hans Von Friedenbatch, composer of the "Swedish Rhapsody." With care and love, he brought me back to life. Though he had many years seniority over me, he wanted to marry me. However, I could not do this, due to my past. Then –

MARLENE: Excuse me, Miss Goose.

JUDY: Yeah?

MARLENE: I'm afraid you have neglected to tell us very much about the tragic details of your past.

JUDY: What do you think I've been doing for the past ten minutes?

MARLENE: That's all well and good, but really the only vaguely tragic detail you have revealed is that you were born in the Yukon, on a sled.

JUDY: Well, isn't that tragic enough for ya?

MARLENE: Well, really.

JUDY: Well, how would you like to be born on a sled?

MARLENE: I have to admit –

JUDY: Can I go on now?

MARLENE: Well, I'm just concerned that –

JUDY: All right already. Jeez. (She straightens her skirt and smiles at the non-existent judge.) I will continue my story, Your Honour. So anyway, where was I –

MARLENE: You could not marry the composer of the "Swedish Rhapsody" due to your tragic past on a sled.

JUDY: Yeah, well something like that. So, I could not marry him, though in my heart I wanted to, therefore the only thing to do was run away to Switz – (realizing she means) Mexico. There I stayed for many years, dissipating. Until finally, in a drunken stupor I met a man who wanted to put me into a show. He was a big producer so I said, "Okay!" But in order to be in this show I'd have to wear a dress. Thus I became a sad and tragic drag queen due to the intenuating circumcisions of my existence. (pause, then looking at the prosecuting attorney) There. How's that?

She begins flirting with the non-existent judge.

MARLENE: Miss Goose, ahh ... Miss Goose, could I please have your attention?

JUDY: Yeah?

MARLENE: May I ask you –

JUDY: Sure.

MARLENE: How you can expect an intelligent adult person in possession of his or her sanity to believe your story.

JUDY: I don't know. That's your problem.

MARLENE: Well, first of all, that is not my problem, Miss Goose; in fact, it is very definitely your problem. It is patently obvious from your badly memorized little performance that your testimony is nothing but a bald-faced lie.

JUDY: Hey! (to judge) Can he say that? (to MARLENE, noticing judge is gone) Where's the judge? I was getting along real swell with him.

Suddenly the back door of the theatre is flung open.

LANA: (from off, as Hermione) Judy Goose.

JUDY: What?

LANA: Judy Goose. Do you remember me?

JUDY: Hey, what's that voice? Where's it coming from?

A woman appears at the back of the courtroom. She is Hermione Rosemount, an ugly middle-aged woman, soberly dressed and wearing a parka.

LANA: It was my voice. I'm sorry to interrupt. My name is Hermione Rosemount. I knew Miss Goose many years ago, before she was Miss Goose. I would like to say a few words.

MARLENE: Judy Goose, do you know this woman?

JUDY: Well, I ... I don't know, I might ...

MARLENE: Hermione Rosemount, will you take the stand.

JUDY: What about me?

MARLENE: We'll get back to you. But it does sound as if this testimony might be very relevant to your case.

JUDY: Well, all right. But I don't understand.

MARLENE: Now, Miss Rosemount, please tell the court how long you have known Miss Goose.

LANA: I have known Miss Goose since she was five years old, and her name was Billy Bunt.

MARLENE: I see. Now was this Billy Bunt that you know, like Miss Goose, born on a sled in the Yukon?

LANA: Well, as strange and fantastical as it may sound, he was. In fact, being born on a sled is, oddly enough, the one detail of Billy's story that is actually true.

JUDY: What's she talking about, the tight-assed bitch, I've never seen her before in my life.

MARLENE: Miss Goose, you will shut up or kindly leave the courtroom.

JUDY: Fuck you. (*She sits down.*)

MARLENE: How did you come to know Billy Bunt?

LANA: Well, Billy's tale is a complex one, and quite tragic in its own way. During his formative years, his elementary school days, I was Billy's guidance counsellor. It's not easy being a guidance counsellor in Whitehorse. Children are children everywhere, of course, but these children always had special problems, and well, Billy's problems were the most special of all.

MARLENE: Is it true that Billy's father beat him?

LANA: No. I'm sorry. That is not true at all. Billy's father was a nice, quiet, kindly man, he used to manufacture sleds, and many a sunny day in Whitehorse would see little Billy pulled along gaily, as it were, by his father's gentle hand.

MARLENE: When did you first perceive that Billy was a problem child?

LANA: Well, his grade three teacher came to me quite concerned because she noticed, first of all, Billy refused to take off his clothes to undress for gym class. We were concerned, of course, that he thought he had some sort of physical deformity. We insisted to little Billy that he needn't worry about taking off his clothes with all the other little boys, because, after all, all little boys looked the same naked. Billy replied, I remember his intent little eyes gazing at us with almost righteous indignation, "All little boys," he solemnly scolded us, "do not look alike naked." (*pause*) It was then that we first knew that something was wrong.

MARLENE: So what did you do then?

LANA: Well, we put little Billy in a special class for exceptional children, we call them, those that don't quite fit in with the others but are unique in their own way. Unfortunately, Billy didn't fit into that class either. In fact, little Billy didn't fit into any class anywhere. It was then that Billy's descent into madness began.

MARLENE: What exactly do you mean by madness?

LANA: Well, in case you haven't noticed – Billy is mad. Not only is Billy a drag queen, living a lie, pretending to be a woman, but somewhere around grade three he went totally bonkers, and I do not use this term lightly.

JUDY: What's she talking about?

MARLENE: Please, Miss Goose.

JUDY: But I don't understand.

MARLENE: Please remain seated.

JUDY sits, obviously worried.

MARLENE: Please continue.

LANA: In grade three, Billy began watching Hercules cartoons. He began to identify dangerously with Newton, Hercules's weak and witty sidekick, so much so that he would go up to boys in class, usually the most handsome and strapping among them, and say, "How's it going, Herc?"

MARLENE: I see, and did these delusions continue?

LANA: Most certainly. Now if you analyze closely Billy's little speech today, you will see that most of what he claims has happened to him, except the birth in the sled, all occurred to Lana Turner in the movie *Madame X*.

MARLENE: I see.

LANA: Yes, Billy, like many modern homosexuals, finds his life so depressing that he must find solace in trashy melodrama. Of course this is unhealthy, but for Billy it has become a fatal obsession. Billy believes, in fact, that he *is* Madame X. He believes that he was rescued from a snowdrift by the composer of the "Swedish Rhapsody," etc. What we have here, in fact, is the tragic end for the child who refused to adjust to normal life and hides in fantasy. Billy is a misfit, and he has finally gone insane.

MARLENE: Is there any hope left for little Billy Bunt?

LANA: None whatsoever. He has descended into the maelstrom of schizophrenia and there is no turning back.

JUDY has started to cry softly in the corner.

MARLENE: Thank you, Miss Rosemount. It must have been difficult for you to come here and tell this sorry tale.

LANA: Yes, well, it was. We guidance counsellors have our trials, too, you know. But just so that one little child out there can be pulled from turning to drugs, excessive sex, or punk-rock music, and become a useful, normal, productive member of society, for the sake of that misguided child for whom there is still some hope, unlike Billy, it is for he/she that I speak.

MARLENE: Thank you again, Miss Rosemount.

LANA: You're welcome.

LANA gets down and walks away, with her usual "martyr" stance. Pause. The prosecutor calls out.

MARLENE: Judy Goose, will you take the stand.

JUDY: (*strangely*) Yeah?

MARLENE: I said, Judy Goose, will you take the stand?

JUDY: (*weirdly*) Sure.

She gets up. Music. Voiceover, as she walks.

JUDY: (*voiceover*) I was real screwed up. This stuck-up old lady said I was crazy. Could it be true? I didn't know for sure, that is, sometimes I sure didn't know what the hell I was thinking. For some reason, I felt real weak and I almost couldn't walk. When I did open my mouth, I didn't know what words were going to come out.

JUDY: Um, I, ummm ...

MARLENE: Miss Goose?

JUDY: (*a shadow of her former self*) Yeah?

MARLENE: What do you have to say now, in the light of the testimony of Miss Rosemount?

JUDY: Well, I ... (*turning to the audience*) Gee, I don't know what to say. This lady says I'm crazy but (*starting to cry*) I'm not crazy, am I? I mean ever since I was a kid I've been different, not like the other kids, but does that mean I'm crazy? I know I like old movies but I didn't know that was a sickness, and I know I like to dress up like a girl but it's really hard being like this, having these feelings ever since you're little and they're not the feelings everybody else has, but they're still your feelings and if you tell people you're afraid they'll just laugh at you and then you feel so alone, you just want to kill yourself and, well, if it's true that I'm crazy because I like old movies and I like to dress up as a girl, well, then maybe the best thing for me to do is kill myself, so I'll do it right now. (*taking out a gun*) Here –

MARLENE: Miss Goose –

JUDY: Here goes ...

She lifts up the gun. There is a struggle among the three for the gun, then the voice on tape interrupts just in time.

VOICE: DRAG QUEENS ON TRIAL.

Blackout. Music.

VOICE: They lived so close to the edge they thought they might fall off.

Lights up.

ALL: (*in a pose*) DRAG QUEENS ON TRIAL.

Blackout.

VOICE: They batted their eyes until they bruised their lids, always praying for that special man to marry them and give them kids –

Lights up.

ALL: DRAG QUEENS ON TRIAL.

Blackout.

VOICE: What will happen? Will Judy Goose kill herself? Will Hermione Rosemount ever have an orgasm? What do you drag queens think?

Lights up.

MARLENE: I think we need a break, darling.

LANA: Oh fuck yes.

MARLENE: Doing the prosecuting attorney is an absolutely thankless role, especially in that scene.

JUDY: And my mascara is running.

LANA: And trying to make myself ugly for that Hermione role is a real trial since I have to squash my natural beauty and sexual *je ne sais quoi*.

MARLENE: I think we should have an intermission.

VOICE: Okay. INTERMISSION. DRAG QUEENS ON TRIAL.

Blackout.

Lights up. The drag queens are caught trying to get offstage.

MARLENE: Honey, put a lid on it, will ya?

LANA: Yeah, yeah, right. (*to audience*) Why don't you go out into the lobby for a Coke or a coffee and please don't come back for at least fifteen minutes, I have this incredible costume change which –

MARLENE: Yeah, someday she's going to suffocate in her own size-D cups.

LANA: If I need any shit from you, Marlene, I'll squeeze your head.

VOICE: DRAG QUEENS ON TRIAL.

ALL: AGHGHGHGHGHGHGHGHGHGGH!

They scream, then sing cheerily.

Let's go out to the lobby
Let's go out to the lobby
Let's go out to the lobby
And have a cigarette, or a Coke, or a beer, or a joint!

Blackout.

ACT TWO

*Lights come up on a forlorn **LANA**, who mouths the words to a tawdry rendition of "Black Coffee," sung by Peggy Lee, or some other suitably tacky number about a woman being abused by a man. When this is over, the lights come up on all three. The queens are at their mirrors again, chatting, getting ready for the final trial scene – LANA's.*

MARLENE: Well, all I can say, Miss Lust, is that you are acting incredibly immature for a girl who's always carrying on like she's Miss Together.

LANA: Look who's talking.

MARLENE: (*to JUDY*) Have you got a cigarette?

JUDY: Yeah.

LANA: Well, if I don't want to phone the doctor back it's my business, slut, not yours.

MARLENE: It's my business because I love you as only one slut can love another, even though I never take money as you do. We're at the bottom of this garbage heap and we have to stick together. Phone him.

JUDY: It's probably only herpes or something.

MARLENE: Only herpes. Herpes is like a major disease, Judy.

JUDY: It's just like warts, isn't it?

LANA: It's not like warts and for your information I already have herpes. (*pause*) Yes, don't look so shocked.

MARLENE: And you never told your sister? After all these years I've been sharing your lipstick?

LANA: You can only get it from licking open sores.

MARLENE: True, I only lick your open sores once a week or so, so I should be fine. Well, now that we know you're herpetic, I'd like my mouthwash back.

LANA: Oh, stop being such a witch. So anyway, the reason I refuse to phone my doctor is because I already have every major disease. The only one left is death.

MARLENE: Pity, they haven't found a cure for that yet.

JUDY: Do we have to talk about this? I'm getting depressed.

MARLENE: That's just it, you dizzy doll, diseases are depressing, but that doesn't mean you shouldn't phone your doctor. Phone him back, or else.

LANA: I won't. The way I look at it is, if I'm going to die, I'm going to die.

MARLENE: Oh, that's a tremendously healthy attitude. You know what? I think you're suicidal.

LANA: Oh, not your psychological analysis, please. Somebody gave me that *I'm OK, You're OK* book and I said, "Honey, look, I think we'd get along a lot better if we both agreed we're two lousy hopeless fucked-up shits."

JUDY: What happened?

LANA: I guess the truth hurts. He never phoned back.

JUDY: Are there men who phone back?

LANA: Yes. They're called heterosexuals.

MARLENE: That also happens to be a pile of fresh, smelly bullshit. I know a lot of straight women who –

LANA: Here she goes again – next thing you'll tell us is they don't know you're a man.

MARLENE: Some of them don't, anyway, and they all have as much trouble as we do with men.

LANA: Listen, bitch, the difference between straight men and gay men is this: straight men make you pay for a movie and a dinner and then don't call you back, right?

JUDY: Yeah, right.

LANA: But gay men make you pay for a movie and a dinner and then fuck you in the ass badly, spill poppers all over your finest gown, rip your nipples off with rusty tit clamps, and then don't phone you back.

MARLENE: Straight women don't have it easier than us. It's men who are the problem.

LANA: It's men who gave me this disease. It's men who killed me.

MARLENE: You're really giving me a pain in the hemorrhoid, darling. You obviously want to die. Or else you'd go to the doctor and find out what's wrong.

JUDY: Why would Lana want to die?

MARLENE: Because she's a sad, not-too-great-looking, rapidly aging drag queen who can't even get into her old dresses anymore.

LANA: At least my back isn't so mashed up with acne scars that I can't wear my low-cut lamé.

MARLENE: You leave my acne scars out of this or I'll tell every bartender in town you're herpetic, and you won't be able to suck them off anymore to get a free drink.

LANA: Frigid bitch!

MARLENE: Cavernous cunt!

LANA: Size queen!

MARLENE: Dinge queen!

LANA: Rice Queen!

MARLENE: (à la Bette Davis in Whatever Happened to Baby Jane?) The bird got out, here's your lunch.

LANA: Oh, Jane, you wouldn't say these awful things to me if I wasn't in a wheelchair.

MARLENE: Butchya *are* Blanche! Ya are! (*pause*) And you are nothing but a ten-dollar-a-blow-job whore.

LANA: That is bullshit. I have never gotten less than twenty dollars for a blow job in my life.

JUDY: (*holding them back*) Wait a minute – for two girls who are supposed to love each other so much, how come I always have to keep you from killing each other.

MARLENE: We have an open relationship. There's always room for hate.

LANA: Just give up and let me die.

MARLENE: I refuse to get involved anymore in this immature melodramatic discussion. Judy is right.

JUDY: Thanks.

MARLENE: If you don't want to call your doctor, fine. It's literally your funeral. And I won't be there.

VOICE: DRAG QUEENS ON TRIAL.

MARLENE: Fuck off.

LANA: Oh dry up.

JUDY: My eyelashes are not sticking. My nail polish isn't dry.

MARLENE: That asshole seems to scream at us earlier and earlier each time.

VOICE: I'm just following the script. I'm prerecorded.

LANA: It's not his fault.

JUDY: Oh, I'm never going to remember all these lines. I hate this scene.

LANA: Well, if you get tongue-tied, I'll just ask myself a question.

VOICE: DRAG QUEENS ON TRIAL. Hurry up!

They go out.

ALL: All right already, we're going – jeez, give it a rest.

They take their places. LANA is on trial. JUDY is the prosecuting attorney. MARLENE is the judge, clerk, and surprise witness, Dr. Dimchick.

MARLENE: (*as judge*) Toronto District Court No. 5,768 now in session.

MARLENE bangs the gavel. LANA looks at the judge, annoyed.

MARLENE: (*as judge*) The court will now come to order.

JUDY: The prosecution calls Lana Lust to the stand.

MARLENE: (as clerk) Lana Lust Lana Lust Lana Lust –

LANA: (turning suddenly) I heard you. (She does a melodramatic toss of her head.) Yes.

MARLENE: (as clerk) Lana Lust, do you swear to tell the whole truth and nothing but the truth, so help you God, or are you going to lie as usual.

LANA: I promise to tell the whole truth to the best of my knowledge for my simple yet passionate heart can allow me to do no less in the face of –

MARLENE: (as clerk) Please be seated.

LANA glares at clerk and sits. Pause.

JUDY: Lana Lust.

LANA: She is I.

JUDY: Lana Lust, you have been accused of being a drag queen. How do you plead.

LANA: I plead ... (pause, for effect) guilty.

A woman screams somewhere in the courtroom.

MARLENE: (as judge) Silence in the courtroom. Someone get that woman to a doctor.

The woman is dragged out. The judge bangs his gavel.

MARLENE: (as judge) You may proceed.

JUDY: Miss Lust. I may call you miss?

LANA: It doesn't much matter what you call me now.

JUDY: A simple yes or no will be ... proficient.

LANA: Sufficient.

JUDY: That's what I said. Now, Miss Lust, I want to ask you a few questions.

LANA: Whatever you wish.

JUDY: First of all (consulting notes): you say ... that you are ... guilty of being a drag queen. Is that true?

LANA: I cannot say otherwise.

JUDY: And why are you guilty?

LANA: Being a drag queen is my life.

JUDY: And why is that?

LANA: Because ... I love to dress as a woman. I always have. It makes life thrilling for me, somehow. Who knows why? But for me, male clothing is boring, restrictive, impractical, it's a contradiction, isn't it –

JUDY: (interrupting) I see. (pause) Do you have sleazy sex with men in back alleys, toilets, steam baths, and other dark and disgusting and dangerous places?

LANA: As often as humanly possible.

JUDY: I see. (shuffling through papers) You admit this?

LANA: Yes, I must. I am Lana Lust and ... I must.

JUDY: I see. (pause) Well ... (finds paper) Do you have sex for money, that is, are you a prostitute?

LANA: Yes.

JUDY: How often.

LANA: Whenever I run out of money.

JUDY: I see. And when is that?

LANA: Well, I ... always seem to be running out of money.

JUDY: Well, Miss Lust, if you admit to these accusations, and you admit to being a drag queen, then it seems that you must be guilty, and there is no choice but for the jury to find you so –

LANA: Wait, I – (She gets up, stops.)

JUDY: What is it?

LANA: I want to say something, that is I ... (sits)

JUDY: Yes.

LANA: Well, it suddenly occurred to me, something about belonging, and well, I always think of Joan Crawford's words at the end of A Woman's Face. I want to have a home and children, she says, and I want to go to market and cheat the grocer and fight with the landlord. I want to belong to the human race. Ironically, I have always identified with –

MARLENE: Lana Lust.

LANA: (gets up, crazed) What's that –

JUDY: I think it's ... the surprise witness, I can't remember her name.

LANA: Omigod –

MARLENE: Lana Lust.

MARLENE enters as Dr. Dimchick. She resembles Margaret Hamilton, the Wicked Witch of the West in The Wizard of Oz, and she wears a lab coat.

MARLENE: Lana Lust, at last I have found you.

LANA: I don't know what she's talking about.

JUDY: Lana Lust, do you know this surprise witness?

LANA: No ... no, I've never seen her before in my life; that is, wait a minute, I think she might be my long-lost sister, who often used to dress up as a doctor, but of course she's out of her mind.

MARLENE: Don't try and be funny, Miss Lust. I am not Miss Lust's crazed sister, though she would prefer you to believe that. No, we had her sister put in a home years ago. Now, thank God, we will be able to have Miss Lust herself put away forever, when my true and factual testimony is finally heard.

JUDY: Miss Lust, will you leave the stand?

LANA: No ... I refuse, this woman is an imposter, a lying, cheating, deceiving imposter. She thinks that just by putting on a lab coat and a stethoscope she can become a doctor, but it takes years of medical school ... (as *MARLENE approaches*) No ... no, stay away from me or I'll ... (*taking out a gun*) I'll shoot!

A reaction in the courtroom.

JUDY: Miss Lust.

MARLENE: Don't worry. (*calmly walking up to LANA*) No weapon is dangerous enough to protect you from the brutal truth. Sit down right now, you depressing, self-defeating, unfortunately dressed, promiscuous slut.

LANA starts to cry and stumbles to her seat in tears. Pause. MARLENE deposits the gun in her pocket and sits down.

JUDY: Dr. Dimchick, how long have you known the defendant?

MARLENE: I have been Miss Lust's personal family physician since she was a tiny, effeminate child. Her name was Davey Dollop then.

JUDY: And what have you come to tell us today?

MARLENE: The simple facts. Miss Lust has been avoiding me, refusing to answer my calls. Well, I have finally caught up with her. The simple facts are these: Miss Lust has contracted the deadly disease AIDS.

LANA: (*a strangled cry*) Ughggh.

MARLENE: I would give her only a few months to live. A few days, if she continues on in her present lifestyle. Her years of loose living, of flaunting authority, have finally caught up with her.

LANA: Ahhh!

MARLENE: Yes, Miss Lust, there's no turning back now. You see, Miss Lust has always favoured promiscuous sex, in which she has been the passive partner. She has swallowed busloads of male sperm, as well as drugging herself into a semi-conscious state every evening in order to loosen her so-called inhibitions, though I firmly doubt that she ever had any in the first place. These activities, combined with the fact that she has been almost constantly under medication for some venereal disease or other, have caused her to contract this fatal illness. There is, in fact, no need to convict Miss Lust, for this human dog shit is going to perish anyway, and for all intents and purposes by her own hand. Like many modern homosexuals, Miss Lust has committed a form of suicide due to her promiscuous habits, and now she must pay the price.

JUDY: What you are saying is that Miss Lust is already just about dead.

MARLENE: That's the long and the short of it. I choose this phrase because it is a pun that Miss Lust, an infamous size queen, would easily understand.

JUDY: Thank you, Dr. Dimchick, your testimony has made many things clear.

MARLENE: You're welcome.

JUDY: You may leave the stand.

MARLENE: I will. I will leave Miss Lust's medical file as Exhibit A. (*She pulls out a chart which has an obviously plunging arrow on it with "DEATH" scrawled all over it.*) And your little dog, too!

Pause. Only LANA's tears can be heard. Then the duet from Wagner's Tristan und Isolde *is heard, with LANA's voice on tape as she moves to the stand.*

LANA: (*voiceover*) So it was true. What I had suspected all along, that my filthy sexual habits had caused my downfall. It was a nightmare, almost too horrible to be real. For a moment, I was so lost and sad and alone that I felt I would collapse there in the courtroom and never recover my senses. I felt like ripping off my wig, my dress, all the symbols of my otherness, and giving myself up to what the doctor had predicted would soon be my almost certain death. Surely every drag queen, nay, every homosexual dreams this nightmare. The sadistic doctor with the facts, the brutal facts, the balance sheet where it says in cold, hard, computer printout – I was a passive partner in sex, as if all my passivity, all my femininity, all my womanliness which I always treasured was the essence of my disease, my heartbreak, my tragedy. I stood up, and looked around the courtroom, and then the strangest thing happened.

A spotlight picks out an attractive young man in the audience.

LANA: (*voiceover*) As I stood up, my eye happened to fall on an attractive boy in the audience. He couldn't have been more than twenty years old and there was something lovely and gentle about his fragile beauty. I sensed that he was confused in his sexual identity, that he was at that turning point in his life when he had to choose between becoming a normal, productive member of society or being a drag queen. Suddenly all my shame, all my terror shattered like glass. Yes, I was promiscuous. Yes, I was even a prostitute. Yes, I had swallowed busloads of sperm in my brief and eventful lifespan. Yes, I was condemned to death, but for that boy, for that lovely confused gentle child, for his sake, I could not succumb to despair. I looked around me at the faces of the people who waited so eagerly for my response. And then slowly, tentatively, for I was sickly now, the physical pain seemed quite real, I began the torturous trek to the witness stand. I knew that all eyes were upon me and I held my head high. And then, somehow, thinking of that lovely, confused boy, there was a lightness to my feet, because I had a mission; after all, people would have to believe me now, for why would a drag queen, condemned to certain death, lie? What, after all, would I have to gain? Finally, I reached the witness stand and sat down proudly, defiantly, almost exultantly. I awaited the prosecutor's question. I would tell everyone. I would tell the world. I would be a saviour. I would triumph even over my own death.

JUDY: Now, Miss Lust, I am going to ask you again, now that you have heard this damaging testimony from Dr. Dimchick, are you still proud of the deed which you in fact admit being guilty of, or have you repented.

LANA: (*weakly*) No.

JUDY: Pardon me?

LANA: I say ... (*louder*) No.

JUDY: (*incredulous*) But how can you –

LANA: I say no, because that is the word I was born with on my lips, the word *no*. Since I was a tiny, yes, effeminate, child, I have always known I was different. So have many others. Unlike those many others, I did not choose the path of conformity, I chose to think for myself and live my own particular lifestyle according to my own particular lights. And if that is wrong, then I will pay for it.

JUDY: Miss Lust, how can you say that, when you have heard positive proof that your habits will lead to your own death?

LANA: Yes, it's strange, isn't it? I suppose I should be repentant, but I'm not. That is what we are like, those who do not live as others do – the different ones, those who do not surrender their minds and souls, their originality and spirituality to the multitude.

JUDY: Don't you think this is a trifle pretentious? Perhaps you forget that you have admitted that you are a common prostitute.

LANA: And who are you, who is anyone to judge? Yes, I am a drag queen, and yes, I am dying of AIDS. Perhaps I have made choices many would not agree with but I followed my heart and did the best I could with my life. For, after all, I have vowed to live dangerously and it has not been an easy vow to take. The life of a homosexual is by nature dangerous. We have always been laughed at, derided, persecuted, hounded, arrested, beaten, maimed, killed – and why? Because we dared to be ourselves. Because we dared to live on the edge, to do those things that other people might be frightened to do, and so often secretly wish to do. Why do you think so many homosexuals have become famous writers, artists, crusaders – because a passion to dare to be different, to live dangerously is the most enthralling disease in the world. And it's catching. Because when you have the disease, you experience no pain. Because the real pain, the real disease is not being true to what's inside, it's in being afraid to be afraid. I have not been afraid to look inside myself, to live on the edge of morality, society, of the world itself and, if I must die for it, so be it. And to all the little boys out there who don't want to wear their little blue booties but pick out the pink ones, to all the little girls who would rather wear army boots than spike heels, to anyone who has ever challenged authority because they lived by their own lights, I say don't turn back. Don't give up. It was worth it.

The courtroom bursts into spontaneous, taped, thunderous applause. LANA smiles humbly. Then the voice on tape.

VOICE: DRAG QUEENS ON TRIAL.

Blackout.

VOICE: The address to you, the jury. First, the prosecuting attorney's speech.

Lights up. All three drag queens play prosecuting attorneys and address the audience.

JUDY: I ask you to –

MARLENE: – think carefully.

LANA: Ladies and gentlemen of the jury –

JUDY: – these pitiful scum –

MARLENE: – who have arrived in court –

LANA: – their skirts above their heads –

JUDY: – their lecherous, disgusting –

MARLENE: – anti-morality –

LANA: – A shock to any decent –

JUDY: – God-fearing –

MARLENE: – law-abiding –

LANA: – *humane* being.

JUDY: All have admitted –

MARLENE: – their crimes –

LANA: – in one way or another.

JUDY: There is nothing to do but –

ALL: – convict them.

LANA: You have been asked here –

JUDY: – to decide –

MARLENE: – if these men are guilty –

LANA: – of being drag queens.

JUDY: Undoubtedly –

ALL: – they are.

LANA: This leaves no recourse –

JUDY: – than for you to call –

MARLENE: – for the stiffest sentence.

LANA: The gas chamber –

MARLENE: – or dismemberment –

JUDY: – might be appropriate.

LANA: Or perhaps the ancient method –

MARLENE: – from which the word *faggot* comes –

ALL: – frying over burning wood.

LANA: This too might be effective.

MARLENE: To protect your children, your families –

JUDY: – your two-car garage –

LANA: – your upwardly mobile lifestyle –

MARLENE: – and to protect you from your own –

JUDY: – secrets –

LANA: – and unconfessed desires –

MARLENE: – we urge –

ALL: – THAT THEY BE BURNED AT THE STAKE!

Blackout.

VOICE: DRAG QUEENS ON TRIAL. The defence attorney's address.

JUDY: These young men are not –

MARLENE: – on trial –

LANA: – for being drag queens –

JUDY: – but rather for being themselves.

MARLENE: If they have erred in –

LANA: – any way –

JUDY: – perhaps it is society's fault –

MARLENE: – for making it so difficult –

LANA: – for the misfit –

JUDY: – to live.

MARLENE: Think –

LANA: – what would you do –

JUDY: – if your son –

MARLENE: – or daughter –

LANA: – turned out to be –

ALL: – A DRAG QUEEN!

Expressions of horror.

ALL: Ughghgh. Arghghgh. AHHHH!

JUDY: Remember –

MARLENE: – it is perhaps not a matter –

LANA: – of choosing pink booties –

JUDY: – over blue ones –

MARLENE: – for a drag queen is born –

LANA: – with pink booties in her heart.

JUDY: There was a long speech –

MARLENE: – I was going to make –

LANA: – but I can't now.

JUDY: I have been too moved –

MARLENE: – by the final drag queen's –

LANA: – simple words.

JUDY: Indeed –

MARLENE: – to condemn these men –

LANA: – is to condemn everything –

JUDY: – brave –

MARLENE: – alive –

LANA: – and dangerous –

ALL: – IN OURSELVES.

Blackout.

Lights up on the drag queens taking off their makeup.

MARLENE: I'm glad that's over.

JUDY: That final scene gives me the creeps.

LANA: How do you think I feel? I'm the one with the AIDS nightmares.

MARLENE: Well, it's all over now, girls.

JUDY: Yeah.

LANA: Another day, another performance.

JUDY: Hey, I just thought of something.

LANA: What, girl – are you missing your Jungle Red, or what.

JUDY: We forgot about them.

MARLENE: Who, doll?

JUDY: The audience.

They all look out.

ALL: Oh yeah.

MARLENE: Well, they're not our problem. They should be able to leave the theatre by themselves.

LANA: I'd like to help that one home, the cute boy that I spotlighted during my big moment.

MARLENE: *Très* tacky, bitch –

LANA: You should talk.

JUDY: Well, you know what I think?

LANA & MARLENE: No, girl.

JUDY: I think we should sing them a song.

MARLENE: What a great idea.

LANA: I like it. Listen, (*as they get up*) the point is, a drag queen always leaves you humming. You may get a lousy blow job, or a bitchy dinner date, but a drag queen always leaves you tits up, humming a tune.

JUDY: What should we sing.

LANA & MARLENE: The only song we know.

ALL: (*singing*)
Forget your troubles, come on, get happy,
You better chase all your cares away
Shout hallelujah, come on, get happy
Get ready for the Judgment Day.

END

KELLY
REBAR

(b. 1956)

Though "the world's longest undefended border" has become a national cliché, and in the years after 9/11 something of a myth, it nevertheless remains an elemental component of Canadian political, psychological, and emotional geography. Canada's complex love-hate relationship with the American behemoth next door involves a passive-aggressive ambivalence about its powerful seductions. How do we – can we ever – measure up to American standards and achievements? How can we – should we bother trying to – resist American wealth and glamour, the smug but enviable self-confidence and infuriatingly effective self-promotion next to which Canadian values and institutions such as politeness, public health care, and hockey pale in comparison? Literally straddling the Canada-U.S. border along the Alberta prairie, the characters of Kelly Rebar's *Bordertown Café* struggle with these issues in the context of a poignant and often hilarious family drama that remains a favourite of Canadian theatregoers.

Rebar was born in Lethbridge and grew up there and in Calgary, where her comedy *Chatters* (1974) was produced at Factory Theatre West when she was just seventeen. After attaining a degree in Film Studies at York University, she returned to Alberta and was offered a commission by Edmonton's Northern Light Theatre. The result, *Checkin' Out* (1981), was a solid hit, with subsequent productions in Ottawa, Vancouver, Thunder Bay, and at Winnipeg's Prairie Theatre Exchange, where it remains the company's most successful production. An offbeat comedy about young, small-town Albertans struggling with low self-esteem and thwarted personal ambition, *Checkin' Out* established Rebar's trademark naturalism and colloquial dialogue, a kind of rough prairie poetry. Its characters' fear of change and ambivalence about leaving home also anticipate the themes of *Bordertown Café*. In 1984, Edmonton's Theatre Network produced *First Snowfall*, a family drama set in Saskatchewan. That year, Rebar also became playwright-in-residence at Prairie Theatre Exchange, which toured Manitoba with her children's play, *All Over the Map*.

Commissioned by Ontario's Blyth Festival, *Bordertown Café* opened at Blyth in 1987 to less-than-rave reviews. The play was substantially rewritten for its Prairie Theatre Exchange premiere the same year, and it proved a major success. Productions in Montreal, Regina, Calgary, Vancouver, and London followed; it was remounted at Blyth in 1988 and toured Ontario. *Bordertown Café* won the 1990 Canadian Authors' Association Award for Drama, and in 1993 it was made into a feature film, written by Rebar and directed by Norma Bailey. The play's popularity endures into its third decade, in small towns and large across the continent, on both sides of the border, marked by productions between 2009 and 2012 in Victoria, British Columbia; Ingersoll, Ontario; and Toledo, Ohio, as well as revivals at Prairie Theatre Exchange and at Blyth.

In 1991, the Blyth Festival produced Rebar's *Cornflower Blue*, a memory play about the prairies. She has also written scripts for the National Film Board, adapting Alice Munro stories and her own plays *Checkin' Out* and *Bordertown Café*. In the 1990s, she worked mostly in series television, writing episodes of *Jake and the Kid* and *Wind at My Back*, as well as a TV adaptation of Munro's *Lives of Girls and Women* (1994). Rebar currently makes her home in Nelson, British Columbia.

In his own way, young Jimmy in *Bordertown Café* faces the archetypal Canadian dilemma: stay home in Canada with all its obvious flaws or join the brain drain, the talent drain, south to the Land of Opportunity. His father is the powerfully encoded Western hero of American popular myth – the cowboy as trucker, living his freedom, riding the roads of Wyoming "in a truck higher'n any ole building we got around here," his mythic status enhanced by his never actually appearing onstage. As an added attraction, Dad offers Jimmy what appears to be the stability and prosperity of his new American home, a big modern house fully equipped with everything, including a capable new wife. In contrast, Marlene is a failed wife and a weak, tentative mother. The home she has made for Jimmy on "the Canadian side of nowhere" is provisional and shabby: half finished, ill equipped, badly decorated. The café itself is neither here nor there, neither truck stop nor restaurant, an economically marginal relic that doesn't even hold the attractions of nostalgia for Jimmy.

Dad, however, drives a harder bargain than at first appears. His cavalier attitude and flexible scheduling make Jimmy's choices a little more difficult. And Jimmy has other concerns that are not so easily left behind. He has his hockey, his desire to help his grandfather get in the harvest, and a powerful emotional connection with Marlene that all the play's comedy cannot finally hide. Woven in and out of Jimmy's self-deprecating self-consciousness – the sweet adolescent gawkiness for which he constantly beats himself up – is a genuine concern for his mother's emotional welfare and quality of life. His most secret fantasies involve making his mother happy. (This boy is almost too good to be true!) She is, after all, barely older than he, and her own horizons are rapidly receding. We watch her struggling with maternal guilt and inadequacy, trying as hard as her son to figure things out. Coping as a single mother in her circumstances is difficult enough, but she also has to operate within an unorthodox family structure where, as she says, "we're none of us what we're supposed to be ... Mum's like my daughter half the time, Jimmy's more of a brother." (Compare this to the more traditional family scenario within which, for example, David French's young men consider their options in *Leaving Home*.)

Marlene's mum is Maxine, chauvinistic stage-American and designated scene-stealer, larger (and louder and funnier) than life. She provides a good deal of the play's energy and much of its cultural comedy. As the family members continually talk over one another, her American inflections merge with their Canadian rural idiom in a rich verbal cacophony and tangled emotional grid that mark this delicately balanced familial détente. Maxine's laconic Canadian husband, Jim, contributes his own revelations at the end, helping to effect his namesake grandson's passage into manhood.

Although the feel-good emotional finale may mask the fact that not much substantial has really changed, the play's bi-national setting and the stage set itself ("a kitchen that bridges public and private use") remain fertile ground for the characters to negotiate personal and cultural identity. As post-colonial critic Homi Bhabha argues in his book *The Location of Culture*, the "in-between space" of the borderlands that Jimmy occupies – between public and private, boyhood and manhood, one world and another – provides an ideal "terrain for elaborating strategies of selfhood."

Kelly Rebar

Bordertown Café

Bordertown Café premiered at the Blyth Festival in Blyth, Ontario, on June 23, 1987, with the following cast:

JIMMY	Kevin Bundy
MARLENE	Laurel Paetz
MAXINE	Lorna Wilson
JIM	Jerry Franken

Directed by Katherine Kaszas
Set and Costume Design by Allan Stichbury
Lighting Design by Kevin Fraser

CHARACTERS

JIMMY, *age seventeen*

MARLENE, *Jimmy's mother, age thirty-four*

MAXINE, *Marlene's mother, age fifty-seven*

JIM, *Marlene's father, age sixty-two*

SCENE

A café on the Canadian side of the Alberta-Montana border. The present [late 1980s.]

SET

The kitchen of the café. It is a kitchen that bridges public and private use. In addition to the trays of dishes and cups, ketchup bottles and relish jars, the lard can, the grill and work area, a small kitchen table with chairs, magazines, bills, and a paperback or two indicate this kitchen is a family centre. The café is old but very clean, organized in its own way. An order window and a swinging door stand at the front of the café. A screen door leads outside. A door or passageway opens to the back suite. JIMMY's bedroom either introduces the back suite, and one must pass through his room to

get to the back, or it is in some way shown to be a room without privacy. The single bed takes up most of the space. Typical teenage boy things are about, and again, there is a tidiness. The closed, tight space of the café is contrasted by a sense of overwhelming prairie sky that surrounds the set.

ACT ONE

The sound of a combine approaching. The sun begins to rise. JIMMY is asleep in his bed. Light enters the kitchen and lends a photographic quality to the place, as if things have been caught in time. The sound of a combine harvester reaches a point, then begins to fade away. As the sound fades, the sunrise approaches its peak. Just as the light seems to hold still, the sound of the combine ceases. JIMMY snaps awake. He gets out of bed and goes into the kitchen to look out through the screen door. The sun carries on, the kitchen loses its quality, and things appear functional. JIMMY goes back to his room and goes back to bed. The sound of a meadowlark is heard. The phone rings. It rings again.

JIMMY: Am I getting that, Mum?

MARLENE enters from the back suite, doing up her robe. She crosses to the phone in the kitchen.

MARLENE: (*answering*) We're awake, Mum. (*realizing her error*) Oh hi. You comin' up? Yeah, 'cept for he's got school startin' today, eh.

JIMMY: (*immediately*) No, I don't, Friday's just registration.

MARLENE: What about?

JIMMY: What about what about?

MARLENE: Oh.

Pause.

JIMMY: Oh what, Mum?

MARLENE: If that's what he wants.

JIMMY: If he's pickin' me up for a haul, I can't go with him, Granddad and me got a crop to get off.

MARLENE: Just sec. (*to JIMMY*) Am I tryna talk?

JIMMY: There's certain considerations.

MARLENE: (*back to the phone*) Up to him.

JIMMY: (*throwing the covers back*) Wait – wait –

MARLENE: 'Kay then, bye.

JIMMY freezes, then falls back to bed. MARLENE hangs up, keeping her hand on the receiver a spell. She crosses to the little kitchen table and lights a cigarette. A tanker can be heard gearing by and fading away. MARLENE waits for it to go. The light makes another transition.

MARLENE: Get up, Jimmy.

JIMMY: Where's he at?

MARLENE crosses to the door to look out. Pause.

JIMMY: Well, if he's just leaving Wyoming now he won't reach the border 'til way past –

MARLENE: Bring me out my curling iron.

MARLENE goes back to the table to place her cigarette down in the ashtray.

JIMMY: Is my dad just leaving Wyoming now, I says.

MARLENE: I'm not beatin' around the bush. I'm gettin' right to the point. Your dad's – just leaving Wyoming now. (*MARLENE takes a quarter from the tip jar and looks toward Jimmy's room.*) And not only that he got married. (*She starts to exit to the front, stopping briefly.*) Make your bed.

She exits. JIMMY jumps out of bed and throws on his jeans. A song comes on the jukebox from out front. JIMMY goes to the kitchen to wait for MARLENE to re-enter.

JIMMY: (*hollering to the front*) And *here* I didn't even know he was goin' with her! (*He realizes the giveaway of his lie and hollers louder to cover it.*) He say who to?!

MARLENE comes back in, heading for the back suite.

MARLENE: (*as if it is all one word*) No, he never – Linda Somebody.

MARLENE sets to making Jimmy's bed. JIMMY follows her into his room to take over from her, but

MARLENE finishes any job she starts and JIMMY is forced to watch, guilt-ridden, and idle.

JIMMY: Well, it don't matter to me, does it matter to you? He got married?

MARLENE: (*disguised*) Does it look like it matters to me? (*continues with the bed*)

JIMMY: (*watching*) Well, that's great.

MARLENE: Colour hair she got?

JIMMY starts to answer but doesn't finish. He watches MARLENE fuss with the bed. He exits back to the suite and returns with a shaving kit and towel. He watches MARLENE fuss with the bedspread. Finally, he speaks.

JIMMY: Quit makin' that bed!

MARLENE: I knew it! Every time your dad comes up to Canada, I end up gettin' yelled at! And I know I shoulda got you a new bedspread four, five years ago, but I didn't!

JIMMY: What!

MARLENE: Didn't, Jimmy, didn't. Should change it to my name, Marlene Didn't. Didn't wanna fix this place up 'cause why would a person wanna sock a bunch of money into a back suite when she's gonna buy the Mathison place when it comes up for sale? Mathison place comes up for sale, did I buy it – ? No, I *didn't*. I don't have the Mathison place and I don't have the fixed-up back suite and now you're – and he's – and this is for a little boy, this bedspread, it's for a little boy.

Pause.

JIMMY: Did Dad say what time he was gettin' here?

MARLENE: Four!

JIMMY: Four?

MARLENE: And you're standing there tellin' me she's got me beat all to heck, this gal.

JIMMY: I got conditioning at four.

MARLENE: I know that without ever layin' eyes on her.

JIMMY: No, Mum.

MARLENE: Eh?

JIMMY: Don't think that.

MARLENE: Well, this is it. How does he think he could do better'n me with the kinda girls he 'sociates with? Answer me that. Oh, those American girls, don't tell me about American girls, I lived down there, I know exactly what they're capable of down there.

JIMMY: This is mattering, Dad getting married.

MARLENE: No it isn't mattering and I'll tell you why it is. (*pause*) See Jimmy, uh.

JIMMY: What?

MARLENE: I – I – I'm not sayin' it's any great shakes livin' here, but there's a lot o' kids out there without a pillow to call their own, they'd think your room there's a palace. (*She has exited back.*)

JIMMY: I got no problems with it neither.

MARLENE: (*off*) And you can stay out the farm any night the week you want.

She enters carrying her curling iron, which she takes to the outlet nearest the table.

JIMMY: I know – I – oh, I was gonna get that.

MARLENE: Gonna, that's another one – Jimmy Gonna and Marlene Didn't, we should move to Nashville and break into an act – speakin' of which I'm not going through the day with Mum song-and-dancing about your dad to me, not today.

JIMMY: I won't say nothing but –

MARLENE: I'm countin' on it.

JIMMY: I have a complication I'd like to air.

MARLENE: Yeah well, he said he'd be here at four.

JIMMY: Coach isn't caring if you're in harvest or not, he said if you wanna play hockey this year you can't miss conditioning. So if he's not carin' about harvest he'll care even less about Dad showin' up –

MARLENE: Just be on that school bus.

JIMMY: But Mum.

MARLENE: (*exiting back*) And get washed.

JIMMY: I'm cut before I even make the team? (*pause*) Mum.

MARLENE: (*off*) What?

JIMMY: This is kind of inconvenient. I can't be takin' off on no haul, I got a crop to get off. I got conditioning. Dad shoulda bin informed. (*pause*) Mum.

MARLENE: (*off*) What?

JIMMY: He won't even *be* here on time, he never is – the guy don't operate on Mountain Standard. But that's okay, Jimmy can count the trucks passin', waitin' on him. (*He takes his kit and towel and starts to head to the front, but stops, wheels around, and addresses the back suite.*) I wanted to start my last year off like a normal human hockey player. The plan was set. The whole time I'm out in that field I'm thinking, Jimmy? – I know you wrecked your

truck, I know it's not exactly smooth in that café, but you bin around Granddad all summer long – just take after him and eat your Puff' Wheat like there's nothing the matter. I figgered today, oh, I'd show up at school, say hi to the guys, register, give the girls a quick once-over to see if there's any changes, and then saunter down to the Doughnut Hole – yes me, Jimmy – saunter, huck a few bottle caps at the garbage can. Uh-huh. Well, shall we scrap that plan, Mum? – Number one, I'm up at the crack of dawn filled to the gills with guilt already for not bein' out in that field.

MARLENE: (*off*) You're gettin' washed up, eh.

JIMMY: "Hey, Jimmy," the guys'll say. "Comin' down to the Hole?" "Sorry, guys, can't." Carve it into my tombstone. "Sorry, guys, can't." (*pause*) Mum?

MARLENE: (*off*) Sorry, guys, can't.

JIMMY: The Hawks' game, a prime example. Game's over, we won, whole team come truckin' in here for Cokes and burgers and who do they find sittin' in that till? Mr. Humiliation, still waitin' on his off-and-on dad to turn up, take him on a haul. Not only could I a' played, I coulda come back and gone to sleep for five hours before his rig pulled up. Oh, but hockey games, they don't matter, sleep? Who needs it? – "Hop on up, kid." If I wanna see the guy, it's in his rig.

MARLENE enters, wearing her uniform. She has her makeup kit and a small, stand-up mirror. She sets up at the kitchen table to do her hair and makeup.

MARLENE: Well, you didn't have to go on those hauls if you didn't want to. Is how I see it.

JIMMY looks to MARLENE until she glances his way.

JIMMY: Didn't want to? Didn't want to, Marlene? A guy would have to be a *fool* not to wanna go on those hauls – those hauls are the highlight of my life! (*pause*) Okay, sure the man tends to run behind from time to time, and I have to miss the odd hockey game – but how many of my friends get to ride in a truck higher'n any ole building we got around here? You know there's not a truck stop here to California don't know my dad? The kinda life that guy has lived? – Well, it's no use even tryna explain it to you, not gonna understand, no girl could, but the life of a trucker, and I mean I bin there and I know, it's better education than anything you learn in school.

MARLENE: Now who is that I'm hearin' talkin', your dad all over again.

JIMMY: (*looking out the back door*) Gives me a chance to get outta here, see for myself there's somethin' besides *nothin'* out some people's windows. Nothin', that's what I gotta look at. We live smack dab in the middle of nowhere – correction, the Canadian side of nowhere. Houses 'at were here're long gone, fillin' station's history, and us? – We're sittin' in this café like we're stuck in the muck.

MARLENE: Your shirt's ironed, it's on the back of my doorknob.

JIMMY: We should get one of those big tractor-trailers and haul this unit outta here, straight into town. Where we can at least be part of life. This – *this* is the last thing a Canadian sees when he leaves home and the first thing an American sees when he arrives.

MARLENE: Hey. Never mind. Gonna be changes. Big ones. Just soon's I get the money.

JIMMY: Gonna Scotch-tape the rips in the leatherette out there, is that it?

MARLENE: Gonna put a decent bathroom in there. (*motioning to the back suite*) Gonna have a bathtub *and* a shower, and I'm gonna do it all up in pink. And that's gonna be the end of goin' out to the farm for a bath. Or standin' in that aluminum box we got now. Gonna get chiffon curtains. Priscillas. Gonna have it lookin' just like the magazines, so just you wait.

Pause.

JIMMY: Mum, I got the money. I'll do it for ya. I got the money in my account right now, I saved a lot this summer, we can getcha a pink bathtub –

MARLENE: Don't want a pink bathtub, want a white one, want pink *accessories*, I want floral design, I want wallpaper, I want it exactly how I got it in my mind and I'm not lettin' you pay for it, I can afford it, I'm just waitin' 'til –

JIMMY: Oh waitin', waitin', waitin' – for what?! – *him* to come back to you? (*He freezes. He shoves the screen door open and stands out back.*) How could I say that to her? How?

MARLENE: Yeah well, I got somethin' to say to you, too.

JIMMY: (*re-enters*) I'll tell you how – it's – it's *him* comin' out in me, it's my dad, just like you said.

MARLENE: Nice try but no go.

JIMMY: I know you wouldn't take him back, I know that – even if he come crawlin'.

MARLENE: Which he did more'n once.

JIMMY: He's nothin' but a good ole boy, never be no more.

MARLENE: That's right.

JIMMY: Even if he just got married.

Pause. The sound of the combine. JIMMY looks outside.

MARLENE: Jimmy.

JIMMY: *Why* does he always have to have a haul up to Canada when Granddad needs me the most? Talk about inconsideration. People, they got no respect for the farmer in this world.

MARLENE: Never mind the world, just let me say.

JIMMY: I should be allowed to have your car today, or Maxine's truck, roar into school, register like a madman, then race my tail back out to the field. Stay at 'er 'til I drop, like Granddad does. But no, me, I sleep in, mouth off, and let Granddad talk me into *havin' Friday off*. Frost is gonna nail our crop but good and I was gonna kick around the Doughnut Hole all day? (*The sound of the combine fades.*) Which now I can't do 'cause my dad's comin' up?

The sound of a pickup truck stopping.

MARLENE: Now here's your grandma's truck, act normal.

JIMMY: Well, how 'bout tellin' me if I'm comin' or goin', Marlene?

MARLENE: And you can quit callin' me "Marlene."

JIMMY: I call Maxine "Maxine."

MARLENE: Maxine's Maxine, I'm me.

JIMMY: *You* call her Maxine.

MARLENE: She's my mother.

JIMMY: And you're my mother.

MARLENE: Way you talk to me I'd never know it.

JIMMY: Just tell me what to do.

MARLENE: Fine.

JIMMY: Fine I tell Dad I got the crop to get off?

MARLENE: Well, you could.

JIMMY: Or fine I tell Granddad my dad's –

MARLENE: Get a move on, you're seventeen and you shouldn't have to be told –

JIMMY: Told what?

MARLENE: And when I was seventeen I had *you*.

JIMMY: Yeah? Well, now I'm seventeen and I got you.

MARLENE: You got me? – I wish I had me when I was your age, I wish I had a mother tellin' me not to go –

JIMMY: On a haul?

MARLENE: It's not a haul he was callin' about, it's not a haul he's got in mind.

JIMMY: Well what?

MARLENE: He wants you to go live down there! With him! And her! In a brand-new house! Happy?

JIMMY: Huh?

MARLENE: Now go get washed for school!

JIMMY: School?

MARLENE: If you're goin'!

JIMMY: Goin'!

MARLENE: I mean it!

JIMMY: What?

MAXINE flings open the back door. She's wearing a windbreaker over her uniform. She throws her purse down.

MAXINE: Hey! Shut your battletraps! Can hear ya all in the parkin' lot.

JIMMY exits to the front.

MARLENE: Jimmy –

MAXINE: Never mind the parkin' lot, they can hear ya in Missoura. And way up in Yellowknife, for that matter – suppose the coffee's not bin turned on? Wait for Maxine to do it, why not.

MAXINE prepares the drip machine. MARLENE starts to follow JIMMY, then stops.

MAXINE: After she's listened to the "Rock of Ages" all night long. Comin' outta your dad's nasal passages – spent half the night on the sofa – then he wonders why I sleep over here so much – gimme one your cigarettes, I'm out.

MARLENE: Just got Canadian. Coupla Lucky's in the junk drawer.

MAXINE opens the drawer, gets a cigarette, takes the lighter out of her brassiere, and lights up. MARLENE lights up another of hers.

MAXINE: Well, I'll tell ya.

MARLENE: That couldn't've bin handled worse.

MAXINE: Those people in Oklahoma never cease to amaze me.

MARLENE: Is Dad comin' in for breakfast?

MAXINE: Yeah, this one of 'em got herself on *Good Mornin' America* for winnin' too many toaster ovens, huh.

MARLENE: (*looking out the back*) I should go runnin' out there.

MAXINE: Give a guess how many.

MARLENE: Nine.

MAXINE: Nine nothin', that squirrel won 783.

MARLENE: What's this we're talkin'?

MAXINE: Those deals your Aunt Thelma uses for that asparagus effort she shoves atcha and calls a meal. "When's the last time you folks sat down together *nice* like this?" – far as I'm concerned that woman as good as killed your Uncle Carl with too many minced baloney sandwiches.

MARLENE: Jimmy! (*to MAXINE*) I don't know how you can be so like that to Dad's family and sweet as pie to any stranger't come in here.

JIMMY: (*comes to the order window*) What?

MARLENE: I – I forget now, never mind.

MAXINE: I had a fourth cousin from Oklahoma.

MARLENE: (*to JIMMY*) Our own's free back there, why you usin' the Men's?

JIMMY: Just like that, up and go?

MAXINE: He was so fat when he died they had to knock out the livin' room window to get his casket out.

JIMMY: Mum.

MARLENE: All I need now is that fat casket story.

MAXINE: That's no lie, his name was Dalton Dooey.

JIMMY: Mum.

MAXINE: Or not Dalton neither, Barney.

MARLENE: (*to JIMMY*) What?

MAXINE: Barney Dalton.

JIMMY: Just like that, I said.

MARLENE: If that's what you want.

MAXINE: I got a black-and-white snapshot o' that casket comin' out the window, don't ask me where.

JIMMY: You weren't even gonna let me in on it, it just come out by chance.

MARLENE: I was tellin' you all along.

JIMMY: You weren't tellin' me anything but to get washed.

MAXINE: My aunt Marietta was there in full force and she weighed a good three hundred herself.

MARLENE: Didn't I say our own's free, why you usin' the Men's?

JIMMY: You were in it when I started out goin' and I'd like to know why you called me out here in the first place.

MARLENE: I didn't mean to.

MAXINE: You kids don't care but that cousin holds the state record down there. He sure does.

JIMMY: For what, Maxine?

MAXINE: Fat.

MARLENE: Mum.

MAXINE: State o' Oklahoma! – Look it up.

MARLENE: Where's a person look that up?

MAXINE: This is it.

JIMMY exits from the order window. MAXINE has begun her morning preparations – getting the food out and ready, garnishes arranged, etc. She continues speaking through the order window.

MAXINE: Put Waylon on!

MARLENE: Never mind Waylon, is your grill on?

MAXINE: (*singing*) "I'd rather be an Okie from Muskokie –"

MARLENE: That's Merle *Haggard's* song, Maxine.

MAXINE: He did time, Merle did.

MARLENE: I'm askin' you not to sing.

MAXINE: (*singing*) "Where they still fly Old Glory down on Main Street."

MARLENE: I'll pay ya to stop. In American funds.

The sound of a combine. MARLENE looks out back. She goes out the door, she comes back in.

MARLENE: Why aren't I knowin' what to do?

MAXINE: (*still with her preparations*) 'Course the farther south you go the fatter people get.

MARLENE: Mum, can you please just not say nothin' for a while?

MAXINE: How come? And why aren't I being let in on it?

Pause.

MARLENE: On what?

MAXINE: On round number 942 you were havin' with that kid.

MARLENE: Don't make it sound like I've done nothin' but fight with him –

MAXINE: These walls tell the story, I'm not sayin' anything original – and as far as that other goes, call me a liar but people from, say, Kansas south, are nine out of ten of 'em that come in here full-fledged porkers. It's the way they eat down there, solid lard casseroles. My mother? She looked like a size-four knittin' needle toward the end, sure, but she was a pudgeball when she was young, she didn't lose that weight 'til she left Texas. Minnesota thinned my mother right down. What you havin' for breakfast, I'm gonna go for a bacon sandwich.

The sound of a tanker. MAXINE throws a slab of bacon onto the grill.

MARLENE: I'll eat with Dad, I guess.

MAXINE: So I tried to call over to wake yas up but you were on the line.

MARLENE: Who was I talkin' to, Mum?

MAXINE: Not me, I couldn't get through.

MARLENE: How long you listen in on that party line?

MAXINE: Hey, I got no time for sweet talk before my mornin' coffee. Which don't pose a threat to your dad. Last time anything nice found its way outta his mouth was when you were born. "Well done," he says, like I just baked a cake.

MARLENE: So you don't know what Don said?

MAXINE: What does he ever say? Comin' to get the kid for a haul, isn't he? – Only boy in the world hasn't seen the left-hand side of his father, just the right – steering. Oh yeah, speakin' o' steering – I think Jimmy should have your car today, first day and all.

MARLENE: Wrecked his truck, should have my car?

MAXINE: Okay, how 'bout my truck then?

MARLENE: Mum, I already said no to him.

MAXINE: You're takin' this little tumble in the ditch too far. So the kid had a bottle o' beer and hit the only vertical object in a hundred-mile radius. As if you never done nothin' dumb when you were that age.

MARLENE: Never wrecked a truck, I'll tell ya.

MAXINE: That's 'cause you left home before you were old enough to reach the gas pedal. You put me through my paces, don't kid yourself. Fifteen years old and that sonovagun strolls in here like

Johnny Cash, charms the daylights outta you and me both.

MARLENE: Okay, fine, never mind.

MAXINE: Gets herself married and taken down to Wyoming, set up in the trailer park, starin' at those narrow walls six outta seven.

MARLENE: Don't tell me about that seventh day, Mum.

MAXINE: Which was all it took.

MARLENE: And now we're into the grilled cheese.

MAXINE: I'm standin' at my grill slappin' my cheese together and who pulls up but Don and Marlene in that ole rig – dumps her off here like a sac' o' potatoes and she's showin' this far a-out.

MARLENE: I wasn't that far "a-out" and I don't appreciate talk like that in this café, I just don't this mornin'.

MAXINE: And you can't blame me because your dad tried to warn you, he seen through Don right from the time that blizzard holed Don up here.

MARLENE: Finished?

MAXINE: Point is you weren't an easy kid to raise, I think Jimmy should take my truck.

MARLENE gathers her makeup and mirror and curling iron and heads to the back.

MARLENE: Jimmy does somethin' wrong it's me who puts her through her paces.

MAXINE: He works hard, Mar.

MARLENE: You're sayin' I've been too strict? Well, that's on my conscience from now 'til kingdom come 'cept for everyone tells me I'm not strict enough and just 'cause I – I say no doesn't mean I always mean it. Bad enough I ground the kid and then pretend I didn't every time he wants to go out – who ever heard of groundin' a kid only when he's home? – okay, so to make up for it I should let him take your truck to school, he's suffered enough.

MAXINE: Well, he has.

MARLENE: What's it matter now anyway?

MAXINE: These are my sentiments exactly. (*watches MARLENE*) Com'ere, honey. (*MARLENE doesn't move. MAXINE goes to her.*) Kids, you know, they want a firm hand when it comes right down to it. They know what's good for 'em. Me, I raised you not knowin' half the time if I was doin' the right thing. Far as that-all goes my mum barely looked up from her gin rummy the day I set the

prairie on fire. Scooter and me burnt away half the state o' Minnesota smokin' roll-me-owns and you wanna know what Mum did? – sent us to the movies. I fixed her, I went ahead and turned out normal. Which boils down to the same thing – you're a darn good mother, quit worryin'.

MARLENE: Was I really, Mum?

MAXINE: (*going to the grill*) Sure, why not?

MARLENE: 'Cause I really need to – to hear that right now.

MAXINE: (*coming back*) Why? – I say somethin' wrong again? – I did, darn it – well, I didn't mean nothin' about all that other, runnin' off to Wyoming, you were a good kid, prat'ly raised yourself, don't pay Maxine any mind, this is just me and my dumb self.

MARLENE: No, Mum, it's me – I'm touchy today, that's all.

MAXINE: (*taking her into her arms*) Aw, honey. What else is new?

MARLENE: Pardon?

MAXINE: You kinda got the market cornered on bein' touchy, let's face it, but how 'bout some ham an' eggs, huh?

MARLENE: You think I'm touchy? Well, I'm not touchy, I'm not the least bit touchy. (*regathers her things to take into the back*) Every time Don calls he's comin' up I get my life dragged up and made out like all I had with him was bad times – well, Max? – there was plenny o' good times down in Wyoming that you don't know about, neither of you two, Jimmy or you. And I'd definitely appreciate it if you'd – because my marriage wasn't a total joke even though my life *is* right now for the very simple reason that I darn well know how to have a good time and I'm gonna start one o' these days and – *boy*. Okay? Well, I got pictures in this back suite, in four different photo albums, *provin'* I had good times in Wyoming.

MAXINE: Oh hey! – Jimmy! – You gotta get your pitcher taken, first day o' school!

MARLENE: (*exiting to the back and returning*) Wanna know a good time, I'll tell you a good time and it was a gas. Don took me to a county fair down there. He won every teddy bear that fella had. Tossin' baseballs in a basket. I was sixteen. Well, didn't those darn teddy bears fill the back seat o' that Chevrolet. That is no exaggeration. It was fun.

MAXINE: Oh, there's no doubt in my mind, back home in Minnesota we had fairs bigger'n anything you'd ever find up here.

MARLENE: I left forty, fifty bears back in Wyoming.

MAXINE: (*doing her garnishes*) Bigger'n the ones in Wyoming, our fairs.

MARLENE: Mum, you never bin to Wyoming, least of all a fair. All those teddy bears and enough *Screen Gem* magazines to sink a ship, I lef' back there.

MAXINE: Jimmy-Jim!

MARLENE: I only brung one o' those bears back home – shoved it into that ole trunk at the las' minute – 'member you gimme that old trunk to take down? – well, that bear? That bear become Jimmy's Floppy.

JIMMY: (*entering from the front*) What year have we time-lapsed into now?

MAXINE: (*to JIMMY*) That trunk weren't mine to give if the truth were known.

MARLENE: Nothin', get dressed.

MAXINE: I snafoofled that trunk off my Aunt Lizzie and she come up the Mississippi River on nothin' but charm.

JIMMY: You mean that old bear I used to practise my slaps with?

MAXINE: She was from Baton Rouge, Louisiana, Lizzie was.

MARLENE: Well, your dad won me that bear.

MAXINE: She dyed her hair red and it turned green.

JIMMY: Dad did?

MARLENE: Your dad could throw a ball.

MAXINE: All Americans can, they're the best baseball players in the United States, 'er the world – I was lead pitcher for my team, that's how good I was.

JIMMY: Geez, Mum, I –

MAXINE: I played for a soda-jerk league.

MARLENE: (*to JIMMY*) You what?

MAXINE: Me and eighteen soda jerks.

MARLENE: No, Mum –

MAXINE: *I* wasn't ever a soda jerk, I just played with 'em.

MARLENE: Jimmy's tryna talk.

MAXINE: But the café I waitressed was right across the street from the drugstore and me and this jerk got talkin' one day and before he knew it I was on his team.

JIMMY: No, I was just gonna say I wouldn'a minded seein' Dad – well, seein' him win you that ... bear. (*exits to the back suite*)

MARLENE: Yeah?

MAXINE: Oh yeah, we had a ball, and as I say, that trunk has a bit o' history all right. (*pause*) 'Course so did Lizzie.

MARLENE: Mum.

MAXINE: Why do you think she headed north? – the weather?

MARLENE: Jimmy wishes he coulda seen his dad and me at that fair.

MAXINE: Oh, it was somethin' all right.

MARLENE: Mum, you weren't there.

MAXINE: I weren't there?

MARLENE: You were standin' right here slappin' your cheese together waitin' for me to show up pregnant, remember.

MAXINE: Yeah well, you got that right.

MARLENE: And he didn't drop me off like a "sac' o' potatoes," either – it was my choice to come back up here, to have my baby north o' that border.

MAXINE: I don't know how I always end up touchin' off these Canadian nerves.

MARLENE: And things would be a whole lot smoother around here if you'd quit callin' anything out the ordinary Canadian.

MAXINE: Well fine, but where's the camera?

MARLENE: And Don come by quite a bit at first, we had a normal marriage off'n on those few times –

MAXINE: First one in the family to get his grade twelve, I'm capturin' it on Kodak.

MARLENE: Okay, so maybe I wasn't a perfect mother, sue me.

MAXINE: It's not in here.

MARLENE: And Don was always showin' up with somethin' for that kid –

MAXINE: Hey, Jimmy!

MARLENE: Droppin' fifty dollars just like that –

MAXINE: It was in this drawer.

MARLENE: That dirt bike alone and top o' the line tanker toys, those don't come cheap and Mum if I go over there and find that camera?

MAXINE: Jimmy, run out to the farm and look for the Instamatic!

MARLENE: I know I haven't – I'm not – and Don's not either but when you're not together it's hard to be alone raisin' a kid and Mum it's right here starin' you in the face.

MAXINE: I can't see for lookin', never could.

MARLENE: That's because you don't keep things in order, I clean this drawer out one day and you're messin' it up the next and I happen to have a bone to pick with you about this very sort o' thing – you were in my unicorn collection yesterday, it was not how I lef' it and you better come clean right now, Max.

MAXINE: (*exiting back*) Found it, Jimmy – never mind!

MARLENE: Right now, Maxine – I mean it, you come marching back right here and you – and – Dad – !

JIM has entered from outside. He takes off his hat. MARLENE turns quickly around to face him.

JIM: Uh-huh.

MARLENE: Dad, I – Don called!

JIM: Oh yeah.

MARLENE: He – wants Jimmy, he wants him to go live down in Wyoming – this is what he says to me on that phone.

Pause.

JIM: In Wyoming, eh.

MARLENE: Live with him and his new wife. (*pause*) Linda.

JIM: Oh yeah.

MARLENE: *Why* didn't I just grab the Mathison place when it was offered? – I *had* the down payment. But *no, I* raise the kid *here* – raise? I didn't even raise him, he just all of a sudden got big and now he's leavin' – he's leavin', Dad.

JIM: All right, simmer down.

MARLENE: Don'll be here at four.

JIM: Number one, he won't be on time. Number two, Jimmy's not moving into that old trailer house o' Don's.

MARLENE: Oh no, Dad, a trailer's not good enough for this gal – Don bought her a brand-new house.

Pause.

JIM: Have you told Jimmy yet?

MARLENE: Sets her up nice – second wife gets what the first wife wants, it's a fact o' life, it's in all the magazines.

JIM: Jimmy, he know yet, Marlene?

MARLENE: Oh, you know me, Dad, I decide to turn the jukebox on, I make his bed like my life depends on it, I end up yellin' it out to him like it was all his fault.

JIM: Oh, Marlene.

MARLENE: I know. Dad, please – please will you – so that he knows and everything like that?

Pause.

JIM: Well, I will, Marlene, I'll talk to him for you. But don't you think he'd –

MARLENE: Yes, I do think he'd rather hear it from me. But I can't talk to that kid, I never could, and you know that.

JIM: Yes, I do.

Pause.

MARLENE: What're you gonna say, so I know?

JIM: Why don't we all three of us sit down here at the table and more or less iron this out together?

MARLENE: Okay, that'd be good I guess.

JIM: I take it you haven't told your mother.

MARLENE: No.

JIM: Let's do ourselves a favour and keep it that way.

JIM heads to the back, rolling up his sleeves to wash.

MARLENE: Dad?

JIM: Eh?

MAXINE: (*enters carrying the camera*) Yeah, you get washed Jim and you can be in the pitcher.

JIM: You're not takin' my picture.

JIMMY: (*entering*) Granddad.

JIM: (*as he exits*) Jimmy.

JIMMY looks after JIM.

MAXINE: Isn't he handsome in that shirt, he's gonna have a swarm o' girls around him today.

JIMMY: Swarm. Right. (*He allows himself to be shuffled out the back door by MAXINE. She barely aims the camera in the right direction before snapping. JIMMY comes inside to sit at the table.*) Only guy in the hemisphere has to have little snaps of his first days of school pinned up over the till for everyone to gawk at.

MAXINE: Never you mind, you get your grade twelve and you and me are gonna get in my pickup and head 'er south.

JIMMY: Mum?

MARLENE: Yeah?

MAXINE: (*going to pour coffee*) We'll see every state in the union.

The sound of the door opening and closing out front. MARLENE glances toward it.

MARLENE: I said, yeah.

MAXINE: And get a souvenir spoon.

JIMMY: Forget it.

MARLENE takes the coffee pot and menus and heads to the front. MAXINE looks to JIMMY. He gets up and goes toward the front, stopping. He goes back to the table.

MAXINE: Hey, Sport.

JIMMY: Yeah?

MAXINE: Tell your Max what's wrong.

JIMMY: Can't.

MAXINE: Yes, you can, you can tell your Max everything.

JIMMY: She don't care.

MAXINE: About what? Don't she care. Huh?

Pause.

JIMMY: I get in her way around here, okay. I'm far too large. For my body. That kinda thing. Not only that but I'm a total klutz act on the farm, I'm a zero winner, an A-one loser – Granddad's always havin' to come bail me out, make me feel small. Does he ever *say* anything? No. He just … stares. If he'd only haul off and lose his temper, just once. Why can't he yell at me or throw the hammer down or spit even? *Why* Max?

MAXINE: He's weird. They both of 'em are, your mother and him. It's that side o' the family, somethin' in the blood – which if you were to ask her royal highness mother-in-law over there she'd claim was blue. Take your Aunt Thelma and that washtub of curdled Jell-O she tries to peddle off as dessert for those goldarn picnics of hers – with that strain of perversion floatin' around in the family? – well, you're bound to be a little backward, Jimmy – but, hey, you and me, we'll show 'em – we're gonna leave the whole silly lot of 'em up here huddled around their hot water bottles and we're gonna see America – from L.A. to New York, zigzaggin' our way down to the South – the Virginias, the Carolinas – oh, you name it – we'll

go see where President Kennedy was buried and Bobby o' course and up to Yankee Stadium –

JIMMY: Yeah, and I wanna see the Yankees and the Mets and the Islanders and the Rangers –

MAXINE: You ain't just a-whistlin' Dixie, kid – we'll see it all and sidestep over to Minnesota so you can see where your Max was born and where she'll be laid to rest when she cashes out for the last time.

JIMMY: You're gettin' buried up here, aren't you?

MAXINE: I'm gettin' buried in American soil!

JIMMY: But what about Granddad?

MAXINE: He can darn well come down there – if you think I'm gonna be a hop, skip, and a jump from her majesty and all this crew up here – *if* any of 'em ever do us the favour of passin' away –

JIMMY: Wait a minute Max, you and Granddad aren't hardly together now – don't you at least wanna be together in the end?

MAXINE: Only one in the family I took a half-likin' to was the old man and he had to be the first one to go. Mind you, it took eleven operations – and your granddad and I are together now, what're you talkin' about?

JIMMY: You're not, Max. Last night was the first time in over a week you didn't sleep here.

MAXINE: You don't like your Max stayin' overnight?

JIMMY: No, I do – I do Max, but Granddad needs you over there.

MAXINE: Oh, he don't need no one.

JIM comes in from the back suite but JIMMY has his back to him and cannot see.

JIMMY: Yeah, he does. 'Cause ya see, a man like Granddad – well, any man – they like to have someone, Max. It's time you understood that about men. That's how we are – they are – they need the security. The emotional security.

MAXINE: That right, Jim?

JIMMY: (*jumping up*) Granddad! – *Geez*, Max – you coulda said somethin' –

JIM takes his place at the table.

MAXINE: Yeah, but uh, a woman – you figger she don't need this here security, is that it?

JIM: Leave the boy.

MAXINE: Huh, Jimmy?

Pause.

JIMMY: Women got it built in as far as I can tell. So if he needs it and she's got it, she should provide him with it, and stay put.

JIM: Pass the milk.

MAXINE: (*going to the grill*) Granddad wouldn't touch that one with a ten-foot pole, huh, Jim?

JIM: Right.

MAXINE: He may be slow but he's not stupid.

JIM: (*to JIMMY*) Time you get to bed?

JIMMY: Not sure.

JIM: Told you to come in off the field by eleven thirty. It was nowhere near eleven thirty time you done all that.

JIMMY: I – I don't need sleep today, it's just registration.

MAXINE: I never slep' when I was his age, I partied all night and worked a double shift to boot – kid's got my stamina, dontcha, Jimmy?

JIMMY: Yep.

MAXINE: What's the capital of Tennessee?

JIM: Not now, Maxine.

MAXINE: We're goin' to Nashville next year, do that place up right, huh, Jimmy-Jim?

JIM: Can your mother see you a minute when her order's done?

MAXINE: Where was Lincoln hung?

JIMMY: He wasn't hung, he was shot.

MAXINE: That's what I meant, shot.

JIMMY: (*to JIM*) See me about what, she tell ya?

JIM: She told me. And I understand she told you, too.

MAXINE: Where was Lincoln shot then?

JIM: Though not in the best way, perhaps. See, Jimmy, your mother –

MAXINE: Where was Lincoln shot!

JIM: (*to JIMMY*) Just tell your grandmother where Lincoln was shot.

JIMMY: Oh – he was shot – uh, was it Edmonton they got ole Lincoln?

Pause. JIMMY signals to JIM to play along.

JIM: Butte, Montana. Custer nailed him.

JIMMY: Was it Custer, Granddad? – or Louis Riel?

MAXINE: Who?

JIM: Got me there, Jimmy.

JIMMY: We give up, Max – where was Lincoln shot?

MAXINE: (*pointing outside*) Out by that burnin' barrel for all you two care. Well fine, but it's a cryin' shame these kids don't know their American history. Sittin' on the most powerful nation in the world and all they wanna do is play hockey.

JIMMY: We know more about you than you know about us.

MAXINE: We? – us? – Hey! – *you're* more American than you are Canadian! – and *I* know my Canadian history! – what there is of it. But I don't forget my American ruts, and you don't neither.

MARLENE: (*entering from the front*) A daily over.

MAXINE: If it wasn't for me you'd know zip about your ruts – capital Zee-I-P.

JIMMY: My what?

MAXINE: Ruts, ruts, where ya come from.

JIMMY: I think she means roots, doesn't she, Granddad?

MAXINE: I said ruts.

JIMMY: Spell that zip again, Max – was that Zed-I-P?

MARLENE: Daily over, eh, Mum.

MAXINE: (*to MARLENE*) And as for you, that ole trunk o' Lizzie's? It was a darn sight more full up when you took it down to Wyoming than it was when I brung it up from Minnesota, wasn't it, Jim. Yes, it was. I come up to this country with what the little boy shot at and missed, that's how I started out my married life – didn't I, Jim? Yes, I did.

JIM: Sit down, Marlene.

MAXINE: And I packed that ole trunk in half an hour.

MARLENE: Daily over.

MAXINE: Kid has to come to *me*, an American, to find out how this half of him ended up here – (*to JIMMY*) What's Granddad talk to you about when you're milkin' those cows every night, huh?

MARLENE: Mum, a daily.

MAXINE: Huh?

JIMMY: I don't know.

MARLENE: Daily, Mum, daily.

JIM: Usually got the radio on durin' chores.

MAXINE: The CBC on in the *barn*. Most educated cows in the county.

JIMMY: District.

MAXINE has finally retreated to the grill area to prepare the order. MARLENE, seated at the table, glances to JIMMY. Then to her dad.

JIM: Jimmy?

JIMMY: Yeah?

JIM: There's a lot o' people tend to think of life as, well, as a road you go down.

MAXINE: (*singing*)

"Zip-a-dee-doo-dah, zip-a-dee-day."

JIM: And in that road, there's sometimes the odd fork that comes up.

MAXINE: "My, oh my, what a wonderful day."

JIM: Well today, you've reached one of those forks and your mother here wants you to consider –

MAXINE: "Plenny o' sunshine, plenny all day – "

JIM: Maxine?

MAXINE: (*singing*)

"Zip-a-dee-doo-dah, zip-a-dee-day!" – What?

JIM: A person can't have a decent say.

MAXINE: Huh?

MARLENE: Leave her, Dad.

JIMMY: Leave her.

MAXINE: (*coming from around the grill*) What? (*Pause. She slithers over to JIM, singing.*) "I'm ... in the mood for love. Simply because you're neeeaaarrr me – " (*She wraps her arms around JIM, kissing him on the head. He remains motionless.*) Isn't he just the best-lookin', heart-thumpin', sexiest man on this great big bowlin' ball called Earth? Huh, Jim? – You handsome brute –huh? – That trip up here with that old trunk on the train? – huh? – 'member? (*to MARLENE*) Four pillow slips is about all I had.

MARLENE: Mum, that fellow looked in a hurry.

MAXINE: I was nineteen and you think you were dumb when you got married, Marlene? – *I* was dumb –I was waitin' tables in this coffee shop and as I say, in walks Jim and his buddy –well, I give a look to Margaret – she's since died – and I says to her, "Kiddo? – I'll give ya my foursome if you gimme that deuce!" – and didn't Jim and his buddy end up draggin' that order on for the better part of an afternoon, huh, Jim?

JIM: Unlike the fellow out front here that wants *his* filled now so he can be on his way.

MAXINE: They were down in Minnesota for a big auction, huh, well, it weren't often you met a fella with manners, so I married him.

JIM: (*to MARLENE*) Tell the gentleman it won't be long.

MARLENE doesn't. She knows JIM is just embarrassed.

MAXINE: I took him home to meet my folks and my mum was sold on him before he hit the livin' room – took his shoes off at the door! Didn't you, Jim?

JIM: May have.

MAXINE: He did.

MARLENE: The daily over, Mum.

MAXINE: Well, my dad, he'd just as soon get rid o' me as have me stay on account of the fact me and Mum fought so terrible and her with that horrible accent, I mean she never shut up from mornin' 'til night, you talk about a screen door in a wind storm, that woman never quit. Pop, he says, – I can hear him to this day – "Well" – he was from down Iowa way – "They-all up in Canada, they *did* join the war before we did" – hands us sixteen dollars and we were married by four o'clock. Right, Jim?

JIM: It seemed like longer. (*pause*) If I were that gentleman out there I'd have second thoughts about returning to this place with the service so slow.

MAXINE: (*to MARLENE*) That slop pail there's got more romance in him than your dad does. (*getting to work*) Prob'ly doesn't even remember meetin' me. Then he has the nerve to take exception if some fella in here pays attention to me.

JIM: I pay attention to you every time you wanted me to I wouldn't have the crop in, never mind off.

MAXINE goes to fill the order – bacon, eggs, hash browns, toast – as JIM takes a serviette, and MARLENE begins to clear the table.

JIM: And it's not that *they* pay attention to her, it's that *she* pays attention to them. Marlene, leave the *dishes*.

MARLENE sits down. A tanker is heard going by.

JIM: As I was saying.

Pause.

JIMMY: (*jumping up*) I know the crop's not off, I know I'm holdin' you up.

JIM stares at JIMMY for a long time. JIMMY sits down.

JIM: Let's just put our cards on the table. Now Don, he tells us he's got a – a wife now, a house, and he's ready to have a son. Well, that's handy, considering his son is soon celebrating his eighteenth birthday.

JIMMY: Why is it *my* fault I'm eighteen too soon? – I can't help it he wasn't ready 'til now –

MARLENE: You're sayin' it's *my* fault?

JIM: Wait a second –

JIMMY: Did I say it was yours, Marlene?

MARLENE: Well, I know that bedspread's for a little boy, I so much as said it was already.

JIM: Bedspread?

MARLENE: I see those plaid spreads every time I flip through that Sears catalogue, but do I order one?

JIM: Let's keep our eye on the ball.

MARLENE: Red and black, green and black, yellow and black, I can't decide, I don't order one.

JIMMY: I don't want a bedspread.

MARLENE: I shoulda got him a VCR.

JIMMY: VCR?

JIM: Now how would that have solved a darn thing?

JIMMY: I got my own money.

MARLENE: I know I made you work till soon's you were old enough to reach it, I know I made you save your money.

JIMMY: I didn't *mind* working till.

MARLENE: Yes, you did.

JIMMY: No, I didn't.

MARLENE: You hated working till.

JIMMY: I loved working till.

MARLENE: Hated.

JIMMY: Loved. (*exits into the back*)

MARLENE: (*looks to JIM*) Dad – I – go after him.

MAXINE: (*through the order window*) So where ya from, buddy?

JIM: Jimmy?

MAXINE: Texas! – My *mother* was from Texas!

JIM: *Why* couldn't he've bin from Saskatchewan?

MAXINE: Lubbock! – You're from Lubbock? (*heading around to the front*) Well, my mother was from Amarillo!

MARLENE: You saw what happened, Dad – you saw what I did – I'm gettin' outta here, I'm headin' down that highway, I'm not bein' heard from again.

JIM: Marlene.

MARLENE: I'm thirty-four and I'm *nowhere*. (*pause*) My life's over, my kid's leavin'. I got nothin' keepin' me here.

JIM: You got a café to run for starters.

MARLENE: What I got it burns down? I got grade nine. Jimmy's gone farther'n me and in more ways'n one. What's he want from me when *he's* the one bin carted all over the western part o' the United States? Knows Texas like the back' his hand – me, I bin to a trailer park in Wyoming and the Woolco Mall in Lethbridge – *I'm* the one should be askin' *him* what to do.

JIM: When it come right down to it, you're still his mother.

MARLENE: I know that and it's about time he grew up and realized it. He's seventeen and – oh, what am I sayin', seventeen isn't very old, it just isn't old enough to leave home.

JIM: No. I know. Neither was fifteen.

> *MARLENE freezes. Pause. She slowly turns around to look at JIM.*

MAXINE: (*off*) Flip those eggs, Mar!

> *Automatically MARLENE moves to the grill to attend to the order.*

JIM: Seemed like one day you were gettin' underfoot in here or beggin' for a ride in the tractor, and the next day, it was you that character was comin' to take across the line.

MARLENE: You can't 'member that.

JIM: Eh?

MARLENE: You were combinin'. You didn't come in off the field to say – say goodbye.

JIM: You knew why that was.

> *Pause.*

MARLENE: Had an idea. Guess I got a better one right now. (*as she sets the order up on the ledge*) Wanna know the first thing to come to me when I hung up that phone this morning? – It was like Jimmy was eleven years old comin' in the door there. All summer long I figgered I was teachin' him how to earn a dollar – oh, he had to have those Cooperalls and me I couldn't see shellin' out a hundert bucks for hockey pants when his last year's still had wear. I make him work till his whole summer in addition to the – the farm – his dad shows up end o' August and takes him down to Texas like it were across the road – I'm supposed to compete with that? Kid comes back full of himself, goes into town with that Cooperall money –

JIM: Okay now.

MARLENE: Here, what's he do but end up at Regency Jewellers – Margie, she tells me after, she says, "Marlene, your son put that $97.50 down on my counter like he was layin' out his life for you." *Why'd* he have to see me lookin' in the window at those diamond-chip earrings? And what I do when he comes through this door with that velvet box in his hand?

JIM: He knows – he knows you liked the earrings.

MARLENE: Not from me showin' it he don't, Dad. (*She looks to the order.*) That order's up and gettin' cold.

> *MAXINE enters talking. She starts to finish the order, realizes that it is up, takes it and is more liberal with the serving and garnishes.*

MAXINE: (*directing her voice to the front*) Well, if it's your first time up this way, buddy, you better get ready to not know how fast you're driving, how hot it is outside, how hard the wind's blowin' or how much gas you're gettin' for your so-called dollar. As for readin' directions on any box or carton – it's all in the wrist action – you'll see a lot a *mode da emploi*'s – means flip it over to English – wrist action – Canadians got real strong wrists, prepares 'em for hockey careers. (*turning to MARLENE*) Mar, take this to my buddy from Texas – I gotta do my garnishes – (*looking out*) Who me? (*MARLENE takes the order out front.*) No, I'm married. (*MAXINE looks ever so assuredly to JIM for an extended pause. Then she looks back out front through the window as she chops her tomatoes, etc.*) I come up in '49. I was nineteen and dumber 'an a dawg, I married a Canadian boy. He farms just over there. I had about a month o' goin' batty in that farmhouse with Miss High-and-Mighty mother-in-law and got myself on here – we owned it prat'ly ever since and believe me, buddy, it owns us. My grandson Jimmy? He's an exceptional boy. He could grill a sandwich age o' eight.

MARLENE: (*entering*) Mum.

JIM: Leave her.

MARLENE: She's gonna start in on Jimmy's hockey.

MAXINE: He's quite the hockey player – scored a hat trick last year.

MARLENE: Watch, she'll show him the puck over the till.

MAXINE: We kep' the puck, it's over the till, if you care to take a look.

MARLENE: Guess who he sees carryin' on in those stands? Mum. Every goal that kid has scored he has to ask me if I seen it, if I seen the puck go in the net.

MAXINE: No, that's not his *sister* in the picture, that's his mother! – Now *she's* not married? – Her, she's had her dad wrapped round her little finger since the day I brung her into the world which was in the state o' North Dakota. I didn't wanna have my baby up here, *you* know what I mean – we were aimin' for Minnesota but we stopped off for coffee in Dakota and I got laughin' so hard I went into labour – didn't I, Jim?

JIM: I don't think laughing actually brought the baby on.

MARLENE: Mum, this fellow I don't know from Sunday now knows how I come into the world.

MAXINE: Uh-huh. (*pause*) You know who you look like standin' there, don't you? Thelma.

MARLENE: Thelma. Thelma, Dad!

MAXINE: With a touch of Her Majesty mixed in there, too, huh, Jim?

MARLENE: She winked! She thinks it's funny!

JIM: Let's just bring Jimmy out here.

MAXINE: Well, I can't understand it – I teach my daughter her presidents age o' nine, I breathe on her, I spit on my Kleenex and wipe the Hershey bar off her face, and what does she turn around and do on me. End up Canadian.

JIM: Maybe we should shoot her.

MARLENE: I don't appreciate bein' told I'm like Aunt Thelma.

MAXINE: Well, no, why would you, it's not a compliment.

JIM: Girls.

MARLENE: And you were in my unicorns yesterday, I know you were Mum – they were all moved around on that dresser and you were in them, weren't you. (*looks to JIM*) Dad?

JIM: (*slowly looks to MAXINE*) Were ... you in Marlene's unicorns by any chance?

MAXINE: No, I wasn't. Just that liver and onions was.

MARLENE: That big fat guy was pawin' through my unicorns?

MAXINE: Not *that* liver and onions. The other one with the bad bleach job, her.

MARLENE: She brings the bad bleach job into my *bedroom.*

MAXINE: She's from Arkansas.

MARLENE: I don't wanna hear about Arkansas.

MAXINE: She's bin bottle jobbin' her hair since Marilyn died.

MARLENE: I don't wanna hear about Marilyn.

MAXINE: I wasn't gonna say nothin' but you asked.

The sound of the front door.

MARLENE: Mum? Can ... you take that new table? And can you top off that Texan's coffee while you're at it?

MAXINE: It's 'cause I showed the bad bleach job her unicorns.

MARLENE: No, it's not.

MAXINE: Her luck was down, that gal. Thought I'd perk her up.

MARLENE: Fine, Mum.

MAXINE: Her poodle died. (*MARLENE says nothing. MAXINE has taken the menus and moved to the exit.*) Mind you it died in 1964 but are you ... mad at your mum?

MARLENE: Mad at myself, Max.

MAXINE: (*exiting*) Get over it.

JIMMY comes in from the back.

JIMMY: Mum?

MARLENE: What?

JIMMY: Never mind.

MARLENE: (*starting to clean*) Got no time for never minds.

JIMMY: Okay, I need the keys to your car.

MARLENE: Pardon?

JIMMY: I gotta go to school one way or the other. If I'm movin' down there I gotta let 'em *know*, don't I? If I'm stayin' here, I gotta *register*. So hand 'em over. (*pause*) Hey, no grade twelve will be on that bus. I want you to know that. Just Jimmy. No one else. I'll be the only one. Apart from girls.

MARLENE: I'm not the one wrecked my truck.

JIMMY: I have to ride the *bus* home at four to sit around *here* and wait for him, eh? – That's what you want? – Me to sit around *here* my only day off?

MARLENE: No, I –

JIMMY: Not able to go to hockey conditioning, not able to even have the *dignity* of drivin' to school on my first day o' grade twelve, *if* I decide to get it?

MARLENE: Okay, I –

JIMMY: I'm sorry, Granddad! – I know I'm actin' like a brat! So keep not sayin' nothin', you're warranted.

MARLENE: Hey, you want a firm hand, you quit makin' it be Dad and just – just *go* live down there.

JIM: Oh, Marlene –

MARLENE: I didn't want him to have that dirt bike, I didn't want him to grow up spoiled, but his dad shows up here with a top o' the line model and *I'm* supposed to make him take it back?

JIM: Marlene, sit down.

JIMMY: *Dirt* bike?

MARLENE: And if you're not gettin' your Canadian grade twelve you better darn well get your American!

JIMMY: I'm not gettin' my American grade twelve, I'm gonna drive truck!

MARLENE: You're doin' what I tell you to!

JIMMY: Well, if I could figger out what that is we'll *both* know!

MARLENE: Keep your voice down in this café! – Look how I'm talkin' to him, Dad – (*glancing to the front at the sound of the door*) There, another table just walked in, satisfied? – and Mum's tellin' my life history to the other one, and that daily over from Texas is takin' it all in.

JIMMY: Granddad –

MARLENE: Not a whole lot I can do about it either.

JIMMY: She needs a holiday.

MARLENE: She? Who's she – the cat's mother? This is how that kid talks to me, like we're not even related, like we're brother and sister, you heard the man.

MAXINE: (*entering*) The Mormon Tabernacle Choir looks like it just walked in and that couple? They're from Edmonton, they seen Wayne Gretzky buyin' a pair o' shoes. In 1984. (*pause*) Grey ones. They both want one my cinnamon buns. (*goes to the grill*) So don't mind me, I just work here.

The sound of the school bus is heard. MARLENE hears it first.

MARLENE: There's the bus here. (*JIMMY goes to grab his jean jacket from his room.*) What do you care if the bus is here if you're takin' Max's truck?

JIMMY stops. MAXINE comes from behind the grill.

JIMMY: I'm takin' Max's truck?

MARLENE: I never said that.

JIMMY: Yes, you did.

MARLENE: I did not.

JIMMY: Yes, you did.

MARLENE: I did not.

JIMMY: I think you did.

MARLENE: I said *if*.

MAXINE: Hey, get while the gettin's good – (*She takes the keys out of her bra and tosses them to JIMMY.*) – and keep your tail outta the ditch, huh.

MARLENE: I didn't say he could have it, I said *if*.

JIMMY: Well, then do I?

MARLENE: You roll your truck and get handed over Max's keys?

JIMMY: I didn't expect to.

MARLENE: What I say don't count.

JIMMY: What *did* you say?

MARLENE: I said *if* I said.

JIMMY: Let's just get that straight.

MARLENE: *If* you're takin' Max's truck, I said!

JIMMY: So now I can't?

MARLENE: I didn't say that.

JIMMY: Yes, you did.

MARLENE: No, I didn't.

JIMMY: Yes, you did.

MARLENE: No, I didn't.

The sound of the bus honking.

MAXINE: Well, this is just like last year.

JIMMY: Am I takin' the bus?

MAXINE: I think he deserves my truck.

JIMMY: Or am I takin' Max's truck?

MAXINE: I think he should.

JIMMY: Mum?

MARLENE: Dad?

MAXINE: That's right Jim, step in.

MARLENE: I'm not sayin' that, Mum.

JIMMY: What *are* you sayin' for the second time!

MARLENE: I'm askin' you, Dad.

MAXINE: She's askin' you, Jim.

MARLENE: I am not, Mum.

JIMMY: Do I or don't I?

MARLENE: Well, take it or leave it –

JIMMY: The bus or the truck?

MARLENE: See what I care –

JIMMY: The bus?

MARLENE: The truck.

MAXINE: How 'bout her car?

JIM: Maxine –

MAXINE: What!

JIM: (*to JIMMY*) Go wave, you won't ride today.

JIMMY: But I rolled my truck!

MARLENE: He's right, Dad.

MAXINE: Hey, we all end up in the ditch sooner or later.

JIM: Just go.

JIMMY: I had those beers! – I don't *deserve* the truck! I don't *want* the truck, don't *give* me the truck!

JIM: *Get*!

> *JIMMY takes a step back. Everyone freezes. JIMMY tears out through the back door.*

MAXINE: Yeah ... so we get talkin' this West Edmonton Mall, huh, and I said to this couple, I said, "You know that shoppin' cenner don't hold a candle to Disneyland," and that Texan he was quick to agree.

> *She has taken the two cinnamon buns and put them on plates. She heads out, taking more menus. JIMMY comes racing back in.*

JIMMY: Okay, this is the kinda total jerk I am. I knew Dad was gonna marry Linda, I knew since July, I kep' it to myself. Day Mum gets clued into it, I be this complete dolt to her, make her feel like sludge for not lettin' me take Max's truck.

> *Pause.*

JIM: Jimmy, it's understandable you didn't want to say anything to your mother.

JIMMY: No, it isn't, is it?

JIM: It is.

JIMMY: Eh?

JIM: Yes, Jimmy.

JIMMY: Oh.

MARLENE: It's – it's fine you didn't tell me, Jimmy. It's fine.

JIMMY: Thanks.

MARLENE: Thanks?

JIMMY: Fine.

MARLENE: How old she, this gal?

Pause.

JIMMY: Beg your pardon?

MARLENE: Old.

JIMMY: I don't really know, any girl over sixteen is old to me.

JIM: Is she a responsible person, your mother means.

MARLENE: If she's just some chick –

JIMMY: Linda? She ... isn't much.

JIM: Jimmy, sit down.

They all take a seat at the table. A long pause.

JIMMY: Actually, no, Linda's all right. I can't help it, she is. And she keeps *him* in line anyway – he even shows up on time for her and everything. We're headin' over to her place and Dad sees this tavern? – Automatically the guy just navigates into the parking lot. Looks over to me, shakes his head, says, "Second thought I don't really need that Budweiser – not if I know what's good for me" – slips it into reverse and we're outta there before we're even in. "Who *is* this girl got you so turned around?" I says and he turns beet red, my own dad. I give him this cuff, eh, and he says, "You're pretty damn cocky kid," and o' course he knows I come by that naturally so that ended that. (*pause*) But so, this Linda, she's really worked wonders – (*to JIM*) Should I 'a said all this. I shouldn't've said all this, should I have?

MARLENE: No, Jimmy, it's ... fine. It's good your dad's like that to her, it's ... good.

JIMMY: Well, I figgered it was.

MARLENE: Then maybe you know about the house, too?

JIMMY: That, I didn't know.

MARLENE: It's in a modern development, it's a big split-level, bedrooms galore, full-size bathroom, prob'ly two even, top o' the line furniture, colonial style he's decked this gal out with.

JIM: Marlene, do you *know* these details?

MARLENE: No, I don't, but I can put two and two together as good as anyone, even *if* I only got junior high.

JIMMY: Did he *say* it was a split-level?

MARLENE: It's nothin' shabby.

JIMMY: Well, no, it wouldn't be, Linda goes in for quality, she had a great apartment, then see, she's been handling all their finances, Dad he signs his paycheques over to her and she put him on this allowance. 'Course with him not drinkin' so much he didn't spend so much and, well, Linda makes a darn good wage herself –

JIM: Quiet, Jimmy.

JIMMY: Pardon?

MARLENE: Well, what's this gal *do*, bank teller?

JIMMY: She – I – it's slipped right from my mind.

MARLENE: Slip it back.

Pause.

JIMMY: She's ... nothin' but a second-rate secretary, prob'ly pours coffee all day, eh.

JIMMY jumps up as he realizes what he has said. MARLENE goes to get the coffee pot and her order pad and exits to the front.

JIMMY: I mean! – not that there's anything wrong with pourin' coffee – Granddad, I didn't mean – look at what we do, think starin' into the north end of a southbound cow's anything to write home about? Huh? Go tell her we're nothin' neither.

JIM: You haven't had an honest breakfast today, have you?

JIMMY: Breakfast? Yes ... no – I don't know.

JIM: Well, sit down and put a decent meal in you.

JIMMY: Sit down? – On what? – This gibbled chair, bent cigarette pack underneath its leg? My thighs are so tense they're gonna take off on their own – look, they're puffin' in an' out – my dad's comin', the crop's not off, you're losin' time like sixty bears and I'm supposed to be a normal human Albertan and eat breakfast? – Well, sorry, Granddad, but Puff' Wheat is just *not* gonna do it right now, not for this cowboy.

JIM: It's a heckuva way for a guy to grow up, you're right.

JIMMY: It's just *total* stress in here, all the time.

JIM: I've noticed that, too.

JIMMY: Granddad, it's not funny, this is my life.

JIM: I know that, Jimmy.

JIMMY: American, Canadian – back, forth – like it *mattered* what a guy was – why couldn't I've bin born in Australia, nowhere *near* the American border? – I go over to Nedchuk's place and *he's* got this complete dream situation – furniture? – totally matches. Sit down to eat and everybody's got their own place? – little doodads on the windowsill.

His dad's got a complete Black & Decker lifestyle down that basement and his mum's all a'fluff her new living-room curtains are a quarter-inch off. (*pause*) That greaseball Nedchuk sits there beefin' a gripe about how he can't blast his stereo. Me, I'm driving home in my truck and I'm thinkin' *what* I wouldn't give for a living-room window – never mind the quarter-inch-off curtains. (*pause*) Okay, I know, I can stay out the farm anytime I want but Max doesn't care about curtains, she's never even over there – Mum cares, but she's afraid to spend a dollar. She's "waitin'."

JIM: Well, that's true.

JIMMY: We should pour cement in this back suite, seal it off.

JIM: Bulldoze the whole café.

JIMMY: Nuke it right off the face of the earth. I'll tell you one thing, I'm not *ever* gettin' married – you can bet the rent on that. I'm gonna build a house. And it's gonna be bought and paid for before I put my wife into it. There's gonna be no make-do, half-done, wait-see about it.

JIM: The girl you're not gettin' married to is sure gonna be set up right.

JIMMY: And it's gonna have a reg'lar kitchen. With appliances rigged up from here to – to – to nowhere. Who am I tryna kid? (*The sound of a tanker going by.*) Let's face it, Granddad, there's … something seriously the matter with me.

JIM: You figger?

JIMMY: I swear to God if people knew the kindsa things find their way into this brain? – they'd have me committed. I cause myself embarrassment, it's no joke.

JIM: Yeah well, I'll admit I've had my suspicions about you.

JIMMY: Eh?

JIM: Sure. Time you were sittin' out in the middle o' the field there for'n hour'n a half. Now what's that kid up to? I thought. Out I go and your mouth was hangin' open and all the rest – you says, "Gonna be a fight tonight, Granddad." Well, the sun was goin' down on this side and the moon was comin' up on this side and you says to me, "A fight which one's prettier." Well, I knew then you didn't think too reg'lar.

JIMMY: Yeah, but, Granddad, it's gotten way worse than that.

JIM: Worse you say.

JIMMY: I start out okay but then before I know it I'm right off the tracks. Like when it's a house I'm gonna build, I get the spot all picked out and settle on a nice little bungalow. But it always happens I'm buildin' the house for Mum instead. And I'll be ridin' along in the combine, or … drivin' my truck, and well, pretty soon that house has something real feasible like eighteen bathrooms – just this ignorant sprawl of a spread that people have to come from miles around just to gawk at. With binoculars. Holidays – I'd take Mum down to L.A. and deck her out with all these clothes – like Dad was always gonna – and she wouldn't have to serve nobody – we'd eat in fancy restaurants and – and, Granddad, there's somethin' awful I gotta tell you.

JIM: What, Jimmy?

JIMMY: I – I didn't have anything to drink the night I rolled my truck. I just *said* I had those three Canadians to gimme an excuse to do such a fried thing. I couldn't just roll it, not me, I had to smack into the telephone pole to boot. Look up and see fifty head o' cattle standin' there starin' at me like I'm dumber 'an they are. I was buildin' the eighteen bathrooms when I rolled my truck, I was takin' Mum to classy restaurants – my mind was wandering, okay? All over the road. And so was the truck. That's the kinda big shot I am. Big shot like my old man. Can't even stay on the road.

JIM: Well, Jimmy, I … don't know *what* to say.

JIMMY: Please don't tell no one.

JIM: That you'd bin grounded all summer 'cause you were stone-cold sober?

JIMMY: Uh, yeah. (*long pause*) Ya know, Granddad, no offence. But you got a way about you that … just seems to narrow in on the idiot side of my personality. Only time I ever feel like I'm on the ball at *all* is when – well – is when I'm with my dad. I can bounce back and forth about goin' on those hauls but I know the minute I hear his rig pull up, I'll just all a' sudden wanna go. I forget everything when I get in that rig. Him and me, we cut-up somethin' terrible. I'm sorry but he's just this hilarious guy, Granddad. And *I'm* pretty funny myself when I'm with him, figger that one out.

JIM: There's nothing wrong with having a good time with your father.

JIMMY: No? Then why do I gotta feel like sludge the minute I come back and see you? You, you're just this perfect human-type guy, never caused no one no trouble when you were a kid – ask anyone in this district, no one'll say a bad word about you – well, try livin' up to that, Granddad.

JIM: Oh, Jimmy, where you got such a silly notion of me –

JIMMY: But no, I can't be your clone, I gotta have a father doesn't even know it's harvest – I can't just up and move with the crop not off. (*pause*) Can I?

JIM: We're almost done. I can get Quint.

JIMMY: Quint?

JIM: Not gonna lie to you. You know I'm no fan of your father's. And it's not my belief that a boy should have to decide something like this in a day's time but that's Don.

JIMMY: I'm not a boy, okay.

JIM: Well, no, but I guess he figures it's better now than not at all.

JIMMY: The fact that he wants me at all is pretty strange – I always thought the most my dad could take o' me was four, five times a year, eh.

Pause.

JIM: Maybe it'll be good for you to get away from all this haywire here. Enjoy yourself for a while. The farm, well, it'll always be here.

JIMMY: Geez, you sound like – aren't you –

JIM: See, Jimmy, when I was about your age –

MAXINE bursts through the door.

MAXINE: I think that couple's communist.

JIM puts his hat on and exits outside. JIMMY follows him as far as the door. MAXINE starts preparing orders.

MAXINE: Me and that Texan got talkin' politics and how it's such a joke up here with three parties and how was I to know they'd belong to the third – well, her chin got that Thelma look and him, he started twitchin' his neck – they're prob'ly so left o' cenner they gotta hold onto the rails to keep from fallin' off. And to think they're headin' into America. Trust Russia to drop 'em down through Edmonton.

JIMMY has moved to his room.

JIMMY: (*to himself*) Well, Granddad's real tore up over all this, isn't he. Mum, she was down on her knees, beggin' me to stay. Guess I'll just have to *pry* myself away from them, break their hearts and move. Aw, there's no way, what am I talkin' about, it's just too late, the damage is done, I've already grown up. Canadian. Am I supposed to just pack up and move? – into that big ... split-level? Be a guy that hangs "a-out." Play their kinda football. I mean, there's no reason for me to – to go, there's just – there's ... *gorgeous* babes down there. American girls. And they're gonna be fallin' at my Canadian feet. Yeah right, Jimmy, you'll be a wipeout down there just like you are up here. I could ... fake it, though.

MAXINE has come toward JIMMY's room.

MAXINE: Fake what?

JIMMY: (*wheels around*) Whataya think of – of America, Max? (*pause*) I might move there, eh.

MAXINE: Sure you might and you can take your Aunt Thelma and Her Majesty with ya – do 'em good to find out what real life is all about – instead o' sittin' up here with milk in their tea, makin' judgments.

JIMMY: I might move there tonight, like.

MAXINE: Huh?

JIMMY: With my dad. Gonna have to say goodbye to this place, isn't that a shame? – Tell a guy – tell a guy why he'd wanna stay *here* when he can move into some swank place down the States. (*MAXINE is stunned. JIMMY looks at her.*) Say somethin', Max. Max.

MARLENE enters from the front.

MARLENE: Two dailies, one ranchman no onions, two ones, one denver and a side o' browns. (*MARLENE looks to MAXINE. MAXINE looks back.*) Side ... o' browns, Mum. (*pause*) Mum.

MAXINE moves to the junk drawer and fumbles for a Lucky. She lights it, having to keep her hand steady. She moves to the kitchen table and sits down. MARLENE looks to JIMMY. He takes the keys out of his pocket and goes out the back door, letting it flap shut. MARLENE goes to the coffee pot and pours MAXINE a cup. Music comes on the jukebox out front to end the act.

ACT TWO

The front of the café. We are now on the other side of the order window and swinging door, and can see into the kitchen. There is a till booth area with rows of Life Savers and chocolate bars. There is a phone by the cash register. Trophies, postcards, and Canadian and American flags are scattered about. Along the counter clusters of serviette canisters, salt and pepper shakers, and sugar containers are evenly placed. Red leatherette stools are up to it. Behind it there is a milkshake maker, pop machine, and coffee maker, etc. There is a booth and a number of tables with a suggestion of the café existing beyond our view. We are looking through the wall and window of the café so that when the characters look toward us they are seeing the highway and prairie.

As another song comes to an end we can hear the sound of the combine fading in and out. The sun is starting to set, and will reach its peak at the close of the play.

A duffle bag, small suitcase, and hockey stick are placed together near the till. JIMMY, his hat on, is sitting sideways on a booth seat. Chocolate bar wrappers and potato chips are on the table. A tanker can be heard gearing up. JIMMY raises himself up slightly to listen. He slouches back down as the tanker gears by.

MAXINE enters from the kitchen. She is in jeans and a sweatshirt, and is carrying Marlene's cigarettes. She places the pack on the counter, puts a coffee mug out, takes the coffee pot from the machine, and pours. She puts the pot back, staring heavily into it.

MAXINE: Readin' this article, oh, where was it. *Reader's Digest.* (*She heads around the counter to sit on a stool, keeping her back to JIMMY.*) Yeah, according to this article ... nine outta ten Americans ... carry guns. (*takes her lighter out and lights a cigarette*) Run across the line and get your Max a package o' Lucky's before I affixicate myself on these of your mother's – I'll handle it if your dad shows up while you're gone.

JIMMY: (*not moving*) I bet you will.

MAXINE: Believe it was in the state of Wyoming, speakin' of Wyoming, that this here nutcase done away with, was it, sixteen families? – on their way to church. He was prob'ly a Vietnam vet, 'course America had no business even *goin'* to Vietnam. Or to any of these other trouble-spot countries, in my opinion. (*takes a drink of coffee*) Not to mention the moon. The moon, in my mind, should remain neutral. We got no business puttin' a claim on it. But violence in America is somethin' the Russians don't have. (*glances over her shoulder to see if JIMMY is paying attention*) Now you know I loved John

Fitzgerald more than the brother I didn't have. The day that news come on the air from Dallas? – I was standin' in there makin' a grilled-cheese sandwich. Yes. You think a Canadian would ever take a shot at their – I mean our prime minister? No. 'Course there were many that wrestled with the idea more'n they should've when Trudeau was in power. (*takes a drag off her cigarette and butts it in disgust*) Now you take television. The stuff they put on down there? Trash. You wanna know the name of a good program on TV and it's been on for twenty, thirty years, and it's *Canadian*, it's not American, it's on the CBC and it's – the – the – it's bin on the years – it's – oh, what the hell's the name o' that show? Well, you know what one I mean, that one. Or how 'bout their national sport, that's a sport? – spittin', chewin', and scratchin' with the odd baseball tossed – and I don't know why you're takin' all this hockey equipment. Hockey isn't nothin' down there, it's not even played.

JIMMY: They play hockey down there.

MAXINE: Well, they *shouldn't*! They're gonna be beatin' yas at your own game before much longer, and then sellin' it back to you, that's the way these people operate, I was raised down there, I know how they think – *me*, us, we're first, we're best, gimme that – you wanna buy it? (*pause*) Jimmy, America is just not the place you think it is. It's not the place it used to be.

JIMMY: Yeah, it seems to've changed an awful lot since this morning even.

MAXINE: What – what happens, this girl sees the light like your mother done and walks out on your dad. Then who's gonna look after you?

JIMMY: I don't need anyone to look after me. I can look after myself, if you haven't noticed.

MAXINE: Everyone needs someone to look after 'em – or I mean, women don't, they got it built-in, but men, they do.

JIMMY has gone to his gear and picked up his hockey stick.

JIMMY: *I* don't. Any chick who gets serious with me is gonna have a few disappointments. (*fakes a slapshot*) 'Cause I'm not the kind to be held down, okay. (*puts the stick down*) Furthermore –

MAXINE: Oh good, I like these furthermores.

JIMMY: I'm takin' her out normal. To the show, to parties, dances – I'm givin' her everything she wants, we're gonna go out for a long, long time – *years* – and really get to know each other and *then* she's gettin' a proper ring, the whole bit – church, reception in the Elks Hall, and a two-week honeymoon. And it will be *decades* before any baby is born to wreck our happiness.

MAXINE: Jimmy.

JIMMY: I'm not rushin' into anything, got the picture?

MAXINE: I guess you're kinda like Granddad when it comes right down to it, huh?

JIMMY: You got it.

MAXINE: Yeah, he knew me a day and a half before we got married.

JIMMY: Well fine, but that's another thing – I'm marrying someone same side o' the *border*.

MAXINE: What side would this be?

The sound of a tanker. JIMMY looks out, seeing if it stops. It gears right on by.

JIMMY: No side.

MARLENE enters. She is wearing jeans and a light sweater. Her appearance changes quite radically when not wearing her uniform. JIMMY wheels around at the sound of the tanker, and sees her enter.

JIMMY: Super, Dad's now five hours late, Marlene.

MAXINE: Is it after nine? (*to MARLENE*) You watchin' *Dallas*?

MARLENE: You ... go ahead and watch it, Mum.

MAXINE: Huh? Oh. (*takes her coffee and heads toward the kitchen*)

JIMMY: I *only* tell my coach I'm not gonna be around this year, I *only* tell all the guys, I *only* been holed up in this café since four lookin' out the window every – (*picks up his hockey stick and sets it back down*) – time a truck goes by.

MAXINE: (*at the door*) You go back to that school on Monday and tell everyone you changed your mind. They'll be so happy they'll throw a party for you.

JIMMY: Max, you seem to have this big idea that I'm someone at that school. I'm no one.

MAXINE: You're more'n your mother was.

JIMMY: Well, I maybe am but I'm not no hero.

MARLENE: I didn't have time for friends when I was rushin' back home to work dinner shift, but never mind, I –

MAXINE: You tell your coach you wanna try out for the team, he'll letcha, star player like you were last year. Huh, Mar?

JIMMY: Star.

MAXINE: You were the best player on the team last year, the *league* – ask your granddad.

JIMMY: Granddad? – All Granddad said was my coordination was improving. I didn't even know my coordination was bad.

MAXINE: It's not, it's excellent, it's cleared right up. I could catch a pop fly when I was a kid, back home in Minnesota – I played with a soda-jerk team, that's how good I was – you get your athaletic ability from my side.

MARLENE: Mum, you don't *have* a side when it comes to Jimmy.

MAXINE: Huh?

MARLENE: He's got my side, and his dad's side.

MAXINE: My side's your side.

MARLENE: Your side's back home in Minnesota – and – and if you're gonna say I'm every inch Aunt Thelma –

MAXINE: Oh, you never forget nothin' do you –

MARLENE: – even though you wiped your American spit all over my face then don't try to inch me out of my own kid's half.

JIMMY looks to MARLENE, then abruptly away.

MAXINE: Whataya pickin' on Maxine for? – I'm tryna talk the kid outta goin'. You don't see your dad in here, do ya?

MARLENE: Dad's got a crop to get off.

MAXINE: I know all about the crop, I bin playin' second fiddle to it since I come up here. And to you. Thelma, and Her Majesty mother-in-law over there – ninety years old and not even a *hint* of poor health. Tellin' me I don't know how to put a meal on the table. Bin doin' it for a livin' all my life, which is somethin' neither of those two know sweet tweet about – living, or makin' one. Sittin' on their royal haunches all their narrow lives – criticizin'. (*exits to the back*)

MARLENE and JIMMY exchange a look.

MARLENE: She's right, you know.

JIMMY: That you take after them?

MARLENE: No, that they're like that – *do* I take after them? I do, don't I – no, I don't.

JIMMY: How should I know and who cares?

MARLENE: Well fine, but I'm not turnin' out like Thelma.

JIMMY: You think Dad's had himself a wreck?

MARLENE: No, I – I don't, Jimmy. Your dad's fine, he's just runnin' a little behind. He hasn't had himself a wreck.

JIMMY: But what if he jack-knifed in his rush to get here?

MARLENE: Well, that much I doubt for the very simple reason that your dad is a professional from the word go. And say it's a shifted load or somethin', well, that's gettin' fixed right this second, they service those big trucks reg'lar on that innerstate. And if it's not that, well, he coulda got away late.

JIMMY: You said he'd be here at four.

MARLENE: I shouldn't've said four, it's my fault. I shoulda just said I don't know. That's what –

JIMMY: What?

MARLENE: Well, that's what I used to do when you were a kid.

JIMMY: You did?

MARLENE: Sure. Or if he'd call when you were out I wouldn't tell you so you wouldn't wait, or if he didn't show up, well, you'd be none the wiser. Then if he did, see, then you got a nice surprise. But I'd like to know why it is you think this is all you'll need down there, this tiny suitcase and that gear.

JIMMY: (*looks to it*) Well, whataya think I should do? Just rip out the whole suite of every bit of evidence I ever lived here? Take all I own so I never have to show my face in here again?

MARLENE: She's gonna think you don't have nothin'! – this is all I ever give ya. Take –take the ghetto blaster at least? – just take it and – oh, what am I sayin', they'll prolly have one, they'll have stereo equipment from here to – (*looking outside*) – that old gas pump.

> MARLENE *has gone to the window to look out.*
> JIMMY *stares out in the direction of the pump as well.*

JIMMY: That pump should be bulldozed.

MARLENE: The pump stays. And so does my ole Texaco star.

JIMMY: *Your* ole Texaco star, that's *my* ole Texaco star.

MARLENE: Used to tell folks, I'd say, you wanna find your way back here, all you gotta do is look for the star.

JIMMY: I never heard you say anything so stunned in your life to *anyone*.

MARLENE: When I was a *kid*. Life was goin' on a little bit before *you* were born, you know. I was the kid around here at one time.

JIMMY: I can't help I was born.

MARLENE: I used to watch those little coloured balls hop around when the gas was pourin' – and if I had my way we'd still have that pop machine out front, that Orange Crush.

JIMMY: It wasn't good for anything but slappin' shots against, and you got no right to put a claim on the pump, or the star. They aren't even ours. We never owned that g'rage.

MARLENE: You see anyone around here care a darn? You see anyone wantin' to buy us out and put up a big Voyajer? It's never gonna be a big draw in here.

JIMMY: You wanna turn a profit, you gotta go one way or the other. Which no one in this family can ever do.

MARLENE: What're you talkin' about?

JIMMY: Turn it back into a truck stop. Or upgrade into a restaurant. Who ever heard of a café on the baldheaded prairie with no place to gas up?

MARLENE: We got those that remember us keepin' us afloat, we got a good clientele – and people make a point of stopping back – thanks to Mum.

JIMMY: A place like this doesn't have a clientele, it's got reg'lars.

MARLENE: That's right, Jimmy. But not everyone wants 'a go to a place 'its build around a salad bar they gotta feel guilty about. Get served parsley with a bran muffin by a waitress named Tom. Like the places up in Calgary. Nice way to bring up a kid. You coulda done worse. There's nothin' fancy about the Bordertown but you'll think more of it when you're gone. Think I liked it before I left? Gang from high school used to pile into their dads' Meteors and come in here for something to do. Well, I had to serve those boys. I was thirteen, fourteen years old. Jack Jaffrey would walk like me, talk like me, act the smart aleck in fronna all his friends? I'd say to Mum, I'm not goin' out there, I'm not no more – then I'd run out to the farm. (*This strikes her funny all of a sudden.*)

JIMMY: Why you laughin'? – I'd like to beat the snot outta that guy.

MARLENE: Well, never mind, poor Mum had to cook, serve, clear, and do till all on her own – that's how rotten I was to her – I'd take off just like that, I'd go down the coulees sometimes and Dad would have to get me. Bring me back. That Jack Jaffrey ended up on drugs, went the hippie route – grew his hair down to his rear-end and hitchhiked down to California.

JIMMY: So, Dad, you don't think he's had a wreck?

MARLENE: No, me, I was still poofin' my hair and wearin' stovepipe pants when I got married.

JIMMY: Yeah well, fine.

MARLENE: Fine what?

JIMMY: Open up a museum in here. Keep the star, keep the pump, plug a Canadian quarter into the jukebox and an American quarter into Maxine, and let her pour forth with a few million stories about her fat cousins in Oklahoma. Or how she come up here in '49. Nineteen and dumber 'an a dawg.

MARLENE: Oh crumb, you said it.

JIMMY: Granddad and me are the only ones know it's the present.

MARLENE: Yeah? That farmhouse don't look too modern.

JIMMY: There's nothin' wrong with that farmhouse, it's got a good foundation.

MARLENE: Got four kinds o' linoleum showin' through on the floor, should put indoor-outdoor down in there.

JIMMY: Granddad's dad built that house, you don't rip that linoleum up, I *like* those other floors showin' through. I suppose I'll come back and you'll've talked Granddad into soakin' every last cent into somethin' him and me don't want.

MARLENE: Whata you care? You're goin' to wall-to-wall plush carpet!

JIMMY: Don't change nothin'!

MARLENE: I won't! I won't get nothin' for myself, I won't get my bathroom –

JIMMY: Never said nothin' 'bout in here!

MARLENE: You want me to bulldoze the pump and star!

The sound of a tanker. They watch for it to gear down. It goes right on by.

JIMMY: Great. Prob'ly chattin' up some chick.

MARLENE: And another thing. Don't you – you – you get what I'm sayin'?

JIMMY: Huh?

MARLENE: Don't you start bein' the – the smart aleck down there, like.

Pause.

JIMMY: I already am one. I'm a chip off the ole block.

MARLENE: You just – if the two of you? I mean it. Are somewhere and what have you. Okay? You think of that – you think of that Linda girl and you ... (*taps her finger on the counter*) you make sure things stay right for her.

JIMMY: How?

MARLENE: Well.

JIMMY: Huh?

MARLENE: No, but I'm sayin' *you* just be responsible when you meet a girl, and what-all.

JIMMY: Meetin' 'em's one thing, gettin' 'em to go out with you's another.

MARLENE: Jimmy?

JIMMY: What?

MARLENE: Don't be ... in a hurry.

Pause.

JIMMY: (*moving away*) Where *is* he, Mum?

MARLENE: Get your grade twelve and you do ... good and do ... good.

JIMMY is looking outside. MARLENE starts to go to him, to touch him, but he turns around and she moves away.

JIMMY: Why isn't Granddad comin' in off the field to say goodbye?

MARLENE: He said so at supper and he's – he's stayin' out there.

JIMMY: He didn't say nothin', I was doin' till – he stayed in there. (*toward the kitchen*) He figures I should be out there workin' 'steada sittin' on my lazy butt in here.

MARLENE: You had to go to school, you had to tell people, the bank.

JIMMY: So I'm here since four afraid to bring the cows in or do my milkin' 'case Dad shows up, sees I'm not chompin' at the bit to hop on up. Granddad has to ask Quint. *Quint*. Pickin' up my slack.

MARLENE: You know what I'm gonna miss? I'm gonna miss, uh, seein' the hockey games, and what-all.

JIMMY: You're kidding?

MARLENE: That hat trick you scored, type-thing, eh. (*pause*) Last year.

JIMMY: Well, what about it?

MARLENE: I'm just sayin'.

JIMMY: Yeah, that was quite the fluke, that night.

MARLENE: Really? Oh. Well, did you want something to eat?

JIMMY: *Eat?*

MARLENE: Eat.

JIMMY: Like what?

MARLENE: Well, food or somethin', whatja have for supper?

JIMMY: Hot beef san'wich.

MARLENE: This gal cook?

JIMMY: Whata you all a' sudden care if I get a balanced diet or not?

MARLENE: You eat reg'lar.

JIMMY: Yeah, I eat *with* 'em, too. I'm just reg'lar around here, like Wally and Quint – that's how *I* eat reg'lar.

MARLENE: Well, what do you *want*?

JIMMY: A salad bar.

MAXINE enters, drinking a Coke.

MAXINE: I seen that one.

MARLENE: Mum, Jimmy wants a salad bar in here.

MAXINE: Why didn'tcha say? – We'll haul that jukebox out and set 'er up there.

MARLENE: I don't want that jukebox hauled out.

MAXINE: Let's knock out a wall.

JIMMY: I don't want a wall knocked out.

MARLENE: He's sayin' I don't feed him reg'lar meals.

MAXINE: We get goin' on this it could be done by Monday.

JIMMY: My dad's had a wreck, she's knockin' out walls.

MARLENE: He hasn't had a wreck and look in that fridge.

JIMMY: Well, it would be just my loser-luck if he *did* have a wreck.

MARLENE: There's a tub o' coleslaw in there day in and day out.

JIMMY: Okay, never mind the coleslaw, never mind the walls.

MAXINE: Your granddad and me nearly had a divorce over that wallpaper – see that buckin' bronc there with the twisted leg? – I took Marlene's brown crayon and coloured that in – when Jim come in from coolin' off over me handin' him the one strip upside down, he took one look at my artwork and – see this roof? (*points up*) He hit it. He was always horrible to live with, even then.

MARLENE: (*leaving to the back*) He doesn't care about the roof, the wallpaper – thirty years old and still holdin' – he doesn't care about anything – *I* didn't feed him reg'lar meals.

JIMMY: (*watches her leave and goes after her*) I do so care!

MAXINE: (*looks to the back, then to JIMMY*) Yeah!

JIMMY: Yeah, *what* Max?

MAXINE: What about the time you fired the hardball through the window there?

JIMMY: If *I* was gonna be five hours late I'd call a guy and *she's* the one that don't care.

MAXINE: Your mother was ready to sell you to the Hutterites for a nickel that day. I'm the one stuck you under the counter 'til she seen the humour. It was me that risked an early death every Christmas climbin' onto the roof to put Sanny Claus up there with his nose blinkin' off and on in thirty below weather. It was me that shovelled the ditch so the kid could play hockey when he come home from school, not his Canadian granddad out in that field.

JIMMY: Granddad said goodbye at supper.

MAXINE: (*grabbing him*) Tell your Max you're not goin' down there, tell her you wanna stay home. (*hugs him*)

JIMMY: (*moving away*) Yeah well, "home."

MAXINE: What about –

JIMMY: (*wheeling around*) What about that Cuisanart I boughtcha? – Eh? Think that come cheap? I sprung two hunderd Canadian for that rig and you haven't even touched it. It sits over at the farm collectin' dust.

MAXINE: I don't do enough cookin' here, I gotta cook there?

JIMMY: And come winter, I wancha to start spendin' more time in that curling rink. Granddad likes that.

MAXINE: I am *not* sittin' ... in *no* curlin' rink with a bunch o' whiny *wives* drinkin' coffee outta a Styrofoam cup.

JIMMY: Oh sure, yet you sit in the hockey rink other side the buildin' watchin' *me* play.

MAXINE: He wants someone to watch him, he's got Marlene.

JIMMY: She liked my hat trick.

MAXINE: She wasn't even there – oh yeah, that's right, she was. (*pause*) Oh boy, that was somethin', that hat trick.

JIMMY: Eh?

MAXINE: You deserved your steak dinner that night, I'll tell ya.

JIMMY: (*picks up his stick and does a shot in slow motion*) You know, I can't even think about that night without feelin' goosebumps. It's almost like it wasn't supposed to happen. I mean, lotsa guys score hat tricks. But, oh, if you woulda known how much I wanted to have a three-goal game. All my life, just please God, let me score a hat trick. Me, I'm the kinda guy gets the odd goal if the other team's lousy. Or if their goalie's got the flu. My mind wanders. I think about my skating, I forget I got a stick. But *that* night, we were *even* playin' against an okay team. And it was one, two, three in the net before I knew what was happening.

MAXINE: You musta had horseshoes up your patootie that night! Huh?

A tanker goes by. JIMMY looks to it.

JIMMY: Yeah. That's all it was. Luck. A fluke.

MAXINE: Huh?

JIMMY: But my dad wouldna known luck from skill, he's never even been to a hockey game. He woulda thought I was great. Had he been there. (*pause*) Max?

MAXINE: Yeah?

JIMMY: I thought he was. He said he was gonna, and I kep' lookin' over by the entrance there thinkin' this man was him, same jacket, eh. You can't see worth a darn on that ice.

MAXINE: You mean *that's* why you played so good?

JIMMY: But it's these darn dispatchers, eh. They hold a trucker up somethin' terrible.

MAXINE: Yeah. I heard that one before.

JIMMY: It's true.

MAXINE: No, I know, you're right.

JIMMY: He tried, he tried real hard to make that game, I know for a fact he did. Linda even said when I was down in July, she told me lotsa stuff. When she first met him, he took out his wallet and showed her my picture. He didn't pretend like he didn't have a son. Like he coulda done. Only thing is the picture was from grade five or somethin', but so – it's a shifted load is all it is right now, and they're servicin' it right this – this minute.

MAXINE: That's probably it.

JIMMY: No, it isn't. (*pause*) Don't take five hours to fix a load. If he's – Max, if – he hasn't even bin married to her a *month.*

MAXINE: Oh, Jimmy, your dad's –

JIMMY: What Max? – what's my dad? – a saint? Huh? No. Well, I clicked in to that a *long* time ago, okay. First time he took me down to Texas, it kinda sunk in. Boy oh boy, he was takin' me to the Lonestar State, I was gonna have somethin' to brag about to the guys when I come back. Mum had me workin' till all summer to save up for those Cooperalls but Dad shows up end o' August – well, somehow his sweet talk to the ladies down there started seemin' a little more'n friendly, put it that way. And the more he talks the more it hits me – math's not my favourite subject but I'm addin' up the years I'm alive with the years he's bin "seeing" this one and that one and it's equalling the same thing – he was two-timin' on Mum before I was even born. After. And probably during. Well, I just couldn't wait to get back here, take out my savings, and – (*pause*) Somehow those dumb little diamond earrings Mum wanted were more important than a pair of Cooperalls. You figger that out. (*MARLENE comes in from the back, but JIMMY cannot see her.*) All day, dumb junk like that keeps comin' to me – like my whole life just decides to show up in my head, in Panavision. And still – *still* Max, I can't help thinkin' how hard Dad's tryin' now and he's got Linda – she's just a way better wife for him than Mum ever was – she's really neat, so easy to talk to, eh, like I can say whatever I want to her, she's a little like you – when she's got somethin' to say? She just says it –

MAXINE: (*noticing MARLENE*) Oh geez, Jimmy –

JIMMY: No, Max, lemme tell you – Linda's got a real way about her. (*MARLENE exits.*) I don't know how Dad managed to get her. Or Mum, for that matter. Women are just like that, they're stupid when it comes to men. But Max, can you see what I mean? – my dad's *finally* givin' me somethin' I *want*. Not some bike or toy that I – I used to leave out in the parkin' lot for some Oldsmobile to back up over. Granddad can say I got no value for the dollar – yeah, Granddad, that's why I *saved* every penny I ever earned *just* so I could blow it on – (*pause*) My dad's bin promisin' me this all my life. Okay, it's a little late. And Mum's not gonna be a part of it. But I quit dreamin' that one a long time ago. And I know I gotta leave the guys, hockey, the farm, Granddad, and Mum but –

MAXINE: What about your Max, gonna miss her?

MARLENE: (*re-entering before JIMMY can answer*) I'll see ya then, Jimmy, I'm goin' out to the farm, eh.

JIMMY: *Pardon*?

MAXINE: The farm?

MARLENE: Yeah, so –

JIMMY: What for?

MARLENE: Whataya think, my bath. (*A tanker goes by.*) There he is.

JIMMY: (*wheels around, willing it to be his dad*) That's not him, Marlene. Did ya hear the rig gear down? No. Is there an engine purrin' out there? No. 'Cause he's not here, he might never get here and you'll be stuck with me. He mighta changed his mind – he don't *phone* me, I'm just supposed to *know*. He maybe decided he doesn't want the kid after all – I miss school, miss hockey, miss everything so I can *wait*. Wait for him like you used to, like you wait for some wonderful thing to happen with your life – some fairy-tale ending – yeah, the unicorn collection is all she thinks about, well, isn't that right on the money, she's never gonna get outta here, she just stays in this café mornin', noon, and night.

MAXINE: Jimmy, your mum goes out.

JIMMY: She doesn't go "a-out." You can't even get her to go to a dance.

MAXINE: She'll come around.

JIMMY: *When*? The woman's only been divorced since I was twelve.

MAXINE: Yeah well, when you were twelve you weren't too keen on your mother even talkin' to a man in here, never mind goin' out with one.

MARLENE: Thank you, Mum.

MARLENE goes to the till area. JIMMY heads to the door, but wheels around.

JIMMY: *How* could I *say* that to her? How? I can't believe I got so little goin' for me I actually say

that-all to her the day I'm leavin' – I don't deserve no father, I don't deserve a home, that's why Dad's not showin' up, he's thinkin' twice about havin' a smart-mouth like me screw up his life again.

MAXINE: Again – you listen here, kid, you didn't screw up his life. *He* screwed up ours, the day she run off with him.

MARLENE: "She" didn't run off with no one. *You're* the one figgered the sun rose and set on Don, he was an American – he was gonna just "have to drop on back next time he was up this way."

MAXINE: I say that to everyone! And I can't help it if you were too shy to talk to him yourself.

MARLENE: Mum, I was fifteen.

MAXINE: You were the *oldest* fifteen-year-old I ever come across. I didn't know what to do with her from the time she was this high. (*pause*) Yes, I liked Don. No, I don't see through people. And I didn't listen to Jim. Like I shoulda. But I seen my girl's eyes light up for the first time the day Don walked in this café. (*looks to JIMMY*) And now he's comin' to take *you* across that border and all you tell your Max is how *she* liked your hat trick. (*JIMMY looks abruptly away from MARLENE.*) How you'll miss Granddad. Am I always gonna be alone in this family?

JIMMY: *Alone*?

The sound of the back door.

MARLENE: Here Dad is now, so you just quit talkin' nuts, Mum, I mean it.

MAXINE: Not talkin' nuts, all this kid thinks to say to me is go sit in the curlin' rink, pay attention to Granddad. Does Granddad ever pay attention to *me*?

JIM walks in, stopping at the door. He is exhausted and dusty.

MAXINE: Huh?

JIM: What's goin' on?

MAXINE: Brings me up here after a day and a half and puts me in that farmhouse with his ditzy mother, gotta change her dress to say hello. Well, my folks didn't *have* sit-down meals. I not only had to raise myself, I had to raise my mum in the bargain. 'Cause my mother was useless. And my dad was no screamin' hell either – *when* he was there. So don't expect me to walk in that farmhouse and balance a china teacup on my knee, too nervous to know what to do but talk.

They all in that family were just too good for me, you none o' ya involve me like I count, never have.

JIM: What she on about this for?

MAXINE: "She" – "leave her" – like I'm some kinda spoiled brat you have to put up with. Husband don't talk to me, doesn't think I'm bright enough. Maxine, she's just a dumb American. S'what you-all think deep down, I know you do.

JIM: Jimmy, what in the hell is goin' on in here?

JIMMY: I hurt Max's feelings real bad, it's all my fault.

MAXINE: *Kid's leavin'*, Jim. *Care?* I'm the only one showin' I do only to find out I'm the only one he's not gonna have a hard time leavin'.

JIMMY: Max, that's not true.

MAXINE: (*to JIM*) You, you're just so afraid all the time o' what I'm gonna do or say if I'm let in on anything. Ever stop to think while you're out in that field that I bin here pushin' forty years and I haven't done nothin' yet?

JIMMY: Max, you done plenny, you're my Max.

MARLENE: Shush, Jimmy.

JIMMY: You shush.

JIM: Memory serves me correct, day I brung you up here you turned around and went right back.

MARLENE looks to JIMMY. JIMMY looks to JIM.

JIMMY: No way.

JIM: Yes, she did. I think walkin' out on me is how you'd put it. Because that's what she did – straight through that field there. Across the border. She had no trouble leaving me.

Pause.

MAXINE: I wouldn't say that. I run my nylon on the barbwire.

JIM: That's right, you did. I was married to her three days, I'd known her five.

MAXINE: Two of which were spent on the train waiting for Saskatchewan to end.

JIM: We got picked up at the station in Lethbridge and –

MAXINE: His dad didn't say one word to us the whole time home. Side by side in that old truck. Me in the middle, a carbon copy on either side, lookin' straight ahead. Walk into that farmhouse expectin' I don't know what and *what* does the woman do but *warm* the teapot. Hands me her best English china just *hopin'* I'd break it, which I did.

JIM: It wasn't her best, it was just some cup I got at the show.

MAXINE: Yeah, but I didn't know that.

JIM: You didn't have to take off.

JIMMY: I can't believe this on the day I'm leavin'.

MAXINE: You didn't have to come after me.

JIM: Well, I did.

Pause.

MAXINE: That's right you did and I'd like to know what for – you-all get along just fine without me.

JIM: I don't know about that.

MAXINE: Huh.

JIM: Said I don't know whereas we would, in fact, get along without you. Maxine.

Pause.

JIMMY: Told ya Max, the man needs ya – it's emotional security.

JIM slowly looks at JIMMY.

JIM: (*to MAXINE*) Speaking of tea.

MAXINE heads to the kitchen to prepare it. Pause.

JIM: Much of a dinner crowd?

MARLENE: Yes.

JIMMY: No. Yes, I mean.

JIM walks over to the gear and case and stares at it. He goes to the window and takes a look out. He takes a deep breath. He takes his hat off and wipes his brow.

JIMMY: I know I shoulda bin out there! I know I didn't even do my chores! You don't have to stand there not tellin' me!

JIM: Well, I didn't expect you to today.

JIMMY: No sooner would I leave he'd show up and how'd he take that? Huh?

MARLENE: Jimmy, don't snap at Granddad, he's gonna wish he never come in.

JIMMY: You snap at Maxine lef', right, and cenner, look how you talk to your own mother, Marlene.

JIM: Here, you kids.

MARLENE: My mother is my mother.

JIMMY: Oh good one, Mum, and who're you? – Way you talk to Max is just pathetic.

JIM: Jimmy, *listen* to yourself son.

JIMMY: Son? – I'm not your son. I never will be, okay? So quit tyin' my stomach up in knots when he's not here yet, and I shoulda bin out in that *field* all along. (*pause*) Good one, Jimmy. Insult Granddad now.

JIM: Never mind.

MARLENE: We're none of us what we're supposed to be in this family. Mum's like my daughter half the time, Jimmy's more of a brother. Guess it's no wonder he's itchin' to go south, eh, Dad? He's got a new and improved father and a perky little secretary real eager to take my place. Gee, you know, Dad, this gal? – she's got a real way about her.

JIMMY: You heard me.

MARLENE: Jimmy can say whatever he wants to her, isn't that great? Wonder if he'll lip her off like he does me. 'Course I'm no one. I pour coffee all day. Raised in the back suite of the Bordertown Café like I had no choice but to tie on an apron, work till, cash out, and close up. Time I was fifteen I could run this place. So what? Is that what I wanted? Who cares what I want – he can show me up all he wants to his dad and her, packin' this piddly little amount like it's *all* I could afford.

JIM: Marlene.

MARLENE: Well, Dad, I give him more'n a hockey stick to show them off.

JIMMY: I don't want her to show them off, I don't want *nothin'* from her, Granddad.

MARLENE: Yes, you do. You want something I just don't *have*. And never will. When I got somethin' to say, I *can't* just say it to you. I'm not her, I'm not the kinda wife your dad needed. I'm not my mother, I'm not Aunt Thelma, I'm no one – just myself. I got a few dollars in the Bank o' Montreal, I got a car, I'm thirty-four years old with fallen arches and a sore back. But you know what? I *like* this place. And any changes I make I wanna make in my own good time. But first, I'm gonna ... tra-vel.

Pause.

JIMMY: *Travel?*

JIM: Travel – ?

MARLENE: Booked my flight today. To Hawaii. And I'm goin'. Come Christmas. Two weeks accommodation. Wardair. You said I needed a holiday. Well, I'm takin' one.

JIMMY: Whataya mean you're goin' to Hawaii? By *yourself*?

MARLENE: Well, this is it.

MAXINE enters with a small pot of tea. She sets it on the counter.

JIMMY: Max, Mum's goin' to Hawaii!

MAXINE: Huh! – How?

MARLENE: Gonna dog-paddle, Mum.

MAXINE: Hawaii? – Hawaii's part o' the United States.

JIMMY: *I'm* not spendin' Christmas with my dad and her. I don't even know them for nothin'. Aren'tcha even gonna invite me home?

MAXINE: I'll get Sanny Claus up and bakes my turkey and we'll have all the reg'lars in – it'll be just the same without her.

JIMMY: You mean we aren't gonna be together ever again? You mean this is it? The guy calls and I'm booted out the door?

MARLENE: Max'll give you a Christmas.

A tanker goes by. JIMMY ignores it.

JIMMY: Mum, listen to reason, you can't go off single like that. There's jerks out there. And – and you're easy prey, especially when you get dressed up.

MARLENE: I won't get dressed up. I'll wear my uniform over there and carry a coffee pot.

MAXINE: Thought you said your mother could do with a good time for a change?

JIMMY: Oh yeah, but don't you think someone should go with her?

JIM: Jimmy should go with you, Marlene. He's right.

JIMMY: No! – I didn't mean *me*.

MARLENE: Well, he could if he ... wants.

Pause.

JIMMY: Want me to?

MARLENE: (*looks to him, then away*) She'll prob'ly have somethin' planned for you down there, a real Christmas, nice homey stuff, fix that place up like you wouldn't believe – your dad'll have so many presents for you under that tree –

JIMMY: Yeah, he's prob'ly planning it all right now, which is why he's so late – but fine, I won't go with you, who cares? I only bin waitin' in this café for the man since I was four – I mean, I mean since *four* – but I'll keep waitin', because it's what you want, I'll just – just – (*takes out his wallet and* fumbles for a piece of paper) – give you this now and take my gear and go stand out on the highway, I'll just get outta your sight, Mum – (throwing the paper at her) – so here, have it, okay? – It's your pink bathroom. It's all paid for, it's looked after, it's what you wanted, it's what you got – white bathtub, pink curtains, flower wallpaper, just like the magazines. You tell the man when he comes Monday, clean, new, modern – exactly how you got it in your head.

Pause.

MAXINE: Kid bought a bathroom. When what she got is fine.

MARLENE: No, it's not fine. A person can hardly turn around in there. There's no place to put my makeup on.

MAXINE: Oh. You're right. The whole suite should be gutted.

MARLENE: No, it shouldn't, just the bathroom.

MAXINE: Just the ... bathroom.

MARLENE: I didn't wanna buy the Mathison house, I wanted to stay *here*. I – I try to teach the kid the value of the dollar, I make him work till, I look in the window at those diamond-chip earrings, I – and now he's put the mon- – the money down on a bathroom.

Pause.

JIMMY: I didn't even *know* you wanted Hawaii, though. I figgered it was just the bathroom you wanted, eh.

MARLENE breaks down completely. JIMMY looks to JIM, to MAXINE, back to MARLENE.

JIMMY: I can't *believe* I didn't think of Hawaii.

MAXINE gets a serviette from the canister and hands it to JIMMY. JIMMY goes to MARLENE to give it to her. She reaches out to get it but grabs onto JIMMY's hand instead. She keeps a distance from him, but brings his hand to her face and holds it there.

JIMMY: You never even *mentioned* Hawaii.

MARLENE rushes to the back suite.

JIM: Go after her, Maxine.

MAXINE exits.

JIMMY: Trust me to come up with a *bathroom*.

JIM: Sit down, Jimmy.

JIMMY sits on one of the stools up to the counter. JIM goes around the counter and reaches under it to a hiding spot. He pulls out a bottle of Canadian Club whisky. JIMMY is floored. He watches as JIM takes two glasses and pours two shots.

JIMMY: Granddad. Are you really doing this?

JIM hands JIMMY a drink. JIMMY takes it.

JIM: I'm a degenerate, there's no gettin' around it.

JIM comes around the counter and sits beside JIMMY. He clinks his glass with JIMMY's. They drink.

JIMMY: Granddad?

JIM: Yep.

JIMMY: Just tell me if I'm doin' the right thing, goin' down there. That's all I wanna know.

JIM: Can't tell you that.

JIMMY: Maxine tells me.

JIM: Do you listen? No. You still pack your kit.

JIMMY: You don't *like* my dad, though. That's sayin' something.

JIM: He's not all bad.

JIMMY: You don't like him, just say you don't like him.

JIM: Not for me to say.

JIMMY: Okay, now *what* don't you like about him? – that he doesn't show up on time, fine. He's not reliable. Now you see where I get it from.

Pause.

JIM: Expecting an answer to that?

JIMMY: Yeah.

JIM: It's a load o' horseshit. (takes a drink) Blood only goes so far. It depends what a person sees around him. Some people, like your dad, they for whatever reason think they need the nonsense in life. That's not your problem.

JIMMY: But Linda, she won't stand for it.

JIM: So you tell me. However, who's to say how long her dent will last. Other hand, to be fair, maybe your dad is ready to quit playin' the man, and start bein' one. Before his son beats him to it. (pause) Which by God I think you already have.

JIMMY gets up to hide his reaction. He goes to the window to look out across the prairie. The sun is very low now and the light in the café is turning gold and pink.

JIM: You ... do a good day's work, Jimmy. I – well, I want you to know I'm proud of you.

JIMMY: (*closes his eyes*) Yeah? (*pause*) How come I lip off my mum so bad?

Pause.

JIM: You get that from your grandmother. Don't worry about your mum. She's had the misfortune of taking after me. So give her time.

JIMMY: I'm runnin' outta time.

JIM: Jimmy, get yourself in the driver's seat. You're lettin' your dad take the reins, take control of your life, waitin' on him like this. You want somethin' outta this bargain, but don't you think he does, too? Eh? If he calls, you give him a time and if he doesn't meet it, well, that's his loss. He'll meet it.

JIMMY: He won't meet it, that's just it.

JIM: Prepare yourself for that. But, Jimmy, don't chase after somethin' unless it's worth having.

JIMMY: That why you chased after Max? You knew?

A long pause.

JIM: I didn't know. I was just turned twenty.

JIMMY: You *didn't* know? – And yet you went and married her?

JIM: Okay.

JIMMY: And then you went after her over that border when she caught her nylon? It just doesn't sound like you, Granddad. I never stopped to think of it before, but marryin' Max so fast and chasin' her across the field, I just thought, boy, *Granddad*?

JIM: I wasn't called Granddad in those days. (*pause*) I was called Jimmy.

JIMMY: Your whole family prob'ly starin' at you out the window.

JIM *sits down.* JIMMY *sits down beside him. They both look out.*

JIM: It was rainin'.

JIMMY: You get all muddy?

JIM: My dad was ready to carve my ass for supper.

JIMMY: Why?

JIM: Well, I hadn't phoned home from Minnesota to say I was bringin' home a wife. He, of course, didn't even approve of me goin' in the first place.

JIMMY: Down the States?

JIM: Actually they thought I was in Manitoba.

JIMMY: What?

JIM: And we were right in the middle of seeding.

JIMMY: You lef' him stranded? *You* left him –

JIM: I wasn't all that keen on work back then.

JIMMY: Huh?

JIM: Chap I met in the Army, from Winnipeg, he had his eye on this Minnesota girl, see. Made the mistake of showin' me her picture. I got it in my head I'd go to Winnipeg, get him to take me down there, introduce us, eh.

JIMMY: You didn't go down for an auction?

JIM: Well, no, that was just the line.

JIMMY: But, Granddad – *Max* still thinks it was just chance, an auction you happened to go down for – didn't you *tell* her – after you were married and stuff?

Pause.

JIM: Well, I've been meaning to. But it's not the sort of thing a person likes to admit to. Especially knowin' it'd be general knowledge to anyone who happened to drop in here for coffee. Goin' all the way to Minnesota on the basis of a two-inch photograph your buddy happens to show you in Halifax?

JIMMY: Halifax? You were in Halifax?

JIM: I was there when the war ended.

JIMMY: Wait a sec', wait a sec' – you mean to say – this is just hittin' me – you bin off the prairies?

Pause.

JIM: Drink up, kid. (*They drink.*) The prairies may be dry, but it was a different kind o' dry in Halifax, when the war ended. We could've done with a little of this then. We couldn't get a bottle o' beer, never mind this.

JIMMY: Why not?

JIM: Banned.

JIMMY: You mean you couldn't celebrate? – What'd you do?

JIM: Well. Not that I was instrumental, but we – we rioted.

JIMMY: *You* rioted?

JIM: Until they threw me in the clinker.

The phone rings. JIMMY jumps.

JIMMY: My dad! (*The phone rings again. JIMMY looks to the back suite.*) I'm gettin' it in here! (*He goes to the phone and stares at it.*)

JIM: Answer it.

JIMMY: (*to himself*) Granddad rioted.

JIM: Pick up the phone.

JIMMY: (*picking up*) Bordertown Café. Hi, Dad.

MAXINE and MARLENE enter.

MARLENE: Where's he at?

JIMMY: (*into phone*) Where you at, Dad? (*cupping the phone*) Hasn't left. Yeah? Oh, is that it, eh? – uh-huh. Yeah well, that happens. Tie you up all day like that. (*cupping the phone*) Truck's just gettin' loaded now.

MARLENE moves to the booth to sit down. MAXINE stays behind the counter. JIM sits as he was. They all stare out, as the sun continues to change.

JIMMY: So I guess you ... never thought to give us a call? No, I know you're callin' now but it's late now – well, never mind, it – it doesn't matter. Eh? Yeah well, this is what Mum was sayin' you said. Pardon? Yeah, I know Linda likes me, why shouldn't she like me, I'm a good guy, eh. Chip off the ole block, right? Eh? Boy, that sounds pretty snazzy, Dad. Twelve hunderd square feet, eh. How many? Boy. *Two* bathrooms? Wow, that's a lot. Uh-huh. Yeah well, I'd like to come down, sure – how big's the living room? Is that right? Is *that* right? (*cupping the phone*) Gotta buy more furniture to fill it up. Family room off the kitchen. (*going back to the phone*) Dad, it sounds just great, I can hardly wait to see it, I'm all packed and – and what was the reason you said you didn't call? Call, Dad, call. Whataya mean why? – because I bin waitin', I had to – to miss hockey, I couldn't do chores for fear of missin' you, and it turns out you weren't even gonna phone to let a guy know? When I got a crop to get off? That wasn't fair, Dad, it just wasn't, and I'm thinkin' maybe I'll take a pass on movin' down there actually. But, uh, uh, how be it I come see you at Christmas? Oh heck, hold on, Christmas is no good, I've already told Mum I'd take her to Hawaii. Yeah well, I checked around and found a deal with Wardair, figured she'd like to see the place – you know how it is, we're not caught up in spending a lot o' money on houses, we'd rather ... travel. Granddad was just tellin' me about Halifax, it's got quite the history, he was there not too long ago – anyhooo – (*cupping the phone*) Can you believe what I'm sayin'? (*going back to the phone*) Tell you what I'm gonna do for ya, Dad. Why don't you just think about droppin' in on me *next* haul so I can know when to be in the café. Like you sayin' next

Friday, well, Friday's a twenty-four hour day and I can't sit around here waitin' for you to show up. Guess my point is in a few weeks I'll be eighteen and – and what it boils down to is you're eighteen years too late, Dad. I gotta be up at four thirty tomorrow, so I'll say good night, you keep in touch, bye. (*He hangs up abruptly. He stares at the phone. He looks up.*) That's *not* what I was gonna say.

MAXINE: We shoulda put booze in that kid's bottle when he was a baby and saved ourselves a lot o' trouble.

MARLENE: It wasn't the liquor, Mum.

JIMMY: Now I'll never see my dad.

JIM: I suspect you'll see more of him.

JIMMY: Mum, I blew it.

MARLENE: Put your stuff in the back suite.

JIMMY: Maybe I should phone back and apologize.

MARLENE: And maybe you shouldn't. (*She holds a look with him. Then she goes to pick up some of his gear.*)

JIM: Listen to your mother. (*JIMMY heads to his things. He picks up the remainder. He looks to JIM.*) I'll finish up tonight, you start in the morning.

MARLENE exits to the back. JIMMY follows her, looking back to him.

JIMMY: That is definitely *not* what I was gonna say. (*exits*)

JIM looks out at the sun setting.

MAXINE: Jim.

JIM: What.

MAXINE: Did you hear that kid talk to his dad?

JIM: Yep.

MAXINE: That's the *American* finally comin' out in him. (*JIM looks to her.*) Huh? – Good ole American gumption.

JIM: (*puts on his hat*) Yeah, I guess that's what it is all right.

Pause.

MAXINE: Well, are you just gonna sit there?

JIM: No. (*gets up and heads to the door*) Gonna get back out to the field.

He goes out, letting the screen door flap behind him. MAXINE looks after him, then goes out through the kitchen.

END

JOAN MACLEOD

(b. 1954)

Joan MacLeod occupies a central place within the generation of Canadian women playwrights who came of age in the 1980s. Like Sharon Pollock, Judith Thompson, Wendy Lill, Sally Clark, and others, she helped redefine the Canadian family play, replacing the primary axis of fathers and sons with fathers or mothers and daughters. As Kelly Rebar did in *Bordertown Café*, MacLeod also deconstructs the nuclear family model more fully, offering new templates for roles, relationships, and responsibilities within the family structure. At the centre of MacLeod's plays are strong female characters who make difficult choices as they find themselves having to reconsider their behaviour in the world. They face eating disorders, the ravages of age, widowhood, and mental disability. They struggle with bullying and the radically alien experiences of others. Over against those challenges they generate powerful imaginative empathy that balances utopian visions with hard-earned realism. *Toronto, Mississippi*, her first full-length success, established MacLeod as a major force in Canadian theatre.

MacLeod was born and grew up in Vancouver, earning degrees in creative writing from the University of Victoria (B.A., 1978) and the University of British Columbia (M.F.A., 1981). While attending a poetry workshop at the Banff Centre in 1984, she met playwright Alan Williams who encouraged her to try her hand at drama. The result was the monologue *Jewel*, which she sent to Tarragon Theatre in Toronto. Tarragon invited her to join its Playwrights Unit in 1985 and subsequently premiered her first four plays. MacLeod remained playwright-in-residence there for six years. Her first produced work, however, was the libretto for a chamber opera, *The Secret Garden*, presented by Toronto's Comus Music Theatre in 1985. Based on the classic children's novel, it won MacLeod a Dora Mavor Moore Award for best new musical.

Jewel premiered at Tarragon in 1987. Set in 1985, it takes the form of a widow's moving valentine to her husband who drowned in the sinking of the oil rig *Ocean Ranger* three years earlier. The woman addresses the dead man in a poignant effort to kick-start her own life again. *Jewel* received nominations for the Floyd S. Chalmers Canadian Play Award, as well as the Dora Mavor Moore Award for best new play. It also marked MacLeod's first (and last) experience as a stage actor when, the day before opening and with no previous experience, MacLeod replaced the actress who had been rehearsing the part. She later reprised the role for radio. Retitled *Hand of God*, the radio adaptation of *Jewel* garnered honourable mention in the prestigious Prix Italia competition, and has been produced in French, German, Danish, and Swedish.

Tarragon also premiered *Toronto, Mississippi* in 1987 and *Amigo's Blue Guitar* in 1990. The latter concerns a political refugee from El Salvador who comes to live with a family in British Columbia's Gulf Islands, his experience of torture and horror challenging their inadequate Canadian liberalism. The play was subsequently produced across western Canada as well as in Ottawa, Chicago, the United Kingdom, and Alaska. The published text of *Amigo's Blue Guitar* won the Governor General's Literary Award for Drama in 1991.

Next came *The Hope Slide* (1992), a one-woman play about an actress who assumes the characters of three dead Doukhobors in an attempt to comprehend the deaths of her friends from AIDS, and to rally her own crumbling hope. The Tarragon production won a Floyd S. Chalmers Canadian Play Award, and the play was produced across Canada. *Little Sister* (1994), a play for young audiences about body image and eating disorders, was co-produced by Vancouver's Green Thumb and Toronto's Theatre Direct. MacLeod's millennial comic drama *2000* (1996) was first produced in Ottawa by the Great Canadian Theatre Company and subsequently in Toronto and Vancouver. Set on the border between city and wilderness in North Vancouver, *2000* combines west-coast mysticism (evoking the ghost of Chief Dan George) with the concerns of an upper-middle-class couple wrestling with mid-life crisis.

The notorious murder of teenager Reena Virk by a group of mostly teenage girls in Victoria led MacLeod to write *The Shape of a Girl*, the monologue of an adolescent girl involved in her own narrative of girl-on-girl bullying and violence. Originally co-produced by Calgary's Alberta Theatre Projects and Vancouver's Green Thumb Theatre in 2001, *The Shape of a Girl* has gone on to become one of MacLeod's most successful and most produced plays. Toured widely by Green Thumb, it has garnered rave reviews wherever it has played, including New York in 2005.

With *Homechild*, first produced by CanStage in Toronto in 2006, and *Another Home Invasion*, co-produced by Tarragon and Alberta Theatre Projects in Calgary in 2009, MacLeod radically shifted generations. A family play, *Homechild* tells the story of orphaned and abandoned young children who were transported from Britain to Canada in the early twentieth century. The central characters, now elderly, relive their traumatic past. In *Another Home Invasion*, another of MacLeod's extraordinary female monologues, eighty-year-old Jean faces a literal home invasion and a more profound metaphorical one as she struggles with her husband's dementia.

In addition to writing for the stage, MacLeod has published poetry and fiction in more than a dozen literary journals, written radio plays and episodes of the TV series *Edgemont*, and adapted *Jewel* and *Amigo's Blue Guitar* for television. Since 2006, she has taught at the University of Victoria, where she is currently Associate Professor of Writing. In 2011, MacLeod won the Elinore and Lou Siminovitch Prize in Theatre for playwriting, Canadian theatre's richest award.

Toronto, Mississippi had its genesis in Joan MacLeod's experience as a childcare worker and life skills instructor for mentally challenged people with Vancouver's Mainstream Society. The fascinating character of Jhana was a composite portrait based on two of MacLeod's women clients: an attractive teen and an older woman obsessed with Elvis. In writing the play MacLeod hoped to "give a real voice" to the mentally challenged and to show what a "joy" a person like Jhana could be. Standing at the thematic centre of the play, Jhana not only challenges our preconceptions about mental disability – or whatever euphemism we use to label this condition – but also invites us to consider whether the other characters, in their own ways, are any less handicapped. All are in some degree damaged, all in need of life-skills lessons. They all need help and, significantly, it is Jhana who dials 9-1-1 for them at the end.

Jhana also occupies the centre of the play's reconstructed family model in ways that echo both *Blood Relations* and *Bordertown Café*. Mentally and physically straddling the border between adult and child, she embodies the ambiguity of the gendered roles each character plays in this version of the exploded post-nuclear family. King, the father (or father the king – also "the King of Rock 'n' Roll," a surrogate Elvis, the powerful testosterone-fuelled American cultural icon) has been replaced by surrogate father Bill, the (feminized Canadian) poet. But Bill also usurps the traditional maternal role. He stays home as primary caregiver while Maddie goes out to work and brings home the income. In the loving but tense mother-daughter relationship, Jhana struggles to define her selfhood and independence while Maddie overcompensates in dealing with her vulnerable daughter's emerging sexuality. Both Maddie and Bill assume that King fails to give Jhana the things she needs from a father. Yet King offers Jhana the most positive reinforcement in the play. While Bill and Maddie insist on reminding Jhana of all that is not possible for her, King tells her, "Sky's the limit for you. Don't forget that." His gift to her, symbolized by the Elvis cape, is the almost magical power to transform herself and her world through imagination. Inspired by him, she constructs that impossible heterotopian place, Toronto, Mississippi (another liminal Canadian-American "bordertown"), where the impossible might just happen.

King is not quite the "fascist" whom Bill fears (quoting from Sylvia Plath's poem "Daddy") that "every woman adores." Nor is Bill himself the ideal father-surrogate. In role-playing life skills with Jhana, playing Elvis to her Priscilla, and Andrew to her real-life horny teenage self, Bill treads dangerous ground, especially when he mixes in his own sexual fantasies and frustrations. And for all his wit, nerdy charm, and good intentions, he turns out to be wrong about some pretty important things. His inadvertently humorous reading of Margaret Atwood leads him to a reductive view of Canadian literature that sees "women as victim" and women's literature as "very despairing" when in fact *Toronto, Mississippi* shows us a young woman who refuses, despite her handicaps, to be in any way a victim. Far from following *The Path of Despair*, as Bill titles his slim volume of poetry, the play takes us on a comic journey to a place rich in possibility.

Toronto, Mississippi

Joan Macleod

Toronto, Mississippi premiered at Tarragon Theatre in Toronto on October 6, 1987, with the following cast:

JHANA	Brooke Johnson
BILL	Jim Warren
MADDIE	Marlane O'Brien
KING	Bruce McFee

Directed by Andy McKim
Set and Costume Design by Sue LePage
Lighting Design by Louise Guinand
Stage Managed by Beth Bruck

CHARACTERS

KING, *Elvis impersonator, Jhana's father, age forty*

JHANA, *moderately mentally handicapped, hyperactive with symptoms of autism, employed at a sheltered workshop, age eighteen*

BILL, *poet, part-time college instructor who boards with Jhana and Maddie, age thirty*

MADDIE, *high school English teacher, Jhana's mother, age forty*

SETTING

A middle-class living room in Toronto.

PLAYWRIGHT'S NOTE

In Jhana's first scene she is slightly "rocking back and forth." It is something she does to comfort herself, and a signal to Bill that she's phasing out a little. This is what Maddie refers to later as "stimming out" and considers inappropriate.

Later in this scene Jhana (pronounced "Jah–nah") says, "We'll all be at workshop. We'll all be at drop-in." The social circle mentally handicapped people move in is often quite small. The people Jhana went to school with are the same people she now works with, bowls with, and goes to drop-in with. Drop-in is a Friday night event for handicapped people at the local community centre.

Jhana later says, "I am mentally handicapped." This is something she does not like having to say. In this case she becomes angry with her mother for making her say it and she yells, "Close the patio door!" Jhana is imitating something her mother said earlier but it's the emotion behind the phrase she's imitating rather than the meaning – something she does often.

Jhana whines offstage about finding her clothes, vacuuming, etc. She is being very lazy about the way she speaks – partly because she finds the tasks at hand uninteresting but also because her mother understands her even when she's talking "silly." If you had to say all your sentences backward for the next half hour it would be very difficult and concentrated work; in a way this is what Jhana has to do all the time. The way she talks naturally is very jumbled but when she is interested in communicating well she can do it; at the very end of the play when she dials 9-1-1 she speaks in perfect sentences.

Jhana is obsessed with her father's visit because she loves him and hasn't seen him for a while. But carrying one thought at a time rather than a half dozen at once is also part of her mental handicap and comes up often. Jhana also often repeats the last line of what her father is saying; she does this to show she is interested but doesn't have a clue what is being talked about. She'll repeat, she'll agree, she'll imitate the emotion she picks up from that person. Her father often talks over her head because he doesn't live with her.

When Jhana says, "Betty died," she refers to the fact that some of the people she went to school with and worked with also have physical handicaps and sometimes a shorter lifespan. Jhana doesn't have this problem but she is much more accustomed to death than the average eighteen-year-old.

The best way to approach Jhana is to find the Jhana within – she's just like any eighteen-year-old but not as slick, and once that discovery's happened there are some mentally handicapped traits that can be added. There is sometimes a flatness to a mentally handicapped person's speech or inappropriate emphasis because what's being said isn't always understood – statements become questions and vice versa. Physically there's "stimming out" and inappropriate physical behaviour. Mentally handicapped people also often have high anxiety rates and low self-esteem; think of a job interview where you don't feel qualified but you fake your way through.

Jhana is hyperactive; her energy is nearly always unrelenting. She is mentally handicapped with only some symptoms of autism – so don't think of Jhana as autistic.

Jhana is based partly on a friend of mine who is a very lovely woman who is also mentally handicapped. The most important thing I can tell you about playing Jhana is that a mental handicap or any handicap is a sad thing, but this life, this particular person, is also a joy.

PROLOGUE

*Black on set, spot on **KING** at microphone, costumed like early Elvis, with a Memphis accent.*

KING: Mrs. Priscilla Presley has just left the building, and believe you me, folks, that is something we can all be grateful for. So now we can kick our heels up, have a good time. I thank you all for coming out tonight, but before I begin a big hello to a special someone who's sitting out there front row centre. I mean, friends and women – they come and go. They certainly have been marching away from me at a steady rate these days. But children ... well it's just a very precious thing to have a child. Ladies and gentlemen, my daughter, my little girl – Lisa Marie Presley. Stand up, honey; don't be scared. She's still real little so let's treat her nice, let's make her feel right at home.

Blackout.

ACT ONE

SCENE 1

Lights up on set.

JHANA is dancing full out to loud, early Elvis music. Eventually she sits and begins rocking back and forth in a trance-like manner. BILL enters and stops her rocking and turns off the music.

BILL: You be Priscilla, and I'll be Elvis.

JHANA: I'm Elvis Presley!

BILL: Five minutes on 9-1-1 and then it's bed. Deal?

JHANA: I'm Elvis Presley!

BILL: You're always Elvis. How about being Lisa Marie?

JHANA: No. Bill's Priscilla. It's funny. Right?

BILL: Why can't we both be Elvis? I hate being her.

JHANA: She isn't dead.

BILL: Good point. So you be Priscilla –

JHANA: You're hating 9-1-1, right?

BILL: Five minutes. When your mom gives us shit for staying up half the night, you can amaze her with 9-1-1. (*role-playing Elvis*) I smell something burning, Cilla. If Graceland burnt ...? Lawdy, lawdy ... C'mon, Jhana.

JHANA: I'm Elvis Presley!

BILL: All right. You win. (*role-playing Priscilla*) Elvis? How many of those pills did you take? You hear me? Are you sick, honey? El?

JHANA: (*role-playing Elvis*) Hi, Priscilla. You're funny, right?

BILL: I'm perfectly fine but you look a little rough. Half-dead if you want to know the truth. I don't care if you are Elvis Presley or the president of the United States. I'm gonna call you an ambulance. Now how on earth do you suppose I do that?

JHANA: 9-1-1.

BILL: Show me.

JHANA: 9-1-1. On her telephone. Pick it up.

BILL: The whole phone?

JHANA: Bill! (*picks up receiver and offers it to BILL*)

BILL: Dial it.

JHANA: Why?

BILL: Look, Jhana. This isn't my idea of a great time either. But you were the one that was all keen on doing this course.

JHANA: She hates it.

BILL: It's only one night a week. You get to hang out at a college, meet guys, learn all kinds of stuff that –

JHANA: It's hard.

BILL: C'mon. You're meeting some new people there, right?

JHANA: We'll all be at the workshop.

BILL: No new faces?

JHANA: We'll all be at drop-in.

BILL: So it's the same old crowd. Lots of old friends there. Right? And life skills is valuable stuff ...

JHANA: (*pointing to television*) *The Love Boat*'s inside.

BILL: It's not on. You were about to call an ambulance before the King of Rock 'n' Roll blew up or passed out ... Sssshhh! That's her.

JHANA: That's her.

> *JHANA dives onto the couch, covers herself with the blanket, and pretends to be asleep. MADDIE enters.*

BILL: How was it?

MADDIE: Lousy. Why's she down here? It's past midnight, Bill.

BILL: She fell asleep.

MADDIE: Faker.

BILL: We were watching *The Love Boat*. I didn't like him much when he picked you up. Where'd he take you?

MADDIE: Downtown. Why's she breathing heavy?

BILL: Filthy dreams.

MADDIE: She's faking. Jhana?

BILL: Didn't you ever pretend you were sleeping when you were little?

MADDIE: She's eighteen years old –

BILL: So that someone would carry you up to bed? Or better yet, you'd be visiting somewhere and get carried out to the car.

MADDIE: This guy tonight. He wasn't 100 per cent horrible. You two have something in common.

BILL: That's impossible.

MADDIE: He writes poetry.

BILL: Everyone's a poet. We'd be visiting my grandfather's place. He wore this black patch on his eye, and I used to think this tunnel of air went right through his head.

MADDIE: C'mon, Jhana.

BILL: He'd carry me outside to my dad's truck. The yard smelled like hay and – I don't know – toilets.

JHANA: (*sits up suddenly*) Toilets!

MADDIE: Faking all along.

JHANA: Princie's gone, Mom, right? (*runs to door*) Bye-bye!

MADDIE: It's October, Jhana. Close the patio door!

JHANA: Close patio door!

MADDIE: Up to bed now, okay?

JHANA: Okay?

MADDIE: Did you clean your room?

JHANA: Did you clean your room?

MADDIE: DID YOU CLEAN YOUR ROOM?

JHANA: Yes.

MADDIE: And brush your teeth?

JHANA: Yes. And brushed your teeth. Princie's dead now, Mom.

MADDIE: We're all aware of that.

JHANA: Elvis Presley was on the bus?

MADDIE: No more nonsense.

JHANA: Not Daddy.

MADDIE: Good night, Jhana.

JHANA: The man on the bus is gone?

MADDIE: Who is the man on the bus?

JHANA: Who is the man on the bus?

MADDIE: And quit the copying. Did you meet someone on the bus today?

JHANA: Yes.

MADDIE: Who?

JHANA: Princie.

MADDIE: I'm not kidding around here, Jhana. Who did you meet?

JHANA: Elvis Presley.

BILL: Elvis Presley on the Woodbine bus? Quick, call the *National Enquirer*.

MADDIE: Bill, just let me handle this, right?

JHANA: Number nine. Number two. The Woodbine bus!

MADDIE: Did you talk to someone on the bus today?

JHANA: Yes I did!

MADDIE: Someone from the workshop? You talked to a man? A man you didn't know?

JHANA: Yes.

MADDIE: Did he touch you?

BILL: A new record –

JHANA: Oh yes.

BILL: For jumping the gun.

BILL arranges two chairs, one behind the other.

MADDIE: Show me where he touched you.

JHANA: Black hair.

MADDIE: He touched your hair? Bloody social workers. I knew you weren't ready for bus training ...

BILL: Okay. I'm the man on the bus.

JHANA: Hi, Billy.

BILL: No. I'm the man on the bus.

JHANA: Hi.

BILL: Hello there.

JHANA: Hello there, black hair.

BILL: I'm the man on the bus with black hair. You just get off work, honey?

JHANA: Elvis Presley.

BILL: I'm the man on the bus, and I look like Elvis Presley?

JHANA: Yes!

BILL: And you like me?

JHANA: (*touching his hair*) Black hair.

BILL: You touch my nice black hair –

JHANA: Yes!

BILL: Do I touch you?

JHANA: No!

BILL: I don't like it when you touch me. (*pause*) SHE molested him, Maddie.

MADDIE: How many times have I told you? What is the only thing we can say on the bus? What do we know from memory?

JHANA: From memory ... January 8th, 1935. Tupelo, Mississippi!

MADDIE: Great. My daughter is going to go bussing off to Niagara Falls by mistake one day, chanting Elvis Presley's birthday. Damn your father.

JHANA: Elvis Presley's birthday!

MADDIE: What have we gone over six hundred times in the past three months. Jhana? C'mon ... I am ...

JHANA & MADDIE: I am Jhana Kelly.

JHANA: I live at three-nine-two Chisholm Avenue.

MADDIE: Three-two-nine.

JHANA: Three-two-nine.

MADDIE: I am ...

JHANA: I am lost.

MADDIE: I am ...

JHANA: I am lost.

MADDIE: And? I am ...

JHANA: I am mentally handicapped.

MADDIE: Please help –

JHANA: Please help me find my way home! (*rocks back and forth*)

MADDIE: Now show me the paper. Where's your purse?

BILL: Lighten up, Maddie.

JHANA dumps out the contents of her purse; she finds some lipstick and applies it meticulously.

MADDIE: Quit stalling, Jhana.

BILL: She's been working at getting that on straight for weeks.

MADDIE: And we've been working at bussing since March.

BILL: Good night. (*He exits.*)

MADDIE: The address, Jhana. It should be written down on the yellow paper in your purse. I'm very upset with –

JHANA: Close the patio door!

SCENE 2

The next morning. BILL and MADDIE are having coffee.

BILL: There is no way you slept through last night.

MADDIE: Good morning to you too, Bill.

BILL: We were all assaulted by Donovan at three o'clock this morning. I mean he was terrible twenty years ago. What if he's having a comeback? (*places a finger on his Adam's apple*) "Hurdy Gurdy Man." The volume made my teeth vibrate. Donovan.

JHANA: (*off*) Mom? The socks are dead. Princie took a new house. Where's the drawer?

MADDIE: In my room. I just folded everything. Wear some socks the same colour as your T-shirt.

BILL: Then at about five they were all out on the front porch throwing up and yelling in this made-up language ... like tongues. Have you ever noticed that a lot of cabs come and go from there? Maybe it's an after-hours place or a whorehouse.

MADDIE: We were always the noisy neighbours – for years. You can imagine living next door to someone like King.

JHANA: (*off*) Mom? The socks are laundried too. Where?

MADDIE: In the clothes basket, Jhana. All paired up.

JHANA: All paired up. Who's vacuuming there now?

MADDIE: You are. The whole upstairs.

JHANA: Why?

MADDIE: Because I said so. We all pitch in.

JHANA: We all pitch in, Bill!

BILL: He called last night.

MADDIE: Who?

BILL: The King of Rock 'n' Roll. He called last night between sets.

MADDIE: He's in town?

BILL: Buffalo. At the Holiday Inn.

MADDIE: The Holiday Inn? You're joking.

BILL: He wants Jhana to come down for the show tonight.

MADDIE: Just like that.

BILL: He didn't talk to her; he wanted to check it out with you first.

MADDIE: She's supposed to get there all on her own?

BILL: She can bribe the driver on the Woodbine bus.

MADDIE: Did he sound all right?

JHANA enters.

BILL: King said to remind you that he is her father and hasn't seen her since June.

JHANA: Her father. Where's Daddy on?

MADDIE: He's in Buffalo.

JHANA: On Buffalo. Where's Daddy on coming here?

BILL: He wants you to go see him. He's not here. He's in another city called Buffalo.

JHANA: Okay. C'mon. Buffalo.

MADDIE: Thanks, Bill.

JHANA: Daddy's on incoming Buffalo! Let's go.

MADDIE: How'd it be if we asked Daddy to come here?

JHANA: Okay!

MADDIE: Bill?

BILL: I'm just a boarder.

MADDIE: We'll phone him when I come home from shopping. He won't be out of bed yet.

JHANA: Okay. Phoning Daddy!

MADDIE: When I come home.

JHANA: C'mon.

MADDIE: When I come home from shopping. And when you finish vacuuming.

JHANA: Okay. Bill's on the vacuum too. In helping.

BILL: I'll give you a hand. If you'll do some of the dusting.

JHANA: And you'll do some of the dusting! Daddy's on incoming Buffalo. Here! (*She exits.*)

MADDIE: We'll ask him for tomorrow. He should have Sunday off.

JHANA: (*off*) Okay!

BILL: When was the last time you saw him?

MADDIE: Easter. I took Jhana up to Ottawa. He looked lousy, kind of overweight.

BILL: Elvis in his later years. What a dedicated impersonator.

MADDIE: He only does the early stuff. In fact, he's the only one who does early Elvis. He thinks Presley really died when he signed with RCA. Did you tell him I was out with someone last night?

BILL: Did you want me to?

MADDIE: Isn't that stupid? We haven't lived together for nearly a decade, but I still love turning the knife. Just a tad.

BILL: I told him you were out with a brilliant young poet.

MADDIE: David?

BILL: Top of the line.

MADDIE: David owns a chain of dry-cleaning stores.

BILL: Pretty tough competition – the King of Rock 'n' Roll.

MADDIE: David isn't competing with King or anyone else, unfortunately. He's nice enough, but sort of a jerk when it came to Jhana. After he met her, he told me she had a sort of grace – in the bovine sense. He writes poems about nature ... as a hobby.

BILL: God help me.

MADDIE: He'd never heard of your book.

BILL: What? The man must live in a cocoon. David the dry-cleaning poet. I like that actually. I think all poets should be dry cleaners.

MADDIE: He knows sweet nothing about kids let alone someone like Jhana. I'll be back in an hour. You don't have to worry about cleaning. I've done piss-all this week. Okay?

BILL nods, and puts early Elvis on the stereo. MADDIE exits. JHANA enters running.

JHANA: Daddy's on Buffalo!

BILL: Yes, ma'am. Before this song ends, you and I are going to do the fastest dusting job ever.

JHANA: Okay.

BILL and JHANA dust to the music. JHANA dances and imitates Elvis.

BILL: Remember how your mom got so pissed off last night about not having the paper in your purse?

JHANA: The paper in your purse. It's in a new house, Bill. On Buffalo. Daddy's on Buffalo. In Princie's mouth.

BILL: Maybe it's lost.

JHANA: Maybe it's lost.

BILL: So what we're going to do is copy out your name, address, and phone number. I'll do the printing if you tell me what to say. Agreed?

JHANA: Okay.

BILL: So, do you have a name or what?

JHANA: Jhana.

BILL: I want the whole thing.

JHANA: Jhana Gladys Kelly.

BILL: You got a phone number, Gladys? I might want to ring you up sometime. I might want to take you on a date.

JHANA: Okay.

BILL: I might want to take you for a beer. Or to a rock concert. How do I do it? What's your phone number, Jhana Gladys Kelly?

JHANA: 692-4444.

BILL: Good. I'll call. What if I want to come to your house. Where do you live?

JHANA: Here.

BILL: I need an address, angel.

JHANA: I live at ... I live at three-nine-three-nine-three-nine. I live at three-TWO-nine Chisholm Avenue.

BILL: You're a wizard.

JHANA: Wizard. She's out on a date. Out on a date on Buffalo.

BILL: What city do you live in?

JHANA: Buffalo.

BILL: Nope.

JHANA: Chisholm Avenue. Tupelo. Tupelo, Mississippi.

BILL: Toronto, angel.

JHANA: Toronto, angel. Toronto, Mississippi.

BILL: Close.

JHANA: You're Andrew, right?

BILL: Never heard of him.

JHANA: At her workshop. Me and Andrew. He's funny, right?

BILL: Andrew's a guy you work with?

JHANA: He's funny. He's drying my face after lunch. Being tall. Right?

BILL: If you say so. You like this guy?

JHANA: Okay. You're Andrew, right? For pretend, Bill.

BILL: Okay. But no funny stuff, Jhana Gladys. You got that? It's after work, and we're just talking. In a café. Okay?

JHANA: Yes.

BILL: So what'll you have. You wanna beer?

JHANA: Diet Coke, please, thank you.

BILL: C'mon. Have a beer. You're old enough.

JHANA: Okay.

BILL: Wow. You give in real easy. Wanna go to bed? Wanna get married?

JHANA: Okay.

BILL: No, Jhana. Not okay. It's our first date. All right?

JHANA: Diet Coke, please, thank you.

BILL: You live at home?

JHANA: Chisholm Avenue.

BILL: You don't talk much. Can't you ask me a thing or two?

JHANA: Okay.

BILL: (*pause*) So …

JHANA: Princie's not south. Buffalo or that. He's dead. Right?

BILL: Can't follow you.

JHANA: He's not on the patio. Not sleeping. It's sunny in his back. Princie.

BILL: Who the hell's Princie?

JHANA: Her dog.

BILL: Whose dog?

JHANA: Jhana Gladys Kelly. Chisholm Avenue.

BILL: Repeat after me: Princie was my dog. He's dead.

JHANA: Princie was my –

BILL: Jesus, what am I saying. You're not supposed to talk about death on a first date. It's against the rules.

JHANA: You're not allowed, Bill!

BILL: So, sweetheart, you like working all right?

JHANA: Sweetheart.

BILL: What do you do exactly?

JHANA: Fine thank you.

BILL: Right.

JHANA: Right! (*pause*) Sweetheart.

BILL: You hungry?

JHANA: (*rehearsed*) Do you like Italian food?

BILL: Sure. Pizza and that is pretty –

JHANA: (*rehearsed*) I like it very much.

BILL: Terrific. We'll eat a king-size.

JHANA: Daddy wears the suits. Right? You don't wear them. Only black. Don't wear a white suit.

BILL: Whatever you say. This is a great pizza. You like it?

JHANA: Diet Coke, please, thank you.

BILL: Top of the line. (*suddenly choking and coughing*) Jesus! It went down the wrong way. Help me.

JHANA: Sweetheart.

BILL: Do something. Please!

JHANA: Andrew's being funny. He's being tall.

BILL: Call someone! What the hell's that number?

JHANA: Nine … She hates 9-1-1!

BILL: I'm dying here, Jhana. How am I gonna date you again?

JHANA: (*picks up receiver*) 9-1-1 on Bill! (*slams it down*)

BILL: That's not how you do it. Okay, fine. Andrew just bought it on an olive. His heart was broken. Death by dating. The defunct Andrew. (*JHANA turns on the stereo.*) Off. Right now, Jhani. You wanna hear about my first love? I was around your age. No. I was sixteen but looked forty. Her name was Diane and she was eighteen and divorced. She also had a dead sister – car wreck I think – which made Diane quite famous locally.

JHANA: Headphones, Bill.

BILL: I'm spilling my guts here. You know, Jhana, if Elvis's last girlfriend had taken a life skills telephone course, the King of Rock 'n' Roll might still be with us. And your father would be making his living singing "Light My Fire."

JHANA: No more 9-1-1!

BILL: Okay. Headphones are swell. (*JHANA puts on headphones and sings phrases of songs, hums.*) Actually Diane and I barely made it past kissing. She was hoping to get back together with her ex. He was haywire. You can read all about it in my first collection: *Love and the Need for Firearms*, unpublished.

JHANA: (*singing*) Shake, shake, and roll. Shake, shake, and roll.

BILL: Oh. It's the first roll in the hay you want to hear about. That's easy – some creature I picked up at the library. I was twenty-seven. She was around ninety. Not romantic enough for you? Well, screw you then, Miss Raw Sexual Energy. No doubt you'll jump another passenger on the Woodbine bus and give him the business.

JHANA: Hi, Bill.

BILL: Hi, angel. Your first time will happen in the best way possible. Where should we make it? July on Yonge Street. Just getting dark. He'll be from … Kenora. Better yet, Lake of the Woods. No. Fuck the northern stuff. He's from Etobicoke and sensitive. Maybe it really will be this Andrew. He'll be a complete wizard when it comes to money – counts back his change. Knows what colour means what amount. Jhana and Andrew – a regular pair. So don't shut down. When Andrew feels your skin, hair, all those hidden and rough places – he'll be able to remake the entire world.

SCENE 3

Spot is up on KING, costumed like Elvis, at microphone, singing an early Elvis song. Lights fade down on KING and come up on set; it is the next night. JHANA, BILL, and MADDIE are getting ready for dinner.

JHANA: The celery is late. Before dinner, Bill, you going to eat it? Like Daddy? (*shows him plate of celery sticks*)

BILL: Did you make that?

JHANA: Yes.

BILL: What's inside there? It looks like porridge.

JHANA: Cheese, Bill. In Daddy's mouth. Where is it lately?

MADDIE: The celery and cheese are perfect. We will eat them before dinner when your father gets here. He isn't late, Jhana. He'll be here in half an hour.

JHANA: Half an hour. He isn't here now.

BILL: Shortly. You look pretty. Is that your dad on your shirt or the real Elvis?

JHANA: Yes. Princie isn't here. He's dead, Bill.

BILL: Sure is.

JHANA: I'm pretty.

BILL: You're absolutely gorgeous. You're gonna knock him out.

JHANA: Knock him out! Mom? He isn't here. He's on the stereo. (*puts on Elvis record*)

MADDIE: This is your father's day off, Jhana. I'll bet the last thing he wants to hear right now is Elvis Presley. Put on one of Bill's Donovan records. He keeps them under his pillow.

BILL: Liar.

JHANA: Liar, Bill. Daddy isn't listening. Is he?

MADDIE: Maybe you should start calling him "Dad." "Daddy" sounds babyish. Don't you think?

JHANA: Don't you think, Bill?

MADDIE: Try it out. "Hi, Dad. Nice to see you."

JHANA: Hi, Dad. Nice to see you, Dad. Celery, Dad. By me. Bill is dead. Dad.

BILL: I am not! Maybe a little tired but –

JHANA: Bill is maybe a little tired, Dad. (*turns up stereo*)

MADDIE: Turn it down! Now, Jhana.

JHANA puts on headphones.

MADDIE: Did you buy the wine?

BILL: In the fridge.

KING enters, wearing regular clothes, carrying a short white cape covered in sequins and an overnight bag.

MADDIE: Good Lord. We have a doorbell you know.

KING: Sssshhh ... (*sneaking up on JHANA and wrapping the cape around her*)

JHANA: Daddy! (*referring to cape*) This is yours too?

MADDIE: (*whispering*) Say "Dad," Jhana.

KING: Hi, Maddie.

MADDIE: You two remember each other?

BILL: We met last winter when I moved in.

KING: Right. How's it going?

BILL: Splendid.

KING: You got a new haircut, Jhana. It's great.

JHANA: It's great, Dad. This is mine, Dad? (*referring to cape*) Elvis Presley is here! He's on my back.

MADDIE: Nice cape.

KING: Some fan gave it to me.

MADDIE: Is the show going okay? I read a review in the Buffalo paper.

KING: You bought a Buffalo paper? That's nice, Maddie.

MADDIE: It's good.

JHANA: It's good, Dad. And it's celery. Made for by me. Dad. (*BILL reaches for a piece of celery.*) Don't!

MADDIE: Your dad can't eat a whole plate. It's for everyone.

JHANA: Eat it, Bill too. Okay, Dad?

KING: Okay. How's school, Jhana?

JHANA: It's working.

MADDIE: Jhani's doing her first placement at a workshop – assembly stuff.

KING: Good for you, darling. You're building cars?

JHANA: Okay. You hate it, Dad.

KING: What?

JHANA: The workshop. You're with the screws in a bag. Screws in a bag. Four of them in a bag.

BILL: Wine?

JHANA: Okay. (*referring to cape*) We're beautiful, Dad.

MADDIE: Just one glass, Jhana. Me too, Bill. Thanks.

>*BILL exits.*

KING: So you put four screws in one bag. What else?

JHANA: Lunch.

KING: And?

JHANA: Coffee. Twice. With Andrew.

KING: Who's Andrew.

JHANA: The boy there. You're liking him, Dad? And me? You're gonna sing?

KING: Maybe after I have a drink. Maybe after supper.

MADDIE: Where's the tour going?

KING: Eastern states. Detroit after this. I brought a list in case anything comes up. You all right, Madelaine?

MADDIE: Fine. Eat your celery, Dad. Jhana's sort of screwing up at the workshop. Right?

KING: Why?

MADDIE: Probably bored. If she does okay there are some great programs she could get into. Jhana? No Elvis, okay? Put on something quiet.

JHANA: Okay, Dad?

KING: Fine. Is school all right?

MADDIE: Same as ever. My grade twelve class is good. Bill's come in a couple of times. He did his thesis on Margaret Atwood, so that's a help. I don't know. I guess I'm a little tired of it.

>*BILL enters with wine and a newspaper.*

KING: Can I see that paper?

BILL: "An invigorating and nostalgic look at – "

KING: I hate that nostalgia shit. That's not why I'm up there.

BILL: But it's a great review. If my last one was half that good –

MADDIE: You've been reviewed more than once?

BILL: Not in the strictest sense but –

KING: I thought you were a professor.

BILL: T.A. One course.

MADDIE: Bill's published a book of poetry. It's very good.

KING: I didn't know people still wrote poetry.

JHANA: (*handing him book*) This is Bill. Dad.

BILL: And I didn't know people would still come out for Elvis.

KING: For eternity, man. Wow. Some picture. I mean it's good and looks like you but it's like there's this knife in your gut. Sixty-eight pages.

MADDIE: That's normal for poetry.

KING: At $11.95. You must be making a mint.

BILL: There is a knife in my gut.

MADDIE: There's a sequence in there called "Black Morning" that made Bill a bit of a celebrity. In fact he's doing a reading from it this week … It's been anthologized, twice … I'm going to check on dinner. (*She exits.*)

KING: How many copies you sell?

BILL: Thirty-seven.

JHANA: Bill's on the book, Dad.

KING: He sure is. That's great, man. Poetry. *The Path of Despair*. What do you know.

BILL: I teach, you know, in Canadian Studies. Literature.

KING: Right.

BILL: Animal as victim, environment as victim, women as victim. That sort of thing. Despair's more of a sideline. Not that they don't overlap. I love women's literature. And it's very despairing, for the most part. This is a very exciting time for female writers in this country. I mean since the time I was born.

KING: Why would that be?

BILL: They just haven't had much of a voice at all, up until now –

KING: Unhappy women have always tended to speak loud and clear around me.

BILL: Right.

KING: I'm out there last night, just talking. And this woman, she's right at the front at this table with two other ladies. (*JHANA tries to sit on his knee.*) That's kinda heavy, darling. How about you and me just holding hands for a while? This woman was real heavy. All dolled up and fat. And sad! Man. I wasn't even halfway through the first set and she started – just weeping at first but then full-blown, hyperventilating tears. Just sobbing away.

BILL: Don't you just get up and sing and shake your hips?

KING: No, I don't.

JHANA: No, Bill.

MADDIE: (*off*) I think we're about ready to eat. Can you give me a hand, Jhana?

JHANA: No.

KING: Help your mom, sweetheart. That's the stuff.

JHANA exits.

BILL: I watched *Blue Hawaii* when I was about seven.

KING: You got a girlfriend?

BILL: Of sorts.

KING: What's "of sorts"? She half fish or something?

BILL: You do sing and shake and that most of the time. Right?

KING: I sing ... tell stories. I have reinvented the man. I've put all the parts back together in a way better suited to survive. He didn't have a very thick skin.

BILL: Thus the weight.

KING: You almost ready out there?

MADDIE: (*off*) Just about.

JHANA: (*off*) Just about, Dad.

BILL: How many of you are there?

KING: Playing the King? Not so many as before. Probably about the same as the number of people writing poetry. Sixty-eight pages. That's a son of a bitch. Don't you think?

BILL: I suppose.

KING: (*in a Memphis accent*) We're in Texas. Way the hell in the middle of nowhere. Very hot. I've been driving. Sonny and Red are in the back, and some asshole we've just met is in the front with me. He's making us stop every twenty minutes or so – taking a piss, taking a picture. There are these clouds in the east, big and thick. Did I say this sort of thing has happened before? I have heard the voice of God twice: once through a blackbird, out back at Graceland; another time while holding a gun against the head of a woman. This is what's whispered while taking aim, "I'm listening. I wasn't before but now I'm all yours." But this is different, man. I am looking at these clouds because they are, you know, pretty good. They're moving fast. Heading south. But when I stare them down, they stop. When I look back toward home, they come

with me. I direct those clouds across the whole fucking sky. Every dream I've ever dreamed has come true a hundred times. I'm always the hero. None of this surprises me.

Blackout.

SCENE 4

After supper the same night. BILL, MADDIE, and KING show the first signs of drunkenness. JHANA sits beside KING.

KING: When you were little, Jhana, around five years old –

JHANA: Five years old, Dad?

KING: We had this old van, all painted up in rainbows and psychedelic shit. I washed it about forty times a week, and I'd put you inside –

JHANA: Yes!

KING: Aim the hose at that pretty face behind the windshield. Remember?

JHANA: Remember!

KING: And you'd fake that I'd knocked you over. You'd wring the water out of your pigtails. Born performers, you and me.

JHANA: You and me, Dad.

KING: Remember touring, sweetheart? The three of us and the band driving across the country? Naw, you were too little then.

JHANA: I'm too little, Dad.

KING: Drink up there, Bill.

BILL: Yes, sir.

KING: Maddie?

MADDIE: Yeah. More. This was my favourite. Driving to Edmonton in the middle of the night. It was about two hundred below and we stopped for coffee –

KING: The Diamond Kitchen.

MADDIE: You remember the horses?

KING: Bunched up around the fence.

BILL: Why would they be outside if it was so cold?

KING: This is the wild west, man! Jhani's real small, and I'm holding her inside this sleeping bag.

JHANA: Me.

KING: You're checking out this big black horse. It's crazy looking and rough 'cause of winter. You're face to face. You just reach out and touch his nose, no fear, none whatsoever.

MADDIE: You thought the northern lights were about the funniest thing ever invented. You'd point at them –

KING: Then just about pee yourself laughing.

JHANA: Pee yourself laughing!

BILL: You know I've been up north too, but the best view I ever had of the lights was from southern Ontario.

KING: (*pause*) What do you know.

MADDIE: Really.

JHANA: Really, Bill.

KING: (*in Memphis accent*) This dog sleeps on the porch all day but when night comes he's got a whole life of his own. Man that's great. Just like us. We're driving through night in this big son of a bitch. Nobody knows what we're doing. Not even the old boys in the back seat.

JHANA: Elvis Presley!

KING: (*same accent*) The one and only, darling.

JHANA: You gonna sing for her?

KING: Who?

JHANA: Jhana Kelly.

> KING *sings one verse of "Are You Lonesome Tonight?" Then* JHANA *cuts him off.*

JHANA: Sing faster!

KING: (*singing*)

You may go to college,
You may go to school,

> JHANA *tries to sing "baby, baby, baby" in the background.*

You may have a pink Cadillac
But don't you be nobody's fool.
Come back baby come back,
Come back baby come back,
Come back baby I want
To play house with you.

MADDIE: Good night, Jhana.

JHANA: (*to KING*) You're sleeping with me?

KING: No, ma'am. But I'll make you breakfast.

JHANA: Dad's making breakfast, Bill.

BILL: Good.

JHANA: Mom? You're sleeping with Bill?

MADDIE: I don't sleep with Bill. I sleep in my own bed. Quit stalling, Jhana. You're being silly. Your dad is staying down here. Everything else is the same as ever.

JHANA: The same as ever.

KING: C'mon, you. Show me your room. Show me what you look like sleeping.

> JHANA *and* KING *exit.*

BILL: I like him, Maddie.

MADDIE: No you don't.

BILL: Why didn't you say he was staying overnight here?

MADDIE: It's no big deal.

BILL: Divorced pals. I think that's wonderful. I really do. (*holds up bottle*) Is there more?

MADDIE: We're all out.

BILL: Maybe you'll be like Elizabeth Taylor … marry the same guy twice. Or Zsa Zsa Gabor. Didn't she do that? You mean we're all out of alcohol? Completely? I'll get more.

MADDIE: It's nearly midnight. And it's Sunday.

BILL: In case you hadn't noticed, Maddie, we have a liquor store right next door.

MADDIE: You're going to buy liquor from the neighbours? That's really low, Bill.

BILL: I can probably buy all sorts of things there. What would you like? Beer? Heroin? Perhaps a film –

MADDIE: You're really serious.

BILL: More white wine? King seems to like it, and he's an alcoholic.

MADDIE: He has it under control. You, on the other hand, are acting like a lunatic.

BILL: If I don't come back –

MADDIE: Bill? You are okay aren't you? You seem really –

BILL: Fun-loving.

MADDIE: I'm serious, Willy.

> BILL *exits.* KING *enters.*

KING: Where's Lord Byron gone?

MADDIE: Hunting down more liquor.

KING: Jhana's real wired, eh?

MADDIE: What else is new.

KING: But great. You're doing a great job and all. Always have.

MADDIE: She's really screwing up at this workshop.

KING: Everyone screws up at their first job.

MADDIE: I didn't.

KING: You making it with Mr. Despair?

MADDIE: People think certain words work magic – "group home," "workshop." They hear that and assume everything's taken care of. Someone from York just did a research project on her. She's moderately mentally handicapped – "moderate." I like that, like the weather when we lived on the coast. Superbly dyslexic – very complicated version of it. Symptoms of autism or soft autism. That's what they're saying now. That's the style. There is a style to everything. But then you'd know all about that.

KING: I'm out of style, Maddie. I'm the greaser at the end of the row while the rest of you are streaking your hair and buying Volvos ... She'll make out.

MADDIE: So you've said. Ever since she was diagnosed.

KING: But it's true, Madelaine. She's done okay.

MADDIE: Bill's great with her. Better than I am, to be perfectly honest. It's not really any of your business, you know, how Bill fits into my life.

KING: My first job was playing a wedding. A lot of the stuff we played through twice because we only knew eight numbers. We'd have been sued except that at weddings everyone's uncle gets pissed and wants to get up onstage and sing "The Impossible Dream." Most bands hate that kind of shit. We encouraged it. You're too hard on yourself about her. You always have been.

MADDIE: I don't have any choice.

KING: You have some –

MADDIE: And don't tell me, King of the Road, about letting things unfold naturally. Her doing okay is a full-time job. For me.

KING: You want me to take her for a while?

MADDIE: Right – to some motel in Detroit. She needs her routine.

KING: We have a routine.

MADDIE: Drinking, getting up at noon. Is she going to stay in your room? Sleep in a twin bed next to you and some barfly: Cindy, Lucy-Ann, Tammi with an *i*. (*pause*) I've always hated the sound of my voice when I talk to you.

KING: There aren't any Cindy-Anns or Tammis right now.

MADDIE: You mean at this particular moment. Here and now. There's probably one or both of them waiting out in the car or in your motel room.

KING: I came on the bus.

MADDIE: I also don't take any of this stuff very seriously anymore. I really don't.

KING: You've made a fist.

MADDIE: Bill delights in making people feel good about themselves. Do you have any idea how great that is for Jhana?

KING: I can imagine.

MADDIE: I mean he's got the confidence of a shoe when it comes to himself but he really does make people feel, you know, pretty good.

KING: He's sort of straight.

MADDIE: Perfect, King.

KING: Perfect. (*touching MADDIE's face*)

MADDIE: You're like your daughter, repeating.

KING: You smell good.

MADDIE: Right. Booze and garlic. Lovely stuff.

KING: You smell like you. The way your pillow used to.

MADDIE: Since when did you lie around sniffing my pillow? Since never.

KING: The Diamond Kitchen. We settle that little girl of ours down in the front of the van. The lights have calmed down, left something thick in the air. We make love against the fence post, and you got a little cut at the top of your leg.

MADDIE: Your memory is very selective.

KING: There should always be something at risk.

MADDIE: The next morning we had a helluva fight. You'd spent practically our last dime on an amplifier and hadn't even told me or –

KING: Fuck the next morning.

MADDIE and KING kiss; then, hearing BILL approaching, they stop. BILL enters unaware of what has just happened.

BILL: The very first movie I saw, I mean in a theatre, was *Blue Hawaii*.

KING: So you said. How'd your mission go?

BILL: It was also about the dumbest fucking movie ever made. Even as a little kid, I thought he was dumb. (*producing a bottle of bright purple wine from under his coat*)

MADDIE: Oh good. Nothing like a little pancake syrup at the end of a day.

BILL: Moody Blue. Brilliant stuff. Where's the crystal? (*He exits.*)

KING: You look about ready to collapse, lady.

MADDIE: He barely drinks, you know.

BILL: (*entering with tall glasses of wine*) You know, Maddie? Our neighbours are good folk. Real salt of the earth.

MADDIE: You're going to get sick, Bill. You get sick mixing beer and water. Remember?

BILL: They're just sitting around, watching a little TV, skinning live animals, that sort of thing. I showed them some poems, explained how I was raised by a family of timber wolves, in the suburbs of Ottawa.

KING: I told Jhana I'd be up again after New Year's.

MADDIE: Then you'd better explain that means you won't be here for Christmas.

BILL: So why do you do it? Why glorify ... No. It's even more bizarre than that. You're a human effigy. I mean at least you could imitate someone who really was a tragic hero. God knows there's enough around.

KING: Elvis was magic, man. Pure and simple.

BILL: Wearing diapers at forty? Giving away fleets of Cadillacs to strangers? And guns. Didn't he spend around a million a week on revolvers and ...

MADDIE: I'm going to clean up a little.

BILL: (*to KING*) Why don't you be Sylvia Plath? "Every woman adores a fascist."

KING: You need a hand?

MADDIE: No. I'm fine. (*She exits.*)

BILL: And all these phony badges and shit from Nixon. He was pretty fucked all around, if you ask me.

KING: (*in the Memphis accent*) I chased every girl I ever met. This one girl was fourteen. Her mother threatened to charge me with rape. She comes in to talk to me after the show. You know something? By the end of our talk, I could've made the mother too.

BILL: You do that very well.

KING: How about some poetry? You write poems about Jhana?

BILL: No.

KING: I'd love to see something like that lying flat on a page.

BILL: I don't write poems about Jhana. I live with her.

KING: She's wearing that cape to bed. That dumb cape I gave her.

BILL: Sometimes she's in overdrive and it's really hard to take. She'll be bitchy to Maddie. Just whining or glued to the TV. She'll talk about Andrew, this guy she's hot on from work, until you can't stand it anymore.

KING: It's over top of her nightgown. That dumb cape.

MADDIE: (*entering*) I'm ready to call it a night.

KING: I'm pretty shot.

BILL: (*to MADDIE*) You need the blankets and stuff out of my room?

MADDIE: It's okay.

BILL: The almighty Elvis. Just a fat old guy, afraid to leave his room.

KING: We're all fat and mean, pal. But even the biggest jerk in the world, when he tucks his kid into bed, he leaves his hand on her forehead a minute 'cause he loves the warmth.

BILL: I don't know how you could do it.

KING: What? Every dream I've dreamed has come true a hundred times. That's the bad ones too, boy. Nightmares the size of China. Going to Jesus. That's what the Southerners call self-destruction and they're fucking ecstatic about it.

BILL: I don't know how –

KING: They're driving drunk, right out of the womb. They're going to Jesus.

BILL: Leaving a kid.

MADDIE: That's between me and King. It's nothing to do with Jhana. Or with you.

KING: I'm going upstairs.

MADDIE: I'll be up in a minute.

> *KING exits. BILL is trying to focus on MADDIE. He's very drunk.*

MADDIE: I'll see you in the morning. Okay?

BILL: Where is it you're going now? Tell me where it is you're going.

MADDIE: I'm going upstairs.

BILL: Where?

MADDIE: Upstairs.

BILL: Tell me where it is you're going.

MADDIE: You're drunk. Goodnight, Willy.

BILL: What will he do? Why is it his mouth and hands ...

MADDIE: You can sleep down here. That might be easier. (*She covers BILL with a blanket.*)

BILL: You're my family?

MADDIE: I know.

BILL: You'll kiss your family on the mouth? (*MADDIE kisses BILL quickly on the forehead.*) Say where it is you're going. Say it after me.

Lights fade.

MADDIE: 'Night. (*She heads for the stairs.*)

BILL: (*singing slightly, gospel style*)

I'm going to Jesus
I just can't wait
running straight to
the arms of Jesus

Blackout.

ACT TWO

SCENE 1

The next morning. Lights up on KING, who is drinking milk from the carton, preparing to leave. JHANA, in her nightgown, surprises him.

JHANA: Dad!

KING: Good morning, sweetheart.

JHANA: (*referring to carton*) You're not allowed. I said you're not.

KING: Yeah? Who are you?

JHANA: Jhana!

KING: Are you the fridge patrol? Are you hell-bent on justice at any cost?

JHANA: (*imitating MADDIE*) We all have to live here, young lady.

KING: (*in the Memphis accent*) Momma. She'd be sleeping pretty as sunrise – right at this particular moment.

JHANA: Sing.

KING: You don't want to hear me sing this early. Trust me. Let me get up now. Okay?

JHANA: Why?

KING: C'mon –

JHANA: You're making her breakfast.

KING: I don't know, Jhana. I don't know if there's time.

JHANA: I'm helping. Dad.

KING: You gonna help me out under the bright lights? Sing for your keep?

JHANA: Okay! And dancing. Everyone's clapping for me. At working I sing, at drop-in.

KING: Drop out, Jhana. It's our only chance, you and me.

JHANA: You and me. Making breakfast. Now.

KING: In Windsor I met one of your pals.

JHANA: Who?

KING: A girl called Bonita.

JHANA: My pal! (*pause*) I don't know her, Dad.

KING: She had a job cleaning up.

JHANA: Steffie cleans up.

KING: Does she now. This Bonita –

JHANA: My pal! Can she come here?

KING: Actually you haven't met her before, Jhani.

JHANA: Why?

KING: What I meant is she's like you.

JHANA: I like her too.

KING: So. At any rate, this Bonita, she'd be around forty and lived at the motel. Took care of everything real good. Even combed out the fringe on the carpet. Imagine that.

JHANA: All right.

KING: She'd just about kill herself that I wouldn't do the "Hawaiian Wedding Song." She came to the show every night. She requested that song every five minutes or so. Bonita. Not as pretty as you. Nearly as smart though.

JHANA: I'm not smart.

KING: You make out okay though? You don't get teased or that anymore? Some rough patches there when you were little. Bonita. Maybe you'll get a real job one day, like her.

JHANA: I have a real job.

KING: Yeah? How much you taking home?

JHANA: Home.

KING: You making any money?

JHANA: I make a paycheque, Dad.

KING: How much?

JHANA: On Fridays. In her purse.

KING: "Hawaiian Wedding Song." That's a load of shit to be singing night after night, isn't it?

JHANA: Okay.

KING: I mean I swore I'd never put on one of those jumpsuits and do that trip. I've always just done him clean, Jhani. Sun Records days, good days. But people come out for the white suits and scarves. The "Hawaiian Wedding Song." And these are lean times. So your old dad, Jhana, he gave in.

JHANA: Gave in, Dad?

KING: That cape I brought you? It was custom made ... for me. But not anymore. No more white suits.

JHANA: No more white suits?

KING: You got her.

JHANA: No more white suits! (*KING puts his coat on.*) Can I come?

KING: No.

JHANA: Where are you going?

KING: After Christmas, Jhana, maybe you and me can take off for a few days, have a little holiday. What do you think?

JHANA: Are you going shopping?

KING: Yeah ... right.

JHANA: I can shop. Okay?

KING: Why don't you stay here and get the ball rolling. I'm going to make you blueberry pancakes but I have to walk a long ways to find those berries. Maybe they're down a ravine, covered in ice. Okay? Bye, bye Jhani. You're my girl.

JHANA: I'm setting the table? Eggs? I can't do them.

KING: Sure you can.

JHANA: I make a mess.

KING: Sky's the limit for you. Don't forget that. (*He exits.*)

JHANA wakes BILL who is sleeping on the couch.

JHANA: (*quietly*) Helping me please, Bill?

BILL: Fuck.

JHANA: Fuck, Bill. You're in there now? In sleeping? C'mon.

BILL: Quiet, Jhana.

JHANA: (*tries to lie on top of BILL*) Mom's in this. See? All tired on Daddy. He's gone. Shopping for me. We need help. You and me.

BILL: Lay off, Jhana.

JHANA: Lay off, Bill. We're like this. We're here!

BILL: What time is it?

JHANA: Cracking the eggs for Daddy. For Dad.

BILL: (*tries to sit up*) Oh God! Do I look the way I always look? Is the right side of my head caved in?

JHANA: I'll be kissing you (*kisses BILL*) better.

BILL: None of that.

JHANA: Andrew's funny, right?

BILL: He's a scream.

JHANA: I'll be kissing you now. (*She tries to kiss BILL again.*)

BILL: (*sitting up quickly*) Careful. There's one way to kiss certain men in the world and another way to kiss all the Bills. Most women know that instinctively.

JHANA: Dad's making pancakes and we're helping. Setting the table. Cracking the eggs. Eggs. Can you do that? The eggs. They're broken. Right?

BILL: I can crack eggs. If you stop talking I'll crack a hundred eggs.

JHANA: It's hard.

BILL: Sure is.

JHANA: Dad's asking for the eggs.

BILL: He's not asking right now. We'll deal with that when it happens.

JHANA: No. He's asking! Bill?

BILL: WHAT!

JHANA: I can't do it. I can't do the eggs.

BILL: Let's go through this. Your dear mother is sleeping happily. The King of Rock 'n' Roll has gone shopping. Good old Bill, who has the worst hangover ever, is supposed to give a lesson on cracking the goddamned eggs.

JHANA: Good old Bill!

BILL: God in heaven.

MADDIE enters.

MADDIE: (*to JHANA*) Hi, honey. (*to BILL*) You look awful.

JHANA: Good old Bill!

BILL: Aren't you two supposed to be at work?

MADDIE: We have a meeting with Jhana's social worker.

BILL: I thought that was Thursday.

MADDIE: That's the assessment at work, not to be confused with next week's meeting with her new one-to-one worker. But today is with Ben at eleven. Remember?

JHANA: Remember?

MADDIE: You say bye to your dad?

JHANA: He's shopping. Pancakes, Mom.

MADDIE: I don't think so.

JHANA: With blueberries. Eggs by Bill with me in helping.

MADDIE: He didn't say goodbye?

JHANA: He's making her breakfast.

MADDIE: I don't know, Jhana. I think he's gone.

JHANA: He's shopping!

MADDIE: I think his bus went about ten minutes ago.

JHANA: Liar. He said.

BILL: (*to MADDIE*) Why don't you look horrible?

JHANA: He's shopping, Bill. For me.

BILL: I know, Jhana. I know all about it.

MADDIE: King always has a beer when he's hung over. First thing in the morning even.

BILL: And he takes the cap off with his teeth.

MADDIE: Belt buckle. Jhana? I'm pretty sure he's gone. We can wait another couple of minutes. But don't get hopeful. He's just lousy at goodbyes.

BILL: Apparently.

MADDIE: (*to BILL*) I don't need that kind of stuff right now.

BILL: Excuse me. Think I'll go crack open a cold one with my eye socket. (*He exits.*)

MADDIE: Just before your dad would head out on tour, I'd lie there all tangled up with him, needing the sound of his breath to fall asleep. Needing to feel everything beat inside him.

JHANA: Gone with Princie, Mom.

MADDIE: But he was a regular Houdini. And I'd wake up to the sound of the van, revving up in the yard, this cold feeling in my gut, pissed off too that he wouldn't let me say goodbye. And he'd argue that these big deal farewells just made me sadder. Maybe that's true but it was also cheating.

JHANA: It's cheating, Mom.

MADDIE: So I'd go in your room, give Chatty Cathy the boot, and I'd crawl into your bed. (*BILL enters.*) Hold on to my perfect little girl. (*holding JHANA*) You were so warm. To hell with that bed of mine that had suddenly become so big and icy. I've got Jhana.

JHANA: Me.

MADDIE: It just makes him upset to say goodbye.

JHANA: I can't without spilling. Dad's mad at me?

MADDIE: He loves you.

JHANA: It's making him sad? At me?

MADDIE: Not you.

JHANA: Dad's happy.

MADDIE: I don't know, Jhana. He's on the bus to Detroit.

JHANA: He's on the bus to Detroit, Bill.

MADDIE: That's the city where his next show is. Why don't you go get dressed and then we can make pancakes together.

JHANA: Okay, Bill?

BILL: I'm not hungry.

JHANA exits.

BILL: When my dad died we were all up at the cottage with him because we knew it was coming. After they came to take away, you know, his body, I lay down beside where he'd been and it was still warm there. This warmth was under the palm of my hand but seeping away. Then all the warmth was gone, and I understood he was dead then. Boom.

MADDIE: Sorry, Willy.

BILL: That isn't the point. It was all right. There was something perfect about the whole thing, his living and dying. So I'm just wondering why you do it?

MADDIE: What?

BILL: Why you're screwing a ghost?

MADDIE: Shut up, Bill.

BILL: No, really. I've been thinking about it, and I think it all stems from your fear of death. Why else continue to haul your ex up out of the cobwebs?

MADDIE: This is bullshit.

BILL: No, this death thing makes sense on another level as well. Because you're also obsessed with a corpse: Elvis Presley. I consider the whole thing fascinating, Maddie. I really do. I mean I know that King has made him immortal now, so that must be like lying down with Jesus or –

MADDIE: Tell me some more about lying down with someone, Bill. When was the last time for you?

BILL: The summer.

MADDIE: What year?

BILL: You met Carolyn. She's been doing a sessional out in the Maritimes. We're in touch.

MADDIE: Perfect. Touching through the mail or over the telephone. Very risky stuff.

BILL: It's tougher for poets. I mean the King of Rock 'n' Roll: tight jeans, possibly a drunkard, depressed. Women are ecstatic about that sort of thing.

MADDIE: Come off it. Your crowd's got its groupies too. This is ridiculous.

BILL: Whoever fantasizes about poets? We're all supposed to be half-starved with tuberculosis, grey skin – not a sexual image.

MADDIE: If something hurt you last night then we should talk about that directly.

BILL: It hurt last night to see you as a groupie.

MADDIE: Jesus. I really can't believe this.

BILL: It hurt to see him with Jhana.

MADDIE: Okay. What else?

BILL: Nothing else.

MADDIE: C'mon, Bill. What happened to your need to confess everything that's ever happened to you.

BILL: I don't do that.

MADDIE: You adore baring your soul. "Maddie, this and this happened when I was in kindergarten. Maddie, I peed myself once at Cubs."

BILL: Okay. It's crossed my mind.

MADDIE: What has?

BILL: I don't mean to imply that I think about it constantly.

MADDIE: It.

BILL: You and me. Something more than, you know, boarder and ... boardee. What are you anyway?

MADDIE: I'm your landlady. And you're my best friend.

BILL: Thank you. It's natural. Living here and all the stuff with Jhana that you'd think about it sometimes, about really getting together.

MADDIE: I don't think about it, Bill. I don't think of you that way.

BILL: Great. As I say it's barely crossed my mind. I mean it's like when I think of making it with the woman next door or with Queen Elizabeth. So much of sex is challenge, it really is –

MADDIE: And I'm grateful for the way you are with Jhani. No. I feel blessed in that department. I really do. And with our friendship –

BILL: So you think of me as what? A talking cocker spaniel? That sort of thing?

MADDIE: Please stop it, Bill.

BILL: I should feel encouraged. If you could fall in love with King, you could fall in love with a gas station. But it makes me bored. This lack of challenge. The whole thing's remarkable. It really is.

KING: (*offstage, singing*)

Since my baby left me –

BILL: Give me a break –

KING: (*singing*)

I found a new place to dwell,
It's down at the end of lonely street
In Heartbreak Hotel

KING enters carrying a large bag of groceries. JHANA enters.

JHANA: My Daddy say Dad!

KING: Who's hungry?

JHANA: Me!

KING: (*sorting through the bag*) Genuine 100 per cent–artificial maple syrup. And just for you ... (*handing JHANA a box of berries*)

JHANA: Blueberries!

KING: Through wind and rain, battles, blight, the frozen-food section of the 7-Eleven. For you, my love – blueberries.

JHANA: See Mom? Daddy's here! Dad.

MADDIE: He sure is. Your dad's full of surprises.

KING: (*to JHANA*) How about going and opening this box. Then sticking those berries in a bowl.

JHANA: Put them in a bowl, Bill.

MADDIE: Your dad asked you to do it, Jhana.

BILL: I'll help.

BILL and JHANA exit.

KING: This blues act in Detroit, she's gonna run another week. I've been put on hold.

MADDIE: And?

KING: I thought it might be nice for Jhana, not to mention the best break you've had this decade.

MADDIE: What?

KING: If I stayed on here. Just for one week.

MADDIE: Then you'd leave.

KING: Run out on the wife and kid all over again. Look, Madelaine, if you don't want me here, just say the word.

MADDIE: When you played Oshawa and had dinner here twice in a row, she thought that meant we were, you know, together again. She'll get too attached to you, Jhana will. Just like before. It's dangerous.

KING: Last night was dangerous. And very sweet.

MADDIE: She's very needy right now.

KING: How's her mother?

MADDIE: Solid as a rock. Always.

KING: I'll get my stuff.

MADDIE: (*pause*) Don't. Don't leave.

KING: Are you sure? Don't you want to check it out with Robert Young in there?

MADDIE: Bill!

BILL: (*off*) What?

MADDIE: King's gonna stay with us a few days. Okay?

BILL: It's your house.

KING: "A house boiled in water and blessed by no one."

BILL: (*entering*) Pardon me?

KING: "A house boiled in water and blessed by no one."

BILL: You read my book.

KING: First thing this morning. Marched up and down *The Path of Despair* – cover to cover.

BILL: Why do you remember that line? Why that one in particular?

KING: You repeated it two hundred times.

MADDIE: You want to go tell your daughter the good news?

BILL: It's like a chorus or refrain. The repeating wasn't an arbitrary decision.

KING: I liked your stuff, Bill. I'm not saying I understand it, but it sure has its moments.

BILL: Don't worry about not understanding. I feel quite strongly about that –

KING: Man, you would've loved the King –

BILL: Poetry is functioning at its best when nobody has a clue what's going on.

SCENE 2

A few days later. **BILL** *is practising out loud for his poetry reading and lecture.*

BILL: Fellow poets and friends. "Black Morning" has been described by critics, or critic as the case may be, as a breakthrough sequence. But breaking through into what, you may well ask. (*pause*) Fuck it. (*in a Memphis accent*) I chased every woman I ever met. Know why? "Black Morning" plunges into a territory (*beat*) better left unexplored. Right. (*Memphis accent*) "Every woman adores a fascist, the boot in the face, the brute brute heart of a brute like you ..." I never stopped cruising. "Black Morning" plunges into and exposes the dark underbelly of that demon called –

JHANA: (*off*) Bill!

JHANA enters, from work, very wired.

BILL: Hi, angel.

JHANA: I'm with the table in the workshop, right? Fat Steffie too. She's mad. She's mad like this. (*shakes hand violently*) Screws go flying! They just fly!

BILL: Steffie has a hard time controlling her muscles –

JHANA: She can't do it –

BILL: Maybe they've changed her medication.

JHANA: She's not on the job!

BILL: Some days she's a whirlwind. Right?

JHANA: A whirlwind, Bill! You can't sing at work. I said DON'T.

BILL: Remember how you had a hard time counting how many screws to put in one bag? For Steffie –

JHANA: Steffie can't –

BILL: Picking something up –

JHANA: Steffie –

BILL: Picking something up is way harder than counting. And putting it in a little bag? It's murder.

JHANA: She can't help it, Bill.

BILL: That's right.

JHANA: She's mad! Hitting at Peter. Mean too. Peter can't get out of his chair. You're scared.

Right? I push Peter for lunch. Don't walk, Bill. Peter can't. Listen to him. (*JHANA groans.*) He talks hard. Like hurting. It doesn't. I'm not Peter, Bill. You're sad? At Peter?

BILL: A little bit.

JHANA: Betty died.

BILL: I remember.

JHANA: She's not at the workshop. People die, Bill. Dogs, television. Steffie's funny too. I'm not scared. (*pause*) Where's my Daddy say Dad.

BILL: I don't know.

JHANA: DAD!

BILL: He's not home, Jhana. Why don't you slow down, kick your shoes off in front of the TV. Relax.

JHANA: RELAX! They're new. New and just coming in – all the little tiny screws. I'm behind Bill. That lady's yelling on me, PAY ATTENTION!

BILL: I could follow you a lot better if you'd slow down –

JHANA: (*stomping her feet in time*) PAY ATTENTION! PAY ATTENTION! PAY ATTENTION! PAY ATTENTION … (*long pause as JHANA notices BILL isn't going to pay attention, then softly*) Hi, Billy. Be Andrew yelling too. Bill, please? Be Andrew.

BILL: Not now, Jhani. They've asked me to do a reading, then a little talk on my process and that. Want to hear some?

JHANA: No. I will keep talking. See? I can sing at lunch. Not at the worktable. That worktable's for working. Everyone watches me. They love this.

BILL: What do you sing?

JHANA: (*imitating Elvis*) Good evening, ladies and … ladies. It's pleasure. Elvis Presley is here! (*singing*)

Love her tender, love her tender Never let her …

Lover her tender, lover her tender Lover her, love her tender …

Are you watching me?

BILL: The world is watching you.

JHANA: Good. Be Andrew. For dinner, Bill. Please?

BILL: For ten minutes. When both hands are at six then you're going to be the audience and I'm going to be the brilliant young poet behind the podium. Got that?

JHANA: Yes! Get out! Out the door, Bill.

BILL exits, then JHANA greets him at the door, role-playing a dinner date.

JHANA: Hello, Andrew.

BILL: Good evening, Miss Kelly –

JHANA: She's Jhana!

BILL: You look lovely.

JHANA: Please eat.

BILL: Don't you want to take my coat first, offer me a place to sit down?

JHANA: Please sit and take your coat.

BILL: How was your day?

JHANA: Funny.

BILL: Why?

JHANA: Steffie hit Peter in the wheelchair! Screws went flying!

BILL: That doesn't sound funny.

JHANA: It's funny. Eat.

BILL: What's for dinner?

JHANA: Cheerios.

BILL: Since when do you eat Cheerios for supper.

JHANA: Since I'm funny.

BILL: Aren't you though. Are you going to make a move? Casually slip an arm around (*BILL puts his arm around JHANA.*) Andrew's mammoth but trembling shoulders?

JHANA: (*JHANA is beginning to act very sexually, but toward herself, not toward BILL.*) I'm funny.

BILL: Are you going to get in there and give Andrew the business.

JHANA: The business.

BILL: You can, Jhana. If you want to, you're allowed. You do understand that, don't you?

JHANA: Kissing him on the mouth?

BILL: Absolutely. And here too. (*touching JHANA's neck*) I'm not saying you should rush in there and jump on him. Take it slow and easy. But you can reach out.

JHANA: Reach!

BILL: If you hold back everything it'll turn sour inside – or worse yet it'll turn into poetry. Then you're really sunk.

JHANA: Kiss his mouth, Bill.

BILL: Not me. That's your job.

JHANA: My job. And here. (*touching BILL's neck*) It's funny. Right? Steffie won't kiss Andrew. Only me.

MADDIE enters.

MADDIE: (to JHANA) Hi, honey!

JHANA: NO!

MADDIE: Nice to see you too. How was your day?

JHANA: She's not allowed, Bill!

BILL: We were just –

MADDIE: What am I not allowed to do?

JHANA: Get out!

MADDIE: My house, kid.

JHANA: We're in private, me and Bill.

BILL: Jhana likes this guy at work and –

JHANA: NO! Make her get out!

MADDIE: Look. You're allowed to talk to Bill on your own but there are polite ways to explain that you're in the middle of something.

JHANA: Get out.

BILL: In fact it's more like pretend dates than just talk or –

JHANA: NO!

MADDIE: Have I interrupted you?

JHANA: NO! (pause) Yes.

MADDIE: You were talking about someone and my coming in made you embarrassed?

JHANA: We're private, me and Bill.

MADDIE: That isn't what I object to. When I come in, you and Bill can move upstairs after you say hi. No one likes being yelled at the second they come in the door.

JHANA: (pause) Sorry, Mom.

MADDIE: It's okay. How was your day?

JHANA: Hi, Mom.

MADDIE: Hi, Jhani.

JHANA: Hi, Bill.

BILL: Hi.

JHANA: How are you, Mom?

MADDIE: Fine.

JHANA: Bill is fine.

BILL: Top notch.

MADDIE: Your reading! Was that today? Jesus, Bill, I meant to –

BILL: It's tomorrow. No big deal.

MADDIE: You're not nervous?

BILL: I've done dozens of these things. Or at least a certain number.

MADDIE: You need an audience?

BILL: God yes. This is a poetry reading – no one will come. And it's in a library, in Pickering.

MADDIE: I meant do you want an audience right now. To practise.

BILL: That's stupid.

MADDIE: I don't mind. Me and Jhana will be the public at large.

JHANA: I'm cooking salad.

MADDIE: Right you are! Jhana makes salad tonight! Jhana makes dessert! How many?

JHANA: Five cup!

MADDIE: One cup of ... come on, Jhani ... oranges ...

JHANA: Oranges!

MADDIE: And?

JHANA: Marshmallows. Tiny, tiny.

MADDIE: One cup ...

JHANA: Coconuts ... pineapple ...

MADDIE: And last but not least!

JHANA: Yes!

MADDIE: What's the white stuff that holds it all together?

JHANA: Milk!

MADDIE: Sour cream!

JHANA: Sour cream!

BILL: Hallelujah!

MADDIE: Five-cup salad! No recipe needed. No fuss, no muss –

JHANA: Five-cup salad!

MADDIE: You know where everything is?

JHANA: The fridge. And cans.

MADDIE: And the coconut is in the cupboard above the sink in a red bag.

JHANA: Red.

MADDIE: The measuring cup is in the dishwasher. You can do all of it by yourself.

JHANA: Don't help her, Bill.

BILL: Best of luck, Jhana. And remember, kid, no matter what happens in there, I loved you.

JHANA: I love you, Bill. And coconut, in a red bag, in the sink.

MADDIE: Above the sink.

JHANA: I love you, Mom.

MADDIE: Me too. Get to work.

JHANA: You're loving Bill?

MADDIE: Yup.

JHANA: She's going to work. I am working for salad and dessert.

MADDIE: And Bill and I are going to have a gigantic glass of Scotch and talk poetry.

JHANA: Poetry! (*She exits.*)

MADDIE: So Jhana wants to sleep with someone at work?

BILL: What happened to her right to privacy?

MADDIE: I changed my mind.

BILL: Just a crush. Lots of talk about kissing.

MADDIE: "Black Morning."

BILL: Right. I'm going to use that quote about my being a voice for women and the responsibility that entails.

MADDIE: Your own voice, Bill. That's all we need.

BILL: It is my voice. Maybe I don't know how to make it sing or shimmy but it is mine.

MADDIE: However sleazy it may seem to you, I need him like breath right now.

BILL: It's your life.

MADDIE: And you're a big part of it. You're my best friend. It's true. Quit taking it like a slap in the face. You're just ... I'm ... I know he's fucked up. But at least he's out there. Trying to do something he feels about. He's always been, you know, very alive.

BILL: I find it remarkable that someone who makes his living pretending to be a dead person is living life to the fullest. Where is he anyway?

MADDIE: He's at the Elvis Museum in Niagara Falls. He might do some stuff for them for the anniversary in August.

BILL: What anniversary?

MADDIE: Elvis's death. Jesus, Bill. I can't believe you wouldn't know that.

BILL: It wasn't like Kennedy. I can't tell you what I was doing at that exact moment.

MADDIE: We were in Whitehorse. This guy called Wade; he came in with the news after the first set. The King is dead.

BILL: When Elvis Presley died I was at Carleton. We thought it was funny.

MADDIE: King hauled Jhana up onstage. Those days I put all my energy into convincing everyone she was normal. A little slow. Jesus. She had a ten-word vocabulary at five. Her first word was "Mom"

and her second word was "pig." Because of this story King had made up about this pig that was a terrific swimmer. But I used to worry about it anyway, mother then pig.

BILL: I'll bet you worried.

MADDIE: While she's up onstage I'm praying she won't open her mouth, won't stim out because of the lights, have a rocking fit because of the drums.

BILL: What'd she do?

MADDIE: Nothing. She loved it. Everyone loved her and was too pissed to notice she wasn't, you know, normal. (*pause*) Bill, promise me this guy at work or some old letch on the bus isn't going to hurt her. Isn't going to take advantage of all that trust.

BILL: She's okay.

MADDIE: Mother then pig.

BILL: I think you are very wonderful with her.

MADDIE: You too, Willy.

BILL: And I have been a bit of an asshole about him staying here. A little bit.

JHANA enters, much slowed down, nearly dreamy.

JHANA: It's perfect, Mom. Cooking in the bowl. It's so pretty. Five-cup salad. In the fridge.

MADDIE: You all done?

JHANA: Done.

MADDIE: No problems?

JHANA: Maybe.

MADDIE: Let's not worry about it now. Come give your old mom a hug.

JHANA: Old Mom. Old, old Mom.

MADDIE: Thanks a lot, kid.

JHANA: Mine.

SCENE 3

*The spot is up on **KING** at the microphone, costumed like Elvis, using the Memphis accent.*

KING: I don't do any requests. Used to be I'd play whatever you asked for but I am now sick to death of everyone wanting what is bad for them, myself included. This also ties into the way I feel about women. I chased every dream going, man. They've run me ragged. All of you have. Listen to me. It's *Louisiana Hayride*, 1954. Something good is happening (*touching chest*) inside here. When

I sing, play guitar, you're with me. Swaying in time, singing along, you know every single word. But what's this now? Something is coming undone inside you. This is not what I mean to do. This also ties into the way I feel about women. All of them wanting to come undone. This is a very sad business and should not be part of the entertainment industry. I am just an entertainer and hold no opinions, political or otherwise. I am also, and get this clear, nobody's path of despair. All right? Listen. (*singing*)

Are you lonesome tonight?

Do you miss me tonight?

Basically I think all of that is a load of shit. I sing that sort of thing fourteen times a night, onstage or rocking inside the arms of some woman. You wanna know the truth, man? Every time I sing it, I believe the whole thing entirely. Like I keep saying, I don't take requests.

Blackout.

SCENE 4

A few days later, MADDIE and JHANA are going through JHANA's report from the workshop.

MADDIE: The top part says they're recommending you do another term at the workshop, that advancement seems premature. In other words, you screwed up and aren't going anywhere. The bottom part breaks everything down and explains why – poor attitude, inconsistent work habits, frequenting washroom as much as ten times in a single morning, distracting other workers ... What are you doing in the bathroom all day?

KING enters.

JHANA: Nothing.

MADDIE: I asked you a question. What are you doing in the bathroom all day?

JHANA: Periods. You're sore in your stomach, Mom. Twice.

KING: Maybe I shouldn't be here.

MADDIE: This is exactly when you should be here. If you have cramps you take a blue pill.

JHANA: A football.

MADDIE: A blue pill shaped like a football.

JHANA: They're in her purse?

MADDIE: What are you doing in the bathroom all day?

JHANA: What are you doing in the bathroom all day?

KING: Maybe she doesn't understand the question, Maddie.

MADDIE: This isn't a joke, Jhana. Are you in there by yourself?

JHANA: Maybe.

MADDIE: This is a job. An honest-to-God grown-up job. You're not a little schoolgirl or –

JHANA: You're not allowed.

MADDIE: I know you're not. You're not allowed to slack off or spend the day sitting on the lid of the toilet.

JHANA: You! You're not allowed to know. Bill said.

KING: What's he got to do with this?

JHANA: I'm trying! Counting four, opening the bags –

MADDIE: What are you going to do if you don't make it at the workshop, Jhana? Have you thought about that?

JHANA: Yes.

MADDIE: Good. Fill me in. What are you going to do for a living?

JHANA: So? I don't care.

MADDIE: What's the big plan?

JHANA: (*hugging KING*) Helping Daddy. Helping Dad.

MADDIE: How is it you're going to help? Carry his guitar?

JHANA: Okay.

MADDIE: Stay up all night with the roadies and sleep until noon?

KING: Madelaine.

JHANA: Okay!

MADDIE: Jesus, Jhani.

JHANA: I'm singing! See? I'm singing beside Daddy.

MADDIE: Good Christ.

JHANA: (*singing*)

Love her tender, love her tender –

MADDIE: ME tender. ME! You don't know the right words. And you have to sing the whole song right through. Those are things you can't do. Those things aren't possible for you.

JHANA: Love HER ME tender. ME!

MADDIE: What do you think, King? Has she got the job?

KING: Come on, Maddie. Get off her back.

JHANA: Andrew likes it. Andrew loves my singing.

MADDIE: Andrew is very disappointed in you right now.

JHANA: He loves me.

MADDIE: He's given you one chance after another this month. If he wasn't so new at it he wouldn't be anywhere near this patient.

JHANA: Andrew loves me.

MADDIE: Andrew is your boss.

JHANA: He's my boyfriend.

MADDIE: He's your supervisor. Quit the nonsense.

JHANA: He loves me.

MADDIE: He is someone that you work for. It has nothing to do with boyfriends or any of that. It has to do with you screwing up at work.

JHANA: Shut up! Make her shut up!

MADDIE: And you're following him around all day. Why are you doing that?

JHANA: He hates you, Mom! Andrew hates you!

MADDIE: Sitting in his car. Is that true?

JHANA: Andrew hates you! And Daddy! Daddy hates you! And me! Hate you, hate you!

MADDIE: Go up to your room until you cool down. Until you can talk decently.

JHANA: You're going to the workshop! You're hating it more and you're not allowed, Mom. Nobody's allowed. (*picking up her coat and heading for the door*)

MADDIE: Where do you think you're going?

JHANA: Where do you think you're going? You, Mom!

MADDIE: I want you back in here and –

JHANA: You, MOM! YOU'RE NOT ALLOWED!

JHANA exits out the front door.

MADDIE: You know how when she's mad she sort of goose-steps but keeps her head down low? I'll bet she's doing that now. Curtains are parting. Someone's saying it's that girl out there. What do they call her? Probably just retarded.

KING: Special. Isn't that the latest?

MADDIE: Naw, just social workers say that, teachers.

KING: Well, that accounts for half the neighbourhood.

MADDIE: Simple. People still say that, I'll bet.

KING: People aren't that out of it, Maddie. Everyone has a cousin or someone who is –

MADDIE: Not everyone has a daughter.

KING: Hey. She's mine too. My family. My little girl.

MADDIE: Do you think I'm too awful to her? I should go out there. She's probably ripping up the neighbour's lawn or something. Taking off like this? That's something she just started this year because she knows it makes me crazy.

KING: She's okay. Just let her cool off.

MADDIE: When I was a kid there was a boy that lived near us in this orange house. I think he had cerebral palsy but really handicapped. Even their house looked different. The colour seemed too bright. You know how when you go away for a while then when you come back everything looks different? Their house looked like that all the time. Sort of charged up but dead – all at once.

KING: Slow down now, Madelaine.

MADDIE: This is my house. People look at my house that way –

KING: You're always so hard on yourself.

MADDIE: My home. I was shitty to her just now. I've got to find her.

KING: Talk to me. Tell me about your day and –

MADDIE: That guy died didn't he? Wade. Remember the guy who sang Elvis all night up in Whitehorse?

KING: Hit by a truck.

MADDIE: Jhana's great in traffic. It took forever to learn but even on the side streets, not a car around for miles. She's checking it out thoroughly from the curb, looking both ways ... I'm going to find her.

KING: You walked her to school until she was fifteen. It's not right, you hanging on like that.

MADDIE: And now she's eighteen and I want to hold on more than ever, protect her from all of them. You bet.

KING: You think everyone is some kind of rapist?

MADDIE: I think it's worse than that. I think everyone out there thinks Jhana's doing just fine.

KING: Weren't you going to get her into a group home?

MADDIE: You're as bad as the rest.

KING: So Jhana's gonna live with you until you're both old and grey. Great, Madelaine, you two seem to get along real well.

MADDIE: Her name's on a list for supervised apartments. Okay?

MADDIE tries to leave, but KING keeps her back.

KING: No. Not okay.

MADDIE: Don't tell me –

KING: She's mine too –

MADDIE: Part-time. Between shows and women and –

KING: Look. I'm not here to fight with anyone.

MADDIE: Then you deal with her. You get her keyed up to make lunch, go to the workshop, do up her buttons right, keep her hair clean, her hands off the men on the bus –

KING: I ask how your day is and you tell me about her.

MADDIE: What time is it?

KING: It's like you've disappeared.

MADDIE: What is it you want from me? I don't know why you stayed on this week if it was just to –

KING: I want to come home.

MADDIE: Yeah right. Then you get to leave again.

KING: I'm talking about staying. Leaving is not part of the picture.

MADDIE: Are you sure?

KING: No ... Let her go stomping around and make the whole fucking neighbourhood crazy.

MADDIE: I get scared there isn't anything left inside that's just me.

KING: Bring me home, Maddie.

MADDIE: I don't even know how to remember things that are all mine. That happened before she was born. Did it change you that way?

KING: I guess so.

MADDIE: Right inside? That happened to you too?

KING: I don't know. I don't examine it all to death the way you do. The way she is has nothing to do with you.

MADDIE: We made her life –

KING: It has to do with oxygen being cut off at birth. That has nothing to do with either of us.

MADDIE: How can that be true –

KING: Don't do this.

MADDIE: If I could've held her inside longer, maybe she'd have been stronger –

KING: We've been over this a thousand times. It doesn't make sense to keep –

MADDIE: Nobody, King, is ever allowed to talk to me about what makes sense.

SCENE 5

The next morning, JHANA and BILL are at the table.

JHANA: She killed me.

BILL: Who did?

JHANA: Mom killed me.

BILL: If your mom killed you, you wouldn't be here to tell me about it. You'd be dead.

JHANA: Princie's dead.

BILL: But not Jhana. You just got in trouble last night for riding around for three hours on the Woodbine bus.

JHANA: It's funny, right?

BILL: Not really. And talking to people you don't know about your troubles isn't such a great idea either. The bus driver that phoned last night –

JHANA: I hate him.

BILL: He was a nice guy, Jhani. He got worried. We all did.

JHANA: Be Andrew please. Be Andrew.

BILL: You have to change your thinking about Andrew. I didn't realize he was, you know ... your boss.

JHANA: Good evening, Andrew, and –

BILL: Rule number one: Don't get hung up on the boss. Rule number two: Don't fall for any guy who ... doesn't see the world in the same way you do. Right? Have you had breakfast yet? I'm starving.

JHANA: Starving. I'm pretty, Bill.

BILL: Yes you are. How about Smitty's? Then maybe we can go along the Danforth and look for something for your mom. Sort of make up for last night.

JHANA: He likes me.

BILL: We can take the subway.

JHANA: Andrew likes me and drying my face.

BILL: I don't doubt that for a minute but he doesn't like to see you outside work or any of that. It isn't possible. You ever tried kissing your elbow? (*demonstrates*) Can't be done. No matter how hard you try. It's impossible.

JHANA: Liar Bill. Steffie's hitting and Peter can't get out of his chair ... Andrew loves me.

BILL: Look. These are the rules and they stink.

JHANA: Stink.

BILL: Fall in love with someone you work with or someone from your school –

JHANA: No! No one likes you, Bill. No, no, no, no. No one. You said I'll be kissing, I'll be phoning Andrew –

BILL: I made a mistake. Okay? Look, Steffie believes that Barry Manilow is going to ask her on a date. And everyone loves teasing Steffie about that. But at the same time you know Barry Manilow isn't really going to take Steffie out anywhere. It's sort of like that with you and Andrew or you and the guy next door, the man on the bus. It isn't really going to happen. So you stick to the guys from your own turf. With Rory or Jason or those brothers with the big heads.

JHANA: I am loving Andrew. Loving him now and you said ... Pig.

BILL: You got it, Jhana. Lots of those around but I didn't invent any of it. In my world Barry Manilow would have to do time putting screws in a bag and you and Steffie would be onstage at Maple Leaf Gardens.

JHANA: Bill?

BILL: You'd sing, strut, tell your story. Everyone seeing you live for the first time.

JHANA: I want a boyfriend.

BILL: I still think that can happen.

JHANA: Be Andrew. Please be Andrew.

BILL: You be Jhana and I'll be Bill.

JHANA: Good evening and ... Bill? Are you sad?

BILL: Yes.

JHANA: At me? Be mad at me, don't.

BILL: You are my favourite girl in the whole world. (*putting his arms around JHANA*) Did you know that?

C'mon. Go put on something fancy. I'm taking you to Smitty's for breakfast.

JHANA: Kiss, kiss, kiss, kiss, kiss. Kiss her mouth, Bill.

BILL: Naw, friends don't do that. They keep clear of that sort of thing.

JHANA: Do it tiny. Once. (*BILL kisses JHANA's cheek.*) Do it tiny again. Kiss her mouth, Bill. Kiss her bigger.

> *BILL looks closely at JHANA. He turns her face toward him, holds her face for a long time, then kisses her fully on the mouth. KING appears on the stairs.*

JHANA: Bigger.

BILL: I can't, sweetheart.

KING: Don't move.

JHANA: My Daddy say Dad.

KING: (*coming downstairs*) Stand up, Jhani. Get away from that couch. (*to BILL*) Get out.

JHANA: Why?

KING: (*to JHANA*) Go upstairs.

JHANA: Going to Smitty's, me and Bill.

KING: (*to BILL*) Get out.

BILL: It isn't like that –

KING: Get the fuck out!

BILL: I was just –

JHANA: You can come, Dad. Going to Smitty's –

KING: Jhana, shut up.

JHANA: Jhana, shut up.

KING: Don't you ever come near my daughter again.

BILL: This is my house too –

JHANA: You're kissing Bill?

KING: (*to JHANA*) Get up those stairs!

BILL: I'll go up your goddamned stairs.

JHANA: I'll go up your goddamned stairs.

BILL: Hey, Maddie!

JHANA: Hey, Maddie!

BILL: (*heading up stairs*) I'm being evicted by a dead pop singer.

> *MADDIE enters.*

KING: You're pushing it, man.

BILL: I've seen you. With both of them. You never get in close enough to be pushed.

MADDIE: What's going on?

KING: He was all over Jhana.

MADDIE: Are you okay?

JHANA: We don't tell people to shut up around here.

MADDIE: What happened?

KING: He's been feeling her up.

MADDIE: I don't believe that.

BILL: Fuck you.

KING: I'm warning you, man –

JHANA: Shut up, shut up! (*BILL heads for the door.*) Can I come?

BILL: This house is too small –

JHANA: I'm small!

KING: You said it.

JHANA: I'll be smaller. See?

MADDIE: Look, if everyone would just –

JHANA: Look at me!

BILL: Now the two of you can go drive to Jesus. Just like the good old days in Moosebone, Alberta.

MADDIE: Jesus, Bill. I just spent half the night lecturing Jhana on running away when she's pissed off –

JHANA: (*crouching down*) I'm small now!

KING: Maybe you didn't hear me, Madelaine. He was all over Jhana when I came down.

BILL: You don't even know who Jhana is.

KING knocks BILL down to the floor.

JHANA: (*running to BILL*) Bill! Up, Bill! Get up!

BILL: I can't just yet.

MADDIE: I'm sorry, Willy.

KING: Ah Christ we're all sorry. Get up.

JHANA: He's hurting. Take a blue pill, Bill. A football. In your stomach.

BILL: Thanks a lot, Jhana.

MADDIE: (*to KING*) Leave. Go pack your stuff.

KING: What?

MADDIE: You're going to do it again anyway. Let's just get it over with. I mean it, King.

KING: I'm doing my best here, Maddie.

MADDIE: It isn't enough.

KING: She's my family.

MADDIE: My family is down on the floor.

JHANA: My Daddy say Dad.

KING: You just stepped over the line, lady.

MADDIE: I know.

KING exits.

JHANA: (*picks up the phone and dials 9-1-1*) My name is Jhana Gladys Kelly. I am mentally handicapped. I live at three-TWO-nine Chisholm Avenue. I live in Toronto. Help me, please, 9-1-1. They are hurt.

EPILOGUE

*Spotlight on **KING**, downstage at the microphone, costumed like Elvis, addressing the audience in the Memphis accent.*

KING: Thank you very much, ladies and gentlemen. You've been a wonderful audience. Before I go, I wanna tell you something nice about my kid. Lisa's out back of the house playing with this ratty dog of her mother's, which I hate. She's trying to make this dog sit and that. She's being real bossy which sort of cracked me up because I mean she's a real little kid. The dog's antsy and being a dog. Finally it does settle down, and you know what she does? She sings to him. She's pretending she's me. Even has the moves down right. It felt great. I mean someone pretending to be me but not to make fun and that. It's nice. But what's even better is that she's my kid, and I just … Lord, just a little. What I'm trying to say is she might love me.

KING walks off stage; the spot is still on the microphone. JHANA enters in her nightgown and Elvis cape, and speaks into the microphone.

JHANA: Hello. HELLO MAPLE LEAF GARDENS! IT'S ME! JHANA! DO YOU LIKE ME? Bill says you can't. C'mon. Try. Elvis is on the mouths of women all the time. She likes it. He sings "Loves ME, loves ME." He is happy and I love him back. You know on the bus? The Woodbine bus? The black hair is in front of you. Don't touch it. You're not allowed. Princie's back is sunny, and I'm laying my head there but not now. (*She tries kissing her elbow.*) See? She's this far away. (*shows the distance with her fingers*) Trying and trying. Bill says you can't. He kisses there for me. Steffie tries this too. No one will know and don't tell. Right? But I am (*arms out to the audience*) kissing you. Now.

Blackout.

END

ANN-MARIE MACDONALD

(b. 1958)

The Canadian Adaptations of Shakespeare Project, an online archive, chronicles more than five hundred theatrical revisions of Shakespeare in Canada over the past two centuries. Adaptations range from John Wilson Bengough's *Hecuba; or Hamlet's Father's Deceased Wife's Sister: A Comic Opera* (1885) and Djanet Sears's *Harlem Duet* (1997), her contemporary take on *Othello* (included in *Modern Canadian Plays*, vol. 2), to Rick Miller's *MacHomer* (1995), a one-man tour de force in which all the roles in *Macbeth* are performed by characters from *The Simpsons*, and Peter Hinton's Aboriginal *King Lear* (2012). Shakespeare's ultra-canonical status, the familiarity of his characters, and the quotability of his dialogue, as well as the cultural capital associated with his name and work make his plays natural targets for appropriation, imitation, and parody.

Given Canada's British heritage and "colonial mentality," in the apt phrase of *Billy Bishop*'s Lady St. Helier, Shakespeare has long held a strong attraction for Canadians. The Stratford Shakespearean Festival put Canadian theatre on the world map in 1953 and has been a dominant, and contentious, element of the Canadian theatrical landscape ever since. Even in francophone Quebec, Shakespeare retains special status. Robert Gurik's allegorical *Hamlet, prince du Québec* (1968) targeted the Shakespeare who embodied for Quebec sovereigntists the hegemony of English-Canadian politics and culture, while Quebec's most famous theatrical son, Robert Lepage, built his international reputation along a series of Shakespearean productions and adaptations, from his bilingual *Romeo and Juliette* in Saskatchewan (1989), to his landmark production of *A Midsummer Night's Dream* at Britain's National Theatre (1992), to *Elsinore* (1997), his solo *Hamlet*.

In *Goodnight Desdemona (Good Morning Juliet)*, Ann-Marie MacDonald rewrites Shakespeare – in iambic pentameter – from a post-colonial Canadian feminist perspective with a variety of comic twists. Through her heroine, Constance Ledbelly, MacDonald raises serious questions (in funny ways) about how academic interpretations of Shakespearean texts may perpetuate distorted ideas and images of women. By transforming Shakespeare's genre from tragedy to comedy, MacDonald interrogates the ways dramatic structures and even theatrical production centres like Canada's Stratford Festival themselves help shape our views of the world. And in drawing a link between genre and gender, she not only addresses but redresses and cross-dresses Shakespeare so that we can never read *Othello* or *Romeo and Juliet* the same way again.

MacDonald was born in 1958 to Cape Breton parents at a Canadian Air Force base in West Germany where her father, an RCAF officer, was stationed. Moving frequently during her childhood, she finished high school in Ottawa, spent a year at Carleton University, and then attended National Theatre School in Montreal. Graduating in 1980, she moved to Toronto to begin working as an actor. She performed with Theatre Passe Muraille and found a home with the feminist theatre company Nightwood. MacDonald collaborated with playwright Banuta Rubess on *Smoke Damage* (1983), a play about the witch burnings; co-wrote with Beverley Cooper *Nancy Prew: Clue in the Fast Lane* (1984), a spoof of the Nancy Drew mysteries; and worked as actor and writer on the important Nightwood collective *This Is for You, Anna* (1985), an intensely theatrical drama about a mother who kills her daughter's murderer. MacDonald was also acting for the screen. She appeared in Robin Phillips's film of Timothy Findley's *The Wars* (1983), was nominated for a Genie Award for her work in *I've Heard the Mermaids Singing* (1987), and received a Gemini Award for Best Supporting Actress for her performance in a TV movie about residential schools, *Where the Spirit Lives* (1989).

Goodnight Desdemona (Good Morning Juliet) was the first play MacDonald wrote on her own. Directed by Banuta Rubess for Nightwood in 1988, it won the Floyd S. Chalmers Canadian Play Award, the Canadian Authors' Association Award, and the Governor General's Literary Award for Drama. It toured Canada in 1990 and has since been regularly produced around the world. In addition to Kate Lynch who premiered the role, notable Canadian Constances have included Clare Coulter, Gina Wilkinson, Nancy Palk, and MacDonald herself in a 2001 revival at Toronto's Canadian Stage. Cherry Jones played Constance in a 1992 off-Broadway production, with Hope Davis as Juliet and Liev Schreiber as Romeo.

Following *Goodnight Desdemona*, MacDonald wrote *The Arab's Mouth* (1990), a Gothic mystery set in Scotland in 1899, first produced by Toronto's Factory Theatre. Substantially rewritten and retitled *Belle Moral: A Natural History*, it was produced at the Shaw Festival in 2005. Tarragon Theatre premiered the chamber opera *Nigredo Hotel* (1992; music by Nic Gotham), for which she wrote the libretto. She also wrote the book and lyrics for *Anything That Moves* (2000), a romantic musical co-produced by Tarragon and Nightwood. MacDonald returned to the collective model as co-creator and performer in both *The Attic, the Pearls, and Three Fine Girls* (Buddies in Bad Times, 1995), a comedy about the reunion of three sisters after their father's death, and its sequel, *More Fine Girls* (Tarragon and Theatre Columbus, 2011).

She has continued to perform in TV episodics such as *Due South*, *The L-Word*, and *Slings and Arrows* as well as onstage. Major roles include Rosalind in *As You Like It* (Canadian Stage, 2005) and Pope Joan in Caryl Churchill's *Top Girls* (Soulpepper, 2008). From 1996 to 2007, she hosted the CBC-TV series *Life and Times*. MacDonald has also had substantial success as a novelist. *Fall on Your Knees* (1996), a family saga set in Cape Breton and New York City, won the Commonwealth Writers Prize and was a pick of Oprah Winfrey's Book Club. *The Way the Crow Flies* (2003), a murder mystery set on a Canadian Air Force base in the 1960s, was shortlisted for the Giller Prize. MacDonald lives in Toronto with her partner, director Alisa Palmer.

Goodnight Desdemona (Good Morning Juliet) rings changes on a familiar dramatic paradigm: the protagonist pursues a mystery, the solution to which is herself. The most famous theatrical instance of this is Sophocles's *Oedipus Rex*. The play climaxes with Oedipus's recognition that he authored his own fate, although Sophocles also makes clear that the gods had known what Oedipus would do even before he was born. The recognition scene reveals an unavoidable and unchangeable truth: this is what the character has always been and must be. His triumph is in recognizing and accepting it, just as Othello recognizes the folly of his false self-conception just before nobly taking his own life (after, of course, taking Desdemona's). "Star-crossed lovers" Romeo and Juliet similarly act out a fate that seems inevitably always to have awaited them.

MacDonald provides a postmodern comic feminist revisioning of this traditional tragic male dramatic model. Simply to reaffirm that things are as they always have been and must continue to be would limit the possibilities for women, given that for much of the history of drama women have been portrayed as weak, passive, and victimized. Feminist playwrights replace "recognition" with "transformation" as the play's central element, argues Helene Keyssar in her book *Feminist Theatre*. Whereas recognition is essentially static, transformation implies an ongoing dynamic process of becoming, emphasizing what may be, rather than what is. At the end of MacDonald's play, Desdemona and Juliet concede to Constance's newfound wisdom, agreeing "To live by questions, not by their solution. / To trade our certainties for thy confusion."

Goodnight Desdemona actually combines the dramas of transformation and recognition. The metaphor of alchemy runs through the play, whereby lead (Ledbelly) is changed into gold, along with other markers of possibility: classic texts are altered, men and women exchange identities, and Constance falls through her wastebasket, like Alice down the rabbit hole, into a Shakespearean wonderland. "For anything is possible, you'll find, / within the zone of the unconscious mind," the Chorus says, where "one plus two makes one, not three." At the same time Constance turns out to be a constant. Behind the persona of the meek Mouse, exploited and humiliated by Professor Night, lives a strong, capable woman who already embodies within herself the qualities of Desdemona the warrior and Juliet the lover. Constance has always been the Author of her own script, a Wise Fool. It just takes these adventures to bring her to recognize that.

Just as MacDonald liberates Desdemona and Juliet from their Shakespearean limitations, the two characters aid and inspire Constance on her journey toward transformation and liberation. Desdemona's fierce behaviour makes Constance realize that the same academe that labels her a crackpot for her Shakespearean theories has obviously been wrong about Desdemona, who is far from a "doomed and helpless victim," leading to one of the great moments in the play as Desdemona and Constance, together, raise their battle cry, "Bullshit!" Whereas Amazonian Desdemona teaches

Constance to know her own strength, lusty, bisexual Juliet unlocks her passion. "Zounds!" exclaims Desdemona, as cross-dressed Juliet embraces Constance while Tybalt ardently carries off cross-dressed Romeo, "Doth no one in Verona sail straight?" The play argues that gender, like so much else, is neither innate nor exclusive but a matter of possibility. MacDonald's requirement for multiple casting, with four actors playing sixteen characters, further drives the play's transformational theme. Watching the quick changes of roles, clothes, and genders in the wild third act destabilizes our notion of a singular fixed identity and reinforces the idea that anyone can be or become anything.

In the end, Constance incorporates into her tripartite identity all the most positive qualities of Desdemona and Juliet while rejecting their "tragic tunnel vision" and celebrating her own (re)birthday. After the final warp effect she finds herself back in her office with nothing physically changed except her quill pen, which has turned to gold. An alchemical transformation has taken place but its minimal nature suggests that Constance's journey has only begun. The goodnight and good morning of the title lead back to the day and the office: there's work to be done. Recognizing her own author(ity) is just the first stage in the ongoing transformational process of becoming Constance.

Goodnight Desdemona (Good Morning Juliet)

Ann-Marie MacDonald

Goodnight Desdemona (Good Morning Juliet) was commissioned and first produced by Nightwood Theatre on March 31, 1988, at Toronto's Annex Theatre with the following company:

OTHELLO, TYBALT, PROFESSOR CLAUDE NIGHT and **JULIET'S NURSE**	Derek Boyes
JULIET, STUDENT, SOLDIER OF CYPRUS	Beverley Cooper
DESDEMONA, RAMONA, MERCUTIO, SERVANT	Diana Fajrajsl
CONSTANCE LEDBELLY	Tanja Jacobs
ROMEO, CHORUS, IAGO, GHOST	Martin Julien

Directed by Banuta Rubess
Set and Costume Design by Denyse Karn
Prop Design by Joan Parkinson
Lighting Design by Dorian Clark
Sound and Original Music by Nic Gotham
Fight Direction by Robert Lindsay
Choreography by Susan McKenzie
Stage Managed by Maria Popoff

PLAYWRIGHT'S NOTE

Direct quotes from Shakespeare are set in italic.

CHARACTERS

DESDEMONA
OTHELLO
JULIET
ROMEO
CONSTANCE LEDBELLY, *an assistant professor at Queen's University*
CHORUS
STUDENT, *"Julie, uh Jill," a student at Queen's University*
IAGO
RAMONA, *a student at Queen's University*
TYBALT
MERCUTIO
PROFESSOR CLAUDE NIGHT, *a professor at Queen's University and boss to Constance Ledbelly*
A SOLDIER OF CYPRUS
JULIET'S NURSE
SERVANT
GHOST

ACT I

THE DUMBSHOW

Three vignettes play simultaneously:
1. *Desdemona's bedchamber:* ***OTHELLO*** *murders* ***DESDEMONA*** *in her bed, by smothering her with a pillow.*
2. *A crypt:* ***ROMEO*** *dead,* ***JULIET*** *unconscious on a slab.* ***JULIET*** *awakens, sees* ***ROMEO****, and kills herself with his rapier.*
3. *Constance Ledbelly's office at Queen's University:* ***CONSTANCE*** *finishes a telephone conversation. She is upset. She hangs up the phone, takes her green-plumed fountain pen from behind her ear, and pitches it into the wastebasket. She then picks up a long, narrow, ancient, leather-bound manuscript, pitches it in after the pen, and exits.*

ACT I

THE PROLOGUE

> *CONSTANCE's office at Queen's University, Kingston. The CHORUS enters CONSTANCE's office*

by a route that suggests he is not bound by the reality of the office walls. He lights a cigarette and speaks the prologue.

CHORUS:
What's alchemy? The hoax of charlatans?
Or mystic quest for stuff of life itself:
Eternal search for the Philosopher's Stone,
Where mingling and unmingling opposites,
Transforms base metal into precious gold.
Hence, scientific metaphor of self:
Divide the mind's opposing archetypes –
If you possess the courage for the task –
Invite them from the shadows to the light;
Unite these lurking shards of broken glass
Into a mirror that reflects one soul.
And in this merging of unconscious selves,
There lies the mystic "marriage of true minds."

He takes the discarded objects from the wastebasket and replaces them on the desk as he says:

Swift Mercury, that changing element,
Portrayed as Gemini, hermaphrodite and twin,
Now steers the stars of Constance Ledbelly,
And offers her a double-edged re-birthday.

He picks up the Manuscript from the wastebasket and replaces it on the desk. An unintelligible inscription on the cover is now apparent.

Here is the key to her Philosopher's Stone –

Indicates Manuscript.

The psychic altar that will alter fate.
But she has not the eyes to see it ... yet.

The CHORUS butts out his cigarette on the floor next to her desk and exits.

ACT I

SCENE i

CONSTANCE's office. CONSTANCE enters her office, absently humming and occasionally singing, "Fairy Tales Can Come True." She wears a coat, boots, and a bright red woollen toque with a pom-pom at the end. She is laden with a bookbag, a Complete Works of Shakespeare, and a stack of dog-eared loose-leaf foolscap. The telephone rings, but CONSTANCE, in the middle of jotting down a particularly salient note on her foolscap, only manages to lay her hand on the phone just as it ceases to ring. She removes her coat, under which she wears a crumpled tweedy skirt-and-jacket suit. She forgets to remove her toque and

wears it throughout the scene. She sits down at her desk, opens a drawer, and takes out a package of Velveeta cheese upon which she nibbles while warming to her subject. Throughout the rest of the scene, *CONSTANCE works aloud on her doctoral thesis: a copious dog-eared document handwritten in green ink on foolscap.*

CONSTANCE:
Pen ...

She searches, then finds her pen behind her ear.

"*Romeo and Juliet* and *Othello*: The Seeds of Corruption and Comedy." Of all Shakespeare's tragedies, *Othello* and *Romeo and Juliet* produce the most ambivalent and least Aristotelian responses. In neither play do the supposedly fate-ordained deaths of the flawed heroes and heroines seem quite inevitable. Indeed, it is only because the deaths do occur that they can be called inevitable in hindsight, thus allowing the plays to squeak by under the designation, "tragedy." In both plays, the tragic characters, particularly Romeo and Othello, have abundant opportunity to save themselves. The fact that they do not save themselves tends to characterize them as the unwitting victims of a disastrous practical joke. Insofar as these plays may be said to be fatalistic at all, any grains of authentic tragedy must be seen to reside in the heroines, Desdemona and Juliet.

A sheaf of papers slides under the office door. CONSTANCE goes to the door and stoops to pick them up just as they begin to slide out again. A little tug of war ensues. Suddenly the door opens against CONSTANCE's head. She stands up to see a young female STUDENT.

STUDENT:
I'm sorry, Miss Ledbelly, I thought you were out.

CONSTANCE:
Oh. Um. I'm in.

STUDENT takes the sheaf from CONSTANCE and writes on it.

STUDENT:
I put the incorrect date on my essay.

CONSTANCE:
Oh. What's today?

STUDENT:
It's the first.

CONSTANCE:
The first what?

STUDENT:
Of the month.

CONSTANCE:
Oh.

STUDENT hands essay back to CONSTANCE.

STUDENT:
I know it's a week past the due date but (*lying*) you remember the extension you gave me, eh?

CONSTANCE:
I did?

STUDENT:
Yes, because I've been ill lately. (*cough-cough*)

CONSTANCE:
Oh yes, well, whatever, that's fine.

STUDENT:
Thanks, Miss Ledbelly.

CONSTANCE:
Wha – uh, what was this assignment?

STUDENT:
"The Effect of Filth on Renaissance Drama."

CONSTANCE:
Good. That sounds just fine, Julie, uh, Jill, uh ... keep up the good work.

STUDENT:
Thanks, Miss. By the way, I like your hair like that. It's really pretty.

CONSTANCE:
Oh.

She vaguely touches her hair below the toque.

Thanks.

Exit STUDENT. CONSTANCE closes the door then, stuffing the student's essay into her bookbag.

Lie thou there. Now where was I?

She takes a bite of Velveeta and settles down to work.

Uh, At ... At the tragic turning point in *Othello* even the hardened fatalist is at pains to suppress a cry of warning, *id est*, "O Othello, O Tragic Man, stop your ears against the false yapping of that cur, Iago. The divine Desdemona, despite her fascination with violence and her love of horror stories, and aside from the fact that she deceived her father to elope with you, is the very embodiment of purity and charity."

CONSTANCE opens her Shakespeare, oblivious to OTHELLO and IAGO, who enter and play out the following scene which she reads silently to herself.

IAGO:
My Lord Othello, *Did Cassio, when you wooed Desdemona, know of your love?*

OTHELLO:
He did from first to last, Iago.
And went between us very oft.

IAGO:
                              Indeed?

OTHELLO:
Indeed? Ay, indeed! Discern'st thou aught in that?
Is he not honest?

IAGO:
                    Honest, my lord?

OTHELLO:
                              Honest? Ay, honest.

IAGO:
My lord, for aught I know.

OTHELLO:
What dost thou think?

IAGO:
                    Think, my lord?

OTHELLO:
                              Think, my lord?
By heaven thou echo'st me,
As if there were some monster in thy thought
Too hideous to be shown. Thou dost mean something.
If thou dost love me, show me thy thought.

IAGO:
My lord, you know I love you.

CONSTANCE takes a previously opened can of Coors Light beer from her desk drawer and sips it.

CONSTANCE:
We are willing to accept Iago's effortless seduction of Othello unto foaming jealousy – the Moor is, after all, an aging warrior, in love with honour and young Desdemona –

CONSTANCE turns a page of Shakespeare. Back to OTHELLO and IAGO.

OTHELLO:
Villain, be sure thou prove my love a whore!
Be sure of it; give me the ocular proof.

IAGO:
Tell me but this:
Have you not sometimes seen a handkerchief
Spotted with strawberries in your wife's hand?

OTHELLO:
I gave her such a one; 'twas my first gift.

IAGO:

I know not that; but such a handkerchief –
I am sure it was your wife's – did I today
See Cassio wipe his beard with.

OTHELLO:

If it be that –

IAGO:

If it be that, or any that was hers,
It speaks against her with the other proofs.

OTHELLO:

Had Desdemona forty thousand lives!
One is too poor, too weak for my revenge.
Damn her, lewd minx! O damn her! Damn her! O!
I will chop her into messes! Cuckold me!

IAGO:

O 'tis foul in her.

OTHELLO:

With mine officer!

IAGO:

That's fouler.

OTHELLO:

Get me some poison, Iago, this night.

IAGO:

Do it not with poison. Strangle her in bed, even the bed she hath contaminated.

OTHELLO:

Good, good! The justice of it pleases. Very good! Now art thou my lieutenant.

IAGO:

I am your own forever.

> *OTHELLO and IAGO embrace, then exit.*

CONSTANCE:

– but we cannot help suspect that all might still so easily be set to rights; and *there's the rub*! For it is this suspicion which corrupts our pure experience of fear and pity at a great man's great plight, and – by the end of the handkerchief scene – threatens to leave us, frankly … irritated.

> *CONSTANCE sips her beer just as the door bursts open. Another young female student, RAMONA, stands in the doorway, all business and very assertive.*

RAMONA:

Hello, Professor, my name is Ramona.

CONSTANCE:

I'm not actually – I'm, I'm just an Assistant Professor.

> *CONSTANCE suddenly remembers her beer, and conceals it.*

RAMONA:

Oh. Well, I wonder if you could pass on a message to Claude for me.

CONSTANCE:

Claude? Oh, you mean Professor Night?

RAMONA:

Yes. Just tell him I won the Rhodes.

CONSTANCE:

Congratulations … Ramona.

RAMONA:

Thanks. By the way, Coors beer is part of the right-wing infrastructure that has brought this hemisphere to its knees.

CONSTANCE:

Oh. Sorry. It … was a gift.

> *Exit RAMONA. CONSTANCE picks up her beer, goes to throw it away, looks around, then drains it furtively and pitches it into the wastebasket.*

CONSTANCE:

In *Romeo and Juliet*, Shakespeare sets the stage for comedy with the invocation of those familiar comic themes, love-at-first-sight, and the fickleness of youth. But no sooner has our appetite for comedy been whetted, when Tybalt slays Mercutio, and poor Romeo proceeds to leave a trail of bodies in his wake.

> *CONSTANCE turns another page of her Shakespeare. Enter TYBALT and MERCUTIO.*

TYBALT:

Mercutio, thou consortest with Romeo –

MERCUTIO:

Consort? What Tybalt, dost thou make us minstrels?
And thou make minstrels of us, look to hear nothing
but discords. Here's my fiddlestick; (indicates sword)
here's that shall make you dance.

> *Enter ROMEO.*

TYBALT:

Romeo, the love I bear thee can afford
No better term than this: thou art a villain.

ROMEO:

Tybalt, the reason that I have to love thee
Doth much excuse the appertaining rage
To such a greeting. Villain am I none.
Therefore farewell. I see thou knowest me not.

TYBALT:

Boy, this shall not excuse the injuries
That thou hast done me; therefore turn and draw.

ROMEO:

I do protest I never injured thee,
But love thee better than thou canst devise
Till thou shalt know the reason of my love;
And so, good Capulet, which name I tender
As dearly as mine own, be satisfied.

MERCUTIO:

O calm, dishonorable, vile submission!
(draws) Tybalt, you rat catcher, will you walk?

CONSTANCE:

If only Romeo would confess to Tybalt that he has just become his cousin-in-law by marrying Juliet. Such is our corrupt response that begs the question, "Is this tragedy?!" Or is it comedy gone awry, when a host of comic devices is pressed into the blood-soaked service of tragic ends?

TYBALT: (*draws*)
I am for you.

ROMEO:

Gentle Mercutio, put thy rapier up.

MERCUTIO:

Come, sir, your passado!

> *TYBALT* and *MERCUTIO* fight.

ROMEO:

Hold Tybalt! Good Mercutio!

> *TYBALT*, under *ROMEO's* arm, thrusts *MERCUTIO* in, and flies.

ROMEO:

Courage, man. The hurt cannot be much.

MERCUTIO:

Why the devil came you between us? I was hurt under your arm. A plague a' both your houses!

> *MERCUTIO exits and dies. Enter TYBALT.*

ROMEO:

Alive in triumph, and Mercutio slain?
He draws.

TYBALT:

Thou wretched boy that didst consort him here,
Shalt with him hence.

> *They fight. TYBALT falls.*

ROMEO:

O I am fortune's fool!

> *Exit ROMEO, TYBALT, and MERCUTIO. CONSTANCE reaches into her bookbag and withdraws a pack of Player's Extra Light cigarettes. It's empty. She spots the CHORUS's cigarette butt on the floor, picks it up, and carefully begins to repair it.*

CONSTANCE:

What if a Fool were to enter the worlds of both *Othello* and *Romeo and Juliet*? Would he be akin to the Wise Fool in *King Lear*? – a Fool who can comfort and comment, but who cannot alter the fate of the tragic hero. Or would our Fool defuse the tragedies by assuming centre stage as comic hero? Indeed, in *Othello* and *Romeo and Juliet* the Fool is conspicuous by his very absence, for these two tragedies turn on flimsy mistakes – a lost hanky, a delayed wedding announcement – mistakes too easily concocted and corrected by a Wise Fool. I will go further: are these mistakes, in fact, the footprints of a missing Fool? – a Wise Fool whom Shakespeare eliminated from two earlier comedies by an unknown author?! *Non obstante*; although a Fool might stem the blundering of Othello and Romeo, the question remains, would he prove a match ... (*She pops the cigarette butt between her lips and hunts for a match.*) for Desdemona and Juliet? Or are these excellent heroines fated to remain tragedies looking for a place to happen? (*Having failed to find a match, she tosses the cigarette butt into the wastebasket, then opens the ancient Manuscript. It is the same length and width as foolscap. She becomes momentarily absorbed in it, trying to decipher it, turning it every which way.*) Nevertheless. I postulate that the Gustav Manuscript, when finally decoded, will prove the prior existence of two comedies by an unknown author; comedies that Shakespeare plundered and made over into ersatz tragedies! It is an irresistible – if wholly repugnant – thought.

> *The office door begins to open silently. Oblivious, CONSTANCE resumes her soft tuneless singing. She takes up her fountain pen once more but discovers it is out of ink. She bends down to her bookbag on the floor to look for a refill and does not see PROFESSOR CLAUDE NIGHT enter on tiptoe. He is about the same age as Constance, is perfectly groomed and brogued, speaks with an Oxford accent, and oozes confidence. He silently perches on her desk. She rises from the depths of her bookbag, sees him, and hits the roof.*

CONSTANCE:

Ah-h-h!

PROFESSOR:

Heh-heh-heh, got you again, Connie.

CONSTANCE:

Heh. Oh, Professor Night, you scared the daylights out of me.

PROFESSOR:

You must learn to relax, my little titmouse. You're working too hard. Speaking of which ... have you got something for me?

> *CONSTANCE stares at him for a moment too long before answering.*

CONSTANCE:

Yes. It's here somewhere.

> *She begins rummaging. PROFESSOR NIGHT picks up her green-ink thesis. He shakes his head. CONSTANCE surfaces from her desk with a thick essay, also handwritten in green ink on foolscap. She sees that he is reading her thesis. She shoots out her hand involuntarily and snatches it from him.*

CONSTANCE:

Don't read that! ... sir ... the ink's not dry.

> *She stuffs her thesis into a drawer of her desk. He wipes his green ink–stained fingers on his handkerchief.*

PROFESSOR:

Still harping on the Gustav Manuscript are you? I hate to see you turning into a laughing stock, Connie. You know you'll never get your doctorate at this rate.

CONSTANCE:

I know ... I guess I just have a thing for lost causes.

PROFESSOR:

You're an incurable romantic, Connie.

CONSTANCE:

Just a failed existentialist.

PROFESSOR:

Traipsing after the Holy Grail, or the Golden Fleece, or some such figment.

CONSTANCE:

Whoever cracks the Gustav code will be right up there with Darwin, Bingham –

PROFESSOR:

– and Don Quixote. The best tenured minds in the world have sought to translate it for the past three hundred years. What gives you the notion you're special?

CONSTANCE:

Oh, I'm not, I'm, I'm not the least bit special, I'm, I'm just one flawed and isolated fragment of a perfect infinite mind like anybody else, I – I think that I exist in that you and I are here chatting with the sense evidence of each other, insofar as we're over there not chatting, no, I'm not special – unique, maybe, in the, in the sense that a snowflake is unique, but no more valuable than any other flake ... It's just that I, I did win the Dead Languages Prize as an undergraduate, and it would be a shame to hide my light under a bushel.

PROFESSOR: (*concealing his curiosity*)

Say you did crack these obscure alchemical hieroglyphs, what if they turned out to be a grocery list or some such rubbish?

CONSTANCE:

I think it's source material that Shakespeare wanted to suppress yet preserve.

PROFESSOR:

And I suppose you've feverishly identified a whole raft of anagrams to support this heresy?

CONSTANCE:

As a matter of fact, yes. If you take the second letter of the eighteenth word of every second scene in *Othello*, and cross-reference them with the corresponding letters in *Romeo and Juliet*, it says: "I dare not name the source of this txt."

PROFESSOR:

"txt"?

CONSTANCE:

Well, "text." I'm missing the letter *e*, it was probably deleted in a later printing.

PROFESSOR:

Your fascination with mystery borders on the vulgar, I'm afraid.

CONSTANCE:

I can't help it. I'm a fallen Catholic. It's left me with a streak of "whodunit."

PROFESSOR:

Well, who did dun it? What became of this mysterious source material?

CONSTANCE:

I think Shakespeare gave it to his elderly friend, Gustav the alchemist, to shroud in an arcane code, and that's what's in here.

PROFESSOR: (*amused*)

Oh, Connie. You have such an interesting little mind.

CONSTANCE:

Thank you, sir.

PROFESSOR:

Hand it over.

> *CONSTANCE thinks he is referring to the Manuscript.*

PROFESSOR:
No, ye gods forfend, not that decrepit tome. The – ahem – your latest commission.

CONSTANCE:
Oh, the essay. Here you go. I hope I've destroyed Professor Hollowfern's book to your satisfaction.

PROFESSOR:
I'm sure it's up to your customarily dizzying standard. Did you remember to give yourself the usual thanks for "irksome proofing of the text"?

CONSTANCE: (*beet red*)
In point of fact, sir, I took the liberty of dedicating it to myself.

PROFESSOR:
That's awfully sweet of you, Connie. (*Looks at essay.*) Tsk, tsk, tsk, your hand gets more cryptic all the time. Like the tracks of some tiny green creature. I do wish you'd learn to type, my dear. I'm weary of doing my own typing, and I daren't trust anyone else with our little secret.

CONSTANCE:
I'm working on it, sir, but my fine motor skills are really poor.

PROFESSOR: (*still scanning the essay*)
Indeed.

CONSTANCE:
I'm ready for my next assignment, Professor. I've sharpened my nib to a killing point.

They share a malicious chuckle.

PROFESSOR:
And dipped it in venom to paralyze the academic foe with one poisonous phrase?

More chuckling.

CONSTANCE:
Just name your victim.

PROFESSOR:
Connie. There remains but one thing you can do for me.

CONSTANCE:
Oh? ... What's that?

He takes a small velvet box from his pocket, opens it, and shows her.

PROFESSOR:
Tell me ... do you like it?

CONSTANCE:
Oh, Professor Night –

PROFESSOR:
Claude.

CONSTANCE:
Oh, Claude ... it's the most beautiful diamond I've ever seen.

PROFESSOR:
Dear Connie. Thank you. I'm the happiest man in the world.

CONSTANCE:
So am I. I can't quite believe it!

PROFESSOR:
Neither will Ramona.

CONSTANCE:
Ramona? ... Oh.

PROFESSOR:
I'm going to miss you, Connie.

CONSTANCE:
Am I going somewhere?

PROFESSOR:
I am, pet. I've decided to take that lecturing post at Oxford myself. Even if it does fall somewhat short of a challenge.

CONSTANCE:
Oh. I thought you might recommend someone less distinguished, say an Assistant Professor, for that job.

PROFESSOR:
That's what I thought too until Ramona won the Rhodes. Now it's Oxford for the both of us, eh what?

CONSTANCE:
What about – Will I still work for you?

PROFESSOR:
I'm afraid not, love. I made Full Professor today, so the pressure's off.

CONSTANCE:
Congratulations.

PROFESSOR:
Not to worry. I've lined up a lovely post for you in Regina.

CONSTANCE:
Thanks.

PROFESSOR:
What's your schedule like day after tomorrow? I hoped you'd help pack my books.

CONSTANCE:
I'd love to but ... that's my birthday ... and I planned on going to the zoo.

PROFESSOR:

Birthday, eh? Chalk up another one for the Grim Reaper. Still twenty-nine and holding are we? Well, many happy re-runs. (*chuckle*) I've got to dash. I'm addressing the Literary Society this evening – which reminds me!

But CONSTANCE has anticipated him and hands him another sheaf of inky green foolscap.

CONSTANCE:

Here's your speech.

PROFESSOR:

Thanks, old girl.

He tugs the pom-pom on her toque then exits.

PROFESSOR:

Oxford ho!

CONSTANCE slowly pulls off her toque and drops it into the wastebasket. She is in shock. This is the nadir of her passage on this earth.

CONSTANCE:

Regina. I hate the Prairies. They're flat. It's an absolute nightmare landscape of absolutes and I'm a relativist, I'll go mad. Diamonds are a girl's best friend. Diamonds are harder than a bed of nails. I can't feel anything. I'm perfectly fine. I'll call the Dean and resign. I'll go back to my apartment and watch the plants die and let the cats copulate freely. I'll order in groceries. Eventually, I'll be evicted. I'll smell really bad and swear at people on the subway. Five years later, I run into Professor Night and Ramona: they don't recognize me. I'm selling pencils. They buy one. Suddenly, I drop dead. They discover my true identity. I'm awarded my doctorate posthumously. Professor Night dedicates his complete works to me and lays roses on my grave every day. My stone bears a simple epithet: "Oh, what a noble mind is here o'erthrown." ... There's no time to lose! I have to start right now if I'm going to sink that low in five years. (*grabs phone, dials*) Hello, give me the office of the Dean! ... Oh yes, I'll hold. (*While holding, she surveys the objects on her desk, picks them up one by one, addresses them, and then tosses them into the wastebasket.*) The bronze wings that my Brownie pack gave me. (*reads inscription*) "To the best Brown Owl in the forest." I flew up more girls than any Brown Owl other than Lady Baden Powell. (*Toss. Picks up a jar that contains something like an anchovy.*) My appendix. It was removed in the summer of love when the rest of my family went to Expo '67. The doctor gave it to me in this baby-food jar. He

thought it would cheer me up. It did. (*Toss. Takes the plumed fountain pen from behind her ear.*) The fountain pen I made from my parakeet, Laurel. She used to sing "Volare." She fell five storeys and died instantly. (*Goes to toss it away, but cannot bear to do so. She replaces it behind her ear, where it stays for the rest of the play. Picks up the Manuscript.*) And this – my fool's gold. Silent mocking oracle. I'll do the world a favour.

CONSTANCE goes to toss it in the wastebasket but her gesture is suddenly arrested in midair and she stares, spellbound, at the inscription on the cover. Harp music and light effects. She blinks and tries to focus, as though the inscription were swimming before her eyes with a disorienting effect. CONSTANCE reads the inscription aloud:

CONSTANCE:

"You who possess the eyes to see
This strange and wondrous alchemy,
Where words transform to vision'ry,
Where one plus two makes one, not three;
Open this book if you agree
To be illusion's refugee,
And of return no guarantee –
Unless you find your true identity.
And discover who the Author be."

CONSTANCE hesitates for a moment, then opens the Manuscript. Its three pages fall out and down into the wastebasket. CONSTANCE sets the cover on her desk, then stoops and reaches into the wastebasket to retrieve the pages. Suddenly her arm jerks downward; she is being pulled down into the wastebasket. "Warp" effects, sound of screeching wind and music.

When the sound and lights return to normal in CONSTANCE's office, she is nowhere to be seen. The phone receiver dangles off the hook. Smoke issues from the wastebasket. The CHORUS's head, a cigarette between his lips, emerges from the wastebasket.

CHORUS:

You've witnessed an impossible event:
A teacher, spinster – "old maid," some would say –
Whose definition of fun and excitement
Is a run of "ibids" in an essay,
Disappears before your very eyes.
Suspend your disbelief. Be foolish wise.
For anything is possible, you'll find,
Within the zone of the unconscious mind.

*His head disappears back into the wastebasket. During the scene change, we hear **OTHELLO** and **IAGO** via their enhanced voiceover:*

IAGO:
Think, my lord?

OTHELLO:
Think, my lord? By heaven thou echo'st.

IAGO:
Indeed?

OTHELLO:
Indeed? Ay indeed!

IAGO:
Think, my lord?

OTHELLO:
Think, my lord? Ay!

IAGO:
Have you not sometimes seen a handkerchief?

OTHELLO:
If it be that –

IAGO:
If it be that –

OTHELLO:
Goats and monkeys!

IAGO:
Indeed.

ACT II

SCENE i

> *OTHELLO's citadel at Cyprus. **OTHELLO** and **IAGO** reprise the end of the "Handkerchief Scene." **DESDEMONA**'s "strawberry-spotted" handkerchief hangs out the back of **IAGO**'s hose.*

IAGO:
Tell me but this:
Have you not sometimes seen a handkerchief
Spotted with strawberries in your wife's hand?

OTHELLO:
I gave her such a one; 'twas my first gift.

IAGO:
I know not that; but such a handkerchief –
I am sure it was your wife's – did I today
See Cassio wipe his beard with.

OTHELLO:
If it be that –

IAGO:
If it be that, or any that was hers,
It speaks against her with the other proofs.

> *CONSTANCE's head peeks out from behind an arras.*

OTHELLO:
Had Desdemona forty thousand lives!
One is too poor, too weak for my revenge.
Damn her, lewd minx! O damn her! Damn her, O!
I will chop her into messes! Cuckold me!

IAGO:
O 'tis foul in her.

OTHELLO:
With mine officer!

IAGO:
That's fouler.

OTHELLO:
Get me some poison, Iago, this night.

IAGO:
Do it not with poison.

> *IAGO hands a pillow to OTHELLO.*

Strangle her in bed.

CONSTANCE:
No!

> *Both **OTHELLO** and **IAGO** turn and stare at her, amazed.*

CONSTANCE:
Um ... you're about to make a terrible mistake ... m'lord.

> *Shocked, and at a loss for words to explain her statement, **CONSTANCE** gathers her courage and timidly approaches **IAGO**.*

CONSTANCE:
Excuse me, please.

> *She plucks the handkerchief from IAGO's hose and gives it to OTHELLO.*

OTHELLO:
Desdemona's handkerchief! (*to* IAGO) Which thou didst say she gave to Cassio!

IAGO:
Did I say that? What I meant to say –

OTHELLO:
O-o-o! I see that nose of thine, but not that dog I shall throw it to!

IAGO:
My lord, I can explain –

CONSTANCE:

Omigod, what have I done?

*She grabs the handkerchief from **OTHELLO** and tries unsuccessfully to stuff it back into **IAGO**'s pocket.*

Look, just forget you ever saw me here, okay?!

*She grabs the pillow and offers it to **OTHELLO**.*

Here.

***OTHELLO** ignores the pillow and proceeds to bind and threaten **IAGO**.*

CONSTANCE: (*aside*)

I've wrecked a masterpiece. I've ruined the play,
I've turned Shakespeare's *Othello* to a farce.
O Jesus, they've got swords! And this is Cyprus;
There's a war on here! O please wake up.
Please be a dream. I've got to get back home!
Back to my cats. They'll starve. They'll eat the plants.
They'll be so lonely. (*to OTHELLO*) Please! I've got
    to go!
Where's the exit!?

OTHELLO:

                          Stay!!!

CONSTANCE:

                          Sure.

OTHELLO:

Forty-thousand lives were not enough
To satisfy my debt to you, strange friend.
I'd keep you on this island till I knew
Which angel beached you on our war-like shores,
And how you gained fair knowledge of foul deeds.

CONSTANCE:

Well. Actually. I've studied you for years.

OTHELLO:

You must be a learnèd oracle.
I'd have you nightly search the firmament,
And daily read the guts of sheep for signs
To prophesy our battles with the Turk.

CONSTANCE:

I only know of your domestic life.

OTHELLO:

And of the murd'rous viper in my breast.
My shame is deeper than the Pontic sea,
Which yet would drown in my remorseful tears,
Whose crashing waves are mute before the
    trumpet cry
Of this atoning heart would tumble Jericho!

CONSTANCE:

Oh well, I wouldn't dwell on it too much.
You'd never have been jealous on your own.

OTHELLO:

O yes, I had forgot. (*to IAGO*) 'Twas all thy fault.
(*to CONSTANCE*) If that you be the mirror of my
    soul,
Then you must learn the story of my life:
Of moving accidents by flood and field,
Of hairbreadth scapes i' th' imminent deadly breach,
Of being taken by the insolent foe –

CONSTANCE:

                          Oh yes, I know.

IAGO: (*aside*)

So know we all the wag and swagger of this tale.

OTHELLO:

In Egypt, kicked I sand into the eyes
Of infidels who thought I made a truce
When I did give to them a pyramid
On wheels they pulled into the garrison.
But I had packed it full with Christian men,
Who slit the savage throat of every Turk.

CONSTANCE:

That sounds like Troy.

IAGO: (*aside*)

                          Not Troy, but false.

CONSTANCE:

And Desdemona fell in love with you,
Because she loved to hear you talk of war.

OTHELLO:

These things to hear she seriously inclined.

CONSTANCE:

I've always thought she had a violent streak,
And that she lived vicariously through you,
But no one else sees eye to eye with me.
Yet I maintain, she did elope with you,
And sailed across a war zone just to live
In this armed camp, therefore – (*aside*) He's not
    a Moor.

IAGO: (*aside*)

Amour? Aha! C'est ça! Et pourquoi pas?!

A flourish of martial music.

OTHELLO:

Here comes the lady. Let her witness it.

*Enter **DESDEMONA** attended by a **SOLDIER** who carries her needlework.*

DESDEMONA:

O valiant general and most bloody lord!

OTHELLO:

O my fair warrior!

DESDEMONA:

        My dear Othello!

CONSTANCE:

Divine Desdemona!

OTHELLO:

        My better self!

OTHELLO and DESDEMONA embrace.

IAGO: (*aside*)

    And my escapèd prey. I'll trap thee yet.

DESDEMONA:

That I love my lord to live with him,
My downright violence and storm of fortunes
May trumpet to the world. My sole regret –
That heaven had not made me such a man;
But next in honour is to be his wife.
And I love honour more than life! Who's this?

Everyone turns and stares at CONSTANCE.

CONSTANCE:

Hi ... Desdemona? ... This is like a dream ...
You're just as I imagined you to be.

CONSTANCE, in awe, reaches out to touch the hem
of DESDEMONA's sleeve and fingers it throughout
her next speech.

I'm Constance Ledbelly. I'm an academic.
I come from Queen's. You're real. You're really real.

DESDEMONA:

As real as thou art, Constance, Queen of
Academe.

CONSTANCE:

Is that my true identity? Gosh. I was just a
teacher 'til today.

DESDEMONA:

A learnèd lady? O most rare in kind.
And does your husband not misprize this
knowledge?

CONSTANCE:

Oh, I'm not married.

IAGO: (*aside*)

        Most unnatural!

OTHELLO:

A virgin oracle! Thanks be to Dian!

DESDEMONA:

Brave agèd maid, to wander all alone!

CONSTANCE:

I'm really more of an armchair traveller.

In fact this is the biggest trip I've made.
I've only ever gone on package tours.

DESDEMONA:

I long to hear the story of your life.

CONSTANCE:

There isn't much to tell. It's very dull.
I'm certain your life's much much more exciting.

DESDEMONA:

This modesty becomes your royal self.
Othello, may she lodge with us awhile?

OTHELLO:

I would she'd never leave these bristling banks.
She hath uncanny knowledge of our lives,
And sees us better than we see ourselves.
(*to CONSTANCE*) So now art thou my oracle and
chaste.

OTHELLO grips CONSTANCE in a bear hug.

OTHELLO: (*to DESDEMONA*)

Hither sent by fortune, she hath saved me
From *perdition such as nothing else could match.*
Make her a darling like your precious eye.
(*aside to CONSTANCE*) You are her greatest friend.
But don't tell why.
(*aside to IAGO*) Deliver up the handkerchief, thou
cur.

OTHELLO takes the handkerchief and presents it
to DESDEMONA.

IAGO: (*aside to OTHELLO*)

I was just testing you, my lord.

Exit OTHELLO and IAGO.

DESDEMONA:

If I do vow a friendship, I'll perform it
to the last article. Othello's honour is my own.
If you do find me foul in this,
Then let thy sentence fall upon my life;
As I am brave Othello's faithful wife.

DESDEMONA seizes CONSTANCE and squeezes
her in a soldierly embrace.

CONSTANCE:

Thanks. (*a blast of trumpets*) Ah-h!

DESDEMONA:

Ah, supper. They have killed a suckling pig in
honour of thee.

CONSTANCE:

        I'm a vegetarian.
That is – I don't eat ... flesh. Of any kind.

DESDEMONA:
Such abstinence is meet in vestal vows,
Therefore in all points do I find thee true.
I'd serve thee, Pedant! Beg of me a boon!
Though it be *full of poise and difficult weight,
And fearful to be granted,* I'll perform it!

CONSTANCE:
There is a problem you could help me with.
I'm not sure how to say this.

DESDEMONA:
                                Speak it plain.

CONSTANCE:
All right, I will. I'm from another world –

DESDEMONA:
Ay, Academe. And ruled by mighty Queens,
A race of Amazons who brook no men.

CONSTANCE:
It's really more like –

DESDEMONA:
                        – Nothing if not war-like!
I'd join these ranks of spiked and fighting shes:
To camp upon the deserts vast and sing
Our songs of conquest, and a dirge or two
For sisters slain on honour's gory field.

CONSTANCE:
If only I could bring you home with me.

DESDEMONA:
I'll anywhere with thee, my friend.

CONSTANCE:
                                That's it,
You see, I can't return until – That is ...
My Queens have charged me with a fearful task:
I must find out my true identity,
And then discover who the author be.

DESDEMONA:
Thou dost not know thyself?

CONSTANCE:
                        Apparently not.

DESDEMONA:
Do none in Academe know who thou art?

CONSTANCE:
Maybe. They call me Connie to my face,
And something else behind my back.

DESDEMONA:
                                What's that?

CONSTANCE:
"The Mouse."

DESDEMONA:
"The Mouse"?

CONSTANCE:
I saw it carved into a lecture stand.

DESDEMONA:
The sculptor dies.

CONSTANCE:
Ironic really, since in my world,
Women are supposed to be afraid of mice.

DESDEMONA:
O fie, that's base! Where be the Amazons?

CONSTANCE:
In fact they're few and far between
And often shoved to th' fringe.

DESDEMONA:
Let's fly to their beleaguered side.

CONSTANCE:
                                My tasks.

DESDEMONA:
The first task is performed already Con,
Thou art an Amazon.

CONSTANCE:
                        I'm not so sure.

DESDEMONA:
As to the second task, the Author find.
There be no authors here, but warriors.

CONSTANCE:
I'm looking for the Author of it all.
How can I put this? Who made you?

DESDEMONA:
                                God made me.

CONSTANCE:
But do you know another name for God?

DESDEMONA:
God's secret name?

CONSTANCE:
                        That's it! God's secret name.

DESDEMONA:
Seek not to know what God would keep a
mystery.

CONSTANCE:
Have you known God to be called Shakespeare?

DESDEMONA:
                                Shake
Spear? He might be a pagan god of war.

CONSTANCE:
This isn't Shakespeare. It must be a source.
Then I was right about the Manuscript!

DESDEMONA:
Manuscript?

CONSTANCE:
                The book that conjured ... this.
It's written by that secret name of God.
If I could find those foolscap pages –

DESDEMONA:
                           – Fool's cap?

CONSTANCE:
About yea long, and written in a code;
They fell into the garbage. So did I.

DESDEMONA:
This Garbage, be it ocean, lake, or sea?

CONSTANCE:
... A sea then – if you like – Sargasso Sea.

DESDEMONA:
I'll call this quest mine own, my constant friend.
Though I should drown in deep Sargasso Sea,
I'll find thine unknown Author and Fool's Cap,
For I do love thee! And when I love thee not,
Chaos is come again.

    A cannon blast. **CONSTANCE** *is badly startled.*
    Battle cries within.

DESDEMONA:
                    The infidel!
This volley heralds battle with the Turk.
Let's to the seawall and enjoy the fray!

CONSTANCE:
Oh no, I can't. I can't stand violence.

DESDEMONA:
If thou wouldst know thyself an Amazon,
Acquire a taste for blood. I'll help thee. Come.

    She takes **CONSTANCE***'s hand and starts to lead*
    her off. **CONSTANCE** *pulls back.*

CONSTANCE:
No, please!!! I won't look. I'll be sick. I can't even
kill a mosquito!

DESDEMONA:
Thou shalt be et alive in Cyprus, Con.
Learn to kill.

CONSTANCE:
No!

DESDEMONA:
That's a fault! Thy sole deficiency.
An errant woman that would live alone,
No husband there, her honour to defend,
Must study to be bloody and betimes.

CONSTANCE:
Please promise me you'll follow your advice.

DESDEMONA:
So will we both. And we be women; not mice.
Come go with me.

CONSTANCE:
                  Okay, I'll be right there.

    DESDEMONA exits.

CONSTANCE:
They can't use real blood, can they?

    Another cannon blast.

CONSTANCE:
                        Omigod!
Oh, Constance, don't be scared, it's just a play,
And Desdemona will look after you.
Desdemona! I am verging on
The greatest academic breakthrough of
the twentieth century!
I merely must determine authorship.
But have I permanently changed the text? –
You're floundering in the waters of a flood;
The Mona Lisa and a babe float by.
Which one of these two treasures do you save?
I've saved the baby, and let the Mona drown –
Or did the Author know that I'd be coming here,
And leave a part for me to play? How am I cast?
As castaway to start, but what's my role?
I entered, deus ex machina,
And Desdemona will not die,
Because I dropped in from the sky ...
Does that make this a comedy?
And does it prove my thesis true?
In that case, I've pre-empted the Wise Fool!
He must be here somewhere – I'll track him down
And reinstate him in the text,
And then I'll know who wrote this travesty,
Since every scholar worth her salt agrees,
The Fool is the mouthpiece of the Author!
It's all so strange ... What's even stranger though –

    She counts the beats of her speech by tapping each
    of the five fingers of one hand onto the palm of
    the other, in time with her words.

CONSTANCE:
I speak in blank verse like the characters:
Unrhymed iambical pentameter.
It seems to come quite nat'rally to me.
I feel so eloquent and ... (*making up the missing*
    beats) eloquent.
My God. Perhaps I'm on an acid trip.

CONSTANCE:

What if some heartless student spiked my beer?!
(*stops counting*) Nonsense. This is my head, this is
my pen, this is *Othello*, Act III, Scene iii.

Sounds of the fray within.

DESDEMONA: (*within*)

Constance, the fray!

CONSTANCE:

Desdemon, I obey!

*CONSTANCE dashes off toward DESDEMONA's
voice.*

ACT II

SCENE ii

*Same. Enter IAGO bearing two buckets of filth on
a yoke.*

IAGO:

Othello seeks to hide the grisly news
That he did almost kill his guiltless wife,
So dares not gut me openly in law,
But decorates my service with a mean and stinking
Yoke. For this, I thank the pedant:
Othello's vestal mascot, Desdemona's cherished
    pet. (*Takes a Manuscript page from his shirt.*)
My wife found this by chance.
It's in no Christian hand, but pigeon pecks –
The script of infidels! Or mayhap not.
Whate'er it be, I will endow it ill,
For it must dovetail with my plot. Let's see:
To 'venge myself upon the bookish mouse,
Regain my former credit with my lord,
And undo Desdemona once again ...
How? How? Aha! Confide myself
Betrayed by pedant's lies, to Desdemona!
For she is of a free and noble nature
That thinks men honest that but seem to be.
I'll tell her Constance is a spy and whore
Would skewer state and marriage on the same
    kabob!
Thus I blind and train my falcon for the job.

*Sounds of the battle off, as CONSTANCE enters.
She does not look well. IAGO withdraws to
shadows, unseen. CONSTANCE collapses on a
rampart and hangs her head between her knees.
DESDEMONA enters with a severed head. Between
the lips of the head is a scroll.*

DESDEMONA:

Constance! Sister! Here's thy boon!
Behold what I have pluckèd off the beach!

CONSTANCE beholds the head and nearly vomits.

'Tis like to be thy fool's cap. Take it. Read.

*CONSTANCE, trying not to make eye contact with
the head, plucks the scroll from between its teeth.
She opens it. A bowel falls out. She forces herself
to read the scroll.*

CONSTANCE:

Hmm ... it's in Sumerian ...

DESDEMONA:

Script of infidels!

CONSTANCE: (*reads*)

"The tapestries and portraits of the main hall.
Five spring lambs, all the horse and woman-flesh ..."
    This isn't it. This is a looting list.

DESDEMONA: (*addressing head*)

Villain! (*tosses head off*)

CONSTANCE is about to faint.

Faint not, my noble heart of Academe.
Envision thy worst foe with open gorge.

CONSTANCE:

But I don't have a foe.

DESDEMONA:

Fie, thou must have!

CONSTANCE:

There's only one on earth whom I resent.
But never did he mean to hurt me.

DESDEMONA:

Nay?

Who be this false foe?

CONSTANCE:

He's Professor Claude Night.

DESDEMONA:

What harm to thee?

CONSTANCE:

I used to work for him.
For ten years I ... assisted him, by writing.
Some articles he would have writ himself,
Had he the time, but he's a busy man.
Now he's got tenure and an Oxford post
I hoped was meant for me.

DESDEMONA:

Ten years of ghostly writing for a thief?
Thy mind hath proved a cornucopia
To slake the glutton, sloth, and he hath cooked
His stolen feast on thy Promethean heat.

CONSTANCE:
You really think so?

DESDEMONA:
                Ay! Thou wast in thrall;
Ten years an inky slave in paper chains!

CONSTANCE:
Yeah.

DESDEMONA:
He wears the laurel wreath that should be thine.

CONSTANCE:
I guess he does.

DESDEMONA:
And commands the legion Academe
From Lecture Stands that he usurped from thee.

CONSTANCE:
What can you do?

DESDEMONA:
            Gird thou thy trembling loins,
And slay Professor Night!

CONSTANCE:
              I'm guilty too:
I helped him in deceiving Queen's for years.

IAGO: (*aside*)
This will serve my turn upon the pedant.

    Exit IAGO.

DESDEMONA:
Thine eyes were shrouded by the demon Night,
And so art thou *more sinned against than sinning.*

CONSTANCE:
Thanks.

DESDEMONA:
But tell me more of life in Academe.
If there be *cannibals that each other eat,*
And men whose heads do grow beneath their
    shoulders?
These things to hear, I seriously incline.

CONSTANCE:
It is quite dog-eat-dog. And scary, too.
I've slaved for years to get my doctorate,
But in a field like mine that's so well trod,
You run the risk of contradicting men
Who've risen to the rank of sacred cow,
And dying on the horns of those who rule
The pasture with an iron cud.
Not that I'm some kind of feminist.
I shave my legs and I get nervous in a crowd –
It's just that ... I was labelled as a crackpot
By the sacred herd of Academe;

And after years spent as a laughingstock,
I finally came to think that it was true.
But, Desdemona, now that I've met you,
I want to stand out in that field and cry, "Bullshit!"

DESDEMONA:
Wherefore? And what, pray tell, may bullshit be?

CONSTANCE:
A kind of lie. For instance, Academe
Believes that you're a doomed and helpless
    victim.

DESDEMONA:
I?

CONSTANCE:
Ay.

DESDEMONA:
Did I not beat a path into the fray,
My vow to honour in thy fool's cap quest?
Did I not flee my father, here to dwell
Beneath the sword Hephaestus forged for Mars?
Will I not dive into Sargasso Sea,
To serve abreast the Amazons abroad?
Will I not butcher any cow that dares
Low lies to call me tame, ay, that I will!
So raise I now the battle cry, *Bullshit!!*

CONSTANCE & DESDEMONA:
Bullshit!!! Bullshit!!! Bullshit!!!

CONSTANCE:
You are magnificent!
Othello should make you his lieutenant.
You're capable of greatness, Desdemona.

    Enter the SOLDIER.

SOLDIER:
What ho! What ho! What ho! What ho! What ho!
Othello, warrior and raconteur,
Would see my lady pedant post-post-haste,
In discourse touching secrets of the state.

CONSTANCE:
Oh, okay. Bye.

DESDEMONA:
            Commend me to my lord.

IAGO enters as CONSTANCE and the SOLDIER
exit. He sneaks up behind DESDEMONA with his
bucket. She sniffs the air.

DESDEMONA:
What putrefaction haunts the island air?
Belike the slaughtered entrails of our meal?

IAGO:
My lady.

DESDEMONA:

        O Iago! And so low?

IAGO:

But that the love I bear my lord forbids,
I'd howl of treachery that tumbled me
From officer, to sweeper of his sewers.

DESDEMONA:

Nay, speak.

IAGO:

        Since you command it, ma'am, I will:
Once prowled I o'er the battlements, a proud
Protective beast to prey upon my lord's
Fell foes. Now creep I fetid conduits,
To paw the slime, a declawed panther, trapped.
And by a cunning mouse.

DESDEMONA:

        What rodent, this?

IAGO:

Was that the Academic with you now?

DESDEMONA:

It was.

IAGO:

        And called in private haste unto my lord?

DESDEMONA:

He makes of her his Delphic prophetess.
Othello said she knows our secret selves.

IAGO:

        Indeed?

DESDEMONA:

Indeed? Ay, indeed. Discernst thou aught in that?
Is she not honest?

IAGO:

        Honest, madam?

DESDEMONA:

Honest? Ay, honest.

IAGO:

        For aught I know.

DESDEMONA:

What dost thou think?

IAGO:

        Think, my lady?

DESDEMONA:

        Think, my lady?
By heaven, thou echo'st me. Thou dost mean
   something.
If thou dost love me, show me thy thought.

IAGO:

It were not for your quiet nor your good,
To let you know my thoughts.

DESDEMONA:

By heaven, I'll know thy thoughts!

IAGO:

Beware, my lady, of the mouse who eats
The lion's cheese while sitting in his lap.

DESDEMONA:

... cheese? ... mouse? – lion? – in his lap? ... to
   eat there? – What?!
Think'st thou I'd make a life of jealousy?

IAGO:

I would I did suspect mere harlotry.

DESDEMONA:

Go to, thou knave!

   DESDEMONA goes to strike IAGO.

IAGO:

O monstrous world! Take note, take note, O world,
To be direct and honest is not safe.

   He goes to exit.

DESDEMONA:

Nay stay. Thou shouldst be honest.

IAGO:

        I obey.

DESDEMONA:

And give the worst of thoughts the worst of words.

IAGO:

She lacks a husband.

DESDEMONA:

So?
   'Tis vestal study that anoints her chaste.

IAGO:

Pray God she be not secretly married.

DESDEMONA:

What dost thou mean?

IAGO:

        A hag may seem a maid,
When she in truth is Satan's bride.

DESDEMONA:

        A witch?

IAGO:

She hath uncanny knowledge of our lives.

DESDEMONA:

She spake of conjuring. And names for God,
Unknown to Christian ears. Of Amazons,
Who brook no men and live alone. Of mice –

IAGO:
– Her own familiar spirits.

DESDEMONA:
Of men, that she changed into sacred cows.

IAGO:
And so did Circe turn Ulysses's friends
To pigs by witchcraft after she had lain with
     them.

DESDEMONA:
She's with Othello now; ye stars forfend,
He be not changed by suppertime! I'll hence!

IAGO:
Stay, ma'am! That is but half her purpose here.
Doth not the pedant prate of fool's cap?

DESDEMONA:
It is a boon that I am honour-bound to find.
I swore upon my life, this to perform.

IAGO:
The devil thus recruits an honest heart.
What's writ upon the fool's cap, in what tongue?

DESDEMONA:
A foreign tongue that's known to her alone.

IAGO:
What if it be an incantation, wrought
By infidels?

DESDEMONA:
                    I saw her read their script.
If it be that –

IAGO:
If it be that, or any heathen tongue,
It speaks against her with the other proofs.

DESDEMONA:
Is she an evil witch they have employed
To conjure up our secrets to their ears?!

IAGO:
The Turk did strike the hour she arrived.

DESDEMONA:
O that the slave had forty thousand lives.
One is too poor, too weak for my revenge!
O why did I embrace her as my friend?!
'Tis monstrous, O!!

IAGO:
I see this hath a little dashed your spirits.

DESDEMONA:
Not a jot. I'll to my lord and dilate all.

IAGO:
Hold! My lord's bewitched and hates me now;
He'll not believe.

DESDEMONA:
                    Then how should we proceed?

IAGO:
Be not forsworn. Fulfill thy boon to her:
Recover her unholy foolish cap,
Her guilt to prove before you strike.

DESDEMONA:
                    And proving guilt,
I'll spit her head upon a pike *for daws to peck at.*
Thou wilt instruct me in the manly work
Of swordplay; doubtless she is expert there,
For all her lack-a-liver timid show!

IAGO:
Patience, I say. Your mind may change.

DESDEMONA:
As well it may. La donna é mobile.

IAGO: (*alarmed*)
Yet watch her, ma'am, *if thou hast eyes to see.*
She did deceive her Queens; *and she may thee.*

> CONSTANCE and OTHELLO *enter in conversation,*
> *unaware of* DESDEMONA *and* IAGO *who draw*
> *back to listen, observe, and comment aside.*

OTHELLO:
As thou dost love me, not a word of this
To Desdemona. She must not suspect.

CONSTANCE:
Don't worry, it will be our little secret.

> *They chuckle.* DESDEMONA *lunges forward but*
> IAGO *pulls her back.*

DESDEMONA:
Look how she laughs already!

> OTHELLO *takes out a large version of the velvet*
> *box that* PROFESSOR NIGHT *had in Act I, Scene i.*

OTHELLO:
Which jewels most delight your female eye?

CONSTANCE:
Diamonds, of course; a girl's best friend.

> OTHELLO *opens the box, takes out a diamond*
> *necklace with a prominent gold clasp, and places*
> *it around* CONSTANCE's *neck.*

DESDEMONA:
Festoons the whore with baubles!

OTHELLO:
The bees of Solomon ne'er counselled half so wise.
Unto thy sweet and hiving breast,
Do I confide the honey of my heart.

DESDEMONA:
Drone on my husband, drone.

CONSTANCE:
                    Don't mention it.

OTHELLO:
Have I e'er told thee of the time I slew
A singing beast in Turkish Antioch?
'Twas on a grassy riverbank where grazed
A golden ox. The beast did tend this ox.
Three heads grew from the shoulders of the beast.
On one the hair was black as ebony,
The other crown was curlèd angel fair,
The third head wore a scarlet cap of wool,
That ended in a foolish bauble bright.
I asked the beast to show the shallow spot
Where it was wont to ford the ox of gold.

CONSTANCE:
In some strange way this beast seems so familiar.

IAGO:
"Familiar"! Yet again "familiar"!
Most potent witch to suckle such a beast!

CONSTANCE:
You say you killed it dead?

OTHELLO:
                The demon fell
And bled a sea of inky green.

CONSTANCE:
                Alas.

DESDEMONA:
She mourns a beast of Turkish Antioch!

OTHELLO:
I left the thing for dead, as I made haste
To find a shallow spot and ford my ox.

CONSTANCE:
Your ox? Ford, your ox? (*aside*) I'm having déjà-vu.
I think we'd better leave each other now.
Your wife may come and think that something's up.

IAGO:
We know what's up, and who will soon go down.

DESDEMONA:
Adulteress! Let me stone her in the square!

OTHELLO:
Adieu, friend, I'll have more of thee anon.

    OTHELLO embraces CONSTANCE vigorously.

IAGO:
As prime as goats, as hot as monkeys.

    OTHELLO releases CONSTANCE and goes to exit.
    He stops, sniffs the air.

OTHELLO:
Iago?

IAGO: (*emerging from the shadows*)
My lord.

OTHELLO:
Look to the morning's night-soil. And keep in the light.

IAGO:
Yes, my lord.

    OTHELLO pats CONSTANCE on the head.

CONSTANCE: (*to OTHELLO*)
'Night 'night.

    As OTHELLO exits, CONSTANCE sees IAGO whisper
    to DESDEMONA before he too exits. CONSTANCE
    conceals the necklace.

DESDEMONA:
Academic!

CONSTANCE:
Oh, Desdemona – hi. I've been meaning to ask you, does Lord Othello keep a Wise Fool here?

DESDEMONA:
The only wise fool is a one that's dead.
I hate a tripping, singing, licensed fool,
That makes a motley of the mighty,
And profanes the sacred with base parody.

CONSTANCE:
Oh.

    DESDEMONA glowers at CONSTANCE.

CONSTANCE:
Are you okay?

DESDEMONA:
I have a pain upon my forehead, here.

CONSTANCE:
Tsk, tsk, tsk, well, I'm not surprised. I saw you talking to that creep, Iago –

DESDEMONA:
"Creep"?

CONSTANCE:
Colloquial for, "base and noisome knave."
I'd stay away from him if I were you.

DESDEMONA:
Wherefore? Hast thou some secret knowledge
of him?

CONSTANCE:
Oh yes. You'd be surprised how much I know.

DESDEMONA:
I think not. I think thou know'st my husband.

CONSTANCE:
I know some things I hope you'll never know.

DESDEMONA:
What passed between my lord and thee just now?

CONSTANCE:
Uh-oh. What did you hear?

DESDEMONA:
Enough to rear
Suspicion's head.

CONSTANCE:
Oh no.

DESDEMONA:
O yes!

CONSTANCE:
Oh well.
Whate'er you do, don't let him know that you suspect.

DESDEMONA:
Nay, he'll know not that I wot aught.
(aside) Goats and monkeys!

DESDEMONA goes to exit.

CONSTANCE:
Boy, Shakespeare really watered her down, eh? ...
I wish I were more like Desdemona.
Next to her I'm just a little wimp.
A rodent. Roadkill. Furry tragedy
All squashed and steaming on the 401
With "Michelin" stamped all over me. It's true:
People've always made a fool of me
Without my even knowing. Gullible.
That's me. Old Connie. Good sport. Big joke. Ha.
Just like that time at recess in grade five:
A gang of bully girls comes up to me.
Their arms are linked, they're chanting as they march,
"Hey. Hey. Get outta my way!
I just got back from the IGA!"
I'm terrified. They pin me down,
And force me to eat a dog-tongue sandwich.
I now know it was only ham ...
O what would Desdemona do to Claude,
Had she *the motive and the cue for passion*

That I have? She would drown all Queen's with blood,
And cleave Claude Night's two typing fingers from
His guilty hands. She'd wrap them in a box
Of choc'lates and present them to Ramona.
She'd kill him in cold blood and in blank verse,
Then smear the ivied walls in scarlet letters spelling "thief"!
To think, I helped him use me: a gull, a stooge,
A swine adorned with mine own pearls,
A sous-chef, nay! a scull'ry maid that slaved
To heat hell's kitchen with the baking stench
Of forty-thousand scalding humble pies,
O Vengeance!!!

DESDEMONA and IAGO enter, sword fighting. IAGO disarms DESDEMONA, his sword poised to strike. CONSTANCE snatches up DESDEMONA's sword and thrusts savagely and repeatedly at IAGO.

Villainy, villainy, villainy!

CONSTANCE disarms IAGO, knocks him down and is poised to skewer him.

May thy pernicious soul rot half a grain a day!

She raises her sword to strike, but DESDEMONA stops her.

DESDEMONA:
Hold! (*DESDEMONA helps IAGO to his feet. He glares at CONSTANCE, shaken.*) 'Twas all in sport.

CONSTANCE:
Oh.

IAGO:
Ay.

CONSTANCE:
Gee. I'm sorry. Um – (*to IAGO*) here's your sword back and everything ... (*retreating*) Have fun.
(*aside*) Dear God, I could have murdered that poor man.
I saw a flash of red before my eyes.
I felt a rush of power through my veins.
I tasted iron blood inside my mouth.
I loved it!

CONSTANCE faints.

DESDEMONA:
If she be false, heaven mocked itself.

Holding her sword at IAGO's throat.

Wretch, be sure thou prove my friend a villainess!
Be sure of it; give me the ocular proof –

IAGO manages to take the Manuscript page from his shirt.

IAGO:

Yet be content!

DESDEMONA:

Make me to see't!

IAGO thrusts the page under her nose.

DESDEMONA:

What's this?

IAGO:

The pedant's fool's cap writ in Turkish code, found by my wife in your underwear drawer!

DESDEMONA releases IAGO.

DESDEMONA:

Damn her, lewd spy! *O damn her, damn her, O!*

IAGO:

O 'tis foul in her.

DESDEMONA:

And to lie with my husband!

IAGO:

That's fouler.

DESDEMONA:

Fool's cap – *confession* – fool's cap – *to confess then die – first to die, then to confess –*

DESDEMONA is about to fall prey to apoplexy when CONSTANCE wakes up and picks something off the hem of DESDEMONA's dress.

CONSTANCE:

My Brownie wings! What are they doing here? I thought I threw them in the garb … age. Oh.

DESDEMONA: (*aside*)

She may be honest yet. I'll try her once In fairness. Then *I'll chop her into messes.*

DESDEMONA impales the foolscap upon the point of her sword.

CONSTANCE: (*aside to DESDEMONA*)

Hey, Desdemona! Look what I just found. My Brown Owl wings!

IAGO:

An owl stands for a witch! It is the shape that Hecate takes at night.

DESDEMONA:

I know who thou art. And I saw what thou didst.

CONSTANCE:

You mean you've found out who I really am?

DESDEMONA nods.

CONSTANCE:

Who?! Who?! Who?!

IAGO:

The owl's cry!

DESDEMONA points her sword with the foolscap at CONSTANCE's face.

DESDEMONA:

Here is the sword of justice. If this be thine, Read the verdict and reveal thyself.

CONSTANCE:

It certainly looks like the real McCoy.

CONSTANCE plucks the foolscap off the sword.

It is! Page one! I must be getting warm.
(*reads*) "Thou'rt cold, and Cyprus is too hot for thee.
Seek truth now in Verona, Italy;
There find a third to make a trinity,
Where two plus one adds up to one not three."
Hmm. How strange.

Warp effects. CONSTANCE starts to be pulled off. DESDEMONA grabs her by the skirt. When the warp effects are over, all that remains of Constance is her skirt, which is speared onto DESDEMONA's sword.

DESDEMONA:

The pedant hath by magic disappeared
To fly unto her evil genius, Brown Owl.
When she returns with fresh enchantments here,
Then must the cause of justice claim her life.
How shall I kill her Iago?

IAGO hands DESDEMONA the pillow.

ACT III

SCENE i

Verona; a public place. MERCUTIO and TYBALT are about to fight. ROMEO looks on, horrified.

MERCUTIO: (*draws*)
Tybalt, you rat catcher, will you walk?

TYBALT: (*draws*)
I am for you.

ROMEO:
Gentle Mercutio, put thy rapier up.

MERCUTIO:
Come, sir, your passado!

They fight. CONSTANCE enters, minus her skirt,
now wearing just her long johns, boots, and tweed
jacket.

ROMEO:

Hold, Tybalt! Good Mercutio!

> *ROMEO is about to fatally intervene in the sword*
> *fight.*

CONSTANCE: (*aside*)

One Mona Lisa down, and one to go.

> *She tackles ROMEO. They fly into the sword fight,*
> *knocking TYBALT and MERCUTIO aside. TYBALT*
> *and MERCUTIO jump to their feet and immediately*
> *point their swords at CONSTANCE while ROMEO*
> *sits on her.*

MERCUTIO:

Shall I lance the pimple? Or rub the quat
To bursting!

TYBALT:

　　　　　Name the house that whelped thee,
　　pup!
What kennel loosed thee hence to interfere
With honour's reck'ning?

ROMEO: (*to TYBALT and MERCUTIO*)

Stay! You fright the wretch.
Speak, boy ... speak, boy.

CONSTANCE: (*aside*)

Boy? (*A moment of decision. She clears her throat*
to a more masculine pitch.)
　　From Cyprus washed I here ashore,
A roving pedant lad to earn my bread
By wit and by this fountain pen, my sword.
A stranger here, my name is Constan- ... tine.
I couldn't let you kill each other, for
Young Juliet and Romeo have wed;
And by th'untying of their virgin-knot,
Have tied new blood betwixt you cousins here.
Tybalt, Romeo is your cousin now,
In law, and so you fellows should shake hands.

> *A dangerous pause, then TYBALT turns to ROMEO*
> *and embraces him.*

TYBALT:

Cousin Montague!

ROMEO:

Kindred Capulet!

> *MERCUTIO and TYBALT embrace CONSTANCE*
> *in turn.*

TYBALT:

Fortunate harbinger!

MERCUTIO:

Madcap youth!

ROMEO:

Brave Greek! (*ROMEO embraces CONSTANCE, but*
lingers a little too long.)
　　(*aside*) *Did my heart love till now?* Forswear it, nay!
For I ne'er saw true beauty till this day!

MERCUTIO:

Now we have put our angry weapons up,
Let's hie to Mistress Burnbottom's to put up
And to sheath our jocund tools of sport.

> *Lewd Renaissance gestures and laughter through-*
> *out the following dreadful jokes.*

TYBALT:

A bawd! And falling apart with'th' pox! Take
　　care –
She'll pay *thee*, and with a French crown too!

MERCUTIO:

Ay, a bald pate, for a little head!

TYBALT:

I'd as lief to pluck a green maid off the street.

MERCUTIO:

Thou'dst feel that green fruit yerking in thy guts,
When that her kinsfolk 'venged her maidenhead!

TYBALT:

She'd never know who'd had her maidenhead,
For I would pass as quickly through the wench,
As any fruit so green, would pass through me!

> *Laughter – CONSTANCE nervously bites her*
> *thumbnail.*

TYBALT:

Do you bite your thumb at me, sir?!

CONSTANCE:

No! I just bite my nails, that's all.

TYBALT:

Do you bite your nails at me, sir?!

CONSTANCE:

No, I swear! Look, I'll never bite them again. This'll
be a great chance for me to quit once and for all.
Thanks.

> *Pause. The boys tense. Will there be a fight?*

TYBALT:

You're welcome.

ROMEO:

Now t'th' baths, new friendship to baptize!

MERCUTIO & TYBALT:

T'th' baths, t'th' baths!

ROMEO: (*to CONSTANCE*)

Come, Greekling, splash with us!

ROMEO, TYBALT, and MERCUTIO hoist CONSTANCE onto their shoulders.

CONSTANCE:

No, wait! I can't! I had a bath today.
(*struggling down*) What's more, I've got a lot of things to do;
I have to buy a lute, a sword, some hose,
And teach a class or two before it's noon,
In time to see a man about a horse.

ROMEO:

I'd see thee mounted well in stallion flesh.
Beware thou art deceived not in a mare.

ROMEO, TYBALT, and MERCUTIO exit.

CONSTANCE:

Thank God they think that I'm a man. (*to God*)
Thank you. O thank you.
How long can I avoid their locker room?
Those guys remind me of the Stratford shows I've seen,
Where each production has a Roman bath:
The scene might be a conference of state,
But steam will rise and billow from the wings,
While full-grown men in Velcro loincloths speak,
While snapping towels at each other.
Why is it Juliet's scenes with her Nurse
Are never in a sauna. Or *King Lear*:
Imagine Goneril and Regan, steaming
As they plot the downfall of their dad,
While tearing hot wax from each other's legs;
Ophelia, drowning in a whirlpool full
Of naked women. Portia, pumping iron –

A woman screams within. Male laughter.

CONSTANCE: (*verge of tears*)

I want to go home.
I want to see my cats. I want to read
Jane Eyre again and never leave the house.
Where's the Fool? Where's the damn Fool?!
How come I end up doing all his work?
I should have waited in the wings
For him to leap onstage and stop the fight,
And then I could have pinned him down
And forced him to reveal the Author's name!
The Author – who must know my true identity.
The Author! who – I have to pee …
There must be a convent around here somewhere.

Exit CONSTANCE.

ACT III

SCENE ii

JULIET and ROMEO's bedchamber. The next day. Bright sunlight. Oppressive heat. JULIET, clad in a Renaissance peignoir set, languishes near the bed and fans herself, while ROMEO sleeps.

JULIET:

Ay me. (*yawn*)

ROMEO: (*half-asleep*)

Was that the lark?

JULIET:

It was the luncheon bell.

ROMEO:

Oh no! (*leaps out of bed*) Julie-e-et, where be my blue doublet?!

JULIET:

Under the bed where thou didst leave it, dear.

ROMEO retrieves his doublet.

JULIET & ROMEO: (*both aside*)

Th'affections of our love's first-sighted blood,
Have in the cauldron of one hot swift night,
All cooled to creeping jelly in the pot.

JULIET:

Wilt thou be gone?

ROMEO: (*on with the doublet*)

Yes, dear. There's some fun going forward at The Gondolier: the fellows and I are getting up a cock-fight, followed by a bear-baiting, then hie us to a public hanging in the piazza, there to take our noonday meal. (*aside*) I mean to find the lovely Greek boy, Constantine, or die.

JULIET:

Goodbye, dear.

ROMEO:

Goodbye. (*ROMEO exits on the run, but stops short just outside.*) Zounds! I had forgot. (*He heads back into the chamber.*) What, Julie-e-et!

JULIET:

What?

ROMEO is frantically searching for something.

ROMEO:

Where be Hector, my turtle?

JULIET:

Belike dead in the chamber pot.

ROMEO: (*verge of tears*)

Dead?! My Hector?!

JULIET: (*verge of tears*)
Dead?! Sayest thou?!

ROMEO:
Nay, thou sayest so!

JULIET:
Nay, I know not. Perchance he lives yet in the water dish.

ROMEO and JULIET both dash to the water dish and retrieve Hector the turtle, whom they share between their two cupped hands.

ROMEO:
Poseidon be thanked! Hector lives to fight another day!

JULIET:
Be Lazarus from this day forth, thou risen turtle.

They shower the turtle with loving kisses.

ROMEO: (*to JULIET*)
I must be gone.

They exchange a cursory peck on the cheek.

JULIET:
Goodbye, dear.

ROMEO:
Goodbye, dear. (*ROMEO attempts to exit with Hector.*)
Let go thy hand, for I must needs be gone,
And Hector goes with me.

JULIET:
     Nay, stays with me.

ROMEO:
He goes.

JULIET:
He stays!

A turtle tug-of-war ensues.

ROMEO:
Goes!

JULIET:
Stays!

ROMEO:
Goes!

Hector is ripped in two.

JULIET:
Ah! Hector! *Look how he bleeds!*

ROMEO:
Warm and new killed. O Hector. *O heavens!*

They weep.

JULIET:
Thou bloody-fingered boy, hast slaughtered him!

ROMEO:
Thou panther-taloned girl, hast rent his shell!

JULIET:
I'll tell my father!

ROMEO:
     So will I tell mine!
O wherefore did I wive a sniv'lling girl?!

ROMEO exits in tears.

JULIET:
O wherefore married I a stripling boy?!

NURSE calls from within.

NURSE:
What Juliet, ladybird, what little maid!

JULIET: (*aside*)
No maid but matron, thus made and unmade.

NURSE enters. She is hot and puffing, and carries a gift-wrapped package.

NURSE:
Another wedding gift for thee, my lamb.
Beshrew this heat, Verona is ablaze!
'T'will be tomorrow fourteen years ago
Since thou wert born upon a wave of heat
That cooked the country, marry, to an ash.
Child look, I have a pretty box for thee.

JULIET doesn't look up.

JULIET:
Say if it take the measure of my corpse?

NURSE:
Nay, 'tis no bigger than a bread chest.

JULIET:
Entomb it with the rest and leave me be,
And when thou hast done so, come weep with me,
Past hope, past care, past help, past tense, O Nurse!!!

JULIET flings herself upon NURSE's bosom and sobs.

NURSE:
There, there, lamb, thou art too soon made a
 bride.
Was Cupid's loving dart too sharp for thee?
Say if Romeo's of unnatural size,
To tear (*as in "tear drop"*) thee so? Or mayhap,
 saints forfend,
Behind his boyish drool there lurks a foaming
 wolf!
A pox on him! Though't be thy wifely load,
To bear his married weight, I'll pry him hence,
With false chancres for thy nether lips.

JULIET:
  Oh, Nurse, 'tis none of these!

NURSE:
                                      What is it then?

JULIET:
  I die of tedium!

NURSE:
  Oh.

JULIET:
  O Hymen, god of marriage, pray undo
  Thy holy work: Make me a maid again!
  To plunge once more in love's first fiery pit,
  To hover there 'twixt longing and content,
  Condemned to everlasting Limbo, O!
  Penance me with new love's burning tongs;
  Spit and sear me slow o'er heaven's flames;
  Grant me an eternity to play with fire!

NURSE:
  By my maid'nhead, what a turn is here.

JULIET:
  O I have naught to live for from today;
  A once-plucked rose that withers ere it's blown;
  Tomorrow sees the change of fourteen years,
  Yet even now my life is ended.

NURSE:
                                      Nay.
  There's much to live for yet.

JULIET:
                                      Name one of much.

NURSE:
  This very night thy wedding feast invites
  Verona to a table that doth groan
  With joy, and creak at new-fit joinery
  Of married Capulet and Montague.

JULIET: (*subsiding sobs*)
  A party? Tonight? I had forgot.

NURSE:
  Be merry. Feast thine eyes on fresh gallants;
  Rekindle loving embers to reheat
  Thy day-old husband when the feast is o'er.

JULIET:
  I will look. And yet not seek to touch.
  Thanks, Nurse. (*aside*) But touched and whetted
    once before,
  Love's first keen edge grows dull with use and
    craves
  Another grinding. (*to NURSE*) Nurse, what shall
    I wear?

ACT III

SCENE iii

  A public place. Enter **CONSTANCE**, *furtive, peering
  at someone, off.*

CONSTANCE:
I've found him. I've found the Fool. He's skulking
around here, carrying a bag full of Manuscript
pages. (*CONSTANCE lurks apart, as a strangely dressed
SERVANT enters with a bag full of foolscap scrolls out-
wardly identical to the Manuscript pages.*)
  (*aside*) I suppose I could just ask him ... no:
    "When in Verona –"

  CONSTANCE pounces on him and pins him down.

  Name the Author, thou elusive Fool!
  What fiendish hack is he that scribbled thee
  And these (*scrolls*) and this (*this world*) unto the
    light of day?!

SERVANT:
Don't hurt me, sir, pray hurt me not and I will talk.

CONSTANCE:
I'm listening.

SERVANT:
My master is the great rich Capulet and he hath writ
all that you see.

CONSTANCE:
Juliet's father, Capulet?

  The SERVANT nods.

CONSTANCE:
Wrote all this? (*She regards the scrolls.*) Wow.

  *CONSTANCE unrolls the scroll and – with great
  expectation – looks at it. But there is no warp. She
  riffles the other scrolls.*

CONSTANCE:
These are just party invitations.

SERVANT:
Ay.

CONSTANCE: (*reading aloud*)
"Signor Capulet is pleased to announce the marriage of his daughter, Juliet, to Romeo of Montague,
and doth request the honour of your company at a
masked ball this night." You're not the Fool.

SERVANT:
Thank you, sir.

CONSTANCE: (*to herself*)
A masked ball for Romeo ... and Juliet ... "a third
to make a trinity" ... I've got to buy a mask!

ACT III

SCENE iv

That night. The masked wedding feast at Capulet Hall. Renaissance party sounds, decorations, a roast suckling pig with apple … Everyone wears a half-mask. Enter ROMEO and JULIET, sulky and annoyed with each other. The SERVANT sings a love song and plays a lute. JULIET scrutinizes him. The song ends.

JULIET:
Boy, wherefore is thy voice so sweet and high?

SERVANT:
For that I sing castrato, lady.

JULIET:
Oh. Hast thou a brother that's a tenor?

SERVANT:
Ay, ma'am. (*points off*) Look where he tunes his instrument.

JULIET: (*exiting*)
So tune I mine, to pitch in sweet duet.

ROMEO:
If only Constantine were here tonight;
This feast were better borne in light of him.
I feigned a mirthful splashing at the baths,
And sought, but could not find him out today.
What if he's gone and barked again for Greece?
If this be so, I'll to my closet straight,
There to forswear all daylight and all food,
To mirror thus the wasting of my heart,
All shrouded in the dark night of my soul.

Enter TYBALT, masked. ROMEO approaches him from behind.

ROMEO: (*aside*)
No mask can hide that sleek Aegean form.
This is my Constant-teen, as I am his.

ROMEO places his hand on TYBALT's bottom. TYBALT whirls about, yanks ROMEO's eye mask forward, and lets it snap back when he recognizes him.

TYBALT:
Ah, Romeo, 'tis thee, my cuz!

TYBALT gives ROMEO a macho slap on the ass and laughs.

ROMEO:
                    Tybalt!
I knew 'twas thee.

ROMEO punches TYBALT, jock-like, on the arm. The friendly brutality goes on until ROMEO sees CONSTANCE enter, wearing a stupid Mouse half-mask.

I'll pummel thee to pulp anon, my cuz,
But now must I put on the gentle host.

ROMEO leaves TYBALT and cautiously approaches CONSTANCE. TYBALT exits.

ROMEO:
Constantine?

CONSTANCE:
Romeo?

ROMEO:
Ay!

CONSTANCE:
Hi.

ROMEO embraces CONSTANCE warmly, taking her off guard.

CONSTANCE:
Oh. (*extricating herself*) Heh.

ROMEO gazes into her eyes.

Um. How do you like being married?

ROMEO:
Speak not of Juliet, 'tis thee I love.

CONSTANCE:
What?

ROMEO drops to one knee and seizes her hand.

ROMEO:
O Constantine, O emperor of my heart!
It is my sex that is thine enemy.
Call me but love, and I'll be new endowed.

CONSTANCE:
It isn't that – good grief, get up.

ROMEO:
Then love me!

He jumps up to kiss her. CONSTANCE escapes.

CONSTANCE:
No, please, I – I'm not that kind of boy.

ROMEO:
What kind of boy?

CONSTANCE:
The kind that can just hop right into bed
With any Tom or Dick or … Romeo.

ROMEO:
Where be these rivals, Tom and Dick?!
Are their sweet lips more to thy taste than mine?

CONSTANCE:

Oh no, I ... suspect that you're beyond compare.

ROMEO:

Then kiss me now and prove suspicion true.
Surrender unto Romeo thy lips,
And let him enter at those ruby gates,
Forever barred against both Tom and Dick.

CONSTANCE: (*about to yield*)

Oh my.

Enter TYBALT, jovial, drinking a Coors Light.

TYBALT: (*aside*)

I'm told the Greek boy, Constantine, doth feast
with us tonight. (*sees CONSTANCE*) Ah.

ROMEO kisses CONSTANCE's neck.

TYBALT: (*aside*)

O! What, an Hellenic deviant?! O fie!

CONSTANCE:

Please, Romeo, you don't understand, I can't do
this, I'm not – I'm – way too old for you!

ROMEO:

A maiden blush bepaints thy hairless cheek.

He strokes her cheek.

Eternal springs the fountain of thy youth;
I'd quench myself at thy Priapic font.

He kisses her neck.

CONSTANCE:

O ... Romeo ...

TYBALT: (*aside*)

And dares this mockery of manhood bent,
Come hither, covered with an antic face,
To fleer and lisp at our solemnity?

CONSTANCE:

Romeo, please, I know your family – they'll be
very upset.

ROMEO:

Boy, *what love can do, that dares love attempt.*
Therefore my kinsmen are no stop to me.

CONSTANCE:

They are to me! I'm not a hero, I'm just a school
teacher.

ROMEO:

And my Socrates that art condemned
In sweet subversion of Verona's youth.
Then die thou not alone. *I'll kiss thy lips.*
Haply some hemlock *yet doth hang on them.*

CONSTANCE:

I don't want to die! –

ROMEO:

O that I were a fountain pen within thy hand,
To spurt forth streams of eloquence at thy
command!

ROMEO kisses CONSTANCE. She yields.

TYBALT: (*aside*)

The villain! He is hither come in spite,
To shame my cousin, Romeo, this night.

Enter JULIET, dishevelled. TYBALT hides his rage.
The kiss ends.

TYBALT: (*to JULIET*)

Gentle cuz, pray rescue Romeo;
He's trapped in tedious discourse with that man.

JULIET:

Romeo, a messenger doth cry.

ROMEO:

Perchance he cries for thee, dear.

CONSTANCE: (*awestruck*)

Juliet?

JULIET:

Ay.

ROMEO:

Juliet, this be Constantine, the Greek –
Blind Cupid's servant, who unveiled our love
For all the world to see.

JULIET:

Oh. Thanks.
(*aside*) The Greek hath taught not just the world
to see,
But also me. Would I were blind again.

CONSTANCE removes her mask and extends her
hand.

CONSTANCE:

I'm truly thrilled to meet you, Juliet.

JULIET: (*aside*)

Hail, Roman Cupid that hath heard my cries,
And sent Greek Eros to benight mine eyes!

JULIET takes CONSTANCE's hand and does not
release it.

JULIET: (*to ROMEO*)

Romeo, a man doth steal thy horse within.

Exit ROMEO, alarmed. Music. JULIET leads
CONSTANCE in a dance throughout the following
dialogue.

JULIET:

Romeo spake of thee as pedant wise.

CONSTANCE:
I wouldn't say I'm really all that wise.
I have done lots of homework on you, though.
For years I've sought to penetrate your source,
And dreamt of meeting you a thousand times –

JULIET:
Awake. Or let me share thy sleep of dreams.
I'd have thee penetrate my secret source,
And know me full as well and deep as thou
Dost know thyself O dreamer, Constantine.

CONSTANCE:
There must be something in Verona's air;
I feel like half my years have dropped away.

JULIET:
The air is redolent with hearts afire;
Their flames all licking at thy new-blown lip,
Consume thy tongue to spark of love alone.

CONSTANCE:
Wow.

JULIET gives a little laugh. CONSTANCE giggles.

CONSTANCE:
May I ask you something?

JULIET:
                                    Anything.

CONSTANCE:
You're the essence of first love –
Of beauty that will never fade,
Of passion that will never die.
Are you afraid of growing old?

JULIET:
No one may remain forever young.
We change our swaddling clothes for funeral
    shrouds,
And in between is one brief shining space,
Where love may strike by chance, but only death
    is sure.

CONSTANCE:
What happens though, if love itself should die?

JULIET:
When love goes to its grave before we do,
Then find another love for whom to die,
And swear to end life first when next we love.

Enter TYBALT and ROMEO from different places.

ROMEO: (*aside*)
I rode not hither on a horse tonight!

TYBALT: (*aside re: CONSTANCE*)
O villain, that would plunder shirt and skirt!

ROMEO: (*aside re: CONSTANCE*)
How swingst thou now, capricious pendulum!

TYBALT: (*aside re: CONSTANCE*)
Now, by the stock and honour of my kin,
To strike him dead, I hold it not a sin.

ROMEO: (*aside*)
Then let a bodice be my winding sheet;
I'll wear a woman's gown until I die,
Sith it's a piece of skirt that likes his eye!

JULIET and CONSTANCE dance by. ROMEO cuts in and continues the dance with CONSTANCE.

JULIET: (*aside*)
I now perceive the slant of Constantine's desire.
He looks to match his stick to light his fire.
And since he savours a two leggèd pose,
I'll into Romeo's closet and steal hose!

TYBALT: (*aside*)
I will withdraw; but this intrusion shall,
Now seeming sweet, convert to bitt'rest gall.

TYBALT crushes his Coors Light can in his fist, tosses it at CONSTANCE's feet, and exits. CONSTANCE pauses in her dance with ROMEO, picks up the can, and recognizes it.

JULIET: (*aside*)
Thou pretty boy, I will ungreek thee yet.
(*intercepting CONSTANCE*)
If I profane with my unworthiest hand –

ROMEO:
Hold! I saw him first.

JULIET:
                                    Thou wouldst corrupt him.

ROMEO:
Sayst *thou?!* Thou that bedded the first doublet
To o'erperch thine orchard walls?

JULIET:
                                    Thou caitiff!
I sicken of thy blubb'ring boyish charm.

ROMEO:
Thou'rt in the green-eyed clutch of envy, sweet.

JULIET:
"Gather ye rosebuds while ye may," Romeo,
For with each new lust, thou creepeth close
Unto the agèd day when soft moist lip
And dewy eye convert to senile rheum.

ROMEO:
Thinkst *thou* to leave a lovely corpse, my dear,
When even now the crows have footed it
In merry measure all about thine eyes?

JULIET:
Oh! I shall tell my father of this insult!

They are both on the verge of passionate tears.

ROMEO:
Be thou assured *my* father will hear of it!

CONSTANCE:
You kids, now that's enough, just settle down,
Involving family here will make things worse.

JULIET: (*weeping*)
I wish I were dead!

ROMEO: (*weeping*)
I wish I had ne'er been born!

CONSTANCE:
Now, that's no way to talk. Apologize,
And count your lucky stars.

ROMEO and JULIET stare at CONSTANCE for a moment.

ROMEO & JULIET: (*to CONSTANCE*)
Our lucky stars?

CONSTANCE:
I need a breath of air. Thanks for the party. It was a ball. Shut up, Constance.

Exit CONSTANCE.

ACT III

SCENE v

CONSTANCE's balcony overlooking an orchard. The SERVANT warbles on the balcony, holding a taper. CONSTANCE enters the balcony, sees something on the floor, bends down, and picks up the CHORUS's half-smoked cigarette butt from her office. She lights her cigarette from the SERVANT's taper and inhales gratefully. Exit SERVANT. Enter JULIET below the balcony, dressed in ROMEO's clothing.

JULIET: (*below*)
But soft! What light through yonder window breaks?
It is the East, and Constantine *the sun!*

CONSTANCE:
Uh-oh.

JULIET:
He speaks.

CONSTANCE:
Romeo? Is that you?

JULIET:
I know not how to tell thee who I am.
My sex, dear boy, *is hateful to myself,*
Because it is an enemy to thee;
Therefore I wear tonight this boyish hose.

CONSTANCE:
Juliet? What are you doing down there? How on earth did you get into the orchard?

JULIET:
With love's light wings did I o'erperch –

CONSTANCE:
I see.
I'm sorry, Juliet, it's not to be,
I'm not at all the man you think I am.

JULIET:
I wot well what thou art, and yet I love.

CONSTANCE:
You do?

JULIET:
Ay.

CONSTANCE:
You mean you know my true identity?

JULIET:
Indeed. Thou art a deviant of Greece.
O Constantine! O wherefore art thou bent?

CONSTANCE:
Shshshsh! Good heavens, keep your voice down please.

JULIET:
Deny thy preference and refuse thy sex;
Or, if thou wilt not, be but sworn my love,
And henceforth never will I be a girl.

CONSTANCE:
I'm not ... a deviant, for heaven's sake.

JULIET:
Not deviant? Art thou then a timid virgin?
Dear boy, I envy thee thy bliss to come.

CONSTANCE:
I may be celibate, but I'm not exactly a virgin.

JULIET:
Tut, boyish bluster. Hast thou tasted woman?

CONSTANCE:
No!

JULIET:
Then are thy vestal senses all intact.
O let Juliet initiate
Thy budding taste of woman's dewy rose.

Learn how the rose becomes a sea of love:
Come part the waves and plumb Atlantic depths.
I'll guide thee to the oyster's precious pearl ...
We'll seek out wat'ry caves for glist'ning treasure,
Spelunk all night until we die of pleasure.

CONSTANCE:
I'm not into that sort of thing.

JULIET:
Then claim another conduit for thy use.

CONSTANCE:
Heavenly days, what's come over you?!
You're supposed to be all innocence.

JULIET:
The time for innocence is sped!
I'll love once more before I'm dead!

CONSTANCE:
Who said anything about dying? You're only fourteen years old.

JULIET:
Thirteen! Tomorrow will I be fourteen.

CONSTANCE:
You will? So will I! I mean, be a year older.

JULIET:
We share the self-same stars! We're truly
matched.

CONSTANCE:
Juliet?

JULIET:
My love?

CONSTANCE:
I'm flattered. And you're very beautiful,
And sweet and passionate, and probably
A – lovely ... lover, but – in point of fact,
I don't – I can't – I must – not. Love you. Juliet.

JULIET:
Wherefore?

CONSTANCE:
Well ... for one thing, you're married.

JULIET:
Hmph.

CONSTANCE:
And we've barely met.

JULIET:
So?

CONSTANCE:
I don't believe in love-at-first-sight.

JULIET:
Say then that thou dost not believe in air!
Or in the solid ground on which we tread!
Nay, love's a force of nature, can't be stopped;
The lightning waiteth not upon my thought
To thus endow it bright; it doth but light!

CONSTANCE:
Nay, love's a bond of servitude;
A trap that sly deceptors lay for fools –
Fools they use then throw away,
Or trade in like a lib'ry book
They've read, then lost, then found beneath the
bed
All coffee-stained and dust-bunnied,
All dog-eared, thumbed, and overdue.

JULIET:
Thou art one that loved and lost.

CONSTANCE:
Well. I will admit I had a crush –
Delayed post-adolescent fantasy.

JULIET:
Seek not to excuse thy one true love.

CONSTANCE:
No. I refuse to say that I felt love
For someone who did grind my mind to pulp,
And lined a gilded birdcage with the dust.
He played the parrot: I fed him great lines,
And he pooped on my head.

JULIET:
                                        Unrequited love.

CONSTANCE:
It certainly was unrequited:
I never pooped back. I could kick myself.

JULIET:
He crushed thy heart as 't'were a pomegranate
Underfoot and thou didst kiss that foot.

CONSTANCE: (*starting to give in*)
Yes.

JULIET:
        And doted on his every whim.

CONSTANCE:
Yes.

JULIET:
        And idolized him from the start.

CONSTANCE:
I loved him from the moment I first saw him
Across the crowded cafeteria.
He looked so dignified, and irritated.

I stood second in the line for lunch.
I saw him check his watch and pinch his nose.
"He has important things to do," I thought,
And so I offered up my place to him.
He thanked me in his cultivated voice,
And asked where one might find a decent cup
    of tea.
I told him I'd be glad to make him one,
And shared with him the last of my Velveeta.
He smiled as he ate my cheese.
I loved that man …

JULIET:
Tell heaven!

CONSTANCE: (*meekly to heaven*)
I loved Claude Night. Love.

JULIET:
                              Declaim!

CONSTANCE:
Love. Love! I love that shit, Claude Night!
Amour – at-first-sight, in plain view, a coup de
    foudre,
La vie en soir, amo, amas, amat!!!
There. I've said it. So what do I do now?

JULIET:
Impale thy cleavèd heart upon a sword!

CONSTANCE:
Yes, O yes!!! I wish I had the nerve
To do it right in front of everyone
While standing in the cafeteria line!
To play a swan song on my arteries,
Anoint the daily special with my veins!

JULIET: (*offering dagger*)
Stab thyself first, then will I stab mine!

CONSTANCE:
Thanks. That's very sweet of you, Juliet.
But not just now. I have to find the Author first;
Or else the Fool to lead me to the bard.

JULIET:
Author? Fool?

CONSTANCE:
               And Self. It is my quest,
And it means more to me than love or death.

JULIET:
What passion is of such ferocity?

CONSTANCE:
The one that killed the cat: curiosity.

JULIET:
I know the Author, Constantine.

CONSTANCE:
You do?

JULIET:
Ay. The Fool told me.

CONSTANCE:
Who is he? What's his name?

JULIET:
Wouldst love me if I told thee who it be?

CONSTANCE:
Until I pass into another world.

JULIET:
Mount unto my closet for a tryst.
I'll trade the name, and claim of thee one kiss.

CONSTANCE:
Okay.

    JULIET goes to exit.

CONSTANCE:
Hey, wait up!

JULIET:
I dare not risk discovery in thy company; we must
go severally. Dost thou espy yon boneyard?

CONSTANCE:
Yes, I see it.

JULIET:
My balcony lies three courtyards to the east of that
unhallowed ground.

CONSTANCE:
Why is it unhallowed?

JULIET:
For that the bones of actors, whores, and pedants
lie there buried and condemned.

    JULIET blows a kiss and exits.

CONSTANCE:
Thanks.

    *Exit CONSTANCE. Enter ROMEO, furtive, in JULIET's
    clothing.*

ROMEO: (*aside*)
I dare not take the front gate for my leave;
My father must not see my woman's weeds.

    Exit. Softly, from off.

ROMEO:
Constantine … it is I, Romiet …

ACT III

SCENE vi

The boneyard. A distant bell tolls midnight. A watchman cries from off, "Twelve o'clock and all is well." Enter CONSTANCE, *scared. Creepy night sounds: crows, distant cries …*

CONSTANCE:
(*singing tunelessly to herself to allay her fear*)
I never saw a ghost in my life, ghost in my life, ghost in my life; I never saw a ghost in my life, 'cause there's no such thing. I never saw a –

Suddenly, ghost sounds: wind, chains, smoke. A skeleton-faced GHOST *emerges through a trap door. He wears* CONSTANCE's *red toque with the pom-pom.* CONSTANCE *turns and sees him, and is terrified.*

CONSTANCE:
Holy Mary, Mother of God! –

GHOST:
A man told me he hadn't had a bite
In three days, so I bit him. I awoke
Today and shot an elephant in my
Pyjamas. How he got there, I know not.
I just flew in from Padua, and zounds,
Are my arms tired!

CONSTANCE:
Who are you?

GHOST:
Who are you-ou-ou?

CONSTANCE:
Where'd you get that hat?

GHOST:
A fo-o-ol's cap.

CONSTANCE:
Is this some kind of joke?

GHOST:
My stock in trade.

CONSTANCE:
A ghostly fool? A jester from the grave?
Are you – ? You couldn't be. What play is this?
Could you be … Yorick?!

GHOST:
                          Na-a-ay. You're it.

CONSTANCE:
You're it?

GHOST:
Alas, poor fool, you know me well.

CONSTANCE:
                          I do?
Don't speak in riddles, tell me what you mean.

GHOST:
I mean you script a woman, and a fool,
It's not a man you seek, the Manuscript …

CONSTANCE:
Do you know something of the Manuscript?!
Do you know who the Author is?

GHOST:
                          A lass.

CONSTANCE:
I know, "alas, alas poor Yorick," so?!
Who wrote this thing?

GHOST:
                          A beardless bard.

CONSTANCE:
                          A boy?

GHOST:
A lass!

CONSTANCE:
          Oh, here we go again, "alas"!
Who is the Author?

GHOST:
                          A Fool, a Fool.

CONSTANCE:
The Fool and the Author are one in the same?

GHOST:
Ha, ha, ha, ha.

CONSTANCE:
What's his name?!

GHOST:
Do not forget. This visitation
Is but to whet thy almost blunted purpose.
Beware of Tybalt.
He hath not a sense of humour.
Adieu, adieu, adieu. Remember me-e-e.

GHOST begins to sink back down the trap.

CONSTANCE:
No, wait! Don't go yet! Yorick!

GHOST:
                          Yo-o-u-u're it.

Exit GHOST. Enter TYBALT.

TYBALT:
Hermaphrodite!

CONSTANCE:
> Who, me? Oh, hi, Tybalt.

TYBALT:
> Greek boy! *The love I bear thee can afford*
> *No better term than this: thou art a villain.*

CONSTANCE:
> There must be some mistake. *Therefore, farewell.*

> *CONSTANCE tries to exit.*

TYBALT:
> *Boy, this shall not excuse the injuries*
> *That thou hast done me; therefore turn and draw.*

CONSTANCE:
> No, please! I haven't done anything!

TYBALT:
> *I am for you!*

> *He draws. Something like an anchovy hangs off the end of his sword. CONSTANCE recognizes it, and plucks it off.*

CONSTANCE:
> Good heavens, this is somebody's appendix ... (*mouthing the word*) mine! No. No, please don't hurt me, please!

TYBALT:
> A l'arme!

> *TYBALT tosses her a sword. She catches it.*

CONSTANCE:
> All right, then, come on! (*swishes her sword*) I trained in Cyprus, you know, come on. (*swish*) Hit me. (*thumping her chest*) Hit me right here.

> *TYBALT lunges. CONSTANCE yelps with fear and fends him off clumsily. Enter ROMEO in women's clothing.*

ROMEO:
> *Hold Tybalt! Good* Constantine*! Put up your swords!*

> *ROMEO comes between the combatants, raising his arms to stop them as in* Romeo and Juliet*; but here, TYBALT's sword, rather than skewering CONSTANCE under ROMEO's arm, gets caught in the flowing fabric of ROMEO's dress. CONSTANCE escapes as the two men struggle. ROMEO runs off. TYBALT looks about, swishes his sword, then runs off after CONSTANCE.*

ACT III

SCENE vii

> *JULIET's balcony and bedchamber. JULIET, still in ROMEO's clothing, waits for CONSTANCE.*

JULIET:
> Ay me.

CONSTANCE: (*from off below*)
> Juliet! Help!

> *JULIET takes a rope ladder from under the bed and throws it down.*

JULIET:
> Catch, love!

> *CONSTANCE struggles up and onto the balcony, still bearing the sword.*

CONSTANCE:
> Tell me the name!

JULIET:
> Give me my kiss!

> *CONSTANCE gives JULIET a chaste peck on the cheek.*

JULIET:
> Where's passion in thy curiosity?

CONSTANCE:
> My life's at stake.

JULIET:
> My heart's on fire.

> *Pause. CONSTANCE works up her nerve and kisses JULIET on the mouth. JULIET takes over. CONSTANCE breaks it off.*

CONSTANCE:
> Ahem. Now who's the Author?

JULIET:
> I did lie.

CONSTANCE:
> You little brat!

> *JULIET picks up CONSTANCE's sword, thrusts it into CONSTANCE's hands, and bares the upper portion of her own left breast.*

JULIET:
> Now wreak atonement here!
> Spear the lie e'en to its bubbling source!

> *JULIET grabs the tip of CONSTANCE's sword and tries to plunge it into her heart. CONSTANCE resists.*

CONSTANCE:

Hang on! There's no need to overreact!

CONSTANCE manages to wrest the sword from JULIET and tosses it over the balcony.

JULIET:

And I cannot rejoice upon thy sword,
I'll die upon my dagger, so!

JULIET takes a dagger and winds up to stab herself. CONSTANCE intervenes.

CONSTANCE:

No!

CONSTANCE wrests the dagger from JULIET, flings it over the balcony, and pins JULIET down.

CONSTANCE:

Now listen here. There's something you don't know.
For safety did I first secrete my sex.
I mean! – I'll have to trust you with the truth.
My name is Constance. I'm a woman.

JULIET:

Oh.

CONSTANCE:

That's right. So that's that.

JULIET:

And art thou of Cyprus?

CONSTANCE:

Not originally.

JULIET:

Then art thou of Lesbos?!

CONSTANCE:

What?! I've never been there in my life.

JULIET:

O most forbidden love of all!

CONSTANCE:

Oh no.

JULIET:

Unsanctified desire, more tragic far
Than any star-crossed love 'twixt boy and girl!

CONSTANCE:

Now wait.

JULIET:

Once more am I a virgin maid.
O take me to thine island's curvèd shore,
And lay me on the bosom of the sand;
There sing to me the psalm that Sappho wrote;
Her hymn to love will be our Song of Songs.

CONSTANCE:

I'm not up on Sappho.

JULIET:

Then we'll compose an epic of our own.

CONSTANCE:

But I'm not – you know – I'm not ... a lesbian. At all. That's just a rumour. I've never been involved with a woman.
Unless you count that one time in grade eight
When Ginnie Radclyffe did my portrait.
Her mother worked, and Ginnie was a cubist.
She said she had to have a detailed tour
Of my physique for authenticity.
Ginnie had such poignant hands and wrists.
But I never painted her.

JULIET:

She died.

CONSTANCE:

She's married now and can't recall a thing.

JULIET:

A portrait hangs unfinished in thy heart.

CONSTANCE:

I know I felt bereft. But that was then.

JULIET:

Make ready now to paint me in her stead.
So mix and frame the colours on this bed.

CONSTANCE:

I don't know how.

JULIET:

Be thou the mirror pool of my desire:
Reflect my love as thou dost ape my form.

CONSTANCE:

Thou wouldst distort the pool, thy looking glass,
With words of love like careless pebbles tossed;
The rippling waters tell a loving lie,
And show my face to thee as 't'were thine own.
Still waters would reflect an agèd crone.

JULIET:

More beauty in thy testament of years,
Than in the face of smooth and depthless youth.
Nay, lovelier by far, now that I see
The sculpting hand of time upon thy brow;
O look on me with eyes that looked on life
Before I e'er was born an infant blind.
O touch me with those hands that held thy quill
Before I learned to read and write my name.
And thus with every look and touch, entwine
My poor young thread into thy richer weave.

CONSTANCE:
Okay.

JULIET:
Tomorrow will they find one corpse entwined,
When, having loved each other perfectly,
Our deaths proclaim one night, eternity.

CONSTANCE:
Eternity ...

JULIET:
I have a vial of poison hidden here; (*concealed in her shirt*)
It will dispatch us with the morning lark.

CONSTANCE:
But for now, the nightingale doth sing.

JULIET leans down and CONSTANCE reaches into her shirt.

CONSTANCE:
What have we here?

CONSTANCE withdraws her hand from JULIET's shirt, holding a Manuscript page.

CONSTANCE:
Oh shit.

She unrolls the scroll and reads:

CONSTANCE:
"Thy demons rest not till they've eaten thee.
Get Desdemon and merge this trinity,
Or never live to see another Birthdy."
I forgot. It's my birthday today.

The warp effect begins. JULIET is terrified.

JULIET:
Constance!

CONSTANCE:
Hang on, Julie-e-et!

The warp ends, to reveal JULIET and CONSTANCE, huddled together, eyes closed, still on JULIET's bed. Nothing, apparently, has changed.

CONSTANCE:
It's all right.

They release one another and scan the room.

CONSTANCE:
False alarm.

They chuckle and lie back again as JULIET begins to rearrange the pillows on the bed. Suddenly she screams –

JULIET:
Ah-h-h-h-h-h-h-!!!

– and leaps back to reveal DESDEMONA, who rises: a phoenix from the pillows.

DESDEMONA:
'Tis strange, i'faith. 'Tis passing wondrous strange.

CONSTANCE:
Desdemona.

DESDEMONA:
O perjured pedant, *thou dost stone my heart.*

CONSTANCE: (*about to introduce JULIET*)
Desdemona, this is –

DESDEMONA takes up a pillow.

DESDEMONA:
Put out the light, and then put out the light.

DESDEMONA brings the pillow down on CONSTANCE's head.

CONSTANCE:
No! Help!!!

Muffled etc. ...

JULIET:
Hold!

DESDEMONA:
Thy fool's cap is a Turkish document,
And thou, base strumpet, hast seduced my lord!

DESDEMONA raises the pillow.

CONSTANCE:
No! No way, I swear!

The pillow comes down again. JULIET grabs another pillow and offers it to DESDEMONA.

JULIET:
Kill me in her stead!

DESDEMONA ignores JULIET.

DESDEMONA:
I saw thee fingering his very jewels!
A diamond necklace that would ransom kings!

Pillow up.

CONSTANCE:
Oh, that!

DESDEMONA:
Down strumpet!

JULIET hits DESDEMONA with the pillow, but DESDEMONA disarms her easily and knocks her flying.

CONSTANCE:
Kill me tomorrow!

DESDEMONA:
It is too late!

> *Pillow down.*

JULIET: (*exiting*)
Help! Murther!

> *CONSTANCE, her head still beneath the pillow, reaches under her shirt, yanks off the diamond necklace, and holds its broad golden clasp before DESDEMONA's eyes.*

DESDEMONA:
Aha! (*reading inscription*) "For gentle Desdemona, upon thy birthday, love Othello."

> *CONSTANCE's hands drop to the bed and go limp.*

DESDEMONA: (*smiling*)
Oh. It is my birthday today. I had forgot. (*to CONSTANCE*) I'm sorry. (*suddenly remembering*) Constance! (*Whips the pillow up.*)
Not dead? Not yet quite dead?

> *A beat, then CONSTANCE takes a huge gasp of air.*

CONSTANCE:
Happy birthday.

> *CONSTANCE takes the pillow from DESDEMONA and whacks her with it, knocking her down.*

TYBALT: (*off*)
Greek boy!

CONSTANCE:
Oh no, it's Tybalt. Pretend I'm dead, and tell Juliet to meet us at the crypt.

> *CONSTANCE lies back on the bed.*

DESDEMONA:
Who?

TYBALT: (*off*)
The worms line up to feast on thee!

CONSTANCE:
Juliet! The lady of the house, she was here a second ago.

DESDEMONA:
I saw no one, save a spindly boy.

> *TYBALT enters over the balcony, sword drawn. CONSTANCE plays dead.*

TYBALT:
Ha!

DESDEMONA: (*pointing to CONSTANCE*)
Dead! Quite dead!

TYBALT:
Well killed! I'll drag him to the charnel house.

DESDEMONA:
Sir, how might I know Juliet?

TYBALT:
She is a young and lovely sylph in flowing rose-hued silk.

> *Exit DESDEMONA. JULIET appears at the balcony in time to see TYBALT dragging CONSTANCE off.*

JULIET: (*aside*)
Constance dead? *Is it e'en so?*

> *Exit TYBALT with CONSTANCE. JULIET raises her dagger aloft.*

JULIET:
Then I defy you stars! Constance, *I will lie with thee tonight.*

> *Exit JULIET.*

ACT III

SCENE viii

> *Beneath CONSTANCE's balcony. Enter ROMEO, still in JULIET's clothing, with rope ladder. Enter DESDEMONA. She watches ROMEO toss one end of the rope ladder over a balustrade above, in an attempt to scale the wall to the balcony.*

DESDEMONA: (*aside*)
By Tybalt's own account, must this be Juliet.
Here is the rose-hued silk ...
But nowhere do I see the lovely sylph.
(*to ROMEO*) What ho, I have a message for you, Lady.

> *ROMEO sees DESDEMONA.*

ROMEO: (*aside*)
O she doth teach the torches to burn bright!

DESDEMONA:
Constance doth await us at the crypt, ma'am.

ROMEO:
I am no ma'am, but man, and worship thee.

DESDEMONA:
We'd make short work of thee in Cyprus, lad.

ACT III

SCENE ix

A crypt and the boneyard surrounding it. The crypt is eerily lit, and the boneyard that surrounds it is darker, à la silhouette. TYBALT arranges CONSTANCE upon a raised slab in the crypt.

TYBALT:
Lie thou there, inverted nature.

He starts to exit, pauses, then turns back.

If curiosity doth stay my leave,
It's of an wholesome scientific kind –
To take the measure of his member.

DESDEMONA, followed by ROMEO, enters the graveyard as TYBALT goes to remove CONSTANCE's long johns.

ROMEO: (*lying on a tombstone*)
Come lie with me upon this marble bed.

ROMEO's voice startles TYBALT away from CONSTANCE.

TYBALT:
I'd not be caught, mine hands upon his hose,
And of his self-same cloth thought to be cut.

Exit TYBALT into the graveyard, as DESDEMONA continues to search for the correct crypt. CONSTANCE sits up.

DESDEMONA:
"Blessed be the man that spares these stones. And cursed be he that moves my bones; William – "

TYBALT sees ROMEO through the gloom and approaches.

TYBALT:
What maiden corse lies fest'ring here for crows to peck?

ROMEO reaches up and pulls TYBALT toward him.

TYBALT:
Ha-ha! No corse but fresh, and laid out for the pecking.

TYBALT picks ROMEO up and carries him off, ardently. CONSTANCE resumes her death pose in response to the sound of someone entering. It is JULIET. She approaches CONSTANCE and raises her dagger, poised to slay herself.

JULIET:
O happy dagger!
This is thy sheath; there rust, and let me die.

JULIET starts her fatal upswing, but before she can stab herself:

CONSTANCE:
Juliet?

JULIET screams.

JULIET:
Not dead?

CONSTANCE shakes her head.

Not yet quite dead?

CONSTANCE:
Not one bit dead.

JULIET:
O Love! O resurrected Love, O Constance!

JULIET, overcome, embraces CONSTANCE, her dagger still in hand. DESDEMONA dashes into the crypt and draws her sword upon JULIET.

DESDEMONA:
Unhand the damsel, thou rapacious knave!

JULIET cowers against CONSTANCE as DESDEMONA rears back, about to lunge.

CONSTANCE:
Hold! Desdemona, this is Juliet, the young lady of the house ... Remember?

DESDEMONA:
Zounds! Doth no one in Verona sail straight?

CONSTANCE:
Juliet, this is Desdemona, an old friend of mine from Cyprus.

JULIET:
With friends like this, thou wantest not for foes.

DESDEMONA:
Dost thou dare impugn my honour, poppet?

JULIET:
Aye, and what if I durst?

DESDEMONA:
Then dare to die!

CONSTANCE:
Wait –

JULIET:
That do I dare any day for love!

DESDEMONA:
Ha.

JULIET:
I twice did nearly slay myself today
For love of her whom thou didst seek to kill.

DESDEMONA:

I love her better than thou canst devise,
For naught I did in hate, but all in honour.

JULIET:

Hateful honour!

DESDEMONA:

Dishonourable love!

JULIET:

'Tis I that Constance loveth best.

DESDEMONA:

Pish, come, Constance, let's hie home.

CONSTANCE:

Home.

JULIET:

Constance will not leave my side.

DESDEMONA:

She hath naught to live for here.

JULIET:

But everything for which to die.

DESDEMONA:

In Cyprus hath she that for which to kill.
(to CONSTANCE) Return with me to Cyprus; take
  this sword,
And dip it deep to drink Iago's gorge.

> *DESDEMONA puts the sword in CONSTANCE's*
> *hand.*

JULIET:

Remain! To one blade, we'll two hearts afix,
Then sail together 'cross the River Styx.

> *JULIET puts the dagger in CONSTANCE's other*
> *hand.*

DESDEMONA:

Nay, come and kill.

JULIET:

Nay, stay and die.

DESDEMONA:

Nay, come!

JULIET:

Nay, stay!

DESDEMONA:

Nay, kill!!

JULIET:

Nay, die!!

CONSTANCE:

Nay, nay!! – Nay. Just … nay … both of you. I've
had it with all the tragic tunnel vision around
here. You have no idea what – life is a hell of a
lot more complicated than you think! Life – real
life – is a big mess. Thank goodness. And every
answer spawns another question; and every question blossoms with a hundred different answers;
and if you're lucky you'll always feel somewhat
confused. Life is – ! … Life is …

A harmony of polar opposites,
With gorgeous mixed-up places in between,
Where inspiration steams up from a rich
Sargasso stew that's odd and flawed and full

Of gems and worn-out boots and sunken ships –
Desdemona, I thought you were different; I
thought you were my friend, I worshipped you.
But you're just like Othello – gullible and violent.
Juliet, if you really loved me, you wouldn't want
me to die. But you were more in love with death,
'cause death is easier to love. Never mind. I must
have been a monumental fool to think that I could
save you from yourselves … Fool …

DESDEMONA:

Nay, thou speakst wise.

JULIET:

                                        Aye, fools were never
  wise.

DESDEMONA:

Could any fool reveal, how we were wont to err?

JULIET:

Or get us to concede, what we will gladly swear?

CONSTANCE:

What's that?

DESDEMONA:

To live by questions, not by their solution.

JULIET:

To trade our certainties, for thy confusion.

CONSTANCE:

Do you really mean that?

> *JULIET and DESDEMONA nod "yes."*

GHOST: (*under the stage*)
Swear. Swear.

DESDEMONA & JULIET:

We swear.

CONSTANCE:

Then I was right about your plays. They were comedies after all, not tragedies. I was wrong about one
thing, though: I thought only a Wise Fool could
turn tragedy to comedy.

GHOST: (*below*)
Ha-ha-ha-ha-ha!

CONSTANCE:
Yorick.

GHOST:
Na-a-ay. You're it.

CONSTANCE:
I'm it? ... I'm it. *I'm* the Fool!

GHOST:
A lass.

CONSTANCE:
A lass!

GHOST:
A beardless bard.

CONSTANCE:
"The Fool and the Author are one and the same"...

GHOST:
Ha-ha-ha-ha-ha!

CONSTANCE:
That's me. I'm the Author!

A golden hand rises up through the surface of the slab upon which CONSTANCE lay. The hand holds a scrolled Manuscript page. CONSTANCE takes the page and unscrolls it.

CONSTANCE:
It says –
"For those who have the eyes to see:
Take care – for what you see, just might be thee."

She looks at DESDEMONA and JULIET.

"Where two plus one adds up to one, not three."
Goodnight Desdemona. Good morning Juliet.

DESDEMONA & JULIET:
Happy birthday, Constance.

The warp ensues. It is a choreographed transformation involving all the actors: the crypt and boneyard turn back into CONSTANCE's office at Queen's. During the transformation, the actors exit and enter with gold-wrapped boxes – birthday presents for CONSTANCE. Their costumes transform as well, until each actor wears an odd combination of her or his various costumes.

When the warp is over, CONSTANCE is alone in her office at Queen's. Both she and the office are precisely as they were at the onset of the first warp at the end of Act I: the phone receiver dangles by its cord, and CONSTANCE is leaning over with just her – hatless – head in the wastebasket. She straightens up and looks about her, a little disoriented. She tentatively touches herself as if to confirm her reality, bringing one hand up to her head. She feels her pen behind her ear, removes it, and looks at it. It has turned to solid gold, feather and all.

ACT III

THE EPILOGUE

Enter the CHORUS holding the GHOST's skeleton mask.

CHORUS:
The alchemy of ancient hieroglyphs
Has permeated the unconscious mind
Of Constance L. and manifested form,
Where there was once subconscious dreamy
    thought.
The best of friends and foes exist within,
Where archetypal shadows come to light
And doff their monster masks when we say
    "boo."
Where mingling and unmingling opposites
Performs a wondrous feat of alchemy,
And spins grey matter, into precious gold.

Lights and music. The company dances.

END

TOMSON HIGHWAY

(b. 1951)

In 1967, George Ryga's *The Ecstasy of Rita Joe* awoke theatre audiences to a new awareness of Aboriginal people and their situation in Canada. Rita, Jaimie, and David Joe were shown to be capable of joy, ambition, disappointment, rage: the whole gamut of thoughts and feelings that whites had always been deemed to have, but which Aboriginal characters, when they appeared onstage at all, were generally denied. But Ryga's Native characters are ultimately imprisoned by despair. Oppressed by a white society that refuses to see them as fully, autonomously human, Rita and Jaimie are doomed. The play reflects the vision of a white writer of conscience berating his own culture and bemoaning its victims. Rita herself, in the first production, was played by a white actress.

Two decades later, Tomson Highway appeared in the vanguard of a group of Aboriginal theatre artists ready to write and perform their own stories. They tell of oppression but also of hope, of tragedies but also of the ordinary daily pleasures and absurdities of life experienced from inside the skin of Aboriginal women and men. For the first time, the Canadian theatre heard Native voices telling Native stories. The voices are distinctly post-colonial, appropriating forms and styles from the dominant culture while incorporating traditional formal and spiritual elements of Aboriginal art and life. In Highway's *The Rez Sisters* and *Dry Lips Oughta Move to Kapuskasing*, the result is a brilliant theatrical synthesis bursting with vitality and speaking to Native and non-Native alike. "You feel as if you've been somewhere after one of these plays," writes critic Lucy Bashford, "as if you're still alive under the armour of twentieth-century life."

Highway's life spans two radically different worlds. Born on a trapline on the remote Brochet reserve in northern Manitoba, the eleventh of twelve children, he spoke only Cree until the age of six when he was sent south to residential school in The Pas. Later, he lived in white foster homes while attending a Winnipeg high school where he was the only Aboriginal student. Developing an interest in classical piano, he enrolled at the University of Manitoba and studied with music professor William Aide, who invited Highway to join his family for a sabbatical year in England. Highway spent 1972–73 touring England and the continent, immersing himself in European culture and civilization. Returning to Canada, he transferred to the University of Western Ontario in London, earning an honours degree in music and a B.A. in English (1975–76). Fast-tracked for a career as a concert pianist, Highway was brought up short by the poverty and alcoholism he saw other Aboriginal people suffering in the cities where he was playing Bartók and Chopin. Unable to reconcile the two worlds, he gave up music and worked for seven years with Native social service agencies in London and Toronto. While still in London he also became involved in James Reaney's play development workshops on *Wacousta* and *The Canadian Brothers*. He saw *The Donnellys*, too, and was struck by Reaney's use of myth, folklore, music, and poetry, and his evocation of a community – elements Highway would later incorporate into his own work.

In the early 1980s, now living in Toronto, Highway started writing theatre pieces for himself and his brother René, a professional dancer, in an attempt to combine Aboriginal life and spirituality with what he called his "high art" training. In 1983, he joined Native Earth Performing Arts, an Aboriginal theatre company founded the year before. He wrote and directed music as well as acting in a series of collective shows for Native Earth, and studied mask and clown techniques for dramatizing the traditional figure of the Trickster. From 1986–90, Highway served as the company's artistic director, nurturing an important group of Native Earth plays through development into production. Meanwhile, he had also begun workshopping a new play of his own with another Ontario company, De-ba-jeh-mu-jig Theatre on Manitoulin Island. In November 1986, Act IV Theatre Company and Native Earth Performing Arts presented *The Rez Sisters*, directed by Larry Lewis at the Native Canadian Centre in Toronto, marking a new era in Canadian theatre.

The Rez Sisters follows seven women on the fictional Wasaychigan Hill reserve on Manitoulin Island, better known as "Wasy" or "the rez," as they work, dream, compare notes on life, and make their way to Toronto to play THE BIGGEST BINGO IN THE WORLD. Pelajia Patchnose fantasizes about paving the dusty rez roads with her winnings. Philomena Moosetail would buy a new toilet, and Veronique St. Pierre, a stove to cook for her mentally disabled daughter. That daughter, Zhaboonigan, was raped by two white guys with a screwdriver. Marie-Adele Starblanket wants a little island with a picket fence for her fourteen kids. Manic Annie Cook and bisexual biker Emily Dictionary round out the group who are shadowed by a seagull – actually Nanabush, the Ojibway Trickster – played by a male dancer (René Highway in the original production). Only Zhaboonigan and Marie-Adele, who is dying of cancer, can see Nanabush and talk to him in Cree. Inspired in part by Michel Tremblay's *Les Belles-Soeurs* but lacking its bitterness, *The Rez Sisters* offers an earthy comic vision of a world in which suffering is a daily reality, but by no means the primary one, and in which sisterhood is very powerful. It won the Dora Mavor Moore award for best new play and received a Governor General's Literary Award nomination, had a triumphant cross-Canada tour, and went to the Edinburgh Festival in 1988. The play and its exciting production established Tomson Highway as a major theatrical talent, and Aboriginal theatre as a potent force on the Canadian scene.

Continuing his work with Native Earth, Highway wrote and played piano on *Aria* (1987), a solo show for Greenland Inuit actress Makka Kleist, further exploring the condition of Aboriginal women. In 1988, he collaborated with brother René on *New Song ... New Dance*, performing on piano as Weesageechik, the Cree Trickster, in a multimedia treatment of the traumas suffered by Aboriginal people displaced from their families and culture. *The Sage, the Dancer, and the Fool* (1989), co-created by Tomson, René, and Billy Merasty, looked at a day in the life of a Native man in the city. Once again the Trickster appears, this time adapting to contemporary urban realities in a show Highway described as a combination of Cirque du Soleil, dance theatre, and powwow.

Dry Lips Oughta Move to Kapuskasing (originally titled *The Rez Brothers*) also appeared in 1989, co-produced by Native Earth and Theatre Passe Muraille, and directed by Larry Lewis. It won the Floyd S. Chalmers Canadian Play Award, as well as Dora Mavor Moore awards for outstanding new play, best production, male lead (Graham Greene), and featured female (Doris Linklater). Following its first showing, Highway was given the Wang Festival Prize for contributions to the literary community. *Dry Lips* next played Winnipeg, then was remounted in 1991 by mega-producer David Mirvish at the National Arts Centre and in a major commercial production at Toronto's lavish Royal Alexandra Theatre. This was the most extravagant production of a Native play to date on any Canadian stage, and confirmation of Highway's mainstream success – although some people felt that bigger did not necessarily make it better.

The eagerly awaited third installment in the "rez" cycle did not appear until 2000, and then only in a student production at the University of Toronto. *Rose* is a large-cast musical set on the Wasaychigan Hill reserve in 1992, featuring many of the same characters as the first two plays. Emily Dictionary takes centre stage again along with some of her female biker pals, and Big Joey returns with plans to open a casino. Bob Rae, premier of Ontario at the time, makes an appearance in a land claims negotiation with band chief Rose, and violence against women is a featured theme once more. In 2004, *Ernestine Shuswap Gets Her Trout* was commissioned and premiered by Western Canada Theatre Company in Kamloops, British Columbia, telling the story of Prime Minister Wilfrid Laurier's 1910 visit to Kamloops, where he received a deputation of local Native chiefs who offered him an account of their concerns and mistreatment. Highway tells the story through four local women of the Shuswap, Okanagan, and Thompson nations. In typical Highway fashion, it's funny, playful, tragic, musical, and sublimely theatrical.

Highway has expressed frustration at the difficulty of getting his plays produced in Canada, in part, he believes, due to the "political correctness" of Canadian companies afraid to cast non-Aboriginal actors in his work. The Japanese, he points out, had no compunction about presenting an all-Japanese cast in the 2001 Tokyo premiere of *Dry Lips*. (See Highway's essay "Should Only Native Actors Have the Right to Play Native Roles?") A notable Canadian exception was Factory Theatre's 2011 revival of *The Rez Sisters*, using white, black, Asian, and Aboriginal performers.

Partly in response to these frustrations, Highway turned to writing fiction and had great success with his first novel, *Kiss of the Fur Queen* (1998). This semi-autobiographical, tragicomic tale follows two brothers from their birth on a trapline through the agonies of residential school to adult life as artists in the city, accompanied all the while by the Trickster. Subsequently, he published three bilingual children's books (in Cree and English), *Caribou Song* (2001), *Dragonfly Kites* (2002), and *Fox on the Ice* (2003). In 2010, Fifth House published Cree versions of *The Rez Sisters* (*Iskooniguni iskweewuk*) and *Dry Lips Oughta Move to Kapuskasing* (*Paasteewitoon Kaapooskaysing tageespichit*). Highway has received eight honorary doctorates as well as a National Aboriginal Achievement Award and the Order of Canada.

Dry Lips is a harsher, more complex, and ambitious play than either *The Rez Sisters* or *Rose*, examining the possibility of spiritual renewal for contemporary First Nations culture in a radical mélange of styles that combines broad comedy with brute tragedy. The rivalry between Big Joey and Zachary Jeremiah Keechigeesik for band funds to support their entrepreneurial projects – Joey's radio station and Zachary's bakery – suggests an economic approach to the reserve's malaise, and finds a comic echo in their sexual rivalry. The conflict between Simon Starblanket and Spooky Lacroix has higher stakes. Simon seeks nothing less than the return of traditional Native spirituality: the resurrection of old dance and drum rituals, and the recuperation of Nanabush. He reaches back to tradition through his engagement to Patsy Pegahmagahbow, stepdaughter of the last medicine woman on the reserve. Simon also wants to reach back through Dickie Bird Halked, whose grandfather was a great medicine man until the priest turned the people against him. But Dickie's uncle Spooky has embraced the religion of the priest, as has his mother, Black Lady Halked. Highway wouldn't seem to have much sympathy for the white man's religion in this battle for the Native soul, except that Spooky Lacroix himself was saved from the hell of alcoholism by Christianity. In the context of the play's central iconic event, that provides a potent argument.

Dry Lips actually features two such events. The first, in flashback, is the nightmarish birth of Dickie Bird in the bar with Kitty Wells wailing on the jukebox, his mother "drunk almost senseless," and his father, Big Joey, running away. Highway seems here to be directly confronting Native people with their own responsibility for their condition, although the play should also be read as a dramatization of some of the (literally) unspeakable consequences of the residential school system (see Wasserman, "God of the Whiteman!"). The result of the mother's drunkenness and the father's evasion is Dickie's fetal alcohol syndrome, made worse by Big Joey's denial of his paternity. Seventeen years later, we see Dickie driven over the edge by his spiritual crisis arising from Spooky's evangelism. The *tableau vivant* that ends the first act illustrates these relationships in a vivid theatrical moment that captures the stylistic audacity of the play. All this leads directly to the second iconic event, Dickie's horrible rape of Patsy, begotten by and enacted with the symbolically loaded crucifix, the phallic weapon with which patriarchal Christianity has ravaged Native culture. And once again Big Joey stands by and does nothing.

In the program for the original production, Highway included an epigraph from Native elder Lyle Longclaws: "before the healing can take place, the poison must first be exposed ..." The ellipses suggest an ongoing, incomplete process, and in *Dry Lips* the process of exposure is painful and ugly. Finally forced to account for his inactions, Big Joey blames Native women for taking "the fuckin' power away from us faster than the FBI [at Wounded Knee] ever did." His fear of women's power is reflected in the other men's frantic responses to the women's hockey team, especially comic chorus characters Pierre St. Pierre and Creature Nataways, and perhaps too in the grotesque male-fantasy forms Nanabush assumes in becoming the three women with their huge breasts, belly, and bum. The rape, the blame, the fear, the exaggerated sexuality all add up to misogyny. Robert Cushman, reviewing the Royal Alex production for the *Globe and Mail*, called *Dry Lips* "the most powerful play I have seen about misogyny." Other commentators, including a number of Aboriginal women, felt that the play itself was misogynist. Highway is appalled at that suggestion. "To me *Dry Lips* is about the return of God as a woman," he told *Toronto Life* magazine. "I wrote it as a hymn – of pain, yes – but a hymn to the beauty of women and the feminine energy that needs to come back into its own if this world is going to survive."

The figure of Nanabush is the most difficult element of the play to comprehend for a non-Aboriginal audience or reader. As Highway explains in his prefatory note, the Trickster, like the languages of Cree and Ojibway, is not bound by gender, so s/he tends to assume exaggerated or contradictory gendered characteristics. S/he is neither solemn nor distant like the central figures in Judeo-Christian theology, but rather clownish, earthy, and immediate. Native playwright and poet Daniel David Moses says, "The trickster is the embodiment of our sense of humour about the way we live our lives. It's a very central part of our attitude that things are funny even though horrible things happen." So Nanabush makes the poster of Marilyn Monroe fart when Dickie Bird tries to kill himself, and Nanabush as Jehovah in drag sits on a mock-heavenly toilet "nonchalantly filing his/her fingernails" as Zachary keens over the terrible wastefulness of Simon's death.

At the end of the play, everything is resolved and nothing is. If the dream-frame suggests that nothing that happened is real, what has been learned? What progress has been made? In another program note, Highway wrote that "dreams – and the dream-life – have traditionally been considered by Native society to be the greatest tool of instruction ..." Zachary awakens to a lesson in his Native language from his wife with the goddess's name and the "magical, silvery Nanabush laugh," to his beautiful laughing baby girl – and to *The Smurfs* on television. Creating a living harmony out of such contradictions is the challenge of Highway's provocative and exhilarating theatre.

Dry Lips Oughta Move to Kapuskasing

Tomson Highway

Dry Lips Oughta Move to Kapuskasing premiered at Theatre Passe Muraille in Toronto on April 21, 1989, produced by Theatre Passe Muraille and Native Earth Performing Arts, with the following cast:

NANABUSH (as the spirit of
GAZELLE NATAWAYS,
PATSY PEGAHMAGAHBOW,
BLACK LADY HALKED,
and HERA KEECHIGEESIK)   Doris Linklater
ZACHARY JEREMIAH KEECHIGEESIK Gary Farmer
BIG JOEY   Ben Cardinal
CREATURE NATAWAYS   Erroll Kinistino
DICKIE BIRD HALKED   Kennetch Charlette
PIERRE ST. PIERRE   Graham Greene
SPOOKY LACROIX   Ron Cook
SIMON STARBLANKET   Billy Merasty

Directed by Larry Lewis
Set and Costume Design by Brian Perchaluk
Lighting Design by Stephane Droege
Music Written & Performed by Carlos del Junco
Choreography by René Highway

CHARACTERS

NANABUSH (*as the spirit of GAZELLE
  NATAWAYS, PATSY PEGAHMAGAHBOW,
  BLACK LADY HALKED, and HERA
  KEECHIGEESIK*)
ZACHARY JEREMIAH KEECHIGEESIK,
 age forty-one
BIG JOEY, *age thirty-nine*
CREATURE NATAWAYS, *age thirty-nine*
DICKIE BIRD HALKED, *age seventeen*
PIERRE ST. PIERRE, *age fifty-three*
SPOOKY LACROIX, *age thirty-nine*

SIMON STARBLANKET, *age twenty*
HERA KEECHIGEESIK, *age thirty-nine*

SPOOKY LACROIX's baby, toward the end of Act Two, can and should be played by a doll wrapped in a blanket. But for greatest effect, ZACHARY's baby at the very end of the play should be played by a real baby, preferably about five months of age.

SCENE

The Wasaychigan Hill Indian Reserve, Manitoulin Island, Ontario. Between Saturday, February 3, 1990, 11:00 p.m., and Saturday, February 10, 1990, 11:00 a.m.

SET

The set for the original production of Dry Lips Oughta Move to Kapuskasing contained certain elements that I think are essential to the play.

First of all, it was designed on two levels, the lower of which was the domain of the "real" Wasaychigan Hill. This lower level contained, onstage left, BIG JOEY's living room and kitchen, with its kitchen counter at the back, and facing downstage, an old brown couch with a television set a few feet in front of it. This television set could be made to double as a smaller rock for the forest scenes. Stage right had SPOOKY LACROIX's kitchen, with its kitchen counter for which BIG JOEY's kitchen counter could double, and its table and chairs.

In front of all this was an open area, the floor of which was covered with Teflon, a material that looks like ice and on which one can actually skate, using real ice skates; this was the rink for the hockey-arena scenes. With lighting effects, this area could also be turned into "the forest" surrounding the village of Wasaychigan Hill, with its leafless winter trees. The only other essential element here was a large jutting rock beside which, for instance, **ZACHARY JEREMIAH KEECHIGEESIK** and **SIMON STARBLANKET** meet, and this rock could be made to glow at certain key points. **PIERRE**'s "little bootleg joint" in Act Two, with its "window," was also created with lighting effects.

The upper level of the set was almost exclusively the realm of **NANABUSH**. The principal element here was her perch, located in the very middle of this area. The perch was actually an old jukebox of a late 1960s or early '70s make, but it was semi-hidden throughout most of the play, so that it could be fully revealed as this fabulous jukebox only at those few times when it was needed; the effect sought after here is of this magical, mystical jukebox hanging in the night air, like a haunting and persistent memory, high up over the village of Wasaychigan Hill. Over and behind this perch was suspended a huge full moon whose glow came on, for the most part, only during the outdoor scenes, which all take place at nighttime. All other effects in this area were accomplished with lighting. The very front of this level, all along its edge, was also utilized as the "bleachers" area for the hockey arena scenes.

Easy access was provided between the lower and the upper levels of this set.

SOUND

The soundscape of Dry Lips Oughta Move to Kapuskasing was mostly provided by a musician playing, live, on harmonica, off to the side. It is as though the dreamscape of the play were laced all the way through with **ZACHARY JEREMIAH KEECHIGEESIK**'s "idealized" form of harmonica playing, permeated with a definite blues flavour. Although **ZACHARY** ideally should play his harmonica, and not too well, in those few scenes where it is called for, the sound of this harmonica is most effectively used to underline and highlight the many magical appearances of **NANABUSH** in her various guises.

LANGUAGE

Both Cree and Ojibway are used freely in this text for the reasons that these two languages, belonging to the same linguistic family, are very similar and also to the fact that the fictional reserve of

Wasaychigan Hill has a mixture of both Cree and Ojibway residents.

Note: Words and passages in Cree and Ojibway are translated in parentheses, except as noted.

PLAYWRIGHT'S NOTE ON NANABUSH

The dream world of North American Indian mythology is inhabited by the most fantastic creatures, beings, and events. Foremost among these beings is the "Trickster," as pivotal and important a figure in our world as Christ is in the realm of Christian mythology. "Weesageechak" in Cree, "Nanabush" in Ojibway, "Raven" in others, "Coyote" in still others, the Trickster goes by many names and many guises. In fact, he or she can assume any chosen guise. Essentially a comic, clownish sort of character, the Trickster role is to teach us about the nature and the meaning of existence on the planet Earth; he or she straddles the consciousness of man and that of God, the Great Spirit.

The most explicit distinguishing feature between the North American Indian languages and the European languages is that in Indian languages (e.g., Cree, Ojibway) there is no gender. Unlike English, French, German, etc., the male-female-neuter hierarchy is entirely absent from Cree, Ojibway, and other First Nation languages. Following this system of thought, the central hero figure from First Nation mythology – theology, if you will – is theoretically neither exclusively male nor exclusively female, or is both simultaneously. Therefore, where in The Rez Sisters Nanabush was male, in this play – "flip side" to The Rez Sisters – Nanabush is female.

Some say that Nanabush left this continent when the white man came. We believe he or she is still here among us – albeit a little the worse for wear and tear – having assumed other guises. Without the continued presence of this extraordinary figure, the core of Indian culture would be gone forever.

ACT ONE

The set for this first scene is the rather shabby and very messy living room and kitchen of the reserve house *BIG JOEY* and *GAZELLE NATAWAYS* currently share. Prominently displayed on one wall is a life-size pin-up poster of Marilyn Monroe. The remains of a party are obvious. On the worn-out old brown couch, with its back toward the entrance, lies *ZACHARY JEREMIAH KEECHIGEESIK*, a very handsome Indian man. He is naked, passed out. The first thing we see when the light comes up – a very small "spot," precisely focused – is *ZACHARY's* bare, naked bum. Then, from behind the couch, we see a woman's leg, sliding languorously into a nylon stocking and right over *ZACHARY's* bum. It is *NANABUSH*, as the spirit of *GAZELLE NATAWAYS*, dressing to leave. She eases herself luxuriously over the couch and over *ZACHARY's* bum and then reaches under *ZACHARY's* sleeping head, from where she gently pulls a gigantic pair of false, rubberized breasts. Then *NANABUSH / GAZELLE NATAWAYS* sashays over to the side of the couch, picks a giant hockey sweater up off the floor, and shimmies into it. The sweater has a huge, plunging neckline, with the capital letter W and the number 1 prominently sewn on. Then she sashays back to the couch and behind it. Pleasurably and mischievously, she leans over and plants a kiss on *ZACHARY's* bum, leaving behind a gorgeous, luminescent lipstick mark. The last thing she does before she leaves is turn the television on. This television sits facing the couch that *ZACHARY* lies on. *NANABUSH / GAZELLE* does not use her hand for this, though; instead, she turns the appliance on with one last bump of her voluptuous hips. Hockey Night in Canada comes on. The sound of this hockey game is on only slightly, so that we hear it as background "music" all the way through the coming scene. Then *NANABUSH / GAZELLE* exits, to sit on her perch on the upper level of the set. The only light left onstage is that coming from the television screen, giving off its eerie glow.

Beat.

The kitchen door bangs open, the kitchen light flashes on, and *BIG JOEY* and *CREATURE NATAWAYS* enter, *CREATURE* carrying a case of beer on his head. At first, they are oblivious to *ZACHARY's* presence. Also at about this time, the face of *DICKIE BIRD HALKED* emerges from the shadows at the "kitchen window." Silently, he watches the rest of the proceedings, taking a particular interest – even fascination – in the movements and behaviour of *BIG JOEY*.

BIG JOEY: (*calling out for GAZELLE who, of course, is not home*) Hey, bitch!

CREATURE: (*At regular intervals he bangs the beer case down on the kitchen counter, rips it open, pops bottles open, throws one to BIG JOEY, all noises that serve to punctuate the rat-a-tat rhythm of his frenetic speech.*) Batman oughta move to Kapuskasing, nah, Kap's too good for Batman, right, Big Joey? I tole you once I tole you twice he shouldna done it he shouldna done what he went and did, goddawful Batman Manitowabi the way he went and crossed that blue line with the puck, man, he's got the flippin' puck right in the palm of his flippin' hand and only a minute and a half to go he just about gave me the shits the way Batman Manitowabi went and crossed that blue line right in front of that brick shithouse of a white man why the hell did that brick shithouse of a white man have to be there ...

ZACHARY: (*talking in his sleep*) No!

CREATURE: Hey!

BIG JOEY raises a finger signalling CREATURE to shut up.

ZACHARY: I said no!

CREATURE: (*in a hoarse whisper*) That's not a TV kind of sound.

BIG JOEY: Shhh!

ZACHARY: ... goodness sakes, Hera, you just had a baby ...

CREATURE: That's a real-life kind of sound, right, Big Joey?

BIG JOEY and CREATURE slowly come over to the couch.

ZACHARY: ... women playing hockey... damn silliest thing I heard in my life ...

BIG JOEY: Well, well ...

CREATURE: Ho-leee! (*whispering*) Hey, what's that on his arse look like lip marks.

ZACHARY: ... Simon Starblanket, that's who's gonna help me with my bakery ...

CREATURE: He's stitchless, he's nude, he's gonna pneumonia ...

BIG JOEY: Shut up.

CREATURE: Get the camera. Chrissakes, take a picture. (*CREATURE scrambles for the Polaroid, which he finds under one end of the couch.*)

ZACHARY: ... Simon! (*jumps up*) What the?!

CREATURE: Surprise! (*camera flashes*)

ZACHARY: Put that damn thing away. What are you doing here! Where's my wife? Hera! (*He realizes he's naked, grabs a cast-iron frying pan and slaps it over his crotch, almost castrating himself in the process.*) Ooof!

BIG JOEY: (*smiling*) Over easy or sunny side up, Zachary Jeremiah Keechigeesik?

ZACHARY: Get outta my house.

CREATURE: This ain't your house. This is Big Joey's house, right, Big Joey?

BIG JOEY: Shut up.

ZACHARY: Creature Nataways. Get outta here. Gimme that camera.

CREATURE: Come and geeeet it! (*grabs ZACHARY's pants from the floor*)

ZACHARY: Cut it out. Gimme them goddamn pants.

CREATURE: (*singing*) Lipstick on your arsehole, tole da tale on you-hoo.

ZACHARY: What! (*straining to see his bum*) Oh lordy, lordy, lordy, gimme them pants. (*He tries to wipe the stain off.*)

CREATURE: Here doggy, doggy. Here poochie, poochie woof woof! (*ZACHARY grabs the pants. They rip almost completely in half. CREATURE yelps.*) Yip!

Momentary light up on NANABUSH / GAZELLE, up on her perch, as she gives a throaty laugh. BIG JOEY echoes this, CREATURE tittering away in the background.

ZACHARY: Hey, this is not my doing, Big Joey. (*As he clumsily puts on what's left of his pants, CREATURE manages to get in one more shot with the camera.*) We were just having a nice quiet drink over at Andy Manigitogan's when Gazelle Nataways shows up. She brought me over here to give me the recipe for her bannock apple pie, cuz, goodness sakes, Simon Starblanket was saying it's the best, that pie was selling like hotcakes at the bingo and he knows I'm tryna establish this reserve's first pie-making business gimme that camera.

BIG JOEY suddenly makes a lunge at ZACHARY but ZACHARY evades him.

CREATURE: (*in the background, like a little dog*) Yah, yah.

BIG JOEY: (*slowly stalking ZACHARY around the room*) You know, Zach, there's a whole lotta guys on this rez been slippin' my old lady the goods but there ain't but a handful been stupid enough to get caught by me.

He snaps his fingers and, as always, CREATURE obediently scurries over. He hands BIG JOEY the picture of ZACHARY naked on the couch. BIG JOEY shows the picture to ZACHARY, right up to his face.

BIG JOEY: Kinda em-bare-ass-in' for a hoity-toity educated community pillar like you, eh, Zach?

ZACHARY grabs for the picture but BIG JOEY snaps it away.

ZACHARY: What do you want?

BIG JOEY: What's this I hear about you tellin' the Chief I can wait for my radio station?

ZACHARY: (*As he proceeds around the room to collect and put on what he can find of his clothes, BIG JOEY and CREATURE follow him, obviously enjoying his predicament.*) I don't know where the hell you heard that from.

BIG JOEY: Yeah, right. Well, Lorraine Manigitogan had a word or two with Gazelle Nataways the other night. When you presented your initial proposal at the band office, you said: "Joe can wait. He's only got another three months left in the hockey season."

ZACHARY: I never said no such thing.

BIG JOEY: Bullshit.

ZACHARY: W-w-w-what I said was that employment at this bakery of mine would do nothing but add to those in such places as those down at the arena. I never mentioned your name once. And I said it only in passing reference to the fact ...

BIG JOEY: – that this radio idea of mine doesn't have as much long-term significance to the future of this community as this fancy bakery idea of yours, Mr. Pillsbury Doughboy, right?

ZACHARY: If that's what you heard, then you didn't hear it from Lorraine Manigitogan. You got it from Gazelle Nataways and you know yourself she's got a bone to pick with ...

BIG JOEY: You know, Zach, you and me, we work for the same cause, don't we?

ZACHARY: Never said otherwise.

BIG JOEY: We work for the betterment and the advancement of this community, don't we? And seeing as we're about the only two guys in this whole hellhole who's got the get-up-and-go to do something ...

ZACHARY: That's not exactly true, Joe. Take a look at Simon Starblanket...

BIG JOEY: ... we should be working together, not against. What do you say you simply postpone that proposal to the Band Council ...

ZACHARY: I'm sorry. Can't do that.

BIG JOEY: (*cornering ZACHARY*) Listen here, bud. You turned your back on me when everybody said I was responsible for that business in Espanola seventeen years ago and you said nothin'. I overlooked that. Never said nothin'.

> ZACHARY *remembers his undershorts and proceeds, with even greater desperation, to look for them, zeroing in on the couch and under it. BIG JOEY catches the drift and snaps his fingers, signalling CREATURE to look for the shorts under the couch. CREATURE jumps for the couch. Without missing a beat, BIG JOEY continues.*

BIG JOEY: You turned your back on me when you said you didn't want nothin' to do with me from that day on. I overlooked that. Never said nothin'. You gave me one hell of a slap in the face when your wife gave my Gazelle that kick in the belly. I overlooked that. Never said nothin'. (*CREATURE, having found the shorts among the junk under the couch just split seconds before ZACHARY does, throws them to BIG JOEY who holds them up to ZACHARY, smiling with satisfaction.*) That, however, was the last time ...

ZACHARY: That wasn't my fault, Joe. It's that witch woman of yours Gazelle Nataways provoked that fight between her and Hera and you know yourself Hera tried to come and sew up her belly again ...

BIG JOEY: Zach. I got ambition ...

ZACHARY: Yeah, right.

BIG JOEY: I aim to get that radio station off the ground, starting with them games down at my arena.

ZACHARY: Phhhh!

BIG JOEY: I aim to get a chain of them community radio stations, not only on this here island but beyond as well ...

ZACHARY: Dream on, Big Joey, dream on.

BIG JOEY: ... and I aim to prove this broadcasting of games among the folks is one sure way to get some pride –

ZACHARY: Bullshit! You're in it for yourself.

BIG JOEY: – some pride and dignity back, so you just get your ass on out of my house and you go tell that Chief your Band Council resolution can wait until next fiscal year or else ...

ZACHARY: I ain't doing no such thing, Joe, no way. Not when I'm this close.

BIG JOEY: (*eases himself down onto the couch, twirling the shorts with his forefinger*) ... or else I get my Gazelle Nataways to wash these skivvies of yours, put them in a box all nice and gussied up, your picture on top, show up at your doorstep and hand them over to your wife.

> *Silence.*

ZACHARY: (*quietly, to BIG JOEY*) Gimme them shorts. (*no answer; then to CREATURE*) Gimme them snapshots. (*still no response*)

BIG JOEY: (*dead calm*) Get out.

ZACHARY: (*seeing he can't win for the moment*) You may have won this time, Joe, but ...

BIG JOEY: (*like a steel trap*) Get out.

> *Silence. Finally ZACHARY exits, looking very humble. Seconds before ZACHARY's exit, DICKIE BIRD HALKED, to avoid being seen by ZACHARY, disappears from the "window." The moment ZACHARY is gone, CREATURE scurries to the kitchen door, shaking his fist in the direction of the already-departed ZACHARY.*

CREATURE: Damn rights! (*strutting like a cock, he turns to BIG JOEY*) Zachary Jeremiah Keechigeesik never shoulda come in your house, Big Joey. Thank God, Gazelle Nataways ain't my wife no more ... (*BIG JOEY merely has to throw a glance in CREATURE's direction to intimidate him. At once, CREATURE reverts to his usual nervous self.*) ... not really, she's yours now, right, Big Joey? It's you she's livin' with these days, not me.

BIG JOEY: (*sits on the couch with his beer, mostly ignoring CREATURE and watching the hockey game on television*) Don't make her my wife.

CREATURE: (*trying to clean up the mess around the couch, mostly shoving everything back under it*) I don't mind, Big Joey, I really don't. I tole you once I tole you twice she's yours now. It's like I loaned her to you, I don't mind. I can take it. We made a deal, remember? The night she threw the toaster at me and just about broke my skull, she told me: "I had enough, Creature Nataways, I had enough from you. I had your kids and I had your disease and that's all I ever want from you, I'm leavin'." And then she grabbed her suitcase and she grabbed the kids – no, she didn't even grab the kids, she grabbed the TV and she just sashayed herself over here. She left me. It's been four years now, Big Joey, I know, I know. Oh, it was hell, it was hell at first but you and me we're buddies since we're babies, right? So I thought it over for about a year... then one day I swallowed my pride and I got up off that chesterfield and I walked over here, I opened your door and I shook your hand and I said: "It's okay, Big Joey, it's okay." And then we went and played darts in Espanola except we kinda got sidetracked, remember, Big Joey, we ended up on that three-day bender?

BIG JOEY: Creature Nataways?

CREATURE: What?

BIG JOEY: You talk too much.

CREATURE: I tole you once I tole you twice I don't mind ...

> *PIERRE ST. PIERRE comes bursting in, in a state of great excitement.*

PIERRE: (*addressing the case of beer directly*) Hallelujah! Have you heard the news?

CREATURE: Pierre St. Pierre. Chrissakes, knock. You're walkin' into a civilized house.

PIERRE: The news. Have you heard the news?

CREATURE: I'll tell you a piece of news. Anyways, we come in the door and guess who ...

BIG JOEY: (*to CREATURE*) Sit down.

PIERRE: Gimme a beer.

CREATURE: (*to PIERRE*) Sit down.

PIERRE: Gimme a beer.

BIG JOEY: Give him a fuckin' beer.

> *But PIERRE has already grabbed, opened, and is drinking a beer.*

CREATURE: Have a beer.

PIERRE: (*talking out of the side of his mouth, as he continues drinking*) Tank you.

BIG JOEY: Talk.

PIERRE: (*putting his emptied bottle down triumphantly and grabbing another beer*) Toast me.

BIG JOEY: Spit it out.

CREATURE: Chrissakes.

PIERRE: Toast me.

CREATURE: Toast you? The hell for?

PIERRE: Shut up. Just toast me.

CREATUR & BIG JOEY: Toast.

PIERRE: Tank you. You just toasted "The Ref."

CREATURE: (*to PIERRE*) The ref? (*to BIG JOEY*) The what?

PIERRE: "The Ref"!

CREATURE: The ref of the what?

PIERRE: The ref. I'm gonna be the referee down at the arena. Big Joey's arena. The Wasaychigan Hill Hippodrome.

CREATURE: We already got a referee.

PIERRE: Yeah, but this here's different, this here's special.

BIG JOEY: I'd never hire a toothless old bootlegger like you.

PIERRE: They play their first game in just a coupla days. Against the Canoe Lake Bravettes. And I got six teeth left so you just keep your trap shut about my teeth.

CREATURE: The Canoe Lake Bravettes!

BIG JOEY: Who's "they"?

PIERRE: Haven't you heard?

BIG JOEY: Who's "they"?

PIERRE: I don't believe this.

BIG JOEY: Who's "they"?

PIERRE: I don't believe this. (*BIG JOEY bangs PIERRE on the head.*) Oww, you big bully! The Wasaychigan Hill Wailerettes, of course. I'm talkin' about the Wasy Wailerettes, who else geez.

CREATURE: The Wasy Wailerettes? Chrissakes ...

PIERRE: Dominique Ladouche, Black Lady Halked, that terrible Dictionary woman, Fluffy Sainte-Marie, Dry Lips Manigitogan, Leonarda Lee Starblanket, Annie Cook, June Bug McLeod, Big Bum Pegahmagahbow, all twenty-seven of 'em. Them women from right here on this reserve, a whole batch of 'em, they upped and they said: "Bullshit! Ain't nobody on the face of this earth's gonna tell us us women's got no business playin' hockey. That's bullshit!" That's what they said: "Bullshit!" So. They took matters into their own hands. And, holy shit la marde, I almost forgot to tell you my wife, Veronique St. Pierre, she went and made up her mind she's joinin' the Wasy

Wailerettes, only the other women wouldn't let her at first on account she never had no babies – cuz, you see, you gotta be pregnant or have piles and piles of babies to be a Wasy Wailerette – but my wife, she put her foot down and she says: "Zhaboonigan Peterson may be just my adopted daughter and she may be retarded as a doormat but she's still my baby." That's what she says to 'em. And she's on and they're playin' hockey and the Wasy Wailerettes, they're just a-rarin' to go, who woulda thunk it, huh?

CREATURE: Ho-leee!

PIERRE: God's truth ...

BIG JOEY: They never booked the ice.

PIERRE: Ha! Booked it through Gazelle Nataways. Sure as I'm alive and walkin' these treacherous icy roads.

BIG JOEY: Hang on.

PIERRE: ... God's truth in all its naked splendour. (*He pops open yet another beer.*) I kid you not, gentlemen, not for one slippery goddamn minute. Toast!

BIG JOEY: (*grabbing the bottle right out of PIERRE's mouth*) Where'd you sniff out all this crap?

PIERRE: From my wife, who else? My wife, Veronique St. Pierre, she told me. She says to me: "Pierre St. Pierre, you'll eat your shorts but I'm playin' hockey and I don't care what you say. Or think." And she left. No. First, she cleaned out my wallet, (*grabs his beer back from BIG JOEY's hand*) grabbed her big brown rosaries from off the wall. Then she left. Just slammed the door and left. Period. I just about ate my shorts. Toast!

CREATURE: Shouldn't we ... shouldn't we stop them?

PIERRE: Phhht! ... (*CREATURE just misses being spat on.*)

CREATURE: Ayoah!

PIERRE: ... Haven't seen hide nor hair of 'em since. Gone to Sudbury. Every single last one of 'em. Piled theirselves into seven cars and just took off. Them back wheels was squealin' and rattlin' like them little jinger bells. Just past tea time. Shoppin'. Hockey equipment. Phhht! (*Again, CREATURE just misses getting spat on.*)

CREATURE: Ayoah! It's enough to give you the shits every time he opens his mouth.

PIERRE: And they picked me. Referee.

BIG JOEY: And why you, may I ask?

PIERRE: (*faking humility*) Oh, I don't know. Somethin' about the referee here's too damn perschnickety. That drum-bangin' young whipperschnapper, Simon Starblanket, (*grabbing yet another beer*) he's got the rules all mixed up or somethin' like that, is what they says. They kinda wanna play it their own way. So they picked me. Toast me.

CREATURE: Toast.

PIERRE: To the ref.

CREATURE: To the ref.

PIERRE: Tank you. (*They both drink.*) Ahhh. (*pause; to BIG JOEY*) So. I want my skates.

CREATURE: Your skates?

PIERRE: My skates. I want 'em back.

CREATURE: The hell's he talkin' about now?

PIERRE: They're here. I know they're here. I loaned 'em to you, remember?

BIG JOEY: Run that by me again?

PIERRE: I loaned 'em to you. That Saturday night Gazelle Nataways came in that door with her TV and her suitcase and you and me were sittin' right there on that old chesterfield with Lalala Lacroix sittin' between us and I loaned you my skates in return for that forty-ouncer of rye and Gazelle Nataways plunked her TV down, marched right up to Lalala Lacroix, slapped her in the face, and chased her out the door. But we still had time to make the deal whereby if I wanted my skates back you'd give 'em back to me if I gave you back your forty-ouncer, right? Right. (*produces the bottle from under his coat*) Ta-da! Gimme my skates.

BIG JOEY: You sold them skates. They're mine.

PIERRE: Never you mind, Big Joey, never you mind, I want my skates. Take this. Go on. Take it.

BIG JOEY fishes one skate out from under the couch.

CREATURE: (*to himself; as he sits on the couch*) Women playin' hockey. Ho-leee!

BIG JOEY and PIERRE exchange bottle and skate.

PIERRE: Tank you. (*He makes a triumphant exit. BIG JOEY merely sits there and waits knowingly. Silence. Then PIERRE suddenly re-enters.*) There's only one. (*silence*) Well, where the hell's the other one? (*Silence. PIERRE nearly explodes with indignation.*) Gimme back my bottle! Where's the other one?

BIG JOEY: You got your skate. I got my bottle.

PIERRE: Don't talk backward at me. I'm your elder.

CREATURE: It's gone.

PIERRE: Huh?

CREATURE: Gone. The other skate's gone, right, Big Joey?

PIERRE: Gone? Where?

CREATURE: My wife, Gazelle Nataways.

PIERRE: ... your ex-wife ...

CREATURE: ... she threw it out the door two years ago the night Spooky Lacroix went crazy in the head and tried to come and rip Gazelle Nataways's door off for cheatin' at the bingo. Just about killed Spooky Lacroix, too, right, Big Joey?

PIERRE: So where's my other skate?

CREATURE: At Spooky Lacroix's, I guess.

PIERRE: Aw, shit la marde, youse guys don't play fair.

BIG JOEY: You go over to Spooky Lacroix's and you tell him I told you you could have your skate back.

PIERRE: No way, José. Spooky Lacroix's gonna preach at me.

BIG JOEY: Preach back.

PIERRE: You come with me. You used to be friends with Spooky Lacroix. You talk to Spooky Lacroix. Spooky Lacroix likes you.

BIG JOEY: He likes you, too.

PIERRE: Yeah, but he likes you better. Oh, shit la marde! (takes another beer out of the case) And I almost forgot to tell you they decided to make Gazelle Nataways captain of the Wasy Wailerettes. I mean, she kind of ... decided on her own, if you know what I mean.

BIG JOEY: Spooky Lacroix's waitin' for you.

PIERRE: How do you know?

BIG JOEY: God told me.

Pause. PIERRE actually wonders to himself. Then:

PIERRE: Aw, bullshit. (exits)

Silence. Then BIG JOEY and CREATURE look at each other, break down, and laugh themselves into prolonged hysterical fits. After a while, they calm down and come to a dead stop. They sit and think. They look at the hockey game on the television. Then, dead serious, they turn to each other.

CREATURE: Women ... Gazelle Nataways ... hockey? Ho-leee ...

BIG JOEY: (still holding PIERRE's bottle of whisky) Chrissakes ...

Fade-out.

From this darkness emerges the sound of SPOOKY LACROIX's voice, singing with great emotion. As he sings, the lights fade in on his kitchen, where DICKIE BIRD HALKED is sitting across the table from SPOOKY LACROIX. DICKIE BIRD is scribbling on a piece of paper with a pencil. SPOOKY is knitting pale-blue baby booties. A Bible sits on the table to the left of SPOOKY, a knitting pattern to his right. The place is covered with knitted doodads: knitted doilies, a tea cozy, a tacky picture of The Last Supper with knitted frame and, on the wall, as subtly conspicuous as possible, a crucifix with pale-blue knitted baby booties covering each of its four extremities. Throughout this scene, SPOOKY periodically consults the knitting pattern, wearing tiny little reading glasses, perched "just so" on the end of his nose. He knits with great difficulty and, therefore, with great concentration, sometimes, in moments of excitement, getting the Bible and the knitting pattern mixed up with each other. He has tremendous difficulty getting the "disturbed" DICKIE BIRD to sit still and pay attention.

SPOOKY: (singing) Everybody oughta know. Everybody oughta know. Who Jesus is. (speaking) This is it. This is the end. Igwani eeweepoonaskeewuk. ("The end of the world is at hand.") Says right here in the book. Very, very, very important to read the book. If you want the Lord to come into your life, Dickie Bird Halked, you've got to read the book. Not much time left. Yessiree. 1990. The last year. This will be the last year of our lives. Clear as a picture. The end of the world is here. At last. About time, too, with the world going crazy, people shooting, killing each other left, right, and centre. Jet planes full of people crashing into the bushes, lakes turning black, fish choking to death. Terrible. Terrible.

DICKIE BIRD shoves a note he's been scribbling over to SPOOKY.

SPOOKY: What's this? (reads with some difficulty) "How ... do ... you ... make ... babies!" (shocked) Dickie Bird Halked! At your age? Surely. Anyway. That young Starblanket boy who went and shot himself. Right here. Right in the einsteins. Bleeding from the belly, all this white mushy stuff come oozing out. Yuch! Brrr! I guess there's just nothing better to do for the young people on this reserve these days than go around shooting their einsteins out from inside their bellies. But the Lord has had enough. He's sick of it. No more, he says, no more. This is it.

DICKIE BIRD shoves another note over. SPOOKY pauses to read.

SPOOKY: Why, me and Lalala, we're married. And we're gonna have a baby. Period. Now. When the world comes to an end? The sky will open up. The clouds will part. And the Lord will come down in a holy vapour. And only those who are born-again Christian will go with Him when He goes back up. And the rest? You know what's gonna happen to the rest? They will die. Big Joey, for instance. They will go to hell and they will burn for their wicked, whorish ways. But we will be taken up into the clouds to spend eternity surrounded by the wondrous and the mystical glory of God. Clear as a picture, Dickie Bird Halked, clear as a picture. So I'm telling you right now, you've got to read the book. Very, very, very important.

DICKIE BIRD shoves a third note over to SPOOKY. SPOOKY reads and finishes.

SPOOKY: Why, Wellington Halked's your father, Dickie Bird Halked. Don't you be asking questions like that. My sister, Black Lady Halked, that's your mother. Right? And because Wellington Halked is married to Black Lady Halked, he is your father. And don't you ever let no one tell you different.

Blackout.

From the darkness of the theatre emerges the magical flickering of a luminescent powwow dancing bustle. As it moves gradually toward the downstage area, a second – and larger – bustle appears on the upper level of the set, also flickering magically and moving about. The two bustles "play" with each other, almost affectionately, looking like two giant fireflies. The smaller bustle finally reaches the downstage area and from behind it emerges the face of SIMON STARBLANKET. He is dancing and chanting in a forest made of light and shadows. The larger bustle remains on the upper level; behind it is the entire person of NANABUSH as the spirit of PATSY PEGAHMAGAHBOW, a vivacious young girl of eighteen with a very big bum (i.e., an oversized prosthetic bum). From this level, NANABUSH / PATSY watches and "plays" with the proceedings on the lower level. The giant full moon is in full bloom behind her. From the very beginning of all this, and in counterpoint to SIMON's chanting, also emerges the sound of someone playing a harmonica, a sad, mournful tune. It is ZACHARY JEREMIAH KEECHIGEESIK, stuck in the bush in his embarrassing state, playing his heart out. Then the harmonica stops and, from the darkness, we hear ZACHARY's voice.

ZACHARY: Hey.

SIMON hears this, looks behind, but sees nothing and continues his chanting and dancing. SIMON chants and dances as though he were desperately trying to find the right chant and dance.

ZACHARY: Pssst!

SIMON: Awinuk awa! (*"Who's this?"*)

ZACHARY: (*in a hoarse whisper*) Simon Starblanket.

SIMON: Neee, Zachary Jeremiah Keechigeesik. Awus! (*"Go away!"*) Katha peeweestatooweemin. (*"Don't come bothering me [with your words]."*)

Finally, ZACHARY emerges from the shadows and from behind a large rock, carrying his harmonica in one hand and holding his torn pants together as best he can with the other. SIMON ignores him and continues with his chanting and dancing.

ZACHARY: W-w-w-what's it cost to get one of them dough-making machines?

SIMON: (*not quite believing his ears*) What?

ZACHARY: Them dough-making machines. What's it cost to buy one of them?

SIMON: A Hobart?

ZACHARY: A what?

SIMON: Hobart. H-O-B-A-R-T. Hobart.

ZACHARY: (*to himself*) Hobart. Hmmm.

SIMON: (*amused at the rather funny-looking ZACHARY*) Neee, machi ma-a, (*"Oh you, but naturally,"*) Westinghouse for refrigerators, Kellogg's for corn flakes igwa (*"and"*) Hobart for dough-making machines. Kinsitootawin na? (*"Get it?"*) Brand name. Except we used to call it "the pig" because it had this ... piggish kind of motion to it. But never mind. Awus. Don't bother me.

ZACHARY: What's it cost to get this ... pig?

SIMON: (*laughing*) Neee, Zachary Jeremiah here you are, one of Wasy's most respected citizens, standing in the middle of the bush on a Saturday night in February freezing your buns off and you want to know how much a pig costs?

ZACHARY: (*vehemently*) I promised Hera I'd have all this information by tonight we were supposed to sit down and discuss the budget for this damn bakery tonight and here I went and messed it all up thank God I ran into you because now you're the only person left on this whole reserve who might have the figures I need what's this damn dough-making machine cost, come on now, tell me!

SIMON: (*a little cowed*) Neee, about four thousand bucks. Maybe five.

ZACHARY: You don't know for sure? But you worked there.

SIMON: I was only the dishwasher, Zachary Jeremiah, I didn't own the place. Mama Louisa was a poor woman. She had really old equipment, most of which she dragged over herself all the way from Italy after the Second World War. It wouldn't cost the same today.

ZACHARY: Five thousand dollars for a Mobart, hmmm ...

SIMON: Hobart.

ZACHARY: I wish I had a piece of paper to write all this down, sheesh. You got a piece of paper on you?

SIMON: No. Just ... this. (*holding the dancing bustle up*) Why are you holding yourself like that?

ZACHARY: I was ... standing on the road down by Andy Manigitogan's place when this car came by and wooof! My pants ripped. Ripped right down the middle. And my shorts, well, they just ... took off. How do you like that, eh?

SIMON: Nope. I don't like it. Neee, awus. Kigithaskin. (*"You're lying to me."*)

ZACHARY: W-w-w-why would I pull your leg for? I don't really mind it except it is damn cold out here.

At this point, NANABUSH / PATSY, on the upper level, scurries closer to get a better look, her giant powwow dancing bustle flickering magically in the half-light. SIMON's attention is momentarily pulled away by this fleeting vision.

SIMON: Hey! Did you see that?

But ZACHARY, too caught up with his own dilemma, does not notice.

ZACHARY: I'm very, very upset right now ...

SIMON: ... I thought I just saw Patsy Pegahma-gahbow ... with this ...

ZACHARY: (*looks, perplexed, in the direction SIMON indicates*) ... do you think ... my two ordinary convection ovens ...

SIMON: (*calling out*) Patsy? ... (*Pause. Slowly, he turns back to ZACHARY.*) ... like ... she made this for me, eh? (*referring to the bustle*) She and her stepmother,

Rosie Kakapetum, back in September, after my mother's funeral. Well, I was out here thinking, if this ... like, if this ... dance didn't come to me real natural, like from deep inside of me, then I was gonna burn it. (*referring to the bustle*) Right here on this spot. Cuz then ... it doesn't mean anything real to me, does it? Like, it's false ... it's driving me crazy, this dream where Indian people are just dropping off like flies ...

NANABUSH / PATSY begins to "play" with the two men, almost as if, with the help of the winter night's magic and the power of the full moon, she were weaving a spell around SIMON and ZACHARY.

ZACHARY: (*singing softly to himself*) Hot cross buns. Hot cross buns. One a penny, two a penny, hot cross buns ...

SIMON: ... something has to be done ...

ZACHARY: (*speaking*) ... strawberry pies ...

SIMON: ... in this dream ...

ZACHARY: ... so fresh and flaky they fairly bubble over with the cream from the very breast of Mother Nature herself ...

SIMON: ... the drum has to come back, mistigwuskeek (*"the drum"*) ...

ZACHARY: ... bran muffins, cherry tarts ...

SIMON: ... the medicine, the power, this ... (*holding the bustle up in the air*)

ZACHARY: ... butter tarts ...

SIMON: ... has to come back. We've got to learn to dance again.

ZACHARY: ... tarts tarts tarts upside-down cakes cakes cakes and not to forget, no, never, ever to forget that Black Forest cake ...

SIMON: ... Patsy Pegahmagahbow ...

ZACHARY: ... cherries jubilee ...

SIMON: ... her stepmother, Rosie Kakapetum, the medicine woman ...

ZACHARY: ... lemon meringue pie ...

SIMON: ... the power ...

ZACHARY: ... baked Alaska ...

SIMON: ... Nanabush! ...

ZACHARY: (*then suddenly, with bitterness*) Gazelle Nataways, K'skanagoos! (*"The female dog!"*)

All of a sudden, from the darkness of the winter night, emerges a strange, eerie sound; whether it is wolves howling or women wailing, we are

not sure at first. And whether this sound comes from somewhere deep in the forest, from the full moon or where, we are not certain. But there is definitely a "spirit" in the air. The sound of this wailing is undercut by the sound of rocks hitting boards, or the sides of houses, echoing, as in a vast empty chamber. Gradually, as SIMON speaks, ZACHARY – filled with confusing emotion as he is – takes out his harmonica, sits down on the large rock, and begins to play a sad, mournful melody, tinged, as always, with a touch of the blues.

SIMON: ... I have my arms around this rock, this large black rock sticking out of the ground, right here on this spot. And then I hear this baby crying, from inside this rock. The baby is crying out my name. As if I am somehow responsible for it being caught inside that rock. I can't move. My arms, my whole body, stuck to this rock. Then this ... eagle ... lands beside me, right over there. But this bird has three faces, three women. And the eagle says to me: "The baby is crying, my grandchild is crying to hear the drum again." (*NANABUSH / PATSY, her face surrounded by the brilliant feathers of her bustle, so that she looks like some fantastic, mysterious bird, begins to wail, her voice weaving in and out of the other wailing voices. As SIMON continues to speak, the wailing begins to fade.*) Then the eagle is gone and the rock cracks and this mass of flesh, covered with veins and blood, comes oozing out and a woman's voice somewhere is singing something about angels and God and angels and God ...

The wailing has now faded into complete silence. ZACHARY finally rises from his seat on the rock.

ZACHARY: ... I dreamt I woke up at Gazelle Nataways's place with no shorts on. And I got this nagging suspicion them shorts are still over there. If you could just go on over there now ... I couldn't have been over there. I mean, there's my wife, Hera. And there's my bakery. And this bakery could do a lot for the Indian people. Economic development. Jobs. Bread. Apple pie. So you see, there's an awful lot that's hanging on them shorts. This is a good chance for you to do something for your people, Simon, if you know what I mean ...

SIMON: I'm the one who has to bring the drum back. And it's Patsy's medicine power, that stuff she's learning from her stepmother, Rosie Kakapetum, that ... helps me ...

ZACHARY: I go walking into my house with no underwear, pants ripped right down the middle, not a shred of budget in sight and wooof! ...

PIERRE ST. PIERRE comes bursting in on the two men with his one skate in hand, taking them completely by surprise. NANABUSH / PATSY disappears.

ZACHARY: Pierre St. Pierre! Just the man ...

PIERRE: No time. No time. Lalala Lacroix's having a baby any minute now so I gotta get over to Spook's before she pops.

SIMON: I can go get Rosie Kakapetum.

PIERRE: Too old. Too old. She can't be on the team.

SIMON: Neee, what team? Rosie Kakapetum's the last midwife left in Wasy, Pierre St. Pierre, of course she can't be on a team.

ZACHARY: (*to PIERRE*) You know that greasy shit-brown chesterfield over at Gazelle Nataways's?

SIMON: (*to ZACHARY*) Mind you, if there was a team of midwives, chee-i? ("*eh!*") Wha!

PIERRE: Gazelle Nataways? Hallelujah, haven't you heard the news?

ZACHARY: What? ... you mean ... it's out already?

PIERRE: All up and down Wasaychigan Hill –

ZACHARY: (*thoughtfully, to himself, as it dawns on him*) The whole place knows.

PIERRE: – clean across Manitoulin Island and right to the outskirts of Sudbury ...

ZACHARY: Lordy, lordy, lordy ...

PIERRE: Gazelle Nataways, Dominique Ladouche, Black Lady Halked, that terrible Dictionary woman, Fluffy Sainte-Marie, Dry Lips Manigitogan, Leonarda Lee Starblanket, Annie Cook, June Bug McLeod, Big Bum Pegahmagahbow –

SIMON: Patsy Pegahmagahbow. Get it straight.

PIERRE: Quiet! I'm not finished ... all twenty-seven of 'em ...

SIMON: Neee, Zachary Jeremiah, your goose is cooked.

PIERRE: Phhht! Cooked and burnt right down to a nice crispy pitch-black cinder because your wife, Hera Keechigeesik, is in on it, too.

ZACHARY, reeling from the horror of it all, finally sits back down on the rock.

SIMON: Patsy Pegahmagahbow is pregnant, Pierre St. Pierre. She can't go running around all over Manitoulin Island with a belly that's getting bigger by the –

PIERRE: Aw, they're all pregnant, them women, or have piles and piles of babies and I'll be right smack dab in the middle of it all just a-blowin' my whistle and a-throwin' that dirty little black thingie around ...

ZACHARY: (*rising from the rock*) Now you listen here, Pierre St. Pierre. I may have lost my shorts under Gazelle Nataways's greasy shit-brown chesterfield not one hour ago and may have lost my entire life, not to mention my bakery, as a result of that one very foolish mistake but I'll have you know that my shorts, they are clean as a whistle, I change them every day, my favourite colour is light blue, and black and crusted with shit my shorts most certainly are not!

SIMON: (*surprised and thrilled at ZACHARY's renewed "fighting" spirit*) Wha!

PIERRE: Whoa! Easy, Zachary Jeremiah, easy there. Not one stitch of your shorts has anything whatsoever to do with the revolution.

SIMON: Pierre St. Pierre, what revolution are you wheezing and snorting on about!

PIERRE: The puck. I'm talkin' about the puck.

ZACHARY: The puck?

SIMON: The puck?

PIERRE: Yes, the puck. The puck, the puck, the puck, and nothin' but the goddamn puck they're playin' hockey, them women from right here on this reserve, they're playin' hockey and nothin', includin' Zachary Jeremiah Keechigeesik's bright crispy undershorts, is gonna stop 'em.

SIMON: Women playing hockey. Neee, watstagatch! (*"Good grief!"*)

PIERRE: "Nee, watstagatch" is right because they're in Sudbury, as I speak, shoppin' for hockey equipment, and I'm the referee! Outta my way! Or the Lacroixs will pop before I get there. (*He begins to exit.*)

ZACHARY: Pierre St. Pierre, get me my shorts or I'll report your bootleg joint to the police.

PIERRE: No time. No time. (*exits*)

ZACHARY: (*calling out*) Did Hera go to Sudbury, too? (*But PIERRE is gone.*)

SIMON: (*thoughtfully to himself, as he catches another glimpse of NANABUSH / PATSY and her bustle*) ... rocks hitting boards ...

ZACHARY: (*to himself*) What in God's name is happening to Wasaychigan Hill ...

SIMON: ... women wailing ...

ZACHARY: (*with even greater urgency*) Do you think those two ordinary convection ovens are gonna do

the job or should I get one of them great big pizza ovens right away?

SIMON: ... pucks ...

ZACHARY: Simon, I'm desperate!

SIMON: (*finally snapping out of his speculation and looking straight into ZACHARY's face*) Neee, Zachary Jeremiah. Okay. Goes like this. (*very quickly*) It depends on what you're gonna bake, eh? Like if you're gonna bake bread and, like, lots of it, you're gonna need one of them great big ovens but if you're gonna bake just muffins –

ZACHARY: – muffins, nah, not just muffins –

SIMON: – then all you need is one of them ordinary little ovens but, like I say, I was only the dishwasher ...

ZACHARY: How many employees were there in your bakery?

SIMON: ... it depends on how big a community you're gonna serve, Zachary Jeremiah –

ZACHARY: – nah, Wasy, just Wasy, to start with –

SIMON: – like, we had five, one to make the dough – like, mix the flour and the water and the yeast and all that – like, this guy had to be at work by six a.m., that's gonna be hard here in Wasy, Zachary Jeremiah, I'm telling you that right now –

ZACHARY: – nah, I can do that myself, no problem –

SIMON: – then we had three others to roll the dough and knead and twist and punch and pound it on this great big wooden table –

ZACHARY: – I'm gonna need a great big wooden table?

SIMON: Hardwood, Zachary Jeremiah, not softwood. And then one to actually bake the loaves, like, we had these long wooden paddles, eh?

ZACHARY: ... paddles ...

SIMON: ... yeah, paddles, Zachary Jeremiah, real long ones. It was kinda neat, actually ...

ZACHARY: ... go on, go on ...

SIMON: Listen here, Zachary Jeremiah, I'm going to Sudbury next Saturday, okay? And if you wanna come along, I can take you straight to Mama Louisa's Pasticerria myself. I'll introduce you to the crusty old girl and you can take a good long look at her rubbery old Hobart, how's that? You can even touch it if you want, neee ...

ZACHARY: Really?

SIMON: Me? I'm asking Patsy Pegahmagahbow to marry me ...

ZACHARY: ... Simon, Simon ...

SIMON: ... and we're gonna hang two thousand of these things (*referring to his dancing bustle*) all over Manitoulin Island, me and Patsy and our baby. And me and Patsy and our baby and this Nanabush character, we're gonna be dancing up and down Wasaychigan Hill like nobody's business cuz I'm gonna go out there and I'm gonna bring that drum back if it kills me.

ZACHARY: (*pause; then quietly*) Get me a safety pin.

SIMON: (*pause*) Neee, okay. And you, Zachary Jeremiah Keechigeesik, you're gonna see a Hobart such as you have never seen ever before in your entire life!

SIMON & ZACHARY: (*smiling, almost laughing at each other*) Neee ...

Blackout.

*Lights come up on the upper level, where we see this bizarre vision of **NANABUSH**, now in the guise of **BLACK LADY HALKED**, nine months pregnant (i.e., wearing a huge, outsized prosthetic belly). Over this, she wears a maternity gown and, pacing the floor slowly, holds a huge string of rosary beads. She recites the rosary quietly to herself. She is also drinking a beer and, obviously, is a little unsteady on her feet because of this.*

*Fade-in on the lower level into **SPOOKY LACROIX's** kitchen. **DICKIE BIRD HALKED** is on his knees, praying fervently to this surrealistic, miraculous vision of the Madonna (i.e., his own mother, which he actually sees inside his own mind). Oblivious to all this, **SPOOKY LACROIX** sits at his table, still knitting his baby booties and preaching away.*

SPOOKY: Dickie Bird Halked? I want you to come to heaven with me. I insist. But before you do that, you take one of them courses in sign language, help me prepare this reserve for the Lord. Can't you just see yourself, standing on that podium in the Wasaychigan Hill Hippodrome, talking sign language to the people? Talking about the Lord and how close we are to the end? I could take a break. And these poor people with their meaningless, useless –

PIERRE ST. PIERRE comes bursting in and marches right up to SPOOKY. The vision of NANABUSH / BLACK LADY HALKED disappears.

PIERRE: All right. Hand it over.

SPOOKY: (*startled out of his wits*) Pierre St. Pierre! You went and mixed up my booty!

PIERRE: I know it's here somewhere.

SPOOKY: Whatever it is you're looking for, you're not getting it until you bring the Lord into your life.

PIERRE: My skate. Gimme my skate.

SPOOKY: I don't have no skate. Now listen to me.

PIERRE: My skate. The skate Gazelle Nataways threw at you and just about killed you.

SPOOKY: What the hell are you gonna do with a skate at this hour of the night?

PIERRE: Haven't you heard the news?

SPOOKY: (*pauses to think*) No. I haven't heard any news.

DICKIE BIRD gets up and starts to wander around the kitchen. He looks around at random, first out the window, as if to see who has been chanting, then, eventually, he zeroes in on the crucifix on the wall and stands there looking at it. Finally, he takes it off the wall and plays with its cute little booties.

PIERRE: The women. I'm gonna be right smack dab in the middle of it all. The revolution. Right here in Wasaychigan Hill.

SPOOKY: The Chief or the priest. Which one are they gonna revolution?

PIERRE: No, no, no. Dominique Ladouche, Black Lady Halked, that terrible Dictionary woman, that witch Gazelle Nataways, Fluffy Sainte-Marie, Dry Lips Manigitogan, Leonarda Lee Starblanket, Annie Cook, June Bug McLeod, Big Bum Pegahmagahbow, all twenty-seven of 'em. Even my wife, Veronique St. Pierre, she'll be right smack dab in the middle of it all. Defence.

SPOOKY: Defence? The Americans. We're being attacked. Is the situation that serious?

PIERRE: No, no, no, for Chrissakes. They're playin' hockey. Them women are playin' hockey. Dead serious they are, too.

SPOOKY: No.

PIERRE: Yes.

SPOOKY: Thank the Lord this is the last year!

PIERRE: Don't you care to ask?

SPOOKY: Thank the Lord the end of the world is coming this year! (*Gasping, he marches up to DICKIE BIRD.*)

PIERRE: I'm the referee, dammit.

SPOOKY: Watch your language. (*grabbing the crucifix from DICKIE BIRD*)

PIERRE: That's what I mean when I say I'm gonna be right smack dab in the middle of it all. You don't listen to me.

SPOOKY: (*puts the little booties back on the crucifix*) But you're not a woman.

PIERRE: You don't have to be. To be a referee these days, you can be anything, man or woman, don't matter which away. So gimme my skate.

SPOOKY: What skate?

PIERRE: The skate Gazelle Nataways just about killed you with after the bingo that time.

SPOOKY: Oh, that. I hid it in the basement. (*PIERRE opens a door, falls in, and comes struggling out with a mousetrap stuck to a finger.*)

SPOOKY: Pierre St. Pierre, what the hell are you doing in Lalala's closet?

PIERRE: Well, where the hell's the basement? (*He frees his finger.*)

SPOOKY: Pierre St. Pierre, you drink too much. You gotta have the Lord in your life.

PIERRE: I don't need the Lord in my life, for God's sake, I need my skate. I gotta practise my figure eights.

SPOOKY: (*begins to put the crucifix back up on the wall*) You gotta promise me before I give you your skate.

PIERRE: I promise.

SPOOKY: (*unaware, he threatens PIERRE with the crucifix, holding it up against his neck*) You gotta have the Lord come into your life.

PIERRE: All right, all right.

SPOOKY: For how long?

PIERRE: My whole life. I promise I'm gonna bring the Lord into my life and keep him there right up until the day I die just gimme my goddamn skate.

SPOOKY: Cross my heart.

PIERRE: All right. Cross your heart.

Neither man makes a move until SPOOKY, finally catching on, throws PIERRE a look. PIERRE crosses himself.

SPOOKY: Good. (*exits to the basement*)

PIERRE: (*Now alone with DICKIE BIRD, half-whispering to him. As PIERRE speaks, DICKIE BIRD again takes the crucifix off the wall and returns with it to his seat, taking*

the booties off in haphazard fashion.*) Has he been feedin' you this crappola, too? Don't you be startin' that foolishness. That Spooky Lacroix's so fulla shit he wouldn't know a two-thousand-year-old Egyptian Sphinxter if he came face to face with one. He's just preachifyin' at you because you're the one person on this reserve who can't argue back. You listen to me. I was there in the same room as your mother when she gave birth to you. So I know well who you are and where you come from. I remember the whole picture. Even though we were all in a bit of a fizzy ... I remember. Do you know, Dickie Bird Halked, that you were named after that bar? Anyone ever tell you that? (*DICKIE BIRD starts to shake. PIERRE takes fright.*) Spooky Lacroix, move that holy ass of yours, for fuck's sakes! (*DICKIE BIRD laughs. PIERRE makes a weak attempt to laugh along.*) And I'll never forgive your father, Big Joey – oops ... (*DICKIE BIRD reacts.*) ... I mean Wellington Halked – for letting your mother do that to you. "It's not good for the people of this world," I says to him, "it's not good for 'em to have the first thing they see when they come into the world is a goddamn jukebox." That's what I says to him. Thank God, you survived, Dickie Bird Halked, thank God, seventeen years later you're sittin' here smack dab in front of me, hale and hearty as cake. Except for your tongue. Talk, Dickie Bird Halked, talk. Say somethin'. Come on. Try this: "Daddy, daddy, daddy." (*DICKIE BIRD shakes his head.*) Come on. Just this once. Maybe it will work. (*He takes DICKIE BIRD by the cheeks with one hand.*) "Daddy, daddy, daddy, daddy." (*DICKIE BIRD jumps up and attacks PIERRE, looking as though he were about to shove the crucifix down PIERRE's throat. PIERRE is genuinely terrified. Just then, SPOOKY re-enters with the skate.*) Whoa, whoa. Easy. Easy now, Dickie Bird. Easy.

SPOOKY: (*Gasping again at the sight of DICKIE BIRD manhandling the crucifix, he makes a beeline for the boy.*) Dickie Bird Halked? Give me that thing. (*He grabs the crucifix with a flourish. Then he turns to PIERRE and holds the skate out with his other hand.*) Promise.

PIERRE: Cross my heart. (*crosses himself*)

SPOOKY: (*replacing the crucifix on the wall and pointing at PIERRE*) The Lord.

PIERRE: The Lord.

SPOOKY hands the skate over to PIERRE. Just then, CREATURE NATAWAYS stumbles in, now visibly drunk.

CREATURE: The Lord!

Picking on the hapless DICKIE BIRD, CREATURE roughly shoves the boy into a chair.

PIERRE: (*holding up both his skates*) I got 'em both. See! I got 'em.

CREATURE: Hallelujah! Now all you gotta do is learn how to skate.

SPOOKY: Creature Nataways, I don't want you in my house in that condition. Lalala is liable to pop any minute now and I don't want my son to see the first thing he sees when he comes into the world is a drunk.

PIERRE: Damn rights!

SPOOKY: You, too, Pierre St. Pierre.

CREATURE: Aw! William Lacroix, don't give me that holier-than-me, poker-up-the-bum spiritual bullcrap –

SPOOKY: – say wha? –

CREATURE: Are you preachin' to this boy, William Lacroix? Are you usin' him again to practise your preachy-preachy? Don't do that, William, the boy is helpless. If you wanna practise, go practise on your old buddy, go preach on Big Joey. He's the one who needs it.

SPOOKY: You're hurting again, aren't you, Creature Nataways.

CREATURE: Don't listen to Spooky Lacroix, Dickie Bird. You follow Spooky Lacroix and you go right down to the dogs, I'm tellin' you that right now. Hairspray, Lysol, vanilla extract, shoe polish, Xerox machine juice, he's done it all, this man. If you'd given William Lacroix the chance, he'd have sliced up the Xerox machine and ate it ...

PIERRE: (*mockingly*) No!

CREATURE: ... He once drank a Kitty Wells record. He lied to his own mother and he stole her record and he boiled it and swallowed it right up ...

PIERRE: Good heavens!

BIG JOEY enters and stands at the door unseen.

CREATURE: ... Made the *Globe and Mail*, too. He's robbed, he's cheated his best friend ...

SPOOKY: Alphonse Nataways! Why are you doing this, may I ask?

CREATURE: Oh, he was bad, Dickie Bird Halked, he was bad. Fifteen years. Fifteen years of his life pukin' his guts out on sidewalks from here to Sicamous, B.C., this man ...

SPOOKY: Shush!

CREATURE: ... and this is the same man ...

BIG JOEY: (*Speaking suddenly and laughing, he takes everyone by surprise. They gasp. And practically freeze in their tracks.*) ... who's yellin' and preachin' about "the Lord!" They oughta retire the beaver and put this guy on the Canadian nickel, he's become a national goddamn symbol, that what you're sayin', Creature Nataways? This the kind of man you wanna become, that what you're sayin' to the boy, Creature Nataways? (*close up to DICKIE BIRD*) A man who couldn't get a hard-on in front of a woman if you paid him a two-dollar bill?

SPOOKY: (*stung to the quick*) And is this the kind of man you wanna become, Dickie Bird Halked, this MAN who can't take the sight of blood least of all woman's blood, this MAN who, when he sees a woman's blood, chokes up, pukes, and faints, how do you like that?

PIERRE, sensing potential violence, begins to sneak out.

BIG JOEY: (*pulls a bottle out of his coat*) Spooky Lacroix, igwani eeweepoonaskeewuk. (*"The end of the world is at hand."*)

PIERRE, seeing the bottle, retraces his steps and sits down again, grabbing a tea cup en route, ready for a drink.

SPOOKY: (*shocked*) Get that thing out of my house!

BIG JOEY: Tonight, we're gonna celebrate my wife, Spooky Lacroix, we're gonna celebrate because my wife, the fabulous, the incredible Gazelle Delphina Nataways, has been crowned captain of the Wasy Wailerettes. The rez is makin' history, Spooky Lacroix. The world will never be the same. Come on, it's on me, it's on your old buddy, the old, old buddy you said you'd never, ever forget.

SPOOKY: I told you a long time ago, Big Joey, after what you went and done to my sister, this here boy's own mother, you're no buddy of mine. Get out of my house. Get!

BIG JOEY: (*handing the bottle of whisky to CREATURE*) Creature Nataways, celebrate your wife.

CREATURE: (*raising the bottle in a toast*) To my wife!

PIERRE: (*holding his cup out to the bottle*) Your ex-wife.

BIG JOEY: (*suddenly quiet and intimate*) William. William. You and me. You and me, we used to be buddies, kigiskisin? (*"Remember?"*) Wounded

Knee. South Dakota. Spring of '73. We parked my van over by that little lake, we swam across, you almost didn't make it and nothin' could get you to swim back. Kigiskisin? So here we're walkin' back through the bush, all the way around this small lake, nothin' on but bare feet and wet undershorts and this black bear come up behind you, kigiskisin? And you freaked out. (*laughs*)

> *PIERRE tries, as best he can, to create a party atmosphere, to little avail. CREATURE nervously watches BIG JOEY and SPOOKY. DICKIE BIRD merely sits there, head down, rocking back and forth.*

SPOOKY: (*obviously extremely uncomfortable*) You freaked out, too, ha-ha, ha-ha.

BIG JOEY: That bear gave you a real spook, huh? (*Pause. Suddenly, he jumps at the other men.*) Boo! (*The other men, including SPOOKY, jump, splashing whisky all over the place. BIG JOEY laughs. The others pretend to laugh.*) That's how you got your name, you old Spook ...

SPOOKY: You were scared, too, ha-ha, ha-ha.

BIG JOEY: ... we get back to the camp and there's Creature and Eugene and Zach and Roscoe, bacon and eggs all ready for us. Christ, I never laughed so hard in my life. But here you were, not laughin' and we'd say: "What's the matter, Spook, you don't like our jokes?" And you'd say: "That's good, yeah, that's good." I guess you were laughin' from a different part of yourself, huh? You were beautiful ...

SPOOKY: That's good, yeah, that's good.

BIG JOEY: (*getting the bottle back from CREATURE and PIERRE*) So tonight, Bear-who-went-and-gave-you-a-real-Spooky Lacroix, we're gonna celebrate another new page in our lives. Wounded Knee Three! Women's version!

PIERRE: Damn rights.

BIG JOEY: (*raising the bottle up in a toast*) To my wife!

SPOOKY: Ha! Get that thing away from me.

PIERRE: Spooky Lacroix, cooperate. Cooperate for once. The women, the women are playing hockey.

CREATURE: To my wife!

PIERRE: Your ex-wife.

CREATURE: Shut up, you toothless old bugger.

SPOOKY: Big Joey, you're not my friend no more.

BIG JOEY: (*Grabs SPOOKY roughly by the throat. CREATURE jumps to help hold SPOOKY still.*) You never

let a friend for life go, William Hector Lacroix, not even if you turn your back on your own father Nicotine Lacroix's spiritual teachings and pretend like hell to be this born-again Christian.

SPOOKY: Let go. Creature Nataways, let go of me! (*to BIG JOEY*) For what you did to this boy at that bar seventeen years ago, Joseph Jeremiah McLeod, you are going to hell. To hell!

> *BIG JOEY baptizes SPOOKY with the remainder of the bottle's contents. Breaking free, SPOOKY grabs DICKIE BIRD and shoves him toward BIG JOEY.*

SPOOKY: Look at him. He can't even talk. He hasn't talked in seventeen years!

> *DICKIE BIRD cries out, breaks free, grabs the crucifix from the wall, and runs out the door, crying. SPOOKY breaks down, falls to the floor and weeps. BIG JOEY attempts to pick him up gently, but SPOOKY kicks him away.*

SPOOKY: Let go of me! Let go!

CREATURE: (*lifting the empty bottle, laughing and crying at the same time*) To my wife, to my wife, to my wife, to my wife, to my wife ...

> *BIG JOEY suddenly lifts SPOOKY off the floor by the collar and lifts a fist to punch his face.*

> *Blackout.*

> *Out of this blackout emerges the eerie, distant sound of women wailing and pucks hitting boards, echoing and echoing as in a vast empty chamber. The lights come up on DICKIE BIRD HALKED and SIMON STARBLANKET, standing beside each other in the "bleachers" of the hockey arena, watching the "ice" area (i.e., looking out over the audience). The bleachers area is actually on the upper level of the set, in a straight line directly in front of NANABUSH's perch. DICKIE BIRD is still holding SPOOKY's crucifix and SIMON is still holding his dancing bustle.*

SIMON: Your grandpa, Nicotine Lacroix, was a medicine man. Hell of a name, but he was a medicine man. Old priest here, Father Boucher, years ago – oh, he was a terrible man – he went and convinced the people old Nicotine Lacroix talked to the devil. That's not true. Nicotine Lacroix was a good man. That's why I want you for my best man. Me and Patsy are getting married a couple of months from now. It's decided. We're gonna have a baby. Then we're going down to South Dakota and we're gonna dance with the Rosebud Sioux this summer. (*sings as he stomps his foot in the rhythm of a powwow drum*) "... and me I don't wanna go to the moon, I'm gonna leave that moon alone. I just wanna dance with the Rosebud Sioux this summer, yeah, yeah, yeah ..." (*breaks into a chant*)

DICKIE BIRD watches, fascinated, particularly by the bustle SIMON holds up in the air.

At this point, ZACHARY JEREMIAH KEECHIGEESIK approaches timidly from behind a beam, his pants held flimsily together with a huge safety pin. The sound of women wailing and pucks hitting boards now shifts into the sound of an actual hockey arena, just before a big game.

ZACHARY: (*to SIMON*) Hey! (*SIMON doesn't hear and continues chanting.*) Pssst!

SIMON: Zachary Jeremiah. Neee, watstagatch!

ZACHARY: Is Hera out there?

SIMON: (*indicating the "ice"*) Yup. There she is.

ZACHARY: Lordy, lordy, lordy ...

SIMON: Just kidding. She's not out there –

ZACHARY: Don't do that to me!

SIMON: – yet.

ZACHARY: (*coming up to join the young men at the "bleachers"*) You know that Nanabush character you were telling me about a couple of nights ago? What do you say I give his name over to them little gingerbread cookie men I'm gonna be making? For starters. Think that would help any?

SIMON: Neee ...

Just then, BIG JOEY enters to get a microphone stand ready for broadcasting the game. ZACHARY goes to stand as far away from him as possible.

ZACHARY: (*looking out over the "ice"*) It's almost noon. They're late getting started.

BIG JOEY: (*yawning luxuriously*) That's right. Me and Gazelle Nataways ... slept in.

CREATURE NATAWAYS comes scurrying in.

CREATURE: (*still talking to himself*) ... I tole you once I tole you twice ... (*then to the other men*) Chrissakes! Are they really gonna do it? Chrissakes!

SPOOKY LACROIX enters wearing a woollen scarf he obviously knitted himself. He is still knitting, this time a pale-blue baby sweater. He also now sports a black eye and Band-Aid on his face. All the men, except PIERRE ST. PIERRE, are now in the "bleachers," standing in a straight line facing

the audience, with *DICKIE BIRD* in the centre, *SIMON* and *SPOOKY* to his immediate right and left, respectively.

SPOOKY: It's bad luck to start late. I know. I read the interview with Gay Lafleur in last week's *Expositor*. They won't get far.

He sees GAZELLE NATAWAYS entering the "rink," unseen by the audience. All the hockey players on the "ice" are unseen by the audience; it is only the men who can actually see them.

SPOOKY: Look! Gazelle Nataways went and got her sweater trimmed in the chest area!

Wild catcalls from the men.

CREATURE: Trimmed it! She's got it plunging down to her ootsee (*"belly button"*).

ZACHARY: Ahem. Smokes too much. Lung problems.

BIG JOEY: Nah. More like it's got somethin' to do with the undershorts she's wearin' today.

ZACHARY: (*fast on the uptake*) Fuck you!

BIG JOEY: (*blowing ZACHARY a kiss*) Poosees. (*"Pussycat." [Zachary's childhood nickname]*)

SPOOKY: Terrible. Terrible. Tsk, tsk, tsk.

PIERRE ST. PIERRE enters on the lower level, teetering dangerously on his skates toward the "ice" area downstage. He wears a referee's top and a whistle around his neck.

PIERRE: (*checking the names off as he reads from a clipboard*) Dominique Ladouche, Black Lady Halked, Annie Cook, June Bug McLeod, Big Bum Pegahmagahbow ...

SIMON: (*calling out*) Patsy Pegahmagahbow, turkey.

PIERRE: Shut up. I'm workin' here ... Leonarda Lee Starblanket, that terrible Dictionary woman, Fluffy Sainte-Marie, Chicken Lips Pegahmagahbow, Dry Lips Manigitogan, Little Hand Manigitogan, Little Girl Manitowabi, Victoria Manitowabi, Belinda Nickikoosimeenicaning, Martha Two-Axe Early-in-the-Morning, Her Royal Highness Gazelle Delphina Nataways, Delia Opekokew, Barbra Nahwegahbow, Gloria May Eshkibok, Hera Keechigeesik, Tall Mary Ann Patchnose, Short Mary Ann Patchnose, Queen Elizabeth Patchnose, the triplets Marjorie Moose, Maggie May Moose, Mighty Moose, and, of course, my wife, Veronique

St. Pierre. Yup. They're all there, I hope, and the world is about to explode!

SPOOKY: That's what I've been trying to tell you!

PIERRE ST. PIERRE, barely able to stand on his skates, hobbles about, obviously getting almost trampled by the hockey players at various times.

BIG JOEY: (*Now speaking on the microphone. The other men watch the women on the "ice"; some are cheering and whistling, some calling down the game.*) Welcome, ladies igwa gentlemen, welcome one and all to the Wasaychigan Hill Hip-hip-hippodrome. This is your host for the big game, Big Joey – and they don't call me Big Joey for nothin' – Chairman, CEO, and proprietor of the Wasaychigan Hill Hippodrome, bringin' you a game such as has never been seen ever before on the ice of any hockey arena anywhere on the island of Manitoulin, anywhere on the face of this country, anywhere on the face of this planet. And there –

CREATURE: – there's Gazelle Nataways, Number One –

BIG JOEY: – they are, ladies –

SPOOKY: – terrible, terrible –

BIG JOEY: – igwa gentlemen ...

CREATURE: ... Chrissakes, that's my wife, Chrissakes ...

BIG JOEY: ... there they are, the most beautiful –

SIMON: ... give 'em hell, Patsy Pegahmagahbow, give 'em hell ...

BIG JOEY: – daring, death –

SIMON: (*to ZACHARY*) ... there's Hera Keechigeesik, Number Nine ...

BIG JOEY: – defying Indian women –

SPOOKY: – terrible, terrible –

BIG JOEY: – in the world –

ZACHARY: – that's my wife –

BIG JOEY: – the Wasy Wailerettes – (*clears his throat and tests the microphone by tapping it gently*)

ZACHARY: ... lordy, lordy, lordy ...

CREATURE: Hey, Gazelle Nataways and Hera Keechigeesik are lookin' at each other awful funny. Something bad's gonna happen, I tole you once I tole you twice, something bad's gonna happen ...

SPOOKY: This is a sign from the Lord. This is THE sign ...

BIG JOEY: Number One Gazelle Nataways, captain of the Wasy Wailerettes, facing off with Number Nine, Flora McDonald, captain of the Canoe Lake Bravettes. And referee Pierre St. Pierre drops the puck and takes off like a herd of wild turtles ...

SIMON: Aw, Spooky Lacroix, eat my shitty shorts, neee ...

BIG JOEY: Hey, aspin (*"there goes"*) Number Six Dry Lips Manigitogan, right-winger for the Wasy Wailerettes ...

ZACHARY: ... look pretty damn stupid, if you ask me. Fifteen thousand dollars for all that new equipment ...

BIG JOEY: ... eemaskamat (*"and steals the puck from"*) Number Thirteen of the Canoe Lake Bravettes anee-i-puck ...

CREATURE: ... Cancel the game! Cancel the game! Cancel the game!

BIG JOEY: ... igwa aspin sipweesinskwataygew. Hey, k'seegoochin! (*"and skates off. Hey, is she ever flying!"*) (*off microphone*) Creature Nataways. Shut up. (*to the other men*) Get that asshole out of here ...

SIMON: Yay, Patsy Pegahmagahbow! Pat-see! Pat-see! Pat-see!

BIG JOEY: (*back on microphone*) How, Number Six Dry Lips Manigitogan, right-winger for the Wasy Wailerettes, soogi pugamawew igwa anee-i puck igwa aspin centre-line ispathoo ana puck ... (*"shoots the puck and the puck goes flying over toward the centre-line ..."*)

CREATURE: (*to SIMON*) Shut up. Don't encourage them ...

BIG JOEY: ... ita (*"where"*) Number Nine Hera Keechigeesik, left-winger for ...

SIMON: (*to CREATURE*) Aw, lay off! Pat-see! Pat-see! Pat-see!

BIG JOEY: ... the Wasy Wailerettes, kagatchitnat (*"catches it"*). How, Number Nine Hera Keechigeesik ... (*He continues uninterrupted.*)

CREATURE: ... Stop the game! Stop the game! Stop the game! ...

ZACHARY: Goodness sakes, there's gonna be a fight out there!

CREATURE continues his "stop the game"; ZACHARY repeats "goodness sakes, there's gonna be a fight out there"; SIMON's "Pat-see!" has now built up into a full chant, his foot pounding on the floor so that it sounds like a powwow drum, his dancing bustle held aloft like a shield. SPOOKY finally grabs the crucifix away from DICKIE BIRD, holds it aloft, and begins to pray, loudly, as in a ceremony. DICKIE BIRD, caught between SIMON's chanting and SPOOKY's praying, blocks his ears with his hands and looks with growing consternation at "the game." PIERRE blows his whistle and skates around like a puppet gone mad.

SPOOKY: The Lord is my shepherd; I shall not want. He maketh me to lie down in green pastures; He leadeth me beside the still waters. He restoreth my soul; He leadeth me in the paths of righteousness for his name's sake. Yea, though I walk through the valley of the shadow of death, I will fear no evil; for Thou art with me. Yea, though I walk through the valley of the shadow of death, I will fear no evil; for Thou art with me ... (*He repeats the last phrase over and over again.*)

Finally, DICKIE BIRD freaks out, screams, and runs down to the "ice" area.

BIG JOEY: (*continuing uninterrupted above all the other men's voices*) ... igwa ati-ooteetum blue line ita Number One Gazelle Nataways, captain of the Wasy Wailerettes, kagagweemaskamat anee-i-puck, ma-a Number Nine Hera Keechigeesik mawch weemeethew anee-i puck. Wha! "Hooking," itwew referee Pierre St. Pierre, Gazelle Nataways isa keehookiwatew her own teammate Hera Keechigeesikwa, wha! How, Number One Gazelle Nataways, captain of the Wasy Wailerettes, face-off igwa meena itootum asichi Number Nine Flora McDonald, captain of the Canoe Lake Bravettes igwa Flora McDonald soogi pugamawew anee-i puck, ma-a ("... *approaching the blue line where Number One Gazelle Nataways, captain of the Wasy Wailerettes, tries to get the puck off her, but Number Nine Hera Keechigeesik won't give it to her. Wha! "Hooking," says referee Pierre St. Pierre, Gazelle Nataways has apparently hooked her own teammate Hera Keechigeesik, wha! How, Number One Gazelle Nataways, captain of the Wasy Wailerettes, facing off once again with Number Nine Flora McDonald, captain of the Canoe Lake Bravettes and Flora McDonald shoots the puck, but"*) Number Thirty-seven Big Bum Pegahmagahbow, defence-woman for the Wasy Wailerettes, stops the puck and passes it to Number Eleven Black Lady Halked, also defence-woman for the Wasy Wailerettes, but Gazelle Nataways, captain of the Wasy Wailerettes, soogi bodycheck meethew ("*gives a mean bodycheck to*") her own teammate

Black Lady Halked woops! She falls, ladies igwa gentlemen, Black Lady Halked hits the boards and Black Lady Halked is singin' the blues, ladies igwa gentlemen, Black Lady Halked sings the blues. (*off microphone, to the other men*) What the hell is goin' on down there? Dickie Bird, get off the ice! (*back on microphone*) Wha! Number Eleven Black Lady Halked is up in a flash igwa seemak n'taymaskamew Gazelle Nataways anee-i puck, holy shit! The ailing but very, very furious Black Lady Halked skates back, turns, and takes aim, it's gonna be a slapshot, ladies igwa gentlemen, slapshot keenatch taytootum Black Lady Halked igwa Black Lady Halked shootiwoo anee-i puck, wha! ("*Wha! Number Eleven Black Lady Halked is up in a flash and grabs the puck from Gazelle Nataways, holy shit! The ailing but very, very furious Black Lady Halked skates back, turns, and takes aim, it's gonna be a slapshot, ladies and gentlemen, Black Lady Halked is gonna take a slapshot for sure and Black Lady Halked shoots the puck, wha!*") She shoots straight at her very own captain, Gazelle Nataways, and holy shit, holy shit, holy fuckin' shit!

All hell breaks loose; it is as though some bizarre dream has entered the arena. We hear the sound of women wailing and pucks hitting boards, echoing and echoing as in a vast empty chamber. The men are all screaming at the same time from the "bleachers," recalling Black Lady Halked's legendary fall of seventeen years ago.

BIG JOEY: (*dropping his microphone in horror*) Holy Christ! If there is a devil in this world, then he has just walked into this room. Holy Christ! (*He says this over and over again.*)

ZACHARY: Do something about her, goodness sakes, I told you guys to do something about her seventeen years ago, but you wouldn't do fuck-all. So go out there now and help her ... (*repeated*)

CREATURE: Never mind, Chrissakes, don't bother her. Let me out of here. Chrissakes, let me out of here! ... (*repeated*)

SPOOKY: ... Yea, though I walk through the valley of the shadow of death, I fear no evil; for thou art with me ... (*repeated*)

SIMON continues chanting and stomping.

PIERRE: (*from the "ice" area*) Never you mind, Zachary Jeremiah, never you mind. She'll be okay. No she won't. Zachary Jeremiah, go out there and help her. No. She'll be okay. No she won't. Yes. No.

Yes. No. Help! Where's the puck? Can't do nothin' without the goddamn puck. Where's the puck?! Where's the puck?! Where's the puck?! (*He repeats this last phrase over and over again.*)

> *Centre and downstage, on the "ice" area, DICKIE BIRD is going into a complete freak out, breaking into a grotesque, fractured version of a Cree chant. Gradually, BIG JOEY, ZACHARY, and CREATURE join PIERRE's refrain of "where's the puck?!" with which they all, including the chanting SIMON and the praying SPOOKY, scatter and come running down to the "ice" area. As they reach the lower level and begin to approach the audience, their movements break down into slow motion, as though they are trying to run through the sticky, gummy substance of some horrible, surrealistic nightmare.*

PIERRE, BIG JOEY, ZACHARY & CREATURE: (*slower and slower as on a record that is slowing down gradually to a stop*) Where's the puck?! Where's the puck?! Where's the puck?! ...

> *SIMON continues chanting and stomping. SPOOKY continues intoning the last phrase of his prayer and DICKIE BIRD continues his fractured chant. Out of this fading sound collage emerges the sound of a jukebox playing the introduction to Kitty Wells's "It Wasn't God Who Made Honky Tonk Angels," as though filtered through memory. At this point, on the upper level, a giant luminescent hockey stick comes seemingly out of nowhere and, in very slow motion, shoots a giant luminescent puck. On the puck, looking like a radiant but damaged Madonna-with-Child, sits NANABUSH, as the spirit of BLACK LADY HALKED, naked, nine months pregnant, drunk almost senseless, and barely able to hold a bottle of beer up to her mouth. All the men freeze in their standing positions facing the audience, except for DICKIE BIRD, who continues his fractured chanting and whimpering, holding his arms up toward NANABUSH / BLACK LADY HALKED. The giant luminescent puck stops at the edge of the upper level. NANABUSH / BLACK LADY HALKED struggles to stand and begins stag-gering toward her perch. She reaches it and falls with one arm on top of it. The magical, glittering lights flare on and, for the first time, the jukebox is revealed. NANABUSH / BLACK LADY HALKED staggers laboriously up to the top of the jukebox and stands there in profile, one arm lifted to raise her beer as she pours it over her belly. Behind her, the full moon begins to glow, blood red. And from the jukebox, Kitty Wells sings:*

As I sit here tonight, the jukebox playing,
That tune about the wild side of life;
As I listen to the words you are saying,
It brings memories when I was a trusting wife.
It wasn't God who made honky tonk angels,
As you said in the words of your song;
Too many times married men think they're still single,
That has caused many a good girl to go wrong.

> *During the instrumental break of the song, DICKIE BIRD finally explodes and shrieks out toward the vision of NANABUSH / BLACK LADY HALKED.*

DICKIE BIRD: Mama! Mama! Katha paksini. Katha paksini. Kanawapata wastew. Kanawapataw wastew. Michimina. Michimina. Katha pagitina. Kaweechee-ik nipapa. Kaweechee-ik nipapa. Nipapa. Papa. Papa. Papa. Papa. Papa. Papa! (*"Mommy! Mommy! Don't fall. Don't fall. Look at the light. Look at the light. Hold on to it. Hold on to it. Don't let it go. My daddy will help you. My daddy will help you. My daddy. Daddy. Daddy."*) (*He crumples to the floor and freezes.*)

> *Kitty Wells sings:*

It's a shame that all the blame is on us women,
It's not true that only you men feel the same;
From the start most every heart that's ever broken
Was because there always was a man to blame.
It wasn't God who made honky tonk angels,
As you said in the words of your song;
Too many times married men think they're still single,
That has caused many a good girl to go wrong.

> *As the song fades, the final tableau has DICKIE BIRD collapsed on the floor between SIMON, who is holding aloft his bustle, and SPOOKY, who is holding aloft his crucifix, directly in front of and at the feet of BIG JOEY and, above BIG JOEY, the pregnant NANABUSH / BLACK LADY HALKED, who is standing on top of the flashing jukebox, in silhouette against the full moon, bottle held up above her mouth. ZACHARY, CREATURE, and PIERRE are likewise frozen, standing off to the side of this central grouping.*

> *Slow fade-out.*

ACT TWO

When the lights come up, DICKIE BIRD HALKED is standing on a rock in the forest, his clothes and hair all askew. He holds SPOOKY's crucifix up to the night sky; he is trying, as best he can, to chant after SIMON STARBLANKET's fashion. As he does, NANABUSH appears in the shadows a distance behind him as the spirit of GAZELLE NATAWAYS, minus the gigantic breasts, but dressed this time as a stripper. She lingers and watches with interest. Slowly, DICKIE BIRD climbs off the rock and walks offstage, his quavering voice fading into the distance. The full moon glows. Fade-out.

Fade-in on SPOOKY LACROIX's kitchen, where SPOOKY is busy pinning four little pale-blue baby booties on the wall where the crucifix used to be, the booties that, in Act One, covered the four extremities of the crucifix. At the table are PIERRE and ZACHARY. PIERRE is stringing pale-blue yarn around ZACHARY's raised, parted hands. Then SPOOKY joins them at the table and begins knitting again, this time a baby bonnet, also pale-blue. ZACHARY sits removed through most of this scene, preoccupied with the problem of his still-missing shorts, his bakery, and his wife. The atmosphere is one of fear and foreboding, almost as though the men were constantly resisting the impulse to look over their shoulders. On the upper level, in a soft, dim light, NANABUSH / GAZELLE can be seen sitting up on her perch, waiting impatiently for "the boys" to finish their talk.

PIERRE: (*in a quavering voice*) The Wasy Wailerettes are dead. Gentlemen, my job is disappeared from underneath my feet.

SPOOKY: And we have only the Lord to thank for that.

PIERRE: Gazelle Nataways, she just sashayed herself off that ice, behind swayin' like a walrus pudding. That game, gentlemen, was what I call a real apostrophe ...

ZACHARY: Catastrophe.

PIERRE: That's what I said, dammit ...

SPOOKY: ... tsk ...

PIERRE: ... didn't even get to referee more than ten minutes. But you have to admit, gentlemen, that slapshot ...

SPOOKY: ... that's my sister, Black Lady Halked, that's my sister ...

PIERRE: ... did you see her slapshot? Fantastic! Like a bullet, like a killer shark. Unbelievable!

ZACHARY: (*uncomfortable*) Yeah, right.

PIERRE: When Black Lady Halked hit Gazelle Nataways with that puck. Them Nataways eyes. Big as plates!

SPOOKY: Bigger than a ditch!

PIERRE: Them mascara stretch marks alone was a perfectly frightful thing to behold. Holy shit la marde! But you know, they couldn't find that puck.

SPOOKY: (*losing his cool and laughing, falsely and nervously*) Did you see it! It fell ... it fell ... that puck went splat on her chest ... and it went ... it went ... plummety plop ...

PIERRE: ... plummety plop to be sure ...

SPOOKY: ... down her ... down her ...

PIERRE: Down the crack. Right down that horrendous, scarifyin' Nataways bosom crack.

The kitchen lights go out momentarily and, to the men, inexplicably. Then they come back on. The men look about them, perplexed.

SPOOKY: Serves ... her ... right for trimming her hockey sweater in the chest area, is what I say.

PIERRE: They say that puck slid somewhere deep, deep into the folds of her fleshy, womanly juices ...

ZACHARY: ... there's a lot of things they're saying about that puck ...

PIERRE: ... and it's lost. Disappeared. Gone. Phhht! Nobody can find that puck.

At this point SPOOKY gets up to check the light switch. The lights go out.

ZACHARY: (*in the darkness*) Won't let no one come near her, is what they say. Not six inches.

PIERRE: I gotta go look for that puck. (*Lights come back on. PIERRE inexplicably appears sitting in another chair.*) Gentlemen, I gotta go jiggle that woman.

Lights go out again.

ZACHARY: (*from the darkness*) What's the matter, Spook!

SPOOKY: (*obviously quite worried*) Oh, nothing, nothing ... (*Lights come back on. PIERRE appears sitting back in his original chair. The men are even more mystified, but try to brighten up anyway.*) ... just ... checking the lights ... Queen of the Indians, that's what she tried to look like, walking off that ice.

PIERRE: Queen of the Indians, to be sure. That's when them women went and put their foot down and made up their mind, on principle, no holds barred ...

A magical flash of lavender light floods the room very briefly, establishing a connection between SPOOKY's *kitchen and* NANABUSH's *perch, where* NANABUSH / GAZELLE *is still sitting, tapping her fingers impatiently, looking over her shoulder periodically, as if to say: "Come on, boys, get with it."* PIERRE's *speech momentarily goes into slow motion.*

PIERRE: ... no ... way ... they're ... takin' up ... them hockey sticks again until that particular puck is found. "The particular puck," that's what they call it. Gentlemen, the Wasy Wailerettes are dead. My job is disappeared. Gone. Kaput kaput. Phhht!

SPOOKY: Amen.

Pause. Thoughtful silence for a beat or two.

ZACHARY: W-w-w-where's that nephew of yours, Spook?

SPOOKY: Dickie Bird Halked?

PIERRE: My wife, Veronique St. Pierre, she informs me that Dickie Bird Halked, last he was seen, was pacin' the bushes in the general direction of the Pegahmagahbow acreage near Buzwah, lookin' for all the world like he had lost his mind, poor boy.

ZACHARY: Lordy, lordy, lordy, I'm telling you right now, Spooky Lacroix, if you don't do something about that nephew of yours, he's liable to go out there and kill someone next time.

SPOOKY: I'd be out there myself pacing the bushes with him except my wife Lalala's liable to pop any minute now and I gotta be ready to zip her up to Sudbury General.

PIERRE: Bah. Them folks of his, they don't care. If it's not hockey, it's bingo she's out playin' every night of the week, that Black Lady of a mother of his.

ZACHARY: Went and won the jackpot again last night, Black Lady Halked did. All fifty pounds of it ...

PIERRE: Beat Gazelle Nataways by one number!

ZACHARY: ... if it wasn't for her, I'd have mastered that apple pie recipe by now. I was counting on all that lard. Fifty pounds, goodness sakes.

SPOOKY: This little old kitchen? It's yours, Zachary Jeremiah, anytime, anytime. Lalala's got tons of lard.

PIERRE: Ha! She better have. Zachary Jeremiah hasn't dared go nowhere near his own kitchen in almost a week.

ZACHARY: Four nights! It's only Wednesday night, Pierre St. Pierre. Don't go stretching the truth just cuz you were too damn chicken to go get me my shorts.

PIERRE: Bah!

SPOOKY: (*to* ZACHARY) Your shorts?

ZACHARY: (*evading the issue*) I just hope that Black Lady Halked's out there looking after her boy cuz if she isn't, we're all in a heap of trouble, I have a funny feeling. (*Suddenly, he throws the yarn down and rises.*) Achh! I've got to cook! (*He goes behind the kitchen counter, puts an apron on, and begins the preparations for making pie pastry.*)

SPOOKY: (*to* PIERRE, *half-whispering*) His shorts?

PIERRE *merely shrugs, indicating* ZACHARY's *pants, which are still held together with a large safety pin.* SPOOKY *and* PIERRE *laugh nervously.* SPOOKY *looks concernedly at the four little booties on the wall where the crucifix used to be. Beat.*

Suddenly, PIERRE *slaps the table with one hand and leans over to* SPOOKY, *all set for an argument, an argument they've obviously had many times before. Through all this,* ZACHARY *is making pie pastry at the counter and* SPOOKY *continues knitting. The atmosphere of faked jocular camaraderie grows, particularly as the music gets louder later on.* NANABUSH / GAZELLE *is now getting ready for her strip in earnest, standing on her perch, spraying perfume on, stretching her legs, etc. The little Tivoli lights in the jukebox begin to twinkle little by little.*

PIERRE: Queen of Hearts.

SPOOKY: Belvedere.

PIERRE: Queen of Hearts.

SPOOKY: The Belvedere.

PIERRE: I told you many times, Spooky Lacroix, it was the Queen of Hearts. I was there. You were there. Zachary Jeremiah, Big Joey, Creature Nataways, we were all there.

From here on, the red, blue, and purple glow of the jukebox (i.e., NANABUSH's *perch) becomes more and more apparent.*

SPOOKY: And I'm telling you it was the Belvedere Hotel, before it was even called the Belvedere Hotel, when it was still called ...

PIERRE: Spooky Lacroix, don't contribute your elder. Big Joey, may he rot in hell, he was the bouncer there that night, he was right there the night it happened.

ZACHARY: Hey, Spook. Where do you keep your rolling pin?

SPOOKY: Use my salami.

PIERRE: (*to SPOOKY*) He was there.

ZACHARY: Big Joey was never the bouncer, he was the janitor.

SPOOKY: At the Belvedere Hotel.

PIERRE: Never you mind, Spooky Lacroix, never you mind. Black Lady Halked was sittin' there in her corner of the bar for three weeks ...

SPOOKY: Three weeks? It was more like three nights. Aw, you went and mixed up my baby's cap. (*getting all tangled up with his knitting*)

ZACHARY: Got any cinnamon?

SPOOKY: I got chili powder. Same colour as cinnamon.

Faintly, the strip music from the jukebox begins to play.

PIERRE: ... the place was so jam-packed with people drinkin' beer and singin' and smokin' cigarettes and watchin' the dancin' girl ...

SPOOKY: Gazelle Nataways, she was the dancing girl ...

The music is now on full volume and NANABUSH / GAZELLE's strip is in full swing. She dances on top of the jukebox, which is now a riot of sound and flashing lights. SPOOKY's kitchen is bathed in a gorgeous lavender light. BIG JOEY and CREATURE NATAWAYS appear at SPOOKY's table, each drinking a bottle of beer. The strip of seventeen years ago is fully re-created, the memory becoming so heated that NANABUSH / GAZELLE magically appears dancing right on top of SPOOKY's kitchen table. The men are going wild, applauding, laughing, drinking, all in slow motion and mime. In the heat of the moment, as NANABUSH / GAZELLE strips down to silk tassels and G-string, they begin tearing their clothes off.

Suddenly, SIMON STARBLANKET appears at SPOOKY's door. NANABUSH / GAZELLE disappears, as do BIG JOEY and CREATURE. SPOOKY, PIERRE, and ZACHARY are caught with their pants down. The jukebox music fades.

SIMON: Spooky Lacroix.

The lavender light snaps off, we are back to "reality," and SPOOKY, PIERRE, and ZACHARY stand there, embarrassed. In a panic, they begin putting their clothes back on and reclaim the positions they had before the strip. SPOOKY motions SIMON to take a seat at the table. SIMON does so.

SIMON: Spooky Lacroix. Rosie Kakapetum expresses interest in coming here to birth Lalala's baby when the time comes.

SPOOKY: Rosie Kakapetum? No way some witch is gonna come and put her witchy little fingers on my baby boy.

SIMON: Rosie Kakapetum's no witch, Spooky Lacroix. She's Patsy Pegahmagahbow's stepmother and she's Wasy's only surviving medicine woman and midwife ...

SPOOKY: Hogwash!

PIERRE: Ahem. Rosie Kakapetum says it's a cryin' shame the Wasy Wailerettes is the only team that's not in the Ontario Hockey League.

ZACHARY: Ontario Hockey League?

PIERRE: Absolutely. The OHL. Indian women's OHL. All the Indian women in Ontario's playin' hockey now. It's like a fever out there.

ZACHARY: Shoot. (*referring to his pastry*) I hope this new recipe works for me.

PIERRE: Well, it's not exactly new without the cinnamon.

SPOOKY: (*to SIMON*) My son will be born at Sudbury General Hospital ...

SIMON: You know what they do to them babies in them city hospitals?

SPOOKY: ... Sudbury General, Simon Starblanket, like any good Christian boy ...

PIERRE: (*attempting to defuse the argument*) Ahem. We got to get them Wasy Wailerettes back on that ice again.

SIMON: (*refusing to let go of SPOOKY*) They pull them away right from their own mother's breast the minute they come into this world and they put them behind these glass cages together with another two hundred babies like they were some kind of scientific specimens –

PIERRE: – like two hundred of them little monsters –

ZACHARY: Hamsters!

PIERRE: – that's what I said dammit –

SPOOKY: – tsk –

PIERRE: ... you can't even tell which hamster belongs to which mother. You take Lalala to Sudbury General, Spooky Lacroix, and your hamster's liable to end up stuck to some French lady's tit.

SIMON: ... and they'll hang Lalala up in metal stirrups and your baby's gonna be born going up instead of dropping down which is the natural way. You were born going up instead of dropping down like you should have ...

PIERRE: Yup. You were born at Sudbury General, Spooky Lacroix, that's why you get weirder and weirder as the days get longer, that's why them white peoples is so weird they were all born going up –

SIMON: – instead of dropping down –

ZACHARY: (*sprinkling flour in SPOOKY's face, with both hands, and laughing*) ... to the earth, Spooky Lacroix, to the earth ...

SPOOKY: Pooh!

PIERRE: ... but we got to find that puck, Simon Starblanket, them Wasy Wailerettes have got to join the OHL ...

SPOOKY: (*to SIMON*) If Rosie Kakapetum is a medicine woman, Simon Starblanket, then how come she can't drive the madness from my nephew's brain, how come she can't make him talk, huh?

SIMON: Because the medical establishment and the church establishment and people like you, Spooky Lacroix, have effectively put an end to her usefulness and the usefulness of people like her everywhere, that's why Spooky Lacroix.

SPOOKY: Phooey!

SIMON: Do you or your sister even know that your nephew hasn't been home in two days, since that incident at the hockey game, Spooky Lacroix? Do you even care? Why can't you and that thing (*pointing at the Bible that sits beside SPOOKY*) and all it stands for cure your nephew's madness, as you call it, Spooky Lacroix? What has this thing (*the Bible again*) done to cure the madness of this community and communities like it clean across the country, Spooky Lacroix? Why didn't "the Lord," as you call Him, come to your sister's rescue at that bar seventeen years ago, huh, Spooky Lacroix? (*pause; tense silence*) Rosie Kakapetum is gonna be my mother-in-law in two months, Spooky Lacroix, and if Patsy and I are gonna do

this thing right, if we're gonna work together to make my best man, Dickie Bird Halked, well again, then Rosie Kakapetum has got to birth that baby. (*He begins to exit.*)

SPOOKY: (*in hard, measured cadence*) Rosie Kakapetum works for the devil.

> *SIMON freezes in his tracks. Silence. Then he turns, grabs a chair violently, bangs it down and sits determinedly.*

SIMON: Fine. I'll sit here and I'll wait.

SPOOKY: Fine. You sit there and you wait.

> *Silence. SIMON sits silent and motionless, his back to the other men.*

PIERRE: Ahem. Never mind, Spooky Lacroix, never you mind. Now as I was sayin', Black Lady Halked was nine months pregnant when she was sittin' in that corner of the Queen of Hearts.

SPOOKY: The Belvedere!

PIERRE: Three weeks, Black Lady Halked was sittin' there drinkin' beer. They say she got the money by winnin' the jackpot at the Espanola bingo just three blocks down the street. Three weeks, sure as I'm alive and walkin' these treacherous icy roads, three weeks she sat there in that dark corner by herself. They say the only light you could see her by was the light from the jukebox playin' "Rim of Fire" by Johnny Cash ...

ZACHARY: "Rim of Fire." Yeah, right, Pierre St. Pierre.

SPOOKY: Kitty Wells! Kitty Wells!

> *The sound of the jukebox playing "It Wasn't God Who Made Honky Tonk Angels" can be heard faintly in the background.*

PIERRE: ... the place was so jam-packed with people drinkin' and singin' and smokin' cigarettes and watchin' the dancin' girl ...

SPOOKY: ... Gazelle Nataways, she was the dancing girl, Lord save her soul ...

PIERRE: ... until Black Lady Halked collapsed.

> *SPOOKY, PIERRE, and ZACHARY freeze in their positions, looking in horror at the memory of seventeen years ago.*

> *On the upper level NANABUSH, back in her guise as the spirit of BLACK LADY HALKED, sits on the jukebox, facing the audience, legs out directly in front. Nine months pregnant and naked, she holds*

a bottle of beer up in the air and is drunk almost senseless. The song "It Wasn't God Who Made Honky Tonk Angels" rises to full volume, the lights from the jukebox flashing riotously. The full moon glows blood red. Immediately below NANABUSH / BLACK LADY HALKED, DICKIE BIRD HALKED appears, kneeling, naked, arms raised toward his mother. NANABUSH / BLACK LADY HALKED begins to writhe and scream, laughing and crying hysterically at the same time and, as she does, her water breaks. DICKIE BIRD, drenched, rises slowly from the floor, arms still raised, and screams.

DICKIE BIRD: Mama! Mama!

From here on, the lights and sound on this scene begin to fade slowly, as the scene on the lower level resumes.

PIERRE: ... she kind of oozed down right then and there, right down to the floor of the Queen of Hearts Tavern. And Big Joey, may he rot in hell, he was the bouncer there that night, when he saw the blood, he ran away and puked over on the other side of the bar, the sight of all that woman's blood just scared the shit right out of him. And that's when Dickie Bird Halked, as we know him, came ragin' out from his mother's womb, Spooky Lacroix, in between beers, right there on the floor, under a table, by the light of the jukebox, on a Saturday night, at the Queen of Hearts ...

SPOOKY: They went and named him after the bar, you crusted old fossil! That bar, which is now called the Belvedere Hotel, used to be called the Dickie Bird Tavern ...

SIMON: (*suddenly jumping out of his chair and practically lunging at SPOOKY*) It doesn't matter what the fuck the name of that fucking bar was! (*The lights and sound on NANABUSH and the jukebox have now faded completely.*) The fact of the matter is, it never should have happened, that kind of thing should never be allowed to happen, not to us Indians, not to anyone living and breathing on the face of God's green earth. (*Pause. Silence. Then dead calm.*) You guys have given up, haven't you? You and your generation. You gave up a long time ago. You'd rather turn your back on the whole thing and pretend to laugh, wouldn't you? (*silence*) Well, not me. Not us. (*silence*) This is not the kind of earth we want to inherit. (*He begins to leave, but turns once more.*) I'll be back. With Patsy. And Rosie. (*He exits. Another embarrassed silence.*)

SPOOKY: (*Unwilling to face up to the full horror of it, he chooses, instead, to do exactly what SIMON*

said: turn his back and pretend to laugh.*) That bar, which is now called the Belvedere Hotel, used to be called the Dickie Bird Tavern. That's how Dickie Bird Halked got his name. And that's why he goes haywire every now and again and that's why he doesn't talk. Fetal alcohol something something, Pierre St. Pierre ...

ZACHARY: (*from behind the counter, where he is still busy making pie crust*) Fetal alcohol syndrome.

SPOOKY: ... that's the devil that stole the baby's tongue because Dickie Bird Halked was born drunk and very, very mad. At the Dickie Bird Tavern in downtown Espanola seventeen years ago and that's a fact.

PIERRE: Aw, shit la marde. Fuck you, Spooky Lacroix, I'm gonna go get me my rest. (*throws the yarn in SPOOKY's face, jumps up and exits*)

SPOOKY sits there with a pile of yarn stuck to his face, caught on his glasses.

ZACHARY: (*proudly holding up the pie crust in its plate*) It worked!

Blackout.

On the upper level, in a dim light away from her perch, NANABUSH / BLACK LADY HALKED is getting ready to go out for the evening, combing her hair in front of a mirror, putting on her clothes, etc. DICKIE BIRD is with her, naked, getting ready to go to bed. SPOOKY's crucifix sits on a night table to the side. In DICKIE BIRD's mind, he is at home with his mother.

DICKIE BIRD: Mama. Mama. N'tagoosin. (*"I'm sick."*)

NANABUSH / BLACK LADY: Say your prayers.

DICKIE BIRD: Achimoostawin nimoosoom. (*"Tell me about my grandpa."*)

NANABUSH / BLACK LADY: Go to bed. I'm going out soon.

DICKIE BIRD: Mawch. Achimoostawin nimoosoom. (*"No. Tell me about my grandpa."*)

NANABUSH / BLACK LADY: You shouldn't talk about him.

DICKIE BIRD: Tapweechee eegeemachi-poowamit nimoosoom? (*"Is it true my grandpa had bad medicine?"*)

NANABUSH / BLACK LADY: They say he met the devil once. Your grandpa talked to the devil. Don't talk about him.

DICKIE BIRD: Eegeemithoopoowamit nim-oosoom, eetweet Simon Starblanket. (*"Simon Starblanket says he had good medicine."*)

NANABUSH / BLACK LADY: Ashhh! Simon Starblanket.

DICKIE BIRD: Mawch eemithoosit awa aymeewatik keetnanow kichi, eetweet Simon Starblanket. (*"Simon Starblanket says that this cross is not right for us."*) (*He grabs the crucifix from the night table and spits on it.*)

NANABUSH / BLACK LADY: (*Grabbing the crucifix from DICKIE BIRD, she attempts to spank him but DICKIE BIRD evades her.*) Dickie Bird! Kipasta-ood! (*"You're committing a mortal sin!"*) Say ten Hail Marys and two Our Fathers.

DICKIE BIRD: Mootha apoochiga taskootch nimama keetha. Mootha apoochiga m'tanawgwatch kisagee-in. (*"You're not even like my mother. You don't even love me at all."*)

NANABUSH / BLACK LADY: Dickie Bird. Shut up. I'll say them with you. "Hail Mary, full of grace, the Lord is with thee ..." Hurry up. I have to go out. (*She prepares to leave.*) "Hail Mary, full of grace, the Lord is with thee ..." (*She gives up.*) Ashhh! Your father should be home soon. (*exits*)

DICKIE BIRD: (*speaking to the now absent NANABUSH / BLACK LADY*) Mootha nipapa ana. (*"He's not my father."*) (*He grabs his clothes and the crucifix and runs out, down to the lower level and into the forest made of light and shadows.*) Tapwee anima ka-itweechik, chee-i? Neetha ooma kimineechagan, chee-i? (*"It's true what they say, isn't it? I'm a bastard, aren't I?"*) (*He is now sitting on the rock where SIMON and ZACHARY first met in Act One.*) Nipapa ana ... Big Joey ... (*to himself, quietly*) ... nipapa ana ... Big Joey ... (*"My father is ... Big Joey."*) (*silence*)

A few moments later, NANABUSH comes bouncing into the forest, as the spirit of the vivacious young PATSY PEGAHMAGAHBOW, complete with very large, oversized bum. The full moon glows.

NANABUSH / PATSY: (*to herself, as she peers into the shadows*) Oooh, my poor bum. I fell on the ice four days ago, eh! And it still hurts, oooh. (*She finally sees DICKIE BIRD huddling on the rock, barely dressed.*) There you are. I came out to look for you. What happened to your clothes? It's freezing out here. Put them on. Here. (*She starts to help dress him.*) What happened at the arena? You were on the ice, eh! You feel like talking? In Indian? How, weetamawin. (*"Come on, tell me."*)

BIG JOEY and CREATURE NATAWAYS enter a distance away. They are smoking a joint and BIG JOEY carries a gun. They stop and watch from the shadows.

CREATURE: Check her out.

NANABUSH / PATSY: Why do you always carry that crucifix? I don't believe that stuff. I traded mine in for sweetgrass. Hey. You wanna come to Rosie's and eat fry bread with me? Simon will be there, too. Simon and me, we're getting married, eh? We're gonna have a baby ...

CREATURE: What's she trying to do?

NANABUSH / PATSY: ... Rosie's got deer meat, too, come on, you like my mom's cooking, eh? (*She attempts to take the crucifix away from DICKIE BIRD.*) But you'll have to leave that here because Rosie can't stand the Pope ...

DICKIE BIRD grabs the crucifix back.

CREATURE: What's he trying to do?

NANABUSH / PATSY: ... give it to me ... Dickie ... come on ...

CREATURE: He's weird, Big Joey, he's weird.

NANABUSH / PATSY: ... leave it here ... it will be safe here ... we'll bury it in the snow ... (*Playfully, she tries to get the crucifix away from DICKIE BIRD.*)

CREATURE: Hey, don't do that, don't do that, man, he's ticklish.

NANABUSH / PATSY: (*As DICKIE BIRD begins poking her playfully with the crucifix and laughing, NANABUSH / PATSY gradually starts to get frightened.*) ... don't look at me that way ... Dickie Bird, what's wrong? ... ya, Dickie Bird, awus ...

DICKIE BIRD starts to grab at NANABUSH / PATSY.

CREATURE: Hey, don't you think, don't you think ... he's getting kind of carried away?

NANABUSH / PATSY: ... awus ...

CREATURE: We gotta do something, Big Joey, we gotta do something. (*BIG JOEY stops CREATURE.*) Let go! Let go!

NANABUSH / PATSY: (*now in a panic*) Awus! Awus! Awus! ...

DICKIE BIRD grabs NANABUSH / PATSY and throws her violently to the ground. He lifts her skirt and shoves the crucifix up against her.

BIG JOEY: (*to* CREATURE) Shut up.

NANABUSH / PATSY: (*screams and goes into hysteria*) ... Simon! ...

> DICKIE BIRD *rapes* NANABUSH / PATSY *with the crucifix. A heartbreaking, very slow, sensuous tango breaks out on offstage harmonica.*

CREATURE: (*to* BIG JOEY) No! Let me go. Big Joey, let me go, please!

BIG JOEY: (*suddenly grabs* CREATURE *violently by the collar*) Get out. Get the fuck out of here. You're nothin' but a fuckin' fruit. Fuck off. (CREATURE *collapses.*) I said fuck off.

> CREATURE *flees.* BIG JOEY *just stands there, paralyzed, and watches.*

> NANABUSH / PATSY, *who has gradually been moving back and back, is now standing up on her perch again (i.e., the "mound" jukebox which no longer looks like a jukebox). She stands there, facing the audience, and slowly gathers her skirt, in agony, until she is holding it up above her waist. A blood stain slowly spreads across her panties and flows down her leg. At the same time,* DICKIE BIRD *stands downstage beside the rock, holding the crucifix and making violent jabbing motions with it, downward. All this happens in slow motion. The crucifix starts to bleed. When* DICKIE BIRD *lifts the crucifix up, his arms and chest are covered with blood. Finally,* NANABUSH / PATSY *collapses to the floor of her platform and slowly crawls away. Lights fade on her. On the lower level,* BIG JOEY, *in a state of shock, staggers, almost faints, and vomits violently. Then he reels over to* DICKIE BIRD *and, not knowing what else to do, begins collecting his clothes and calming him down.*

BIG JOEY: How, Dickie Bird. How, astum. Igwa. Mootha nantow. Mootha nantow. Shhh. Shhh. (*"Come on, Dickie Bird. Come. Let's go. It's okay. It's okay. Shhh. Shhh ..."*) (*Barely able to bring himself to touch it, he takes the crucifix from* DICKIE BIRD *and drops it quickly on the rock. Then he begins wiping the blood off* DICKIE BIRD.) How, mootha nantow. Mootha nantow. How, astum, keeyapitch uplsees ootee. Igwani. Igwani. Poonimatoo. Mootha nantow. Mootha nantow. (*"Come on, it's okay. It's okay. Come on, a little more over here. That's all. That's all. Stop crying. It's okay. It's okay ..."*) (*DICKIE BIRD, shaking with emotion, looks questioningly into* BIG JOEY's *face.*) Eehee. Nigoosis keetha. Mootha

Wellington Halked kipapa. Neetha ... kipapa. (*"Yes. You are my son. Wellington Halked is not your father. I'm ... your father."*)

> *Silence. They look at each other.* DICKIE BIRD *grabs* BIG JOEY *and clings to him,* BIG JOEY *reacting tentatively at first, and then passionately, with* DICKIE BIRD *finally bursting out into uncontrollable sobs. Fade-out.*

> *Out of this darkness gunshots explode. And we hear a man's voice wailing, in complete and utter agony. Then comes violent pounding at a door. Finally, still in the darkness, we hear* SIMON STARBLANKET's *speaking voice.*

SIMON: Open up! Pierre St. Pierre, open up! I know you're in there!

PIERRE: (*still in the darkness*) Whoa! Easy now. Easy on that goddamn door. Must you create such a carpostrophe smack dab in the middle of my rest period?

> *When the lights come up, we are outside the "window" to* PIERRE ST. PIERRE's *little bootleg joint.* PIERRE *pokes his head out, wearing his night clothes, complete with pointy cap.*

PIERRE: Go home. Go to bed. Don't be disturbin' my rest period. My wife, Veronique St. Pierre, she tells me there's now not only a OHL but a NHL, too. Indian women's National Hockey League. All the Indian women on every reserve in Canada, all the Indian women in Canada is playin' hockey now. It's like a fever out there. That's why I gotta get my rest. First thing tomorrow mornin', I go jiggle that puck out of Gazelle Nataways. Listen to me. I'm your elder.

> SIMON *shoots the gun into the house, just missing* PIERRE's *head.*

SIMON: (*dead calm*) One, you give me a bottle. Two, I report your joint to the Manitowaning police. Three, I shoot your fucking head off.

PIERRE: All right. All right. (*He pops in for a bottle of whisky and hands it out to* SIMON.) Now you go on home with this. Go have yourself a nice quiet drink. (SIMON *begins to exit.* PIERRE *calls out.*) What the hell are you gonna do with that gun?

SIMON: (*calling back*) I'm gonna go get that mute. Little bastard raped Patsy Pegahmagahbow. (*exits*)

> *Pause.*

PIERRE: Holy shit la marde! (*pause*) I gotta warn him. No. I need my rest. No. I gotta warn that boy. No. I gotta find that puck. No. Dickie Bird's life. No. The puck. No. Dickie Bird. No. Hockey. No. His life. No. Hockey. No. Life. Hockey. Life. Hockey. Life. Hockey. Life. Hockey. Life. Hockey. Life ...

Fade-out.

Lights up on **SPOOKY LACROIX**'s *kitchen.* **CREATURE NATAWAYS** *is sitting at the table, silent, head propped up in his hands.* **SPOOKY** *is knitting, with obvious haste, a white christening gown, of which a large crucifix is the centrepiece.* **SPOOKY**'s *Bible still sits on the table beside him.*

SPOOKY: Why didn't you do something? (*silence*) Creature. (*Silence.* **SPOOKY** *stops knitting and looks up.*) Alphonse Nataways, why didn't you stop him? (*silence*) You're scared of him, aren't you? You're scared to death of Big Joey. Admit it. (*silence*)

CREATURE: (*quietly and calmly*) I love him, Spooky.

SPOOKY: Say wha?!

CREATURE: I love him.

SPOOKY: You love him? What do you mean? How? How do you love him?

CREATURE: I love him.

SPOOKY: Lord, have mercy on Wasaychigan Hill!

CREATURE: (*rising suddenly*) I love the way he stands. I love the way he walks. The way he laughs. The way he wears his cowboy boots ...

SPOOKY: You're kidding me.

CREATURE: ... the way his tight blue jeans fall over his ass. The way he talks so smart and tough. The way women fall at his feet. I wanna be like him. I always wanted to be like him, William. I always wanted to have a dick as big as his.

SPOOKY: Creature Alphonse Nataways! You know not what you say.

CREATURE: I don't care.

SPOOKY: I care.

CREATURE: I don't care. I can't stand it anymore.

SPOOKY: Shut up. You're making me nervous. Real nervous.

CREATURE: Come with me.

SPOOKY: Come with you where?

CREATURE: To his house.

SPOOKY: Whose house?

CREATURE: Big Joey.

SPOOKY: Are you crazy?

CREATURE: Come with me.

SPOOKY: No.

CREATURE: Yes.

SPOOKY: No.

CREATURE: (*suddenly and viciously grabbing* **SPOOKY** *by the throat*) Cut the goddamn bullcrap, Spooky Lacroix! (**SPOOKY** *tries desperately to save the christening gown.*) I seen you crawl in the mud and shit so drunk you were snortin' like a pig.

SPOOKY: I changed my ways, thank you.

CREATURE: Twenty-one years. Twenty-one years ago. You, me, Big Joey, Eugene Starblanket, that goddamn Zachary Jeremiah Keechigeesik. We were eighteen. We cut our wrists. Your own father's huntin' knife. We mixed blood. Swore we'd be friends for life. Frontenac Hotel. Twenty-one years ago. You got jumped by seven white guys. Broken beer bottle come straight at your face. If it wasn't for me, you wouldn't be here today, wavin' that stinkin' Bible in my face like it was a slab of meat. I'm not a dog. I'm your buddy. Your friend.

SPOOKY: I know that.

CREATURE tightens his hold on SPOOKY's throat. The two men are staring straight into each other's eyes, inches apart. Silence.

CREATURE: William. Think of your father. Remember the words of Nicotine Lacroix.

Finally, **SPOOKY** *screams, throwing the christening gown, knitting needles and all, over the bible on the table.*

SPOOKY: You goddamn fucking son of a bitch!

Blackout. Gunshots in the distance.

Lights up on **BIG JOEY**'s *living room and kitchen.* **BIG JOEY** *is sitting, silent and motionless, on the couch, staring straight ahead, as though he were in a trance. His hunting rifle rests on his lap.* **DICKIE BIRD HALKED** *stands directly facing the life-size pin-up poster of Marilyn Monroe, also as though he were in a trance. Then his head drops down in remorse.* **BIG JOEY** *lifts the gun, loads it, and aims it out directly in front. When* **DICKIE BIRD** *hears the snap of the gun being loaded, he turns to look. Then he slowly walks over to* **BIG JOEY**, *kneels down directly in front of the barrel of the gun, puts it in his mouth, and then slowly reaches over and gently, almost lovingly, moves* **BIG JOEY**'s hand away from the trigger, caressing the older man's hand as he does. BIG JOEY slowly looks up at DICKIE BIRD's face, stunned. DICKIE BIRD puts his own thumb on the trigger and pulls. Click. Nothing. In the complete silence, the two men are looking directly into each other's eyes. Complete stillness. Fade-out. Split seconds before complete blackout, Marilyn Monroe farts, courtesy of MS. NANABUSH: a little flag reading "poot" pops up out of Ms. Monroe's derriere, as on a play gun. We hear a cute little "poot" sound.

Out of this blackout emerges the sound of a harmonica; it is ZACHARY JEREMIAH KEECHIGEESIK playing his heart out. Fade-in on PIERRE ST. PIERRE, still in his nightclothes but also wearing his winter coat and hat over them, rushing all over the "forest," ostensibly rushing to BIG JOEY's house to warn DICKIE BIRD HALKED about the gun-toting SIMON STARBLANKET. He mutters to himself as he goes.

PIERRE: ... Hockey. Life. Hockey. Life. Hockey.

ZACHARY appears in the shadows and sees PIERRE.

ZACHARY: Hey!

PIERRE: (*not hearing ZACHARY*) ... Hockey. Life. Hockey. Life ...

ZACHARY: Pssst!

PIERRE: (*still not hearing ZACHARY*) Hockey. Life. Hockey. Life. (*pause*) Hockey life!

ZACHARY: (*finally yelling*) Pierre St. Pierre!

PIERRE: (*jumps*) Hallelujah! Have you heard the news?

ZACHARY: The Band Council went and okayed Big Joey's radio station.

PIERRE: All the Indian women in the world is playin' hockey now! World Hockey League, they call themselves. Aboriginal Women's WHL. My wife, Veronique St. Pierre, she just got the news. Eegeeweetamagoot fax machine. (*"Fax machine told her."*) It's like a burnin', ragin', blindin' fever out there. Them Cree women in Saskatchewan, them Blood women in Alberta, them Yakima, them Heidis out in the middle of your Specific Ocean, them Kickapoo, Chickasaw, Cherokee, Chepewyan, Choctaw, Chippewa, Wichita, Kiowa down in Oklahoma, them Seminole, Navajo, Onondaga, Tuscarora, Winnebago, Micmac-paddy-wack-why-it's-enough-to-give-your-dog-a-bone! ... (*Getting completely carried away, he grabs his crotch.*)

ZACHARY: Pierre. Pierre.

PIERRE: ... they're turnin' the whole world topsy-turkey right before our very eyes and the prime minister's a-shittin' grape juice ... (*A gunshot explodes in the near distance. PIERRE suddenly lays low and changes tone completely.*) Holy shit la marde! He's after Dickie Bird. There's a red-eyed, crazed devil out there and he's after Dickie Bird Halked and he's gonna kill us all if we don't stop him right this minute.

ZACHARY: Who? Who's gonna kill us?

PIERRE: Simon Starblanket. Drunk. Power mad. Half-crazed on whisky and he's got a gun.

ZACHARY: Simon!

PIERRE: He's drunk and he's mean and he's out to kill. (*another gunshot*) Hear that!

ZACHARY: (*to himself*) That's Simon? I thought ...

PIERRE: When he heard about the Pegahmagahbow rape ...

ZACHARY: Pegahmagahbow what?

PIERRE: Why, haven't you heard? Dickie Bird Halked raped Patsy Pegahmagahbow in most brutal fashion and Simon Starblanket is out to kill Dickie Bird Halked so I'm on my way to Big Joey's right this minute and I'm takin' that huntin' rifle of his and I'm sittin' next to that Halked boy right up until the cows come home. (*exits*)

ZACHARY: (*to himself*) Simon Starblanket. Patsy ...

Blackout.

Out of this blackout come the gunshots, much louder this time, and SIMON's wailing voice.

SIMON: Aieeeeee-yip-yip! Nanabush! ...

Fade-in on SIMON, in the forest close by the large rock, still carrying his hunting rifle. SIMON is half-crazed by this time, drunk out of his skull. The full moon glows.

SIMON: ... Weesageechak! Come back! Rosie! Rosie Kakapetum, tell him to come back, not to run away, cuz we need him ...

NANABUSH / PATSY PEGAHMAGAHBOW's voice comes filtering out of the darkness on the upper level. It is as though SIMON were hearing a voice from inside his head.

NANABUSH / PATSY: ... her ...

SIMON: ... him ...

NANABUSH / PATSY: ... her ...

Slow fade-in on NANABUSH / PATSY, standing on the upper level, looking down at SIMON. She still wears her very large bum.

SIMON: ... weetha (*"him or her" – i.e., no gender*) ... Christ! What is it? Him? Her? Stupid fucking language, fuck you, da Englesa. Me no speakum no more da goodie Englesa, in Cree we say "weetha," not "him" or "her," Nanabush, come back! (*Speaks directly to NANABUSH, as though he or she were there, directly in front of him; he doesn't see NANABUSH / PATSY standing on the upper level.*) Aw, boozhoo how are ya! Me good. Me berry, berry good. I seen you! Just seen you jumping jack-ass thisaway ...

NANABUSH / PATSY: (*as though he or she were playing games behind SIMON's back*) ... and thataway ...

SIMON: ... and thisaway and ...

NANABUSH / PATSY: ... thataway ...

SIMON: ... and thisaway and ...

NANABUSH / PATSY: ... thataway ...

SIMON: ... and thisaway and ...

NANABUSH / PATSY: ... thataway ...

SIMON: ... et cetra, et cetra, et cetra ...

NANABUSH / PATSY: et cetERA. (*pause*) She's here! She's here!

SIMON: ... Nanabush! Weesageechak! (*NANABUSH / PATSY peals out with a silvery, magical laugh that echoes and echoes.*) Dey shove dis ... whach-you-ma-call-it ... da crucifix up your holy cunt ouch, eh? Ouch, eh? (*SIMON sees the bloody crucifix sitting on the rock and slowly approaches it. He kneels directly before it.*) Nah ... (*laughs a long, mad, hysterical laugh that ends with hysterical weeping*) ... yesssss ... noooo ... oh noooo! Crucifix! (*spits violently on the crucifix*) Fucking goddamn crucifix, yesssss ... God! You're a man. You're a woman. You're a man? You're a woman? You see, nineethoowan poogoo neetha (*"I speak only Cree"*) ...

NANABUSH / PATSY: ... ohhh ...

SIMON: ... keetha ma-a? (*"How about you?"*) Nah. Da Englesa him ...

NANABUSH / PATSY: ... her ...

SIMON: ... him ...

NANABUSH / PATSY: ... her ...

SIMON: ... him! ...

NANABUSH / PATSY: ... her! ...

SIMON: ... all da time ...

NANABUSH / PATSY: ... all da time ...

SIMON: ... tsk, tsk, tsk ...

NANABUSH / PATSY: ... tsk, tsk, tsk.

SIMON: If, God, you are a woman/man in Cree but only a man in da Englesa, then how come you still got a cun ...

NANABUSH / PATSY: ... a womb.

With this, SIMON finally sees NANABUSH / PATSY. He calls out to her.

SIMON: Patsy! Big Bum Pegahmagahbow, you flying across da ice on world's biggest puck. Patsy, look what dey done to your puss ... (*NANABUSH / PATSY lifts her skirt and displays the blood stain on her panties. She then finally takes off the prosthetic that is her huge bum and holds it in one arm.*) Hey! (*NANABUSH / PATSY holds an eagle feather up in the air, ready to dance. SIMON stomps on the ground, rhythmically, and sings.*) "... and me I don't wanna go to the moon, I'm gonna leave that moon alone. I just wanna dance with the Rosebud Sioux this summer, yeah, yeah, yeah ..." (*SIMON chants and he and NANABUSH / PATSY dance, he on the lower level with his hunting rifle in the air, she on the upper level with her eagle feather.*) How, astum, Patsy, kiam. N'tayneemeetootan. (*"Come on, Patsy, never mind. Let's go dance."*)

We hear ZACHARY JEREMIAH KEECHIGEESIK's voice calling from the darkness a distance away.

ZACHARY: Hey!

But SIMON and NANABUSH / PATSY pay no heed.

NANABUSH / PATSY: ... n'tayneemeetootan South Dakota? ...

SIMON: ... how, astum, Patsy. N'tayneemeetootan South Dakota. Hey, Patsy Pegahmagahbow ... (*He finally approaches her and holds his hand out.*)

NANABUSH / PATSY: (*holds her hand out toward his*) ... Simon Starblanket ...

SIMON & NANABUSH / PATSY: ... eenpaysageeitan (*"I love you to death"*) ...

ZACHARY finally emerges tentatively from the shadows. He is holding a beautiful, fresh pie. NANABUSH / PATSY disappears.

ZACHARY: (*calling out over the distance*) Hey! You want some pie?

SIMON: (*silence; calling back*) What?! (*Not seeing ZACHARY, he looks around cautiously.*)

ZACHARY: I said. You want some pie?

SIMON: (*calling back, after some confused thought*) What?

ZACHARY: (*approaches SIMON slowly*) Do you want some pie?

SIMON: (*Silence. Finally, he sees ZACHARY and points the gun at him.*) What kind?

ZACHARY: Apple. I just made some. It's still hot.

SIMON: (*long pause*) Okay.

Slowly, NANABUSH / PATSY re-enters the scene and comes up behind SIMON, holding SIMON's dancing bustle in front of her, as in a ceremony.

ZACHARY: Okay. But you gotta give me the gun first. (*The gun goes off accidentally, just missing ZACHARY's head.*) I said, you gotta give me the gun first.

Gradually, the dancing bustle begins to shimmer and dance in NANABUSH / PATSY's hands.

SIMON: Patsy. I gotta go see Patsy.

ZACHARY: You and me and Patsy and Hera. We're gonna go have some pie. Fresh, hot apple pie. Then, we go to Sudbury and have a look at that Mobart, what do you say?

The shimmering movements of the bustle balloon out into magical, dance-like arches, as NANABUSH / PATSY manoeuvres it directly in front of SIMON, hiding him momentarily. Behind this, SIMON drops the base of the rifle to the ground, causing it to go off accidentally. The bullet hits SIMON in the stomach. He falls to the ground. ZACHARY lets go of his pie and runs over to him. The shimmering of the bustle dies off into the darkness of the forest and disappears, NANABUSH / PATSY manoeuvring it.

ZACHARY: Simon! Simon! Oh, lordy, lordy, lordy ... Are you all right? Are you okay? Simon. Simon. Talk to me. Goodness sakes, talk to me Simon. Ayumi-in! (*"Talk to me!"*)

SIMON: (*barely able to speak, as he sinks slowly to the ground beside the large rock*) Kamoowanow ... apple ... pie ... patima ... neetha ... igwa Patsy ... n'gapeetootanan ... patima ... apple ... pie ... neee. (*"We'll eat ... apple ... pie ... later ... me ... and Patsy ... we'll come over ... later ... apple ... pie ... neee."*) (*He dies.*)

ZACHARY: (*kneels over SIMON's body, the full moon glowing even redder*) Oh, lordy, lordy ... Holy shit! Holy shit! What's happening? What's become of this place? What's happening to this place?

What's happening to these people? My people. He didn't have to die. He didn't have to die. That's the goddamn most stupid ... no reason ... this kind of living has got to stop. It's got to stop! (*talking and then just shrieking at the sky*) Aieeeeeee-Lord! God! God of the Indian! God of the white man! God-Al-fucking-mighty! Whatever the fuck your name is. Why are you doing this to us? Why are you doing this to us? Are you up there at all? Or are you some stupid, drunken shit, out-of-your-mind-passed-out under some great beer table up there in your stupid fucking clouds? Come down! Astum oota! (*"Come down here!"*) Why don't you come down? I dare you to come down from your high-falutin' fuckin' shit-throne up there, come down and show us you got the guts to stop this stupid, stupid, stupid way of living. It's got to stop. It's got to stop. It's got to stop. It's got to stop. It's got to stop ...

He collapses over SIMON's body and weeps. Fade-out.

Toward the end of this speech a light comes up on NANABUSH. Her perch (i.e., the jukebox) has swivelled around and she is sitting on a toilet having a good shit. He or she is dressed in an old man's white beard and wig, but also wearing sexy, elegant women's high-heeled pumps. Surrounded by white, puffy clouds, he or she sits with her legs crossed, nonchalantly filing his or her fingernails. Fade-out.

Fade-in on BIG JOEY's living room and kitchen. BIG JOEY, DICKIE BIRD HALKED, CREATURE NATAWAYS, SPOOKY LACROIX, and PIERRE ST. PIERRE are sitting and standing in various positions, in complete silence. A hush pervades the room for about twenty beats. DICKIE BIRD is holding BIG JOEY's hunting rifle. Suddenly, ZACHARY JEREMIAH KEECHIGEESIK enters, in a semi-crazed state. DICKIE BIRD starts and points the rifle straight at ZACHARY's head.

CREATURE: Zachary Jeremiah! What are you doing here?

BIG JOEY: Lookin' for your shorts, Zach?

From his position on the couch, he motions DICKIE BIRD to put the gun down. DICKIE BIRD does so.

ZACHARY: (*to BIG JOEY*) You're unbelievable. You're fucking unbelievable. You let this young man, you let your own son get away with this inconceivable act ...

CREATURE: Don't say that to him, Zachary Jeremiah, don't say that ...

ZACHARY: (*ignoring* CREATURE) You know he did it and you're hiding him what in God's name is wrong with you?

SPOOKY: Zachary Jeremiah, you're not yourself ...

PIERRE: Nope. Not himself. Talkin' wild. (*Sensing potential violence, he sneaks out the door.*)

BIG JOEY: (*to* ZACHARY) He don't even know he done anything.

ZACHARY: Bullshit! They're not even sure the air ambulance will get Patsy Pegahmagahbow to Sudbury in time. Simon Starblanket just shot himself and this boy is responsible ...

SIMON rises slowly from the ground and "sleep-walks" right through this scene and up to the upper level, toward the full moon. The men are only vaguely aware of his passing.

BIG JOEY: He ain't responsible for nothin'.

ZACHARY: Simon Starblanket was on his way to South Dakota where he could have learned a few things and made something of himself, same place you went and made a total asshole of yourself seventeen years ago ...

CREATURE: Shush, Zachary Jeremiah, that's the past ...

SPOOKY: ... the past ...

CREATURE: ... Chrissakes ...

ZACHARY: What happened to all those dreams you were so full of for your people, the same dreams this young man just died for?

SPOOKY: (*to* BIG JOEY, *though not looking at him*) And my sister, Black Lady Halked, seventeen years ago at that bar, Big Joey, you could have stopped her drinking, you could have sent her home, and this thing never would have happened. That was your son inside her belly.

CREATURE: He didn't do nothing. He wouldn't let me do nothing. He just stood there and watched the whole thing ...

SPOOKY: Creature Nataways!

CREATURE: I don't care. I'm gonna tell. He watched this little bastard do that to Patsy Pegahmagahbow ...

BIG JOEY: (*suddenly turning on* CREATURE) You little cocksucker!

DICKIE BIRD hits CREATURE on the back with the butt of the rifle, knocking him unconscious.

SPOOKY: Why, Big Joey, why did you do that?

Silence.

ZACHARY: Yes, Joe. Why?

Long silence. All the men look at BIG JOEY.

BIG JOEY: (*raising his arms, as for a battle cry*) "This is the end of the suffering of a great nation!" That was me. Wounded Knee, South Dakota, spring of '73. The FBI. They beat us to the ground. Again and again and again. Ever since that spring, I've had these dreams where blood is spillin' out from my groin, nothin' there but blood and emptiness. It's like ... I lost myself. So when I saw this baby comin' out of Caroline, Black Lady ... Gazelle dancin' ... all this blood ... and I knew it was gonna come ... I ... I tried to stop it ... I freaked out. I don't know what I did ... and I knew it was mine ...

ZACHARY: Why? Why did you let him do it? Why? Why did you let him do it? Why? Why did you let him do it? Why? Why did you let him do it? (*finally grabbing* BIG JOEY *by the collar*) Why?! Why did you let him do it?!

BIG JOEY: (*breaking free from* ZACHARY's *hold*) Because I hate them! I hate them fuckin' bitches. Because they – our own women – took the fuckin' power away from us faster than the FBI ever did.

SPOOKY: (*softly, in the background*) They always had it.

Silence.

BIG JOEY: There. I said it. I'm tired. Tired. (*He slumps down on the couch and cries.*)

ZACHARY: (*softly*) Joe. Joe.

Fade-out.

Out of this darkness emerges the sound of SIMON STARBLANKET's chanting voice. Away up over NANABUSH's perch, the moon begins to glow, fully and magnificently. Against it, in silhouette, we see SIMON, wearing his powwow bustle. SIMON STARBLANKET is dancing in the moon. Fade-out.

Fade-in on the "ice" at the hockey arena, where PIERRE ST. PIERRE, in full referee regalia, is gossiping with CREATURE NATAWAYS and SPOOKY LACROIX. CREATURE is knitting, with great difficulty, pink baby booties. SPOOKY is holding his new baby, wrapped in a pale-blue knit blanket. We hear the sound of a hockey arena just before a big game.

PIERRE: ... she says to me: "Did you know, Pierre St. Pierre, that Gazelle Nataways found Zachary Jeremiah Keechigeesik's undershorts under her chesterfield and washed them and put them in a box real nice, all folded up, and even sprinkled her perfume all over them and sashayed herself over to Hera Keechigeesik's house and handed the box over to her? I just about had a heart attack," she says to me." And what's more," she says to me, "when Hera Keechigeesik opened that box, there was a picture sittin' on top of them shorts, a colour picture of none other than our very own Zachary Jeremiah Keechigeesik ... (*Unseen by PIERRE, ZACHARY approaches the group, wearing a baker's hat and carrying a rolling pin.*) ... wearin' nothin' but the suit God gave him. That's when Hera Keechigeesik went wild, like a banshee tigger, and she tore the hair out of Gazelle Nataways which, as it turns out, was a wig ..." Imagine. After all these years. "... and she beat Gazelle Nataways to a cinder, right there into the treacherous icy doorstep. And that's when 'the particular puck' finally came squishin' out of them considerable Nataways bosoms." And gentlemen? The Wasy Wailerettes are on again!

CREATURE: Ho-leee!

SPOOKY: Holy fuck!

PIERRE: And I say shit la ma ... (*finally seeing ZACHARY, who is standing there listening to all this*) ... oh my ... (*turns quickly to SPOOKY's baby*) ... hello there, koochie-koochie-koo, welcome to the world!

SPOOKY: It's not koochie-koochie-koo, Pierre St. Pierre. Her name's "Kichigeechacha." Rhymes with Lalala. Ain't she purdy!

Up in the "bleachers," BIG JOEY enters and prepares his microphone stand. DICKIE BIRD enters with a big sign saying "WASY-FM" and hangs it proudly up above the microphone stand.

PIERRE: Aw, she'll be readin' that ole Holy Bible before you can go: "Phhht! Phhht!"

PIERRE accidentally spits in the baby's face. SPOOKY shoos him away.

SPOOKY: "Phhht! Phhht!" to you too, Pierre St. Pierre.

CREATURE: Spooky Lacroix. Lalala. They never made it to Sudbury General.

SPOOKY: I was busy helping Eugene Starblanket out with Simon ...

SPOOKY / PIERRE: ... may he rest in peace ...

ZACHARY: Good old Rosie Kakapetum. "Stand and deliver," they said to her. And stand and deliver she did. How's the knitting going there, Creature Nataways?

CREATURE: Kichigeechacha, my goddaughter, she's wearin' all the wrong colours. I gotta work like a dog.

PIERRE: (*calling up to DICKIE BIRD HALKED*) Don't you worry a wart about that court appearance, Dickie Bird Halked. I'll be right there beside you tellin' that ole judge a thing or two about that goddamn jukebox.

SPOOKY: (*to CREATURE*) Come on. Let's go watch Lalala play her first game.

He and CREATURE go up to the "bleachers" on the upper level, directly in front of NANABUSH's perch, to watch the big game.

PIERRE: (*reading from his clipboard and checking off the list*) Now then, Dominique Ladouche, Black Lady Halked, Annie Cook, June Bug McLeod ... (*He stops abruptly for BIG JOEY's announcement, as do the other men.*)

BIG JOEY: (*on the microphone*) Patsy Pegahmagahbow, who is recuperating at Sudbury General Hospital, sends her love and requests that the first goal scored by the Wasy Wailerettes be dedicated to the memory of Simon Starblanket ...

CREATURE and SPOOKY, with knitting and baby, respectively, are now up in the "bleachers" with DICKIE BIRD and BIG JOEY, who are standing beside each other at the microphone stand. PIERRE ST. PIERRE is again skating around on the "ice" in his own inimitable fashion, warming up. ZACHARY, meanwhile, now has his apple pie as well as his rolling pin in hand, still wearing his baker's hat. At this point the hockey arena sounds shift abruptly to the sound of women wailing and pucks hitting boards, echoing and echoing as in a vast empty chamber. As this hockey game sequence progresses, the spectacle of the men watching, cheering, etc., becomes more and more dream-like, all the men's movements imperceptibly breaking down into slow motion until they fade, later, into the darkness. ZACHARY "sleepwalks" through the whole lower level of the set, almost as though he were retracing his steps back through the whole play. Slowly, he takes off his clothes item by item until, by the end, he is back lying naked on the couch where he began the play, except that this time it will be his own couch he is lying on.

BIG JOEY: ... And there they are, ladies igwa gentlemen, there they are, the most beautiful, daring, death-defying Indian women in the world, the Wasy Wailerettes! How, Number Nine Hera Keechigeesik, CAPTAIN of the Wasy Wailerettes, face-off igwa itootum asichi Number Nine Flora McDonald, captain of the Canoe Lake Bravettes. Hey, soogi pagicheeipinew "particular puck" referee Pierre St. Pierre ... (*"and referee Pierre St. Pierre drops the 'particular puck' ..."*)

CREATURE: Go Hera go! Go Hera go! Go Hera go! ... (*repeated all the way through – and under – BIG JOEY's commentary*)

BIG JOEY: ... igwa seemakwathay g'waskootoo (*"and takes off"*) like a herd of wild turtles ...

SPOOKY: Wasy once. Wasy twice. Holy Jumpin' Christ! Rim ram. Goddamn. Fuck, son of a bitch, shit! (*repeated in time to CREATURE's cheer, all the way through – and under – BIG JOEY's commentary*)

BIG JOEY: ... Hey, aspin Number Six Dry Lips Manigitogan, right-winger for the Wasy Wailerettes, eemaskamat Number Thirteen of the Canoe Lake Bravettes anee-i "particular puck" ... (*"... Hey, and there goes Dry Lips Manigitogan, right-winger for the Wasy Wailerettes, and steals the 'particular puck' from Number Thirteen of the Canoe Lake Bravettes ..."*)

DICKIE BIRD begins chanting and stomping his foot in time to CREATURE's and SPOOKY's cheers. Bits and pieces of NANABUSH / GAZELLE NATAWAYS's strip music and Kitty Wells's "It Wasn't God Who Made Honky Tonk Angels" begin to weave in and out of this sound collage, a collage which now has a definite pounding rhythm to it. Over it all soars the sound of ZACHARY's harmonica, swooping and diving brilliantly, recalling many of NANABUSH's appearances throughout the play. BIG JOEY continues uninterrupted.

BIG JOEY: ... igwa aspin sipweesinskwataygew. Hey, k'seegoochin! How, Number Six Dry Lips Manigitogan igwa soogi pugamawew anee-i "particular puck" ita Number Twenty-six Little Girl Manitowabi, left-winger for the Wasy Wailerettes, katee-ooteetuk blue line ita Number Eleven Black Lady Halked, wha! defence-woman for the Wasy Wailerettes, kagatchitnat anee-i "particular puck" igwa seemak kapassiwatat Captain Hera Keechigeesikwa igwa Hera Keechigeesik mitooni eepimithat, hey, kewayus graceful Hera Keechigeesik, mitooni Russian ballerina eesinagoosit. Captain Hera Keechigeesik beeline

igwa itootum straight for the Canoe Lake Bravettes' net igwa shootiwatew anee-i "particular puck" igwa she shoots, she scores ... almost! Wha! Close one, ladies igwa gentlemen, kwayus close one. But Number Six Dry Lips Manigitogan, right-winger for the Wasy Wailerettes, accidentally tripped and blocked the shot ... (*"... and skates off. Hey, is she ever flying. Now, Number Six Dry Lips Manigitogan shoots the 'particular puck' toward where Number Twenty-six Little Girl Manitowabi, left-winger for the Wasy Wailerettes, is heading straight for the blue line where Number Eleven Black Lady Halked, wha! defence-woman for the Wasy Wailerettes, catches the 'particular puck' and straightaway passes it to Captain Hera Keechigeesik and Hera Keechigeesik is just a-flyin', hey, is she graceful or what, that Hera Keechigeesik, she looks just like a Russian ballerina. Captain Hera Keechigeesik now makes a beeline straight for the Canoe Lake Bravettes' net and shoots the 'particular puck' and she shoots, she scores ... almost! Wha! Close one, ladies and gentlemen, real close one. But Number Six Dry Lips Manigitogan, right-winger for the Wasy Wailerettes, accidentally tripped and blocked the shot ..."*)

BIG JOEY's voice begins to trail off as CREATURE NATAWAYS marches over and angrily grabs the microphone away from him.

BIG JOEY: ... How, Number Nine Flora McDonald, captain of the Canoe Lake Bravettes, igwa ooteetinew anee-i "particular puck" igwa skate-oo-oo behind the net igwa soogi heading along the right side of the rink ita Number Twenty-one Annie Cook ... (*"... How, Number Nine Flora McDonald, captain of the Canoe Lake Bravettes, grabs the 'particular puck' and skates behind the net and now heading along the right side of the rink where Number Twenty-one Annie Cook ..."*)

CREATURE: (*off microphone, as he marches over to it*) Aw shit! Aw shit! ... (*He grabs the microphone and, as he talks into it, the sound of all the other men's voices, including the entire sound collage, begins to fade.*) ... That Dry Lips Manigitogan, she's no damn good. Spooky Lacroix, I tole you once I tole you twice she shouldna done it she shouldna done what she went and did godawful Dry Lips Manigitogan they shouldna let her play, she's too fat, she's gotten positively blubbery lately, I tole you once I tole you twice that Dry Lips Manigitogan oughta move to Kapuskasing, she really oughta, Spooky Lacroix. I tole you once I tole you twice she oughta move to Kapuskasing, Dry Lips oughta move to Kapuskasing! Dry Lips oughta move to Kapuskasing! Dry Lips oughta move to Kapuskasing! Dry Lips oughta move to Kapuskasing Dry Lips oughta move to Kapuskasing Dry Lips oughta move to Kapuskasing Dry Lips oughta move to Kapuskasing Dry Lips oughta move to Kapuskasing Dry Lips oughta move to Kapuskasing ...

*And this, too, fades into first a whisper, magnified on tape to other-worldly proportions, then into a slow kind of heavy breathing. On top of this we hear **SPOOKY**'s baby crying. Complete fade-out on all this lights and sound, except for the baby's crying and the heavy breathing, which continue in the darkness. When the lights come up again, we are in **ZACHARY**'s own living room (i.e., what was all along **BIG JOEY**'s living room and kitchen, only much cleaner). The couch **ZACHARY** lies on is now covered with a "starblanket" and over the pin-up poster of Marilyn Monroe now hangs what was, earlier, **NANABUSH**'s large powwow dancing bustle. The theme from The Smurfs television show bleeds in. **ZACHARY** is lying on the couch face down, naked, sleeping, and snoring. The television in front of the couch comes on and The Smurfs are playing merrily away. **ZACHARY**'s wife, the "real" **HERA KEECHIGEESIK**, enters carrying their baby, who is covered completely with a blanket. **HERA** is soothing the crying baby.*

ZACHARY: (*talking in his sleep*) ... Dry Lips ... oughta move to ... Kapus ...

HERA: Poosees.

ZACHARY: ... kasing ... damn silliest thing I heard in my life ...

HERA: Honey. (*bends over the couch and kisses ZACHARY on the bum*)

ZACHARY: ... goodness sakes, Hera, you just had a baby ... (*Suddenly, he jumps up and falls off the couch.*) Simon!

HERA: Yoah! Keegatch igwa kipagee-cheep'skawinan. (*"Yoah! You almost knocked us down."*)

ZACHARY: Hera! Where's my shorts?!

HERA: Neee, kigipoochimeek awus-chayess. (*"Neee, just a couple of inches past the rim of your asshole."*)

ZACHARY: Neee, chimagideedoosh. (*"Neee, you unfragrant kozy": Ojibway.*) (*He struggles to a sitting position on the couch.*)

HERA: (*correcting him and laughing*) "ChimagideeDEESH." (*"You unfragrant KOOZIE."*)

ZACHARY: All right. "ChimagideeDEESH."

HERA: And what were you dreaming abou ...

ZACHARY: (*finally seeing the television*) Hey, it's *The Smurfs*! And they're not playing hockey da Englesa.

HERA: Neee, machi ma-a tatoo-Saturday morning Smurfs. Mootha meena weegatch hockey meetaweewuk weethawow Smurfs. (*"Well, of course, The Smurfs are on every Saturday morning. But they never play hockey, those Smurfs."*) Here, you take her. (*She hands the baby over to ZACHARY and goes to sit beside him.*) Boy, that full moon last night. Ever look particularly like a giant puck, eh? Neee ...

Silence. ZACHARY plays with the baby.

ZACHARY: (*to HERA*) Hey, cupcake. You ever think of playing hockey?

HERA: Yeah, right. That's all I need is a flying puck right in the left tit, neee ... (*But she stops to speculate.*) ... hockey, hmmm ...

ZACHARY: (*to himself*) Lordy, lordy, lordy ... (*HERA fishes ZACHARY's undershorts, which are pale blue in colour, from under a cushion and hands them to him. ZACHARY gladly grabs them.*) Neee, magawa nipeetawitoos (*"Neee, here's my sharts ..."*)

HERA: (*correcting him and laughing*) "NipeetawiTAS." (*"My SHORTS"*)

ZACHARY: All right. "NipeetawiTAS." (*Dangles the shorts up to the baby's face and laughs. Sing-songy, bouncing the baby on his lap.*) Magawa nipeetawitas. Nipeetawitas. Nipeetawitas. Nipeetawitas ...

*The baby finally gets dislodged from the blanket and emerges, naked. And the last thing we see is this beautiful naked Indian man lifting this naked baby Indian girl up in the air, his wife sitting beside them watching and laughing. Slow fade-out. Split seconds before complete blackout, **HERA** peals out with this magical, silvery **NANABUSH** laugh, which is echoed and echoed by one last magical arpeggio on the harmonica from offstage. Finally, in the darkness, the last sound we hear is the baby's laughing voice, magnified on tape to fill the entire theatre. And this, too, fades into complete silence.*

END

JUDITH THOMPSON

(b. 1954)

Nothing else in the Canadian theatre prepares us for the strange and savage intensity of Judith Thompson's world. Her characters wear their psyches and their emotions on their sleeves. They talk about and sometimes act out – "really" or in their minds, although the distinction is not always clear – their deepest insecurities, fantasies, and fears. They live on the edge of madness and sometimes over the edge. All Thompson's plays explore what she calls "the huge chasm" between the rational everyday self we like to think comprises our life, and the dangerous, primeval places where so much of our real life goes on. At the same time, her characters often desperately seek something like spiritual grace or salvation. A lapsed Catholic and daughter of a psychology professor, Thompson infuses her characters with an obsessive need to reconcile the innate violence of their unconscious life – the animal, the dark side, or whatever other metaphors she uses for the id – with the equally profound pull toward some unnameable transcendent pole of experience. All this is forged in a language remarkable for its vivid colloquial qualities and haunting imagery. Thompson is considered by many to be the most exciting playwright in the English-Canadian theatre, and *Lion in the Streets* remains one of her most powerful and disturbing plays.

Born in Montreal, Thompson grew up in Kingston, Ontario. She attended Catholic schools and by age eleven was acting in plays directed by her mother, an English teacher. After a B.A. at Queen's University (1976), where her father was head of the psychology department, she went on to the acting program at Montreal's National Theatre School. There, during a summer job as a social worker with adult protective services, Thompson met a mentally handicapped woman on whom she modelled a character she began to perform in her mask class. Writing monologues to develop the character she called Theresa, Thompson eventually built a play around her. After graduating theatre school in 1979 and acting for a year, Thompson premiered *The Crackwalker* at Theatre Passe Muraille in 1980.

This remarkable first play scrapes the lower depths of Kingston, where two couples struggle to construct normal lives for themselves in the face of mental limitations, abuse, environmental degradation, and their own irrational terrors. Superficially naturalistic, *The Crackwalker*, like all Thompson's plays, continually fractures its own realist surface with a kind of psycho-surrealism. Often in monologues, the characters' deepest fears break through into their speech, a vulgar, supercharged colloquial language that is one of the great strengths of Thompson's dramas. The play also embodies Thompson's spiritual impulse.

"Sucking off queers down the Lido for five bucks," Theresa is perceived by her boyfriend as the Madonna, and that perception transforms her. *The Crackwalker* had only moderate success in its Toronto debut, but in 1982 a highly praised production by Montreal's Centaur Theatre, subsequently remounted in Toronto, garnered rave reviews. The play has since been widely and regularly produced.

White Biting Dog (1983), first performed at Tarragon Theatre where most of Thompson's plays have premiered, won the Governor General's Literary Award for Drama in 1984. The play concerns a young man rescued from suicide by a dog; the experience gives him a mission to save his dying father's life by reconciling his father and adulterous mother. The quest for grace and the problematic nature of love and home are themes that recur throughout Thompson's work.

She wrote and developed *I Am Yours* while playwright-in-residence at Tarragon, and it won the Floyd S. Chalmers Canadian Play Award in 1988. *I Am Yours* explores with hallucinatory intensity the deep desire to be loved and possessed, the psychic damage that can be caused when that desire remains unrealized, and the costs of possession itself. Battles rage between sisters, between husbands and wives, between children and their living and dead parents, as well as an unborn/newborn child and those who claim it as their own. The play's subsequent productions included a Québécois translation in Montreal titled *Je suis à toi* (Théâtre de la Manufacture, 1990).

Also in 1987, her CBC radio play *Tornado* won the ACTRA Award for Best Radio Drama. The powerful story of an epileptic woman on welfare who is conned by a middle-class social worker into giving up her newborn, *Tornado* was collected along with *The Crackwalker* and *I Am Yours* in a volume titled *The Other Side of the Dark* (1989), which garnered Thompson her second Governor General's Award. Another radio drama, *White Sand* (1991), a study of racist demagoguery, won the B'nai B'rith Media Human Rights Award.

Thompson directed the premiere of *Lion in the Streets* in 1990, winning another Chalmers. A French version, *Lion dans les rues*, played Montreal in 1991. She has never stopped rewriting the play: the version printed here contains a revised Sherry-Edward scene and, following it, a new alternate scene involving Ben and his mother. Thompson adapted and directed *Hedda Gabler* at the Shaw Festival in 1991, then returned to Tarragon with *Sled* (1997), a play about innocence and loss set in the Canadian North, featuring a kidnapping, murders, ghosts, pornography, the northern lights, and the usual Thompsonian possibility of redemption. In *Perfect Pie* (2000), two childhood friends from rural Ontario reunite in middle age. As the women recall their younger selves, the play flashes back and forth, weaving social ostracism, epilepsy, a train crash, and pie-baking.

Toronto's Canadian Stage premiered *Habitat* (2001), a play about the stresses that result when a group home for troubled teens is established in a residential neighbourhood. Thompson returned to Tarragon with the characteristically intense *Capture Me* (2004), which follows a young teacher stalked by her abusive former husband. In *Enoch Arden in the Hope Shelter* (2005), two homeless people in a Toronto shelter for the mentally ill play out their relationship in the context of Tennyson's 1864 love poem "Enoch Arden" and Richard Strauss's 1897 musical score for it. *Such Creatures* (Theatre Passe Muraille, 2010), nominated for the Governor General's Literary Award, intertwines the monologues of a troubled Toronto teen and a dying Holocaust survivor recalling her own adolescence in Auschwitz.

Thompson's most successful twenty-first century play, *Palace of the End* (2008), links three searing monologues about the Iraq War: notorious American soldier Lynndie England at Abu Ghraib prison; British arms inspector David Kelly after his suicide; and an Iraqi dissident, her family tortured by Saddam Hussein and herself killed by an American bomb. *Palace of the End* premiered at the Canadian Stage Company after earlier versions appeared in Edinburgh and Los Angeles. It subsequently played to great acclaim in New York and London and across Canada, winning Thompson the prestigious Susan Smith Blackburn Prize (the first Canadian dramatist to be so honoured) and the Amnesty International Freedom of Expression Award. In 2007, she was awarded the Canada Council's Walter Carsen Prize for Excellence in the Performing Arts.

Her screenwriting includes a study of domestic violence, *Life with Billy* (1994), for CBC-TV, and an adaptation of Susan Swan's novel about a girls' boarding school, *The Wives of Bath*, for the feature film *Lost and Delirious* (2000), directed by Léa Pool. She also adapted her own *Perfect Pie* for a 2002 film. A mother of five children, Thompson has taught in the School of English and Theatre Studies at the University of Guelph since 1993.

In interviews, Thompson frequently employs vivid physical metaphors of invasion and possession to describe her creative processes and the plays that emerge from them. An idea enters her unconscious "the same way a disease begins ... and starts to reproduce itself in the nucleus of your cells." She develops characters by "stepping into the[ir] blood." She imagines her own mild epilepsy as "a screen door swinging between the unconscious and the conscious mind," putting her "in contact with the dark." ("It's like they forgot to nail in the storm windows in my head.") The shock of her plays, she says, derives less from their language, sex, and violence than from our buried fears: "It's this animal we all have tucked away in the corner of our unconscious, and it is very frightening to see the cage unlocked."

The text of *Lion in the Streets* opens with a stage direction explaining that the character we would see onstage if we were in the theatre, a nine-year-old girl played by an adult, is actually a ghost. It says she was killed by a man seventeen years earlier, and she does not yet know she is dead. This information would not be available to us if we were watching the play. Only gradually would we come to understand, as does Isobel herself, that she has been murdered, and that the "home" to which she is trying to return is both the scene of the crime, where she will finally confront her killer, and the "heaven" to which she will ascend "in her mind."

Thompson's strategy is to disorient us, to jolt us out of our normal expectations of the world and make us see the frightening reality that lies beneath the benign appearance of things. Surface appearance is the "pickshur" of which, Isobel assures us, we shouldn't be scared because we know it as we know her. She is our neighbour; she plays with our kids in our parks. But this is *not* our familiar neighbourhood; it's some strange and terrifying limbo where souls live in torment. On her journey through this purgatory, Isobel will observe a variety of lives. Like her, unobserved, we'll see the darkness beneath the bright surface and learn about our need to create such comforting pictures (the need for lyin' in the streets). We'll catch glimpses of the lions of anger and fear and of repression and denial that lie in wait not just in the streets but in the abysses of the human heart.

In the opening sequence Isobel, too, is dominated by the lion of rage and violence, growling threats to kill the children who torment her. Rescued by Sue, Isobel will spend much of the rest of the play alternately seeking such a saviour and offering herself as one. "I am your HARMY! I am your SAINT!" she will declare, a soldier of virtue like St. George, out to slay the dragon with her "great crooked stick." But at the end she will forgo the way of violence and revenge in an extraordinary leap of faith generated, at least in part, by the bestial behaviour she observes on her journey.

Isobel first watches Sue, whose humiliating experience at the dinner party is a nightmare brought to life, one of the many scenes that exist on the border between expressionism and naturalism, at once hallucinatory and all too real. As the polite surface of the party fractures, fearful images break through: phone sex, the striptease, colon cancer. Laura, the hostess who mocks Sue, turns out to be no more secure herself. Her overwrought reaction in the "sugar meeting" suggests that middle-class privilege offers no respite from personal demons. Socio-economic status does matter, as we see in Rhonda's violent response to Laura's condescending accusations. Yet in the next scene, class issues seem relatively superficial alongside Joanne's fear of death, her desire to dress up the horrible reality of her illness by emulating the pre-Raphaelite picture of Ophelia, who "dies good." Formal religion masks similar fears. The scene between David and Father Hayes is a revelation of guilt, regret, and unfulfilled desire. Act Two extends the ideas of the first act in the intense confrontations between Christine and Scarlett, Michael and Rodney, and Sherry and Edward.

Edward's terrifying, violent misogyny leads inevitably to Isobel's showdown with Ben and the play's stunning conclusion. Does *Lion in the Streets* sanction the idea that women who are victims of violence should turn the other cheek and forgive their aggressor? Thompson says the decision is Isobel's, not hers. Just as Isobel ascends "in her mind" to heaven, she herself resolves the battle between "the forces of vengeance and forgiveness warring inside her." She has come to realize that "to have your life" you have to take control of it yourself; no one can do it for you. She has learned how to take back her life by watching those whose lives lie beyond their control, in the claws and maws of their terrible beasts.

Judith Thompson

Lion in the Streets

Lion in the Streets was first produced by Tarragon Theatre at the du Maurier Theatre Centre in Toronto as part of the du Maurier World Stage Theatre Festival in June 1990, with the following cast:

ISOBEL	Tracy Wright
NELLIE, LAURA,	
ELAINE, CHRISTINE,	
and **SHERRY**	Jane Spidell
RACHEL, LILY,	
RHONDA, ELLEN,	
and **SCARLETT**	Ann Holloway
SCALATO, TIMMY,	
GEORGE, DAVID, RODNEY,	
and **BEN**	Stephen Ouimette
MARTIN, ISOBEL'S FATHER,	
RON, FATHER HAYES,	
and **MICHAEL**	Andrew Gillies
SUE, JILL,	
JOANNE, BECCA,	
and **JOAN**	Maggie Huculak

Directed by Judith Thompson
Set and Costume Design by Sue LePage
Lighting Design by Steven Hawkins
Sound Effects by Evan Turner
Music by Bill Thomson
Stage Managed by Nancy Dryden

CHARACTERS

ISOBEL, *the ghost of a Portuguese girl, age nine*
NELLIE
RACHEL
SCALATO *the children*
MARTIN
SUE, *age thirty-eight*

ISOBEL'S FATHER
TIMMY, *Sue's son*
LAURA
BILL, *Timmy's father, Sue's husband*
LILY
GEORGE
MARIA, *Isobel's mother*
RON
JILL
RHONDA
JOANNE
DAVID
FATHER HAYES
CHRISTINE
ELLEN
SCARLETT
RODNEY
MICHAEL
EDWARD
SHERRY
BEN
JOAN, *Ben's adoptive mother*

ACT ONE

*The ghost of **ISOBEL**, deranged and very ragged looking, runs around and around in a large circle, to music, terrified of a remembered pursuer: in fact, the man who killed her in this playground seventeen years before the action of the play. There are autumn leaves all over the playground, and the kids who approach her all have large hand-fuls of leaves, which they throw at her. At this point, **ISOBEL** does not know she is a ghost, but she knows that something is terribly wrong. She is terrified.*

ISOBEL: Doan be scare. Doan be scare. (*turns to audience*) Doan be scare of this pickshur! This pickshur is niiiice, nice! I looove this pickshur, this pickshur is mine! (*gesturing behind her*) Is my house, is my street, is my park, is my people! You know me, you know me very hard! I live next house to you, with my brother and sisters, Maria, Luig, Carla, and Romeo, we play, we play with your girl, your boy, you know me, you know me very hard. But ... when did tha' be? Tha' not be now! Tha' not be today! I think tha' be very long years ago, I think I be old. I think I be very old. Is my house but is not my house, is my street but is not my street, my people is gone, I am lost. I am lost. I AM LOOOOOOOOOST!!

Four children – two girls and two boys – laugh and approach ISOBEL.

NELLIE: Take a bird why doncha?

RACHEL: Go back with the nutties to the nuttyhouse!

SCALATO: She looks like a crazy dog!

MARTIN: (*barks*) Hey!

All bark.

ISOBEL: Peoples! Peoples, little boy little girl peoples! Hey!

ISOBEL walks toward them.

MARTIN: What's she doin'?

NELLIE: She's coming over here!

RACHEL: She's gonna get us!

ISOBEL: You, girl, you help to me. I am lost you see! You help!

NELLIE: She smells.

RACHEL: You should dial 9-1-1 so the police could help you.

SCALATO: Where do you live?

MARTIN: With all the other pork and cheese west of Christie Street?

RACHEL: Martin, that's not nice.

ISOBEL: (*overlapping*) Portuguese, Portuguese, yes ... I catch a bus! Is there a bus, bus maybe? To take me to my home? You know a bus?

SCALATO: No buses here.

ISOBEL: Yah, bus right here, bus right here, number ten, eleven, I take with my mother to cleaning job, where this bus?

SCALATO: I said there's no buses here, you ugly little SNOT.

ISOBEL: (*points*) You! YOU bad boy you bad boy, say Isobel, BAD.

SCALATO: Why don't you get your ugly little face outta here, snot?

MARTIN: Snotface!

ISOBEL: Shut up, boy, shut up, I kill you, I kill you, boy.

SCALATO: Hey, she's gonna kill me!

RACHEL: She's a witch.

ISOBEL tosses rocks at them.

MARTIN: She's throwin' rocks! Hey, she's throwin' rocks!

NELLIE: STOP IT.

RACHEL: Stop throwin' rocks or we'll tell the police!

ISOBEL: You BAD boy you BAD I will kill you!

SCALATO: (*jumping off and attacking her*) You just try it you goddamned faggot!! Faggot! Faggot!! (*hitting her*)

ISOBEL: (*growling like a dog*) G-r-r-r-r. G-r-r-r-r.

They circle one another.

MARTIN: What's she doing?

NELLIE: I don't like her.

ISOBEL and SCALATO scrap and the others join in. SUE, wearing a grey sweatsuit, is walking home from a meeting, when she spies the fight and rushes up.

SUE: Hey! Hey hey hey, stop that right now! (*pries them apart*) HEY! Listen! What is going on??

ISOBEL: I KILL YOU, BOY!

SCALATO: She started it!

MARTIN: She was throwing rocks at us!

RACHEL: She's crazy.

ISOBEL leaps toward SCALATO. SUE catches her. She falls to the ground.

SUE: Little girl? Little girl!

ISOBEL: (*overlapping*) I kill that stupid boy.

SCALATO: She started it, lady.

MARTIN: I'm getting out of here.

SCALATO: Me, too.

NELLIE & RACHEL: Wait for me!!

SCALATO: You chicken, Martin! You suck!

ISOBEL: I kill that stupid boy! (*beat*) I no like those boys.

SUE: I'm sorry if they hurt you.

ISOBEL: They no want play with me. Why they no want play with me? Why all the kids no want play with Isobel? Ha?

SUE: Ohhh ... sometimes kids are just ... mean that way, Isobel, when I was little kids were mean like that to me once.

ISOBEL: Kids? Mean, no play to you?

SUE: That's right. We had just moved to a new town, Cornwall actually, near Montreal? Well, my sisters and I went for a walk around the neighbourhood and these big boys on bikes started firing arrows at us.

ISOBEL: Boys on bikes?

SUE: That's right, just like those nasty boys!

ISOBEL: Nasty boys, to you too! Mean to you!!

SUE: That's right. And those arrows, they hurt! They really hurt!! And I was the oldest so I told my sisters, "Just cry, just start to cry and then maybe they'll feel sorry for us," so we all started to cry.

ISOBEL: Cry.

SUE: But you know what? It didn't work! They kept shooting those arrows anyways. They were just mean.

ISOBEL: Mean boys shoot arrows. Haaah!

SUE: AND suddenly, a bigger boy, about sixteen, came along and made them stop, and you know, he was like an angel to us, an angel who came down from the sky on his big blue bicycle. I've never forgotten that.

ISOBEL: Never forgetting.

SUE: Nope. I guess I'm your helper today.

ISOBEL: Helper.

ISOBEL'S FATHER: (*on porch*) Hey! Is-o-bel.

SUE: Isobel, is that your father?

ISOBEL: Father. My father. Eu pensava que té tinha perdedo!

ISOBEL'S FATHER: (*ordering ISOBEL to go around to the back door*) Vai pela porta das traseiras.

SUE: Hello. (*ISOBEL'S FATHER grunts.*) My name is Sue Winters and I don't know if you're aware of it, but some of the boys in the neighbourhood have been, well, I'd say doing some not very nice teasing of your daughter. I just ... thought ... you might ... (*ISOBEL'S FATHER goes in, slamming the door.*) Poor

man probably works all day in construction and then all night as a janitor in some Bay Street office building. What a life. (*exits*)

ISOBEL: My father? My father is not there. My father is dead. Yes, was killed by a subway many many years; it it breathed very hard push push over my father; push over to God. Hi, my father.

Music. Lights come up just a bit. SUE is in her son TIMMY's room, in the dark. TIMMY is in bed. ISOBEL watches.

SUE: And so the giant starfish saved the drowning boy.

TIMMY: What was the starfish's name?

SUE: The starfish's name? Uh ... Joey. It was Joey.

TIMMY: Mummy? Why isn't magic true? I want magic to be true.

SUE: Well. It is true, in a way, it ...

TIMMY: No, it's not. It's not true. And ya know what else?

SUE: What, darling?

TIMMY: I think tonight's the night.

SUE: That what, Tim?

TIMMY: That we're all gonna die. Tonight's the night we're gonna die.

Music. A dinner party, around a table. ISOBEL is there, invisible. The conversation is simultaneous.

LAURA: There was nothing to do! Nothing to bloody do but sing in the church choir!! And go to baked-bean suppers!! The snow at one point was actually up to the second-floor window.

BILL: No, she had the gall to ask my male students to "please leave the room," for her senior seminar. She did "not wish to be dominated by men." Where did that leave me, I asked her?

LILY: No no no, you have to pat the dough, pat it for ohh a good five minutes, then put it in the microwave for one, then take it out, then pat it again.

GEORGE: St. Paul said, "We are as vapour," what is it? Like "vapour vanisheth" or – something. "We are no more." So I got up this notion of Martians – being these – wisps of vapour ... no, you see your problem is you want the aliens to be like you, you are anthropomorphizing, you ...

LAURA: That's so boring. That's so knee-jerk boring.

BILL: And she launched into the most savage tirade –

SUE rushes in, dressed in her sweatsuit and sneakers. Everyone turns and freezes, except BILL, who continues to talk until SUE's third "Bill."

SUE: Bill ... Bill ... Bill!! We have to talk!

BILL: Sue! Hi! Who's with the boys?

SUE: Mum came over. Bill, I need to talk, NOW.

LAURA: Would you like a drink, Sue? We have ...

GEORGE: Yeah, come in and sit down ...

SUE: No, no thank you, I just ... want to talk to my husband.

ISOBEL: My helper, Suuuuusan!

BILL: Oh – okay, Sue, I'll just finish this conversation. Anyway –

SUE: He thinks he's going to die.

BILL: Who?

SUE: Timmy! Your son! He –

BILL: What, did he say that tonight? Oh, that's just kids, he's –

SUE: BILL, come home, your son is very depressed his father is never there, why are you never never ...

BILL: Sue, PLEASE, we'll talk about it later, okay? So as I was saying, Laura ...

SUE: Come with me.

BILL: I'll come in a while. I'll just finish this conversation, and then I'll come, okay?

SUE: YOU COME WITH ME NOW!

BILL: Sue.

SUE: Bill, I need you, please, why won't you come?

BILL: Why won't I come? Why won't I come? Because ... (*walks over to the others*) I'm ... not ... I am not coming home tonight.

SUE: Bill! Stop it, this is private –

BILL: It is not private, Sue, nothing we do is private for Chrissake, you tell your friends everything, they all – know everything – about us, don't they? How many times we had sex in the last month.

LAURA: I don't think that's true, Bill.

GEORGE: I haven't heard anything.

SUE: Bill, I think you're being very unreasonable.

There is an awkward pause in which BILL and SUE lock eyes.

LAURA: (*to LILY and GEORGE*) Well, it's a lovely night out there. Why don't the three of us go for a walk?

BILL: No.

SUE: You stay and finish up that wonderful-looking chocolate paté, Laura, I'm sure you spent a lot of time on it. I'll just get Bill's coat and we'll go on home.

BILL: There is ... somebody else, Sue. And I will be going home with her.

GEORGE: I think we've all had a little too much to drink, why don't we just ...

SUE: Don't worry, guys, this isn't real. He's just drunk, he's just trying to scare me because we had this argument about the new sofa – Come on, honey, let's go home. Who is it. Who is it, Bill? She's not here, is she? You didn't, you didn't bring her to my neighbours', OUR friends' dinner party, to which I was invited. Laura! Laura, for God's sake.

LILY: It's me. (*SUE laughs.*) Why do you think I'm joking?

SUE looks at LILY, then looks at BILL.

SUE: Bill??

BILL: This is – Lily.

LILY: How do you do, Susan?

SUE: Don't you call me by my name, you FAT–!! Please, I don't think you know what you're doing. This is not just me, this is a family, a family, we have two children.

LILY: I'm sorry.

SUE: Bill you are not leaving your children.

BILL: Sue, please.

SUE: YOU TOOK A VOW! In a CHURCH in front of a priest and my mother and your mother and your father and you swore to LOVE and honour and cherish till DEATH US DO PART, till DEATH US DO PART, BILL, it's your WORD, your WORD.

BILL: I am breaking my word.

SUE: No!

BILL: YOU turned your back on me!! You you – look at you in that ... sweatsuit thing you're not – I mean look at her, really, you're you're you're a kind of ... cartoon now, a ... cartoon mum a ... with your daycare meetings and neighbourhood fairs, you know what I mean, Laura! Your face is a drawing, your body, lines. The only time, the only time you are alive, electric again is ... when you talk on the phone, to the other mums, there's a flush in your face, excitement, something rushing through your body, you laugh, loudly, you make all those wonderful female noises, you cry, your voice, like ... music, or in the park, with Timmy and John, while they cavort with the other children at the drinking fountain, spraying the water and you talking and talking with all the mothers, storming, storming together, your words like crazy swallows, swooping and pivots and ... landing ... softly on a branch, a husband, one of us husbands walk in and it's like walking into ... a large group of ...

LILY: You see, I love ... his body, Sue. I mean, I really love it. I love to suck it. I love to kiss it, his body is my God, okay? His body –

SUE slaps LILY twice.

SUE: YOU ... DON'T LIVE ON THIS STREET. You don't belong in this neighbourhood. (*LILY restrains herself from slapping SUE back.*) Where did you meet this ... woman? On the street? (*BILL starts to try to answer.*) In a house of prostitution? I demand to know –

LILY: I fucked him on the telephone, Susan, many many times.

SUE: That is a disgusting ... lie.

LILY: Come on, Suzy, don't you remember? You caught him a couple of times, on the downstairs phone with his pyjamas around his ankles, he told me!

SUE: (*the wind totally out of her*) I thought he was making ... obscene phone calls.

BILL: Hello.

LILY: Hi, there.

BILL: You got back to me quickly.

LILY: Fucking right.

BILL: Fucking right.

LILY: Your voice makes me crazy.

BILL: My voice.

LILY: I'm wet, Bill, wet just from hearing your voice.

BILL: What are you wearing?

LILY: Black silk underwear, red spiked heels, black lace bra.

BILL: Yeah? And what do you want? What do you want?

LILY: I want to suck your big cock, Bill, would you like me to do that? Would you like me to suck your big cock?

BILL: Oh baby, baby.

LILY: And then I want you to fuck me from behind all night long, can you do that? Can you do that for me, Bill?

BILL: Yes, yes, oh yes! Yes! Yes!

LILY: Oh Bill!

SUE: BILLLLLLLLLLLLLLLLLLLLLL!!!!!!! (*She physically attacks LILY.*) Aghhhh! Listen, you, if you take my husband away from me and my children I will ... kill you, I will I will ... come when you are sleeping and I will pull your filthy tongue out of your filthy mouth. And then I will ... feed it to our cat.

BILL: Susan.

SUE: (*forced laugh*) I didn't mean that, I really didn't. I'm sorry, everybody, this is all just so ridiculous and embarrassing and I'm sure we'll all laugh about it someday I KNOW we will, but um ... Bill? Won't you just ... give me a chance? To show you? That I can? Be sexy? 'Cause I can, you know, much much more so than THAT creepy shit ... Don't you remember? Don't you remember before we were married how you loved to watch me dance? Come on, you did! Remember remember that wedding, Kevin and Leslie's? I wore that peach silk that you loved so much that dress drove you crazy! And after after the wedding we were in that room in the Ramada Inn over the water and I danced? You lay on the bed and you just ... watched me, you loved it, I ... whooshed whooshed in that dress, back and forth to this thing on the radio back and oooh and back and you were laughing and and (*laughs*) and whoosh. (*Music beats louder, filling the room, and SUE begins a slow striptease.*) And whoosh ... and ... close to you, you're hard ... and far away and ... turn ... and whooosh ... and ... let ... my ... hair ... down ... you – love my hair whoosh and ... zipppper ... whoooo down so slowwwww turn and turn ... you watching lying on the bed and ease ... off my shoulders you love my shoulders, elegant ohhh, Billy, and down. Over my body the soft silky down and whoooooooooooooooo whooOOOOOOOO, Billy. Take me home, Billy, take me home and let's make mad passionate love! Please.

> *BILL and LILY leave. GEORGE and LAURA pick up SUE's clothing and bring it to her. LAURA dresses her.*

LAURA: Honey, I'm sorry.

SUE: Aghh, don't feel sorry for me, it's fine, everything will be fine because ... his colon cancer's gonna come back, don't you think? Dr. Neville said he had a sixty-forty chance it will. And she'll drop him, for sure, don't you think? And he will let me nurse him, I will ... feed him broth, with a spoon, like I did my mum, and I will hold, I will hold his sweet head in my chest till till his lips are black and his eyes ... like bright dead stars and he is dead and I will stay I will stay, with his body, in the hospital room because I did love that body ... oh, I did love – that – body once.

ISOBEL: Susan, Susan, Susan. The boy with the arrow ha' killed you, ha? Where's your helper now? Oh Susan, you can't help me now, you can't take me home. (*to the audience*) Hey! Who gonna take me home? You? You gotta car? What kinda car you got? Trans Am? What about bus tickets? You gotta bus tickets? C'mon. Come on. COME ON. SOMEBODY. What I'm s'posed to do, ha? Who gonna take me home? Who gonna take me home?

ISOBEL finds a watching place. A few hours later, at LAURA and GEORGE's, LAURA clears the table.

LAURA: Poor Suzy. Poor poor Suzy.

GEORGE: (*half-asleep*) Yeahh. Chee.

LAURA: God, that is the worst thing I have ever seen happen to anybody.

GEORGE and LAURA laugh hysterically and imitate SUE in the previous scene.

GEORGE: Whoosh! That peach silk, oh baby, take me home.

LAURA: Take me home, Bill. Let's make mad passionate love. (*stops imitating SUE*) I don't know, I mean I know she needs a friend badly, I am her friend, I mean, I love her. George, how can you laugh? This is important. If she calls me tomorrow, what should I say? I'm just going to say, I'm going to say, "SUZY? I feel really badly for you and I think you're a wonderful person but you will have to look somewhere else for –"

GEORGE: Nice.

LAURA: GEORGE, you KNOW –

GEORGE: You always say she's your best friend, Laura, "my BEST –"

LAURA: She is! But, George, are you forgetting Maria? I had a nervous breakdown because of that woman and her problem, how could you FORGET?

GEORGE: I was on the book tour, Loo.

LAURA: I told you about it a hundred times, how could you forget?

GEORGE: I was on the book tour – Loo.

LAURA: George, you are so insensitive, I can't believe this. I told you about it one hundred times. How can you forget?

GEORGE grabs a tablecloth and wraps it around his head, like a shawl, speaking in a Portuguese accent.

GEORGE: How could I forget, how could I forget?

LAURA: George.

GEORGE: Looka this. Me? I donta forget nothing.

LAURA: George, I'm going to bed. Molly gets up in two hours and it's always me that gets up with her, of course.

She walks around the circle. Now GEORGE speaks as MARIA, ISOBEL's mother. ISOBEL recognizes her.

GEORGE / MARIA: LAURA.

LAURA: George! Come to bed.

GEORGE / MARIA: LAURA.

LAURA: Maria.

MARIA: I am ... so sorry to be coming to your house, maybe you busy, I don't know –

LAURA: No, no, please come in, Maria, I'm just – reading the paper, the kids are at school and –

MARIA starts shaking violently and keening. She looks like she is in shock.

LAURA: Maria? ... uh ... Maria? Are you all right? You look – why don't you sit down. Here. Sit down. Can I get you a drink of water?

MARIA starts to keen with grief, quite quietly.

MARIA: Eeeeeeee –

LAURA: Maria? Maria ... are you all right? Maria, Maria, please tell me ... what's ...

MARIA: ... think ... I think ... Antonio –

LAURA: Your husband? Something happened to your husband? (*MARIA continues to keen.*) It's okay, Maria, you don't have to tell me if you don't –

MARIA: Five o'clock in the morning I cook: smelt and three scramble eggs, nice bread, coffee. For Antony must work long day, construction on highway, long day in the sun, he come from his shower to kitchen, but he don't want. He gotta rat in his stomach that day he say, make a joke, don't want my cooking, eat a little bitta bread and just small glass of milk and he go, catch his subway. I fold. I fold clothes one pile for Antony, one pile for me, one for Maria, Romeo, Isobel, and Luig, my hands fold the clothes but my ... (*gesture indicating self or soul*)

LAURA: Sure, you go on automatic – I –

MARIA: Like I fold myself, too, and I go in his body, maybe, you know, his ... hand, to wipe off his face when he hot and too sweat, I am there. (*She walks operatically downstage to deliver the rest of the speech, which should be like an aria.*) I am foldin' a light sheet of blue then, and sudden, I can see through his eye, am at subway, in him, he stands on the platform, is empty, empty, and I am his head, circles and circles like red birds flying around and around, I am his throat, tight, cannot breathe enough air in my body, the floor, the floor move and sink in, rise up, rise like a wall, like a killin' wave, turn turn me in circles with teeth in circles and under and over I fall!

ISOBEL falls on an imaginary track in front of her mother.

MARIA: I fall on the silver track, nobody move, I hearing the sound. The sound of the rats in the tunnel, their breath like a basement, these dark rats running running toward me, I am stone, I am earth, cannot scream, cannot move, the rats tramp ... trample my body flatten and every bone splinter like ...

We hear the sound of a strong wind as the "Sugar Meeting" is being set up on the stage. By the end of the sound of the wind, LAURA is at her table, addressing the meeting.

LAURA: Good evening, everybody.

GEORGE: Good evening.

RON: Hi, Laura.

LAURA: I, uh, might as well get straight down to business. As head and sole member of the menu research committee, I have spent some three weeks doing ... a great deal ... of ... research, and even a little detective work ...

RON and GEORGE are talking to one another.

LAURA: ... and I would like to make my presentation tonight without too much interruption, thank you.

GEORGE: Go for it.

RON: No problem.

LAURA: POINT ONE. Sugar: I strongly recommend that we make a concerted effort to eradicate all sugar from the children's diet. Sugar is an over-stimulant, sugar is empty calories, sugar rots ...

RON: Uh, I have to say, that, while I agree, sure, too much sugar is not a good thing, that once in a while ...

LAURA: Would you let your four-year-old smoke "once in a while"?

A murmur from the crowd.

RON: (*with a little laugh*) I don't really think you can equate ...

ISOBEL rises and walks into the meeting.

LAURA: Sugar is a known carcinogen, Ron, I have a study right here ...

JILL: Lettuce is a known carcinogen, for God's sake!

ISOBEL: Hey! Boys! Girls! Looka this! I think tha' they can't see me! They no see Isobel! Wha' happen? Wha' happen?

JILL: Okay as chairperson, I say – let's cut the comments and raise our hands for questions. Laura? You want to go ahead?

LAURA: Yes, thank you, Jill. Uh. (*clears her throat*) It has come to my attention ... (*GEORGE groans.*) Excuse me, I have to ask you why you groaned like that, George, did I say something wrong?

JILL: George, penalty for groaning out of turn, just kidding.

GEORGE: No, no, I'm sorry, I just, I don't know, I just ... have a kind of a hard time with "meeting ... talk" ... "it has come to my attention."

LAURA: Well, I'm very sorry, George, if you have a better way of –

JILL: That was uncalled for, George, really.

RON: George, your mother's calling you.

General laughter.

JILL: Let's let Laura continue, please, so we can get out of here ...

ISOBEL: I think I invisible!

LAURA: Thank you, Jill. I have NOTICED, if you don't like "it has come to my attention," I have noticed that in this nursery school they are ... subtly, and I'm sure unwittingly, encouraging an addiction to sugar in our children.

RHONDA: Hey, that's not true.

LAURA: Rhonda, I'm SAYING it's not intentional …

RHONDA: The kids are not …

LAURA: PLEASE LET ME TALK.

JILL: Go ahead, Laura, please.

LAURA: I have noticed that sugar is used as a reward. If you're good we'll make cookies tomorrow. If you tidy up you get chocolate cake as a reward. You are creating … unwittingly, I concede, you are creating TOMORROW'S COKE ADDICTS … TO –

RHONDA: EXCUSE ME, I HAVE TO SAY THAT, AS THE CAREGIVER, I RESENT THIS.

LAURA: Rhonda, I'm not accusing just you, I think you are fabulous with the kids, it's our whole society …

RHONDA: I am not creating drug addicts.

JILL: Rhonda, Laura does not mean any of this personally, I think that's …

LAURA: I'm saying it's a small step from sugar addiction to –

RON: Excuse me, I have to say, all food is sugar …

LAURA: REFINED SUGAR IS FAST-ACTING, RON, IT BURDENS THE PANCREAS.

GEORGE: I think you are taking this a little too seriously, Laura, we're just talking about a few cookies now and then for heaven's sake.

LAURA: WE ARE TALKING ABOUT A LIFETIME ADDICTION AND I DON'T THINK IT SHOULD BE TAKEN LIGHTLY.

JILL: Laura, are you willing to listen to a response from Rhonda?

LAURA: Sure.

RHONDA: I would just … like to say that I, also have done … a great deal of studying, diet and menu and that, and I fully agree with Laura that sugar is … something to be avoided, IF YOU CAN. Listen, if I'm giving the kids yogourt, they won't eat it without honey they won't, so I figure, a bit of honey is worth getting the yogourt down 'em …

LAURA: BULLSHIT, THAT IS ABSOLUTE UNADULTERATED BULLSHIT.

RHONDA: I beg your pardon, Laura?

LAURA: You don't know what you're saying, Rhonda.

RHONDA: If you don't trust me, Laura …

LAURA: Rhonda …

RHONDA: I do not encourage sugar, I do not hold it up as a reward, ever, I have never done that.

LAURA: You're lying, Rhonda.

RON: WAIT A MINUTE, HOLD ON JUST A …

LAURA: SHUT UP, RON. LISTEN. LISTEN TO ME, RHONDA. I FOUND OUT THAT JUST LAST FRIDAY, LAST FRIDAY, AS A REWARD, YOU TOOK SIX KIDS, INCLUDING MY TWINS, TO A DOUGHNUT SHOP. YOU TOOK THEM TO A DOUGHNUT SHOP AND BOUGHT THEM EACH A JELLY DOUGHNUT. I think I screamed for five minutes when the twins told me that, I just couldn't believe it, they started harassing me every five minutes, "Mum, if we're good, can we have a jelly doughnut?" I don't think they'd ever HEARD OF JELLY DOUGHNUTS BEFORE THAT!! I find it unconscionable, UNCONSCIONABLE, that a jelly doughnut would be the sole purpose of an excursion.

RHONDA: Um, I can explain that. It was a Friday, right, and I happen to get severe cramps with my period, right? And I was very sick that day and the kids had bad bad cabin fever, well …

LAURA: (*overlapping*) And the Friday before that it was Popsicles, Rhonda, I'm not blaming you, I'm saying you need to be re-educated, we all do, smelling the flowers is a reason to go for a walk, not getting a poisonous body-destroying drug …

RHONDA: LET MEEEEE TALLLLLK. LET ME TALK, LET ME TALLLLLLLLLLLK!! I feel … nailed to the wall by you, lady, nailed right to the fucking wall. I have to say and something else I have to say is that I think you are … are very … inconsiderate … of feelings! I brought up two kids on what I feed your kids, and they turned out just fine, are you telling me what I feed my kids isn't good enough for your kids? You know the funny thing is, Laura, you may be a bitch on wheels, but lookin' at all the rest of you, Laura? At least you're honest, you are. Youse others, what you're thinkin' is … it really doesn't matter what they get at the day care, the real learning is at home, that's where youse teach your kids to become – huh. Here I am saying "youse," I haven't said that since I was a kid! that's how flustered I am – at home you teach your kids … to be … higher kind of people, higher kind of people don't eat Kraft slices and tuna casserole, I've seen that kinda laugh in your voices, all of you, when you say, "Oh, they had tuna casserole," I seen, I have seen the roll in your eyes at the grace before meals, or the tidy-up song, or the stars we give out for citizen of the week, you think, oh well, the kid is happy, well cared for, we can undo all that and we can make the kids high people like ourselves, better people, more better people than the poor little teacher who reads ROMANCE, yes, yes, JILL MATHINS, I saw you showin' my book, my novel to RON there and Cathy and havin' a big giggle, you think I didn't see that? You think the books you read are deeper more ... higher, well, it's the same story, don't you see that? What's makin' me cry in my book is, when ya come right down to it, is exactly the same thing that's makin' you cry in your book, oh yes, oh yes and I'll tell you something, I'll tell all of you, I GREW UP ON THAT. I grew up on jelly doughnuts and butter tarts, and chocolate ice cream, and I happen to think they're a wonderful thing. I happen to agree with the mice and the cockroaches and the horses and birds that treats are a wonderful thing, you need treats, you need treats in this life, each bit of a treat can wipe out a nasty word, every bite of a jelly doughnut cleans out your soul, it is a gift from GOD, a wonderful gift from GOD, and I for one ... I for one ... I ... for ... your eyes, eh? Your eyes are all the same colour and shape like a picture, a ... freaky art picture, all the same in a row like dark soldiers raisin' your ...

ISOBEL shoots everybody there except RHONDA with her finger. There are real shot sounds although ISOBEL is imagining this.

ISOBEL: (*big laugh, then struts*) Rho-HONDA! Bebbe! Beautiful belle! I have killed those dirty bastards, babe, I have killed them dirty dead. I am your harmy, Rhohonda! And you! You gonna take me home!

ISOBEL falls and wraps herself around RHONDA's feet. Music. A restaurant. DAVID takes his place behind the bar. Another person is sitting alone at a table. RHONDA and her friend, JOANNE, meet for drinks. They are laughing. ISOBEL watches.

RHONDA: Oh man, is this Singapore Sling fantastic.

JOANNE: My Fuzzy Navel is warm. Hot!

RHONDA: SEND it back! We're paying through the teeth for these drinks. Waiter, take this thing back!

JOANNE: No, I like it this way, honest, Rhonda, I do.

DAVID: Is there a problem with your cocktail?

JOANNE: No no no no, please ...

DAVID: I could take it back –

JOANNE: No.

RHONDA: Are you sure?

JOANNE: I'm sure.

DAVID: Okaaay.

RHONDA: Ohhh Christ, I'd like to just sit and drink all afternoon to tell you the truth.

JOANNE: I thought you quit heavy drinkin'.

RHONDA: I did. I'm just ... down in the dumps.

JOANNE: Why, ya on your time?

ISOBEL: Is this my home? This is not my home!

RHONDA: No no no, I get happy then, no, it's just ... work.

JOANNE: Yeah, jeez, I'm glad I'm not workin', it made me crazy, what's goin' on? The kids at the day care gettin' to ya?

RHONDA: No no, it's not the kids, the kids are great, it's the parents.

JOANNE: Uh-oh. That same B-I-T-C-H?

RHONDA: No, she was quite good this time, strangely enough, it's another one.

JOANNE: They all look like bitches to me in their leather pants. Stuck up, puttin' their kids in forty-five-dollar shoes, I looked at the price of them Reeboks for kids – the other day when I picked you up I saw three of those kids had those shoes on, I couldn't believe my eyes.

RHONDA: Yeah, well, they're pretty well off, but I don't hold that against them, I mean, who wouldn't be if they had the chance, right?

JOANNE: Well, that's a good point, SO ...

RHONDA: We had this meeting, okay?

JOANNE: RHONDA. Excuse me!

RHONDA: What?

JOANNE: (*intake of breath*) ... I don't know.

RHONDA: What do you mean?

JOANNE: I mean ... no, I don't know.

RHONDA: Joanne.

JOANNE: I mean ... oh God, I wasn't going to tell nobody –

RHONDA: You're pregnant again?

JOANNE: No no no no, if only, I ...

RHONDA: JOANNE, I'M YOUR BEST FRIEND.

JOANNE: YOU'RE MY BEST FRIEND?

RHONDA: Yes, you know that!

JOANNE: THEN SWEAR ON YOUR MOTHER'S LIFE.

RHONDA: What?

JOANNE: That you will do what I'm gonna ask you.

RHONDA: Joanne, what is this?

JOANNE: Just ... swear.

RHONDA: I'm not swearing on my mother's life without knowing what it is, she's got enough problems ...

JOANNE: Okay, your husband's life.

RHONDA: Okay, I swear on the asshole's life. There. Now what?

JOANNE: You remember ... I had this pain in my back?

RHONDA: Yeah, for the last few months, every time ya bend down.

JOANNE: SEARING pain, every time I moved ...

RHONDA: ... Okay ...

JOANNE: Well, remember I told you I went to that specialist and he said he was gonna do some tests?

RHONDA: Right, uh-huh.

JOANNE: Well –

RHONDA: You gotta go in and have an operation and you want me to take your kids, no problem, of COURSE I'll take them, Jo, for God's –

JOANNE: (*overlapping*) No. No, I mean, you might have to take the kids but that's only ... part of it.

RHONDA: Joanne, I really don't like guessing games.

JOANNE: Shadows ... that's what they call them, and ... it is ... the very worst thing it could be, and the ... kind, the kind is of the bone.

RHONDA: Oh boy.

JOANNE: Yeah.

RHONDA: (*whispers*) Jo ...

JOANNE: Don't ... don't touch me. I'll go hysterical, please.

RHONDA: YOU ... want a cigarette?

JOANNE: Yeah. (*RHONDA lights one and gives it to her.*) Ya know, I have to go to the bathroom, like, real bad but I'm not gonna go, ya know why? 'Cause every time ... I sit down to pee I feel my whole life drainin' out of me, just draining out with the pee, goin' ... outta me, into the water down in the pipes, and under the ... friggin' ... GROUND. That's where I'll be, Rho, that's where I'm gonna ... (*fights to regain her composure*) I'll come home with the groceries? Like after dark? and I'll see Frank and the kids through the window, in the livin'-room, right? Watchin' TV, or drawing on paper,

cuttin' out stuff, whatever, and I'll stand on the porch and watch 'em, just ... playing ... on the floor, and I think ... that's life, that's life goin' on without me, it'll be just like that, only I won't be here with the groceries, I'll be under the ground under the ground with my flesh fallin' offa my face and I just can't take it. You know in that picture? That picture I had in my bedroom growing up?

RHONDA: UHH –

JOANNE: My aunt and uncle sent me that from England, the poster it's OPHELIA, from this play by Shakespeare, right? And she she – got all these flowers, tropical flowers, wild flowers, white roses, violets, and buttercups, everything she loved and she kinda weaved them all together. Then she got the heaviest dress she could find ... you know how dresses in the olden days were so long and heavy, with petticoats and that? And she got this heavy heavy blue dress, real ... blue and then she wrapped all these pretty pretty flowers round and round her body, round her head, and her hair, she had this golden, wavy hair, long, and then she steps down the bank, and she lies, on her back, in the stream. She lies there, but the stream runs so fast she's on her back and she goes. It pulls her along so fast and she's lookin' at the sky and the clouds, and she's singing little songs – "I'm lookin' over a four-leaf clover" – and being pulled so fast by clear cold water, pulled along, and she's not scared, she's not scared at all, she's calm, so happy! And just ever so slowly her dress gets heavier, right? Then, then, she gets caught on a stick, like a branch, of a willow tree, and her dress pulls her down, soft, she's still singin', down deep deep deep to the bottom of the stream and with all these "fantastic garlands," these beautiful flowers all around her – "one's for the roses that blew down the lane" – she dies, Rhon, she dies ... good. She dies good.

RHONDA: That's ... something.

JOANNE: I want to die like that. But ... I don't ... want to do it all alone, I mean, I want you to help me, with the flowers, and with the dress, and my hair, I want you to make sure the willow branch is there, and the stream is right, and maybe ... maybe that ... Frank ... sees, I ... wouldn't mind him seein' ... me in that stream, with the flowers, and the heavy blue dress ... I wouldn't mind if you took maybe some pictures of me like that and then you could have them printed and given out at the funeral, something like that ... just, you know, two by four, colour, whatever, it's the one thing that would make it all right – it's the one thing ...

RHONDA: I just ... I don't know, Jo, you know I'd do anything to make it all right ...

JOANNE: Well, this is what I want, Rhonda, it's really really really what I want. Are you going to help me?

RHONDA: I uh – think you need to see a counsellor, Jo, you know they have counsellors that ... specialize in these ... situations, I'm surprised your doctor didn't ...

JOANNE: You think I'm crazy.

RHONDA: No no, Joanne, I just think that ... your situation is so hard that you are not quite yourself, I mean this is not ... you, the Joanne I know is practical, she ... you should believe in the treatments, Jo, they do work sometimes, they really do, and the Joanne I know – would never ask a friend to help ... her ... is one of the most thoughtful people that I know, of other people and how the hell, how the hell do you think that I could live with that after, eh?? I mean it's all very lovely and that, your picture, in your room, but that's a picture, that's a picture, you dim-wit! The real of it would be awful, the stalks of the flowers would be chokin' you, and the smells of them would make you sick, all those smells comin' at you when you're feelin' so sick to begin with, and the stream, well, if you're talking about the Humber River or any stream in this country you're talkin' filth, in the Humber River you're even talkin' sewage, Jo, you're talkin' cigarette packages and used condoms and old tampons floating by, you're talking freezin', you'd start shakin' from head to toe, you're talkin' rocks gashin' your head, you're talkin' a bunch of longhairs and goofs on the banks yellin' at you, callin' you "whorebag," sayin' what they'd like to do to you, you're talkin' ... and where would you get a dress like that, eh? You'd never find the one in the picture, Jo, it'd be too tight at the neck and the waist, it'd be a kind of material that itches your skin, even worse wet, drives you nut-crazy, the blue would be off, wouldn't look right, your shoes wouldn't match, you could never find the same colour, Joanne. You can't become a picture, do you know what I mean? I mean you can't ... BE ... a picture, okay?

They freeze. ISOBEL runs from her watching place, around the circle, screaming. She has realized, listening to JOANNE, that she is not lost but dead, murdered seventeen years before.

ISOBEL: AAHHHHHHHHHHH!! I am dead! I have been bones for seventeen years, missing, missing, my face in the TV and newspapers, posters, everybody lookin' for, nobody find, I am gone, I am dead, I AM DEADLY DEAD! Down! It was night, was a lion, roar!! With red eyes: he come closer (*silent scream*) come closer (*silent scream*) ROAR tear my throat out ROAR tear my eyes out ... ROAR I am kill! I am kill! I am no more! (*music; to JOANNE*) We are both pictures now. WHO WILL TAKE US? WHO WILL TAKE US TO HEAVEN, HA?

Lights down. Cathedral bells ring. DAVID is outside, walking down the street.

DAVID: God, that customer dying of bone cancer. I didn't even want to touch her glass. I don't know, she had that look, that dead look. I mean, I almost felt hostile.

ISOBEL: (*inside the cathedral*) I WANT TO GO TO HEAVEN NOW! (*She sees a life-size statue of the Virgin Mary and approaches it.*) Holy Mary, Mother of God. Will you take Isobel to heaven now, please? (*She lies at the base of the statue, her hand touching its foot.*)

DAVID: God, that cathedral is beautiful. Funny, I've passed it every day on my way out from work and I've never really looked at it. Look at the stonework, those *spires* – (*He opens the church doors and enters. The doors slam behind him.*) Oh I love this it's so ... the air is so ... holy it *is*, look at those bird-bath things full of holy water, I love it, it's so primitive. (*splashes some on his face*) In the name of the Father ... the Son, and the Holy –

FATHER HAYES: Good evening. (*DAVID shrieks, startled. His shriek echoes.*) It's all right, it's all right. Have you come for ...

DAVID: Confession. I've come for confession, eight thirty, yes? I'm not too late, am I, see, I just finished work, and ...

FATHER HAYES: Not too late, of course not. (*goes into his part of the confessional*)

DAVID: (*to himself*) I guess just – God, I don't remember a THING about what to do!!

We hear the wooden barrier being opened, and the priest begins the Latin prayer.

FATHER HAYES: In the name of the Father, and the Son, and the Holy Spirit.

DAVID: (*overlapping*) Oh God, he's saying something –

FATHER HAYES: May the Lord be in your heart and help you to confess your sins with true sorrow. Let us listen to the Lord as he speaks to us: I will give them a new heart and put a new spirit within them; I will remove the strong heart from their bodies and replace it with a natural heart, so that they will live according to my statutes, and observe and carry out my ordinances; thus they shall be my people and I will be their God.

DAVID: (*overlapping*) I think it's Latin, isn't that against Papal Law? I should report him to the Vatican and have him defrocked, here goes nothing – (*FATHER HAYES finishes the prayer.*) AHH – FORGIVE ME, FATHER, FOR I have sinned. It has been ... four weeks since my last confession. These are my sins? ... OKAY, told Barb I'd be there last night for dinner with her and the niece and nephew – didn't show up, didn't phone, nothing, was in a mad PASH with my hockey player. I was very cruel to Daniel Thursday, saw him at Billy's – the club? And I don't know, the way he was looking at me drove me CRAZY, CRAZY, he was mooning! Well, I walked up to him and told him to "quit mooning, I'd rather see your hairy ass than that pathetic face, face it!" I said, "Face it, you old fag, you have been dumped, DUMPED!" That was really mean, that's gotta be more than a venial sin, AND THEN, then, yesterday, I walked through a park? And I saw a large group of poor children playing, and I just thought they were trouble; I wondered why God had put them in the world, really, isn't that unkind? THEN today I saw a fat lady eating an ice cream cone and I said, I think quite audibly I said "disgusting," oh AND I did not stand up in the subway, the incredibly packed subway, for a hugely pregnant lady and her kid, I just didn't feel like it. Quite the catalogue, eh? Oh and another thing, I've lied to you already. I haven't been to confession in fifteen years, haven't stepped in a church in fifteen years, just ... did it on a whim, don't ask me why I was passing by on my way ...

FATHER HAYES: AND you felt the hand of GOD?

DAVID: Well ... it was just a whim – really ...

FATHER HAYES: David.

DAVID: How do you know my name?

FATHER HAYES: David, I know your name better than I know my own.

DAVID: Wait a minute, wait a minute, I think maybe this is some odd coincidence because although my name is DAVID, I don't actually know you at all, so ...

FATHER HAYES: There's nothing odd about it, David, you were an altar boy for me two years,

for two years you served, in 1957 and 1958 at St. Bernard's in Moncton, New Brunswick. Remember?

DAVID: Moncton? We were around there for a couple of years –

FATHER HAYES: You were a believer, David, the other boys were just forced into it by their parents, you believed in every statue every –

DAVID: Father Hayes? You – are Father Hayes?

FATHER HAYES: I am.

DAVID: You're still alive?

FATHER HAYES: I think.

DAVID: But you were so old even way back then!

FATHER HAYES: Not really.

DAVID: I remember you now. I remember you did look old, because you stooped, and you had white hair already, didn't you?

FATHER HAYES: Indeed, I was prematurely white ...

DAVID: White hair and ... and ... red eyes.

FATHER HAYES: I ... suffered from allergies, hay fever. I'm sorry if it frightened you.

DAVID: I guess maybe it did frighten me a bit, Father, but you know how young boys are –

FATHER HAYES: I am sorry, but, but ...

DAVID: No no, I ... look, I uh –

FATHER HAYES: David, I want ...

DAVID: ... don't mean to be impolite but I'd like you to be honest with me, sort of man to man, I ... I always got the impression that you were looking at me much more than you looked at the other boys, am I right?

FATHER HAYES: Well ...

DAVID: I felt ... I felt as though your eyes were devouring me.

FATHER HAYES: No, no, no ...

DAVID: No?? I'm gay, Father, you can be honest with me. I'll forgive you, I mean you never actually did anything, you never even touched me, you just ... looked. You kept looking at me – tell me, tell me the truth.

FATHER HAYES: It was not what you think, no, no, please –

DAVID: Confess to me Father, come on, come on ...

FATHER HAYES: I make my confessions on a regular ...

DAVID: Have you confessed this sin?

FATHER HAYES: No, no, I haven't, but –

DAVID: God loves sinners who confess, Father, you taught me that, as long as you speak up and you're sorry as hell, you're okay, you still got your ticket to heaven, but you won't you won't, Father, if you don't tell me, you'll wither in LIMBO! I suffered, I need you to tell me! CONFESS ...

FATHER HAYES: I'm due to a christening. I have to shave first, there's a big party, I –

DAVID: You would christen a baby with this sin, bobbing on the surface, bobbing? Confess, you son of a bitch. Con –

FATHER HAYES: Forgive me, Father, for I have sinned.

DAVID: All right.

FATHER HAYES: I looked at you, David, because ... I ... because ... I wanted ... to ... remember ... you.

DAVID: Remember me?

FATHER HAYES: Because ... of what was to happen, in the water: oh OH when the day arrived, when the picnic came round, in July, that Canada Day picnic? I had a bad feeling, I had ... a very bad feeling indeed. We all piled out of the cars: families, priests, nuns, altar boys, piled out and lugged all those picnic baskets to tables under trees. The grown-ups all fussed with food and drink while the kids, all of you children, ran, ran in your white bare feet to the water, throwing stones and balls, and a warning sound, terrible, the sound of deep nausea filled my ears and I looked up and saw you, dancing on the water, and I saw a red circle, a red, almost electric circle, dazzling round and round like waves, spinning round your head and body. I thought, watch, watch that boy, on this day he will surely drown, he *will*. David, I knew that you would die. And all because of the chicken. The twenty-nine-pound chicken brought there by Mrs. Henry grown on her brother's farm, everyone had talked and talked about that chicken, who would carve that chicken, Mrs. Henry took it out, you skipped along the shore, she laid it on the table, "FATHER HAYES, YOU GO AHEAD AND CARVE, AND DON'T MAKE A MESS OF IT OR YOU WON'T SEE ME AT MASS NEXT SUNDAY." Everyone laughed, laughed, the men, the men drinking beer, watching me, sure they're thinking, "Watch him carve like a woman," most men hate priests, you know this is a fact, I could see them thinking cruel thoughts under hooded eyes and practised grins; my sin was the sin of pride! The sin of pride, David, I started to carve, didn't want to look up,

lest I wreck the bird. You see at that moment that chicken was worth more, indeed worth more ... than your LIFE, David, I SHUT OUT the warning voice and I – carved. I carved and carved and ran into trouble, real trouble I remember thinking, "Damn how does any person do it, it's a terrible job," people behave as if it's nothing, but it's terrible, I kept at it, I wouldn't give up, I wouldn't look up till I'd finished, and I finished carving, and I had made a massacre. The men turned away, the women ... murmured comfort, and before I looked up I had a hope, a hard hope, that you were still skipping on the rocks and shouting insults to your pals, all hands reached for chicken and bread, potato salad, chocolate cake, I looked, I looked up, and your hand from the sea, your hand, far away, was reaching, reaching for me far away ... oh no! I ran, and tripped, fell on my face, ran again, I could not speak, ran to the water and shouted as loud as I could but my voice was so tiny; I saw your hand, ran to the fisherman close, he wasn't home, his fat daughter and I, in the skiff, not enough wind, no wind, paddling paddling, you a small spot, nothing, then nothing, the sun burns our faces, our red red faces.

DAVID: And I ... was ... never found?

FATHER HAYES: And now ... you have come!! You have finally come!!

DAVID: And what have I come for?

FATHER HAYES is sleeping.

DAVID: Uh ... Father? Uh – listen ... I'm sorry. I'm sorry but I never died. You got the wrong guy, I knew you ... some other time – I mean, shit, I wish I had died, I only wish, it would have made my life so much more interesting ... I grew up, I grew up. Listen, if I had drowned in the sea, in Moncton, New Brunswick, a beautiful perfect young boy, if I was ... pulled by the sea if I reached and was lost, and all those people felt this loss, a loss all their lives, mother father brothers and sister friends, a dark ache, somewhere in their chest for what could have been, they could all imagine, you see, what could have been, Father Father? I forgive you, I forgive you, Father, it was nice on the water, you know? It was neat, so calm, as I slipped underneath I wasn't scared, I'll tell ya. I wasn't scared a bit. The water was so ... nice!!

Music. ISOBEL dances, joined by the cast one by one until they are all dancing fully. Cast dance off one by one leaving ISOBEL, who freezes. Blackout.

ACT TWO

Sounds of kids playing in a park. A group of mothers chat. ISOBEL watches.

CHRISTINE: How's your pregnancy going, dear?

Lion roar.

ISOBEL: I hear the LION, I hear the lion ROAR!!

ELLEN: Wonderful! I finally feel … good for something. LEO, SHARE IT. Share it please.

CHRISTINE: Not me, NOT me, when I was pregnant I felt as useful as a cow. A large, stupid …

ELLEN: Christine!!

CHRISTINE: EMMA! Five more minutes, honey! Mummy's got to go to work! Well, considering I despised the man whose child I was carrying –

ELLEN: I suppose that would … alter things – GOOD CATCH, Leo!

SUE: Hi guys. Timmy, just five minutes. Remember, your father's coming to get you at five.

CHRISTINE: Sue, I love that blouse! Really suits you!

ELLEN: Gorgeous!

SUE: Thank you, I'm organizing a bake sale, if you can believe it, for the community centre over on Ash Street. PLEASE say you'll bake, or sell tickets, even a promise to buy –

ISOBEL: I must tell these peoples, I must tell them now!

ELLEN: Forget me, I'm a diabetic! I can't even look at the stuff.

SUE: Tim! Why don't you try the swing? You love swings.

CHRISTINE: Okay, put me down for fudge brownies, *if* my kids don't eat them first. (*GEORGE enters with a kid's bicycle.*) George! How's the book going?

GEORGE: Well, well, very well indeed!! And how's the busiest freelancer in town? Bradley, don't push so hard!

CHRISTINE: Overworked and underpaid.

GEORGE: What else is new? (*RON enters.*) Ron! Why aren't you at your office?

ELLEN: We're telling!

GEORGE: Good. Bradley!

SUE: Tim? Why don't you try the swing?

CHRISTINE: RON, did you get my note? EMMA, PUT IT BACK!

RON: Yes, I did, I – I – I –

ISOBEL: (*hitting them*) Shut up, boy! Shut up, girl! I say, I say it's time!! He's in the streets, get them out, he's in the streets, save your children, take their hand, take their leg.

SUE: Isobel! I saw this girl before, she –

ISOBEL: I say shut up! I say LISTEN TO ME NOW! Can you no hear? Listen! Can you nooo –

All freeze except SUE, who crosses slowly toward the children.

SUE: Timmy?

ISOBEL: (*goes to her*) The lion is here, in your streets. He is trying to kill you, to kill all of your children. He really really is. (*She picks up a great crooked stick, which she will carry until she says, "I love you" to BEN in the final scene.*) Watch me! (*laughs*) I am your HARMY! (*laughs*) I am your SAINT! I am your HARMY! Watch me, watch me (*a war cry*) I WILL KILL THE LION NOW!!

Thunderstorm as SUE shouts, "TIMMMYY!!" and the others ad lib to their children, e.g., "Quick, you don't want to get wet!" All exit. A kid's bike is left onstage. Blackout.

Lights up on CHRISTINE walking toward SCARLETT's basement apartment, "tracked" by ISOBEL.

ISOBEL: This girl, Christine, Christine, this girl, SHE will take me to the lion, yes, for she … she is very hard. Harrrrd. HARRRRRRRD!!

CHRISTINE: 116 Carlisle. Lord, what a stench. What could that be? (*knocks*)

SCARLETT: Come in!

CHRISTINE: Scarlett Deer?

SCARLETT: That's my name, don't wear it out, has to last a lifetime!!

CHRISTINE: I'm Christine Pierce from the *Telegraph*. We talked on the phone.

SCARLETT: Have a seat.

CHRISTINE: Thank you. Nice place.

SCARLETT: What, this hole? Sorry if it stinks, I cooked chicken today an' ever since I ate it I been fartin' up a storm. Dead chicken farts, that's what my brother always said.

CHRISTINE: Scarlett, I don't have a lot of time, so is it all right if I ask you some questions?

SCARLETT: Sure, How does it feel to be an ugly geek? Fine thank you, fuck you very much.

CHRISTINE: Scarlett, advanced cerebral palsy is a serious handicap. Don't you feel that living on your own is dangerous?

SCARLETT: Would you like to live in a freakhouse?

CHRISTINE: Well, Scarlett, I –

SCARLETT: Freedom, freedom girl, I'd rather fuckin' rot on the floor of my own home than be well fed and cared for in a freakhouse.

CHRISTINE: What you're saying, then, is that above all things, you cherish freedom. That you would rather risk –

SCARLETT: Once when my volunteers were sick? All of 'em were sick, right? And I just wanted to see what the hell I would do? I lay in my own shit and piss for three days.

CHRISTINE: Good Lord, what –

SCARLETT: I coulda phoned somebody, my parents live down the street, but I just wanted to see ... I wanted to see how long I'd survive, I wanted to see if I could do it.

CHRISTINE: Well, who did you eventually –

SCARLETT: My mother, my poor mother. And it makes me sick, sick, because what will I do when they die? They're old you know, they're gonna die soon.

CHRISTINE: What will you do?

SCARLETT: I'll die on the floor in my shit and piss.

CHRISTINE: Scarlett, do you have any hobbies; that is, what do you do between volunteers, do you have favourite soap operas or game shows, or –

SCARLETT: I screw my brains out.

CHRISTINE: (a weak laugh) No seriously, Scarlett.

SCARLETT: You think I'm kiddin'? You think I sit around and watch game shows and, uh, stare out the window waitin' for the next volunteer? No way, girlie, I git it ONNN.

CHRISTINE: You're ... sexually active, then?

SCARLETT: Shocked, aren't you, pretty pea?

CHRISTINE: No.

SCARLETT: YOU ARE TOO, YOU LYING BITCH!!

CHRISTINE: All right, I will admit, I am ... surprised. I suppose the public perception of handicapped people is somewhat – skewed.

SCARLETT: You think you're better'n me, dontcha?

CHRISTINE: Oh Scarlett, really I ...

SCARLETT: Well, I'll tell you somethin', Christine, my boyfriend wouldn't rub your titty. And you think he's handicapped? No way, babe, I'm not fucking a freak.

CHRISTINE: Well, I'm very happy for you, really Scarlett.

SCARLETT: Bullshit, you think it's sick.

CHRISTINE: No, honestly, Scarlett, I don't! I think everybody deserves to have a happy sex life.

SCARLETT: Yeah? Wanna hear more?

CHRISTINE: Sure!

SCARLETT: But don't print this part in your article, right, just the crap about how noble I am copin' on my own and that shit, and how good the United Church is helpin' me out, all that shit, right?

CHRISTINE: Scarlett, I won't print anything that you don't want me to. I despise journalists that do that kind of thing. I want you to think of me as a friend. Maybe we could even go out sometime, catch a movie, or go to dinner ...

SCARLETT: Sure, if you like.

CHRISTINE: So! How did it all start with your boyfriend?

SCARLETT: It all started one night, I'd just been watching TV for sixteen hours straight, from eight in the morning, right? And that's hard on the eyes, I was bone tired. So I go to bed, I look out the window and there's no moon, right? And I lie there for hours, can't sleep, itchy, bored, just wishin' I was dead, as usual, when I hear, my door open.

CHRISTINE: Were you frightened?

SCARLETT: I couldn'ta cared. I thought it was, you know, a guy with a knife, come to carve me up. I thought good, great, what a way to go. I laughed thinkin' a Monica, she's my morning volunteer, thinkin' a her comin' in findin' me dead – so I wait to be cut, but I don't hear nothin', nothin', I figure he's in his socks, not a sound then ... he sits on the edge of my bed, and and and, and then he start ... he start ... he start ... touchin' my foot, just touchin' my foot so soft, and nice, and I ... laugh. I laugh and laugh, and, Christine, I don't think I ever laughed so long and so long in my life.

CHRISTINE: Who was it?

SCARLETT: That's the question, isn't it, Chris? Who the hell is it?

CHRISTINE: Did he ... ever come again?

SCARLETT: He come every time there isn't no moon, in like a big cat sit on the bed, and me, like a big piece of fruit (*Dance music starts. She gets up.*) explodin' in the heat, exploding up and out the whole night, I can MOVE when my boy comes (*She twirls.*) I am movin', I know I am, I am turnin' and swishin' and holdin' ...

> *A MAN enters. He and SCARLETT dance romantically around the set. He leaves her back in her chair, immobile, and exits.*

SCARLETT: ... like eels, you ever seen eels? Lamprey eels, brilliant light, moving fast fast, they swim from the Saint John River down to Montego Bay to spurt their young, I swim like that coloured-up, bright and fast when my boy comes, swirlin' and movin' in the dark no moon ...

CHRISTINE: Hey, is he handsome?

SCARLETT: I tole you there's no moon.

CHRISTINE: You mean you haven't –

SCARLETT: He's my midnight man, you dick! My midnight man, he is my midnight man, get it? You can't SEE night, you can't SEE when there's no moon, why? Why do you think it's so big to see your boyfriend two eyes, nose, a mouth, what the diff, what the hell is the –

CHRISTINE: I must go, I ... have an appointment.

SCARLETT: You're not gonna print that.

CHRISTINE: I have a job, Scarlett, I have a child to support ...

SCARLETT: I'll slit your throat if ya print that.

CHRISTINE: Goodbye.

SCARLETT: (*grabs CHRISTINE's clothing*) PLEASE!! PLEASE!! Please, Christine, my old lady and old man, they're old, my mum's had a stroke, my dad's got M.S., this'd kill 'em, please!!

CHRISTINE: That is not my business, Scarlett, Scarlett, let go of me, LET GO!

SCARLETT: Reverend Pete and everybody down the church, they'd think I was a slut, they'd send me to the freakhouse.

> *They struggle.*

CHRISTINE: Let me go!!

SCARLETT: (*falls on top of CHRISTINE*) You're gonna kill me, you're gonna kill me.

CHRISTINE: (*rolls her off and onto the floor*) You are trying to obstruct the freedom of the press, lady.

SCARLETT: You can't do this, you can't do this!

CHRISTINE: (*frees herself and gets away*) I'm sorry. I'm doing it.

SCARLETT: I'll see you in hell!!

> *This stops CHRISTINE.*

CHRISTINE: What?

SCARLETT: I said you'll go right to hell for this!!

CHRISTINE: I don't believe in hell.

SCARLETT: Joke's on you, girl, 'cause I'm in it, right now, live from hell, and if you do this, you're gonna be burning here with me, maybe not today, maybe not tomorrow but soon, soon, you'll be whizzing down the highway with a large group of handsome friends to some ski resort or other, and your male driver will decide to pass on the right, you will turn over and over, knocking into each other's skulls breaking each other's necks like eggs in a bag, falling through windshields, it's gonna rain blood and I will open my big jaws and swallow youuuu! YOU will spend the rest of eternity inside me. Inside my ... body and ooooh time goes slowwwww ...

CHRISTINE: You're crazy.

SCARLETT: I am waiting for you, Chrissy, I'm waiting for you, Chrissy, I am waiting for you, Chrissy, I am ...

CHRISTINE: STOP THAT. Stop that craziness NOW, there is no such thing, there is no such thing as any of that ANY of it. You live and you die in your own body and you go up to heaven or just nowhere.

SCARLETT: Into the middle of Scarlett ...

CHRISTINE: You don't know ANYTHING.

SCARLETT: Inside my big wet behind ...

CHRISTINE: Stop it. Stop saying those things.

SCARLETT: In the bummy of a big dead fish ...

CHRISTINE: Stop it, I said stop it now.

SCARLETT: Your left arm and your head too, Chrissy, gonna be severed, you'll be all over the highway, and your mean little soul will ...

CHRISTINE: (*beats SCARLETT to the ground, screaming*) STOP IT! STOP IT! (*kicking her*) STOP IT! STOP IT!

> *CHRISTINE collapses. SCARLETT breathes with difficulty.*

CHRISTINE: Oh no. Oh no. Scarlett, are you okay? You're okay. You're okay. Your mother will be by soon or a volunteer and, and I'll call, I, I, I'll call an ambulance. You shouldn't have made me do that,

Scarlett. You shouldn't have made me kick you like that. The way you, you, you talked to me like that. Like, like, like you belong. In the world. As if you belong. Where did you get that feeling? I want it. I need it. (*pause, about to exit*) I need it.

SCARLETT: OOOOOOH! Come down and kiss me, put your tongue in my mouth!! Come on, NOW, RIGHT now, there's no one around, right now, on the ground, do me, kiss me, come down and kiss me, like a lion, so hot right here right now, swirl, swirl me twirl, twirl me, make me light, light exploding into ... (*laughs*)

> *CHRISTINE returns, swooping down like a condor, and gives SCARLETT the kiss of death. SCARLETT, thinking it is her lover, responds passionately and then, without air, dies.*

ISOBEL: (*to CHRISTINE, touching her*) SLAVE! You are a slave of the lion! You lie with him, you laugh, you let him bite your neck, you spread your legs. You will take me to him now.

> *Music, blackout. Lights up on CHRISTINE's office. She is moving things in an angry way.*

ISOBEL: Shhh. I wait for the lion!!

> *RODNEY, an early-middle-aged man with a stoop, CHRISTINE's research assistant, comes in and waits until she addresses him. He has an armload of papers.*

CHRISTINE: Yes, Rodney, what is it?

RODNEY: I've ... uh ... brought the research material you asked for.

CHRISTINE: Good. Great. Thank you ... how was your weekend?

RODNEY: Quiet.

CHRISTINE: Rodney. Rodney – Rodney I told you I wanted stats on C.P., cerebral palsy, not just "handicapped people." I wanted information on cerebral palsy!

RODNEY: You did NOT specify cerebral palsy, Christine.

CHRISTINE: Oh yes, I most certainly did, I said –

RODNEY: I have it on tape, Christine!

CHRISTINE: Rodney! Are you or are you not a professional researcher?

RODNEY: Yes.

CHRISTINE: Well then, start doing professional work! NOW! Or you are out. Is that understood? IS THAT UNDERSTOOD?

RODNEY: ... of ... course ...

> *CHRISTINE exits. RODNEY is at his desk.*

RODNEY: You will NOT EVER SPEAK TO ME THAT WAY AGAIN, CHRISTINE, YOU WILL NOT TREAT ME AS AN OBJECT, do you understand? Is that understood? IS THAT UNDERSTOOD?? (*knock on the door*) Yes? Hello. May I help you?

MICHAEL: Yes, I'm looking for a Rodney LeHavre – I was directed to this office.

RODNEY: I ... am ... Mr. LeHavre.

MICHAEL: Rodney?

RODNEY: Do I know you?

MICHAEL: Michael ... Lind ... from St. George's, '60 to '64. How are you? You remember me, don't you?

RODNEY: Michael ... Lind? No. No, I'm afraid I don't, I'm sorry. Were you in my class?

MICHAEL: Yeah, yeah, we were good friends for a while even, don't you remember? Come on. We played chess. You were a great player. You taught me ... how to play. You must remember.

RODNEY: Chess.

MICHAEL: I guess you don't remember. I'm sorry. I was sure that you'd remember. I ... I ... (*backing out*)

RODNEY: Would you like to come in and sit down? I can take ten minutes I think. Would you like to sit down?

MICHAEL: Oh, oh, okay, if you don't mind ...

RODNEY: No. A cup of coffee ... I could – get the secretary – Sherry – to –

MICHAEL: (*laughs*) You've got to remember the fly collection. It was really hot. July, I think. We caught it must have been fifty houseflies, and, and we stuck them with Elmer's glue, to a piece of bristol board. To a big piece of bristol board. And labelled them in Latin. Don't you remember? You must remember.

RODNEY: Wait a minute ... wait a minute ... yeah, yeah, and we even named them, didn't we? Didn't we name each one?

MICHAEL: Yeah, yeah ... I'll never forget. You even named one Clarence. I thought it was brilliant.

RODNEY: Right! And yours were all names like Fred, Joe, Cindy, weren't they? Right!

MICHAEL: And yours were all royalty – Elizabeth, Margaret, Clarence. God!

RODNEY: God. A fly collection. So what did we *do* with it?

MICHAEL: I think ... we had it arranged ... to show someone. A colleague of my father's. Someone in insect ...

RODNEY: Entomology.

MICHAEL: Yeah, that's it. And it was raining or something ...

RODNEY: Pouring, yes, pouring, and all the flies –

RODNEY & MICHAEL: – FELL OFF THE BRISTOL BOARD!

RODNEY: God. Michael Lind. Michael LIND! I'm sorry.

CHRISTINE: (*off*) Rodney I need that material as SOON as possible, please!

MICHAEL: Well, I see that you have to get back to work, I'd better go ... ahhh ... just before I go, there's one thing. I ... uh ... this is going to sound strange, but ... I've been having ... sort of ... dreams ... about ... back then, I ... have them a lot –

RODNEY: Oh?

MICHAEL: Yes, only ... I always wake up at the same spot, fairly distressed, actually, and ... I just ... wondered ... if you could ... help me ... remember ... what actually happened. Back then ... when we were ... kids. Do you think you could –

RODNEY: Sure, I could try ...

MICHAEL: Okay, let's start at the beginning. It was something to do with chess.

RODNEY: Chess.

MICHAEL: You loved to play chess you ... brought me to your house after school, it was a Tuesday, I think, cold, we went through a shortcut it said "Pedestrians Only," I thought it said "Protestants Only" and I was terrified. (*RODNEY laughs.*) And we went to your room, with all the paper airplanes hanging from the ceiling all over the room! And we lay on the floor. Do you remember? You remember lying on the floor? Rodney, your carpet. Your carpet was brown and orange, sort of circles or something. There was the sound of a snow blower outside. My queen. You took my queen. And then, and then, Rodney, didn't we laugh, or or or or ... some touch some touch, Rodney, and you made a strange sound. What was that sound. Please help me! I need to go back there. I need to go back there, you see? You were the only – friend that I – we

saw the world the same way. Remember? We saw the world the same way. I want to go back there. (*caresses his shoulder*) I want to go back there ...

RODNEY: I want to go back there, too. I want to go back there, too.

MICHAEL and RODNEY embrace. RODNEY makes the sound. MICHAEL pulls him back and throws him to the ground.

MICHAEL: QUEER!! Queer queer queer queer queer queer QUEER! FAIRY SISSY LITTLE CREEP!! DON'T YOU EVER ever remember again. YOU have WRECKED my life, your slimy memory, using me over and over and over again like an old porno magazine you will RELINQUISH that memory you will wipe it OUT, YOU understand?

RODNEY: You're crazy, you need psychiatric ...

MICHAEL: You will NOT remember me again because if you do, if you do, I will feel it, oh yes, and I will come and I will kill you. I could feel you remembering, almost daily, I would be in the middle, the middle of a crucial business meeting all the way in Vancouver and suddenly I would feel you ... holding my memory, turning it over and over, folding it, caressing it, reliving it, SPEWING, spewing your filth all over me. How, how I always wondered, how could you do it in the middle of the day? Did you do it here, at work, at this desk is this where you –

RODNEY: Anywhere I can, Michael. You see, my life has been terribly disappointing.

MICHAEL: You will ... free me –

RODNEY: Of course. I'll try, but memory ... does seem to have a will of its own, I can't really help what –

MICHAEL hits him. They fight, rolling and punching, and end up on the floor. Very, very slowly MICHAEL raises his head and extends his tongue. RODNEY does the same. They come together and their tongues touch. It is an ecstatic moment for both of them. MICHAEL pulls out a knife. RODNEY takes it from him and cuts his throat. MICHAEL dies. Music. The actor playing MICHAEL gets up and exits. ISOBEL goes to RODNEY and touches him, then RODNEY gets up and straightens himself.

RODNEY: "Hello, welcome to St. George's. My name is Rodney LeHavre, grade seven, and you're ...? Michael Lind! Welcome! You just came from Vancouver? I have a cousin there! Do you play chess?" Chess, every day ... chess, Monday,

Tuesday, Wednesday, Thursday, chess, with … Michael … at school, at my house, at his house, in his room, lying on our stomachs staring at the chess board, he sticks his tongue out at me because he had just captured my queen and then I stuck my tongue out back at him and he moved forward just a bit till his tongue was touching mine, and my whole life jumped into my tongue, we didn't move, just lay there touching tongues, "Would you boys like some tuna sandwiches?" his mother, the best mother in the world with her red bangles and Bourbon Sour at six, "Okay, Mrs. Lind, thanks!" And we had a secret, an atomic secret nobody else in the whole entire world knew that we had touched tongues, oh OH, wrote his name, MICHAEL, over and over one thousand times one thousand times; on the fifth day, the fifth day after, I'm at the blackboard doing math, very good at math, superb mind for mathematics, the other boys jealous, always been jealous of my superior brain throwing spitballs, used to that, yelling, "Froggy, froggy frog," because of my francophone name, used to that, I turn, I catch his face, white, darkened so quickly like a sky, he caught, he knew, suddenly he knew, Michael, that he had been playing chess with the loser, "FROGGY, HEY, FROGGY" they scream, "HEY, FROG." He stands up! They look expectantly, is the new kid going to defend his friend? What's he going to say, I say to myself, "Oh thank you, Michael, thank you, thank you, the first to ever defend me oh what what are you going to say to defend me?" He takes a breath, I'm holding mine, he smiles he speaks he says, "Is he a frog … OR A TOAD!!" They laugh and laugh and laugh screaming their laughter, slapping their desks, shaking their fists, triumphing a new member of the PACK!! Is he a frog, or a toad – Am I a frog or am I a toad?

SHERRY enters.

SHERRY: RODDEE! RODDEEE!! Baby Bunny.

ISOBEL: She!

SHERRY: You'll never guess what I have! Milk chocolate bar with lots of gushy cream in it. Two squares for you, and two squares for me.

ISOBEL: She!

SHERRY: One hundred and forty calories a square, who gives a shit. I heard Christine chewin' ya out, what a fuckin' cow.

ISOBEL: She … I see, I smell the spray, the lion's spray …

SHERRY: (*notices that RODNEY is very upset*) What happened?

SHERRY runs from RODNEY's office back home to the apartment she shares with her boyfriend of two years, EDWARD, an out-of-work actor. When she comes in, he is practising a tap routine for an audition. Newspapers are all over the floor.

SHERRY: Je-SUS, I'm peed off – I'm standing on the escalator, right? Goin' down to the subway? My back hurts, I don't feel like takin' the stairs? So I'm standin' there when this woman shoves by me right into the wall and goes, "Can't *you* move? Some people are in a hurry!" And I just STAND there like a fucking WETWIPE with my mouth open, FUCK, if I see that bitch again –

EDWARD: That's very interesting, Sherry.

SHERRY: Whatcha workin' on, that dance tryout thing?

EDWARD: Uh, no. I'm fixing the faulty wiring with my feet, it's magic, Sherry, really! Right through the –

SHERRY: Ah jeez, you're not mad at me again are ya? Whad I do now?

EDWARD: I don't know, Sherry, what did you do now?

SHERRY: I get off work at five thirty, Ed, it's ten to six what the hell am I supposed to do? Fly home?

EDWARD: I phoned work at four o'clock, Sherry, and Arlene said that you had left for the day.

SHERRY: Oh well, THAT – I was havin' a coffee and a piece of cake with Rodney, he –

EDWARD: Don't lie, please.

SHERRY: I was, Eddie, ask Rodney, ask –

EDWARD: You've rehearsed them all.

SHERRY: Listen to me! Rodney had some kind of fit today, Christine just about called the cops he was yelling and screaming at nobody all afternoon – he's right nuts.

EDWARD: It is a skillful liar it is.

SHERRY: Don't call me "it."

EDWARD: I beg your pardon?

SHERRY: Have you been drinking? Or doin' coke or some shit? You have, haven't you? You –

EDWARD: We're out of toilet paper.

SHERRY: No, there's more right under the –

EDWARD: No there's NOT!

SHERRY: All right, I'll go and get some now –

EDWARD: YOU'LL stay right where you are, Sherry. Please. PLEASE, I'm asking you. Don't leave me alone – here – I don't want to be alone.

SHERRY: Aww, Eddie, you know I love you, don't you.

EDWARD: If – if you're not happy with my performance in bed ... I wish you'd just ... tell me and – and –

SHERRY: Honey, I love your performance in bed.

EDWARD: You don't really, do you?

SHERRY: Listen, I was just tellin' Arlene today you got the best hands of I bet any guy there is on the whole fuckin' planet!

EDWARD: You were?

SHERRY: The way you touch me, Eddie, Christ, I feel like a whole bouquet, you know? A bouquet of red flowers just ... poppin' open, poppop pop pop pop just like on one of them nature specials. I love makin' love with you, I think about it all day, half the time my pants are wet thinkin' about you.

EDWARD: They're not, really?

SHERRY: They are. Feel ... feel that. (*puts his hand under her dress*) Oh honey, I want you to make love to me. Please?

EDWARD: (*kissing her*) Oh! Oh! I've been thinking about you too, all day, every day.

SHERRY: Oh Eddie, I want you.

EDWARD: You want me ...?

SHERRY: Did you not get that part in the TV series? About the runaway kid or whatever? Is that why you're – Eddie what's wrong? Did I say something wrong?

EDWARD: YOU ARE A FLAMING ASSHOLE!

SHERRY: Eddie!

EDWARD: Who are you dreaming about every night?

SHERRY: What?

EDWARD: Every night you're moaning like an animal in heat, who?

SHERRY: What?

EDWARD: Who are you dreaming about, Sherry?

SHERRY: Nobody! I'm not dreaming about – nobody.

EDWARD: WHO ARE YOU DREAMING ABOUT?

SHERRY: Just forget it, I'm going over to Arlene's, I'll see you later.

EDWARD: You tell me who you are dreaming about or I will cancel the wedding.

SHERRY: Eddie.

EDWARD: I will ... TODAY, if you don't stop lying to me treating me like a fucking maggot –

SHERRY: I'm not lying to you, Ed, please, just –

EDWARD: I'll cancel the wedding! I'll phone up Father Hayes and I'll cancel the whole fucking thing.

SHERRY: I paid nine hundred dollars for that dress, Eddie.

EDWARD: I don't give a flying fuck what you paid for it.

SHERRY: EDDIE, my mum's got her ticket from Florida, my sisters –

EDWARD: I don't give a hot damn miss –

SHERRY: OKAY OKAY OKAY OKAY, you're right, you're right. There is someone I'm dreaming about ... it's ... uh ... it's ...

EDWARD: Now we are cookin' with GAS, Sherry. This is what I always knew in my heart, never DARED with all this feminist shit going down. Come on, come on, tell me, if I'm going to be your husband I want to know it all.

SHERRY: Tell you. Tell ... you ...?

EDWARD: You were walking home from the subway, yes?

SHERRY: Yes.

EDWARD: About one thirty in the morning, yes?

SHERRY: Yes. Well. I had been at my great aunt's doin' –

EDWARD: I don't give a fuck where you were, Sherry, you were walking home, one thirty in the morning, right?

SHERRY: Right.

EDWARD: And you hear steps behind you.

SHERRY: Steps.

EDWARD: Clack clack clack like cowboy boots.

SHERRY: Clack. Clack.

EDWARD: And a voice ...

SHERRY: Like a housefly.

EDWARD: A VOICE.

SHERRY: Asks me if I had been seein' that ... porno show down the street.

EDWARD: And you said ...

SHERRY: I didn't say, Ed, I walked faster.

EDWARD: But your heels were so high, so provocative, that you turned on your ankle.

SHERRY: I sprained my ankle.

EDWARD: And he grabbed you.

SHERRY: By the arm!

EDWARD: He was all man.

SHERRY: Oh no! No!

EDWARD: And then what happened, Sherry? What happened then?

SHERRY: You know what happened, Ed.

EDWARD: I forget, Sherry. Tell me again. Tell me again, come on, come ON, or I ... cancel ...

SHERRY: You know what happened.

EDWARD: ORICANCEL ...

SHERRY: He threw me between two houses, Ed.

EDWARD: And you are breathing fast. And hot.

SHERRY: And he smashed my head against the firewall, Ed.

EDWARD: You dream about that, don't you, Sherry?

SHERRY: And he told me he was going to kill me.

EDWARD: His voice. MASTERFUL ...

SHERRY: And he held my throat and he ...

EDWARD: And he ...

SHERRY: Please, Eddie. Please please, I am asking you ... I can't do this again, I cannot go through it for you, Eddie. I'm tired, I'm ...

EDWARD: And? And?

SHERRY: And I fought like a cat, Ed, you know that! I scratched him and bit him and twisted and screamed but he –

EDWARD: But he ...?

SHERRY: He –

EDWARD: He –

SHERRY: Eddie please ...

EDWARD: Say it!!!

SHERRY: NO!

EDWARD: Say it now, Sherry.

SHERRY: Eddie!

EDWARD: You *are* the snake.

SHERRY: No.

EDWARD: Because the snake tempts others to sin, uh-huh? SATAN tempts others to sin. Say it, Sherry. Come on, "I am the snake," come on, "I am the snake," "I am the snake," come on, COME ON.

SHERRY: I ... am ... the snake.

EDWARD: With the diamond back, glittering.

SHERRY: Yeah. I am. The snake. With the back.

EDWARD: Oh yes!! You ARE the snake, baby, come on, "I am the snake!"

SHERRY: I am. The snake! I am the snake! I am the snake! I AM THE SNAKE I AM THE SNAKE I AM THE SNAKE I AM THE SNAAAAAAAAKE!

SHERRY breaks down in tears. She collapses on the floor. EDWARD cleans up and then sits down.

SHERRY: Eddie? Will you come with me tomorrow then to Ashley's to pick out a pattern? Like I've made the appointment and everything, Ed, and after all, you are going to have to live with the dishes. I mean, I know guys hate goin' in there, all guys do, but everyone that gets married goes to Ashley's, everyone that gets married –

EDWARD: All right. But nothing with flowers on it. I just want something clean, maybe – white, with a black stripe.

SHERRY thinks, changes her mind, then turns away. ISOBEL enters the room and offers her hand to SHERRY, who takes it gratefully. Arm in arm, they walk away from SHERRY and EDWARD's apartment to a graveyard. At first ISOBEL is helping SHERRY, but by the time they reach the graveyard, it is SHERRY who helps ISOBEL find her grave, and gently lays her down, and disappears.

PLAYWRIGHT'S NOTE

The next section has two scene options.

SCENE OPTION 1

In the graveyard, sitting on another tombstone, is BEN, the man who killed ISOBEL seventeen years before.

BEN: There's one thing, you know. There's one thing that I always ... wanted to tell somebody and that is that ... I done her a favour. I was – kindly – yeah, see, I pull her outta the car and throw her on the cement in front of the warehouse there's a streetlight and ... and she says to me she says,

"Please," she says, "Please no strangle, I so … scared of strangle," in this voice of breath just … purely of breath so I stopped, eh? I did. I stepped out of the twister 'cause that's what it's like, when you're doin' something like that, you're inside a twister and to step out, is like … liftin' a dishwasher, eh, but I did. So I go back of the warehouse and I picked up a brick and I hit her – 'cause she touched me okay? She touched me, right?

ISOBEL approaches with her weapon.

Scene Option 1 continues after Scene Option 2.

SCENE OPTION 2

In the graveyard a group of mourners exits, leaving BEN and his mother, JOAN, alone.

JOAN: Dear, you're looking quite uncomfortable, shall we go?

BEN: Yeah, yeah, let's go. No. No. Let's stay here. Here, sit on a tombstone why dontcha? (*reading*) "Harvey J. Walker, 1920–1973." What's that make him?

JOAN: Dear, it's getting quite chilly, don't you think?

BEN: It's summer, Joanie!

JOAN: Yes dear, but there is a wind! I'm afraid my silly old hair will just –

BEN: JOAN! I wanna siddown and pay my respects. SIDDOWN! SIT DOWN!

JOAN: (*sitting down awkwardly*) All right. Somebody hasn't watered these impatiens in a very long time. Poor old Father Hayes, I will miss him.

BEN: He was an old fruit.

JOAN: Benny he was not, how can you say that about Father Hayes?

BEN: Because he talked like a fruit; he walked like one, too.

JOAN: Now now, you don't mean that.

BEN: I sure as hell do.

JOAN: BEN, PLEASE, your language!!

BEN: So, whaddya been up to, Joan, lots a charity work, what?

JOAN: Yes, I'm still working in the shop, at the hospital.

BEN: What about bridge, you still play bridge?

JOAN: Oh yes, every week, heavens, I guess it's been every week for the last … fifteen years. Ben I wish you would call me Mum.

BEN: I can't. I told you that before.

JOAN: You are my son. We've had you since you were three weeks old for heaven's sake.

BEN: I don't give a shit. You're Joan, I like you, you're just not my mother.

JOAN: You break my heart, Christine still calls me Mum.

BEN: Christine's different.

JOAN: How? How is Christine different?

BEN: 'Cause … she's … like you, see; she's the same. Her mother was some kinda student or something, her father a professor or some shit, me, I wasn't from nothin', I'm different, I'm different from you, see?

JOAN: I love you, Ben, I hope you …

BEN: Don't say that word.

JOAN: I'm sorry, but it's true, I love every hair on your sweet head …

BEN: Joan.

JOAN: And I will till the day I die.

BEN: DO YOU LOVE ME?

JOAN: Well yes, I just –

BEN: Do you love me?

JOAN: Terribly.

BEN: Well then, gimme some money.

JOAN: I beg your pardon?

BEN: I need a loan. About sixty thousand bucks. And I need it tonight.

JOAN: Oh, so that's why you agreed to come with me to Father Hayes's funeral, stupid me, I actually thought …

BEN: Shut up, I came because I knew it meant something for you, I hadn't seen you in a while –

JOAN: Eight months.

BEN: Yeah well, I was busy.

JOAN: You're only seeing me because you want money.

BEN: Shut up, don't give me that shit …

JOAN: It's obviously true, Ben.

BEN: Okay, it's true. Can you get the money?

JOAN: What do you need it for?

BEN: I said can you get it?

JOAN: I don't know, Ben, I don't know until you tell me what you need it for.

BEN: Okay I'm leaving.

JOAN: Ben WAIT, WAIT. (*crying*) I'm sorry.

BEN: WELL, don't cry, I hate it when an old woman cries, it's friggin' gross, youse are ugly enough to begin with but when you start with the water ...

JOAN: Ben, that's enough.

BEN: I'm just being straight, Joan, come on, the old "visage" is NOT what it used to be, HEY, you can take a little tease, can't ya?

JOAN: Well, I know I've aged, dear, but I didn't think –

BEN: You're old and ugly. But you're okay. Wanna smoke?

JOAN: No thank you, Ben, you know I don't.

BEN: The cancer thing, right, right, well, I don't give a shit myself, so I'm gonna smoke myself sick.

JOAN: Ben, why do you say you don't care?

BEN: 'Cause I'm a sittin' duck. Unless you give me that cash money now, I'll be dead news anyways, so what do I care.

JOAN: I don't follow you, Ben.

BEN: I'm saying that there's people after me, Joanie, bad bad dudes, these jokers don't think nothin', nothin' of blowin' a guy's head off and stickin' him in a trunk.

JOAN: Oh Benny, how did you get involved with these ...

BEN: Don't ask questions, Joanie, for crying out loud, I did time in a federal penitentiary, I did twenty years in friggin' Collins Bay, the place is crawlin' with creeps, they follow you out ...

JOAN: Why are they ... after you?

BEN: Why are they after me? Why are they after me? You are askin' me why they are after me? Why do you think?

JOAN: Well goodness, anybody who knows anything knows you did not kill that little girl, all the magazines wrote about the suppressed evidence, and impossibility of the time factor, everybody knows it was a miscarriage of justice –

BEN: I know that you know that, butcha think the turkeys know that? Hey, they just gotta feel upper than somebody, right? They're the lowest on the social ladder they gotta have somebody lower, that's me, scum of the earth.

JOAN: Oh Benny.

BEN: You never thought I done it.

JOAN: Not for a second.

BEN: May I ask why?

JOAN: Because – because – you would fall asleep only in my arms till you were six years old.

BEN: ONLY IN YOUR ARMS.

JOAN: And you brushed my hair, your favourite pastime in the world was for us to lie on the bed and you would brush and brush my hair, my hair was long then, black ...

BEN: I still like brushin' chicks' hair.

JOAN: I always knew, I always knew it wasn't you.

BEN: I know. I know you always knew that.

JOAN: I am your mother ...

BEN: NO!

JOAN: I AM.

BEN: You are not! You are ... my guardian, LIKE a mother to me, not my mother. My mother is probably some whore living outta Dominion bags now.

JOAN: Oh Benny.

BEN: Are you gonna give me the cash?

JOAN: Just ... please, please tell me what it's for? Please, darling?

BEN: Surgery. Changin' my face so those jokers won't know me, then I'm gonna start in on the pasta, the milkshakes, gain fifty pounds, then dye the hair red.

JOAN: But surely that won't cost –

BEN: LET ME FINISH, Christ, did ya ever let anybody finish anything?

JOAN: I'm sorry.

BEN: You better be. Now where was I ...

JOAN: About why you need so much –

BEN: Okay, after the looks change, I go into business. I got a idea for a business gonna make me a millionaire. Alls I gotta do is have some cash up front.

JOAN: Ben, dear, I don't mean to be discouraging, but I've watched so many of these schemes of yours –

BEN: What?

JOAN: Fail!!

BEN: They didn't fail! They didn't fail, they just didn't work 'cause of people rippin' me off, 'cause my heart was too big!! Well, this time I learned my lesson, I know, I know to be ruthless, okay?

JOAN: Well, I don't think you have to be "ruthless," I mean Walter was a brilliant businessman, but he was never never –

BEN: (*spits*) HE WAS A SON OF A BITCH.

JOAN: Walter loved you, Benny.

BEN: Don't you mention that man's name, the man was a pig.

JOAN: Ben, you are talking about your father, my husband.

BEN: NOT MY FATHER NOT MY FATHER, YOU only saw one face, Joanie, one WALTER face, the other face was secret, between him and me, only I saw the ...

JOAN: Oh Ben, how can you –

BEN: He he he he he used to force me ...

JOAN: He forced you to do what?

BEN: Well ... forget it.

JOAN: Ben, please, I don't understand what you –

BEN: WHY DO YOU THINK THIS BOY IS HELL, I was hell for you from the time I was seven, killin' the cats, wrecking the car, sellin' your stereo, WHY? 'Cause my mother was a fifteen-year-old kid from Gerrard and Parliament with stringy hair ... who couldn't say her alphabet? You think it's that? Why do you think it is, Joanie, why do you think I am hell?

JOAN: I think that when we told you that you were adopted, you were crushed and we were never able to help you.

BEN: No. So whaddya think it is, Joan?

JOAN: ... Something ... Walter ...?

BEN: Yeah. Yeah. Yeah ... something Walter said.

JOAN: You are saying that he ... did something to you – he struck you?

BEN: Joanie, bein' hit, I wouldn'ta minded, hell it was a relief when it was that. It's ... the other ...

JOAN: It's not true.

BEN: You never noticed anything, NOTHIN' strange? Whyd'ja think, whyd'ja think he left the bed every night?

JOAN: To have a snack, he ... always said that he had had a ... snack.

BEN: (*laughs*) Yeah right.

JOAN: I'm ... really in a state of shock.

BEN: Believe me, Joan.

JOAN: I thought I knew Walter so well ...

BEN: Yeah.

JOAN: OH GOD. My little boy, my poor little ...

BEN: Poor Joanie, no one told her. No one ever told her that 95 per cent of the human population is maggots. You got fooled into thinkin' life was nice tea parties and hot cocoa after skatin' and tuckin' your kids in and singing a pretty song about the fuckin' moon ... 'Member that rabbit I used to have?

JOAN: Honey.

BEN: Yeah, Honey, well, Honey always made me think of you, you know, with those big wide-apart eyes, believe everything thinkin' everything is nice, so trusting, she was so trustin' it made me mad, you know? Like why do you trust me, don't you know I could pull your eyes out? You should hop away when my hands are in your cage, hop away, you stupid pest, don't just stand there. With those eyes.

JOAN: Is that why you –

BEN: I DON'T LIKE STUPIDITY.

JOAN: Oh dear.

BEN: Look, Joan, I'm short on time here, so do we have a deal?

JOAN: Sixty ... thousand ...?

BEN: You got it.

JOAN: Oh Ben. Oh Ben. Walter. I am shattered to know that my Walter –

BEN: Hey. Would I lie to you, Joanie? Just to score some cash? Come on ...

JOAN: Now I know, Ben, I know ...

BEN: Whaddya know.

JOAN: Her picture, in the papers on all those posters, that picture, her eyes, she had unusually trusting, wide apart –

BEN: Back off, I'm tellin' ya, Joanie –

JOAN: YOU HATE TRUSTING EYES because – they reminded you of me and how ... I trusted Walter, how I let it go on, how dumb I was how dumb I was, you were killing me, killing – WALTER! It's all my fault!! That little girl's death is all my fault!

BEN: There's one thing, you know. There's one thing that I always ... wanted to tell somebody and that is that ... I done her a favour. I was – kindly – yeah, see, I pull her outta the car and throw her on the cement in front of the warehouse there, and ... I put my hands around her neck and she says to me she says, "Please," she says, "Please no strangle, I so ... scared of strangle" in this ... voice of breath just ... purely of breath and I stopped, eh? I stepped out of the twister 'cause that's what it's like, Joanie, when you're doin' somethin' like that you're inside a twister and to step out, is like ... liftin' two hundred pounds but I did 'cause she touched me, okay? She touched me right – she was me, right? She was me, under Walter, asking him askin' him, please, Daddy, please, please, Daddy, so I done what I always wanted Walter to do, what I always wished, what I wished every night, I got a brick a plain red brick, yeah, killed her with a brick, smashed her little face in. To this day I can't watch them Brick commercials, you know, the furniture warehouse? No money down – turn the set right off, right off for the night. Hey! Did I really used to brush your hair?

He puts his head in her lap. She extricates herself and backs off in horror. ISOBEL approaches with her weapon.

Scene Option 1 and Scene Option 2 both resume at this point in the play:

ISOBEL: BEN ... ja ... men. (*He looks.*) BEN ja men BEN ja men.

BEN: Who are you?

ISOBEL: Is ... o ... bel.

BEN: Isobel.

ISOBEL: July. Isobel in July, July the one, remember? Don't you remember? CANADA Day Day for CANADA Birthday. I selling tickets tickets on a Chrysler car, for boys' and girls' club, one dollar fifty for a ticket. I have five tickets left. Don't you remember? I see you in park. It is raining. In my park I ask you, "You want to buy ticket on a Chrysler car?" You say, "Yes, yes, I buy all five all five tickets. Come into my car, come into my silver car with dark red seats, come into my car. I will give you the money for the tickets I have the money in my car," you said ...

BEN: I'm hallucinatin'.

ISOBEL: I'm Isobel.

BEN: You're a picture.

ISOBEL: I'm Isobel.

BEN: What ... do you want?

ISOBEL: I have come.

BEN: What do you want?

ISOBEL: I am here.

BEN: WELL, GO AWAY! You hear me? GO AWAY.

She is about to kill him with the stick, the forces of vengeance and forgiveness warring inside her. Forgiveness wins.

ISOBEL: I love you.

BEN: NO!!

ISOBEL: You took my last breath!

BEN: Christ, I'm sick, I'm so sick.

ISOBEL: I want back my life. Give me back my life!

The players enter singing a religious-sounding chorale with a sense of sadness and triumph. They place a veil on ISOBEL's head, the actor playing BEN joining them.

ISOBEL: (*an adult now*) I want to tell you now a secret. I was dead, was killed by lion in long silver car, starving lion, maul maul maul me to dead, with killing claws over and over my little young face and chest, over my chest, my blood running out, he take my heart with. He take my heart with, in his pocket deep, but my heart talk. Talk and talk and never be quiet never be quiet. I came back. I take my life. I want you all to take your life. I want you all to have your life.

Players sing a second, joyful chorale, walking off. ISOBEL ascends, in her mind, into heaven. The last thing we see is her veil.

END

SALLY
CLARK

In an emblematic scene in Sally Clark's *Moo* (1988), the title character is confined to an insane asylum, strapped into a straitjacket, having been committed on false pretences by her husband and kept there through the unwitting connivance of a male doctor. A parallel scene in *Life Without Instruction* sees seventeenth-century painter Artemisia Gentileschi tortured by an interrogator in front of the man who raped her. Such scenarios are played over and over in Clark's drama. Nearly all her female protagonists are accused and tormented, judged mad or guilty by men and the surreal patriarchal systems they administer. Engaged in uneven power struggles, Clark's women endure various abuses and many end up suffering violent death. Yet the plays are very funny and the women almost all extraordinary, tough, and outspoken. Artemisia, the heroine of what Clark calls her "revenge comedy," uncharacteristically manages to triumph. She occupies the most positive pole on the spectrum between classic victim and feminist rebel that marks the fascinating and disturbing paradox of Sally Clark's black comedy.

Born and raised in Vancouver, Clark went to Toronto to pursue a career as a painter. She received her B.A. in fine arts from York University in 1975, continued studying painting at the New School of Art in Toronto, and showed her work at a number of galleries. She also began writing plays, earning honourable mention in a 1976 competition run by Playwrights Co-op.

Her one-act *Ten Ways to Abuse an Old Woman* was first produced in 1983 by Toronto's Buddies in Bad Times at its Rhubarb Festival of new theatre. A powerful, very dark comedy about an addled old woman abused by her middle-aged daughter and son-in-law, the play sports the quintessential Sally Clark title and a protagonist whose pursuit of her own reality drives others to distraction. Theatre Passe Muraille produced Clark's first major effort, *Lost Souls and Missing Persons* (1984). The middle-class heroine of this sprawling comedy wanders away from her empty marriage on a trip to New York, ending up bereft of her language, her identity, and eventually her life. Both plays suggest that a woman can be happy only if she loses her mind.

Vancouver's Tamahnous Theatre produced *Trial* in 1985, Clark's adaptation of Kafka's nightmarish novel of paranoia and bureaucracy, restaged with major revisions as *The Trial of Judith K.* by Toronto's Canadian Stage in 1989. Judith Kaye, a sexually repressed corporate loans officer, stands in for Josef K. in an updated, sometimes silly version of

Kafka's tale that moves inexorably to the same chilling conclusion. *Moo* premiered in Calgary in 1988 and won a Floyd S. Chalmers Canadian Play Award in Toronto in 1990. The play traces a woman's scandalous, obsessive, all-consuming passion for her "rotter" of a husband and lover over half a century. In 1989, Tarragon produced *Jehanne of the Witches*, a complex metatheatrical retelling of the Joan of Arc story. Associated with the matriarchal paganism of pre-Christian Europe, Clark's Jehanne is also friends with Gilles de Rais, aristocratic pederast and reputed mass murderer of children – thought to have inspired the infamous character Bluebeard – portrayed in the original production by Sky Gilbert. The play turns out to be Gilles's production, with one of his boys in the role of Jehanne.

Life Without Instruction was commissioned by Toronto's Nightwood Theatre and first produced by Theatre Plus in 1991. A Québécois translation played Montreal's La Licorne under the title *La Vie sans mode d'emploi* (1993). *Saint Frances of Hollywood*, Clark's take on the twisted life of actress Frances Farmer, premiered at Calgary's Alberta Theatre Projects in 1994. *WASPS*, a sex farce about a librarian, opened in Toronto in 1996 and was subsequently directed by Clark herself in Vancouver. In *The Widow Judith* (1998), Clark developed one of the Biblical stories that Artemisia paints in *Life Without Instruction*. And in *Wanted*, a young woman makes her chaotic way through the Yukon gold rush. It premiered at Whitehorse's Nakai Theatre in 2003 and toured the Yukon.

Clark has been playwright-in-residence at Buddies in Bad Times (1983–84), Theatre Passe Muraille (1985–86), Nightwood (1987), the Shaw Festival (1988), the University of Cincinnati (1996), and Berton House in Dawson City, Yukon (2000). She spent 1991 in residence at the Canadian Centre for Advanced Film Studies where she made a short film of *Ten Ways to Abuse an Old Woman*. In 2010, she published her first novel, *Waiting for the Revolution*, the story of a young female artist's university years during the hippie era. Clark has continued to paint and exhibits her work frequently in Vancouver, where she makes her home.

Just as Sharon Pollock does with Lizzie Borden and Ann-Marie Mac-Donald with Shakespeare's characters, Clark writes revisionary history in *Life Without Instruction*. Artemisia Gentileschi (1593–1652) was an Italian baroque artist, daughter of painter Orazio. She did go to court with her father to ask that Agostino Tassi be forced to marry her because he had raped her. She also went on to become one of the few notable female painters of her era, and *Judith Slaying Holofernes* became her most famous canvas. Artemisia's life and work have received a great deal of critical and artistic attention in recent years, much of it, not surprisingly, from a feminist perspective.

"Perspective" is in fact what Orazio asks Tassi to teach his daughter in the play, and the rape is only the first of the lessons Artemisia learns about what it means to be female, and a female artist, in a man's world. From her culture's patriarchal perspective, she can be a daughter and wife, a slut and a whore, and little else. The story of Judith and Holofernes begins the same way: powerless Judith is to be powerful Holofernes's concubine.

But of course the Biblical Judith turns the tables. And in Clark's version of Artemisia's life, her portrait of the artist as a young woman, Artemisia does, too – more or less.

Like so many of Clark's other theatrical women, Artemisia conspires in her own sexual and social entanglements. She doesn't in any way invent or invite or embellish the rape; the chilling trial scenes remind us of the additional victimization that rape victims often experience at the hands of the law. But for a variety of reasons Artemisia maintains a complicated relationship with Tassi and the other repulsive men of his "bohemian" circle. She and Tassi are far more interesting characters than the Judith and Holofernes the same two actors perform in the painting-within-the-play. We also see how the play's only other women, Tutia and Lisa, find it in their best interests to side with men.

In her usual fashion, Clark takes what might in other hands be played as melodrama and turns it into black comedy and even farce. But in this unusual case, her female protagonist gets the last laugh. Artemisia revenges herself on Tassi by immortalizing him in her painting as the slain Holofernes. In the final scene, Artemisia holds the sexual power as well. (See Sherrill Grace's "*Life Without Instruction*: Artemisia and the Lessons of Perspective" for fascinating readings of the final stage direction and the play as a whole.) The verdict of art history also comes down on Artemisia's side. The men in the play, big shots in the Italian art scene in their time, are today little more than footnotes in the chronicle of Artemisia Gentileschi's life and work.

Life Without Instruction

Sally Clark

Life Without Instruction premiered at Theatre Plus, Toronto, on August 2, 1991, with the following cast:

ARTEMISIA GENTILESCHI and **JUDITH**	Pamela Sinha
ORAZIO GENTILESCHI and **RATZO**	Benedict Campbell
AGOSTINO TASSI and **HOLOFERNES**	Tom McCamus
TUTIA	Brenda Robins
COSIMO QUORLI	Conrad Coates
GIAMBATTISTA STIATESSI	Damon D'Oliveira
LISA	Chick Reid
OLD MAN	Al Kozlik
INTERROGATOR	Ephraim Hylton and Richard Binsley
TONY	Antony Audain

Directed by Glynis Leyshon
Set and Costume Design by Phillip Clarkson
Lighting Design by Lesley Wilkinson
Stage Managed by Sheila Z. Buchanan

CHARACTERS

ARTEMISIA GENTILESCHI, *Italian painter of the Caravaggio school, daughter of* **ORAZIO,** *age fifteen*

ORAZIO GENTILESCHI, *father of* **ARTEMISIA,** *painter, follower of Caravaggio, age forty*

AGOSTINO TASSI, *close friend of* **ORAZIO,** *age thirty*

TUTIA, *chaperone to* **ARTEMISIA,** *age twenty-five*

COSIMO QUORLI

GIAMBATTISTA STIATTESI

JUDITH

HOLOFERNES

RATZO

LISA

OLD MAN

INTERROGATOR

TONY, *ARTEMISIA's husband*

PLAYWRIGHT'S NOTE

This play can be performed by eight actors: three women and five men. The Biblical scenes are played as follows: **ARTEMISIA** *as* **JUDITH,** **TASSI** *as* **HOLOFERNES,** *and* **ORAZIO** *as* **RATZO.**

SETTING AND STAGING

There are no changes in costume between the Italian scenes and the Biblical scenes. The costumes for the play should be in the style of Caravaggio paintings, Italian early seventeenth century. The first act of the play takes place in Rome in 1610. The second act takes place six months later.

ACT ONE

SCENE 1

HOLOFERNES's TENT. A man and woman lounging on a large mattress with many cushions. They lie underneath a purple net canopy that is studded with jewels. The man, HOLOFERNES, is amorously drunk.

HOLOFERNES: Do you love me, Judith?

JUDITH: Of course I love you, my lord.

HOLOFERNES: You say that as though you're obeying orders. You're not my servant, Judith. You're a free woman. Your god and my god. We will rule together. Now, do you really love me?

JUDITH: Yes, I do.

HOLOFERNES: I sent everyone out so we could be alone. Not a very wise manoeuvre, is it?

JUDITH: Pardon?

HOLOFERNES: I am at your mercy.

JUDITH: Oh, my lord.

HOLOFERNES: You could do anything to me.

JUDITH: Oh, my lord.

HOLOFERNES: Why don't you start by kissing me? (*JUDITH hesitates.*) Don't you want to?

JUDITH: Yes, of course. It's just that I've been in mourning for three years.

HOLOFERNES: Why did you change into these? (*fingers JUDITH's clothes*) Are you setting a trap for me?

JUDITH: No – of course not.

HOLOFERNES: That's a very beautiful dress you're wearing, Judith. (*runs fingers along JUDITH's bodice*) It seems odd to wear such enticing clothes and still be so shy. (*gazes at her*) God, you're beautiful. (*about to embrace her – stops himself*) I refuse to make the first move. I'm tired of women claiming I rape them. You say you love me. Then, do something about it. Kiss me. (*JUDITH kisses him.*) You can do better than that. There's a passion in you, Judith. I can see it. Why are you hiding from me? (*kisses her*)

JUDITH responds.

HOLOFERNES: (*breaks away*) Now, you kiss me.

JUDITH kisses him passionately. Lights down.

Lights up on JUDITH and HOLOFERNES, lying on the mattress. Both are naked. The man is in a deep sleep. JUDITH gets up and quickly puts on clothes. She goes to the opening in the tent.

JUDITH: (*whispers*) Tutia. (*pause*) Tutia!

Silence. JUDITH's maidservant, TUTIA, enters. She is holding a basket. She stands expectantly. JUDITH goes off to one side.

JUDITH: Oh Lord God of Israel, strengthen me. I must despise him. On behalf of my people, fill my heart with rage that I may do what I have promised.

She reaches for a large sword by the bed and holds it over her head. HOLOFERNES moans.

JUDITH: Oh God! (*starts trembling, brings the sword back down to her side, looks over at TUTIA*) Tutia! (*sternly*) Hold his body down.

TUTIA positions herself to hold his body down. JUDITH raises the sword over HOLOFERNES's head.

HOLOFERNES: Judith?

JUDITH brings the sword down like a cleaver onto HOLOFERNES's neck.

Blackout.

SCENE 2

The young girl who played JUDITH casually tosses the head of HOLOFERNES up in the air. She is a bit bored. ORAZIO, a man aged forty, is off to one side behind an easel. He is painting her. The young girl adopts a pose where she cradles the head in her lap.

ORAZIO: That's right. Look down. (*He opens a curtain. Light falls on one side of the girl's face – a Caravaggio effect.*) Perfect! Now hold it. (*starts painting*) Ah Bella, you'll never leave me, will you?

ARTEMISIA: Can I scratch my nose?

ORAZIO: Not yet.

ARTEMISIA: It itches. Why should I leave?

ORAZIO: Girls your age get restless. They don't want to be around old men like me.

ARTEMISIA: That's what Tutia says.

ORAZIO: What?! She's got her nerve.

ARTEMISIA: She says I should get married. She says it would be wrong if I lived with you all my life.

ORAZIO: I don't care what people think. Do you?

ARTEMISIA: I never meet them. You never let me out.

ORAZIO: (*throws down brush*) Now, that simply is not true! You're going to be a great painter. You don't have time to gallivant around Rome, meeting people!

ARTEMISIA: The least you could do is give me a commission.

ORAZIO: You're not ready yet.

ARTEMISIA: When?

ORAZIO: Soon. (*pause*) You know, you could "sort of" get married.

ARTEMISIA: Sort of?

ORAZIO: You could marry someone old who didn't have long to live. He'd die and leave you comfortably well off. So it wouldn't be as if you were actually married to him.

ARTEMISIA: Sounds creepy. Why can't I marry someone young? A painter like me?

ORAZIO: You'd wind up having his babies and mixing his paints. Painters are ruthlessly selfish.

ARTEMISIA: Oh.

ORAZIO: Yes! I've got it. Yes, it's there! (*stands back from easel*) That's what it is. A frozen moment in time. All moments combining to form one moment – the essence of everything that came before and will follow after. And I have captured it. At this moment, in my painting, Bella, you are perfection itself. Nothing can change that. (*sighs*) I am an artist, Bella, because I hate change.

ARTEMISIA: Let's see. (*goes over to the painting and is disappointed*) It looks just like me.

ORAZIO: Yes. I've finally captured you.

ARTEMISIA: But it should look like Judith. I was trying to be Judith.

ORAZIO: I wondered why you had that strange expression on your face. I just ignored it.

ARTEMISIA: You made me look like a little girl. Why did you even bother telling me I was Judith?

ORAZIO: It's just a story. Clients like Biblical themes.

ARTEMISIA: What's the point of painting the story if you don't believe it?

ORAZIO: I was painting you.

ARTEMISIA: You should paint the story.

ORAZIO: Trying to tell me how to paint now, are you. Remember, Missy, everything you learned, you learned from me.

ARTEMISIA: I know. (*pause*) I think I need another teacher.

ORAZIO: What?!

ARTEMISIA: You want me to be the best. Then please, let me study with Caravaggio.

ORAZIO: Not that again!

ARTEMISIA: But Caravaggio is –

ORAZIO: Don't say that name in my studio!

ARTEMISIA: Caravaggio!! Caravaggio!! (*dances around*)

ORAZIO: Stop it! Stop it this instant!!

ARTEMISIA: (*sing-song*) C-a-a-r-a-v-a-a-g-g-i-o!!

ORAZIO: ALL RIGHT! ALL RIGHT! I'll find you a teacher.

ARTEMISIA: Cara-?

ORAZIO: NO! (*pause*) Someone else.

ARTEMISIA: Who, Daddy? He's got to be good. I want the best –

ORAZIO: (*studies the painting*) Don't nag. (*smiles*) If you ever leave, I'll have you here. I've captured your soul, Bella. You're in my canvas forever.

ARTEMISIA: I'll have to put you in my painting then.

ORAZIO: Make me young, Bella. Paint me young.

ARTEMISIA: (*laughs*) Daddy!

SCENE 3

Art studio. ORAZIO and his friend, AGOSTINO TASSI, stagger in. They are both drunk. TASSI looks like HOLOFERNES.

ORAZIO: Come here. I want to show you something.

TASSI: No.

ORAZIO: Whaddya mean, no?

TASSI: I don't want to see it.

ORAZIO: What the hell is that supposed to mean!

TASSI: We go out. We get drunk. You drag me back to your studio and I'm supposed to tell you how great your work is. Well – I'm fucking sick of it. Your work is shit.

ORAZIO: You're just saying that because you're drunk. (*tries to haul him over to easel*)

TASSI: No. I'm not.

ORAZIO: Your work isn't so great either, you know.

TASSI: At least I'm not stupid enough to think I'm a painter. I have one craft and I master it. Drawing. That's what's really wrong with your paintings. You can't draw. Your colour sense is godawful but the main problem is you can't draw.

While TASSI is talking, ORAZIO takes the canvas off the easel and thrusts it in front of TASSI.

ORAZIO: (*announces*) Judith Beheading Holofernes!

TASSI: Christ! What'd you do to me?!

ORAZIO: Don't take it personally, Tassi.

TASSI: That's my goddamn head in her lap!

ORAZIO: I thought I better show you first. It's a commission.

TASSI: Severed heads. Everyone's painting severed heads these days. Why the fascination? And why does it have to be my head. It's unlucky, for Chrissake!

ORAZIO: Actually, your head was the reason for the commission.

TASSI: Who would do that?!

ORAZIO: You can't think of anyone?

TASSI: I can think of a whole bunch of people but none of them have any money.

ORAZIO: Your sister-in-law's husband.

TASSI: Oh. The Old Man. (*looks at painting*) Where did you find that little lardo?

ORAZIO: I beg your pardon.

TASSI: The model. A real dog.

ORAZIO: She has a certain spiritual beauty.

TASSI: (*scrutinizes painting*) I wouldn't fuck her if my life depended on it.

ORAZIO: AAAAGGGH! (*goes to hit TASSI*)

TASSI: (*ducks*) Ratzo – Ratzo – What's the matter! Look, I'm sorry. Are you having an affair with this broad?

ORAZIO: SHE'S MY DAUGHTER! YOU NIT!!

TASSI: Oh. (*pause*) God, she looks just like you. Sorry. I didn't know you had a daughter. I've met your sons. Why haven't I met her?

ORAZIO: She keeps close to the house.

TASSI: What do you do? Lock her up. Did the Old Man put in a special request for your daughter, too?

ORAZIO: Well – it was – hem – a deal we had – it fell through.

TASSI: You mean you –

ORAZIO: Good God! Nothing so sordid. Marriage.

TASSI: To that old letch. That's worse.

ORAZIO: I don't want her to marry the first young boob she lays eyes on.

TASSI: What else is she supposed to do.

ORAZIO: You don't understand. Bella is not like other girls. She's well – she's precocious. (*starts rummaging for another canvas*)

TASSI: You don't say.

ORAZIO presents another canvas to TASSI.

TASSI: Oh please, Ratzo. I'm just not in the mood to look at –

ORAZIO: (*thrusts TASSI at canvas*) *Susannah and the Elders!*

TASSI: (*stares at it*) I didn't know you painted nudes.

ORAZIO: You don't like it.

TASSI: There's a living body here. It's not your usual shit, Ratzo. This is a well-observed human form. My God, Ratzo, after all these years of being a third-rate Caravaggio, can it be possible that –

ORAZIO: I was doing light and dark long before he was. He stole my ideas!

TASSI: Jesus, sorry to bring all that up again. But, this is good. Except the perspective is all off. What are those two black lumps over her head?

ORAZIO: Elders.

TASSI: Trees? They don't look like trees.

ORAZIO: No. *Elders!* Old guys. That's me, you idiot!

TASSI: You don't flatter yourself.

ORAZIO: No. (*looks at it closely*) I don't. The other one's not done yet.

TASSI: She has a delightful body.

ORAZIO: Who?

TASSI: The model. Really firm. Good tits. I love it when they point up. All that hope and optimism in that firm little breast pointing up. Then, of course, they get old and grumpy and the breasts sag down to their navel and life is hell.

ORAZIO: Oh yes. How is your wife?

TASSI: Dead.

ORAZIO: What?

TASSI: Yeah. She died.

ORAZIO: Didn't she –

TASSI: Ratzo, you sly old bugger – you want to know the dirt. She ran off with her lover and she died.

ORAZIO: Did he kill her?

TASSI: Not intentionally. Too much sex.

ORAZIO: Really?

TASSI: How should I know. She ran off and now she's dead. I couldn't care less. Who's the model –

ORAZIO: You don't draw nudes.

TASSI: Who said I was going to draw her. Who is she?

ORAZIO: No one you know. (*flips a cover over the painting*) I wanted your opinion of the work.

TASSI: I was just getting to it. (*removes cover*) This painting, Ratzo, is the best painting that you have ever done. Your colour sense here is superb.

Usually your colours are all muddy. And the body – well – it is magnificent!

ORAZIO: (*sighs, and puts the cover back over the painting*) Thanks.

TASSI: You don't seem very happy about it.

ORAZIO: I didn't paint it.

TASSI: What.

ORAZIO: My daughter painted it.

TASSI: Your daughter. (*pause*) You're being funny, aren't you?

ORAZIO: No.

TASSI: You taught your daughter how to paint?!

ORAZIO: I didn't mean to. When Prudentia died, Bella wouldn't leave my side. Followed me around the studio like a little dog. She helped me with my painting. Then, she started to do her own work.

TASSI: She's good.

ORAZIO: Good? She's brilliant! I taught her everything she knows. (*pause*) So why is she so much better than me? (*breaks down*) I taught her my colours. But she uses her own. And they're better.

TASSI: Maybe she's been seeing Caravaggio.

ORAZIO: I don't let her out of my sight!

TASSI: I was just kidding, Ratzo. Get a grip on yourself.

ORAZIO: She will be better, though. She will be the best. She is my revenge on that son of a bitch.

TASSI: It's not too late. You could still apprentice one of your sons.

ORAZIO: What are you talking about?

TASSI: She'll get married and have kids and forget all about painting. You're wasting your time.

ORAZIO: But she has genius!

TASSI: That may be true. But what does this painting say? It's a girl's painting. It's well-crafted but it's empty. You've locked her away from the world and now you expect her to have something to say about it.

ORAZIO: But –

TASSI: You don't want her to lose her innocence. Put her in a nunnery and have done with it. (*takes a swig of wine, starts to leave*)

ORAZIO: You're right. She does need to learn about the world.

TASSI: She needs to learn perspective.

ORAZIO: You could teach her, couldn't you?

TASSI: You don't want her to get married.

ORAZIO: No.

TASSI: My price is high.

ORAZIO: For a friend?!

TASSI: She's an ugly girl.

ORAZIO: You dare to insult my dead wife?!

TASSI: Your wife was gorgeous, Ratzo. This girl looks like you. Plug ugly.

ORAZIO punches TASSI, knocks him out. TASSI falls in a heap on the floor.

ORAZIO: Omigod! Tassi! (*slaps him*) I didn't kill you, did I? (*rolls him over with his foot*) Christ! I need a drink.

He grabs a bottle of wine, gets the Judith painting, props it on the floor near him, and, using TASSI as a cushion, lies against him. He gazes at the painting.

ORAZIO: Bella. (*falls asleep*)

Lights down. ARTEMISIA pokes her head in. She is wearing a nightgown. She enters with a candle and stares at TASSI. She puts the candle down, grabs some paper and a pencil lying around in the studio, and proceeds to draw TASSI's head.

SCENE 4

The studio. ARTEMISIA is painting TUTIA.

TUTIA: (*telling a story*) "And Romeo looked around the crowd of young girls – their eyes glittering under their masks. And there in the centre was the most beautiful girl he had ever beheld."

ARTEMISIA: How could he tell she was beautiful if she had a mask on?

TUTIA: Oh, that's right. "Well, the girls all removed their masks and there in the centre of the circle was the most beautiful girl Romeo had ever beheld."

ARTEMISIA: What makes someone beautiful?

TUTIA: You're either born that way or you're not.

ARTEMISIA: My father says I'm beautiful.

TUTIA: Your father loves you very much.

ARTEMISIA: It's funny, you know, Tutia. 'Cause I don't feel beautiful.

TUTIA: No kidding.

ARTEMISIA: I feel big and clumsy.

TUTIA: Well, you're growing.

ARTEMISIA: I feel as if I'll never stop. Look how big my hands are.

TUTIA: And your feet.

ARTEMISIA: Do you think Juliet was big like me?

TUTIA: (*hastily*) No! I mean – she was probably smaller.

ARTEMISIA: Yes. I think so, too. She feels like a small person to me. My mother was big.

TUTIA: You were only a little girl. How would you know.

ARTEMISIA: I was nine. I remember exactly what she looked like.

TUTIA: You should ask your father to take you out more often. Wouldn't you like to go to a ball like Juliet's?

ARTEMISIA: A ball?

TUTIA: That's what most girls your age do. Your father should –

ORAZIO sits bolt upright from a pile of drapery.

TUTIA: (*sees him – gasps*) AH! (*clutches her heart*)

ARTEMISIA: (*takes no notice*) Afternoon, Daddy.

ORAZIO: (*with great pronouncement*) You are going to have instruction.

ARTEMISIA: You found me a teacher?! Who?!

ORAZIO: Instruction in the art of perspective. Taught by the best draughtsman in all of Rome. Agostino Tassi. (*He gets up carefully and starts to stagger out the door, moaning.*)

ARTEMISIA: Oh, thank you, Daddy! But he's not a painter. Don't you think –

ORAZIO: (*waves her off*) Not another word. I have decided. (*leaves*)

TUTIA: You might have told me he was here.

ARTEMISIA: Sorry. I forgot.

TUTIA: You'll have to get a new dress.

ARTEMISIA: Why?

TUTIA: For your classes.

ARTEMISIA: You don't wear good clothes when you paint.

TUTIA: You do when Agostino Tassi is your teacher. He's so handsome.

ARTEMISIA: Oh. Do you think so?

TUTIA: Oh yes, he's very clever, too. And he's a widower. You could marry him.

ARTEMISIA: Are you crazy?

TUTIA: Wouldn't you like to marry Signore Tassi?

ARTEMISIA: He's a friend of my father's. He's old.

TUTIA: He's only thirty and he has all his teeth.

ARTEMISIA: (*lays down paint brush*) Come on. Let's play "Judith." (*goes over and pulls TUTIA off the model stand*)

TUTIA: You're too old to play games. Your father would have a fit if he –

ARTEMISIA: I can't do anything anymore! I can't play games! I can't go out by myself because I'm too old and I'm supposed to be a lady. What's the point of being a lady if you can't do anything!!

TUTIA: Stop complaining. You have more freedom than most girls your age. Most girls wouldn't be frittering away their time painting. Most girls would be doing chores. Helping their mothers.

ARTEMISIA: (*starts to cry*) It's not my fault my mother's dead!

TUTIA: Oh Bella, I'm sorry. I didn't mean it that way. Please stop crying. We'll play the game. (*ARTEMISIA shakes her head "no."*) "In the town of Bethulia, there lived a young woman whose name was Judith. She was very beautiful but it was hard to tell because she wore black all the time. Those ugly black widow's weeds totally covered up her delicate features – her tiny feet and trim little –"

ARTEMISIA: "She was very large. She had huge massive shoulders and big huge hands. Judith was about six feet tall. But that was all right because her dead husband was even bigger. He was six foot five. No one would marry Judith because she was too big for them. Even though she was beautiful."

TUTIA: She was not big! It doesn't say anywhere in the Bible that Judith was big.

ARTEMISIA: She'd have to be pretty big to saw off a man's head.

TUTIA: She cut it neatly in two strokes. The way you slaughter a pig.

ARTEMISIA: No. She must have sawed it off. Like she was cutting wood.

TUTIA: I don't know why you focus on the most disgusting part of the story.

ARTEMISIA: That's the best part.

TUTIA: That's not the best part. The seduction of Holofernes is the best part. "The Assyrian general, Holofernes, had jet-black hair, a jet-black beard and flashing blue eyes. He was a wicked, evil man. Totally unscrupulous and very attractive to women. He was very tall. At least six foot seven."

ARTEMISIA: He was not!

TUTIA: I'm telling the story now. "His army held the town of Bethulia under siege to try and force the Jews to pay homage to Ozymandias. Holofernes's men were very evil. If they saw a young woman on the street –" (*ARTEMISIA pretends to be walking down the street.*) "They would loosen her headdress to defile her." (*pulls ARTEMISIA's hair*)

ARTEMISIA: OW!

TUTIA: "Strip her thigh to shame her." (*rips off ARTEMISIA's art smock*)

ARTEMISIA: Hey! That's my smock.

TUTIA: You can fix it. You need a new one, anyway. "*And* profane her womb to disgrace her." (*She yanks ARTEMISIA to her and throws her on the ground.*)

> *ARTEMISIA screams. ORAZIO appears in the doorway, clutching his head.*

ORAZIO: WHAT THE HELL IS GOING ON HERE!!

ARTEMISIA: Oh hi, Daddy.

TUTIA: (*straightens herself out*) Signore Gentileschi.

ARTEMISIA: We were just playing, Daddy.

ORAZIO: WHAT SORT OF –

TUTIA: Actually, we were practising scenes for Bella's next painting.

ORAZIO: The rape of the Sabine women? I'll not have you –

ARTEMISIA: No. *Judith.*

TUTIA: Bella admires your painting so much, Signore, that she wants to do one as well.

ORAZIO: Oh. A pretty strange way to go about it. Your classes start tomorrow, Bella. Go fix your smock.

ARTEMISIA: Yes, Daddy. (*She leaves.*)

TUTIA: Signore Gentileschi. (*She starts to leave.*)

ORAZIO: (*grabs her arm*) Give us a kiss. (*pulls her to him*)

TUTIA: No, Ratzo. This really isn't right. (*ORAZIO kisses TUTIA.*) I'm very worried about Bella. She spends too much time alone.

ORAZIO: That's why you're here. (*continues kissing her*)

TUTIA: I have my family to look after. My baby.

ORAZIO: Want another one?

TUTIA: This is serious, Ratzo. Sometimes, I go by the studio and Bella's talking to herself. She's at

that age. If you're not careful, she'll start to get fanciful.

ORAZIO: Fanciful?

TUTIA: Crazy.

ORAZIO: Oh come off it! My daughter's not crazy.

TUTIA: She has a very vivid imagination.

ORAZIO: That's good. Good for her art. (*He starts undoing TUTIA's clothes.*)

TUTIA: Is that all you ever think about! Art!

ORAZIO: No. I wouldn't say so. (*fondles TUTIA's breasts*)

TUTIA: It's not natural the way you're bringing up that girl. You're turning her into a freak.

ORAZIO: Bella has talent. Why shouldn't she be allowed to use it. (*buries his head in TUTIA's breasts*)

TUTIA: Frank and Carlo and Marcus might also have talent. Why don't you train them?

ORAZIO: (*raises his head*) That is beside the point. (*He buries his head back in TUTIA's breasts.*)

TUTIA: (*grabs ORAZIO by the hair*) What you've done is unnatural!

ORAZIO: All right. Let's be natural, then. (*He hoists TUTIA over his shoulder and staggers over to a mattress in his studio.*)

TUTIA: She should meet people her own age. She needs to be introduced to society. A party, or perhaps a ball.

ORAZIO: A ball's a fine idea. (*plunks TUTIA down*)

TUTIA: Is that a promise? You'll take her to a ball?

ORAZIO: Mmmm? Oh, all right. (*throws himself down on her*)

TUTIA: That's wonderful. You've made me very happy. (*She heaves ORAZIO off her easily.*)

ORAZIO: I could make you a lot happier.

TUTIA: You're sweet. (*She runs out.*)

SCENE 5

> *ORAZIO and TASSI.*

ORAZIO: Be gentle with her.

TASSI: That might be difficult. She might not like it.

ORAZIO: Praise her paintings.

TASSI: If you think that would help.

ORAZIO: Oh yes – a little praise goes a long way with her. You see, she's not used to other men.

TASSI: I should hope not.

ORAZIO: Well, she's spent all her time with me so she only knows my style.

TASSI: Pardon me?

ORAZIO: I have a different way of doing things than you. I believe in giving lots of encouragement. I know you're more the bullying type. Don't bully her. She won't like it.

TASSI: Look, don't tell me how to do my job.

ORAZIO: I'm sorry. I've interfered enough.

TASSI: It would probably be best if you went out for the whole day.

ORAZIO: The whole day? Is that necessary? (*pause*) I suppose it's better that I'm not around to distract. The first time will be the hardest. (*starts to leave – turns around*) I hope she likes you. (*He leaves.*)

TASSI looks puzzled.

SCENE 6

The studio. TUTIA sits near the model stand.

TASSI: (*enters, looks at TUTIA*) Who are you?

TUTIA: Tutia. I live here.

TASSI: Not in the studio.

TUTIA: No. I live downstairs.

TASSI: Then what are you doing in the studio?

TUTIA: Well – ah – to chaperone, of course.

TASSI: Why?

TUTIA: Well – a young girl always has a chaperone.

TASSI: When she goes out, yes. But in her own home?

TUTIA: I can't leave her alone with you.

TASSI: Did Signore Gentileschi ask you to stay?

TUTIA: Well, no. But he's very absent-minded. I'm sure he's expecting me to stay.

TASSI: Why? What do you think I'm going to do?

TUTIA: Well – it's not right.

TASSI: You think I'm going to seduce his daughter?!

TUTIA: Well – ah –

TASSI: THIS IS OUTRAGEOUS! I AM THE BEST FRIEND OF THE MAN WHO OWNS THIS HOUSE! THIS HOUSE THAT YOU HAPPEN TO BE LODGED IN!! AND YOU ACCUSE ME!!! (*splutters with rage*) I'm not getting paid for these lessons – you know. I'm only doing this out of friendship. I mean – you've seen the girl! REALLY! (*starts to leave*) Well, that's it! I'm leaving. You can tell Ratzo what you've done. And good luck. He's not very pleasant when he's angry.

TUTIA: (*catches his arm*) I'm sorry I offended you. Please stay and teach your class. I'll leave.

TASSI: You look tired. Orazio works people too hard. He probably has you up at all hours night and day.

TUTIA: Yes. He does.

TASSI: Orazio employs your husband, too?

TUTIA: No. He's in Tuscany looking for work.

TASSI: (*ushers TUTIA out the door*) You get some beauty sleep. If you were Orazio's daughter, it would be quite another matter.

TUTIA: (*giggles*) Oh now –

TASSI kisses her hand, and closes the door on her.

SCENE 7

The lesson. AGOSTINO TASSI is in the studio. ARTEMISIA enters.

ARTEMISIA: How do you do, Signore Tassi. (*curtseys; looks around*) Where's Tutia?

TASSI: No need to be so formal. I'm not your mathematics teacher. I'm your art teacher. And art is life. Is that not right?

ARTEMISIA: I don't have a mathematics teacher.

TASSI: Don't be so literal. Art is life. Would you agree with that?

ARTEMISIA: I hadn't thought about it.

TASSI: You should. Lesson number one: Think. Agostino. (*He holds out his hand.*)

ARTEMISIA: Oh – I – ah – my father will think I'm being rude if I call you by your first name. Have you seen my chaperone?

TASSI: No. I haven't. Lesson number two: Your father is not the only man in the world. Here is another. (*holds out hand*) Agostino Tassi. And your name?

ARTEMISIA: You know my name. She should be here.

TASSI: Your name.

ARTEMISIA: Artemisia Gentileschi. But everyone calls me Bella.

TASSI: Give me your hand. (*ARTEMISIA gives it reluctantly. TASSI fondles it.*) Artemisia. What a beautiful name.

ARTEMISIA: Yes, it's from the Greek goddess of the hunt. She –

TASSI: Yes, yes, I know all that. Artemisia, you must learn that when a man says something nice, you don't suddenly talk his ear off. If someone gives you a compliment, take it. Because they're going to be few and far between. So – you say, "Thank you." We'll try it again.

ARTEMISIA: Why should they be few and far between?

TASSI: You're no beauty.

ARTEMISIA: I'm not?

TASSI: No, of course not. You look shocked. You've been paying too much attention to your father. Fathers see with different eyes. Do you know why your father hired me?

ARTEMISIA: To teach me drawing.

TASSI: No. To teach you perspective.

ARTEMISIA: Yes. Drawing and perspective.

TASSI: Don't be sullen. Perspective isn't just drawing. It's a way of looking at the world. Everyone agrees that they will learn to look at the world in the same way and when you learn to see the way everyone else does, then that's perspective.

ARTEMISIA: I thought perspect–

TASSI: Parallel lines meet at the horizon.

ARTEMISIA: I thought parallel lines never met.

TASSI: As I said, I'm not your math teacher. That is one of the rules of perspective.

ARTEMISIA: But it's wrong!

TASSI: You think you're very important. If you were standing in a meadow a hundred feet away from a man and he looked at you, from his point of view you would be very small and not important at all. That's perspective. So when I tell you you're a big ugly girl, believe me. Because that also is perspective. An objective point of view.

ARTEMISIA: Why are you so mean to me?

TASSI: I hate to see someone go through life deluded. Now, let's look at some of your work. (He starts to pull out Susannah and the Elders.)

ARTEMISIA: No! (She places herself in front of it.)

TASSI: Why not?

ARTEMISIA: I don't want to show you my work.

TASSI: Don't be spoiled. There are worse things in life than being a big lump. Are you going to get out of my way or do I have to move you myself.

(ARTEMISIA remains standing.) All right. (He grabs her and picks her up. ARTEMISIA struggles. He places her to one side.) You're better looking with a bit of colour to your cheek. Don't get enough excitement at home. (looks at painting) I don't know why you didn't want me to see it. It's quite a good painting.

ARTEMISIA: I know it's a good painting.

TASSI: Is that a fact.

ARTEMISIA: Yes. It is. And if you don't mind, I'd like you to look at something else. (She goes to move it.)

TASSI: I do mind. And it's not as good as you think it is. The two Elders are ridiculously placed. They're almost on top of her. Wait a minute. You've changed his face.

ARTEMISIA: How would you know. You've never seen it before.

TASSI: (peers at it) And you've never seen me before. But if that's the case, why am I in your painting?

ARTEMISIA: That's not you!

TASSI: No? (moves in closer) Have you been spying on me, Artemisia?

ARTEMISIA: No.

TASSI: I'm flattered that you decided to immortalize me. I had no idea you found me that attractive.

ARTEMISIA: I don't. In my painting, you're an Elder.

TASSI: So, you work from life.

ARTEMISIA: Pardon?

TASSI: Well, that's me. I don't look at all old there. And that's your father. You've made him look old. And a bit dim, too. Do you think your father's stupid?

ARTEMISIA: Of course not!

TASSI: I think he's stupid. I wouldn't let a man like me near my daughter. So – if that's him and that's me, then that beautiful naked woman must be you. You look a lot better with your clothes off.

ARTEMISIA: That's not me!

TASSI: The face is yours and those hands are definitely yours. Huge. So I presume the rest is you. Cowering in naked splendour from those two old men. What are you afraid of, Artemisia?

ARTEMISIA: I'm not afraid of anything.

TASSI: You've painted me and your father as conspirators plotting against you. Do you really think your father lusts after you?

ARTEMISIA: Of course not!

TASSI: Why did you paint him that way?

ARTEMISIA: I just used his face. Stop reading meaning into it!

TASSI: What a beautiful body you have. The skin is milky. And that breast – (*He runs his finger along the painting, looking at ARTEMISIA while he does so.*) Exquisite. You're blushing, Artemisia.

ARTEMISIA: No, I'm not.

TASSI: Yes. You are. You see, the skin here has a rosy glow to it. (*He runs his finger along ARTEMISIA's cheek.*) Not like the skin here. (*runs his finger down and around her neck*) You've captured your skin tones very well. Oh. Blushing again. It's funny. You portray me as a man lusting after you and here I am, suddenly obsessed with your body. There is a power in your painting, Artemisia.

ARTEMISIA: Is there?

TASSI: You like it when I talk about your art. (*He kisses her neck.*)

ARTEMISIA: It's what you were hired to do.

TASSI: Maybe I was hired to do something else.

He kisses her passionately. ARTEMISIA is too surprised to resist. Still kissing her, he puts his hand up her skirt. ARTEMISIA tries to push his hand away. They struggle. TASSI pins ARTEMISIA down and yanks her skirt up.

ARTEMISIA: NO! (*She struggles and screams.*)

TASSI: (*claps his hand over her mouth*) Your father's left you here alone. Surely that should tell you something. (*ARTEMISIA bites his hand.*) OW! (*He loosens his grip on her.*)

ARTEMISIA tries to get away. TASSI grabs her, stuffs a paint rag in her mouth, pins her down, and rapes her.

Lights down.

SCENE 8

ARTEMISIA is curled up in a ball to one side. She rocks back and forth. The door rattles. She looks up in terror.

TUTIA: (*off*) Bella? Are you in there? The door's locked.

ARTEMISIA stares at the door. A key turns in the lock. TUTIA rushes in, looks around, does not initially see ARTEMISIA, turns to leave, and sees her.

TUTIA: Bella? (*ARTEMISIA stares at her.*) Bella, are you all right? (*goes over to her, sees her clothes are torn, etc.*) Omigod! That bastard! That bloody bastard!

ARTEMISIA: (*quietly and without emphasis*) Where were you? Why weren't you here?

TUTIA: (*embraces ARTEMISIA*) Oh, you poor dear. It must have been awful. Did it hurt? (*ARTEMISIA nods. TUTIA fusses over ARTEMISIA's clothes.*) Your beautiful new dress. (*ARTEMISIA stares mournfully at her.*) Now, don't worry, we can fix it. You didn't encourage him, did you? (*ARTEMISIA looks blank.*) Smile at him? Flirt with him?

ARTEMISIA: First he told me I was ugly. Then he started kissing me.

TUTIA: You let him kiss you?!

ARTEMISIA: Romeo kisses Juliet.

TUTIA: Romeo is going to marry Juliet. Did he say anything about marriage before he started kissing you?

ARTEMISIA: He said he was obsessed with my body.

TUTIA: That's it?

ARTEMISIA nods. ORAZIO can be heard offstage.

ORAZIO: (*off*) Bella!

TUTIA & ARTEMISIA: (*together*)

(*TUTIA*) Omigod! (*rushes up and locks the door*)

(*ARTEMISIA*) He can't see me like this!

TUTIA: Ssssh.

ORAZIO: (*at the door*) Bella? Are you in there?

TUTIA: Bella's downstairs.

ORAZIO: Oh. (*sound of footsteps walking away*) Bella?

ARTEMISIA: I'll have to tell him.

TUTIA: No! (*pause*) He'll go after Tassi and Tassi will say you encouraged him and it'll be your word against his and, believe me, that man has a mouth on him. God! He's probably telling people now.

ARTEMISIA: What am I going to do?

TUTIA: (*paces*) If only I'd caught him! We could have forced him to marry you.

ARTEMISIA: I don't think I'd want to marry him.

TUTIA: You could have been engaged and then broken it off.

ARTEMISIA: But why?

TUTIA: He wouldn't tell people his fiancée's a whore.

ARTEMISIA: Oooh.

TUTIA: But it's too late. I wasn't there. (*pause*) Unless, of course, it happens again. Was it only the one lesson your father arranged?

> *TUTIA and ARTEMISIA exchange a conspiratorial look.*

SCENE 9

> *TASSI's apartment. A young girl lounges in a chair in the room. TASSI enters, exhausted. He looks up, sees the girl, and gives a start.*

TASSI: LISA?

LISA: Surprised to see me.

TASSI: Well – you're – ah – married now.

LISA: That old fart. He can't get it up more than once a day.

TASSI: Does he know where you are?

LISA: Of course not. I've gone out.

TASSI: He might guess.

LISA: When did you become so cautious?

TASSI: I'm tired of lawsuits.

LISA: You forgot my birthday and I want my present. (*smiles and advances on him*)

TASSI: How old are you, now? Sixteen?

LISA: Fourteen. You know exactly how old I am.

TASSI: You seem older. (*LISA removes a stocking.*) I had a very interesting day, today.

LISA: (*not interested*) Really.

TASSI: I met a young girl who was entirely innocent.

LISA: What a bore. (*removes other stocking*)

TASSI: A frightening experience. Not a bore at all. She was like a large child.

LISA: Like me?

TASSI: You were never a child.

LISA: She won't be innocent for long.

TASSI: I don't know why you have such a low opinion of me. Anyway, her father hired me to seduce her.

LISA: What father in his right mind would do that!

TASSI: He's not in his right mind. He's an artist.

LISA: He probably wants you to marry her.

TASSI: I don't think so. He knows me too well.

LISA: It might be a trap. He might be planning to catch you at it.

TASSI: No. That doesn't make sense. (*Pause – he starts to laugh.*)

LISA: What's so funny?

TASSI: Well – he was fairly cryptic in his request. (*laughs*) I mean – it is possible that he simply wanted me to teach her perspective. (*laughs*) We were both pretty drunk. Omigod! (*hysterical laughter*)

LISA: What happened to your hand?

TASSI: Occupational hazard.

LISA: Here. I'll kiss it all better. (*starts to kiss his hand*)

TASSI: No – LISA – really. Stop. I'm not in the mood. (*breaks away*) Don't you feel any remorse at all about your sister?

LISA: No. I hated her. She was a bitch. Did you really kill her?

TASSI: I hired someone.

LISA: Oh. That doesn't count.

TASSI: She's dead, isn't she.

LISA: Yes, but it would have been better if you'd done it yourself.

TASSI: I'm sorry.

LISA: That's all right. Let's make love, now.

TASSI: It's not true, you know.

LISA: What.

TASSI: I didn't murder your sister. I didn't hire anyone, either.

LISA: I don't care.

TASSI: I know. (*pause*) Fascinating.

LISA: Don't get so high and mighty with me. You wanted her dead. You might as well have killed her.

TASSI: There's a huge gulf between the desire and the action.

LISA: It's too late to tell me that. (*She removes her clothes.*)

> *TASSI watches her, sighs. LISA shoves TASSI onto the bed. A loud knocking on the door. TASSI and LISA sit bolt upright.*

TASSI & LISA: (*together*)

(*TASSI*) Your husband!

(*LISA*) My husband!

TASSI pushes LISA out of bed, grabs her clothes, and shoves her out of a side exit. More knocking. TASSI opens the door in a nonchalant fashion. ORAZIO stands in the doorway.

TASSI: Shit. (*tries to close the door*)

ORAZIO: (*walking in*) That's not much of a greeting. We didn't set a time for the next lesson.

TASSI: Another one?

ORAZIO: Yes. My daughter wants you back.

TASSI: Pardon?

ORAZIO: She says you haven't begun to teach her what she needs to know.

TASSI: She didn't really say that, did she?

ORAZIO: Yes. It's a little insulting, you know, Tassi.

TASSI: This is extraordinary.

ORAZIO: I mean, I think I'm a pretty good teacher. But I suppose she's right. There's no point in only one class. What did you cover?

TASSI: Oh – ah, one-point perspective. And worm's-eye view. We explored that thoroughly.

ORAZIO: Then, you've got two-point and bird's-eye for the next lesson. Creating forms in space for the third.

TASSI: She's probably well on her way to creating a form in space.

ORAZIO: She couldn't do it without you, Tassi. Same time next week, then. (*claps him on the back and leaves*)

SCENE 10

The studio. ARTEMISIA is wearing a very provocative dress. She looks very intent, as though about to perform some secret rite.

ARTEMISIA: "Judith prayed to God to give her strength to defeat Holofernes. Bring to pass, O Lord, that his pride may be cut off with his own sword. Let him be caught in the net of his own eyes in my regard and do Thou strike him by the graces of the words of my lips. Give me constancy in my mind that I may despise him and fortitude that I may overthrow him. For this will be a glorious monument for Thy name, when he shall fall by the hand of a woman."

She squirts perfume all over herself, puts on too much makeup, and fixes her hair while she speaks.

ARTEMISIA: "And she washed her body and anointed herself with the best ointment and plaited the hair of her head. (*She tries to plait her hair, gives up, and lets it fall loose.*) And clothed herself with the garments of her gladness and put sandals on her feet and took her bracelets and lilies and earlets and rings and adorned herself with all ornaments."

She puts masses of jewellery on and looks at herself in the mirror.

ARTEMISIA: "And the Lord also gave her more beauty: because all this dressing up did not proceed from sensuality but from virtue. And therefore, the Lord increased this her beauty so that she appeared to all men's eyes incomparably lovely."

ARTEMISIA stands as though in a trance.

Lighting changes for Judith scenes.

SCENE 11

HOLOFERNES's camp. HOLOFERNES, TASSI, and RATZO.

RATZO: It's about that Hebrew woman, sire.

HOLOFERNES: Yes – why hasn't she been brought to me? Why am I always the last person to know?

RATZO: I asked them not to. Not till I'd spoken to you first.

HOLOFERNES: You've got your nerve!

RATZO: Sire, I'm not subject to female charms and –

HOLOFERNES: Why not. Being a eunuch shouldn't deprive you of an aesthetic sense.

RATZO: I mean – sire – I don't trust this woman. She claims that she will help us conquer her town. Now, why would she do that. She's got this cock-and-bull story about how her God is angry at her people and wants to punish them.

HOLOFERNES: Why is her God angry?

RATZO: Oh – I don't know – they've been eating the wrong food. She's eating the right food. She will lead us straight to her people and as long as she eats the right food, it's okay.

HOLOFERNES: It sounds ridiculous.

RATZO: It *is* ridiculous. But the problem is – everyone believes her.

HOLOFERNES: Why?

RATZO: She's very beautiful, sire. She's got them all charmed. And when she tells her story, for some weird reason, it sounds convincing. I think it would be best if you didn't see her.

HOLOFERNES: Send her in.

RATZO: But, sire –

HOLOFERNES: Don't tell me what to do. Send her in!

RATZO leaves and brings in JUDITH.

SCENE 12

JUDITH enters and prostrates herself before HOLOFERNES.

JUDITH: My lord.

HOLOFERNES: You are the Hebrew woman from Bethulia?

JUDITH: (*still prostrate*) Yes, my lord.

HOLOFERNES: And you choose to serve Ozymandias?

JUDITH: Yes, my lord.

HOLOFERNES: You may rise. What's your name?

JUDITH: (*rises and looks at him*) My name is Judith, my lord.

HOLOFERNES: You're trembling. Don't be afraid. I've never harmed anyone who chose to serve Ozymandias. Simply those who defy him. Your people would have been safe if they hadn't insulted us. Give me your hand. (*JUDITH does so reluctantly.*) People have to meet me halfway. You're not ready yet, are you?

JUDITH: I don't understand, my lord.

HOLOFERNES: (*drops her hand*) Later. If you're such a devout Hebrew, how do you plan to serve both gods?

JUDITH: I worship Jehovah in heaven and Ozymandias on earth.

HOLOFERNES: A clever answer. You're very shrewd.

JUDITH: But it is the truth, my lord. I swear by Ozymandias it is so. May he strike me dead if I lie.

Pause.

HOLOFERNES: Then again, if you don't believe in him, he couldn't strike you dead, could he?

JUDITH: That's blasphemy, my lord.

HOLOFERNES: Not really. Ozymandias is simply the king who rules Ninevah. He'd like to be worshipped and so, as part of my job, I worship him. The other part of my job is that I have to make everyone else worship him. That is more difficult.

JUDITH: So you don't really believe Ozymandias is a god?

HOLOFERNES: Given the choice, I prefer my gods to be invisible. Visible gods have an annoying habit of thinking up things for me to do. But you still haven't answered my question. How can you betray your god?

JUDITH: I am not betraying Him. He is very angry with my people. They are planning to break into the forbidden food supplies. Jehovah has sent me to punish them through you.

HOLOFERNES: Is food that important?

JUDITH: Yes.

HOLOFERNES: Does this god – this Jehovah – does he actually talk to you?

JUDITH: Yes. He gave me a prophecy. "I am to do things with you that will be the wonder of the world wherever men hear about them."

HOLOFERNES: Hmmm. (*smiles*)

JUDITH: I am to stay in your camp and each night before dawn I am to go out into the valley and pray to Jehovah.

HOLOFERNES: I don't think you should go out alone.

JUDITH: My maid can come with me then. Jehovah will tell me when my people have committed this sin. Then I will return and you may lead out your whole army and you will meet with no resistance. They will follow you like sheep. We will set up your throne in the heart of Jerusalem.

HOLOFERNES: If you do as you have promised, Jehovah shall be my god as well. (*to RATZO*) Food and drink for our guest!

JUDITH: I'm afraid I can't eat your food, my lord. If I broke my food vow, Jehovah would not talk to me. I have my own provisions. (*indicates basket*)

HOLOFERNES: It isn't much. What if you run out? (*motions for RATZO to leave*)

JUDITH: I won't run out until I have done what my lord has planned.

HOLOFERNES: That sounds sinister.

JUDITH: I only meant, my lord, that together you and I will accomplish a great deal very quickly.

HOLOFERNES: Then, let us begin tonight! (*pulls her onto the bed*)

JUDITH: My lord!

HOLOFERNES: Oh stop calling me that! (*kisses her*)

JUDITH: (*struggling*) No! Please! You must stop!

HOLOFERNES: (*stops*) You have nothing to fear from me, Madame. I didn't know you found me so unattractive.

JUDITH: I admire you a great deal, my lord. Still, everything must come at its appointed time.

HOLOFERNES: When's that? Doomsday.

JUDITH: Soon. My lord, will you give orders for me to be allowed out each day before dawn? That is the best time for me to talk to Jehovah.

HOLOFERNES: Very well. (*He claps his hands. RATZO enters.*) Ratzo, please conduct the Hebrew woman to her tent. She will go to the guards before dawn and ask to be allowed out to pray. Tell the men to let her pass.

RATZO gives HOLOFERNES a questioning look and leaves.

JUDITH: Thank you, my lord. (*bows*)

HOLOFERNES withdraws. Lights change. TUTIA enters.

TUTIA: Whew! What's that stink!

ARTEMISIA: Perfume. Don't you ever knock.

TUTIA: Christ, what's happened to you. You look like a slut.

ARTEMISIA: What?

TUTIA: Bangles up to your elbows. (*removes them*) Do up your bodice. (*starts hoisting up ARTEMISIA's dress*) Your breasts are about to fall out.

ARTEMISIA: I'm supposed to seduce him, aren't I?

TUTIA: Seduce him?! You'll scare the living daylights out of him. Wash your face.

ARTEMISIA: He'll be here any minute.

TUTIA: I don't care. Wash your face. (*ARTEMISIA washes off her makeup.*) Are you sure you want to go through with this?

ARTEMISIA: Yes.

TUTIA: You seem pretty nervous.

ARTEMISIA: He's late! Why isn't he here yet?

TUTIA: Maybe he's not coming. Maybe we should just leave well enough alone.

ARTEMISIA: But this was your idea!

TUTIA: He might not have told anyone. And if there're no repercussions.

ARTEMISIA: Repercussions?

TUTIA: Babies.

ARTEMISIA: Omigod!

TUTIA: Yes. I meant to mention that. You've got long fingers so that's a good sign.

ARTEMISIA: Pardon?

TUTIA: Women with long fingers don't get pregnant as easily as women with short fingers. But then again, there's the element of surprise. You weren't expecting it. And somehow, those are the ones that usually take. When was your period?

ARTEMISIA: Two weeks ago.

TUTIA: Omigod! Not today! Bolt the door!

ARTEMISIA: What?!

TUTIA: Bad day today. Definitely not the day!

There's knocking at door. TUTIA races up to bolt it. ARTEMISIA pulls her back.

ARTEMISIA: No! He started it and I'm going to finish it. (*She opens the door and curtseys to TASSI who walks in.*) Signore Tassi.

TASSI: Signorina Gentileschi. And Signora Liotta. (*bows*)

ARTEMISIA: So, Tutia, if you hurry, you'll be able to catch up with Father. Tell him we're running low on burnt sienna, please.

TUTIA: Oh, all right. (*leaves*)

TASSI: So, you've asked me back for a command performance. Anything special you'd like me to do?

ARTEMISIA: Um – ah – you're the teacher. You should decide what I need to learn next.

TASSI: How delightfully ambiguous. Are you suggesting what I think you are?

ARTEMISIA: Perhaps.

TASSI: Well, forget it. It won't happen again.

ARTEMISIA: It won't?

TASSI: No. There are some duties in life that are simply too onerous.

ARTEMISIA: Onerous?

TASSI: Too much hard work.

ARTEMISIA: Raping me was hard work?!

TASSI: Damn right it was. Look at my hand. It still hasn't healed. I think you should apologize.

ARTEMISIA: I should apologize?!

TASSI: I'm waiting. (*ARTEMISIA lunges at him, rips his shirt.*) Hey! Don't rip my clothes. How'd you like it if I ripped your dress.

ARTEMISIA: Just try it! I dare you! You snivelling little pimp!

> *TASSI grabs her bodice and tears it open. ARTEMISIA grabs TASSI's belt and tries to pull his pants down.*

TASSI: WHAT THE HELL!

> *They struggle and fall on the ground. ARTEMISIA works it so TASSI is in a very compromising position.*

ARTEMISIA: Perfect! (*grabs TASSI and won't let him get away*) HELP! HELP! RAPE!! DADDY!! DADDY!!

TASSI: Holy Jesus! (*He struggles to get up.*)

> *ARTEMISIA clamps on to him and screams. ORAZIO and TUTIA rush in. TUTIA is carrying a broom.*

ORAZIO: Omigod! (*crosses himself*)

> *TUTIA hits TASSI with the broom.*

TASSI: OW! (*dodges blows*) Fine! I'll leave. (*He rushes to the door.*)

ORAZIO: (*bolts door*) YOU B-A-A-A-STARD.

TASSI: It's not what you think. She set it up.

ORAZIO: Who? My daughter?! LIAR!! (*He grabs TASSI's throat and pulls out a knife.*)

TASSI: Sorry. Didn't mean that.

ARTEMISIA: Don't kill him, Daddy.

ORAZIO: Why not?

ARTEMISIA: He did propose to me.

TASSI & ORAZIO: WHAT?!

ARTEMISIA: And I accepted.

TASSI: Jesus! (*puts his head in his hand*)

ORAZIO: (*lets TASSI go*) Oh, Bella, how could you!

ARTEMISIA: He is a friend of yours, Daddy, and he said he loved me very much and we'd have one of those old-fashioned engagements. Nozze di riparazione.

TUTIA: Marriage by capture. It's all the rage now, sir.

ORAZIO: (*to TASSI*) Is this true?

TASSI: Well – there is my wife.

ORAZIO: (*draws knife*) You said she was dead.

TASSI: Yes, of course I did, didn't I? Well – I'm sure she is. Dead, that is. (*to ARTEMISIA*) Is this a long engagement?

ARTEMISIA: Yes.

TASSI: Well – if she isn't dead now, one of us will be by the time I marry your daughter. (*laughs uneasily*)

ORAZIO: You're such a kidder.

TASSI: Joke's on me this time, Ratzo. I really don't deserve your daughter.

ORAZIO: Come, let's celebrate! Put your clothes back on and we'll grab a bottle of my best wine and drink! To marriage by capture!

ARTEMISIA: Yes! To marriage by capture!

> *Blackout.*

ACT TWO

SCENE 1

> *Six months later. The studio. TASSI is sprawled out on the studio mattress in the "Holofernes" pose. His shirt is off and he has fallen asleep. ARTEMISIA enters, quietly, so as not to wake him. She sees a sword hanging on the wall. She very carefully takes it down from the wall.*

TASSI: Mmmmm. (*moves slightly*)

> *ARTEMISIA freezes. She waits for a few moments, then goes over to TASSI. She lifts the sword up and poises it over TASSI's throat.*

TASSI: (*wakes up, sees ARTEMISIA*) HOLY CHRIST!

> *He raises his arm and grabs ARTEMISIA's sword hand, making her drop the sword.*

ARTEMISIA: Oh sorry, I was just thinking.

TASSI: Do you have to do it with a sword at my throat! JESUS!

ARTEMISIA: It won't work. She won't be able to do it on her own. She'll need the maid. Let's see now. Lie back again. (*picks up sword*)

TASSI: GET THAT FUCKING SWORD AWAY FROM ME!

ARTEMISIA: Did I frighten you?

TASSI: NO! (*pause*) I'm just not used to waking up with a sword at my neck, held by a woman with a very intent look on her face. Call me crazy, but it makes me nervous. What's this for, anyway?

ARTEMISIA: I'm doing a painting of Judith.

TASSI: And I'm Holofernes? (*ARTEMISIA nods.*) OH NO! THAT'S IT! NOT ME! I hate that story. You're not using my face! (*goes over to drawing*) Doesn't even look like me. (*He tears the drawing in half. ARTEMISIA gasps. He throws the pieces on the floor.*) You're not putting me in that painting and that's final!

ARTEMISIA: What right have you to –

TASSI: (*puts on shirt*) I'm your fiancé. Love, honour, and obey.

ARTEMISIA: But –

TASSI: Christ! You shouldn't have let me sleep so long. We gotta go!

ARTEMISIA: Where? What are you talking about?

TASSI: Picnic. Do your bodice up. I don't want my friends to think I'm marrying a slut. (*kisses her and leaves*)

> ARTEMISIA straightens her clothes. As she is about to leave, she grabs pieces of her drawing, rolls them together, and hides them under the bed.

SCENE 2

> The picnic. ARTEMISIA, TASSI, COSIMO, GIAMBATTISTA, LISA, and her husband, who shall be referred to as OLD MAN.

OLD MAN: This liver isn't chopped fine enough. It's got gristly bits that catch in my teeth.

LISA: Poor baby. I didn't know you still had teeth.

OLD MAN: (*smiles beneficently at her*) Ah, my love. So, you will get the butcher to grind it finer in the future.

LISA: Certainly, my dove.

OLD MAN: Excuse me a moment. My digestion is not what it used to be. (*leaves*)

LISA: Ground glass.

ARTEMISIA: What?

LISA: (*ignores her; to TASSI*) The glass isn't working. Maybe, I've ground it too fine. But if it were bigger, he'd see it. (*GIAMBATTISTA coughs, splutters.*) Oh, don't worry. Once in a while does no harm at all.

COSIMO: (*to ARTEMISIA*) You've got great tits. (*ARTEMISIA blushes, looks away.*) Well, ya do. She's got great tits, Tassi. Who'd have thought my daughter would have great tits.

ARTEMISIA: Your daughter?

COSIMO: Hey, Giambattista, don't you think we look alike?

GIAMBATTISTA: No.

LISA: She's got your hairy arms, Cosimo. (*ARTEMISIA looks at her arms.*) Trust me. They're hairy. How can you stand it, Tassi. She looks like a gorilla.

TASSI: I think hairy arms are very attractive.

LISA: Does she have hair all over her stomach, too?

TASSI: (*warningly*) LISA.

COSIMO: (*to ARTEMISIA*) Do you? (*strokes her arm*)

ARTEMISIA: Please. Take your hands off me. (*COSIMO continues mauling her.*) Agostino.

TASSI: Yes, Artemisia.

ARTEMISIA: Please.

COSIMO: But I'm his best man. We share everything.

LISA: She really is bourgeois, isn't she. (*to ARTEMISIA*) Shall I spell it out for you. I love Cosimo (*kisses him*) and Cosimo loves me. I could love Giambattista but he won't let me and I'm very, very good friends with Agostino here. We were better friends until you came along. But you see – those bourgeois principles of yours – one man, one woman – well, it's very divisive. Isolating yourselves in a little cocoon. What about the rest of the world? Giambattista here. Now, he loves Agostino. And what sort of man would Agostino be if he didn't return that love from time to time. You're being very selfish, Artemisia. You want Agostino all to yourself. And that's wrong. We're all one big loving family here.

> OLD MAN enters.

LISA: Except for him.

OLD MAN: Did I miss something?

LISA: No, darling. Why don't you have a nice little nap and when things get exciting, I'll wake you up.

OLD MAN: All right. (*lies down to sleep*)

LISA: Bad heart. Can't take the strain of my lifestyle but he likes to watch.

ARTEMISIA: (*to TASSI*) Is this true?

TASSI: He's an old man.

ARTEMISIA: No. Her. This man. (*gestures to GIAMBATTISTA*)

GIAMBATTISTA: Agostino and I were once lovers. Does that disturb you?

ARTEMISIA: Yes!

LISA: How small-minded of you.

TASSI: (*to ARTEMISIA*) I thought you wanted to be an artist.

ARTEMISIA: Yes, but what does this –

TASSI: Then, you have to explore your senses. You have to experience life to the fullest. You can't remain on the outside, forever. Innocence can only take you so far. You want to be a great painter, don't you.

ARTEMISIA: What if I wind up like her.

LISA: What's wrong with me!

TASSI: You might. That's a risk you have to take.

LISA: What the hell's wrong with me!

COSIMO & TASSI: Nothing, dear.

OLD MAN wakes up and stares at ARTEMISIA.

OLD MAN: Say, are you related to Orazio the painter?

LISA: Quick off the mark, as always.

ARTEMISIA: Yes. I'm his daughter.

COSIMO: No. You're my daughter!

OLD MAN: (*astonished*) Sonofabitch!

ARTEMISIA: Pardon?

OLD MAN: I was supposed to marry you. Your name's Bella, right?

ARTEMISIA: That's my father's name for me. Yes.

OLD MAN: Your father said you weren't ready yet. You look pretty ripe to me. That fruit's been plucked, eh, Tassi. (*nudges him*)

ARTEMISIA: My father would never arrange such a thing.

OLD MAN: Which? Marrying me or getting plucked. Not to be rude, Missy, but I think he arranged both. You don't put a cat like Tassi with your prize pigeon without expecting to lose a few feathers. (*chortles away*)

GIAMBATTISTA: Have some more chopped liver.

OLD MAN: Oh – now – I've had plenty. (*eyes ARTEMISIA up and down lasciviously*) Well – now, isn't that interesting. That's two you've stolen from me, Tassi. Oh well, better to lose this one right away than to marry her and then lose her. Maybe I'll try and steal her back.

LISA: Why don't you go back to sleep, dear.

OLD MAN: DON'T TELL ME WHEN TO FALL ASLEEP.

ARTEMISIA: That's not true what you said about my father! He's not like that!

COSIMO: Yeah, I've got better taste than that.

OLD MAN: He's a friend of Tassi's. What do you expect?

ARTEMISIA: He'd never do those things!

TASSI: Your father's a hypocrite. It's fine for him and it's fine for me, but it's not all right for you. You're supposed to be purer than pure – good as gold. Why do you have to maintain a standard of virtue. Nobody else does. Least of all your father. (*snickers*) Ha! The bordellos he's dragged me into – grungy little hovels – whores with names like Black Maria and Spanish Flea. Lately, he's come up in the world. Tutia's quite respectable.

ARTEMISIA: Stop! Stop this! It's not true!

GIAMBATTISTA: Agostino, stop. I think she's had enough.

TASSI: (*to ARTEMISIA*) You can flirt with danger but you can't live with it. When I told you life was art – you thought I was being facetious. I am in deadly earnest.

ARTEMISIA: I can't live this way.

TASSI: Then you'll never be great. You have to live on the edge to be great.

LISA: Like Caravaggio.

TASSI: Like Caravaggio!

ARTEMISIA: (*to TASSI*) Why aren't you great, then?

GIAMBATTISTA: She's direct.

TASSI: I am. It's not my fault if the world at large hasn't heard of me.

ARTEMISIA: She's a great painter, too, I suppose.

TASSI: Lisa is one of my best pupils, aren't you, dear?

LISA: Yes. I'm very good. In fact, I have some drawings I'd like you to look at. Privately.

TASSI: Perhaps, later.

LISA: No. I want you to look at them now. I need help with my foreshortening. (*to ARTEMISIA*) Have you had that lesson, yet? It's one of his best. Although the introduction to perspective is interesting. "If I were a man standing a hundred feet away from you –"

TASSI: Hem! (*tries to take her off*)

LISA: Gets them every time. (*She leaves with TASSI.*)

COSIMO: Well, how about it?

ARTEMISIA: How about what?

COSIMO: How about a little kiss for your old dad.

GIAMBATTISTA: Lay off her, Cosimo.

COSIMO: Lisa said –

GIAMBATTISTA: I don't care what Lisa said. Lay off her!

COSIMO: Easy for you to say. Women aren't your special interest group. He gets paid. I do it for pleasure.

OLD MAN: It's a pity we missed each other, my dear. You have just the right amount of spunk. Lively – yet not vicious. Lisa has a bit too much spunk for my taste. What enormous hands you have. (*takes one of ARTEMISIA's hands*)

COSIMO: Yes – they are rather large, aren't they. (*takes the other*)

> *The two men exchange glances. ARTEMISIA tries to snatch her hands away. She is still held by the two men. GIAMBATTISTA pulls out a knife and advances on COSIMO, who promptly drops ARTEMISIA's hand. The OLD MAN also backs off. TASSI enters with LISA.*

TASSI: That won't be necessary. (*goes over to ARTEMISIA*) My darling, I think it's time we went home.

OLD MAN: (*to ARTEMISIA*) I'll have you on canvas, then. (*ARTEMISIA and TASSI start to leave.*) You, too, Tassi. In fact, you're the reason for the painting.

TASSI: Ratzo's painting?

OLD MAN: You've seen it, then. I wanted your head, Tassi, and Ratzo volunteered to paint it for me. Salome, John the Baptist, head on a platter. Not too subtle but it suited my mood. But Ratzo couldn't bear to paint his little Bella as a temptress. So he suggested Judith.

TASSI: Why that little shit.

OLD MAN: There's nothing he wouldn't do for a buck. He must have finished it by now.

TASSI: (*to ARTEMISIA*) Your father mention anything about a dowry?

ARTEMISIA: No.

OLD MAN: Are you kidding?! You won't get a dowry from Ratzo. He wouldn't give me one.

TASSI: How much did he want for the painting?

OLD MAN: Well, he wanted the world but I talked him down.

TASSI: How much?

OLD MAN: Three hundred ducats.

TASSI: I'll sell it to you for two hundred.

OLD MAN: I hate to cheat a friend.

TASSI: It's my head. And my fiancée. I'm entitled to a dowry. Don't you agree, my dear?

ARTEMISIA: Oh – ah – I don't know –

TASSI: We'll deliver it tomorrow night.

OLD MAN: I wouldn't want to start a quarrel.

TASSI: I'm only taking what's rightfully mine. (*leaves with ARTEMISIA*)

SCENE 3

ARTEMISIA and TASSI are lying on a bed.

ARTEMISIA: You're trying to make a whore of me.

TASSI: It's just a lifestyle. You take things so seriously.

ARTEMISIA: I couldn't sleep with those men. Never.

TASSI: You don't have to. You can live exactly the way you like.

ARTEMISIA: And you?

TASSI: I live the way I like.

ARTEMISIA: Have you – ah – slept with all those people?

TASSI: Not the Old Man. I don't think anyone sleeps with the Old Man. Not even Lisa.

ARTEMISIA: Who does Lisa sleep with?

TASSI: Whoever's around, I imagine.

ARTEMISIA: Were you ever – around?

TASSI: You're not going to be jealous, are you? That would be very boring. You can't own people, Artemisia. I love you but I can't guarantee that I'll always be faithful to you. Any more than you can.

ARTEMISIA: But you're faithful to me now?

TASSI: More or less.

ARTEMISIA: Which is it?

TASSI: Let's not be tedious. Nobody's perfect. Not me. Not you. Not even your father.

ARTEMISIA: I don't like what you said about my father.

TASSI: Can't help it. It's true.

ARTEMISIA: Did he really ask you to rape me?

TASSI: "Rape" is an ugly word. And misleading. (*undoes her bodice*)

ARTEMISIA: Did he?

TASSI: He knew the sort of man I was. Anyway, you should be honoured.

ARTEMISIA: Pardon?

TASSI: He's treated you like a son. He's taught you his craft and now he wants you to live like a man. (*ARTEMISIA looks puzzled.*) On my twelfth birthday, my father bought me the services of his favourite whore. His tastes ran to overripe women, so it wasn't exactly a pleasant experience. But it was necessary.

ARTEMISIA: Why?

TASSI: It's a fact of life. Women never get a proper introduction to the facts of life. Your father has done you this immense service and you don't even appreciate it.

ARTEMISIA: He's been lying to me my whole life!

TASSI: I told Ratzo it was a waste of time to train you. Women will never be as clear-headed as men. I fucked the whore but I didn't marry her. You want to marry the whore.

ARTEMISIA: The whore? (*pause*) Or the pimp.

TASSI: (*looks at her sharply, then stops himself*) You act as though life is a personal affront. I simply follow my instincts.

ARTEMISIA: Like a dog.

TASSI: Yes. Like a dog. (*fondles her*) I see my master's linen, lying on a bed. White and newly starched. I creep up, grab a crisp white corner in my mouth. (*He grabs her sleeve with his mouth.*) And I pull. Gently at first. (*tugs at her sleeve*) And then, I yank it (*pulls her onto the floor*) off the bed and I roll around in it. I roll around and around –

> *ARTEMISIA and TASSI roll around on the floor. ARTEMISIA starts giggling.*

TASSI: And around and around. (*stops; he is on top of her*) Imbuing it with my scent until it's mine.

> *They kiss.*

SCENE 4

The studio. ORAZIO is pacing back and forth. ARTEMISIA enters and walks by him.

ORAZIO: (*blocks her path*) You didn't come home last night.

ARTEMISIA: So. (*tries to get by*)

ORAZIO: (*stops her*) You ditch your chaperone – you go out on this picnic and you disappear for the night.

ARTEMISIA: (*pulls away*) I'll live as I please.

ORAZIO: Not in my house, you won't!

ARTEMISIA: Then I'll live with Agostino.

ORAZIO: NO! You can't stay at his house. Not till you're married. It looks bad.

ARTEMISIA: Why? It makes me look like a whore?

ORAZIO: Don't say that word!

ARTEMISIA: Why not? You sell me to the highest bidder. I might as well be one. Maybe Spanish Flea will lend me some of her clothes.

ORAZIO: Who?

ARTEMISIA: You know Spanish Flea, Daddy.

> *TUTIA enters.*

ORAZIO: No. Of course, I don't.

ARTEMISIA: LIAR! HYPOCRITE!!

ORAZIO: Bella!

TUTIA: I'm sure she doesn't mean it, Signore. Young girls are very excitable.

ARTEMISIA: Shut up, you bitch!

> *TUTIA gasps.*

ORAZIO: You apologize to Tutia!

ARTEMISIA: NO! Ask her why she wasn't at the picnic.

TUTIA: I didn't know you were going! Little Julio had colic and was screaming his lungs out. So, it's not as if I spent a pleasant Sunday –

ORAZIO: A misunderstanding, then. In future, Tutia, please accompany them.

TUTIA: Yes, Signore.

ARTEMISIA: (*disgusted*) Oh spare me the Signore act. You two were probably having it off.

TUTIA: WHAT?!

ORAZIO: Hem! Who was with you on this picnic?

ARTEMISIA: All your friends, Daddy. That horrible old man you tried to sell me to –

ORAZIO: Pardon?

ARTEMISIA: The man who commissioned the *Judith* painting.

ORAZIO: Oh yes – have you seen it? I can't find it, anywhere.

ARTEMISIA: Who else was there? The old man's wife – Lisa. I guess she beat me to it. Giambattista, Cosimo –

ORAZIO: Cosimo?! He's a sex fiend. You spent the afternoon with him?!

ARTEMISIA: I spent the afternoon with all of them, Daddy. Individually and all at once.

ORAZIO: WHAT!

ARTEMISIA: Agostino says it's the way you live. So why shouldn't I try it. Like father, like daughter.

ORAZIO: WHAT! These are lies! That bastard! I'll –

ARTEMISIA: At least he doesn't pretend to be something he's not. After years of lies, it's nice to meet an honest man.

ORAZIO: HONEST?! ARE YOU CRAZY! Bella – you must believe me.

ARTEMISIA: You go with him on his whoring. Tell the truth.

ORAZIO: Well. (*looks at* TUTIA)

ARTEMISIA: Tell the truth.

ORAZIO: Yes. I do.

TUTIA: Orazio! Those filthy diseases!

ORAZIO: What difference does it make! You never let me get near you. Bella, it's what men do. You're not supposed to take it seriously.

ARTEMISIA: Fine. I won't. I'll do it, too. As Tassi's wife, it will be my pleasure.

ORAZIO: You can't marry him!

ARTEMISIA: But, Daddy, he's my fiancé. He's the man you chose for me.

ORAZIO: I didn't choose him! I caught him with his pants down!

ARTEMISIA: But, Daddy, it was all your idea. My first lesson –

ORAZIO: What are you talking about?

ARTEMISIA: He raped me at my first class. You arranged it.

ORAZIO: This is outrageous!! He raped you in front of Tutia?!

ARTEMISIA: Tutia wasn't there.

TUTIA edges toward the door.

ORAZIO: What?! But she's supposed to stay with you.

ORAZIO and ARTEMISIA look at TUTIA.

TUTIA: Well – now – nobody said how long, Signore.

ORAZIO: YOU!

TUTIA: I was going to stay but then he accused me of being suspicious of him and he was your best friend and you'd get furious with me and my baby needed to be fed and well, I couldn't do that in his presence and he seemed like a nice man, being your friend and all –

ORAZIO: YOU!!!

TUTIA: (*hysterical*) You arranged the lessons with him. You should have known better!

ORAZIO: I did! That's why I asked you to stay!!

TUTIA: Well – my baby –

ORAZIO: SHUT UP ABOUT THE FUCKING BABY!!!

TUTIA: Well, now Bella's engaged so the problem's solved.

ORAZIO: And whose idea was that! (*TUTIA looks sheepish.*) YOURS?!

TUTIA: Well – no, not exactly –

ORAZIO: God! I'd like to wring your neck. This viper at my breast. This is what happens when you try to be kind. I take in a lodger and presto! the fangs go right into the heart.

TUTIA: You're charging enough for the apartment.

ORAZIO: You're making lots on the side. What did Tassi pay you? Nice dress.

TUTIA: You'd never buy me one, you dirty old cheapskate!

ORAZIO: You bitch! You whore! Where's my painting!

TUTIA: What painting?

ORAZIO: Don't play innocent with me. My Judith. Who'd you let in last night?

TUTIA: I didn't let anyone in. If you go out and leave the gate unlatched, it's not my fault if people come in!

ORAZIO: People?! Who?!

TUTIA: Just Signore Cosimo. (*pause*) And a few friends.

ORAZIO: You let total strangers in to rob me?!

TUTIA: Cosimo's a friend of yours. Tassi sent him to pick up the dowry.

ORAZIO: AAAAAAGH!!!

TUTIA: Anyway, it wasn't any of my business –

ORAZIO: (*flies into a rage and chases* TUTIA) NONE OF YOUR BUSINESS!!! I'LL KILL YOU GODDAMMITT!!! THEN WE'LL SEE WHOSE BUSINESS IT IS!!! (*He lunges at her.* TUTIA *shrieks and runs out.*) I'M SUING YOU! I'LL HAVE YOU PUT IN JAIL!! CHEAP RENT THERE! (*laughs maniacally*) THAT BASTARD! HE STOLE MY DAUGHTER AND NOW HE STEALS MY PAINTING! WELL – HE'S NOT GETTING AWAY WITH IT! DO YOU HEAR ME!! NONE OF IT! NOT ANY MORE! I'M SUING HIM FOR THEFT AND FOR RAPE!

ARTEMISIA: You can't do that!

ORAZIO: Why? Are you afraid your fiancé won't stand up under public scrutiny? DAMN RIGHT HE WON'T!!

ARTEMISIA: I'll deny the rape!

ORAZIO: Tassi will deny it, too, and then you'll come out looking like a whore.

ARTEMISIA: He wouldn't do that.

ORAZIO: Let's just put him to the test, shall we?

ARTEMISIA: No! Please!!

ORAZIO: Why not? Afraid you'll lose your fiancé.

ARTEMISIA: He'll return the painting. There's no need to press charges.

ORAZIO: No. Your honour's at stake and I'm going to defend it!

ARTEMISIA: But nobody knows it's lost.

ORAZIO: You think the people at that picnic aren't gossiping about you. He degrades you to his level, then he doesn't have to marry you.

ARTEMISIA: Please! Don't do this! You'll shame me!

ORAZIO: I'll make him pay for what he's done to you!

ARTEMISIA: But I love him!!

ORAZIO: (*slaps her*) Don't you ever say that again!

SCENE 5

INTERROGATOR, ARTEMISIA, and ORAZIO.

INTERROGATOR: (*exasperated*) Did he rape your daughter or didn't he?!

ORAZIO & ARTEMISIA: (*together*)

(*ORAZIO*) Of course he did!

(*ARTEMISIA*) No! He didn't!!

INTERROGATOR: (*to ORAZIO*) There's no point proceeding if she denies the rape.

ORAZIO: (*to ARTEMISIA*) You can't do this to me. Tell him the truth.

ARTEMISIA: Signore Tassi and I are engaged to be married.

ORAZIO: Over my dead body!

ARTEMISIA: (*glares at ORAZIO*) If necessary!

INTERROGATOR: Excuse me, but did you and Signore Tassi engage in – erhem – sexual intercourse?

ARTEMISIA & ORAZIO: (*together*)

(*ARTEMISIA*) Yes!

(*ORAZIO*) She was raped!

INTERROGATOR: (*to ARTEMISIA*) How many times?

ORAZIO & ARTEMISIA: (*together*)

(*ORAZIO*) Many, many times!

(*ARTEMISIA*) I can't say offhand. A lot.

INTERROGATOR: (*confused*) She was raped many, many times?

ORAZIO: She screamed rape and Tutia and I caught him!

INTERROGATOR: Ah. (*to ARTEMISIA*) Did you scream rape?

ARTEMISIA: Yes – but I don't want to press charges.

ORAZIO: I'm the one pressing charges. She has nothing to do with it!

INTERROGATOR: Please, Signore Gentileschi, we could all save ourselves a lot of trouble. The charges of theft could still stand but as for the rape – since the defendant denies even knowing your daughter and your –

ARTEMISIA: Pardon?

ORAZIO: You heard him. Your fiancé says he doesn't know you.

ARTEMISIA: Is this true?

INTERROGATOR: When we arrested him, yes. We worked on him for a bit and he finally admitted that he'd heard of you. (*pause*) That you'd – erhem – acquired a certain notoriety. But that is neither here nor there, since you also deny the rape.

ARTEMISIA: Tassi raped me.

ORAZIO: Bella! (*hugs her*)

ARTEMISIA pushes ORAZIO away angrily.

INTERROGATOR: Now, are you sure about this? Because –

ARTEMISIA: Yes. I'm sure. I'll make my statement.

INTERROGATOR: Perhaps, in the interests of delicacy, your father should leave the room.

ORAZIO: (*starts to leave*) Yes.

ARTEMISIA: I want him to stay. I want him to know exactly what happened.

ORAZIO: (*stops in his tracks*) Oh.

INTERROGATOR: Well, let's begin then. (*to ORAZIO*) No interference, please. (*to ARTEMISIA*) When did he rape you?

ARTEMISIA: At my first art class. Just before Easter.

INTERROGATOR: How did he rape you?

ARTEMISIA: Well – you know. He held me down and he raped me.

INTERROGATOR: Did he hold you down with one hand? Or two hands? Did he pull your legs apart with his hands? Did he tie you up? Did he lie you down flat or did he press you up against a wall?

ORAZIO & ARTEMISIA: (*together*)

ORAZIO gasps.

(*ARTEMISIA*) Excuse me?

INTERROGATOR: We have to know every detail. We have to know what each part of his body was doing at each moment.

ARTEMISIA: Why?

INTERROGATOR: To see if you are telling the truth. To see if you were in fact raped. If it was intercourse, his body parts would be in different places. You see, there is a technique to rape and we need to see if you describe it correctly.

ARTEMISIA: Oh. (*pause*) Well, it was my first class. He made several comments about my paintings. He pointed to one of the nudes and said it was my body. I denied it but he kept looking at it and then looking at me –

INTERROGATOR: No. The rape. Just tell us about the rape. Not the preamble.

ARTEMISIA: Oh. Well. He locked the door – then he grabbed me and threw me on the bed and –

INTERROGATOR: Where were his hands?

ARTEMISIA: One hand was holding my hands together. The other hand was holding my body down.

INTERROGATOR: So you were flat on the bed.

ARTEMISIA: Yes.

INTERROGATOR: And he was on top of you.

ARTEMISIA: Yes. He pushed his knees between –

INTERROGATOR: One knee or two?

ARTEMISIA: One knee. Between my thighs so I couldn't close them. Then, he lifted up my skirts. (*pause*) With great difficulty. Then he let go of my hands and stuffed a paint rag in my mouth. I tried to push him away but by this time he had pushed my thighs apart with both knees and his penis was about to enter me. He pushed and rammed it in. Is this what you want to hear?

ORAZIO is listening in a state of agony.

INTERROGATOR: Yes.

ARTEMISIA: It burned against me and I screamed in pain but I had the rag in my mouth so no one could hear me. He withdrew his penis and as he was about to put it back in, I squeezed my thighs together so hard that I tore off a piece of his flesh.

ORAZIO sighs, as if to faint.

INTERROGATOR: (*nods*) Hmmm. Very good.

ARTEMISIA: He did not make anything of this and continued with his business. I started to bleed. (*ORAZIO faints.*) That frightened him so he stopped.

ARTEMISIA and the INTERROGATOR slap ORAZIO's face to bring him to.

INTERROGATOR: A lot of blood?

ARTEMISIA: Yes.

INTERROGATOR: Hmmm. Well, thank you very much, Signorina Gentileschi. We will be bringing in two midwives to examine you.

ORAZIO: (*revives*) The bastard!

INTERROGATOR: Your daughter will be brought to court in five days' time to testify in front of the defendant. We're hoping that a confrontation will reveal the truth.

ORAZIO: (*walks out with the INTERROGATOR*) He's telling lies about her. My Bella. She's very obedient. Very virtuous. Just a little high-strung.

INTERROGATOR: I understand. I have a daughter, too.

They leave. ARTEMISIA is left alone onstage. She stares off into space.

Light changes.

SCENE 6

HOLOFERNES and his slave, RATZO.

HOLOFERNES: I haven't seen that Hebrew woman about.

RATZO: She stays in her tent all day.

HOLOFERNES: There's no need for that.

RATZO: Count yourself lucky, master. You don't want that one in your bed.

HOLOFERNES: I think I'll have a little get-together for the slaves.

RATZO: Oh no, master.

HOLOFERNES: A banquet. Tonight. Something small yet sumptuous. Now, we can't leave the Hebrew woman out of the festivities, can we? Go. Persuade her to join us. Don't tell her it's for slaves. She might be offended.

RATZO: Please, master. This one is trouble. I can guarantee it.

HOLOFERNES: GO!

SCENE 7

RATZO, JUDITH, and TUTIA.

RATZO: Ah – Madame Judith.

JUDITH: Yes.

RATZO: Holofernes requests the pleasure of your company at a feast tonight. It is to be your initiation as one of the handmaidens of Ozymandias.

JUDITH: Oh.

RATZO: I wouldn't refuse if I were you.

JUDITH: Who am I to refuse my lord. Whatever pleases Him, I will do it at once and it will be a joy to me until the day of my death.

RATZO: That's a yes? Fine. Eight o'clock. (*leaves*)

TUTIA: Oh, Madame Judith, we'll be ruined. I knew staying in the tent would do no good. We should never –

JUDITH: Tutia. Prepare my food. Pack it in the basket with the cloth. Don't forget my wine.

TUTIA: That's not wine.

JUDITH: They don't know that.

TUTIA: Do you have a plan?

JUDITH: I hope so. Wait outside the tent if you can. We'll be going out for our usual stroll.

TUTIA: Do you think Holofernes will let you?

JUDITH: If all goes well, he might even be joining us.

SCENE 8

THE BANQUET. HOLOFERNES's tent. HOLOFERNES, COSIMO, GIAMBATTISTA, LISA, RATZO, JUDITH, and OLD MAN.

HOLOFERNES: Isn't she beautiful! Isn't she the most exquisite creature on the face of the earth!

COSIMO: Why don't you fuck her and get it over with.

HOLOFERNES: What a terrible thing to say. (*to JUDITH*) Don't listen to him, my darling. These Assyrian men are very crude. Are Hebrew men as crude as well?

JUDITH: Some.

GIAMBATTISTA: Are Hebrew men as beautiful as their women?

LISA: I don't think she's so beautiful. She's very large.

HOLOFERNES: That's because you are very small. With the brain of a gnat. You are a slave but Judith will be my queen.

LISA: (*to JUDITH*) He's said that before. (*imitates*) "You will be my queen."

HOLOFERNES: I never said such a thing! Don't even think to compare yourself! Judith is a princess. She is good, kind, and wise. (*to JUDITH*) You're an angel. (*JUDITH looks away.*) Yes. You are. You are my guardian angel and I adore you. (*takes her hand and kisses it*) Will you protect me tonight? (*to group*) I embarrass her. See how she blushes.

OLD MAN: I wouldn't mind a Hebrew woman myself. (*to JUDITH*) Do you have any sisters?

HOLOFERNES: Enough! You should be satisfied with the woman you have. (*indicates LISA*)

OLD MAN: She didn't satisfy you. Why do I have to put up with her.

LISA: Because you're old and you're ugly. That's why.

OLD MAN: (*to HOLOFERNES*) Did she talk like that to you?

COSIMO & HOLOFERNES: (*together*)

(*COSIMO*) Always.

(*HOLOFERNES*) Never!

GIAMBATTISTA: (*to JUDITH*) Holofernes is truly smitten with you. I've never seen him like this before. Don't hurt him.

JUDITH: Hurt him?

GIAMBATTISTA: Break his heart.

JUDITH: His heart will remain in one piece.

COSIMO: (*to JUDITH*) Have some more wine. We're all getting smashed here and you've hardly touched yours. (*starts to pour wine into JUDITH's glass*)

JUDITH: I brought my own wine. (*takes her glass away*)

COSIMO: Holofernes isn't stingy. Have some of ours.

JUDITH: NO! I mean – I have to drink my own wine.

COSIMO: It's an odd colour for wine. (*sniffs it*) Smells like – (*takes JUDITH's glass*)

JUDITH: You mustn't drink it!

COSIMO: (*takes a sip*) This isn't wine. It's grape juice.

HOLOFERNES: What?

JUDITH: It's Hebrew wine, my lord. It's very sweet.

COSIMO: It's not fair that we should get absolutely pissed and she should sit there watching.

JUDITH: Hebrew wine is just as potent. But I admit, I haven't drunk much. (*raises her glass*) I will drink now, my lord, because my life means more to me today than in all the days since I was born.

LISA: That's overdoing it a bit, isn't it.

GIAMBATTISTA: You haven't said you loved our master.

HOLOFERNES: She speaks in poetry.

GIAMBATTISTA: Or riddles.

LISA: It's not riddles. I like riddles.

HOLOFERNES: (*raises glass*) To Judith! Drink up, my darling. We've a long night ahead of us.

SCENE 9

HOLOFERNES's tent. RATZO is standing by the door. JUDITH and HOLOFERNES are lying on a mattress underneath a purple canopy.

HOLOFERNES: (*very drunk*) This Ozymandias stuff. It's all bullshit, you know. (*to RATZO*) Don't listen to me, Ratzo. Your master's drunk. He doesn't know what he's saying. (*to JUDITH*) I know exactly what I'm saying. Why should anyone worship a man. It's stupid. I wish I could believe in a god the way you do.

JUDITH: You make it sound as though it's strictly arbitrary.

HOLOFERNES: It is. Why else are there so many people believing in so many gods.

JUDITH: There's just one. Jehovah.

HOLOFERNES: And Ishtar, Isis, Nuit, Ninmah, Kubala. Now I think there probably is just one. But why kill each other over a name. God! I'm so bored with war. It's not who I really am. It's just a life I fell into. I'm good at it.

JUDITH: I'm sure you are, my lord.

HOLOFERNES: Oh no – not this "my lord" stuff. Please – not tonight. I want it to be just you and me. Alone. (*pause*) Ratzo, you're dismissed.

RATZO: But, master, I could serve the wine.

HOLOFERNES: Ratzo!

RATZO: As you wish. (*He leaves.*)

HOLOFERNES: Do you love me, Judith?

Lights down.

SCENE 10

ARTEMISIA stares off into space. GIAMBATTISTA sneaks up behind her.

GIAMBATTISTA: Artemisia?

ARTEMISIA gasps, freezes. GIAMBATTISTA comes up behind her, grabs her, claps his hand over her mouth.

GIAMBATTISTA: Don't scream. Promise me you won't scream. It's very important. Agostino has to talk to you. He asked me to take you to him. (*releases hand cautiously*)

ARTEMISIA: I'm not visiting him in prison!

GIAMBATTISTA: They let him out for a walk around the grounds. Come to the gate with me. He has to talk to you. It's urgent.

ARTEMISIA: He said he didn't even know me!

GIAMBATTISTA: He wouldn't do it if he didn't have some better plan in mind. I know him.

ARTEMISIA: Maybe you're as deluded as I am about him.

GIAMBATTISTA: (*holds out his hand*) Come!

SCENE 11

Evening. Grounds outside the prison. ARTEMISIA and GIAMBATTISTA enter and walk around nervously.

TASSI: Pssst. Darling, over here. (*ARTEMISIA walks over to TASSI, reluctantly.*) Why are you accusing me of such things? I thought we had an understanding.

ARTEMISIA: I told the truth. You said you didn't even know me!

TASSI: (*horrified*) Is that what they told you?

ARTEMISIA: Yes. You mean, you –

TASSI: Of course not. You see, they didn't arrest me because of you. They arrested me because of my wife.

ARTEMISIA: You're still married?!

TASSI: No. She's dead. Now, she was a horrible person and I'm not sorry. But that's the problem, see. Because she was so horrible, they think I killed her.

ARTEMISIA: How did she die?

TASSI: A band of thieves broke into her house. They robbed her and then they murdered her. I was in Naples at the time. But people think I hired these men.

ARTEMISIA: Lisa is your wife's sister, isn't she?

TASSI: Yeah, what about it?

ARTEMISIA: You had an affair with her.

TASSI: I swear I didn't kill my wife! You must believe me!

ARTEMISIA: Do you think Lisa hired them?

TASSI: God! I never thought of that. It's possible. The problem is – the longer I'm in jail, the more time they'll have to manufacture evidence against me. If I admit to raping you, they'll put me away for five years –

ARTEMISIA: Five years?!

TASSI: Yes. Didn't your father tell you that?

ARTEMISIA: I couldn't stop him from pressing charges!

TASSI: You could have denied the rape. But it's all right. Don't blame yourself. I think we can still salvage the situation. You'll have to say that someone else raped you.

ARTEMISIA: I can't do that. I've already told them what happened.

TASSI: Say you made a mistake. It was Cosimo instead. It all happened in the dark and you mistook Cosimo for me.

ARTEMISIA: But it happened in broad daylight. I can't take back what I said.

TASSI: You're worried about what people might say.

ARTEMISIA: People are already talking. I've been publicly declared a whore. By your friends.

TASSI: That was Cosimo. You can get your revenge on him by –

ARTEMISIA: No! I won't do it.

TASSI: A small leap of faith. All I ask of you is this small leap of faith and you can't do it. You don't trust me.

ARTEMISIA: I trust you.

TASSI: Then why are you taking your father's side against me!

ARTEMISIA: I have to tell the truth.

TASSI: Why? To please your father? He's put you up to public ridicule! He only pressed charges because of the bloody painting! He couldn't care less about you. It's his money he's worried about.

ARTEMISIA: No! That's not true!

TASSI: Why is he prosecuting me, now? DAMN IT! He hired me to rape you. IT WAS A JOB!

ARTEMISIA: (*faltering*) You don't love me.

TASSI: What would be the point! You're in love with your father! Go ahead. Testify against me. You and your father deserve each other! (*He leaves.*)

ARTEMISIA: Please, Agostino!

TASSI: (*shouts in the dark*) LET NO MAN PUT ASUNDER!

SCENE 12

The trial. TASSI on one side. ARTEMISIA on the other. The INTERROGATOR presides, played by the same actor who played the OLD MAN. ORAZIO, TUTIA, COSIMO, GIAMBATTISTA, and LISA are present.

INTERROGATOR: Do you, Artemisia Gentileschi, hereby swear that your statement of March 11th is true?

ARTEMISIA: I do.

INTERROGATOR: Do you maintain that the defendant, Agostino Tassi, raped and deflowered you?

ARTEMISIA: I do.

TASSI: Many, many times.

COSIMO and LISA titter.

INTERROGATOR: Please – no interruptions from the defendant.

TASSI: But, Your Honour, I am simply repeating the charges as they stand. According to Signore Gentileschi, I raped his daughter many, many times. As, I am sure, did a number of men before me.

More titters.

INTERROGATOR: Silence. Signorina Gentileschi, is there anything you wish to change in your testimony?

ARTEMISIA: No.

INTERROGATOR: You swear you are telling the truth.

ARTEMISIA: Yes. Tutia will vouch for me.

INTERROGATOR: Signora Liotta says she doesn't know whether you were raped or not.

ARTEMISIA: What?! Tutia!

TUTIA: (*scratches herself*) I wasn't there.

ARTEMISIA: But you know what happened. My clothes!

TUTIA: You could have torn them yourself. (*ARTEMISIA is astonished.*) You spend a couple of weeks in jail and see how you feel. Your father should have thought twice –

ARTEMISIA: Tutia – please!

TUTIA: And don't say he didn't mean to do it! That old bugger gets away with blue murder and he always says he didn't mean it. (*scratches furiously – picks something off herself*) Damn! I knew it! Lice!

She throws it away. People in the vicinity scurry away.

INTERROGATOR: We don't like to do this but it appears to be necessary.

He pulls out the torture instrument – "Les sybilles" – thumbscrews that go around the fingers.

ORAZIO: You're going to torture my daughter?! Why don't you torture that bastard! (*points to TASSI*)

INTERROGATOR: (*while adjusting instrument*) We've tried it. Torture is completely ineffectual on a man of his character. The defendant has aggressively maintained that he didn't know your daughter. However, we had a brief conversation with his friend, Giambattista Stiatessi, and he confirmed that they were acquainted.

TASSI: (*to GIAMBATTISTA*) WHAT!

GIAMBATTISTA shrugs.

INTERROGATOR: Anyway, Signore Gentileschi, these are mild instruments. They merely serve to get the truth out of her. (*to ARTEMISIA*) Now, do you swear you are telling the truth? You were a virgin before you met Signore Tassi? (*adjusts screws*)

ARTEMISIA: Aaaagh! YES!

INTERROGATOR: YOU WERE A VIRGIN?

ARTEMISIA: YES!!

INTERROGATOR: (*to ORAZIO*) I apologize for the repetitive nature of my questioning and please excuse me if I sound abrupt. (*shouts*) WERE YOU A VIRGIN!

ARTEMISIA: AAAAAAGH! YES, YES I WAS A VIRGIN!!!

INTERROGATOR: AND DID AGOSTINO TASSI DEFLOWER YOU?

ARTEMISIA: Yes! Yes. He did.

INTERROGATOR: HE DID WHAT?

*The **INTERROGATOR** tightens the screws periodically.*

ARTEMISIA: AAAAGH! HE RAPED AND DEFLOWERED ME!!

INTERROGATOR: Did Agostino rape you?

ARTEMISIA: YES!!

INTERROGATOR: Did any other man rape you?

ARTEMISIA: AAGH! NO!

INTERROGATOR: And everything you've said is true.

ARTEMISIA: IT'S TRUE! IT'S TRUE! IT'S TRUE! (*leans over to TASSI, holds up thumbscrews*) THIS IS MY ENGAGEMENT RING AND THESE ARE YOUR PROMISES!!!

INTERROGATOR: Yes, well, thank you, I think that's sufficient. (*He undoes the thumbscrews.*) Perhaps we should torture Signore Tassi as well. For old times' sake, the rack.

TASSI: All right. I'll tell you exactly what happened. In full detail. (*pause*) It's true. I knew Artemisia Gentileschi. How could you not know her. She was notorious. Orazio was away a lot so she used to turn tricks in the studio.

ORAZIO & TUTIA: (*together*)

(*ORAZIO*) What!

(*TUTIA*) Omigod!

ARTEMISIA: It's not true!

TASSI: Fitted it out for each client. The Judith set was the patron's favourite.

TUTIA: So, that's why you always wanted to play Judith!

ARTEMISIA: TUTIA! He's lying. Agostino!

TASSI: Though some people preferred her Salome. But that's another story. At that time, I hadn't met her. I was good friends with her father, Orazio.

ORAZIO: VIPER!

TASSI: He begged me to give her art classes. Mainly to give her something else to do with her time. I don't blame her for whoring. Everyone knows Ratzo is a dirty old skinflint who wouldn't give a dying man a dime.

TUTIA: Yeah! You old piker!

ORAZIO: LET ME AT HIM! I'LL GIVE HIM HIS DIME!!

ORAZIO is restrained by COSIMO and GIAMBATTISTA.

TASSI: Artemisia told me that she started selling herself when her father went to Padua on a three-month commission and left her without any food or money.

ORAZIO: LIES!!

ARTEMISIA: STOP HIM! HE CAN'T SAY THESE THINGS!!

INTERROGATOR: (*pounds gavel*) SILENCE! ALLOW THE DEFENDANT TO CONTINUE!

TASSI: I arrived for the class. I was surprised that we were alone. Apparently, Orazio had left Tutia to chaperone but Signorina Gentileschi had sent her away.

ARTEMISIA: Why are you lying? Please, Agostino!

TUTIA: Is he talking about the first or second lesson?

TASSI: Your Honour, I find it hard to concentrate with all these interruptions. Could we please restrain the plaintiff?

INTERROGATOR: (*to ARTEMISIA*) Silence or we will gag you.

TASSI: Signorina Gentileschi was dressed provocatively but I pretended not to notice.

ARTEMISIA: (*stands up*) But everything he says is a lie!

INTERROGATOR gags ARTEMISIA.

TASSI: Perhaps something to hold her to the chair.

COSIMO dashes up with a long scarf. He ties ARTEMISIA to the chair. The INTERROGATOR looks at him doubtfully.

TASSI: I asked her to bring out her pencils. She said she kept them in a very special place and I could draw one out, if I wished. She then drew up her skirt to reveal a range of pencils, held in place by a garter – (*coughs*) – hem! strapped to her thigh. I reached out to take one and she laughed and pulled her skirt down. I thought that was the end of the matter and moved away. She then grabbed my hand and said, "I'll guide you. You'll want one that has a soft point." Well – she – ah – took my hand and – need I continue?

The INTERROGATOR and the entire court are leaning forward with avid interest. ORAZIO is open-mouthed. ARTEMISIA makes protesting noises.

INTERROGATOR: Please. I mean – yes, do continue.

TASSI: She drew my hand up her skirt and proceeded to amuse herself.

ORAZIO: THESE ARE LIES!! BASE SLANDER!!

ARTEMISIA makes noises through the handkerchief.

INTERROGATOR: (*to ORAZIO*) SILENCE or you leave the court! (*to TASSI*) Continue.

TASSI: I quickly withdrew my hand. I said her behaviour was disgusting and that I would tell her father. She replied, "Oh, that stingy old fart. If I'm going to put out, then I better get paid. And if he won't pay me, I'll find someone who will."

INTERROGATOR: What did she mean by "put out"?

TASSI: I believe she was referring to certain services rendered.

INTERROGATOR: Such as?

TASSI: She posed for his paintings. Nudes. Admittedly, not many. Orazio was afraid of gossip. I inferred from the remark that they had an incestuous relationship.

ORAZIO, ARTEMISIA & TUTIA: (*together*)

ORAZIO gasps, clutches his heart, faints.

ARTEMISIA struggles, kicks the chair, makes as much noise as possible.

(*TUTIA*) Omigod!

GIAMBATTISTA goes to ORAZIO.

GIAMBATTISTA: Sir, are you all right? (*tries to revive him*)

TUTIA: He's not dead, is he? (*slaps ORAZIO's face*)

TASSI: See! This is what comes of telling the truth!

ORAZIO: (*revives, sees TUTIA*) Get away from me, you stupid old cow!

COSIMO: (*stands up*) TASSI'S WRONG.

ORAZIO: Finally!

COSIMO: Artemisia and Ratzo did not commit incest. Because (*pause*) I am Artemisia's father. Many years ago, Ratzo's wife, Prudentia –

ORAZIO: God! (*faints again*)

TUTIA: (*gasps*) Oh no! Really?!

COSIMO: But it's true. We look alike and everything. She's a right slutbag. Gets that from me. When she started her brothel – I was her first customer!

INTERROGATOR: Will someone please remove this revolting person from the room.

GIAMBATTISTA takes COSIMO out.

COSIMO: But it's true! Tassi didn't rape her! I did! That's how great families are made. Gotta keep the blood pure!

The door slams behind COSIMO. GIAMBATTISTA returns. TASSI has his head in his hands. ORAZIO starts to come to.

INTERROGATOR: (*to TASSI*) Is that man a close friend of yours?

TASSI: An acquaintance.

INTERROGATOR: (*to ARTEMISIA*) Have you anything to say to all this? (*ARTEMISIA stares at him.*) Oh sorry. (*He removes her gag.*)

ARTEMISIA: And the scarf, please.

The INTERROGATOR unties her. ARTEMISIA tries to rush at TASSI. With some difficulty the INTERROGATOR keeps her in the witness box.

GIAMBATTISTA: (*stands up*) She's innocent!

TASSI: (*lurches in the chair*) What the –

GIAMBATTISTA: Look, I love Agostino very much but I can't stand by and watch him destroy this girl's life. Agostino is lying. He and Artemisia must have had a fight. Agostino is very vindictive when he's angry, but I know he doesn't mean what he's said.

TASSI: Bullshit!

GIAMBATTISTA: He loves Artemisia. He told me so himself. You can imagine how this hurt me. I thought our love was –

INTERROGATOR: So, Artemisia didn't run a brothel?

GIAMBATTISTA: No.

TASSI: Don't believe him! He's only saying this to get back at me!

INTERROGATOR: Did Agostino rape her?

GIAMBATTISTA: He told me he did. But he did it out of love.

ARTEMISIA & TASSI: BULLSHIT!

GIAMBATTISTA: All I know is this. Agostino loves Artemisia and wants to marry her but he had a lot of problems so he couldn't.

LISA: Are you calling me a problem!

GIAMBATTISTA: The whole case should be dropped. Agostino should give back the painting and the two of them should get married.

ARTEMISIA & TASSI: (*together*)

(*ARTEMISIA*) I'll never marry that snivelling liar!

(*TASSI*) I'll never marry that conniving whore!

LISA: He can't marry anyone. He's married to me!

ARTEMISIA: WHAT?!

INTERROGATOR: Aren't you supposed to be dead?

LISA: Do I look dead to you, Buster!

INTERROGATOR: Which wife are you?

LISA: How many does he have!

ARTEMISIA: Trust me?! Ha!!

ARTEMISIA jumps up over the enclosure and runs over to TASSI, who backs away.

TASSI: No! She's lying! She's not my wife! OW!

ARTEMISIA attacks TASSI, kicks him and bites him.

ORAZIO: (*to LISA*) But your husband?

LISA: He died last week. And if you think I'm going to buy your lousy painting, forget it!

ORAZIO: But the money! Who's going to pay –

LISA & TUTIA: (*together*)

(*LISA*) Not me, that's for sure! I don't want your ugly daughter on my wall.

(*TUTIA, to ORAZIO*) Serves you right! You miserable old fart! (*kicks him*)

ORAZIO: Who are you calling ugly!

LISA: Your daughter, dumb ass!

ORAZIO rushes to attack LISA.

TASSI: (*still struggling with ARTEMISIA*) HOLY CHRIST! GET HER OFF ME!!

LISA: (*tries to haul ARTEMISIA off*) Get your filthy paws off my husband!!

ARTEMISIA: Your husband?!! (*fights with LISA, pulls at her hair*)

ORAZIO: (*attacks TASSI*) YOU BASTARD!!! SELL THE PAINTING TWICE OVER!! ONCE TO A DEAD MAN!! AND THEN TO SOMEONE ELSE!!

TASSI: HELP!!! GIAMBATTISTA HELP!!

GIAMBATTISTA goes to help TASSI who punches GIAMBATTISTA in the nose.

WHAT'D YOU OPEN YOUR BIG MOUTH FOR!! YOU TRAITOR!! COSIMO!! GET IN HERE!!

COSIMO rushes back in. He attacks GIAMBATTISTA. Bedlam ensues. Chairs are thrown.

INTERROGATOR: (*shouting above chaos*) LOCK THEM UP!! LOCK THEM ALL UP!!

SCENE 13

The studio. There is a gilt frame around the HOLOFERNES set, as though a painting is resting against it. A piece of drapery falls from top to bottom, acting as a canopy. ARTEMISIA carries a long sword. She is practising sword moves. She hears people coming. She hides. TASSI and ORAZIO stagger in. They are hauling in ORAZIO's Judith.

TASSI: (*plunks it down*) There! Your fucking painting's back. Sign here, please. (*pulls out paper, hands it to ORAZIO*)

ORAZIO: What?

TASSI: Proof that I returned it. (*ORAZIO signs.*) Thank you. (*He starts to leave.*)

ORAZIO: Tassi.

TASSI: What?

ORAZIO: I'm worried about Bella.

TASSI: Oh, fuck off, Ratzo. Just fuck right off!

ORAZIO: I can't talk to anyone else about this.

TASSI: That's because we all hate you. (*starts to leave*)

ORAZIO: Bella's gone mad. (*TASSI stops.*) She took all her paintings and she locked them in her room. And now, she lurks.

TASSI: She lurks.

ORAZIO: Well – yeah. I haven't seen her but I can feel her. Lurking.

TASSI: I did not drive your daughter mad.

ORAZIO: You publicly humiliated her.

TASSI: You made it public, Ratzo. I was simply defending myself. If I'd confessed, I would have been locked up for five years – which, I guess, is precisely what you wanted. It was okay for me to rape your daughter, but not okay to marry her.

ORAZIO: You're a low-life, Tassi.

TASSI: No lower than you.

ORAZIO: Maybe not. But I, at least, have aspirations. Giambattista's cousin Tony has agreed to marry Bella.

TASSI: How very boring for her. (*ORAZIO gives him a dirty look.*) But very respectable. She'll get a lot of work done. Won't be much amusement at home. She'll have to paint. Anyway, count your blessings. Your daughter's going to be an artist, after all. And you don't have me as a son-in-law.

ORAZIO: Let's drink to it. (*He rummages around for a bottle of wine which is on the HOLOFERNES set.*) Here's to Art!

TASSI: Here's to not being a son-in-law!

They drink.

ORAZIO: Do you think I'm despicable.

TASSI: We're two of a kind, Ratzo.

ORAZIO: I was simply trying to do what's best for her. I didn't want her to waste her talent. You would have destroyed her.

TASSI: Maybe.

ORAZIO: She hates me now.

TASSI: That's not surprising.

ORAZIO: She hasn't spoken to me since the trial. But when she's my age she'll know why I did it. (*pause, takes a swig*) I'm willing to wait. (*They drink.*) She was so innocent. It's awful when they lose their innocence.

TASSI: Yeah.

ORAZIO: (*stands up*) To Bella! She will be the greatest painter in all of Rome. She will surpass Caravaggio!

TASSI: Caravaggio's dead, Ratzo.

ORAZIO: What?

TASSI: He died over a year ago in a knife fight.

ORAZIO: WHAT?!

TASSI: Nobody liked to tell you, Ratzo. It was your mission in life to hate him. So we all kept the bad news from you.

ORAZIO: Who killed him?

TASSI: Oh well – now, that's another awkward – ah –

ORAZIO: You killed him, didn't you!

TASSI: Well – yeah – I got mad. He was cheating at cards again and I hate it when –

ORAZIO: YOU KILLED CARAVAGGIO?! THE MAN WAS A GENIUS AND YOU KILLED HIM!!

TASSI: You never liked him, Ratzo. Anyway, you have Bella.

ORAZIO: YOU WOULD HAVE KILLED HER, TOO!! YOU'RE A MONSTER!!

ORAZIO punches TASSI in the face and knocks him out. He takes a long swig of wine and passes out, collapsing in a heap. ARTEMISIA comes out from her hiding place. She is carrying a sword. She walks over to TASSI and prods him with the sword. *TASSI groans, comes to, sees **ARTEMISIA** and tries to get up.*

ARTEMISIA: (*stops him with the sword*) I thought so. A coward.

TASSI: Artemisia – please!

ARTEMISIA: Flirt with danger but only if you have all the weapons. I'm on the edge now, Agostino. THE CUTTING EDGE!!

She raises the sword.

Blackout.

SCENE 14

*JUDITH and her maid, **TUTIA**. **JUDITH** is carrying the basket. **HOLOFERNES**'s head is wrapped in the red and white checked cloth in the basket. **JUDITH** and **TUTIA** move furtively.*

HEAD: Judith.

JUDITH stops, freezes in her tracks.

TUTIA: (*goes on ahead, stops*) What's the matter, ma'am?

JUDITH: Did you hear something, Tutia?

TUTIA: No. Come on. The town gates are up ahead.

They walk again.

HEAD: Judith.

JUDITH: Tutia, give me a few moments alone.

TUTIA: You have to talk to Jehovah?

JUDITH: Just leave me alone.

TUTIA withdraws. JUDITH looks in the basket. She lifts the cloth off the head.

HEAD: Judith. (*JUDITH drops the cloth back over the head.*) I love you, Judith.

JUDITH lifts the cloth up again. She gazes in morbid fascination.

HEAD: I love you, Judith. Keep me with you. Put my head on your pillow. I'd love to see you in the morning. Eyes blurred with sleep. That sweet fresh dead look that people have. Those few precious moments of the soul.

JUDITH: (*gasps, covers head*) Tutia!

TUTIA: Ma'am?

JUDITH runs past TUTIA and stands in front of the town gate.

JUDITH: OPEN THE GATE! OPEN THE GATE!! (*pulls head by the hair out of her basket*) THE HEAD OF HOLOFERNES! PRAISE GOD! PRAISE HIM! Praise Jehovah who has conquered our enemies by my hand tonight. HANG THIS HEAD UP FOR ALL TO SEE! LET HOLOFERNES'S MEN SEARCH AND FIND HIM HERE!!!

TUTIA runs up and joins JUDITH.

TUTIA: Calm down, ma'am. It's going to be all right.

JUDITH: (*fevered*) THE HEAD OF HOLOFERNES!!! SLAIN BY MY HAND!! THE HAND OF A MERE WOMAN –

One of the guards comes down from the gate. TUTIA takes the head from JUDITH and hands it to him.

TUTIA: That's very good, ma'am. Now, let's go to your tent. You've had a busy time.

JUDITH: THE HEAD OF HOLOFERNES –

TUTIA leads JUDITH off.

SCENE 15

*The studio. **ARTEMISIA** stands over **TASSI**, sword raised to strike. She looks at **TASSI** and allows him to escape. She walks over to **ORAZIO**. She is still carrying the sword. She kicks **ORAZIO**, who grunts. **ARTEMISIA** boots him again.*

ORAZIO: OW! Bella?

ARTEMISIA: Judith, Daddy. My name is Judith now. You've got your wish. Your Judith has come back to you. (*She raises the sword.*)

ORAZIO: Aaah! (*He clambers out of the way.*)

ARTEMISIA: (*stalks him*) What's the matter, Daddy? Don't you want your Judith anymore?

ORAZIO: Where's Tassi?

ARTEMISIA: (*laughs*) Oh – I've taken care of him. (*She walks over to **ORAZIO**'s painting and points to it with the sword.*) This is your moment. Frozen in time. This is who I am in your eyes? Was I ever really like that? That agreeable? That content? (*walks over to the **JUDITH** set*) Now THIS is a painting. *My Little Daughter Bella About to Chop a Head Off.* (*She pulls the canopy off the gilt frame to reveal her painting,* Judith Beheading Holofernes.) Why don't you paint one like that, Daddy.

ORAZIO: My God! Is that your new painting?

ARTEMISIA: Yes. (*laughs*) I have taken my revenge on Agostino Tassi. He is dying as we speak. An ignominious and gruesome death. Dying for all eternity and all the world shall be witness.

ORAZIO: What?

ARTEMISIA: (*crying*) You've done what you set out to do, Daddy. I'm not your little girl anymore. I'm something else. Something truly unspeakable. An artist! GODDAMN YOU!! (*She throws the sword down and leaves.*)

ORAZIO: Bella! Come here this instant! (*pause*) Bella? Bella, I order you to come back! (*pause*) Bella!

He breaks down sobbing, looks up at the frame.

SCENE 16

ORAZIO backs away in awe. A group of people gather and stare at the painting. LISA and GIAMBATTISTA are off to one side.

LISA: And did you see what she did.

GIAMBATTISTA: Heard about it. Haven't been able to see it.

LISA: It's on public exhibit.

GIAMBATTISTA: It's packed with people. I'll have to wait till the furor dies down. What's it look like?

LISA: Well – she's got him lying there with his throat slit, bleeding like a pig, and she's painted herself hacking away at him.

GIAMBATTISTA: How does he look?

LISA: Very surprised.

GIAMBATTISTA: No. No, nude! How does he look nude?

LISA: You've seen him nude.

GIAMBATTISTA: We've all seen him nude. But how did she paint him? Did she make him look sexy?

LISA: She made him look like a side of beef.

GIAMBATTISTA: Great! He'll never live it down.

LISA: (*whispers*) Talk of the town.

GIAMBATTISTA: (*whispers*) Talk of the town.

CROWD: (*whispers*) Talk of the town.

SCENE 17

ARTEMISIA and her husband, TONY, are in bed. They are lit only by the slide projection of the painting Judith Beheading Holofernes *above the headboard of the bed.*

TONY: I'm not having that painting hanging over my head! In fact, as your husband, I forbid you –

ARTEMISIA: And as my lover?

TONY: Pardon?

ARTEMISIA: As my lover, how would you feel about it, then?

TONY: It puts me off. I can't concentrate.

ARTEMISIA: What's the matter, Tony? Don't I moan enough for you?

TONY: You don't love me!

ARTEMISIA: I'm trying to love you.

TONY: Damn it! It's not the same thing.

ARTEMISIA: It's the best I can do.

TONY: What's wrong with me?

ARTEMISIA: There's nothing wrong with you, Tony. You're a sweet loving husband.

TONY: And you don't want that, do you. You want someone like Tassi.

ARTEMISIA: Agostino is dead for me.

TONY: You'll never be free of him. What do you want me to do? Who do you want me to be? (*flings himself down on her and tries to claim his conjugal rights*) What do I have to do to make you love me!

ARTEMISIA lies back, her head upside down, facing the audience in the "Holofernes" position.

TONY: Make you love me! MAKE YOU LOVE ME! MAKE YOU LOVE ME!!

END

A SELECTIVE BIBLIOGRAPHY OF SOURCE MATERIAL

I. Selected Websites and Journals

There is a huge amount of material on Canadian theatre available online, though the rapidly changing nature of the digital world means that material you may be able to find on the Web today may be gone tomorrow. Googling a play, playwright, actor, or director will give you immediate access to a good deal of online information, often including their own website. Ditto for YouTube, a valuable resource for accessing scenes from productions and playwright interviews. But not everything can easily be found via the common search engines. The websites listed here provide important information about Canadian theatre, and many have links to other excellent sites. All were active as of July 2012.

Atlantic Canada Theatre Site:
www.lib.unb.ca/Texts/Theatre/index.html

Canadian Adaptations of Shakespeare Project:
www.canadianshakespeares.ca

Canadian Association for Theatre Research:
www.catr-acrt.ca

Canadian Theatre Critics Association:
www.canadiantheatrecritics.ca

Canadian Theatre Encyclopedia:
www.canadiantheatre.com

Canadian Theatre Record:
http://canadiantheatrerecord.torontopubliclibrary.ca

Chalmers Public Theatre Resource Collection:
www.stratford.library.on.ca/chalmers2.htm

L.W. Conolly Theatre Archives at University of Guelph:
www.lib.uoguelph.ca/resources/archival_&_special_
collections/the_collections/digital_collections/
theatre

Theatre Museum Canada:
www.theatremuseumcanada.ca

The primary journals in the field of Canadian theatre studies are *Canadian Theatre Review*, which began publication in 1974; *Theatre Research in Canada* (formerly *Theatre History in Canada*), published since 1980; and *alt.theatre*, in existence since 1998. The journal *Canadian Drama* ran from 1975 to 1990, and *Theatrum* lasted from 1985 to 1995.

II. Backgrounds, Surveys, and General Studies

Anthony, Geraldine, ed. *Stage Voices: Twelve Canadian Playwrights Talk about Their Lives and Work*. Toronto: Doubleday, 1978.

Appleford, Rob, ed. *Aboriginal Drama and Theatre*. Critical Perspectives on Canadian Theatre in English, vol. 1. Toronto: Playwrights Canada, 2005.

Aquino, Nina Lee, and Ric Knowles, eds. *Asian Canadian Theatre: New Essays on Canadian Theatre*, vol. 1. Toronto: Playwrights Canada, 2011.

Astle, Robert. *Theatre without Borders*. Winnipeg: Signature, 2002.

Atkey, Mel. *Broadway North: The Dream of a Canadian Musical Theatre*. Toronto: Natural Heritage, 2006.

Barton, Bruce, ed. *Collective Creation, Collaboration, and Devising*. Critical Perspectives on Canadian Theatre in English, vol. 12. Toronto: Playwrights Canada, 2008.

———, ed. *Developing Nation: New Play Creation in English-Speaking Canada*. Toronto: Playwrights Canada, 2009.

Bennett, Susan, ed. *Feminist Theatre and Performance*. Critical Perspectives on Canadian Theatre in English, vol. 4. Toronto: Playwrights Canada, 2006.

Benson, Eugene, and L.W. Conolly. *English Canadian Theatre*. Toronto: Oxford UP, 1987.

———, eds. *The Oxford Companion to Canadian Theatre*. Toronto: Oxford UP, 1989.

Bessai, Diane. *Playwrights of Collective Creation*. Toronto: Simon & Pierre, 1992.

Brask, Per, ed. *Contemporary Issues in Canadian Drama*. Winnipeg: Blizzard, 1995.

Brisset, Annie. *A Sociocritique of Translation: Theatre and Alterity in Quebec, 1968–1988*. Trans. Rosalind Gill and Roger Gannon. Toronto: U of Toronto P, 1996.

Brookes, Chris. *A Public Nuisance: A History of the Mummers Troupe*. St. John's: Institute of Social and Economic Research, Memorial Univ. of Newfoundland, 1988.

Brydon, Diana, and Irena R. Makaryk, eds. *Shakespeare in Canada: "A World Elsewhere"?* Toronto: U of Toronto P, 2002.

Burnett, Linda, ed. *Theatre in Atlantic Canada*. Critical Perspectives on Canadian Theatre in English, vol. 16. Toronto: Playwrights Canada, 2010.

Carson, Neil. *Harlequin in Hogtown: George Luscombe and Toronto Workshop Productions*. Toronto: U of Toronto P, 1995.

Chapman, Vernon. *Who's in the Goose Tonight? An Anecdotal History of Canadian Theatre*. Toronto: ECW, 2001.

Conolly, L.W. *The Shaw Festival: The First Fifty Years*. Don Mills: Oxford UP, 2011.

———, ed. *Canadian Drama and the Critics*. Rev. ed. Vancouver: Talonbooks, 1995.

Cushman, Robert. *Fifty Seasons at Stratford*. Toronto: McClelland & Stewart, 2002.

Davis, William B. *Where There's Smoke: Musings of a Cigarette Smoking Man*. Toronto: ECW, 2011.

Day, Moira, ed. *West-Worlds: Celebrating Western Canadian Theatre and Playwriting*. Regina: Canadian Plains Research Centre, 2011.

Donohoe, Joseph I. Jr. and Jonathan M. Weiss, eds. *Essays on Modern Quebec Theatre*. East Lansing: Michigan State UP, 1995.

Filewod, Alan. *Collective Encounters: Documentary Theatre in English Canada*. Toronto: U of Toronto P, 1987.

———. *Committing Theatre: Theatre Radicalism and Political Intervention in Canada*. Toronto: Between the Lines, 2011.

———. *Performing Canada: The Nation Enacted in the Imagined Theatre*. Kamloops, BC: Univ. College of the Cariboo, 2002.

———, ed. *Theatre Histories*. Critical Perspectives on Canadian Theatre in English, vol. 13. Toronto: Playwrights Canada, 2009.

Gallagher, Kathleen, and David Booth, eds. *How Theatre Educates: Convergences and Counterpoints with Artists, Scholars and Advocates*. Toronto: U of Toronto P, 2003.

Garebian, Keith. *A Well-Bred Muse: Selected Theatre Writings, 1978–1988*. Oakville, ON: Mosaic, 1991.

———, ed. *William Hutt: Masks and Faces*. Oakville, ON: Mosaic, 1995.

Gilbert, Helen, and Joanne Tompkins. *Post-Colonial Drama: Theory, Practice, Politics*. London: Routledge, 1996.

Glaap, Albert-Reiner, with Rolf Althorp, ed. *On-Stage and Off-Stage: English Canadian Drama in Discourse*. St. John's: Breakwater, 1996.

Grace, Sherrill, and Albert-Reiner Glaap, eds. *Performing National Identities: International Perspectives on Contemporary Canadian Theatre*. Vancouver: Talonbooks, 2003.

Grace, Sherrill, and Jerry Wasserman, eds. *Theatre and AutoBiography: Writing and Performing Lives in Theory and Practice*. Vancouver: Talonbooks, 2006.

Green, Lynda Mason, and Tedde Moore, eds. *Standing Naked in the Wings: Anecdotes from Canadian Actors*. Toronto: Oxford UP, 1997.

Hadfield, D.A. *Re: Producing Women's Dramatic History: The Politics of Playing in Toronto*. Vancouver: Talonbooks, 2007.

Hengen, Shannon. *Where Stories Meet: An Oral History of De-ba-jeh-mu-jig Theatre*. Toronto: Playwrights Canada, 2007.

Hodkinson, Yvonne. *Female Parts: The Art and Politics of Female Playwrights*. Montreal: Black Rose, 1991.

Houston, Andrew, ed. *Environmental and Site-Specific Theatre*. Critical Perspectives on Canadian Theatre in English, vol. 8. Toronto: Playwrights Canada, 2007.

Hurley, Erin. *National Performance: Representing Quebec from Expo 67 to Céline Dion*. Toronto: U of Toronto P, 2011.

Jennings, Sarah. *Art and Politics: The History of the National Arts Centre*. Toronto: Dundurn, 2009.

Johnston, Denis. *Up the Mainstream: The Rise of Toronto's Alternative Theatres*. Toronto: U of Toronto P, 1991.

Johnston, Sheila M.F. *Let's Go to the Grand! 100 Years of Entertainment at London's Grand Theatre*. Toronto: National Heritage, 2001.

Kennedy, Brian. *The Baron Bold and the Beauteous Maid: A Compact History of Canadian Theatre*. Toronto: Playwrights Canada, 2005.

Kerr, Rosalind, ed. *Queer Theatre in Canada*. Critical Perspectives on Canadian Theatre in English, vol. 7. Toronto: Playwrights Canada, 2007.

Knowles, Ric. *Reading the Material Theatre*. Cambridge: Cambridge UP, 2004.

———. *Shakespeare and Canada: Essays on Production, Translation, and Adaptation*. Brussels: P.I.E.-Peter Lang, 2004.

———. *The Theatre of Form and the Production of Meaning: Contemporary Canadian Dramaturgies*. Toronto: ECW, 1999.

Knowles, Ric, and Ingrid Mündel, eds. *"Ethnic," Multicultural, and Intercultural Theatre*. Critical Perspectives on Canadian Theatre in English, vol. 14. Toronto: Playwrights Canada, 2009.

Knutson, Susan, ed. *Canadian Shakespeare*. Critical Perspectives on Canadian Theatre in English, vol. 18. Toronto: Playwrights Canada, 2010.

Levin, Laura, ed. *Theatre and Performance in Toronto*. Critical Perspectives on Canadian Theatre in English, vol. 21. Toronto: Playwrights Canada, 2011.

Loiselle, André. *Stage-Bound: Feature Film Adaptations of Canadian and Québécois Drama*. Montreal: McGill-Queen's UP, 2003.

Longfield, Kevin. *From Fire to Flood: A History of Theatre in Manitoba*. Winnipeg: Signature, 2001.

McKinnie, Michael. *City Stages: Theatre and Urban Space in a Global City*. Toronto: U of Toronto P, 2007.

———, ed. *Space and the Geographies of Theatre*. Critical Perspectives on Canadian Theatre in English, vol. 9. Toronto: Playwrights Canada, 2007.

Martz, Fraidie, and Andrew Wilson. *A Fiery Soul: The Life and Theatrical Times of John Hirsch*. Montreal: Véhicule, 2011.

Maufort, Marc. *Transgressive Itineraries: Postcolonial Hybridizations of Dramatic Realism*. Brussels: P.I.E.-Peter Lang, 2003.

Maufort, Marc, and Franca Bellarsi, eds. *Crucible of Cultures: Anglophone Drama at the Dawn of a New Millennium*. Brussels: P.I.E.-Peter Lang, 2002.

Maufort, Marc, and Caroline De Wagter, eds. *Signatures of the Past: Cultural Memory in Contemporary North American Anglophone Drama*. Brussels: P.I.E.-Peter Lang, 2008.

Miller, Mary Jane. *Turn Up the Contrast: CBC Television Drama Since 1952*. Vancouver: UBC Press, 1987.

Moore, Mavor. *Reinventing Myself: Memoirs*. Toronto: Stoddart, 1994.

Morrow, Martin. *Wild Theatre: The History of One Yellow Rabbit*. Banff: Banff Centre, 2003.

Moynagh, Maureen. *African-Canadian Theatre*. Critical Perspectives on Canadian Theatre in English, vol. 2. Toronto: Playwrights Canada, 2005.

Much, Rita, ed. *Women on the Canadian Stage: The Legacy of Hrotsvit*. Winnipeg: Blizzard, 1992.

Nardocchio, Elaine. *Theatre and Politics in Modern Quebec*. Edmonton: U of Alberta P, 1986.

New, William H., ed. *Dramatists in Canada: Selected Essays*. Vancouver: UBC Press, 1972.

Nothof, Anne, ed. *Theatre in Alberta*. Critical Perspectives on Canadian Theatre in English, vol. 11. Toronto: Playwrights Canada, 2008.

Perkyns, Richard. *The Neptune Story: Twenty-Five Years in the Life of a Leading Canadian Theatre*. Hantsport, NS: Lancelot, 1989.

Pettigrew, John, and Jamie Portman. *Stratford: The First Thirty Years*. 2 vols. Toronto: Macmillan, 1985.

Plummer, Christopher. *In Spite of Myself: A Memoir*. NY: Alfred A. Knopf, 2008.

Podbrey, Maurice. *Half Man, Half Beast: Making a Life in Canadian Theatre*. Montreal: Véhicule, 1997.

Prentki, Tim, and Jan Selman. *Popular Theatre in Political Culture: Britain and Canada in Focus*. Portland: Intellect, 2000.

Ratsoy, Ginny, ed. *Theatre in British Columbia*. Critical Perspectives on Canadian Theatre in English, vol. 6. Toronto: Playwrights Canada, 2006.

Rewa, Natalie. *Scenography in Canada: Selected Designers*. Toronto: U of Toronto P, 2004.

———, ed. *Design and Scenography*. Critical Perspectives on Canadian Theatre in English, vol. 15. Toronto: Playwrights Canada, 2009.

Rubin, Don, ed. *Canada on Stage: Canadian Theatre Review Yearbook*. Toronto: CTR Publications, 1974–88.

———, ed. *Canadian Theatre History: Selected Readings*. Toronto: Playwrights Canada, 2004.

Rudakoff, Judith, ed. *Questionable Activities: Canadian Theatre Artists Interviewed by Canadian Theatre Students*. 2 vols. Toronto: Playwrights Union of Canada, 1997.

Rudakoff, Judith, and Rita Much. *Fair Play: 12 Women Speak: Conversations with Canadian Playwrights*. Toronto: Simon & Pierre, 1990.

Ruffo, Armand Garnet, ed. *(Ad)dressing Our Words: Aboriginal Perspectives on Aboriginal Literatures*. Penticton, BC: Theytus, 2001.

Saddlemyer, Ann, and Richard Plant, eds. *Later Stages: Essays in Ontario Theatre from the First World War to the 1970s*. Toronto: U of Toronto P, 1997.

Salverson, Julie, ed. *Community Engaged Theatre and Performance*. Critical Perspectives on Canadian Theatre in English, vol. 19. Toronto: Playwrights Canada, 2011.

———, ed. *Popular Political Theatre and Performance*. Critical Perspectives on Canadian Theatre in English, vol. 17. Toronto: Playwrights Canada, 2010.

Scott, Shelley. *Nightwood Theatre: A Woman's Work Is Always Done*. Edmonton: AU Press, 2010.

Stephenson, Jenn, ed. *Solo Performance*. Critical Perspectives on Canadian Theatre in English, vol. 20. Toronto: Playwrights Canada, 2010.

Stuart, E. Ross. *The History of Prairie Theatre: The Development of Theatre in Alberta, Manitoba, and Saskatchewan, 1833–1820*. Toronto: Simon & Pierre, 1984.

Theatre Memoirs: On the Occasion of the Canadian Theatre Conference. Toronto: Playwrights Union of Canada, 1998.

Tompkins, Joanne, ed. *"Theatre and the Canadian Imaginary." Australasian Drama Studies* 29 (Oct. 1996).

Usmiani, Renate. *Second Stage: The Alternative Theatre Movement in Canada*. Vancouver: UBC Press, 1983.

Vogt, Gordon. *Critical Stages: Canadian Theatre in Crisis*. Ottawa: Oberon, 1998.

Wagner, Anton, ed. *Contemporary Canadian Theatre: New World Visions*. Toronto: Simon & Pierre, 1985.

———, ed. *Establishing Our Boundaries: English-Canadian Theatre Criticism*. Toronto: U of Toronto P, 1999.

Walker, Craig Stewart. *The Buried Astrolabe: Canadian Dramatic Imagination and Western Tradition*. Montreal: McGill-Queen's UP, 2001.

Wallace, Robert. *Producing Marginality: Theatre and Criticism in Canada*. Saskatoon: Fifth House, 1990.

Wallace, Robert, and Cynthia Zimmerman, eds *The Work: Conversations with English-Canadian Playwrights*. Toronto: Coach House, 1982.

Weiss, Jonathan M. *French-Canadian Theater*. Boston: Twayne, 1986.

Whittaker, Herbert. *Whittaker's Theatre: A Critic Looks at Stages in Canada and Thereabouts, 1944–1975*. Ed. Ronald Bryden with Boyd Neil. Greenbank, ON: The Whittaker Project, 1985.

Zimmerman, Cynthia. *Playwriting Women: Female Voices in English Canada*. Toronto: Simon & Pierre, 1994.

III. Individual Playwrights and Plays

Note: Wherever a book in this section has already appeared as an entry in Part II, I have used a short form here. *Canadian Theatre Review* is abbreviated *CTR*.

GEORGE RYGA and *The Ecstasy of Rita Joe*

Abu-Swailem, Abder-Rahim. "The Agony of Rita Joe in George Ryga's *The Ecstasy of Rita Joe*." *Commonwealth Essays and Studies* 16.1 (1993): 70–76.

———. "The Dance of Memory: George Ryga's *The Ecstasy of Rita Joe*." *Commonwealth Essays and Studies* 21.2 (1999): 63–73.

Balachandran, K. "Cultural Problems in George Ryga's *The Ecstasy of Rita Joe*." *Atlantic Literary Review* 7.1 (2006): 88–95.

Barber, James. "Rita – An Exhausting Emotional Experience." *Vancouver Province*, 25 Nov. 1967. 38.

Bennett, Susan. "Who Speaks? Representations of Native Women in Some Canadian Plays." *Canadian Journal of Drama and Theatre* 1.2 (1991): 13–25.

Birnie, Peter. "Performers Shine in 40th Anniversary Production." *Vancouver Sun*, 30 Nov. 2007. H2.

Boire, Gary. "Theatres of Law: Canadian Legal Drama." *Canadian Literature* 152/153 (Spring–Summer 1997): 124–44.

———. "Tribunalations: George Ryga's Postcolonial Trial 'Play.'" *ARIEL* 22 (Apr. 1991): 5–20.

———. "Wheels on Fire: The Train of Thought in George Ryga's *The Ecstasy of Rita Joe*." *Canadian Literature* 113–14 (Summer–Fall 1987): 62–74.

Carson, Neil. "George Ryga and the Lost Country." *Canadian Literature* 45 (Summer 1970): 33–40. Rpt. *Dramatists in Canada*, ed. New. 155–62.

Chamberlain, Adrian. "Native Strife Sadly Remains Topical Drama." *Victoria Times-Colonist*, 14 Oct. 2005. D5.

Chevrefils, Marlys, and Appolonia Steele, eds. *The George Ryga Papers*. Calgary: U of Calgary P, 1995.

Cohen, Nathan. "A Non-Production of a Non-Play." *Toronto Star*, 25 Nov. 1967. 30.

Conolly, L.W., ed. *Canadian Drama and the Critics*. 41–44, 55–68.

Crew, Robert. "More Agony Than Ecstasy in *Rita Joe*." *Toronto Star*, 12 Nov. 1989. C10.

Donnelly, Pat. "High Energy Approach in *Rita Joe*." *Montreal Gazette*, 10 Mar. 1989. C6.

Donnelly, Tom. "Theater Journal: Two Views." *Washington Post*, 9 May 1973. F4.

Gilman, Marvin. "Fennario and Ryga: Canadian Political Playwrights." *Australasian Drama Studies* 29 (Oct. 1996): 180–87.

Grace, Sherrill. "The Expressionist Legacy in the Canadian Theatre: George Ryga and Robert Gurik." *Canadian Literature* 118 (Fall 1988): 47–58.

Grant, Agnes. "Canadian Native Literature: The Drama of George Ryga and Tomson Highway." *Australian-Canadian Studies* 10.2 (1992): 37–56.

Hay, Peter. "George Ryga: Beginnings of a Biography." *CTR* 23 (Summer 1979): 36–44.

———. "The Psychology of Distortion: A Rebuttal of Christopher Innes." *Theatre History in Canada* 7 (Spring 1986): 119–24.

Hoffman, James. *The Ecstasy of Resistance: A Biography of George Ryga*. Toronto: ECW, 1995.

Innes, Christopher. *Politics and the Playwright: George Ryga*. Toronto: Simon & Pierre, 1985.

Johnson, Chris. "Amerindians and Aborigines in English Canadian and Australian Drama, 1606–1975." *Canadian Drama* 10.2 (1984): 167–87.

Kucherawy, Dennis. "Play Stirs New Controversy." *Vancouver Province*, 30 Nov. 1981. B6.

Langston, Patrick. "Four Decades Later, Heartbreaking Rita Joe Still Resonates." *Ottawa Citizen*, 3 May 2009. B4.

Maracle, Lee. "A Question of Voice." *Vancouver Sun*, 6 June 1992. D9.

Martinez, Jill. "An Interview with George Ryga." *Journal of Canadian Fiction* 35/36 (1986): 106–21.

McCracken, Rosemary. "Young Cast Electrifies Play." *Calgary Herald*, 5 Apr. 1984. D1.

Moore, Mavor. *4 Canadian Playwrights*. 68–75.

———. "Introduction." *Two Plays by George Ryga*. Winnipeg: Turnstone, 1982. 1–7.

Parker, Brian. "The Ballad-Plays of George Ryga." *The Ecstasy of Rita Joe and Other Plays*. Toronto: New Press, 1971. vii–xx.

Parker, Dorothy. "George Ryga." *Profiles in Canadian Literature.* 4th ser. Ed. Jeffrey M. Heath. Toronto: Dundurn, 1985. 61–68.

Pell, Barbara. "George Ryga's 'Hail Mary' and Tomson Highway's *Nanabush*: Two Paradigms of Religion and Theatre in Canada." *Theatre Research in Canada* 27 (Fall 2006): 245–59.

Popkin, Henry. "*The Ecstasy of Rita Joe*: A Drama of American Indian Life." *Christian Science Monitor*, 11 June 1973. 12.

Portman, Jamie. "*Ecstasy of Rita Joe* Still Manages to Shock and Scourge." *Vancouver Province*, 12 Apr. 1976. 10.

Richards, Jack. "World Premiere Lays Bare Tragedy of Canadian Society." *Vancouver Sun*, 24 Nov. 1967. 6.

Rubin, Don. "George Ryga: The Poetics of Engagement." *On-Stage and Off-Stage: English Canadian Drama in Discourse*, ed. Glaap. 224–39.

Ryga, George. "Theatre in Canada: Three Statements." *Canadian Theatre History*, ed. Rubin. 348–61.

Saddlemyer, Ann. "Crime in Literature: Canadian Drama." *Rough Justice: Essays on Crime in Literature.* Ed. Martin L. Friedland. Toronto: U of Toronto P, 1991. 214–30.

Shales, Tom. "An Acting Indian Chief." *Washington Post*, 10 May 1973. C1.

———. "*Ecstasy of Rita Joe.*" *Washington Post*, 3 May 1973. B1.

Skene, Reg. "*Ecstasy of Rita Joe* a Powerful Piece of Theatre." *Winnipeg Free Press*, 26 Nov. 1981. 55.

Wagner, Vit. "Indian Actors Proud to Dramatize Native Tragedy." *Toronto Star*, 3 Nov. 1989. D15.

Wardle, Irving. "A Pogrom in Canada." *The Times* (London), 23 Sept. 1975. 12.

Wasserman, Jerry. "George Ryga." *Canadian Writers Since 1960.* 2nd ser. *Dictionary of Literary Biography*, vol. 60. Ed. W.H. New. Detroit: Gale, 1987. 320–24.

———. "'It's the Do-Gooders Burn My Ass': Modern Canadian Drama and the Crisis of Liberalism." *Modern Drama* 43 (Spring 2000): 32–47.

Watson, David, and Christopher Innes. "Political Mythologies: An Interview with George Ryga." *Canadian Drama* 8.2 (1982): 160–72.

Wilson, Peter. "*Rita Joe* Still Leads to More Anger than Ecstasy." *Vancouver Sun*, 19 Mar. 1992. C1.

Worthington, Bonnie. "Ryga's Women." *Canadian Drama* 5 (Fall 1979): 139–43.

Zichy, Francis. "*Rita Joe* in New York: An Interview with Gordon McCall." *NeWest Review* 10 (Summer 1985): 15–17.

MICHEL TREMBLAY and *Les Belles-Soeurs*

Note: Only English-language books, articles, and reviews are listed below; a much more substantial body of commentary on Tremblay is available in French.

Abrams, Tevia. "Théâtre du Rideau-Vert Opens New Season with *Les Belles-Soeurs.*" *Montreal Gazette*, 29 Aug. 1968. 24.

Ackerman, Marianne. "Sweet Jesus! Who's That, Ma?" *Saturday Night* 103 (June 1988): 40–47.

Anthony, Geraldine, ed. *Stage Voices.* 275–90.

Antosh, Ruth B. "The Hermaphrodite as Cultural Hero in Michel Tremblay's Theatre." *Essays on Modern Quebec Theatre*, ed. Donohoe and Weiss. 207–22.

Babington, Doug. "The Shared Voice of Michel Tremblay." *Queen's Quarterly* 99 (Winter 1992): 1074–81.

Bednarski, Betty. "'Sameness' and 'Difference' in *Les Belles-Soeurs*: A Canadian Spectator's Reflections on Two Polish Productions of Michel Tremblay's Play." *International Journal of Francophone Studies* 13.2 (2010): 315–25.

Bolster, Charles. "*Les Belles-Soeurs* a Microcosm of Quebecois Society." *Edmonton Journal*, 17 May 1980. B16.

Bosley, Vivien. "Diluting the Mixture: Translating Michel Tremblay's *Les Belles-Soeurs.*" *TTR Traduction, Terminologie, Rédaction* 1.1 (1988): 139–45.

Cardy, Michael. "Varieties of Anger in Some Early Plays of Michel Tremblay." *Romance Studies* 31 (Spring 1998): 5–17.

Chadbourne, Richard. "Michel Tremblay's 'Adult Fairy Tales': The Theatre as Realistic Fantasy." *Québec Studies* 10 (Spring–Summer 1990): 61–68.

Chapman, Geoff. "*Soeurs* Cast Lights Up Social Comment." *Toronto Star*, 3 June 1991. B3.

Conlogue, Ray. "A Celebration of Woman's Progress." *Globe and Mail*, 2 Mar. 1993. A11.

———. "Keeping Tremblay's Masterpiece Relevant." *Globe and Mail*, 6 Apr. 1999. C3.

Conolly, L.W. ed. *Canadian Drama and the Critics.* 308–16.

Corbeil, Carole. "The Aging of Tremblay's *Les Belles-Soeurs.*" *Globe and Mail*, 28 June 1984. E2.

Cushman, Robert. "Staging a Slice of Quebec Life – 30 Years Later." *National Post*, 9 Apr. 1999. B12.

Dickinson, Peter. *Here Is Queer: Nationalisms, Sexualities, and the Literatures of Canada.* Toronto: U of Toronto P, 1999. Ch. 4.

Donnelly, Pat. "Never a Dull Moment; Production Is More Relevant than Ever." *Montreal Gazette* 2 Apr. 2009. D4.

————. "Tremblay's *Les Belles-Soeurs* in Yiddish Underscores City's Rich Ethnic Diversity." *Montreal Gazette*, 30 May 1992. E13.

Dorsinville, Max. "The Changing Landscape of Drama in Quebec." *Dramatists in Canada*. Ed. W.H. New. 179–95.

Findlay, Bill. "Translating Tremblay into Scots." *Theatre Research International* 17.2 (Summer 1992): 138–45.

Gobin, Pierre. "Michel Tremblay: An Interweave of Prose and Drama." *Yale French Studies* 65 (1983): 106–23.

Harvie, Jennifer. "The Real Nation? Michel Tremblay, Scotland, and Cultural Translatability." *Theatre Research in Canada* 16 (Spring–Fall 1995): 5–25.

Heller, Zelda. "Tremblay's *Belles-Soeurs* Landmark in Quebec Theatre." *Montreal Star*, 25 May 1971. 64.

Hicks, Colin. "Imagination Import: Reception and Perception of the Theatre of Québec in the United Kingdom." *Performing National Identities*, ed. Grace and Glaap. 145–59.

Hurley, Erin. *National Performance*. Ch. 4.

Kapica, Jack. "The Incredible Saga of *Les Belles-Soeurs*, or … How a Writer Found Fame Could Be a Costly Gain." *Montreal Gazette*, 27 Oct. 1973. 25.

Kareda, Urjo. "*Les Belles-Soeurs* a Breath of Life." *Toronto Star*, 4 Apr. 1973.

Kelly, Brendan. "A Gem in Any Language," *Financial Post*, 5 Oct. 1992. S7.

Kennedy, Brian. *The Baron Bold and the Beauteous Maid*. Ch. 4.

Killick, Rachel. "In the Fold? Postcolonialism and Quebec." *Romance Studies* 24 (Nov. 2006): 181–92.

Knelman, Martin. "The Outlandish *Joual* World of Michel Tremblay." *Saturday Night* 90 (May 1975): 79–83.

Koustas, Jane. "From Gélinas to Carrier: Critical Response to Translated Quebec Theatre in Toronto." *Studies in Canadian Literature* 17.2 (1992): 109–28.

Loiselle, André. "Film-Mediated Drama: André Brassard's **Film** *Il était une fois dans l'Est* as a Pivot in Michel Tremblay's Dramaturgy." *Essays in Theatre* 10 (May 1992): 165–80.

Malina, Marten. "Rideau Vert Opens New Season with Play by André Brassard." *Montreal Star*, 29 Aug. 1968. 38.

Malone, Paul. "'Good Sisters' and 'Darling Sisters': Translating and Transplanting the Joual in Michel Tremblay's *Les Belles-Soeurs*." *Theatre Research in Canada* 24.1 (2003): 39–57.

Martin, Michèle. "Modulating Popular Culture: Cultural Critics on Tremblay's *Les Belles-Soeurs*." *Labour / Le Travail* 52 (Fall 2003): 109–35.

McQuaid, Catherine. "Michel Tremblay's Seduction of the 'Other Solitude.'" *Canadian Drama* 2 (Fall 1976): 219–23.

"Michel Tremblay Casebook." *CTR* 24 (Fall 1979): 11–51.

Monahan, Iona. "Dynamic Quebecers Triumph: Parisians Bow to *Les Belles Soeurs*." *Montreal Star*, 23 Nov. 1973. B8.

Nestruck, J. Kelly. "Songs Bring New Life to Michel Tremblay's 1968 Play." *Globe and Mail*, 3 Apr. 2010. R12.

Nicholls, Liz. "Romanians Fall in Love with *Les Belles-Soeurs*." *Edmonton Journal*, 23 Sept. 1994. E4.

Portman, Jamie. "London's *Belles Soeurs* Bubbles." *Montreal Gazette*, 8 Mar. 1977. 42.

Quig, James. "The Joual Revolution: Playwright Michel Tremblay." *The Canadian Magazine*, 14 May 1977. 16–19.

Rabillard, Sheila. "The Seductions of Theatricality: Mamet, Tremblay, and Political Drama." *Australasian Drama Studies* 29 (Oct. 1996): 33–42.

Rae, Lisbie. "Tremblay at P'tit Bonheur, 1982–1985." *Canadian Drama* 13.1 (1987): 1–26.

Ripley, John. "From Alienation to Transcendence: The Quest for Selfhood in Michel Tremblay's Plays." *Canadian Literature* 85 (Summer 1980): 44–59.

Rudakoff, Judith. "Michel Tremblay." *Profiles in Canadian Literature*. 6th ser. Ed. Jeffrey M. Heath. Toronto: Dundurn, 1987. 65–72.

Sabbath, Lawrence. "New Run Proves Greatness of *Les Belles-Soeurs*." *Montreal Star*, 20 June 1974. B15.

Salter, Denis. "Who's Speaking Here? Tremblay's Scots Voice." *CTR* 74 (Spring 1993): 40–45.

Smith, Donald. *Voices of Deliverance: Interviews with Quebec and Acadian Writers*. Trans. Larry Shouldice. Toronto: Anansi, 1986. 205–41.

Swoboda, Victor. "Michel Tremblay's Belles-Soeurs Put on Their Flamenco Skirts." *Montreal Gazette*, 16 Sept. 2006. E9.

Thomson, Laurel. "*Les Belles-Soeurs*, with a Newfie Twist." *Sherbrooke Record*, 16 Nov. 2004. 9.

Twigg, Alan. *For Openers: Conversations with 24 Canadian Writers*. Madeira Park, BC: Harbour, 1981. 151–61.

Usmiani, Renate. "The Bingocentric Worlds of Michel Tremblay and Tomson Highway: *Les Belles-Soeurs* vs. *The Rez Sisters*." *Canadian Literature* 144 (Spring 1995): 126–40.

————. *Michel Tremblay*. Vancouver: Douglas & McIntyre, 1982.

————. "Michel Tremblay." *Canadian Writers Since 1960*, 2nd ser. *Dictionary of Literary Biography*, vol. 60. Ed. W.H. New. Detroit: Gale, 1987. 342–52.

———. *The Theatre of Frustration: Super Realism in the Dramatic Work of F.X. Kroetz and Michel Tremblay*. NY: Garland, 1990.

Wagner, Vit. "Tremblay's Stamp Resonates." *Toronto Star*, 2 Apr. 1999. D6.

Walker, Craig. *The Buried Astrolabe*. Ch. 4.

Weiss, Jonathan M. *French-Canadian Theatre*. 27–48.

Whittaker, Herbert. "*Les Belles-Soeurs* Milestone Play." *Globe and Mail*, 4 Apr. 1973. 13.

Wyman, Max. "*Les Belles Soeurs*: A Gem of Comic Commentary." *Vancouver Sun*, 4 Mar. 1976. 37.

DAVID FRENCH and *Leaving Home*

Anthony, Geraldine, ed. *Stage Voices*. 234–50.

Bemrose, John. "Romancing the Rock." *Maclean's* 101 (31 Oct. 1988): 58–59.

Carson, Neil. "Towards a Popular Theatre in English Canada." *Canadian Literature* 85 (Summer 1980): 62–69.

Coe, Richard. "Toronto's Theatre Scene." *Washington Post*, 28 June 1972. E5.

Conolly, L.W., ed. *Canadian Drama and the Critics*. 87–98, 128–34, 238–45.

Cushman, Robert. "Returning Home a Generation Later." *National Post*, 12 May 2007. 22.

Dafoe, Christopher. "*Leaving Home* Will Strike Home." *Vancouver Sun*, 13 Nov. 1973. 35.

French, David. "David French Looks at His 17-Year Love Affair with the Mercer Family." *Toronto Star*, 15 Oct. 1988. F3.

Glaap, Albert-Reiner. "Family Plays, Romances, and Comedies: Aspects of David French's Work as a Dramatist." *On-Stage and Off-Stage: English Canadian Drama in Discourse*, ed. Glaap. 161–74.

Gross, Konrad. "Looking to the Far East? Newfoundland in David French's Mercer Tetralogy." *Down East: Critical Essays on Contemporary Maritime Canadian Literature*. Ed. Wolfgang Hochbruck and James O. Taylor. Trier: WVT, 1996. 247–63.

Jewinski, Ed. "Jacob Mercer's Lust for Victimization." *Canadian Drama* 2 (Spring 1976): 58–66.

Johnson, Chris. "David French." *Canadian Writers Since 1960*. 1st ser. *Dictionary of Literary Biography*, vol. 53. Ed. W.H. New. Detroit: Gale, 1986. 191–94.

———. "Is That Us? Ray Lawler's *Summer of the Seventeenth Doll* and David French's *Leaving Home*." *Canadian Drama* 6 (Spring 1980): 30–42.

Johnston, Denis. *Up the Mainstream*. Ch. 5.

Kareda, Urjo. "Introduction." *Leaving Home* by David French. Toronto: New Press, 1972. v–ix.

———. "Tarragon Theatre's Dynamic Play: Quite Exceptional." *Toronto Star*, 17 May 1972.

Maufort, Marc. "Celebrating Paradises Lost: Echoes of Eugene O'Neill in David French's 'Mercer Cycle.'" *Études Canadiennes / Canadian Studies: Revue Interdisciplinaire des Études Canadiennes en France* 49 (Dec. 2000): 97–107.

Mullaly, Edward. "Canadian Drama: David French and the Great Awakening." *The Fiddlehead* 100 (Winter 1974): 61–66.

Neary, Peter. "Of Many-Coloured Glass: Peter Neary Interviews David French." *Canadian Forum* 53 (Mar. 1974): 26–27.

Noonan, James. "The Comedy of David French and the Rocky Road to Broadway." *Thalia* 3 (Fall–Winter 1980–1981): 9–16.

Nothof, Anne. "David French and the Theatre of Speech." *Canadian Drama* 13.2 (1987): 216–23.

Nunn, Robert. "The Subjects of *Salt-Water Moon*." *Theatre History in Canada* 12 (Spring 1991): 3–21.

Ouzounian, Richard. "Prodigal Sons Return." *Toronto Star*. 4 May 2007. D9.

Taylor, Kate. "Soulpepper Plays It Safe with First Canadian Script." *Globe and Mail*, 7 May 2007. R5.

Thalenburg, Eileen, and David McCaughna. "Shaping the Word: Guy Sprung and Bill Glassco." *CTR* 26 (Spring 1980): 30–43.

Tyson, Bryan F. "Swallowed Up in Darkness: Vision and Division in *Of the Fields, Lately*." *Canadian Drama* 16.1 (1990): 23–31.

Wallace, Robert, and Cynthia Zimmerman, eds. *The Work*. 304–16.

Whittaker, Herbert. "Some Fine Domestic Brawling." *Globe and Mail*, 17 May 1972. 18.

———. "Kate Reid as Mother Dominates *Leaving Home*." *Globe and Mail*, 15 Nov. 1973. 14.

Zimmerman, Cynthia. "David French." *Profiles in Canadian Literature*. 4th ser. Ed. Jeffrey M. Heath. Toronto: Dundurn, 1982. 117–23.

JAMES REANEY and *Sticks and Stones: The Donnellys, Part I*

Anthony, Geraldine, ed. *Stage Voices*. 139–64.

Atwood, Margaret. "James Reaney." *Brick* 82 (2009): 160–61.

Bessai, Diane. "Documentary into Drama: Reaney's Donnelly Trilogy." *Essays on Canadian Writing* 24–25 (1982–83): 186–212.

Bowering, George. "Reaney's Region." *Essays on Canadian Writing* 24–25 (1982–83): 1–14.

Browne, Colin. "Reaney's *Twelve Letters*: A Portrait of the Artist as a Young Boy." *Essays on Canadian Writing* 24–25 (1982–83): 100–30.

Campbell, Wanda. "Alchemy in Ontario." *Canadian Literature* 151 (1996): 102–17.

_____. "To Flow Like You: An Interview with James Reaney." *Windsor Review* 29 (Spring 1996): 9–21.

Carson, Neil. "Canadian Historical Drama: Playwrights in Search of a Myth." *Studies in Canadian Literature* 2 (1977): 213–25.

Conlogue, Ray. "*Sticks and Stones*." *Globe and Mail*, 27 June 1989. A17.

Conolly, L.W., ed. *Canadian Drama and the Critics*. 145–55, 167–86, 302–07.

Crew, Robert. "Haste Blackens Donnellys." *Toronto Star*, 22 June 2005. D4.

Day, Moira. "James Reaney." *Canadian Writers, 1920–1959*. 1st ser. *Dictionary of Literary Biography*, vol. 68. Ed. W.H. New. Detroit: Gale, 1986. 282–90.

Dragland, Stan, ed. *Approaches to the Work of James Reaney*. Downsview, ON: ECW, 1983; rpt. of James Reaney Special Issue. *Essays on Canadian Writing* 24–25 (1982–83).

_____. "James Reaney's 'Pulsating Dance In and Out of Forms.'" *The Human Elements*. Ed. David Helwig. Ottawa: Oberon, 1978. 112–33.

Gerry, Thomas M.F. "'Imagining Out Things': The Act of Vision in James Reaney's *Alphabet*." *University of Toronto Quarterly* 70.4 (2001): 857–68.

Grandy, Karen. "Playing with Time: James Reaney's *The Donnellys* as Spatial Form Drama." *Modern Drama* 38 (Winter 1995): 462–74.

Huebert, Ronald. "James Reaney: Poet and Dramatist." *CTR* 13 (Winter 1977): 125–28.

Hutchman, Laurence. "Interview with James Reaney." *River Review* 3 (1997): 171–88.

Johnston, Denis. *Up the Mainstream*. Ch. 5.

Jones, Manina. "'The Collage in Motion': Staging the Documentary in Reaney's *Sticks and Stones*." *Canadian Drama* 16.1 (1990): 1–22.

_____. *That Art of Difference: 'Documentary-Collage' and English-Canadian Writing*. Toronto: U of Toronto P, 1993.

Kenney, Patricia. "James Reaney: Playmaker." *On-Stage and Off-Stage: English Canadian Drama in Discourse*. Ed. Albert-Reiner Glaap. 214–23.

Knowles, Ric. "Replaying History: Canadian Historiographic Metadrama." *Dalhousie Review* 67 (1987): 228–43.

Lee, Alvin. *James Reaney*. NY: Twayne, 1969.

Lee, Alvin, and Eleanor R. Goldhar. "James Reaney." *Profiles in Canadian Literature*. 4th ser. Ed. Jeffrey M. Heath. Toronto: Dundurn, 1985. 17–28.

Ludwick, Patricia. "One Actor's Journey with James Reaney." *Essays on Canadian Writing* 24–25 (1982–83): 130–37.

McKay, Jean. "Interview with James Reaney." *Essays on Canadian Writing* 24–25 (1982–83): 138–50.

Meyer, Bruce, and Brian O'Riordan. "James Reaney: Horses, Buggies, and Cadillacs." *In Their Words: Interviews with Fourteen Canadian Writers*. Toronto: Anansi, 1984. 56–70.

Miller, Mary Jane. "The Use of Stage Metaphor in *The Donnellys*." *Canadian Drama* 8.1 (1982): 34–41.

Morrow, Martin. "Donnellys Get Sympathetic Treatment." *Calgary Herald*, 10 Aug. 1996. C8.

New, W.H., ed. *Dramatists in Canada*. 114–44.

Noonan, James. "The Critics Criticized: An Analysis of Reviews of James Reaney's *The Donnellys* on National Tour." *Canadian Drama* 3 (Fall 1977): 174–82.

_____. "Foreword" and "Concluding Essay." *The Donnellys* by James Reaney. Victoria: Press Porcépic, 1983. 1–8, 275–88.

Nothof, Anne. "Variant Tellings: The Reconstruction of Social Mythology in James Reaney's *The Donnellys*." *International Journal of Canadian Studies* 10 (Fall 1994): 1–15.

Parker, Brian. "Is There a Canadian Drama?" *The Canadian Imagination: Dimensions of a Literary Culture*. Ed. David Staines. Cambridge, MA: Harvard UP, 1977. 152–87.

Parker, Gerald. "History, Story, and Story-Style: James Reaney's *The Donnellys*. *Canadian Drama* 4 (Spring 1978): 150–59.

_____. *How to Play: The Theatre of James Reaney*. Toronto: ECW, 1991.

_____. "'The Key Word ... Is "Listen"': James Reaney's 'Sonic Environment.'" *Mosaic* 14 (Fall 1981): 1–14.

_____. "Melodrama and Tragedy in James Reaney's Donnelly Trilogy." *Essays on Canadian Writing* 24–25 (1982–83): 165–85.

Perkyns, Richard. "The Innocence of the Donnellys: James Reaney's Three-Ring Circus." *Canadian Drama* 3 (Spring 1977): 162–73.

Reaney, James. *Fourteen Barrels from Sea to Sea*. Erin, ON: Press Porcépic, 1977.

_____. "James Reaney Looks Towards a National Repertory." *Theatre History in Canada* 6 (Fall 1985): 218–26.

_____. "A Letter from James Reaney: Halloween." *Black Moss* 2.1 (Spring 1976): 2–10.

_____. "Ten Years at Play." *Canadian Literature* 41 (Summer 1969): 53–61; rpt. *Dramatists in Canada*, ed. New. 70–78.

———. "'They are Treating Us Like Mad Dogs': A Donnelly Biographer's Problem." *Biography and Autobiography: Essays on Irish and Canadian History and Literature*. Ed. James Noonan. Ottawa: Carleton UP, 1993. 247–52.

———. "Your Plays Are Like Movies – Cinemascope Ones." *Canadian Drama* 5 (Spring 1979): 32–40.

Reaney, J. Stewart. *James Reaney*. Toronto: Gage, 1977.

Ricou, Laurie. *Everyday Magic: Child Languages in Canadian Literature*. Vancouver: UBC Press, 1987. Ch. 8.

Roberts, Eric. "*Sticks and Stones*: History, Play, and Myth." *Canadian Drama* 4 (Fall 1978): 160–72.

Ruebsaat, Norbert. "*Sticks and Stones*." *Globe and Mail*, 14 Aug. 1996. C1.

Walker, Craig Stewart. *The Buried Astrolabe*. Ch. 1.

———. "James Reaney's *The Donnellys* and the Recovery of 'the Ceremony of Innocence.'" *Australasian Drama Studies* 29 (Oct. 1996): 188–96.

Woodman, Ross. *James Reaney*. Toronto: McClelland & Stewart, 1972.

GEORGE F. WALKER and *Zastrozzi: The Master of Discipline*

Almonte, Richard. "Must a Black Text Always Be Written by a Black Author? Race, Authorship, Ethics, and the Plays of Andrew Moodie and George F. Walker." *Essays on Canadian Writing* 75 (2002): 142–58.

Bemrose, John. "Satan with a Sword." *Maclean's* 100 (25 May 1987): 55.

Birnie, Peter. "*Zastrozzi: The Master of Discipline*." *Vancouver Sun*, 25 July 2007.

Borkowski, Andrew. "Theatre of the Improbable: George F. Walker." *Canadian Forum* 70 (Sept. 1991): 16–19.

Brown, Joe. "*Zastrozzi*." *Washington Post*, 11 Feb. 1988. C4.

Conlogue, Ray. "A Triumph of Gothic Comedy." *Globe and Mail*, 14 May 1987. C3.

Conolly, L.W., ed. *Canadian Drama and the Critics*. 207–16, 297–301.

Corbeil, Carol. "A Conversation with George Walker." *Brick* 58 (Winter 1998): 59–67. Rpt. *George F. Walker*, ed. Lane. 114–27.

Crew, Robert. "Swashbuckler Still Has Charms." *Toronto Star*, 27 Aug. 2009. E10.

———. "*Zastrozzi* Returns in Splendid Form." *Toronto Star*, 14 May 1987. F3.

Galloway, Myron. "*Zastrozzi* Cast Superb." *Montreal Star*, 28 Nov. 1978. A12.

Gass, Ken. "Introduction." *Three Plays by George Walker*. Toronto: Coach House, 1978. 9–15. Rpt. *George F. Walker*, ed. Lane. 1–7.

"George F. Walker." *Contemporary Literary Criticism: Yearbook 1989, vo*l. 61. Ed. Roger Matuz. Detroit: Gale, 1990. 422–34.

Hadfield, Dorothy. "The Role Power Plays in George F. Walker's Detective Trilogy." *Essays in Theatre* 16 (Nov. 1997): 67–84.

Haff, Stephen. "Slashing the Pleasantly Vague: George F. Walker and the Word." *Essays in Theatre* 10 (Nov. 1991): 59–69. Rpt. *George F. Walker*, ed. Lane. 75–84.

Hallgren, Chris. "George Walker: The Serious and the Comic." *Scene Changes* 7 (Mar.–Apr. 1979): 23–25.

Johnson, Bryan. "*Zastrozzi* Wields a Satanic Rapier." *Globe and Mail*, 3 Nov. 1977. 17.

Johnson, Chris. *Essays on George F. Walker: Playing with Anxiety*. Winnipeg: Blizzard, 1999.

———. "George F. Walker: B-Movies Beyond the Absurd." *Canadian Literature* 85 (Summer 1980): 87–103. Rpt. *George F. Walker*, ed. Lane. 8–23.

———. "George F. Walker Directs George F. Walker." *Theatre History in Canada* 9 (Fall 1988): 157–72.

———. "George F. Walker." *Post-Colonial English Drama: Commonwealth Drama since 1960*. Ed. Bruce King. NY: St. Martin's, 1992. 82–96.

Johnston, Denis W. "George F. Walker: Liberal Idealism and the Power Plays." *Canadian Drama* 10.2 (1984): 195–206. Rpt. *George F. Walker*, ed. Lane. 37–50.

———. *Up the Mainstream*. Ch. 3.

Knowles, Ric. "The Dramaturgy of the Perverse." *Theatre Research International* 17 (Fall 1992): 226–35.

Lane, Harry, ed. *George F. Walker*. Critical Perspectives on Canadian Theatre in English, vol. 5. Toronto: Playwrights Canada, 2006.

Lane, William. "Introduction." *The Power Plays by George F. Walker*. Toronto: Coach House, 1984. 9–14.

———. "Introduction." *Zastrozzi: The Master of Discipline*. Toronto: Playwrights Co-op, 1979. 3–6.

Mallet, Gina. "Theatre Finds Strength with Style." *Toronto Star*, 3 Nov. 1977. F1.

Morrow, Martin. "*Master of Discipline* a Young Person's Play." *Calgary Herald*, 31 Oct. 1992. C5.

Nestruck, J. Kelly. "A Little Air and the Show Would Soar." *Globe and Mail*, 25 Aug. 2009. R1.

Oliver, Edith. "*Zastrozzi*." *The New Yorker* 57 (1 Feb. 1982): 116–17.

Orr, Tom. "*Zastrozzi* Not for the Faint." *Seattle Times*, 10 Mar. 1994. E8.

Read, Nicholas. "*Zastrozzi*." *Vancouver Sun*, 7 Oct. 1986. C6.

Reid, Kerry. "Muddy Vengeance Story in *Zastrozzi.*" *Chicago Tribune*, 9 Feb. 2012.

Rich, Frank. "Serban Directs *Zastrozzi* at the Public." *New York Times*, 18 Jan. 1982. C14.

Sinclair, Gregory J. "Live from Off-Stage." *Canadian Forum* 65 (Aug.–Sept. 1986): 6–11.

Usmiani, Renate. *Second Stage*. 35–38.

Walker, Craig. *The Buried Astrolabe*. Ch. 5.

Wallace, Robert. "George F. Walker." *Profiles in Canadian Literature*. 6th ser. Ed. Jeffrey M. Heath. Toronto: Dundurn, 1987. 105–12.

———. "Looking for the Light: A Conversation with George F. Walker." *Canadian Drama* 14.1 (1988): 22–33. Rpt. *George F. Walker*, ed. Lane. 51–60.

Wallace, Robert, and Cynthia Zimmerman, eds. *The Work*. 212–25. Rpt. *George F. Walker*, ed. Lane. 24–32.

Wasserman, Jerry. "Introduction." *Somewhere Else: Four Plays by George F. Walker*. Vancouver: Talonbooks, 1999. 5–6.

———. "'Making Things Clear': The *Film Noir* Plays of George F. Walker." *Canadian Drama* 8.1 (1982): 99–101. Rpt. *George F. Walker*, ed. Lane. 33–36.

Wynne-Jones, Tim. "Acts of Darkness," *Books in Canada* 14 (Apr. 1985): 11–14.

JOHN MacLACHLAN GRAY with ERIC PETERSON and *Billy Bishop Goes to War*

Anderson, Ian. "Coming Home from Billy Bishop's War." *Maclean's* 94 (16 Mar. 1981): 17, 20.

Arnott, Brian. "The Passe Muraille Alternative." *The Human Elements*. Ed. David Helwig. Ottawa: Oberon, 1978. 97–111.

Atkey, Mel. *Broadway North: The Dream of a Canadian Musical Theatre*. Ch. 24.

Bemrose, John. "Billy Soars Again." *Maclean's* 111 (28 Sept. 1998): 69–70.

Bessai, Diane. "Discovering the Popular Audience." *Canadian Literature* 118 (Fall 1988): 7–28.

———. *Playwrights of Collective Creation*, 179–214. Rpt. *Solo Performance*, ed. Stephenson. 19–28.

Birnie, Peter. "Billy Bishop Soars Again on the Wings of Youth." *Vancouver Sun*, 1 Nov. 2008. F15.

Bolin, John S. "The Very Best of Company: Perceptions of a Canadian Attitude towards War and Nationalism in Three Contemporary Plays." *American Review of Canadian Studies* 23.3 (1987): 309–22.

Conolly, L.W., ed. *Canadian Drama and the Critics*. 217–26.

Corbeil, Carole. "*Billy Bishop* Lands Safely." *Globe and Mail*, 13 Jan. 1982. 17.

Cruise, David. "John Gray, Writer." *Atlantic Insight* 5 (Aug. 1983): 22–27.

Donnelly, Pat. "Like Its Subject, Theatre Classic Is a High Flyer." *Montreal Gazette*, 19 Feb. 2011. E13.

Galloway, Myron. "Life Is a One-Man Show [Eric Peterson]." *Montreal Star*, 24 Feb. 1979. D8.

Gray, John. "Preface." *Billy Bishop Goes to War*. Vancouver: Talonbooks, 1981. 5–16.

Gray, John, and Ginny Ratsoy. "Satire, Monologue, and the Creation of Indigenous Mythology: *Billy Bishop Goes to War*." *Playing the Pacific Province: An Anthology of British Columbia Plays, 1967–2000*. Ed. Ginny Ratsoy and James Hoffman. Toronto: Playwrights Canada, 2001. 141–45.

Gussow, Mel. "Capital Sees *Billy Bishop Goes to War*." *New York Times*, 13 Mar. 1980. III, 20.

Heinrich, Jeff. "Billy Bishop Doesn't Get Old, He Changes with the Times." *Montreal Gazette*, 12 Feb. 2011. E3.

Johnson, Bryan. "*Billy Bishop Goes to War*: Flying Ace a Soaring Success." *Globe and Mail*, 14 Feb. 1979. 13.

Kerr, Walter. "*Billy Bishop* Flies In." *New York Times*, 30 May 1980. III, 3.

Knelman, Martin. "Dancing in the Sky with Billy Bishop." *Saturday Night* 94 (June 1979): 50–51.

Lardner, James. "Lighter Than Air." *Washington Post*, 6 Mar. 1980. D1.

MacIntyre, Jean. "Language and Structure in *Billy Bishop Goes to War*." *Canadian Drama* 13.1 (1987): 50–59.

———. "The Male-Bond World of John Gray's Musicals." *Canadian Drama* 16.1 (1990): 123–28.

Mallett, Gina. "*Billy Bishop* Deserves Some Medals." *Toronto Star*, 14 Feb. 1979. C3.

Miller, Mary Jane. "*Billy Bishop Goes to War* and *Maggie and Pierre*: A Matched Set." *Theatre History in Canada* 10.2 (1989): 188–98.

Morrow, Martin. "Canada's Billy Bishop Still Flying High." *Calgary Herald*, 24 Oct. 1992. D1.

Nestruck, J. Kelly. "Thirty Years On, Billy Bishop Soars Onstage." *Globe and Mail*, 15 Aug. 2009. R13.

Nickson, Liz. "Canada: Bombing on Broadway." *CTR* 35 (Winter 1982): 138–42.

Ouzounian, Richard. "Delightful Bishop Called Up Again." *Toronto Star*, 27 Jan. 2010. E2.

Steed, Judy. "John Gray's Progress." *Toronto Life*, 15 (May 1981): 66, 97–103.

———. "Mike and Eric and Chris and John: The Night Mike Nichols Met Billy Bishop." *The Canadian Magazine* (26 May 1979): 2–6.

Sullivan, Dan. "*Billy Bishop Goes to War* and Likes It." *Los Angeles Times*, 17 Oct. 1980. VI, 1.

Taylor, Kate. "Billy Bishop Still Flying High." *Globe and Mail*, 26 Sept. 1998. C9.

Twigg, Alan. "John Gray: Filius." *For Openers: Conversations with 24 Canadian Writers*. Vancouver: Harbour, 1981. 97–106.

Usmiani, Renate. *Second Stage*. 67–71.

Wagner, Vit. "Billy Bishop Hasn't Lost His Old Charm." *Toronto Star*, 25 Sept. 1998. D13.

Wallace, Robert, and Cynthia Zimmerman, eds. *The Work*. 44–59.

Wardle, Irving. "*Billy Bishop Goes to War*." *The Times* (London), 21 Aug. 1980. 9.

Wasserman, Jerry. "Flying Low into Another Tour of Duty: Jerry Wasserman Speaks With John Gray." *Books in Canada* 28 (Feb. 1999): 25–27.

Wyman, Max. "From the Wild, Blue Yonder to the Great, White Way." *Vancouver Magazine* 12 (July 1979): 65–71.

Yardley, M. Jeanne. "Unauthorized Re-visions of the Billy Bishop Story." *Textual Studies in Canada*, 3 (1993): 86–96.

DAVID FENNARIO and *Balconville*

Abley, Mark. "The Shabby Intimacy of Daily Life." *Maclean's* 94 (13 Apr. 1981): 66.

Ashley, Audrey M. "Play Provides Biting Humour, Raw Language." *Ottawa Citizen*, 6 Nov. 1979. 59.

Bagnall, Janet. "At Home in Verdun with David Fennario." *Montreal Gazette*, 23 Feb. 1997. D5–6.

Benazon, Michael. "From Griffintown to Verdun: A Study of Place in the Work of David Fennario." *Matrix* 19 (1984): 25–34.

Blades, Margaret W. "Anglophobes, Francophobes, and the Language Question in *Balconville*." *Selecta* 12 (1991): 8–12.

Blazer, Fred. "Bilingual Drama Is Universal." *Globe and Mail*, 10 Feb. 1979. 37.

Burke, Tim. "Art in *Balconville* Mirrors Chunk of Life at Its Grittiest." *Montreal Gazette*, 16 Feb. 1980. 93.

Byrnes, Terence. "The Matrix Interview: David Fennario." *Matrix* 48 (1996): 11–17.

Collet, Paulette. "Fennario's *Balconville* and Tremblay's *En Pièces détachées*: A Universe of Backyards and Despair." *Canadian Drama* 10 (Spring 1984): 35–43.

Conlogue, Ray. "Tough-Guy Playwright from the Point." *Globe and Mail*, 4 Oct. 1980. E1.

Conolly, L.W., ed. *Canadian Drama and the Critics*. 227–37.

Desson, Jim, and Bruce K. Filson. "Where Is David Fennario Now?" *CTR* 46 (Spring 1986): 36–41.

Donnelly, Pat. "Fennario's *Balconville* Has Changed, But Stands the Test of Time." *Montreal Gazette*, 11 Jan. 1992. C3.

Fennario, David. *Banana Boots*. Vancouver: Talonbooks, 1998.

———. *Without a Parachute*. Toronto: McClelland & Stewart, 1974.

Gilman, Marvin. "Fennario and Ryga: Canadian Political Playwrights." *Australasian Drama Studies* 29 (Oct. 1996): 180–87.

Gonick, Cy. "David Fennario: A Revolutionary Playwright." *Canadian Dimension* 21 (Apr. 1987): 22–27.

Grigsby, Wayne. "The Bard from Balconville." *The Canadian Magazine*, 20 Jan. 1979: 16–18.

Hays, Mathew. "Building on the Balconville Block." *Globe and Mail*, 11 Oct. 2005. R3.

Horenblas, Richard. "David Fennario: Burning Houses Down." *Scene Changes* 8 (Mar. 1980): 26–29.

Jaffe-Berg, Erith. "Enacting Translation in Multilingual Theatre." *Translation Perspectives* 12 (2003): 77–92.

King, Dierdre. "The Drama of David Fennario." *Canadian Forum* 60 (Feb. 1981): 14–17.

Knelman, Martin. "Bilingualism Among the Hopeless." *Saturday Night* 94 (Nov. 1979): 101–04.

Koustas, Jane. "Imagi / Nation: Fennario, Friel, and the Staging of Language and Identity in Quebec." *Canadian Journal of Irish Studies* 33.1 (2007), 41–47.

Mallet, Gina. "Montreal Play Brings Slum to Life." *Toronto Star*, 4 Oct. 1979. B1.

Milliken, Paul. "Portrait of the Artist as a Working-Class Hero: An Interview with David Fennario." *Performing Arts in Canada* 17 (Summer 1980): 22–25.

Nunn, Robert C. "The Interplay of Action and Set in the Plays of David Fennario." *Theatre History in Canada* 9 (Spring 1988): 3–18.

Page, Malcolm. "David Fennario's *Balconville*: Document and Message." *On-Stage and Off-Stage: English Canadian Drama in Discourse*, ed. Glaap. 138–47.

Podbrey, Maurice. *Half Man, Half Beast: Making a Life in Canadian Theatre*. Ch. 5.

Radz, Matt. "Back to the Balconies." *Montreal Gazette*, 1 Oct. 2005. H2.

Ravel, Aviva. "David Fennario." *Canadian Writers Since 1960*. 2nd ser. *Dictionary of Literary Biography*, vol. 60. Ed. W.H. New. Detroit: Gale, 1987. 60–64.

Reid, Gregory J. "David Fennario Turned Rhapsodist: The Rebirth of the Author in Performance." *Essays in Theatre* 18.1 (1999): 63–77.

———. "Mapping Jouissance: Insights from a Case Study in the Schizophrenia of Canadian Drama." *Comparative Drama* 35.3–4 (2001): 291–319.

Salter, Denis. "Six Characters in Search of a Hero." *CTR* 69 (Winter 1991): 87–91.

Wallace, Robert, and Cynthia Zimmerman, eds. *The Work*, 293–303.

Wardle, Irving. "Nationalist Tension and Physical Congestion." *The Times* (London), 3 Apr. 1981. 11.

SHARON POLLOCK and *Blood Relations*

Akihiko, Senda. "Toyko: Festival of Canadian Drama." *CTR* 83 (Summer 1995): 69–71.

Bessai, Diane. "Introduction." *Blood Relations and Other Plays* by Sharon Pollock. Edmonton: NeWest, 1981. 7–9.

———. "Sharon Pollock's Women: A Study in Dramatic Process." *Amazing Space: Writing Canadian Women Writing*. Ed. Shirley Neuman and Smaro Kamboureli. Edmonton: Longspoon / NeWest, 1986. 126–36. Rpt. *Sharon Pollock*, ed. Nothof. 44–67.

———. "Women Dramatists: Sharon Pollock and Judith Thompson." *Post-Colonial English Drama*. Ed. Bruce King. NY: St. Martin's, 1992. 97–117.

Chung, Kathy K.Y. "'A Different Kind of the Same Thing': Narrative, Experiential Knowledge, and Subjectivity in Susan Glaspell's *Trifles* and Sharon Pollock's *Blood Relations*." *Theatre Research in Canada* 20.2 (1999): 159–80.

Clark, Bob. "Sharon Pollock Has an Axe to Grind." *Calgary Herald*, 24 Sept. 2009. E3.

Clement, Susan, and Esther Beth Sullivan. "The Split Subject of *Blood Relations*." *Upstaging Big Daddy: Directing Theater As If Gender and Race Matter*. Ed. Ellen Donkin and Susan Clement. Ann Arbor: U of Michigan P, 1993. 53–66.

Conlogue, Ray. "'These Plays Are Not Translated into French': Lizzie Borden Comes to Quebec." *Globe and Mail*, 11 June 1986. D5.

———. "Victorian Production Bustles into Confusion." *Globe and Mail*, 2 Oct. 1981. 22.

Conolly, L.W., ed. *Canadian Drama and the Critics*. 135–44, 259–76, 317–23.

Cushman, Robert. "Murder Most Complicated." *National Post*, 23 May 2003. M10.

Dunn, Margo. "Sharon Pollock: In the Centre Ring." *Makara* 1 (Aug.–Sept. 1976): 2–6.

Gilbert, Reid. "Sharon Pollock." *Profiles in Canadian Literature 6*. Ed. Jeffrey M. Heath. Toronto: Dundurn, 1986. 113–20.

Grace, Sherrill. "Creating the Girl from God's Country: From Nell Shipman to Sharon Pollock." *Canadian Literature* 172 (2002): 92–111.

———. "Imagining Canada: Sharon Pollock's *Walsh* and *Fair Liberty's Call*." *Performing National Identities*, ed. Grace and Glaap. 51–69. Rpt. *Sharon Pollock*, ed. Grace and La Flamme. 133–50.

———. *Making Theatre: A Life of Sharon Pollock*. Vancouver: Talonbooks, 2008.

———. "Pollock's Portraits of the Artist." *Theatre Research in Canada* 22.2 (2002): 124–38.

———. "Sharon Pollock's *Doc* and the Biographer's Dilemma." *Theatre and AutoBiography*, ed. Grace and Wasserman. 275–88.

Grace, Sherrill, and Michelle La Flamme, eds. *Sharon Pollock*. Critical Perspectives on Canadian Theatre in English, vol. 10. Toronto: Playwrights Canada, 2008.

Hofsess, John. "Families." *Homemaker's* 15 (Mar. 1980): 41–60.

Holder, Heidi J. "Broken Toys: The Destruction of the National Hero in the Early History Plays of Sharon Pollock." *Essays in Theatre* 14 (May 1996): 131–45. Rpt. *Sharon Pollock*, ed. Nothof. 100–27.

Jones, Ann. *Women Who Kill*. NY: Fawcett, 1981.

Kerr, Rosalind. "Borderline Crossings in Sharon Pollock's Out-Law Genres: *Blood Relations* and *Doc*." *Theatre Research in Canada* 17 (Fall 1996): 200–15. Rpt. *Sharon Pollock*, ed. Grace and La Flamme. 69–80.

Knowles, Ric. "Replaying History: Canadian Historiographic Metadrama." *Dalhousie Review* 67 (1987): 228–43.

Kürtösi, Katalin. "Women Playing Women in Sharon Pollock's *Blood Relations*." *Reading(s) from a Distance: European Perspectives on Canadian Women's Writing*. Ed. Charlotte Sturgess and Martin Küester. Augsburg: Wissner, 2008. 91–98.

Loiselle, André. "Paradigms of 1980s Québécois and Canadian Drama: Normand Chaurette's *Provincetown Playhouse, juillet 1919, j'avais 19 ans,* and Sharon Pollock's *Blood Relations*." *Québec Studies* 14 (1992): 93–104.

Metcalfe, Robin. "Interview with Sharon Pollock." *Books in Canada* 16 (Mar. 1987): 39–40.

Miner, Madonna. "'Lizzie Borden Took an Ax': Enacting *Blood Relations*." *Literature in Performance* 6 (Apr. 1986): 10–21.

Much, Rita. "Theatre by Default: Sharon Pollock's Garry Theatre." *CTR* 82 (Spring 1995): 19–22. Rpt. *Sharon Pollock*, ed. Grace and La Flamme. 48–53.

Nicholls, Liz. "Lizzie Borden's Axe Has the Chops in *Blood Relations*." *Edmonton Journal*, 23 Jan. 1998. C5.

Nothof, Anne. "Crossing Borders: Sharon Pollock's Revisitation of Canadian Frontiers." *Modern Drama* 38 (Winter 1995): 475–87. Rpt. *Sharon Pollock*, ed. Nothof. 81–99.

———. "Interview with Sharon Pollock." *Sharon Pollock: Essays on Her Works*, ed. Nothof. 167–79.

———, ed. *Sharon Pollock: Essays on Her Works*. Toronto: Guernica, 2000.

———. "Staging the Intersections of Time in Sharon Pollock's *Doc, Moving Pictures,* and *End Dream.*" *Theatre Research in Canada* 22.2 (2001): 139–50. Rpt. *Sharon Pollock,* ed. Grace and La Flamme. 123–32.

Nunn, Robert C. "Sharon Pollock's Plays: A Review Article." *Theatre History in Canada* 5 (Spring 1984): 72–83. Rpt. *Sharon Pollock,* ed. Nothof. 26–43.

Ouzounian, Richard. "Borden Play Delivers Thrills." *Toronto Star,* 23 May 2003. C10.

Page, Malcolm. "Sharon Pollock: Committed Playwright." *Canadian Drama* 5 (Fall 1979): 104–11. Rpt. *Sharon Pollock,* ed. Nothof. 12–25.

Pollock, Sharon. "Canada's Playwrights: Finding Their Place." *CTR* 34 (Spring 1982): 34–38. Rpt. *Canadian Theatre History,* ed. Rubin. 389–93.

———. "Dead or Alive? Feeling the Pulse of Canadian Theatre." *Theatrum* 23 (Apr – May 1991): 12–13. Rpt. *Sharon Pollock,* ed. Grace and La Flamme. 41–43.

———. "Many Brave Spirits." *Theatre Memoirs.* 13–17.

_____. "Playwright: Parasite or Symbiont?" *Theatre and AutoBiography,* ed. Grace and Wasserman. 295–300.

———. "Reflections of a Female Artistic Director." *Women on the Canadian Stage,* ed. Much. 109–14. Rpt. *Sharon Pollock,* ed. Grace and La Flamme. 44–47.

———. "Revisiting My Bloody Relationships." *Calgary Herald,* 18 Sept. 2009. 40.

Rudakoff, Judith, and Rita Much. *Fair Play.* 208–20.

Saddlemyer, Ann. "Crime in Literature: Canadian Drama." *Rough Justice: Essays on Crime in Literature.* Ed. Martin L. Friedman. Toronto: U of Toronto Press, 1991. 214–30.

Salter, Denis. "(Im)possible Worlds: The Plays of Sharon Pollock." *The Sharon Pollock Papers: First Accession.* Ed. Apollonia Steele and Jean F. Tener. Calgary: U of Calgary P, 1989. xi–xxxv. Rpt. *Sharon Pollock,* ed. Grace and La Flamme. 13–32.

Stone-Blackburn, Susan. "Feminism and Metadrama: Role-Playing in *Blood Relations.*" *Canadian Drama* 15 (1989): 169–78. Rpt. *Sharon Pollock,* ed. Nothof. 68–80.

Striff, Erin. "Lady Killers: Feminism and Murder in Sharon Pollock's *Blood Relations* and Wendy Kesselman's *My Sister in This House.*" *New England Theatre Journal* 8 (1997): 95–109.

Taylor, Kate. "Lizzie Borden, How Could You?" *Globe and Mail,* 23 May 2003. R4.

Walker, Craig. *The Buried Astrolabe.* Ch. 3.

Wallace, Robert, and Cynthia Zimmerman, eds. *The Work.* 115–26.

Wasserman, Jerry. "Daddy's Girls: Father-Daughter Incest and Canadian Plays by Women." *Essays in Theatre* 14 (Nov. 1995): 25–36. Rpt. *Sharon Pollock,* ed. Grace and La Flamme. 54–68.

———. "Remembering Agraba: Canadian Political Theatre and the Construction of Cultural Memory." *Signatures of the Past,* ed. Maufort and De Wagter. 101–14.

Wylie, Herb. "'Painting the Background': Metadrama and the Fabric of History in Sharon Pollock's *Blood Relations.*" *Essays in Theatre* 15 (May 1997): 191–205. Rpt. *Sharon Pollock,* ed. Grace and La Flamme. 81–97.

Zichy, Francis. "Justifying the Ways of Lizzie Borden to Men: The Play Within the Play in *Blood Relations.*" *Theatre Annual* 42 (1987): 61–81.

Zimmerman, Cynthia. *Playwriting Women.* 60–98.

———. "Sharon Pollock: Transfiguring the Maternal." *Theatre Research in Canada* 22.2 (2001): 151–60. Rpt.114–22. *Sharon Pollock,* ed. Grace and La Flamme, 114–22.

_____. "Towards a Better, Fairer World: An Interview with Sharon Pollock." *CTR* 69 (Winter 1991): 34–38.

SKY GILBERT and *Drag Queens on Trial*

Barnidge, Mary Shen. "Secrets / Drag Queens on Trial." *Chicago Reader.* 26 July 1990.

Berto, Tony. "'Seeking Clues of Queerness': Researching Contemporary Canadian Queer Theatre." *Theatre Histories,* ed. Filewod. 189–97.

Boni, Franco. "An Interview with Sky Gilbert." *Rhubarb-o-Rama! Plays and Playwrights from the Rhubarb! Festival.* Ed. Franco Boni. Winnipeg: Blizzard, 1998. 16–20.

Gilbert, Sky. "Closet Plays: An Exclusive Dramaturgy at Work." *CTR* 59 (Summer 1989): 55–58.

———. "Diary of a (Reluctant) Radical." *This Magazine* 30 (May–June 1997): 34–37.

———. "Drag and Popular Culture." *CTR* 58 (Spring 1989): 42–44.

_____. *Ejaculations from the Charm Factory: A Memoir.* Toronto: ECW, 2000.

———. "Playwright's Foreword." *Painted, Tainted, Sainted: Four Plays* by Sky Gilbert. Toronto: Playwrights Canada, 1996. 15–17.

_____. "Political Theatre: Because We Must; Reflections." *CTR* 117 (Winter 2004): 25–28.

_____. "Writing Gay: Is It Still Possible?" *Queer Theatre in Canada,* ed. Kerr. 256–64.

_____, and Jim Giles. "The Other Side of Alternative Theatre: An Interview with Sky Gilbert." *How Theatre Educates,* ed. Gallagher and Booth. 182–88.

Grignard, Christopher. "Monstrous Ejaculations: Sky Gilbert's *Ejaculations from the Charm Factory: A Memoir*." *CTR* 120 (2004): 50–56.

Halferty, J. Paul. "Queer and Now: The Queer Signifier at Buddies in Bad Times Theatre." *Theatre Research in Canada* 27.1–2 (2006): 123–54. Rpt. *Queer Theatre in Canada*, ed. Kerr. 239–55.

Kaplan, Jon. "Female Ethos and Drag Queen Life." *Now* 5.8 (Oct. 1985): 21.

Kastner, Susan. "Sky Queen." *Toronto Star*, 9 Oct. 1994. C1, 11.

Mietkiewicz, Henry. "*Drag Queens on Trial* Is Not for the Faint-Hearted." *Toronto Star*, 20 Oct. 1985. G4.

Scott, Jay. "Drag Queens Tackle Stereotypes." *Globe and Mail*, 21 Oct. 1985. C12.

Vaughan, R.M. "Arguments in Motion." *Books in Canada* 23 (Apr. 1994): 16–19.

———. "Bullet-Proof Heels, 3 A.M. ... and Other Problems: An Introduction." *Painted, Tainted, Sainted: Four Plays* by Sky Gilbert. 11–13.

Wallace, Robert. "Making Out Positions: An Introduction." *Making, Out: Plays by Gay Men*. Toronto: Coach House, 1992. 11–40.

———. "No Turning Back: An Introduction." *This Unknown Flesh: A Selection of Plays by Sky Gilbert*, Toronto: Coach House, 1995. 11–26.

———. "Theorizing a Queer Theatre: Buddies in Bad Times." *Contemporary Issues in Canadian Drama*. Ed. Brask. 136–59.

Webb, Margaret. "What's Eating Sky Gilbert?" *Toronto Life* 31 (Mar. 1997): 45–48.

Whitehead, Jay. "Discovering the Relevance of Drag Culture in 'Bible Country.'" *alt.theatre* 3.4 (Mar. 2005): 7–9.

KELLY REBAR and *Bordertown Café*

Ashley, Audrey. "Family Relationships Simmer in Humorous Cross-Border Comedy at Blyth Festival." *Ottawa Citizen*, 24 June 1987. F2.

Chamberlain, Adrian. "Drama in the Diner." *Victoria Times-Colonist*, 19 Sept. 2009. D5.

Conlogue, Ray. "New *Bordertown Café* Serves Up Absorbing Drama." *Globe and Mail*, 15 Oct. 1988. C13.

Crook, Barbara. "Troupe Brings Bordertown Family to Life." *Ottawa Citizen*, 18 July 1988. A17.

Donnelly, Pat. "Café Conveys Spirit of West." *Montreal Gazette*, 8 Apr. 1988. D1.

———. "Playwright a Dramatic Success." *Montreal Gazette*, 6 Apr. 1988. B5.

Keahey, Deborah. *Making It Home: Place in Canadian Prairie Literature*. Winnipeg: U of Manitoba P, 1998. 26–34.

Loiselle, André. *Stage-Bound*. Ch. 4.

McCormick, Marion. "A Good Play Is Still the Thing." *Montreal Gazette*, 18 Apr. 1988. D1.

Morrow, Martin. "Author of Hit Café Play Insists She's Serving Pure Invention." *Calgary Herald*, 23 Apr. 1990. D1–2.

———. "Play Delivers Sad Message about Modern Fathers." *Calgary Herald*, 25 Feb. 1990. E1.

Prokosh, Kevin. "Playwright Planted Prairie Populism at PTE." *Winnipeg Free Press*, 12 Nov. 2009. D3.

———. "Prairie Playwright." *Winnipeg Free Press*, 19 Sept. 1987. 29.

Sadowski-Smith, Claudia. *Border Fictions: Globalization, Empire, and Writing at the Boundaries of the United States*. Charlottesville: U of Virginia P, 2008. Ch. 4.

Salter, Denis. "Introduction." *New Canadian Drama* 3. Ed. Denis Salter. Ottawa: Borealis, 1984. vii–xiii.

Skinner, C.J. "*Bordertown Café*." *CTR* 65 (Winter 1990): 60–61.

Thiessen, Vern. "*Bordertown Café*." *Prairie Fire* 11.3 (1990): 98–99.

JOAN MacLEOD and *Toronto, Mississippi*

Belliveau, George. "Investigating British Columbia's Past: *The Komagata Maru Incident* and *The Hope Slide* as Historiographical Metadrama." *BC Studies* 137 (Spring 2003): 93–106.

Birnie, Peter. "Actress Shines in Classic." *Vancouver Sun*, 7 Mar. 2009. F11.

Chapman, Geoff. "Unpredictable MacLeod Brings Rich Writing to Real-Life Worries." *Toronto Star*, 5 Mar. 1992. E8.

Conlogue, Ray. "*Toronto, Mississippi* Well Worth a Visit." *Globe and Mail*, 7 Oct. 1987. C8.

Crew, Robert. "Play Talks to Handicapped via Elvis." *Toronto Star*, 2 Oct. 1987. E12.

Derksen, Céleste. "BC Oddities: Interpellation and/in Joan MacLeod's *The Hope Slide*." *CTR* 101 (Winter 2000): 49–52.

Dykk, Lloyd. "Playwright Tackles Heartaches, Heroes." *Vancouver Sun*, 14 Nov. 1988. D6.

Kirchhoff, H.J. "The Reincarnation of Joan MacLeod." *Globe and Mail*, 28 Mar. 1992. C6.

Lacy, Liam. "Potboiler Turns Out to Be a Comedy." *Globe and Mail*, 1 Mar. 1989. C9.

MacLeod, Joan. "Interview with Joan MacLeod." *Capilano Review* 2.12 (1994): 68–90.

McIlroy, Randal. "Production Decidedly Daring." *Winnipeg Free Press*, 30 Nov. 1990. 37.

Morrow, Fiona. "My Plays Are All about Family." *Globe and Mail*, 14 Mar. 2009. R12.

Nothof, Anne. "The Construction and Deconstruction of Border Zones in *Fronteras Americanas* by Guillermo Verdecchia and *Amigo's Blue Guitar* by Joan MacLeod." *Theatre Research in Canada* 20 (Spring 1999): 3–15.

Ratsoy, Ginny. "Dramatizing Alterity: Relational Characterization in Postcolonial British Columbia Plays." *Embracing the Other: Addressing Xenophobia in the New Literatures in English*. Ed. Dunja M. Mohr. Amsterdam: Rodopi, 2008. 295–306.

Rudakoff, Judith, and Rita Much. *Fair Play*. 190–207.

Scott, Shelley. "Hell Is Other Girls: Joan MacLeod's *The Shape of a Girl*." *Modern Drama* 45.2 (2002): 270–81.

Smith, Gary. "A Barnburner of a Play." *Hamilton Spectator*, 24 Jan. 2009. E4.

Wasserman, Jerry. "Introduction." *The Shape of a Girl / Jewel* by Joan MacLeod. Vancouver: Talonbooks, 2002. 7–11.

———. "Joan MacLeod and the Geography of the Imagination." *Performing National Identities*, ed. Grace and Glaap. 92–103. Rpt. *Theatre in British Columbia*, ed. Ratsoy. 153–64.

Zacher, Scotty. "Dysfunction Junction, What's Your Function?" *Chicago Theatre Beat*, 24 Nov. 2010.

ANN-MARIE MacDONALD and *Goodnight Desdemona (Good Morning Juliet)*

Bemrose, John. "Theatre: Shakespearean Folly." *Maclean's* 103 (29 Jan. 1990): 66.

Burnett, Linda. "'Redescribing a World': Towards a Theory of Shakespearean Adaptation in Canada." *CTR* 111 (Summer 2002): 5–9.

Conlogue, Ray. "New Roles for Classic Heroines." *Globe and Mail*, 4 Apr. 1988. C9.

Coulbourn, John. "Good Day for Shakespeare." *Toronto Sun*, 24 Mar. 2001.

Crew, Robert. "Desdemona Delicious Fun." *Toronto Star*, 29 Mar. 1990. C3.

Curran, Beverley. "Mingling and Unmingling Opposites: Bending Genre and Gender in Ann-Marie MacDonald's *Goodnight Desdemona (Good Morning Juliet)*." *He Said, She Says: An RSVP to the Male Text*. Eds. Mica Howe and Sarah Appleton Aguiar. London: Fairleigh Dickinson UP, 2001. 211–20.

Cushman, Robert. "Tragically, These Heroines Remain Who They Are." *National Post,* 27 Mar. 2001. B6.

Djordjevic, Igor. "*Goodnight Desdemona (Good Morning Juliet)*: From Shakespearean Tragedy to Postmodern Satyr Play." *Comparative Drama* 37.1 (2003): 89–115.

Donnelly, Pat. "Centaur's New *Goodnight Desdemona* Is an Erudite Comedy about Shakespeare." *Montreal Gazette*, 2 Nov. 1991. E6.

Dvorak, Marta. "Goodnight William Shakespeare (Good Morning Ann-Marie MacDonald)." *CTR* 79–80 (Summer–Fall 1994): 128–33.

Fortier, Mark. "Shakespeare with a Difference: Genderbending and Genrebending in *Goodnight Desdemona*." *CTR* 54 (Spring 1989): 47–51.

———. "Undead and Unsafe: Adapting Shakespeare (in Canada)." *Shakespeare in Canada*, ed. Bryden and Makaryk. 339–52.

Friedman, Sharon. "The Feminist Playwright as Critic: Paula Vogel, Ann-Marie MacDonald, and Djanet Sears Interpret *Othello*." *Feminist Theatrical Revisions of Classic Works: Critical Essays*. Ed. Sharon Friedman. Jefferson: McFarland, 2009. 113–34.

Gussow, Mel. "O Juliet, O Desdemona: Wherefore Is Everyone?" *New York Times*, 22 Oct. 1992.

Hadfield, D.A. *Re: Producing Women's Dramatic History*. Ch. 6.

Harrington, Louise. "'Excuse me while I turn this upside-down': Three Canadian Adaptations of Shakespeare." *British Journal of Canadian Studies* 20.1 (2007): 123–42.

Hengen, Shannon. "Towards a Feminist Comedy." *Canadian Literature* 146 (Fall 1995): 97–109.

Hoile, Christopher. "Ann-Marie MacDonald's Delightful Confection *Goodnight Desdemona (Good Morning Juliet)*." *Theatre World*, 12 Apr. 2001.

Knowles, Ric. "*Othello* in Three Times." *Shakespeare in Canada*, ed. Brydon et al. 371–94.

———. "Reading Material: Transfers, Remounts, and the Production of Meaning in Contemporary Toronto Drama and Theatre." *Essays on Canadian Writing* 51–52 (1993–94): 258–95.

Kolinska, Klara. "'If the Bard Were Still Jung': Reading for One('s)Self in Ann-Marie MacDonald's *Goodnight Desdemona (Good Morning Juliet)*." *Shakespeare and His Collaborators over the Centuries*. Eds. Pavel Drabek, Klara Kolinska, and Matthew Nichols. Newcastle upon Tyne: Cambridge Scholars, 2008. 203–10.

MacDonald, Ann-Marie, and Kathleen Gallagher. "Intellectual Passions, Feminist Commitments, and Divine Comedies: A Dialogue with Ann-Marie MacDonald." *How Theatre Educates*, ed. Gallagher and Booth. 247–68.

Mackay, Ellen. "The Spectre of Straight Shakespeare: New Ways of Looking at Old Texts in *Goodnight Desdemona* and *Mad Boy Chronicle*." *CTR* 111 (Summer 2002): 10–14. Rpt. *Canadian Shakespeare*, ed. Knutson. 69–76.

Matthews, Sara, ed. "Special Issue on Ann-Marie MacDonald." *Canadian Review of American Studies* 35.2 (2005): 125–249.

Morrow, Martin. "Roll over Shakespeare, This Spoof Is a Real Hoot." *Calgary Herald*, 10 Oct. 1998. 19.

Novy, Marianne. "Saving Desdemona and/or Ourselves: Plays by Ann-Marie MacDonald and Paula Vogel." *Transforming Shakespeare: Contemporary Women's Re-Visions in Literature and Performance*. Ed. Marianne Novy. NY: St. Martin's, 1999. 67–85.

Porter, Laurin R. "Shakespeare's 'Sisters': Desdemona, Juliet, and Constance Ledbelly in *Goodnight Desdemona (Good Morning Juliet)*." *Modern Drama* 38.3 (1995): 362–77.

Prokosh, Kevin. "Attack on Bard Yields Wild, Wonderful Trip." *Winnipeg Free Press*, 8 Nov. 1991. D41.

Rampton, James. "On the Fringe: *Goodnight Desdemona (Good Morning Juliet)*; Grace Theatre at the Latchmere, London." *The Independent* (London), 23 July 1997. 15.

Rozett, Martha Tuck. *Talking Back to Shakespeare*. Cranbury, NJ: Associated U Presses, 1994. Ch. 5.

Rudakoff, Judith, and Rita Much. *Fair Play*. 127–43.

Schaffeld, Norbert. "'A wondrous feat of alchemy': A Post-Jungian Reading of Ann-Marie MacDonald's Play *Goodnight Desdemona (Good Morning Juliet)*." *The Golden Egg: Alchemy in Art and Literature*. Eds. Alexandra Lembert and Elmar Schenkel. Berlin: Glienicke; Cambridge: Galda & Wilch, 2002. 115–29.

Scott, Shelley. "Desdemona, Juliet, and Constance Meet the Third Wave." *Resources for Feminist Research* 31.3–4 (2006): 29–41. Rpt. *Canadian Shakespeare*, ed. Knutson. 146–57.

———. *Nightwood Theatre: A Woman's Work Is Always Done*. Edmonton: AU Press, 2010.

Snyder, Laura. "Constance Ledbelly's Birthday: Construction of the Feminist Archetype of the Self in Ann-Marie MacDonald's *Goodnight Desdemona (Good Morning Juliet)*." *Text & Presentation: The Journal of the Comparative Drama Conference*. Supplement 2 (2006): 43–55.

Stevenson, Melanie A. "Othello, Darwin, and the Evolution of Race in Ann-Marie MacDonald's Work." *Canadian Literature* 168 (Spring 2001): 34–54.

Stone-Blackburn, Susan. "Recent Plays on Women's Playwriting." *Essays in Theatre* 14.1 (1995): 37–48.

Taylor, Kate. "Say Goodnight Desdemona, Already." *Globe and Mail*, 24 Mar. 2001. R19.

Walker, Craig. "Moral Adaptations: How Ann-Marie MacDonald's *The Arab's Mouth* Became *Belle Moral*." *CTR* 131 (Summer 2007): 61–67.

Wilson, Ann. "Critical Revisions: Ann-Marie MacDonald's *Goodnight Desdemona (Good Morning Juliet)*." *Women on the Canadian Stage*, ed. Much. 1–12. Rpt. *Feminist Theatre and Performance*, ed. Bennett. 71–79.

Yachnin, Paul, and Brent Whitted. "Canadian Bacon." *Shakespeare in Canada*, ed. Bryden and Makaryk. 255–73.

TOMSON HIGHWAY and *Dry Lips Oughta Move to Kapuskasing*

Alexie, Sherman. "Spokane Voices: Tomson Highway Raps with Sherman Alexie." *Aboriginal Voices* 4 (Jan.–Mar. 1997): 36–41.

Anderson, Allyson. "Reincarnating Fatherhood in Aboriginal Fiction." *Canadian Woman Studies* 26 (Winter–Spring 2008): 179–87.

Baker, Marie Annharte. "Angry Enough to Spit But with Dry Lips It Hurts More Than You Know." *CTR* 68 (Fall 1991): 88–89.

Bashford, Lucy. "*Dry Lips Oughta Move to Kapuskasing*." *Malahat Review* 91 (June 1990): 109–10.

Bennett, Susan. "Who Speaks? Representations of Native Women in Some Canadian Plays." *Canadian Journal of Drama and Theatre* 1.2 (1991): 13–25.

Billingham, Susan. "The Configurations of Gender in Tomson Highway's *Dry Lips Oughta Move to Kapuskasing*." *Modern Drama* 46.3 (2003): 358–80. Rpt. *Queer Theatre in Canada*, ed. Kerr. 112–33.

Burnham, Clint. "Lips, Marks, Lapse: Materialism and Dialogism in Tomson Highway's *Dry Lips Oughta Move to Kapuskasing*." *Open Letter* 8 (Summer 1994): 19–30.

Chang, Oswald Yuan-Chin. "Tomson Highway's 'The Rez' Plays: Theatre as the (E)Merging of Native Ritual through Postmodernist Displacement." *Nebula* 5.4 (2008): 129–44.

Chapman, Geoff. "Royal Treatment for *Dry Lips*." *Toronto Star*, 14 Apr. 1991. C1.

Conlogue, Ray. "An Emotionally Riveting *Dry Lips*." *Globe and Mail*, 24 Apr. 1989. A17.

Crew, Robert. "Hope Flickers in Disturbing Probe of Native Spirit." *Toronto Star*, 23 Apr. 1989. C1.

Crook, Barbara. "A Few Slips Twixt Audience and *Lips*." *Vancouver Sun*, 25 Mar. 1995. H8.

Curran, Beverley. "Invisible Indigeneity: First Nations and Aboriginal Theatre in Japanese Translation and Performance." *Theatre Journal* 59.3 (2007): 449–65.

Cushman, Robert. "From Ideal to Painfully Real." *Globe and Mail*, 15 Apr. 1991. C3.

da Cunha, Rubelise. "The Unending Appetite for Stories: Genre Theory, Indigenous Theatre, and Tomson Highway's Rez Cycle." *Canadian Journal of Native Studies* 29.1–2 (2009): 165–82.

Davison, Carol Margaret. "The Matrix Interview: Tomson Highway." *Matrix* 46 (1995): 2–7.

Dickinson, Peter. *Here Is Queer: Nationalisms, Sexualities, and the Literatures of Canada.* Toronto: U of Toronto P, 1999. Ch. 7.

Donnelly, Pat. "Greene a Scene-Stealer in *Dry Lips*." *Montreal Gazette*, 23 Mar. 1991. E12.

Enright, Robert. "Let Us Now Combine Mythologies: The Theatrical Art of Tomson Highway." *Border Crossings* 11 (1992): 22–27.

Filewod, Alan. "Averting the Colonial Gaze: Notes on Watching Native Theater." *Aboriginal Voices: Amerindian, Inuit, and Sami Theater.* Ed. Per Brask and William Morgan. Baltimore: Johns Hopkins UP, 1992. 17–28.

———. "Receiving Aboriginality: Tomson Highway and the Crisis of Cultural Authenticity." *Theatre Journal* 46 (Oct. 1994): 363–73. Rpt. *Aboriginal Drama and Theatre*, ed. Appleford. 37–48.

Folkerth, Wes. "Goodfellows: Hockey, Shakespeare, and Indigenous Spirits in Tomson Highway's *Dry Lips Oughta Move to Kapuskasing*." *Canadian Shakespeare*, ed. Knutson. 199–205.

Fraser, Marian Botsford. "Contempt for Women Overshadows Powerful Play." *Globe and Mail*, 17 Apr. 1991. A13.

Godfrey, Stephen. "Trip from Comedy to Drama Is a Worthwhile, if Bumpy, Ride." *Globe and Mail*, 9 Mar. 1991. C8.

Grant, Agnes. "Canadian Native Literature: The Drama of George Ryga and Tomson Highway." *Australian-Canadian Studies* 10.2 (1992): 37–56.

Hannon, Gerald. "Tomson and the Trickster." *Toronto Life* (Mar. 1991): 28–31, 35–44, 81–85.

Highway, Tomson. "Fact Does Not Interest Me Near As Much As Fantasy." *Theatre and AutoBiography*, ed. Grace and Wasserman. 306–08.

———. "On Native Mythology." *Theatrum* 6 (Spring 1987): 29–31. Rpt. *Canadian Theatre History*, ed. Rubin, 420–23; *Aboriginal Drama and Theatre*, ed. Appleford. 1–3.

———. "Should Only Native Actors Have the Right to Play Native Roles?" *Prairie Fire* 22 (Fall 2001): 20–26.

Hodgson, Heather. "Survival Cree, or Weesakeechak Dances Down Yonge Street." *Books in Canada* 28 (Fall 1999): 2–5.

Honegger, Gitta. "Native Playwright: Tomson Highway." *Theater* 23 (Winter 1992): 88–92.

Hunt, Nigel. "Tracking the Trickster." *Brick* 37 (Fall 1989): 58–60.

Imboden, Roberta. "On the Road with Tomson Highway's Blues Harmonica in *Dry Lips Oughta Move to Kapuskasing*." *Canadian Literature* 144 (Spring 1995): 113–24.

Innes, Christopher. "Dreams of Violence: Moving Beyond Colonialism in Canadian and Caribbean Drama." *Theatre Matters: Performance and Culture on the World Stage.* Ed. Richard Boon and Jane Plastow. Cambridge: Cambridge UP, 1998. 76–96.

Johnston, Denis W. "Lines and Circles: The 'Rez' Plays of Tomson Highway." *Canadian Literature* 124–125 (Spring–Summer 1990): 254–64.

Knowles, Ric. "Reading Material: Transfers, Remounts, and the Production of Meaning in Contemporary Toronto Drama and Theatre." *Essays on Canadian Writing* 51–52 (1993): 258–95.

La Flamme, Michelle. "Highway to the Valley." *CTR* 151 (Summer 2012): 151–55.

Loucks, Brian. "Another Glimpse: Excerpts from a Conversation with Tomson Highway." *CTR* 68 (Fall 1991): 9–11.

Lundy, Randy. "Erasing the Invisible: Gender Violence and Representations of Whiteness in *Dry Lips Oughta Move to Kapuskasing*." *(Ad)dressing Our Words*, ed. Ruffo. 101–24.

Macfarlane, Heather. "Beyond the Divide: The Use of Native Languages in Anglo- and Franco-Indigenous Theatre." *Studies in Canadian Literature* 35.2 (2010): 95–109.

Maufort, Marc. *Transgressive Itineraries.* 148–57.

Morgan, William. "The Trickster and Native Theater: An Interview with Tomson Highway." *Aboriginal Voices: Amerindian, Inuit, and Sami Theater.* Ed. Per Brask and William Morgan. Baltimore: Johns Hopkins UP, 1992. 130–38.

Morra, Linda M., and Deanna Reder, eds. *Troubling Tricksters: Revisioning Critical Conversations.* Waterloo: Wilfrid Laurier UP, 2010.

Moses, Daniel David. "The Trickster Theatre of Tomson Highway." *Canadian Fiction Magazine* 60 (1987): 83–88.

Nestruck, J. Kelly. "A Diverse Cast, with No Reservations." *Globe and Mail*, 9 Nov. 2011. R1.

Nothof, Anne. "Cultural Collision and Magical Transformation: The Plays of Tomson Highway." *Studies in Canadian Literature* 20.2 (1995): 34–43.

Pell, Barbara. "George Ryga's 'Hail Mary' and Tomson Highway's *Nanabush*: Two Paradigms of Religion and Theatre in Canada." *Theatre Research in Canada* 27 (Fall 2006): 245–59.

Petrone, Penny. *Native Literature in Canada: From the Oral Tradition to the Present.* Toronto: Oxford UP, 1990. 170–75.

Portman, Jamie. "Native Play's Impact Dulled by Buffoonery." *Calgary Herald*, 25 Apr. 1989. D3.

Preston, Jennifer. "Weesageechak Begins to Dance: Native Earth Performing Arts Inc." *TDR* 36 (Spring 1992): 135–59.

Rabillard, Sheila. "Absorption, Elimination, and the Hybrid: Some Impure Questions of Gender and Culture in the Trickster Drama of Tomson Highway." *Essays in Theatre* 12 (Nov. 1993): 3–28. Rpt. *Aboriginal Drama and Theatre*, ed. Appleford. 4–31.

Scott, Jay. "*Dry Lips*' Loss of Intimacy Transforms Visceral Images into Picturesque Tableaux." *Globe and Mail*, 21 Apr. 1991. 9.

Shackleton, Mark. "Can Weesageechak Keep Dancing? The Importance of Trickster Figures in the Work of Native Earth Dramatists, 1986–2000." *Performing National Identities*, ed. Grace and Glaap. 278–88.

Smyth, Michael. "Native Play Triumphs." *Winnipeg Free Press*, 15 Apr. 1991. 16.

Solga, Kim. "The Line, the Crack, and the Possibility of Architecture: Figure, Ground, Feminist Performance." *Theatre Research in Canada* 29 (Spring 2008): 1–28.

Steed, Judy. "Tomson Highway: My Way." *Toronto Star*, 24 Mar. 1991. D1–2.

Taylor, Drew Hayden. "Storytelling to Stage: The Growth of Native Theatre in Canada." *TDR* 41 (Fall 1997): 140–52.

Tompkins, Joanne, and Lisa Male. "'Twenty-One Native Women on Motorcycles': An Interview with Tomson Highway." *Australasian Drama Studies* 24 (Apr. 1994): 13–28.

Usmiani, Renate. "The Bingocentric Worlds of Michel Tremblay and Tomson Highway: *Les Belles-Soeurs* vs. *The Rez Sisters*." *Canadian Literature* 144 (Spring 1995): 126–40.

Wasserman, Jerry. "'God of the Whiteman! God of the Indian! God Al-fucking-mighty!' The Residential School Legacy in Two Canadian Plays." *Journal of Canadian Studies* 39 (Winter 2005): 23–48.

———. "Where the Soul Still Dances: The Blues and Canadian Drama." *Essays on Canadian Writing* 65 (Fall 1998): 56–75.

Wigston, Nancy. "Nanabush in the City." *Books in Canada* 18 (Mar. 1989): 7–9.

Wilson, Ann. "Tomson Highway, Interview." *Other Solitudes: Canadian Multicultural Fictions*. Ed. Linda Hutcheon and Marion Richmond. Toronto: Oxford UP, 1990. 350–55.

Zufferey-Boulton, Isabelle. "A Fugue for Three Voices: Q Art Theatre's Production of *Ernestine Shuswap Gets Her Trout*." *alt.theatre* 5 (June 2008): 21–25.

JUDITH THOMPSON and *Lion in the Streets*

Adam, Julie. "The Implicated Audience: Judith Thompson's Anti-Naturalism in *The Crackwalker*, *White Biting Dog*, *I Am Yours*, and *Lion in the Streets*." *Women on the Canadian Stage*, ed. Much. 21–29. Rpt. *Judith Thompson*, ed. Knowles. 41–46.

Armstrong, John. "Sharp Cast and Razor Wit Help to Hone Tale of Animal Savagery." *Vancouver Sun*, 18 Nov. 1991. C2.

Barnett, Claudia. "Judith Thompson's Ghosts: The Revenants that Haunt the Plays." *CTR* 114 (Spring 2003): 33–37. Rpt. *Judith Thompson*, ed. Knowles. 92–97.

Bemrose, John. "Lionhearted Drama." *Maclean's* 103 (19 Nov. 1990): 69.

Berson, Misha. "Taking Aim at the Bourgeoisie." *Seattle Times*, 31 Mar. 1995. G14.

Bessai, Diane. "Women Dramatists: Sharon Pollock and Judith Thompson." *Post-Colonial English Drama: Commonwealth Drama Since 1960*. Ed. Bruce King. NY: St. Martin's, 1992. 97–117.

Burliuk, Greg. "Judith Thompson's Lion Bites Hard." *Kingston Whig-Standard*, 16 Oct. 1999. 42.

Conlogue, Ray. "Drama Succeeds by Baring Its Teeth." *Globe and Mail*, 8 Nov. 1990. C1.

Cushman, Robert. "Exploring a Limitless Domain of Human Misery." *Globe and Mail*, 4 June 1990. C8.

Donnelly, Pat. "Trail of an Angry Ghost." *Ottawa Citizen*, 21 Oct. 2000. D10.

Filewod, Alan, and Allan Watts, eds. *Judith Thompson Casebook. CTR* 89 (Winter 1996).

Hadfield, D.A. *Re: Producing Women's Dramatic History*. Ch. 3.

Hancock, Brecken Rose. "Taking a Walk with Judith Thompson: Flânerie Tames the Lion in the Streets." *Studies in Canadian Literature* 32 (Jan. 2007): 34–61.

Harvie, Jennifer. "Constructing Fictions of an Essential Reality or 'This Pickshur Is Niiiice': Judith Thompson's *Lion in the Streets*." *Theatre Research in Canada* 13 (Spring–Fall 1992): 81–93. Rpt. *Judith Thompson*, ed. Knowles. 47–58.

———. "(Im)Possibility: Fantasy and Judith Thompson's Drama." *On-Stage and Off-Stage: English Canadian Drama in Discourse*, ed. Glaap. 240–56.

Hemming, Sarah. "There Goes the Neighborhood." *The Independent* (London), 14 Apr. 1993. 14.

Holloway, Ann. "Hedda & Lynndie & Jabber & Ciel: An Interview with Judith Thompson." *The Masks of Judith Thompson*, ed. Knowles. 134–46.

Hunt, Nigel. "In Contact with the Dark." *Books in Canada* 17 (Mar. 1988): 10–12. Rpt. *The Masks of Judith Thompson*, ed. Knowles. 1–5.

Kirchhoff, H.J. "A Lion in Winnipeg." *Globe and Mail*, 19 Jan. 1995. E2.

Knowles, Ric. "The Fractured Subject of Judith Thompson." *Lion in the Streets* by Judith Thompson. Toronto: Coach House, 1992. 7–10.

———, ed. *Judith Thompson*. Critical Perspectives on Canadian Theatre in English, vol. 3. Toronto: Playwrights Canada, 2005.

———, ed. *The Masks of Judith Thompson*. Toronto: Playwrights Canada, 2006.

Maufort, Marc. "Poetic Realism Reinvented: Canadian Women Playwrights and the Search for a New Theatrical Idiom." *Canadian Studies* 42 (1997): 27–38.

———. *Transgressive Itineraries*. Ch. 1.

Morrow, Martin. "Sage Theatre Debuts with a Lacerating Lion." *Calgary Herald*, 13 Sept. 1998. C6.

Nightingale, Benedict. "Off the Tourist Itinerary in Ontario: *Lion in the Streets*." *The Times* (London), 21 Apr. 1993.

Nunn, Robert. "Crackwalking: Judith Thompson's Marginal Characters." *Siting the Other: Re-Visions of Marginality in Australian and English-Canadian Drama*. Ed. Marc Maufort and Franca Bellarsi. Brussels: P.I.E.-Peter Lang, 2001. 311–23.

———. "Spatial Metaphor in the Plays of Judith Thompson." *Theatre History in Canada* 10 (Spring 1989): 3–29. Rpt. *Judith Thompson*, ed. Knowles. 20–40.

Pressley, Nelson. "Ugliness and the Beast." *Washington Post*, 24 Jan. 2000. C5.

Rafelman, Rachel. "What I Show Are Simple Moments of Truth." *Globe and Mail*, 1 Dec. 1990. C2.

Read, Robyn. "Who Is the Stranger? The Role of the Monstrous in Judith Thompson's *Capture Me*." *Theatre Research in Canada* 24.1–2 (2003): 187–201. Rpt. *Judith Thompson*, ed. Knowles. 111–22.

Rosborough, Linda. "Grim Play Emotionally Draining." *Winnipeg Free Press*, 13 Jan. 1995. D5.

Rudakoff, Judith. "Under the Goddess's Cloak: reCalling the Wild, enGendering the Power." *Women on the Canadian Stage*, ed. Much. 115–30.

Rudakoff, Judith, and Rita Much. *Fair Play*. 87–104. Rpt. *The Masks of Judith Thompson*, ed. Knowles. 27–42.

Steed, Judy. "Thompson Different from Her Characters." *Globe and Mail*, 11 Feb. 1982. E5.

Thompson, Judith. "Beyond the U.S.A., Beyond the U.K.: A View from Canada." *Women Writing Plays: Three Decades of the Susan Smith Blackburn Prize*. Ed. Alexis Greene. Austin: U of Texas P, 2006. Rpt. *The Masks of Judith Thompson*, ed. Knowles. 127–33.

———. "Epilepsy & the Snake: Fear in the C. Process." *CTR* 89 (Winter 1996): 4–7. Rpt. *Masks of Judith Thompson*, ed. Knowles. 79–84.

———. "'I Will Tear You to Pieces': The Classroom as Theatre." *How Theatre Educates*, ed. Gallagher and Booth. 25–34. Rpt. *The Masks of Judith Thompson*, ed. Knowles. 103–11.

———. "'It's My Birthday Forever Now': Urjo Kareda and Me." *CTR* 113 (Winter 2003): 11–14. Rpt. *The Masks of Judith Thompson*, ed. Knowles. 112–17.

———. "One Twelfth." *Language in Her Eye: Views on Writing and Gender by Canadian Women Writing in English*. Ed. Libby Scheier et al. Toronto: Coach House, 1990. 263–67. Rpt. *The Masks of Judith Thompson*, ed. Knowles. 23–26.

———. "That Stinking Hot Summer." *Theatre Journal* 62 (Dec. 2010): 505–10.

———. "Why Should a Playwright Direct Her Own Plays?" *Women on the Canadian Stage*, ed. Much. 104–08. Rpt. *The Masks of Judith Thompson*, ed. Knowles. 52–55.

Toles, George. "'Cause You're the Only One I Want': The Anatomy of Love in the Plays of Judith Thompson." *Canadian Literature* 118 (Fall 1988): 116–35. Rpt. *Judith Thompson*, ed. Knowles. 1–19.

Tomc, Sandra. "Revisions of Probability: An Interview with Judith Thompson." *CTR* 59 (Summer 1989): 18–23. Rpt. *The Masks of Judith Thompson*, ed. Knowles. 6–13.

Toscano, Michael. "Look at Humanity's Dark Side Holds Up under Spotlight." *Washington Post*, 31 Oct. 2002. T21.

Wachtel, Eleanor. "An Interview with Judith Thompson." *Brick* 41 (Summer 1991): 37–41. Rpt. *The Masks of Judith Thompson*, ed. Knowles. 43–49.

Wagner, Vit. "Thompson's Duet a Theatre Triumph." *Toronto Star*, 15 Nov. 1990. B5.

Walker, Craig Stewart. *The Buried Astrolabe*. Ch. 6.

Wilson, Ann. "Canadian Grotesque: The Reception of Judith Thompson's Plays in London." *CTR* 89 (Winter 1996): 24–28.

———. "The Culture of Abuse in *Under the Skin*, *This Is for You, Anna*, and *Lion in the Streets*. *Contemporary Issues in Canadian Drama*, ed. Brask. 160–70.

Winston, Iris. "Lion Roars with Sense of Surreal." *Ottawa Citizen*, 9 Nov. 1990. D2.

Zimmerman, Cynthia. "A Conversation with Judith Thompson." *Canadian Drama* 16.2 (1990): 184–94. Rpt. *The Masks of Judith Thompson*, ed. Knowles. 14–22.

———. *Playwriting Women: Female Voices in English Canada*. 176–209.

Life Without Instruction

‌ways Stick to Facts." *Theatre and* ‌ny, eds. Grace and Wasserman. 321–23.

‌eface / Introduction to 'Ten Ways to Abuse ‌ld Woman.'" *Windsor Review* 30 (Spring ‌997): 23–25.

Conlogue, Ray. "I Hate Political Correctness." *Globe and Mail*, 21 Oct. 1989. C1, C3.

———. "Life Without Instruction." *Globe and Mail*, 5 Aug. 1991. C3.

Donnelly, Pat. "Playwright Sally Clark Making Her Mark in Quebec." *Montreal Gazette*, 22 Apr. 1993. F7.

Godard, Barbara. "(Re)Appropriation as Translation." *CTR* 64 (Fall 1990): 22–31.

Grace, Sherrill. "*Life Without Instruction*: Artemisia and the Lessons of Perspective." *Theatre Research in Canada* 25.1–2 (2004): 116–35.

Hadfield, D.A. *Re: Producing Women's Dramatic History*. 115–82.

Kirchhoff, H.J. "The Trials – and Plays – of Sally Clark." *Globe and Mail*, 8 Aug. 1991. A10.

Knowles, Ric. *The Theatre of Form and the Production of Meaning*. 155–58.

Rudakoff, Judith. "Under the Goddess's Cloak: reCalling the Wild, enGendering the Power." *Women on the Canadian Stage*, ed. Much. 115–30.

Rudakoff, Judith, and Rita Much. *Fair Play*. 74–86.

Wagner, Vit. "Clark's Life Is Full of Ripe Contradiction." *Toronto Star*, 4 Aug. 1991. C2.

———. "Painter-Turned-Playwright Trying to Portray Heroines Warts and All." *Toronto Star*, 13 Jan. 1989. E17.

Professor of English and theatre at the University of British Columbia, Jerry Wasserman has written and lectured widely on Canadian theatre. Books include *Spectacle of Empire: Marc Lescarbot's Theatre of Neptune in New France* and *Theatre and AutoBiography* (with Sherrill Grace). He has over two hundred professional acting credits on stage and screen, and has reviewed more than fifteen hundred plays for CBC Radio, the *Province* newspaper, and his website, Vancouverplays.com. Jerry is a recipient of the Killam Teaching Prize (1998), the Dorothy Somerset Award (2005), and the Sam Payne Award (2012), honouring a lifetime of achievement in the performing arts.